Ded

To the many preachers of the whole counsel of God

who every Lord's Day strive to preach,

with power and proportion but without apology,

a

scripturally-grounded

rational,

God-centered, and

theologically-articulate sermon

to the glory of God,

the author sincerely and thankfully

dedicates this book.

Inscription for a Pulpit

"The hungry sheep look up, and are not fed."
The hungry sheep, that crave the living Bread,
Grow few, and lean, and feeble as can be
When fed not Gospel but philosophy,
Not love's eternal story, no, not this,
But apt allusion, keen analysis,
Discourse well framed—forgot as soon as heard—
Man's thin dilution of the living Word.

O Preacher, leave the rhetorician's arts;
Preach Christ, the Food of hungry human hearts;
Hold fast to science, history, or creed,
But preach the Answer to our human need,
That in this place, at least, it may be said
No hungry sheep looks up and is not fed.

—Robert Hammond Adams (1883-1975)

Contents

Introduction 9

Part One

One: The Need for a Scripturally-Grounded Pulpit 13

Two: The Need for a Rational Pulpit 31

Three: The Need for a God-Centered Pulpit 55

Four: The Need for a Theologically Articulate Pulpit 99

Five: The Need for a Godly Pulpit 115

Six: The Need for a Protestant Pulpit 127

Seven: The Need for an Evangelistic Pulpit 159

Eight: The Need for a Reformed Pulpit 177

For Further Reading 193

Part Two

Introduction 197

One: "Where Does God Live?" 199

Two: "Jesus' Great Invitation" 211

Three: "Jesus' Strange Question" 225

Four: "Choosing to Live on the 'Joy Side' of the Christian Life" 237

Five: "The Immeasurable Greatness of the Love of God" 253

Six: "Martin Luther's Text" 269

Seven: "The Relevance of Christ's Cause" 281

Eight: "Christ Has Redeemed Us!" 293

Nine: "Seeing Him Who Is Invisible" 309

Ten: "What Will Happen When Jesus Comes Again?" 323

Subject Index 339

Persons Index 345

Scripture Index 348

Introduction

This book is for preachers and men aspiring to become preachers. Never has the need been greater for Spirit-anointed preachers who can stand in the pulpits across the world and with power 'rightly handle' the unsearchable riches of the Word of God. Regrettably, men aspiring to the gospel ministry today are being told that they must make themselves proficient not primarily in the knowledge of Holy Scripture and sound theology but in many non-theological areas—business administration, personnel management, communication skills, counseling, and so forth. Failure in these areas, it is being said, will have a lasting negative effect upon one's ministry.

There is no question, of course, that proficiency is these areas can be quite useful to the preacher, and the acquisition of this proficiency is never intentionally to be shunned in ministerial preparation. But in their zeal to become effective business administrators, personnel managers, or good communicators, the ordained preacher and the ministerial candidate must *never* begin to think that they can neglect to acquire and to hone to a razor-sharp edge their biblical/theological skills, for it is this area of their training above all others that will provide them the content of their message and will determine in large measure the degree to which their preaching, teaching, and counseling ministries will be true to the Word of God, will thus enjoy God's evident blessing, and will be taken seriously by those who hear them.

It is to assist both the ordained preacher and the ministerial candidate that I offer in Part I the following collection of addresses. The first four I gave to about seventy-five ministers and about half again as many ministerial candidates of the Church of Scotland during Rutherford House Week in Glasgow, Scotland in May 1986. The fifth (which I adapted from an ordination sermon I heard the Reverend Doctor Robert S. Rayburn preach some twenty-five years ago) and seventh addresses I gave to around fifty pastors in May 2000 at the Pastors' Conference sponsored by the Metropolitan

Tabernacle in London, England. The sixth address I gave in March 2001 to around three hundred pastors and church leaders at the Connecticut Valley Conference on Reformed Theology convened in Wethersfield, Connecticut. And the eighth address I gave to around eight hundred pastors and church leaders in June 2001 at the School of Theology also sponsored by the Metropolitan Tabernacle in London, England. Each lecture has been edited, with the third and sixth being somewhat enlarged over the form in which I gave them originally because of the significance of the topics.

The ten sermons in Part II I offer only to illustrate the kinds of sermon that I think Protestant and Reformed pastors should be preaching from their pulpits, namely, sermons that are biblically grounded, rational, God-centered, theologically accurate, and that focus on some specific condition of the Fall and provide a Christological solution. I do not intend to suggest for a moment that they are paragons of preaching. Pastors may use these sermons in any way they deem appropriate and need not cite me as their source.

I now offer this book to my brother preachers and to my brothers aspiring to the Christian ministry with the prayer that these addresses and sermons will help them, at least in a small way, both to determine the trajectory of their preaching ministries and to offer up to their Redeemer a pulpit ministry approved of God.

Robert L. Reymond
September 2003

Part One

Eight Lectures

Chapter One

The Need for a Scripturally-Grounded Pulpit

Throughout its long history the one true church founded on the apostles and prophets, with Jesus Christ himself being its chief cornerstone, has believed and confessed that the one living and true God has revealed himself, not only in creation and providence, not only in Jesus Christ, but also *verbally* or informationally – in Old Testament times through his servants the prophets and in New Testament times through the apostles of Christ. Furthermore, the church has confessed that this verbal or informational revelation, under the Spirit's superintendence (which is technically called inspirationn), was infallibly preserved in written form in the Scriptures of the Old and New Testaments, this inscripturation being done in such a way that the two Testaments, taken together in their unitary wholeness, although written by men, may be designated legitimately as the written Word of God.

The Holy Scripture itself is replete with this claim, as the Bible student with only a Sunday School education knows. The many occurrences of the phrase, 'Thus the Lord says' in the Old Testament, both Jesus' testimony to the Old Testament's divine authority (Matt 5:17-18; John 10:35) and his pre-authentication of the several portions of the New Testament (John 14:25-26; 16:12-15), and the epistolary declarations in 1 Corinthians 2:11-13, 2 Timothy 3:16-17, and 2 Peter 1:20-21, 3:15-16 all bear ready testimony to the revelatory character of the Holy Scriptures.

Of special interest to the ministerial candidate may be the fact that it is this conception of the matter that is set forth in the great creeds of the church. The *Westminster Confession of Faith,* for example, after affirming that natural revelation is not sufficient to produce that knowledge necessary for salvation, declares that 'it pleased the Lord, at sundry times, and in divers manners, to reveal himself, and to declare that [revelation] his will unto his church'; then, the same Confession affirms, 'for the better preserving and propagating of the truth,' it pleased God 'to commit the same [revelation] wholly unto writing; which maketh the Holy Scripture to be most necessary; those former ways of God's revealing his will unto his people being now ceased' (I.i). The *necessity* of Scripture for both theology and ministry, in short, is grounded in two facts: the *insufficiency* of natural revelation and the *cessation* of special revelation. Because these two conditions obtain, this great Confession declares, the Holy Scriptures, carefully defined as the books of the Old and New Testaments, having been 'given by inspiration of God; are the *only* rule for faith and life (I.ii). After referring to the Holy Scriptures in I.iv and I.v in so many words as 'the word of God,' the Confession continues in I.vi: 'The whole counsel of God, concerning all things necessary for his own glory, man's salvation, faith, and life, is either expressly set down in Scripture, or by good and necessary consequence may be deduced from Scripture: unto which nothing at any time is to be added, whether by new revelations of the Spirit, or traditions of men.' Because the Bible was 'immediately inspired' of God and was preserved throughout the ages by his singular care and providence, the Bible in the original languages is therefore to be regarded as the final authority 'in all controversies of religion' (I.viii). And in its sentences we are to rest because 'none other but the Holy Spirit speaks in the Scripture' (I.x).

These teachings of the *Westminster Confession of Faith* are in no way to be construed as unique within Protestant confessionalism. Rather, this Confession simply lent its voice to the consentient testimony of many confessions before it, confessions not simply of Presbyterianism but of Protestantism as a whole. If the *Westminster Confession of Faith* is more explicit in some particular regards than earlier confessional statements, it is simply to its credit and its glory as a precise and articulate statement of faith. Its explicitness in no way goes beyond or alters the intentions of the earlier creeds, nor are its statements the 'hardening' expressions of a retrograde seventeenth-century Protestant 'scholasticism', as some recent theologians have charged. Without fear of refutation, I may state categorically that both the Bible's own testimony to itself and the combined testimonies of the great creeds of Christendom that have touched at all upon the nature and attributes of Scripture declare that the Bible is the inspired, infallible, inerrant Word of God to men.

Not every scholar, it is true, has yielded to the Bible's claim concerning itself. One can still hear it often said that there are scientific, historical, geographical, and ethical blunders within the Bible's pages. To these overt and explicit objections to biblical inerrancy and to the Bible's divine authority as a whole, the Christian minister will have to be able to respond, as his spiritual forebears did before him, with careful research and accurate exegesis (Tit 1: 9-11). Thus, by resolving the alleged contradictions between biblical statements, by correcting false readings of its historical and geographical statements, and by setting forth what the Scriptures actually assert in the areas of science, history, and morality, the Christian minister can disarm opposition by laying to rest specious objections to the Scripture's truthfulness.

Most objections to the inspiration and authority of Scripture which the average minister will hear will be fairly explicit and not very sophisticated in nature – on the order of the complaint: 'The Bible contains contradictions.' These objections, as I just suggested, can be normally answered by direct, 'unsophisticated' responses based on the Scriptures themselves. Good books are available to the minister to assist him in his response to the lists of alleged contradictions in Scripture (which lists, by the way, are embarrassingly archaic). But in recent times more sophisticated objections, reflecting certain theories concerning religious language and language *per se,* have been registered against the whole idea of a verbal revelation. The ministerial candidate should not be unduly overwrought regarding them. They too can be and have been answered. Consider two such objections, the first drawn from the theological realm, the second from the secular realm.

Religious truth will always be existential truth

The first objection contends that religious truth by its very nature will always be existential truth – that is, subjective 'truth for me, the human existent'. Because written or spoken language will always be caught in the web of historical relativity and thus is inadequate as a conveyor of religious truth to meet the soul's subjective demand for religious certainty, at best, it is said, language serves as a *Hinweis – a* pointer – to the 'existential truth encounter' lying behind the actual words and experienced *nonverbally* by the human existent.

The theologically trained minister will recognize in this objection to an objective verbal or propositional revelation the dogmatic pronouncement of classic neo-orthodoxy. As one facet of that impressive enterprise of the 1920s, 1930s, and 1940s, it takes its place in the broader vision of that theological novelty which, under the influence of the Kantian distinction between the 'phenomenal' and 'noumenal' realms, maintained the 'qualitative distinction between God and man, between eternity and time'. Kant had argued that the *phenomenal* realm is the 'knowable' world and is controlled by pure reason, while the *noumenal* realm is the realm of God, freedom, and immortality and is governed by practical reason (faith). Accordingly, the neo-orthodox theologians contended that, while eternity might 'touch' time as a tangent touches a circle, it never enters into time. While God, true enough, existentially 'speaks' to men, this 'revelation' always lurks outside of and behind history (*Historie*) in what the proponents of this view referred to as 'primal' history (*Urgeschichte*), and is never to be identified with the words of the Bible or any other book in the A=A sense of the word. This objection, in a word, views the Bible as a (flawed) record of God's revelation to men but not the revelation itself. Revelation is always a non-verbal *direct theophany* outside of ordinary history, and religious truth is always personal or existential truth – the effect of an existential crisis encounter between God and the individual human existent.

What shall we say to this objection against the historic Protestant doctrine of Scripture as the very Word of God? I would say at least three things.

First, whatever one may personally think about the verbal or propositional character of special revelation, he should at least be willing to admit that *Scripture itself affirms that one form of divine disclosure assumed precisely this character.* James Barr, himself certainly no friend of the evangelical doctrine of Scripture, concedes as much in his book, *Old and New in Interpretation.* In an appendix to this book Barr observes that 'In modern revelational theologies [by this term he refers to the neo-orthodox theologies], it is a stock argument against fundamentalism [by this term he refers to evangelical theology] to say that it depends on a propositional view of revelation, while the right view of revelation is one of encounter, events, history or the like'.[1] But Barr, because he believes that one's position must be based upon 'an exegesis of the texts as they are',[2] is compelled to acknowledge that the evangelical has read his Bible correctly when he affirms that one form of divine revelation is verbal or propositional:

> In so far as it is good to use the term 'revelation' at all, it is entirely as true to say that in the OT, revelation is by verbal communication as to say that it is by acts in history. We have verbal communication both in that God speaks directly with men and in that men learn from other and earlier men through the verbal form of tradition. When we speak of the highly 'personal' nature of the OT God, it is very largely upon this verbal character of his communication with man that we are relying. The acts of God are meaningful because they are set within this frame of verbal communication. God tells what he is doing, or tells what he is going to do. He does nothing unless he tells his servants the prophets (Amos 3:7). A God who acted in history would be a mysterious and supra-personal fate if the action was not linked with this verbal conversation.[3]
>
> There is some reluctance to face the fact of this verbal communication because it is supposed that an apologetic problem is involved. We think that we cannot imagine verbal communication between God and man, and we worry about terrible consequences which would ensue in the Church, and of serious damage to the rationality of our presentation of Christianity, if it were admitted that such verbal communication is important.
>
> But, in the first place, these apologetic considerations should not prevent us from speaking historically about the character of the ancient literature. When we speak of the importance of verbal

1. James Barr, *Old and New in Interpretation* (New York: Harper and Row, 1966), 201.
2. Barr, *Old and New in Interpretation*, 77.
3. Barr, *Old and New in Interpretation*, 78f.

> communication, we are talking as historical-literary scholars about the character of the literature and the forms of expression which it displays. It may well be that as historical scholars we cannot give an adequate account of these phenomena; but we can seek to give an adequate account of how they were understood to be, and of the way in which they dominate the form-patterns of the literature.[4]

> We may express the matter in this way: that whatever acts and encounters formed the experience of man with God in the OT, the tangible form which they take is that of verbal, linguistic, literary statement. It is this that provides the *content* of all the acts and encounters, and provides the discrimination between one and another and the elements of purpose and personal will. Thus the experience of Israel and its prophets and others crystallizes in the form of sentences and literary complexes which are the articulate form (and thus the knowable form) of the way in which God has related himself to them.[5]

In his article, 'Revelation Through History in the Old Testament and in Modern Theology' *(Interpretation,* April 1963; reprinted in *New Theology, No. I),* Barr states this conviction even more strongly:

> We come to those texts which have supplied the basic examples for the idea of revelation through history, such as the Exodus story. If you treat this record as revelation through history, you commonly speak as if the basis were the doing of certain divine acts (what, exactly, they were is often difficult to determine), while the present form of tradition in its detail and circumstantiality is 'interpretation' of these acts, or 'meditation' upon them, or theological reflection prompted by them. Thus one may hear the great revelatory passage of Exodus 3 described as 'interpretation' of this divine act of salvation, or as an inference from the fact that God had led Israel out of Egypt.

---

4. Barr, *Old and New in Interpretation*, 79.
5. Barr, *Old and New in Interpretation*, 80.

But I cannot make this scheme fit the texts, for this is not how the texts represent the Exodus events. Far from representing the divine acts as the basis of all knowledge of God and all communication with him, they represent God as communicating freely with men, and particularly with Moses, before, during, and after these events. Far from the incident at the burning bush being an 'interpretation' of the divine acts, it is a direct communication from God to Moses of his purposes and intentions. This conversation, instead of being represented as an interpretation of the divine act, is a precondition of it. If God had not told Moses what he did, the Israelites would not have demanded their escape from Egypt, and the deliverance at the Sea of Reeds would not have taken place.

We may argue, of course, from a critical viewpoint that the stories of such dialogues arose in fact as inference from a divine act already known and believed, and for this there may be good reasons. All I want to say is that if we do this we do it on critical grounds and not on biblical grounds, for this is not how the biblical narrative represents the events.[6]

[As to] direct verbal communication between God and particular men on particular occasions. Such direct communication is, I believe, an inescapable fact of the Bible and of the OT in particular. God can speak specific verbal messages when he wills, to the men of his choice. But for this, if we follow the way in which the OT represents the incidents, there would have been no call of Abraham, no Exodus, no prophecy. Direct communication from God to man has fully as much claim to be called the core of the tradition as has revelation through events in history. If we persist in saying that this direct, specific communication must be subsumed under revelation through events in history and taken as subsidiary interpretation of the latter, I shall say that we are abandoning the Bible's own interpretation of the matter for another which is apologetically more comfortable.

---

6. James Barr, 'Revelation Through History in the Old Testament and in Modern Theology,' *Interpretation,* April 1963; reprinted in *New Theology*, No. I, 65.

> And here I want, if I may use an inelegant phrase, to call a particular bluff. It has been frequently represented to us in modern times that there is a 'scandal' in the idea of revelation through history [the reader should realize that, from the neo-orthodox perspective, it is this 'scandal' which is the 'scandal' of the gospel which challenges the modern mind and thus is a desirable thing – RLR], and that the acceptance of it is something seriously difficult for the modern mind, including that even of theologians. The contrary seems to me to be obviously the case.... The reason why we use it so much is the very reverse: far from being a central stumbling block to our minds, it is something we use because it is a readily acceptable idea within our theological situation; thus it is one which, in our use of the Bible, enables us to mitigate the difficulty of elements which are in fact infinitely more scandalous, elements such as the direct verbal communication of which I have been speaking, or prophetic prediction, or miracles.[7]

These quotations are sufficient to make my point. What Barr is saying is that the neo-orthodox scholar should admit that the view of revelation espoused by the evangelical is the view espoused by the Bible itself and that his rejection of the 'evangelical view' is based upon extra-biblical philosophico-critical grounds with which he is comfortable rather than on biblical grounds. It would seem that the evangelical has read his Bible more carefully than the neo-orthodox theologian, if Barr is to be believed! This is the first thing I would say.

Second, we must insist that the epistemological basis which neo-orthodoxy offers to justify its claim to religious knowledge has all of the apologetic weaknesses of every 'leap of faith' theology, specifically, the radical subjectivism and the irrationality inherent within every non-verbal religious experience. The human religious existent who would espouse the epistemological views of neo-orthodoxy

---

7. James Barr, 'Revelation Through History in the Old Testament and in Modern Theology,' 70.

can never be sure that the non-verbal subjective religious encounter concerning which he boasts was with God and not with Satan. How does he know it is a true and not a false religious experience? What reason can he offer to justify his *verbal* explication of his non-verbal religious experience? And why should anyone believe him?

Finally, we can summon to our aid here the judgment which more recent theological history has rendered respecting these conclusions. What has happened to classic neo-orthodoxy? After the radical Bultmannianism of the 1940s and 1950s had carried its epistemological implications to their logical conclusions by denying, through its program of 'demythologizing' the Jesus of the New Testament, the very possibility of discovering any significant historical facts about him, and by virtually transforming theology into a Heideggerian existential anthropology, it has itself been displaced by the post-Bultmannian 'new quest' of the 1960s, 1970s, and 1980s for the *historical* Jesus once again. You see, a theological vision that talked much about the mighty acts of God in history but refused to identify any historical event as an act of God, that talked much about the Christ of faith but refused to identify Jesus of Nazareth directly with this Christ at any point, and that talked much about the Word of God to man but refused to identify the Bible or any other book directly with this Word of God, could not for long fire the imagination or answer the hard questions of thinking people. And a gospel whose Christ is a 'phantom', whose cross is merely a symbol, and whose resurrection occurs only in 'primal history' but not in the actual history where men experience pain and death and long for deliverance from them simply has no staying power in it. Increasing uneasiness with precisely the absence of the historical element in the existentialism of neo-orthodoxy has provoked the impetus behind the 'new quest for the historical Jesus' conducted by much post-Bultmannian critical New Testament scholarship. And it is a striking commentary on how badly classic neo-orthodoxy with its concept of revelation as non-historical and existential has fared to note that, whereas Bultmann entitled his existential 'life of Jesus' in 1926 simply *Jesus,* Gunther Bornkamm, one of Bultmann's students, entitled his own 1956 'life of Jesus' *Jesus of Nazareth,* the very title of which reflects the remarkable shift away from the existential theologies which dominated the academic scene some decades ago. The man aspiring today to a ministry grounded in the Holy Scriptures as God's Word to needy people need not fear that the affirmations and contentions of neo-orthodoxy cannot be answered. They can be and have been more than adequately rebutted by solid evangelical scholarship that has time and again shown that it is neo-orthodoxy that has been weighed in the balance and found wanting.

Human language is incapable of expressing literal truth

The second objection to the notion of a verbal or propositional revelation from God to man – much more radical and clearly more secular than the former objection we just considered – contends that human language by its very nature is simply incapable of expressing literal truth. One advocate of this theory, Wilbur Marshall Urban, in his book *Language and Reality,* writes: 'Strictly speaking, there is no such thing as literal truth in any absolute sense, for there is no such thing as absolute correspondence between expression and that which is expressed...'.[8] Urban insists that to have wholly non-symbolic truth 'is really impossible in view of the very nature of language and expression. If there

---

8. Wilbur Marshall Urban, *Language and Reality* (London: George Allen & Unwin, 1961), 382.

were such a thing as wholly non-symbolic truth, it could not be expressed.'[9]

This theory of language is based on the premise that human language evolved to its present state from the so-called original grunts of earliest man, and had a totally sensory origin. All terms, in other words, derive their meaning from the sensory world. Consequently, all language is symbolic. Literal meanings, particularly for metaphysics, are impossible because words can never be completely detached from their sensory origin.

What is one to say concerning such a radical theory? First, I would say that such a theory of language is self-defeating. To show this, one has only to ask the proponent of the theory, which theory he has expressed in language, 'Is your theory as you have framed it literally true?' If he says that it is not, one need not accept it, and that is the end of the matter. But if he affirms that it is literally true, one only needs to note that, if his statement of the theory is literally true, the theory itself is false, for as a proposition set forth in language it contradicts and thus falsifies the very assertion which it makes – namely, that language cannot express literal truth. If he should say that his statement is the one exception to the thesis it proposes, one can urge again that this self-serving claim still nullifies the theory. If he should reply to the original question that, while the theory is not literally true, it is (in keeping with the theory itself) *symbolically* true, one only needs to ask, 'Symbolically true of what?' Since anything he says in response, according to his own view, could only be symbolically true of something else *ad infinitum,* his infinite symbolic explanatory regress renders impossible the theorist's effort to justify his first assertion ('The theory is symbolically true').

I would reply, second, that no one who thinks seriously

---

9. Urban, *Language and Reality*, 446.

about this matter at all can really live comfortably with the notion that language cannot communicate literal truth or that it is an illegitimate vehicle for the expression of literal truth. Sane, honest persons discourse every day around the world in political, economic, and social situations. They intend, apart from the obvious figures of speech such as metaphors in their speech, that their language be understood and received as literally true by their listeners. They, in turn, assume that the words spoken to them will normally be literally true. If they do not understand one another's meanings, they ask for clarification, and if they have reason to suspect the truthfulness of the words spoken to them, there are means at their disposal to verify or to falsify them. In other words, people just do not assume that language is freighted with so many inherent theoretical difficulties respecting 'that which is to be expressed' that its value as a vehicle for literal truth is reduced to zero. Stated another way, humans simply do not believe that their verbalizing efforts are so burdened with ambiguous symbols that their words cannot state what they literally mean or that their words cannot state literal truth.

Now if we take all this for granted, and properly so, with regard to human discourse, how much more plausible is the notion that the infinite, personal God can communicate literal truth to us verbally or propositionally. If God is omnipotent, surely he can speak literal non-symbolic truth to humans without his intention being warped or becoming freighted with distorting and nullifying ambiguities in the revelatory process. In fact, according to Scripture this is precisely what he has done – he has spoken literal truth to people. And if God created man originally for the purpose of fellowship with him, as he says he did, it is fair to assume that God would create man with the capacity both to comprehend God's literal truth coming to him *ab extra* and in turn to respond verbally with no loss or distortion of the truth in the verbal interchange. This is simply to place language as to its origin and significance within the framework of the teaching of Scripture itself. The Scriptures teach that man is the crowning creation of God. As such, all of man's abilities are of divine origination. Specifically, the Scriptures assert in no uncertain terms that human language, far from having its origin in so-called primitive man's first grunts, is a gift from God. To Moses, who advanced his lack of eloquence as an excuse for refusing God's call, God responded: 'Who has made man's mouth? . . . Is it not I, the LORD?' (Exod. 4:11) Surely, God is the Source and Originator of language, and he created man in his own image in order that he and they might be able to speak literal truth to each other. And the Christian has good and ample reasons for believing that the Scriptures are a trustworthy record of at least a portion of that entire divine-human dialogue. The ministerial student can learn these reasons, if he does not already know them, at any number of orthodox seminaries that are available to him.

The unbeliever, of course, as we have already noted, is ready with his objections to the very idea of God speaking to humans. Even if he could, they have asked, is it not possible that those who first heard him misunderstood or misconstrued his message to them, and if so, how can one ever be sure that they did not misunderstand his word to them? Yes, theoretically they could have misunderstood his truth to them and thus have unintentionally misrepresented it to others. But that is precisely the reason that God the Holy Spirit 'carried [the prophets] along' as they spoke and superintended the writers of Holy Scripture as they permanently recorded his word to them – in order that they would record his word to them and to others without error (1 Cor 2:13; 2 Pet 1:20-21).

But what about us 'uninspired men', they ask? Does not the fact that we can misunderstand the Scriptures nullify any value that they might otherwise have as a vehicle for literal truth? After all, they point out, individuals, interpreting the same biblical passage, have come to opposite conclusions. In other words, they ask, even if the Bible were an inspired revelation from God to men, does not the fact that men interpret it so differently and can actually misunderstand it nullify its value as a vehicle for literal truth? What shall we say to these questions? Well, it is true that some men do argue that because the Bible can be misinterpreted, its value as a record of literal truth is nullified. For example, William Temple, Archbishop of Canterbury, thought so. In his *Nature, Man and God*, he declares that even if God had revealed himself in a verbal way (he personally believes that he did not), the value of this revelation as a verbal communication would be destroyed because of the possibility of man's misunderstanding its intent.[10] In other words, because men can misunderstand a verbal revelation, such a mode of revelation, Temple alleges, is valueless. But if Temple is correct, it can be pointed out, on this same principle the worth of his own book is vitiated: because it may be misunderstood, it too is valueless as a statement of literal truth. But apparently Temple did not believe that the possibility that men might misunderstand his book destroys its value. Otherwise, he would not have written it.

This should be sufficient as a response to Temple's allegation concerning the value of a verbal truth claim. But more can and must be said. While it true that men can and have misunderstood the Scriptures, sometimes even to their own destruction (2 Pet 3:16), it simply is not true that the Bible is a 'wax nose' that can be 'punched and shaped' to

---

10. William Temple, *Nature, Man and God* (London: Macmillan, 1934), 310-11.

mean anything that the interpreter wants it to mean. For example, the statement, 'God so loved the world that he gave his one and only Son that whoever believes in him shall not perish but have eternal life,' is clear and plain: the Son of God, the Father's gift of love to undeserving men, will save from eternal perdition and give eternal life to anyone who puts his trust in him. This verse does not and cannot be made to mean that Esar-hadon, King of Assyria, so loved the world that he gave his son for it, or that the world so loved God that it did something for him, or that trust in Jesus Christ will bring one to eternal perdition. The meaning of words and the laws of grammar and logic are too unflinchingly rigid to tolerate any such nonsense. And I feel quite sure that the person who would maintain that John 3:16 could indeed mean any or all of these things would not want his hermeneutical rules applied to his own words; otherwise, his words could be construed as supporting the idea of a literally true verbal revelation from God to man!

Now, of course, it is true that men can and do interpret the Scriptures differently – indeed, so differently at times that they have come to opposite conclusions regarding the meaning of a given Scripture statement. How do we explain this? And does this not destroy the value of the Holy Scriptures as God's written revelation to men? What shall we say about this? Well, we must be rational enough and courageous enough simply to declare that both interpretations cannot be right. They may both be wrong, but they cannot both be right. One interpretation, if not both, needs to be corrected by a rigid application of the canons of grammatical/historical hermeneutics, bearing always in mind the great '*analogy* of Scripture' principle that Scripture must interpret Scripture. This is what we as ministers must say. But the one thing that we must not say is that language cannot convey precise literal meaning from one mind to another and that therefore even contradictory interpretations may both be right! I will say more about this last point in the next chapter, but for now suffice it to say that, far from being incapable of expressing literal truth, language is not only the most capable vehicle by which literal truth may be communicated from one mind to another – it is the *only* vehicle for communicating literal truth to other minds. For truth can only be expressed propositionally, but propositions cannot be framed apart from language. It is as simple as this: deny to language the capacity to communicate literal truth and one rejects the only means of communicating literal truth from one mind to another. Any denial of this must assume linguistic form, as we have already had occasion to note, and in the end, of course, only self-destructs if it claims to be literally true.

I have one final comment to make in response to this second major objection. It is this: every theory that would endorse the idea that literal truth cannot be revealed or communicated propositionally from God to man because language *per se is* incapable of such, is ultimately an attack against Jesus Christ. For in the 'days of his flesh' Jesus Christ taught the multitudes, using the known language of Aramaic, claiming as he did so that he was imparting eternal truth (for example, John 8:26, 40). Consequently, the issue comes down finally to this: every denial of the possibility of a literally true verbal revelation from God to man strikes directly at Jesus Christ in his role as Prophet and Teacher, for he claimed to be the Deliverer of just such a revelation. And those who would be loyal to him must be willing to affirm not only that God can and has revealed himself but also that he has done so in propositional fashion – and in inscripturated fashion at the point of the Christian Scriptures.

This propositional or informational revelation the

preacher must make the *bedrock* of the instructional aspect of his ministry if he would have a teaching ministry approved of God, for it is only as he teaches and preaches truth originating from God himself that he can speak with authority and demand that his audience give heed to what he says.

How firm a foundation, ye saints of the Lord,
Is laid for your faith in his excellent Word!
What more can he say than to you he hath said,
To you who for refuge to Jesus have fled?

Chapter Two

The Need for a Rational Pulpit

In the first chapter I urged that language in general is capable of communicating absolute and literal truth from God to man, and that divine revelation in particular can be framed in non-existential, verbal or propositional terms. I suggested that the church has always held that it has good reason to believe that God did, in fact, speak in propositional terms to Moses and the prophets in Old Testament times and to the apostles and prophets during the apostolic age, inspiring men to commit to *inscripturated* form throughout this revelatory process that portion of his revealed will that he deemed essential to the ongoing spiritual health of his people. This inscripturated revelation the church claims it possesses in the inspired Hebrew/Christian Scriptures. I am assuming that every preacher and every ministerial candidate reading this book believes this as well. If my assumption is not unfounded, then I may also assume that every preacher and every ministerial candidate reading this book understand that it is from this inscripturated revelational material that the preacher of the gospel must derive his *theology,* that is, what he believes and teaches others to believe – about God's ways and works.

Now 'theology' by definition means '*rational* discourse about God'. But for a lot of reasons which we will not go into here, a large dose of the *irrational* has been introduced, not least from neo-orthodox influence, into theology today, even evangelical theology – with the result that real disdain is often heaped upon any and every effort to *systematize* the teaching of the Word of God. Whereas systematic theology used to be regarded as the 'queen of the sciences', today, as Gordon H. Clark comments, it 'hardly rises to the rank of a scullery maid'.[1]

To counteract this drift, even among Bible-believing preachers, away from rational discourse about God, in this chapter I want to analyse two commonly-held and oft-expressed opinions which reflect this drift. So important are right conclusions respecting these opinions that I do not hesitate to say that wrong conclusions here will vitiate all that the minister of the gospel, in his role as teacher, would propound as 'truth', and will ultimately dull, if not totally blunt, the 'cutting edge' of the entire Christian claim to a true knowledge of God. Indeed, if every minister of the gospel were consistently to hold wrong conclusions respecting these opinions, Christianity's inherent right, as the legitimate claimant to divine truth, to be heard by intelligent persons would be fatally compromised. I refer, first, to the question of the nature of the relationship between God's knowledge, on the one hand, and our knowledge of God derived from his written revelation to us on the other, and second, to the role which paradox should be granted in our systematic formulation of the truth derived from God's written revelation to us. To these issues then let us turn with minds submissive to the revelation which God has given to us, for only by such submission can we avoid the dire consequences just envisioned.

God's knowledge and man's knowledge never coincide at any single point.

With respect to the first of our present concerns, the issue more pointedly put is this: are the content of God's knowledge and the content of man's knowledge that is derived from Scripture ever the same? One can find many

1. Gordon H. Clark, *In Defense of Theology* (Milford: Mott Media, 1984), 3.

reputable and otherwise good theologians and ministers today who would insist that God's knowledge of a truth and man's knowledge of the same truth, acquired even from God's revelation to him, will never coincide at any single point. The relationship between these 'two contents' is said to be 'analogical' and not 'univocal'.

Definitions of these two terms are, of course, in order. By these terms is normally intended the precise meaning of a given predicate when applied to separate subjects. A given predicate applied to separate subjects *univocally* would intend that the subjects possess the predicate in a precisely *identical* sense. The opposite of univocism is *equivocism* which attaches a given predicate to separate subjects in a completely *different* or unrelated sense. Now between univocism and equivocism is *analogy*. A predicate employed analogically intends a relationship between separate subjects based upon a comparison or proportion, a relationship which is neither completely similar (univocism) nor completely dissimilar (equivocism) but partly the same, partly not the same. With these definitions before us, we are able to sharpen our earlier question this way: Are the content of God's knowledge and the content of man's knowledge that is gained from God's verbal revelation *univocal* (the same), *equivocal* (different), or *analogical* (partly alike, partly not alike)?

Thomas Aquinas (1224-74) was one of the first Christian theologians formally to deal with this issue in any significant way (see his *Summa Contra Gentiles,* XXXII–XXXIV). He was not the first, of course, to address the issue of the nature of knowledge and the functions and limits of language. Augustine (354-430), for example, had grappled with these issues in his treatise, *De Magistro,* and incidentally had come to radically different conclusions from those of Thomas. But in the latter's treatment Thomas declared that nothing can properly be predicated of God and man in a univocal sense. To do so and to say, for example, that God and man are both 'good' and to intend by 'good' the same meaning, was, for Thomas, to ignore the difference between the essences respectively of God the Creator (his existence is identical with his essence) and of man the creature (his existence and his essence are two different matters). But Thomas saw too that to intend an equivocal meaning for 'good' would lead to complete ambiguity and epistemological scepticism. Therefore, Thomas urged the way of proportionality or analogy as the *via media* between the Scylla and Charybdis of univocism and equivocism. In other words, the assertion, 'God and man are both good,' means analogically that man's goodness is proportional to man as God's goodness is proportional to God, but it also means that the goodness intended cannot be the same goodness in both cases. In sum, of this Thomas was certain: nothing can be predicated of God and man in the univocal sense. Rather, only analogical predication is properly possible when speaking of the relationship between them.

But now a problem arises, for what is it about any analogy which saves it from becoming a complete equivocism? Is it not the univocal element implicit within it? For example, if I assert that an analogy may be drawn between an apple and an orange, do I not intend to suggest that the apple and the orange, obviously different in some respects, are the same in at least one respect? Why, otherwise, would I be drawing attention to the relationship between them? While it is true that the one respect in which I perceive that they are similar will not be immediately apparent to anyone else without further explanation on my part, it should be clear nonetheless to everyone, if I assert that they are analogous one to the other, that I believe that in some sense a univocal feature exists between them – in this case, it may be that I have in mind that they are both fruit, or that they are both spherical, or that they both have extension in space or have mass. But whatever I intend, I at least intend to suggest that, for all their differences, they have at least something in common. The predicate indicates something that is equally true of both. What I am urging here is that the success of any analogy turns on the strength of the univocal element in it. Or as E. J. Carnell said in his *An Introduction to Christian Apologetics*, the basis for any analogy is non-analogical, that is, univocal.[2] Thomas' dilemma is that he wants to have his cake and eat it too. He wants to affirm the analogous relationship between God and man on the one hand, but he denies all univocal coincidence in predication respecting them on the other. But if he affirms the relationship between God and man to be truly analogous, he cannot consistently deny that in some sense a univocal element exists between them. Or if he denies all univocal coincidence in predication between God and man, he cannot continue to speak of the predicative relationship between them as one of analogy. As a matter of fact, Gordon H. Clark argued through the years that Thomas' doctrine of the *analogia entis* (analogy of being) between God and man is actually not analogical at all but really an equivocism. If Clark is correct, and I am persuaded that he is, Thomas' natural theology, which was grounded in his understanding of the *analogia entis*, is also defective, for he was, of necessity, working with two different meanings for the word 'existence' as that single predicate applies to God and to sensory data; thus his argument from the existence of sensory data to the existence of God commits the error of equivocating, that is, using a single word with two different meanings in the same argument.

---

2. E. J. Carnell, *An Introduction to Christian Apologetics* (Grand Rapids: Eerdmans, 1948), 147.

Having sensitized the reader to the particular problem inherent in any analogical predication which would deny a univocal element, I would now like to turn attention to our own time, for after all, we are people of the twenty-first century. How are *we* to respond to this issue? What should you and I say when asked about the relationship between the content of God's knowledge and the content of our human knowledge which is based upon (or derived from) God's verbal revelation to us? I propose that we address this matter by considering the pronouncements of Professor Cornelius Van Til of revered and recent memory. I was privileged to study under him and admire him greatly for his labours of over half a century to work out an apologetic methodology consistent with the Reformed faith.

Throughout his exposition of the Reformed faith and his corresponding explication of an apologetic method consistent with it, Van Til made it always his goal to be true to a single and initial *ontological* vision – the *distinction* between the Creator and the creature. Throughout his writings, striving always to remain consistent with his understanding of this single ontological distinction, again and again Van Til insists that man's knowledge is and can only be *analogical* to God's knowledge.[3] What this means for Van Til is the express rejection of any and all qualitative coincidence between the content of God's mind and the content of man's mind. That is to say, according to Van Til, not only is God's knowledge prior and necessary to man's knowledge which is always secondary and derivative knowledge if it is true knowledge (with this I am in total agreement), not only is God's knowledge self-validating whereas man's knowledge is dependent upon God's prior

---

3. See, for example, his *The Defense of the Faith* (Philadelphia: Presbyterian and Reformed, 1955), 56, 65, and his *Common Grace* (same publisher, 1954), 28.

self-validating knowledge for its justification (with this I am also in agreement), but also for Van Til this means that *man qualitatively knows nothing as God knows a thing.*

In his *An Introduction to Systematic Theology*, Van Til writes: 'All human predication is analogical reinterpretation of God's pre-interpretation. Thus the incomprehensibility of God must be taught with respect to *any* revelational proposition'.[4] In his 'Introduction' to Warfield's *The Inspiration and Authority of the Bible*, Van Til declares:

> When the Christian restates the content of Scriptural revelation in the form of a 'system' such a system is based upon and therefore analogous to the 'existential system' that God himself possesses. Being based upon God's revelation it is on the one hand, fully true and, on the other hand, at no point identical with the content of the divine mind.[5]

In a *Complaint* filed against the presbytery which voted to sustain Gordon Clark's ordination examination, to which Van Til affixed his name as a signatory, it was declared a 'tragic fact' that Clark's epistemology 'has led him to obliterate the qualitative distinction between the contents of the divine mind and the knowledge which is possible to the creature'.[6] The *Complaint* also affirmed: 'We dare not maintain that [God's] knowledge and our knowledge coincide *at any single point.*'[7] It is important to note here that it is not the way that God and man know a thing that the *Complaint* declares is different. Both the complainants and Clark agreed that God knows everything by eternal intuition whereas men

---

4. Cornelius Van Til, *An Introduction to Systematic Theology* (unpublished syllabus), 17, emphasis his.

5. B.B. Warfield, *The Inspiration and Authority of the Bible* (Philadelphia: Presbyterian and Reformed, 1948), 33.

6. *Minutes* of the Twelfth General Assembly of the Orthodox Presbyterian Church, 1945, 15.

7. *Minutes*, 14, emphasis original.

learn what they know (excluding certain innate ideas) discursively. Rather, insists Van Til and certain of his students, it is the *content* of man's knowledge that is qualitatively distinct from God's knowledge.

Because of his particular ontological vision Van Til insists that all verbal revelation coming from God to man (and this, of course, includes the Bible) will of necessity be 'anthropomorphic', that is, it must assume 'human form' in order to be understood at the level of creaturely finite comprehension. But Van Til is equally insistent that this divine self-revelation, by the Spirit's enabling illumination, can produce in men a 'true' knowledge of God, although their knowledge of him will be only 'analogical' to God's knowledge of himself. That is to say, their knowledge of God, although true, will never correspond to God's knowledge of himself at any single point! How Van Til can regard this 'never corresponds' knowledge as 'true' knowledge is, to say the least, a serious problem. Perhaps he means that the Creator is willing to regard as 'true' the knowledge that men derive from his self-revelation to them even though it is not univocal knowledge at any single point, because due to man's finiteness he had to pitch his revelation to men at the level of their creaturely finite comprehension. God's verbal revelation to men, in other words, since it is 'creature-oriented' (that is, 'analogical'), is not a univocal statement of his understanding of himself or of anything else and thus can never produce anything higher than a creaturely ('analogical') comprehension of God or of anything else. If this is what Van Til means, and I cannot think of another alternative, I fail to see how Van Til with his explicit rejection of the univocal element (see his 'corresponds at no 'single point') in man's so-called 'analogical' knowledge of God can rescue such knowledge from being in actuality a total equivocism and no true knowledge at all. Nor do I see how he can rescue God from the irrationality in regarding as true what in fact (if Van Til is correct) he knows all the while coincides at no single point with his own knowledge which is both true and the standard of truth.

Against all this, Clark contended more than once that Van Til's position leads to total human ignorance. Listen to Clark's own words:

> If God knows all truths and knows the correct meaning of every proposition, and if no proposition means to man what it means to God, so that God's knowledge and man's knowledge do not coincide at any single point, it follows by rigorous necessity that man can have no truth at all.[8]

He further argues:

> If God and man know, there must with the differences be at least one point of similarity; for if there were no point of similarity it would be inappropriate to use the one term *knowledge* in both cases.... If God has the truth and if man has only an analogy [this 'analogy' containing no univocal element], it follows that he (man) does not have the truth.[9]

Clark illustrates his point this way:

> If...we think that David was King of Israel, and God's thoughts are not ours, then it follows that God does not think David was King of Israel. David in God's mind was perchance prime minister of Babylon. To avoid this irrationality...we must insist that truth is the same for God and man. Naturally, we may not know the truth about some matters. But if we know anything at all, what we

---

8. Gordon H. Clark, 'Apologetics,' *Contemporary Evangelical Thought*, edited by Carl F. H. Henry (New York: Harper-Channel, 1957), 159.
9. Gordon H. Clark, 'The Bible as Truth,' *Bibliotheca Sacra* (April 1957), 163ff.

> know must be identical with what God knows. God knows the truth, and unless we know something God knows, our ideas are untrue. It is absolutely essential therefore to insist that there is an area of coincidence between God's mind and our mind. One example, as good as any, is the one already used, viz., David was King of Israel.[10]

Clark concludes:

> If God is omnipotent, he can tell men the plain, unvarnished, literal truth. He can tell them David was King of Israel, he can tell them he is omnipotent, he can tell them he created the world, and...he can tell them all this in positive, literal, non-analogical, non-symbolic terms.[11]

Of course, as far as the extent or quantity of their respective knowledge data is concerned, Clark readily acknowledged that God knows more and always will know more than man. This hardly even needs saying. But if we are to preserve for man any knowledge at all, Clark urged, we must insist that if God and man both truly know anything, then what they know must have some point of correspondence as far as the content of their knowledge is concerned. I wholeheartedly concur, and believe that Francis Schaeffer's dictum is right on target: men, Schaeffer says, may indeed have 'true though not exhaustive knowledge'.

At this point the reader may believe it appropriate to enlist the aid of a catena of biblical references that seems to support Van Til's contention that God's knowledge and man's knowledge are always and at every point qualitatively distinct. Van Til himself suggested that Deuteronomy 29:29, Job 11:78, Psalm 145:3, Isaiah 40:28, 55:8-9, Matthew 11:27, Luke 10:22, John 1:18, 6:46, Romans 11:33, and 1 Timothy

---

10. *The Philosophy of Gordon H. Clark,* edited by Ronald H. Nash (Philadelphia: Presbyterian and Reformed, 1968), 76-77.
11. *The Philosophy of Gordon H. Clark,* 78.

6:16 support his contention that with respect to any revelational proposition God still remains, even after the revelatory act, the incomprehensible God.[12] Of course, if these verses do teach this, then what is being asserted is that these verses are primarily concerned with an *epistemological* issue, specifically, that they affirm the *analogical* nature and limits of human knowledge of the incomprehensible God. I suggest, however, that a close examination of these verses will disclose that, while they do not deny the immeasurable wisdom and knowledge of God, they are primarily concerned with the *soteriological* issue, that is, they are underscoring man's need of propositional revelation if he is savingly to know God, a saving knowledge which *can* be gained by men, but *only* in the redemptive/revelatory complex made possible by God for sinful, needy man. Job 11:78, Psalm 145:3, Isaiah 40:28, Romans 11:33, and 1 Timothy 6:16, while certainly affirming the infinity of God, need simply mean that men, beginning with themselves and refusing the benefit of divine revelation, cannot, as Paul so forcefully declares in 1 Corinthians 1:21, come to God through their own wisdom, or said somewhat differently, that men will always be dependent upon divine informational revelation for a true and saving knowledge of God. Franz Delitzsch captures the essence of the intention of these verses when he comments on Psalm 145:3:

> ...of [Yahweh's] 'greatness' . . . there is no searching out, *i.e.* it is so abysmally deep that no searching can reach its bottom (as in Isa. xl. 28, Job xi. 7 sq.). *It has, however, been revealed,* and is being revealed continually, and is for this very reason thus celebrated in ver. 4.[13]

---

12. *Minutes* of the Twelfth General Assembly of the Orthodox Presbyterian Church, 1945, 12.

13. Franz Delitzsch, *Biblical Commentary on the Psalms,* III, 389, emphasis supplied.

As for Deuteronomy 29:29, Matthew 11:27, Luke 10:22, and John 1:18, 6:46 (see verse 45), these verses actually teach that men can know God and his thoughts truly to the degree that he reveals himself in his spoken word. Finally, Isaiah 55:8-9, far from depicting 'the gulf which separates the divine knowledge from human knowledge',[14] actually holds out the real possibility that men may know God's thoughts and urges them to turn away from their own thoughts and to learn God's thoughts from him. Consider carefully the context: in verse 7 God calls upon the wicked man to forsake his way and thoughts. Where is he to turn? To the Lord, of course (vv. 6-7). Why should he forsake his way and thoughts? 'Because,' says the Lord, 'my thoughts are not your thoughts, neither are your ways my ways' (v. 8). The entire context, far from affirming that God's ways and thoughts are beyond the capacity of men to know, to the contrary, expressly calls upon the wicked man to turn away from his ways and thoughts and instead to seek God's ways and thoughts. In doing so, the wicked man gains ways and thoughts which, just as the heavens transcend the earth, transcend his own. These verses in Isaiah 55 teach then the very opposite of what they are often thought to teach. Far from teaching that an unbridgeable gulf exists between God's thoughts and our thoughts, they actually call upon the wicked man, in repentance and humility, *to seek and to think God's thoughts after him.* Again, Franz Delitzsch, in my opinion, rightly interprets these verses:

> The appeal, to leave their own way and their own thoughts, and yield themselves to God the Redeemer, and to his word, is...urged on the ground of the heaven-wide difference between the ways and thoughts of this God and the despairing thoughts of men (Ch. xl. 27, xlix. 24), and their aimless labyrinthine ways.... On what side the heaven-wide elevation is to be seen, is shown by what

14. *Minutes* of the Twelfth General Assembly of the Orthodox Presbyterian Church, 1945, 12.

> follows. [God's thoughts] are not so fickle, so unreliable, or so powerless.[15]

My analysis of these verses of necessity has been brief, but the reader may be assured that none of these verses teaches that man's knowledge of God can be only at best 'analogical', in the Van Tilian sense, to God's knowledge. To the contrary, some of them expressly declare that in dependence upon God's propositional self-revelation in Scripture, men can know some of God's thoughts truly, that is, univocally (though of course not exhaustively), that is, that they can know a revealed proposition in the same sense that God knows it and has revealed it.

None of this is intended to suggest that there are no non-literal figures of speech in Scripture. Of course there are. The Bible is filled, for example, with metaphorical terms. But metaphors have literal meanings, and once the appropriate canons of grammatical/historical hermeneutics have determined the precise literal meaning of a metaphor, I would insist that its meaning is precisely the same for God and for man.

The preacher of God's Word should, as should all Christians, be overwhelmed by the magnitude of this simple truth that we take so much for granted: *The eternal God has deigned to share with us some of the truths that are on his mind. Poor undeserving men such as we he condescends to elevate by actually sharing with us a portion of what he knows.* What an exalted calling then is God's call to chosen men to serve him as his earthly flock's pastor/teachers. It is their privilege to communicate, not their own, but God's divine thoughts which alone can deliver men from their fickle, labyrinthine, powerless thoughts and ways. Men *can* know God's mind to the degree that he has revealed

---

15. Franz Delitzsch, *Commentary on Isaiah*, II, 358.

it propositionally to them in Scripture. Accordingly, since the Scriptures require that saving faith be grounded in *true knowledge* (see Rom 10:13-14), the church must vigorously oppose any linguistic or revelational theory, however well-intended, which would take from men the only ground of their knowledge of God and, accordingly, their only hope of salvation. Against the theory of human knowledge that would deny to it the possibility of univocal correspondence at any point with God's mind as to content, I would urge that we come down on the side of Christian reason and work with a theory of knowledge that insists upon the possibility of at least some identity between the content of God's knowledge and the content of man's knowledge.

Christian truth will often, if not always, be paradoxical in appearance.

Now I want to turn the reader's attention to the second major issue to be considered in this chapter, namely, the place which we should assign to paradox in systematic theological formulation. I wish to begin by stating that I take for granted that the Christian reader wholeheartedly believes (1) that God is rational, that is, that God is logical, that he thinks and speaks in a way that reflects the so-called 'laws' of logic – the law of identity (A is A), the law of non-contradiction (A is not non-A), and the law of excluded middle (A is either A or non-A) – just as all other rational minds do, (2) that his knowledge is self-consistent, and (3) that he cannot lie (Tit. 1:2; Heb. 6:18). Accordingly, just because God is rational, self-consistent, and always and necessarily truthful, I would insist that we should assume that his inscripturated propositional revelation to us – the Holy Scriptures – is of necessity also rational, self-consistent, and true. (In the light of our just concluded discussion, I would even insist that the truth which God's revelation intends to convey to us is, in addition, *univocal* truth.) That this view of Holy Scripture is a common Christian conviction is borne out, I would suggest, in the consentient willingness by Christians everywhere to affirm that there are no contradictions in Scripture. The church, on a wide scale, has properly seen that the rational character of the one living and true God would of necessity have to be reflected in any propositional self-revelation which he determined to give to men, and accordingly has confessed the entire truthfulness (inerrancy) and non-contradictory character of the Word of God.

Now while the evangelical church – that large portion of Protestant Christendom which believes that the Bible is the Word of God – everywhere and unhesitatingly confesses this, not all of its theologians and preachers have endorsed this conviction. While many Bible-believing theologians and preachers *unwittingly* do so, many other Bible-believing theologians and preachers *self-consciously* affirm that the Scriptures, even when correctly interpreted, will represent their truths to the human existent – even the *believing* human existent – in paradoxical terms, that is, in terms which (so it is said), while not *actually* contradictory, are nevertheless not only *apparently* contradictory but also *cannot possibly be reconciled before the bar of human reason.* It is commonly declared, for example, that the doctrines of the Trinity, the person of Christ, God's sovereignty and human responsibility, unconditional election and the sincere offer of the gospel, and particular redemption and the universal offer of the gospel are all biblical paradoxes – each advancing antithetical truths which are unmistakably taught in the Word of God but which cannot possibly be reconciled before the bar of human reason.[16]

---

16. See George W. Marston, *The Voice of Authority* (Philadelphia: Presbyterian and Reformed, 1960), 16, 17, 21, 70, 78, 87.

James I. Packer affirms the presence of such paradoxes in Scripture in his *Evangelism and the Sovereignty of God*, although he prefers the term 'antinomy' to 'paradox':

> ...we have to deal with...antinomy in the biblical revelation.... What is an antinomy? ...an antinomy – in theology, at any rate – is...not a real contradiction, though it looks like one. It is an *apparent* incompatibility between two apparent truths. An antinomy exists when a pair of principles stand side by side, seemingly irreconcilable, yet both undeniable.... [An antinomy] is insoluble.... What should one do, then, with an antinomy? Accept it for what it is, and learn to live with it. Refuse to regard the apparent contradiction as real....[17]

Van Til even declares that, because man's knowledge is 'only analogical' to God's knowledge, *all Christian truth will finally be paradoxical*, that is, all Christian truth will ultimately appear to be contradictory to the human existent. Ponder his exact words:

> A word must...be said about the question of antinomies.... They are involved in the fact that human knowledge can never be completely comprehensive knowledge. Every knowledge transaction has in it somewhere a reference point to God. Now since God is not fully comprehensible to us *we are bound to come into what seems to be contradictions in all our knowledge. Our knowledge is analogical and therefore must be paradoxical.*[18]
>
> I have contended that we must think more concretely and analogically.... *All the truths of the Christian religion have of necessity the appearance of being contradictory.... We do not*

---

17. James I. Packer, *Evangelism and the Sovereignty of God* (Chicago: Inter-Varsity Press, 1961), 18-25.
18. Cornelius Van Til, *The Defense of the Faith* (Philadelphia: Presbyterian and Reformed, 1955), 61, emphasis supplied.

> *fear to accept that which has the appearance of being contradictory*.... In the case of common grace, as in the case of every other biblical doctrine, we should seek to take all the factors of Scripture teaching and bind them together into systematic relations with one another as far as we can. But *we do not expect to have a logically deducible relationship between one doctrine and another.* We expect to have only an *analogical* system.[19]

What should one say respecting this oft-repeated notion that the Bible will often (always, according to Van Til) set forth its (unmistakably taught) truths in irreconcilable terms? To say the least, one must conclude, if such is the case, that it condemns at the outset as futile even the *attempt* at *systematic* (orderly) theology that Van Til calls for in the last source cited, since it is impossible to reduce to a system irreconcilable paradoxes which steadfastly resist all attempts at harmonious systematization. One must be content simply to live theologically with a series of 'discontinuities'.

Now if nothing more could or were to be said, this is already problematical enough because of the implications such a construction carries regarding the nature of biblical truth. But more can and must be said.

First, the proffered definition of 'paradox' (or antinomy) as two truths which are both unmistakably taught in the Word of God but which also cannot possibly be reconciled before the bar of human reason is itself inherently problematical, for the one who so defines the term is suggesting by implication that either he knows by means of an omniscience that is not normally in the possession of men that no man is capable of reconciling the truths in question or he has somehow universally polled every man who has ever lived, is living now, and will live in the future and has discovered

---

19. Cornelius Van Til, *Common Grace and the Gospel* (Philadelphia: Presbyterian and Reformed, 1973), 165-66, emphasis supplied.

that not one has been able, is able, or will be able to reconcile the truths. But it goes without saying that neither of these conditions is or can be true for any man. Therefore, the very assertion that there are paradoxes, so defined, in Scripture is seriously flawed by the terms of the definition itself. There is no way for any man to know if such a phenomenon is present in Scripture. Merely because any number of scholars have failed to reconcile to their satisfaction two given truths of Scripture is no proof that the truths cannot be harmonized before the bar of human reason. And if just one scholar *claims* to have reconciled the truths to his own satisfaction, his claim *ipso facto* renders the definition both gratuitous and suspect.

Second, while those who espouse the presence in Scripture of paradoxes are solicitous to point out that these paradoxes are only *apparent* and *not* actual contradictions, they seem to be oblivious to the fact that, if actually non-contradictory truths can *appear* as contradictories and if no amount of study or reflection can remove the contradiction, there is no available means to distinguish between this 'apparent' contradiction and a real contradiction. Since both would appear *to the human existent* in precisely the same form – contradictories – and since neither will yield up its contradiction to study and reflection, how does the human existent know for certain that he is embracing only a seeming contradiction and not a real contradiction?

Third, and if the former two difficulties were not enough, this last point, only rarely recognized, should deliver the *coup de grace* to the entire notion that irreconcilable (only 'apparent,' of course) contradictions exist in Scripture: once one asserts that truth may legitimately assume the form of an irreconcilable contradiction, *he has given up all possibility of ever detecting a real falsehood.* Every time he rejects a proposition as false because it 'contradicts' the teaching of Scripture or because it is in some other way illogical, the proposition's sponsor only needs to contend that it only *appears* to contradict Scripture or to be illogical, and that his proposition is one of the terms (the Scripture may provide the other) of one more of those paradoxes which we have acknowledged have a legitimate place in our 'little systems', to borrow a phrase from Tennyson. But this means both the end of Christianity's uniqueness as the revealed religion of God since it is then liable to – nay, more than this, it *must* be open to – the assimilation of any and every truth claim of whatever kind, and the death of all rational faith.

Now it begs the question to respond to this crisis in truth detection by insisting that in this situation one must simply believe what the Bible says about these other claims to truth and reject those that contradict the Bible, if one has already conceded that the Bible itself can and does teach that truths may come to the human existent in paradoxical terms, that is, in irreconcilable contradictory terms. Why should either proposition of the 'declared' contradiction be preferred to the other when applying Scripture to a contradicting truth claim? Why not simply live with one more unresolved antithesis? The only solution to this madness is to deny to paradox, if understood as an *irreconcilable* contradiction, a legitimate place in a Christian theory of truth, recognizing it for what it is – the offspring of an irrational age. If *there is to be an offence to men in Christianity's truth claims, it should be the ethical implications of the cross of Christ and not the irrationality of contradictories proclaimed to men as being both true.*

By nothing said thus far have I intended to deny that the living God, upon occasion, employed paradoxes (understood as apparent but *reconcilable* contradictories) in his spoken

Word to man. But he did so for the same reason that men employ them – as a literary device to invigorate the thought being expressed, to awaken interest, to intrigue, to challenge the intellect, and to shock and frustrate the lazy mind. But I reject the notion that any of God's truth to men will always appear to the human existent as contradictory. Specifically, I reject the notion that the cardinal doctrines of the faith – the Trinity, the person of Christ, the doctrines of grace – when proclaimed aright to men must be proclaimed as contradictory constructs. What a travesty – to perpetrate the notion that the great and precious doctrines which are central and vital to Christian faith and life are all, at heart, a veritable nest of irreconcilable 'discontinuities'!

Now I readily concede that it is possible for an erring exegete so to interpret two statements of Scripture that he *thinks* that they teach contradictory propositions. But I totally reject the idea that he will have interpreted the statements correctly. Either he misinterpreted one statement (maybe both) or he tried to relate two statements, given their specific contexts, which were never intended to be related to one another. To affirm otherwise, that is, to affirm that Scripture statements, when properly interpreted, can teach that which for the human existent is both irreconcilably contradictory and yet still true, is to make Christianity and the propositional revelation upon which it is based for its teachings irrational, and strikes at the rational nature of the God who speaks throughout its pages. God is Truth itself, Christ is the Logos of God, neither can lie, what they say is self-consistent and noncontradictory, and none of this is altered in the revelatory process. It does the cause of Christ no good, indeed, only positive harm results, when the core teachings of Scripture are portrayed by Christ's friends, not only to the non-believing mind but even to the Christian mind, as at heart a 'precious list of contradictories'.

But what about the examples cited earlier? What about the Trinity? Does not the classical doctrine of the Trinity present, if not a real contradiction, at least an apparent one? In order to illustrate how the systematician should go about his work, while my answer here must be somewhat brief, I will run the risk of oversimplification for the sake of showing why the widely-touted, so-called paradox of the Trinity – namely, that three equals one and one equals three – is in fact not one at all. Let it be said unequivocally at the outset, if the numerical adjectives 'one' and 'three' are intended to describe in both cases the same noun so that the theologian or preacher intends to say that one God equals three Gods and three Gods equal one God (or one person equals three persons and three persons equal one person) in the same way that one might say that one apple equals three apples and three apples equal one apple, that this is not an *apparent* contradiction. This is a *real* contradiction which not even God can resolve! But of course, this is not what the church teaches by its doctrine of the Trinity, although this representation is what is advanced all too often not only by lay people but by certain theologians who should know better. No orthodox creed has ever so represented the doctrine as far as I have been able to discern. In fact, it is apparent to me that all of the historic creeds of the church have been exceedingly jealous to avoid the very appearance of contradiction here by employing one noun – 'God' or 'Godhead' – with the numeral 'one' and another noun – 'persons' – with the numeral three. The church has never taught that three Gods are one God or that one person is three persons but rather that 'in the unity of the Godhead there are three persons' (*Westminster Confession of Faith,* II. iii), the Father, the Son, and the Holy Spirit, and that while each is wholly divine, no one person totally comprehends all that the Godhead is hypostatically. I grant that some of the factors which insure the unity of the Godhead may be unknown to us. But I would insist that when the Bible refers to the Father or the Son or the Holy Spirit, it intends that we think of persons or distinct centres of self-consciousness within the Godhead, whereas when it employs the imprecise and flexible title 'God', it refers either to the Godhead construed in its unitary wholeness (for example, Genesis 1:26) or to one of the persons of the Godhead, specifically which one to be determined by the context (for example, 'God' in Romans 8:28 refers to the Father; 'God' in Romans 9:5 refers to the Son). Thus construed, the doctrine of the Trinity does not confront us with even an apparent contradiction, much less a real one. The triune God is complex but not a contradiction!

Similarly, the Christian church has never creedally declared that Christ is one person and also two persons or one nature and also two natures. Rather, the church has declared that the Lord Jesus Christ, 'being the eternal Son of God, became man, and so was and continues to be God and man, *in two distinct natures and one person* forever' *(Westminster Shorter Catechism,* Question 21, emphasis supplied). The person of Christ as well is complex but he is not a contradiction!

In this chapter I have not been urging a Cartesian rationalism which presupposes the autonomy of human reason and freedom from divine revelation, a rationalism which asserts that it must begin with itself in the build-up of knowledge. But make no mistake about it – I am calling here for a *Christian* rationalism which forthrightly affirms that the divine revelation which it gladly owns and makes the bedrock of all its intellectual efforts is internally self-consistent, that is, non-contradictory. And I urge the preacher and the ministerial candidate reading these words to strive for nothing less than the same consistency in both their theological formulations and their preaching deduced from that revelation. This will mean careful reflection and a doggedness in their labours as students of the Word of God as they seek to understand the individual truths of revelation and to harmonize these truths into a systematic whole. But this labour, admittedly difficult, is infinitely to be preferred to the suggestion of all too many theologians and preachers that we must assume that the Scriptures will necessarily contain unresolvable paradoxes. Not to set before oneself the goal of quarrying from Scripture a *rational* theology is to sound the death knell, not only to systematic theology, but also to all theology that would commend itself to men as the truth of the one living and true God.

Most perfect is the law of God,
  restoring those that stray;
His testimony is most sure,
  proclaiming wisdom's way.

The precepts of the Lord are right;
  with joy they fill the heart;
The Lord's commandments all are pure,
  and clearest light impart.

The fear of God is undefiled
  and ever shall endure;
The statutes of the Lord are truth
  and righteousness most pure.

Chapter Three

The Need for a God-Centered Pulpit

Every preacher will have either a God-centered or a man-centered theology. Of course, if the Bible is given its due, his theology will be God-centered, and the gospel he preaches will uphold the sovereign grace of God in all its purity. He will reject every suggestion that men originate anything ultimately determinative for their salvation. He will have discovered from his training and study that, according to Scripture, the chief end of God is to glorify and to enjoy himself forever, and that the chief end of man accordingly is also to glorify God and to enjoy him forever. He will have learned from Scripture that God loves himself with all his heart, soul, mind, and strength, that he himself is at the centre of his affections, that the impulse that drives him and the thing he pursues in everything he does is his own glory! The instructed preacher will know that God created all things *for his own glory* (Isa 43:7, 21), that he chose Israel *for his renown and praise and honour* (Jer 13:11), that it was *for his name's sake and to make his mighty power known* that he delivered his ancient people again and again after they had rebelled against him (Ps 106:7-8), and that it was *for the sake of his name* that he did not reject them (1 Sam 12:20-22), spared them again and again (Ezek 20:9,14, 22, 44), and had mercy upon them and did not pursue them with destruction to the uttermost (Isa 48:8-11). He will have learned from Scripture that it was *for his own glory* that God did all these things (Ezek 36:16-21, 22-23, 24-32). He will know too that Jesus came the first time *to glorify* God (John 17:4, 6), that every detail of the salvation which he enjoys God arranged in order to provoke in him *the praise of his glorious grace* (Eph 1:6, 12, 14), and that Jesus is coming again '*to be glorified* in his saints on that day, and *to be marvelled at* among all who have believed' (2 Thess 1:9-10).

Recognizing in the earthly *execution* of his divine plan the centrality of God's determination to glorify himself in all that he does, the biblically-taught preacher, standing in the tradition of Paul, Augustine, and the great Reformers of the sixteenth century, will not hesitate also to declare that that same determination – to *glorify himself* – is central to God's eternal plan. Accordingly, he will not hesitate to declare, in the words of the *Westminster Confession of Faith,* that 'God from all eternity did, *by the most wise and holy counsel of his own will,* freely and unchangeably ordain whatsoever comes to pass' (III.i, emphasis supplied), and that 'by the decree of God, *for the manifestation of his own glory,* some men and angels are predestinated unto everlasting life, and others foreordained to everlasting death' (III.iii, emphasis supplied) – surely, without controversy, one of the 'deeps' of the divine wisdom.

Concerning those of mankind in the group predestinated unto life, the biblical preacher will *gladly* proclaim that 'God, before the foundation of the world was laid, *according to his eternal and immutable purpose, and the secret counsel and good pleasure of his will,* hath chosen in Christ, unto everlasting glory, *out of his mere free grace and love,* without any foresight of faith or good works, or perseverance in either of them, or any other thing in the creature, as conditions, or causes moving him thereunto; and *all to the praise of his glorious grace*' (III.v).

Concerning 'the rest of mankind', the preacher faithful to God's Word will *solemnly* teach that 'God was pleased, *according to the unsearchable counsel of his own will,* whereby he extendeth or withholdeth mercy as he pleaseth, *for the glory of his sovereign power over his creatures,* to pass by; and to ordain them to dishonour and wrath for their sin, *to the praise of his glorious justice*' (III.vii).

Of course, these two groups making up the totality of mankind, he will teach, do not arrive at their divinely-determined destinies arbitrarily with no interest on God's part in what they would believe or how they would live before they got there, for he is aware that 'as God hath appointed the elect unto glory, so hath he, by the eternal and most free purpose of his will, *foreordained all the means thereunto*' (lll.vi), such as the Son's atoning work, his own effectual calling of the elect, the Spirit's regenerating work by which faith and repentance are wrought in the human heart, and justification and sanctification.

And he is aware that while it is certain that God's determination to pass by the rest of mankind (the doctrine of preterition) is grounded solely in the unsearchable counsel of his own will, he is aware that it is equally certain that God's determination to ordain those whom he passed by to dishonour and wrath (the doctrine of condemnation) took into account the human condition which alone deserves his wrath – the fact of their sinful ways.

This eternal purpose (Eph 3:11), the biblical preacher will proclaim, God began to initiate by his work of creation. He will also teach that, since the creation of the world to this very moment, God has continued to execute his purpose to bring glory to himself through the providential exercise of his almighty power, unsearchable wisdom, and infinite goodness, his providence extending itself to all his creatures and all their actions; 'even to the first fall, and all other sins of angels and men, and that not by a bare permission, but such [permission] as hath joined with it a most wise and powerful bounding, and otherwise ordering and governing of them, in a manifold dispensation, *to his own holy ends*' (V.iv). Adam's sin, he will teach, 'God was pleased, according to his wise and holy counsel [which counsel occurred before the foundation of the world], to permit, *having purposed to order it to his own glory*' (VI.i).

By his sin Adam fell from his original state of integrity and so 'became dead in sin, and wholly defiled in all the parts and faculties of soul and body' (VI.ii). And the biblical preacher will declare that, because Adam was the covenantal (federal) representative head of his race by divine arrangement, his first sin was imputed (and his corruption thereafter was conveyed) to all mankind descending from him by ordinary generation (VI.iii). Accordingly, all mankind (with the sole exception of Christ who did not descend from Adam by *ordinary* generation), the biblical preacher will insist, God regards as sinners in Adam. And because of both their position in Adam and their own sin and corruption all men are continually falling short of the glory of God (Rom 3:23) and are under his sentence of death. But in accordance with his elective purpose, the biblical preacher with great delight will also proclaim, God is pleased to save the elect by Christ's atoning death in their behalf and in their stead, and by his Spirit's application of the benefits of Christ's redeeming virtues to them. And though the elect do assuredly believe in Christ to the saving of their souls, yet they contribute nothing *ultimately* determinative of that salvation. Salvation from beginning to end belongs ultimately and wholly to the Lord, *to the praise of his glorious grace.* All of these articles of faith the biblical preacher will hold to be true to the teachings of Holy Scripture. He will, in short, espouse the Reformed Faith.

'If this is the case, men are neither free nor responsible agents.'

Opponents of the Reformed Faith, both within and without the church, insist that if all of this is true, a horrible and insoluble problem emerges. Specifically, if God himself has foreordained whatever comes to pass, the only logical conclusion that one may draw is that men are not really free; and if men are not really free when they are faced with incompatible courses of action but are divinely determined to make the choices they do, then their sinful choices must ultimately be traced to God. And if this is so, how can God escape the charge of being the 'author of sin', and how can he justly hold men responsible for their unbelief and disobedience?

Arminian theologians generally have argued that this problem alone ought to be sufficient to show the unbiblical character of Reformed thinking. J. Kenneth Grider, citing Arminius, argues that Reformed thinking in these regards is 'repugnant to God's wise, just, and good nature, and to man's free nature' and 'makes God "the author of sin".'[1] In his bibliography Grider commends to the reader a widely acclaimed volume of essays, edited by Clark Pinnock, entitled *Grace Unlimited*,[2] which espouses the Arminian theology. Pinnock himself is convinced that God cannot justly hold men responsible for their sins under such conditions as those described by Reformed preachers. He presents a sustained rejection of any form of predestination which infringes on human freedom in the chapter he contributed to the volume, entitled 'Responsible Freedom and the Flow of Biblical History'.

---

1. J. Kenneth Grider, 'Arminianism,' *Evangelical Dictionary of Theology* (Grand Rapids: Baker, 1984), 79-81.
2. Clark Pinnock (ed.), *Grace Unlimited* (Minneapolis: Bethany Fellowship, 1975).

Pinnock's thesis

Repudiating by name the insights of such notable Reformed scholars as Loraine Boettner, J. I. Packer, and John Gerstner, Pinnock marshals alongside of his own interpretation of the scriptural data in support of his position the opinions of Mortimer J. Adler, Gordon D. Kaufman, Walther Eichrodt, Antony Flew, Karl Barth, and Karl Rahner, none of whom unfortunately are even evangelical, not to mention Arminian, in their doctrinal outlook. (This fact alone ought to make his reader somewhat wary of Pinnock's conclusion.) But supported by such men, Pinnock maintains throughout his chapter that men are free moral agents undetermined by the divine will. He regards human freedom to be 'one of the deepest of all human intuitions' and a 'fundamental self-perception'. He states that 'universal man almost without exception talks and feels as if he were free', and furthermore that 'human freedom is the precondition of moral and intellectual responsibility'.[3] Pinnock is persuaded that 'when a theory comes along, whether philosophical, theological, or psychological, which endeavors to deny this intuition of freedom, it is up against a basic human self-perception that will eventually overwhelm it'.[4]

His proposal

In order to have the real picture of God's dealings with the human race 'borne home to us in a fresh way', Pinnock proposes that we 'retell the biblical story and allow it to create its own impression upon us'.[5] When we do this, all determinism, fatalism, and what Pinnock (following Kaufman) calls 'blueprint-predestination' will 'fall away' and 'the clear biblical witness to significant human freedom' will impress itself upon us.[6]

---

3. Pinnock, *Grace Unlimited*, 95.
4. Pinnock, *Grace Unlimited*, 96.
5. Pinnock, *Grace Unlimited*, 97.
6. Pinnock, *Grace Unlimited*, 97.

Now as incredible as it may seem it is nonetheless true that Pinnock's 'retelling the biblical story' fails to include any references at all to the numerous didactic passages of Scripture where divine predestination in general and divine sovereignty in salvation in particular are clearly taught in so many words. Rather, he restricts his exposition of Scripture to Genesis 1–12, and more specifically only to a brief consideration of four themes he finds therein: (1) the creation of man, (2) Adam's fall, (3) what he calls 'the cycle of cumulative degeneration' which pervaded mankind after Adam's fall, and (4) God's 'counteractive grace'.

His treatment of the four themes

With respect to the first theme he thinks is relevant – man's creation, Pinnock is certain, because of man's image-bearing character, that man 'has been made...capable...of self-determination', and that man as *imago Dei* is a 'creature who through the exercise of his freedom would be able to shape his own future'. According to Pinnock, Genesis portrays Adam as 'enjoying free will in the fullest sense, acting without any coercion'.[7]

The entrance of sin into mankind – Pinnock's second theme – resulted when Adam misused his divinely-given freedom. By his wilful rebellion, writes Pinnock, Adam 'vetoed God's will' and contravened God's purpose for him. In no sense, Pinnock insists, can one suggest that God predestinated man's fall without blaspheming God. To the contrary, Pinnock asserts that Adam's fall sprang wholly from his own free choice to disobey God. *In no sense* was man's rebellion against God the result of God's sovereign will.[8]

The question now arises, did Adam's sin in any way affect his descendants? Certainly not in, any biological or legal

7. Pinnock, *Grace Unlimited*, 98. 8. Pinnock, *Grace Unlimited*, 100-2.

sense, writes Pinnock. The 'cumulative degeneration' following upon Adam's sin – Pinnock's third theme – he explains as the result of the 'warped social situation' which now confronts every man with the temptation to misuse his freedom and which invariably perverts all men. According to Pinnock, this is the *only* construction of the doctrine of original sin which the Bible will tolerate.[9]

Into the arena of man's 'cumulative degeneration,' the result solely of man's misuse of his moral freedom, God injects his overtures of 'counteractive grace' (illustrated by God's call of Abraham in Genesis 12) as his response to man's misuse of his freedom.[10] Elucidating his view of God's gracious activity, Pinnock declares that God does not have a secret plan 'according to which he only desires to save some'.[11] Rather, he wills the salvation of all, and 'it was for the whole world that [Christ] was delivered up'.[12] However, God's will is not always done, Pinnock continues, because he will not force his grace upon any man. Hence, 'people perish because they reject God's plan for them...and *for no other reason.*'[13] Pinnock considers it blasphemy to assert that man's rebellion against God is '*in any sense* the product of God's sovereign will or primary causation'.[14]

This then is the theological construction advanced by Pinnock to explain the presence of human sin and to ground the basis upon which God may justly hold men responsible for their transgressions against his holy laws. By way of summary, Pinnock urges that God has created men with free wills and hence with the power to choose with equal ease between incompatible courses of action. God also determined to permit them to choose the way of death if

---

9. Pinnock, *Grace Unlimited*, 104-5. 10. Pinnock, *Grace Unlimited*, 107.
11. Pinnock, *Grace Unlimited*, 105. 12. Pinnock, *Grace Unlimited*, 106.
13. Pinnock, *Grace Unlimited*, 106, emphasis supplied.
14. Pinnock, *Grace Unlimited*, 102, emphasis original.

they so desire. Of course, he urges men to choose life and is delighted when some do so, but the decision is wholly theirs. Therefore, when men do disobey him, concludes Pinnock, God may justly hold them responsible for their sin.

While every Arminian will not agree with every detail of Pinnock's exposition, it is still true that the conclusions he draws reflects the classic Arminian position which uniformly grounds human responsibility in *freedom* to sin on man's side and *permission* to sin on God's side. It is important that the reader clearly see that these two tenets form the heart of the Arminian doctrine of human responsibility.

Clearly, the Reformed position (popularly called Calvinism) and Arminianism are antithetical visions of God's relationship to human actions and cannot both be correct. The former traces all things ultimately to God (hence we speak of a 'God-centered' theology); the latter relates God to human actions only in a 'permissional' way, every choice for or against Christ ultimately springing from the 'free' human will (hence we speak of a 'man-centered' theology). Which position does the Bible endorse?

Pinnock's solution is both unbiblical and irrelevant. From several different perspectives Pinnock's position (and Arminianism to the degree that Pinnock accurately reflects it) is markedly unbiblical and therefore untrustworthy. I am not suggesting, of course, that Pinnock intentionally sets out to mislead. One cannot read his contribution to the volume without being moved by the fervour and conviction with which he writes. His passionate concern to teach truth is obvious in every paragraph. And one can only admire the tenacious way in which he rigidly applies the law of non-contradiction when he writes:

> It is surely a real contradiction...to assert (1) that God determines all events, and (2) that man is free to accept or reject his will. Fortunately Scripture does not require us to attempt logical gymnastics of this kind. It does not teach that God 'determines' all things.[14]

He also correctly attacks the oft-heard evangelical pronouncement that God's sovereignty and man's freedom, both said to be equally true, simply present us with a 'paradox' or 'antinomy'.[15] It is regrettable that some Reformed thinkers have not perceived as clearly as Pinnock that these propositions comprise a *real* contradiction and not just an *apparent* contradiction which God demands that we believe to be true. As we saw in the last chapter, it does a man little good to be informed that this contradiction is only apparent and not real (how his informant is able to distinguish between the two is not at all clear) since it is still a contradiction which he is told he must believe. And once he believes that contradictories can both be true at the same time, he can never detect a real falsehood. These observations by Pinnock are on the plus side. So I say again, I am not questioning at all Pinnock's sincerity or his conviction that he writes from the standpoint of biblical truth. I simply believe that Pinnock is wrong – drastically so – in his understanding of what the Bible teaches concerning the significant issues which he attempts to analyse in his chapter in *Grace Unlimited*. The following critical evaluation will demonstrate why it is that Pinnock's construction totally fails as a truly Christian understanding of God's relation to human events.

---

14. Pinnock, *Grace Unlimited*, 109, fn. 17.
15. Pinnock, *Grace Unlimited*, 101.

His failure to solve the basic problem

As we have seen, Pinnock believes, with Arminian thought in general, that unless one postulates on God's part a *laissez-faire* posture toward man's choices and actions and on man's part the complete freedom to choose one from two or more incompatible courses of action God becomes the responsible cause of sin and thus renders himself incapable – at least in justice – to call men to account for their sins.

Pinnock's construction, however, assuming its correctness for the sake of argument, does not accomplish what it claims to do, namely, distance God from all involvement in man's choices. This may be perceived from three different perspectives. First is the *legal* perspective. Consider the following illustration: if I, knowing his intention beforehand, *permitted* my child to break the law, claiming as the ground for my own exoneration from all responsibility for the crime that, though it is true that I knew of his intention and did not prevent him, I warned him of the penalty for wrongdoing and that it was he, exercising his freedom (which I gave him), who chose the unlawful course of action, human consensus would hold, on the ground of my knowledge of his planned course of action and my failure to prohibit him by all lawful force, that I am an 'accessory before the fact'. So in the case of God: if he determined that he would permit men to sin if they want to, and determined too that he would do nothing to interfere with their God-given freedom to do so, knowing beforehand however, as he knows all things by divine prescience,[16] that if permitted to do so men would certainly sin, again human consensus must rightly conclude that his informed permission makes God also an 'accessory before the fact'.

Second is the *moral* problem raised by the 'hands-off'

16. Pinnock denies that God knows the future – a drastic road to take just to protect man's freedom!

attitude toward human activity which Pinnock proposes for God. B. B. Warfield underscores this problem when he observes:

> It is an immoral act to make a thing that we cannot or will not control. The only justification for making anything is that we both can and will control it. If a man should manufacture a quantity of an unstable high-explosive in the corridors of an orphan asylum, and when the stuff went off should seek to excuse himself by saying that he could not control it [or had determined that he would not], no one would count his excuse valid. What right had he to manufacture it, we should say, unless he could [or would] control it? He relieves himself of none of the responsibility for the havoc wrought, by pleading inability [or unwillingness] to control his creation.
>
> To suppose that God has made a universe – or even a single being the control of which he renounces, is to accuse him of similar immorality. What right has he to make it, if he cannot or will not control it? It is not a moral act to perpetuate chaos. We have not only dethroned God; we have demoralized him.[17]

Then there are the *theological* problems implicit in Pinnock's quasi-deistic description of God's relationship to human actions as being that of mere permissionism. Gordon H. Clark has noted that *bare permission* to do evil, as opposed to *positive causality*, does not relieve God of involvement *in some sense* in man's sin, inasmuch as it was God who made man with the ability to sin in the first place.[18] After all, who made the world? Surely God could have made both it and man differently, or at the very least he could have made man with the freedom to do only good, as is the

---

17. B.B. Warfield, 'Some Thoughts on Predestination,' *Christian Workers Magazine* (December 1916), 265-67.
18. Gordon H. Clark, *Religion, Reason and Revelation* (Philadelphia: Presbyterian and Reformed, 1961), 205.

condition of the glorified saints in heaven, could he not? Surely an omnipotent God could have prevented man from sinning, could he not? Since the answer to these questions is obvious, it is transparently clear that if God only permits a man to sin, he is not totally unrelated to the event when that man does sin. John Calvin indicates his awareness that some theologians in his day were seeking to make the same distinction as does Pinnock between God's decretive will and his permission, but he will have none of it. He writes:

> ...they have recourse to the distinction between will and permission. By this they would maintain that the wicked perish because God permits it, not because he so *wills. But why shall we say permission unless it is because God so wills?* Still, it is not in itself likely that man brought destruction upon himself through himself, by God's mere permission and without any ordaining. As if *God did not establish the condition in which he wills the chief of his creatures to be!* I shall not hesitate to confess with Augustine that 'the will of God is the necessity of things; and that what he has willed will of necessity come to pass.'[19]

This is already serious enough to illustrate the irrelevancy of Pinnock's solution to the problem of human sin. But there is a second factor that Pinnock has failed to face. As Clark declares:

> The idea of permission is possible only where there is an independent force [beyond the permitter's control]. But this is not the situation in the case of God and the universe. Nothing in the universe can be independent of the Omnipotent Creator, for in him we live and move and have our being [a fact not even Pinnock would wish to deny, for Clark is merely citing Scripture]. Therefore, the idea of [bare] permission makes no sense when applied to God.[20]

---

19. John Calvin, *Institutes of the Christian Religion* (III.xxiii, 8), emphasis supplied.
20. Gordon H. Clark, *Religion, Reason and Revelation*, 205

Still further, it must also be noted that if God 'permits' men to make the choices they do, he does it either willingly or unwillingly. If he permits men to make the choices they do *unwillingly*, then one can only conclude that something is more powerful than God and thus one 'loses' God altogether, or rather he places the more powerful thing that countermands God's will on God's throne in his stead. But if God *willingly* permits men to make the choices they do, *knowing* as he knows all things that they will make wrong choices, and refuses to prevent them from making those choices, then Pinnock's assertion of divine permission as half of the solution to the problem of sin does not provide the solution it is supposed to yield. Indeed, if God knows they will make wrong choices before they do so (Pinnock denies such knowledge to God), then *their future acts are certain and can be nothing other than certain*, and again 'bare permission' is shown to be an irrelevancy.

Finally, there are the theological problems implicit in his claim that men have free wills or the power to choose with equal ease either of incompatible courses of actions. There simply is no such thing as a will which is detached from and totally independent of the person making the choice – suspended, so to speak, in mid-air and enjoying some extra-volitional vantage point from which to determine itself. Men choose the things they do because of the complex and limited persons that they are. They cannot will to walk on water with any success or flap their arms and fly. Their choices in such matters are restricted by their physical capabilities. Similarly, their moral choices are also determined by the total make-up of who they are. And the Bible informs us that men, among other things, are now sinners, who by nature *cannot* bring forth good fruit (Matt 7:18), by nature *cannot* be subject to the law of God (Rom 8:7), by nature *cannot* discern truths of the Spirit of God (1

Cor 2:14), and by nature *cannot* come to Christ (John 6:44, 45, 65). To do any of these things, they must receive powerful aid coming to them *ab extra*. So there simply is no such thing as a free will.

But assuming, again for the sake of argument only, that man's will is *normally* free, even Pinnock will not deny that forces, unknown to them, can influence, even coerce men to choose one rather than another course of action. The weather, for instance, at least sometimes unknown to us, affects how we feel, which in turn determines our choices. Diseases present in our body of which we are unaware (for example, brain tumours) can cause us to make irrational decisions. Parents long dead, through their teaching and example in our formative years, often unbeknown to us, still wield a powerful determining influence upon us in our adult years (see Proverbs 22:6). The problem which arises then is this: How can any man know for sure, when he has chosen a specific course of action, that he was completely free from and uncoerced by some external or internal cause?

> The conclusion is evident, is it not? In order to know that our wills are determined by no cause, we should have to know every possible cause in the entire universe. Nothing could escape our mind. To *be conscious* of *free will therefore requires omniscience.* Hence there is no consciousness of free will: what its exponents take as consciousness of free will is simply the unconsciousness of determinism.[21]

These facts point up the inadequacy and irrelevancy of Pinnock's solution to the problem he sets out to solve, namely, how God can hold men responsible for their deeds. Divine permission and human freedom simply do not resolve the difficulties which Pinnock assumes they do.

---

21. Clark, *Religion, Reason and Revelation*, 229, emphasis supplied

His faulty norm for theological construction

Pinnock is apparently little bothered by the idea of deriving his doctrine of human freedom from what *people* think, say, and feel about themselves. Because they have the intuition that they are free, apparently for Pinnock not only must they be free, but also this perceived freedom, so he thinks, is an 'important clue' to the very nature of reality itself.[22] It pains me to say it, but it is not only a pretty sorry affair for a Christian theologian to derive his view of man from man's own description of himself, but it is also an exceedingly dangerous approach to the formulation of doctrine to base any doctrine on man's intuition rather than on God's authoritative Word to man. Today people think of themselves as basically good as well as free, as having been, so to speak, 'immaculately conceived', and not the sinful transgressors that the Scriptures declare them to be. Are we to conclude that they are essentially good because they have this intuition about themselves? To ask the question is to answer it. Even a cursory reading of the Bible will disclose how far from the truth is this 'human intuition', this 'fundamental self-perception' about themselves (see Gen 6:5; Ps 58:3; Jer 17:9; Luke 11:13; Rom 3:10-18, 23; Gal 5:19-21; Eph 2:1-3; 4:17-19). And just as they are in error with regard to their claim to native goodness, so people are equally far from the truth, as we shall now see from Scripture, when they affirm that they are free agents, in no sense under God's sovereign decree, and insist that their freedom is and can be the 'only precondition' of their moral and intellectual responsibility.

What does the Bible say?

The Bible nowhere suggests that people are free from God's decretive will. In fact, everywhere it affirms just the contrary.

22. Pinnock, *Grace Unlimited*, 65.

It teaches that God's will and his providential execution of his eternal purpose determines all things. This is why Calvin wrote:

> *God's will is, and rightly ought to be, the cause of all things that are.* For if it has any cause, something must precede it, to which it is, as it were, bound; this is unlawful to imagine. For God's will is so much the highest rule of righteousness that whatever he wills, by the very fact that he wills it, must be considered righteous. When, therefore, one asks why God has so done, we must reply: because he has willed it. But if you proceed further to ask why he so willed, you are seeking something greater and higher than God's will, which cannot be found.[23]

This is in accord with the plain teaching of Scripture. In fact, it is amazing how willing the Bible is to affirm God's 'holy, wise, and powerful preserving and governing all his creatures and all their actions'. Certainly the Bible is more willing to do so than those preachers who altogether deny such a relationship, thinking when they do so that they do God service by their denial. The reader would do well to ponder the following biblical data.

The one living and true God, the Bible says, is the absolutely sovereign Ruler of the universe (Pss 103:19; 115:3; 135:6). Beside the fact that it is God who created the universe in the first place, the Bible teaches that by his providence he oversees both it and all things in it. He works *all* things after the counsel of his will (Eph 1:11). He causes *all* things to work together for good (conformity to Christ's image) for those who love him, for those who are called according to his purpose (Rom 8:28). From him and through him and to him are *all* things (Rom 11:36; 1 Cor 8:6) – from the raising up and deposing of earthly kings to the flight and fall of the tiny sparrow (Dan 4:31-32; Matt 10:29), from

---

23. John Calvin, *Institutes,* III. xxiii, 2; emphasis supplied.

the determination of the times and boundaries of the earth's nations to the number of hairs on a man's head (Acts 17:26; Matt 10:30). Long ago King David recognized these truths when, blessing God, he exclaimed:

> Thine, O LORD, is the greatness and the power and the glory and the victory and the majesty, indeed everything that is in the heavens and the earth; thine is the dominion, O LORD, and thou dost exalt thyself as head over all. Both riches and honor come from thee, and thou dost rule over all, and in thy hand is power and might; and it lies in thy hand to make great, and to strengthen everyone. Now therefore, our God, we thank thee, and praise thy glorious name. But who am I and who are my people that we should be able to offer as generously as this? For all things come from thee, and from thy hand we have given thee (1 Chr 29:11-14)

King Jehoshaphat likewise declared God the absolute Sovereign: 'O LORD, the God of our fathers, art thou not God in the heavens: And art thou not ruler over all the kingdoms of the nations? Power and might are in thy hand so that no one can stand against Thee' (2 Chr 20:6).

The Scriptures are filled with illustrations of God's sovereignty, relating his divine purpose and predetermination to all the events of the world – the evil no less than the good, tracing them all back to God's eternal, wise, and good design to glorify himself and his Son (Eph 3:11; Acts 2:23; Rom 8:29). The following illustrations, far from being an exhaustive list, should suffice to place God's absolute control over all things beyond all legitimate doubt. As the reader reflects upon them, it would be well if he bore in mind the helpful observation of Geerhardus Vos:

> Both election and preterition are by preference viewed in the Old Testament as they emerge in the actual control of the issues of history. It is God acting in result of his eternal will rather than willing in advance of his temporal act that this stage of revelation

describes to us. Keeping this in mind, we perceive that preterition is as frequently and as emphatically spoken of as its counterpart [election], not only in national and collective relations, but also with reference to individuals. In the New Testament, while the historical mode of viewing the decree as passing over into realization is not abandoned, the eternal background of the same, as it exists above all time, an ideal world in God, is more clearly revealed.[24]

Old Testament illustrations

1. All the main characters of Genesis – Noah, Abraham, Isaac, Jacob, and Joseph – God chose according to his gracious purpose unto their positions of blessing (Gen 6:8; 12:1-3; 17:19-21; 21:12-13; 25:23; 45:7-8; cf. Neh 9:6-7).

2. Joseph declared that the wicked treatment which he had received at the hands of his brothers had been an essential part of the divine plan to save the family of Jacob during the intense famine which was to come some years later (Gen 45:7-8; 50:20).

3. Job, living most likely during the patriarchal age, affirmed God's sovereignty over all men and all of life when he responded to his 'worthless physician' friends in Job 12:7-25 as follows:

> In his hand is the life of every creature and the breath of all mankind.... To God belong wisdom and power; counsel and understanding are his.... To him belong strength and victory; both deceived and deceiver are his. He leads counsellors away stripped and makes fools of judges. He takes off the shackles put on by kings.... He silences the lips of trusted advisors and takes away the discernment of elders. He pours contempt on nobles and disarms the mighty.... He makes nations great, and destroys them. He enlarges nations, and disperses them. He deprives the leaders of the earth of their reason.... He makes them stagger like drunkards.

---

24. Geerhardus Vos, 'The Biblical Importance of the Doctrine of Preterition,' *The Presbyterian* 70, 36 (September 5, 1900), 9-10; see also H. Bavinck, *The Doctrine of God* (Grand Rapids: Baker, 1971), 339-44.

4. During the events leading up to the Exodus from Egypt, God represented himself as the one who makes man 'dumb or deaf, or seeing or blind' (Exod. 4:11). He also informed Moses that he would harden Pharaoh's heart in order that his power to deliver Israel might have ample opportunity to be placed in the boldest possible relief (Ex 4:21; 7:3; 9:12; 10:1; 10:20; 11:10; 14:4; 14:8; 14:17; see also Ps 105:25).

We are often told that God hardened Pharaoh's heart only *after* Pharaoh had hardened his own heart, God's hardening activity to be viewed then as *judicial* hardening. But there is nothing in the entire context to suggest that this is the proper approach to this *crux interpretum*. It is true, of course, that Pharaoh would already have had a sinner's heart, but that fact alone does not require that we must say that Pharaoh would necessarily have hardened his heart against Israel after the first confrontation (Ex 7:6-13). In God's providence, he could have been persuaded from the confrontation itself that the better wisdom dictated permission to let Israel go. But a careful examination of the biblical text will show that God declared to Moses, even before the confrontation between Moses and Pharaoh commenced, that he would harden Pharaoh's heart (Ex 4:21; 7:3). And the text indicates that the first time Pharaoh hardened his heart, he did so 'just as the LORD had said' (Ex 7:13). Paul would later declare that, in his hardening activity, God was exercising his sovereign right as the Potter to do with his own as he pleased (Rom 9:17-18, 21). In the Exodus context, God, in fact, declared that the reason behind his raising Pharaoh up and placing him on the throne of Egypt (or allowing him to remain upon the throne, as some translators render the Hebrew) was in order to show Pharaoh his power and in order to proclaim his own name throughout the earth (Ex 9:16; see Rom 9:17). It is evident from both Exodus and Romans that Pharaoh and Egypt were at the disposition of an absolute Sovereign.

5. God declared that he would so control the hearts of men that none would desire an Israelite's land when the latter appeared before him three times a year (Ex 34:24).

6. During the conquest of Transjordan, Moses represented God again as the hardener of kings' hearts: 'Sihon...was not willing for us to pass through his land; for the LORD your God hardened his spirit and made his heart obstinate, in order to deliver him into your hands' (Deut 2:30).

7. On the eve of Canaan's conquest, Moses informed Israel that God had chosen them to be a people for his own possession by an election (see Hosea 13:5; Amos 3:2) based not upon Israel's merit but upon God's condescending love and grace. (See Deut 4:37; 7:6-8; 8:18; 9:4-6; 10:15; I would advise the reader to read these passages before he continues further.)

8. During the conquest of Canaan, 'there was not a city which made peace with the sons of Israel except the Hivites living in Gibeon; they took them all in battle. For it was of the LORD to harden their hearts, to meet Israel in battle in order that he might utterly destroy them, just as the LORD had commanded Moses' (Josh 11:19-20).

9. During that strange period in Israel's history when the judges ruled the land, Samson's lustful infatuation with the Philistine woman of Timnah, we are informed, 'was of the LORD, for he was seeking an occasion against the Philistines' (Judg 14:4).

10. Eli's wicked sons, the Bible says, did not listen to their father's sage advice which would have saved them, 'for the LORD desired to put them to death' (1 Sam 2:25).

11. During Absalom's rebellion against David, although Ahithophel's counsel to Absalom was militarily superior to Hushai's, Absalom nonetheless decided to follow Hushai's advice, 'for the LORD had ordained to thwart the good counsel of Ahithophel, in order that the LORD might bring calamity on Absalom' (2 Sam 17:14).

12. Rehoboam's failure to heed the people's plea for relief from the yoke of heavy taxation and oppressive labour, that resulted in the division of the united kingdom 'was a turn of events from the LORD' (1 Kgs 12:15).

13. Later in Israel's history Amaziah of Judah did not heed the warning issued to him by Joash of Israel 'for it was from God, that he might deliver them into the hand of Joash because they had sought the gods of Edom' (2 Chr 25:20).

14. Such passages as the above illustrate the truth of Proverbs 21:1: 'The king's heart is like channels of water in the hand of the LORD; he turns it wherever he wishes.' (For additional illustrations, see Judges 7:22; 9:23; 1 Samuel 18:10-11; 19:9-10; 2 Chronicles 18:20-22; Ezra 1:1-2; 7:27; I would advise the reader to read these passages before he proceeds further.)

15. The Psalmist declares that the number of a man's days is ordained by God when as yet there is none of them (Pss 31:15; 39:5; 139:16).

16. The Psalmist traces the blessings of salvation to divine election when he sings: 'Blessed is the man whom thou choosest and causest to approach unto thee' (65:4).

17. The Psalmist also exclaims: 'Our God is in the heavens; he does whatever he pleases' (115:3). Again, he declares: 'Whatever the LORD pleases, he does, in heaven and in earth, in the seas and in all deeps' (135:6).

18. The wise man of Proverbs 16 acclaimed God's sovereign rule over men when he declared: 'The plans of the heart belong to man, but the answer of the tongue is from the LORD' (v. 1); again, 'The LORD has made everything for himself, even the wicked for the day of evil' (v. 4); yet again, 'The mind of man plans his ways, but the LORD directs his steps' (v. 9); and finally, 'The lot is cast into the lap, but its every decision is from the LORD' (v. 33). (See, for similar statements, Proverbs 19:21; 20:24; 21:30-31; I would advise

the reader to read these verses before he proceeds further.)

19. Isaiah declared God's awesome sovereignty over Assyria when he wrote that under God's sovereign governance Assyria would come against Israel because of the latter's transgressions, even though Assyria 'does not intend nor does it plan so in its heart' (10:6-7).

20. The same prophet declared that all things happen in accordance with God's eternal and irresistible decree: 'Surely, as I have planned, so it will be, and as I have purposed, so it will stand.... For the LORD Almighty has purposed, and who can thwart him?' (14:24, 27). 'I make known the end from the beginning, from ancient times, what is still to come. I say: My purpose will stand, and I will do all that I please.... What I have said, that will I bring about; what I have planned, that will I do' (46:10, 11).

21. Through the same prophet God declared that it is he, the Lord, who forms and creates darkness, 'causing peace and creating calamity; I, the LORD, do all these things' (45:7).

22. Echoing the same theme, Amos rhetorically queried: 'When a calamity comes to a city, has not the LORD caused it?' (3:6)

23. Through Habakkuk God revealed to Judah that he was going to bring the Neo-Babylonians into the land to chasten Judah for her sins (1:5-6), again pointing up his sovereign governance of the hearts of kings and of nations.

24. Daniel united his own to the consentient testimony of the prophets before him when he informed Nebuchadnezzar on the basis of a heavenly vision (4:17) that 'the Most High is ruler over the realm of mankind; and bestows it on whomever he wishes' (4:31-32). Then after his humbling experience, the chastened Babylonian king blessed the Most High with the following words: 'His dominion is an everlasting dominion, and his kingdom endures from generation to generation. And all the

inhabitants of the earth are accounted as nothing, but he does according to his will in the host of heaven and among the inhabitants of the earth; and no one can ward off his hand or say to him, "What have you done?" ' (vv. 34-35).

25. Perhaps no declaration sums up the attitude of the Old Testament witness to God's awesome sovereignty over men and nations more majestically than Isaiah 40:15, 17, 22, 23:

> Surely the nations are like a drop in a bucket;
> they are regarded as dust on the scales;
> he weighs the islands as though they were fine dust.
> Before him all the nations are as nothing;
> they are regarded by him as worthless and less than nothing.
> he sits enthroned above the circle of the earth,
> and its people are like grasshoppers ....
> he brings princes to naught
> and reduces the rulers of this world to nothing.

These Old Testament statements make it abundantly clear that God is absolutely sovereign in his world, that his sovereignty extends to the governance of all his creatures and all their thoughts and actions, and that his governance of man in particular down to the minutest detail is in accord with his most wise and holy purpose for both the world and his children whom he created.

New Testament illustrations

It should already be evident from the examples cited from the Old Testament that God is hardly the detached Deity that is suggested by the Arminian teaching which contends that God is related only in a 'permissional' sense to the deeds of men and nations. But the New Testament, as Vos suggested, is even more didactically explicit than the old in its insistence upon God's sovereignty over life and salvation. Consider the following examples:

1. Immediately after being rejected by certain cities of Galilee, Jesus prayed: 'I praise thee, O Father, Lord of heaven and earth, that thou didst hide these things from the wise and intelligent and didst reveal them unto babes. Yes, Father, for thus it was wellpleasing in thy sight' (Matt 11:25-26).

2. He also said: 'Every plant that my heavenly Father has not planted will be pulled up by the roots' (Matt 15:13).

3. On another occasion Jesus expressly taught that no one can come to him unless the Father (1) 'draws' him (John 6:44), (2) 'teaches' him to come (John 6:45), and (3) 'engifts' him with the saving approach to Jesus (John 6:65). (See also John 17:2, 6, 9, 11, 12.)

4. John traced Israel's rejection of Jesus to God's work of blinding and hardening (John 12:37-40). (See in this connection also Isaiah 6:9-10; Mark 4:11-12; Romans 9:18-24; 11:32.)

5. Again, Jesus said: 'You did not choose me, but I chose you to go and bear fruit – fruit that will last' (John 15:16). And in the same vein, on another occasion he said: 'Many are invited, but few are chosen' (Matt 22:14).

6. Before Pilate Jesus declared: 'You could have no authority against me, except it were given you from above' (John 19:11).

7. Peter declared unequivocally that the treatment and death by crucifixion perpetrated on the Son of God by godless men were in accordance with 'the predetermined plan and foreknowledge of God' (Acts 2:23). Here is indisputable evidence from Scripture that God's eternal decree included the foreordination of evil. (See also in this connection Matthew 18:7; 26:24; Mark 14:21; Luke 17:1; 22:22.)

8. The entire early church in Jerusalem gladly affirmed God's sovereignty over all of life, and specifically reaffirmed that all that Herod, Pilate, the Roman soldiers,

and the Jewish religious leaders had done to Jesus was in accordance with 'whatever thy hand and thy purpose predestined to occur' (Acts 4:24-28).

9. Three times in Acts Luke explicitly traces the salvation of certain Gentiles to the election and prevenient work of God (Acts 13:48; 16:14; 18:27).

10. In the extended passage in Romans 8:28-39 Paul traces all redemptive blessing ultimately to God's sovereign foreknowledge (to be understood as covenantal love, not mere prescience) and predestination: 'Those whom God foreknew [foreloved], he also predestined.' 'Who will bring any charge against those whom God has chosen?,' he then rhetorically asks.

11. In Romans 9, a passage which calls for extended discussion, in view of Israel's high privileges as the Old Testament people of God and the lengths to which God had gone to prepare them for the coming of the Messiah, Paul addresses the naked anomaly of Israel's official rejection of Christ. He addresses this issue at this point for two reasons: first, he is aware, if justification is by faith alone (as he had argued earlier), with the racial connection of a man accordingly being irrelevant to justification, that one could ask: 'What then becomes of all the promises which God made to Israel as a nation? Haven't they proven to be ineffectual?' He knows that, unless he can answer this inquiry, the integrity of the Word of God would be in doubt, at least in the minds of some. This in turn raises the second possible question: 'If the promises of God proved ineffectual for Israel, what assurance does the Christian have that those divine promises implicit in the great theology of Romans 3–8 won't also prove to be finally ineffectual?' Accordingly, he addresses the issue of Israel's unbelief. His explanation in one sentence is this: God's promises to Israel have not failed simply because God never promised to save every

Israelite; rather, God promised to save the elect (true) 'Israel' within Israel (9:6). He proves this by underscoring the fact that from the beginning not all the natural seed of Abraham were accounted by God as 'children of Abraham' – Ishmael was excluded from being a child of promise by sovereign elective divine arrangement (9:7-9).

Now it is likely that few Jews of Paul's day would have had much difficulty with the exclusion of Ishmael from God's gracious covenant. But someone might have argued that Ishmael's rejection from the beginning as a 'son' of Abraham was due both to the fact that, though he was Abraham's seed, he was the son of Hagar the servant woman and not the son of Sarah, and to the fact that God knew that he would 'persecute him that was born after the Spirit' (see Gen 21:9; Ps 83:5-6; Gal 4:29). In other words, it could be argued, God drew the distinction between Isaac and Ishmael not because of a sovereign divine election of the former, but because they had two different earthly mothers and because of Ishmael's subsequent hostility to Isaac. The fact of two mothers is true enough, and indeed it is not without *figurative* significance, as Paul himself argues in Galatians 4:21-31. But Paul sees clearly that the principle which is operative in Isaac's selection over Ishmael is one of sovereign divine discrimination and not one grounded in human circumstances. Lest this elective principle which governed the choice of Isaac (and all the rest of the saved) be lost on his reader, Paul moves to a consideration of Jacob and Esau. Here there were not two mothers. In their case there was one father (Isaac) and one mother (Rebeccah) and, in fact, the two boys were twins, Esau as Ishmael being the older. Too, the discrimination was made prior to their birth, *before* either had done anything good or bad. Paul argues (9:11-13):

> ...before the twins were born or had done anything good or bad – in order that God's purpose according to election might stand: not by works but by him who calls – she was told, 'The older will serve the younger.' Just as it is written: 'Jacob I loved, but Esau I hated.'

Clearly, for Paul both election ('Jacob I loved') and reprobation ('Esau I hated') are to be traced to God's sovereign discrimination among men.

Now the Arminian contends, because Romans 9:13 is a quotation of Malachi 1:2-3 which was written at the end of Old Testament canonical history, that God's election of Jacob and his rejection of Esau are to be traced to God's prescience of Edom's sinful existence and despicable historical treatment of Israel (Ezek 35:5). But this interpretation introduces an element that is foreign to Paul's entire argument in Romans 9 and totally distorts his point. This is evident for at least three reasons:

(1) The Malachi context is against it. The very point the prophet is concerned to make is that, in spite of Jacob's (Israel's) similar history to that of Esau (Edom) in so far as covenant faithfulness is concerned, God continued to love Jacob and to reject Esau.

(2) To inject into Paul's thought here the notion of human merit or demerit as the ground for God's dealings with the twins is to ignore the plain statement of Paul: 'before the twins were born or had *done anything good* or *bad* – in order that God's purpose according to election might stand: *not by* works but by him who calls – she was told....'

(3) To inject into Paul's thought here the notion of human merit or demerit as the ground for God's dealings with the twins is also to make superfluous and irrelevant the following anticipated objection to Paul's position captured in the questions: 'What then shall we say? Is God unjust?' No one would even think of accusing God of injustice if he had

related himself to Jacob and Esau on the basis of human merit or demerit. But it is precisely because Paul had declared that God related himself to the twins, not on the basis of human merit but solely in accordance with his own elective purpose, that he anticipated the question: 'Well, does this not make God arbitrarily authoritarian and unjust?' It is doubtful whether any Arminian will ever be faced with the question that Paul anticipates here, simply because the Arminian doctrine of election is grounded in God's prescience of men's faith and good works. It is only the Calvinist, who insists that God relates himself to the elect 'out of his mere free grace and love, without any foresight of faith or good works, or perseverance in either of them, or any other thing in the creature, as conditions, or causes moving him thereunto; and all to the praise of his glorious grace' (*Westminster Confession of Faith*, III.v), who will face this specific charge that God is unjust.

The Arminian also has to struggle with Paul's response to this question concerning God's justice, for using Moses as the type of the elect man and Pharaoh as the type of the nonelect man, Paul declares: '[Salvation] does not depend on man's will or effort, but on God who shows mercy.... Therefore, God has mercy on whom he wants to have mercy, and he hardens whom he wants to harden' (9:16, 18). By these remarks Paul makes it abundantly clear again that God's dealings with men are grounded in decretive, elective considerations which brook no recourse to human willing or human working. This is placed beyond all legitimate controversy by the following anticipated question: 'One of you will say to me: "Then why does God still blame us? For who resists his will?"' To this Paul simply rejoins:

> who are you, O man, to talk back to God? Shall what is formed say to him who formed it, 'Why did you make me like this?' Does not the Potter have the right to make out of the same lump of clay

> some vessels for honor and some for dishonor? [Surely he has the right, does he not], if, determining to show his wrath and to make his power known [see same verbs in 9:17] God endured with much longsuffering vessels of wrath prepared for destruction [as he did with Pharaoh throughout the period of the plagues], even in order to make the riches of his glory known to vessels of mercy prepared in advance for glory? (Rom. 9:20-23)

God's Word has not failed regarding Israel, Paul argues in sum, because God's dealings with men are not ultimately determined by anything they do but rather are determined by his own sovereign elective purpose. Therefore, Christians too may be assured that, God having set his love upon them from all eternity by his sovereign purposing arrangement, nothing will be able to separate them from the love of God that is in Christ Jesus (Rom 8:28-39).

12. In another context Paul writes: 'By [God's] doing you are in Christ Jesus' (1 Cor 1:30), which effectual work he views as the outworking of divine election (1:23-28).

13. Paul enunciated God's sovereignty over and predestination of men unto salvation in no uncertain terms in doxological form in Ephesians 1:3-14:

> Blessed be the God and Father of our Lord Jesus Christ, who has blessed us with every spiritual blessing in the heavenly places in Christ, just as *he chose us in him before the foundation of the world,* that we should be holy and blameless before him. In love *he predestinated us* to adoption as sons through Jesus Christ to himself, according to the kind intention of his will, to *the praise of the* glory *of his grace,* which he freely bestowed upon us in the Beloved.... In him also we have obtained an inheritance, *having been predestinated according to his purpose who works all things after the counsel of his* will, in order that we...might be *for the praise of his glory* (emphasis supplied).

14. Paul insists still further that 'God has chosen [the Christian] from the beginning for salvation' (2 Thess 2:13), and that God saved the Christian 'not according to works, but according to his own purpose and grace which was granted [the Christian] in Christ Jesus from all eternity' (2 Tim 1:9).

15. As a final example, Peter contrasts those who disobey, 'unto which disobedience,' he says, 'they were appointed,' with those who believe, whose faith he traces to the fact that they are a 'chosen generation' (1 Pet 2:8-9).

More examples could be cited (for example, 2 Thess 2:11; Rev 17:17) all to the same effect, showing that God is represented in Scripture as both the sovereign Ruler over the world and all its creatures and the sovereign Saviour of men.

It is transparently clear from these illustrations and didactic passages that Pinnock and Arminianism in general are in grave error when they reject the Calvinist view of predestination which teaches that God's sovereign decree determines men's actions and destinies. Clearly, the Bible teaches that God, for the manifestation of his glory, predestined some men and angels to everlasting life and foreordained others to everlasting death.

Why God is not the author or chargeable cause of sin

If God has decreed all that comes to pass, as these verses surely teach, if God, by his most holy, wise, and powerful providence, governs all his creatures and all their actions, how is one to understand these verses so that God is not made the author of sin and so that man is left responsible for his sin?

God, the decreeing 'first cause'; man, the spontaneous 'second cause'.

As we face these questions, it is important at the outset, if we are to be biblical, that we affirm with no equivocation that God has ordained whatever comes to pass. As the *Westminster Confession of Faith* declares, God is the sole ultimate 'First Cause' of all things (V.ii). Calvin forthrightly taught that God's will 'is, and rightly ought to be, the cause of all things that are'.[25] But God is neither the author of sin nor the chargeable cause of sin for two reasons. The first reason is this: while he has certainly decreed all things, God has also decreed that all things would come to pass *according to the nature of 'second caus*es', either (1) *necessarily,* as in the case of planetary motion, (2) *freely,* that is, voluntarily with no violence being done to the will of the creature, as in the case of the archer in 1 Kings 22:17-35, who from his point of view randomly shot his arrow but in doing so mortally wounded the disobedient king in accordance with the prophet's word, or (3) *contingently,* that is, with due regard to the contingencies of possible future events, as in his informing David what Saul and the citizens of Keilah *would do* to him if David remained in the city of Keilah (1 Sam 23:9-13), so that *whatever sinfulness ensues proceeds only from men and angels and not from God.* Far from God's decree violating the will of the creature or taking away his liberty or contingency, God's decree established that what they would do they would (normally) do freely *(Westminster Confession of Faith*, III.i; V.ii, iv).

The occurrence of this word 'freely' here may surprise some readers. How can the Reformed pastor speak of man's 'freedom' if God has decreed his every thought and action? The solution is to be found in the meaning of the word. Reformed theology does not deny that men have wills or

---

25. John Calvin, *Institutes,* III.xxiii, 2.

that men exercise their wills countless times a day. To the contrary, Reformed theology happily affirms both of these propositions. What Reformed theology denies is that a man's will is ever free from God's decree, his own intellection, limitations, parental training, habits, and (in this life) the powers of sin. In sum, there is no such thing as the *liberty of indifference*; no man's will is an island unto itself, undetermined to any degree by the aforementioned factors. This is so obvious that it should not be necessary even to say it.

Furthermore, Reformed theology is not opposed to speaking of man's 'free will', 'freedom', or 'free agency' (the phrases may be found in the *Westminster Confession of Faith* and in the writings, for example, of A. A. Hodge, John Murray, and Gordon Clark, whose Reformed convictions are unquestioned), provided the Arminian construction of the liberty of indifference is not placed upon the phrases. According to Reformed theology, if an act is a *voluntary* act, that is, if it is done *spontaneously* with no violence being done to the man's will, then that act is a *free* act.[26] This is happily acknowledged in order to preclude the conclusions of a Hobbesian or a Skinnerian determinism that would insist that man's will is mechanistically, genetically, or chemically forced or determined to good or evil by an absolute necessity of nature. What all of this means is this: if at the moment of willing, the man *wanted* to do the thing being considered, then Reformed theology declares that he acted *freely*. There is, Reformed theology would affirm, a *liberty of spontaneity*. It is in this sense that I used the term 'freely' earlier. To illustrate: was Adam aware of God's prohibition and warning respecting the tree of the knowledge of good and evil at the moment he ate its

---

26. See A. A. Hodge, *Outlines of Theology* (Edinburgh: Banner of Truth Trust, 1972), 287-88.

fruit? Reformed theology says yes. Did Adam have the capacity and power to do God's *preceptive will* respecting the fruit? Reformed theology says yes. Did Adam want to eat the fruit? Reformed theology says yes. Was Adam forced to eat the fruit against his will? Reformed theology would say no. Therefore, because Adam acted knowingly, willingly, spontaneously, with no violence being done to his will, Reformed theology insists that he was a free and responsible agent in his transgression. But if someone should ask: was Adam free from God's eternal decree, Reformed theology would say no. Could Adam have done differently? Again, from the view of the divine decree, the answer is no. To answer these questions any other way is simply to nullify the Scripture's teaching to the effect that God purposed before the foundation of the world to save a multitude of sinners who would fall in Adam (see *Westminster Confession of Faith,* V.iv; VI.i; IX.ii). Henry Stob has said all this succinctly and superbly in his *Ethical Reflections*:

> Calvinists are not 'free willists'. They assert indeed that man is free, that he is a moral agent not caught up in the wheel of things or determined by mere natural antecedents. But they apprehend that this is something else than freedom of the will. Man is free, *i.e.,* he can under ordinary circumstances do what he wills to do. But the will is not free, *i.e.,* there is no extra-volitional vantage point from which the will can determine itself. Man's will responds to his nature, which is what it is by sin or by the sovereign grace of God. All of which leaves responsibility fully grounded, for *nothing more is required for holding a man accountable than his acting with the consent of his will, however much this may be determined.*[27]

27. Henry Stob, *Ethical Reflections* (Grand Rapids: Eerdmans, 1978), 152, emphasis supplied.

Thus because God decreed that all things would come to pass *according to the nature of second causes,* which means that in the case of men they would act freely and spontaneously, whatever sin they commit proceeds from them and not from God. He does not sin, nor is he the author of sin. Only second causes sin.

God the sovereign cause; man the responsible cause

But for another reason it is clear that God is not the chargeable cause of sin and that man alone is responsible for his sin. This may be shown by a careful analysis of the *meaning of* and *necessary condition for* responsibility, a word that many talk about but which few bother to think much about.

With regard to the meaning of the word, as its main element suggests, 'responsibility' has reference to the obligation to give a response or an account of one's actions to a lawgiver. To illustrate, when a judge hears a case concerning an automobile accident involving two cars, he attempts to determine who is 'responsible', that is, which one of the two drivers bears the obligation arising from a traffic violation to give an account to the traffic court. In short, a man is a responsible moral agent if he can and will be required to give an account to a lawgiver for any and all infractions he commits against the law imposed upon him by the lawgiver. Whether or not he has free will in the Arminian sense of that term (the liberty of indifference) is irrelevant to the question of responsibility. To insist, as does Pinnock, that without free will a man cannot lawfully be held responsible for his sin completely fails to appreciate the meaning of the word. *Free will, as understood by the Arminian, has nothing to do with the establishment of responsibility*. What makes a person 'responsible' is whether there is a lawgiver over him who has declared that he will give an accounting to the lawgiver for his thoughts, words, and actions. Hence, if the divine Lawgiver determined that men will give a personal account to him for their thoughts, words, and actions, then they are responsible agents whether free in the Arminian sense or not. In other words, *far from God's sovereignty making human responsibility impossible, just because God is their absolute Sovereign men are accountable to him.* In short, the existence of a sovereign God neither removes nor lessens but rather establishes human responsibility. If the sovereign God has determined that men shall answer to him for their thoughts, words, and actions, then his determination *ipso facto* makes them responsible to him for their thoughts, words, and actions.

A full biblical treatment of the grounds of human responsibility would also include treatments of (1) man's innate knowledge of God's law, and (2) the doctrine of original sin. Men are chargeable causes of the sins they commit if they *know* to do the good but do not do it, even if they are unable to do it (Luke 12:47; Rom 8:7). Men are also responsible to God for Adam's sin by the principle of representative headship and legal imputation (Rom 5:12-19). Clearly, free will is in no sense the precondition of my responsibility for imputed sin, but responsible for Adam's sin, Paul teaches, I am nevertheless. It is not my purpose to enlarge further on these aspects of human responsibility. I think enough has been said, however, to demonstrate that free will in the Arminian sense is not the necessary precondition of a man's responsibility for his sin. A lawgiver is the necessary precondition of responsibility.

It will now be evident from the above analysis of the precondition of responsibility why God, on this ground, cannot be the chargeable or responsible cause of sin. Men are responsible because there is a Lawgiver over them who will call them to account for their sins (Rom 14:12). But there is no lawgiver over God to whom he is accountable. Contrary to what some might think, he is not obligated to keep the ten commandments. The ten commandments are his revealed precepts for men. The ten commandments do not even apply to him. He cannot dishonour his father and his mother, he cannot steal, he cannot lie, he cannot covet, etc. And because he is the absolute Sovereign over the universe, he cannot be called to account for anything he does or ordains someone else to do. Because he is sovereign, whatever he does in accordance with his eternal purpose is proper just because he does it. Did he decree the horrible crucifixion of Christ? The Bible says he did. Then it was proper that he do so. Did he predestinate some men in Christ before the foundation of the world to be his sons while he foreordained others to dishonor and wrath for their sins? The Bible says he did. Then it was proper that he do so. Did he determine that he would call men to account for their transgressions against him? The Bible says he did. Then it is proper that God regard them as the chargeable, responsible causes of their sin.

We have now spelled out the reasons why Reformed preachers unhesitatingly affirm God's predestination of all things in general and his sovereignty in salvation in particular, while denying to men free will in the Arminian sense of free will. The first is simply the clear Biblical teaching (see the many illustrations cited) that God has in fact decreed all things. The second is that God ordained that all things would come to pass according to the nature of second causes, either necessarily, freely, or contingently, with no violence being done to the will of the creature. The third is the meaning of responsibility and the clear Reformed perception that divine sovereignty, far from being an impediment to human responsibility as the Arminian imagines, is ultimately the necessary precondition for it.

A Biblical Theodicy

One final issue must be addressed in light of the position which I have espoused in this chapter. It is this: given the fact that God decreed as part of his eternal plan that all men would sin (Rom 11:32-36) and that only some men would be saved, why did he do it?

My answer, of necessity, must be brief, but I would suggest the following as the only possible direction in which to look for a biblical and thus a defensible theodicy: *the ultimate end which God decreed he regards as great enough and glorious enough that it justifies both the divine plan itself and the ordained incidental evil arising along the foreordained path to his plan's great and glorious end.* But is there, indeed, can there, be such an end? Yes, indeed there is such an end. Paul can declare: 'I consider that our present sufferings[28] [which are ordained of God] are not worth comparing with the glory that will be revealed in us'; and again: 'our light and momentary troubles are achieving for us an eternal glory that far outweighs them all' (Rom 8:18; 2 Cor 4:17; 1 Cor 2:7). And what is that anticipated and destined end for us? Someday the elect will be conformed to the image of Christ – our *highest* good according to Romans 8:28-29. But our conformity to Christ's likeness is not the 'be all and end all' of God's eternal purpose. We have not penetrated God's purpose sufficiently if we conclude that *we* are the centre of God's purpose or that his purpose terminates finally upon accomplishing *our* glorification. Rather, we must understand that our glorification is only the means to a higher, indeed, the *highest* end conceivable – 'that God's Son [not Adam] might be the firstborn [that is, might occupy the place of highest honor] among many brothers' (Rom 8:29), and all to the

---

28. The reader is referred to 2 Corinthians 11:23-33 and 12:7-10 for a sampling of Paul's sufferings.

praise of God's glorious grace (Eph 1:6, 10, 12, 14; 2:7).

My point in mentioning Adam in the above sentence is this: from the comparison which Paul draws between Adam and Christ in Romans 5:12-19 as representative heads of two covenant arrangements, it is necessary to postulate that had Adam successfully passed his probation, he would have been *confirmed* in holiness, moving from the state of being able to sin (*posse peccare*) to a state of not being able to sin (*non posse peccare*), and all his descendants would have received by legal imputation *his* confirmed holiness. But then his descendants, you and I, learning of the outcome of his test, would have needed gratefully to look to Adam, still living among us, as our 'Saviour' from sin and death. God would then have been required eternally to share his glory with the creature, and his own beloved Son would have been denied the mediatorial role which led to his messianic lordship over men and to his Father's glory which followed (see Phil 2:6-11). Accordingly, God decreed to 'permit [the fall], having purposed to order it to his own glory' *(Westminster Confession of Faith,* VI.i).

As for 'the others', someday the non-elect, irrevocably hardened in their rebellion against God, will endure God's wrath for their sin in eternal perdition, and this 'to the praise of his glorious justice'. Consider: of Pharaoh, who is the Old Testament type and Pauline example of the non-elect man, God declares: 'I raised you up for this very purpose, that I might display my power in you and that my name might be proclaimed in all the earth' (Ex 9:16; Rom 9:17). It is evident from this divine declaration that Pharaoh, the enemy of God and of God's people, served the divine purpose in being instrumental to the display of God's power and his ultimate exaltation in the earth, and also in providing the backdrop against which God could, by contrast, 'make the riches of his glory known to the objects of his mercy, whom he prepared in advance for glory' (Rom 9:23).

Consider another example: In the Revelation (19:1-4), after eschatological 'Babylon the Great,' the symbolic epitome of Satanic and human evil, is destroyed, heaven is filled with the exultant shout of a great multitude:

> Hallelujah! Salvation and glory and power belong to our God, for true and just are his judgments. He has condemned the great prostitute who corrupted the earth by her adulteries. He has avenged on her the blood of his servants.
>
> And again they shout: 'Hallelujah! The smoke of her goes up for ever and ever'.

Here we have it – the *ultimate end* of all things in heaven and on earth: the unabridged, unqualified *glorification of God himself* in the praises of his saints for his judgments against their enemies and for the corresponding display to them who equally deserved the same judgments – of his great grace to them in Christ Jesus. And *that* end God regards as sufficient reason to decree what he has, including even the entrance of evil into the world!

A criticism of specific errors

It only remains for me to direct some closing remarks by way of criticism to Pinnock's understanding of the four themes he extracted from Genesis. I will then be finished, he will have been sufficiently refuted, and God's glory will have been preserved intact.

Adam's creation and fall

Pinnock is entirely correct, of course, when he affirms forthrightly both the historical space/time creation and fall of Adam. In a day when the historicity of these events is being denied on every hand such forthrightness is refreshing indeed. Pinnock is to be given high marks for his faithfulness to the biblical witness relating to these events. But with respect to the former event, except for the obvious fact that God sovereignly asserted his right to determine all of the details of the creation and to impose the restrictions that he did upon Adam, the Genesis record does not enter into the question of divine determinism in any didactic fashion one way or the other. Whether or not the first pair were free from divine determinism has to be decided by a direct statement of God on the matter. This the Bible does give to us in its generalizing statements, not in Genesis it is true, but in many other places, as we have already seen (see, for example, Rom 11:32-36). Pinnock's insistence that Adam was entirely free from all divine influence, deriving this perception from the *imago Dei* character of man, begs the question. He offers not one word of exegesis to sustain his declaration that the *imago* is to be defined in terms of freedom *from* God's decretive will.

With respect to the fall of man, what Pinnock refuses to face anywhere in his chapter is the fact that the fall of man, not to mention the creation of man as well, was preceded, indeed eternally so, by salvific decision-making on God's part (see Eph 1:3-4). By this decision-making, sometimes referred to by Reformed thinkers as 'the covenant of redemption', God determined before the creation of the world, in keeping with his eternal purpose (Eph 3:11), to effect an atonement by Christ Jesus which would reverse the effects of the space/time fall. Since this is so, it follows necessarily that the fall of man was an integral fact in the eternal and immutable purpose of God. Not to affirm so is either to permit contradictories to stand unresolved in our theological thinking or to reduce the meaning of the great *pro* ('before') verbs in the passages that teach eternal election to zero.

Man's cumulative degeneration

It is in this area that Pinnock commits one of his most serious errors. As we have seen, Pinnock denies the legal imputation of Adam's sin to the race. But Romans 5:12-19 expressly teaches precisely this fact. The reader may consult John Murray's treatment of these verses in his commentary, *The Epistle to the Romans*,[29] for a full exposition, but suffice it to say here that any interpretation of these verses which would reject legal imputation shatters on the unflinching rock of exegesis and calls into question the legal imputation of Christ's righteousness to sinners which is the other half – the 'so also' half – of Paul's great comparison between Adam and Christ. While it is certainly true that a 'warped social situation' is a contributing factor in man's universal morass of sin, that factor alone hardly suffices as the sole explanation of the biblical description of the condition of man since the fall (see Rom 1:18-32; 3:10-18; 1 Cor 2:14; Eph 2:1-3; 4:17-18). If all that Adam's act of disobedience did was to open up by way of example an alternative path for men to follow which would take them away from God's purpose for them (Pinnock's explanation), this is hardly an adequate explanation of the fact that *all men have followed his example.*

God's counteractive grace

The Bible is quite explicit regarding what man's response to God's overtures of grace would be if it were left to man to determine it. He would find them foolishness (1 Cor 2:14) and would refuse to submit to them (Rom 8:7). And a form of grace that would only place salvation before lost men, God knowing all the while that as sinners they are incapable of receiving it apart from powerful divine aid that he would

---

29. John Murray, *The Epistle to the Romans* (Grand Rapids: Eerdmans, 1959), I, 178-206.

not extend, is no grace at all. It would be a charade and a mockery of man's helpless condition . But God's grace not only makes salvation available; it also actually saves men! Salvation is from the Lord (Jonah 2:9) – this is the consentient theme of Scripture. Man contributes nothing that is ultimately determinative of his salvation – *not good works* (Eph 2:8-9; 2 Tim 1:9; Tit 3:5) because he has none that will commend him savingly to God's favour (Isa 64:6; Rom 3:10-18, 23), *not faith* (Acts 11:18; 13:48; 16:14; 18:27; Phil 1:29) because he has a mind that '*does not* subject itself to the law of God [that is depravity], *neither is it able* to do so [that is inability]' (Rom 8:7; 1 Cor 2:14), *not the exercise of will* (John 1:12-13; Rom 9:16) because his unregenerate will is in bondage to sin (Rom 6:17, 19, 20; 7:14-25) and is dead toward God (Eph 2:1). From beginning to end the Scriptures teach that men, when they come to God savingly, come because God effectually calls them to himself: 'Blessed is the man whom thou choosest and causest to approach unto thee, that he may dwell in thy courts' (Ps 65:4). Men do not come, as Pinnock would teach, ultimately because *they will* to do so; they come because *God* wills that they should will to do so. The triune God alone saves men, and to God alone rightly belongs all the glory, just as it has been written: 'Let him who boasts, boast in the Lord' (1 Cor 1:31).

I began this chapter by saying that if the Scriptures are given their due, a man's theology will be God-centered because God's glory is central to himself. I believe that I have shown this. Plainly, the sovereign God has foreordained whatever comes to pass for his own glory, and controls all his creatures and all their actions for his own glory in order to accomplish his own wise and holy ends, and is alone the Saviour of men. Though men make choices and initiate actions that either honour or violate God's revealed preceptive will for them, never is God's decretive will thwarted, his wise design frustrated, or his eternal purpose checkmated. And while unbelieving men and many sincere but mistaken Christians would deny to God his sovereign right to decree all things or would seek to share his glory with him, the Christian mind informed by Scripture will humble itself before the God of Scripture and gladly sing:

'Tis not that I did choose thee, for, Lord, that could not be;
This heart would still refuse thee, hadst thou not chosen me.
Thou from the sin that stained me hast cleansed and set me free;
Of old thou hast ordained me, that I should live to thee.

'Twas sov'reign mercy called me and taught my op'ning mind;
The world had else enthralled me, to heav'nly glories blind.
My heart owns none before thee, for thy rich grace I thirst;
This knowing, if I love thee, thou must have loved me first.

And this:

I sought the Lord, and afterward I knew
He moved my soul to seek him, seeking me;
It was not I that found, O Saviour true,
No, I was found of thee.

Thou didst reach forth thy hand and mine enfold;
I walked and sank not on the storm-vexed sea,
'Twas not so much that I on thee took hold,
As thou, dear Lord, on me.

I find, I walk, I love, but, O the whole
Of love is but my answer, Lord, to thee;
For thou wert long beforehand with my soul,
Always thou lovedst me.

Chapter Four

The Need for a Theologically Articulate Pulpit

In his second letter to Timothy, Paul wrote: 'The things you have heard me say in the presence of many witnesses entrust to *reliable* men who will also be *qualified* to teach others' (2:2; emphasis supplied). He further urged the church not to be hasty in ordaining men to the gospel ministry before they had undergone ministerial trial (1 Tim. 5:22), insisting in Titus 1:4–2:1 that along with the other requirements essential to the teaching eldership (see 1 Tim. 3:1-7; Tit. 1:5-9) he who would be a pastor/teacher must be 'able to exhort in *sound doctrine* and to refute those who contradict' his teaching (Tit. 1:9; emphasis supplied). Clearly, the great apostle mandates a theologically articulate ministry for the church.

The responsibility to prepare himself theologically through rigorous study is as great for both the man already in and the man aspiring to the ministry today as it was in Paul's day – perhaps even greater; for while it is true that today he can 'stand on the shoulders', so to speak, of twenty previous centuries of Spirit-wrought insight into the Holy Scriptures, not only is he faced today with the ever-increasing avalanche of secular humanism in a world whose unbelieving population is even more numerous now than there were even people in the world when our Lord first issued his Great Commission two thousand years ago, but also he must combat *within* the church, in addition to the many ancient heresies which still abound on every hand, the myriad new forms of overt and covert opposition to the true teaching of Scripture.

It is absolutely essential that the church of our generation train a vast contingent of qualified men who will be able to draw from the Scriptures, through the best canons of exegesis and hermeneutics, what the Bible teaches and to proclaim and to apply that teaching powerfully and winsomely to the present condition.

In response to the third question of the *Westminster Shorter Catechism,* 'What do the Scriptures principally teach?', the Westminster Assembly approved the following answer: 'The Scriptures principally teach, what man is to believe concerning God, and what duty God requires of man.' By its response, the Assembly underscored the two requisites for a healthy, vital church in any age, namely, an apprehension of the Scripture's teaching and obedience to it. Only when the church is taught what it is to believe, and obeys what it has been taught, will it manifest the glory of God and enjoy him and his blessing as it should.

The value of a system of belief

Now not only does Scripture but all human experience as well demonstrates that a man's *behaviour* in the long run corresponds with his *beliefs* and, humanly speaking, is determined by them. Paul realized this, as evidenced by the fact that in all of his letters his summon to Christians to a high and holy walk is preceded by and grounded in the proclamation of sound doctrine that logically inspires and compels that walk. This fact points up the necessity for every man who would be an 'expert builder' in the church (1 Cor 3:10) to impart *sound* doctrine to those whose very souls are under his care. But then, how equally necessary it is, in order to do this, that the one who would indoctrinate others with a given *body* of truth should acquire a mastery of that sound doctrine himself; for it will ever be true, as Benjamin Warfield wrote in 1887:

> A mutilated gospel produces mutilated lives, and mutilated lives are positive evils. Whatever the preacher may do, [his] hearers will not do without a system of belief; and in their attempt to frame one for the government of their lives out of the fragments of truth which [the indifferent] preacher will grant them, is it any wonder if they should go fatally astray?... it is not given to one who stands in the pulpit to decide whether or no he shall teach, whether or no he shall communicate to others a system of belief which will form lives and determine destinies. It is in his power only to determine what he shall teach, what system of doctrine he shall press upon the acceptance of men; by what body of tenets he will seek to mold their lives and to inform their devotions.... And this is but another way of saying that *the systematic study of divine truth...is the most indispensable preparation for the pulpit.* Only as the several truths to be presented are known in their relations can they be proclaimed in their right proportions and so taught as to produce their right effects on the soul's life and growth.[1]

Three Illustrations from Christology

Let me illustrate what I mean when I say that there is an urgent need in our time for a generation of preachers who have acquired a *systematic* grasp of divine truth. I will solicit three concrete common examples of theological error from the locus of Christology which, in my opinion, could be avoided if the pastor/teacher would acquire a sound belief *system.*

'He is very God of very God'

I think that Christians will agree that nothing is more central to the system of Christian truth than the doctrine of the person of Christ. It is perhaps the doctrine of the Incarnation more than any other that evangelicals generally have

---

1. B. B. Warfield, 'The Indispensableness of Systematic Theology to the Preacher,' *Selected Shorter Writings of Benjamin B. Warfield,* edited by John E. Meeter (Nutley: Presbyterian and Reformed, 1973), II, 287-88; emphasis supplied.

concerned themselves to understand, to proclaim, and to defend. They are acutely aware that if any wrong thought about this altogether miraculous and transcendent wonder must necessarily cast a shadow over the soul that entertains it – if any defective view about his character must inevitably take its toll upon the life of the soul (although such harmful effects may not always be discernible immediately), then it is of paramount importance that the church propagate sound doctrine respecting him. If he who 'for us men and for our salvation' came from heaven and endured our suffering, paid the penalty for our sins, bore our curse, and died our death, is not both God and man in the fullest and unabridged sense of those two descriptive words, then he cannot re-establish fellowship between the holy God and sinful man. Athanasius saw this clearly at Nicaea in A.D. 325; therefore, he argued unrelentingly that, though he was true man, the incarnate Son is of one and the same substance (*homoousios*) with God the Father, that is, fully God as well.

So also today evangelical Christians are equally solicitous to include Christ's full deity within their system of belief.

But among their many well-intended descriptive phrases of him as true God is the Nicene phrase, 'very God of [*ek*] very God.' Since the phrase is often heard from evangelical pulpits today as a description of Jesus, one would assume that the preacher knows its background. Evidence would suggest, however, that many evangelical pastors think that the phrase is simply the literary device, on the analogy of the phrases, 'King of kings' and 'Lord of lords,' which denotes the superlative degree. But only slight reflection will demonstrate that, if that were its meaning, the second occurrence of 'God' would have to be a plural and lower case, the second occurrence of 'very' then being inappropriate, the resultant phrase achieved by these changes being 'God of gods'. But since this is not the way the phrase is turned, it cannot intend merely the exaltation of the Son as God above all the false gods which men fashion and worship.

I wonder how many evangelical preachers know that, when the Nicene Fathers included that phrase in their creedal description of the Son, as evidence from their writings indicates, they intended to declare that the Son *derived* his deity, through the Father's eternally continuing act of begetting, from the deity of the Father, and that he was not therefore God *in himself*. Influenced as they were by their peculiar understanding of the eternal generation of the Son 'with the consequent subordination of the Son...to the Father in modes of subsistence as well as of operation' (Warfield), the Nicene Fathers, I would submit, were giving away with one hand what they were solicitous to achieve against the Arians with the other, for they were denying to the Son one essential attribute of deity – that of self-existence, and in the process were affirming that the *same* essence, depending upon the person being considered, could be both 'unbegotten' (the Father) and 'begotten' (the Son).

In the sixteenth century John Calvin, while he happily acknowledged the Son's subordination to the Father as to order, vigorously contended against all essential subordination of the Son to the Father. He insisted that the Son, as to his godness, was 'God in himself *(autotheos)*. His immediate opponent was one Valentinus Gentilis, but a similar subordination is implicit in the language, if not in the theology, of the ancient Creed as well. Calvin realized that such a representation of the intra-divine relationship between the persons of the Trinity detracts from the glory of the Son and wounds the doctrine of the Trinity at its heart:

> How will the Creator, who gives being to all, not have being from himself, but borrow his essence from elsewhere? For whoever

> says that the Son has been given his essence from the Father denies that he has being from himself.[2]
>
> We say that it is a detestable invention that essence is proper to the Father alone, as if he were the deifier of the Son.[3]
>
> We say...that the Godhead is absolutely of itself. And hence also we hold that the Son, regarded as God, and without reference to person, is also of himself; though we also say that regarded as Son, he is of the Father.[4]

'To the credit of Calvin,' John Murray writes in this connection, 'he did not allow his own more sober thinking to be suppressed out of deference to an established pattern of thought when the latter did not commend itself by conformity to Scripture and was inimical to Christ's deity thereby.'[5] As a result of his loyalty to Scripture in this regard, Calvin takes his place, alongside of Tertullian, Athanasius, and Augustine, among those in the history of the development of the doctrine to whom the church is indebted for formulating for the church its doctrine of the Trinity. And by so doing, Calvin, the pastor/teacher, also set those who would hold the office of pastor/teacher the finest example of a Christian mind determined to be captive to the Word of God at all costs.

Calvin's insight has been around for over four centuries now, and these facts are treated in standard textbooks on the history of Christian doctrine, yet still today evangelical preachers continue to use a phrase in their description of Christ which detracts from his full deity and propagates by implication serious theological error.

---

2. John Calvin, *Institutes,* I.xiii, 23.
3. John Calvin, *Institutes,* I.xiii, 24.
4. John Calvin, *Institutes,* I.xiii, 25.
5. John Murray, 'Systematic Theology,' *Westminster Theological Journal,* XXV (May 1963), 141.

'He "emptied himself of all but love"'

A second equally serious theological error, which denies to the *incarnate* Son of God the unabridged deity which is his as very God in himself, is committed today when many evangelical pastor/teachers describe the effects which his assumption of human nature had upon his deity. All too often they teach a kenotic Christology. Very likely most evangelical Christians have never even heard of the kenosis theory. It was first formally propounded by G. Thomasius in 1857, and has been perpetuated, with variations on the theme, by A. M. Fairbairn, F. Godet, Charles Gore, A. B. Bruce, H. R. Mackintosh, Oliver Quick, Vincent Taylor, and others, including men whose names are revered by evangelicals, such as A. H. Strong and H. C. Theissen. The theory in general propounds the view that God the Son 'emptied' or divested himself of one or more of his divine attributes when he assumed human flesh, such as omnipresence and omniscience.

Reading a study in Christology some time ago entitled *More Than Man* by Russell F. Aldwinckle, I came across this comment:

> Whether we use the word kenosis or not...the fact remains that Jesus of Nazareth does not exercise all the functions of deity, *nor was He in His historical actuality in the full possession and exercise of what we have called the metaphysical attributes....* if God is to become man, God must adapt himself to the limitations of the finite creature.... This means that Christian theology must work with a concept of divine self-limitation.[6]

Consider for a moment the Son's attribute of omnipresence. On several occasions I have asked evangelical pastors the following question: 'After the Incarnation had

6. Russell F. Aldwinckle, *More Than Man* (Grand Rapids: Eerdmans, 1976), 192; emphasis supplied.

occurred, did the Second Person of the Holy Trinity still possess the attribute of omnipresence or was he confined to the human body of Jesus?' More of them than I would like to report opted for the latter construction, the necessary implication being that in the Incarnation God the Son divested himself of his attribute of being always and everywhere immediately present in his created universe. But divine attributes are not characteristics that are separate and distinct from God's essence that he can set aside like one might remove a garment of clothing at the end of a busy day. Rather, it is precisely the sum total of God's attributes that constitutes the very essence of his deity and, speaking ontologically, that expresses his divine glory. To hold that God the Son actually emptied himself in his state of humiliation of even one divine attribute is tantamount to contending that he who 'enfleshed' himself as Jesus of Nazareth, while perhaps 'more than man,' is not quite God either. But as Bishop Moule pointed out long ago, a Saviour not quite God 'is a bridge broken at the farther end'.

The uniform New Testament representation of the outcome of his incarnation is that God the Son, without ceasing to be what he is as God, took into union with himself what he was not, making our human nature his very own. Though Jesus displayed all of the characteristics of men generally, sin excepted, he also claimed on numerous occasions to be the eternal I AM (John 8:58), claiming omnipresence for himself in Matthew 18:20 and 28:20, evidencing omniscience in John 1:47; 2:25; 4:29; and 11:11-14, exercising almighty power in, for example, the stilling of the storm (Mark 4:39), and asserting divine authority in forgiving sins (Mark 2:10). The writer of Hebrews goes so far as to declare that even while offering himself up for our sins on the cross Jesus was, at that very time, also upholding all things by the word of his power (1:3)!

While we can never afford to ascribe to church fathers, councils, or creeds the same authority we gladly accede to the Holy Scripture itself, it can easily be demonstrated that a kenotic Christology was never a part of historic orthodoxy. For example, Cyril of Alexandria, who led the orthodox opposition against Nestorius at the Council at Ephesus in A. D. 431, in a letter to Nestorius wrote

> [The eternal Word] subjected himself to birth for us, and came forth man from a woman, without casting off that which he was.... although he assumed flesh and blood, he remained what he was, God in essence and in truth. Neither do we say that his flesh was changed into the nature of divinity, nor that the ineffable nature of the Word of God was laid aside for the nature of the flesh; for he is unchanged and absolutely unchangeable, being the same always, according to the Scriptures. For although visible and a child in swaddling clothes, and even in the bosom of his Virgin Mother, he filled all creation as God, and was a fellow-ruler with him who begat him, for the Godhead is without quantity and dimension, and cannot have limits.[7]

Twenty years later in A. D. 451, the Council of Chalcedon, whose creedal labours produced the Christological definition that fixed the boundaries of all future discussion, declared that Jesus possessed 'two natures without confusion, without change, without division, without separation, the distinctiveness of the natures being by no means removed because of the union, but the properties of each nature being preserved....'

Calvin is hardly being heterodox, then, as the Lutherans have charged, when he wrote:

---

7. From 'The Epistle of Cyril to Nestorius with the XII Anathematisms,' A *Select Library of Nicene and Post Nicene Fathers of the Christian Church*, edited by Schaff and Wace (Grand Rapids: Eerdmans, 1956 [second series]), XIV,202.

> Another absurdity... – namely, that if the Word of God became incarnate, [he] must have been confined within the narrow prison of an earthly body, is sheer impudence! For even if the Word in his immeasurable essence united with the nature of man into one person, we do not imagine that he was confined therein. Here is something marvellous: the Son of God descended from heaven in such a way that, without leaving heaven, he willed to be born in the virgin's womb, to go about the earth, to hang upon the cross, yet he continuously filled the earth even as he had done from the beginning![8]

The *Heidelberg Catechism* even grants explicit Reformed creedal status to this position when it declares in Question 48:

> since [Christ's] Godhood is illimitable and omnipresent, it must follow that it is beyond the bounds of the human nature it has assumed, and yet none the less is in this human nature and remains personally united to it.

It is patently clear, then, both from Scripture and church history that kenotic Christology is a blemish – doctrinal acne on the face of Christian orthodoxy. Our watchword as evangelicals must be 'No more kenoticism!'

We must note in passing that, far from the Reformed position being heterodox, it is actually the Lutheran representation of the person of Christ, in which our Lord's human nature, by virtue of its union with his divine nature, 'acquires' infinite attributes and is virtually divinized, that 'forms,' in the words of Charles Hodge, 'no part of Catholic Christianity'.[9]

---

8. John Calvin, *Institutes,* II.xiii, 4.
9. Charles Hodge, *Systematic Theology,* II, 418.

'The finite can contain the infinite'

My mention of the Lutheran representation of the person of Christ, which must hold that 'the finite is capable of containing the infinite' with its peculiar understanding of the *communicatio idiomatum,* brings me to my third example of theological imprecision among evangelical Christians – another form of affirming the same error.

While evangelicals are solicitous with a jealousy approaching that of the Zealot to contend for the full unabridged deity of Jesus Christ over against all aberrations which would deny or attenuate it in any way, I do not find them as careful to safeguard his humanity from heterodoxy. While most, if not all, evangelicals would never affirm, as do the Lutherans, (1) that the divine Logos, by virtue of the union of his divine and human natures in his one person, communicated the attributes of his deity to his humanity so that the human nature of our Lord is physically ubiquitous and (2) that it was, accordingly, his human nature which he 'emptied' of its divine characteristics in the incarnation, I am afraid that I have seen the same erroneous *communicatio* affirmed of his humanity in the area of knowledge by virtue of another medium, namely, his resurrection, by evangelical preachers even in the Reformed community.

Let me be more precise. I have heard it said many times and have tried to correct the error just as often – that while our Lord, it is true, did not know all things *as a man* during 'the days of his flesh' on earth – he himself said as much in Mark 13:32 – he must surely know everything now as a man *since* his resurrection and ascension.

But such thinking grants powers to the event of resurrection which it simply does not have and was never intended to have. While our bodies, sown in mortality, dishonour, weakness, and that state that comports with the conditions of this fallen world, by virtue of the resurrection will be raised in immortality, glory, honour, and that state that comports with the conditions of the post-resurrection existence, the resurrection itself does not and cannot 'divinize' humanity in any sense of the word. Similarly for Christ, his resurrection in no sense transformed the essential manness which was his prior to his resurrection into something other or different from manness. He was true man before his resurrection and is and will remain so – all that man is, with all that is involved in being man – through all the ages and into the eternity of the eternities. But this means, if we take the limitations of human finitude with the deadly seriousness that the Definition of Chalcedon did when it spoke of Christ's 'two natures [being] without confusion, without change...the distinctiveness of the natures being by no means removed because of the union, but the properties of each nature being preserved,' that Christ *as a man* must remain finite in knowledge forever. With the trenchant insight which we are accustomed to associate with his name, Benjamin Warfield writes in this regard:

> The Reformed theology which it is our happiness to inherit, has never hesitated to face the fact [that all that man as man is, that Christ is to eternity] and rejoice in it, with all its implications. With regard to knowledge, for example, it has not shrunk from recognizing that Christ, as a man, had a finite knowledge and must continue to have a finite knowledge forever. Human nature is ever finite, it declares, and is no more capable of infinite *charismata,* than of the infinite *idiomata* or attributes of the divine nature; so that it is certain that the knowledge of Christ's human nature is not and can never be the infinite wisdom of God itself. The Reformed theology has no reserves, therefore, in confessing the limitations of the knowledge of Christ as man, and no fear of overstating the perfection and completeness of his humanity.[10]

---

10. B. B. Warfield, 'The Human Development of Jesus,' *Selected Shorter Writings of Benjamin B. Warfield,* 1: 162.

So much for our examples. From our consideration of these three aspects of the church's doctrine of Christ's person, I have suggested that doctrinal aberrations still circulate within evangelical Christianity with respect to this most fundamental and cardinal doctrine of the Faith which the preacher could avoid through a *systematic* harmonization of his doctrinal beliefs.

Space does not permit treatment of the many other doctrinal deviations presently being propagated by and among evangelicals away from the unerring benchmark of Holy Scripture. But I urge every pastor/teacher and any and all who would aspire to that sacred office to 'be diligent to present yourselves approved to God, a workman who does not need to be ashamed, rightly handling the word of truth' (2 Tim. 2:15), in order both to know and to teach sound doctrine and to counteract helpfully and effectively the influence of such erroneous teachings as the following:

(1) the increasing apostasy away from the doctrine of biblical inerrancy among churches and seminaries historically evangelical and even Reformed in their commitment;

(2) such anti-Christian Christologies as are being set forth in such works as *The Myth of God Incarnate* and in the Jesus Seminar;

(3) the perverse Pelagian forces both within and without the church that denounce the necessity for divine grace, either preveniently or at all, for salvation, and that encourage men to believe that they can and must make themselves acceptable to God by their own efforts;

(4) the previous heresy's half-sister, Arminianism, (a) whose view of election renders God impotent to decree anything but his own actions and even then only in reaction to the so-called free and undetermined actions of the sinful creature, (b) whose representation of the design of the atonement as unlimited depicts not a victorious but a

defeated Christ who died for multitudes of men who still suffer eternal perdition, and (c) whose order of application of Christ's saving benefits to the sinner grounds the reception of those benefits ultimately in the decision of the creature, all of which means that God is required to share his divine glory in salvation with the sinner; and

(5) the rampant lawless ecclesiasticism that today demands that women and homosexuals be ordained to the office of church elder, that works for the right of women to abort on demand their unwanted unborn children, and that advocates and underwrites with Christian money, in the name of the so-called 'Christian-Marxist ideal' of social justice, political revolution and terrorist upheaval around the world.

On and on we could go cataloguing still other doctrinal declensions in modern Christendom away from the norm of Scriptural truth. But let me conclude with a pastoral appeal.

A pastoral appeal

I say it with sadness, but in my opinion it is true nonetheless that at a time when opportunities for the church of Jesus Christ to make real advances were never better, a theological illiteracy which invites the rise of wholesale heresy pervades the church, traceable both to apostate clergymen and to a distressing lack of theologically articulate spokesmen among evangelicals capable of correcting the maladies that afflict the church.

Do not misunderstand me. There is no paucity of preachers. But the burning question is, how many are really theologically qualified to minister in this day? In his brief article on 'The Indispensableness of Systematic Theology to the Preacher,' previously quoted, Warfield relates that Professor Flint of Edinburgh, in closing his opening lecture to his class, now many years ago, took occasion to warn his theological students of what he perceived to be an imminent danger. There was a growing tendency, he said, to

> deem it of prime importance that they should enter upon the ministry, accomplished preachers, and of only secondary importance that they should be scholars, thinkers, theologians. 'It is not so,' he is reported as saying, 'that great or even good preachers are formed. They form themselves before they form their style of preaching. Substance with them precedes appearance, instead of appearance being a substitute for substance. They learn to know truth before they think of presenting it.... They acquire a solid base for the manifestation of their love of souls through a loving, comprehensive, absorbing study of the truth which saves souls.' In these winged words [Warfield comments] is outlined the case for the indispensableness of Systematic Theology for the preacher. It is summed up in the proposition that it is through the truth that souls are saved, that it is accordingly the prime business of the preacher to present this truth to men, and that it is consequently his fundamental duty to become himself possessed of this truth....[11]

Our attitude toward the wonderful 'strangeness' and challenges of Holy Scripture should be the same as Moses' immediate reaction to the sign of God's presence at the burning bush: 'I will turn aside and see this great sight.' With Calvin we must say: 'Let us learn, by the example of Moses, as often as God invites us to himself by any sign, to give *diligent* heed, lest the proffered light be quenched by our own apathy.'[12]

I take for granted from the fact that you the reader have proceeded with me to these concluding remarks that you are interested in and committed to the acquisition of a sound theology. Covenant with God to *learn* all that you can from

---

11. B. B. Warfield, *Selected Shorter Writings of Benjamin B. Warfield,* 2: 280.
12. John Calvin, *Commentary* on Exodus 3:3, emphasis supplied.

his inscripturated revelation to his church about what men are to believe concerning him, his Christ, and his great salvation (how can they escape if they neglect it?), and what duty God requires of them, and to *preach* what he teaches you to the dear church for whom Christ died, for the improvement of its health and the equipping of his children for those good works which God himself has decreed for it. And while it will ever be the case that it is he alone who can give the increase, bathe your entire labour for him in the fervent prayer that you may be used to plant his Word and to water it in the souls of needy men. May our prayer as preachers always be:

Shine thou upon us, Lord, True Light of men, today,
And through the written word thy very self display,
That so from hearts which burn with gazing on thy face
Thy little ones may learn the wonders of thy grace.

Breathe thou upon us, Lord, Thy Spirit's living flame,
That so with one accord our lips may tell thy Name.
Give thou the hearing ear, fix thou the wand'ring thought,
That those we teach may hear the great things thou hast wrought.

Speak thou for us, O Lord, in all we say of thee,
According to thy Word let all our teaching be,
That so thy lambs may know their own true Shepherd's voice,
Where'er he leads them go, and in his love rejoice.

Live thou within us, Lord; thy mind and will be ours;
Be thou belov'd, adored, and served with all our pow'rs,
That so our lives may teach thy children what thou art,
And plead, by more than speech, for thee with ev'ry heart.

Chapter Five

The Need for a Godly Pulpit

It is my intention to restrict my remarks in this lecture to what I believe is the most *crucial* piece of advice which anyone in my place could give to any Christian minister laboring today in the gospel ministry. It is the advice which the apostle Paul gives to Timothy in 1 Timothy 4:7: Γύμναζε...σεαυτὸν πρὸς εὐσέβειαν, *Gumnaze...seauton pros eusebeian.* The NIV translates these four words: "Train yourself to be godly." The NKJV translates them: "Exercise yourself to[ward] godliness." In his commentary on First Timothy George W. Knight III comments on this statement as follows:

> Γυμνάζω [*Gumnazō*, from which we derive our English words, "gymnast" and "gymnasium"] means literally "exercise naked, train" and is used also figuratively "of [the exercise or training of] mental and spiritual powers"...γυμνάζειν [*gumnazein*, "to train"] is required of the minister. [The reflexive pronoun] σεαυτόν [*seauton*] "yourself," brings the [present] imperative [for that is what Γύμναζε, *Gumnaze*, is] forcefully to bear on Timothy....
>
> Εὐσέβεια [*Eusebeia*]...is best rendered as "godliness" here...this word and others from the same root refer to awe and reverence, which imply a worship that befits that awe and a life of active obedience that befits that reverence. "[This] εὐσέβεια [*eusebeia*] is...a εὐσέβεια [*eusebeia*] rooted in...Jesus Christ. It is...a distinctly Christian εὐσέβεια [*eusebeia*], which is not just an external form but which has an inner power (2 Tim. 3:5). That inner power is appropriated in Christ (cf. 2 Pet 1:3)" (Knight is citing himself here).
>
> ...[the preposition] πρός [*pros*] should be understood to indicate

> that εὐσέβειαν [*eusebeian*] is that *in* which one exercises, and not just that toward which one exercises [which is the idea suggested by the NKJV]...One may speak paraphrastically of exercising one's godliness with the purpose of being more godly. Therefore, the εὐσέβεια [*eusebeia*] that one has in Christ is to be developed by γυμνάζειν [*gumnazein*] in εὐσέβεια [*eusebeia*].

Now aware as I am that I may have already told you more about this statement than you really wanted to know—I am reminded here of the story of the little boy who asked his mother who was busy at the time to tell him about pelicans. She pointed out to him that she was very busy cooking supper and urged him to ask his father, to which suggestion he replied: 'I didn't want to know that much'—may I still suggest from Knight's exposition of the text that Paul in paraphrase is simply commanding Timothy: 'Since you would instruct others in godliness, do not neglect but rather *continually* devote *yourself* to the systematic cultivation and earnest exercise of your own spiritual life.' In sum, he is commanding Timothy to be a 'man of God' (2 Tim 3:17),[1] that is, a 'man possessed by God' or a 'godly man'.

Given the times in which we live, all the more urgently must this advice be pressed upon people entering Christ's service today, for godliness or holiness of life is a necessary prerequisite of any true fragrance of spiritual prosperity in Christian service, and what John Owen of Coggeshall said of true godliness in the mid-seventeenth century must be truer still today: 'It is a comely thing,' he writes, 'to see a Christian weaned from the world, minding heavenly things,

---

1. This term occurs 76 times in the Old Testament as a designation of a true prophet—36 times for Elisha, 15 times for the unnamed prophet in 1 Kings 13, with the other 25 times divided as follows: 7 times of Elijah, 5 times of Moses, 4 times of Samuel, 3 times of David, 2 times of Shemaiah, and 4 times of other unnamed prophets of God. The genitive could denote either possession, that is, 'God's man,' or description, that is, 'godly man.'

green and flourishing in spiritual affections, and it is the more lovely because it is so rare' (*Works*, 7, 453).

However much the earnest and systematic cultivation of the spiritual life may be the deepest aspiration of Christian saints generally, even more is it a *duty* to be impressed upon those of us who hold the teaching and ruling office in Christ's church. For without that inner life which is produced only by much time spent in the consideration of and meditation upon the Word of God in purposeful self-examination, and before the presence of the Lord in earnest prayer, we who hold ordination to the Christian ministry will never obtain that blessed ministry which the Puritan writers described as 'powerful', 'painful', that is, laborious, and 'useful'—that high ministry to which one must eagerly aspire if the call of Almighty God to the teaching ministry has truly been written large upon his heart. This is so, I believe, for the following three reasons, which reasons make up the burden of this address:

In the first place, only a flourishing spiritual life and a genuine walk in godliness with God will fortify the ordained teaching minister in times of discouragement. I sincerely believe that the ministerial failure, 'burnout' and 'dropout' about which we read and hear all too often today is to be traced directly to the minister's failure to maintain personal intimate fellowship with the triune God. Because of the press of his myriad other ministerial duties, all too often he allows the cultivation of his spiritual walk with God—this training in godliness—to drop out of his daily vocational routine. Now mark well, dear pastors, the minister of God who eliminates this exercise from his daily round immediately places his ministry in peril.

It is hard for new ministers to comprehend fully the nature of the service upon which we in the ministry have embarked. In particular, it is difficult for them to appreciate the extent of the difficulties and discouragements which attend the pastor's teaching and labors in the gospel ministry. In a letter to a recently ordained friend, John Newton wrote (*Letters*, 49):

> ...a distant view of the ministry is generally very different from what it is found to be when we are actually engaged in it...if the Lord were to show us the whole beforehand, who that has a due sense of his own insufficiency and weakness, would venture to engage [himself in it]?...The ministry of the Gospel, like the book which the Apostle John ate, is a bitter sweet: but the sweetness is tasted first, the bitterness is usually known afterwards, when we are so far engaged that there is no going back.

The gospel ministry in general and the teaching ministry in particular is indeed a high privilege but also a hard calling, its executors not only divinely chosen *in* but often also divinely chosen *to* the furnace of affliction. Martin Luther wrote concerning the ministry:

> The labors of the ministry will exhaust the very marrow of your bones, [and] hasten old age and death.

And he captures for us his own personal awareness of the spiritual extremities and struggles of the teaching ministry and his constant need of the Lord's presence with him in his famous Pastor's Prayer which is depicted in a frame that hangs on the wall of the reception area at Knox Theological Seminary in Fort Lauderdale. Permit me to remind you what Luther prayed:

> O Lord God, thou hast made me a pastor and teacher in the church. Thou seest how unfit I am to administer rightly this great and responsible office; and *had I been without thy aid and counsel I would surely have ruined it all long ago*. Therefore do I invoke thee. How gladly do I desire to yield and consecrate my heart and

> mouth to this ministry! I desire to teach the congregation. I too desire to learn and to keep thy Word my constant companion and to meditate thereupon earnestly. Use me as thy instrument in thy service. *Only do not thou forsake me, for if I am left to myself, I will certainly bring it all to destruction*. Amen.

The Puritan pastor, John Flavel, adds to Luther's thought his opinion:

> [The engagements of the ministry] are fitly compared to the toil of men in harvest, to the labours of a woman in travail, and to the agonies of soldiers in the extremity of a battle (*Works*, 6, 568).

This is so, he says,

because the issues and consequences of the work of the ministry are so great,

because the opposition is so powerful [coming sometimes even from peers who would urge the subordination of truth to denominational prosperity and unity],

because the outcome of the pastor's labor is so completely beyond his control, and

because, '...sin and Satan unravel almost all we do, the impressions we make on our people's souls in one sermon vanishing before the next' (*Works*, 6, 569).

Consider for a moment the ministry of Richard Greenham, who labored in an English country parish near Cambridge for twenty years in the late sixteenth century. He was a diligent, faithful, and gifted servant of God and the gospel. Rising at 4 a. m. each week day he would preach a daybreak sermon to catch the flock before they left for the fields. His godliness and insight as a Christian counselor attracted needy people from afar. Yet, in spite of his faithful and earnest ministry and eminent gifts and in spite of the success he enjoyed in ministering to those who came to him from *other* parishes, his ministry among his own people was virtually fruitless. As reported by James I. Packer, he said to his successor, 'I perceive no good wrought by my ministry on any but one family.' And observers at the time wryly concurred: 'Greenham has pastures green,' they said, 'but flocks full lean' (*Evangelical Quarterly*, 52, [1980], 6).

I am sincerely trusting, of course, that you pastors are not sharing Richard Greenham's lot, but of this I *am* sure: you will know so many separate occasions of failure and discouragement in the gospel ministry that you will be no stranger to grief. The burdens are so great, the troubles so constant, the failures so painful, that unless you are personally thriving in your devotion to the Lord, delighting in *his* love and fellowship, enjoying intimacy with him in prayer, and generally having the gospel proven to you again and again in the secret places of your own heart, your ministry will not well endure the shocks that will come to it. But if you are walking closely with your Lord and if you are surrounded and protected by daily experiences of his love and presence, you *will* find strength to endure every trial and to overcome every obstacle, and your ministry will not be undone by its discouragements but rather will persevere in the midst of difficulty and in this way bring even greater honor to Christ.

The second reason why the diligent cultivation of personal godliness is so essential to every preacher of the gospel's verities is that only a flourishing spiritual life and walk with God will protect him from the perils of success in the ministry. I am confident that you pastors have been well-equipped for service in the ministry of the church. And I am assuming that God has equiped you to be effective servants of the gospel and of the church. Doubtless, you have good minds, winsome personalities, and the ability to communicate effectively, and therefore I believe that, if not now, over time all of you will become sought-after preachers, teachers, and counselors. But take note of what I am about to say.

What success and popularity you will find attending your ministry will certainly increase your opportunity to be useful in the kingdom of God, but *such success will also expose you to the great temptation of pride.* However much we all may admit that it is necessary for ministers to remain humble, alas, it remains true, as the godly John Newton once wrote (*Works*, 52):

> There will be almost the same connection between popularity and pride, as between fire and gunpowder; they cannot meet without an explosion, at least not unless the gunpowder [of pride] is kept very damp.

And unless your heart is being constantly impressed, through self-examination and meditation in God's Word, with the true and odious darkness of your *own* old man, with the weakness of your will, with the utter necessity of the mercies of God and the aid of his Spirit upon which you must depend if any good is to come from your ministry, your successes will lead you astray, turn your eyes away from the Lord to yourself, and spoil your ministry insofar as it would have any capacity to exalt Christ and to build his church. The Lord himself has said in both the Old and New Testaments: 'I resist the proud, but give grace to the humble' (Prov 3:34; Jas 4:6). But if by earnest and regular devotion as a servant of God you are cultivating that pure poverty of spirit and meekness of heart in which the Lord of grace and mercy delights, the success that attends your labors will not undo your ministries but will simply give you cause to praise the name of the Lord and to trust him to use you even more.

Third, and finally, the cultivation of personal

godliness—'training oneself to be godly'—is crucial to all true ministry because only a flourishing spiritual life and walk with God will lend the needed power and effectiveness to one's labor in the gospel. We all know many talented men in the ministry whose work produces little or no fruit because God is blowing a cold wind across their churches. The problem with these men is not that they have no natural gifts, for they are often eminent in such gifts; nor is the problem necessarily that they are proud or harboring some other great sin in their hearts for reason of which God is withholding his blessing. The problem is that they are personally simply spiritually dull and listless; there is no Spirit-wrought animation in their devotion to God, no earnestness, no zeal, no inexpressible joy in God, and no tears shed over their people's sin and condition.

We in the gospel ministry may have the highest academic and professional competence, but the work of our ministry cannot be sustained by any aggregate of natural gifts, however splendid. Such gifts alone cannot compensate for the lack of a Spirit-enkindled heart. We are to be perennially 'charismatic' in the sense that we are to be continually 'fanning into flame' the Spirit's engiftings by our longing for godliness and a personal spiritual walk before God (2 Tim 1:6). For if we have a dull listless walk with God our auditors will not take our teaching very seriously.

We may tell them as often as we want that sin is terrible, but our own indifferent example, if it is there, will neutralize the desired effect of our words.

We may tell them as often as we want that the love of God ought to make their hearts sing for joy, but our own listless demeanor, if there, will undo our exhortations.

We may tell them as often as we want that there ought to be a deep abiding love among the brethren in the church, but our own arid experience, if there, will prevent them from rejoicing with their brothers and sisters who rejoice or from truly weeping with their brothers and sisters who weep in distress and sorrow.

No, my beloved yoke-fellows in the ministry of the gospel, God honors that ministry that blazes with the passion and fire of a Spirit-filled heart, and he pours out his power upon that ministry

in which the teaching and pleading come from the broken heart and are accompanied by tears,

in which the encouragement is not in promises only but in the sharing of the servant's own experiences of God's faithfulness and mercy, and

in which its counsel is animated by a deep and obvious devotion to God, by true love for people, and by genuine concern for their eternal state and the salvation and sanctification of their souls.

But whence comes that tender, earnest, zealous heart which so powerfully animates the greatly used servant of the gospel? It does not reside natively in your breast, I assure you, as you all surely already know. *It comes from many experiences with God*—from great exercises of heart and mind in heavenly things, in the cultivation of spiritual affections in the Word of God and in prayer, in spending time with God, or, in Paul's simple words, in "training oneself to be godly."

I remind my seminary classes rather often of Robert Murray McCheyne's words: 'The greatest need my flock will ever have is to see their pastor walking before them in holiness.' May God's Spirit etch McCheyne's sentiment indelibly upon the tablet of your heart as you stand before your flock and as you labor among them!

And as we train ourselves more and more in godliness we will more and more glory, as did the apostle Paul, only in the cross of Christ (Gal 6:14). We will discover that there is no place for boasting in ourselves. About himself Paul affirmed: 'I cannot boast' (1 Cor 9:6), 'I will not boast about myself' (2 Cor 12:5), 'We do not preach ourselves' (2 Cor 4:5), and 'May I never boast except in the cross of our Lord Jesus Christ' (Gal 6:14). He described himself as 'the least of the apostles' (1 Cor 15:9), the worst of sinners (1 Tim 1:15), and 'less than the least of all God's people' (his 'less than the least' here is ἐλαχιστότερος, *elachistoteros*, a comparative piled on top of a superlative, suggesting deep self-abasement) (Eph 3:8). He regarded himself as a slave of Christ (Rom 1:1; Gal 1:10; Phil 1:1), of God (Titus 1:1), and of the saints (2 Cor 4:5).

Indeed, if we glory in *anything* about ourselves, we should glory not in our strengths but in our weaknesses so that Christ's power may rest upon us: 'That is why, for Christ's sake,' writes Paul, 'I delight in weaknesses, in insults, in hardships, in persecutions, in difficulties. For when I am weak, then I am strong' (2 Cor 12:9-10). God does not need or want men, regardless of the number and strength of the talents with which he has engifted them, who believe they can and should conduct their ministries in their strength. What God wants is a few weak men, for when they are weak in themselves, then he can make them strong in him.

We should strive, accordingly, as did Paul, to give all glory to God for everything that God by his grace and power enables us to accomplish for the cause of Christ (1 Cor 1:26-31; 10:31). This simply means—echoing the first answer of the *Westminster Shorter Catechism*, 'Man's chief end is to glorify God and enjoy him forever'—that *our greatest passion in life should be to learn to know God better than we know anyone or anything else in this world and to enjoy God more than we enjoy anyone or anything else in this world*, for only in such devotion will our lives publicly display as they should the glory of God and thus give as they should all glory to him.

Seven hundred and some years even before Paul, Isaiah cried: 'Depart..., go forth from Babylon! Touch no unclean thing! Come out from her and *be pure, you who carry the vessels of the Lord*' (52:11). Beloved fellow-laborers in the gospel ministry, for the health and sake of your flocks whom Christ purchased with his own blood, I call upon you, in the simple words of the great Apostle: 'Train yourself to be godly.' If you do that, dear friend, your flocks will ever bless God that he permitted you to walk for a while among them and to have taught them about heavenly things not only by your preached and taught word but also by your godly example.

Take time to be holy, speak oft with thy Lord;
  abide in him always, and feed on his Word.
Make friends of God's children; help those who are weak;
  forgetting in nothing his blessing to seek.

Take time to be holy, the world rushes on;
  Spend much time in secret with Jesus alone.
By looking to Jesus, like him thou shalt be
  Thy friends in thy conduct his likeness shall see.

Take time to be holy, let him be thy guide,
  and run not before him, whatever betide.
In joy or in sorrow, still follow thy Lord,
  and, looking to Jesus, still trust in his Word.

Chapter Six

The Need for a Protestant Pulpit

In my Sunday School class at Coral Ridge Presbyterian Church, Fort Lauderdale, Florida in September of 1999 I observed that one who knows the teachings of Roman Catholicism on justification must conclude that the Judaizers in the first-century church—Luke's 'believers belonging to the party of the Pharisees' (Acts 15:1, 5) who should have been disciplined because of their nomist teaching but instead not only were tolerated by but were even employed to run errands for the Jerusalem leadership (Gal 2:12)—against whose distortion of God's law-free gospel Paul wrote his letter to the Galatians, were Rome's forerunners. Roman Catholicism, as did the Judaizers earlier, confesses Jesus of Nazareth to be the Messiah, the divine Son of God, the risen and exalted Lord, the Giver of the Spirit, in whose name is salvation. Roman Catholicism, as did the Judaizers earlier, also confesses that Christ sits today on his Father's throne in heaven and that he will return someday in great power and glory to raise the dead and to judge the world. But Roman Catholicism, as did the Judaizers earlier, also contends that a vital faith alone in the perfect obedience and finished work of Jesus Christ accomplished in the sinner's behalf is not sufficient for his justification or right standing before God. In addition to trusting in Christ's saving work the sinner must himself perform good works, which infused works of righteousness, though initiated by grace, are nonetheless *meritorious* and contribute to his final justification. The Roman Catholic counter-reformation Council of Trent (1545-1563) states in its Sixth Session, Chapter XVI, on the fruits of justification:

> ...to those *who work well unto the end* and trust in God, eternal life is to be offered, both as a grace mercifully promised to the sons of God through Christ Jesus, and as a reward promised by God himself, *to be faithfully given to their good works and merits*...nothing further is wanting to those justified [in Rome's sense of the word] to prevent them from being considered to have, *by those very works* which have been done in God, fully satisfied the divine law according to the state of this life and *to have truly merited eternal life*. (emphasis supplied).[1]

I noted too for the class that such unevangelical, anti-Pauline nomism—one may justly label this nomism a form of 'legalism'—Rome has never repudiated. Indeed, Rome continues to this day to urge upon the world the teachings of Trent,[2] thus evidencing its own apostate condition. Paul

---

1. The Council of Trent expressed itself on justification in its Sixth Session (January, 1547) with sixteen chapters and thirty-three canons of anathemas. Chapters one through nine stress humankind's incapacity to save itself but confirm the necessity for the cooperation of human free will, including the resolve to receive the sacrament of baptism and to begin a new life. Chapters ten through thirteen affirm that justifying grace may be increased through obedience to God's commandments and deny that predestination to salvation can be known with certainty. Chapters fourteen through sixteen declare that justifying grace is forfeited by infidelity or by other grievous sins and must be recovered through the sacrament of penance, and that salvation is given to the justified person not only as gift but also as reward since he has meritoriously fulfilled God's law by good works performed in a state of grace.
2. Lest one conclude that Rome does not take Trent's deliverances seriously anymore, he should consider the following citation from the 1994 publication, the *Catechism of the Catholic Church*: citing the Council of Trent (Sixth Session, Chapter VII, 1547), it declares: 'Justification is not only the remission of sins, but also *the sanctification and renewal of the interior man*' (para. 1989, emphasis supplied). It also states: 'Justification is conferred in Baptism' and by it God '*makes us inwardly just* by the power of his mercy' (para. 1992, emphasis supplied). This

condemned the Judaizers' teaching in his day,[3] and were he living today I believe that he would denounce in equally condemnatory terms the teachings of Rome as well.

---

catechetical deliverance and the following statement of Pope John Paul II, made in his 1995 address commemorating the 450th anniversary of the Council of Trent, should be sufficient to demonstrate that Rome does indeed still espouse Trent's teaching on justification:

> Thus, with the Decree of Justification—one of the most valuable achievements for the formulation of Catholic doctrine—the council intended to safeguard the role assigned by Christ to the Church and her sacraments in the process of sinful man's justification.

3. Paul twice calls down God's 'anathema' on the Judaizers who were 'trying to pervert the gospel of Christ' by their law-ridden 'gospel, which is really no gospel at all' (Gal 1:8-9). His words deserve citation:

> ...even if we or an angel from heaven should preach a gospel other than the one we preached to you, let him be eternally condemned [ἀνάθεμα ἔστω, *anathema estō*]! As we have already said, so now I say again: If anybody is preaching to you a gospel other than what you accepted, let him be eternally condemned [ἀνάθεμα ἔστω, *anathema estō*]!

The first thing that must be noted from Paul's statement is that for him the gospel—justification by faith alone in Christ's saving work—was already a *fixed* message needing no additions or alterations to it in the mid-first century when he first came to the Galatian region and proclaimed it. Neither he nor an angel from heaven could alter it in any way or to any degree without falling under divine condemnation. The implication of Paul's statement here is clear: irrespective of *whatever else* they may believe—including even *every* tenet of the Apostles' Creed—they who would teach others that in order to be justified before God and thus go to heaven when they die they must, in addition to trusting Christ's saving work, 'keep the law,' that is, perform meritorious good works of their own, are in actuality 'false brothers' and stand under God's condemnation. Rome's Tradition, which has corrupted the law-free gospel with its many additions, falls under such condemnation. In fact, the sad truth is that from the post-apostolic age to the present time many church fathers and many church communions,

One of the members of my class asked me: 'Since its teachings are so obviously non-Pauline, why does Rome teach what it does about justification?' My answer that morning was brief due to time: 'Rome has followed its Tradition and that Tradition has been for the most part bad Tradition.' But believing that many Protestants (and, I sincerely believe, Roman Catholics as well) need to hear more about these matters, I have expanded upon that answer here.

I must begin by saying, sadly, that where the Holy Scripture and classical Protestantism have placed their *solus* ('alone') in soteriology (see their *sola gratia*, *solus Christus*, *sola fide*, *soli Deo gloria*), Roman Catholic theology has continued to place its *et* ('and').

Rome's 'And' in the Accomplishment of the Atonement

The Bible and classical Protestantism teach that Christ's saving work at Calvary was a 'once for all' atoning work which he alone accomplished. Christ's cross-work satisfied divine justice once and for all with respect to the sin of all those for whom he died, as witnessed by Holy Scripture and by the fact that God raised him from the dead, and it does not require any repetition:

> Romans 6:10: 'The death he died, he died to sin *once for all* [ἐφάπαξ, *ephapax*].'

---

in addition to the Roman Catholic Church, have proclaimed "a different gospel" and thus stand under Paul's apostolic anathema.

As for the word 'anathema' (ἀνάθεμα, *anathema*), it is derived from the preposition ἀνά (*ana*, 'up'), the verb τίθημι (*tithēmi*, 'to place or set'), and the -μα (*-ma*) noun ending conveying passive voice significance. Hence it refers to 'something set or placed up [before God]' and is the New Testament synonym of the Old Testament חֵרֶם (*cherem*, 'devoted') principle of 'devoting' or handing something or someone over to God for his disposal, usually to destruction.

Hebrews 7:27: ‘Unlike the other high priests, he does not need to offer sacrifices day after day.... he sacrificed for their sins *once for all* [ἐφάπαξ, *ephapax*] when he offered himself.’

Hebrews 9:12: ‘He did not enter by means of the blood of goats and calves; but he entered the Most Holy Place once for all [ἐφάπαξ, *ephapax*] by his own blood, having obtained eternal redemption.’

Hebrews 9:25-26, 28: ‘Nor did he enter heaven to offer himself again and again...now he has appeared *once for all* (ἅπαξ, *hapax*] at the end of the ages to do away with sin by the sacrifice of himself...so Christ was sacrificed *once for all* [ἅπαξ, *hapax*] to take away the sins of many people.’

Hebrews 10:10-14: ‘...we have been made holy through the sacrifice of the body of Jesus Christ *once for all* [ἐφάπαξ, *ephapax*].... But when this priest had offered for all time one sacrifice for sins, he sat down at the right hand of God. Since that time he waits for his enemies to be made his footstool, because by one sacrifice he has made perfect forever those who are being made holy.’

1 Peter 3:18: ‘For Christ died for sins *once for all* [ἅπαξ, *hapax*], the righteous for the unrighteous, to bring you to God.’

And the author of Hebrews informs us that once we have received the forgiveness of sins by Christ’s ‘once for all sacrifice,’ ‘there is no longer any sacrifice for sins’ (Heb 10:18)

In spite of these clear biblical affirmations, however,

Rome teaches that the Roman Catholic priest must continue to sacrifice Christ for sins after baptism in and by what Rome calls the 'unbloody sacrifice' of the Mass.[4] Now the Roman Catholic priest can only be a priest either in the order of Aaron whose sacrifices can never take away sin (Heb 10:11) or in the order of Melchizedek—one or the other—since the Scriptures recognize no other priestly orders and since they do not legitimately exist contemporaneously. Which one? Would you believe that Gratian's *Decretum* I. xxi and Peter Lombard's *Sentences* IV. xxiv. 8-9 both declare that the Roman priest serves as a priest in the Aaronic order, as does the 1994 *Catechism of the Catholic Church*:

> The liturgy of the Church...sees in the priesthood of Aaron and the service of the Levites...a prefiguring of the ordained ministry of the New Covenant. ...At the ordination of priests, the Church prays: 'Lord...you shared among the sons of Aaron the fullness of their father's power.' (paragraphs 1541-42)

But that priestly order was superseded by the priestly order of Melchizedek and rendered null and void by that priestly

---

4. In the second chapter of its Twenty-Second Session (September, 1562) the Council of Trent declares: '... inasmuch as in this divine sacrifice which is celebrated in the mass is contained and immolated [offered in sacrifice] in an unbloody manner the same Christ who once offered himself in a bloody manner on the altar of the cross, the holy council teaches that this is truly propitiatory.... For, appeased by this sacrifice, the Lord grants the grace and gift of penitence and pardons even the gravest crimes and sins. For the victim is one and the same, the same now offering by the ministry of priests who then offered himself on the cross.... The fruits of that bloody sacrifice...are received most abundantly through this unbloody one [and] it is rightly offered not only for the sins, punishments, satisfactions and other necessities of the faithful who are living, but also for those departed in Christ but not yet fully purified.'

order which was founded upon a 'better covenant' (Heb 7:22) and 'better promises' (Heb 8:6), which introduced a 'better hope' (Heb 7:19), and which served with 'better sacrifices' (Heb 9:23) 'the greater and more perfect tabernacle that is not man-made, that is to say, not a part of this creation' (Heb 9:11). About the Aaronic priestly system the author of Hebrews distinctly states:

> <u>Hebrews 7:11:</u> 'If perfection could have been attained through the Levitical priesthood..., why was there still need for another priest to come—one in the order of Melchizedek, *not in the order of Aaron*?'
>
> <u>Hebrews 8:6-7:</u> '...the ministry Jesus has received is as superior to [the Aaronic ministry] as the covenant of which he is the mediator is superior to the old one. For if there had been nothing wrong with that first covenant, no place would have been sought for another.'
>
> <u>Hebrews 9:9, 13-14:</u> '...the gifts and sacrifices being offered [in the Aaronic order] were not able to clear the conscience of the worshiper...[their offerings made the worshiper only] outwardly clean. How much more, then, will the blood of Christ...cleanse our consciences from acts that lead to death, so that we may serve the living God.'
>
> <u>Hebrews 10:1, 12:</u> '[The Aaronic sacrifices which can never take away sin, Heb 10:11] can never...make perfect those who draw near to worship. But when [Christ] had offered *for all time* one sacrifice for sins, he sat down at the right hand of God...because by one sacrifice he has made perfect forever those who are being made holy.'

Should Rome claim that its priests are also serving in the order of Melchizedek, then the priest should realize that he serves an earthly order created out of whole cloth that has no scriptural warrant. Jesus Christ, being 'holy, blameless, pure, set apart from sinners, exalted above the heavens' (Heb 7:26), is the *only* high priest in the order of Melchizedek, who as such is a priest *forever* (Heb 5:6; 6:20; 7:3, 17, 21), who possesses an '*indestructible* life' (Heb 7:16) and a '*permanent* priesthood' (Heb 7:24), who is 'able to save *completely* those who come to God through him, because he *always* lives to intercede for them' (Heb 7:25), and who, unlike the high priests of the Aaronic order, 'does not need to offer sacrifices day after day, first for his own sins, and then for the sins of the people' since 'he sacrificed for their sins *once for all* when he offered himself' (Heb 7:27-28), that is, when 'he entered the Most Holy Place *once for all* by his own blood, *having obtained eternal redemption*' (Heb 9:12). In other words, there is no further need for an earthly priesthood to continue to offer a carnal sacrifice to God, either animal or human. And nowhere does Scripture teach that Christ appointed within the Church a special order of priests to offer him again and again to the Father in and by the Mass. What Christ the heavenly high priest has done is to make his people—*all* of them—'priests to serve his God and Father' (Rev 1:6; 5:10; 20:6), indeed, he has made them a '*holy* priesthood, offering spiritual sacrifices acceptable to God through Jesus Christ' (1 Pet 2:5) and a '*royal* priesthood' that they 'may declare the praises of him who called [them] out of darkness into his wonderful light' (1 Pet 2:9). Such people need no other priest before God than the one high priest Jesus Christ who is the propitiation for their sins and their Advocate before the right hand of the Father (1 John 2:1-2). Finally, if ministers of Jesus Christ have a 'priestly duty' in this present age—and they surely do!—it is the 'priestly duty' about which Paul writes in Romans 15:16, namely, the 'priestly duty of proclaiming the gospel of God, so that the Gentiles might become an offering acceptable to God, sanctified by the Holy Spirit' (see Isaiah 66:20), which is precisely the one duty which is *not* listed under the tasks of the priest in the index of the *Catechism of the Catholic Church* (790). Charles Hodge correctly observes on Romans 15:16:

> In this beautiful passage we see the nature of the only priesthood which belongs to the Christian ministry. It is not their office to make atonement for sin, or to offer a propitiatory sacrifice to God, but by the preaching of the gospel to bring men, by the influence of the Holy Spirit, to offer themselves as a living sacrifice, holy and acceptable to God. It is well worthy of remark, that amidst the numerous designations of the ministers of the gospel in the New Testament, intended to set forth the nature of their office, they are never officially called priests. *This is the only passage in which the term is even figuratively applied to them*, and that under circumstances which render its misapprehension impossible. They are not mediators between God and man; they do not offer propitiatory sacrifices. Their only priesthood, as Theophylact says, is the preaching of the gospel,...and their offerings are redeemed and sanctified men, saved by their instrumentality. (Emphasis supplied)[5]

Is it any wonder that John Calvin declared that Rome is 'attempting something ingenious: to shape one religion out of Christianity and Judaism and paganism by sewing patches together' (*Institutes*, 4.19.31), and that the illegitimate Roman priesthood, as it goes about its offerings of an 'unbloody sacrifice' in the myriad Masses it offers daily,

---

5. Charles Hodge, *Commentary on the Epistle to the Romans* (Reprint of revised 1886 edition; Grand Rapids: Eerdmans, 1955), 439.

blasphemes the *once for all* cross work of Christ, suppresses the eternal power of his cross work to save sinners once and for all, wipes out the true and unique death of Christ, robs men of the benefit of his death, and nullifies the true significance of the Lord's Supper (*Institutes*, 4.18.2-7).

Moreover, Rome instructs the communicants in the Mass that they should regard the bread and the wine after their consecration by the priest as having become God the Son himself and that they should bow down and worship that which hands have made.[6] This is idolatry. Regarding all such teaching the Scriptures are silent; the Lord's Supper is a sacramental *remembrance*, not a sacerdotal *reenactment*, and certainly not a transubstantiation of the creature into the Creator.

---

6. In the fourth and fifth chapters of its Thirteenth Session (October, 1551) the Council of Trent declared that 'by the consecration of the bread and wine a change is brought about of the whole substance of the bread into the substance of the body of Christ our Lord, and of the whole substance of the wine into the substance of his blood,' and that therefore 'the faithful of Christ may...give to this most holy sacrament in veneration the worship of *latria*, which is due to the true God...For we believe that in it the same God is present of whom the eternal Father...says: *And let all the angels of God adore him.*'

The *Westminster Confession of Faith*, XXIX/vi, declares: 'That doctrine which maintains a change of the substance of bread and wine into the substance of Christ's body and blood (commonly called transubstantiation), by consecration of a priest, or by any other way, is repugnant not only to Scripture alone, but even to common sense and reason; overthroweth the nature of the sacrament; and hath been, and is, the cause of manifold superstitions, yea, of gross idolatries.' This language may be considered by some as intemperate, but the doctrine it enunciates, it should be recognized, is Protestantism in its purest confessional expression. But how many professing Protestants are publicly saying this today? Very few, I fear.

Rome's 'And' in the Application of Redemption

Rome does the same again when it places its 'and' in the sphere of the *application* of salvation. The Bible teaches that Christ, by his Word and Spirit, applies the benefits of his redemption to his own, but Rome adds the 'meritorious' work of Mary to this applicational work of the Godhead. In his papal encyclical *Redemptoris Mater* issued on March 25, 1987, Pope John Paul II teaches that Mary, having been assumed bodily into heaven and being absolutely pure and sinless (1) cooperates in her Son's work of redemption, (2) unceasingly intercedes for believers and for the world,[7] (3) protects God's people and the nations, and (4) reigns as Queen of the Universe. He writes:

> Mary's motherhood continues unceasingly in the Church as the mediation which intercedes, and the Church expresses her faith in this truth by invoking Mary 'under the titles of Advocate, Auxiliatrix, Adjutrix, and Mediator.' (39)
>
> We believe that the Most Holy Mother of God, the new Eve, the Mother of the Church, carries on in heaven her maternal role with regard to the members of Christ, cooperating in the birth and development of divine life in the souls of the redeemed. (47)
>
> She is also the one who, precisely as the 'handmaid of the Lord,' cooperates unceasingly with the work of salvation accomplished by Christ, her Son. (49)

---

7. Do Roman Catholics not understand that to believe that Mary can hear the prayers of the millions of Catholic faithful who are praying to her at any one time in the myriad languages of the world, that she can keep each prayer infallibly related to its petitioner, and that she can present these myriad petitions as they are prayed to her Son is to ascribe the divine attributes of omniscience to her? Do they not understand that they have deified her?

> Mary, though conceived and born without the taint of sin, participated in a marvelous way in the sufferings of her divine Son, in order to be Coredemptrix of humanity.

In this encyclical, by giving to Mary the titles he does, from Mediatrix to Morning Star, from Advocate to Adjutrix, from Protector to Perfect Model, Pope John Paul II has taken the attributes and accomplishments rightly attributable only to the Father, to Christ and to the Holy Spirit and has applied them to the sinful creature. Nevertheless, he believes that this emphasis on Marian devotion and on 'Mary's role in the work of salvation' will help the divided churches on their path toward unity:

> By a more profound study of both Mary and the Church, clarifying each by the light of the other, Christians who are eager to do what Jesus tells them—as their Mother recommends (cf. Jn. 2:5)—will be able to go forward on 'this pilgrimage of faith.' Mary, who is still the model of this pilgrimage, is to lead them to the unity which is willed by their one Lord and so much desired by those who are attentively listening to what 'the Spirit is saying to the Churches' today (Rev. 2:7, 11, 17). (30)

Moreover, in the conclusion of his encyclical letter *Veritatis Splendor* (*The Splendor of Truth*) Pope John Paul II calls upon all the bishops of the Catholic Church to entrust themselves, not to Jesus Christ, but to Mary, 'the Mother who obtains for us divine mercy' (para. 118, 120).

The sad reality, however, is that there is no biblical warrant for such Marian devotion anywhere in Scripture. Nowhere does the Bible exalt Mary in the manner that Rome does. In fact, the Gospel record suggests that she erred at times when she attempted to inject herself into her son's ministry, for which Jesus always firmly reproved her (Luke 2:48-50; John

2:3-4; Matthew 12:49-50; Mark 3:34-35). According to the Matthean and Markan passages just cited our Lord, upon hearing that his mother and brothers were calling for him, pointed to his *disciples* and declared: 'Here are my mother and my brothers. For *whoever* does the will of my Father in heaven is my brother and sister and mother.' In Luke 8:21 he declared: 'My mother and brothers are those who hear God's word and put it into practice.' When a woman on another occasion said to him, 'Blessed is the womb that bore you and the breasts that nursed you,' he expressed the same sentiment: 'On the contrary [Μενοῦν, *Menoun*], blessed are those who hear the word of God and obey it' (Luke 11:27-28). By these declarations Jesus implies that Mary's physical relationship to him as his biological mother, while not unimportant to him, was not all-important either. His disciples' doing the will of God, that is, hearing and obeying God's word, was what ultimately mattered to him, for such submission places one in Christ's *spiritual* family that transcends any and every earthly familial relationship. His disciples Christ loved, cherished and honored as his 'family' above even his biological family, including Mary his mother. Which is just to say that his true disciples comprise the only 'family' Jesus recognizes.

Moreover, Rome's idolatrous view of Mary is anything but a unifying feature in its theology. To the contrary, its unbiblical exaltation of Mary continues to be one of the major blocks to reunification of the church as it diminishes the uniqueness of Christ's saving work, weakens the sense of immediate access to Christ that is every Christian's birthright, and undermines the Pauline *solus Christus* and *sola fide* of justification. In a word, Roman Catholicism has become the most populace cult in Christendom—the Marian cult.

Rome's 'And' in Ecclesiology

Rome does the same again when it teaches that the proper object of saving faith is Christ and the Roman church (which it would appear for most Catholics becomes faith in the Roman church and its sacraments): William F. Lynch, who describes the uniqueness of Roman Catholicism precisely in terms of its perception of the Roman church as the ongoing incarnation of Christ, writes that 'the Church claims resolutely, scandalously, to be Christ himself.'[8] 'For the Catholic,' Richard John Neuhaus writes, 'faith in Christ and faith in the Church are one act of faith.'[9] Joseph Ratzinger speaks of the Roman church as 'a single subject with Christ.'[10] And the *Catechism of the Catholic Church* asserts that 'Christ and his Church...together make up the 'whole Christ' (*Christus totus*).'[11] Accordingly, Friedrich G. E. Schleiermacher, the father of modern theological liberalism, rightly observed many years ago: 'For Protestants the individual's relationship to the Church depends upon a relationship to Jesus Christ, whereas in Catholicism the reverse is true.'[12] This is just to say that, according to Rome, to have *implicit* faith that whatever the church teaches is true and to submit to its teaching, even though Scripture is

---

8. William F. Lynch, 'The Catholic Idea,' in *The Idea of Catholicism*, edited by Walter Burghardt and William F. Lynch (Expanded edition; Cleveland: World, 1964), 58-9.
9. Richard John Neuhaus, 'The Catholic Difference,' in *Evangelicals and Catholics Together: Toward a Common Mission*, edited by Charles Colson and Richard John Neuhaus (Dallas: Word, 1995), 216.
10. Joseph Ratzinger, *Introduction to Christianity* (London: Burns & Oates, 1969), 179.
11. *Catechism of the Catholic Church* (Ligouri, Missouri: Ligouri, 1994), paragraph 795.
12. Friedrich G. E. Schleiermacher, *The Christian Faith* (New York: Harper Torchbooks, 1963), 103.

silent on or opposed to such teaching and even though one may not even know what the church teaches, is to have *explicit* faith in Jesus Christ. Rome urges its faithful that they need not fear committing themselves with implicit faith to the church's teachings since the church's Magisterium cannot err in matters necessary to salvation because, as the continuing 'whole Christ,' it is being guided by the Holy Spirit. Therefore, whatever dogma it proclaims, even if that dogma cannot be found in the written Word of God, should still be accepted as a sure oracle of God.

Such teaching is erroneous in the extreme. The Scriptures teach that the church in all its teaching must be subject to the written Word of God and that the Holy Spirit guides the church only by means of the written Word. This means that the church, with a sole appeal to the Holy Spirit's guidance, cannot safely go its own way without the written Word. John Calvin, the sixteenth century Reformer, warned against this isolated appeal to the Holy Spirit as a colossal error that has done great harm to the church:

> ...it is easy to conclude how wrong our opponents act when they boast of the Holy Spirit solely to commend with his name strange doctrines foreign to God's Word—*while the Spirit wills to be conjoined with God's Word by an indissoluble bond*, and Christ professes this concerning him when he promises the Spirit to his church...[Christ] forbade anything to be added to his Word or taken away from it. It is this inviolable decree of God and of the Holy Spirit which our foes are trying to set aside when they pretend that the church is ruled by the Spirit apart from the Word.[13]

---

13. See John Calvin, *Institutes of the Christian Religion*, edited by John T. McNeill and translated by Ford Lewis Battles (Philadelphia: Westminster, 1960), IV.8.13 (emphasis supplied).

Rome grounds these teachings in its *theological* extrapolation from the *biblical* metaphor of the church as the 'body of Christ' with Christ as its 'head' that the church is *objectively* the mystical prolongation of the Incarnation and as such has Christ's authority to issue its *Roma locuta, causa finita est*—'Rome has spoken, the matter is settled'—in doctrine. Hence for Rome the church is the proper object of faith. The New Testament, however, employs more than eighty metaphors for the church,[14] and the burden of proof rests upon Rome to show that this image is the one image among them that is to be construed not metaphorically but literally. Moreover, in the New Testament the church always preaches Christ and never self-reflectively itself (see, for example, John 1:12; 3:16; Acts 5:42; 8:5; 9:20, 22; 18:5, 28; 26:22-23; 28:23, 31; Rom 10:13; 1 Cor 12:3; Col 1:28), that is to say, the church's gospel is always theocentric and christocentric and never ecclesiocentric. In the New Testament it is always Christ, never the church, who is the single subject of salvific activities: it is he who loved (Eph 5:2), he who died for (Rom 5:6), he who gave himself for (Tit 2:14), he who suffered for (1 Pet 2:21), he who redeemed (Gal 3:13), he who quickens (John 5:21), he who washes (Rev 1:5), he who grants repentance to (Acts 5:31), he who gives eternal life to (John 10:28), he who gives peace to (John 14:27), and he who nourishes and cherishes (Eph 5:29) the church. In the New Testament the church's call to faith is always a summons to trust in Christ as Messiah and Lord, as Redeemer and Savior (Acts 2:21; Rom 10:13). Never does the New Testament church in its proclamation self-reflectively represent itself in these roles as the object of saving faith.[15] Indeed, faith itself in Christ is never

14. See Paul Minear, *Images of the Church in the New Testament* (Philadelphia: Westminster, 1960).

15. The Nicaeno-Constantinopolitan formula of A. D. 381, 'We believe

represented in the New Testament as the gift of the church but as the gift of God (Eph 2:8-9; Phil 1:29). Finally, in the New Testament 'all authority' has been given, not to the church, but to Christ (Matt 28:19), and the church is to be subject to him. One must conclude with sadness that Rome's 'high' ecclesiology, created in the interest of establishing its ecclesial stability and unshakeability, has correspondingly resulted in its 'low' soteriology.

Rome's 'And' in Eschatology

Rome does the same again when it teaches that men receive justification through faith in Christ *and* their meritorious works *and* by earning indulgences. Rome teaches that the great mass of Christians, who are only imperfectly 'justified' in this life, dying in communion with the church, go to purgatory after death where they 'undergo purification [by suffering in the fires of purgatory], so as to achieve the holiness necessary to enter the joy of heaven' (*Catechism of the Catholic Church*, para 1030).[16] This latter teaching, based on a strained exegesis of 2 Maccabees 12:46, 1

---

in one holy catholic and apostolic church' (Πιστεύομεν εἰς μίαν ἁγίαν καθολικὴν καὶ ἀποστολικὴν ἐκκλησίαν, *Pisteuomen eis mian hagian katholikēn kai apostolikēn ekklēsian*) was intended by these early church fathers to affirm that Christians believe that there is such a church in the world, not that such a church is a saving object of trust alongside God the Father, God the Son, and God the Holy Spirit.

16. On this subject the Creed of the Council of Trent (1564), a summary of Trent's doctrines and a creedal test to which, upon demand, every faithful Catholic must subscribe, states: 'I, N., firmly hold that there is a purgatory, and that the souls detained therein are helped by the prayers of the faithful. I likewise hold that the saints reigning together with Christ should be honored and invoked, that they offer their prayers to God on our behalf, and that their relics should be venerated. I firmly assert that images of Christ, of the Mother of God ever Virgin, and of the other saints should be owned and kept, and that due honor and veneration should be given to them. I affirm that the power of indulgences

Corinthians 3:15, 1 Peter 1:7 and Jude 22-23, may be found in seed form in Tertullian where prayers for the dead are mentioned, in Origen who speaks of a purification by fire at the end of the world by which all men and angels are to be restored to favor with God, and in Augustine who did express doubt about some aspects of it. But it was specifically Gregory the Great who 'reigned' on the papal throne from A. D. 590 to 604 who 'brought the doctrine into shape and into such connection with the discipline of the church, as to render it the effective engine of government and income, which it has ever since remained.'[17] It was finally formulated into and proclaimed an article of faith at the Councils of Florence (1439-1445) and Trent (1545-1563). The Vatican's quite recent deliverance on indulgences, its *Enchiridion Indulgentiarum*, declares that the church will no longer sell indulgences as it did in the Middle Ages; *now Catholics are going to have to earn them by their good works!*

Protestants quite rightly reject entirely Rome's doctrines of indulgences and purgatory as being unscriptural. To suggest that a finite sinful creature could by his suffering for a finite number of years expiate the infinite disvalue of his sin against the true and holy God is a pernicious error of massive proportions. Not only is it 'another one of those foreign growths that has fastened itself like a malignant tumor upon the theology of the Roman Catholic Church,'[18] but also it is a doctrinal promulgation devised in the interest of sustaining the Roman Catholic priestcraft and the entire

---

was left in the keeping of the Church of Christ, and that the use of indulgences is very beneficial to Christians.' In light of what I will say later about relics, it is very important to note here that Trent endorsed the veneration of relics.

17. Charles Hodge, *Systematic Theology* (Grand Rapids: Eerdmans, n. d.) III, 770.

18. R. Laird Harris, *Fundamental Protestant Doctrines* [booklet], V, 7.

indulgence system of that church which, I would suggest, is its chief source of income.[19]

Rome teaches, because it believes that 'a perennial link of charity exists between the faithful who have already reached their heavenly home, those who are *expiating their sins* [*sic!*] in purgatory and those who are still pilgrims on earth' (emphasis supplied),[20] that Christians still living on earth can aid sufferers in purgatory to get to heaven by obtaining 'indulgences' (remissions of sin before God) in their behalf. An elaborate doctrinal scheme underlies this teaching. Because the pope, it is said, holds 'keys' given to him by Christ, these keys are obviously keys to something. To what? Rome teaches that the church is in possession of a 'treasury of supererogatory merit' (*thesaurus supererogationis meritorum*) consisting of the infinite worth of Christ's redemptive work, 'the prayers and good works [of supererogation] of the Blessed Virgin Mary' which are 'truly immense, unfathomable, and even pristine in their value before God,' as well as 'the prayers and good works [of supererogation] of all the saints' who by their good works 'attained their own salvation and at the same time cooperated in saving their brothers in the unity of the Mystical Body' (see Pope Paul VI's *Indulgentiarum doctrina*, 5).[21]

---

19. At first blush one might conclude that the Romish teaching on purgatory would be so shocking to the Catholic mind that a steady departure from the Catholic church for Protestantism on this account alone would continually occur as Rome makes known to its young its teaching on purgatory. But further reflection on the fact that Rome's doctrine of purgatory contributes in its own way to fallen man's pride as it informs him that after death he will contribute to the accomplishment of his own salvation by means of his *expiating* suffering for his sins explains why men accept Rome's teaching on this terrible doctrine: the doctrine conforms to the thinking of their Pelagian hearts.

20. See *Catechism of the Catholic Church*, paragraphs 1471-79.

21. John Calvin dealt in his *Institutes*, 3.14.13-17, with the vanity of

According to Romish dogma the pope has the authority to declare the terms of indulgences, and in exchange for the faithful Catholic's doing what the indulgence requires of him the pope dispenses out of this 'treasury of the Church,' through the administation of the priests, the merits of Christ, of Mary and of the saints in behalf of and for the benefit of loved ones suffering in purgatory. This teaching points up as plainly as any teaching could that Rome teaches that salvation is grounded in Christ's merit plus Mary's and the saints' good works which also have merit before God, plus their own expiatory suffering in purgatory—all the expression of its philosophy of the *analogia entis* in the sphere of soteriology.

With respect to the indulgence system itself, Philip Schaff, professor of church history at Union Seminary, New York, notes in his discussion of Rome's sale of indulgences in the Middle Ages that the expression *plena* or *plenissima remissio peccatorum* ('full remission of sins') occurs again and again in papal bulls granting such indulgences.[22] Such

---

believing that there can be 'works of supererogation', by showing from Scripture (1) that the one who speaks of 'supererogatory' works misunderstands the sharpness of God's demand and the gravity of sin, (2) that even the perfect fulfillment of our obligation would bring us no glory since we would have done 'no more than what we ought to have done' and are still only 'unworthy servants [Δοῦλοι ἀχρεῖοι, *Douloi achreioi*]' (Luke 17:10), (3) that, since God is entitled to all that we are and have, there can be no supererogatory works, and (4) that when we employ Aristotle's and Aquinas's 'four kinds of causes', since the *efficient cause* of our receiving eternal life is God the Father's freely given love for us, the *material cause* Christ and his obedience through which he acquired righteousness for us, the *instrumental cause* our Spirit-given faith in Christ, and the *final cause* the demonstration of God's justice and the praise of his glorious grace, it is plain that in no respect can *our* works serve as the cause of our or anyone else's righteousness or holiness.

22. Philip Schaff, *History of the Christian Church* (Grand Rapids: Eerdmans, reprint of 1910 edition), VI, 756-7.

indulgences, confined mainly to the Germanic peoples of Europe, were granted for all sorts of purposes: for crusades against the Turks, for the building of churches, hospitals, and bridges, and for the repair of dikes. Among the more famous indulgences for the building of German churches were those for the rebuilding of the Cathedral of Constance, the building of the Dominican church in Augsburg and the St. Annaberg church, and the restoration of the Cathedral of Treves. And there were the indulgences granted for the building of St. Peter's Basilica in Rome. In this last case, according to Martin Luther, Tetzel the indulgence hawker, by the authority of Leo X, offered indulgences for the 'complete absolution and remission of all sins,' both for the living and the dead. Tetzel even declared that no sin—not even the sin of violating the Virgin Mary, if such a thing were possible, or a sin that one was *planning* to commit—was too great to be covered by the indulgence! Needless to say, such preaching led to great licence.

Always one-third to one-half of all indulgence money collected in these nations—from Switzerland and Austria to Norway and Sweden—would go to Rome. These vast sums of money were handled by the powerful banking house of the Fuggers for a five-percent commission for changing the money, transmitting the money to Rome, and overseeing the money chests there. And this practice was carried out in spite of the fact that Peter, Rome's purported 'first pope', had declared to his readers: '...it was not with perishable things such as silver and gold that you were redeemed from the empty way of life...but with the precious blood of Christ, a lamb without blemish or defect' (1 Pet 1:18-19).

Special indulgences were granted also to those who collected Christian relics. With the collection, for example, of the eight thousand, one hundred, and thirty three relics at Halle billions of days of indulgence were associated. To be more exact, the indulgences granted for the veneration of these relics were good for pardons totaling thirty nine million, two hundred and forty five thousand, one hundred and twenty years, and two hundred and twenty days of suffering in purgatory! In the best known of his satirical treatises, 'An Admonition, Showing the Advantages which Christendom Might Derive from an Inventory of Relics,'[23] John Calvin, the sixteenth century Reformer—endlessly and monotonously to accomplish his desired effect—out of the four thousand dioceses, thirty thousand abbacies, forty thousand monasteries, and the multitude of parishes and chapels throughout Europe enumerates the relics of which he was aware *in only six or so German cities, three or so cities in Spain, fifteen in Italy, and between thirty or forty in France* which were exposed for the veneration of the people. Since this treatise is not readily available to the Christian reading public, permit me to list some of the relics he mentions.

With respect to Christ these relics included his teeth, his hair, his sandals, and his blood, not to mention the manger in which he was laid at birth, the swaddling clothes in which he was wrapped, the cradle in which his mother later laid him, the altar on which he was circumcised, and his foreskin —displayed at three (!) different sites simultaneously; a picture of him when he was twelve years old, a pillar against which he leaned while disputing in the Temple, the water pots employed in his first miracle including some of the wine he created on that occasion, five pieces of the bread he created when he fed the five thousand, and the earth on

23. John Calvin, 'An Admonition, Showing the Advantages which Christendom Might Derive from an Inventory of Relics,' in *Selected Works of John Calvin: Tracts and Letters*, translated by Henry Beveridge and edited by Henry Beveridge and Jules Bonnet (Reprint; Grand Rapids: Baker, 1983), 287-341.

which he stood when he raised Lazarus from the dead; the branch he purportedly carried when he rode into Jerusalem, the tail of the ass on which he rode, the table of the last Passover, some of the bread he broke on that occasion, the knife which was used to cut up the Paschal Lamb, two cups, one in a church near Lyons and one in an Augustinian monastery, both purported to have contained the sacrament of his blood, three dishes—at Rome, at Genoa, and at Arles—all purported to have been the dish in which the Paschal Lamb was placed, the linen towel—one at Rome and another at Acqs (with the mark of Judas' foot on it)—with which he wiped the apostles' feet; the money which Judas received to betray Jesus and the steps of Pilate's judgment-seat (the steps Luther climbed); his cross the fragments of which if gathered together, Calvin estimated, would require more than three hundred men to carry; the tablet which Pilate ordered affixed over the cross—but displayed both at Rome and at Tholouse simultaneously; fourteen nails purported to be the nails driven into his hands and feet, the soldier's spear—but displayed at Rome, also at Paris, also at Saintonge, and still a fourth at Selve; the crown of thorns, a third part of which is at Paris, three thorns of which are at Rome, one at Vincennes, five at Bourges, three at Besançon, and three at Köningsberg, an unknown number in Spain, and twelve in almost as many cities in France; the robe in which Pilate clothed Christ located in at least four different sites; the reed placed in his hand as a mock scepter, the dice which were used to gamble for his robe but in appearance resembling more what we know today than what was known in Roman times, and the sponge containing vinegar mixed with gall which was offered to him at the cross; the napkin wrapped around his head in burial—but on display in eight different cities simultaneously, and a piece of the broiled fish Peter offered him after his resurrection, not to mention the numerous claims of possessing his footprints as well as crucifixes that grew beards, that spoke, and that shed tears.

With regard to Mary, two churches claimed to possess the body of her mother, while three churches claimed to possess one of her hands. The churches displayed Mary's hair, her combs, pieces of her wardrobe, four pictures of her purported to have painted by Luke, a very valuable wedding ring purported to have been Mary's, and even vials of her milk, with so many towns, so many monasteries, so many nunneries laying claim here that, as Calvin writes, 'had she continued to nurse during her whole lifetime, she scarcely could have furnished the quantity which is exhibited.'

Six different churches claimed to possess the finger John the Baptist used when he pointed his disciples to Christ, while others claimed to possess his sandals, his girdle, the altar on which he purportedly prayed in the desert, and the sword that was used to cut off his head.

With regard to the apostles, the church at Lyons claimed to possess the twelve combs of the twelve apostles. Half of Peter's and Paul's bodies was said to be at St. Peter's, half at St. Paul's in Rome, while the heads of both were purportedly located in yet a third church. This did not stop other cities from claiming to have Peter's cheekbone, many bones belonging to both, and one claimed to have Paul's shoulder. Rome claimed to have the sword Peter used to cut off Malchus' ear, the 'throne' on which he sat, the robe in which he was attired when he officiated at and the altar at which he said Mass, the chain with which he was bound, and the pillar on which he was beheaded. Regarding the rest of the apostles, the church of Tholouse claimed to have six of their bodies, namely, those of James the Greater, James the Less, Andrew, Philip, Simeon, and Jude. But Andrew had another body at Melfi, Philip and James the Less had each another body at Rome, and Simeon and Jude had second bodies at St. Peter's. Bartholomew's body was exposed both at Naples and at Rome simultaneously. Three different churches claimed to have the body of Matthias, with a fourth claiming to possess his head and an arm. Most were purported to have body parts on display throughout the realms.

The church even boasted of possessing relics of an angel—the dagger and shield of the angel Michael!

I will not weary you any longer by detailing an account of the thousands of other relics to which Rome laid claim—the Ark of the Covenant and Aaron's rod, the bones of Abraham, Isaac, and Jacob, the bodies of the Magi and of the Bethlehem 'Innocents,' the body of Stephen and those of other lesser known martyrs—only some of which Calvin methodically itemized in turn.

It only remains for me to remind you, first, that Rome instructed the common people in Calvin's time that they should revere these relics and employ them in their approach to and worship of God, and, second, that nothing has really changed since Calvin's day. For example, one is still shown in the Church of St. Peter in Chains in Rome the chain that allegedly bound Peter; one is shown in the Church of St. John Lateran in Rome the *Scala Sancta* that Christ allegedly climbed in his trial before Pilate (this church also claims to possess the heads of Peter and Paul); one is still shown and allowed to kiss in the Santa Chiara Cathedral in Naples the alleged vial of the martyred San Gennaro's powdered blood that supposedly 'liquifies' every first Saturday in May and on September 19, the saint's feast day; one may still visit the 'weeping' Madonnas in Civitavecchia, Italy, in Benin, France, in Rincon, Puerto Rico, in Wicklow, Ireland, and in scores of other places, and receive Rome's miracles from these pilgrimages.

Little wonder that the unthinking masses adore them all

as miracle workers and mediators between God and man!

All of these 'and's' are outworkings of Rome's philosophico/theological commitment to its Tradition, specifically to Thomas Aquinas' vision of the 'analogy of being' (*analogia entis*) between nature and grace and between creation and God, the former of which Rome regards, over against Reformation theology, as being still fundamentally good in spite of the Genesis fall. For myself, standing with the Reformers who contended that the first principle of all true theology is the fact that 'God is there and he has spoken uniquely and with finality in Holy Scripture,' while I often disagree with the Swiss theologian Karl Barth, I do agree with him completely when he wrote: 'I regard the *analogia entis* as the invention of Antichrist, and think that because of it one can not become Catholic.'[24] For it is indeed the invention of Antichrist when one adds anything to the great *sola's* of the Bible and the Reformation. The 'and' in 'grace and...,' 'Christ and...,' or 'faith and...' evokes the apostolic curse and leads to the soul's damnation (Gal 1:6-9; 5:2-6; Rom 11:6)!

I do not deny, of course, that Protestantism has its faults[25] and perhaps in some quarters even some idolatry. But from formal *systematic* idolatry, I would contend, Protestantism as a doctrinal system is virtually free. This cannot be said for Roman Catholicism: 'Romanism in perfection is a gigantic system of Church-worship, Sacrament-worship, Mary-worship, saint-worship, image-worship, relic-worship,

---

24. Karl Barth, 'Foreword,' *Church Dogmatics*, translated by G. T. Thomson (Edinburgh: T. & T. Clark, 1936), I/1, x.

25. Roman apologists have incorrectly viewed modern theological liberalism and Barthianism as the natural fruits of the Protestant Reformation. Nothing could be further from the truth. Rome's own insistence on human free will and human freedom has contributed decisively to theological liberalism while Barthianism is a perversion of Reformation thought, indeed, a "new modernism."

and priest-worship,—...it is, in one word, a *huge organized idolatry*.'[26]

Accordingly, although there is no reason to believe that Pope John Paul II would heed my (or any other Protestant's) urgings since he reaffirmed his confidence in Trent's deliverances on justification as recently as 1995, if I had a fifteen-minute private audience with him I would respectfully attempt to take him to Galatians 1:8-9 and urge him, first, to recognize that according to Paul the content of God's law-free gospel was already fixed by A. D. 49—indeed, it was already taught in the Old Testament (Gen 15:6; Psalm 32:1-2; see Rom 4:1-8)—and, second, for the sake of his own soul and the souls of the people of his communion, to repudiate the long stream of later additions which Romanism has added through the centuries to God's gospel of justification by faith alone, especially the Council of Trent's unevangelical, nomist, anti-Pauline teaching on justification, taking the church thereby away from the 'sincere and pure devotion' (ἁπλότητος, *haplotētos*) which is in the Christ (2 Cor 11:3). And I would stress, because of these idolatrous additions, that he and all other Catholics are in peril of losing their souls.

I know that some readers will bristle at and be put off by my last remarks as being not only highly judgmental and irrational but also unbridled stridency and serious error since, they would remind me, the pope and the Roman Catholic faithful regularly confess their faith using the Apostles Creed, the Nicene Creed, the Niceno-Constantinopolitan Creed, the Definition of Chalcedon, and the Athanasian Creed. This observation is true enough, and I commend Rome for revering these early Creeds as valiant efforts to state and to protect the full unabridged deity of Jesus Christ and thus the triune character of the one living

26. J. C. Ryle, *Warnings to the Churches*, 158, emphasis in the original.

and true God. But what is overlooked is that these early creeds are not *evangelical* creeds, that is, creeds explicating soteric matters. As I just intimated, they were framed in the context of the Trinitarian and Christological debates in the fourth and fifth centuries and are sorely underdeveloped and virtually silent on soteriological matters. As has been often pointed out, there is nothing in them that the Judaizers whom Paul confronted in his letter to the Galatians could not also have endorsed. Nevertheless, Paul condemned the Judaizers in the strongest terms possible because they were preaching 'another gospel which is not another' when they corrupted his doctrine of justification by faith alone. Quite obviously, according to Paul there is no *saving* value in holding to an 'orthodox view' of the *person* of Christ if one is at the same time also holding to an 'unorthodox view' of the *work* of Christ. Which is just to say that the question of who Jesus is cannot be separated salvifically from the question of what he has done for us. And if Philip Melanchthon is right when he said, 'This is to know Christ: to know his benefits,' then one must even conclude that Rome does not even know correctly who Christ really is!

In order that I might make myself crystal clear here—and what I am now about to say may shock the reader but I assure him that I do not say it for its shock value—I would contend that one can believe from his heart that every statement of the Apostles' Creed, the Nicene Creed, the Niceno-Constantinopolitan Creed, the Definition of Chalcedon, and the Athanasian Creed is true and *still be lost*, if in order to be saved he is trusting to any degree in his own character, and/or if he believes that he must contribute at least some good works toward his salvation, and/or if he is trusting in Christ plus anyone or anything else. Church history is filled with too many examples of such 'believers' for us to ignore this fact, and they who so believe do so at the peril of their own souls. Martin Luther as an Augustinian monk confessed his faith many times during his monkish days using the Apostles' Creed, but according to Scripture until he cast himself in simple faith on Christ's saving work alone for his justification before God he was lost. John Calvin in his early years had the same experience.

Until these men cast themselves in simple trust upon Christ alone they were unsaved. So one must clearly see that there is a danger in reciting even the revered, time-honored, truth-laden Apostles' Creed if one assumes that by simply believing its tenets one is thereby necessarily saved. For it is possible to believe the Apostles' Creed, and all the other Christological creeds as well, but also believe at the same time that if one would go to heaven when one dies one must still put some kind of an 'and' or a 'plus' of his own good works after Christ's perfect work of obedience. But they who would trust in the work of Christ *plus* their own 'good works' that possess, they are informed by Rome if they are Roman Catholics, 'congruent merit' before God, *and/or* in the 'pristine righteousness' and intercessory work of Mary and Rome's designated saints, *and/or* in their pilgrimages to Rome's designated holy sites, *and/or* in their earning of indulgences, according to Paul, as the Judaizers did before them, have made Christ's cross-work of no value to them (ὑμας οὐδὲν ὠφελήσει, *humas ouden ōphelēsei*, Gal 5:2); they have been alienated from Christ (κατηργήθητε ἀπὸ Χριστοῦ, *katērgēthēte apo Christou*, 5:4a); they have fallen away from grace (της χάριτος ἐξεπέσατε, *tēs charitos exepesate*, 5:4b); they have abolished the offense of the cross (κατήργηται τὸ σκάνδαλον τοῦ σταυροῦ, *katērgētai to skandalon tou staurou*, 5:11); they are trusting in a 'different gospel which is no gospel at all' (1:6-7), and they are doing so at the peril of their souls, because they show thereby that they have never been truly regenerated by the Holy Spirit (or they would submit to the teaching of Holy Scripture alone[27]) but are still lost in their sin.[28]

I am quite aware that if today a minister leads a quiet life, leaves the unconverted world and misinformed Catholics alone, and preaches so as to offend no one, many will call him a 'fine churchman'. I am equally aware that when one expresses such opinions as I have expressed in this address today there will be many who will say: 'He is no churchman; rather, he is a schismatic.' I remain unmoved by such an accusation and believe that the Day of Judgment will show who were the true churchmen and who were not. For myself, I am convinced that they are the truest friends of Jesus Christ and his church who labor most for the preservation of the truth of the apostolic gospel even though they may be regarded in their own time as 'firebrands' and 'troublers in Israel.' So because Pelagianism, including in particular the modified form it takes today in Roman Catholicism, is always an attack on the *sola gratia, solus Christus*, and *sola fide* soteric principles, claiming as it does that man deserves at least some measure of credit for effecting his salvation, if not in its initiation, at least in his cooperation with initiating grace, and because Rome has given confessional Protestants

---

27. In light of John 4:41-42, 8:47, 1 Thessalonians 2:13, and 1 John 4:9-10, *Westminster Confession of Faith*, XIV/ii, reminds us that the Christian who has saving faith 'believeth to be true whatsoever is revealed in the word, for the authority of God himself speaking therein'.

28. This is why the practice of some so-called 'Protestant' evangelists who send their Roman Catholic converts back to the Roman Catholic Church is such a deplorable and scandalous compromise of the truth of the gospel. So-called 'cooperative evangelism' that seeks Roman Catholic support for 'evangelical' crusades does great harm in that it leaves every community in which it occurs in confusion as to what the true gospel is and where one should go to hear its proclamation. Such 'cooperative evangelism' should be vigorously opposed by those who love the gospel that the apostles preached.

no reason to anticipate any theological concessions on its part since its church doctrine is an interwoven 'seamless robe' which can brook no concessions without mortally damaging the whole, I would contend that the true church of Jesus Christ must ever be on guard to insure that the *sola gratia, solus Christus*, and *sola fide* soteric principles of Holy Scripture and of Paul specifically continue to be proclaimed as the sole ultimate way of salvation.

Furthermore, all the more is this vigilant proclamation necessary today since one has only to visit the great cathedrals of Europe, hear the Masses being said, and witness for himself the rows and rows of purchased burning candles 'praying' for the souls in purgatory, or visit Fatima in Portugal, as I have, or Lourdes in southern France and observe the Roman Catholic superstitions evidenced there every day, and then try to find a Protestant church in those cities in order to hear the pure preaching of God's Word to realize that a doctrinal reformation is as sorely needed today within Christendom as it was in the sixteenth century in order to capture once again the glorious truth of the Pauline gospel of justification by grace alone through faith alone in Christ's preceptive and penal obedience.

Such a reformation will come and can come only through *public* doctrinal conflict with Rome, openly pitting both in books, monographs, and pamphlets, and in sermons from the pulpit, first, the carefully exegeted, hermeneutically sound salvific teaching and world-and-life view of Holy Scripture against the superstitions and idolatries of Roman Catholic Tradition, and second, a sound knowledge of Rome's historical origins against its pretensions.[29] Protestants

---

29. This second point reminds me of Robert L. Dabney's insightful comments in his address, 'Uses and Results of Church History,' in *Discussions: Evangelical and Theological* (Reprint; London: Banner of Truth, 1967), 2.13, made upon his induction into the professorship of

should not be afraid of such conflict, for the theological genius of the Reformation is really a summons to return to the simplicity of the apostolic gospel: from looking away from the institutional church to Christ, from looking away from Mary and Rome's many other intercessors to Christ the sole Advocate, from looking away from the 'unbloody' Mass to the immeasurable worth of Christ's 'once for all' bloody self-sacrifice, from looking away from the meritoriousness of our alleged good works to God's justification of the ungodly on the sole basis of Christ's doing and dying. In a day when the Roman Catholic Church is receiving 'great press' in the Western media and growing throughout the world, it is high time for evangelical Protestant preachers and theologians publicly and firmly—*but civilly and warmly*—to distinguish again the Protestant faith from that of Roman Catholicism. For upon the doctrinal distinctives of classic Protestantism—its great *solas*—hang the destinies of immortal souls.

---

ecclesiastical history and polity at Union Seminary, Hampden-Sidney, Virginia in 1854:

> ...the best arguments against bad institutions are drawn from their history. The readiest way to explode unreasonable pretensions is to display their origin. Such an auditory as this need only be reminded that the battle against popery in the Reformation was fought on scriptural and historical grounds. Many of the most mortal stabs which Luther gave to mischievous popish institutions were by simply telling the ignorant world where and when they arose. And when the two hosts were regularly marshalled for controversy, there speedily came forth that great work, the parent of Protestant church history, the *Magdeburg Centuries* [thirteen volumes published from 1559 to 1574 under the editorship of Matthias Flacius—RLR]. This work, which was little more than a digest of ecclesiastical events, proved a grand historical argument against popery, and its effects were so deeply felt that Rome put forth her utmost strength in opposition to it, in the annals of Caesar Baronius. And now there is no better argument against popery than a simple history of its growth.

Chapter Seven

The Need for an Evangelistic Pulpit

> In the presence of God and of Christ Jesus, who will judge the living and the dead, and in view of his appearing and his kingdom, I give you this charge: Preach the Word; be prepared in season and out of season; correct, rebuke and encourage—with great patience and careful instruction. For the time will come when men will not put up with sound doctrine. Instead, to suit their own desires, they will gather around them a great number of teachers to say what their itching ears want to hear. They will turn their ears away from the truth and turn aside to myths. But you, keep your head in all situations, endure hardness, do the work of an evangelist, discharge all the duties of your ministry (2 Tim. 4:1-5).

A new vocation within the ranks of the ministry has appeared in our time. They who pursue this vocation—and they are deadly seriously about it—call themselves and are called by others "church futurists." As perceptive students, with unusual understanding, of the age in which we live and of the social and cultural trends which are developing with lightning speed all around us, these people are forecasting—in light of the woeful biblical illiteracy which has invaded the church—what pastors and church leaders must do if their churches are to cope with and survive in this post-modern, deconstructionist culture of the twenty-first century which has developed within the last thirty or forty years. I have read some of their books, know their dire predictions, and have given some thought regarding their remedies.

I would urge the evangelical church not to take these futurists' prognostications too seriously for two reasons: First, they are only men absent the gift of infallible prescience and foreknowledge of the future. At best, therefore, their predictions and solutions can be only short-range ones. Second, I believe they have failed to diagnose what the real problem facing the church is, and therefore their remedies do not and cannot address the church's real ills. They tell us that the church's problems today stem primarily from the new cultural situation in which the church finds herself: never has the church had to cope with a 'post-Christian' culture before, this massive 'pop' culture of illegal drugs, the moral corruption and immorality of the entertainment industry, the animosity of the world's mass media toward Christian spiritual and moral values, the legalization of abortion on demand and the legitimization of homosexuality and homosexual marriage, and just the general apathy of the Western populace toward spiritual things. In other words, the problem, we are led to believe, is primarily *outside* the church and the church must find new ways to adapt itself to these new cultural patterns if it would address itself to the problem and thus survive. But, do you know, my friends, as I see it, the problem is *not* out there. God's hand is not short that he cannot defeat his strongest foe! Why, with one man he can put ten thousand to flight! No, the problem is not outside the church and never has been. The problem is within, with the church's radical unbelief, apostate denominations, and the substitution of the true, pure gospel of Jesus Christ for jaded facsimiles of the gospel. As Pogo in the American comic strip by that name would say, 'We has met the enemy, and it is us!'

If my assessment of this matter is correct, what would I suggest that the Bible-believing church do? Well, as a 'futurist' I too lack infallible foreknowledge of the future. So I will not offer you my suggestions. But Paul, writing under divine inspiration, *was* an infallible, indeed, the greatest, 'futurist' of them all. And with divine insight he predicted:

> There will be terrible times in the last days [and we are in those last days and have been since the first coming of Christ]. People will be lovers of themselves, lovers of money, boastful, proud, abusive, disobedient to their parents, ungrateful, unholy, without love, unforgiving, slanderous, without self-control, brutal, not lovers of the good, treacherous, rash, conceited, lovers of pleasure rather than lovers of God—having a form of godliness but denying its power (2 Tim 3:1-5).

Accordingly, he continued:

> *the time will come* when men will not put up with sound doctrine. Instead, to suit their own desires, *they will gather around them* a great number of teachers to say what their itching ears want to hear. *They will turn their ears away* from the truth and turn aside to myths. (2 Tim 4:3-4)

All this is essentially what he had said earlier to Timothy: '...in future times some will abandon [ἀποστήσονταί, *apostēsontai*] the Faith and follow deceiving spirits and things taught by demons' (1 Tim 4:1).

These are perfect descriptions of the condition that exists both in the world and in the church today. It cannot be improved upon. What should the church do in such times? What should the evangelical, Bible-believing pastor do? What should *you* do, dear pastors?

I know of no other passage in all of Scripture that is a more appropriate source for the answers to these questions than 2 Timothy 4:1-5: St. Paul's charge to Timothy. Its solemnity and the urgent tone of its nine exhortations—the first eight of which spell out aspects of the Christian pastor's ministry and attitudes which must characterize him in his work, with the ninth simply summarizing the whole—underscore the awesome seriousness of the work of the ministry upon which you pastors have embarked.

In the spirit of the Apostle Paul, then, who charged

Timothy in the presence of God and of Christ Jesus, who in the glory and power of his kingdom will soon appear to judge the living and the dead, I similarly charge you to do the same nine things Paul charged Timothy to do. What are these duties?

First, preach (or "herald") the Word of the living God. The verb used here (κηρύσσειν, ***kērussein***) means 'proclaim aloud and publicly, make known as a herald'. This means that there must be a 'herald' quality about your preaching if it is to be Christian preaching. God honors the preaching that blazes with the passion and fire of a Spirit-filled 'herald heart'. He pours out his power upon that preaching

in which the preacher's proclamation comes from the broken heart and is accompanied by tears,

in which the preacher's encouragement is not in promises only but in the sharing of his own experiences of God's faithfulness and mercy, and

in which the preacher's counsel is animated by a deep and obvious devotion to God, by a true love for his people, and by a genuine concern for their eternal state and the salvation and sanctification of their souls.

And what Paul calls 'the Word' in verse 2 he calls 'sound doctrine' in verse 3 and 'the truth' in verse 4. Preach then the divinely inspired Word to your congregations, proclaim its sound doctrine to your flocks, 'herald' its truth and nothing but its truth from your pulpits and from your Sunday School lecterns! And let's be clear about one thing: This is what it really means to be Reformed: just to be *radically* biblical in your preaching and teaching.

Second, be prepared in season and out of season to preach the Word, that is to say, be about the task of proclaiming the Word of God whether the times are perceived to be right for it or not, whether you feel like doing it or not, and whether your congregation and auditors want to hear it or not. Continually preach the Word and only the Word of God without compromising its glory, power, and strength!

Third, correct those who are in error, whether in doctrine or life, by God's Word, and endeavor to convince them of their error and pull them back from it.

Fourth, rebuke those who persist in their error, whether in doctrine or life, and tell them that they persist in it at the peril of the health of their eternal souls.

Fifth, encourage, that is to say, appeal to your listeners to respond in faith to your exhortations, corrections, and rebukes drawn from God's Word to us from another world.

But take special note that Paul's qualifying phrase at this juncture—'with great patience and careful instruction'—appears to modify not just this last imperative but also all three of the preceding imperatives. Which is just to say, correct your people with great patience and careful instruction; rebuke your people with great patience and careful instruction; and encourage your people with great patience and careful instruction.

Paul now gives the reason for these charges in verses 3 and 4. Do these things, he says, because—as we have already noted—because of the regrettable tendency of people in general and professing believers in particular to fall away from the truth in deference to 'myths', that is, into things which are *not* true, *not* historical, *not* real.

Sixth, keep your head in all situations, that is, be balanced and self-controlled. This imperative, the only one in the midst of a catena of aorist imperatives, is a present imperative suggesting that, whereas the other duties are 'occasional' in that you will do them as the occasions and needs arise, yet in *all* things and at *all* times and under *all* conditions you must be continually and constantly level-headed. Your congregation will expect this in their pastor/teacher.

Seventh, endure hardship. Endure hardship, as Paul exhorted Timothy earlier in 2:3, like a good soldier of Christ Jesus who ever resists entanglements in any affairs that would inhibit his service to his heavenly Commander-in-Chief, like an athlete who knows that he will not receive the victor's wreath unless he competes according to the rules, like the farmer who knows he must work hard if he would receive a share of the crops.

Eighth, and Paul's last specific command: 'do the work of an evangelist [ἔργον ποίησον εὐαγγελιστοῦ, *ergon poiēson euangelistou*]' that is, 'do the work of announcing, proclaiming the good news about Jesus' saving benefits' and summon Jews and Gentiles, men and women, rich and poor, young and old, boys and girls, to faith in him even though you may be working in a somewhat settled situation with churches all around you and not in the new and unevangelized territories of 'the regions beyond'.

Now here I want to stress something that is of great importance for the preacher today. The English verb 'to evangelize' and its related nouns 'evangelist' and 'evangel' derive from the Greek verb εὐαγγελίζεσθαι, *euangelizesthai* (or εὐαγγελίζειν, *euangelizein*) ('to proclaim or to herald good news') and its cognate nouns εὐαγγελιστής, *euangelistēs*, Eph 4:11; Acts 21:8; 2 Tim 4:5 ('proclaimer or herald of good news') and εὐαγγέλιον, *euangelion* ('good news') and are employed often in the

New Testament to describe in one way or the other the church's commission. The verb εὐαγγελίζομαι, *euangelizomai*, occurs once in Matthew, ten times in Luke's Gospel, fifteen times in his Acts, twenty-three times (if we include the two occurrences in Hebrews) in the Pauline literature, three times in 1 Peter, and two times (εὐαγγελίζειν, *euangelizein*) in the Revelation (the verb is not found in Mark, John, James, 2 Peter, 1, 2, 3 John, or Jude). But the noun εὐαγγέλιον, *euangelion*, is found four times in Matthew, eight times (if one includes the long ending) in Mark, twice in Acts, sixty times in the Pauline literature, once in 1 Peter and once in the Revelation. This is, of course, fairly common knowledge. But what is not commonly recognized is that the verb εὐαγγελίζεσθαι, *euangelizesthai*, had a linguistic history both in the Septuagint as the translation of forms from the Hebrew verb root בשׂר, *bsr* ('to proclaim good news') and in pagan Greek literature before it ever came into the New Testament. Of particular interest to us are its occurrences in the latter part of Isaiah's prophecy:

Isaiah 40:9:
Go up on a high mountain,
O Zion [the church today], *herald of good tidings* [ὁ εὐαγγελιζόμενος, *ho euangelizomenos*].
Lift up your voice with strength,
O Jerusalem, *herald of good tidings* [ὁ εὐαγγελιζόμενος, *ho euangelizomenos*],
lift it up, do not be afraid,
say to the towns of Judah,
'Behold your God [comes as the Mighty One and will feed his flock like a shepherd]!'

Isaiah 52:7 (which Paul cites in Romans 10:15 as being descriptive of the New Testament gospel proclamation):

How beautiful on the mountains
are the feet *of those who bring good news* [εὐαγγελιζόμενου, *euangelizomenou*],
who proclaim peace,
who bring good tidings [ὁς εὐαγγελιζόμενος ἄγαθα, *hos euangelizomenos agatha*],
who proclaim salvation,
who say to Zion,
'Your God reigns!' (which is just to say, 'The kingdom of God has come!')

Isaiah 61:1:
The Spirit of the Sovereign Lord is on me,
because he has anointed me
to preach good news [εὐαγγελίσασθαι, *euangelisasthai*, which translates לְבַשֵּׂר] to the poor.

These verses show that Isaiah's concept of the 'good news' of 'peace' and 'salvation' that these 'beautiful feet' bring to spiritually impoverished people entails the proclamation of Yahweh's coming to Zion and his enthronement there on Zion with the implied ultimate dethronement of all the gods of paganism (see Isaiah's 'Behold your God!' and 'Your God reigns!').

His enthronement on Zion also holds out the promise of his people's release from exile, for which idea one may go to Isaiah 61:1-2 (which prophecy Jesus declared in Luke 4:17-21 was fulfilled in and by his mission):

The Spirit of the Sovereign Lord is upon me,
because the Lord has anointed me
to preach good news [εὐαγγελίσασθαι, *euangelisasthai*] to the poor.
He has sent me to bind up the brokenhearted,
to proclaim freedom for the captives
and release from darkness for the prisoners,
to proclaim the year of the Lord's favor.

Consequently, 'peace', 'righteousness', 'salvation', 'freedom from exile for captives', 'release from darkness', and 'the Lord's favor'—all to be found in the 'kingdom or reign of God'—are all present in the content of the 'heralding of the good news' to the 'poor' from the Old Testament (Septuagintal) perspective.

In pagan Greco-Roman literature the plural form (only) of εὐαγγέλιον, *euangelion*, is a technical term used within the context of the Caesar cult to designate the announcement of the birth or accession of an emperor or the achieving of a great victory. The coming of a new ruler meant the promise of peace and a new start for the world. An inscription from around 9 B.C. found in Priene on the coast of Asia Minor illustrates well these points when it speaks of Octavian Caesar (Augustus) who became the first Roman emperor in 31 B.C.:

> The providence which has ordered the whole of our life, showing concern and zeal, has ordained the most perfect consummation for human life by giving to it Augustus, by filling him with virtue for doing the work of a benefactor among men, and by sending in him...a saviour for us and those who come after us, to make war to cease, to create order everywhere...; the birthday of the god [Augustus] was the beginning for the world of the *glad tidings* [εὐανγελίων, *euangelion*] that have come to men through him....[1]

Here the 'glad tidings' refer to 'joyous news' of the birthday of the 'god', Augustus Caesar, who, purportedly filled with virtue, would be the world's 'savior' and make wars to cease

1. *Priene Inscriptions*, edited by F. Hiller von Gärtringen, 105, 40f. Note the similarity between the last sentence of the Priene inscription and the opening statement, 'The beginning of the good news,' in Mark 1:1. See also H.G. Liddell and R. Scott, εὐαγγέλιον [*euangelion*], *A Greek-English Lexicon*, revised by H.S. Jones (Oxford: Clarendon, 1940), with *Supplement* (1968), and G.H.R. Horsely, *New Documents Illustrating Early Christianity* (North Ryde: The Ancient History Documentary Research Center, 1981-), 3.12-15.

and usher in universal order (peace).

Is it any wonder then that when the New Testament age of fulfillment opened with the appearance of Jesus the true God and true Messiah, we find Mark speaking of 'the beginning of the good news' (Mark 1:1) and John the Baptist and Jesus both proclaiming the coming of the *reign of God* (Matt 3:2; 4:17)?

Accordingly, the New Testament usages of the verbs εὐαγγελίζεσθαι, *euangelizesthai* ('to evangelize, announce') and κηρύσσειν, *kērussein* ('to proclaim as a herald') highlight the *confrontational* character of the kingdom of God as it is exhibited in the present reign of Jesus Christ, for the gospel comes to us as an invading Word from another world into this one. Moreover, Christ's present reign is not simply one reign alongside others. Distinct in its nature from all other kingdoms—as distinct as a man is from beasts (see Dan 7:2-14)—his kingdom of grace is

> the only kingdom that decisively attests that life is more ultimate than death, that mercy can outreach the arenas of sin and guilt, and that the sphere of God is greater than the realms of hell. It signals the satisfaction of all legitimate human need, the triumph of divine mercy, humanity living life fit for eternity, the homecoming of the renewed community of God. It is the kingdom that cannot be frustrated by the puppet kingdoms of Satan but that explains them for what they really are. It is the enduring kingdom amid others that rise only to have their half day and then perish.
>
> ...the coming of Jesus of Nazareth [two thousand years ago] advance[d] the prophetic promise of the eschatological kingdom into the sphere of fulfillment—if not total fulfillment, yet nonetheless realization in a crucially significant way....
>
> Jesus in his own person is the embodied sovereignty of God. He lives out that sovereignty in the flesh. He manifests the kingdom of God by enthroning the creation-will of God and demonstrating his lordship over Satan. Jesus conducts himself as Lord and true King, ruling over human hearts, ruling over demons, ruling over

> nature at its fiercest, ruling over sickness, conquering death itself. With the coming of Jesus the kingdom [of God] is not merely immanent; it gains the larger scope of incursion and invasion. Jesus points to his release of the victims of Satan, and to his own devastation of demons and the demonic, as attesting that "the kingdom of God has come upon you" (Mark 12:28). He reveals God's royal power in its salvific activity.[2]

And by his death, resurrection, and ascension Christ has inherited the title above all titles—that of Lord (Phil 2:9-11). Now in the first-century Roman world the word κύριος, ***kurios*** ('lord') was regularly used to denote the politico-social superior above all other superiors, even the Roman emperor. From the Roman perspective there was only one lord of the world, the Roman Caesar. But according to the Christian proclamation, not only Caesar but also all other kings have a rival Lord, the majesty of whose person, the might of whose power, and the authority of whose crown out-rival the majesty, might, and authority of all the lesser lords of this earth, and before whom every knee will bow someday and every tongue will confess someday his Lordship to the glory of God the Father.

Therefore, doing the 'work of an evangelist' (2 Tim 4:5) is not simply telling people the so-called 'plan of salvation', that is, 'how to be saved', though it can and will include this. To 'evangelize' is to proclaim, to announce, to herald from the housetops that Jesus Christ, who passed through death and resurrection to heaven's enthronement, is King of kings and Lord of lords and that his kingdom in its grace modality has come. And to announce that Jesus Christ reigns as King and Lord of the universe is to announce to all the self-acclaiming Caesars of this world that they do not. To

---

2. Carl F. H. Henry, 'Reflections on the Kingdom of God,' *Journal of the Evangelical Theological Society*, 35/1 (March 1992), 42.

proclaim Christ's Lordship is to *confront* all the petty pretensions of the religious and secular pagan lords of this world with *his* true and sovereign Kingship which demands heart submission from every member of the human race. As Paul asserts in Romans, his apostleship in the service of God's gospel concerning his Son was divinely intended 'to call people from all the Gentiles to the obedience that comes from faith' in Jesus Christ (Rom 1:1-5).

Nor is the 'proclamation of the gospel' merely the recounting of the details of a salvific system whereby people are saved, that is, the delineating of an *ordo salutis* or an *ordo applicatio*, though it should and will eventually get around to this at some point. No, the proclamation of the gospel is most directly the proclamation that the crucified and risen Jewish Messiah is King and Lord of the universe who now reigns from heaven, and that in that capacity he has *authoritatively* summoned the whole world to repent of its idolatrous pretensions to works-righteousness (Acts 17:30) and to obey him through placing faith in his active and passive obedience for men and for their salvation (Rom 1:5). Only in such entrustment will one find the *shalom* of God, 'righteousness', 'salvation', 'freedom from the exile of sin', 'release from spiritual darkness', and 'the Lord's favor'.

Nor is the 'proclamation of the gospel' merely the 'offering' or 'sharing' of Christ's saving benefits to those who apathetically (that is, who have no sense of their spiritual poverty) may or may not want them (it should *never* be this; this is preaching 'cheap grace'). Paul would no more have said to his auditors, 'If you would like to have an experience of living under an emperor, you might try the Jewish Messiah,' than Caesar's herald would have said: 'If you would like an emperor, you might try Nero.' Just as Caesar's herald would have announced: 'Nero has ascended the throne of Rome and has been crowned as your emperor. Submit to his imperial authority, and disobey him upon pain of death,' so also by his gospel Paul proclaimed: 'Christ by his obedient life and sacrificial death has become the Lord of the universe and your sovereign King! Submit to him if you would be delivered from the bonds of sin that enslave you, and disobey him upon pain of eternal death!' In short, the gospel, that is, the 'good news' concerning God's Son, is the proclamation that through the death and resurrection of a very human—even a Jewish—life the living God in the person of Jesus Christ has become the sovereign King and Savior of the world and demands the repentance and the obedience that flows from faith in him. And only to those who *from the heart* submit to his authority and trust in his saving work will he grant the gift of eternal life. All others, in his wrath, he will destroy.[3]

By the 'folly' of the cross—regarded by the world as folly because a Roman cross is the last place in the whole wide world where one would think to find God—God has reversed the world's values, turning its shame into glory and all human glory into shame. By the folly of the cross he has outsmarted the wise, by the weakness of the cross he has overpowered the strong. But how? Hundreds of Jews had been crucified by the Romans in that first century. Why was his crucifixion so special? Because of who he was and because of what happened on the third day after his crucifixion.

Who was he? Not just the son of David and thus earthly royalty but also the Messianic Son of Man and the divine Son of God, the majesty of whose person outrivals all the pomp of all the earthly kings who have ever lived combined, and the might of whose power is infinite, upholding all things even as he hung upon the cross making purification for our sins, who was publicly declared to be the Son of God by

---

3. I am indebted to N.T. Wright, *What Saint Paul Really Said* (Grand Rapids: Eerdmans, 1997), 41-5, for some of the insights of this section.

what happened next, namely, by his resurrection from the dead.

By his resurrection Christ's crucifixion for our sins was turned into a great victory. By his resurrection Jesus has gone through death and emerged victoriously on the other side. His resurrection means that Christ really is God's anointed King and Lord. He has brought to light life and immortality. The Age to Come has already come in its saving power. And the gospel is the announcement of that great victory. But it is the announcement of even more than that! It goes beyond the simple glad tidings that Jesus Christ reigns today as Lord and King. It also announces that the sinner who trusts Christ's active and passive obedience will receive the forgiveness of sins and right standing before God and will live forever. This is just to say that the gospel is to be enunciated precisely in terms of the doctrine of justification by faith alone in Jesus Christ, the King and only Savior of men. And because he lives and reigns, we too shall someday live and reign, and the very cosmos itself will someday be restored to its paradisiacal state at his return and the resurrection of our bodies. By his cross and resurrection Jesus Christ has inherited that title above all titles—the title of Lord.

The gospel then, my brothers, is indeed a royal announcement—the King's proclamation of the appearing of a great Victor and of an equally great victory over sin and death. And to make light of God's forgiveness by the cross to any degree is to make light of the great price God paid in order to do away with sin. Trivializing the gospel by portraying it as something that men may choose or reject with impunity *if* they please, *as* they please, *when* they please, *how* they please, is to cast its precious pearls before swine who do not recognize its character or its value. And I fear we do that when we simply stress that heaven and eternal life are gifts, and then offer these gospel blessings without stressing at the same time that the grace that gives both them and all other good things freely and without cost demands out of gratitude everything—total submission to his Lordship and our discipleship! Let's not be party to turning the announcement of the great victory of the King of kings into cheap grace by urging men to 'try Jesus' in the same way they might try a Coca Cola: 'Try him; you'll like him!' We must make men understand again *in this age* that they refuse to bow before this heavenly Emperor at the peril of their eternal souls, that they will know only eternal misery and woe if they continue in their rebellion against him, and that they will know this misery and woe at his hands!

To 'evangelize' then means to proclaim faithfully the 'gospel', that is, to proclaim the whole truth about Jesus Christ both as *Savior* and as *Lord.* And the aim of evangelism should be to bring to conversion those who hear the gospel, that is, to bring them to repentance toward God and to faith in Jesus Christ as your Savior and Lord.

Ninth—and now we come to Paul's summation of his commands to Timothy—discharge *all* the duties of your ministry. That is to say, fully and completely discharge not only these eight specific duties but also any and all other ministerial responsibilities to which Christ, the Lord of the church, may call you. You will find many of them delineated in Paul's first letter to Timothy. Moreover, a faithful minister of the gospel will not only do the work of an evangelist but he will also train his flock to evangelize, for according to Paul it is your responsibility to 'prepare God's people for works of service' (Eph 4:11-12). If I were to hazard a guess, I would say that perhaps the most glaring failure of most pastors today is in this area of training their people to evangelize their friends and neighbors. Are you doing it?

Standing now today, as I do, in this distinguished pulpit

of world-wide reputation, I can say that you, dear pastors, have my sincere admiration and respect. I have quickly learned to love you. And I am confident that you have the admiration, respect, and love of your congregations. I charge you, therefore, do nothing to destroy their admiration and respect. We all know of instances where highly placed church leaders have brought disrepute to the name of Christ. Pray for these fallen brothers, weep for them, but do not follow their shameful ways! To the contrary, so labor in your pastoral charge that Christ will be able to say to you when you stand before him someday:

> Well done, *good* and *faithful* servant! You have been faithful with a few things; I will put you in charge of many things. Come and share your Master's happiness!

In conclusion, wherever you go, whatever you do, in all of your conversations of life, make much of the life and blood of Jesus Christ, make his cross and his resurrection the centerpiece of your pulpit ministry and your pastoral service for him, and God will richly bless you, for Christ has said, 'My Father will honor the one who serves me' (John 12:26).

I want to relate a story in closing. Some time back I viewed the 1993 Academy Award movie of the year, *Schindler's List*, the Steven Spielberg story of Oskar Schindler, the Nazi war profiteer, who shortly after the German invasion of Poland in 1939 began to use the Jews of the Krakow ghetto as workers in his pots and pans factory. At first he saw them only as chattel to be used to line his own pockets, which he did quite successfully, becoming exceedingly rich. But as the war dragged on, and as he increasingly witnessed Nazi atrocities being inflicted against the Jews of Poland, increasingly did he begin to use his own wealth to bribe Nazi officials and army officers to give him more and more Jews for his factory that the Nazis had turned into a munitions factory, and that became a model of non-productivity in the Nazi war effort. Though it virtually bankrupted him personally, he saved over twelve hundred Jews from certain death in the gas chambers.

I recount this story line only to say that I was struck by some statements put in his mouth toward the end of the movie. The war has just ended, and having worked for the Third Reich, both he and his Jewish factory workers realize that the Allied authorities might search for him. As he bids farewell to them, they present him with a letter signed by each of them which they hope will help him before the Allied authorities.

At this moment Schindler suddenly becomes very sober and quietly says: 'I could have done more. I could have done more!' He begins to sob. 'I could have done more. I didn't do enough. This car—why did I keep the car? Ten people right there. Ten people. Ten more people.' Pulling off his lapel pin, he exclaims, 'The pin. Two people. This is gold. Two more people. One more. I could have bought more people! But I didn't.' His knees crumble and he sobs heavily.

As his words—'I could have done more! Why did I keep the car? Ten people right there. The pin. This is gold. Two people. One more. I could have bought more people. But I didn't'—seared themselves into my mind as I sat in the darkness of that theater, I suddenly became convicted that many Christians—I among them—are going to be asking similar questions at the Great White Throne Judgment: 'Why did I not do more to reach the lost for Christ? Why did I think I had to have that more expensive house, that more expensive car? Why did I not use more of my resources for the cause of Christ?' More poignantly, 'Why was I not more committed to Christ's cause? Why did I esteem self-preservation so highly?' In that Great Day I fear that many of us will have no answers to salve our smitten consciences.

May God raise up in our day, while divine patience still grants us time, a multitude of men and women who will follow in Paul's footsteps and boldly dare to go into this lost and dying world where no man has ever gone before with the liberating gospel of God!

Lift high the cross,
the love of Christ proclaim,
Till all the world
adore his sacred name.

Chapter Eight

The Need for a Reformed Pulpit

In this address I want you to consider with me a notion that prevails virtually everywhere today, the notion that Christianity, as a way of life, makes no real life-transforming demands on its adherents—that to be Christian in name only is sufficient as far as commitment is concerned—and what should be done about it.

Why do I say that this notion prevails virtually everywhere today? Well, it is an indisputable fact that the modern church, tolerating as it does all kinds of heresies to exist with impunity within its walls, has become doctrinally pluralistic. Accordingly, a *doctrinal nominalism* prevails almost everywhere among the laity—a 'who cares about doctrine' attitude—eloquently captured recently in the bold statement by a so-called American 'Christian' weight-loss priestess: 'Women don't care about the Trinity. They just want to lose weight.'

The same must also be said with regard to the modern church's ethical walk. An *ethical nominalism*—a disconnect between grace and the holy life—abounds in the church today. Regrettably, a fair characterization would have to adjudge many church members as worldly and carnal: while they pay lip service to the Savior's work in their behalf, evidence would indicate that no real love for the Savior animates their attitudes and actions for, thinking relativistically, they openly break his commandments, desecrate the Lord's Day; take his name rarely in witness but often in vain, with the sins of fornication, adultery, immorality and unbiblical divorce flourishing among them almost as much as these sins do outside the church's pale.

It is no different when we assess the modern church for its zeal for God and for holy things: too many professing Christians have little zeal for Christ and for the cause of truth, and have become spiritually lethargic, cold, and lacking in that Spirit-animated vibrancy that ought to characterize Christians generally. Accordingly, an *ecclesial nominalism* is rampant in which allegiance to the church as the family of God and the communion of saints is rare and undernourished. I think it is fair to conclude that many church members 'have lost their first love', if they ever had it. Too many of them are in a spiritual malaise because of the seduction of modern secularity. And too many are Christians in name only, mere 'spectators' as far as the church's divinely-ordained mission to the world is concerned. In a word, the modern church is in desperate need of revival and reformation. It must be confronted with the fact that Christianity, if false, is of no importance, if true, is of infinite worth and importance, but the one thing it cannot be is only nominally important. How are we pastors to confront this problem in our time?

I know that you pastors are struggling mightily to plant and/or to grow churches in your cities, towns and villages. But why should you bother? May I suggest that you should not be planting and growing churches simply in order that your church's 'brand name' can 'get a cut of the soul-winning action'. To do so would be to display the worst kind of party spirit and sectarianism. May I suggest that you should be laboring to reverse the trend I just described and to make a distinctive and lasting contribution to the life of the church as a whole. May I also suggest that in order to reverse the present trend your only justification for planting and growing churches anywhere is that you plant and grow, not 'truly', not 'thoroughly', but just *simply* and *distinctly* Reformed-church witnesses to the truth of God. If you don't do this—

and I am not suggesting for a moment that you are not trying to do this—if your interests are just to plant broad evangelical church witnesses, if your intention is just to duplicate the work that others are also doing, your energy and resources would be better spent in other lands where there is no Christian witness at all, for I believe that the old question 'Why should one person hear the gospel twice when many have never heard it once?' still has an impeccable logical power about it. So I say again, only if you intend to make a unique contribution to the health and growth of the Kingdom of God where you live should you continue to plant and to grow your churches.

Do you have such a contribution to make? I definitely think you do. Given the fact that the established church is doctrinally and morally adrift, is in a sick and weakened spiritual condition with signs everywhere of its deterioration, such as low church attendance, its influence is negligible on *national* life and morals. But in several ways our Reformed distinctives provide precisely the cure for what ails the church today. The promulgation of our distinctives, warmly and winsomely, is therefore vitally important if the Christian church is to survive the hammer blows it is receiving from our secular, decadent, post-modern culture. In this address I want to mention two areas where your voices need to be raised, raised loudly, and raised continually until you have affected the whole church and have been instrumental in bringing reformation to the church for the glory of God alone.

Reformed Church Growth

The first area I want you to consider with me is church growth. I want to begin here by saying that, while it may never have occurred to you, our Reformed doctrinal distinctives are absolutely essential for true church growth. This may indeed sound strange since in our time Reformed churches are known more for their emphasis on doctrine than for their evangelism and church growth. Nevertheless, I would urge that Reformed theology is absolutely necessary to these achievements. And history itself reminds us that the vast majority of the great missionaries and evangelists of the past have been Calvinists, such as John Bunyan, the Puritans, George Whitefield, nearly all the leaders of the Great Awakening (the Wesleys are the exceptions here, being tagged by J. I. Packer for their efforts as 'confused Calvinists'), Charles Spurgeon, the leaders of the modern missionary movement from William Carey and the Baptists in England, Henry Venn and the Church of England, Jonathan Edwards and Adoniram Judson in America, to the Church of Scotland. We have a God-honored legacy here and much therefore to say to our generation.

The problem in our day is twofold: On the one hand, *we are seeing a waning confidence within Evangelicalism in the message of the gospel*. In the United States—I can speak more authoritatively about the condition of the church there than I can about the condition of the church in Britain—the evangelical church shows signs of losing confidence in the convincing and converting power of the gospel message. Why else would preachers trade the bold and accurate proclamation of the Gospel in exchange for pragmatic managerial techniques to build the church unless they had lost confidence in the Gospel's power to change lives and to transform society? That is why increasing numbers of churches hear and prefer sermons on family life and psychological health. We are being overtaken by what Os Guinness has called the managerial and therapeutic revolutions. The winning message, it seems, is the one which helps people solve their *temporal* problems and improve their self-image, and makes them feel good about themselves. In such a cultural climate, preaching on the law, sin and repentance, and the cross has all but disappeared, even in evangelical churches. The old gospel is not popular. So the church has become 'user friendly', 'consumer oriented', and the gospel is watered down to appeal to the consumers. As a result the church is being inundated with the plague of 'cheap grace', to use Dietrich Bonhoeffer's expression. Today's 'gospel' is all too often a 'gospel' without cost, without repentance, without commitment, without discipleship, and thus 'another gospel' and accordingly no gospel at all, producing at best 'spectator Christians', Christians in name only, all traceable to the fact that this is how too many people today have come to believe that the church must be grown.

On the other hand, *we are seeing a waning confidence within Evangelicalism in preaching as the means by which the gospel is to be spread.* Spirit-animated preaching is increasingly being viewed as outdated and ineffective 'Bible thumping'. As a result, preaching is giving way, at least in the United States, to multi-media presentations, drama and dance, 'sharing times', innocuous sermonettes on self-esteem, and pathetic 'how to...in three easy steps' devotionals. So churches have borrowed techniques from the advertising industry to grow themselves. Telemarketing, in particular, has taken the place of personal one-on-one evangelism, and cell groups are now the darling of the church growth movement. And the infusion of the popular culture into many churches in the forms of applause for the church's 'performers' and sappy contemporary music gives evidence of the diminution of those churches' vision of God and suggests that in their eagerness to be relevant they have become only more and more desperate! Churches so infected, look to the multiplication of programs to bring about their growth; they sponsor conferences and seminars on every conceivable topic under the sun; they subdivide their congregations down into marrieds, singles, single-parent, divorced, thirty-something, twenty-something, teens, unemployed, child-abused, drug-addicted, and so on, attempting to arrange programs for them all. This preoccupation with the needs of individual 'selves' is so pronounced that the salient purpose of the church—to know and to worship God and to make him known in all his holiness and love to a lost world—is obscured by the 'what can God do for me' mentality of this 'me' generation. And while there is nothing necessarily unseemly in these attempts to meet the needs of these groups as long as these efforts do not diminish the primacy of biblical preaching in the life of the church, one might still justifiably wonder if the perception that this is what one *must* do in order to minister effectively in the twenty-first century is not in itself a manifestation of waning confidence in the universal appeal and power of the gospel. And once a person joins such a church, conventional wisdom has it, the church and the minister must meet his every felt need. Accordingly, the pastor/teacher in the United States has become more and more a manager, a facilitator, a motivator, even a 'rush chairman', promising the newcomer that all his needs will be met—everything but a herald of the whole counsel of God who marches to the beat of the transcendent Drummer, and this all because we are losing confidence in preaching God's Word as the primary means for the growth of the church and the individual Christian.

What is the cure to this malady? A restored confidence in the Reformed doctrine of the sovereignty of God in salvation! When polished, self-confident, show-boat-type preachers, for example, draw attention to themselves by using music that appeals to the emotions, story-telling, hysteria and hype and appeal to their viewers' 'sense of self-worth' in order to produce 'decisions', it is evident that they don't understand the depravity of man, either their own or their audience's, or they would not act this way. Why do we say this? Because a biblical understanding of the depravity of man and the necessity of God's sovereign initiative in salvation produces abject humility in a preacher and the very antithesis of human self-confidence, namely, confidence in God alone.

Read 1 Corinthians 1:26-31 and let Paul instruct you anew that the truth of God's election destroys human pride and removes all boast before God. Learn anew that only God can convert a sinner, that only God can grow a saint, that no one can boast in this matter of salvation because God does it all (see 1 Cor 3:5-7). Neither the preacher nor the convert can take any credit. Salvation is all God's doing. 'It is because of him that we are in Christ Jesus' (1 Cor 1:30); 'salvation belongs to the Lord' (Jon 2:9). Accordingly, the church needs to be reassured that it can preach the simple, unadorned, unglamorized, unglittery gospel message of the cross, knowing that God will use it to save souls and build his church.

Then read 1 Corinthians 2:1-5 and let Paul instruct you anew that preaching does not need to be spruced up by the use of the finest Greek oratorical skills or modern communication methodologies. Neither does the gospel message need appended to it the philosophical cogitations of an Aristotle or an Aquinas or Freud's analyses of human nature. And here we are bold to say that it is the Reformed theology alone which supplies the necessary theological underpinning which makes true dependence upon God in gospel proclamation possible. When will true reformation come to the church? I say with confidence that it will only come when through all our failures we ministers stop resorting to and relying upon our natural and oratorical skills and clever organizational techniques in order to force church growth and start preaching again with Spirit-animated power God's simple pristine Word from another world to ours and relying upon God's Spirit to do his work.

Martin Luther once said: 'While I drink my little glass of Wittenberg beer the gospel runs its course and overthrows empires.' Now that is truly the finest and most comforting thing I have ever heard said about beer. What Luther meant, of course, is that he understood that a man's conversion is not something that can be humanly 'induced'. He understood that *he* could not change the world. And he knew that once the seed of the Word is sown and watered, the new life comes into being only by stepping aside and letting God's Spirit do his work. Therefore, after preaching Luther could cheerfully and trustfully step down from the pulpit; he didn't need to go on incessantly bellowing and roaring across the countryside. He could joyously drink his little glass of Wittenberg beer and trust in God to work. In all too many cases today we do not sin by doing too little work. On the contrary, many of us ought to ask ourselves whether we are still capable in God's name of simply trusting him to work. Take my word for it, dear brothers, you can actually serve and worship God by occasionally lying flat on your back after proclaiming the gospel and the unsearchable riches of Christ, getting rid of your everlasting need to produce, and simply trusting God to do his work.

None of this that I have just said here, of course, is intended to suggest even for a moment that Reformed preachers may use bad grammar or should be anti-intellectual or idle. If one were to draw such a conclusion from what I have said, it would indicate that he knows little or nothing about the content and substance of the Reformed faith, for anyone who knows anything at all about the Reformed faith will know that it is anything but anti-intellectual and a motivator to sloth. It demands the very best from us in every area of life. But what I do intend to say is that the Reformed understanding of the gospel with its biblical implicates of human depravity, unconditional election, particular atonement, irresistible grace, and perseverance in holiness must not be watered down or ignored in the interest of church growth, and that it will only be when we unceasingly and uncompromisingly proclaim the message of 'Christ and him crucified' and the whole counsel of God that true reformation and true church growth will come to the church.

You see, all true reformation and genuine spiritual renewal comes from Christ alone. True reformation is not worked up by human effort. The last church in the world to be visited by spiritual renewal will be the church which thinks it can produce it. In one sense, reformation is not even prayed down, though much effectual prayer has always been behind the great periods of spiritual awakening which the church has periodically known. No, the source of all true reformation is none other than Christ, the Baptizer of his people. It is he and he alone who can reform and renew his church. And all effectual prayer on the part of God's people *before* his outpouring of blessing is only the response of a particular heart attitude which he has graciously infused within them. And what attitude is that? A lowly spirit and a broken and contrite heart! The church of Jesus Christ needs the gale of the reforming, quickening, enkindling Spirit of Christ sweeping through it today, calling it back to forsaken revealed truths, strengthening its limbs, infusing it with boldness and courage, and empowering it to great deeds. And if that gale is not presently ours, it is doubtless because *we* are not sufficiently low in the dust before him, seeking his forgiveness for placing our confidence in 'broken cisterns that can hold no water' and for forsaking the pristine, powerful proclamation of Christ and his cross.

We should all be reminded that our God looks not primarily at the outward—at our fine attire and our Emily Post or Amy Vanderbilt manners. He looks primarily at our hearts. And what does he see when he looks beyond *our* fine dress and *our* best social decorum? Does he see hearts, to employ here an old Dutch Reformed phrase, that have 'spent time at Sinai' as well as at Calvary, that have been made conscious that apart from being bathed in his grace and mercy our hearts are deceitful above all things and desperately wicked? Does he see hearts beating in true humility before him? Does he see hearts that understand that without him they can do nothing good? Or have we forgotten our own Reformed theology? Is it possible that he sees proud and haughty spirits within us, insisting on doing things our way? Does he see hearts that have not yet come to the end of themselves? Does he see hearts that are willing to try one more 'how to' manual on church growth before they sink in humble desperation before him and cry out for his help and blessing?

Do we desire to see genuine reformation and spiritual renewal occur in our midst and in the church at large? Surely we do! Then we must continually cry out to him, publicly from our pulpits and privately from our closets, for that brokenness of spirit before him that alone he honors with his animating presence. Let us importune heaven for new depths of humility before him that he might regale us with his power from on high! And let us strive to be true to the Reformed faith in our church planting and church growth methods! Not to do so will incur the divine displeasure for hypocrisy.

Reformed Worship

The second area I want you to consider with me is the matter of worship. Every theology produces a particular kind of worship and a particular kind of piety behind that worship. How one thinks about God, you see, will affect how one worships and how one walks before him. Our Reformed worship tradition has a number of things to say to our generation of Christians about this matter.

Our worship tradition must first remind our generation that the worship of God is the most important of all the Christian's duties. That's the primary reason why one should go to church: to worship God. In today's church climate this is a radical idea, I know. Nevertheless, we should go to church, *not* to evangelize, *not* to provide a comfortable 'consumer-friendly' setting for the unchurched, *not even* primarily for the benefit that fellowship with other Christians surely brings, and definitely *not* just for lectures and devotionals, but in order to worship God. We should also understand that the missionary task is not the most important task the church has either. Missionary effort exists among the nations, as John Piper reminds us in his *Let the Nations be Glad*, only because worship of the true God among them doesn't!

Second, we must convince our generation of Christians that the Reformed tradition's 'regulative principle' regarding worship should be the governing principle of all Christian worship, that is to say, that Christians must do in worship only those things which God commands, clearly perceiving that 'what is not commanded is forbidden' and just as self-consciously rejecting the dictum that 'what is not expressly forbidden is permissible' (see Gen 4:4-5; Lev 10:1-2; Num 16-17; 2 Chron 26:16-19; Jer 19:5; Matt 15:9; Mark 7:6-13; John 4:22-24; 14:6; Col 2:20-23; *Westminster*

Confession of Faith, I, 6; XX, 1-8). In this connection it must also be said that we must be careful not to elevate some cherished *cultural tradition* to the level of a worship principle to which all other Christians must adhere. The Reformed approach to worship will produce a worship that is biblical, spiritual, simple, weighty, and reverent. It will produce a worship centered upon God, substantial and life-transforming. It will prohibit a worship that is superficial in character, complicated by ritual, stimulated by props and flippant in tone.

Anyone who will take the time to study the matter will have to conclude that worship in evangelical churches today is, speaking generally, approaching bankruptcy. There is neither rhyme nor reason, much less biblical warrant, for the order of and much that goes on in many evangelical church services today. The fact of the matter is, much evangelical 'worship' is simply not true worship at all. For decades now evangelical churches have been conducting their services for the sake of unbelievers. Both the revivalistic service of a previous generation and the 'seeker service' of today are shaped by the same concern—appeal to the unchurched. Not surprisingly, in neither case does much that might be called Christian worship occur. As a result, many evangelicals who have been sitting for years in such worship services are finding their souls drying up, and they have begun to cry for something else. Accordingly, they have become vulnerable to the appeal of the *mysterium* of hierarchical liturgical services. This is why some today are 'on the Canterbury trail' or defecting to Greek Orthodoxy and to Roman Catholicism. Others who have simply been spectators for years in their worship services are getting caught up in the people-involving, albeit shallow, worship of charismatic services.

The answer to these problems in contemporary worship

will not be found by adopting the style of an ecclesiastical tradition foreign to our Reformed tradition. Some Reformed ministers, I fear, have seen the above defections as a call to imitate their 'more successful rivals'. So they have adopted the perceived 'winning formulae' of these attracting churches. Consequently, today one can walk into many Reformed churches, at least in America, on the Lord's Day and not know for sure whether one will worship in a traditional or contemporary, liturgical or non-liturgical, formal or revivalistic fashion. This is regrettable, I believe, and in the long run damaging to the promulgation of the Reformed faith. After all, we cannot expect to carry Reformed 'water' in non-Reformed 'buckets'. The real cure to the problems in contemporary worship will be found in the simple, spiritual, substantial and serious worship of the Reformed faith and liturgy. In Christ the worshiper enjoys fellowship with the one living and true God who, *even for believers*, according to the author of Hebrews, is a 'consuming fire'.

Consequently, while Christian worship should certainly be joyous and filled with gladness (Ps 149:2), the author of Hebrews urges that it must also be conducted 'with reverence and awe [μετὰ εὐλαβείας καὶ δέους, *meta eu labeias kai deous*]' (Heb 12:28-29). The triune God of the Reformed faith is an awe-inspiring, absolutely sovereign, infinitely just and infinitely gracious, incomprehensible Deity. He will not long be known as such or served as such by a people fed rote ritual or revivalistic preaching or emotional choruses and gospel songs. Our God must be worshiped with the renewed mind. Faith in him requires understanding. And the understanding of our congregations grows primarily as it is nourished by the singing of hymns and psalms and by the prayers and preaching of our public worship services. Therefore, we cannot adopt forms of worship that are either simply 'liturgical' or theologically shallow and expect to remain for long biblically sound and Reformed. Our theology, like all systems of theology, must have a form of worship through which it is expressed and communicated. Neglect that form of worship and our theology will cease to be meaningful to us. What then should our worship be like? What should it include?

Such worship will emphasize and feature the well-read public reading of Holy Scripture, the only infallible rule of faith and practice, and biblically based, hermeneutically sound expository preaching of that Scripture, as interpreted by the classic Reformed confessions.

Such worship will also include contemplation of God's holy Law in keeping with the law-gospel paradigm in order to aid the worshiper in his understanding of his vileness before God and to promote its use as a guide for Christian conduct. Our carnal and antinomian age is in desperate need of a healthy dose of the Law of God. Evangelical Christians have become morally lazy, excuse-ridden, and relativistic. It is the Reformed tradition, above all others, which has given prominence to reading and meditating on the Law of God. If you doubt this, just consult the *Westminster Confession of Faith*, XVI/i-ii and XIX/v-vi, and the *Larger Catechism* (Questions 97-148) *and Shorter Catechism* (Questions 41-81). Regular contemplation in our worship services of God's holy Law as the covenant way of life would do much to cure our churches of their carnal, spectator kind of Christianity and to restore true personal piety, parental and children's responsibilities, and the Protestant work ethic in, and the spiritual reclamation of, our lands.

Such worship will include intelligent prayers to the Almighty in the name of Christ, which means that you pastors must not only give time and thought to your own public prayers but that you must also insure that any ruling elder whom you ask to lead the assembly in public prayer will pray God-honoring prayers as well. Such prayers should include adoration of God, confession of sin, and petitions in behalf of congregational and individual needs.

Such worship will include theologically sound congregational singing. For this I personally recommend for the American church the *Trinity Hymnal*. It will also include the much-neglected singing of the psalms which express the full range of human emotions in worship. The biblical psalms are realistic in a way that many hymns are not and that choruses can hardly ever be. They also contrast the righteous and the wicked and highlight the conflict between them and thereby encourage a bold, militant spirituality such as our Huguenot and Puritan forefathers knew and lived by. For this I recommend, particularly for churches for whom regular psalm-singing would be a new thing, the *Trinity Psalter*.

Such worship will include periodically the faithful and reverent observance of the ordinances of the church, namely, baptism and the Lord's Supper.

Such worship will also stress Sabbath observance. Any attempt at recovering a Reformed spirituality would do well carefully to study the best of the Puritan literature on the observance of the Lord's Day. Observance of the Lord's Day not only provides unhurried time for prayer, reading of Scripture and meditation all day long, but also becomes the day around which all the rest of the week is organized. You see, if one knows he is going to devote a day to spiritual concerns and the elimination of secular distractions, he will also know that he must organize the remaining six days in such a way that his other obligations will be met.

Finally, such worship will *not* include church announcements which have nothing to do with the worship of God and which actually interfere with congregational worship.

* * * * *

To sum up what we have said, our Reformed tradition has exactly the medicine that will heal what ails the secular worldly church today. Particularly will it cure the church over time, in my opinion, of its rampant doctrinal, ethical, and ecclesial nominalism and 'spectatorism'. Our Reformed confidence in the preached gospel in the power of the Holy Spirit as the power of God unto salvation can put an end to the foolish manipulative techniques employed in all too many church planting and church growth efforts today by those who call themselves evangelicals. Our Reformed regulative principle of worship will restore God-centered worship and piety and overthrow the mysticism and superficiality of what passes for worship in many liturgical and charismatic quarters today. And a Reformed liturgy can bring an end to the chaos evident in the rampant man-centered liturgies that exist in too many churches today.

How important is it, then, to plant and to grow Reformed churches? I believe it is absolutely and vitally important. There is no greater work in which one could be involved. So let's not hide our Reformed light, graciously given to us in Holy Scripture, under a bushel. Let's give everything we are and have in demolishing the stronghold of nominal Christianity by the establishing of Reformed witnesses to God's truth that will endure for all generations. No less than the survival of biblical Christianity is at stake.

Our God, our help in ages past,
our hope for years to come,
Our shelter from the stormy blast,
and our eternal home.
Under the shadow of your throne
your saints have dwelt secure,
Sufficient is your arm alone,
and our defence is sure!

For Further Reading

I would recommend that preachers of the gospel should read *all* of the following books on preaching:

Adams, Jay, *Preaching with Purpose* (Zondervan)

Carrick, John, *The Imperatives of Preaching* (Banner of Truth)

Chapell, Bryan, *Christ-Centered Preaching* (Baker)

Clowney, Edmund, *Preaching Christ from All the Scriptures* (Presbyterian and Reformed)

Greidanus, Sidney, *Preaching Christ from the Old Testament* (Eerdmans)

Kistler, Don (ed.), *Feed My Sheep* (Soli Deo Gloria)

Larsen, David, *The Company of the Preachers* (Kregel)

Lloyd-Jones, Martyn, *Preaching and Preachers* (Zondervan)

Logan, Sam (ed.), *The Preacher and Preaching* (Presbyterian and Reformed)

Piper, John, *The Supremacy of God in Preaching* (Baker)

Robinson, Haddon, *Biblical Preaching* (Baker)

Spring, Gardner, *The Power of the Pulpit* (Banner of Truth)

Spurgeon, Charles, *Lectures to My Students* (Christian Focus Publications)

Stott, John, *Between Two Worlds* (Baker)

PART TWO

Ten Sermons for Purposes of Illustration

Introduction

As I have argued in this book, every Christian sermon should be scriptural, rational, God-centered, and theologically articulate. But it must also have the following two characteristics beyond these requisite characteristics if it is to pass muster as a Christian sermon: First, for a sermon just to be a *sermon* and not simply a lecture or an address it must be *preached* in the power of the Spirit and normally within the context of the church and also normally within a worship service of the church. This means, conversely, that when people attend church they should not be given a lecture. They should hear a Spirit-animated sermon in which the Word of God is expounded and proclaimed. Second, if it is a *Christian* sermon that they hear, the sermon must address some effect of the Fall in mankind (this feature of the sermon is called by some homileticians the sermon's 'fallen condition focus'), and it must provide a Christological solution to that effect. Otherwise, the sermon will be just a moralism filled with platitudes and neither a *sermon* nor a *Christian* sermon at all. As he prepares his sermon the preacher must make sure that his sermon has these two additional characteristics, and he must be able to identify clearly in his own mind what the sermon's 'fallen condition focus' (FCF) is, and he must make sure that the sermon provides the appropriate Christological solution (CS) to that problem.

The following ten sermons are not intended to represent the finest in sermonic craftsmanship; I am quite aware that there are far greater crafters of sermons than I. They are intended only to exemplify the characteristics of the pulpit sermon for which I have argued in the eight lectures of this book. However, I do long to hear sermons from Protestant and Reformed pulpits around the world that reflect the scriptural grounding, rationality, God-centeredness, and theological articulation that I try to portray in my sermons. The reader must judge, of course, whether they reflect these characteristics. But whatever he finally concludes regarding my sermons, I would argue still that preachers must craft and preach sermons that have the characteristics for which I have argued in this book if they expect to enjoy the blessing of God on their pulpit ministries.

Sermon One

This sermon is textual, its main and its sub-points being drawn exclusively from Isaiah 57:15. I adapted it from a sermon preached some years ago by Gordon MacDonald. Its FCF is mankind's *ignorance* of where God can be found, and its CS is humble submission to and trust in Jesus Christ.

"Where Does God Live?"

Texts: 2 Chronicles 26:3-5, 16-21 (to be ready earlier in the service); Isaiah 6:1-7, particularly Isaiah 57:15

> For this is what the high and lofty One says—he who lives forever, whose name is holy: I live in a high and holy place, but also with him who is contrite and lowly in spirit, to revive the spirit of the lowly and to revive the heart of the contrite.

Prayer for Illumination: Thank you, heavenly Father, for these inspired insights from your Word. Grant us the ears truly to hear them, remove the scales from our eyes that we may behold wondrous things out of your Law, and open our hearts to believe and to love them. I pray these things, for the glory of Jesus, Amen.

* * * * *

The uniqueness of the Christian gospel is in its reassuring promise and guarantee that one can know the one living and true triune God in a rich and real sense that confounds the comprehension of the unbeliever. The car bumper sticker one occasionally sees is somewhat trite that reads, "God is not dead, I talked to him this morning." But we understand the theology behind a statement like that, don't we? You see, our God *is* alive, and we believe that we can know him, fellowship with him, and converse with him!

Now this reality of knowing God is a central thrust of Holy

Scripture, and in our last text, Isaiah 57:15—an Old Testament verse which is beautifully New Testament as well in scope and concept—Isaiah is passionately concerned that people know who his God is, what he is like, and specifically, where he dwells.

So, to the question that a little boy or girl might ask, "Daddy, Mommy, where does God live?" Isaiah declares: "He lives in two places: He lives in the high and lofty place, and he lives in the place of the contrite." Here are the two themes of our text: *Where* does God live? He lives in lofty places, and he lives in lowly places. In *these* two places our God can be found. In *only* these two places does he make his presence known.

Before we go any farther, may I ask you: Does Isaiah's reminder that these are the only two places where our God lives disturb you at all? I think it should. I confess, as I reflect on Isaiah's statement, that I become greatly agitated in my spirit by his reminder that God lives in the high and lofty place and he lives in the lowly place, because I know I simply do not appreciate as I should what it means

- ♦ either to approach God and to *worship* him in the lofty place where he dwells in his terrible, holy transcendence,
- ♦ or to *feel* genuine wretchedness and heartfelt contrition in the lowly place where he descends in his gracious condescendence.

And I would dare say, beloved friends, that you too—perhaps even most Christians today—are in a similar condition. You see, most professing Christians today prefer to approach God in worship on *middle* ground that is neither lofty for God nor lowly for them. But, my beloved, middle ground is simply not where God lives. There is *no middle ground* in *this* relationship, and *if* that is where we poor creatures of sin think we are standing today with God—on middle ground with him—I must warn us all that we are not in fellowship with the true and living God at all, for he is simply not there. Standing on middle ground we are standing all alone, talking to an idol we have created in our minds with whom we can feel comfortable and who requires nothing of us, but we are not talking with the true and living God!

Today I want you to explore with me the two places where our text says God lives. Come with me to the text and let's mine it together for its life-giving ore. I want to say no *more* than it says, but I want to say *all* that it does say. It has been my prayer that God's Spirit would speak to our hearts through it.

Consider with me, first, the theme of God's loftiness. Isaiah begins by affirming three true but incredibly difficult concepts for us to grasp about our God:

A. He is high and lofty;
B. He inhabits eternity; and
C. His name is holy.

Let me try to help us understand these three truths by relating each concept to the earthly Israelite monarchy.

First, being "high and lofty" means, at the very least, that God who is "spirit, infinite, eternal, and unchangeable in his being, wisdom, power, holiness, justice, goodness, and truth," is *above* us, *infinitely* above us!

He is our absolute Sovereign; we are his subjects. And just as the earthly king in Israel sat elevated and exalted above those who approached him in his throne room, so also God sits—high and exalted—above us, just as we read in Isaiah 6:1 moments ago: "I saw the Lord seated on a throne, high and exalted."

Then listen to these words of Isaiah in the middle of his book—in chapter 40:

> Surely the nations are like a drop in a bucket;
>   they are regarded as dust on the scales;
>   He weighs the islands as though they were fine dust.
> Before him all the nations are as nothing;
>   they are regarded by him as worthless and less than nothing.

"To whom will you compare me, or who is my equal?" asks the Holy One. "Do you not know? Have you not heard? The LORD is the everlasting God, the Creator of the ends of the earth"

I think I hear Isaiah saying by these three passages—at the beginning, the middle, and the end of his prophecy: "You better get it straight, Jerusalem: Your God is above you. You are not his equal by an infinite degree, and you had better never forget it."

Over thirty years ago A. W. Tozer wrote something that speaks to all this in his book, *The Knowledge of the Holy*. I believe his assessment is still frighteningly true today:

> A condition has existed in the church for some years and is steadily growing worse. I refer to the loss of the concept of [God's] majesty from the popular religious mind. The church has surrendered her once lofty concept of God and has substituted for it one so low, so ignoble, as to be unworthy of thinking, worshiping men.
>
> The low view of God entertained almost universally among Christians [today] is the cause of a hundred lesser evils everywhere among us. With our loss of the sense of [the] majesty [of God] has come the further loss of religious awe and consciousness of the divine Presence. We have lost our spirit of worship and our ability to meet God in adoring silence. Modern Christianity is simply not producing the kind of Christian who can appreciate or experience true life in the Spirit. The words, "Be still, and know that I am God," mean next to nothing to the self-confident, bustling worshiper in this period of the twentieth century.

Is Tozer right? I believe he is. Christians simply do not tremble before God today as they should.

Men, women, do you recognize that God is your sovereign—infinitely high and exalted above you? It is necessary to your spiritual health and mental well-being, as well as to every true worship experience, that you do.

Second, Isaiah says our God inhabits eternity.

Can you grasp this truth? Have you ever tried to define "time," not to mention attempting to define "eternity"? My senior colleague in the department of systematic theology at Covenant Theological Seminary in St. Louis, Missouri for some years was Dr. J. Oliver Buswell, Jr., who religiously required his students year after year to memorize his definition of time and eternity. "Time" he said, "is the mere abstract (or ideational) possibility of the before and after relationship in durational sequence," and eternity is simply "infinite time," that is, time (so defined) extrapolated in both directions to infinity.

Now do you understand? No? Well, don't feel bad. For even if you did, I know that none of us here can fully comprehend a self-conscious, personal being who *never* had a beginning, who has *always* existed. We are so time-oriented. Isaiah would live to see four kings come to the throne of Judah in the brief span of his own prophetic ministry, and then die—some a miserable death. But his God—ah, his God inhabited eternity. *Before* the mountains were brought forth, *before* the foundations of the earth were laid, *even from everlasting to everlasting*, his God was already and is always there and always will be there—*above* the passing of kings from thrones, *above* the shifting circumstances and vicissitudes of life. Our God inhabits eternity, my friends. He is always there—for you.

Third, Isaiah says that our God's name is holy, which means, at the very least, that *he* is holy.

What does it mean to say that God is holy? Permit me to try to help us grasp this concept about our God by two different Scriptural allusions.

First, let's go back to Isaiah 6 for a moment: Note the creatures who fly about the throne of God extolling the thrice-holy God day and night with their song. They are unfallen, sinless creatures. Nevertheless, with four of their six wings they cover themselves. Why? Because of the unapproachable light of God's all-glorious holiness about which they sing antiphonally without ceasing.

Then second, recall Uzziah about whom we read earlier in 2 Chronicles 26:16-21. In this poor man we see what happens to the creature who dares to walk into God's holy presence uninvited, acting as though it were his perfect right to be there.

This is true of us as well. Just as we cannot look for a moment at the brilliant, boiling light of the sun with our naked eyes without destroying them, so also we cannot in our raw state look at the God who dwells in the unapproachable light of his all-consuming holiness without doing irreversible and eternal harm to ourselves.

Now all of this should deeply disturb us, for how often have you, have I, have we—"Uzziah-like"—

- entered into the very presence of God in worship,
- sat before his powerful, wonderful Word from another world as we are doing now, and
- handled things—such as the communion elements—that he declares are holy,
- all the while presuming that it is our perfect right to be in his presence apart from his grace?

When you came to church today, what was on your mind? Did you come to worship the high and lofty God, who inhabits eternity, whose name is holy? Did you come to be lifted up to heaven by the prayers and praises in Zion and to sit under the precepts of God's Word? Or did you come simply to be gripped again somehow by that religious feeling that church attendance often invokes or to be entertained by the music or the preacher, just as the people of Ezekiel's day came to him to be entertained? Listen to God's description of his people in Ezekiel 33, and ask yourself, "Do his words describe me?"

> As for you, son of man, your countrymen are talking together about you by the walls and at the doors of the houses. My people come to you, as they usually do, and sit before you to listen to your words. With their mouths they express devotion, but their hearts are greedy for unjust gain. Indeed, *to them* you are nothing more than one who sings love songs with a beautiful voice and plays an instrument well, for they hear your words but do not put them into practice. But when all that you say comes true, and it surely will, then they will know that a prophet had been among them (33:30-33).

Is it possible, dear friends, that some of you came simply to be entertained by the preacher's words or to visit and to fellowship with friends, with no real thought that this place is to be primarily a house of worship and prayer? Is it possible that we have not given God his rightful due? Where is honest, reverential awe of the living God in the twentieth-first-century church? Where is the trembling that should occur as we read of his threatenings to the one who does not love and serve him? Where is the man—is he here? Where is the woman—is she here? Where is the boy, where is the girl, are they here? Where are they, I ask, who are conscious that they are—right now—in the presence of the lofty, holy God who inhabits eternity and who is a consuming fire to his enemies?

The story is told of Alfred Smith, one-time governor of New York State, who was prevailed upon, on one occasion, to speak at a convention banquet attended almost entirely by out-of-state conventioneers who, as the writer who tells the story says, obviously had at best "a supercilious, condescending, semi-inebriated half-interest in him." It was evident to all who possessed even a modicum of appreciation for the conditions of the moment that Gov. Smith was being treated by them as some kind of "fun joke." This was confirmed when the toastmaster, after a flippant, jocose introduction, climaxed his remarks with "And now, boys, I give you a great guy, Al Smith." Now Governor Smith was the last man in the world to insist on empty form or idle ceremony, but sensing an affront to his office, he responded briefly and tersely:

> Gentlemen, when I was a little boy on the East Side, my father took me one day to a great civic parade. I held his hand tightly and thrilled as battalion after battalion of infantry marched passed to stirring drum and martial music. Suddenly, my father stiffened, and I felt almost electricity pass from his hand to mind. "Son," he said, "take off your hat! The Governor of New York is passing by." I took off my hat. Gentlemen, the Governor of New York bids you goodnight.

And he left the platform and walked out the door.

Are there times, do you suppose, dear hearts, are there times when God simply wants to walk out on congregations—perhaps at times even on this one—who think they can meet God on "middle ground" that is comfortable—where he is simply a "good guy"—rather than meet him in adoring silence, and with the reverential fear that befits the undeserving sinner standing in the presence of infinite majesty? Have we come to think of our God so much as our buddy and our pal that he is no longer our *God*—the high and lofty One? I think I hear Isaiah saying:

"Get it straight, Jerusalem. You better not play around with the everlasting God, who dwells in the most prominent place, whose name is holy!"

We have considered now the "lofty place" where God sits upon his heavenly throne in incomparably awesome transcendence. We have seen that Isaiah tells us three basic facts about our God's loftiness: first, that he sits enthroned in the high and lofty place; second, that he inhabits eternity as the God who knows neither beginning nor ending, and third, that his name is holy, which means that *he* is holy—so transcendently holy that even *sinless* seraphs have to cover themselves in his presence, so transcendently holy that no *sinful* man can stand uninvited for an instant of time in his presence. Hence we must be ever aware that we sinful creatures of this world are not his equal and that we have no right to approach him in worship in our raw natural state.

Are you ready for "Chapter Two"? Consider with me now the second theme of Isaiah 57:15: the theme of God's lowliness.

Where does God live? As I just noted, Isaiah says that our God lives in the high and lofty place. This fact is disturbing enough, for it means that we cannot come into his presence at all apart from gracious aid coming to us. He is beyond our "reach"—infinitely so—unless we have an Advocate of some kind who can bridge the infinite distance between us. But the second part of Isaiah's statement disturbs me equally as much as the first, for I confess that there are large times in my life, as I said earlier, when I prefer to meet God on "middle ground," and I am simply not comfortable when I am reminded that the only other place he lives is in the place of the *contrite* and that if

I would meet him at all, *I* must first meet him there.

Let's look carefully at this second portion of the text and again mine it for its treasured ore. The first thing I want us to note is that the Hebrew word translated "contrite" here literally means "crushed," and it describes one who has been *spiritually crushed.* "Crushed"! One understands with his mind what "contrite" means, but one *feels* with his entire being what "crushed" means. "Crushed" suggests "pain," "remorse," "brokenness," "dejection," "at the end of oneself." And *who* are the "crushed" in Isaiah 57:15? The "crushed" are those who have come to grips honestly with the total, ultimate sinfulness of themselves.

Isaiah 6 again helpfully illustrates this for us. When Isaiah saw the Son of God in all his glory and heard the seraphs singing of his transcendent holiness that fills the whole earth, he cried, "Woe is me [that is, I stand under divine judgment], for I am undone. For my eyes have seen the King, the Lord of Hosts."

This is very instructive. What Isaiah is telling us is that he had never seen himself as he really was until he had seen the awesomely terrible glory of the holy God, and when he did come to grips with the incredible moral dimensions of the living God, *he felt crushed by the inescapable weight of the sheer godness of God*—the weight of his glorious grandeur, particularly the grandeur of his holiness.

What is the lesson in this for you and for me? It is this: When we truly understand who God is, what he is like, and where he dwells, we suddenly realize that we fall infinitely short of his expectations for us. We can no longer be happy with ourselves. We know we need to recalibrate our opinion about ourselves. We know we must leave our comfortable "middle ground." We realize that we don't belong before him by right of birth or of place or of nature in our raw, natural state. We suddenly realize that no worship experience—I repeat, *no* worship experience—is genuine apart from this sense of "crushedness," that no worship experience is real apart from the recognition that one is nothing before God unless he is bathed in the mercy of God in Christ. I suddenly understand that I must *really* mean it when I sing,

And from my smitten heart with tears,
two wonders I confess:
the wonders of redeeming love
and *my unworthiness*.

The second thing I would note here is that Isaiah's declaration is really just a further revelation of God's infinite grace, for when he comes to you in *your* "crushedness," *you will find him with you there, crushed and broken too*.

Will you look with me at Isaiah 53:5? Isaiah informs us in this verse that in God's incredible love for you, when he, in the person of his Son, came to dwell with you, he came as the One who "was bruised for your transgressions, who was *crushed* [the same Hebrew word] for your iniquities" at Calvary.

Now what design, what purpose, lies behind Christ's willingness and desire to come and to dwell with the lowly and contrite in spirit as himself *the* crushed one? We must be extremely careful when we answer this question, for we have no right to determine for him his reasons for doing what he does. We must let *him* always inform *us* of his motives for doing what he does. And here he clearly does inform us. Look at the text again. He states quite clearly that he comes to contrite ones in order to *revive* them, to quicken them, to raise them up, to give them new life and new hope.

In this single, simple statement, we are informed of the source of all true spiritual life in the church. It is to be found in Christ alone. *True* spiritual life, indeed, *all* true spiritual renewal, comes from none other than the crucified and risen Christ, the high and lofty One who is himself the Baptizer of his people (Matt 3:11; John 1:33). It is he and he alone who can revive and quicken the crushed of this world. And his outpouring of revivification and quickening, Isaiah informs us, comes only to one with a particular heart attitude that has been graciously implanted within him. And what is that heart attitude? Hear the High and Lofty One again: It is singularly significant that he states that he comes not only to the *crushed* but also to those *lowly in spirit* to revive them. I tell you, beloved, the church of Jesus Christ needs the gale of the reviving Spirit of Christ *sweeping* through her limbs today, *calling* her back to forsaken revealed truths, *lifting up* her fallen hands, *strengthening* her weakened knees, *fanning* her smoking flax back into a bright and warming flame, *infusing* her with boldness and courage, and *empowering* her to attempt great deeds for God. If that gale is not presently ours, it is doubtless because we are not sufficiently low in the dust before him. Are you in a state that may justly be labeled "lowly in spirit"? If not, guess what's wrong. You are not sufficiently low before him and hungering and thirsting after *his* righteousness, for if you were, our Lord has declared that God will fully satisfy your hunger and your thirst.

My friends, I must remind you that your God looks not primarily at your outward dress but at your hearts. I must ask you, what does he see when he looks beyond your dress and your best social decorum? Does he see hearts conscious that apart from his grace they are deceitful above all things and desperately wicked? Does he see hearts beating in true humility before him? Does he see hearts that understand that without him one can do nothing good? Or does he see proud and haughty spirits, insisting on their own autonomy and on having their own way? Dear ones, do you want genuine renewal in your church? I'm sure you do. Then cry out to him not only today but also continually for that lowliness of spirit before him that alone he honors with his presence. Importune heaven for new depths of humility before him in order that he might revive you and regale you with his power from on high! For we have his word on this matter both in the Old and New Testaments: "God opposes the proud but gives grace to the humble" (Prov. 3:34; James 4:6). Spirit of the living Christ, descend upon this church, I pray, and humble us in the dust before you!

I close now with a final summary about this text as a whole. Dear friends, I have informed you, in the most fragile of words, what Isaiah says about the places where God lives. He lives in *the high and lofty place* where he sits in dreadful transcendence, where our only proper response is to worship and to adore him through the merits of Christ's doing and dying. And he lives in his amazing condescendence in *the lowly place* among the spiritually crushed people of this globe who bow before him in contrition and humility and cry out for his gifts of grace in Christ. So, both to believer and to unbeliever gathered in this place today, I would admonish you: In *these* two places find your God, for only in these two places does he live and only in these two places will you find him, for they are where he dwells!

Let us pray:
O blessed triune God, Father, Son, and Holy Spirit, who dwells in that transcendently holy light that no man can approach in his natural state and live, who dwells in the high and lofty place, who inhabits eternity, and whose name is holy, yet who keeps covenant to the thousandth generation of those who love you:

Today, having considered the places where you live, we thank you that we can know you—the infinite God—personally, even in the midst of our knowledge of our own unworthiness and sin, and even as we know that, when the desires of your great heart have been so freely opened to us, we have been so slow to worship you in reverence and awe.

Today we thank you for the mighty truths that you have flashed, even if only momentarily, before our eyes from this text in Isaiah. We pray for your gracious presence in our lives, that, drawn by the sweetness of your grace and the bliss of your beauty, we may turn our eyes and hearts away from the deceptive and dying, but oh so alluring, lights of this world. May we know you enough to long after you, and longing for you, may we know you even better. Indeed, grant us such heart desire for you that our greatest passion in life will be to know you better than we know anyone or anything else in this world and to enjoy you more than we enjoy anyone or anything else in this world—more than our spouses, more than our children, more than our homes, more than our jobs.

Give us while we sit before you now, acknowledging the depth and the greatness of our own unworthiness and of our many sins and shortcomings, the awareness of the great ocean of your love sweeping over us and covering our sin. Be with us throughout our days. Turn our sadnesses to joy, quiet our inner turmoil, and give us your peace that passes all understanding. We ask all this through our Lord Jesus Christ, Amen.

Sermon Two

This sermon is textual, based as it is on Matthew 11:25-30. Of all the sermons in Part II it is the most technical, providing in several footnotes (which, of course, are not to be preached) information for the sake of reference.

The sermon's FCF is mankind's weariness and sin-burden, and its CS is Jesus' universal invitation to all who are tired and weary to come to him as the alone revealer of God for rest, removal of their burden, and salvation. Not only does the sermon instruct the Christian about Jesus' person but also it makes an evangelistic appeal to the lost.

"Jesus' Great Invitation"

We teach our students at Knox Seminary that every biblical passage has within it a "fallen condition focus." That is to say, every passage contains within it a reference to some human condition that is the result of mankind's lapse into sin. This fallen condition may be corporate or individual; it may be political immorality on the part of the state or outright transgression or iniquity on the part of the sinner; it may be pride or unbelief, it may be physical or mental illness; it may be sorrow or grief or loneliness or a hundred other things. But whatever it is, the preacher should make sure that he identifies that "fallen condition" in the text and sets it clearly forth. He should then provide the *Christological* solution to that condition. If he does not provide this second part, *anything else* his sermon would recommend by way of remedy for that fallen condition is not only cruel and misguided but also simply a moralistic platitude, and *the sermon ceases to be a Christian sermon at all.*

Today my sermon's "fallen condition focus," taken directly from the biblical text, is mankind's weariness from wrestling with the burden of sin, and its Christological solution, also drawn directly from the biblical text, is Jesus' universal invitation to all who have grown weary in that struggle to come in simple child-like trust to him, the only revealer of God the Father, for their rest, for the removal of their burden, and for the gift of eternal life. Please turn in your copy of God's Word to the sermon text, follow along as I read it to you, and then keep your Bibles open as I expound the passage.

Text: Matthew 11:25-30: a close parallel is in Luke 10:21-22

> At that time [And what time was that? At the very time when entire cities and that generation were rejecting him] Jesus said: "I praise you, Father, Lord of heaven and earth, because you have hidden these things [about me] from the wise and learned [the spiritual "know-it-alls"], and revealed them to little children. Yes, Father, for this was your good pleasure.
>
> "All things have been committed to me by my Father. No one knows the Son except the Father, and no one knows the Father except the Son and those to whom the Son chooses to reveal him.
>
> "Come to me, all you who are *weary and burdened*, and I will give you rest. Take my yoke upon you and learn from me, for I am gentle and humble in heart, and you will find rest for your souls. For my yoke is easy and my burden is light."

What a precious text this is! What great doctrine and what a comforting promise it contains! As we approach it now in our study, let us

> think of it carefully, study it prayerfully,
> deep in our hearts let its oracles dwell;
> study its history, slight not its history,
> for none ever loved it too fondly or well.

Prayer for Illumination

Dear Lord Jesus Christ, our ever-faithful, never-failing Friend and Savior, today we come to you with all our burdens and sorrows and look to you to give us that rest and the peace that passes understanding that only you can give. Instruct us by your Spirit not only about yourself but also about our heavenly Father. And may we find in that blessed instruction our solace in the coming days of trial and dread, days when men's hearts are failing them for fear. This I pray in your most holy, dreadful, but infinitely gracious name, Amen.

* * * * *

The Fallen Condition—Weariness from our Struggle with Sin

Let us all now turn to the passage I just read. In it Jesus pinpoints the fallen condition we want to consider when he addresses the people generally as "weary and burdened." Surely this is a "fallen condition." Whence comes this spiritual and often mental weariness? Well, every human being struggles with his sin. He may not describe the opponent in his struggle by the term *sin*, but every person is at least conscious that there is a great divide between what he knows he *ought to be* and what he knows he *actually is*—a psychological "Fall," as it were. And he is troubled by that divide and he struggles to remove or at least to reduce its breadth, for every person in his heart of heart wishes he were morally better than he is and wants to improve himself. All one has to do to confirm this fact is to go to the sections on self-help books either in Borders or Barnes & Noble; there one will find hundreds of titles on such matters. Or check the Yellow Pages for local psychiatrists and therapists. Yes, self-improvement is indeed a major concern with people. Even Hollywood has capitalized on this human longing with its comedies *Analyze This* and *Analyze That* starring Robert DeNiro and *Anger Management* starring Jack Nicholson.

Of course, unless the Holy Scripture has instructed them these people will not know how serious their spiritual condition is, how broad that great divide is, and how impossible by their own efforts is their removal or reduction in the slightest of the breadth of that psychological divide. Now these people may conclude that this last assertion of mine is quite intemperate, but then they do not know that the Word of God provides a lengthy list of moral "cannots" that are true of them. For example, the Bible teaches that

- these people do not face the fact that "a bad tree *cannot bear* good fruit" (Matt 7:18), and that they are, as we all are natively, "bad trees."
- They do not know that unless a person is born from above, he *cannot* even *see*, much less "*enter* the kingdom of God" (John 3:3, 5).
- They do not know that "*no one can come* to Jesus Christ unless the Father draws him" and "enables him" to come (John 6:44, 45).
- They do not know that they "*cannot accept* the Spirit of truth, because they neither see him nor know him" (John 14:17).
- They do not know that they cannot bear any true moral fruit on their own, for according to Jesus: "No branch can bear fruit by itself; it must remain in the vine. *Neither can you bear fruit unless you remain in me*. I am the vine...apart from me *you can do nothing*" (John 15:4-5).
- They do not know that "the sinful mind...*does not submit* to God's law [that's what theologians call moral depravity]; nor *can it do so* [that's what they call moral inability]. Those controlled by the sinful nature *cannot please* God" (Rom 8:7-8).
- They do not know that "the person without the Spirit *does not accept* the things that come from the Spirit of God, for they are foolishness to him [there it is again, moral depravity], and he *cannot understand* them [there it is again, moral inability], because they are discernable only through the Spirit's enabling" (1 Cor 2:14).
- They do not know that "*no one can say*, 'Jesus is Lord,'" and really mean it, "except by the Holy Spirit" (1 Cor 12:3).
- They do not know that they "*cannot [even] tame* their [own] tongues" that are "restless evils, full of deadly poison" (James 3:8).

- They do not know that *no one can learn* the "new song" of truth that is sung around the throne of God except he be redeemed (Rev 14:3).

No, they do not know that it is as impossible for them to improve their character or to act in a way that is distinct from their native corruption as it is, as Jeremiah declares, for "the Ethiopian to change his skin or the leopard to change his spots" (13:23).

In sum, without being aware of it, these people are incapable of the understanding, the affections, and the will to act which, taken together, enable one to be subject to the law of God, to respond to the gospel of God, and to love God.

So they go on feeling unhappy about themselves and their divided moral condition and continue to struggle against the powers of sin that rage and wage war within them and that make them captive to the law of sin that dwells within them (Rom 7:23). And the extreme and horrible irony in their go-it-alone struggle against their divided selves, again unknown to them, is that *their very struggle is itself sinful* in that the very essence of their anxious concern to improve themselves on their own is their imagining that they are wiser than God, that they must remember things that God has forgotten, and that they must do for themselves what God is unwilling to do or incapable of doing for them. What is this but going to their own "broken cisterns that can hold no water" instead of to the Lord who is the "fountain of living water" (Jer 2:13)? And if they continue seriously and long enough in that self-struggle, they will be brought by their weariness to the spiritual and emotional depths where they cry with the convicted Saul of Tarsus: "O wretched man that I am! Who will deliver me from this body of death?" (Rom 7:24)

There it is, dear hearts: the Bible's maturest expression of the weariness of the soul that comes from trying to improve and better oneself in the struggle with the burden of sin. And if you are here today and are in that self-help struggle, please know that I feel sorry, very sorry, for you. My heart goes out to you, I weep for you, for I know that you will never improve yourself to your own satisfaction, that you will wear yourself out in your struggle, and that you will die a spiritual failure, regardless of what other successes you may achieve in life, if you continue on your own to struggle to remove the breach within.

But I know something else: I know what the solution to your struggle is, not because I am smarter than you are, but because Jesus tells me what it is. And my prayer all week long has been that God will grant you today that special pair of ears that Jesus talked about when he said: "Let him who has ears to hear, let him hear," in order that you may truly discover what that solution is. So pay attention now to what I am about to say.

The Christological Solution to This Struggle

If Matthew 28:18-20 is Jesus' "Great Commission," then Matthew 11:28 is surely Jesus' "Great Invitation." Here Jesus issues the invitation: "*Come to me*, all you who are weary and burdened, and I will give you rest." Jesus' invitation here provides the *formal* New Testament parallel to God's own Old Testament invitation in Isaiah 45:22, as is clear if one places the two invitations in their several parts beside each other as follows:

God states in Isaiah 45:22: "Turn to me, all the ends of the earth, and I will save you."

Jesus states in Matthew 11:28: "Come to me, all you who are weary and burdened, and I will give you rest."

Here Jesus places himself centrally and at the forefront of this invitation as the great healer of all of mankind's spiritual, mental and emotional problems. His invitation is *universal* in its all-encompassing comprehensiveness: "*all* you who are weary and burdened." That includes everyone here. And his invitation is *unqualified* in its promise to grant the blessing of rest to all who come to him ("and *I will* give you rest"). It contains no qualifying clauses. Such an invitation would be nothing less than grossly audacious—indeed, it would be indicative of the mental disease known as delusions of grandeur—were it to come from the lips of any other person. No pastor, however great his gifts, abilities, and fame, has ever dared to issue such an invitation. Nor would it ever enter his mind to do so. Were he to do so, the entire world would scoff at him and would have the right to ask him, "How do you have the temerity to say such a thing?" And if he continued in issuing his invitation, the world would have the right to judge him to be insane. And yet millions and millions of Christians through the ages have testified that such an invitation is perfectly proper and quite appropriate coming from the lips of Jesus, for they have discovered that *he* can keep and has indeed kept his promise to them.

Now on what legitimate grounds could he issue such a universal invitation? How could *this* man keep such a promise? Well, because of the truth of the assertions he makes preceding his promise to succor all who come to him. By his prior assertions Jesus implicitly claims for himself a place of power and privilege as the "Son" of the "Father" that places him altogether on the level of deity. By his prior assertions—assertions, by the way, that the learned Princeton theologian Benjamin B. Warfield declared contained "in some respects the most remarkable [utterance] in the whole compass of the four Gospels"[1] and that the equally learned Princeton theologian Geerhardus Vos judged to be "by far the most important seat of the testimony which Jesus bears to his sonship" as well as being "the culminating point of our Lord's self-disclosure in the Synoptics"[2]—by these assertions, I say, we are brought face to face with some of the most wonderful words Jesus ever spoke and several of the greatest claims he ever made.

Therefore, I invite you now to follow my exposition of the passage and discover for yourself that Matthew 11:25-30 (as well as its parallel in Luke 10:21-22) confronts us with some of the most remarkable utterances and one of the most compelling promises Jesus ever made.

---

1. Benjamin B. Warfield, *The Lord of Glory* (Reprint of 1907 edition; Grand Rapids: Baker, 1974), 82-3; see also 118-19.
2. Geerhardus Vos, *The Self-Disclosure of Jesus* (Reprint of 1926 edition; Phillipsburg, N. J.: Presbyterian and Reformed, 1978), 143.

The Passage's Four Great Parallels

My exposition will focus on what I am calling "the four great parallels"—can you find them?—that Jesus draws between God as "the Father" and himself as "the Son" of Matthew 3:17 (Mark 1:11; Luke 3:22). The *unique* and *intimate* nature of the Father-Son relationship Jesus asserts here of himself—higher than which it is impossible to conceptualize unless it be in certain of the utterances of the Fourth Gospel, such as "I and the Father are one" (10:30)—comes to expression precisely in terms of these parallels and provides the answer to my earlier questions, namely, Why would Jesus place himself so centrally and at the forefront of this invitation as the great healer of all of mankind's spiritual, mental and emotional problems? And on what legitimate grounds could he issue such a universal invitation?

The first parallel that Jesus draws is the *mutual absolute lordship that the Father and he the Son each possesses*, the Father's lordship expressed in Jesus' descriptive words in 11:25: "Father, Lord of heaven and earth," his own lordship expressed in his words in 11:27: "All things [in heaven and on earth] have been committed to me by my Father." He makes the same claim, you may recall, in his Great Commission when he states: "All authority in heaven and on earth has been given to me" (Matt 28:18). Here Jesus claims to be, as a result of his Father's investing him with the messianic task, earth's King of kings and Lord of lords, whose royal diadem out-rivals all the combined crowns and tiaras of all the kings and queens, of all the dictators and petty Caesars of this world. In a sentence, Jesus teaches that he is in charge of all things!

The second parallel that he highlights is the *exclusive, mutual knowledge that the Father and he the Son each has of the other.* Jesus declares in 11:27: "No one knows the Son except the Father, and no one knows the Father except the Son." The first thing we note here is his dual employment of the same Greek verb (*epiginōskei*) to describe the Father's knowledge of the Son and the Son's knowledge of the Father, which verb with its attached preposition means "knows exactly, completely, through and through."[3] And the second thing to note is Jesus' emphasis upon the *exclusiveness* of this mutual knowledge reflected by his twice-used phrase, "no one knows *except*" (*ei mē*).[4] Only a moment's reflection will show that the nature of this exclusive knowledge which Jesus claims to have lifts him above the sphere of the ordinary mortal and places him "in a position, not of equality merely, but of absolute reciprocity and interpenetration of knowledge with the Father."[5] Geerhardus Vos observes:

> That essential rather than acquired knowledge is meant follows...from the correlation of the [parallel] clauses: the knowledge God has of Jesus cannot be acquired knowledge [it must, from the fact that it is God's knowledge, be direct, intuitive, and immediate—in a word, divine—knowledge, grounded in the fact that the Knower is divine[6]]; consequently the knowledge Jesus has of God cannot be acquired knowledge either [it too must be direct, intuitive, and immediate—in a word, divine—knowledge], for these two are placed entirely on a line. In other words, if the one is different from human knowledge, then the other must be so likewise.[7]

The only conclusion that this correlation of the two clauses justly warrants is, first, that God has his exclusive and penetrating knowledge of the Son because he is God, the Father of the Son, and, second, that Jesus has his exclusive and penetrating knowledge of the Father because he is God, the Son of the Father.

---

3. BAGD, 291, 1a.
4. The exclusiveness of Jesus' knowledge is not invalidated by his following remark, "and to whomever the Son wills to reveal him," since the very point of his statement is that other men must acquire their saving knowledge of the Father *from him*. They can acquire it *in no other way* (John 14:6), whereas his knowledge of the Father is intrinsic to the filial relationship he sustains to his Father.
5. Benjamin B. Warfield, "The Person of Christ According to the New Testament," *The Person and Work of Christ* (Philadelphia: Presbyterian and Reformed, 1950), 65.
6. See George Eldon Ladd, *A Theology of the New Testament* (Grand Rapids: Eerdmans, 1974), 166.
7. Vos, *The Self-Disclosure of Jesus*, 149.

The third parallel, which rests upon the second, comes to focus in Jesus' assertion of *the mutual necessity of the Father and of him the Son each to reveal the other if men are ever to have an acquired saving knowledge of them*. This parallel is highlighted by Jesus' declaration in 11:25 that the Father had hidden (*ekrupsas*) from the spiritual "know-it-alls" the mysteries of the Kingdom that are *centered in him the Son* and had *revealed* (*apekalupsas*) them to "babies" (such as Peter to whom Jesus said in Matthew 16:17: "...flesh and blood has not revealed this to you, but my Father who is in heaven."), and his statement in 11:27 that "no one knows the Father except the Son and those to whom the Son chooses to *reveal* [*apokalupsai*] him." I call your attention again to Jesus' dual employment here of the same Greek verb (*apokaluptō*) to describe the activities of the two: The Father *reveals* the Son; the Son *reveals* the Father.

The fourth parallel Jesus draws is that of the *mutual absolute sovereignty the Father and he the Son each exercises in dispensing his revelation of the other*. The Father's sovereignty in this regard is displayed in Jesus' words in 11:26: "...for this was your *good pleasure* [*eudokia*]," the Son's sovereignty is displayed in his words in 11:27: "to whomever the Son *wills* [*boulētai*] to reveal him." A higher expression of parity between the Father and the Son with respect to the possession of the divine attribute of sovereignty in the dispensing of saving knowledge is inconceivable. Jesus teaches here that no sinful creature has a right to such revelation. If the creature ever learns about the Son it is because the Father has sovereignly determined in his grace to reveal him. If he ever learns about the Father it is because the Son has sovereignly determined in his grace to reveal him!

Warfield is surely justified when he summarizes Jesus' absolutely amazing utterance here in these words:

> ...in it our Lord asserts for Himself a relation of practical equality with the Father, [who is] here described in most elevated terms as the "Lord of heaven and earth" (v. 25). As the Father only can know the Son, so the Son only can know the Father: and others

> may know the Father only as He is revealed by the Son. That is, not merely is the Son the exclusive revealer of God, but the mutual knowledge of Father and Son is put on what seems very much a par. The Son can be known only by the Father in all that He is, as if His being were infinite and as such inscrutable to the finite intelligence; and His knowledge alone—again as if He were infinite in His attributes—is competent to compass the depths of the Father's infinite being. He who holds this relation to the Father cannot conceivably be a creature.[8]

Ned B. Stonehouse, professor of New Testament at Westminster Theological Seminary, in his *The Witness of Matthew and Mark to Christ*, similarly writes:

> Here [in Matt 11:25-27] Jesus claims such an exclusive knowledge of the Father, and a consequent exclusive right to reveal the Father (both corresponding with the Father's exclusive knowledge and revelation of the Son), that nothing less than an absolutely unique self-consciousness, on an equality with that of the Father, is involved.[9]

Also in his *The Witness of Luke to Christ* Stonehouse asserts:

> Most clearly of all, perhaps, the claim to divine Sonship in a form excluding subordination altogether [of the Son to the Father] is found in Luke x. 22, which closely parallels Mt. xi. 27. The Son's knowledge of the Father and the Father's knowledge of the Son are set forth with such exact correspondence and reciprocity, and are moreover made the foundations of their respective sovereign revelational activity, that all subordination is excluded, and the passage constitutes an unambiguous claim of deity on the part of the Son.[10]

---

8. Warfield, *The Lord of Glory*, 82-3; see also 118-19.
9. Ned B. Stonehouse, *The Witness of Matthew and Mark to Christ* (Philadelphia: Presbyterian Guardian, 1944), 212.
10. Ned B. Stonehouse, *The Witness of Luke to Christ* (London: Tyndale, 1951), 167.

Application of the Parallels to Jesus' Invitation

We have now laid bare the contextual reasons for Jesus' invitation to weary men to come to him, and *only* to him, for their rest. It only remains for us to apply what we have seen.

Such a parity of the Father and the Son as that which is implicit in the four great parallels of this passage provides the basis upon which our Lord grounds his great invitation to the weary and burdened to come to him as the Revealer of the Father, for his invitation follows immediately upon his claim that *he alone knows the Father*: "Because I alone know the Father and I alone can reveal him," he declares in effect, "come to *me*, his revealer, and learn about him from *me*, the only source of such knowledge." With his infinite knowledge as God the Son of God the Father, he the Son is alone capable of revealing to men his Father.

But why, someone asks, is such knowledge of the Father necessary or even important? Jesus promised *rest* to those who came to him. Why in my struggle must I learn about the Father? Why in my struggle should I be interested in knowing him? Because, Jesus says in John 17:3: "This is eternal life: to know God the Father, the only true God, and Jesus Christ whom he sent." Only in such knowledge will any person find his sin removed and thereby the spiritual and mental rest he seeks!

So now I must ask you: Have *you*, tired and weary one, heeded his invitation and have you come—I mean, really come in trustful repose—to Jesus Christ for your rest? Have you come humbly, not as his equal or as his teacher, but as a seeker who is at the end of yourself in order to become his disciple? Have you taken his yoke upon you, that is, have you begun to sit at his feet as his disciple and to learn about his Father, and are you learning from him daily about his Father? Only as you do so will you "find rest for your souls."

Why do you delay? You have no need to hold back or to fear *this* divine Teacher, for *this* Teacher is gentle and humble in heart, his yoke is easy, and the burden of discipleship that he places upon you is *infinitely* lighter than the burden of sin you presently bear. So respond now to his invitation. Come to him, I implore you, and find that rest that can be found nowhere else—

- that rest that can be found only in him,
- that rest that alone can deliver you from the guilt and power of sin and hell,
- that rest that alone can save you for a life of fruitfulness and heaven.
- Come to him now, I beg you, tired and weary one, and trust his teaching to meet your every need.

Let us pray:
Our Father and our God, from whom we learn about Jesus and about whom we learn from Jesus, your revealing Son:

We joyously confess anew that your Son by his Spirit is indeed the only true and trustworthy Teacher concerning you, the only true God, and Jesus Christ whom you sent into the world to give us rest and everlasting life.

We confess that we have not lived in accordance with his teaching about you as faithfully as we should have, for we have all too often sought out many of our own inventions to alleviate our spiritual hunger. We have all too often hewn out for ourselves broken cisterns that can hold no water to satisfy our spiritual thirst, and we have all too often turned away from you who alone are the fountain of living water. But we acknowledge today that you have made us for yourself, and that our souls are ignorant and restless until you fill them by that knowledge of you and of your Son that alone brings us eternal felicity, hope, and rest.

Grant, in light of the great claims that Jesus made in the passage we considered today, that for the rest of our lives we will come to him and his Word and to no other when we would know more about you.

This we ask not only for his glory and cause but also for our own souls' spiritual and mental health. We pray these things in Jesus' name. Amen.

Sermon Three

By the four simple points of this sermon I retell the gospel story about the healing of Bartimaeus and apply it to a Christian audience. Preachers can do a great deal with the Evangelists' stories of Jesus if they reflect on them and find ways to retell their gospel stories with imagery and to bring in details that may have escaped the average reader. Of course, preachers should always be concerned to avoid distortions of the story in order to produce theatrical or contrived effects. They should always endeavor to preach scripturally, rationally, God-centeredly, and with theological accuracy.

For any sermon to be a truly Christian sermon it must also have both a FCF and a CS solution to the condition. As he prepares his sermon the preacher should be able to identify clearly in his mind what the sermon's FCF is and make sure that the sermon provides the Christological solution. Otherwise, the sermon will not be a *Christian* sermon. The FCF of this sermon is the universal spiritual blindness that has affected the entire race and the CF is Christ's power to remove such blindness and grant spiritual sight to the spiritually blind.

"Jesus' Strange Question"

Text: Mark 10:46-52, esp. vs 51

> Then they came to Jericho. As Jesus and his disciples, together with a large crowd, were leaving the city, a blind man, Bartimaeus (that is, the son of Timaeus), was sitting by the roadside begging. When he heard that it was Jesus of Nazareth, he began to shout, "Jesus, Son of David, have mercy on me!" Many rebuked him and told him to be quiet, but he shouted all the more, "Son of David, have mercy on me!" Jesus stopped and said, "Call him." So they called to the blind man, "Cheer up! On your feet! He's calling you." Throwing his cloak aside, he jumped to his feet and

came to Jesus. "What do you want me to do for you?" Jesus asked him. The blind man said, "Rabbi, I want to see." "Go," said Jesus, "your faith has healed you." Immediately he received his sight and followed Jesus along the road.

Prayer for Illumination

O Christ of God, speak to us today through this portion of your blessed Word. May my words capture the exact intention of the Spirit when he inspired the Evangelist to write these words. And grant to all here today that *special* set of ears that you had in mind when you said: "Let him who has ears to hear, let him hear." May we hear your Word today indeed, and may we respond to it according to your will as we ought to do. We pray, in your mighty and powerful name, Amen.

* * * * *

Men, less gifted than a William Shakespeare, might simply say: "Seize every opportunity when it comes your way or you'll always regret it." Shakespeare himself said it this way:

There is a tide in the affairs of men,
    Which, taken at the flood, leads on to fortune;
Omitted, all the voyage of their life
    Is bound in shallows and in miseries.
        —Brutus, in *Julius Caesar*, Act II, Scene iii, lines 216-19.

But the Holy Spirit declares more eloquently and directly than ever could a Shakespeare: "Today, if you hear his voice, harden not your heart. For now is the time of God's favor, today is the day of salvation."

1. Such a "crisis day" or "defining moment" one day confronted the life of Bartimaeus, the blind beggar.

That particular day doubtless began inauspiciously for Bartimaeus, like thousands of days before.

- Bartimaeus was awakened by the damp dawn cold creeping through the moth-eaten blanket he used both for bedding and a cloak.

- The fact that it was still dark didn't bother him, however, for he was blind. But the cold—how he despised that early morning cold!

- But being the practical man that his condition had forced him to become, he determined to make the best of his insomnia and to get a head start on his blind compatriots by getting to the city gate earlier than they and thereby obtaining the best spot for begging. "That Jedidiah," he thought to himself with no little relish, "is forever trying to get the spot nearest the gate. But today it is going to be different, very different. I'll get there ahead of him."

- With haste Bartimaeus shoveled into his mouth the piece of stale bread and the small block of goat's cheese which he had purchased the evening before from the previous day's proceeds from begging, washing it down with some equally stale beer. Then he left the hovel he called home and groped his way through the narrow lanes of Old Jericho that he had passed along a thousand times before leading to the city gate.

- As he stumbled toward his "place in the morning sun" he cursed again the day that his mother had been told, "You have given birth to a manchild." And he cursed that later day, now some ten years past, when fever had struck and left him temporarily dissipated but permanently blind.

- The sun was beginning to rise as he settled himself at the gate of Jericho, and "not a bit too soon," he thought to himself, for already the merchants and traveling caravans were beginning to pass into the new city in order to sell their wares in the city's open market.

- Through that cool April morning Bartimaeus sat and begged for alms. Occasionally a kind merchant dropped a *lepton* into his cup; and once a couple of Roman soldiers dropped a coin in front of him in the dust and told him he could have it if he could find it. How they howled as he and his fellow beggars scrambled to find it. "That wretch Mehujael!" he said half aloud as he reflected moments later on the incident. Not being blind, you see, the beggar Mehujael had found it and claimed it for his own. "This is definitely not going to be a good day," Bartimaeus muttered to himself.

- Suddenly he began to hear the approaching commotion and hubbub of what he thought at first was another caravan. But as the noise grew louder, he was able to determine that an enormous crowd of people was moving toward him on foot. Over the crescendoing din he cried out, "What's going on? Someone tell me what's going on." His heart leaped into his throat, and he momentarily froze when a passing voice cried out, "Jesus of Nazareth is passing by."

- His pulse quickened. He had heard of this one. He had heard that this Jesus was able to heal the sick, to make the lame to walk, and to restore sight to the blind. He had even heard that upon occasion Jesus had raised the dead. He knew too that the Old Testament had predicted that the Messianic Age would be an age of great blessing, particularly so for the blind. In this regard D. A. Carson has rightly observed in his commentary on *Matthew* (233) that

> the Messianic Age was to be characterized as a time when 'the eyes of the blind [would be] opened'.... If Jesus was really the Messiah, the blind reasoned, then he would have mercy on them; and they would have their sight.

So Bartimaeus, displaying his faith in Jesus as the Messiah by employing the messianic title that was popular in some branches of Judaism, began to cry out: "Jesus, *Son of David*, have mercy on me!"

- Some in the passing crowd rebuked him and tried to silence him: "Beggar, hold your tongue." But he cried all the more: "Son of David, have mercy on me." Suddenly a nearby voice said, "Cheer up, on your feet, beggar, he's calling for you."

- Throwing his cloak aside, he scrambled to his feet and groping his way forward, he stumbled to Jesus. This, he was convinced, was his "flood tide" moment, and he was not going to let it pass with no effort on his part to take advantage of it!

2. What about Jesus? Was he in fact the Messiah? And what had his day thus far been like?

- With regard to the first of these questions, a careful reading of the Gospel data will convince any fair-minded investigator that, as far as the four Evangelists were concerned, Jesus was indeed the Messiah, even the long-promised *divine* Messiah of the Old Testament. My own personal research into this question, laid out in my *Jesus, Divine Messiah*, has convinced me beyond a shadow of doubt that the historic affirmation of the Church in this regard is completely biblical and true.

- With regard to the second question—what had Jesus' day been like thus far?—one needs to recall that for some days now Jesus had been making his way down the eastern side of the Jordan, his Great Galilean ministry having been concluded, and the hour of his departure from this world was now drawing near.

- Mark informs us that there was something about Jesus' demeanor at this time that astonished his disciples and struck awe in the crowd that followed him (10:32). His face had been for days set as a flint toward Jerusalem.

- Earlier that morning Jesus had crossed the Jordan River from the East and had started up the long graded incline toward the city of Jericho in the distance.

- Perhaps he looked off to his left and saw in the distance the buildings of Qumran. If he did, I can imagine a smile may have flickered across his face as, with a divine omniscience, he thought of those scrolls hidden away in clay jars in the caves of Qumran, which would not be discovered until our day, in 1947—scrolls which would dispel many critical contentions and theories about the Old Testament canon.

- Perhaps he recalled the day when his ancient ancestress, Rahab the harlot, by faith had helped the spies of Israel and had saved herself and her household from the destruction of ancient Jericho.

- Perhaps he thought of his ancient namesake, that first Joshua, son of Nun, who had led the people of God into the land and had seen the walls of old Jericho fall down and on that occasion had led Israel to its first victory in Canaan.

- We can't know for sure about *these* things, but we *do* know that he was thinking of the baptism of fire that awaited him at Jerusalem. These thoughts deeply stirred him, but it did not turn him aside from his appointed task. Nothing was going to keep him from his appointment with the destiny that his Father's eternal plan itself had determined for him. Nothing was going to stop him from that!

- But wait! Did I say that nothing was going to stop him in his steady gait up to Jerusalem? As he was leaving the city of old Jericho, the Evangelist tells us that suddenly Jesus stopped in his tracks and stood still. What had stopped him? *He had heard a cry for mercy!* Someone was asking for his help, a request he always honors.

- He called for the petitioner to draw near to him, and Bartimaeus came. I like the directness of Mark's statement: "Bartimaeus came to Jesus." Have you come to Jesus? Have you asked him for his saving help, for his cure of your spiritual blindness? I hope so! I sincerely hope so! For if you haven't sought his help in this regard your greatest need has never yet been met.

3. So there they stood facing each other.

- Infinite need in the presence of infinite supply! Infinite poverty petitioning infinite provision! The physical darkness of blindness on the one hand, the spiritual Light of the World on the other!

- I imagine a hush fell across the crowd as they waited to see what Jesus would do. But to their surprise he didn't *do* anything. Rather, he spoke. But they were not words of consolation or hope that fell from his lips. Rather, he asked the blind man a simple, direct question: "What do you want me to do for you?" Isn't that a strange question? Whether you do or not, I must tell you, I at first found it very strange.

- One at first wants to cry out: "Isn't it obvious, Jesus, what he wants? Why are you toying with him like that? Quit playing this cat and mouse game with him!"

- But we can be sure that Jesus was not playing games with him. And we can be sure that Jesus knew what Bartimaeus needed, better even than Bartimaeus knew it. But did Bartimaeus know what he needed?

- Doubtless, our Lord intended his strange question to force the beggar to look deep within himself, beyond his surface needs, and to drive him to consider the implications of any request he would make of the Savior.

- You see, Bartimaeus could have responded to Jesus' question any number of ways. He could have responded

  senselessly, that is, he could have said: "Nothing, really; I just wanted to be able to say that I shook the hand of a celebrity"; or he could have answered

  selfishly, for within that very hour Jesus had asked his disciples the very same question and had received a very selfish answer from them (Mark 10:36-37). Like James and John, Bartimaeus might have said: "I want you to make me the most important, the most successful beggar in town—one might even say, the 'king of beggars,' so that the other beggars will respect me"; or he could have answered

symptomatically (rather than "curatively"), for, you see, if he was looking only at the symptoms of his problem, considering only his poverty, he would ask only for money. But his poverty was only a symptom of a much deeper problem; his poverty was only the effect of a more terrible cause, namely, his blindness.

♦ We learn from Mark's record, of course, that Bartimaeus actually responded in none of these ways. Rather, he responded

seriously: "Rabbi, I want…."

"But wait, Bartimaeus, what do you want? Before you complete your response, do you understand, if you finish your response in the only way that addresses your deepest need, that your days of begging are over. You will have to become a productive citizen." Apparently, he understood this, for without hesitation he cried, "Rabbi, I want to see." And immediately Jesus healed him, and we read that Bartimaeus followed Jesus in the way.

♦ Bartimaeus understood his obligations toward Jesus better than many Christian do. He understood that Jesus' healing touch meant a transformed life that would carry lifelong implications, that he would have to give up begging and get a productive job, that he would have to be ever grateful to the messianic Lord who cured him, and that, having known the life of a beggar, he would ever after have to be compassionate toward other beggars.

♦ Many years ago I took my children to see their first movie. It was the musical version of Charles Dicken's *A Christmas Story* entitled *Scrooge* starring Albert Finney in the title role.

The movie took us on Scrooge's journey with the three spirits from Christmas Past to Christmas Present to Christmas Future. Then we watched as Scrooge awoke Christmas morning to discover that his journey had all been a dream. But he had learned well the lesson the spirits had taught him. He immediately began joyously to exhibit his new-found Christmas spirit, buying the goose for Bob Cratchet, going to his nephew's house for Christmas dinner, and showing generosity to the poor.

After the movie was over, on our way home in the car I felt I had to instruct my children that while it was a lovely movie, they had to understand that the story was essentially teaching by implication that one goes to heaven when he dies because he does good works and that in this it was very wrong. However, I noted that the movie had a redeeming feature: it quite powerfully portrayed the change that comes to the life of every man or woman whom Christ has truly converted. The Christian is one who indeed has a "past" and who is now a different person with new affections and new purposes.

4. Now I must ask you: Has Christ touched you? Has he healed you spiritually?

♦ Has he granted you *spiritual* sight? If he has done so, do you understand that you have been bought with a price and that you are not your own? Do you understand that since you have been shown mercy, you must show mercy to others the rest of your life? Have you given your life to Jesus Christ? Have you been captured by the cause of Christ?

♦ Think of Paul's commitment for a moment. He, earlier a self-righteous Pharisee and a persecutor of the church, became after Christ confronted him on the Damascus Road a man "Christ-possessed,"

who had "resolved to know nothing among men but Jesus Christ and him crucified" (1 Cor 2:2);

who declared that "for him, to live is Christ" (Phil 1:21);

who so lived that "in everything [Christ] might have the preeminence" (Col 1:18);

who gloried only in the cross (Gal 6:14);

who "considered whatever was to his profit [before his conversion] as 'loss' for the sake of Christ"; what is more,

who considered everything as "loss compared to the surpassing greatness of knowing Christ Jesus my Lord, for whose sake [he said], 'I have suffered loss of all things [apparently his parents had disinherited him; all his old teachers and friends had disowned him]. I consider them 'dung' [he continued] that I may gain Christ and be found in him, not having a righteousness of my own that comes through the Law, but that which is through faith in Christ—the righteousness that comes from God and is by faith" (Phil 3:7-9);

who said: "One thing I do: Forgetting what is behind, and straining toward what is ahead, I press on toward the goal to win the prize for which God has called me heavenward in Christ Jesus" (3:13-14); and

who could testify toward the end of his life as a missionary: "I consider my life worth nothing to me, if only I may finish the race and complete the task the Lord Jesus has given me—the task of testifying to the gospel of God's grace" (Acts 20:24). Quite plainly, self-preservation was not the number one priority on Paul's list. Christ's cause was his number one priority.

- Quite evidently, all of the native gifts, worldly learning, physical and mental energies, tireless zeal, personal genius, and unflagging persistence which he had directed earlier to the elevation of the "traditions" of Judaism, he now consecrated to a new end—to declare the fullness of the blessing of the gospel of Christ.

Christian, should it be any different for any of us? I would respond resoundingly with an unqualified "No!" If you disagree and think your God and Lord will be satisfied with your used "seconds" in his service, you must be able to justify your response someday before the high tribunal of heaven. And I can assure you, you will not be able in that day to answer the Judge once in a thousand times.

If one day Jesus Christ asked you by his Spirit, "What do you want me to do for you?" and you pled for his mercies and he granted them to you and forgave you, then you now in response should do no less than did the healed Bartimaeus: you should "follow Jesus along the road." I trust that you are doing so.

Let us pray:
Dear Lord and Savior, Great Healer of mankind: We thank you for saving us, for healing us of our spiritual blindness. We confess that had you not come our way one day we would still be in our sin, for we know now that we could have never healed ourselves. We know we owe everything to you.

Help us to realize anew that we were only blind beggars in your sight before you came to us and healed us. Stir our hearts and create within us new levels of devotion, and help us never to forget that it is now our task to tell other blind beggars where they too can receive their sight. We ask this for your cause and for your glory. Amen.

Sermon Four

While this sermon is not overly doctrinal, it is still essentially Reformed and theologically sound—characteristics of the Christian sermon about which the preacher must always be concerned. Drawing upon some ideas that I found years ago in a sermon by Helmut Thielicke, it is a simple, direct, three-point sermon, addressing a very real need in the life of the average Christian—the need to discover what it is about which he should rejoice every day of his life and how he may acquire this joy.

Its FCF is the joylessness that affects so many Christians, and its CS is the lasting joy that Christ gives them in their knowledge of who they are in him and what God has done for them by him.

"Choosing to Live on the 'Joy Side' of the Christian Life"

Text: Luke 10:17-20; Matthew 11:25ff.

> I was watching Satan fall like lightning from heaven. I have given you authority to trample on snakes and scorpions [Jesus did not intend literal snakes here but all the Enemy's powers of darkness] and to overcome all the power of the enemy; nothing will harm you. However, *do not rejoice* that the spirits submit to you, but *rejoice* that your names are written in heaven.

Prayer for Illumination

Great and Holy Father: bless my preaching today about a truth that is, *perhaps above almost any other*, needful for Christians to understand and to grasp in the present hour when men's hearts are failing them for fear. You know the condition of every heart gathered here before you. Grant that I, professing to have been instructed in the Kingdom of God, may bring forth from the storehouse of your Word things new and old to help troubled hearts. I pray, for the sake of our souls, in Christ's name. Amen.

* * * * *

Dear hearts, if one virtue should characterize the life of every Christian it should be joy! The Psalmist commands: "Rejoice in the Lord, O you righteous" (Ps 33:1). Jesus said: "These things I have spoken to you that my joy may be in you and that your joy may be full" (John 15:11). To the Thessalonians Paul wrote: "Rejoice always,...for this is the will of God in Christ Jesus for you" (1 Thes 5:16, 18). To the Philippians Paul wrote: "Rejoice in the Lord always; again I will say, rejoice" (Phil 4:4). And he tells us that one of the fruit of the Spirit in the Christian life is joy (Gal 5:22). And to his readers Peter wrote: "Without having seen him you love him; though you do not now see him you believe in him and rejoice with unutterable and exalted joy" (1 Pet 1:8).

Yet, in spite of these biblical injunctions and scores of others I could have cited, many Christians today are not very joyous people, and that's too bad since joylessness is a bad testimony for Christ before the world. Christians of all people, you surely know, have something about which truly to rejoice. Indeed, we are really the only ones who have anything eternally significant in which to rejoice. The living God is our Father and Provider. Jesus Christ is our Savior. The great Comforter—the Spirit of truth—dwells within us. Our sins have been forgiven. We are righteous in the sight of the Judge of all the earth. And we are on our way to heaven. So we have more truly to rejoice about than any other group of people on the face of the whole earth. But, as I said, many Christians aren't rejoicing in their spiritual possessions. In fact, the evidence would indicate that *our churches are filled with unhappy, disillusioned, joyless people* in regard to their Christian faith and experience. One has only to read George Barna's 1990 book, *The Frog in the Kettle*, published by Regal, or William D. Hendricks' 1993 Moody title, *Exit*

Interviews: Revealing Stories of Why People Are Leaving the Church (the last three chapters are "must" reading for every pastor) to bear this out for himself. Commenting in the October 24, 1992 issue of the *Dallas Morning News* on the fact that the evangelical movement in North America is now losing more members annually through the "back door" than it is gaining through the "front door," Charles Colson declared: "If [the evangelical movement] were a business, we'd be contemplating Chapter 11 [bankruptcy]." And a major cause of the church's hemorrhaging of Christians back into the world is the joylessness that is rampant among us. In my own years of ministry I've talked to many discouraged church people—many of them my converts and personal friends of mine—who have admitted they've not known a vital, joyous walk with Christ for ten, twenty, even thirty years. And *for a Christian to lack Christian joy is a distressing condition indeed.*

So I want us to think this morning about this virtue of Christian joy, this precious fruit of the Spirit. More specifically, I will be encouraging you to choose, from this day forward, every day of your life, *to live on the "joy side" of the Christian life.* Write that statement down somewhere right now. Here it is again: "Today I choose to live on the 'joy side' of the Christian life." Now the first thing I want us to think together about is this question:

1. In what should we Christians rejoice?

Turn with me again to Luke 10, and when you get there note first that in the first 16 verses Jesus is giving instructions to his appointed servants before he sends them forth to the work. With these instructions completed, he sends his seventy-two appointees "two by two ahead of him to every town and place where he was about to go." Some time later, Luke informs us, "the seventy-two returned *with joy* and said, 'Lord, even the demons submit to us in your name.'" Take careful note now. In response to their exuberant acclamation Jesus calmly replied in verses 19-20:

> I was watching Satan fall like lightning from heaven [as you carried out your work]. I have given you authority to trample on snakes

> and scorpions [referring here not to literal snakes but to the Arch-Enemy's powers of darkness] and to overcome all the power of the enemy; nothing will harm you. However, *do not rejoice* that the spirits submit to you, but *rejoice* that your names are written in heaven.

Do you understand what Jesus was saying to them? He was saying: "Don't rejoice in your powers that have brought you such triumphs! Find your real and lasting joy rather in the fact that God is your Father, that I am your Savior, and that you are mine." In other words: "Don't make your successes in life that which really 'turns you on' in your Christian experience—even your spiritual successes."

Why would Jesus say that? I think, for two reasons: first, because he knows that if you derive your joy from the successes flowing out of *your* labors that source of joy will soon give birth in your thinking to the idea that you must work for the sake of his approval. You will begin to feel the need for personal proficiency in everything, which will foster in turn the "I must win the point at any cost" attitude and the manipulation of others, as well as other notions such as

> I must score big and score standing up;
> I must gain the upper hand;
> I must carry the day no matter what it takes;
> I must prevail over others;
> I must get the advantage of others;
> I must get the better of others;
> I must always outdo, out-rival, dominate, and beat the competition;
> I must take precedence over and be superior to others;
> and I must *simply try harder* when I fail;
> all which are wrong attitudes.

Second, Jesus knows your days will experience their disappointments and discouragements as well. Even your Christian service will know its "days of dismay" and idleness and you are going to take some major "hits" along the way. And if you are going to find your joy in life in your successful labors for Christ, you will spend a good many of your days in this present evil age in discouragement and despondency.

So Jesus is telling all of us who serve him what he taught John Milton through his blindness, namely, that "they also serve who *only* stand and wait," and that we should find our ultimate and lasting joy not in what *we* do for *him* but rather in what *he* has done for *us!*

Make it your habit, Jesus declares, *not* to rejoice in what *you* have done for the Lord, for even after you have done all that God commands you to do, you have but done your duty and are only unworthy servants. Rather, rejoice in what God in Christ has done for you. And when you do that—and it may take some practice before you get the hang of it—you will find that rejoicing in God your Savior will quickly give birth in your thinking to such glorious ideas as divine grace, the worth of the Cross, divine mercy, infinite compassion, forgiveness, divine acceptance in spite of earthly failure, acquittal, reconciliation, pardon, God's love, divine providence, eternal life, redemption, perfect righteousness, eternal bliss, eternal victory over death, going to heaven when you die, and God working out the "all things" of Romans 8:28 for your good.

And aren't these the really important things in the Christian's life? Isn't Jesus telling us here where the "joy side" of the Christian life is to be found? I think he is. And apparently he expects us to live on the "joy side" of the Christian life every day because he *commands* us to rejoice in our God and in the fact that our names are written in the Lamb's book of life! Now the second thing I want you to note is that

2. Jesus in his earthly ministry practiced what he preached. If you want a living Exemplar, indeed, the perfect illustration, of living on the "joy side" of life and how this "blessed confidence" works its tranquil way out in a human life, we have only to look at the Lord Jesus himself. What tremendous pressures there must have been within him, tempting him to hectic, nervous, impulsive, indeed explosive activity. He saw, as no one else ever saw, with an infinite and awful nearness, all the injustice, terror, dread, and beastliness in the world, the agony of the dying man, the anguish of his wounded conscience, and the unspeakable horrors of the hell awaiting the impenitent. He saw and heard and felt all this with the heart of a compassionate Savior, which means that he did not merely take note of human distress and misery as with a tabulating machine but he actually suffered distress and misery to immeasureable depths. Would this not have filled his every waking hour and robbed him of sleep at night? Must he not begin immediately to set the *entire* world ablaze—in *his* own time—with talk about him, to win people, to work and to work furiously, unceasingly, frenzily, unrestingly, before the night comes when no man can work? That is what we could well imagine the earthly life of the Son of God to have been like if we were to think of him in our current human terms.

But how utterly different was the actual life of Jesus! Though the burden of the whole world unquestionably lay heavy upon his shoulders, though the sin of the world's continents of people with all their desperate needs was dreadfully near to his heart, though suffering and sinning were going on behind closed doors in chambers, on street corners, in castles and in slums, known and seen only by the Son of God, though such immeasurable misery and wretchedness cried aloud for a divine Physician, he always had time to stop and talk to the individual:

- he associated with publicans, lonely widows, and despised prostitutes;
- he moved among the outcasts of society;
- he appeared not to be bothered by the fact that these were not strategically important people, that they had no prominence, that they were not key figures or society's "movers and shakers," but *only* the unfortunate, lost children of the Father in heaven;
- he seemed to ignore with a sovereign indifference the great so-called "world-historical perspective" of his mission in Jerusalem when it came to an insignificant, blind and smelly beggar, a Mr. Nobody, who was nevertheless dear to the heart of God and needed to be saved.

Moreover, because Jesus knew which way God had providentially set the "switches," the words he spoke were *never* prepared, tactical propaganda speeches. The propaganda of humankind and the "spin" of even well-intentioned Christian people that are so much with us today, even when they masquerade as a kind of evangelism and become an enterprise of the church, are always based on the Pelagian notion that success and failure, fruit and harvest are dependent upon our human activity or lack thereof, upon our imagination or lack thereof, upon our energy and intelligence or lack thereof. Therefore, the church must ever guard itself against becoming merely a *busy* enterprise, and pastors too must beware of becoming simply religious administrators

devoid of power,
dried up as far as spiritual substance is concerned, and
trying to force spiritual growth by carnal means.

No, Jesus was not a mere propagandist. And there is one fact which shows that he was not, and that fact is that *for him, speaking to his Father in prayer was more important than speaking to men*, no matter how great the crowds that gathered around him, even when they would make him king. Just when you think that he would surely seize the moment and accept their offer, that he would surely strike while the iron is hot and mold the masses to his purpose, he "passes through their midst" and withdraws into the silence of communion with his Father.

Why was it that he spoke with such calm authority, as the scribes and Pharisees did not? Because he was rhetorically gifted? Because he was dynamic? No, though he was no doubt rhetorically gifted and dynamic. Rather, he spoke to men with authority

- because *always* he had spoken first with his Father,
- because *always* he came to men out of communion with the Father with the *joyous* confidence that springs from knowing that his Father does all things well.

In a real sense he found his *joy in eternity*. That's why he was and is so disturbing to humankind. He lived in communion with God. His powerful speech flowed from his joyous prayer life; and the very reason he could afford to pray so diligently and give his best, his most opportune hours, to communion with the Father, is that he knew that while he rested serenely and joyfully in the Father's bosom, it was not that nothing was happening but that in doing this he was rather giving place to the really important thing—namely, letting his *Father* work out his will in and by him.

Because Jesus knew that he must serve his neighbor (literally, those nearest him then and there) he could confidently leave to his Father's care the things farther away. By being obedient in his corner of the highly provincial precincts of Nazareth and particularly of Jerusalem he allowed himself to be fitted into the great salvific mosaic whose Planner and Maker is God, a mosaic that involved for him a hideous Cross. That's why he had time for individuals: *he knew that all of history—especially his history—is in the hands of his Father*. And that is why joy and not fretful unrest went forth from him.

In sum, Jesus lived what he taught his disciples in Luke 10:20. For note that Luke immediately informs us in verse 21 after his admonition to his disciples:

> *At that time* Jesus, *full of joy through the Holy Spirit*, said: "I praise you, Father, Lord of heaven and earth, because you have hidden these things from the wise and learned, and revealed them to little children. Yes, Father, for this was your good pleasure."

At that time Jesus, being "anointed with the oil of *gladness* above his fellows," possessed an inexhaustible treasury of heavenly joy through the Holy Spirit. At what time was that? From verses 13-15 and the parallel in Matthew 11:25 we learn the context of Jesus' remark: *At the very time* that his ministry had been *rejected* and had failed to produce repentance in the cities of Korazin, Bethsaida, and Capernaum—the very cities in which most of his miracles had been performed—Jesus joyously said, "I praise you, Father...."

How could he do this? How was he able to praise his heavenly Father when entire cities were rejecting him? Because, dear hearts, our Lord was not looking ultimately to men's *acceptance* for his joy, but rather, he endured the cross, scorning its shame, "for the *joy* that was set before him" (Heb 12:2) in doing his Father's will. That is to say, he found his joy in his relationship with his heavenly Father and his Father's will for him, even though the divine will involved for him the hideous Cross of woe and abandonment.

Are you a Christian today? Do you know Christ as your Savior and Lord who is your righteousness, and have you experienced the forgiveness of sin? Are you on your way to heaven? Then, because of these things "rejoice in the Lord always; and again I will say it, Rejoice!" (Phil 4:4) "Rejoice always,...for this is the will of God in Christ Jesus for you" (1 Thes 5:16, 18).

You have heard all your Christian life, I suspect, that the shortest verse in the Bible is John 11:35: "Jesus wept." Well, in one sense it is but in another sense it isn't. It *is* in the English versions of our Bible, but the shortest verse in the original Greek versions of our Bible is 1 Thessalonians 5:16: "Rejoice always!" You see, the Greek takes sixteen letters to say "Jesus wept" but uses only fourteen letters to say "Rejoice always!" I find that fascinating: In a sense the good news of the gospel is captured in these four words: "Jesus wept"; "Rejoice always!" The former two sum up his entire ministry for us as the man of sorrows. And because he walked the *Via Dolorosa*, we can "rejoice always," rejoicing in who he is and what he did for us, not in what we are in our raw natural state or in what we have done or are doing for him! *Herein is true joy: To rejoice in one's relationship with Jesus Christ, for that will never change.*

Now the last thing I want us to think about is

3. How we can *learn* to "choose to live on the 'joy side' of the Christian life".

How can we achieve this blessed experience of living joyously everyday when our lives are so attached to fretful busyness and worry? After all is said and done, I think you will agree this *is* our problem.

I will suggest a prescription for this problem even though I know that such a prescription in a sermon can and often does have something shady about it, particularly if it gives the impression that there are certain little tricks, which if one learns them, he will learn the "art" of joyous living—as if joy were an "art" at all! No, *joy comes from just being quiet and receptive when God speaks about what he has done for you and who you are as a result of his working!* So what I have to say now I say only to help us to stop "conjuring up" joys that will always be false joys if they are humanly contrived. Here's my prescription. Are you ready?

The next time you are on a plane or sitting alone in your living room or on your patio, when the portable telephone beside you is silent for a moment and your appointment book is beyond your reach, and *it is quiet*, try for once not to reach for the next file folder or for the newspaper or for the crossword puzzle or for the remote on your TV. Take a deep breath and whisper the words of the *Gloria Patri*:

> Glory be to the Father, and to the Son, and to the Holy Ghost;
> As it was in the beginning, is now, and ever shall be,
> World without end, Amen.

And then ponder these words meditatively:

Glory be to the Father! Say to yourself: "Glory be to him who with his fatherly love has brought me to this quiet moment in my day's work, who has entrusted to me this special silent time with him, and who in the last analysis is the one who makes the final decision regarding my phone calls, every appointment today, and every decision I am now obliged to make!"

Glory be to the Son! Say to yourself: "The Son I'm praising here in my quietude is none other than Jesus Christ my Lord who died for me. Dare I—for whom he suffered such pain, for whom he opened the gates of heaven—dare I go on frittering my life away on trifles and futilities? Must not the *one* thing needful that Mary chose be constantly present before my mind, and must *it* not show up the relative non-importance of the many things in which I am engaged today? After all, for what did Christ die? Did he die for my cash register, my bank account, my balance sheet, my stock portfolio, for the roving eye of the boss whom I am desperately trying to please, for my television set? Did he not rather die for *me*, for *me* personally, and not only for me but also for my fellow Christian who will be sitting beside me next Sunday who is struggling with some burden and who needs encouragement? And did he not die for my children whom I hardly ever see? And speaking of my children, did he die for their food and clothing or did he die for their souls whom I hardly even seem to know at all because the 'many things' that Martha chose are always getting between me and their eternal souls." Ah, beloved, detach yourself from life's "lesser things" and meditate upon him and his life's doing and dying for you and for your children and get your priorities straight! In doing that you will know joy!

Then think: *Glory be to the Holy Spirit!* Ask yourself in that meditative moment: "Do I ever fall silent before him in order that this blessed Holy Comforter within me may fill my mind with himself and give me a sense of the true priorities in life, particularly the fruit of Christ's joy?"

Now ponder this statement: *As [the triune God's divine glory] was in the beginning, [it] is now, and ever shall be, world without end.* Here you are suddenly encompassed by the sheer "godness" of God, surrounded and overshadowed by an everlasting faithfulness you can trust, and rooted upon a foundation that the shifting sands of daily routine can never provide. And having reminded yourself of God's *eternal* glory, perhaps you will become newly aware of the truth of the first answer of the *Westminster Shorter Catechism*, that "[your] chief end is to glorify God and *enjoy him forever*," which means that your *greatest* passion in life should be to learn to know God better than you know anyone or anything else and to *enjoy* him more than you enjoy anyone or anything else.

If you do this repeatedly, and other such meditative exercises like it, during the day, you will soon find that such exercises are not simply mantras or mystical rigmarole, and much less inward flights of fancy by which you simply escape the daily routine. Oh, no! You will go back to your work renewed, you will become a *joyous*

Christian. For then you will be distinguishing what is eternal from what is temporal, what is significant from what is insignificant, what is real from what is false. You will begin to live out the words of the hymn verse that you have sung so often:

> Does sadness fill my mind? A solace here I find:
> May Jesus Christ be praised.
> Or fades my earthly bliss? My comfort still is this:
> May Jesus Christ be praised.

Ah, what an unspeakable joy comes from knowing that in the midst of man's mischief, in the midst of his vain scheming and bad speculations, his shaping and misshaping, his activisms and failures, that God is still on his throne and that a *divinely* planned stream of events deserving of my joyous praise is still flowing silently on in my life!

And what an indescribable consolation it is *to know* that in spite of all of the confusions of men in their personal lives and in the politics of today's world, in spite of all the many dodges and futilities which only take men farther away from God's desire for them—*to know* that *in spite of all these things* nothing can or will divert God from accomplishing his purposes for us—*to know* that, despite all the chaos, all the stupidities, all the sin of man, through all the labyrinths of history and the confusions of *our* own lives, there yet runs the thread of God's immutable purpose for us. He knows what he wants of us, and he *is doing* in and for us exactly what he wills. One day, no doubt, when we stand before God's throne on the last day and look back on our lives from that vantage point, we shall say with amazement and surprise:

- "If only I had known when I stood at the grave of my loved one and everything seemed to come to an end for me,
- "if only I had known when I learned of that malignant disease and was informed that it was terminal,
- "if only I had known when the little financial world I had created for myself fell apart around my feet,

- "if only I had known at that moment that God was only carrying out his wise design and perfect plan for me through all my woes,
- "if only I had known that in the midst of my troubles and despair *his* harvest was ripening, and everything was pressing on toward *his* last kingly day—
- "if only I had known this, I would have been more calm and confident, I would have been more cheerful and much more tranquil, I would have been more composed, yes, and even joyous."

Ah, my beloved, woe to the nervous activity of those of little faith who never learn to look away from themselves to their God for their joy! Woe to the anxiousness and busyness of those who never pray and who have never learned to turn their problems over to the one who feeds the sparrow and knows when it falls. Martin Luther once said: "While I drink my little glass of Wittenberg beer the gospel runs its course." Now that is truly the finest and most comforting thing I have ever heard said about beer. What Luther meant is that he understood that *he* could not change the world with all *his* fretful busyness. He knew that after he had preached God's Word he could step down from the pulpit and fall silent; he didn't need to go on incessantly bellowing and roaring across the countryside. He knew he could step aside, quietly drink his little glass of Wittenberg beer, and trust in God's Word to tear down the Enemy's empires and to do God's work of "kingdom building." In all too many cases today we preachers do not sin by doing too little work. On the contrary, *many of us ought to ask ourselves whether we are still capable in God's name of being idle and letting God do his work.* Take my word for it, dear hearts, you can actually serve and worship God simply by lying flat on your back occasionally, getting away from your everlasting need to produce, and just trusting God to do his work.

The person who has grasped the truth that God is caring for him even when it is not evident that he is doing so, who is capable, often in spite of all *his* failed labors, to maintain a serene and joyous existence, and who therefore lies down and soundly sleeps in Jesus' care—that man is doing not only the most godly thing but also the wisest thing he could ever do for his own physical and spiritual health.

So do not rejoice in your professional successes, dear hearts. Today and everyday choose rather to live on the "joy side" of the Christian life: to rejoice in your God, in what he has savingly done for you, and in what *he* has made and is making you to be in his beloved Son!

Let us pray:

Father, deliver us from the frantic, helter-skelter hustle and bustle which the world would want to impose upon us and in doing so destroy us, and from the exhausting, draining belief that *we* must somehow, all by ourselves, save ourselves, the world, and everyone else in it. Help us to rest and trust in you, the giver of life and peace and lasting joy, more than we have in the past.

Give us Jesus' joy and laughter today, not because of what we think we have done well or what we think we have done better than someone else, and not even ultimately because of what we have done for you at all, but give us *great joy* today because of *whose* we are and *who* we are in Jesus Christ and *what* he has done for us, and because our names are written in the Lamb's ledger in heaven with a "Paid in full" stamped across the page. I say again, Father, give us Christ's joy and laughter today. Enable us to say with Habakkuk:

Though the fig tree should not blossom nor grapes appear on the vines,

Though the produce of the olive tree should fail and the fields yield no food,

Though the flock should be cut off from the fold and there be no herd in the stalls,

Yet I will still choose to live today on the "joy side" of the Christian life and rejoice in the God of my salvation.

Enable any discouraged brother or sister here today to rejoice in who he is in Christ and to say in his sense of rejection, discouragement, failure, or whatever it is that is bothering him:

I thank you, Father, Lord of heaven and earth, for who I am right now—who I am in Christ—and what he has done and is doing for me. Thank you, Father, that my name is written in the Lamb's book of life in heaven. In Jesus' mighty name I pray, Amen.

Sermon Five

This sermon is textual, based as it is upon John 3:16. As a textual sermon its points are drawn directly from the biblical text, underscoring simply what the text itself says. Of course, I develop and elaborate the several points. The sermon illustrates my attempt carefully to expound this verse in such a way that what I say is scripturally grounded, rational, God-centered, and theologically accurate, and at the same time does not bore the audience as I move through this very familiar text. Its FCF is the eternal perdition facing all men apart from Christ and its CS is trust in Christ for salvation.

A word about the alliteration of the sermon points. There is always a danger in alliteration and it is this: If the alliteration becomes so all-important that it overpowers the biblical text and makes the text say what it does not say, then it should not be used. But there is nothing wrong with alliteration as long as it captures and conveys the intention of the text. I do not think my alliteration here distorts the text in any way. A good alliteration may even stimulate the audience and make it easier for the people to remember the sermon points.

I read 2 Chronicles 33:1-13 earlier in the service concerning Manasseh's sin and God's grace because I return to its history at the end of the sermon.

"The Immeasurable Greatness of the Love of God"

Text: John 3:16

> For God so loved the world that he gave his one and only Son, that whoever believes in him shall not perish but have everlasting life.

Prayer for Illumination

Jesus, thou Joy of loving hearts,
thou Fount of life, thou Light of men,
From the best bliss that earth imparts
we turn unfilled to thee again.

Dear Lord Jesus Christ, we come to you today as redeemed prodigal children, drawn once again, *by your grace*, away from the folly of thinking that we can live without you and drawn back, *by your mercy*, to your consolations that are new every morning and *by the wonder* of your love that has forgiven us so very much.

Now I ask you, O faithful Savior, to prosper the message of your grace in this place as I proclaim your unsearchable riches. Grant once again that your Holy Spirit will work by and with the preached Word in stony hearts and transform them into hearts that love and desire to serve you.

For these things I humbly cry to you, in your strong name, O mighty, merciful Savior. Amen.

* * * * *

Christian hymnody is filled with poetic efforts to express the immeasurable greatness of the love of God. We can all think of hymns such as "Love divine, all loves excelling, Joy of heaven, to earth come down" that seek to do this. Or this one:

O the deep, deep love of Jesus—vast, unmeasured, boundless, free
Rolling as a mighty ocean in its fullness over me.
Underneath me, all around me, is the current of thy love,
Leading onward, leading homeward, to my glorious rest above.

O the deep, deep love of Jesus, Love of every love the best!
'Tis an ocean vast of blessing, 'tis a haven sweet of rest.
O the deep, deep love of Jesus, 'tis a heav'n of heav'ns to me.
And it lifts me up to glory, for it lifts me up to Thee.

Or this one:

The love of God is greater far than tongue or pen can ever tell;
It goes beyond the highest star and reaches to the lowest hell.
The guilty pair bowed down with care, God gave his Son to win;
His erring child he reconciled, and pardoned from his sin.

Could we with ink the ocean fill and were the skies of parchment made,
Were every stalk on earth a quill, and every man a scribe by trade,
To write the love of God above would drain the ocean dry,
Nor could the scroll contain the whole tho' stretched from sky to sky.

O, love of God, how rich and pure! How measureless and strong!
It shall forever more endure—'Tis saints' and angels' song!

But no uninspired hymn, however sublime its poetry, however exalted and lovely its mental conceptions, excels the simple majesty of or brings greater assurance to the human heart than the apostle John's simple inspired declaration:

> For God so loved the world that he gave his one and only Son, that whoever believes in him shall not perish but have eternal life.

It is the immeasurable greatness of the love of God for his fallen world about which John teaches his readers in this beloved verse of the Christian church. And it is this verse that I ask you to consider with me today.

Now, of course, our little one-syllable English word "God," translating the two-syllable Greek word *theos*, is the obvious grammatical subject of this biblical affirmation. But if we move too quickly over this small word, thinking about it only in terms of its being a point of grammar or just a noun, and do not reflect upon it, we shall not take the first needful step in understanding our text. We must endeavor to appreciate this word with regard to its intended referent.

In other words, when we come to John 3:16 and see this noun "God," our minds should immediately be flooded with the wondering awareness that the God about whom John writes here is the one living and true Lord God Almighty, more specifically, the God and Father of our Lord Jesus Christ (for John speaks of "his Son")—infinite in his majesty and ineffaceable exaltation, stainlessly perfect in his holiness, righteousness, and flaming purity—whom the heaven of heavens cannot contain, to whom the earth is as the small dust on the balance, and before whom all the nations are like a drop in a bucket, indeed, before whom all the nations are like nothing, who regards them as worthless and as less than nothing (Isa 40:15-17).

He has need of nothing, nor can his unsullied blessedness be in any way affected—whether by way of increase or decrease—by any act of the creatures of his hand. What *we* call infinite space is but a speck on the horizon of his contemplation. What *we* call countless millennia and aeons are in his sight but as yesterday when they are past. Apparelled in unapproachable glory and majesty and girded with matchless strength, his will is the resistless law of all existences to which their every motion conforms. Righteousness and judgment are the foundations of his throne.

Now it is *this* God, mind you, this God about whom simply to say that he is the Lord of all the earth is to say so *little* that it is to say virtually nothing at all—it is *this* God of whom our text speaks. And if we are to discern its intention, we must bear all this fully in our minds.

Now our text tells us concerning this great God—the Almighty God and Father of our Lord Jesus Christ, the First Person of the triune Godhead—that he *loves*. Of necessity, then, his love is as boundless, majestic, pure, stainless, and unfathomable as he is. Accordingly, it is the immeasurable greatness of the *love* of this God, as we have already noted, that receives the emphasis of the verse. This is evident from the word order itself in the original text, reading literally, "For *so loved* God the world." John throws the two words "loved" and its adverbial modifier "so"—"so loved"—forward in the sentence before everything else—even before the word "God"—for our contemplation. Note then that John does not just say: "...*loved* God the world," but rather, "...*so loved* God the world."

Now what does John tells us about the love of this God in this text? I would suggest that he tells us the following seven things, and developing these ideas for your mind's holy contemplation will occupy our time in this sermon. God the Father's love, John tells us here, is

extraordinary in the object of its affection,
expressive in its actions,
expensive in its sacrifice,
extensive in its offer,
exclusive in its bestowment,
exceptional in its work, and
exhaustless in its benefits.

Let's look now at each of these features of God's love in turn.

First, John would have us know that God's love is *extraordinary in the object of its affection*—he loved, John tells us, "the world." Many will ask here, "Why should it be thought extraordinary that he should love the world? Why *wouldn't* he love this world, for consider how many people there are who live in it. Would not the sheer *number* of people—some seven billion plus of us today—move the great heart of God to love this world?" But, you know, dear friends, the mere uncounted multitudes of men are hardly a reason for God's loving it, for as great as this conception is, the mere measure of the number of mankind cannot compel the love of God to action. All the multitudes of humankind—what is their mere finite sum, however immense, compared to the infinitude of God? Do we praise the blacksmith's brawn in the slightest by declaring it capable of supporting a mustard seed in his outstretched hand? Of course not. Similarly, the mere *number* of people in this world is too small to be the standard for measuring the greatness of God's love. Conceive of the multitudes of mankind as vastly as you may, their number remains ever a poor measure—an inappropriate index—by which to comprehend the immeasurable love of God. (Warfield)

If it is not then the number of men in this world that gauges for us the extraordinariness of God's love, why then do I say that this world is an extraordinary choice of his love?

> We must let the Scriptures themselves tell us, and primarily that Apostle to whom we owe this great declaration. Nor does he fail to tell us; and that without the slightest ambiguity. The "world," he tells us—that we are not to love—is just the synonym of all that is evil and disgusting [which is why we are not to love it]. There is nothing in it that can attract God's love.... It is not that God's love is so great that it is able to extend over the whole of a big world; it is rather that His love is so great that it is able to prevail over His own holy hatred and abhorrence of sin and love the world that lies in the evil one. "World" here is not a term of [demographic] extension so much as it is a term of [ethical] intensity. Its primary connotation is ethical, and the point of its employment is not to suggest that the world is so big that it takes a great deal of love to embrace it all, but that the world is so bad that it takes a great kind of love to love it at all, and much more to love it as God...loved it when He gave His son for it. The passage is intended to arouse in our hearts a wondering sense of the marvel and the mystery of the love of God for the sinful world—conceived here, not quantitatively but qualitatively as, in its very distinguishing characteristic, sinful. Search the universe through and through and you will find no marvel so great, no mystery so unfathomable, as this, that the great and good God, whose perfect righteousness flames in indignation at the sight of every iniquity, and whose absolute holiness recoils in abhorrence in the presence of every impurity, yet loves this sinful world, yes, has so loved it that He has given His one and only Son to die for it. It is this marvel and this mystery that our text would carry home to our hearts. (Warfield)

God the Father's love is indeed a very extraordinary thing, I say, when we take due note that it set itself upon *this* lost, ruined, guilty world. What was there in this world that should compel him to love it so? There was *nothing* lovable in it. *No* fragrant flower of corresponding love for him grew in it anywhere, but rather only the weeds of enmity toward him, and hatred toward his truth, disregard of his law, and rebellion against his commandments. *Nothing and no one* upon the face of the earth *merits* his love. Human kind deserves only his displeasure. There are seven billion plus reasons today he should detest it. Yet God loved this world with a love that was so deep, so wide, so strong, so incredible, so immeasurable—so beyond all human imagining—that even inspiration found it difficult to compute its measure in human terminology, and hence the Holy Spirit gave us that wondrous little word "so"—"he *so* loved"—and left us to attempt to comprehend the measurement of it.

Second, God's love, John tells us, was *expressive in its action*—God so loved, he writes, "that he gave." One night before one of his musicals was to open, Oscar Hammerstein pushed past Mary Martin, his singing star, in the soft red glow of the semi-darkness of the curtained stage and pressed into her hand a slip of paper. On it were these words:

> A bell is not a bell unless you ring it,
> A song is not a song unless you sing it, and
> Love is not love unless it gives itself away.

words which later were to become the basis of one of the hit numbers in the uncut version of his "The Sound of Music."

Similarly, God's love was not just in word. Indeed, real love is never just a noun. It is always a verb. God did not simply shout to us from heaven that he loved us. He loved this world of *sinful* people and expressed his love for it in a very tangible concrete way. He reached out and touched our world with his love, indeed, he *embraced* it as Hosea embraced his adulterous wife Gomer. And it is my earnest prayer, if he has never yet touched you personally, that before this service is over, you will have come personally to know his loving embrace and will have been personally drawn down into the infinite depths of his affection.

Third, God's love was *expensive in its sacrifice*—God so loved...that he gave "his one and only Son" to save sinners. Like Mary who broke the alabaster bottle of perfume—her most valuable possession—and filled the house with its sweet aroma, so God the Father gave the alabaster box of his own beloved Son, breaking him in death upon the cross that the fragrance of his saving benefits might pervade an entire world.

None of us ever had such a Son as our heavenly Father had.

Ours are the sinful sons of men; his the pure Son of God, the Father's other self, one with himself. When God gave his Son, he gave God himself, for Jesus is in his eternal nature not less or other than God. When God gave God for us he gave himself. What more then could he give? He gave his all; he gave himself. Who can measure this wondrous love!

Judge, you fathers here, how you love your sons. Could you give them to die for your enemy? Judge, you fathers who have only one son, does it not seem that God loved us even better than he loved his one and only Son? For many a father has given a son to the service of his country and many a mother's son has become a casualty of war. But we regard theirs as honorable deaths. But to what did God give his Son—to some profession in the pursuit of which he might always enjoy his company? To some service which men would respect? To an honorable death? No, no! He gave his Son to exile among men, he sent him down to hunger and thirst amid poverty so dire that he had no place to lay his head, he sent him down to the scourging and the crowning with thorns, to the giving of his back to wicked smiters and his cheeks to those who plucked out his beard. And finally, the Father gave his Son up to death on the cross—a type of execution so ignoble and reprehensible that it was reserved for the meanest and lowest criminal types. Roman law even excluded the Roman citizenry normally from death by crucifixion—and he gave him up to the awful loneliness expressed in "the strangest utterance that ever ascended from earth to heaven" (Murray), that cry of dereliction: "My God, my God, why have you forsaken me?" We hesitate to say it, but say it we must: in those hours at Calvary, God the Father became a sonless Father, and God the Son a fatherless Son—for us men and for our salvation. Oh, wondrous reach of love that God would give his one and only Son to the divine abandonment and to the dread suffering of a Roman cross for us—a Roman cross, the last place in the whole wide world where one would look to find his God and expect to find a saving transaction!

Fourth, God's love is *extensive in its offer*—"that *whoever*." Here John moves to his explanation for the Father's largess to sinners of the gift of his Son. "...that whoever...." That little word, "whoever," small as it is, is a word that in itself has no limit. It is a large enough chariot that it will carry everyone who is encompassed by it all the way from earth to heaven. Whoever hears or reads this sermon! Whoever in this world! That's its meaning. So God's love is indeed *extensive in its offer*—"...that *whoever*..."!

But—and this brings us to our fifth point—God's love is *exclusive in its bestowment*. This exclusivity of bestowment is underscored in our text in *two* ways: by its word "believes" and by its tiny modifying phrase "in him." Let's look at both of these restricting thoughts.

First, we are not taught here that God gave his Son for those who obey his law, for that none of us could ever do. And if even one of us could earn our own salvation, then righteousness would come by the law and Christ would not have come (Gal 3:21).

Nor does our text declare that God will save those who will both believe in Christ and *also* try to keep his law. Some, as J. Gresham Machen pointed out, believe that going to heaven is like going across a river in a rowboat. If one pulls only on the "oar of faith" he will simply go around in a circle; if he pulls only on the "oar of works" he will simply go around in a circle in the opposite direction. But if he pulls on both oars he will move across the river to the other side. Now that would be a fine illustration, Machen noted, if we were going to heaven in a rowboat! But we are not. Whoever would go to heaven must turn from his labors and cast himself in faith upon Jesus who is alone the Savior of sinners.

Nor does our text say that he gave his Son to save all who experience terrible despair and bitter remorse. Some people, you know, believe that they will go to heaven because they have known such despair and remorse here on earth. But many others do not feel such emotions who nevertheless *are* the Lord's own, and many feel such wretched depression who are *not* Christians at all. What does Augustus Toplady's hymn that we often sing say?

> Could my zeal no respite know,
> Could my tears forever flow,
> All for sin could not atone,
> Thou must save and thou alone.

What does Horatius Bonar's hymn say?

> Now what I feel or do can give me peace with God;
> Not all my prayers and sighs and tears can bear my awful load.

Nor does our text state that God gave his Son that every man will certainly and finally be saved. No, a large percentage of mankind will not be saved and are condemned already.

John's declaration makes it crystal clear that God must find one specific condition in all who would be saved, and that condition is *trust*—a trust that looks entirely away from all one's own self-help efforts at salvation and all one's pretensions of good works. So the word "believes" excludes works—even works of righteousness—and restricts the bestowment of God's love to those in whom are the condition of trust. How about you? Are you trusting in your alleged good works? I hope not! To do so is death!

Second—now mark well—the exclusiveness of God's love as to its bestowment is not found simply in that restrictive word "believes" or "trusts." Some years ago a popular song, you may recall, was entitled "I believe." One of the verses said, "Every time I hear a newborn baby cry, or touch a leaf or see the sky, then I know why I believe." But the song never stated what one believed or in whom one believed. John, however, declares clearly the object of saving faith: "that whoever believes *in him*," that is, in God's Son.

So we see that the exclusiveness of the bestowment of God's love is found not only in the word "believes"—that word alone circumscribes the "whoever" a great deal for it excludes all human works—but it is found also in the phrase "in him," which phrase restricts salvation exclusively to those who trust God's Son. Whoever believes *in him*—and only *him*—will be saved. With these two little words "in him"—and I do not say this with a triumphalist spirit or in prideful boast—all the other religions of the world are adjudged to be useless insofar as saving anyone is concerned. Muslims will not be saved by their devotion to Allah. Buddhists and Hindus will not go to heaven by their religious devotion. Christ-rejecting Jews who follow the teachings of Judaism will never know God's forgiveness. And professing Christians who look for salvation not only to Jesus for their acceptance before God but also to the righteousness of Mary, to the reputed righteousness of the other saints, and to their expiation of their own sin in Purgatory will not see God for they have made the cross of Christ of no effect; they have fallen away from grace.

Here we have the single greatest offense of Christianity among men today—the exclusivity of the Evangelical's claim that salvation belongs only to those who trust Christ alone! No wonder men hate biblical Christianity! But Jesus said: "I am the way and the truth and the life. No one comes to the Father but by me" (John 14:6). Peter declared: "Salvation is found in no one else, for there is no other name under heaven given to men by which we must be saved" (Acts 4:12). Paul states: "there is one God and one mediator between God and man, the man Christ Jesus" (1 Tim 2:5). John affirms: "He who has the Son has life; he who does not have the Son of God does not have life" (1 John 5:12).

And bear in mind that when these faithful preachers declared these things, they were fully aware of the other religions in the world, but they declared Christ's saving uniqueness nonetheless. This means that not just self-acclaimed atheists will go to hell! Most people who go to hell will be religious people, theists of one sort or another, those who believe in some god. But in order to be saved, John declares, Christ and Christ alone must become the object of one's reliance and confidence. Apart from faith in Christ there is no salvation. Are you trusting him alone? Is Jesus' doing and dying alone sufficient for you? I certainly pray so.

Sixth, God's love is *exceptional in its work*—How so? Now mark well, this point underscores why all that I have said thus far is so terribly important: "that whoever believes in him *shall not perish*." Even in this much-loved verse a dark shadow falls across our path as we move through it. It is the shadow that the word "perish" casts. Perdition! What is it to perish? It is to lose all hope, all light in the blackness of darkness, all peace, all joy, all bliss after death, and all these things forever. It is to know no love at all, and to experience only conscious eternal torment forever and ever with the devil and his angels. And it is to have to stare forever into the lidless, unblinking eye of a disapproving God who is a consuming fire. So God's love accomplishes the exceptional work of saving men from the horrible conditions of perdition.

But there is *another index* of his love's exceptional work: Imagine, if you will, a man who has been guilty of all the lusts of the flesh to as deep a degree as is possible for any man to sink. Suppose that he is so detestable that he is only fit to be treated like a moral leper by the entire world. If that man turns in true faith to Jesus Christ, in that moment he shall at once be cleansed from his defilement, be forgiven, and be granted new life like that of a newborn infant. What an exceptional work of grace!

Imagine this same man from another perspective. Suppose he has hated Christ and despised the gospel all his life, has consciously and openly repudiated every cardinal doctrine of the Christian faith, and has given his entire professional lifetime of thirty, forty, fifty years and devoted all of his possessions to the destruction of our most precious faith—such as Usama bin Ladin who masterminded the infamous September 11, 2001 attack on the World Trade Center in New York City. Were this man, at death's door, truly to repent of his sins and turn to Christ, the moment he trusted God's Son he would at once be forgiven and received into heaven. What exceptional work God's love accomplishes through the sinner's simple response in trust to what Jesus did at Calvary!

God's love for us in Jesus Christ—and I should stress, *only* that love—saves us and saves us forever from the dreadful end contemplated under that word "perish."

Finally, God's love is *exhaustless in its benefits*—and this truth underscores the eternal glory of our salvation—"but have everlasting life." God gives the believer "life that is everlasting." What is such life but

life that shall last throughout our all too short three-score-years-and-ten,
life that shall last us should we live to be a hundred,
life that will still be flourishing when we stare into the mouth of the grave whatever our age,
life that will still be strongly abiding in us when we have departed from our bodies and leave them rotting in their coffins,
life that will still be shining brightly when our bodies are raised from death in the Eschaton,
life that will last as long as God himself lives,
life that will last until God dies and angels sing a funeral dirge over the grave of God, and that will never happen.

The person who has entrusted himself to the arms of Christ our Good Shepherd may be assured of the triune God's *exhaustless* care and safekeeping. For Jesus declared:

> "The one who comes to me I will never cast out" (John 6:37-40). And

> "My sheep will never perish...no one will snatch them out of my hand. No one is able to snatch them out of my Father's hand" (John 10:28-29).

Moreover, writes Paul,

> "[the Father] who did not spare his own Son but delivered him up for us all, how shall he not with him also *freely* give us all things" needful for our everlasting salvation (Rom 8:32). And

> "[The Father] who is rich in mercy, because of his great love with which he has loved us, even when we were dead in trespasses, made us alive together with Christ (by grace you have been saved) " (Eph 2:4-5). Therefore, we may be assured that

> "He who has begun a good work in [us] will continue to perform it until the day of Jesus Christ" (Phil 1:6), because

"[Christ] is able to save forever those who come to God through him, because he [has an unchangeable priesthood and] ever lives to makes intercession for them" (Heb 7:25). Accordingly, Peter reassures us,

"You are kept by the power of God through faith for the salvation ready to be revealed in the last times" (1 Pet 1:5).

In sum, we are eternally secure—in God's immeasurable love. I am not afraid that I might slip through his fingers and be finally lost because my name is engraved on the palms of his hands in his own blood.

Well, there you have it: a plain, simple, straightforward exposition of John 3:16. What a mighty attribute is this attribute of the love of God who so loved the world that he gave his one and only Son that whoever believes in him shall not perish but have everlasting life! What a mighty work his love did for us through the gift of his Son at Calvary! Do you know personally this gift of the Father's love? Have you placed *your* trust in Christ? I trust that all of you have done so. If not, I implore you to do so now.

Dorothy Sayers says somewhere that even if the gospel story were not true, it is so wondrous that one could find himself wishing that it were. If it is not true, I myself will go to hell wishing the gospel story were true. But it *is* true. Do I hear someone saying to me:

> Oh, would it were the case that what you say is true—that God loves and will accept a sinner such as I just as I am when I entrust myself to his mercies in Jesus Christ. But how do I know—can I know—that God really acts this way?

Fair enough, so I take you back to the history I read earlier:

> In his distress, [wicked] Manasseh sought the favor of the Lord his God, and humbled himself greatly before the God of his fathers. And when he prayed to him, the Lord was moved by his entreaty and listened to his plea; so he brought him back again to Jerusalem and to his kingdom.

What amazing love!
What marvelous love!
What matchless love!

Let us pray:
In this moment in our lives, O blessed Father, we thank you for your immeasurable love for us. In response to it,

we would flee to no other refuge than your Son Jesus,
we would wash in no other fountain than his redeeming blood,
we would build on no other foundation than his perfect Word,
we would receive from no other our fullness, and
we would rest in no other for our souls' relief from sin
and sin's misery.

Grant that all who hear or read this sermon are indeed trusting in your beloved Son, mankind's only Savior. If some listener or reader is not yet trusting him, draw him or her by your Spirit now, I pray, to a saving faith in Jesus. In whose matchless name we pray, Amen.

Sermon Six

This is a Reformation Day sermon. In the United States, Protestant and Reformed churches celebrate the Reformation on the last Sunday of October, the Sunday nearest October 31—the day when Martin Luther nailed his "Ninety-Five Theses" to the door of the Castle Church at Wittenberg. It reflects the theology I long to hear being proclaimed again from Protestant and Reformed pulpits throughout the world.

The sermon is textual, highlighting the single text of Romans 1:17. In another sense it is a biographical sermon, taking the reader on a journey through Luther's early struggles to understand this verse finally to his exultant conclusion that Paul was teaching by it the biblical doctrine of justification by faith alone. The sermon's FCF is man's sin and need for righteousness, captured by Luther's question, "How can I find a gracious God," and its CS is the imputed righteousness of Christ propounded in the Pauline doctrine of justification by faith alone.

"Martin Luther's Text"

Text: Romans 1:16-17

> I am not ashamed of the gospel, for it is the power of God for salvation for everyone who believes, for the Jew first and also for the Greek. For in it the righteousness of God is revealed from faith to faith, as it is written: "The righteous shall live by faith."

Prayer for Illumination

Ever-merciful Father and never-failing Friend: heartened by your promises to us, we bring our praises, however imperfect, to join in that great song of praise, honor, glory, and blessing sung in heaven that is directed toward your blessed Son who was slain in our behalf and who rose again for our justification.

Grant to me now the ability to proclaim your Word to us from another world and grant your Spirit's anointing to this assembly that their ears may truly hear your Word taught. May they heed my words in this hour as Heaven's message to them; keep them from trivializing my words into simple entertainment.

Give to us what you know we need, make my words and this time full of blessing and a harvest yield of high good to each of us.

All these things we ask for our own souls' health and for the glory and cause of Jesus Christ our Lord. Amen.

* * * * *

I want to begin my remarks with a citation from Martin Luther himself about his spiritual struggles as an Augustinian monk:

> ...in the same year [1519] I had begun to lecture on the Psalms again, believing that with my classroom experience in lecturing on the letters of Paul to the Romans, to the Galatians, and on the Letter to the Hebrews, I was now better prepared. All the while I was aglow with the desire to understand Paul in his letter to the Romans. But up till then it was...the single expression in Chapter 1:17 concerning "the righteousness of God" that blocked the way for me. For I *hated* that expression "righteousness of God," since I had been instructed by the usage and custom of all the teachers to understand it according to the scholastic philosophy as the "formal and active righteousness" by which God proves himself righteous by punishing sinners and the unjust.
>
> Although I was a holy and blameless monk...I did not love, indeed, I hated the righteous God...and...murmuring greatly, I was angry with God, and said: "As if, indeed, it is not enough that miserable sinners, eternally lost through original sin, are crushed by every kind of calamity by the law of the Decalogue, without having God add pain to pain...by the gospel also threatening us with righteousness and wrath!" Thus I raged with a fierce and stubborn conscience. Nevertheless, I beat importunately upon Paul at that place [Romans 1:17], most ardently desiring to know what Paul wanted.

These words Martin Luther wrote twenty-six years later in 1545 in his "Preface" to the Latin edition of his *Works*, to which "Preface" we will return later.

Now if we can associate Romans 13:13-14 with the conversion experience of Augustine and 1 Timothy 1:19 with Jonathan Edwards' conversion, we can surely associate Romans 1:17 in a very special way with the life of the great Protestant Reformer, Martin Luther, which verse teaches so clearly that the gospel's "good news" is that God's righteousness, which we sinful human beings so desperately need because we have none of our own, he freely gives to anyone and everyone who trusts in the preceptive and penal obedience of the Lord Jesus Christ alone.

I want us to consider the influence of this verse on Martin Luther's life. We shall see that in a real way it became his life text. To see this we must take an excursion into a bit of Reformation history; I am trusting that there is a bit of the history buff in all of you.

His Monastic Life at Erfurt

Martin Luther was born November 10, 1483 in Eisleben, Germany (which was, by the way, his death city as well). He began his professional academic life in 1501, at the age of eighteen, studying philosophy and law at the University of Erfurt. This was more his father's desire for him than his own. But although he excelled in his studies and gave every promise of becoming a successful lawyer, taking the B.A. and M.A. degrees there, Luther throughout this entire period of time was deeply troubled in soul at the thought that one day he would have to argue, not someone's else, but his own case before the Great Judge of all the earth and to give an account of himself before him. But how could *he* appear, he asked himself, before the high tribunal of the infinitely holy God with his impure heart?

Having been frightened about his time in his life almost to death by a terrifying thunderstorm during which he vowed to St. Anne that he would become a monk, and to prepare himself for that awful meeting someday with God, Luther, against all the pleadings of his astonished friends, on August 17, 1505, then twenty-one years old, suddenly left the university and entered the Augustinian Cloister in Erfurt, not so much to study theology, he says, as to save his soul. One can visit this cloister today and see Luther's cell-like bedroom and the cloister chapel where he officiated at his first Mass.

Immediately Luther gave himself rigorously and with unflagging zeal to the monastic life. He fasted and prayed, he tortured himself and devoted himself to the most menial of tasks. Above all, he adhered to the medieval church's sacrament of penance, confessing even the most trivial of perceived faults, for hours on end, until his superiors wearied of his soul-searching exercises and ordered him to cease confession until he had committed some sin worth talking about. Luther would write later to the Duke of Savoy:

> I was indeed a pious monk and followed the rules of my order more strictly than I can express. If ever a monk could obtain heaven by his monkish works, I should certainly have been entitled to it. Of this all the friars who have known me can testify. If it had continued much longer, I should have carried my mortifications even to death, by means of my watchings, prayers, reading and other labor.

Still, Luther found no peace of heart or mind.

When the monkish wisdom advised him to satisfy God's righteous demands by meritorious works, he thought: "But what works can come from a heart like mine? How can I stand before the holiness of my Judge with polluted works—polluted as they are at their very source?"

During this period of spiritual agonizing, God sent to Luther a wise spiritual father in the person of John Staupitz, the vicar-general of the Augustian Order for all Germany. "Why are you so sad, brother Martin?" Staupitz asked him one day.

"Ah," replied Luther, " I do not know what will become of me.... It is vain that I make promises to God; sin within me is ever the stronger."

To this Staupitz replied:

> [Dear Martin,] more than a thousand times have I sworn to our holy God to live piously, and I have never kept my vows. Now I swear no longer, for I know that I cannot keep my solemn promises. If God will not be merciful towards me for the love of Christ and grant me a happy departure when I must quit this world, I shall never with the aid of all my vows and all my good works stand before him. I must perish.
>
> Why, dear Martin, do you torment yourself? Look at the wounds of Jesus Christ, to the blood that he has shed for you; it is there that the grace of God will appear to you. Instead of torturing yourself on account of your sins, throw yourself into the Redeemer's arms. Trust in him—in the righteousness of his life—in the atonement of his death. Do not shrink back.... Listen to the Son of God. He became a man to give you the divine favor.

But how, Luther asked him, could he hear the Son of God? Where could *he* hear the voice of God's Son? In the church's tradition? "In the Bible," said the vicar-general, "let the study of the Scriptures be your favorite occupation." And it was thus that Luther, who had only first seen a Bible in his law days shortly before entering the cloister, began to study the Scriptures, especially the letters of Paul, a privilege that you and I take so much for granted today.

His Trip to Rome

But the divine work begun by Staupitz was not finished. The conscience of the young Augustinian monk, in spite of all his efforts in self-denial, had still not yet found peace with God. In 1510, five years after he had become a monk and two years after he had, upon Staupitz's recommendation, begun to teach the Bible at Elector Frederick of Saxony's new university at Wittenberg, Luther was sent to Rome on church business by his Order.

Going not only as an emissary for his Order but also as a pilgrim, when Luther caught sight of Rome in the distance—the site to which Paul's letter to the church at Rome was written and the capital city of Roman Catholicism—he tells us that he fell to his knees and raised his hands in ecstasy, exclaiming: "I greet you, holy Rome, thrice holy from the blood of the martyrs." No sooner did he arrive than he began, as time and official business permitted, to make the rounds of the churches, shrines, and relics, believing all the superstitions that were told to him at each site, and even regretting, he says, that his parents were not already dead because he could then have assured them against Purgatory by all of his acts of penance.

Yet Rome was not the city of light and piety Luther had imagined it would be. Very quickly he perceived that the Mass, at which he thought the body and blood of Christ were being offered up by the priests as a sacrifice for sin—still the center of his religious devotion—was being made a laughing stock by many priests. Once, while he was repeating one Mass, the priests at the adjoining altar rushed through seven of them, calling out to Luther: "Quick, quick, send our Lady back her Son." In the company of some distinguished ecclesiastics, Luther heard them ridiculing the rite, laughing and with apparent pride boasting how, when they were standing at the altar repeating the words that were supposed to transform the bread and wine into the very body and blood of Christ, they said instead, no doubt in solemn intonations: "*Panis es, et panis manebis; vinum es, et vinum manebis*" ("Bread you are, and bread you will remain; wine you are, and wine you will remain"). Then they laughingly explained that they would elevate the host and the people would bow down and worship the creaturely elements. Luther was shocked beyond words at what was to him at that time such freely confessed blasphemy!

Then there occurred the famous incident told many years later by Luther's son, Dr. Paul Luther, and preserved in a manuscript in the library at Rudolfstadt. In the Church of St. John Lateran in Rome there is a set of medieval stone stairs, said to have been the stairs leading up to Pilate's house in Jerusalem and thus once trod upon by the Lord himself, which stairs Luther was told had been miraculously transported to Rome. For this reason they were called the *Scala Sancta* or "Holy Stairs." It was customary for pilgrims to ascend these stairs on their knees, praying as they ascended and kissing the bloodstains that supposedly appeared at certain intervals. Remission of years of punishment in Purgatory was promised to all who performed this arduous exercise.

His father, Paul Luther writes, began to crawl up those stairs as many others had done before him. But as he ascended the staircase, the words of Romans 1:17: "The righteous will live by faith," suddenly came forcefully to his mind. They seemed to echo over and over again: "The righteous will live by faith." "The righteous will live by faith." The old superstitions and the new biblical theology began to wrestle within him:

"By fear," argued Luther.
"By faith," said Paul.
"By meritorious works," the scholastic fathers had taught him.
"By faith," said the Apostle.
"By agonizing suffering," argued Luther and those on the steps beside him by their actions.
"By faith," spoke God the Holy Spirit, the Author of Scripture, to his heart.

Luther rose in wonder from the steps up which he had been dragging himself, shuddering at the superstition and folly in which he had been engaged. Now he began to realize that God justifies human beings by faith alone. Slowly he turned on "Pilate's Staircase" and returned to the bottom. He went back to Wittenberg, and while not without still some spiritual struggle, in time, as his son said, "He took, 'The righteous will live by faith,' as the foundation of all his doctrine."

Of that "staircase experience" J. H. Merle d'Aubigne, the great nineteenth century historian of the Reformation, writes:

> This powerful text [Romans 1:17] had a mysterious influence on the life of Luther. It was a creative sentence both for the Reformer and the Reformation. It was in these words God then said: "Let there by light!" When Luther rose from his knees on Pilate's Staircase, in agitation and amazement at those words which Paul had addressed fifteen centuries before to the inhabitants of that same metropolis—Truth, till then a melancholy captive fettered in the church, rose also to fall no more.

This was the real beginning of the sixteenth-century Reformation—for Luther's *personal* reformation necessarily had to precede his effort to reform medieval Christendom's false theology. The latter began seven years later on October 31, 1517 when he posted his "Ninety-Five Theses" on the door of the Castle Church at Wittenberg. This act eventually led to his excommunication from the Roman Catholic Church by Pope Leo X in January 1521, and eventually brought him before Emperor Charles V at the Diet of Worms in April of that same year. At that assembly, in response to the two questions: "Are these your writings? And will you, or will you not, recant?" after an all-night vigil in prayer he put both the world's and the church's mighty ones to flight with his immortal declaration:

> Since your most serene majesty [Charles V] and your high mightinesses require from me a clear, simple, and precise answer, I will give you one, and it is this: I cannot submit my faith either to the pope or to the councils, because it is clear as the day that they have frequently erred and contradicted each other. Unless therefore I am convinced by the testimony of Scripture, or by the clearest reasoning—unless I am persuaded by the passages I have quoted—and unless they thus render my conscience bound by the Word of God, I cannot and I will not retract, for it is unsafe for a Christian to speak against his conscience. Here I stand, I can do no other; may God help me! Amen!

Theological Exposition

Do you remember how I began this sermon—citing Luther's ragings against God because he thought not only the righteousness of God in the law but also the righteousness of God in the gospel condemned him? I will now complete his remarks:

> At last, by the mercy of God, meditating day and night, I gave heed to the context of the words, namely, "He who *by faith* is righteous shall live." There I began to understand that the righteousness of God is that by which the righteous lives by the gift of God, namely, by faith...[that] the righteousness of God

> revealed by the gospel is the righteousness with which the merciful God justifies us by faith.... Here I felt that I was altogether born again and had entered Paradise itself through open gates.... And as previously I had detested with all my heart these words, "the righteousness of God," I began from that hour to value and to love them, as the sweetest and most consoling words in the Bible. In very truth, that place in Paul [Romans 1:17] was for me truly the gate to Paradise.

Dear friends, the burning question for Martin Luther in the sixteenth century was "How can I find a gracious God?" (*Wie kriege ich einen gnädigen Gott?*), or as Bildad's ancient question phrases it: "How can a man achieve right standing before God?" (Job 25:4) The church of the medieval period had taught for centuries that right standing before God was achieved through the Spirit's *inward* work of grace in the human heart, that is to say, through the sacrament of baptism, inner renewal, works of penance to address post-baptismal sins, and the grace of sanctification that is never complete in this life and thus Christians must go to Purgatory to make expiation for their sins. Candor requires that I inform you that that church is still with us today, with no change in its false soteriology, in spite of Vatican I and II, from that time to our own, declaring again as recently as its 1994 *Catechism of the Catholic Church* that "justification is...the sanctification and renewal of the interior man."

Today we have observed how Luther struggled for an answer to Bildad's question and tried to find the answer in his own works of penance that never brought peace, and we have seen how he finally came to a true and proper understanding of Romans 1:17 and found the very gates of heaven opened wide to him in that verse. Through his struggles and careful study of Scripture Martin Luther came to understand

1. that the *only* man with whom the infinitely holy God can have *direct* fellowship is the perfect Godman, the only mediator "between God and man, the man Christ Jesus" (1 Tim 2:5), and that it is only as sinful people place their trust in Christ's saving

work and are thereby regarded by God as "in Christ" that the triune God can have any fellowship with them;

2. that the only way to protect the *solus Christus* ("Christ alone") of salvation is to insist upon the *sola fide* ("faith alone") of justification, and the only way to protect the *sola fide* of justification is to insist upon the *solus Christus* of salvation;
3. that saving faith is to be directed to the doing and dying of Christ alone and not to the good works or inner experience of the believer;
4. that the Christian's righteousness before God today is *in heaven* at the right hand of God in Jesus Christ, and *not on earth* within the believer;
5. that the ground of our justification is the vicarious work of Christ *for* us, not the gracious work of the Spirit in us;
6. that the faith-righteousness of justification is not personal but vicarous, not infused but imputed, not experiential but forensic, not psychological but legal, not our own but a righteousness alien to us, and not earned but graciously given through faith in Christ, which faith is itself a gift of grace; all which means
7. that justification by faith is not to be set off over against justification by works as such but over against justification by *our* works, for justification is indeed grounded in Christ's alien active and passive obedience in our stead, which we receive by faith alone.

These tenets meant for Luther practically or existentially, as he says, that

> a Christian is at once a sinner and a saint; he is wicked and pious at the same time. For so far as our persons are concerned, we are in sins and are sinners in our own name. But Christ brings us another name, in which there is the forgiveness of sins, that for his sake sins are remitted and pardoned. So both statements are true: There are sins, for the old Adam is not entirely dead as yet; yet the sins are *not* there. The reason is this: For Christ's sake God does

> not want to see them. I have my eyes on them. I feel and see them well enough. But there is Christ, commanding that I be told that I should repent, that is, confess myself a sinner and believe the forgiveness of sins in his name. For repentance, remorse, and knowledge of sin, though necessary, is not enough; faith in the forgiveness of sins in the name of Jesus must be added. But where there is such faith, God no longer sees any sins; for then you stand before God, not in your name but in Christ's name. He adorns you with grace and righteousness, although in your own eyes and personally you are a poor sinner, full of weakness and unbelief.[1]

And it is this teaching on justification, Luther contended in the *Schmalkald Articles* of 1537, that

> must be believed and cannot be obtained or apprehended by any work, law, or merit…nothing in this article [of faith] can be given up or compromised, even if heaven and earth and things temporal should be destroyed…. On this article rests all that we teach and practice against the pope, the devil, and the world. Therefore we must be quite certain and have no doubts about it. Otherwise all is lost, and the pope, the devil, and all our adversaries will gain the victory.

Conclusions and Summons

While I trust that most of you here are genuinely converted and are true Christians, I must urge you to examine yourselves now to make sure that you are trusting solely in the active and passive obedience of Jesus Christ for your forgiveness and needed righteousness before God. For make no mistake about it: the day will come when you and I will stand naked before God, and in that day the issue of in whom or in what we trusted here for our salvation will be all-important. Unable to "answer him once in a thousand times" you and I in that Great Day will be stripped of all the things in which we may have placed our confidence in this world. We will stand before the throne of God in that day without title, without money, without

1. Martin Luther, *What Luther Says: An Anthology*, edited by Ewald M. Plass (St. Louis, Missouri: Concordia, 1959), 1:522.

property, without reputation, without personal prestige—in utter poverty in ourselves. And unless we have been forgiven of our sins and are enrobed in the imputed righteousness of Jesus Christ, God will consign us to eternal perdition for our sins.

Beloved friends, if you have never completely repudiated your own efforts at self-salvation and have never totally trusted the Savior's righteous life and sacrifical death alone for your salvation, I beg of you, *do both right now*! For not by works of righteousness that you and I will ever do will we be saved. Christ is our only hope for heaven. Trust him now, for it is by faith alone in Christ's doing and dying that we are justified before God.

Let us pray:

O great God of the Reformers, of Martin Luther, John Calvin, John Knox, and the many other spiritual giants that roamed the earth in those days:

I thank you for your servant, Martin Luther, and for the great truth of Holy Scripture, "The righteous will live by faith," that your Holy Spirit used to draw him to yourself and to grant him peace.

I pray that even now, if any here in this place have not cast themselves by faith solely, wholly, and only upon your saving mercies exhibited in Jesus Christ, that today—right now—your Holy Spirit will quicken them and move them to trust his saving work. For Jesus' sake, I pray. Amen.

Sermon Seven

This sermon is topical, based on the context of 1 Corinthians 2:2. Some of its ideas I obtained from a sermon that I read a good many years ago by Martyn Lloyd-Jones.

Its FCF is the perception that many people have that the church of Jesus Christ and its message of the Cross have become irrelevant in this post-Christian age, and its CS to this perception is the truth that Paul urges in the text—that as long as people need saving and as long as Christ alone is the Saviour of the world, then the Church's message remains the most relevant proclamation in the world, and it must continue to make the message of his Cross the centrepiece of its ministry to mankind.

"The Relevance of Christ's Cause"

Text: 1 Corinthians 2:2

> I have resolved to know nothing among you but Jesus Christ and him crucified.

Occasionally it is a good thing to take stock of why we come to church, why we are doing what we do, and to ask, Does the church of Jesus Christ still have anything really relevant to say to our country and to the world? More specifically, do the Bible and the Christian gospel hold out any real answers to the needs of our world? Permit me to be even more direct for a moment: Does this church still need to exist? Has the reason for its founding been satisfied? Is its continued existence no longer a necessity? Some of you here this morning may be wondering:

> What am I doing here in this place this morning? Am I wasting my time attending and supporting this church? Does this church still serve any useful purpose in this community? Is there any need for me to continue to make the arduous sacrifice which I am asking of myself and of my family?

Well, if Paul thought it necessary to admonish the Galatians not to grow weary in well-doing (6:9), then such questions, I would submit, are not a waste of time to consider because there are many in our time—both within and without the church—who are indeed expressing grave doubts about the church's relevance in the world. Let me illustrate what I mean by recounting two events, one borrowed and one personally experienced.

Illustration #1—the borrowed one: In one of Dr. Martyn Lloyd-Jones' books he tells of a large religious conference he attended which was being held in the city of Glasgow in Scotland. As is often done, for some extraordinary reason when such conferences are held, the Lord Provost of the City had been invited to attend the inaugural meeting and to welcome and address the conference for a few minutes. As reported by Dr. Lloyd-Jones, this is the essence of what he said:

> All of you men assembled here today are very learned theologians, and confessedly I am not. I am a plain man. I am a man of affairs and I do not understand your theology and all these church things. In fact, I am not interested in your theology, and personally I believe you are wasting a lot of time when you argue among yourselves about your theology. What *I* want to know—in fact, what a lot of people like me want to know—is simply this: How can I love my neighbor? That is what we want to know from you. We are not interested in your great theology. We just want to know—indeed, the common man simply wants to know—How can I love my neighbor?

Now if you have had a course in Christian personal and social ethics you will immediately recognize that man's total doctrinal illiteracy, for you know that the Bible and theology are directly related to an interest in love for one's neighbor. In fact, you know that unless a transcendent and absolute authority requires us to love our neighbors and to do so in such a way that we will do it even to our own hurt, no other reason can possibly be given to obligate any of us to do anything at all for anyone else other than for ourselves. But this is not the point of my citing the illustration at this moment. Do you see my present point? It illustrates that for this man, the church, with its Bible and its theology, was a complete irrelevancy unless it could address what for him was the wholly secular matter of "how to live at peace with one's neighbor."

Illustration #2—the more directly personal one: Several years ago, one weekend my wife and I decided we would drive down to Key West for a day or two of relaxation. The Orthodox Presbyterian Church has a church there and its preacher, Bill Welzien, who is a chalk-talk artist, goes to Mallory Pier on the west side of the island each evening on Monday, Wednesday, and Friday (he has trained a church member to go on Tuesday, Thursday, and Saturday, but quite often on these evenings he goes also) when the hundreds of tourists gather to watch the sun set in the west. Bill attracts a crowd with his artistry, and then preaches the gospel. Knowing this, my wife Shirley and I made it a point of being there on Friday evening and we stood in the crowd and prayed for him as he sketched his drawing and proclaimed the gospel to the crowd.

In the middle of his presentation, a man who was pushing through the crowd in his attempt to get to an attraction further down the pier, yelled to this preacher with a great deal of huff: "What do you think you are doing? Why don't you go out and find a real job?"

Do you see it? Can you not feel the biting sarcasm in the man's remark? To this man, and to many people like him, the church is an irrelevancy. He was suggesting that Bill would have spent his time much more profitably studying to become a doctor, an engineer, a school or business administrator, a chef, an environmental designer, an educator—yes, even a lawyer—than studying to enter the Christian ministry.

So I want us to consider these very basic questions today:

- ♦ Does the church of Jesus Christ have anything really relevant to offer mankind?

- ♦ And should you obligate yourself to continue your membership and witness or should you all quietly "roll up your tent" and slip, hopefully unnoticed, into the night?

I want us to address these questions head-on this morning

From the extended passage we read a few moments ago, it is apparent that here, at least, was a man committed to Jesus Christ. Paul was

a man "intoxicated" by Christ,

a man under orders,

a man captured by the cause of Christ,

Paul, at least, regarded his Lord's cause as *infinitely* relevant to all men in all ages. But why? Was he right? And why should we follow his lead?

Let's begin our answer to these "why's" by considering Paul's striking word "resolved" ("decided, determined") in his "I have resolved" in 1 Corinthians 2:2. What lay behind and motivated this resolution? What does that word suggest?

I. Well, first, it suggests serious reflection on his part; it suggests that what Paul was proclaiming **he had not come to haphazardly or accidentally**. What he had decided to proclaim to the Corinthians was quite obviously a deliberate decision on his part.

One gets the impression that, having looked at the whole situation in which he found himself and having carefully assessed all the facts, he had come to the deliberate determination to know nothing among men but the crucified Christ, that is, to make him the centerpiece of his proclamation.

No, Paul's proclamation of Christ was no accident.

II. Nor was his resolve to proclaim the gospel of God to the Corinthians a mid-course correction in his ministry trajectory. Let me explain what I mean. He had not come to this resolve, as some well-intending scholars have concluded, as a *corrective* action to a perceived failure of his ministry at Athens.[1] To understand this suggestion, we must go back some six years, to Paul's time in Athens before he went to Corinth (Acts 17:15-34).

These scholars, some of whom are evangelical, argue that Paul

---

1. For example, William M. Ramsay, *St. Paul, The Traveller and the Roman Citizen* (New York: G. P. Putnam's Sons, 1896), 252; Jack Finegan, *Light from the Ancient Past* (Princeton: Princeton University Press, 1959), 358; Merrill C. Tenney, *New Testament Survey* (Grand Rapids: Eerdmans, 1961), 287.

concluded from the perceived "poor showing" of his address on Mar's Hill in Athens that his mission strategy had been unwise if not downright compromising in its content.[2] And therefore, he had resolved on his way to Corinth never again to preach anything but the cross. But F. F. Bruce, with rich insight, declares:

> At Athens, as formerly as Lystra, the Paul of Acts does not expressly quote Old Testament prophecies which would be quite unknown to his audience: [but neither does he] argue from "first principles" of the kind that formed the basis of various systems of Greek philosophy; [rather,] his exposition and defence of his message are founded on the biblical revelation and they echo the thought, and at times the very language, of the Old Testament writings. Like the biblical revelation itself, his speech begins with God the creator of all, continues with God the sustainer of all, and concludes with God the judge of all [all three concepts were offensive to the Greek mind—RLR] (*Paul*, 239).

When one notes too that Paul's address was interrupted by the Council when he mentioned the resurrection of Jesus (so that what is reported in Acts is little more than his introduction), and bears in mind at the same time that Paul "by this time was no novice in Gentile evangelization, experimenting with this approach and that to discover what was effective" (*Paul*, 246), Paul will have been sufficiently absolved of any and all missiological wrongdoing in the eyes of all but his most antagonistic interpreters.

So again, we conclude that his resolve to proclaim Christ was not a new experiment because previous trial methods had failed.

III. Nor should we trace his resolve to proclaim the cross of Christ to mere ignorance on his part, that is, to the bald-faced fact that he simply did not know anything else to talk about.

Make no mistake about it; his resolve was not due to ignorance of anything else to proclaim. If his purpose had been to be received favorably by the people of his day, Paul knew perfectly well *what* to talk about, and he *could* have talked about it.

---

2. According to some of these scholars, Paul's message in Athens was more a "theology of glory" than a "theology of the cross".

A. Paul knew that his proclamation of the crucified Christ was a stumbling block to the Jews. And we can be assured that Paul knew, when he went to the synagogues of the Diaspora, that if he would only insist upon the intrinsic worth of circumcision before God, he would be welcomed by the Jews there with open arms. He knew perfectly well that if he had expounded the Law to them and had debated, even endlessly, with them about the minutiae of the alleged 613 laws of Torah, he would have become the darling of the synagogues of the Diaspora.

Why then didn't he spend his time doing that? He could have, you know. He had been a Pharisee of Pharisees and knew Judaism backwards and forward, in and out. Well, he tells us. In fact, he gives us his answer in many places, but consider just two Pauline statements in this regard, both from Galatians:

- 2:16: "By observing the law [that is, by relying on one's own efforts to satisfy the demands of the law for righteousness] no one will be justified before God," and

- 3:10: "All who rely on observing the law are under a curse, for it is written: "Cursed is everyone who does not continue to do everything written in the Book of the Law."

In other words, reliance on law-keeping leaves one still under the Law's curse, lost, groveling in the dust before God, and unsaved. "I did not preach the law to you," Paul is saying, "because, being weak as it was through the flesh, it could not save you. It can only condemn the sinner and leave him under the wrath of Almighty God."

B. Then, Paul knew too that the proclamation of the crucified Christ was to the Greeks foolishness. They were looking for "wisdom." And so they talked about their philosophies.

Why then didn't Paul talk philosophy to the Greeks? He could have, you know. He was in the best sense of the phrase, a true "Renaissance Man." He could speak at least four languages. He knew Greek thought so well that he was not afraid to throw down the gauntlet and to challenge its worth with his disdainful query:

> "Where is the wise man? Where is the scholar? Where is the philosopher of this age? Has not God made foolish the wisdom of the world?" (1 Cor 1:20).

So why wasn't he high on Greek philosophy and human wisdom? Well, he tells us. He gives us four reasons in the passage we read together earlier.

First, he was not high on worldly wisdom because the best, most powerful ratiocinations of human wisdom, he says, in spite of what many apologists would have us believe, have never with all their intellectual powers and efforts ever found God who is after all, as the ultimate Who's Who in the universe, the most important single datum one should know. Read 1 Corinthians 1:21 again.

Second, he was not impressed with the wisdom of the world because it was going to come to nothing, along with this world's rulers. Read 1 Corinthians 1:19 and 2:6 again.

Is it possible that someone here still believes that the United Nations or a national political party or some group of statesmen somewhere, sometime, are going to solve the ills of this world? Are you aware that many of the most reflective thinkers of our time acknowledge that men have no ultimate answers to give concerning human ills? Let me quote just two:

Count Tolstoy, one of the great novelists of this century, author of War and Peace, said at the end of his life: "The meaningless absurdity of life is the only incontestable knowledge accessible to man." How tragic, illustrating the bankruptcy of mere human intellectual effort!

Bertrand Russell, philosopher and mathematician, winner of the Nobel Prize for Literature in 1950, wrote before his death: "All the labor of the ages and all the noonday brightness of human genius are destined to extinction in the vast death of the solar system, and the whole temple of man's achievement must inevitably be buried beneath the debris of a universe in ruins." Again, how tragic! Where did all of Russell's unbelieving brilliance take him? To God and to any eternal consolations? No, he was an atheist. How little was he benefited by all of his learning!

Third, Paul had no confidence in the wisdom of this world to better the world morally because it had failed to change the ancient world and men's hearts. All one has to do to confirm this is to read Romans 1:18ff. And we can be certain that the wisdom of this world will fail to change our generation for the better as well. Listen to Arnold Toynbee, brilliant philosopher of history (but not a Christian), who wrote a twelve-volume *History of the World*. In the last volume, entitled *Mankind and Mother Earth*, he writes this:

> There is a morality gap in the development of mankind. Man constantly extends his physical power over the environment, but he is unable to improve his social arrangements correspondingly, still less to subdue his destructive passions. Technology is the only field of human activity in where there has been progress.

Did you get his point? Human wisdom has effected no improvement in the race's morality.

Fourth, Paul was not high on talking about the wise men of the world because he had someone else, infinitely superior in every way to Socrates, Plato, Aristotle, and the Roman Caesars to talk about it. Why talk about them when he could talk about the King of kings, the Lord of lords, even Jesus Christ?

And who is he? Not just a great politician or a great statesman or a great philosopher. He is the long promised Messiah of God. He is the Lord of Glory (1 Cor 2:8)—the ever-blessed Second Person of the Holy Trinity, the *majesty* of whose person and the *might* of whose power out-rivals the pomp and circumstance of all the kings and petty Caesars of the earth—who had come to earth to die for men and who had risen from the dead on the third day after death.

Ladies and Gentlemen: Why talk *about* mere men when he could talk *to* mere men about him—the incarnate Son of God?

All right, someone may say, talk about Christ if you must, but why must you talk to men about him being "crucified" for us? Why do you have to talk about Christ *crucified*? Why can't we simply deconstruct him and eliminate the cross so that with Bultmann he becomes the "kerygmatic Christ" summoning us out of our illusory existence in the world into authentic existence? Or with Tillich the "bearer of the New Being"? Or with Rahner the "unique, supreme case of the total actualization of human destiny"? Or with Goulder the "man of universal destiny"? Why talk about that horrid, repulsive Roman cross?

Because – now hear me and hear me well! – because his doing and his death at Calvary comprise the only way to be reconciled to an angry God, to have one's sins forgiven, to have one's deepest longings fulfilled and satisfied.

Because his atoning work on the cross is the only thing that will change men's hearts and make men new.

Nothing else saves! Nothing else meets the real needs of mankind and nothing else ever will.

That's why Paul was a "man possessed," a man "intoxicated by Christ." That's why he had resolved to proclaim Christ and him crucified. That's why he would write elsewhere:

- Philippians 1:21: "...for me, to live is Christ."
- Colossians 1:18: "...in everything Christ should have the preeminence"
- Galatians 6:14: "God forbid that I should glory, save in the cross of our Lord Jesus Christ"
- Philippians 3:7-9: "I consider whatever was to my profit as 'loss' for the sake of Christ; what is more, I consider everything as 'loss' compared to the surpassing greatness of knowing Christ Jesus my Lord, for whose sake, I have suffered loss of all things [apparently his parents has disowned him; all his old teachers and friends had forsaken him]. I consider them as 'dung' that I may gain Christ and be found in him, not having a righteousness of my own that comes through the law, but that which is through faith in Christ."
- Acts 20:24: "I consider my life worth nothing to me (self-preservation was not an issue that ranked high on Paul's list of priorities) if only I may finish the race and complete the

> task the Lord Jesus has given me—the task of testifying to the gospel of God's grace."

There is simply no other way to heaven! Jesus Christ alone is the Way, the Truth, and the Life. No man comes to the Father but through him.

There is no other name under heaven, given to men, by which we may be saved.

There is no other mediator between God and man.

Christian man, Christian woman, I must ask you: Do you understand that you have the most relevant message in the world? You possess the only ultimate remedy for your neighbor's spiritual needs and for his fears, frustrations, and the miseries of this life. And most compellingly, you hold the only answer to his guilt before God? Have no doubts about that! I call upon you then to step out and boldly let your faith in Christ be known.

Elders, with Paul make Christ and his cross the centerpiece of this church's ministry. Make much of Christ's blood, for it alone is sufficient to quiet God's wrath toward sinful people! Don't fear that another will have some opinion and worldview more trustworthy than your own. They do not, for there are none!

Two final questions: If you do not do it in this community, then who will do it? And if you do not begin to do it now, then when will you begin?

Pray with me please:

Our Father and our God,
We thank and praise you for this worship service. I pray that you would turn us—drawn by your blessed Holy Spirit—away from the broken cisterns of this world which can hold no life-sustaining water but which charm so easily the hearts and minds of fallen men, to that Fountain which you have opened for sin and uncleanness, that Fountain which you have filled with the blood drawn from Immanuel's veins, beneath which flood, we sinners plunged, loose all our guilty stains.

We joyously confess anew and afresh that Jesus is indeed

the Joy of our uplifted hearts,
the Fount of our eternal hope, and
the only Balm for sin-infested men,

This morning, from the *best* bliss which earth imparts, we turn *unfilled* to him again.

Holy Father, forgive us for failing to comprehend all that we are and have in your precious Son, our blessed Savior. And renew a right spirit in us.

How dull of mind we are in failing to realize more fully than we do that Jesus is indeed

our hidden source of calm repose,
our all-sufficiency in life's dread hours,
our help and refuge from our foes—
that we are his and he is ours;

How dark our souls are in refusing as we often do to believe that Jesus' name indeed is full salvation,

that it keeps us safe with Thee above,
that it our souls' true comfort brings, with power and peace
and joy and love;
that with his name are freely given pardon, holiness, and heaven.

How decadent of heart we are to refuse to act in faith upon the blessed fact that Jesus is indeed

our rest in toil, our ease in pain,
in war our peace, in loss our gain,
our smile beneath the tyrant's frown,
in shame our glory and our crown;

How deceitful our thinking in so often failing to see that Jesus is

in want our plentiful supply,
    in weakness our almighty power,
in bonds our perfect liberty,
    our light in Satan's darkest hour,
our help and stay whenever we call,
    our life in death, our heaven, our all.

May our stubborn minds this morning be moved never again to wonder, "Is Christ and his gospel important or relevant? What is there for us in him?" With Peter, may we say, "To whom shall we go if not to Jesus, for he and he alone has the gift of eternal life."

May your beloved Son ever be the joy and the rejoicing of our hearts, and O our God, never, never allow us to outlive our love for him! We pray in his matchless name. Amen.

Sermon Eight

This sermon, like the sermon on John 3:16, is textual. Each point is drawn directly from the text. It too illustrates my concern always to proclaim a scriptural, rational, God-centered, and theologically articulate sermon. The sermon's FCF is the curse of God and its CS is Christ's substitionary atonement and his accomplished full and free redemption by which he bore God's curse in the stead of his people.

Note that I do not hesitate to make appeals throughout to the audience to flee to Christ for deliverance from God's curse. Thus it is an evangelistic sermon at heart.

"Christ Has Redeemed Us!"

Text: Galatians 3:10-13

> All who rely on observing the law are under a curse, for it is written: "Cursed is everyone who does not continue to do everything written in the Book of the Law." Clearly no one is justified before God by the law, because, "The righteous will live by faith." The law is not based on faith; on the contrary, "The man who does these things will live by them." Christ redeemed us from the curse of the law by becoming a curse for us, for it is written: "Cursed is everyone who is hanged on a tree."

Prayer for Illumination:
We acknowledge before you, our great and sovereign God, that to satisfy our spiritual thirst we have all too often hewn out for ourselves broken cisterns that can hold no water, and we have all too often turned away from you who alone are the fountain of living water. I pray for your pardon for this folly, and beseech you that you will prosper the proclamation of the gospel of grace this day in every land and language, more specifically in the evangelical churches of

this city and most particularly here and now in this place as we proclaim the unsearchable riches of Christ.

I ask you now for your help as I preach the glorious gospel. Hide me in its own outshining, that no voice may be ultimately heard, no blessing experience, no power felt save that which comes from it through your Spirit.

Grant again, as you have so often done before, that your Holy Spirit may brood over the confusion of every human heart here as he did over the primeval chaos, and out of *our* darkness bring forth light and out of our chaos bring forth beauty, peace, and order.

For all these things we humbly cry to you, in the strong name of our mighty Savior, Jesus Christ our Lord. Amen.

* * * * *

Some Bible verses almost *dare* the preacher to find a sermon in them (such as 1 Chronicles 26:18), while others almost preach themselves through the mere reading of them to the congregation. My sermon text today (one of the latter kind) is the last of the four verses that I just read to you—a verse that captures in a unique way most if not all of the essential aspects of Christianity's glorious law-free gospel, a verse that just to read it is to convey and to confront any audience with much gospel truth. I refer to Galatians 3:13. Please turn with me to it again. Under divine inspiration the apostle Paul writes: "Christ redeemed us from the curse of the law by becoming a curse for us, for it is written: 'Cursed is everyone who is hung on a tree.'"

I am from the "old school" of homiletics. I will tell you what I am going to do—thus the people on the front row will get it. Then I will do it—the people on the second row will then get it. And when I am through, I will tell you again what I have done—then the people on the third row will get it, and the people on the front row will never forget it!

Today I will expound this verse using the following headings:

1. The ***Fundamental Fact*** behind the Cross
2. The ***Stupendous Sight*** on the Cross
3. The ***Paramount Purpose*** for the Cross
4. The ***Awesome Acccomplishment*** of the Cross
5. The ***Trustworthy Testimony*** about the Cross

Look with me at this text and follow my exposition of it, won't you? And lest you begin to think after my first two points that this will be an exceptionally long sermon, let me assure you that my development of points one and two are longer separately than points three through five combined. Now the first thing our text does is to confront us with the dire straits in which the entire human race, considered apart from Christ, finds itself. I call it:

1. "The Fundamental Fact Behind the Cross" — "the curse of the law."

The law Paul speaks of here is summarily set forth in the Ten Commandments, which ten in turn are captured by the two great love commandments to love God and our neighbour. But at this moment Paul speaks not about the content of the law but about the "curse" of that law.

A. Now, dear hearts, you may be assured that the law of God is holy, just, and good (Rom 7:12), indeed even spiritual (Rom 7:14), but it is an unforgiving taskmaster! Its slightest infraction brings its curse upon the perpetrator of the trespass, for Deuteronomy 27:26, which Paul cites in the preceding verse (Gal 3:10), states categorically: "Cursed is everyone who does not continue to do *everything* which is written in the Book of the Law." *Not* to do and/or not to continue to do from the heart even its slightest requirement is to sin against God, for "sin is *any* want of conformity unto, or transgression of, the law of God."

B. But this means that the "curse of the law" is actually the curse of God himself, which fact underscores that *it is really from God that men must be saved*. And since God is the righteous Lawgiver, men must understand that the law's curse is and always will be supremely just, for God is and always will be supremely just. Moreover, when *God* curses, it is a curse of the weightiest kind. When *he* curses, it is a curse indeed.

Dear friends, there is something so terrible in the very idea of the omnipotent God pronouncing a curse upon the transgressor of his law that one's blood curdles at the thought of it. A father's curse of a son is terrible, but it is nothing compared to the awful malediction of the Almighty Father. To be cursed by human society is no small calamity either, but to be cursed by God is a thing of sheer terror, for eternal sorrow, anguish, and everlasting woe lie in that curse; for in hell—where even any semblance of order is disorder and where even its light is the blackness of darkness forever—there is only horror, torment, and woe. Our sin infuriates God, and one day, so say the prophets Nahum (1:2, 5, 8) and Malachi (4:1), God

> ...will take vengeance on his adversaries and pour out his wrath upon his enemies...the mountains will quake at him, the hills will melt, the earth will burn at his presence, the world, and all that dwell therein. Who will stand before his indignation? Who will abide the fierceness of his anger? For he will pursue his enemies into darkness...Behold, the day will come that will burn as an oven, and all the proud and those that do wickedly will become stubble and that day will burn them up, says the Lord of hosts.

Now the Bible is quite clear that in Adam's first transgression we *all* sinned (Rom 5:12)—Jews and Gentiles, men and women, rich and poor, young and old. We sinned against God's holy law and are continually falling short of his glorious righteousness (Rom 3:23). None of us is righteous, not even one! Read the Apostle Paul's litany of indictments—fourteen in all—against us in Romans 3 if you doubt this. As a result, in our raw, natural state we are *all* sinners. Our sin nature is so overpowering and blinding that it can and does defeat and take captive even the strongest human will among us that would oppose it. Accordingly, we have *all* spurned God's voice and rejected his pleas, we have *all* responded to the overtures of his common grace and of his eternal love for us with enmity and abject obstinacy.

Our transgressions of God's law are unmitigatingly inexcusable, utterly indefensible and fully deserve his punishment. Our sin is not only real evil, morally wrong, the violation of God's law, and therefore, detestable, odious, ugly, disgusting, filthy, loathsome, and ought not to be, but it is also the contradiction of God's perfection, cannot but meet with his undiluted disapproval and wrath, and is *damnable* in the strongest sense of the word because it *dishonors* God. God *must* react with holy indignation. He *cannot* do otherwise. And when I say God "cannot" here, we come face to face (as John Murray reminds us)

> with a divine "cannot" that bespeaks *not* divine weakness but everlasting strength, *not* reproach but inestimable glory. He cannot deny himself. To be complacent towards that which is the contradiction of his own holiness would be a denial of himself. So God's wrath against sin is the correlate of his holiness. And this is just to say that the justice of God demands that sin receive its retribution. The question to be squarely faced then is not at all: How can God, being what he is, send people to hell? The real question is, How can God, being what he is, not sent people to hell but rather save them from hell?

C. But perhaps someone is asking at this juncture, will God *really* punish the sinner for his sin? I will only say here that it is all too clear from Holy Scripture that *he will do so indeed*, for it cannot be denied that he has already demonstrated that he will. Holy Scripture teaches that

- God cast the angels who sinned against him out of heaven and delivered them into everlasting chains of darkness, to be reserved until the great judgment day when he will consign them to the lake of fire forever (Jude 6); that

- he destroyed the antediluvian world of mankind because the wickedness of mankind against him then was great in the earth, with every imagination of the thoughts of every person being only evil continually (Gen 6-8); that

- he rained fire and brimstone upon Sodom because the Sodomites were wicked and exceedingly evil before the Lord (Gen 19:24); and that someday

- he will turn all the nations who have forgotten him and spurned his law and rejected his overtures of grace into hell (Ps 9:17).

But *more than these*—now please hear me, dear hearts—*more than all the other demonstrations of his wrath throughout all the world and throughout all of recorded history* the death of Jesus Christ on the cross most clearly shows that God *will* punish impenitent men for their sin. I say this because if ever there were a time when one might expect that God would have withheld his wrath, it would have been against his own beloved Son because there was no one in the whole universe so dear to God as his own Son and because his Son had no sin of his own. But when God made his Son the Sinbearer for his elect, it "pleased the Lord to bruise him" (Isa 53:10). This is why I say that if any single event demonstrates that God will punish the lawbreaker it is the death of his own dear and sinless Son when he stood in the stead of sinners. *If anything in all the world is then an exhibition of divine wrath on earth against sin, that is, of the sinner's damnation, it is the crucifixion of Jesus Christ, God's own beloved Son, at Calvary*. Thomas Kelly, the hymn writer, understood this:

> Ye who think of sin but lightly nor suppose the evil great
> here may view its nature rightly, here its guilt may estimate.
> Mark the sacrifice appointed, see who bears the awful load;
> 'tis the Word, the Lord's Anointed, Son of Man and Son of God.

As sinners then by nature, by habit, and by practice, in our raw, natural state we stand under the law's curse and condemnation, and the wrath of God abides upon us all. And the Bible says that the only way that was open to God to save us was by the Incarnation of God the Son through his wondrous conception in the womb of the Virgin Mary and being born of her and then going to his death at

Calvary. The Bible knows of no other reason for the Incarnation or for Calvary.

With the *fundamental fact* before us of the curse of the law—which *ought* to be of the greatest concern to everyone within the sound of my voice since it applies to every single human being considered apart from Christ—we now turn to the next feature of our text. I refer to

2. The Stupendous Sight on the Cross — Christ "hanging on a tree"

A. Why is such a sight absolutely amazing, totally staggering, utterly, titanically stupendous? Because of who it is who is hanging there—the incarnate Second Person of the Godhead, the Lord of glory, the Creator of all things, who for us men and for our salvation became the "Godman"—the majesty of whose person and the might of whose power out-rival the majesty and power of all the kings of the earth combined, and who today wears a diadem and who owns a title that announce to all the petty Caesars of this world that he is King of kings and Lord of lords and that it is he who rules the world and that they do not.

Think about this stupendous sight with me for a few moments. Now before I say anything else about it, I must point out to you that Christ's cross-work is the church's "holy of holies"; it is sacred ground, and we must take off the sandals of our minds, and speak—if we speak at all—in hushed tones as we approach it, for our Lord's cross-work is "the most solemn spectacle in all history, a spectacle unparalleled, unique, unrepeated, and unrepeatable" (Murray). Beholding it,

> here we are spectators of a wonder the praise and glory of which eternity will not exhaust. It is the Lord of glory, the Son of God incarnate, the God-man, drinking the cup given him by the eternal Father, the cup of woe and of indescribable agony.

B. But, do you know, my friends, his cross-work was only the climactic part of his entire downward human life-cycle.

At his birth our Lord—the infinite, eternal, and unchangeable Second Person of the Godhead—took upon himself the form of servant, having been "made of a woman, made under the law" (Gal 4:4). And if taking on, *not* sinful flesh but the *form* of sinful flesh, was not humiliating enough for the Son of God, what do you think the angels of heaven must have thought when they saw their great Creator

1. born in a cattle stall in Bethlehem, for some of them were summoned to sing that night, you will recall, but not to the earth's mighty but to lowly shepherds in the field. They must have found that spectacle incomprehensible.

2. Then as the days and years moved on, they saw a drama unfold which must have over-loaded ever circuit in their mind's ability to compute the ways of God. For one day word came to them that their Lord was sweating, as it were, great drops of blood in Gethsemane, and one of them was dispatched to strengthen him in his agony.

3. Hours later even more astonishing news reached them. The incarnate Christ, the Lord of glory, was bleeding out his life on the cross of Calvary. That surely was the bottom, the very worst! Surely all their legions would be summoned to stop this horrid injustice and to relieve him from his agony!

4. But no! The next thing they heard was even worse: Suddenly from his dying lips came what John Murray has described as "the most *mysterious* utterance that ever ascended from earth to heaven"—"My God, my God, why have you forsaken me?" We almost hesitate to say so. But it must be said. That cry of dereliction evinces God in our nature forsaken of God. The cry from the accursed tree speaks of nothing less than the abandonment that is the wages of sin. Contrary to much thinking that would rationalize away or sentimentalize his abandonment, be assured that it was very real—heartbreakingly so. And there is no analogy of this abandonment anywhere. There is no

reproduction or parallel of it in the experience of archangels or of the greatest saints. The faintest parallel would crush the holiest of men and the mightiest of the angelic host. The God whose whole impulse is to wash away the tears from the eyes of his people refused to alleviate the agonizing pain or to wash away the tears of his own much-loved Son. Rather, he forsook him, and for a *brief* time—which period of time was infinite in its salvific significance—and for the *first* time in all eternity God the Father became a Sonless Father and God the Son became a Fatherless Son!

5. And that's how it was for our precious Lord from the beginning to the end of his earthly life—down, down, ever down! The tremendous step down from his heavenly throne to the stable, the incredible journey from the stable to the cross, the stupendous journey on the cross from the first immolations of the spikes in his hands and feet to his abandonment by God and his woeful cry of dereliction!

The angels must have asked themselves: "Will this never, never end? How low must he go? How low does he have to go?" And then they witnessed the depths of his humiliation, for he who is the very Lord of life, who said, "I am the resurrection and the life," endured the last physical penalty of the wages of sin. He slumped forward and *died*—under the curse of God!

Tell me, ye who hear him groaning, was there ever grief like his?
Friends thro' fear his cause disowning, foes insulting his distress;
Many hands were raised to wound him, none would interpose to save;
But the deepest stroke that pierced him was the stroke that Justice gave.

6. No human being there that day really fully understood who he was or what was going on because his full identity was buried beneath layer after layer of humiliation—Martin Luther speaks of the divine *incognito*, the unknown Christ, dying there; John Calvin speaks of the *hidden* Christ dying there at Calvary—

layered as his deity was beneath his servanthood, beneath his humanness, beneath his cursed death on the cross, beneath his abandonment by God. He is so obscure there at Calvary that even his disciples do not recognize him. They lose their faith and their hope and forsake him too. And why? *Because a Roman cross is the last place in the whole wide world where a man would look for God.* There was nothing that looked less like God was in it than that repulsive hideous form slumped on the cross—the last rags of clothing torn from him, his beard pulled out, his back lacerated from the beating, those horrible thorns pressed mercilessly down upon his brow, those long terrible Roman spikes driven through his hands and feet, the spear thrust in his side! There was *nothing*, I submit, that looked less like a divine act than that transaction which was working itself out at Calvary that day!

Will you not have to agree with me, then, beloved, that the cross of Christ is the most stupendous sight, the most incomprehensibly incredible sight that any mortal ever beheld or ever could behold—the Creator of the world and all things in it—including us men—the very Lord of Glory allowing himself to be taken by wicked human hands and crucified on a Roman tree under the curse of God himself!

"Why all this?" you ask. This question brings us to my next point:

3. The Paramount Purpose for the Cross to bear our curse!
"Why all this?" you ask? Well, there at the cross God made Christ, as he hung on the tree, "a curse for us," for "cursed is everyone who hangs upon a tree." He did all that he did there,

A. Not primarily to give mankind an example of self-effacing, self-sacrificing love that we should emulate, but to do something that no one else could even faintly emulate, even, effect a substitutionary atonement for sin.

B. I spoke a moment ago of the great transaction that God was working out at Calvary. We had sinned and the curse of God's law and the threat of eternal death hung over us like the mythical sword that hung by a hair over Damocles. Only our plight was not mythical! It was dreadfully real. We could do nothing to save ourselves. So God sent his perfect Son to die *in our stead* to bear our curse *in our place* and to die our death! At Calvary, Paul says, he was "made a curse for us." He lovingly paid a debt he did not owe—being sinless as he was—because we all owed a debt—being the sinners that we are—we could never pay. "God made him who knew no sin to be sin for us, that we might become the righteousness of God in him!" Here is the very heart and core of our most holy faith—the great *substitutionary* work of atonement accomplished by Christ at Calvary. Jesus being our substitute, God laid his full vengeance for our sin upon him. God emptied into him the quiver of his wrath. He fired every last arrow of his holy recoil against our sin into the person of his Son who lovingly, meekly, voluntarily bore our curse in our stead.

Now what did he accomplish by that work? Our text speaks of

4. The Awesome Accomplishment of that Cross-Work—and all who are regenerate Christians should rejoice in it!—"*Christ* has redeemed us!"

Christ did not simply *try to* redeem us. No, he actually and fully redeemed all those for whom he died! *He* did it all, it is finished! He accomplished full and free redemption for us by his great cross work! And I have this day the high privilege of proclaiming the good news of Christ's law-free gospel to you. And here it is, expressed in the fragile, simple words of J. Proctor's children's hymn:

Nothing either great or small,
  Nothing, sinner, no;
Jesus did it, did it all,
  Long, long ago.

"It is finished!" Yes, indeed,
  Finished, ev'ry jot;
Sinner, this is all you need—
  Tell me, is it not?

When he, from his lofty throne,
    Stooped to do and die,
Everything was fully done,
    Hearken to his cry.

Weary, working, burdened one,
    Wherefore toil you so?
Cease your doing; all was done
    Long, long ago.

Till to Jesus' work you cling
    By a simple faith,
"Doing" is a deadly thing,
    "Doing" ends in death.

Cast your deadly "doing" down,
    Down at Jesus' feet;
Stand in him, in him alone,
    Gloriously complete!

All the other religions of the world say, Do and live. Biblical Christianity says, Live and do!

All the other religions of the world say, Do and be saved. Biblical Christianity say, Be saved and do!

All the other religions of the world, including even a number of denominations within professing Christendom, say, "Something in my hands I bring." Biblical Christianity alone says: "Nothing in my hands I bring; simply to thy cross I cling."

So man, whoever you are, be done with *your* deadly doing. Repent of your idolatrous dependence upon yourself. Repudiate all your religious rituals and all your pretensions to good works.

Woman, if you are here, wherever you are, be done with all *your* doing to make God like you. Lay down all the filthy rags of your righteousness and take up the unsullied robes of Christ's perfect righteousness.

Simple trust in Christ's finished work alone will save you forever. Christ will save anyone here and give you the gift of eternal life when you place your trust in him, for does not the inspired apostle tell us in this very passage that "the just will live by faith"? If you cast yourself in faith upon Christ as the Alpha and Omega, the first and last, the beginning and end of your salvation—though you are the most damnable, polluted sinner on earth—not a sin of yours shall remain upon you after your believing. God, about whom it must be said that nothing escapes his omniscient eye, will look upon you and see you as pure in his sight as new-fallen snow, for he will have placed all your sin upon his great Scapegoat Son who carried it away by his death into the land of forgetfulness.

So if you would be saved, you must add to the obedient work of the Savior Jesus Christ absolutely nothing—"*Jesus* paid it all; all to *him* we owe. Sin had left a crimson stain; *he* washed it white as snow."

Now how do I know all this is true? I know it is true because—and here I come to the final point in our text—because of

5. The *Trustworthy Testimony* about the Cross

Do you see it in the text: *"for it is written* [in Deuteronomy 21:23], 'Cursed is everyone who hangs upon a tree!'"

There on the tree he fully bore my curse, "for it is written."

There on the tree he fully paid my penalty for sin, "for it is written."

There on the tree he died my death, "for it is written."

There on the tree he loved me and gave himself for me, "for it is written."

So now I must ask, has he redeemed you? Are you part of the "us" in this text? If you've never trusted him *alone*,

if you've never placed all your hopes, for time and for eternity, on his glorious work at Calvary,

if Christ is not your *only* hope today,

if you are still putting your hope in your church membership and your baptism, the sad answer to that question is no.

But if you have turned *completely* away from *your* doing to *his* dying and have trusted him alone and only him, yes—a thousand times yes—you are redeemed! Halellujah!

Well, dear friends, there you have the text as I have worked it out for you today. It speaks of

1. The **fundamental fact** behind the cross—the curse of the law

2. The **stupendous sight** on the cross—Christ on the tree

3. The **paramount purpose** for the cross—Christ was made a curse for us

4. The **awesome accomplishment** by that cross—Christ redeemed us

5. The **trustworthy testimony** about the cross—"it is written."

In an art gallery in Europe there is a painting of a chess game. Seated on one side of the board is a young man whose clothes are in disarray and his hair is disheveled; he has the look of absolute surrender! Seated on the other side of the board is the artist's conception of the Devil who sits with a leer on his face, confident that he has defeated his opponent. The young man has been playing with the Devil, and underneath the painting is the word: "Mate." The young man has just surrendered the game to the Devil. One day a famous chess player entered the gallery, saw the painting, became fascinated with it, and studied it for a long time. Suddenly, through the corridors of the gallery was heard his shout: "Young man, I've found a move. There's only one move but there is a move that you can make to defeat the Devil!"

The point of this illustration is obvious, isn't it? There is one move—only one—that you can make if you would be delivered from the terrible curse of the law about which we have been preaching and would achieve right standing before God, and that is to flee in faith to the saving Christ of God who alone can save you and to cast yourself upon his mercy for his forgiveness and the bestowment of his righteousness. If you have never trusted in his finished work at Calvary alone, do it right now, I beg you in Christ's name.

Let us pray:

God of all mercy and grace: By your Spirit take us now, first to the cross and help us to behold afresh the One who hung and suffered there in our stead. In the radiance of Jesus' glory and grace, strip us, as never before, of every pretense of a righteousness of our own which we would urge as the ground of our acceptance before you.

May we truly understand that our hearts are desperately wicked in your sight, and may we see our works-righteousness for what it is, namely, as filthy rags before you.

May we contemplate again the evil of our sin and abominate it, not first because it damns *us* but because it so dreadfully dishonors *you*.

Then take us to our blessed Savior's tomb and

in its emptiness show us anew the proof that his vicarious offering has been accepted in our stead;

in its emptiness assure us afresh that the claims of divine justice have been satisfied;

in its emptiness reveal again to us that in Christ we rose, in his life we live, in his victory over death we triumph, and in his ascension we are glorified.

And beholding him so, forgive us, Father, for our ever thinking that the labor of our hands was sufficient in your sight to win for us a home with you in heaven.

Teach us afresh that Christ's work alone is all-sufficient to save us from our sins. And may we always rely upon his power, walk in his love, depend upon his grace, and be conformed to him.

I humbly plead that you will now bring forth fruit for all eternity from my proclamation of this message of your grace today. May someone here today be moved by your Spirit to close with God. I pray, in Christ's holy name, Amen.

Sermon Nine

This sermon is topical, stressing the influence Moses' vision of God had upon him and the influence that a similar experience with God can have upon us. Its points are five, not alliterative but rather just statements declaring straightforwardly in sentence form how "seeing him who is invisible" affected Moses. Its FCF is man's waywardness and listlessness apart from God and his need for spiritual direction, and its CS is "seeing him who is invisible" with the eyes of true faith that will impart to the wayward person a "new affection" with its "expulsive power." Once again, I attempt to draw all of the sermon's main and subsidiary points, as well as its conclusions, either from the text itself or from implications in the text in order that the sermon will be scriptural, rational, God-centered, and theologically accurate.

"Seeing Him Who Is Invisible"

Text: Hebrews 11:24-27

> *By faith* Moses, when he had grown up, refused to be known as the son of Pharaoh's daughter. He chose to be mistreated along with the people of God rather than to enjoy the pleasures of sin for a short time. He regarded disgrace for the sake of Christ as of greater value than the treasures of Egypt, because he was looking ahead to his reward [of "a better country, that is, a heavenly one," according to vs 16]. *By faith* he left Egypt, not fearing the king's anger; he persevered because he saw him who is invisible.

Prayer for Illumination

Almighty Father, may your Spirit move upon our hearts as we consider now this portion of your Word to us from another world.

May we
think of it carefully,
study it prayerfully,
deep in our hearts let its oracles dwell;
ponder its mystery,
slight not its history,
for none ever loved it too fondly or well.

This I ask in that name that charms the angels of heaven and strikes fear in the hosts of darkness, even the name of Jesus Christ, our Lord. Amen.

* * * * *

Dr. Bob Jones, Sr., the founder and first president of Bob Jones University, often said to his students: "Every successful person I have ever known came at some time in his life under the dominating power of some great idea that made him what he was."

What did Dr. Jones mean by this statement? He was saying that if you succeed in this world it is going to be because at some point in your life you are going to read something, or hear something, or see something, or get an idea about something that grips your very heart and soul down to the very depths of your being and thus changes your entire outlook on life. In this sermon I will contend that this transformation is the effect of "the expulsive power of a new affection." And if you are never gripped by such a "new affection" you are destined to live all your life "bound in the shallows" of mediocrity.

Talk to any great person anywhere in the world who ever did anything worthwhile and ask him: "How did you get where you are," and he will tell you:

"Well, one day I heard somebody say 'such and such,'" or

"One day I came across such and such an idea in a book," or

"One day I was walking along and suddenly the idea struck me that if I did such and such, I could do so and so, and that idea consumed me and would not let me go."

Let me give you an example. If you could ask the first Henry Ford how it was that he became the successful car manufacturer that he did, he would tell you, "Well, one day the thought came to me that if I had an assembly line and taught each man on that line to do just one job and to do it well rather than many jobs, I could mass produce my cars and thereby reduce their price so that the common man could buy one. That simple idea of an assembly line revolutionized and nationalized my manufacturing business." And I might add, it transformed the industrial world in America.

The same is true in the realm of the Spirit. For example, in the case of Dr. Jones, he tells us that the most profound thought he ever had was a very simple truth that came to him one day as a little eleven-year-old country boy walking down a dusty road in southeast Alabama. Suddenly it occurred to him that—now here it is: get it—*he had to live somewhere forever*. Of course, he had heard this truth before. His mother had taught it to him. His Sunday School teachers had taught it to him. The Bible itself had taught it to him. But it had never really gripped him before that he was going to have to live somewhere *forever*. Let Dr. Jones tell this in his own words:

> It dawned on me in a flash that I had to live somewhere forever. I said to myself, "It doesn't matter whether I want to live or not. I may prefer to die and sleep a dreamless sleep in the silent dust, but I cannot do that. I have to live somewhere forever. I've got to live as long as God Almighty lives. I've got to live until God dies. I've got to live until angels sing a funeral dirge over the grave of God. And that will never be. Like it or not, I've got to live forever. Therefore, *since I've got to live, I had better learn how to live*."

It was that simple truth, he often said, that stayed him on his course the rest of his life and that motivated him in all that he did and said.

The life secret of every successful person would be well worth knowing, wouldn't it? To learn how he accomplished the things he did and triumphed over all the obstacles confronting him?

We would all be richer, wouldn't we, if we could learn the secret of a John Calvin or a William Gladstone or an Arthur Wellesley, the

"Iron Duke" of Wellington, or a George Washington or an Abraham Lincoln or a David Livingstone or a Borden of Yale or a Charles Spurgeon or a Martyn Lloyd-Jones?

Incidentally, this is the reason you should read biographies and autobiographies of great Christians—to discover the truths that made them great, in the confident hope that these same truths will assist you in setting the trajectory of your pilgrimage here.

Now while we will never know the life secret of every successful person, I would still insist, dear friends, that whether he or she be statesman, industrialist, merchant, warrior, artist, poet, athlete, or preacher—you can count on it—*at some point in his or her life every one of them came under the dominating power of some great idea or truth that transformed his or her life.*

So it was with Moses. In our text the Author of Hebrews informs us of the life secret of one far greater than all of the people I mentioned earlier. Here he is—the world's great lawgiver, a great political organizer as the founder of the Mosaic theocracy, a statesman and leader of men, a scholar, a poet, a prophet—indeed, the one person above all others in the Old Testament who typified most clearly the great Prophet, Jesus Christ, whom he announced, for he himself declared: "The LORD your God will raise up for you a prophet *like me* from among you, from your brothers—it is to him you shall listen" (Deut 18:15).

What a man! What was his secret for success? What was the great truth that dominated his life? Here it is, stated quietly simply by the Author of Hebrews in the words of Hebrews 11:27b: "…for he *persevered* as seeing him who is invisible."

Let's analyze that statement for a moment. It says that Moses *saw* the unseeable, he visualized the invisible. How did he do that? Well, he obviously saw "him who is invisible" with the 20/20 vision of a strong and vital faith, for twice in this short passage the Author affirms of Moses that what he did for God he did "by faith". And it was this "seeing him who is invisible" that gave to Moses his life-transforming "new affection." It has ever been so: men who have come to know God have always acquired this "new affection" that has transformed and revolutionized their lives.

Augustine acquired this "new affection" when, disillusioned after nine years in the Manichaean sect with its failed answers to life and with his own wayward existence, he picked up his New Testament one day and read at random Romans 13:14: "Clothe yourselves in the Lord Jesus Christ, and do not think about how to gratify the desires of the sinful nature." He tells us in his *Confessions* that he closed the New Testament and told his friends he had become a Christian. He went on to become Bishop of Hippo in North Africa and one of the greatest Christian thinkers of all time.

Martin Luther acquired this "new affection" in his "tower experience" at Wittenberg when he came to understand the meaning of the phrase "the righteousness of God" in Romans 1:17 and thereby was finally delivered from his hostility to God. He writes in his "Preface" to the Latin Edition of his *Works*:

> At last, by the mercy of God, meditating day and night, I gave heed to the context of the words, namely, "He who by faith is righteous shall live." There I began to understand that the righteousness of God is that by which the righteous lives by a gift of God, namely, by faith...[that] the righteousness of God revealed by the gospel is the righteousness with which the merciful God justifies us by faith.... Here I felt that I was altogether born again and had entered Paradise itself through open gates.... And as previously I had detested with all my heart these words, "the righteousness of God," I began from that hour to value and to love them, as the sweetest and most consoling words in the Bible. In very truth, that place in Paul was for me truly the gate to Paradise.

Calvin acquired this "new affection" when he was converted, about the details of which he says very little. He writes in his "Preface" to his *Commentary on the Psalms*:

> I tried my best to work hard [in the study of law], yet God at last turned my course in another direction by the secret rein of his providence. What happened first, since I was too obstinately addicted to the superstitions of Popery to be easily extricated from so profound an abyss of mire, was that God by an unexpected conversion [*subita conversione*] subdued and reduced my mind

> to a teachable frame. And so this taste of true godliness...set me on fire with such a desire to progress [in godliness] that I pursued the rest of my studies [in law] more coolly....

So it has ever been with God's great saints: It was "seeing him who is invisible" in Isaiah 6 that made Isaiah the great evangelical prophet that he became; it was "seeing him who is invisible" in Acts 9 that made Paul the great missionary theologian that he became. It should be obvious to us then that this experience of "seeing him who is invisible" is a very significant matter, and I want us to spend some time today thinking about it with the hope and confident expectation that God will use this same truth in our lives.

More specifically, I want us to consider five ways how "seeing him who is invisible," that is, how looking to and loving the one living and true God supremely affected Moses' life. I want us to note what "seeing the invisible God" enabled Moses to do, to the end that we ourselves will desire such a relationship and be transformed as he was and be empowered to attempt great things for God as he did.

First, let's underscore the obvious. The Bible says: "By faith Moses left Egypt." "Seeing him who is invisible" with the eyes of faith, then, enabled Moses to lead God's people out of Egypt.

Now apart from some "new affection" that would impart its expulsive power this would have been no *little* thing or *easy* thing—maybe even an *impossible* thing for Moses to do. To forsake

resplendent royalty,
unbounded luxury,
unlimited material resources,
ease and sensual pleasure,
honor below that only of Pharaoh himself, and the prospect of becoming himself one day Pharaoh of all Egypt—

how could he give all that up? What moved him to do so? The answer: the living God had invaded his life. Moses "saw him who is invisible." God had become real to him!

Believe me, dear hearts, when God truly becomes real to a man or woman, God—in and of himself—becomes more precious to that one than anything else this world has to offer. Everyone and everything else joins the ranks of "lesser things." When you have "seen him who is invisible" you will want to know him better than anyone or anything else in life. This is what David meant when he said: "The Lord is my chosen portion and my cup. . . . The boundary lines have fallen for me in pleasant places; surely I have a delightful inheritance" (Ps 16:5-6).

Walking with God enables a man to forsake house and father and mother and brother and sister and children and lands. I read again recently Howard Taylor's biography of Hudson Taylor, his father, who founded the China Inland Mission (now the Overseas Missionary Fellowship). I would encourage you to read it and you will see a magnificent example of what I mean about how walking with God enables a man to forsake everything for him.

Christian man, Christian woman, listen to me! If you are not willing to forsake all for Christ, you need a healthy dose of "seeing him who is invisible." Until you do, you will never know the unspeakable joy, the peace that passes understanding, and the sheer thrill of walking, as did Moses, with the invisible God. Young man, young woman, have you seen him who is invisible yet? You cannot live forever on the vision of God your parents have. Sooner or later you must close with him personally.

Second, "seeing him who is invisible" empowered Moses to break the habits of a lifetime. Look with me at Hebrews 11:24-26:

> By faith Moses, *when he was grown up* [that is, *when he had come of age*], refused to be called the son of Pharaoh's daughter, choosing rather to be mistreated with the people of God than to enjoy the fleeting pleasures of sin.

This means that Moses forsook Egypt at an extremely difficult time in his life—"*when he had come of age.*"

Just when his Egyptian mentors believed that he should and would begin to shoulder some of the responsibilities of the Egyptian court and Egyptian statecraft for which he had been trained all his life, he forsook Egypt.

Just at the time when his instructors expected him to take up the tasks for which they had trained him, that is to say, "*when he had grown up,*" Moses renounced all allegiance to Egypt and declared that he was on the side of the enslaved Israelites.

Here is a man who had been trained to lead Egypt, who had learned the elite life of the court and the Egyptian ways of waging war, whose every wish had been someone's command, who had lived in the blaze of earthly splendor *a long, long time*.

You ask, "How long had he known that life?" Well, for a full forty years and they were his *formative* years. It is difficult to take up a new life purpose and a new direction in life after one's formative years have prepared him for something else. But when God invaded Moses' world and became real to him, that is to say, when Moses "saw him who is invisible," a totally "new affection" moved Moses to give up Egypt even though he had come to years and to maturity.

I tell you, dear friends, God is able, as in Moses' case, to break the power of the training and habits of a lifetime. No habit, no commitment, no lesser life purpose can stand before him. Once we really see "him who is invisible" *one* time with the eyes of a true and living faith and come to understand that he is our Sovereign Lord, we, as did Moses, will experience a "new affection" and its "expulsive power" that will move us to forsake the world's purposes for us and to be done with all the lesser things of this world in lieu of the cause, the purpose, and the high calling of God in Jesus Christ! We will go—happily, willingly, voluntarily—*anywhere, any time, at any cost* to do his bidding. Have you seen him? Do you understand he is your Sovereign Lord? Has he become the object of your "new affection"?

Third, "seeing him who is invisible" enabled Moses to act for the benefit of others in spite of great personal risk to himself. Listen again to the Author of Hebrews:

> By faith Moses refused to be called the son of Pharaoh's daughter (Heb 11:24).

What does that mean? It means that one day he informed Egyptian officialdom: "I am ***not*** an Egyptian; I am a Hebrew. I am ***not*** the son of Hat-shep-sut; I am a son of Levi."

Pharaoh's daughter, I think we may presume, was furious at Moses' lack of appreciation for all that she had done for him. She probably sought ways to inflict upon him her wrath to salve her wounded pride.

Also we read: "By faith Moses left Egypt, not being afraid of the anger of the king." So we *know* that Pharaoh was furious. Moses' perceived betrayal of his family and his homeland incurred Pharaoh's bitter enmity and hostility. *Moses lost favor with Pharaoh forever.*

Ah, beloved, to leave the world for Christ and for truth in this age still results in incurring its enmity and hostility. Martin Luther learned this. When he posted his "Ninety-Five Theses" on the door of the Castle Church at Wittenberg on October 31, 1517, that act eventually led to his excommunication from the Roman Catholic Church by Pope Leo X in January 1521, and it eventually brought him before Emperor Charles V at the Diet of Worms in April of that same year, at which assembly, in response to the two questions: "Are these your writings? And will you, or will you not, recant?" after an all-night vigil in prayer he put both the world's and the church's mighty ones to flight with his immortal declaration:

> Since your most serene majesty [Charles V] and your high mightinesses require from me a clear, simple, and precise answer, I will give you one, and it is this: I cannot submit my faith either to the pope or to the councils, because it is clear as the day that they have frequently erred and contradicted each other. Unless therefore I am convinced by the testimony of Scripture, or by the clearest reasoning—unless I am persuaded by the passages I have quoted—and unless they thus render my conscience bound by the Word of God, I cannot and I will not retract, for it is unsafe for a Christian to speak against his conscience. Here I stand, I can do no other; may God help me! Amen!

I have often reflected on the eleven words in Luther's powerful testimony: "…it is unsafe for a Christian to speak against his conscience." Some among both his friends and his detractors would have said to him: "Martin, apparently you don't understand: *you are not safe now*! Don't you know that these men hold in their hands the power of death? Don't you know they can burn you? How then do you have audacity, the temerity, to say: '…it is unsafe…,' in your refusal to recant?" "Because," Luther would have said: "'because I spent last night in prayer with 'him who is invisible,' and I got my priorities straight. I know these men can kill me; I'm not crazy. But I know too that they can only destroy the body; they cannot destroy my soul. I fear him more who is invisible because he can destroy both body and soul in hell. That is the reason I say it is not safe for a Christian to speak against his conscience."

And that is what spending time with the invisible God will do for a man or a woman facing great trial. That is the reason the political and religious dictators of this world despise Christians and would rid the world of them if they could. "Seeing him who is invisible" expulsively empowers Christian saints with a new affection to stand against the tyrannies of these petty Caesars and to say: "We cannot obey you when you ask us to disobey or to recant our God." Let me remind you of what Jesus said to his disciples: "If you were of the world, the world would love you as its own; but because you are not of the world, but I chose you out of the world, therefore, the world hates you" (John 15:19).

How often during my years as a pastor have I seen young men and young women forsake all for Christ and immediately their former friends have forsaken them. Jesus said it would be this way.

Not as often, thank God, but still all too often have I seen some of them return to the fleshpots of Egypt, under the pressures and allurements that only the world can bring to bear. Jesus also said it would be this way too: there will be those, he said, who "endure only for a time, but when tribulation and persecution arise because of the word, immediately their love will cool and they will fall away" (Matt 13:21; 24:12).

Oh, how real the invisible God must have been to Moses for

him to "endure" first a world power's hostility and then his own people's insults and rebellion for forty years! Are you willing to incur the hatred of Jesus' enemies for Jesus' sake? Are you willing to risk all for Jesus Christ? If not, you need to "see him who is invisible."

Fourth, "seeing him who is invisible" enabled Moses to *choose* a life of hardship over against a life of fleeting pleasures. Look with me at Hebrews 11:25: "Moses *chose* to be mistreated with the people of God rather than to enjoy the fleeting pleasures of sin."

I have stressed the word "chose" for the Author of Hebrews uses it in verse 25. Moses' life of trial was not something that was thrust upon him against his will. He ***chose*** it, the Author of Hebrews tells us. Moses clearly saw the alternatives and he chose the *reproach* of Christ rather than the wallowing in the "dog vomit" that this world offers and then calls it excitement and pleasure.

Moses' choice was going to mean forty years of continuing hardship. His choice was going to mean a long, long road from the banks of the Nile to the heights of Pisgah where he would only view the Promised Land but would not enter into it. Nevertheless, he chose the life of hardship over against his former life of fleeting pleasures. How did he know the pleasures of sin were fleeting? Because he had seen "him who is invisible" and had acquired a "new affection" for the everlasting powers of the age to come.

So he *chose* to endure Pharaoh's hostility and rage.

He *chose* to endure the Israelites' murmurings in the wilderness of Sin and at Sinai and at numerous other places.

He *chose* to give up Egypt's pleasures and treasures to take up the trials and afflictions and reproaches of the Messiah's ministry.

How could he choose such suffering over against the treasures and pleasures of Egypt? I hope you know the answer by now to this question. But if you don't, let me repeat it again: because he had seen "him who is invisible," because God had invaded his world, because God had become real to him, because he had acquired a "new affection." Now I need to ask you: "How long are *you* going to limp between these two alternatives? Get off of the fence. Choose today whom you will serve. If the gods of this world are deserving of your service—which they are not—then serve them. But if the triune God of Christianity is Lord—which he is—then serve him."

Finally, "seeing him who is invisible" enabled Moses properly to estimate the worth and rewards of time and eternity. Note Hebrews 11:26: "He regarded disgrace for the sake of Christ as of greater value than the treasures of Egypt."

On the one hand, we are told, Moses looked squarely at Egypt's power and treasures. He saw no earthly hardships there; rather, he saw only pleasures, riches, and earthly glory. But wait, in the light of eternity he clearly saw something else: he saw that all these things were only temporary. He clearly perceived that this world's pleasures were fleeting; he saw that were he to gain the whole world, it would profit him nothing if he lost his own soul.

On the other hand, he clearly saw disgrace and hardships with an enslaved, unruly people; he saw trials, hardships and affliction ahead. But wait again. He looked beyond all these things to the "reward" awaiting him of a heavenly city whose builder and maker is God. He saw him who is invisible with the 20/20 vision of a living faith; he saw the glories of the heavenly city; and he saw the pleasures that are at God's right hand forevermore.

And so Moses *chose* to live for the *invisible* things of eternity rather than for the *visible* things of time. He came to understand, as Paul says, that we should "fix our eyes not on what is seen, but on what is unseen. For what is seen is temporary, but what is unseen is eternal" (2 Cor 4:18). Having seen God, he chose rather to be with his "new affection"—the invisible God—with all the hardships that path would eventually entail than to remain with Egypt at its fleeting best.

Egypt here is a type of the world. Moses' new affection drove him to God and his purposes for him and away from the world and its purposes for him. For which world are you living? The world of the fleeting seen or the world of the everlasting unseen? Jim Eliot insightfully reminds us: "He is no fool who gives up that which he cannot keep to gain that which he cannot lose."

Conclusion

As I begin to close, my beloved, I believe that *you* know in the depth of your heart that Moses made the right choice. And if you will acknowledge that, you know that you should make a similar choice. True, today the pharaohs have their tombs and their monuments. Moses could have had and doubtless would have had one or two as well, but he has none. Rather, his body lies today in an unknown grave somewhere in the land of Moab in a valley opposite Beth Peor (Deut 34:6).

But don't feel sorry for Moses, for while it is true that Moses has no giant pyramidic sepulchre for tourists to gaze at or into, he has a better place today by far. Incidentally, those pyramids are not much to look at; I've seen them and they're only big piles of weather-beaten stones. Today Moses occupies a place of high honor among God's great heroes of the Faith. And look at Moses in his tangible appearance on the Mount of Transfiguration, discussing with Jesus his approaching death at Calvary. What a privilege! I say again, don't feel sorry for Moses. This is why I say that, having seen him who is invisible, Moses made the ***right*** choice. Of course,

- having seen him who is invisible, his was also a ***serious*** choice—serious because of the issues of eternal life and eternal death that it entailed; and
- having seen him who is invisible, his was a ***costly*** choice—costly because of the sacrifice his choice imposed upon him; but
- having seen him who is invisible, he made a ***glorious*** choice—glorious because of the role he modeled ever after for us and because of the glorious inheritance awaiting him in the heavenly city—a reward, by the way, that is laid up for us as well in heaven—an inheritance, incorruptible, undefiled, and that does not fade away—indeed, a reward laid up for all who love and long for his appearing!

Now think with me one more moment about all this. We have even a better opportunity to see the invisible God today than did

Moses, for the invisible God has revealed himself in the flesh to us. Paul informs us in Colossians 1:15 that Christ is the visible "image of the invisible God." Have you seen him with the eyes of faith? Do you know him as your Savior and Lord? Have you forsaken all to follow him? I pray God you have!

Now I close: And in the simplest, most fragile of words, I will tell you what the secret of Moses' success was. I will tell you one more time what the great truth was that impacted Moses' mind and heart and that empowered him with a dominating new affection. It is this: he saw him who was invisible and accordingly he put living for eternal things ahead of living for the temporal baubles and trifling "hand-me-downs" of this world of time. Have you come to see, with Moses, that

> Only one life! 'Twill soon be passed.
> Only what's done for Christ will last!

May God impact our lives by this simple truth with the same power with which he impacted Moses!

May today—right now—we come under the dominating power of the new affection intrinsic in the experience of "seeing him who is invisible"—the affection that imparts to all who see him a life-transforming expulsive power to choose the reproach of the Lord Jesus Christ as being of greater worth than *all* of the treasures of this world.

May God enable us to see "him who is invisible" with the same clear 20/20 vision of a living, vital faith that Moses was given!

Let us pray:
O great King of the ages, immortal, invisible, God only wise: to you be honor and glory forever and ever. By your Spirit enable us to see you with eyes of faith today, and grant to us by this vision of faith the expulsive power of a completely new affection that transforms us, equips us, energizes us, dominates us, and leads us forth to accomplish great exploits for you and your church. This I ask, in Jesus' name. Amen!

Sermon Ten

This sermon is topical in nature. That is to say, its points are not drawn from a specific text as with the previous two sermons but are drawn from a rather free-ranging choice of textual material available throughout the New Testament. Its FCF is the rampant confusion and fear in the minds of people about their and this world's future, and its CS is the biblical teaching about Christ's second coming and what it will involve. Again, my over-arching concern is to be biblical, rational, God-honoring, and theologically accurate. Once again, I press upon the audience the claims of Christ and urge Christians to remain faithful to him until he returns.

"What Will Happen When Jesus Comes Again?"

Text: I Corinthians 15:21-26

> ...since death came through a man, the resurrection of the dead comes also through a man. For as in Adam all die, so in Christ all will be made alive. But each in his own turn: Christ, the firstfruits; then *when he comes*, those who belong to him. Then the end will come, when he hands over the kingdom to God the Father after he has destroyed all dominion, authority, and power. For he must reign until he has put all his enemies under his feet. The last enemy to be destroyed is death....

Prayer for Illumination

Dear heavenly Father, compassionate Lord Jesus Christ, blessed Holy Spirit: We thank you for the opportunity to study your precious Word together, to *discern* what it has to say about end-time eventualities.

Grant that we may clearly perceive that vain will be our efforts unless we

grow in grace,
increase in knowledge, and
labor to make ourselves more ready for that great Day of Harvest awaiting us.

By our attendance upon your Word tonight, enable us

to know you more perfectly,
to adore you more fully, and
to determine to serve you more single-mindedly.

We bring our hungry hearts to you and implore you to fill them with your choicest gifts, not the least of which is wisdom and understanding.

We bring our blind understanding to you and plead that you would drive away our ignorance.

We bring to you all the unwholesome paths of sin in which we wandered last week and would beg you to hedge up our ways lest we walk in these same paths this week and bring our undoing and your displeasure upon us.

We confess the ease with which we become entangled in the poisonous springs of error from which we are all too willing to drink but which can never quench our thirsting souls. So guide us, we pray, lest we become entangled in error and Satan's hidden traps and secret snares.

We dare to believe, as we ask all these things, that you will answer our prayers, because Jesus is our Savior from sin. So purify our hearts, cleanse and clear our minds, that we may learn more about the future as the Bible depicts it.

And I ask all of these things in that name that charms the angels, strikes fear in Satan's host, and draws you, our heavenly Father, away from wrath to rapturous overtures of grace, even Jesus Christ our Lord. Amen.

* * * * *

A great amount of confusion is rampant in evangelical Christianity in our time concerning biblical eventualities. Some scholars, urging a kind of "realized eschatology," inform us that all the prophecies of the Old and New Testament were fulfilled by the time of the destruction of Jerusalem in A.D. 70. Such a view leaves too many questions unanswered, such as how the saints are finally perfected, how sickness and death are overcome, and how the redemption of the body and the glorification of creation are finally achieved. Other scholars inform us, just to the contrary, first, that all the Old Testament prophecies concerning Israel's future blessedness yet await their fulfillment in a decidedly Jewish millennium following this current church age, and second, that hardly any of the prophecies of the book of the Revelation have been fulfilled yet, indeed, that Revelation 4-22 speaks of things yet to come. As a result the airwaves, especially in America, and many Christian publications are filled with bizarre depictions of end-time eventualities that are intended to scare people silly and to "frighten them to Christ." From my study of Holy Scripture I have concluded that neither of these extremes is true. And the purpose of this sermon is to attempt to bring some clarity to this confusion. Naturally one sermon can never respond to all the issues that have been raised, but it can go some distance to advance the discussion in a sane and sensible way.

Today I will call your attention to several Bible verses. Let's begin with this one: On the night of his betrayal, Jesus consoled his disciples in the upper room by saying to them:

> In my Father's house there are many rooms; if it were not so, I would have told you. I am going there to prepare a place for you. And if I go and prepare a place for you, *I will come back* and take you to be with me that you also may be where I am (John 14:2-3).

Then the very first promise he sent back to his disciples by angels from heaven after he departed this world at his ascension was this:

> Men of Galilee,...why do you stand here looking into the sky? This same Jesus, who has been taken from you into heaven, *will come back* in the same way you have seen him go into heaven (Acts 1:11).

Then throughout his Thessalonian correspondence the apostle Paul teaches that Jesus is coming again. In fact, each chapter in 1 Thessalonians ends with an allusion to the return of Christ:

In 1:10 Paul says that Christians should be "waiting for God's Son from heaven";

In 2:19 he says that Christians such as you here in this church will be their faithful pastor's "hope, joy, and crown in which he will glory in the presence of our Lord Jesus *when he comes*";

In 3:13 he prays that his Thessalonian readers' hearts will be strengthened so that they will be "blameless and holy in the presence of our God and Father *when the Lord Jesus comes with all his holy ones*";

In 4:16: he declares: "For *the Lord himself will come down from heaven*, with a loud command, with the voice of the archangel and with the trumpet call of God, and the dead in Christ will rise first."

And in 5:23 Paul says that he prays that his readers "would be kept blameless—body, soul, and spirit—at the coming of our Lord Jesus Christ."

In 2 Thessalonians 1:7-10 Paul gives us an extended description of Christ's return:

> ...when the Lord Jesus is revealed from heaven in blazing fire with his powerful angels, he will punish those who do not know God and do not obey the gospel of our Lord Jesus. They will be punished with everlasting destruction and shut out from the [approving] presence of the Lord and from the majesty of his power *on the day he comes* to be glorified in his holy people and to be marveled at among all those who have believed.

In 2 Thessalonians 2:1-12 Paul gives an even more extended treatment of Christ's return and certain events that will precede it.

In Titus 2:13 he states: "...we [Christians] wait for the blessed hope—the glorious appearing of our great God and Savior, Jesus Christ."

And in Hebrew 9:26, 28 we read: "[Christ] has appeared once

for all at the end of the ages to do away with sin by the sacrifice of himself...and *he will appear a second time*, not to bear sin, but to bring salvation to those who are waiting for him."

So there can be no question that, according to Holy Scripture, someday *Jesus is coming again*.

Now let's get something settled at the very outset of this sermon about the issue of *when* Christ is coming. I don't know when he is coming, and—in spite of all the bizarre things being said today about Christ's soon coming—no one else knows either.

It may be at morn, when the day is awak'ing,
When sunlight through darkness and shadow is breaking,
That Jesus will come in the fullness of glory,
To receive from the world his own.

It may be at midday, it may be at twilight,
It may be, perchance, that the blackness of midnight
Will burst into light in the blaze of his glory,
When Jesus receives his own.

But while we do not know *when* he is coming, we do know for certain *that* he is coming and that certain things must occur *before* he comes. For example, we read in 2 Thessalonians 2 of the great falling away of the church [I would suggest that we may be seeing this as a work in progress], and the appearing of the man of sin. Until then, our cry can only be:

O Lord Jesus, how long, how long
Ere we shout the glad song:
Christ returneth! Hallelujah!
Hallelujah! Amen.

But if we cannot say *when* Jesus will come, we can surely say something with absolute certainty about *what* will happen when he comes again. And it this topic that I want to address in this sermon: "What will happen when Jesus comes again?" Let's look at some of these things for a few minutes, and because Scripture clearly teaches these things I can assure you, even before we look at them, that you can know for certain that they will come to pass.

1. The World Will Be Taken by Great Surprise (1 Thes 5:2-3; Matt 24:36-39, 42-44; Mark 13:33-37)

First, according to Holy Scripture, when Jesus comes again the world *will be taken by great surprise*, for "the day of the Lord will come like a thief in the night. While people are saying, 'Peace and safety,' destruction will come on them suddenly, as labor pains on a pregnant woman, and they will not escape" (1 Thes 5:2-3).

Our Lord himself taught: "As it was in the days of Noah, so will it be at the coming of the Son of Man...[for just as Noah's generation] knew nothing about what would happen until the flood came and took them all away, so also...*the Son of Man is coming at an hour when the world does not expect him.*"

And Peter declared in 2 Peter 3:3-4, 10 that "in the last days scoffers will come, scoffing and following their own evil desires. They will say, 'Where is this "coming" he promised? Ever since our fathers died, everything goes on as it has since the beginning of creation.' ...*But* [Peter says,] the day of the Lord *will come* like a thief. The heavens will disappear with a roar; the elements will be destroyed by fervent heat, and the earth and everything in it will be laid bare."

Yes, when Christ returns, many people will be greatly surprised, but "you, my brothers and sisters," writes Paul, "are not in darkness, so that this day should surprise you as a thief. You are all sons and daughters of light and sons and daughters of the day. We do not belong to the night or to the darkness. So then, let us not be like others, who are asleep, but let us be alert and self-controlled...putting on faith and love as a breastplate, and the *hope* of salvation as a helmet...Therefore encourage one another and build each other up, just as in fact you are doing" (1 Thes 5:4-11). That is to say, Christians will not be taken by complete surprise when Jesus comes, because they will have been expecting him to return.

2. There Will Be a Glorious Resurrection of the Dead (Acts 24:15 ; 1 Thes 4:16; 1 Cor 15:51-57)

Second, as we read earlier, in connection with the world's *great surprise* at Christ's return, there will be an accompanying *glorious resurrection of the dead*. Look at

Acts 24:15: "...there will be a resurrection [note: ***a*** resurrection] of both the righteous and the unrighteous."

1 Corinthians 15:51-57 "...Behold, I tell you a mystery: We will not all sleep, but we will all be changed—in a flash, in the twinkling of an eye, at the last trumpet. For the trumpet will sound, *the dead will be raised* imperishable, and we will all be changed. For the perishable must clothe itself with the imperishable, and the mortal with immortality. When the perishable has been clothed with the imperishable, and the mortal with immortality, then the saying that is written will come true, 'Death has been swallowed up in victory.' 'Where, O death, is your victory? Where, O death, is your sting?'"

Have you ever tried to imagine what that day and that great event are going to be like? In his sermon, "The Resurrection of the Body," William Elbert Munsey, the nineteenth-century Southern evangelist, let his sanctified imagination reflect on that day as he eloquently declared:

> The last day will come. The sun will drag along the jarring heavens and refuse to shine. The stars will hide their faces, and the moon will roll up in the heavens red as blood, and hang her crimson livery upon the wing of the night. Earth will tremble upon her axis, and huge mountains will crash in ruins.
>
> A might angel with a face like the sun, clothed with clouds, and crowned with a rainbow, and shod with wings of fire, will cleave the heavens in his lightning track, and descending with his right foot upon the troubled sea, and his left foot upon the quaking earth, will lift his hand to Heaven, and swear by the judge of the quick and the dead that the time has finally come.
>
> The trump of God will then sound. Its resonant thunders will roll through all the lengths and breadths of death's vast empire, and its old walls and arches crammed with buried millions will fall in crashing ruins. The dry-boned king will drop his scepter ringing

> in fragments upon the damp pavements of the grave, and fly howling from his tottering throne. The antiquated dead will start into life from their ashy urns and funeral pyres. Pyramids of granite and crypts of marble will be rent in twain to let the rising bodies come. Mummies will fling off the trappings of centuries, and pour forth from their vaulted chambers. Revivified dead will stream from their dungeons. Abbeys, cathedrals, grottoes, caverns and cemeteries will become vocal with life. Wanderers will shake off the winding sheets of sand, and rise from the face of the world's deserts. Human bones will break away from their coral fastenings; and whole oceans will heave and swell with teeming millions.
>
> The battlefields of the world—Troy and Thermopylae, Talavera and Marengo, Austerlitz and Waterloo, Marathon and Gettysburg; the battlefields of Europe, Asia, Africa, and the Americas—will reproduce their armies, and crowd the world with revivified legions. Indian maidens will leap from the dust of our streets, and our houses overturning will let their chiefs to judgment. Abraham will shake off the dust of Machpelah and arise with Sarah by his side. David will come forth, harp in hand. The Reformer of Geneva and the Apostle of Methodism will come side by side.
>
> Our village churchyards and family burial grounds will be deserted. All will come: patriarchs, prophets, Jews and Gentiles, Christians and heathen, bond and free, rich and poor—fathers, mothers, children, sisters, brothers, husbands, wives—all from Adam down will come forth. And all the saved in that moment all around the world all together will hail redemption's grand consummation, with one grand anthem, whose choral thunders, rolling along all the paths of space, will shake the universe with its bursting chorus: "O death, where is thy sting? O grave, where is thy victory?"

Yes, indeed, there will be a glorious resurrection of all the dead when Jesus returns to earth.

You say to me, how can this be? How can flesh and bones that have rotted and turned back to dust, that even may have been torn apart and eaten and digested by wild animals and the fish of the sea, be resurrected? My answer here is simply this: in the words of the inspired apostle, "we eagerly await a Savior from heaven, the Lord

Jesus Christ, who, *by the power that enables him to bring everything under his control*, will transform our lowly bodies so that they will be like his own glorious body" (Phil 3:20). Did you hear Paul's words: "...by the power that enables him to bring everything under his control." There's your answer to the *how* of the resurrection, and in this answer our minds should find their rest.

3. A Grand Reunion Will Follow

Third, after this glorious resurrection occurs, then there will be a *grand reunion*. We say we live in the land of the living, and we do. But in another sense, we live in the land of the dying. We live in a world of goodbyes. Hardly a day goes by but what we don't have to say goodbye to spouses and to friends whom death takes away from us. But then—ah then—we will see our saved loved ones again. I will see my precious mother who loved the Lord dearly. You will see your saved loved ones too. And most important, we all will see Christ. Listen to some words from 1 Thessalonians 4:15-18:

> According to the Lord's own word, we tell you that we who are still alive, who are left till *the coming of the Lord*, will certainly not precede those who have fallen asleep. For the Lord himself *will come down from heaven*, with a loud command, with the voice of the archangel and with the trumpet call of God, and the dead in Christ will rise first. After that, we who are still alive and are left will be caught up *together with them* in the clouds *to meet the Lord* in the air. And so we will be with the Lord forever. Therefore, encourage each other with these words.

Have you been encouraging one another with this fact of the grand reunion that we will someday know and experience with our deceased friends and loved ones? You should, you know. The next time you catch one of your brothers or sisters in the doldrums, remind him or her that Jesus is coming back and that a glorious resurrection and a grand reunion with loved ones we will all experience someday. It will lift their spirits like nothing else will! Christ's return is, you know, the Christian's blessed hope.

4. A Grave Accounting

Fourth, if there is to be a *grand reunion*, there is also to be *both* for the ungodly and unbelieving *and* for Christians a *grave accounting*. The Bible teaches this so often that only the spiritually perverse will miss this truth. Listen to the words of Jesus:

Matthew 24:45-51: "Who then is *the faithful and wise* servant, whom the master has put in charge of the servants in his household to give them their food at the proper time? It will be good for that servant whose master finds him doing so when he returns. I tell you the truth, he will put him in charge of all his possessions. But suppose that servant is *wicked* and says to himself, 'My master is staying away a long time,' and he then begins to beat his fellow servants and to eat and drink with drunkards. The master of that servant will come on a day when he does not expect him and at an hour he is not aware of. He will cut him to pieces and assign him a place with the hypocrites, where there will be weeping and gnashing of teeth."

Matthew 25:14-30: And in his parable of the talents, Jesus tells of the servant who invested his master's five talents and gained five more and of the servant who invested his master's two talents and gained two more, both of whom received the master's accolade: "Well done, *good and faithful servant*. You have been faithful with a few things; I will put you in charge of many things. Come and share your master's happiness." But Jesus concludes this parable by having the master say to the servant who hid his talent and did not use it: "You *wicked, lazy servant*! ...you should have put my money on deposit with the bankers so that when I returned I would have received it back with interest. Take the talent from him and give it to the one who has the ten talents. For everyone who has will be given more, and he will have an abundance. Whoever does not have, even what he has will be taken from him. And throw that worthless servant outside, into the darkness, where there will be weeping and gnashing of teeth."

In other words, my beloved brothers and sisters, Jesus expects you to use your gifts—whatever they may be, how many or few they may be—in his cause, and if you don't, you will be sorry someday that you didn't!

Then, Paul declares:

Romans 2:16: "[The day will come] when God will judge men's secrets through Jesus Christ."

Romans 14:10b-12: "For we will all stand before God's judgment throne. It is written: 'As surely as I live,' says the Lord, 'every knee will bow before me; and every tongue will confess to God.' So, then, each of us will give an account of himself to God."

1 Corinthians 3:10-15: "By the grace God has given me, I laid a foundation as an expert builder, and someone else is building on it. But each one should be careful how he builds. For no one can lay any foundation other than the one already laid, which is Jesus Christ. If any man builds on this foundation using gold, silver, costly stones, wood, hay, or straw, his work will be shown for what it is, because the Day will bring it to light. It will be revealed with fire, and the fire will test the quality of each man's work. If what he has built survives, he will receive his reward. If it is burned up, he will suffer loss; he himself will be saved, but only as one escaping through the flames."

2 Corinthians 5:9-11: "So we make it our goal to please him, whether we are at home in the body or away from it. For *we must all appear before the judgment seat of Christ*, that each one may receive what is due him for the things done while in the body, whether good or bad. Since, then, we know what it is to fear the Lord, we try to persuade men."

Ah, dear hearts, you must not think that God will receive careless, worldly, carnal Christians who have lived for themselves in the same manner he will receive the great saints who have served him night and day. John instructs us to "continue in him, so that when he appears we may be confident and unashamed before him at his coming" (1 John 2:28). Dear friends, I think often about that Great Day and my own accounting. And I ask myself:

If he should come today
    and find I had not told
one soul about my heavenly friend,
    whose blessings all my way attend,
what will he say? What will he say?

If he should come today
    and find my heart so cold,
My faith so very weak and dim,
    I had not even looked for him,
what will he say? What will he say?

Some time back I succumbed to all the hype and went to see the 1993 Academy Award movie of the year, *Schindler's List*, the Steven Spielberg story of Oskar Schindler, the Nazi war profiteer, who shortly after the German invasion of Poland in 1939 began to use the Jews of the Krakow ghetto as workers in his pots and pans factory. At first he saw them only as chattel to be used to line his own pockets, which he did quite successfully, becoming exceedingly rich. But as the war dragged on, and as he increasingly witnessed Nazi atrocities being inflicted against the Jews of Poland, increasingly did he begin to use his own wealth to bribe Nazi officials and army officers to give him more and more Jews for his factory that the Nazis had turned into a munitions factory, that became a model of non-productivity in the Nazi war effort. Though it virtually bankrupted him personally, he saved over twelve hundred Jews from certain death in the gas chambers.

I recount this story line only to say that I was struck by some statements put in his mouth toward the end of the movie. The war has just ended, and having worked for the Third Reich, both he and his Jewish factory workers realize that the Allied authorities might search for him. As he bids farewell to them, they present him with a letter signed by each of them, that they hope will help him before the Allied authorities.

At this moment Schindler suddenly becomes very sober and quietly says: "I could have done more. I could have done more!" He begins to sob. "I could have done more. I didn't do enough. This car—why did I keep the car? Ten people right there. Ten people. Ten more people." Pulling off his lapel pin, he exclaims, "The pin. Two people. This is gold. Two more people. One more. I could have bought more people! But I didn't." His knees crumble and he sobs heavily.

As his words—"I could have done more! Why did I keep the car? Ten people right there. The pin. This is gold. Two people. I could have bought more people. But I didn't."—as his words, I say, seared themselves into my mind as I sat in the darkness of that theater, I suddenly became convicted that many Christians—I among them—are going to be asking similar questions at the Great Assize in heaven: "Why did I not do more to reach the lost for Christ? Why did I think I had to have that more expensive house, that more expensive car? Why did I not use more of my resources for the cause of Christ?" More poignantly, "Why was I not willing to go myself?" In that Great Day when we all give an accounting of our lives lived here, I fear that many of us will have no answers to salve our smitten consciences.

5. A Grievous Separation of the Saved and Lost (Chapter 4—Christians; Chapter 5—others; see also Matthew 25:31ff; 2 Thessalonians 1:6-10).

Fifth, and finally, after the *grave accounting* there will be for all eternity a grievous separation of the saved from the lost. This is glad news for the saved for it means that we will be delivered from the very presence of sin and evil, but this is sad news for the lost, for after Jesus comes there is no way to escape it. The Bible knows nothing about a universal salvation that will finally bring all mankind to heaven. Our Lord himself taught in Matthew 25:31-46:

> When the Son of Man comes in his glory, and all the angels with him, he will sit on his throne in heavenly glory. All the nations will be gathered before him, and he will separate the people one from another as a shepherd separates the sheep from the goats. He will put the sheep on his right and the goats on his left. Then the King will say to those on his right, "Come, you who are blessed by my Father, take your inheritance, the kingdom, prepared for you since the creation of the world"...Then he will say to those on his left, "Depart from me, you who are cursed, into the eternal fire prepared for the devil and his angels.... And they will go away to eternal punishment, but the righteous to eternal life."

Clearly, someday a *grievous separation* among mankind will occur. The New Testament teaches in more than fifty passages the ultimate bifurcation of mankind between the two destinies of heaven and hell. I provide this list of passages in my *Systematic Theology* (1083, fn 24). Look them up and see for yourself. And Christ alone can save you for the one and deliver you from the other. So trust him now to save you.

Conclusion and Application

There you have it: my sermon's five points that, for all the mystery in which Jesus' second coming is still shrouded, we *know* beyond any and all doubt will surely happen:

1. The *great surprise* the world will experience when he returns,
2. The *glorious resurrection* of all the dead,
3. The *grand reunion* of living and dead saints,
4. The *grave accounting* that we all shall give to God, and
5. The *grievous separation* of the saved and lost.

Is this doctrine of the second coming of Christ simply "pie in the sky" teaching—irrelevant and impractical? Hardly. After his discussion of the resurrection of the body in 1 Corinthians 15, Paul writes:

> Therefore, my dear brothers [and sisters], stand firm. Let nothing move you. Always give yourselves fully to the work of the Lord, because you know that your labor in the Lord is not in vain (1 Cor 15:58).

And John informs us:

> Now are we the sons of God, and it does not yet appear what we shall be, but we know that when he appears we shall be like him, for we shall see him as he is. And *everyone who has this hope in him purifies himself just as he is pure* (1 John 3:2-3).

The best illustration of which I am aware of John's assertion that true saints will make sure they are pure when Jesus comes T. Roland

Philips, the Baltimore Presbyterian pastor, tells on himself in his early ministry as a young man. In his first pastorate a young lady in his church became engaged but had to carry on her courtship with her fiancé by letter because he was working in another city. One day she came to Pastor Philips and told him that her fiancé was coming to visit her and she invited him to her home to meet him. The day came and Pastor Philips went to her home. He said he was overwhelmed at the obvious preparations that had been made for the occasion. Friends and relatives were all present, dressed in their finery. Everything was spotless, the aroma of lovely flowers filled the home, and the bride-to-be was dressed in a lovely, spotless dress. Then, he said, the worst idea he ever had came to him: he slipped out the back door, made his way around to and up the front steps, and he rang the door bell. He said he saw through the curtained glass at the side of the door the room start into life. He saw the mother of the future bride gently nudging the young lady toward the front door. And he watched the bride-to-be smoothing her spotless dress one last time. Then she opened the door and saw her pastor grinning at her. She burst into tears, and exclaimed: "O pastor, how could you do this to me?" He said he never felt so bad in all his life. But, he said, he also saw in that split-second expectant, pure look of the young lady the best picture he could ever have of what the church of Jesus Christ should be like as it awaits its Lord's coming.

But you say, "I have waited and waited for him to come. I have longed and prayed for him to come for a long, long time and he has not come. I am getting so wearied waiting for him to return."

Let me close with a final story about "Greyfriars Bobby," not a boy but Auld John Gray's "wee Skye terrier." Bobby had deeply bonded to his master, so much so that when his master died, Bobby followed his coffin to the Greyfriars Churchyard in Edinburgh, Scotland, and when everyone else left the gravesite Bobby lay down on his master's grave and waited for his master to return. His waiting became a legend in the city. Then one day Bobby died, and the authorities arranged for a monument to be built in Bobby's memory. The inscription on Bobby's monument reads:

> A tribute to the affectionate fidelity of Greyfriars Bobby. In 1858 this faithful dog followed the remains of his master to Greyfriars Churchyard and lingered near the spot until his death in 1872.

1858 to 1872! Fourteen years! If a tiny dog can show such devotion and fidelity to its dead master, how much more should we remain faithful to our living Lord who will indeed come back some day to receive us to himself! 'Therefore, let us not grow weary in doing good, for at the proper time we will reap a harvest if we do not give up' (Gal 6:9).

Let us pray

O most merciful Christ: To whom shall we come with our prayers but to you, for wherever else we would go to receive the desires of our hearts are broken cisterns that can hold no water, idols that can neither profit nor help us.

You alone have the words of eternal life. We praise you that there is eternal life in our union with you.

We thank you again for the blessed privilege of studying your Word about what will happen when you come again. If someone here needs to close with you now about his sin, grant him the miracle of regeneration to do it. Convince him of his sin and misery, enlighten his mind in the knowledge of Christ, and renew his will. Enable him to embrace you for his salvation, as you are offered freely in the gospel.

If someone here has a particular anxiety, may he or she find your grace sufficient, working strength and consolation where they are lacking and providing correction and rebuke where they are needed.

Lord, quicken us all by your Word and Spirit that we may become more holy, more earnest, more Christ-like, more fit to be partakers of the inheritance of the saints in light as we await your coming from heaven.

All these things we ask for your sake, in whose majestic name we bring our petitions. Amen.

Subject Index

alliteration 253
analogy 33
antinomy *see* paradox
apostles 13, 31, 124, 150, 156fn
Arminianism 59, 63, 78, 82-3, 85, 87, 89-91, 111-12
atonement 95, 111, 130, 135, 185, 273, 302-3
authority of Christ 106, 143, 169-71, 218, 243
authority of Scripture 13-15, 107, 156fn
baptism 128fn, 132, 191, 277, 305
Barthianism 152fn
Bartimaeus, healing of 225-32
blindness, spiritual 225, 230
Bultmannianism 22
Calvinism 63, 83, 85, 88, 180
Catechism, Heidelberg 108
Christ, person of 29, 45, 50, 52, 101-4, 109, 111, 154, 217
Christology 101, 105, 107-8, 111, 154-5, 195, 211
church, relevance of 281-4, 290
church growth 178-82, 184-6, 192
commandments 91, 128fn, 177, 258, 295
condemnation 57, 129fn, 262
conscience 133, 175, 276, 317-18
contrition 205-8
conversion 173, 184, 231, 313
corruption 58, 160
covenant 81, 93, 95, 132-3, 190
creation 13, 26, 57, 61, 94-5, 107, 133, 152, 323
creeds 14-15, 51, 103, 107, 129fn, 153-5
cross of Christ 22, 49, 106, 108, 123, 130, 132fn, 136, 149, 155, 171-2, 174, 181, 183, 186, 234, 245, 259-60, 263, 284-9, 293-307
    see also death of Christ
death 22, 56, 58, 62, 85, 93, 102, 118, 133, 143, 145fn, 168-9, 171-2, 175, 325, 329-40
death of Christ 58, 79, 130, 136, 169, 171, 246-7, 259-60, 263, 263, 278, 280, 289, 298, 301-3, 305, 321
    see also cross of Christ

degeneration 61-2, 96
deity of Christ 102-7, 109, 153, 221, 302
demythologization 22
depravity 97, 183, 185, 214
destruction 55, 67, 119, 130fn
determinism 60, 69, 87, 95
disobedience 59, 85, 96
doctrine 17, 47, 50, 57, 70, 90, 99-104, 111, 136fn, 141-2, 143fn, 144, 145fn, 157, 159, 161-3, 177, 180, 182, 275
ecclesiasticism 112
ecclesiology 140, 143
eldership 99, 112
election 45, 57-8, 72, 75-6, 80-4, 95, 111, 183, 185
equivocism 33
eschatology 143, 168, 325
eternity 17, 56, 84, 110, 168, 201-2, 244, 320
ethics, Christian 282
evangelism 156fn, 164-9, 173, 180-1, 187
evil 66, 72, 76, 79, 87, 92-4
exegesis 15, 18, 96, 100, 143
existentialism 17, 22
faith 14-15, 17, 21-2, 28, 30, 44, 49, 50, 56-7, 80, 63, 85, 97, 127, 129fn, 138, 140-3, 146fn, 152-5, 156fn, 157-8, 161, 163-4, 170-3, 189-90, 234, 261, 262-3, 266, 269, 275-8, 280, 289, 290, 305-6, 309, 312-17, 320, 322
faithfulness 82, 123, 162, 247
fall 57, 61, 93-6, 152, 195, 213
fallen condition focus (FCF) 197, 211, 225, 237, 253, 269, 293, 309, 323
fatalism 60
forgiveness 131, 172, 185, 245, 263, 278-80, 289, 306
free will 61-3, 68-9, 87-91, 128fn, 152fn
freedom 17, 52, 59-66, 69-70, 86-8, 95, 152fn, 166-7, 170
fundamentalism 17
glorification 92, 94
glory of God 14, 55-8, 72, 84-5, 92-4, 97, 100, 103, 106, 110, 112, 124-5, 127, 171, 179, 206, 246-7, 256, 297, 299
godliness 115-17, 119-20, 122-3, 161
goodness of God 34, 57
grace 50, 55-6, 58, 61-2, 75, 83-4, 88, 93, 94, 96-7, 98, 111, 114,

grace *(cont)* 121, 124, 127-8, 132fn, 146fn, 152, 155-7, 168-70, 172-3, 177, 181, 185-6, 206, 208, 220, 234, 263, 264, 265, 273, 277, 278, 279, 290, 296, 298, 307, 338
heresy 99, 111-2, 177
hermeneutics 28, 43, 100
history 15, 17-22, 72, 75, 82, 154, 158fn, 180, 271
holiness 93, 116, 123, 143, 146fn, 182, 185, 202-4, 206, 256, 258, 272, 297
Holy Spirit, work of 26, 122, 135, 141, 156, 184, 192, 197, 247, 277, 278
humanism 99
humility 42, 121, 183, 186, 208
idolatry 136, 139, 152-3, 157
ignorance 199
immorality 66, 160, 177
immortality 17, 110, 172, 329
incarnation 101-2, 105-9, 140, 142
indulgences 143-8, 155
inerrancy 15, 45, 111
see also inspiration of Scripture
injustice 82
inspiration of Scripture 13-15, 160
Israel 19, 55, 74-7, 79-80, 82, 84
Jews 81, 164, 171, 174-5, 262, 285-6, 334
joy 237-51, 292, 315
Judaizers 127, 129, 154-5
judgment of God 94, 127, 156, 175, 235, 256, 271, 279-80, 297, 332-5
justice 57, 65, 83, 93, 112, 130, 146fn, 297, 307
justification 57, 80, 127-8, 129fn, 130, 139, 143, 153-5, 157-8, 172, 269, 275, 278, 279, 286, 313
kenosis 105, 107-8
kingdom of God 77, 121, 159, 162, 166-9, 179, 214
knowledge 32-3, 36-44, 46, 52, 87, 90, 109-10, 218-21
language, human 23-6, 28-9, 31, 33
law of God 53, 62, 65, 68, 90, 97, 128, 129fn, 181, 190, 214, 234, 258, 261, 270, 286, 289, 293-9, 302, 306
life, eternal 28, 56, 78, 85, 128, 134, 142, 146fn, 171-2, 222, 255, 264-5, 266, 292, 304, 311, 321, 335, 338
liturgy 188-9, 192
loftiness of God 199-201

Lord's Day 177, 189, 191
Lord's Supper 136, 191
lordship of Christ 218
love of God 28, 56, 75, 80-4, 98, 114, 120, 122, 206, 246, 253-67, 296, 307
majesty of God 201, 256, 288, 299
Marian devotion 137-9
Mass 132, 134-6, 157-8, 274
mercy 55, 57, 83-4, 93, 98, 123, 128fn, 138, 162, 168, 186, 206, 230, 233, 265, 306
merit 75, 82, 128, 145-6, 155
Messiah 229, 288
Messianic Age 228
mind 28-9, 36-7, 39-40, 43-4, 50, 69, 97-8, 104, 121, 175, 189, 291-2
ministry 11-12, 14, 23, 30, 99, 113, 115, 117-23, 125, 132fn, 133, 135, 138, 159, 161, 173-4
miracles 21, 151
morality 15, 160, 288
neo-orthodoxy 16-17, 21-23, 31
nomism 127-8, 153
obedience 100, 115, 127, 128fn, 139, 146fn, 155, 157, 170-2, 271, 278, 279
omnipresence 105-6, 108
omniscience 47, 69, 105-6, 137fn, 305
pain 22
see also suffering
paradox 44-9, 51, 53, 64
Pelagianism 156
penance 272, 274, 277
perdition, eternal 28, 93, 112, 263-4, 280, 335-6
permissionism 66-9, 78
philosophy 285, 286-7
power of God 55, 57, 72-4, 84, 93-4, 106, 123-4, 127, 132, 162, 169, 171, 184, 192, 266, 288, 299
power of gospel 180, 182, 192
prayer 114, 117-18, 120, 123, 137fn, 143fn, 144-5, 185, 189-91, 243-4
predestination 56, 59-61, 80, 84-5, 91, 128fn
Presbyterianism 15
preterition 57, 72
pride 121, 145fn, 183
priest 131-6, 144, 146, 274

promises of God 80-1, 128, 133, 168, 217
prophecy 20
prophets 13, 18-19, 26, 31, 77, 82, 86, 312, 314
Protestantism 15, 130, 136fn, 145fn, 152, 158
providence 13-14, 57, 71, 74, 85, 167, 313
psalms, use of 189, 191
purgatory 143-6, 148, 157, 263, 274, 277
Qumran 230
rationalism 52
reason 17, 44-5, 47-8, 52
redemption 131, 134, 137, 303-5, 323
    covenant of 95
    particular 45
Reformation, the 271, 276
reformation, to the church 178-9, 183, 185-6
Reformed faith 36, 58-9, 184, 186, 189
Relics, of saints 143-4fn, 147-51, 274
repentance 42, 57, 142, 171, 173, 181, 279
reprobation 82
responsibility, human 45, 60, 63, 65-6, 70, 85, 87-91, 99
rest 212, 216, 222-3
resurrection 22, 109-10, 149, 169, 171-2, 174, 329-31, 336
revelation 13-14, 16-21, 23, 27-9, 31-3, 36-8, 41, 43-6, 50, 52-3, 72, 114, 220-1, 285, 322
reverence 115, 188-9, 204
righteousness 53, 71, 96, 127, 146fn, 155, 167, 170, 234, 245, 256, 258, 261, 263, 269, 270-1, 273, 276-80, 286, 289, 296, 303, 304, 306-7, 313
Roman Catholicism 127-30, 132, 137-40, 144, 152, 156-8, 188, 273
sacrifices 131-5, 158, 321
salvation 14, 19, 44, 55-6, 58, 61-2, 76, 78, 80, 83-4, 91, 94, 97, 102, 111-12, 114, 123, 127, 128fn, 137-8, 141, 145-6, 154, 156-7, 162, 166-7, 169-70, 182-3, 192, 226, 250, 260-6, 277-8, 280, 291, 299, 301, 304-7, 328, 335, 338
sanctification 57, 123, 128fn, 162, 277
second coming of Christ 325-38
sermon requirements 195
sin 57-9, 61-3, 65-8, 77, 85-6, 88-91, 93, 95-8, 102, 106, 119, 122, 128fn, 130-5, 138, 144-7, 156, 168, 170-2, 177-8, 181, 191, 209, 211, 213, 214, 222-3, 242, 258, 272, 277-80, 295-8, 300-3, 305,

sin *(cont)* 307, 319, 335, 338
original sin 62, 90, 95, 270
soteriology 130 143, 146, 154, 156-7, 277
sovereignty of God 45, 61, 64, 71-3, 76-81, 84-5, 89-91, 97, 168, 182, 201, 220
suffering 92, 102, 138, 143-4, 145fn, 146, 242, 260, 275, 319
see also pain
temptation 62, 121
theology 11, 14, 21-22, 31, 46, 55, 63, 80, 97, 103, 105, 113, 130, 139, 144, 152, 187, 275, 282, 284
liberal 140, 152fn
natural 35
Reformed 86-8, 110, 180, 183, 186, 190, 269
systematic 32, 44, 47, 53, 112-3
time 17
tradition 14, 18-20, 56, 129fn, 130, 152, 157, 187-90, 192, 273
transcendence of God 200, 205
Trent, Council of 127, 128fn, 129fn, 136, 143-4fn, 153
Trinity 45, 50-2, 103-4, 106, 154
trust 262, 266, 304-6
see also faith
truth 14, 16-17, 23-7, 29-33, 39-40, 43-53, 63-4, 68, 70-81, 100-1, 107, 111-3, 119, 137, 156-7, 159, 161-3, 173, 178, 185, 192, 214, 215, 263, 275, 290, 312, 317, 322
unbelief 59
univocism 33
weariness 213, 215
Westminster Confession of Faith 14-15, 51, 56, 86-8, 93, 136fn, 156fn, 187-8, 190
Westminster Shorter Catechism 52, 100, 124, 190, 247
will of God 14, 31, 56-7, 60-2, 64, 67-8, 70-2, 78, 83-5, 95, 97, 114, 139, 244, 245, 248
will of man 19, 63, 83, 86-8, 91, 97, 121
see also free will
wisdom, human 286-8
works 56, 83-4, 97, 114, 127-8, 129fn, 143-6, 154-5, 158, 170, 173, 261, 262, 272-3, 275, 278, 280, 304, 307
worship 103, 115, 133, 136, 151-3, 182, 184, 187-92, 199, 201, 203, 206, 249
wrath of God 57, 84, 91, 93, 171, 286, 290, 296-8, 303

Persons Index

Adler, Mortimer J. 60
Aldwinckle, Russel F. 105
Aquinas, Thomas 33, 34, 35, 146fn, 152, 183
Aristotle 146fn, 183
Arminius 59
Athanasius 102, 104
Aubigne, J. H. Merle d' 275
Augustine 33, 56, 104, 144, 271, 312-3
Augustus Caesar 167
Barna, George 238
Baronius, Caesar 158fn
Barr, James 17, 18, 19-20, 21
Barth, Karl 60, 152
Boettner, Lorainne 60
Bonar, Horatius 262
Bonhoeffer, Dietrich 181
Bornkamm, Gunther 23
Bruce, A. B. 105
Bruce, F. F. 285
Bultmann, Rudolf 23, 288
Bunyan, John 180
Buswell, J. Oliver, Jr. 201
Calvin, John 67, 71, 86, 103, 104, 107-8, 113, 135, 141, 145-6fn, 148, 150, 151, 155, 301, 313
Carey, William 180
Carnell, E. J. 35
Carson, D. A. 228
Charles V, Emperor 276, 317
Clark, Gordon 32, 35, 37, 39, 40, 66, 67, 87
Colson, Charles 239
Cyril of Alexandria 107
Dabney, Robert L. 157-8fn
Delitzsch, Franz 41, 42-3
Dickens, Charles 232
Dunn, James D. G. 285
Edwards, Jonathan 180, 271
Eichrodt, Walther 60
Eliot, Jim 320
Fairburn, A. M. 105
Finegan, Jack 284fn
Flacius, Matthias 158fn
Flavel, John 119
Flew, Antony 60
Flint, Robert 112
Ford, Henry 310-1
Freud, S. 183
Gärtringen, F. Hiller von 167fn
Gentilis, Valentinus 103
Gerstner, John H. 60
Godet, F. 105
Gore, Charles 105
Goulder, Michael 289
Gratian 132
Gray, Auld John 337
Greenham, Richard 119, 120
Gregory the Great 144
Grider, J. Kenneth 59
Guinness, Os 180
Hammerstein, Oscar 259
Harris, R. Laird 144fn
Hendricks, William D. 238
Henry, Carl F. H. 169fn
Hodge, A. A. 87
Hodge, Charles 108, 135, 144fn
Horsely, G. H. R. 167fn
John Paul II, Pope 129, 137-8, 153

Jones, Bob, Sr. 310, 311
Jones, H. S. 167fn
Judson, Adonirum 180
Kant, Immanuel 17
Kaufman, Gordon D. 60
Kelly, Thomas 298
Knight, George W. 115-16
Ladd, George Eldon 219fn
Ladin, Usama bin 264
Leo X, Pope 276, 317
Liddell, H. G. 167fn
Lloyd-Jones, Martyn 282
Lombard, Peter 132
Luther, Martin 118, 147, 155, 158fn, 184, 249, 269-80, 301, 313, 317-18
Luther, Paul 274-5
Lynch, William F. 140
MacDonald, Gordon 199
Machen, J. Gresham 261
Mackintosh, H R. 105
Marston, George W. 45fn
Martin, Mary 259
McCheyne, R. M. 123
Melanchthon, Philip 154
Milton, John 241
Minear, Paul 142fn
Moule, Handley 106
Munsey, William Elbert 329
Murray, John 87, 96, 104, 260, 297, 299, 300
Nestorius 107
Neuhaus, Richard John 140
Newton, John 118, 121
Origen 144
Owen, John 116
Packer, J. I. 46, 60, 120, 180
Paul VI, Pope 145
Philips, T. Roland 336-7
Pinnock, Clark 59, 60, 61, 62-3, 64-70, 85, 89, 94, 95, 96, 97
Piper, John 187
Proctor, J. 303
Quick, Oliver 105
Rahner, Karl 60, 289
Ramsay, William M. 284fn
Ratzinger, Joseph 140
Rayburn, Robert S. 12
Russell, Bertrand 287
Ryle, J. C. 153fn
Sander, E. P. 285
Savoy, Duke of 272
Sayers, Dorothy L. 266
Schaeffer, Francis 40
Schaff, Philip 146
Schindler, Oskar 174-5, 334-5
Schleiermacher, Friedrich 140
Scott, R. 167fn
Shakespeare, William 226
Smith, Alfred 204
Spielberg, Steven 174, 334
Spurgeon, C. H. 180
Staupitz, John 272-3
Stob, Henry 88
Stonehouse, Ned B. 221
Strong, A. H. 105
Taylor, Howard 315
Taylor, Hudson 315
Taylor, Vincent 105
Temple, William 27
Tenney, Merrill C. 284fn
Tertullian, 100 144
Tetzel, John 147
Theissen, H. C. 105
Theophylact 135
Thielicke, Helmut 237
Thomasius, G. 105
Tillich, Paul 289

Tolstoy, Leo 287
Toplady, Augustus 261
Toynbee, Arnold 288
Tozer, A. W. 200-1
Urban, Wilbur Marshall 23-4
Van Til, Cornelius 36, 37, 38, 39, 40, 43, 46, 47
Venn, Henry 180
Vos, Geerhardus 72-3, 78, 217, 219
Warfield, Benjamin B. 37, 65, 66, 100-1, 103, 110, 112-13, 217, 219fn, 220-1, 257, 258
Welzien, Bill 283
Wesley, Charles 180
Wesley, John 180
Whitefield, George 180
Wright, N. T. 171fn

Scripture Index

Genesis
1-12 61
1:26 52
4:4-5 187
6–8 297
6:5 70
6:8 73
12 62
12:1-3 73
15:6 153
17:19-21 73
19:24 298
21:9 81
21:12-13 73
25:23 73
45:7-8 73
50:20 73

Exodus
3 19
4:11 26, 74
4:21 74
7:6-13 74
7:13 74
9:12 74
9:16 74, 93
10:1 74
10:20 74
11:10 74
14:4 74
14:8 74
14:17 74
34:24 74

Leviticus
10:1-2 187

Numbers
16-17 187

Deuteronomy
2:30 75
4:37 75
7:6-8 75
8:18 75
9:4-6 75
10:15 75
18:15 312
21:23 305
27:26 295
29:29 40, 42

Joshua
11:19-20 75

Judges
7:22 76
9:23 76
14:4 75

1 Samuel
2:25 75
12:20-22 55
18:10-11 76
19:9-10 76
23:9-13 86

2 Samuel
17:14 75

1 Kings
12:15 76
22:17-35 86

1 Chronicles
26:18 294
29:11-14 72

2 Chronicles
18:20-22 76
20:6 72
25:20 76
26:3-5 199
26:16-19 187
26:16-21 199, 203
33:1-13 253

Ezra
1:1-2 76
7:27 76

Nehemiah
9:6-7 73

Job
11:7-8 40-1
12:7-25 73
25:4 277

Psalms
9:17 298
16:5-6 315
31:15 76
32:1-2 153
33:1 238
39:5 76
58:3 70
65:4 76, 97
83:5-6 81
103:19 71
105:25 74
106:7-8 55
115:3 71, 76
135:6 71, 76
139:16 76
145:3 40-1
145:4 41
149:2 189

Proverbs
3:34 121, 209
16:1 76
16:4 76
16:9 76
16:33 76
19:21 76
20:24 76
21:1 76
21:30-31 76
22:6 69

Isaiah
6 203, 207, 314
6:1 199, 201
6:9-10 79
10:6-7 77
14:24 77
14:27 77
40 201
40:9 165
40:15 78
40:17 78
40:22 78
40:23 78
40:28 40-1
43:7 55
43:21 55
45:7 77
45:22 216
46:10-11 77
48:8-11 55
52:7 165
52:11 125
53:5 208
53:10 298
55:6-7 42
55:8-9 40, 42
57:15 199, 200, 206, 207
61:1-2 166
64:6 97
66:20 135

Jeremiah
2:13 215
13:11 55
13:23 215
17:9 70
19:5 187

Ezekiel
20:9 55
20:14 55
20:22 55
20:44 55
33 204
33:30-33 204
35:5 82
36:16-32 55

Daniel
4:17 77
4:31-32 71, 77-8
4:34-35 78
7:2-14 168

Hosea
13:5 75

Amos
3:2 75
3:6 77
3:7 18

Jonah
2:9 97, 183

Nahum
1:2 296
1:5 296
1:8 296

Habakkuk
1:5-6 77

Malachi
1:2-3 82
4:1 296

Matthew
3:2 168
3:11 208
3:17 218
4:17 168
5:17-18 13
7:18 68, 214
10:29 71
10:30 72
11:25 218, 220, 244
11:25ff 237
11:25-26 79
11:25-27 221
11:25-30 211, 212, 217
11:26 220
11:27 40, 42, 218, 220, 221
11:28 216
12:49-50 138-9
13:21 318
15:9 187
15:13 79
16:17 220
18:7 79
18:20 106
22:14 79
24:12 318
24:36-39 328
24:42-44 328
24:45-51 332
25:14-30 332
25:31ff 335
25:31-46 335
26:24 78
28:18 218
28:18-20 216
28:19 143
28:20 106

Mark
1:1 168
1:11 218
2:10 106
3:34-35 138-9
4:11-12 79
4:39 106
7:6-13 187
10:32 229
10:36-37 231
10:46-52 225
12:28 169
13:32 109
13:33-37 328
14:21 79

Luke
2:48-50 138-9
3:22 218
4:17-21 166
8:21 139
10:1-16 239
10:13-15 244
10:17-20 237
10:19-20 239
10:20 244
10:21 244
10:21-22 212, 217
10:22 40, 42, 221
11:13 70
11:27-28 139
12:47 90
17:1 79
17:10 146fn
22:22 79

John
1:12 142
1:12-13 97
1:18 40, 42
1:33 208
1:47 106
2:3-4 138-9
2:5 138
2:25 106
3:3 214
3:5 214
3:16 28, 142, 253, 255, 266, 293
4:22-24 187
4:29 106
4:41-42 156
5:21 142
6:37-40 265
6:44-45 68, 79, 214
6:45 426:46 40, 42
6:65 68, 79
8:26 29
8:40 29
8:47 156
8:58 106
10:28 142
10:28-29 265
10:30 218
10:35 13
11:11-14 106
11:35 245
12:26 174
12:37-40 79
14:2-3 325
14:6 187, 219fn, 263
14:17 214
14:25-26 13
14:27 142
15:4-5 214
15:11 238
15:16 79
15:19 318
16:12-15 13
17:2 79
17:3 222
17:4 55
17:6 55, 79
17:9 79
17:11-12 79
19:11 79

Acts
1:11 325
2:21 142
2:23 72, 79
4:12 263
4:24-28 80
5:31 142
5:42 142
8:5 142
9:20 142
9:22 142
11:18 97
13:48 80, 97
15:1 127
15:5 127
16:14 80, 97
17:15-34 284
17:26 71
17:30 170
18:5 142

Acts *(cont)*
18:27 80, 97
18:28 142
20:24 234, 289
21:8 164
24:15 329
26:22-23 142
28:23 142
28:31 142

Romans
1:1 124
1:1-5 170
1:16-17 269
1:17 269, 270, 271, 275, 277, 313
1:18ff 288
1:18-32 96
2:16 333
3 296
3-8 80
3:10-18 70, 96, 97
3:23 58, 70, 97, 296
4:1-8 153
5:6 142
5:12 296
5:12-19 90, 93, 96
6:10 130
6:17 97
6:19-20 97
7:12 295
7:14 295
7:14-25 97
7:23 215
7:24 215
8:7 68, 90, 96, 97
8:7-8 214
8:18 92
8:28 52, 71, 241
8:28-29 92
8:28-39 80, 84
8:29 90, 92
8:32 265
9 80-2
9:5 52
9:6 81
9:7-9 81
9:11-13 81
9:13 82
9:16 83, 97
9:17 74, 84, 93
9:17-18 74
9:18 83
9:18-24 79
9:20-23 84
9:21 74
9:23 94
10:13 142
10:13-14 44
10:15 165
11:6 152
11:32 79
11:32-36 92, 95
11:33 40-1
11:36 71
13:13-14 271
13:14 313
14:10b-12 333
14:12 90
15:16 134-5

1 Corinthians
1:19 287
1:20 287
1:21 41, 287
1:23-28 84
1:26-31 124, 183
1:30 84
1:31 97
2:1-5 183
2:2 233, 281, 284
2:6 287
2:7 92
2:8 288
2:11-13 13
2:13 26
2:14 68, 96, 97, 214
3:5-7 183
3:10 100
3:10-15 333
3:15 143-4
8:6 71
9:6 124
10:31 124
12:3 142, 214
15:9 124
15:21-26 323
15:51-57 329
15:58 336

2 Corinthians
4:5 124
4:17 92
4:18 320
5:9-11 333
11:3 153
11:23-33 92fn
12:5 124
12:7-10 92fn
12:9-10 124

Galatians
1:6-7 155
1:6-9 152
1:8-9 129fn, 153
1:10 124
2:12 127
2:16 286
3:10 286, 295
3:10-13 293
3:13 142, 294
3:21 261
4:4 300
4:21-31 81
4:29 81
5.2 155
5:2-6 152
5:4 155
5:11 155
5:19-21 70
5:22 238
6:9 281, 338
6:14 123, 124, 234, 289

Ephesians
1:3-4 95
1:3-14 84
1:6 52, 93
1:10 93
1:11 71
1:12 56, 93
1:14 56, 93
2:1 97
2:1-3 70, 96
2:4-5 265
2:7 93
2:8-9 97, 143
3:8 124
3:11 57, 72, 95
4:11 164
4:11-12 173
4:17-18 96
4:17-19 70, 96
5:2 142
5:29 142

Philippians
1:1 124
1:6 265
1:21 234, 289
1:29 97, 143
2:6-11 93
2:9-11 169
3:7-9 234, 289
3:13-14 234
3:20 331
4:4 238, 245

Colossians
1:15 322
1:18 234, 289
1:28 142
2:20-23 187

1 Thessalonians
1:10 326
2:13 156
2:19 326
3:13 326
4:15-18 331
4:16 326, 331
5:2-3 328
5:4-11 328
5:16 238, 245

C000138335

To/
Mike

with thanks for seeing me off,
and for all the happy times in
the department

Chris

July 1997

The Clinical Psychologist's Handbook of Epilepsy

It is becoming increasingly recognised that epilepsy is no longer the sole domain of the medical profession. In particular, over recent years the contribution made by psychologists to the understanding and treatment of this disorder has developed enormously. *The Clinical Psychologist's Handbook of Epilepsy* addresses those psychological aspects of epilepsy that are important for both assessment and management.

Following a brief introduction to epilepsy, its causes, classification and investigation, the topics addressed in detail by the book include: neuropsychological assessment; memory deficits in epilepsy, their assessment and rehabilitation; the impact of anti-epileptic medication on cognition and behaviour; psychological disturbance associated with epilepsy; behaviour problems in children with epilepsy and the impact of epilepsy in people with learning disabilities.

The book contains contributions from experts in the field and provides a review of the latest research findings. It will be a valuable handbook and a practical guide for all clinical psychologists, and other clinicians, working in, or new to, the field of epilepsy.

Christine Cull is a Clinical Psychologist with the Learning Disabilities Service, Mid Anglia Community Health NHS Trust. **Laura Goldstein** is Senior Lecturer in Neuropsychology at the Institute of Psychiatry and Honorary Consultant Clinical Psychologist for the Neuropsychiatry/Epilepsy Unit, Maudsley Hospital, London. Both have published widely in the field of epilepsy.

The Clinical Psychologist's Handbook of Epilepsy

Assessment and Management

Edited by Christine Cull
and Laura H. Goldstein

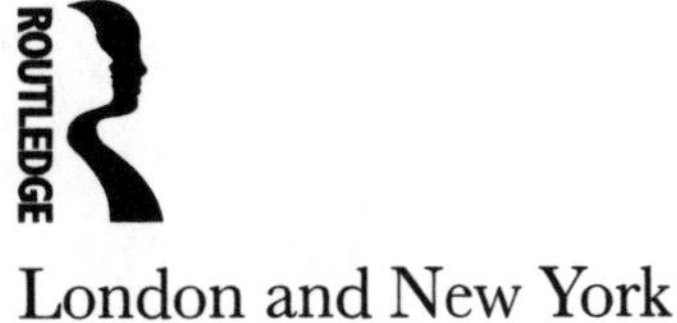

London and New York

First published 1997
by Routledge
11 New Fetter Lane, London EC4P 4EE

Simultaneously published in the USA and Canada
by Routledge
29 West 35th Street, New York, NY 10001

Typeset in Baskerville by Routledge
Printed and bound in Great Britain by Creative Print and Design (Wales), Ebbw Vale

British Library Cataloguing in Publication Data
A catalogue record for this book is available from the British Library

Library of Congress Cataloguing in Publication Data
The clinical psychologist's handbook of epilepsy: assessment and management/edited by Christine Cull and Laura H. Goldstein.
Includes bibliographical references and index.
1. Epilepsy – Psychological aspects. 2. Clinical psychology.
I. Cull, Christine, II. Goldstein, Laura H. (Laura Hilary).
RC372.C55 1997 96–52980
616.8'53 – 21 CIP

ISBN 0–415–13050–6 (hbk)
ISBN 0–415–13051–4 (pbk)

Contents

List of Illustrations viii
Notes on Contributors ix
Preface xiii
Acknowledgements xv

Introduction 1

1 An introduction to epilepsy 4
What is epilepsy? 4
Epidemiology 4
Causes of epilepsy 5
Prognosis 8
Classification of seizure disorders 9
Investigations 12
Treatment 13
Conclusions 16

2 Neuropsychological assessment 18
Memory and temporal lobe lesions 18
Executive functions and frontal lobe lesions 22
Intellectual ability 24
Cognitive deterioration 24
Other factors influencing cognitive performance 25
Practical guide 27
Conclusions 30

3 Epilepsy and memory 35
Memory complaints 35
Risk factors 37
Other memory studies 41
Rehabilitation 44

Memory assessment 45
Intervention 48
Conclusions 49

4 Assessment for surgery 54
Introduction 54
The contribution of neuropsychological assessment 55
Specific surgical interventions and pre- and post-operative neuropsychology 57
Practical guide 67
Psychosocial issues 71

5 The role of anti-epileptic drugs: their impact on cognitive function and behaviour 77
Investigation of drug effects 77
Review of drug effects 82
Conclusions 91
Implications for clinical practice 91

6 Psychological responses to epilepsy: their development, prognosis and treatment 96
Introduction 96
Prevalence of psychological problems in epilepsy 98
The contribution of the clinical psychologist to the management of psychological problems in epilepsy 104
Summary 108

7 Psychological control of seizures 113
The beginnings of a psychological understanding of seizure occurrence 113
Approaches to the psychological management of seizures 115
Non-epileptic seizures 121
Practical guide 124
Conclusions 126

8 Quality of life 130
Introduction 130
Quality of life and the patient with epilepsy 131
Measurement of QoL in patients with epilepsy 134
Summary 143

9 Neuropsychological and cognitive assessment of children with epilepsy 149
Cognitive function of children with epilepsy 149

The multifactorial framework of disability 151
Assessment of children – practical considerations 155
Conclusion 162

10 Assessment and management of behaviour problems in children 167
Neurobiological factors 168
Pharmacological factors 171
Psychosocial factors 173
The multi-aetiological approach 175
Assessment and treatment: clinical considerations 176
Future developments 180

11 Epilepsy and learning disabilities 184
The prevalence of epilepsy in learning disabilities 184
The sequelae of epilepsy in learning disabilities 185
The role of the clinical psychologist in the practical management of people with epilepsy and learning disabilities 192
Conclusion 198

12 The way forward 203
Neuropsychology 203
Psychological interventions 206
Anti-epileptic drugs (AEDs) 208
Quality of life (QoL) 208
Behaviour problems in children 209
Learning disabilities 209
Family issues 210
Conclusions 210

Appendix 213
Neuropsychological, cognitive and developmental tests 213
Contributors' addresses 215

Index 217

Illustrations

FIGURES

4.1 A photomicrograph of the hippocampus to show the subfields CA1, CA2, CA3 and CA4 61
8.1 Global evaluation (Case 1) 139
8.2 Individual profile (Case 1) 140
8.3 Global evaluation (Case 2) 140
8.4 Individual evaluation (Case 2) 141
11.1 A conceptual model of factors influencing learning 186

TABLES

1.1 Drugs currently used to treat epilepsy in the UK 14
3.1 Memory systems 36
4.1 Numbers of surgical procedures carried out before 1985 and between 1986–1990 55
4.2 Pre-operative investigations 56
6.1 Potential multiaetiological risk factors for psychosocial and psychiatric consequences of epilepsy 97
6.2 Assessment of behavioural functioning in people with epilepsy 106
8.1 Contributory factors to impaired QoL in people with epilepsy 131
8.2 Areas of concern identified by patients with epilepsy 134

Contributors

Gus Baker graduated from the University of Liverpool with a Masters Degree in Clinical Psychology in 1988 and completed his PhD in 1992. He is a Clinical Lecturer in Neuropsychology and Health Psychology at the University Department of Neurosciences in Liverpool. Dr Baker is also a Consultant Clinical Neuropsychologist at the Walton Centre for Neurology and Neurosurgery, where he works in a multidisciplinary team providing both clinical and surgical services for people with epilepsy. He has published widely on the psychosocial consequences of living with epilepsy, and is a member of the Outcomes Commission for the International League Against Epilepsy and executive member of the Mersey Region Epilepsy Association.

Christine Cull is a Clinical Psychologist with the Mid Anglia Community Health NHS Trust in the Learning Disabilities Service. She is also an Honorary Senior Lecturer in Clinical Psychology at the Institute of Psychiatry, London. Dr Cull has worked with people with epilepsy in a variety of clinical settings, and currently is particularly interested in the psychosocial sequelae of epilepsy in people with learning disabilities. She has published on a variety of topics, including anti-epileptic drug effects on cognition and behaviour, behaviour problems in children with epilepsy, and seizure self-control.

Colin Espie is Professor of Clinical Psychology in the Department of Psychological Medicine, University of Glasgow, where he is also Course Director of the West of Scotland post-graduate training course in clinical psychology. Current research interests include the assessment and management of sleep disorders in various populations, health issues in people with learning disabilities, and the measurement of outcomes in people with epilepsy. Professor Espie has held numerous research grants and published widely in these areas.

Maria Fowler has worked extensively in the field of epilepsy and behaviour as Principal Educational Psychologist at St Piers Lingfield in Surrey, a school for children and young adults with epilepsy and other special needs. She has specialised in learning disabilities with an interest in developmental and cognitive neuropsychology, and has undertaken research on the effects of anti-epileptic drugs on behaviour. Other interests include rehabilitation in frontal lobe dysfunction, education and subtle seizures, self-control of seizures and cognitive slowing in epilepsy. She has published in all these areas.

Ruth Gillham holds an Honorary Senior Clinical Lectureship at the University of Glasgow. She is also a Consultant Neuropsychologist at the Institute of Neurological Sciences in Glasgow, where she is involved in the assessment and treatment of people with neurological problems. Dr Gillham's research interests and publications in the field of epilepsy include the effect of anti-epileptic drugs on cognition and the psychological management of seizures.

Laura Goldstein is a Senior Lecturer in Neuropsychology at the Institute of Psychiatry in London. She is also an Honorary Consultant Clinical Psychologist at the Bethlem Royal and Maudsley NHS Trust, where she has provided a clinical psychology service to the Neuropsychiatry/Epilepsy Unit for over nine years. Dr Goldstein previously worked in the epilepsy surgery programme at the Maudsley Hospital. Her epilepsy-related research interests include neuropsychological and psychosocial sequelae of epilepsy as well as psychological treatments for people with epilepsy, and she has published in these areas. She is involved in the post-qualification training of clinical psychologists and runs the Diploma in Clinical Neuropsychology course at the Institute of Psychiatry.

Anna Kendrick completed her PhD (*Repertory Grid Technique in the Assessment of Quality of Life*) at the Institute of Neurology, London. Her main research interest has been in the development of an epilepsy-specific measure of quality of life. She has also conducted research on the effects of anticonvulsant medication and nutrition on cognition and mood. She has recently published on the use of repertory grid technique as a model for assessing quality of life. Dr Kendrick is currently employed as an Associate Lecturer with the Open University in Wales, teaching on the post-foundation 'Introduction to Psychology' course.

Susan Oxbury, a Consultant Clinical Psychologist, is head of the Department of Clinical Neuropsychology at the Radcliffe Infirmary,

Oxford. She has developed the neuropsychology service to the Oxford Epilepsy Surgery programme for both adults and children. Her particular interests are temporal lobe surgery and the relationship between hippocampal pathology and neuropsychological function, long-term neuropsychological and psychosocial outcome in children following surgery for epilepsy, and studies of severe amnesia. She has published in all these areas.

Audrey Paul is a Research Psychologist in the Epilepsy Unit of the Western Infirmary, Glasgow. She is currently writing up her PhD on stereotyped behaviours in people with learning disabilities and epilepsy and has recently produced an educational video on epilepsy for use with clients. She was the 1996 winner of the Gowers Prize for young health professionals working in the field of epilepsy.

Pamela Thompson is Head of Psychology and Rehabilitation Services at the National Society for Epilepsy, Honorary Consultant Psychologist at the National Hospital for Neurology and Neurosurgery, and Lecturer in Psychology at the Institute of Neurology, University of London. From 1978, her clinical and research activities has been devoted to psychological aspects of epilepsy. Research work has included memory problems, neuropsychological and psychosocial aspects of surgical treatment and, more recently, family stress. She has also co-written a book for people with epilepsy, their families and carers.

Preface

Epilepsy is a relatively common neurological disorder, which traditionally has been the domain of the medical profession (general practitioners, neurologists, neurosurgeons and psychiatrists). However, it is becoming increasingly clear that other professional groups have a valuable role to play in the assessment and treatment of epilepsy and its psychosocial sequelae. In this particular text we are concerned with one of those professions, namely, clinical psychology.

Clinical psychologists have been working in this field for many years, and from the work carried out to date, it is clear that, as a profession, we can make a major contribution to the understanding of epilepsy, its assessment and treatment. Our aim, therefore, in editing this volume is to bring together current expertise and knowledge in order to provide a readily accessible source of information for psychologists coming to the field for the first time, for those with some experience, and for other interested professionals.

CC
LHG

Acknowledgements

We would like to take this opportunity to acknowledge our debt to Professor Michael Trimble (Institute of Neurology, London) and Dr Peter Fenwick (Institute of Psychiatry, London), who, within our respective careers, have stimulated our interest and influenced our work in the field of epilepsy.

We are also extremely grateful to Gail Millard for her good-natured and efficient processing of numerous modified manuscripts. It is thanks to her that this book is seeing the light of day. Of course, the support and encouragement of our respective husbands (Roger and David) and families has been incalculable.

CC
LHG

Introduction

Clinical psychologists work in a variety of settings where they may encounter individuals with epilepsy (e.g. child guidance clinics, child development clinics, general practice, services for older people and learning disabilities) as well as in child or adult neurology and neurosurgery services. Traditionally, in a clinical setting, psychologists have been asked to carry out assessments of neuropsychological functioning and to repeat assessments over time to evaluate cognitive decline. However, clinical psychologists are increasingly being asked to become involved in the treatment of individuals with epilepsy, in particular those who are thought to display seizures for which there are identifiable psychological factors. They are also becoming involved in the treatment of people with non-epileptic seizures. In addition, in the last twenty years, psychologists have been undertaking epilepsy-related research from an increasingly wide range of perspectives. These have involved the assessment of anti-epileptic drug effects on behaviour and cognition, investigations into the psychosocial sequelae of epilepsy, examinations of the relationship between environment and seizure occurrence, non-medical (i.e. psychological) approaches to seizure management, the assessment of cognitive and psychosocial functioning pre- and post-surgery for epilepsy, and the factors that affect the quality of life of those with epilepsy.

Our aim here is to present a collation of this work, reviewing the available literature to date and highlighting its broad-ranging implications. In this way it is hoped that this text will be of value to researchers and practising clinicians alike.

We start off with those areas which have traditionally been the domain of the clinical psychologist, and about which relatively more is known, notably neuropsychological assessment (Chapter 2); epilepsy and memory (Chapter 3) and assessment related to surgery (Chapter 4).

Chapter 4 considers not only what is known about pre- and post-operative cognitive/neuropsychological procedures, but also what is known about changes in psychosocial functioning and assessment of this. In any assessment, part of the clinician's skill is to evaluate the reliability of their findings, and the extent to which factors other than the critical variable of interest may have a contributing role to play. In this respect, in Chapter 5 we consider one of those factors, the impact of anti-epileptic drugs on cognitive functioning and behaviour. This is also of importance, as claims that AEDs do not have adverse effects on behaviour and cognition are an important marketing strategy for drug developers.

Chapter 6 addresses the relationship between epilepsy and psychological disorders in adults, reviewing the literature and exploring the psychologist's contribution to the assessment/treatment of such disorders.

It is becoming increasingly clear in the literature that seizure occurrences, be they spontaneous epileptic seizures or pseudoseizures (non-epileptic seizures) may be affected by factors in both the person's external and internal environments, and that psychological approaches can be used beneficially in both the assessment and management of such seizures, as can be seen in Chapter 7.

A diagnosis of epilepsy can have a major impact on the individuals themselves – their self-image, their expectations for the future, not to mention their family and friends and, in the broadest sense, on their quality of life. It is only in recent years that this issue has been addressed in relation to epilepsy, and this is the topic of Chapter 8.

Thus far we have concerned ourselves mainly with epilepsy as it affects adults. The next two chapters deal with children. The first is on neuropsychology and cognitive assessment (Chapter 9), as the assessment of children presents a different set of challenges and the need to use different measures to that of adult neuropsychology. Behaviour problems are commonly associated with a diagnosis of epilepsy in childhood, and can be of such severity that residential schooling may seem the only solution to an apparently insurmountable problem. Chapter 10 deals with this issue, focusing on assessment and management, having considered the prevalence and aetiology of such problems.

Epilepsy occurs more commonly in people with learning disabilities than in the normal population, and most frequently in those with severe/profound learning disabilities. Surprisingly, this group has been the focus of very little research interest. In an attempt to redress the balance, research is reviewed in Chapter 11 with respect to the psychological implications of epilepsy for people with learning disabilities, and its contribution to our understanding of epilepsy in people with learning disabilities is highlighted. The practical implications for psychologists working with individuals with both learning disabilities and epilepsy are explored. In Chapter 12 we summarise issues raised in the book and consider future developments. Finally, as several chapters discuss the use of neuropsychological tests, we provide the reader with an Appendix containing names and sources of materials referred to, especially those in Chapters 2, 3, 4 and 9. However, before all of this, we felt that it would be of value to present in Chapter 1 a brief overview of the disorder of epilepsy itself.

We have endeavoured throughout the text to use terminology that is not pejorative or demeaning. For example, we refer to 'people with epilepsy' rather than 'epileptics', since, while the term may be an appropriate description of seizures, it only serves to perpetuate inappropriate stereotypes when applied to people.

Christine Cull
Laura H. Goldstein

Chapter 1

An introduction to epilepsy

Christine Cull and Laura H. Goldstein

WHAT IS EPILEPSY?

Epilepsy is . . .

> a chronic disorder characterised by recurrent seizures
>
> (Gastaut 1973)

and a seizure is . . .

> an occasional, an excessive and a disorderly discharge of nerve tissue
>
> (Hughlings Jackson in Taylor 1958)

that is, an episode of altered behaviour and/or consciousness, which can take many forms, but which results from an abnormal electrical paroxysmal discharge in cerebral neurones. Types of epileptic seizures will be described later in this chapter but, a clinical diagnosis of epilepsy is made if two epileptic seizures occur within a two-year period.

EPIDEMIOLOGY

Epilepsy is a common neurological disorder, occurring in 5:1000 children (Cowan *et al.* 1989) and in 4–7:1000 adults (Hauser and Annegers 1993), such that in the UK it has been estimated that there are approximately 350,000 people with a diagnosis of epilepsy (Brown and Betts 1994). The prevalence of epilepsy is reported to be ten times that of multiple sclerosis and a hundred times that of motor neurone disease (Brown *et al.* 1993).

New cases reported each year are in the region of 20–70 per 100,000 (Hauser and Annegers 1993), the highest rates occurring in infants and young children and in the elderly (Brown *et al.* 1993). The incidence is consistently found to be higher in males than females, although in most studies the difference fails to reach statistical significance (Hauser and Annegers 1993).

CAUSES OF EPILEPSY

Everybody has the potential to have an epileptic seizure. When considering the aetiology of seizures, Lishman (1987) emphasises however that epilepsy must be thought of as a symptom rather than a disease. He also indicates that for many people the cause of the disorder may never be identified. The proportion of cases of unknown aetiology may account for as many as two-thirds of cases (see Lishman 1987). He indicates that the majority of such seizures are generalised (either absence or tonic-clonic) in nature, and that in most cases the presence of a focal component to the seizures will indicate the existence of a discrete structural brain lesion. In addition, an hereditary component is found more commonly for seizures of unknown origin than for seizures that occur in the presence of readily identifiable brain lesions.

Where causes can be identified, they may be varied in nature. Lishman (1987) reviews these causes, and categorises them as seizures due to birth injury or congenital malformations, due to brain damage, infections, cerebrovascular disease, tumours, neurodegenerative disorders, drugs or toxins, or metabolic disorders. Chadwick (1994) distinguishes between acute symptomatic seizures that are the result of some metabolic disorder or cerebral insult, and remote symptomatic seizures that reflect some form of persisting brain damage. Hopkins (1987), on the other hand, considered two main classes of aetiology – predisposing and precipitating factors – and this subdivision will be used here.

Predisposing factors

When considering predisposing factors, it is important to remember that these may not be independent of each other. Thus, a genetic predisposition towards epilepsy may involve either the inheritance of a convulsive threshold, or of a condition associated with epilepsy (see Anderson and Hauser 1993). Lishman (1987) indicates that family loadings seem to be more marked with certain types of seizures, but he cautions that the potential to have an epileptic seizure is present throughout the population, given the right precipitating circumstances.

Developmental brain abnormalities that predispose to seizures may or may not be inherited. Porencephaly, microgyria (and other abnormalities of the cortex), tuberous sclerosis and arteriovenous malformations are other congenital malformations that may be associated with the development of epilepsy. In addition, the person may have acquired structural brain abnormalities that then predispose to epilepsy. With respect to epilepsy arising from birth injury, Lishman (1987) indicates that pregnancy and delivery complications may produce brain damage and lead to epilepsy. Particularly relevant here is damage that produces anoxia or cerebral haemorrhage. Illnesses early in infancy (e.g. cardiorespiratory disorders, infections or metabolic disorders) may also produce seizures. The occurrence of febrile convulsions, possibly with status epilepticus, may give rise to anoxic damage and the formation of scar tissue. This so-called 'mesial temporal sclerosis', which consists of gliosis of mesial temporal lobe structures, is commonly found in patients with temporal lobe epilepsy. Whilst this was initially thought to occur unilaterally in most cases, data revealing the more frequent bilateral presence of abnormality is now appearing (Incisa della Rochetta *et al.* 1995).

In terms of post-traumatic epilepsy, head injury carries a high risk for the subsequent development of seizures. In cases of closed head injury, the underlying neuropathology may include the formation of scar tissue (gliosis) with focal cerebral atrophy. The incidence of epilepsy will be about 5 per cent once the immediately post-traumatic seizures have been excluded (Jennett 1975). Post-traumatic seizures may not appear for several years after injury even though more than half of those going on to develop epilepsy after head injury will do so in the first year post-injury. Where there has been an open head injury, with skull penetration or fracture, there is a much higher incidence of post-traumatic epilepsy (e.g. Russell and Whitty 1952). Post-traumatic seizures may prove difficult to treat, and have important implications for rehabilitation following head injury. Their development must be considered when estimating compensation following head injury.

Certain infections of the central nervous system are likely to be associated with the development of epilepsy. Thus encephalitis or cerebral abscesses are more likely to lead to the development of epilepsy than is meningitis (Lishman 1987). In certain parts of the world, parasitic cysts play an important role. Epilepsy may also develop as a consequence of subtle brain involvement during childhood mumps or whooping cough, although this may be hard to determine in individual cases. In older patients, neurosyphilis should be ruled out as a cause of seizures.

Again, in older patients, cerebral arteriosclerosis and episodes of hypertensive encephalopathy may be important aetiological factors.

Lishman (1987) indicates that a cerebral embolus is more likely to lead to epilepsy than are either a thrombosis or a cerebral haemorrhage; however, any cerebral infarct may provide a focus for the subsequent development of seizures. With ageing, the increased incidence of dementia may also be accompanied by the development of epilepsy, and seizures may occur in 25–33 per cent of cases of Alzheimer's disease and in Huntington's and Creutzfeldt-Jakob disease (see Shorvon 1988). Demyelinating neurodegenerative disorders such as multiple sclerosis may accompany seizure onset in adults, whereas in children degenerative disorders such as tuberous sclerosis may be causative. The development of seizures in a previously healthy adult may reveal the existence of a brain tumour. Sumner (1969) indicated that in 20 per cent of cases of cerebral tumour, the first symptom may be the onset of seizures.

Precipitating factors

A number of factors can be shown to precipitate seizures. Many of these are due to toxic conditions or metabolic disturbances, with an interaction between these. Thus, in addition to alcohol and rapid withdrawal from other drugs, Lishman (1987) notes the wide range of substances that may be associated with seizures. These include barbiturates, amphetamines, ergot alkaloids and steroids, as well as exposure to lead and the chlorinated hydrocarbons found in some pesticides. In addition, certain antipsychotic and antidepressant agents may lower seizure thresholds, thus making them more likely to occur.

A wide range of metabolic causes have been found for seizures. These may include porphyria, and occasionally hypoglycaemia, as well as uraemia, hypernatremia and hypercalcaemia. Electrolyte disturbances, such as those occurring in eclampsia may also be associated with seizure occurrence.

Certain external stimuli may precipitate seizures. Thus, there are accounts of reading, music, flashing lights, TV screens, loud sounds and other such events precipitating seizures (see Chapter 7 for further discussion of so-called reflex epilepsies).

Changes in the sleep–wake cycle have also been shown to precipitate seizures, as has sleep deprivation, and some seizures occur on waking. For seizures which occur in sleep and arise from the frontal lobes, the precipitating factor is the transition between different stages of sleep. Rapid alterations in arousal level in the waking state may also be associated with seizure occurrence (see Chapter 7).

In some women with epilepsy, seizure occurrence is related to the menstrual cycle. So-called catamenial epilepsy, where there is an increase in seizure frequency pre- or perimenstrually in the majority of menstrual cycles, has been shown to occur in anything from 9–72 per cent of women with drug resistant epilepsy (Crawford 1991).

Other precipitating factors may take the form of illnesses and intercurrent infections. The possibility that psychological factors may influence seizure occurrence will be considered in Chapter 7.

Overall in terms of the epidemiology related to aetiology, Sander *et al.* (1990) found that in newly diagnosed patients with seizures, tumours were a rare cause of seizures in people younger than 30 years of age, accounting for only 1 per cent of the sample studied; however in adults between the ages of 50 to 59 years, 19 per cent of cases were attributed to the presence of a tumour. Vascular disease accounted for 49 per cent of cases of epilepsy in elderly individuals. In general, cerebral infection was the cause in 2 per cent of cases and traumatic brain injury was found in 3 per cent of the sample. Alcohol was the most likely single cause of what Chadwick (1994) termed acute symptomatic seizures, accounting for 6 per cent of these, with the highest incidence occurring in adults aged between 30 and 39 years old.

PROGNOSIS

Chadwick (1994) reviewed a number of studies that have considered prognostic indices for seizure remission. Prognostic factors may include age at onset of epilepsy, duration of epilepsy before the onset of treatment, seizure type and aetiology and although Chadwick indicated that none of the studies to date permit adequate quantification of the relative weights that each of these factors may play in overall prognosis, age at onset of seizures seems to be the most important factor, with seizures beginning in the first year of life carrying a poor prognosis. In addition, the absence of early brain damage and the absence of evidence of generalised seizure activity are positive indications of good outcome. The interested reader is referred to his useful paper for more details.

It is important to note that a diagnosis of epilepsy carries with it increased risk of mortality, perhaps some two or three times higher than expected for the general population (Chadwick 1994). The risk is highest in the first year of life, and in individuals with tonic-clonic and frequently occurring seizures. Sudden unexpected death in people with epilepsy is a matter of concern as is accidental death due to drowning, with patients with epilepsy needing to take precautions over bathing and swimming arrangements. Accidents involving falling or burns as a result of seizures are problematic but rarely result in death.

CLASSIFICATION OF SEIZURE DISORDERS

Different classification systems of seizure disorders exist, focusing either on the type of seizure or on the type of epilepsy. One is therefore symptom-based, while the other is disorder-based.

The classification of seizures by the International League Against Epilepsy (ILAE) ignores underlying anatomical features of seizures and does not take into account age and gender in its seizure classification (see Neppe and Tucker 1992). It broadly divides seizures into partial (simple and complex), generalised and unclassified epileptic seizures. For a fuller discussion of seizure classification, see Dreifuss and Henriksen (1992) and Chadwick (1994).

Partial seizures

Partial seizures are subdivided into simple and complex partial seizure types. In simple partial seizures there is no alteration of consciousness. Seizures begin in a localised brain area with the sensations evoked dependent upon the part of the brain that is involved. Simple partial seizures are subdivided into *motor* (any part of the motor cortex can be involved), *somatosensory* (with sensory, somatosensory, gustatory or vertiginous symptoms), *autonomic* (with vomiting, flushing, sweating) and *psychic* (dysphasia, dysmnesia, déjà vu, jamais vu) seizures.

In complex partial seizures, there is a characteristic alteration of consciousness, and the person demonstrates automatic behaviour (automatisms), which takes the form of more or less co-ordinated involuntary activity occurring either during the seizure or immediately after it, and for which the person is usually amnesic. Automatic behaviour may take the form of eating actions (chewing, swallowing), gestures, ambulation and verbal utterances. Complex partial seizures most commonly arise from the mesial temporal lobe structures, although approximately one-third of such seizures have their origin in the frontal lobes. Prior to a complex partial seizure, the person may experience an aura, which is a simple partial seizure and which often serves as a warning of a more serious impending seizure. Auras for seizures arising in the temporal lobes include epigastric auras, described as a feeling that starts in the stomach and which rises up to the throat, feelings of fear, déjà vu and jamais vu. Both simple and complex partial seizures can develop into generalised seizures with the resulting seizures being known as secondary generalised seizures.

Generalised seizures

There are a number of types of generalised seizures. Primary generalised seizures manifest themselves immediately and there is a simultaneous spread of the seizure throughout the cortex.

In *absence seizures* (previously called petit mal), there is an abrupt onset with cessation of ongoing activity and the person may demonstrate a vacant appearance, either with or without an upward movement of the eyes. The attacks may last for up to thirty seconds, with an abrupt end and no postictal confusion. Occasionally, automatisms such as lip-smacking or chewing may occur, causing confusion with complex partial seizures.

Tonic-clonic seizures (previously called grand mal) are rarely preceded by a warning, although there may be a prodromal change in mood in some cases. There is a sudden contraction of muscles with tongue biting, urinary incontinence and absence of breathing, and this is then followed by clonic convulsive movements which are symmetrical, rhythmic, and which decrease in amplitude over time. Seizures will last no more than 2–3 minutes. Following tonic-clonic seizures, the person may remain unconscious for a variable length of time and may then sleep deeply. *Tonic seizures* may occur without the clonic component, and similarly *clonic seizures* may occur on their own.

Myoclonic seizures take the form of single/multiple jerking movements, which may be generalised to the face, trunk or one or more limbs or muscle groups. These contractions occur especially on falling asleep or waking, and occur as part of an idiopathic generalised epilepsy or as part of a mixed seizure disorder such as the Lennox-Gastaut syndrome. They are also seen in Creutzfelt-Jakob disease.

Atonic seizures are characterised by a decrease in muscle tone such that there will be head drop, jaw slackening, and the person will fall to the ground. These are often known as drop attacks but need to be distinguished from drop attacks that occur in narcolepsy/cataplexy.

Of particular concern in individuals with generalised seizures is the development of Lennox-Gastaut syndrome, usually presenting between the ages of one and six years, and which is accompanied by the existence of learning difficulties. It may follow on from infantile spasms (also a form of generalised seizures), but the aetiologies are manifold. The seizure types seen in this disorder may typically include atonic and absence seizures, but they may also be myoclonic in nature. As the person gets older, complex partial and generalised tonic-clonic seizures may become the predominant symptom pattern. Multifocal spikes and spike-wave disturbance are seen on EEGs in individuals with Landau-Kleffner syndrome, which, like Lennox-Gastaut syndrome, presents in childhood and is characterised by acquired aphasia.

A number of types of seizure are unclassified, resulting from insufficient data, and these may include many of the seizure types occurring in infancy. Of particular importance is the need to distinguish epileptic seizures from non-epileptic seizures, especially as both types may occur in the same person. Non-epileptic seizures may take a number of forms (see, for example, Betts and Boden 1992), although disagreement over this exists. There is consensus that such seizures may occur when environmental gains are present (although motivation is likely to be unconscious) and they are frequently triggered by stress. They often look similar, but not identical, to epileptic seizures and seldom result in injury. Diagnosis requires careful post-seizure neurological examinations (checking pupillary and plantar reflexes), the measurement postictally of the hormone prolactin in the blood, and a careful analysis of the function of these attacks in the person's life. Some studies suggest raised incidence of a history of sexual abuse in females with non-epileptic seizures (see Chapter 7).

The occurrence of *status epilepticus* is of particular importance. This refers to continuous seizure activity with no recovery between successive tonic-clonic seizures. As a consequence of the cessation of respiration during the tonic phase of the seizure, the person is at risk of anoxic brain damage and cognitive deterioration (see Chapters 2 and 3). Occasionally, absence status or complex partial status may occur and may also require verification by EEG monitoring (see Treiman 1993 for more details).

In contrast to the ILAE classification of seizures, a classification of epilepsies was approved by the same body in 1970 and revised in 1989. As discussed by Dreifuss and Henriksen (1992), the classification distinguishes primarily between *idiopathic* or *primary epilepsy* (i.e. genetic epilepsy) and *symptomatic* or *secondary epilepsy* resulting from structural or metabolic disorders. In cases of idiopathic epilepsy, there may be a family history of a similar disorder, age at onset of seizures may be young, there will be no structural abnormalities, and the background EEG will be normal.

The term cryptogenic epilepsy is used within this classification to describe secondary epilepsy of unknown cause. Cryptogenic and symptomatic epilepsies are less benign than idiopathic types. Dreifuss and Henriksen (1992) indicate that partial and generalised seizures may fall into either category of idiopathic or symptomatic epilepsies, and describe several examples of these.

INVESTIGATIONS

EEG

The electroencephalogram or EEG, as it is commonly referred to, is a record of cerebral electrical activity measured via electrodes. The standard procedure is a scalp recording, where sixteen to twenty electrodes are placed on the scalp in a standard pattern (or montage) covering both hemispheres and all surface regions of the brain. The activity of the brain is recorded as wave tracing which varies in form, amplitude and frequency, and the EEG provides information about the pattern of activity emanating from each part of the brain. This information can be used to confirm a diagnosis of epilepsy and may contribute to the seizure classification. Recordings of this kind generally take place over a short period of time (less than one hour) during which the subject has to keep quite still, and will rarely coincide with a seizure happening. When there is still doubt about the diagnosis and/or seizure type, recordings during sleep or longer recordings may be preferred, and the latter recordings may involve video-EEG monitoring (telemetry), or ambulatory EEG monitoring.

Telemetry takes place in a controlled environment, where the subject is free to move around with the electrodes in place, but is constantly monitored by a video camera. Thus, behavioural observations can be matched with changes occurring in the EEG. Alternatively, the EEG can be recorded on to a tape in a portable cassette recorder; a smaller number of electrodes are used, which are placed very unobtrusively so that individuals can carry on with their normal daily activities. This ambulatory monitoring allows for much longer periods of recording, although the quality of the information gathered is less detailed.

When surgery is being considered, more invasive recordings may be made, either on the surface of the cortex itself or from deeper structures in the brain (depth recordings), as these will yield more reliable 'noise free' information and permit recording of EEG changes that may not be detectable from routine scalp recordings.

For a more detailed discussion of the EEG, the reader is referred to Binnie (1993).

Brain imaging

In most cases, EEG investigations will be sufficient. However, where an organic aetiology needs to be identified or excluded, or where surgery is being considered, further information will be required. There are a number of methods by which 'images' of the brain, in respect of structure and function, can be obtained.

Both CT (Computerised Tomography) scans and MRI (Magnetic Resonance Imaging) can be used to detect abnormalities of structure – such as tumours, vascular lesions and atrophy – that may be of aetiological significance, although it is generally accepted that MRI is superior in this respect (Polkey and Binnie 1993). In particular, MRI is being used increasingly to examine abnormalities of the hippocampus often found in complex partial seizures arising from mesial temporal lobe structures.

PET (Positron Emission Tomography) and SPECT (Single Photon Emission Computerized Tomography) are used to investigate cerebral function and measure blood flow (PET also measures metabolic rate). Their use includes demonstrating functional abnormalities in affected areas of brain, demonstrating the point from which focal seizures emanate (Polkey and Binnie 1993), and in some instances distinguishing between types of abnormality with similar structural presentations (Kendall 1993).

TREATMENT

It is perhaps worth pointing out that not all epilepsies/seizures will necessarily be treated, for example, if the particular epilepsy syndrome diagnosed is self-limiting, if the seizures are not severe or debilitating, or if the patient does not wish to receive treatment (Richens and Perucca 1993).

Drugs

For those where treatment is indicated, the first approach considered is pharmacological management. The drugs currently in use in the UK are shown in Table 1.1. While some drugs are more effective for particular seizure types than others, and other drugs may be contraindicated in particular types of seizure/epilepsy, the drug–seizure match is actually very limited and, in practice, research suggests that most drugs work for most seizure types. As far as possible, prescribing will be guided by seizure type in the first instance, followed by considerations regarding side effects (Richens and Perucca 1993). Where possible, a single drug will be used, but it may sometimes be necessary to use a second drug if none of the appropriate medications work effectively as a sole treatment. In situations where this is the case, the present trend is towards 'rational polypharmacy' – that is, using two drugs with different modes of action, rather than ones which target the same neurotransmitter system (Brown and Betts 1994). It is now accepted that three drugs are likely to be of little benefit over two (Richens and Perucca 1993). The reader interested in the mechanism of action of anti-epileptic drugs (AEDs), or a more detailed discussion of prescribing habits, is referred to Richens and Perucca (1993).

Although doses of AEDs will be quoted in drug trials and patients' notes, what may be important when judging the effectiveness of AEDs in controlling seizures in an individual case is the blood serum concentration of the drug. This will usually be quoted with reference to a therapeutic range. Whether or not drug serum levels fall in this range may depend upon patients' metabolism, compliance in taking the medication, and the interaction between that AED and other AEDs or other drugs being taken concurrently. Occasionally, serum levels will be too high and the patients will become 'toxic', demonstrating a wide range of side effects specific to the AED. A reduction in drug dose should reverse such symptoms, which may well include cognitive impairment and double vision.

Table 1.1 Drugs currently used to treat epilepsy in the UK

	Generic name	*Trade name*
Licensed for monotherapy use	Phenobarbitone	Gardenal
	Primidone	Mysoline
	Phenytoin	Epanutin
	*Carbamazepine	Tegretol
	*Sodium Valproate	Epilim
	Ethosuximide	Zarontin
	Clonazepam	Rivotril
	Lamotrigine	Lamictal
Licensed for add on use only	Vigabatrin	Sabril
	Gabapentin	Neurontin
	Topiramate	Topamax
	Clobazam	Frisium

* Also available in slow-release preparations.

In any one individual, serum drug levels are known to vary throughout the day when the AED is taken in a divided dose regimen. Thus, drug levels will be at their highest (or peak) value soon after drug ingestion, and at their lowest (or trough) level just before the next dose is due. The introduction of controlled release preparations, necessitating only a single dose per day, minimises the degree of variation in serum drug levels.

For some patients, adverse effects of AEDs (e.g. skin rashes with carbamazepine, low sodium levels) may precipitate drug changes in the same way as might poor seizure control. Clinical experience indicates that patients' seizure control may often initially improve following admission to hospital because medication is taken more regularly than at home, and stress levels may be lower.

The effectiveness of AEDs has improved over the years and new drugs are being developed all the time; however, seizure control is obtained in only approximately 80 per cent of those people being treated for epilepsy (Richens and Perucca 1993), leaving the remainder who continue to display refractory seizures despite optimal drug treatment, some 7,000 new patients each year (Brown and Betts 1994).

For those patients who continue to have seizures, there are two alternatives to be considered. The more conventional consideration is surgery, while a newer alternative being explored is the area of psychological approaches to the treatment of seizures. This is discussed in detail in Chapter 7.

Surgery

As mentioned, surgery may be an option for some patients with intractable seizures which are drug resistant. The aim of surgery is to control the seizures by removing the area of pathology and surrounding tissue (resective surgery). This may involve sections of the temporal lobes, or (less commonly) the frontal lobes, or may necessitate a full lobectomy. The alternative is to limit the impact of the seizures by altering the function of the brain in some way (functional surgery) – for example, by removing a whole hemisphere, or by cutting the links (or part of the links) between the two hemispheres, i.e. the corpus callosum (callosotomy).

The careful selection of patients for surgery means that outcome for surgery is improving, but it is not without its drawbacks that may occur in some patients, such as short-term or lasting neurological complications, cognitive deterioration, and behavioural deterioration. Furthermore, in some patients, seizures may continue unchanged.

Success rates vary, depending in part on the type of surgery undertaken. Thus, approximately 40 per cent of patients may be seizure-free after temporal lobe resection, and approximately 60 per cent of patients will experience at least a 50 per cent reduction in seizure frequency following callosotomy. For a fuller discussion of surgical procedures and outcome, the reader is referred to Polkey and Binnie (1993).

Despite the improving success rates of surgery, it is clear that it is not a successful procedure in a substantial minority of patients, and further, there is another group of people for whom surgery is not a viable option. Again, psychological approaches to seizure management may be appropriate for these people (see Chapter 7).

CONCLUSIONS

The broad-ranging impact of epilepsy in terms of its aetiology, investigation, treatment and effect on daily life indicates the potential scope of involvement for clinical psychologists. These issues will be dealt with in greater detail in the following chapters.

REFERENCES

Anderson, V. E. and Hauser, W. A. (1993) 'Genetics', in J. Laidlaw, A. Richens and D. Chadwick (eds) *A Textbook of Epilepsy* (4th edn), Edinburgh: Churchill Livingstone.

Betts, T. and Boden, S. (1992) 'Diagnosis, management and prognosis of a group of 128 patients with non-epileptic attack disorder: Part 1', *Seizure* 1: 19–26.

Binnie, C. D. (1993) 'Electroencephalography', in J. Laidlaw, A. Richens and D. Chadwick (eds) *A Textbook of Epilepsy* (4th edn), Edinburgh: Churchill Livingstone.

Brown, S. and Betts, T. (1994) 'Epilepsy – a time for change?', *Seizure* 3: 5–11.

Brown, S., Betts, T., Chadwick, D., Hall, B., Shorvon, S. and Wallace, S. (1993) 'An epilepsy needs document', *Seizure* 2: 91–103.

Chadwick, D. (1994) 'Epilepsy', *Journal of Neurology, Neurosurgery and Psychiatry* 57: 264–77.

Cowan, L. D., Bodensteinder, J. B., Leviton, A. and Doherty, L. (1989) 'Prevalence of the epilepsies in children and adolescents', *Epilepsia* 30: 94–106.

Crawford, P. (1991) 'Catamenial seizures', in M. R. Trimble (ed.) *Women and Epilepsy*, Chichester: Wiley.

Dreifuss, F. E. and Henriksen, O. (1992) 'Classification of epileptic seizures and the epilepsies', *Acta Neurologica Scandinavica* 86 (Suppl. 140): 8–17.

Gastaut, H. (1973) *Dictionary of Epilepsy*, World Health Organisation: Geneva.

Hauser, W. A. and Annegers, J. F. (1993) 'Epidemiology of epilepsy', in J. Laidlaw, A. Richens and D. Chadwick (eds) *A Textbook of Epilepsy*, Edinburgh: Churchill Livingstone.

Hopkins, A. (1987) 'The causes and precipitations of seizures', in A. Hopkins (ed.) *Epilepsy*, London: Chapman and Hall.

Incisa della Rochetta, A., Gadian, D. G., Connelly, A., Polkey, C. E., Jackson, G. D., Watkins, K. E., Johnson, C. L., Mishkin, M. and Vargha-Khadem, F. (1995) 'Verbal memory impairment after right temporal lobe surgery: Role of contralateral damage as revealed by 1H magnetic resonance spectroscopy and T2 relaxometry', *Neurology* 45: 797–802.

Jennett, B. (1975) *Epilepsy After Non-missile Head Injuries* (2nd edn), London: Heinemann.

Kendall, B. (1993) 'Neuroradiology', in J. Laidlaw, A. Richens and D. Chadwick (eds) *A Textbook of Epilepsy* (4th edn), Edinburgh: Churchill Livingstone.

Lishman, W. A. (1987) *Organic Psychiatry* (2nd edn), Oxford: Blackwell Scientific Publications.

Neppe, V. M. and Tucker, G. J. (1992) 'Neuropsychiatric aspects of seizure disorders', in S. C. Yudofsky and R. E. Hales (eds) *The American Psychiatric Press Textbook of Neuropsychiatry* (2nd edn), Washington: American Psychiatric Press.

Polkey, C. E. and Binnie, C. D. (1993) 'Neurosurgical treatment of epilepsy', in J. Laidlaw, A. Richens and D. Chadwick (eds) *A Textbook of Epilepsy* (4th edn), Edinburgh: Churchill Livingstone.

Richens, A. and Perucca, E. (1993) 'Clinical pharmacology and medical treatment', in J. Laidlaw, A. Richens and D. Chadwick (eds) *A Textbook of Epilepsy* (4th edn), Edinburgh: Churchill Livingstone.

Russell, W. R. and Whitty, C. W. M. (1952) 'Studies in traumatic epilepsy. 1: Factors influencing the incidence of epilepsy after brain wounds', *Journal of Neurology, Neurosurgery and Psychiatry* 15: 93–8.

Sander, J. W. A., Hart, Y. M., Johnson, A. L. and Shorvon, S. (1990) 'Newly diagnosed epileptic seizures in a general population', *Lancet* 336: 1267–71.

Shorvon, S. D. (1988) 'Late onset seizures and dementia: a review of epidemiology and aetiology', in M. R. Trimble and E. H. Reynolds (eds) *Epilepsy, Behaviour and Cognitive Function*, Chichester: Wiley.

Sumner, D. (1969) 'The diagnosis of intracranial tumours', *British Journal of Hospital Medicine* 2: 489–94.

Taylor, J. (ed.) (1958) *Selected Writings of John Hughlings Jackson, Vol. 1: On Epilepsy and Epileptiform Convulsions*, New York, Basic Books.

Treiman, D. M. (1993) 'Status epilepticus', in J. Laidlaw, A. Richens and D. Chadwick (eds) *A Textbook of Epilepsy* (4th edn), Edinburgh: Churchill Livingstone.

Chapter 2

Neuropsychological assessment

Laura H. Goldstein

The rich literature dealing with different aspects of neuropsychological assessment in epilepsy stems particularly from the need to evaluate patients carefully prior to neurosurgical treatment of their seizures (see Chapter 4). For patients not being considered for neurosurgery, a neuropsychological assessment of a patient with epilepsy is most likely to focus on the delineation of the person's intellectual strengths and weaknesses, with respect to a particular brain lesion, possibly evaluating potential cognitive deterioration (Goldstein 1991). The need may remain, in the absence of good neuroimaging data, to corroborate evidence gained from electroencephalograms (EEGs) with neuropsychological data to predict the location of an epileptic focus. The difficulties in making such predictions will be discussed below. In addition, the factors that may affect neuropsychological performance will be discussed, and suggestions will be made for developing a testing protocol.

MEMORY AND TEMPORAL LOBE LESIONS

Whilst a detailed account of the memory impairments to be found in patients with epilepsy is provided in Chapter 3, the current discussion will outline the limitations in trying to identify the lateralisation of an epileptic focus on the basis of memory impairments.

The literature on memory deficits in individuals with complex partial seizures arising from mesial temporal lobe structures, previously classified as temporal lobe epilepsy (TLE) has parallels with data from neurosurgically treated individuals who have had varying but unilateral excisions of mesial temporal lobe structures. Summaries of surgical outcomes suggest that after unilateral left and right temporal lobectomy there is decreased ability to learn and recall verbal and visuospatial material respectively (e.g. Jones-Gotman 1987). However, this situation is not always replicable in patients with TLE, and a number of studies have failed to find between-groups material-specific deficits dependent upon the side of epileptic focus (Goldstein 1991). Reasons for such failures may have included the difficulty in preventing the verbalisation of visuospatial material (Berent *et al.* 1980) or having used too simple test materials (Loiseau *et al.* 1983). Many studies use subject groups being evaluated for surgery and the exclusion of patients with well-controlled seizures may also have affected results.

More recently, Lee *et al.* (1989) noted that the Verbal and Visual Memory Indices of the Wechsler Memory Scale-Revised (WMS-R) do not differentiate right- from left-TLE patients, and that Visual Paired Associates of the WMS-R do not discriminate between patients with lateralised brain lesions (Chelune and Bornstein 1988). Further, they found that some visuospatial tests (delayed recall of the Rey-Osterreith complex figure and Form Sequence Learning, involving recognition of a series of unfamiliar geometric shapes from an array containing the target and distracter designs) were not very sensitive to the effects of right temporal lobe (TL) damage. The use of complex, unfamiliar, difficult-to-verbalise visuospatial test materials is advocated when attempting to elicit right TL effects.

Loring *et al.* (1989) also criticised the Verbal-Visual Index discrepancy of the WMS-R in that it incorrectly predicted the laterality of a previous temporal lobectomy in an unsatisfactorily high number of cases. Accuracy for left temporal lobectomy cases was higher than for right-sided ones. This may result from the verbalisable nature of the Visual Paired Associates stimuli.

Loring *et al.* (1988) attempted to predict side of onset of seizures in temporal lobectomy candidates, using tests reported by Lee *et al.* (1989). Accurate predictions of laterality of focus were more likely to be achieved when there were consistent dissociations between performance on verbal and visuospatial tasks for all the measures of material specific learning, rather than for single measures. Thus, a comprehensive battery must be employed if lesion lateralisation is to be attempted with any reliable chance of success. In a similarly cautionary manner, Williamson *et al.* (1993) reported that neuropsychological assessment yielded predictions of lateralisation that were in agreement with the side of seizure origin in only 73 per cent of cases. When testing produced discordant or non-lateralising results, patients tended to have right TL foci. The greater accuracy in predicting left-sided foci was attributed to the strong verbal (i.e. left hemisphere) nature of most assessments.

A substantial number of studies, however, do provide evidence of material specific deficits in lateralised TLE. Often delayed recall memory tasks reveal between-groups differences where immediate recall measures do not (see Goldstein 1991), although immediate, as well as delayed, recall and per cent retention of the Logical Memory passages from the old Wechsler Memory Scale (WMS) were found to be impaired in patients with left- as opposed to right-TL seizure foci (Sass *et al.* 1992a). Saling *et al.* (1993) found that patients with left rather than right hippocampal sclerosis (HS) were particularly impaired on learning the hard pairs of the Paired Associate Learning Test; the right-sided group scored essentially within normal limits. No between-groups differences were found on immediate or delayed recall of the Logical Memory passages.

In several studies, the Selective Reminding Test (SRT: Buschke 1973) has yielded promising results. Westerveld *et al.* (1994) recommended its use for identifying patients with dominant TLE, as they are reported to perform more poorly than patients with right TLE (Sass *et al.* 1990; Ribbler and Rausch 1990). Similarly Lee *et al.* (1989) found that verbal learning measures (SRT, supra-span learning) were sensitive to the effects of left-sided pathology.

Despite difficulties in designing adequate testing materials, visuospatial memory deficits have been detected in right-TLE patients. Helmstaedter *et al.* (1991) employed a visual design learning test, wherein nine 5-line hard-to-name designs had to be reconstructed using wooden sticks, within six learning trials. Patients with right- or bilateral-TL foci showed poorer immediate recall and learning capacity than left-TLE individuals. Sass *et al.* (1992a) found that patients with right TLE were impaired relative to left-TLE subjects on the immediate recall of the WMS Visual Reproduction subtest, although between-groups differences were not found on delayed or per cent retained measures.

Recognition memory in patients with TLE has also been examined. Seidenberg *et al.* (1993) focused on the types of recognition errors made on the California Verbal Learning Test (CVLT). Unoperated TLE patients with left-sided focus were less able than right-sided patients to discriminate target words from distracters, they had a positive response bias and made more false positive errors. Ellis *et al.* (1991) found that TLE subjects did not differ from controls in their ability to recognise words using the Recognition Memory Test, whereas right- and left-sided TLE patients were impaired relative to controls (but not to each other) on the face recognition subtest. Right-sided TLE patients were impaired at recognising familiar faces; the left-sided group had difficulty naming them.

Although it is not usually good practice to undertake a neuropsychological assessment shortly after a patient has suffered a seizure, this may assist in the identification of the side of focus. Andrewes *et al.* (1990) tested verbal and visuospatial recognition memory in patients with left or right TLE. Interictal measures (obtained at least twenty-four hours after a seizure) failed to show between-groups differences, whereas in eight patients subsequently tested within one hour of a seizure, seven showed a pattern of deficits that would be expected on the basis of the side of lesion.

Language functions and the temporal lobes

Mayeux *et al.* (1980) had suggested that what some patients report as memory impairments may in fact be word-finding difficulties. They compared small groups of patients with left or right TLE or generalised seizures on the WAIS, the WMS, the Benton Visual Retention Test, the Rey-Osterreith figure, the Boston Naming Test (BNT) and the Controlled Oral Word Association test. Whilst the groups did not differ on the memory measures, the left-TLE group was weak in terms of confrontation naming. Several measures of memory and intelligence were found to be highly correlated with naming ability.

In addition, Mungas *et al.* (1985) reported that left-TLE patients were impaired on phonemic-cued recall, and hypothesised that linguistic deficits might affect verbal memory performance in left TLE. Ellis *et al.* (1991) found that left-TLE patients were impaired relative to right-TLE and control subjects on the National Adult Reading Test and that although both patient groups were impaired on the Graded Naming Test, the left-TLE group was more impaired than the right-sided group. On the Test of Reception of Grammar (TROG), both patient groups were impaired relative to controls, with a trend for greater impairment to be seen in the left-TLE group.

Sass *et al.* (1992b) reported an impairment on the BNT and slightly lower Verbal IQs in left-TLE individuals. Immediate and delayed recall on the Logical Memory passages correlated with BNT scores for the left-TLE subjects but not for the right-sided group. Hermann *et al.* (1988a) examined patients with dominant lobe TLE; performance on the CVLT was generally predicted by scores on the BNT and verbal fluency. Aural and reading comprehension also influenced CVLT scores.

In a further study by Hermann *et al.* (1992), left-TLE patients scored significantly lower than right-TLE patients on visual naming, sentence repetition, reading and aural comprehension and on the Token Test, but not on verbal fluency and spelling, although the findings were in the same direction. Poorer performance on visual naming was associated with poorer memory in both TLE groups.

It is important to distinguish between those memory tests that are and are not correlated with performance on language tests. Saling *et al.* (1995) noted that unrelated paired associates and the post-interference trial of the Rey Auditory Verbal Learning Task do not correlate with results of language assessment; these tests may differentiate better between patients with left and right HS than those that correlate with language skills.

Hermann *et al.* (1988b, 1992) suggested that while naming ability does seem to influence performance on verbal memory measures, anomia is unlikely to account for poor memory ability. Rather, they suggested that underlying both impairments is a general retrieval difficulty. They concluded that there is a distribution of language competence across right- and left-TLE groups, with the left-TLE group overall doing worse, but that the effects of the variability in language competence (particularly visual naming) in the two groups are similar in terms of the consequences for memory functions.

EXECUTIVE FUNCTIONS AND FRONTAL LOBE LESIONS

Considerably less has been written about executive functions and their disruption by frontal lobe epileptic foci.

Corcoran and Upton (1993) compared performance on tests of verbal fluency and on the Stroop Test between patients with frontal epileptic (FE) foci or TL foci, or who had HS. Impairments on both of these tests were expected in the FE group. A significantly poorer performance was found for the word fluency measures (but only in comparison to the HS group – the frontal and temporal groups performed equivalently) with the left-frontal patients producing fewer words than the right-frontal patients. There was only a non-significant trend for the FE group to be less efficient on the Stroop test, with a further non-significant trend for the left-frontal patients to have longer interference condition response times.

More has been written about the Wisconsin Card Sorting Test

(WCST). This test has traditionally been considered sensitive to damage to dorsolateral prefrontal and orbitofrontal cortex. Studies have also shown this test to reflect the presence of TLE. Thus Hermann *et al.* (1988a) reported that 74 per cent of the non-dominant TLE patients and 39 per cent of the patients with dominant TLE foci performed on the test in a manner that would usually be characterised as 'frontal'. High numbers of WCST perseverative errors by TLE patients (irrespective of lateralisation of focus) were reported by Horner *et al.* (1996).

Corcoran and Upton (1993), using Nelson's modification of the WCST, found their patients with HS took longer than the other groups to complete the task, and made more perseverative and category errors than the temporal and frontal groups, and temporal group alone respectively. The HS group also completed fewer categories than the temporal but not the frontal groups. Seventy-five per cent of the HS cases were classified as performing in a 'frontal' manner, making at least 50 per cent perseverative errors. Right-sided HS was associated with more category errors and a longer task completion time than left-sided HS. Corcoran and Upton attributed the poor performance of the HS patients to the working memory component of the WCST, and the poor classification of the FE group's performance as 'frontal' to the mixed location of their foci within the frontal lobes.

Factors affecting WCST performance in TLE patients have also been noted to include side of focus, age at onset of epilepsy (Strauss *et al.* 1993) and mood (Seidenberg *et al.* 1995).

It has also been demonstrated that word fluency, the number of questions (total and pseudo-constrained) asked in the Twenty Questions test, Stroop test interference time, bimanual gestures, motor sequencing and performance on the Trail Making Test are sensitive to left FE, while cost estimation, Porteus Maze completion time, the number of category errors made on the modified WCST, and in an increased number of errors on Part B of the Trail Making Test are more sensitive to right FE (Upton and Thompson 1996).

The assessment of cognitive deficits of patients with FE is, therefore, problematic. Some of this difficulty may result from variable lesion location within the frontal lobes and from the recognition that seizure activity may generalise rapidly from one frontal lobe to the other, so that an epileptic focus in one hemisphere may produce dysfunction in the other. In addition, the similarity in performance between patients with FE and TLE may be explained by the connections between the temporal and frontal regions and by the fact that temporal lobe seizures may spread via the frontal regions, producing dysfunction of these areas. Clinicians must therefore be cautious in using so called 'frontal-lobe' tests when trying to localise an epileptic focus (Corcoran and Upton 1993).

INTELLECTUAL ABILITY

In relatively unselected patients with epilepsy, IQ is generally found to be within or just below the average range, unless it is known that more widespread brain damage exists. Data on IQ is rather confounded in many studies where the samples are being worked-up for temporal lobectomy (see Chapter 4).

Some attention has been paid as to whether the discrepancy between Verbal and Performance IQ is particularly informative in cases of epilepsy (e.g. Ossetin 1988). Brain damage, medication or subclinical epileptic activity (see below) may slow response on timed tests, and may thereby reduce Performance IQ measures. An early age at onset of epilepsy may well result in disrupted schooling, and consequently in lowered Verbal IQ. A tendency towards lower Verbal IQ with left TLE and towards lowered Performance IQ with right TLE may nonetheless be found (Goldstein and Polkey 1993). IQ measures may however be more useful as background measures of functioning than for predicting the localisation of an epileptic focus.

COGNITIVE DETERIORATION

Assessments may be undertaken to evaluate the presence or otherwise of cognitive decline. Whilst this is not necessarily found (Selwa *et al.* 1994), Brown and Vaughan (1988) have described an 'epileptic dementia'. They suggested that in a highly selective group of patients with severe epilepsy, males may be at a higher risk than females of showing significant cognitive deterioration. This may be a 'fronto-temporal' type decline in cognitive abilities, particularly involving the left cerebral hemisphere. Specific neuropathological conditions may also underlie cognitive decline in epilepsy (e.g. Lafora Body disease, progressive myoclonic epilepsy or Rasmussen's encephalitis – see Dreifuss 1992), as may *status epilepticus* (see below). Judicious use of test psychometric properties must be used in evaluating true cognitive decline in the context of the person's medical history.

OTHER FACTORS INFLUENCING COGNITIVE PERFORMANCE

Mood and age at onset of epilepsy can influence neuropsychological profiles, as can a number of other factors although together these may not have enormous predictive value (Hermann *et al.* 1988a; Strauss *et al.* 1995).

Neuropathology

Understanding the impact that differing types of neuropathology can have on test performance may help the interpretation of patients' otherwise confusing test profiles. Thus, for example, the presence of HS has been shown to be associated with a history of febrile convulsions, an earlier onset of regular seizures and with poorer IQ levels when compared with tumour-like malformations or non-specific pathology in patients undergoing temporal lobectomy (McMillan *et al.* 1987). In addition, whereas individuals with right- or left-sided HS did not show any between-groups differences on limited measures of verbal or visuospatial memory (see also Saling *et al.* 1993), patients with left-sided tumour-like malformations displayed performance consistent with the side of the pathology. Thus, patients who suffered febrile convulsions as children and later developed TLE may have intellectual deficits as adults. Oxbury (see Chapter 4) considers in greater detail studies of memory impairment in adults with unilateral HS. It is difficult to separate out the longer history of seizures and the presence of HS when trying to identify the cause of the cognitive deficits, but for individuals with a longer history of intractable epilepsy and possibly increased severity of brain damage, there may be less opportunity for functional reorganisation (Goldstein 1991).

Seizure-related variables

Generalised seizures have been associated with greater cognitive impairment than partial seizures (e.g. Giordani *et al.* 1985), and multiple seizure types are more detrimental than single seizure types (Seidenberg *et al.* 1986). Aldenkamp *et al.* (1992), using computerised assessments found that patients with generalised seizure activity were impaired on tests of language, whereas patients with partial epilepsy or whose seizure classification was unclear were most impaired in terms of response speed. A lifetime total of more than 100 tonic-clonic seizures or a single lifetime episode of *status epilepticus* has been associated with a lowering in IQ and other cognitive functions (Dodrill 1986).

In terms of seizure frequency, Dikmen and Matthews (1977) indicated that high frequency of partial seizures was associated with poorer performance on a range of measures from the Halstead Reitan battery and the WAIS. At worst risk for poor performance were individuals with a long history of seizures; early age at seizure onset has generally been found to be associated with weaker cognitive abilities (see Dodrill 1992; McMillan *et al.* 1987; Strauss *et al.* 1995, but see also Chapter 3). It is important to note, however, that even at the time of the first few seizures, prior to the commencement of treatment, memory and sustained attention may be compromised (Kälviäinen *et al.* 1992). Both in groups and individual cases, a reduction in seizure frequency is accompanied by an improvement in cognitive performance (Seidenberg *et al* 1981; Goldstein *et al.* 1992) Over a prolonged period of retesting, there is no clear evidence that patients with TLE will necessarily show a deterioration in cognitive functioning (Selwa *et al.* 1994).

Neuropsychological assessment results may also be affected by the presence of interictal discharges. When these can be shown to affect cognitive processes, this is known as Transitory Cognitive Impairment (TCI). The demonstration of TCI depends upon the type of neuropsychological task employed and on the nature of the discharges. Binnie and Marston (1992) report that in most studies concerned with this phenomenon, about 50 per cent of patients with frequent subclinical discharges were found to demonstrate TCI (cf. Aldenkamp *et al.* 1992). This is more likely to be seen with demanding tasks that test the patient at the level of their ability and may include choice reaction time, signal detection, information processing, short-term memory and memory span tasks (ibid.). In addition, generalised 3 Hz spike-and-wave discharges of at least three seconds duration are most likely to lead to detectable TCI.

TCI is most likely to occur when the discharges are present during or possibly just before the stimulus presentation (Binnie and Marston 1992, but see Provinciali, *et al.* 1991). Binnie (1988) and Kasteleijn-Nolst Trenité *et al.* (1990) have demonstrated a significant association between the localisation of discharges (e.g. right versus left TL) and the material specificity of the impairment (visuospatial versus verbal). TCI is of relevance during neuropsychological assessment since the pattern of deficits elicited may not be 'permanent' and may be amenable to pharmacological treatment (Binnie and Marston 1992). A range of abilities such as speed and accuracy of reading and mental arithmetic (Kasteleijn-Nolst

Trenité *et al.* 1988), performance on subtests of children's intelligence tests (Sieblink *et al.* 1988) and even driving (Binnie 1993) have been shown to be affected by subclinical discharges.

Therefore, test interpretation may be affected by TCI. However, the practical difficulties of trying to evaluate such a phenomenon in routine clinical practice via simultaneous video and EEG recording, and then analysis of EEG traces corresponding to testing phases, will generally rule out such purity of test interpretation. Careful observation of the patient during testing, in particular for lapses in performance, may at least help with the identification of previously undetected minor seizures.

It is also conceivable that some cognitive tasks, in selected individuals, will induce epileptic activity. These 'secondary psychogenic seizures' (Fenwick and Brown 1989) are discussed in Chapter 7, but include examples of arithmetic-induced seizures as well as reading epilepsy. Finally, not only may epileptic activity affect neuropsychological performance, but the converse may also be true (e.g. Boniface *et al.* 1994).

Other variables

Strauss *et al.* (1995), in a multicentre study, found that Full Scale IQ was 1.35 times higher in patients with extratemporal as opposed to temporal lobe disturbance. Patients with left-sided seizures were 1.6 times more likely to be intellectually impaired than those with right-sided seizures. Atypical speech representation was also associated with decreased performance.

PRACTICAL GUIDE

In interpreting test results, one needs to take into account the patient's mood, underlying neuropathology and seizure related variables as discussed above. In addition, it is important to consider the patient's anti-convulsant medication as discussed in Chapter 5, as well as the psychometric properties of the tests and their sensitivity to change. The absence of adequate norms for people with learning difficulties may impede this process.

The purpose of the assessment will be important in determining the components to be included. An initial assessment after a new diagnosis of epilepsy will establish a baseline against which any future assessments can be compared. Thus, it should assess a wide range of cognitive abilities. All assessments should be informed by the results of investigations such as EEGs and neuroimaging, to determine whether the cognitive profile is consistent with what is known about the patient's epilepsy. Qualitative as well as quantitative interpretations of performance will be needed (Goldstein 1991).

All assessments should include a general measure of intelligence in addition to specific tests of cognitive functioning.

In terms of memory assessment, measures of recognition, recall and learning (where possible of verbal and visuospatial material) should be included. However, local norms are needed in order to be confident about identifying deficits. Comparison of performance across tests may be problematic because of the incomparability of normative samples. This is relevant, for example, when comparing scores on the WAIS-R and WMS-R (Atkinson 1991) and between other memory tests such as the WMS-R and the CVLT (Randolf *et al.* 1994). Without taking such differences into account, inconsistencies in deficient performance may be obtained. While the list learning task from the Adult Memory and Information Processing Battery does not include the recognition components of the CVLT, British norms have been collected. Its ability to distinguish between the effects of right and left TLE remains to be investigated. The SRT offers promise, although non-American norms may not be widely available. A new test of recognition memory, the Doors and People Test may be valuable for patients with lateralised TLE, on the basis of post-lobectomy data (Morris *et al.* 1995). The Rivermead Behavioural Memory Test is not sufficiently sensitive to lateralised memory deficits due to epilepsy (Goldstein and Polkey 1992a), but includes useful measures of prospective memory.

It is important to include measures of language, such as reading, naming, fluency and comprehension. Newer tests such as the Speed and Capacity of Language Processing require evaluation in patients with epilepsy. Measures of attention, and in particular the more ecologically valid Test of Everyday Attention may also have a role to play. Executive dysfunction assessment might include the tests discussed earlier and the Behavioural Assessment of Dysexecutive Syndrome.

Evaluation of mood (anxiety, depression) is also important in this context, particularly because of the high association between anxiety, depression and epilepsy. Mood questionnaires (e.g. the Hospital Anxiety and Depression Scale, Zigmond and Snaith 1983) should be selected that do not contain too many items that refer to physical symptoms that could be due directly to epilepsy.

One increasingly available option for neuropsychological assessments is the use of computerised test batteries. These offer the advantages of precise timing of stimulus presentation and response, improved scoring and the possibility of an increased range of scores, although the qualitative data from an interactive assessment is lost (Thompson 1991), as is scope for being able to break down instructions or 'test the limits' of ability. Many batteries do not yet have sufficient reliability and validity data. Thompson (1991) regards computerised neuropsychological assessment as extending the range of assessment techniques rather than replacing traditional methods. A particularly useful application has been for the detection of TCI, where simultaneous assessment and EEG/video recording can make possible the precise determination of the effect of discharges on cognition (see also Rugland *et al.* 1991).

A computerised battery widely used in Europe for patients with epilepsy is FePSY (e.g. Alpherts and Aldenkamp 1990). This includes simple and choice reaction time tests, rhythm discrimination, finger tapping, a visual search task, measures of vigilance, a WCST-like test, spatial and verbal memory tests and split visual field tasks. Increasingly, good normative data are becoming available, although none are yet available for the effects of lesion laterality as opposed to overall type of epilepsy. There are no parallel versions of the tests.

Finally, it may be helpful to obtain an impression of the patients' own perceptions of their cognitive impairment. This may be done using questionnaires, which have generally focused on memory, such as the Subjective Memory Questionnaire (Bennett-Levy *et al.* 1980; Goldstein and Polkey 1992b), the Head Injury Postal Questionnaire (Sunderland *et al.* 1983) adapted for patients with epilepsy (Corcoran and Thompson 1992) and the Memory Observation Questionnaire (McGlone 1994). A broader-based Multiple Ability Self-Report Questionnaire (MASQ: Seidenberg *et al* 1994) focuses on five domains of cognitive function, (i.e. language, visual memory, verbal memory, visuoperception and attention) and has been validated for use with patients with unilateral TLE; between-groups differences arise on the language and verbal and visual memory subscales. Modest but significant correlations were reported between MASQ scores and objective performance, particularly for left-TLE patients. Other questionnaires such as the Cognitive Failures Questionnaire (Broadbent *et al.* 1982) and the DEX (part of the Behavioural Assessment of Dysexecutive Syndrome), assessing behaviour problems characteristic of the dysexecutive syndrome, require validation for use with patients with epilepsy.

CONCLUSIONS

The neuropsychological assessment of a person with epilepsy remains complex and requires the clinical psychologist to have both a working knowledge of the disorder and the available test materials in order to design and interpret an assessment that will be of help for the patient. Further studies are needed that compare performance of patients across a range of similar tests in order to help the practitioner know which scores really constitute evidence of cognitive impairment.

REFERENCES

Aldenkamp, A. P., Gutter, T. and Beun, A. M. (1992) 'The effect of seizure activity and paroxysmal electroencephalographic discharges on cognition', *Acta Neurologica Scandinavica* Suppl. 140: 111–21.

Alpherts, W. C. J. and Aldenkamp, A. P. (1990) 'Computerised neuropsychological assessment of cognitive functioning in children with epilepsy', *Epilepsia* 31 (Suppl 4): S35–40.

Andrewes, D. G., Puce, A. and Bladin, P. F. (1990) 'Post-ictal recognition memory predicts laterality of temporal lobe seizure focus: comparison with post-operative data', *Neuropsychologia* 28: 957–67.

Atkinson, L. (1991) 'Concurrent use of the Wechsler Memory Scale-Revised and the WAIS-R', *British Journal of Clinical Psychology* 30: 87–90.

Bennett-Levy, J., Polkey, C. E. and Powell, G. E. (1980) 'Self-report of memory skills after temporal lobectomy: the effect of clinical variables', *Cortex* 16: 543–57.

Berent, S., Boll, T. J. and Giordani, B. (1980) 'Hemispheric site of epileptogenic focus: cognitive, perceptual and psychosocial implications for children and adults', in R. Canger, F. Anglieri and J. K. Penry (eds) *Advances in Epileptology*, New York: Raven Press.

Binnie, C. D. (1988) 'Seizures, EEG discharges and cognition', in M. R. Trimble and E. H. Reynolds (eds) *Epilepsy, Behaviour and Cognition*, Chichester: Wiley.

—— (1993) 'Significance and management of transitory cognitive impairment due to subclinical EEG discharges in children', *Brain and Development* 15: 23–30.

Binnie, C. D. and Marston, D. (1992) 'Cognitive correlates of interictal discharges', *Epilepsia* 33 (Suppl. 6): S11–17.

Boniface, S. J., Kennett, R. P., Oxbury, J. M. and Oxbury, S. M. (1994) 'Changes in focal interictal epileptiform activity during and after the performance of verbal and visuospatial tasks in a patient with intractable partial seizures', *Journal of Neurology, Neurosurgery and Psychiatry* 57: 227–8.

Broadbent, D. E., Cooper, P. F., Fitzgerald, P. and Parkes, K. R. (1982) 'The cognitive failures questionnaire (CFQ) and its correlates', *British Journal of Clinical Psychology* 2: 1–16.

Brown, S. W. and Vaughan, M. (1988) 'Dementia in epileptic patients', in M. R.

Trimble and E. H. Reynolds (eds) *Epilepsy, Behaviour and Cognitive Function*, Chichester: Wiley.

Buschke, H. (1973) 'Selective reminding for analysis of memory and learning', *Journal of Verbal Learning and Verbal Behaviour* 12: 543–50.

Chelune, G. J. and Bornstein, R. A. (1988) 'WMS-R patterns among patients with unilateral brain lesions', *The Clinical Neuropsychologist* 2: 121–32.

Corcoran, R. and Thompson, P. (1992) 'Memory failure in epilepsy: retrospective reports and prospective findings', *Seizure* 1: 37–42.

Corcoran, R. and Upton, D. (1993) 'A role for the hippocampus in card sorting?' *Cortex* 29: 293–304.

Dikmen, S. and Matthews, C. G. (1977) 'Effects of major motor seizure frequency on cognitive-intellectual function in adults', *Epilepsia* 18: 21–9.

Dodrill, C. B. (1986) 'Correlates of generalised tonic-clonic seizures with intellectual, neuropsychological, emotional and social function in patients with epilepsy', *Epilepsia* 27: 399–411.

—— (1992) 'Interictal cognitive aspects of epilepsy', *Epilepsia* 33 (Suppl. 6): S7–10.

Dreifuss, F. E. (1992) 'Cognitive function – victim of disease or hostage to treatment?' *Epilepsia* 33 (Suppl. 1): S7–12.

Ellis, A. W., Hillam, J. C., Cardno, A. and Kay, J. (1991) 'Processing of words and faces by patients with left and right temporal lobe epilepsy', *Behavioural Neurology* 4: 121–8.

Fenwick, P. C. B. and Brown, S. W. (1989) 'Evoked and psychogenic epileptic seizures. I. Precipitation', *Acta Neurologica Scandinavica* 80: 535–40.

Giordani, B., Berent, S., Sackellares, J. C., Rourke, D., Seidenberg, M., O'Leary, D. S., Dreifuss, F. E. and Ball, J. T. (1985) 'Intelligence test performance of patients with partial and generalised seizures', *Epilepsia* 26: 37–42.

Goldstein, L. H. (1991) 'Neuropsychological investigation of temporal lobe epilepsy', *Journal of the Royal Society of Medicine* 84: 460–5.

Goldstein, L. H. and Polkey, C. E. (1992a) 'Behavioural memory after temporal lobectomy or amygdalo-hippocampectomy', *British Journal of Clinical Psychology* 31: 75–81.

—— (1992b) 'Everyday memory after unilateral temporal lobectomy and amygdalo-hippocampectomy', *Cortex* 28: 189–201.

—— (1993) 'Short-term cognitive changes after unilateral temporal lobectomy or unilateral anygdalo-hippocampectomy for the relief of temporal lobe epilepsy', *Journal of Neurology, Neurosurgery and Psychiatry* 56: 135–40.

Goldstein, L. H., Patel, V., Aspinall, P. and Lishman, W. A. (1992) 'The effect of anti-convulsants on cognitive functioning following a probable encephalitic illness', *British Journal of Psychiatry* 160: 546–9.

Helmstaedter, C., Pohl, C., Hufnagel, A. and Elger, C. E. (1991) 'Visual learning deficits in nonresected patients with right temporal lobe epilepsy', *Cortex* 27: 547–55.

Hermann, B. P., Wyler, A. R. and Richey, E. T. (1988a) 'Wisconsin Card Sorting Test performance in patients with complex partial seizures of temporal lobe origin', *Journal of Clinical and Experimental Neuropsychology* 10: 467–76.

Hermann, B. P., Wyler, A. R., Steenman, H. and Richey, E. T. (1988b) 'The interrelationship between language function and verbal learning/memory performance in patients with complex partial seizures', *Cortex* 24: 245–53.

Hermann, B. P., Seidenberg, M., Haltiner, A. and Wyler, A. R. (1992) 'Adequacy of language function and verbal memory performance in unilateral temporal lobe epilepsy', *Cortex* 28: 423–33.

Horner, M. D., Flashman, L. A., Freides, D., Epstein, C. M. and Bakay, R. A. (1996) 'Temporal lobe epilepsy and performance on the Wisconsin Card Sorting Test', *Journal of Clinical and Experimental Neuropsychology* 18: 310–13.

Jones-Gotman, M. (1987) 'Commentary: Psychological evaluation – testing hippocampal function', in J. Engel Jnr (ed.) *Surgical Treatment of the Epilepsies*, New York: Raven Press.

Kälviäinen, R., Äikiä, M., Helkala, E-L., Mervaala, E. and Riekkinen, P. J. (1992) 'Memory and attention in newly diagnosed epileptic seizure disorder', *Seizure* 1: 255–62.

Kasteleijn-Nolst Trenité, D. G. A., Bakker, D. J., Binnie, C. D., Buerman, A. and van Raaij, M. (1988) 'Psychological effects of subclinical epileptiform discharges. I: Scholastic skills', *Epilepsy Research* 2: 116–8.

Kasteleijn-Nolst Trenité, D. G. A., Sieblink, B. M., Berends, S. G. C., van Strien, J. W. and Meinardi, H. (1990) 'Lateralised effects of subclinical epileptiform EEG discharges on scholastic performance in children', *Epilepsia* 31: 740–6.

Lee, G. P., Loring, D. W. and Thompson, J. L. (1989) 'Construct validity of material-specific memory measures following unilateral temporal lobe ablations', *Psychological Assessment* 1: 192–7.

Loiseau, P., Strube, E., Broustet, D., Battelochi, S., Gomeni, C. and Morselli, P. L. (1983) 'Learning impairment of epileptic patients', *Epilepsia* 24: 183–92.

Loring, D. W., Lee, G. P., Martin, R. C. and Meador, K. J. (1988) 'Material specific learning in patients with partial complex seizures of temporal lobe origin: convergent validation of memory constructs', *Journal of Epilepsy* 1: 53–9.

—— (1989) 'Verbal and visual memory index discrepancies from the Wechsler Memory Scale-Revised: cautions in interpretation', *Psychological Assessment* 1: 198–202.

McGlone, J. (1994) 'Memory complaints before and after lobectomy: do they predict memory performance or lesion laterality?' *Epilepsia* 35: 529–39.

McMillan, T. M., Powell, G. E., Janota, I. and Polkey, C. E. (1987) 'Relationships between neuropathology and cognitive functioning in temporal lobectomy patients', *Journal of Neurology, Neurosurgery and Psychiatry* 50: 167–76.

Mayeux, R., Brandt, J., Rosen, J. and Benson, D. F. (1980) 'Interictal memory and language impairment in temporal lobe epilepsy', *Neurology* 30: 120–5.

Morris, R. G. M., Abrahams, S., Baddeley, A. D. and Polkey, C. E. (1995) 'Doors and People: visual and verbal memory following unilateral temporal lobectomy'. *Neuropsychology* 9: 464–9.

Mungas, D., Ehlers, C., Walton, N. and McCutchen, C. B. (1985) 'Verbal learning differences in epileptic patients with left and right temporal lobe foci', *Epilepsia* 26: 340–5.

Ossetin, J. (1988) 'Methods and problems in the assessment of cognitive function in epileptic patients', in M. R. Trimble and E. H. Reynolds (eds) *Epilepsy, Behaviour and Cognitive Function*, Chichester: Wiley.

Provinciali, L., Signorino, M., Censori, B., Ceravolo, G. and Del Pesce, M. (1991) 'Recognition impairment correlated with short bisynchronous epileptic discharges', *Epilepsia* 32: 684–9.

Randolf, C., Golds, J. M., Zorora, E., Cullum, C. M., Hermann, B. P. and Wyler, A. (1994) 'Estimating memory function: disparity of Wechsler Memory Scale-Revised and California Verbal Learning Test indices in clinical and normal samples', *The Clinical Neuropsychologist* 8: 99–108.

Ribbler, A. and Rausch, R. (1990) 'Performance of patients with unilateral temporal lobectomy on selective reminding procedures using either related or unrelated words', *Cortex* 26: 575–84.

Rugland, A-L., Henriksen, O. and Bjørnes, H. (1991) 'Computer-assisted neuropsychological assessment in patients with epilepsy', in W. E. Dodson, M. Kinsbourne and B. Hiltbrunner (eds) *The Assessment of Cognitive Function in Epilepsy*, New York: Demos.

Saling, M., O'Shea, M. and Berkovic, S. F. (1995) 'Verbal memory in temporal lobe epilepsy: cognitive influences on task-specific effects', *Epilepsia* 36 (Suppl. 3): S93–4.

Saling, M., Berkovic, S. F., O'Shea, M. F., Kalnins, R. M., Darby, D. G. and Bladin, P. F. (1993) 'Lateralisation of verbal memory and unilateral hippocampal sclerosis: evidence of task-specific effects', *Journal of Clinical and Experimental Neuropsychology* 15: 608–18.

Sass, K. J., Spencer, D. D., Kim, J. H. Westerveld, M., Novelly, R. A. and Lencz, T. (1990) 'Verbal memory impairment correlates with hippocampal pyramidal cell density', *Neurology* 40: 1694–7.

Sass, K. J., Sass, A., Westerveld, M., Lencz, T., Rosewater, K. M., Novelly, R. A., Kim, J. H. and Spencer, D. D. (1992a) 'Russell's adaptation of the Wechsler Memory Scale as an index of hippocampal pathology', *Journal of Epilepsy* 5: 24–30.

Sass, K. J., Sass, A., Westerveld, M., Lencz, T., Novelly, R. A., Kim, J. H. and Spencer, D. D. (1992b) 'Specificity in the correlation of verbal memory and hippocampal neuronal loss: dissociation of memory, language and verbal intellectual ability', *Journal of Clinical and Experimental Neuropsychology* 14: 662–72.

Seidenberg, M., Beck, N., Geisser, M., Giordani, B., Sackellares, J. C., Berent, S., Dreifuss, F. E. and Boll, T. J. (1986) 'Academic achievement of children with epilepsy', *Epilepsia* 27: 753–9.

Seidenberg, M., Haltiner, A., Taylor, M. A., Hermann, B. B. and Wyler, A. (1994) 'Development and validation of a Multiple Ability Self-Report Questionnaire', *Journal of Clinical and Experimental Neuropsychology* 16: 93–104.

Seidenberg, M., Hermann, B., Haltiner, A. and Wyler, A. (1993) 'Verbal recognition memory performance in unilateral temporal lobe epilepsy', *Brain and Language* 44: 191–200.

Seidenberg, M., Hermann, B., Noe, A. and Wyler, A. R. (1995) 'Depression in temporal lobe epilepsy: interaction between laterality of lesion and Wisconsin Card Sort Performance', *Neuropsychiatry, Neuropsychology and Behavioural Neurology* 8: 81–7.

Seidenberg, M., O'Leary, D. C., Berent, S. and Boll, T. (1981) 'Changes in seizure frequency and test-retest scores in the WAIS', *Epilepsia* 22: 75–83.

Selwa, L. M., Berent, S., Giordani, B., Henry, T. R., Buchtel, H. A. and Ross, D. A. (1994) 'Serial cognitive testing in temporal lobe epilepsy: longitudinal changes with medical and surgical therapies', *Epilepsia* 35: 743–9.

Sieblink, B. M., Bakker, D. J., Binnie, C. D. and Kasteleijn-Nolst Trenité, D. G. A. (1988) 'Psychological effects of subclinical epileptiform EEG discharges in children II. General intelligence tests', *Epilepsy Research* 2: 117–21.

Strauss, E., Hunter, M. and Wada, J. (1993) 'Wisconsin Card Sorting performance: effects of age of onset of damage and laterality of dysfunction', *Journal of Clinical and Experimental Neuropsychology* 15: 896–902.

Strauss, E., Loring, D., Chelune, G., Hunter, M., Hermann, B., Perrine, K., Westerveld, M., Trenerry, M. and Barr, W. (1995) 'Predicting cognitive impairment in epilepsy: findings from the Bozeman epilepsy consortium', *Journal of Clinical and Experimental Neuropsychology* 17: 909–17.

Sunderland, A., Harris, J. E. and Baddeley, A. D. (1983) 'Do laboratory tests predict everyday memory? A neuropsychological study', *Journal of Verbal Learning and Verbal Behaviour* 22: 341–57.

Thompson, P. J. (1991) 'Integrating computerised and traditional neuropsychological assessment techniques', in W. E. Dodson, M. Kinsbourne and B. Hiltbrunner (eds) *The Assessment of Cognitive Function in Epilepsy*, New York: Demos.

Upton, D. and Thompson, P. J. (1996) 'General neuropsychological characteristics of frontal lobe epilepsy', *Epilepsy Research* 23: 169–77.

Westerveld, M., Sass, K. J., Sass, A. and Henry, H. G. (1994) 'Assessment of verbal memory in temporal lobe epilepsy using the selective reminding test: equivalence and reliability of alternate forms', *Journal of Epilepsy* 7: 57–63.

Williamson, P. D., French, J. A., Thadani, V. M., Kim, J. H., Novelly, R. A., Spencer, S. S., Spencer, D. D. and Mattson, R. H. (1993) 'Characteristics of medial temporal lobe epilepsy: II. Interictal and ictal scalp electroencephalography, neuropsychological testing, neuroimaging, surgical results and pathology', *Annals of Neurology* 34: 781–7.

Zigmond, A. S. and Snaith, R. P. (1983) 'The hospital anxiety and depression scale', *Acta Psychiatrica Scandinavica*, 67: 361–70.

Chapter 3

Epilepsy and memory

Pamela J. Thompson

MEMORY COMPLAINTS

An association between epilepsy and memory disorders has been reported for centuries. Indeed, early commentators perceived memory decline as an inevitable consequence of having seizures:

> unless the disease be arrested we soon discover that the intellectual faculties begin to fail. The memory is one of the first that shows impairment.
>
> (Sieveking 1861)

Today, while memory difficulties are not seen as an invariable symptom of epilepsy, complaints of disturbed memory represent the most frequently reported cognitive problem by patients. Broughton *et al.* (1984) reported that 50 per cent of a sample of outpatients with epilepsy complained of significant memory problems. In a larger survey involving 760 people with epilepsy we found 54 per cent rated their memory as a moderate or severe nuisance. This contrasted with a nuisance rating of 23 per cent in a control group (Thompson and Corcoran 1992).

A complaint of poor memory, however, may represent different things to different people. In our survey, this became clear from the individual comments made by participants. For instance, one woman wrote of her memory:

> Events that happen involving me which stick out in other people's minds, I have no recollection of at all much to the surprise of friends because that particular event could only have been a year ago.

Another person commented:

> Much can be done to hide the memory problems but the difficulty of

remembering names is so embarrassing and it makes socialising difficult.

All participants in our study completed a questionnaire relating to the frequency of everyday memory failures. The major difficulties reported by subjects and their observers were similar in the epilepsy and the control group, although the frequency was greater for the respondents with epilepsy. The most troublesome failure reported was the 'tip of the tongue' phenomenon, followed by having to go back to check and then losing items (Thompson and Corcoran 1992). Inspection of the responses suggested other cognitive problems, including language difficulties and organisational problems, may underlie or contribute to some of the reported difficulties. Even where a breakdown of memory underlies everyday failures, many different types of deficit might be implicated, as memory is not a unitary phenomenon (see Table 3.1; Baddeley *et al.* 1995).

Most of the formal studies of memory functioning in epilepsy have involved assessing the formation of long-term memories. The majority of these report some impairments in epilepsy groups compared to controls or normative test data. For instance, Halgren and colleagues (1991) report findings from sixty-one general neuropsychological referrals. Twenty-three were reported as having selective memory deficits for verbal or non-verbal material, while twelve were assessed to have a global memory deficit. In an earlier, larger study, Loiseau *et al.* (1988) also reported a high level of memory problems.

Table 3.1 Memory systems

Name	*Characteristic*
Episodic	Memory for personally experienced events
Short-term memory	Small capacity < 30 sec
Long-term memory	Vast capacity > 30 sec
Semantic	Stored knowledge about the world = facts, rules, concepts, independent of time
Implicit/Procedural	Acquisition and recollection does not require conscious recall, e.g. motor skills
Remote Memory	Experiences from distant past
Prospective Memory	Remembering to do things in the future

RISK FACTORS

Investigators have attempted to assess what factors place individuals with epilepsy at risk for memory difficulties.

Aetiology

Brain damage is probably the most potent factor underlying memory problems. Epilepsy can be caused by a variety of pathological processes (see Chapter 1). Some of these clearly cause memory impairments independently of seizures. With improved neuroimaging techniques, an increasing number of cases are found to have brain pathology, for example, cortical dysgenesis and hippocampal sclerosis.

Not surprisingly, pathologies involving temporal lobe structures have been most frequently associated with memory deficits and laterality of pathology with material specific memory deficits. Although this theme is developed further in Chapters 2 and 4, the most consistent finding is a verbal memory deficit in association with dominant temporal lobe pathology (Hermann *et al.* 1987); some authors report deficits with right sided cases, although this is less consistently reported (Helmstaedter *et al.* 1991; Cohen 1992).

Type of epilepsy

Early studies reported that patients with complex partial seizures of temporal lobe origin were more impaired on tests of memory than individuals with generalised epilepsy. This finding may well be related to the underlying pathology, but also to other aspects of the seizure disorder. In our recent research, individuals with frontal lobe epilepsy demonstrated memory disturbance on formal testing. The memory test performance of seventy-four patients with frontal lobe epilepsy was compared with fifty-seven patients with temporal lobe epilepsy. Memory tests included measures of recall, learning and recognition for both verbal and visuospatial information. The scores on the verbal version of the Recognition Memory Test significantly differentiated the groups, although scores on other memory measures did not. Furthermore, the left frontal and right temporal groups were equally impaired on the Design Learning test from the Adult Memory and Information Processing Battery.

Age at onset and duration

Early studies reported an inverse relationship between age at onset and impairment on memory tests. Dikmen *et al.* (1975) studied two groups of patients who were matched for duration and frequency of tonic clonic seizures, but differed with regard to age at onset. Patients with onset below five years were more impaired on the majority of tasks. Kalska (1991) reported that subjects whose epilepsy started below ten years had lower memory quotients and lower IQs than those with later onset.

Some studies have not found any relationship between age of onset and memory function (Delaney *et al.* 1980; Halgren *et al.* 1991; Hermann *et al.* 1988). Loiseau *et al.* (1988) found that onset during adolescence was associated with the greatest risk of memory impairment. Corcoran and Thompson (1993) noted patients who complained most about their memory were significantly older at seizure onset than patients who did not complain. Halgren *et al.* (1991) found that twelve patients with a global memory deficit were seventeen years older when they developed epilepsy than patients with normal memory.

The duration of epilepsy is obviously related to the age of onset. Delaney *et al.* (1980) reported longer duration of epilepsy was associated with greater impairments on memory tests. Hermann and colleagues (1988) did not find any relationship between tests of verbal memory and duration of epilepsy. Clearly, the impact of these variables will be influenced by other factors such as aetiology and seizure control (see also Chapter 2 for further discussion).

Seizures

Memory loss for the duration of a seizure is a feature of most complex partial and generalised attacks. Where seizures occur several times daily, they may be expected to disrupt an individual's ability to register information and form memories for ongoing events.

Disturbances of memory may also arise in association with brief epileptic discharges, so called subclinical seizures, which may have no visible features but are detectable on EEG recordings. This has also been discussed in Chapter 2. These can occur frequently, with hundreds or thousands of episodes a day. Clearly, in such cases, disruption of memory and other functions is to be expected. Furthermore, there is some evidence that epileptic discharges from mesial temporal structures detectable only via implanted depth electrodes have a disruptive impact on memory. Bridgeman *et al.* (1989) reported five patients who underwent memory testing while such discharges were recorded during implantation. Impairments were noted on memory tests, but not on other measures of cognitive functioning.

There are reports in the literature of amnesic seizures, defined as recurrent paroxysmal memory loss with an alteration in consciousness. During the attack the person appears normal and continues activities, including speaking, and personal identity would be retained. Such episodes, however are reported retrospectively and may be difficult to distinguish from transient global amnesia (Kapur 1993).

Recovery from seizures can be variable and in some individuals, neuropsychological assessment undertaken in close proximity to complex partial seizures or generalised attacks may underestimate an individual's memory functioning. Halgren *et al.* (1991) described how patients assessed as much as two days following a bout of complex partial seizures performed significantly less well on tests of learning and memory than two weeks following the episodes (see also Chapter 2).

Whether seizures themselves accelerate forgetting, however, is less clear. In a recent investigation we attempted to explore this issue (Bergin *et al.* 1995). Fifty-eight patients with refractory partial seizures undergoing video EEG telemetry were administered memory tests shortly after the telemetry commenced; memory was reassessed two days later. Thirty patients had at lease one seizure during this period. Patients who had seizures forgot no more than patients who had no seizures. There was no correlation between memory performance and the timing of seizures, or the number of seizures. These findings indicate isolated seizures do not generally cause patients to forget material they have recently learned.

Other research studies have assessed the relationship between estimates of seizure frequency and memory test performance. Loiseau *et al.* (1983) divided 200 subjects into those who had been seizure free for two or more years, those with no more than one seizure in the past two years, and finally those who had had twelve or more seizures in the past year. The authors concluded that seizure frequency analysed in this way was not a factor which influenced memory ability.

Kalska (1991) reported little memory decline in a longitudinal study with a ten year follow-up. During the course of the study, 40 per cent of the patients experienced generalised seizures, twenty-one had ten or fewer seizures and seven patients did not have any seizures. All patients underwent seven subtests of the Wechsler Memory Scale. The mean initial Wechsler Memory Quotient was 91.9 and at ten years 96.8.

Improvement occurred in 30.4 per cent of the patients, while only 5.8 per cent deteriorated.

In addition to Dodrill's (1986) finding that patients who had experienced more than one hundred tonic-clonic seizures, or who had experienced an episode of convulsive *status epilepticus*, performed less well than other patients on a variety of tests, including some measures of memory, Treiman and Delgado-Escueta (1983) reported patients experiencing severe memory problems after an episode of non-convulsive status. One case, a 53-year-old man, experienced a week-long episode of complex partial status after abrupt discontinuation of carbamazepine. Even four months later he had severe memory problems. Victor and Agamamolis (1990) reported a 65-year-old man who suffered an episode of generalised *status epilepticus*. On recovery, he was found to have a moderately severe anterograde and retrograde amnesia which persisted until he died thirty months later.

During absence and partial *status epilepticus*, a range of cognitive disturbances have been reported. Outwardly, an individual may not seem to be behaving too abnormally. Detailed assessment, however, can reveal gross memory disturbance. Such states are more frequent than previously thought; as many as fifteen per cent of individuals with intractable epilepsy may experience at least one episode (Shorvon 1994).

Individuals with atonic and tonic seizures are at risk for head injuries resulting from their seizures. Over time, repeated minor head injuries result in changes in brain function, particularly of the frontal regions which may produce memory deficits. In patients with intractable epilepsy, we have found an association between head injuries and deterioration in intellectual ability and memory.

Anti-epileptic drugs

In recent years there has been much research on the effects of anti-epileptic drugs on cognitive abilities, including memory functioning. Overall, medication in high dosages or when prescribed in combination may influence test performance, although it is the author's impression that this is secondary to more general cognitive effects rather than a specific effect on memory processing (Thompson and Trimble 1996; this volume Chapter 5).

Surgery

A number of surgical options exist for patients with intractable epilepsy. Temporal lobectomy represents the most frequently undertaken procedure and research exists spanning many decades on its impact on memory functioning. (Thompson and Trimble 1996; this volume Chapter 4).

Mood

Depressed mood and elevated levels of anxiety have been reported in patients with epilepsy. There is evidence from other psychological research that negative mood can have an impact on neuropsychological test performance (Calev *et al.* 1986). We have found higher levels of depression to be a predictor of poor memory test performance, particularly on measures of verbal recall (Corcoran and Thompson 1993).

OTHER MEMORY STUDIES

Remote memory

Surprisingly little research has been undertaken assessing the ability of patients with epilepsy to retrieve past memories. Ratti *et al.* (1992) tested fifteen patients with temporal lobe epilepsy on a remote memory questionnaire, and compared their response with fifteen controls matched for age and educational level. The authors report that remote memory was impaired in the epilepsy group, with no difference between patients with right or left temporal lobe seizures. Barr *et al.* (1990) tested remote memory in patients who had undergone anterior temporal lobe resections. Subjects were tested for recognition of famous faces, recognition of names of television programmes, recall of generic and specific factual knowledge and memory for public events that had occurred after the subjects had reached the age of ten. They were also given questions relating to autobiographical knowledge. The left temporal lobectomy group performed significantly less well than the right lobectomy and control groups.

Upton *et al.* (1992) tested autobiographical remote memory in thirty-five patients with the Autobiographical Memory Interview (AMI; Kopelman *et al.* 1989). In this investigation, no significant correlation was found between memory test performance and subjective ratings of memory competence scores. The data were not analysed in regard to seizure variables such as nature or frequency of attacks. Tests of autobiographical memory such as the AMI provide a qualitative assessment of the richness of an individual's memories. It can be difficult, however, to verify answers or quantify the amount of detail remembered. Furthermore, many questions on the AMI do not have relevance for younger subjects as it was standardised on an older sample (mean age 55 years).

Bergin *et al.* (in preparation) recently explored the performance of three groups of patients with epilepsy on a remote memory questionnaire. The questionnaire assessed knowledge of public events which had occurred since 1980. The epilepsy groups comprised thirty-three patients with temporal lobe seizures, thirty-three with extratemporal lobe seizures and ten with primary generalised seizures. Thirty control subjects were also tested. Patients with temporal lobe epilepsy performed significantly less well on the questionnaire than all other groups. Patients with extratemporal primary generalised epilepsy did not differ from controls. Performance on the questionnaire was not determined by verbal IQ, educational achievement or drug treatment, but was related to the number of generalised convulsions which had occurred since 1980. Moderate correlations existed between scores on the questionnaire and performance on tests of verbal memory.

Prospective memory

In our survey of everyday memory problems in epilepsy, it was clear from replies received that patients reported some prospective memory errors, for example, forgetting to undertake tasks they had intended to do, and forgetting to take their tablets. This is probably a common sort of memory complaint which subjects volunteer to their clinicians. Prospective memory is very important, but it is seldom tested clinically in patients with epilepsy. This is partly because it is logistically difficult to devise tests that match the complexities of real life situations.

Bergin and colleagues (in preparation) studied forty patients with intractable temporal lobe seizures who were undergoing a period of video EEG telemetry as part of their pre-surgical assessment programme. The prospective memory task given to the subjects was to answer a written question regarding likely seizure occurrence at four predetermined times (9.30, 12.30, 3.30 and 6.30). Patients were asked to fill in the chart as close as possible to the allocated time. Completion of the task was undertaken in full view of the camera and video tapes were subsequently reviewed to determine when charts were filled in. A scoring system in percentages was devised, with patients gaining maximum points if they made the entry within ten minutes of the appropriate time, and with a reduction in score with time elapsed from this time. Three patients failed to make any predictions and all subsequently confirmed that they had understood the requirements of the study but had completely forgotten about the task. Twenty-five patients scored more than 50 per cent, and the remaining twelve patients less than this.

All three patients who failed to make any prediction had right temporal lobe epilepsy, and patients with right temporal lobe epilepsy as a group tended to perform more poorly than other patient groups. Eighteen patients had one or more seizures during the three-hour period immediately preceding the scheduled entry. The likelihood of the chart being completed, however, was not affected by a seizure occurring during this time period. Indeed, twelve of the patients actually scored as well or better for the entries after an attack than they did following periods when they did not have seizures. Patients who reported weak memory in response to three everyday memory questions tapping memory tended to perform poorly on the prospective task described above. No control group was included in the study; this would have been logistically difficult. For this reason, we have no evidence regarding the efficacy of our patients' memory in relation to other individuals.

Memory questionnaire studies

Some studies have explored memory functioning in epilepsy using subjective questionnaires via which the respondents report the nature and frequency or severity of everyday failures. We use a version of the Everyday Memory Questionnaire (EMQ) devised by Sunderland *et al.* (1983) in our studies referred to in this chapter. Bennett-Levy *et al.* (1980) employed the Subjective Memory Questionnaire (SMQ) in patients who had undergone unilateral temporal lobectomy. Patients rated their memory as poorer than controls.

Memory questionnaires, however, have been criticised as only weak correlations are reported with more traditional neuropsychological tests (Hermann 1984). We found a significant relationship between the EMQ and measures of verbal recall, but not with other memory measures (Corcoran and Thompson 1993). However, memory questionnaire content does not always seem to be tapping the same functions as memory tests and a better relationship has been reported between questionnaire scores and more behavioural measures of memory (Goldstein and Polkey 1992).

REHABILITATION

There are few research studies in the literature which focus upon the effectiveness of rehabilitation. This seems surprising given the importance of an efficient memory for the optimum management of a person's epilepsy. Patients have to remember appointments, to take tablets, to document seizure frequency and to monitor the effectiveness of treatment. If an individual's memory is unreliable, then the physician may be presented with a less than accurate picture of the individual's seizure control on clinic visits. People with epilepsy may be a good target for memory training as generally memory problems are less devastating than for amnesic cases, which have been the main focus of studies in the rehabilitation literature. In addition, patients with epilepsy generally retain insight into their difficulties. Many people with epilepsy live independently and are less likely than more severely affected patients to have a 'carer' at hand to act as an external support for a weak memory.

Reports on memory training in epilepsy are scarce. Aldenkamp and Vermeulen (1991) report group sessions which involve training in the use of memory aids. The group met for six sessions every two weeks. The authors note that the nature of the group changed over time, initially being quite didactic and later taking on a more supportive therapeutic role. Small improvements in memory functioning were noted, but the authors conclude that even small changes in memory can result in a significant increase in a person's level of independence.

Corcoran and Thompson (in press) have undertaken a study which explored the usefulness of a self-help manual based on the nature of a patient's own memory complaints. Within the study, they explored whether a tailor-made self-help memory manual was effective and whether there was any advantage to having some therapist contact as part of the programme. Twenty-seven subjects participated in the study. All had rated their memory as being a moderate or serious nuisance in a previous study. An eighteen-item checklist of everyday memory failures was used as the main outcome measure and also a relative or an individual who came into daily contact with the subjects completed comparable memory scales. In addition, rating scales of mood were employed. The outcome of the intervention was a little disappointing, as not all of the subjects completed the various parts of the study.

Overall, it did seem certain patients benefited more than others. In particular, those individuals reporting moderate memory difficulties seemed better able to utilise the memory training strategies outlined than individuals who had serious memory problems and those who were depressed.

MEMORY ASSESSMENT

The nature of any memory assessment will depend on the question being asked. This may relate to whether a memory deficit exists which is compatible with a known lesion, or with electrophysiological lateralising data in a prospective surgical candidate (Chapter 4). The question may relate to whether a drug-induced memory difficulty exists (Chapter 5). In this chapter, I will focus on memory assessment in an individual who is complaining of memory problems, with a view to some rehabilitative input.

Where there is any concern that ongoing epileptic activity may be a relevant factor, memory testing is best undertaken with simultaneous EEG recording. Furthermore, to obtain a measure of an individual's emotional state, a screening questionnaire of mood is useful. We routinely employ the Hospital Anxiety and Depression Scale (Zigmond and Snaith 1983).

Assessment for rehabilitation purposes needs to include a broad range of measures of memory. It will be important to look at what aspects of memory are impaired, if any, but more important to see what system or systems may be working well. The majority of memory tests available to the clinician measure the learning and retention of new information (Baddeley *et al.* 1995; this volume, Chapter 2). Focusing on the formation of new memories, measures employed should tap immediate and delayed registration of material and also learning capacity over trials. Ideally, this should include memory for different types of material, although usually this is limited to verbal and visuospatial information. A drawback of many of the available tests is that few are available in more than two parallel forms which reduces the reliability of repeated assessments.

Below are a number of commercially available tests (mentioned also in Chapters 2 and 4). We routinely employ the Adult Information Processing Battery and the Recognition Memory Test. More details, therefore, are given for these measures.

The Wechsler Memory Scale – Revised (WMS-R)

The Wechsler Memory Scale represents the most widely-used memory test battery. The original version was criticised on a number of grounds, and the scale has been revised and many of the shortcomings have been addressed, but only one version of the test is available.

Recognition Memory Test

This recognition memory test is quite widely used in the UK. It has two subtests, one involving memory for words and one for faces. The test is easy to administer and the recognition paradigm has an advantage over measures of learning and recall in that test performance is less susceptible to the adverse influence of anxiety and depression. Weaknesses of the test include the photographic detail that could be coded verbally (Kapur 1987), the tendency for subjects to perform close to ceiling level on the verbal version (Mayes 1995), and recent evidence that the word or face discrepancy scores do not necessarily discriminate between right- and left-sided temporal lobe lesions (Morris *et al.* 1995a).

The Adult Memory and Information Processing Battery

This test consists of four measures of memory and two of concentration and information processing. The measures of memory can be subdivided into those tapping verbal memory (prose recall and word list learning) and non-verbal memory (abstract design recall and abstract design learning). The verbal learning test uses the same format as the Rey Auditory Verbal Learning Test. The entire battery is available in two versions and the measures of design retention and story retention have a delayed recall component. Norms for a UK sample are available, although there is some criticism that the standardisation sample is rather small.

The California Verbal Learning Test

This test provides a number of measures, not only of learning capacity, but also of organising strategies and susceptibility to different kinds of interference. There is also a recognition measure.

The Rivermead Behavioural Memory Test

Designed to have more ecological validity than most other memory tests, subtests of this measure include recalling a name, story recall, recognition of faces and of pictures, route learning and recall in addition to questions on personal orientation. It is not specifically materially sensitive however to lateralised temporal lobe lesions (Goldstein and Polkey 1992).

Doors and People Test

This new battery provides measures of learning, recall and recognition of visual and verbal material. Data relating to its sensitivity in surgically-treated patients with epilepsy are now available (Morris *et al.* 1995b).

Other tests

Whichever memory measures are selected, they should never be administered in isolation. It is necessary to assess other aspects of cognitive functioning, including language ability, perceptual skills and organisational and attentional capacity. Reported memory deficits may be secondary to other problems such as organisational difficulties. In addition, if rehabilitative input is being planned, then a memory deficit may be reduced when other cognitive resources are assessed to be well developed.

Remote memory

Adequate assessment of remote memory is difficult and there are fewer tests available.

Autobiographical Memory Interview (AMI)

This measure consists of two subtests. One taps personal memories, including facts about background, childhood, young adulthood and the recent past. Questions include names of schools attended, friends, addresses, journeys, and so forth. The second part focuses on autobiographical incidents and taps event memory using a cuing technique.

The Dead or Alive Test

This is a measure of memory for famous people. Subjects have to indicate whether a given person is dead or alive, and if dead, to indicate how and when they died. Currently it includes famous people from the 1960s to the 1990s (Kapur *et al.* 1989).

Memory questionnaires

A useful complement to memory assessment is the administration of an everyday memory questionnaire. We routinely employ one originally designed by Sunderland *et al.* (1983). Responses obtained provide an idea of the nature and extent of memory deficits experienced on a daily basis. A relatives' version also exists. Other questionnaires are mentioned in Chapter 2.

INTERVENTION

The results of any memory assessment need to be discussed with the patient and their family. This feedback in itself can have a beneficial impact. Individuals may be relieved by the confirmation that a memory difficulty does exist, but that it is not going to get progressively worse. For instance, this would be the case in an individual with well-controlled seizures, but with known left hippocampal sclerosis. For the young person who is struggling academically to achieve a standard comparable to their siblings, confirmation of a memory deficit may result in a reappraisal by the family and redirection to courses with little or no reliance on written examinations.

Sessions can be offered to focus on strategies which might help reduce the impact of a weak memory. Strategies are usually divided into internal and external measures (Baddeley *et al.* 1995). The former include the use of visual imagery whereby individuals may imagine mental pictures involving the information to be remembered. This can be useful in individuals with a verbal memory impairment, particularly where their assessed visual memory is good. Mental imagery can be helpful for remembering a few important names, for example, a bizarre image can be made in association with a name. Other visual strategies include the method of loci and the peg method. Verbal rhymes and first letter mnemonics may be helpful for some people. In general, internal strategies can be mentally taxing and, in my experience, patients find them difficult to employ in their everyday lives. However, it can be fun in rehabilitation sessions to focus on some of these strategies. For instance, a young woman with a post-surgical verbal memory deficit had great difficulty learning lists of words, even with repeated trials. She was, however, able to learn a list of ten things to do – such as go to the dentist, buy some pasta, return a book to the library, etc. – by utilising the method of loci. She would visualise the rooms in her parent's house and make a bizarre image in each room to do with the item to be remembered. Two months after this she was still able to recall all ten items!

External memory aids are the most widely used and are generally the most valuable for patients with epilepsy. Techniques can be divided into aids to assist information storage and cuing devices which prompt people to remember to do things. It is surprising how many patients with impaired memory do not use diaries. Training in the use of a diary or filofax can have a significant impact on their everyday lives. The young woman with the verbal memory deficit discussed above has significantly reduced the impact of her memory deficit by at least daily reference to her filofax. Another young man with significant memory difficulties found his handicap lessened by using a computerised diary and personal organiser.

One of the most valuable external memory aids for people with epilepsy is the drug wallet. Many people find this device helps them remember to take their tablets and also not to take too many. Drug wallets usually consist of seven small containers, one for each day of the week. The compartments can be filled once a week at set times. The seven individual containers are removable so that if the person goes out for the day they do not have to take the complete container with them. Drug wallets can be obtained from local chemists and are not expensive.

For others with memory difficulties, the results of the broader neuropsychological assessment may be of help. For instance, a young man who has a very weak memory, but who has good planning and organising abilities, undertook a year's residential placement which was aimed at improving his independent living skills. On his rehabilitation programme, explicit steps were taken to improve his memory by capitalising on his good organisational skills (see Appendix to this chapter).

CONCLUSIONS

Memory loss is a feature of most epileptic seizures. Many individuals with epilepsy experience difficulties inter-ictally, and complaints of poor memory represent the most frequent reason for a referral for a neuropsychological assessment. In this chapter, research studies were reviewed which have demonstrated memory difficulties in at least subgroups of patients. Most studies focus upon the ability to remember new information, with much less work exploring other aspects such as remote and prospective memory or the efficacy of rehabilitative work. In the second part of the chapter, assessment techniques were presented and rehabilitation strategies discussed. Much more rehabilitative work is needed to enable patients to reduce the negative impact of a memory deficit upon their capacity for independent living.

APPENDIX

An example of a memory rehabilitation programme

John has significant memory difficulties; he finds it hard to remember things he has done and things he has talked about. Despite this he possesses good planning and organisational skills.

Proposed management strategies

1 John is encouraged to take notes of key points of discussions during meetings so that he can remember the work he has done from one week to the next.
2 John now has a filofax/personal organiser which has been personally tailored. This includes the following sections:
   Programme sheets on which he records his daily activities alongside a record of his seizures.
   'Don't Forget' sheets on which he makes notes of things he needs/wants to remember to do.
   A section in which he records the actions he agrees to do during programme review meetings.
   A section in which he records key notes from meetings and workshops.
   Accounts sheets on which he records his daily spending as part of his budget plan.
   Names, addresses and telephone numbers.
   John is encouraged to make frequent use of this organiser as a memory aid.
3 John has a number of identified places in which he keeps important papers/documents.

4 As John finds remembering large chunks of information difficult, important information should be presented in a simple, precise and sequenced way. Discussions should also be concluded by a summary of key points.
5 John needs structure to his day in order for things to become routine and so that the development of his organisational skills can be further encouraged.

REFERENCES

Aldenkamp, A. P. and Vermeulen, J. (1991) 'Neuropsychological rehabilitation of memory function in epilepsy', *Neuropsychological Rehabilitation* 1: 199–214.

Baddeley, A. D., Wilson, B. A. and Watts, F. N. (1995) *Handbook of Memory Disorders*, Chichester: Wiley.

Barr, W., Goldberg, E., Wasserstein, J. and Novelly, R. (1990) 'Retrograde amnesia following unilateral temporal lobectomy', *Neuropsychologia* 28: 243–55.

Bennett-Levy, J., Polkey, C. E. and Powell, G. E. (1980) 'Self-report of memory skills after temporal lobectomy: the effects of clinical variables', *Cortex* 18: 513–57.

Bergin, P. S., Thompson, P. J., Fish, D. R. and Shorvon, S. D. (1995) 'The effect of seizures on memory for recently learned material', *Neurology* 45: 236–40.

—— (in preparation) 'Prospective memory in epilepsy'.

Bridgeman, P. A., Malamut, M. A., Sperling, M. R., Saykin, A. J. and O'Connor, M. J. (1989) 'Memory during subclinical hippocampal seizures', *Neurology* 39: 853–6.

Broughton, R. J., Goberman, A. A. and Roberts, J. (1984) 'Comparison for psychosocial effects of epilepsy and narcolepsy/cataplexy: a controlled study', *Epilepsia* 25: 423–33.

Calev, A., Konn, Y., Shapira, B., Kugelmass, S. and Lever, B. (1986). 'Verbal and non-verbal recall by depressed and euthymic affective patients', *Psychological Medicine* 16: 789–94.

Cohen, M. (1992) 'Auditory, verbal and visuospatial memory in children with complex partial epilepsy of temporal lobe origin', *Brain and Cognition* 20: 325–6.

Corcoran, R. and Thompson, P. (1993) 'Epilepsy and poor memory. Who complains and what do they mean?', *British Journal of Clinical Psychology* 32: 199–208.

—— (in press) 'Memory difficulties in epilepsy: assessing the benefit of self-help procedures', *Seizure*.

Delaney, R. C., Rosen, A. J., Mattson, R. H. and Novelly, R. A. (1980) 'Memory function in focal epilepsy: a comparison of non-surgical, unilateral and temporal lobe and frontal lobe samples', *Cortex* 16: 103–17.

Dikmen, S., Matthews, C. G. and Harley, J. P. (1975) 'The effect of early versus late onset of major motor epilepsy upon cognitive intellectual performance', *Epilepsia* 16: 73–81.

Dodrill, C. B. (1986) 'Correlates of generalised tonic clonic seizures with intellectual, neuropsychological, emotional and social function in patients with epilepsy', *Epilepsia* 27: 399–411.

Goldstein, L. H. and Polkey, C. E. (1992) 'Behavioural memory after temporal lobectomy or amygdalo-hippocampectomy', *British Journal of Clinical Psychology* 31: 75–82.

Halgren, E., Stapleton, J., Domalski, T., Swartz, B. E., Delgado-Escueta, A. V. and Walsh, G. O. (1991) 'Memory dysfunction in epilepsy: patient as a derangement of normal physiology', in D. Smith, D. Treiman and M. Trimble (eds) *Advances in Neurology, Vol. 55: Neurobehavioural Problems in Epilepsy*, New York: Raven Press.

Helmstaedter, C., Pohl, C., Hufnagel, A. and Elger, C. E. (1991) 'Visual learning deficits in non-resected patients with right temporal lobe epilepsy', *Cortex* 27: 547–55.

Hermann, D. J. (1984) 'Questionnaires about memory', in J. E. Harris and P. E. Morris (eds) *Everyday Memory, Actions and Absent-mindedness*, London: Academic Press.

Hermann, B., Wyler, A., Richey, E. and Rea, J. (1987) 'Memory function and verbal learning ability in patients with complex partial seizures of temporal lobe origin', *Epilepsia* 28: 547–54.

Hermann, B. P., Wyler, A. R., Steenman, H. and Richet, E. T. (1988) 'The interrelationship between language function and verbal learning/memory performance in patients with complex partial seizures', *Cortex* 24: 245–53.

Kalska, K. (1991) 'Cognitive changes in epilepsy. A ten year follow-up', in L. Nordberg (ed.) *The Finnish Society of Sciences and Letters. Commentationes Screntarun Socialium* 44.

Kapur, N. (1987) 'Some comments on the technical acceptability of Warrington's Recognition Memory Test', *British Journal of Clinical Psychology* 26: 144–6.

—— (1993) 'Transient epileptic amnesia – a clinical update and reformulation', *Journal of Neurology, Neurosurgery and Psychiatry* 56: 1184–90.

Kapur, N., Young, A., Bateman, D. and Kennedy, P. (1989) 'A long term clinical and neuropsychological follow-up of focal retrograde amnesia'. *Cortex* 25: 671–80.

Kopelman, M. D., Wilson, B. A. and Baddeley, A. D. (1989) *Autobiographical Memory Interview*, Bury St Edmunds: Thames Valley Test Co.

Loiseau, P. and Signoret, J. L. (1988) 'Memory and epilepsy', in M. R. Trimble, and E. H. Reynolds (eds) *Epilepsy, Behaviour and Cognitive Function*, Chichester: Wiley.

Loiseau, P., Struber, E., Broustet, D., Battellochi, S., Gaueni, C. and Morselli, P. L. (1983) 'Learning impairment in epileptic patients', *Epilepsia* 24: 183–92.

Mayes, A. (1995) 'The assessment of memory disorders', in A. D. Baddeley, B. A. Wilson and F. N. Watts (eds) *Handbook of Memory Disorders*, Chichester: Wiley.

Morris, R. G., Abrahams, S. and Polkey, C. E. (1995a) 'Recognition memory for words and faces following unilateral temporal lobectomy', *British Journal of Clinical Psychology* 34: 571–6.

Morris, R. G., Abrahams, S., Baddeley, A. D. and Polkey, C. E. (1995b) 'Doors and people: visual and verbal memory following unilateral temporal lobectomy', *Neuropsychology* 9: 464–9.

Ratti, M., Galimberti, C., Manni, R. and Tantara, A. (1992) 'Remote memory impairment in temporal lobe epilepsy', *Seizure* 1 (suppl. A): 14/11.
Shorvon, S. D. (1994) *Status Epilepticus. Its Causes and Treatment*, Cambridge: Cambridge University Press.
Sieveking, E. H. (1861) *On Epilepsy and Epileptiform Seizures*, London: John Churchill.
Sunderland, A., Harris, J. E. and Baddeley, A. D. (1983) 'Do laboratory tests predict everyday memory? A neuropsychological study', *Journal of Verbal Learning and Verbal Behaviour* 22: 341–57.
Thompson, P. J. and Corcoran, R. (1992) 'Everyday memory failures in people with epilepsy', *Epilepsia* 33 (Suppl. 6): S18–20.
Thompson, P. J. and Trimble, M. R. (1996) 'Neuropsychological aspects of epilepsy', in I. Grant and K. Adams (eds) *Assessment of Neuropsychiatric Disorders* (2nd edn), San Diego: Oxford University Press.
Treiman, D. M. and Delgado-Escueta, A. V. (1983) 'Complex partial status epilepticus', in A. V. Delgado-Escueta, C. G. Wasterlain, D. N. Treiman and R. J. Porter (eds) *Advances in Neurology. Vol. 34: Status Epilepticus*, New York: Raven Press.
Upton, D., Corcoran, R., Fowler, A. and Thompson, P. J. (1992) 'Autobiographical memory in epilepsy', *Seizure 1* (Suppl. A): 14/10.
Victor, M. and Agamamolis, D. (1990) 'Amnesia due to lesions consigned to the hippocampus: a clinical pathological study', *Journal of Cognitive Neuroscience* 34: 246–57.
Zigmond, A. S. and Snaith, R. P. (1983) 'The Hospital Anxiety and Depression Scale', *Acta Psychiatrica Scandinavica* 67: 361–70.

Chapter 4

Assessment for surgery

Susan Oxbury

INTRODUCTION

Of the 0.5 per cent of people with active epilepsy in the UK, 20 per cent continue to have seizures despite adequate treatment with anti-epileptic drugs. Of these, it is estimated that 30–40 per cent have focal seizures, i.e. about 15–20,000 people. Surgical treatment will be an option for some of them.

Focal seizures arise from over-activity in a group of neurones (the focus), which is often the site of structural pathology or abnormal brain tissue. Much of the surgical treatment of epilepsy is based on the concept that if the focus can be removed, the seizures will cease. Surgery is only offered to those people who have disabling, medically resistant seizures, (the definition of disabling will vary according to the individual's circumstances and lifestyle) and in whom removal of the pathology/epileptogenic zone will not cause unacceptable neurological or neuropsychological deficit.

Types of surgery

Various operations are increasingly being performed (see Table 4.1 compiled from Engel's (1993) published data). The first three operations in the table are designed to remove the source of the epilepsy, whereas corpus callosotomy is intended to interrupt fibres and hence to inhibit the spread of seizure activity.

The number of children included in Engel's survey is not reported. However, there is increasing emphasis on earlier surgery for epilepsy at younger ages in the hope of giving freedom from the deleterious effects of seizures and medication during the formative years.

Table 4.1 Numbers of surgical procedures carried out before 1985 and between 1986–1990

	Before 1985	*1986-1990*
Total operations	3,446	8,234
Types: Temporal lobe excisions	68%	67%
Extra-temporal excisions	24%	18%
Hemispherectomy	3%	5%
Corpus callosotomy	6%	10%

Pre-operative investigations

The offer of surgery depends upon the outcome of investigations undertaken by a multi-disciplinary team. Investigations are directed towards establishing firstly the probability that surgery will markedly reduce seizure frequency, and the likelihood of producing a deleterious effect on the patient's physical, cognitive and/or behavioural state. A wide range of investigations are available (Table 4.2). Which are used, depends upon various factors including the type of surgery under consideration, the probable nature of the pathology underlying the epilepsy syndrome, and the age and cognitive ability of the patient. Different epilepsy surgery groups use different investigational programmes (Engel and Ojemann 1993) but seem to achieve similar outcome from surgery.

The contributions of neuropsychological assessment and sodium amytal tests are discussed in detail below.

THE CONTRIBUTION OF NEUROPSYCHOLOGICAL ASSESSMENT

The aims of neuropsychological assessment in epilepsy surgery programmes are broadly: (a) to determine whether the neuropsychological profile is consistent with the lateralisation and localisation of the pathology and/or the epileptogenic area to be excised; (b) to predict the risk to memory and other cognitive functions of the proposed surgery; (c) to evaluate neuropsychological outcome; (d) to contribute information relevant to psychosocial or educational issues; and (e) for audit and research to further knowledge relating to all these issues. Most psychologists would agree that (b), the prediction of neuropsychological outcome

Table 4.2 Pre-operative investigations

Area of investigation	*Types of investigation*
Clinical Neurology (What is the nature of the epilepsy syndrome?)	Clinical History Physical Examination
Electroencephalography (Do seizures start from a consistent focus?)	Routine scalp recording – awake and asleep Recording with special extracranial electrode placements (e.g. sphenoidal) +/- drug activation Ictal recordings - ambulatory using cassette recorder - seizure/EEG correlation using video-telemetry with extracranial or intracranial extracerebral (subdural strips or extradural pegs or foramen ovale) or intracranial-intracerebral (depth) electrodes
Brain Imaging (Where is the pathology likely to underlie the epilepsy?)	Magnetic Resonance Imaging (MRI) - routine for gross pathology (e.g. tumour) - thin slice contiguous for 'subtle' pathology (e.g.dysplasia) and volumetrics - T2 relaxometry - spectroscopy Computerised Tomography (CT) - mainly for detecting calcification
Functional Imaging (Where are the focal metabolic brain changes associated with seizure onset?)	Single Photon Emission Computed Tomography (SPECT) - for detecting focus of seizure onset (increased uptake of isotope injected at seizure onset) Positron Emission Tomography (PET) using radioactive glucose - for detecting interictally hypometabolic cerebral areas indicative of dysfunction Functional Magnetic Resonance Imaging (MRI-f) - for mapping cortical areas subserving major functions (e.g. hand movement, language) - for mapping seizure onset zone
Neuropsychiatry (Are there pre-operative features which increase the risk of post-operative depression or psychosis?)	Clinical history
Neuropsychological Assessment	
Sodium Amytal Tests	Intracarotid injections Selective injections such as posterior cerebral artery

and the risks to cognitive and memory function, is a fundamental and crucial part of their role.

SPECIFIC SURGICAL INTERVENTIONS AND PRE- AND POST-OPERATIVE NEUROPSYCHOLOGY

Our knowledge of brain and behaviour relations has gained much from post-operative studies of cognitive function in patients who have undergone surgery for epilepsy. However, findings from post-operative studies alone cannot be taken to mean that impairment found post-operatively is always the result of surgery, since it may have been present before; or, on the other hand, that the same pattern must be apparent pre-operatively for the neuropsychological profile to be concordant with the site and side of the proposed surgery.

In this chapter, I shall concentrate on pre-operative neuropsychology and on those post-operative studies which include pre-operative assessment and are thus able to reflect change over operation, including the different surgeries for both adults and children.

Temporal lobe (TL) excisions

TL operations may differ in the extent of removal of neocortex and medial structures (hippocampus, amygdala, hippocampal gyrus). The most common procedure is en bloc anterior temporal lobectomy, whereby 4–6 cm of the anterior TL is excised together with medial structures in a single block. In some centres, removal is somewhat smaller in the language dominant side, sparing the superior temporal gyrus. Excisions may be tailored to the individual either by mapping EEG abnormalities and/or areas which disrupt language during surgery, or according to the presence of known pathological tissue. Selective amygdalohippocampectomy (SAH) removes the epileptogenic medial TL areas (hippocampus, amygdala and parahippocampal gyrus) with minimal disruption of neocortex. A small anterior lobectomy giving access to medial structures for removal is sometimes advocated (anteromesiotemporal lobectomy).

Intelligence

IQ is usually in the average range in TL surgery patients. Some centres have considered an IQ below seventy a contraindication to surgery as it suggests more widespread or multifocal damage and thus poor localisation of seizure onset, but this restriction is now less often applied.

Verbal/Performance IQ discrepancies do not consistently distinguish between left and right TL surgery patients (Hermann *et al.* 1995a; see also Chapter 2). Oxbury and Oxbury (1989) found that groups of patients with left or right hippocampal sclerosis (HS) had Performance IQ slightly but not significantly higher than Verbal IQ, with the difference somewhat greater in the left group. A large discrepancy in favour of Verbal IQ in a patient with left TL pathology is probably unusual.

Post-operatively modest increases in IQ may be observed, particularly when seizure outcome is good, possibly more frequently after non-dominant than dominant TL surgery. This may reflect improved function of the non-operated hemisphere (Powell *et al.* 1985).

Cerebral dominance and language function

Determining side of language dominance is important because atypical language dominance will influence interpretation of pre-operative neuropsychological findings and prediction of cognitive outcome from surgery, thereby affecting decisions about whether surgery is safe. It is accomplished by means of intracarotid sodium amytal testing (ISA), which is used routinely in TL surgery candidates in 80 per cent of centres (Snyder *et al.* 1990).

Approximately 90 per cent of right-handed TL patients, and 75 per cent of those with left- or mixed-hand preference, have left hemisphere language dominance (Loring *et al.* 1990). The others have either right hemisphere language dominance or bilateral language representation. The latter is inferred if there is significant language disturbance after both injections and is partly a matter of criteria for definition. It does not necessarily imply equal representation of language in both hemispheres, or that the same functions are represented in both hemispheres (Oxbury and Oxbury 1984; Snyder *et al.* 1990).

Temporal lobectomy candidates do not usually have clinically obvious language disturbance or dysphasia. When this is present, damage beyond anterior TL structures is possible. Some patients, prior to left temporal lobectomy, particularly those with severe HS, appear much less competent linguistically than visuospatially. However, some pre-operative comparisons of left and right TL groups have not revealed significant differences on the Boston Naming Test (BNT), verbal fluency or individual subtests of the Multi-lingual Aphasia Examination (MAE) (Davies *et al.* 1995; Hermann and Wyler 1988;

Hermann *et al.* 1991; Stafiniak *et al.* 1990), although Hermann and Wyler's left TL group was more impaired than the right when subtests were grouped (see also Chapter 2).

In general, lasting disturbance of language function does not follow dominant temporal lobectomy. Thus, Hermann and Wyler (1988) and Hermann *et al.* (1991) found no significant losses on the MAE, but improvement in the comprehension and verbal fluency subtests; Davies *et al.* (1995) found no loss on the BNT and improved verbal fluency. There may be a mild, usually brief, post-operative dysnomia immediately post surgery. Stafiniak *et al.* (1990) using the BNT reported significant decline at two to three weeks after left temporal lobectomy in patients without early risk to brain function (e.g. febrile convulsions, perinatal distress).

Six to 10 per cent of patients do, however, develop persistent aphasia after dominant temporal lobectomy (Pilcher *et al.* 1993). Mostly this is attributable to some people having language zones extending more anteriorly than others. Intra-operative functional mapping can define the anterior limit of the language zones so that the resection can then be tailored. Smaller lobectomies or SAH should also lessen the risk.

Memory

The importance of medial TL structures in anterograde memory function has long been established. The case of HM who developed severe and lasting amnesia after bilateral removal of these structures (Scoville and Milner 1957) is well known. It is also well established that laterality and material specific deficits are seen in patients after unilateral TL surgery. Thus, verbal memory deficits are reliably found in patients who have had left dominant operations (Frisk and Milner 1990) and non-verbal memory deficits in those who have had right non-dominant operations (Smith and Milner 1981), but less reliably so. The extent of hippocampal removal and the type of test paradigm are important factors related to these findings (Jones-Gotman 1991).

In recent years, TL epilepsy research has focused on two main questions. First, what is the status of memory function in patients with unilateral HS (Sagar and Oxbury 1987), since this is the most common single pathology underlying TL epilepsy, and can neuropsychological assessment aid in the diagnosis of this condition? Second, in what circumstances do aspects of memory deteriorate as a result of surgery and can this be avoided (Dodrill *et al.* 1993)? Verbal memory has been studied to a much greater extent than non-verbal memory. Verbal memory decline after left TL surgery may sometimes be quite marked and troublesome; in contrast, patients seldom complain of spatial memory impairment.

The first question can be addressed by investigating the relationship between pre-operative memory and *either* neuronal loss in the hippocampus, which can be established by histopathological examination of the excised specimen post-operatively, *or* by various hippocampal measures seen on pre-operative brain imaging (MRI). These methods have been reviewed by Baxendale (1995). Attempts to answer the second question have investigated the relationship between pre- and post-operative change in memory scores and such factors as pathology, extent and site of removal, pre-operative neuropsychological status and seizure outcome.

The specific nature of the task must be taken into account when considering the relationship between verbal memory and the laterality of HS (Saling *et al.* 1993). The tests most frequently used are those requiring recall of semantically related verbal material usually presented only once (story recall) and those involving learning over several trials of word pairs or word lists which include unrelated material. Several studies have reported no pre-operative difference in immediate or delayed story recall between groups with left or right HS, (McMillan *et al.* 1987; Oxbury and Oxbury 1989; Saling *et al.* 1993) or no relationship between prose recall and degree of HS in either left or right groups (reviewed by Saling *et al.* 1993), although the left HS group was inferior to the right on delayed recall in the study by Miller *et al.* (1993).

Some studies have examined the relationship using neuronal counts in specific hippocampal subfields. Sass *et al.* (1992) found no correlation between immediate and delayed story recall and hippocampal subfields, but in the left group per cent retained correlated with both CA3 and the hilar zones (see Figure 4.1). Matkovic *et al.* (1995a) found a correlation between delayed paragraph recall and CA1 in the right group. MRI hippocampal volume and story recall were not correlated in the study of Trenerry *et al.* (1993). Lencz *et al.* (1992) found a correlation with left hippocampal volume only for per cent retained.

Verbal learning tasks have been more promising in distinguishing patients with left or right HS. Thus, Matkovic *et al.* (1995a), Miller *et al.* (1993), Rausch and Babb (1993) and Saling *et al.* (1993) have all reported differences between left and right groups with varying degrees of HS on paired associate learning and Sass *et al.* (1994) on the Selective Reminding Test. Neuronal counts correlated with verbal

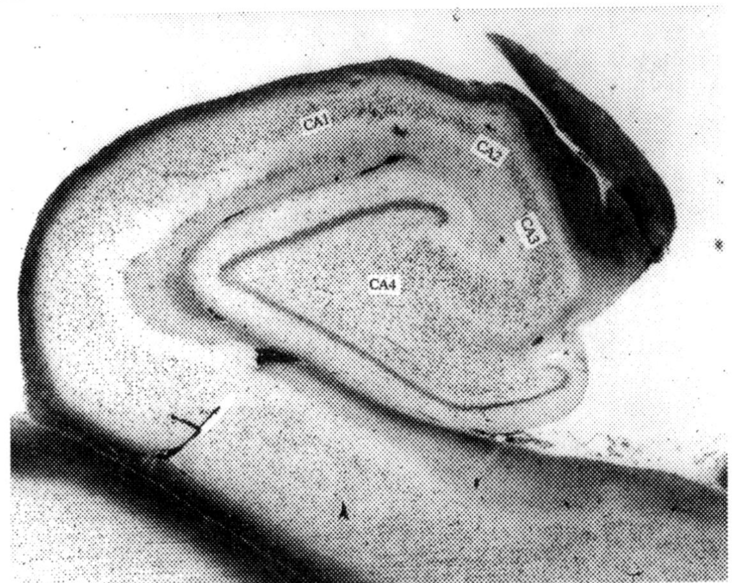

Figure 4.1 A photomicrograph of the hippocampus to show the subfields CA1, CA2, CA3 and CA4

learning in left hippocampus but not right: counts in CA3 and hilar (CA4) zones correlated with selective reminding (Sass *et al.* 1994); CA4 counts correlated with paired associate learning (Matkovic *et al.* 1995a). Although MRI volumes did not correlate with the Rey Auditory Verbal Learning or with the Selective Reminding Test (Trenerry *et al.* 1993; Lencz *et al.* 1992), a left versus right difference in patients with HS defined by MRI volume was found in a word list learning task (Jones-Gotman 1996).

Overall, verbal learning appears to be more specifically associated with left (dominant) hippocampus than does story recall, which frequently fails to distinguish left and right HS groups.

Differences between left and right HS patients in non-verbal memory are rarely reported. However, Matkovic *et al.* (1995b) found a specific correlation between CA4 in the right hippocampus, but not the left, and Benton Visual Retention Test scores. Delayed Rey figure recall correlated with hippocampal neuronal counts in both left and right groups. MRI hippocampal volumes correlated with neither visual reproduction nor a spatial learning task (Lencz *et al.* 1992; Trenerry *et al.* 1993). However, Jones-Gotman (1996) found a right versus left difference between HS groups defined by MRI volumes, on her design learning task.

The risk of reduced verbal memory resulting from left dominant TL surgery is well documented, whereas reduction in non-verbal memory after right TL surgery is less consistently reported (Chelune *et al.* 1991). For left dominant operations, patients with the most intact pre-operative verbal memory appear to be most at risk (ibid.). This is related to the pathological status of the excised tissue. If the excised hippocampus is severely sclerotic, the patient will be likely to have impaired verbal memory prior to surgery and to experience less change over surgery. Conversely, a more intact hippocampus is associated with better pre-operative verbal memory and its excision with a more significant decline (Hermann *et al.* 1995b; Oxbury and Oxbury 1989; Sass *et al.* 1994). Hermann *et al.* found extent of verbal memory loss after left temporal lobectomy to be related to age of onset of epilepsy. This is also likely to be related to pathology, since early onset epilepsy is frequently associated with severe HS (Sagar and Oxbury 1987). Comparable relationships for pathology in right TL and non-verbal memory are not clearly established, but Trenerry *et al.* (1993) demonstrated an association between post-operative decline in visual learning and excision of a relatively non-atrophic right hippocampus, as judged by MRI volumetrics.

Memory change has not been found to be associated with extent of TL excision for total resection, or for extent of medial or cortical resection (Katz *et al.* 1989; Wolf *et al.* 1993). Nevertheless, smaller excisions, if effective for the epilepsy, would seem to be desirable. SAH was designed for this reason and shown to be successful for patients with severe HS. For verbal memory, Verbal IQ and non-verbal memory, Oxbury *et al.* (1995) found better neuropsychological outcome in left HS surgery patients after SAH than after temporal lobectomy, although the better verbal memory has subsequently proved to be the least robust of these findings. Goldstein and Polkey (1992) found no difference in self-reported memory between groups of patients who had undergone SAH compared to standard temporal lobectomy. Goldstein and Polkey (1993) found SAH resulted in slightly less impairment in some cognitive functions than did temporal lobectomy. Improvement in function thought to be mediated by the opposite hemisphere was less after the smaller resection. In these latter two studies, unlike the Oxbury *et al.* study, the two surgical groups were not entirely comparable since they were not matched for pathology, and the criteria for selection for type of operation included pre-operative neuropsychology.

Severe amnesia

There is a small risk that unilateral temporal lobectomy will cause a severe amnesic syndrome (Loring *et al.* 1994; Scoville and Milner 1957). It is associated with a pre-existing abnormality in the medial structures of the non-operated TL (Warrington and Duchen 1992). Pre-operative ISA memory tests are now used to investigate the memory function (and thereby the pathological status) of the not-to-be-operated TL. If memory is inadequate when the side of proposed surgery is inactivated by amytal, then excision of the medial structures may be contraindicated.

Children and temporal lobe excisions

Although many centres now report outcome of TL surgery in children from two to sixteen years of age, remarkably little has been published on detailed pre- and post-operative neuropsychological evaluation. Exceptions are Meyer *et al.* (1986) and Adams *et al.* (1990).

Pre-operatively, neither Meyer *et al.* nor Adams *et al.* found discriminating neuropsychological differences between left and right TL children in either IQ patterns or memory. In the latter study, both left and right groups had a Performance IQ greater than Verbal IQ, particularly those whose excision specimens showed HS. Both groups were poor at verbal paired associate learning, story recall and delayed recall of the Rey figure.

Meyer *et al.*'s group consisted of fifty children followed up after periods ranging from six months to ten years. They reported no overall IQ change, but a shorter interval between seizure onset and surgery was associated with IQ increase. There were no changes in IQ in Adams *et al.*'s forty-four children at six months after en bloc temporal lobectomy. Later follow-up, however, has shown small gains in IQ in those with good seizure outcome (the majority).

Language was assessed in the Adams *et al.* study. Six weeks after left surgery, children had slightly, but significantly, lower scores than pre-operatively on the Oldfield Wingfield naming test. This had recovered at six months. No changes were evident on the Test of Reception of Grammar or Shortened Token Test. In the right group, significant improvement was seen on TROG at six months.

The WMS Memory Quotient did not change overall in Meyer *et al.*'s series, but girls improved while boys worsened slightly. Verbal and non-verbal subtests, however, were not analysed separately in relation to laterality of surgery. Adams *et al.* (1990) found decreased verbal memory following left operation, but no change in either group on delayed reproduction of the Rey figure. Later follow-up has shown more improvement than deterioration in memory scores, not necessarily predictable in terms of laterality or modality. Nevertheless, as in adults, verbal memory is at risk in children having left TL surgery. Pre-operative level and pathology are relevant factors. A significant post-operative decrement can be a continuing disability in schooling.

Frontal lobe (FL) and other extra-temporal excisions

FL excisions constitute the largest single group of extra-temporal operations, but are less frequently performed than TL excisions: 18 per cent and 11 per cent in the series of Penfield and of Olivier, respectively, as compared to 56 per cent and 74 per cent TL operations (Olivier and Awad 1993). Based on post-operative studies alone, FL excision patients show several impairments, for example, in conditional learning (Petrides 1990) and impulsive behaviour (Miller 1992).

Few studies have systematically studied frontal lobectomy patients both pre- and post-operatively. Furthermore, different areas or subsystems within the FL are likely to be associated with different functions, making the problem harder to dissect. Milner (1988) reported pre-operative test performance and post-operative seizure outcome in patients who underwent FL removals. Pre-operative deficits were not consistently seen except in word fluency in the left group, whose seizures were subsequently controlled by surgery.

The author is not aware of any specific pre- and post-operative reports which help to identify those patients who are particularly vulnerable to decline following surgery. An important factor, as with other excisions, is likely to be that of whether the tissue removed is pathological, or intact and functional.

Pre- and post-operative studies of children having FL surgery are also lacking. Jones-Gotman (1990) describes a children's design fluency task and gives examples of abnormal performance in children tested post-operatively only: highly perseverative prolific output, highly perseverative low output, and rule breaking. She suggests this task be used pre-operatively.

Non-frontal extra-temporal excisions form even smaller groups. Neuropsychological assessment should start with standard broad-based evaluation and be expanded to cover functions known to be associated with the area to be excised. Where this encroaches upon language areas, functional mapping is essential.

Hemispherectomy

Most of those undergoing hemispherectomy are children with a history of infantile hemiplegia and intractable epilepsy or who have acquired Rasmussen's syndrome. The rationale is that the massively damaged non-functional hemisphere from which the epilepsy is coming can be removed without increasing the pre-existing neurological impairment. There are several different surgical techniques, from complete anatomical removal to leaving the hemisphere in situ but disconnecting it from the rest of the brain (functional hemispherectomy); some combine partial removal with partial disconnection.

Hemispherectomy for early static damage

These children have severe damage to one hemisphere from an early age (including foetal). Cognitive function has developed in the good hemisphere with generally most functions represented but usually below the average range. The Oxford series has shown no particular Verbal/Performance IQ pattern prior to surgery and usually little discrepancy between these scores. Intractable seizures are often accompanied by difficult behaviour and both behaviour and cognitive function may be deteriorating by the time surgery is considered. Family life is often seriously disrupted (Beardsworth and Adams 1988).

An early review of ten cases of Adams' modified hemispherectomy (Beardsworth and Adams 1988) showed seizure outcome to be good, motor function largely unaffected, and behaviour and family life improved with cessation of seizures. Some children showed significant and continuing cognitive gains with the passage of time and behavioural improvements were recorded at clinical follow-up in approximately 75 per cent (Oxbury *et al.* 1995).

Rasmussen's syndrome

This syndrome, which affects previously normal children, usually begins in the first decade of life with uncontrolled focal seizures and progresses over a variable period of time with development of hemiplegia and cognitive deterioration. The disease is considered to affect one hemisphere only, but generalised cognitive deterioration usually occurs. If the onset is in the left hemisphere before the age of six, language usually develops in the right hemisphere, but may make less satisfactory 'transfer' after this age. Taylor (1991) discusses the dilemma of whether to proceed to left surgery before full transfer of speech to the right hemisphere, with the hope of alleviating the continuous seizures, or whether to wait until transfer has happened, while the child suffers the detrimental effects of seizures.

Corpus callosotomy

This operation disconnects the cerebral hemispheres, rather than excising pathology or epileptogenic tissue, and thereby inhibits the rapid generalisation of seizure activity from one hemisphere to the other. This may reduce the frequency of seizures, especially drop attacks, but rarely abolishes them. Callosotomy may be partial or total, anterior or posterior. Usually the anterior two-thirds is divided first, followed by later completion of callosotomy if seizures are not improved.

Adults

Pre-operative abilities span a wide range, from normal to considerably impaired. There is no particular pattern and there may be damage to, or epileptic foci in, either hemisphere. Therefore, neuropsychological assessment needs to be broad-ranging, carefully evaluating those functions at risk. ISA is essential to establish cerebral dominance.

Neuropsychological features of the various disconnection syndromes resulting from callosal section include diminished speech or mutism, apraxia or neglect of left limbs, hemispheric competition in which the two hands may act antagonistically ('alien hand'), and the classical posterior disconnection syndrome in which visual or tactile information entering the non-dominant hemisphere cannot be responded to verbally. Factors related to the occurrence and permanence of these syndromes are discussed by Pilcher *et al.* (1993).

Memory decline may occur following posterior, but not anterior, section, and may be associated with inclusion of the hippocampal commissure in the posterior section (Phelps *et al.* 1991).

Children

Lassonde *et al.* (1990) concluded that corpus callosotomy in children does not affect long-term cognitive, social or motor behaviour, and that neuropsychological improvement was associated with seizure control. The absence of long-term sequelae of the classical disconnection deficits in children operated under 12 years of age suggests that the young brain adjusts more easily to callosotomy.

PRACTICAL GUIDE

It will be clear from the previous sections (and Chapter 2) that assessment of patients prior to surgery for epilepsy must be a broad-based neuropsychological examination covering tests of general intelligence, language function, visuospatial and perceptual ability, frontal lobe/executive/attentional tasks and several aspects of memory and learning in both the verbal and the non-verbal domains. Jones-Gotman *et al.* (1993) have compiled an exhaustive list of the tests used by psychologists from many centres.

Adults

The following is a suggested protocol for use with adults:

1 Wechsler Adult Intelligence Scale – Revised (WAIS-R).
2 Tests of language function: Multilingual Aphasia Examination (MAE) or selected subtests, e.g. Sentence Repetition, Word Association, augmented by a naming test, Oldfield-Wingfield Object Naming, Graded Naming Test or Boston Naming Test, and a comprehension task such as the Shortened Token Test.
Reading and Spelling – e.g. Schonell Graded Word Reading and Spelling tests.
3 Where indicated, additional visuospatial perceptual tasks, such as the Visual Object and Space Perception Battery (VOSP).
4 Tests intended to examine executive function, such as Wisconsin Card Sorting Test, Trail Making, Stroop, Cognitive Estimates.
Every psychologist is aware of the behavioural and personality problems experienced by some individuals with FL damage, the most florid syndrome resulting from bilateral damage with a milder picture seen after unilateral damage. Thus, it is important to assess, even informally, a patient's ability to plan and structure his or her activities and to interact with others, so that post-operative change or

lack of it may be recorded. An interesting single case showing a strategy application disorder after unilateral lobectomy, is described by Goldstein *et al.* (1993).

5 Tests of memory and learning (important for all patients, especially for TL patients). In the verbal domain: immediate span, both digits and sentences (from WAIS-R or MAE); story recall (e.g. Logical Memory from WMS) with delayed recall; verbal learning, list learning such as the Selective Reminding Test, Rey Auditory Verbal Learning Test, or California Verbal Learning Test (CVLT), Paired Associates from WMS. In the non-verbal sphere: immediate recall, Corsi block tapping span and Benton Visual Retention; Rey Osterrieth figure or Taylor equivalent with delayed recall; ideally, a non-verbal learning task such as design or maze learning.

The choice of a test battery is important. Only when this has been used over a period of time will the psychologist begin to build up experience with different types of patients, so it is important to stick with one's original set at least for a period of time.

Children

Similar principles, with additional considerations, apply for assessment of children. The extent to which the aims of neuropsychological assessment, as discussed earlier in this chapter, are appropriate or can be met will differ depending on the age and developmental level of the child. Since present knowledge of long-term neuropsychological outcome from surgery in children is scanty, the possibility of making predictions is reduced. Educational attainment tests should be added to the battery, to give an indication of the effect of the epilepsy and/or the underlying pathology on the child's school progress.

In very young, or very delayed children the aim of pre-operative assessment may be careful baseline assessment of developmental level, perhaps with special emphasis on language development. Alternatively, the initial aim may be to monitor development over a period of time and to document developmental arrest or regression. These may be important factors in the decision to recommend surgery, since concern about possible cognitive effects of operation will be less potent if a child with intractable seizures is already losing skills. Indeed, in such cases it is hoped that the removal of pathology, and cessation or amelioration of seizures, will halt the decline, so allowing the child to make progress.

In children between the ages of six and twelve years and of average intelligence much less is known about the degree to which psychological functions are lateralised or localised than it is in adults. Language is usually thought to have lateralised by the age of six and earlier damage may affect cerebral dominance. Little is known about surgical risks to memory, cognition and their future development in this age group. The concept of greater plasticity in the child, and hence an improved chance of recovery from cognitive deficit resulting from surgery attributable to other brain areas taking over function, is often raised in discussion of young children. However, plasticity is unlikely to be absolute and the 'crowding' effect may place limits on the final level of cognitive development. In the child over twelve years, the neuropsychological issues can reasonably be assumed to be similar to those in adults. These issues and a range of suggested tests have been reviewed elsewhere (Oxbury 1997).

A test battery should include:

1 Tests of general developmental level or intelligence such as Griffiths or Bayley Developmental Scales, WPPSI-R or WISC-III, depending on age and developmental level.
2 Tests of language function: Naming, Verbal fluency, STT and/or TROG, comprehension vocabulary, British Picture Vocabulary Scale; possibly additional children's language tests, e.g. Clinical Evaluation of Language Fundamentals (CELF).
3 Additional visuospatial tests, e.g. from the British Ability Scales.
4 Children's norms are available for the Wisconsin Card Sorting Test and Trail Making. Whether these tasks measure FL function in children is not known. Children may fail for a variety of reasons, and in any case these functions may develop fairly late in maturation. Nevertheless, results could be of interest, especially in the context of long-term follow-up.
5 Memory tests are important and should cover the same ground as in adults. The Wide Range Assessment of Memory and Learning (WRAML) has several suitable subtests but the disadvantage of no equivalent forms. Story recall (Beardsworth and Bishop 1994) is useful. Spreen and Strauss (1991) give children's norms for several verbal learning tasks (e.g. Paired Associates and Selective Reminding). The non-verbal memory tests suggested for adults are standardised for children (see also Chapter 9).

Sodium amytal tests

These tests are designed to anaesthetise one hemisphere (or part of one hemisphere) while language and memory functions of the other hemisphere are assessed. Cerebral language dominance must be established prior to surgery. Adequate memory function of the not-to-be-operated hemisphere must be demonstrated when TL surgery is proposed. In addition, memory failure, when the side of proposed surgery is tested (by injection into the contralateral hemisphere), is taken to confirm pathology in the hippocampus on this side (Carpenter *et al.* 1996).

The usual method is to inject sodium amytal into the internal carotid artery through a catheter inserted via the femoral artery – intracarotid sodium amytal (ISA). ISA causes contralateral hemiplegia and, in the dominant hemisphere, aphasia lasting a few minutes. Test protocols vary very considerably in terms of dose, whether both hemispheres are tested on the same day or separate days, tests of language and memory, and interpretation of results (see Rausch *et al.* 1993). Protocols for testing language and memory are described in Oxbury and Oxbury (1984) and Carpenter *et al.* (1996).

In Oxford, ISA is routinely used in patients over twelve years. Children under twelve tolerate the procedure less well (Jones-Gotman 1990). When crucially important, language dominance can usually be tested in younger children, but results of memory tests, particularly after dominant hemisphere injection, are unreliable (Williams and Rausch 1992).

Post-operative assessment

Full post-operative neuropsychological follow-up is important and its usefulness as a measure of outcome depends upon the quality of the pre-operative assessment. For both adults and children the measurement of any changes, deficits or improvements, will add to knowledge about the risks and benefits of surgery. They are also useful in psychosocial or educational counselling. Assessments should be repeated at intervals, ideally over several years in the case of children, to monitor development and long-term effects. The implications for research are obvious. Without both pre- and post-operative evaluation, knowledge relating pre-operative neuropsychological factors to lateralisation, localisation and type of pathology, or to predict neuropsychological, developmental and other outcomes cannot advance (Hermann 1990; Dodrill *et al.* 1993).

Methodological considerations must be borne in mind. Effects of practice on test performance and use of alternative test versions are important issues. This constitutes a very real problem in the case of assessment of memory since previous exposure to material purporting to measure new learning may falsify the results. Developmental issues are important. The question remains as to whether it is possible to devise tests for children which can reliably measure the neuropsychological functions evaluated in adults or, perhaps more appropriately, chart the development of these functions over time.

The Oxford protocol includes full pre-operative neuropsychological assessment, including ISA, brief re-assessment of language and memory at six to eight weeks after surgery, and full post-operative neuropsychological assessment at six months, two years and five years.

PSYCHOSOCIAL ISSUES

Consideration of surgical outcome goes beyond that of seizure relief and cognitive outcome. Broader psychosocial functioning should also be evaluated. Areas investigated in studies of psychosocial function vary considerably but commonly include: employment; dependency/independence; interpersonal relationships, inside and outside the family; personal adjustment factors such as self image, sexual functioning (see Dodrill *et al.* 1991). Methodological problems make comparison between studies difficult. These include different areas evaluated; types of measurement (questionnaire, rating scales, factual information); variable follow-up intervals both within and between studies. Nevertheless, some general conclusions may be drawn.

The factor most related to improved psychosocial outcome is relief from seizures. Some studies have found significant improvement only in those patients who experience complete seizure relief. Although others have found the degree of improvement related to the degree of seizure control (Vickrey *et al.* 1991), Hermann *et al.*'s (1992) study re-emphasises the greater beneficial effect of complete seizure relief as compared to 75 per cent reduction in seizure frequency.

Other factors related to improved psychosocial outcome are pre-operative employment status, with those chronically unemployed least likely to benefit, degree of family support and adequacy of pre-operative psychosocial adjustment (Hermann *et al.* 1992).

As for children, Lindsay *et al.*'s (1984) study describing the benefits of seizure relief in all areas of psychosocial adjustment remains a classic. In our more recent Oxford series of children having TL surgery before leaving school, 80 per cent of those who had left education and were seizure free at the five-year follow-up were employed, compared to only 23 per cent of those who still experienced seizures.

Finally, virtually all of these studies have involved patients having TL and, to a lesser extent, other focal resections. Findings may not be applicable to those having other procedures such as hemispherectomy or callosotomy.

REFERENCES

Adams, C. B. T., Beardsworth, E. D., Oxbury, S. M., Oxbury, J. M. and Fenwick, P. B. C. (1990) 'Temporal lobectomy in 44 children: outcome and neuropsychological follow-up', *Journal of Epilepsy* 3 (Suppl. 1): 157–68.

Baxendale, S. A. (1995) 'The hippocampus: functional and structural correlations', *Seizure* 4: 105–17.

Beardsworth, E. D. and Adams, C. B. T. (1988) 'Modified hemispherectomy for epilepsy: early results in 10 cases', *British Journal of Neurosurgery* 2: 73–84.

Beardsworth, E. D. and Bishop, D. (1994) 'Assessment of long term verbal memory in children', *Memory* 2: 129–48.

Carpenter, K. N., Oxbury, J. M., Oxbury, S. M. and Wright G. D. S. (1996) 'Memory for objects presented early after intra-carotid sodium amytal: a sensitive clinical neuropsychological indicator of temporal lobe pathology', *Seizure* 5: 103–8.

Chelune, G. J., Naugle, R., Lüders, H. and Awad, I. A. (1991) 'Prediction of cognitive change as a function of pre-operative ability status among temporal lobectomy patients', *Neurology* 4: 477–85.

Davies, K. G., Maxwell, R. E., Beniak, T. E., Destafney, E. and Fiol, M. E. (1995) 'Language function after temporal lobectomy without stimulation mapping of cortical function', *Epilepsia* 36: 130–6.

Dodrill, C. B., Batzel, L. W. and Fraser, R. (1991) 'Psychosocial changes after surgery for epilepsy', in H. Lüders (ed.) *Epilepsy Surgery*, New York: Raven Press.

Dodrill, C. B., Hermann, B. P., Rausch, R., Chelune, G. J. and Oxbury, S. (1993) 'Neuropsychological testing for assessing prognosis following surgery for epilepsy', in J. Engel Jnr (ed.) *Surgical Treatment of the Epilepsies* (2nd edn), New York: Raven Press.

Engel, J. (1993) 'Overview: who should be considered a surgical candidate?', in J. Engel Jnr (ed.) *Surgical Treatment of the Epilepsies* (2nd edn), New York: Raven Press.

Engel, J. and Ojemann, G. A. (1993) 'The next step', in J. Engel Jnr (ed.) *Surgical Treatment of the Epilepsies* (2nd edn), New York: Raven Press.

Frisk, V. and Milner, B. (1990) 'The relationship of working memory to the immediate recall of stories following unilateral temporal or frontal lobectomy', *Neuropsychologia* 28: 121–35.

Goldstein, L. H. and Polkey, C. E. (1992) 'Everyday memory after unilateral temporal lobectomy or amygdalohippocampectomy', *Cortex* 28: 189–201.

—— (1993) 'Short term cognitive changes after unilateral temporal lobectomy or unilateral amygdalohippocampectomy for the relief of temporal lobe epilepsy', *Journal of Neurology, Neurosurgery and Psychiatry* 56: 135–40.

Goldstein, L. H., Bernard, S., Fenwick, P. B. C., Burgess, P. W. and McNeil, J. (1993) 'Unilateral frontal lobectomy can produce strategy application disorder', *Journal of Neurology, Neurosurgery and Psychiatry* 56: 274–6.

Hermann, B. P. (1990) 'Psychosocial outcome following focal resections in childhood', *Journal of Epilepsy* 3 (Suppl. 1): 243–52.

Hermann, B. P. and Wyler, A. R. (1988) 'Effects of anterior temporal lobectomy on language function: a controlled study', *Annals of Neurology* 23: 585–8.

Hermann, B. P., Wyler, A. R., and Somes, G. (1991) 'Language function following anterior temporal lobectomy', *Journal of Neurosurgery* 74: 560–6.

Hermann, B. P., Wyler, A. R. and Somes, G. (1992) 'Pre-operative psychological adjustment and surgical outcome are determinants of psychosocial status after anterior temporal lobectomy', *Journal of Neurology, Neurosurgery and Psychiatry* 55: 491–6.

Hermann, B. P., Gold, J., Pusakulich, R., Wyler, A. R., Randolph, C., Rankin, G. and Hoy, W. (1995a) 'Wechsler Adult Intelligence Scale-Revised in the evaluation of anterior temporal lobectomy candidates', *Epilepsia* 36: 480–7.

Hermann, B. P., Seidenberg, M., Haltiner, A. and Wyler, A. R. (1995b) 'Relationship of age of onset, chronological age, and adequacy of pre-operative performance to verbal memory change after anterior temporal lobectomy', *Epilepsia* 36: 137–45.

Jones-Gotman, M. (1990) 'Presurgical psychological assessment in children: special tests', *Journal of Epilepsy* 3 (Suppl): 93–102.

—— (1991) 'Presurgical neuropsychological evaluation for localisation and lateralisation of seizure focus', in H. Lüders (ed.) in *Epilepsy Surgery*, New York: Raven Press.

—— (1996) 'Psychological evaluation for epilepsy surgery', in S. Shorvon, F. Dreifuss, D. Fish and D. Thomas (eds), *The Treatment of Epilepsy*, Oxford: Blackwell Science.

Jones-Gotman, M., Smith M-L. and Zatorre, R. J. (1993) 'Neuropsychological testing for localising and lateralising the epileptogenic region', in J. Engel Jnr (ed.) *Surgical Treatment of Epilepsies* (2nd edn), New York: Raven Press.

Katz, A., Awad, I. A., Kong, A. K., Chelune, G. J., Naugle, R. I., Wyllie, E., Beauchamp, G. and Lüders, H. (1989) 'Extent of resection in temporal lobectomy for epilepsy. II. Memory changes and neurologic complications', *Epilepsia* 30: 763–71.

Lassonde, M., Sauerwein, H., Geoffroy, G. and Décarie, M. (1990) 'Long-term neuropsychological effects of corpus callosotomy in children', *Journal of Epilepsy* 3 (Suppl. 1): 279–86.

Lencz, T., McCarthy, G. and Bronen, R. A. (1992) 'Quantitative magnetic resonance imaging in temporal lobe epilepsy: relationship to neuropathology and neuropsychological function', *Annals of Neurology* 31: 629–37.

Lindsay, J., Ounsted, C. and Richards, P. (1984) 'Long-term outcome in children with temporal lobe seizures. V. Indications and contraindications for neurosurgery,' *Developmental Medicine and Child Neurology* 26: 25–32.

Loring, D. W., Meador, K. J., Lee, G. P., Murro, A. M., Smith, J. R., Flanigin, H. R., Gallagher, B. B. and King, D. W. (1990) 'Cerebral language lateralization: evidence from intracarotid amobarbital testing', *Neuropsychologia* 28: 831–8.

Loring, D. W., Hermann, B. P., Meador, K. J., Lee, G. P., Gallagher, B. B., King, D. W., Murro, A. M., Smith, J. R. and Wyler, A. R. (1994) 'Amnesia after unilateral temporal lobectomy: a case report', *Epilepsia* 35: 757–63.

McMillan, T. M., Powell, G. E., Janota, I. and Polkey, C. E. (1987) 'Relationships between neuropathology and cognitive functioning in temporal lobectomy patients', *Journal of Neurology, Neurosurgery and Psychiatry* 50: 167–76.

Matkovic, Z., Oxbury, S. M., Hiorns, R. W., Morris, J. H., Carpenter, K. N., Adams, C. B. T. and Oxbury, J. M. (1995a) 'Hippocampal neuronal density correlates with pre-operative verbal memory in patients with temporal lobe epilepsy', *Epilepsia* 36 (Suppl. 3): S121.

Matkovic, Z., Oxbury, S. M., Hiorns, R. W., Morris, J. H., Carpenter, K. N., Adams, C. B. T. and Oxbury, J. M. (1995b) 'Hippocampal neuronal density correlates with pre-operative non-verbal memory in patients with temporal lobe epilepsy', *Epilepsia* 36 (Suppl 3): S93.

Meyer, F. B., Marsh, R., Laws, E. R. Jr. and Sharbrough, F. W. (1986) 'Temporal lobectomy in children with epilepsy', *Journal of Neurosurgery* 64: 371–6.

Miller, L. A. (1992) 'Impulsivity, risk-taking, and the ability to synthesize fragmented information after frontal lobectomy', *Neuropsychologia* 30: 69–79.

Miller, L. A., Munoz, D. G. and Finmore, M. (1993) 'Hippocampal sclerosis and human memory', *Archives of Neurology* 50: 391–4.

Milner, B. (1988) 'Patterns of neuropsychological deficit in frontal lobe epilepsies', *Epilepsia* 29: 221.

Olivier, A. and Awad, I. A. (1993) 'Extratemporal resections', in J. Engel Jnr (ed.) *Surgical Treatment of the Epilepsies* (2nd edn), New York: Raven Press.

Oxbury, J. M. and Oxbury, S. M. (1989) 'Neuropsychology, memory and hippocampal pathology', in E. H. Reynolds and M. R. Trimble (eds) *The Bridge between Neurology and Psychiatry*, London: Churchill Livingstone.

Oxbury, J. M., Adams, C. B. T., Oxbury, S. M., Carpenter, K. N. and Renowden, S. A. (1995) 'En bloc temporal lobectomy v. selective amygdalohippocampectomy as treatments for intractable epilepsy due to hippocampal sclerosis', *Journal of Neurology, Neurosurgery and Psychiatry* 59: 200.

Oxbury, S. M. (1997) 'Neuropsychological evaluation – children', in J. Engel and T. A. Pedley (eds) *Epilepsy: A Comprehensive Textbook*, Philadelphia: Lippincott-Raven.

Oxbury, S. M. and Oxbury, J. M. (1984) 'Intracarotid amytal test in the assessment of language dominance', in F. C. Rose (ed.) *Progress in Aphasiology: Advances in Neurology 42*, New York: Raven Press.

Oxbury, S. M., Zaiwalla, Z., Adams, C. B. T., Middleton, J. A. and Oxbury, J. M. (1995) 'Hemispherectomy in childhood: serial neuropsychological follow-up and prolonged improvement', *Epilepsia* 36 (Suppl. 3): S24.

Petrides, M. (1990) 'Nonspatial conditional learning impaired in patients with unilateral frontal but not unilateral temporal lobe excisions', *Neuropsychologia* 28: 137–49.

Phelps, E. A., Hirst, W. and Gazzaniga, M. S. (1991) 'Deficits in recall following partial and complete commissurotomy', *Cerebral Cortex* 1: 492–8.

Pilcher, W. H., Roberts, D. W., Flanigan, H. F., Crandall, P. H., Wieser, H. G.,

Ojemann, G. A. and Peacock, W. J. (1993) 'Complications of epilepsy surgery', in J. Engel Jnr (ed.) *Surgical Treatment of the Epilepsies* (2nd edn), New York: Raven Press.

Powell, G. E., Polkey, C. E. and McMillan, T. M. (1985) 'The new Maudsley series of temporal lobectomy. I: Short term cognitive effects', *British Journal of Clinical Psychology* 24: 109–24.

Rausch, R. and Babb, T. L. (1993) 'Hippocampal neuron loss and memory scores before and after temporal lobe surgery for epilepsy', *Archives of Neurology* 50: 812–17.

Rausch, R., Silfvenius, H., Wieser, H-G., Dodrill, C. B., Meador, K. J. and Jones-Gotman, M. (1993) 'Intra-arterial amobarbital procedures', in J. Engel Jnr (ed.) *Surgical Treatment of the Epilepsies* (2nd edn), New York: Raven Press.

Sagar, H. J. and Oxbury, J. M. (1987) 'Hippocampal neurone loss in temporal lobe epilepsy: correlation with early childhood convulsions', *Annals of Neurology* 22: 334–40.

Saling, M. M., Berkovic, S. F. and O'Shea, M. F. (1993) 'Lateralization of verbal memory and unilateral hippocampal sclerosis: evidence of task-specific effects', *Journal of Clinical and Experimental Neuropsychology* 15: 608–18.

Sass, K. J., Westerveld, M. and Buchanan, C. (1994) 'Degree of hippocampal neuron loss determines severity of verbal memory decrease after left anteromesiotemporal lobectomy', *Epilepsia* 35: 1179–86.

Sass, K. J., Sass, A., Westerveld, M., Lencz, T., Novelly, R. A., Kim, J. H. and Spencer, D. D. (1992) 'Specificity in the correlation of verbal memory and hippocampal neuron loss: dissociation of memory, language and verbal intellectual ability', *Journal of Clinical and Experimental Neuropsychology* 14: 662–72.

Scoville, W. and Milner, B. (1957) 'Loss of recent memory after bilateral hippocampal lesions', *Journal of Neurology, Neurosurgery and Psychiatry* 20: 11–21.

Smith, M. L. and Milner, B. (1981) 'The role of the right hippocampus in the recall of spatial location', *Neuropsychologia* 19: 781–93.

Snyder, P. J., Novelly, R. A. and Harris, L. J. (1990) 'Mixed speech dominance in the intracarotid sodium amytal procedure: validity and criteria issues', *Journal of Clinical and Experimental Neuropsychology* 12: 629–43.

Spreen, O. and Strauss, E. (1991) *A Compendium of Neuropsychological Tests*, New York: Oxford University Press.

Stafiniak, P., Saykin, A. J., Sperling, M. R., Kester, D. B., Robinson, L. J., O'Connor, K. J. and Gur, R. C. (1990) 'Acute naming deficits following dominant temporal lobectomy', *Neurology* 40: 1509–12.

Taylor, L. B. (1991) 'Neuropsychologic assessment of patients with chronic encephalitis', in F. Andermann (ed.) *Chronic Encephalitis and Epilepsy, Rasmussen's Syndrome*, Boston: Butterworth–Heinemann.

Trenerry, M. R., Jack, C. R., Ivnik, R. J., Sharbrough, F. W., Cascino, G. D., Hirschorn, K. A., Marsh, W. R., Kelly, P. J. and Meyer, F. B. (1993) 'MRI hippocampal volumes and memory function before and after temporal lobectomy', *Neurology* 43: 1800–5.

Vickrey, R. D., Hays, R., Rausch, R., Engel, J. Jr and Brook, R. H. (1991) 'Quality of life after surgical treatment of epilepsy', *Epilepsia* 32 (Suppl. 1): 57.

Warrington, E. K. and Duchen, L. W. (1992) 'A re-appraisal of a case of persistent global amnesia following right temporal lobectomy: a clinico-pathological study', *Neuropsychologia* 30: 437–50.

Williams, J. and Rausch, R. (1992) 'Factors in children that predict memory performance on the intracarotid amobarbital procedure', *Epilepsia* 33: 1036–41.

Wolf, R. L., Ivnik, R. J., Hirschorn, K. A., Sharbrough, M. D., Cascino, G. D. and Marsh, W. R. (1993) 'Neurocognitive efficiency following left temporal lobectomy: standard versus limited resection', *Journal of Neurosurgery* 76: 76–83.

Chapter 5

The role of anti-epileptic drugs

Their impact on cognitive function and behaviour

Ruth Gillham and Christine Cull

A common concern voiced by people with epilepsy is that their anticonvulsant medication is affecting their memory. This is reflected in the growing interest in the impact of anti-epileptic drugs (AEDs) on aspects of behaviour other than seizures. Indeed, all new AEDs are now evaluated for cognitive/behavioural side effects, and the lack of such effects is a major selling point for manufacturers.

While epilepsy can be associated with a variety of cognitive/behavioural deficits, the clinical psychologist may be asked to comment on the extent to which an AED may be compromising an individual's functioning on formal cognitive testing or on a day-to-day basis, over and above the effects of the seizure disorder itself. The psychologist may be asked to evaluate the impact of any drug change, or to contribute to the planning of drug trials evaluating the effects of new AEDs, in addition to which, the person with epilepsy may wish to discuss the impact of their medication.

In order to make sense of the available literature, the interested clinician needs to be aware of the issues involved in the investigation of drug effects, and the different study designs that have been employed, which we will consider before presenting a brief review of the area.

INVESTIGATION OF DRUG EFFECTS

Study designs

The investigation of drug effects in individuals with epilepsy is problematic. First, this is because one has to take into account all the other variables which may also effect cognition/behaviour such as aetiology, age at onset and duration of the seizure disorder, seizure type and frequency, and type of EEG abnormality. Second, the type of study design that one might use is constrained by ethical issues and the clinical needs of the patient.

Studies of *normal volunteers* eliminate the impact of potentially contaminating epilepsy variables, and allow for methodologically sound designs, often using double-blind placebo cross-over comparisons. However, these are usually single dose studies, or, at most, conducted over a period of two weeks' constant usage at subclinical doses. Thus, there are clearly difficulties in generalising the results to individuals who have to take the drugs for many years. Any effects noted may be transient, but in normal volunteer studies there is no way of evaluating this. A healthy volunteer is not analogous to a patient with epilepsy in that there must be differences between their underlying neural and neurochemical substrates, or both would be producing seizures. Thus, extrapolation from this group to a neurologically different group may not be warranted. Therefore, while such a design has predominantly methodological advantages, the applicability of the results to patients with epilepsy is questionable.

In view of this, the most useful information is likely to come from studies of people with epilepsy, where a number of different designs (longitudinal, cross-over, cross-sectional, or drug/dose concentration studies) are used.

All *longitudinal designs* share in common the use of repeated assessments over time, with individuals acting as their own controls. The most common of these is an *add-on* study in which a new AED is added to a regimen which already includes at least one other AED.

Such designs are often adopted in the investigation of new compounds, used as adjunctive therapy in patients with a refractory seizure disorder. However, since about 80 per cent of patients have their seizures effectively controlled (Brodie 1985), this group is a minority. Many such patients will have complex partial seizures which, by definition, will be associated with focal pathology and may have neuropsychological sequelae. In addition many subjects will have experienced numerous changes in dose and drug combination, which themselves may produce cognitive impairment. Thus, any generalisations made from this group of patients with epilepsy must be tentative. In addition, results may be contaminated by the effect of the new drug on seizure frequency, and by any interaction between the drugs.

It is possible to examine the effects of medication in previously untreated individuals who are taking an AED for the first time. Although the results may be contaminated by the effect of the drug on seizure frequency, such patients do not have a long neuropsychological-deficit producing history and have no previous history of AED treatment, which is clearly advantageous.

Conversely, *drug deletion* studies may be undertaken, involving rationalisation of a multi-drug regimen (which may bring about an improvement in seizure frequency), or, alternatively, the complete withdrawal of AEDs in individuals who have been seizure-free for two years or more, so eliminating the effects of seizure type and frequency. Improvements in performance following withdrawal are taken as evidence that the withdrawn AED was affecting cognitive functioning.

Other longitudinal studies have explored the effect of a change in medication *(drug substitution)*, presumably in an attempt to improve seizure frequency and this may be a confounding factor. While any change in functioning may be attributable to the new drug, it is equally possible that it is the result of the withdrawal of a more toxic or sedative compound.

All of the above designs may be placebo controlled where a matched group of subjects are given a placebo rather than the active medication (although this would not be ethically acceptable in studies of newly diagnosed patients). Both patient and investigator are required not to know who is on what particular regimen (i.e. to be blind). While this is a more methodologically rigorous approach, there are practical issues in maintaining 'blindness' and ethical issues about not allowing patients access to a potentially effective treatment, which means that such studies can only be of limited duration. In studies of new patients, however, it is possible to undertake a double-blind comparison of different drugs.

The simplest study is *cross-sectional* and compares groups of subjects on different AEDs without any treatment changes. However, sources of bias are large: there may well be reasons why a patient has been prescribed one drug and not another, such as the clinician's beliefs about efficacy, previous treatment failures, and even age and gender. For example, sodium valproate (which can produce weight gain) and phenytoin (which can produce facial changes) may be less popular amongst younger women than carbamazepine. Sample sizes must be large, or groups carefully matched, to control for variables such as aetiology, lifetime seizure frequency and previous drug history. The advantage of this design is that it can be carried out in any epilepsy clinic, with the person assessing cognitive factors being blind to treatment, but no complex blinding procedures being necessary. As tests are administered once, learning and practice effects are not an issue. At the end of the day, however, even if there are significant differences between the groups, it will still be difficult to be sure that these are attributable to the drug and the drug alone (Dodrill 1992).

The most methodologically sound design is a *double-blind randomised cross-over* study in which patients are randomly assigned to treatment with one or another drug, or placebo, with both investigator and patient being blind. After a set period of time the new treatment is removed, there may be a brief wash-out phase, and the alternative treatment is then introduced for the same length of time. Assessments take place before any drug is introduced and after a period of time on each agent. Such studies usually involve the use of add-on drugs and thus suffer from the disadvantages outlined previously in terms of the generalisability of the results. Again, ethical and clinical demands dictate that these can only take place over a limited period of time.

A further approach to exploring the cognitive/behavioural impact of AEDs is to look at drug dose/concentration effects (as determined by the concentration of the drug in blood serum (see Chapter 1)). Thus, patients on the same drug but at different serum blood levels may be compared, or performance within the same individual at low and high serum levels. Alternatively, correlational analyses may be carried out between the performance measure and serum levels.

From the above, therefore, it can be seen that there is a wide variety of designs that can be used, none of which are without disadvantages.

Assessment tools

It is also important to take into account the measures used. Early reports in the literature were largely anecdotal. However, as interest in the area grew, so more standardised tests have been used. Cognitive measures have included IQ tests such as the Wechsler scales, or neuropsychological batteries such as the Halstead-Reitan (used predominantly in the USA). Clearly, there are potential difficulties with such measures in a longitudinal study, depending on the test–retest interval and the contribution of practice effects to the outcome. Further, the use of tests designed primarily as neuropsychological measures may yield limited information, as the effects of drugs may be different to those of structural brain damage. Consequently, many investigators have developed their own test batteries resulting in as many different batteries as there are studies, hindering between study comparison.

Most cognitive test batteries try to incorporate measures of memory, psychomotor performance and information processing. The aspects of memory easiest to measure are short term tasks such as Digit Span, which can be repeated without too much learning effect. Recall of passages of prose or word list learning require alternative forms to be available for repeated use. 'Psychomotor' is defined variously: studies from the USA have tended to use it as a composite term, meaning cognitive function, with speed and motor skill included. In Europe, it tends to be reserved for motor tasks such as simple or choice reaction time, and tapping rate. In general, psychomotor tasks, require equipment and this causes a great deal of variability between centres, hindering generalisations from one study to another. 'Information processing' or 'central processing' is an even looser term that subsumes a great many functions and is tested in many different ways. Common tasks which might be included in this category are the Stroop Test and the Digit Symbol subtest from the WAIS-R.

Problems in interpretation of studies

Further complicating matters, Dodrill (1992) asserts that impairments in cognitive functioning may have been wrongly attributed to drug effects because of inappropriate data analysis methods. These include a lack of appreciation of the *selection factors* operating in cross-sectional studies (as described previously), which consequently are not taken into account in the final analysis; *statistical errors* can also contribute to a misinterpretation of the data (including, particularly, the erroneous use of parametric tests, giving credence to a few statistical differences that may have occurred by chance, and running too many statistical tests for the number of subjects or the number of measures). The impact of *seizure frequency* is rarely evaluated in these studies and may in fact be more significant than the AED effects. Dodrill also asserts that the type of *psychological measure* used may determine whether significant results are found or not, in that timed tasks are more likely than untimed tests to be sensitive to drug effects.

In many of the earlier studies there was an implicit but untested assumption that patients were actually taking their medication. More recent studies often report serum drug level concentrations, which may be one way of assessing compliance, and, as mentioned previously, may be a parameter of interest in itself.

The implications of all this are that in reading published studies of cognitive/behavioural effects of AEDs, the clinician should:

- read the whole study thoroughly, not just the results, in order to identify any methodological problems;

- read more than one study to gain a balanced perspective;
- consider the generalisability of the results to the particular issues being addressed.

REVIEW OF DRUG EFFECTS

As there are a number of recent reviews on this topic (Aldenkamp and Vermeulen 1995; Devinsky 1995; Dreifuss 1992; Kälviäinen *et al.* 1996), this review will be limited and will be used to illustrate some of the problems described above.

Older anti-epileptic drugs

Phenobarbitone (PHB)

Historically, phenobarbitone has been associated with behavioural problems, including excitement, aggression, hyperactivity, short attention span, irritability, distractibility, tearfulness and increased motor activity (Hirtz and Nelson 1985), which can occur in up to 75 per cent of those taking this medication (Committee on Drugs 1985). However, in terms of the impact of PHB on cognitive function, the picture is much less clear, partly because very few studies have actually been carried out despite the fact that PHB has been in use since 1912.

Sixteen seizure-free patients (adults and children) were assessed on ten measures of intelligence, vigilance, attention, memory, learning, manual dexterity, sensory discrimination and visuomotor performance (Gallassi *et al.* 1992) before withdrawal from PHB, six months later following a 50 per cent reduction in dose, and again three and twelve months after withdrawal. Only on the Trail Making Test, and before withdrawal, was their performance significantly worse than that of normal volunteers.

Phenytoin (PHT)

Phenytoin is a frequently used AED; it is relatively cheap and widely available in the developing world.

Dodrill (1975) studied seventy patients on PHT monotherapy, who completed the Halstead-Reitan battery, WAIS, Trail Making Test, name writing and strength of grip tests. Comparisons were then made between individuals with low (N=34) as opposed to high (N=36) serum drug levels, and between those who were showing clinical signs of toxicity (N=24) and those who were not (N=46). Groups with high serum levels, or who were clinically toxic, performed more poorly on all tasks than the low and non-toxic groups. Statistical differences were found on eight measures in the serum level comparison, and four in the toxicity comparison, all of which had a major motor component. This data was reanalysed by Dodrill and Temkin (1989), covarying for motor speed, as a result of which the previously obtained statistically significant differences disappeared, suggesting that PHT primarily has its effect on motor speed.

Studying the withdrawal of PHT in patients on a polytherapy regimen, Duncan *et al.* (1990) administered a battery of tests – including the Digit Symbol Substitution Task, a Letter Cancellation Task, Digit Span, Serial Subtraction and Tapping rate – at a practice session prior to study entry, at baseline, at the end of the drug reduction period, and four weeks after withdrawal. The twenty-one subjects showed a significant improvement on a Letter Cancellation Task and Tapping rate. The authors concluded that removal of PHT is associated with an improvement in attention, concentration and simple co-ordinated hand movements.

Gallassi *et al.* (1992) also reported on seven individuals being withdrawn from PHT, using the same design as described previously. Significant differences in favour of the control group were found on two measures prior to withdrawal, and one measure following a 50 per cent reduction in PHT, but no differences after withdrawal.

Thus studies suggest that PHT may have detrimental effects on performance, although the extent to which this may be just a motor speed effect is not always evaluated.

Interestingly, undesirable effects have been reported at serum levels well within, and even at the low end of, the therapeutic range, whereas it has previously been accepted that such effects are more likely to be seen at high serum drug levels (Thompson and Trimble 1982). A more recent study of children disputed this. Aman *et al.* (1994) tested fifty children, whose seizures were well controlled on PHT, at high and low serum level concentrations. Once extraneous factors such as age and seizure type were controlled by statistical modelling, fluctuations in PHT in the order of 50 per cent appeared to have no statistically significant effect on performance.

Sodium valproate (VPA)

Recent studies exploring the impact of withdrawing VPA from either seizure-free patients or those on a polytherapy regimen suggest that VPA may have some detrimental effects. In the studies reported by Gallassi *et al.* (1992), VPA was withdrawn from twelve seizure-free patients. Before withdrawal a healthy control group performed better on a Reaction Time task, the Trail Making Test, Finger Tip Number Writing and Digit Span. After 50 per cent withdrawal, a difference was still apparent on the Trail Making Test and, three months after withdrawal, on a spatial memory task. However, Duncan *et al.* (1990) found that removal of VPA was associated only with improvement on one measure, a tapping task.

A comparison between conventional and controlled release (VPA-CR) preparations has been undertaken in children, comparing their performance on tests of vigilance and attention while taking VPA, and then after four weeks of treatment with VPA-CR. There were no significant differences between the two conditions, and furthermore there was no correlation between performance and plasma drug levels for either VPA or VPA-CR (Brouwer *et al.* 1992).

Carbamazepine (CBZ)

Of all the AEDs mentioned so far, CBZ has been thought to be the least detrimental, in terms of cognitive functioning. Thus, in Gallassi *et al.*'s (1992) study, eleven patients were completely withdrawn from CBZ, and at each of the four assessments there were no differences between the performance of this group and that of a control group.

Duncan *et al.* (1990) found an improvement in tapping rate in fifteen patients having CBZ withdrawn from their AED regimen. However, a significant increase in seizure frequency in this group makes the results difficult to interpret.

Reinvang *et al.* (1991) studied twenty-two subjects on a stable CBZ monotherapy regimen. They were tested twice (following a pre-test) at 8 a.m. or 8 p.m. and noon when the serum concentrations were significantly higher than at 8 a.m. or 8 p.m. Measures included the WAIS, motor speed, reaction time, attention, and memory. Few significant differences between the high and low serum level conditions were found, but there were faster response times in the high serum level condition on two measures, suggesting improved functioning. Interestingly, Aman *et al.* (1990) have also found an improvement in relation to peak serum concentrations of CBZ on tests of attention and motor steadiness in children.

The slow release preparation of CBZ has been studied by Aldenkamp *et al.* (1987) in a single-blind cross over comparison with conventional CBZ. They found a tendency toward consistently higher performance in the slow release condition, especially on tests of memory and visual information processing. On a small battery of automated tests that were administered four times on each day of testing, there were also less fluctuations in performance with the slow release than the conventional preparation, thus resulting in a more stable pattern of performance throughout the day.

Benzodiazepines

There is an extreme paucity of information on the effects of the benzodiazepines most commonly used in epilepsy, notably clonazepam and clobazam.

Scott and Moffett (1986) tested thirty patients on the Stroop test before the initiation of clobazam at 20–30 mg/day as adjunctive therapy, and thereafter at one month, three months and six months, at which times there was a significant improvement in test performance. This was attributed to the addition of clobazam. Interpretation is hampered by the marked reduction in seizure frequency and the role of practice.

No significant change in cognitive function or mood was observed in seventeen people with uncontrolled seizures who were being withdrawn from clonazepam by Chataway *et al.* (1993).

To the authors' knowledge, there are no other recent studies in people with epilepsy. There is thus a need for further research since both clobazam and clonazepam have been associated with behavioural difficulties in some children with epilepsy (Commander *et al.* 1991; Sheth *et al.* 1994).

Newer anti-epileptic drugs

The difficulty in interpreting many of these studies is that the AED is being used as adjunctive therapy in patients with refractory epilepsy; thus, the effect on seizure frequency is unlikely to be negligible.

Vigabatrin (VGB)

Cognitive effects

McGuire *et al.* (1992) compared the performance of fifteen patients taking add-on VGB with fifteen patients whose AEDs remained the same. Over a four-week period no significant cognitive effects of VGB were noted. Gillham *et al.* (1993) also found no significant difference between VGB and placebo in twenty-one patients who participated in a double-blind randomised crossover trial, where VGB or placebo was added to their existing regimen. Subjects were assessed on a battery of nine measures, four times over a twelve-week period in each phase of the study.

A few detrimental effects have been reported, but these may not be clinically significant. Thus, Grunewald *et al.* (1994) compared twenty-two subjects before and twenty weeks after taking VGB, with twenty-three subjects before and twenty weeks after placebo, and reported significantly poorer performance in the VGB group on two measures (motor speed and memory) despite an improvement in seizure frequency. However, this was out of a total of sixteen possible comparisons and it is unclear whether the authors controlled for Type One errors.

Perhaps the largest study carried out to date, in terms of subject numbers, has been that of Dodrill *et al.* (1995). Subjects were assessed before and eighteen weeks after treatment with 1g VGB (N=36), 3g VGB (N=38), 6g VGB (N=32) or placebo (N=40) on eight tests. A worsening performance was found with increasing doses of VGB on one task only, a Letter Cancellation Test.

No detrimental effects were found in fourteen patients who had taken VGB over a period of eighteen months by Bittencourt *et al.* (1994); however, seizure control also improved over this time.

So far, vigabatrin would appear to have no significant effects on cognitive function, at least in patients with difficult-to-control seizures. However, well-controlled double-blind studies are still needed to compare the cognitive effects of VGB with other AEDs (Meador 1995).

Behavioural effects

The impact of VGB on behaviour has been assessed predominantly by self-rating scales/questionnaires, including the General Health Questionnaire (Gillham *et al.* 1993); a mood adjective checklist and the

Hospital Anxiety and Depression questionnaire (Grunewald *et al.* 1994), and mood rating scales, the Profile of Mood States, and the Washington Psychosocial Seizure Index (Dodrill *et al.* 1995). In none of these studies were any of the scales significantly affected in the subjects taking VGB. Thus, in the majority of subjects, VGB appears to have no detrimental effects. In some patients, however, there is an idiosyncratic adverse reaction, whereby they may develop a psychotic-like state, or other severe behaviour disturbance (Sander and Hart 1990; Brodie and McKee 1990). Indeed, in Grunewald *et al.*'s (1994) study, two patients had to discontinue treatment because of depression although this condition was reversible on discontinuation of treatment.

Lamotrigine (LTG)

Cognitive effects

Lamotrigine is the newest AED to be licensed in the UK for monotherapy, but the majority of studies have been carried out using LTG as adjunctive therapy in seizure refractory individuals.

Smith *et al.* (1993) undertook a randomised double-blind crossover study comparing LTG with placebo taken for eighteen weeks each in eighty-one patients (children and adults). Cognitive assessment took place before treatment and at the end of each treatment phase using the Stroop test, number cancellation, Critical Flicker Fusion, and a choice reaction time task. There were no differences between LTG and placebo on any measures. Similarly, Banks and Beran (1991) found no evidence that LTG produces undesirable cognitive side-effects.

One major area of interest with LTG has been its suppression of interictal spiking. In up to 50 per cent of patients with sub-clinical epileptiform discharges, recordable by EEG, there is associated Transitory Cognitive Impairment (TCI) (Binnie 1994); LTG provides effective control over subclinical seizures without adversely affecting cognitive function and therefore, if TCI is prevented, a general improvement in cognitive function might be expected. A study is in progress to evaluate this further.

There are anecdotal reports that LTG may have beneficial effects on the cognitive functioning of children and young adults with severe learning disabilities (Hosking *et al.* 1993; Uvebrant and Bauziene 1994), although such reports are difficult to evaluate, as they are also associated with improved seizure frequency.

Behaviour

Lamotrigine also appears to have beneficial effects on well-being and quality of life. Smith *et al.* (1993) asked patients to complete a variety of mood and self-esteem measures. Subjects reported being significantly more happy and having a greater sense of perceived control when on LTG than placebo, independently of any improvements in seizure control.

Gillham *et al.* (1996) have observed that patients taking LTG report significantly less depression and negative mood than those not on LTG, as assessed by a newly devised self-rating scale.

Beneficial effects of LTG on the behaviour of children with learning disabilities have been reported both anecdotally (Uvebrant and Bauziene 1994), and in studies using standardised rating scales (Fowler *et al.* 1994).

Other new AEDs

Only very preliminary results of the cognitive/behavioural effects of other new AEDs in people with epilepsy are available at the time of writing.

Oxcarbazepine has been available for almost ten years, but is not licensed in the UK. In one UK study, McKee *et al.* (1994) did not demonstrate any significant cognitive effects.

Gabapentin has been evaluated by Arnett and Dodrill (1995), again with no evidence of cognitive effect; preliminary results for Topiramate (Brooks *et al.* 1995) are also negative.

Finally, Tiagabine is currently being evaluated in a multi-centre monotherapy study in the UK and Australia, using cognitive tests and quality of life measures. Results of this study will not be available until 1997, but in a previous add-on study Sveinbjornsdottir *et al.* (1994) showed no cognitive effect.

While initial results for the newer AEDs look promising, more time is needed to evaluate them fully.

Drug comparisons

While it is of some value to examine the effects of individual AEDs, it is difficult to make comparisons between drugs on this basis, although such information is likely to be of more use to both clinicians and patients. It is easier to make sense of studies where comparisons between drugs have been undertaken within the same time frame, using the same test battery, administered by the same personnel.

A number of such studies have been undertaken, and the AEDs most frequently used include PHB, PHT, CBZ and VPA.

To compare CBZ, PHB and PHT, Meador *et al.* (1990) carried out an ambitious randomised, double-blind, triple crossover comparison. Fifteen subjects with complex partial seizures received each drug for three months each. At the beginning of each phase, subjects were withdrawn from their pre-existing medication and started on gradually increasing doses of the drug for that treatment phase. Psychological testing was carried out at the end of each treatment phase consisting of Digit Span, Selective Reminding Test, Digit Symbol Substitution Test, Finger Tapping, Grooved Pegboard and Choice Reaction Time. In the analysis, AED blood levels and seizure frequency were used as covariates, and the only significant difference that emerged was on the Digit Symbol Substitution Test, performance of which was significantly worse in the PHB group. The authors concluded that CBZ, PHT and PHB are comparable in respect of their neuropsychological effects.

In their study of withdrawal of PHT, CBZ and VPA, Duncan *et al.* (1990) also reported that there were no significant differences between the three groups in terms of changes in performance over time. Thus, all three drugs may adversely affect motor function, although there was also a suggestion that PHT is more likely to affect attention and concentration than CBZ or VPA.

The effects of CBZ and VPA have also been found to be comparable after twelve months of treatment in newly diagnosed children, with no significant changes in either cognitive function or behaviour (Stores *et al.* 1992).

Three further studies have also reported no differences, or insignificant differences, between such AEDs and their effects on cognitive function (Craig and Tallis 1994; Meador *et al.* 1993; Verma *et al.* 1993).

However, differences have also been reported. Gillham *et al.* (1990) compared patients taking CBZ, or VPA or PHT with each other, with untreated patients with epilepsy, and with control subjects without epilepsy. CBZ tended to produce the greatest psychomotor impairment and PHT produced the most memory impairment. The biggest differences tended to be between the patients with epilepsy and the control subjects without epilepsy, an indication that whatever effects AEDs might have on cognitive function, they are of less significance than the effect of the disorder itself.

Forsythe *et al.* (1991) randomly assigned sixty-four previously untreated children to either CBZ, PHT or VPA treatment and administered a battery of psychometric tests at baseline, and on three subsequent occasions during the following year. CBZ was associated with poorer scores on memory tests than either PHT or VPA. The study was not blind and the influence of seizure frequency is not clear.

In a study by Bittencourt *et al.* (1992), patients taking PHT or VPA performed worse than controls on a memory test, and patients on CBZ performed worse on the Stroop Test. The authors concluded that the results indicated relatively minor effects of the AEDs on cognitive function.

A major contribution to the evaluation of cognitive function in epilepsy has been the development of a computerised battery specifically for patients with epilepsy. Aldenkamp *et al.* (1994) used FePSY (see Chapter 2) to compare PHT and CBZ in an open, non-randomised, parallel group study. Results showed lower performance in the PHT group on tests measuring motor speed and speed of central processing systems, and information processing.

A study of newly diagnosed patients randomly allocated to treatment with either PHT or CBZ also showed differences. Pulliainen and Jokelainen (1994) tested patients before treatment and after six months, comparing the practice effect with a control group being tested on the same schedule. Both AEDs, but the PHT group in particular, showed a much smaller practice effect.

It will be seen from the above that the evidence for specific profiles for the three first-line drugs is equivocal. The studies reviewed are very different in design, in sample type, and in test battery, and so it is difficult to make an overall generalisation.

Monotherapy versus polytherapy

Drug reduction has been found to have beneficial effects on cognitive function and behaviour, although it is most likely that this has been mediated through beneficial effects on seizure frequency, rather than the AEDs per se (e.g. Ludgate *et al.* 1985). It is further asserted that adverse effects are more likely to be seen with polytherapy rather than monotherapy (Meador 1994), although the impact of drugs used in rational combinations has yet to be evaluated.

CONCLUSIONS

Meador (1994) summarises current opinion with regard to the cognitive effect of AEDs thus:

> all of the established AEDs can produce cognitive side effects, which are both increased with polypharmacy and with increasing dosage and anticonvulsant blood levels. However, cognitive side effects are usually modest with AED monotherapy . . . Further, these effects are offset in part by reduced seizure activity . . . there is no convincing evidence of clinically significant cognitive side effects of AEDs.
>
> (Meador 1994: S12)

Even so, it is still possible for individuals to experience idiosyncratic adverse effects that might not be expected from reading the literature, and it is important to be alert to the possibility of these.

Many of the studies available to date focus on a fairly limited range of subjects, as was alluded to earlier, and do not explore the impact of AEDs in the elderly or people with learning disabilities, and thus the applicability of results to these not insubstantial groups of people is not known. However, it is hoped that in the future, along with improving methodology, such issues will be addressed.

IMPLICATIONS FOR CLINICAL PRACTICE

Any evaluation of the impact of AEDs on the functioning of a particular individual (whether it be a change in the drug or dose of the drug) will inevitably mean that at least two assessments have to be undertaken. This should be taken into account in the choice of tests to be used as they need to be suitable for repeated administration. It will also be important to separate out motor speed from other cognitive measures, to ensure that any effects are not wrongly attributed. Any assessment should include some investigation of aspects of behaviour and quality of life. Clearly any measures used should be appropriate to the developmental level of an individual.

In interpreting test results, the clinician needs to be aware of all medications that a patient is taking, whether they are in a controlled release preparation or not, the dose, and time between drug ingestion and assessment in order to identify whether the AED is at a peak or trough level. A serum drug level assay of blood taken at the time of testing would also be very useful as a way of assessing compliance, and whether or not the levels are within or above the therapeutic range, as a toxic blood level can have detrimental effects on functioning, such as lethargy and slowness. The clinician should also take into account any change in seizure frequency between assessments and the time between the last seizure and test administration.

We would suggest that the challenge now for clinical psychologists is to make a constructive contribution to discussions concerning the impact of AEDs on an individual's functioning, which should be based not just on the literature but on evidence gained directly from their own assessments.

REFERENCES

Aldenkamp, A. P. and Vermeulen, J. (1995) 'Phenytoin and carbamazepine: differential effects on cognitive function', *Seizure* 4: 95–104.

Aldenkamp, A. P., Alpherts, W. C. J., Moerland, M. C., Ottevanger, N. and Van Parys, J. A. P. (1987) 'Controlled release carbamazepine: cognitive side effects in patients with epilepsy', *Epilepsia* 28: 507–14.

Aldenkamp, A. P., Alpherts, W. C., Diepman, L., van't-Slot, B., Overweg, J. and Vermeulen, J. (1994) 'Cognitive side-effects of phenytoin compared with carbamazepine in patients with localization-related epilepsy', *Epilepsy Research* 19: 37–43.

Aman, M. G., Werry, J. S., Paxton, J. W. and Turbott, S. H. (1994) 'Effects of phenytoin on cognitive–motor performance in children as a function of drug concentration, seizure type, and time of medication', *Epilepsia* 35: 172–80.

Aman, M. G., Werry, J. S., Paxton, J. W., Turbott, S. H. and Stewart, A. W. (1990) 'Effects of carbamazepine on psychomotor performance in children as a function of drug concentration, seizure type, and time of medication', *Epilepsia* 31: 51–60.

Arnett, J. L. and Dodrill, C. B. (1995) 'Effects of gabapentin on cognitive functioning and mood', *Epilepsia* 36 (Suppl. 3): S32.

Banks, G. K. and Beran, R. G. (1991) 'Neuropsychological assessment in lamotrigine treated epileptic patients', *Clinical and Experimental Neurology* 28: 230–7.

Binnie, C. D. (1994) 'Cognitive impairment – is it inevitable?' *Seizure* 3 (Suppl. A): 17–21.

Bittencourt, P. R. M., Mazer, S., Marcourakis, T., Bigarella, M. M., Ferreira, Z. S. and Mumford, J. P. (1994) 'Vigabatrin: clinical evidence supporting rational polytherapy in management of uncontrolled seizures', *Epilepsia* 35: 373–80.

Bittencourt, P. R., Mader, M. J., Bigarella, M. M., Doro, M. P., Gorz, A. M., Marcourakis, T. M. and Ferreira, Z. S. (1992) 'Cognitive function, epileptic syndromes and anti-epileptic drugs', *Arquivos de Neuro-Psiquiatria* 50: 24–30.

Brodie, M. J. (1985) 'The optimum use of anticonvulsants', *The Practitioner* 229: October.

Brodie, M. J. and McKee, P. J. W. (1990) 'Vigabatrin and psychosis', *Lancet* 335: 1279.

Brooks, J., Sachedo, R. and Lim, P. (1995) 'Topiramate: neuropsychometric assessments', *Epilepsia* 36 (Suppl. 3): S273.

Brouwer, O. F., Pieters, M. S. M., Edelbroek, P. M., Bakker, A. M., VanGeel, A. A. C. M., Stijnen, Th., Jennekens-Schinkel, A., Lanser, J. B. K. and Peters, A. C. B. (1992) 'Conventional and controlled release valproate in children with epilepsy: a cross-over study comparing plasma levels and cognitive performances', *Epilepsy Research* 13: 245–53.

Chataway, J., Fowler, A., Thompson, P. J. and Duncan, J. (1993) 'Discountinuation of clonazepam in patients with active epilepsy', *Seizure* 2: 295–300.

Commander, M., Green, S. H. and Prendergast, M. (1991) 'Behavioural disturbances in children treated with clonazepam', *Developmental Medicine and Child Neurology* 33: 362–4.

Committee on Drugs (1985) 'Behavioural and cognitive effects of anticonvulsant therapy', *Paediatrics* 76: 644–7.

Craig, I. and Tallis, R. (1994) 'Impact of valproate and phenytoin on cognitive function in elderly patients: results of a single-blind randomized comparative study', *Epilepsia* 35: 381–90.

Devinsky, O. (1995) 'Cognitive and behavioral effects of anti-epileptic drugs', *Epilepsia* 36 (Suppl. 2): S46–65.

Dodrill, C. B. (1975) 'Diphenylhydantoin serum levels, toxicity, and neuropsychological performance in patients with epilepsy', *Epilepsia* 16: 593–600.

—— (1992) 'Problems in the assessment of cognitive effects of anti-epileptic drugs', *Epilepsia* 33 (Suppl. 6): S29–32.

Dodrill C. B. and Temkin, N. R. (1989) 'Motor speed is a contaminating factor in evaluating the "cognitive" effects of phenytoin', *Epilepsia* 30: 453–7.

Dodrill, C. B., Arnett, J. L., Sommerville, K. W. and Sussman, N. M. (1995) 'Effects of differing dosages of vigabatrin on cognitive abilities and quality of life in epilepsy', *Epilepsia* 36: 164–73.

Dreifuss, F. E. (1992) 'Cognitive function – victim of disease or hostage to treatment?' *Epilepsia*, 33 (Suppl. 1): S7–12.

Duncan, J. S., Shorvon, S. D. and Trimble M. R. (1990) 'Effects of removal of phenytoin, carbamazepine, and valproate on cognitive function', *Epilepsia* 31: 584–91.

Forsythe, I., Butler, R., Berg, I. and McGuire, R. (1991) 'Cognitive impairment in new cases of epilepsy randomly assigned to either carbamazepine, phenytoin, or sodium valproate', *Developmental Medicine and Child Neurology* 33: 524–34.

Fowler, M., Besag, F. and Pool, F. (1994) 'Effects of lamotrigine on behavior in children', *Epilepsia* 35 (Suppl. 7): 69.

Gallassi, R., Morreale, A., DiSarro, R., Marra, M., Lugaresi, E. and Baruzzi, A. (1992) 'Cognitive effects of anti-epileptic drug discontinuation', *Epilepsia* 33 (Suppl. 6): S41–4.

Gillham, R. A., Blacklaw, J., McKee, P. J. W. and Brodie, M. J. (1993) 'Effect of vigabatrin on sedation and cognitive function in patients with refractory epilepsy', *Journal of Neurology, Neurosurgery and Psychiatry* 56: 1271–5.

Gillham, R. A., Williams, N., Wiedmann, K. D., Butler, E., Larkin, J. G. and

Brodie, M. J. (1990) 'Cognitive function in adult epileptic patients established on anticonvulsant monotherapy', *Epilepsy Research* 7: 219–25.

Gillham, R., Baker, G., Thompson, P., Birbeck, K., McGuire, A., Tomlinson, L., Echersley, L., Silveira, C. and Brown, S. (1996) 'Standardisation of a self-report questionnaire for use in evaluating cognitive, affective and behavioural side-effects of anti-epileptic drug treatments', *Epilepsy Research* 24: 47–55.

Grunewald, R. A., Thompson, P. J., Corcoran, R., Corden, Z., Jackson, G. D. and Duncan, J. S. (1994) 'Effects of vigabatrin on partial seizures and cognitive function', *Journal of Neurology, Neurosurgery and Psychiatry* 57: 1057–63.

Hirtz, D. G. and Nelson, K. B. (1985) 'Cognitive effects of anti-epileptic drugs', in T. A. Pedley and B. S. Meldrum (eds) *Recent Advances in Epilepsy*, New York: Churchill Livingstone.

Hosking, G., Spencer, S. and Yuen, A. W. C. (1993) 'Lamotrigine in children with severe developmental abnormalities in a paediatric population with refractory seizures', *Epilepsia* 34 (Suppl. 6): 42.

Kälviäinen, R., Äikiä, M. and Riekkinen Sr, P. J. (1996) 'Cognitive adverse effects of anti-epileptic drugs', *CNS Drugs* 5: 358–68.

Ludgate, J., Keating, J., O'Dwyer, R. and Callaghan, N. (1985) 'An improvement in cognitive function following polypharmacy reduction in a group of epileptic patients', *Acta Neurologica Scandinavica* 71: 448–52.

McKee, P. J., Blacklaw, J., Forrest, G., Gillham, R. A., Walker, S. M., Connelly, D. and Brodie, M. J. (1994) 'A double-blind, placebo-controlled interaction study between oxcarbazepine and carbamazepine, sodium valproate and phenytoin in epileptic patients', *British Journal of Clinical Pharmacology* 37: 27–32.

Meador, K. J. (1994) 'Cognitive side effects of anti-epileptic drugs', *Canadian Journal of Neurological Science* 21: S12–16.

—— (1995) 'Cognitive effects of vigabatrin', *Epilepsia* 36 (Suppl. 3): S31.

Meador, K. J., Loring, D. W., Huh, K., Gallagher, B. B. and King, D. W. (1990) 'Comparative cognitive effects of anticonvulsants', *Neurology* 40: 391–4.

Meador, K. J., Loring, D. W., Abney, O. L., Allen, M. E., Moore, E. E., Zamrini, E. Y. and King, D. W. (1993) 'Effects of carbamazepine and phenytoin on EEG and memory in healthy adults', *Epilepsia* 34: 153–7.

McGuire, A., Duncan, J. and Trimble, M. R. (1992) 'Effects of vigabatrin on cognitive function and mood when used as add-on therapy in patients with intractable epilepsy', *Epilepsia* 32: 128–34.

Pulliainen, V. and Jokelainen M. (1994) 'Effects of phenytoin and carbamazepine on cognitive functions in newly diagnosed epileptic patients', *Acta Neurologica Scandinavica* 89: 81–6.

Reinvang, I., Bjartveit, S., Johannessen, S. I., Hagen, O. P., Larsen, S., Fagerthun, H. and Gjerstad, L. (1991) 'Cognitive function and time-of-day variation in serum carbamazepine concentration in epileptic patients treated with monotherapy', *Epilepsia* 32: 116–21.

Sander, J. W. A. S. and Hart, Y. M. (1990) 'Vigabatrin and behaviour disturbances', *Lancet* 335: 57.

Scott, D. F. and Moffett, A. (1986) 'On the anticonvulsant and psychotropic properties of clobazam: a preliminary study', *Epilepsia* 27: S42–4.

Sheth, R. D., Goulden, K. J. and Ronen, G. M. (1994) 'Aggression in children treated with clobazam for epilepsy', *Clinical Neuropharmacology* 17: 332–7.

Smith, D., Baker, G., Davies, G., Dewey, M. and Chadwick, D. W. (1993) 'Outcomes of add-on treatment with lamotrigine in partial epilepsy', *Epilepsia* 34: 312–22.

Stores, G., Williams, P. L., Styles, E. and Zaiwalla, Z. (1992) 'Psychological effects of sodium valproate and carbamazepine in epilepsy', *Archives of Disease in Childhood* 67: 1330–7.

Sveinbjornsdottir, S., Sander, J. W., Patsalos, P. N., Upton, D., Thompson, P. J. and Duncan, J. S. (1994) 'Neuropsychological effects of tiagabine, a potential new anti-epileptic drug', *Seizure* 3: 29–35.

Thompson, P. J. and Trimble, M. R. (1982) 'Anticonvulsant drugs and cognitive functions', *Epilepsia* 23: 531–44.

Uvebrant, P. and Bauziene, R. (1994) 'Intractable epilepsy in children. The efficacy of lamotrigine treatment, including non-seizure – related benefits', *Neuropediatrics* 25: 284–9.

Verma, N. P., Yusko, M. J. and Greiffenstien, M. F. (1993) 'Carbamazepine offers no psychotropic advantage over phenytoin in adult epileptic subjects', *Seizure* 2: 53–6.

Chapter 6

Psychological responses to epilepsy

Their development, prognosis and treatment

Gus A. Baker

INTRODUCTION

In this chapter, the various psychological problems associated with a diagnosis of epilepsy will be considered. Such responses can include high levels of anxiety and depression, low self-esteem, poor sense of control, aggression and some more serious disturbances such as psychosis. The prevalence of such problems will be examined, evidence about their aetiology will be reviewed, and consideration will then be given to the contribution of the clinical psychologist to their assessment and treatment. The focus of this chapter will be upon adults with epilepsy; consideration of behavioural problems in children with epilepsy are discussed in Chapter 10. Rather than providing an exhaustive account of these variables, which would fill a book on its own, this chapter will serve as an introduction, highlighting the main issues.

There are a number of possible reasons why people with epilepsy may develop behavioural and emotional problems and these can be summarised as follows:

(a) the effects of a damaged brain;
(b) the adverse effects of anti-epileptic medication;
(c) the effects of living with a stigmatising disorder.

Historically, the emphasis has tended to be on searching for relationships between structural brain damage and dysfunction as causes of behavioural problems, for example, between psychopathology and specific seizure types, epilepsy duration and seizure localisation (Gibbs *et al.* 1948; Gastaut *et al.* 1955; Gloor *et al.* 1982; Leiderman *et al.* 1990). However, Hermann and Whitman (1991), reviewing a multiaetiological model of psychopathology in epilepsy (see Table 6.1), conclude that the explanatory power of what they term the 'neuroepilepsy' factors is only modest.

Recently, increasing emphasis has been placed on the adverse effects of anti-epileptic drugs as contributory factors in the development and maintenance of behavioural disorders in epilepsy (Dodrill and Batzel 1986; Cull and Trimble 1989). The least researched explanation for behavioural problems in epilepsy relates to the impact of living with a chronic illness, particularly one which is stigmatising and to which a negative social label is attached (Scambler and Hopkins 1986; West 1986; Conrad and Schneider 1992; Jacoby 1994).

It is difficult to disentangle the relative effects of these factors, but if we accept the idea that structural brain damage underlies all

Table 6.1 Potential multiaetiological risk factors for psychosocial and psychiatric consequences of epilepsy (adapted by Hermann and Whitman 1986)

Neurobiological	*Psychosocial*	*Medication*
	Epilepsy - related	
Age at onset	Locus of control	Monotherapy versus polytherapy
Duration of disorder	Fear of seizures	
Seizure type	Adjustment to epilepsy	Presence/absence of barbiturates
Degree of seizure control	Parental overprotection	
Ictal/interictal EEG changes	Perceived stigma	Folate deficiency
Seizure severity	Perceived discrimination	Hormonal/endocrine
Presence/absence of structural effects brain changes		Medication-induced alterations in monoamine metabolism
Phenomenological aspects of seizures	*Non-epilepsy related*	
	Stressful life events	
	Financial stress	
Neuropsychological functioning	Employment status	
	Social support	Medication-induced alterations in cerebral metabolism
Efficiency of cerebral metabolism	Years of education	
Alterations in neurotransmitters		CNS dose-related side effects of medication

behavioural problems, then the clinical psychologists' role in their treatment is limited. However, given the accumulating evidence of the importance of medication and social variables, then the clinical psychologist has a significant part to play in the assessment and amelioration of such problems.

PREVALENCE OF PSYCHOLOGICAL PROBLEMS IN EPILEPSY

Epilepsy and anxiety

For a number of years, anxiety has been cited as a common, if not the most common, consequence of the unpredictable nature of some epilepsies (Arnston *et al.* 1986; Collings 1990). A number of studies investigating the incidence of anxiety in people with epilepsy using the Hospital Anxiety and Depression (HAD) Scale (Zigmond and Snaith 1983) have reported rates of between 25–33 per cent in patients with resistant epilepsy (Smith *et al.* 1991; Baker *et al.* 1996). Betts (1992) has argued, however, that although many patients are fearful of their seizures only a relatively small number develop a true phobic anxiety resulting in social isolation. Further, a number of studies which have investigated the relationship between epilepsy and anxiety have been confounded by failure to define or differentiate between state and trait anxiety (Betts 1981). Many patients experience anxiety as a result of the diagnosis of epilepsy and the ensuing adjustment. Anxiety may also occur as an integral part of the pre-ictal, ictal and post-ictal aspect of an individual's seizure. Some patients have attacks that are associated with, or precipitated by, anxiety (Betts 1981).

The link between epilepsy and anxiety may be understood in terms of a number of potential sources: first, the fear of having a seizure and the belief that seizures may lead to death (Scambler and Hopkins 1986; Mittan and Locke 1982); second, the stigmatising condition of epilepsy may result in higher levels of anxiety and depression. Arnston *et al.* (1986) found their measure of perceived stigma to be related to a number of psychological variables including anxiety, although a causal link is yet to be established (Scambler 1989). In a recent community study there was clear evidence of a relationship between level of seizure activity and psychological functioning, with individuals with frequent seizures having significantly higher rates of anxiety and depression than those with infrequent or no seizures (Jacoby *et al.* 1996). Tenuous links have also been made between perceived discrimination, adjustment to epilepsy and psychopathology, with some patients experiencing anxiety as a result of their determination to conceal their condition.

Anecdotal evidence would suggest a reciprocal relationship between anxiety and epilepsy in that the more anxious the patient is the more likely they are to have a seizure, and the more seizures they have the more anxious they become.

Epilepsy and depression

A series of studies on the relationship between epilepsy and depression in patients with resistant seizures report that depression is more common among people with epilepsy than normal controls or other neurological conditions (Robertson *et al.* 1987). Rates of depression in a population without epilepsy have been reported to vary between 2–4 per cent (Sullivan 1995). Recent studies of a hospital-based and a community-based population report incidence rates of clinical depression, using the Hospital Anxiety and Depression scale, of between 10–15 per cent (Smith *et al.* 1991; Baker *et al.* 1996), while a previous hospital-based study of 666 patients attending a neurology clinic suggested a rate of 16 per cent, including 5 per cent who later committed suicide (Currie *et al.* 1971). Indeed, suicide in people with epilepsy is approximately four to five times more common than in the general population, and twenty-five times more common in people with temporal lobe epilepsy (Matthews and Barabas 1981).

Determining the causes of this depression has been troublesome, with a number of conflicting studies implicating either biological or environmental predisposing factors. Some authors have proposed that depression is as a result of abnormalities in neurochemical functioning, for example, dopamine, noradrenalin, or folic acid levels (Robertson *et al.* 1987), while others have suggested that it is a reaction to living with a stigmatising disorder (Scambler and Hopkins 1986). Dodrill and Batzel (1986) argue that depression is more common in people with multiple seizure types and frequent seizures, whereas Smith *et al.* (1991) have argued that patient-perceived seizure severity may be more important than seizure frequency or seizure type in predicting depression. In patients with resistant epilepsy, what might be important therefore is not the frequency of seizures but their severity. Betts (1992) has argued that reactive and endogenous depression may coexist in people with epilepsy, and as such there may be a number of causes for depression. The potential relationship between epilepsy, depressive feelings and depressive illness may be classified in the following way.

- Depressive reaction to acquiring the label of epilepsy;
- Depressive reaction to social/family problems of epilepsy;
- Prodromal depressive feelings before a seizure;
- Depressive feelings as an aura;
- Depressive feelings as an ictal experience;
- Post-ictal depressive feelings;
- Depressive twilight state;
- Epileptic depressive delirium;
- Endogenous depression unrelated directly to seizures, but possibly to their increase in frequency;
- Depressive symptoms occurring in association with other mental illnesses particularly a paranoid or schizophrenic psychosis.

The depressive symptoms reported by people with epilepsy have been both somatic and psychotic, but a study comparing depressed people with epilepsy and depressed controls using the Hamilton rating scale and a brief psychiatric rating scale found that the epilepsy subjects reported similar prevalence rates of endogenous depressive traits (e.g. psychomotor retardation), but more psychotic behaviours (e.g. hallucinations) and fewer neurotic traits (e.g. somatisation) (Mendez *et al.* 1986).

Depression can be self-reinforcing and the associated sequelae, such as loss of confidence, low self-esteem and agoraphobia, can also be disabling and last longer than the depression itself. In addition, it has been noted that the effects of anticonvulsant drugs may impair learning and therefore interfere with normal coping responses to stress, including depression (Betts 1981). In a recent study by Jacoby *et al.* (1996), later age at onset of seizures, seizure activity and duration of epilepsy were significant predictors of depression suggesting that, for many adults developing seizures, there are important social consequences of becoming labelled 'epileptic', for example, in relation to their ability to function in the role of an employee or family supporter. These recent findings will have implications for determining how we address the problem of depression in people with epilepsy.

Epilepsy and aggression

Historically, aggression has been associated with epilepsy, despite the lack of well-controlled studies investigating the incidence and prevalence of aggressive behaviour in this condition (Fenwick 1986). Previous studies investigating interictal aggressive behaviour have been flawed by a number of methodological problems including poor design, unclear definitions and lack of standardisation (Thompson 1988). A current review of the literature would suggest that there is no evidence that directed aggression may occur as an ictal behaviour manifestation. Where violence has been witnessed in adults with epilepsy, it has usually been as a response to constraint by others during the post-ictal stage of a stereotypical seizure. Nor is there any evidence to suggest that epilepsy is more common in violent or aggressive people, or that violence or aggression are more common in people with epilepsy (Treiman 1990). Given that aggression is not necessarily a consequence of epilepsy, it would seem important to determine the antecedents, behaviour and consequences of aggressive acts and treat them as any other behavioural problem.

Epilepsy and psychosis

There has been a number of conflicting studies investigating the incidence and prevalence of psychosis in people with epilepsy. In a study of fourteen general practices, Pond and Bidwell (1959) found 29 per cent of their sample had a history of psychiatric illness, but none had been, or were, psychotic. In contrast, a number of outpatient studies (Currie *et al.* 1971) reported an incidence of between 2–5 per cent. In an earlier study of sixty-nine patients with a schizophrenia-like psychosis, 80 per cent were found to have focal EEG abnormalities in the temporal lobe (Slater and Beard 1963), leading the authors to conclude that the characteristics of the psychoses accompanying epilepsy were distinct from functional psychosis. This finding has not, however, been confirmed in subsequent prospective studies (Perez and Trimble 1980) although there have been a number of case reports where patients have presented with a post-ictal psychosis following excessive seizure activity involving the limbic system (Waxman and Geshwind 1975). Such psychotic episodes tend to be of limited duration and may be prevented by the prophylactic use of anti-psychotic medication. Alternatively, Landolt (1958) proposed a theory of 'forced normalisation' where an improvement in interictal epileptiform activity was found to be correlated with the initation or exacerbation of psychosis, although the number of reported cases are few.

The relationship between epilepsy and psychosis is unclear (Devinsky 1992) and this has resulted from a number of methodological problems in previous research, including selection bias and a lack of homogeneity in the psychosis syndrome (Toone 1981). Undoubtedly, this has led to an overestimation of the incidence and prevalence of psychosis in epilepsy (Hauser and Hesdorffer 1990). A small number of people with epilepsy will present with psychoses and there is a suggestion that their symptoms may well be as a result of an underlying epileptic process linked with lesions in the limbic system structures (Trimble 1988). Devinsky (1992), reviewing the behavioural consequences of epilepsy, has suggested that there are a number of risk factors for psychosis, and these include left temporal seizure focus, bilateral seizure foci, structural pathology and left-handedness. Further controlled population-based research is clearly necessary to overcome such pitfalls and clarify the relationship between psychosis and epilepsy.

Epilepsy and self-esteem

Low self-esteem is well recognised as a clinical component of several psychiatric conditions including anxiety and depression, and self-esteem has been found to be significantly lower in people with epilepsy than those without (Collings 1990). Scambler (1989) has suggested that this is a result of the perceived level of stigma associated with the condition. For instance, a number of authors have demonstrated how perceptions of stigma of epilepsy were more strongly influenced by self-perceptions than by other more objective measures of epilepsy (e.g. seizure frequency), although in some of the studies the patient groups were hospital-based and samples may have been biased (Stanley and Tillotson 1982; Ryan *et al.* 1980). Jacoby (1994) indicated that people with well-controlled epilepsy were still stigmatised by their condition suggesting that the diagnosis, and not necessarily the frequency or severity of seizures, is important in understanding the stigma in epilepsy. Collings (1995), in a community study, has proposed that people with epilepsy tend to evaluate themselves negatively and this may be related to 'perceived stigma' as a result of the physician's diagnosis which converts them from a normal person to an 'epileptic' (Scambler 1989). Collings (1995) found that there was significant evidence of low self-esteem among patients with epilepsy specifically in terms of people with epilepsy downgrading themselves for success, competence and adaptation to life. Many of those surveyed reported that their self-esteem would be improved if they did not have epilepsy; whilst intuitively this makes sense, there had been no opportunity to test this belief. Particular areas of low fulfilment in this group were social relationships, peace of mind and employment. In contrast, Hills and Baker (1992) found that people with epilepsy reported higher levels of self-esteem than a normative sample. One explanation for their findings is that people with epilepsy are able, through a series of psychological processes, to protect themselves from the stigmatising effects of their condition. A second explanation may relate to the differences in the clinical populations studied, particularly in the frequency and severity of seizures. Low self-esteem in epilepsy may be the result of a number of potential sources including overprotection, perceived stigma and the failure to fulfil expectations.

Epilepsy and mastery (locus of control)

As has been repeatedly emphasised, epilepsy is a disorder characterised by a loss of control (Matthews *et al.* 1982). For a significant number of people with epilepsy, seizures may occur anywhere, at any time, with little or no warning. The threat of a sudden and unpredictable loss of control (and consciousness) has been thought to comprise an essential dimension of epilepsy (Matthews and Barabas 1981; Arnston *et al.* 1986). Indeed, compared with other chronic conditions, epilepsy is associated with a significantly greater external locus of control (Matthews and Barabas 1981). A small number of people will be able to predict their seizure occurrence and for them behavioural management techniques may be of help (see Chapter 7).

Having epilepsy may predispose an individual to develop an external locus of control (Zeigler 1982; Hermann and Whitman 1991). Unpredictability and the associated psychological complications of epilepsy may induce the sufferer to believe that they have little real control over many important and basic events in their lives, perceiving events to be attributable more to the effects of luck, chance, fate or others. Research indicates that such beliefs may render the individuals more susceptible to psychopathology, particularly clinical depression (Lefcourt 1976), which reduces the ability to manage the demands of everyday living. Wallaston and De Villas (1980) reported that patients with epilepsy perceived themselves as having significantly lower levels of internal locus of control when compared with a group of people without epilepsy, while Matthews and Barabas (1981) found high levels of external locus of control to be associated with anxiety, low self-esteem, feelings of helplessness and a higher risk of suicide in people with epilepsy.

Whilst evidence demonstrates the relationship between epilepsy and an external locus of control, there is little understanding of its development or maintenance. It seems reasonable to hypothesise that parenting behaviour, the severity and frequency of seizures and the patients' perceptions of themselves and their disorder all play an important role in understanding why many patients with epilepsy have an external locus of control. A recent study by Gehlert (1994) investigated the relationship between seizure control and perceptions of control and found that, in a sample of 143 people with epilepsy, seizure control could predict attribution style for bad events but not for good events. The author concludes that for people with epilepsy the occurrence of seizures may be so pervasive that it can negatively influence the way they perceive many events in their lives, and that a good event is any event not marred by a seizure. This finding supports previous research that highlights the impact that an unpredictable event (seizure) can have on an individual's perceived control over many aspects of their lives.

THE CONTRIBUTION OF THE CLINICAL PSYCHOLOGIST TO THE MANAGEMENT OF PSYCHOLOGICAL PROBLEMS IN EPILEPSY

Managing all the various psychological factors associated with epilepsy is crucial to making a positive adjustment to the condition. Such emotional and behavioural problems may become important determinants of motivation to comply with anti-epileptic medication and successful adaptation to a change in lifestyle. Little attention has been paid to the non-medical management of epilepsy, but this may be as a result of the small number of specialist centres world-wide providing a multi-disciplinary approach to the assessment and treatment of epilepsy, and the methodological flaws of studies determining the efficacy of such an approach (Goldstein 1990). Non-medical/surgical approaches to the management of epilepsy can be divided into two broad categories: those aimed at reducing seizure frequency and those which target the psychological adjustment of the individual with epilepsy. Techniques aimed at reducing seizure frequency through non-medical approaches will be discussed in Chapter 7.

The importance of the role of the clinical psychologist as a member of a multi-disciplinary team in the assessment and treatment of epilepsy has been well documented although at what stage they should intervene is less clear. Given that some people will develop psychological problems as a result of the diagnosis of epilepsy, then it would seem appropriate that psychological intervention should be made available at that point. For some families it may not be until several years later that difficulties arise as a result of the impact of the epilepsy, and therefore, a psychological service should be routinely available in epilepsy out-patient clinics.

People with epilepsy should be fully investigated to consider what factors may be important in determining the development and maintenance of psychological problems associated with their condition. Obviously some factors will be amenable to psychological treatment, whereas other more severe symptoms may require pharmacological treatment in addition to psychological therapy.

Clinical anecdotal evidence suggests that the most appropriate treatment for people with epilepsy is cognitive behavioural therapy, but this and other treatment programmes, including long term psychotherapy, have yet to be investigated. Indeed, studies of the efficacy of psychological treatments is warranted, although these should be conducted in the context of a randomised clinical trial as opposed to small group studies or single case studies. Although the evidence for the efficacy of psychological treatment programmes in epilepsy is limited, there is evidence for the success of behavioural treatments in other chronic conditions (Illis 1994). Some studies have shown that psychoeducational programmes of two and seven days duration have proved to be effective (Helgeson *et al.* 1990). In this chapter, the author will concentrate on approaches to improving psychosocial adjustment.

Psychological assessment

In order to establish the nature of the psychological problems that are being presented, in-depth clinical interviewing will be necessary and this may involve the individual and their family, as many behavioural problems associated with epilepsy will occur in the context of the family home. There are a number of psychological assessments used routinely that may be helpful in the initial assessment these are listed in Table 6.2.

Anxiety management

A variety of relaxation strategies might be applied in the management of seizures because of the recognition that anxiety may act as a seizure precipitant and that people with epilepsy are more likely to have increased rates of anxiety when compared with the normal population. Progressive muscle relaxation techniques have been used, with some success, in patients who are able to identify heightened physiological arousal prior to seizure onset and who experience anxiety interictally (e.g. Rousseau *et al.* 1985, see Chapter 7). While there is substantial

Table 6.2 Assessment of behavioural functioning in people with epilepsy

Measure	*Authors*
Hospital Anxiety and Depression Scale	Zigmond and Snaith 1983
Self Esteem Scale	Rosenberg 1965
Family Environment Scale	Moos & Moos 1981
Impact of Epilepsy Scale	Jacoby *et al.* 1993
Profile of Mood Scale	McNair *et al.* 1981
Cognitive Effects Scale	Aldenkamp *et al.* 1995
Minnisota Multiphasic Personality Inventory	Dikmen *et al.* 1983
Mastery Scale	Pearlin & Schooler 1978

anecdotal evidence that people with epilepsy will benefit from anxiety management, there are few substantial randomised studies to support the efficacy of such techniques in the management of this condition.

Individual counselling and education

The process of adjusting to epilepsy is complex with people with epilepsy having to make many changes as a result of the diagnosis and subsequent treatment. According to Scambler (1993), there are five dimensions to the process of adjustment: accommodation, rationalisation, concept of self, sociability and fulfilment. In the course of adjustment, people with epilepsy will have to deal with the fear of their seizures, make sense of their medical history (sometimes having to generate their own theories about its cause) and try to minimise the negative impact of epilepsy on their own self-worth. For some people with epilepsy, the condition may have adverse effects on their relationship with others, and for this reason they may conceal their condition and at the same time compromise any potential achievements in a number of social roles.

It is important, therefore, for people with epilepsy and their families to have a greater understanding about their epilepsy and demystify any beliefs they might have about their condition. Thus, clinicians have a significant role in influencing the process of accommodation by being aware of the timing of the communication of a diagnosis of epilepsy, as often the diagnosis marks the beginning of a protracted and sometimes lifelong process of adjustment to having epilepsy. A number of authors have highlighted the role of the clinician in the adjustment process, through rational drug therapy combined with treatment for the possible psychological or psychiatric sequelae of epilepsy (Hermann and Whitman 1991; Scambler 1993).

A number of concerns that people with epilepsy have about their condition could be resolved if acknowledged and discussed. It is important to ensure that the person with epilepsy and their family are encouraged to discover for themselves much of the necessary information they require to make sense of their condition and its management; this process of empowerment will be beneficial in the process of adjustment (Mittan 1986). The epilepsy support agencies will also have a role in educating and supporting the individual with epilepsy and their family. There are both local and national organisations covering the whole of the United Kingdom.

The importance of recognising the connections between people's misconceptions about seizures and psychosocial functioning has been well documented (Mittan 1986). Hills and Baker's (1992) research is also relevant in this context in that they demonstrated how possession of accurate information about epilepsy was significantly related to levels of well-being. People with epilepsy who were better informed about the management and treatment of their condition perceived themselves as being in more control and subsequently had significantly better psychological profiles than those who were less informed.

Cognitive-behavioural therapy

Cognitive-behavioural therapy involves shaping the way people think, feel and behave. The rationale for using this approach for people with epilepsy would be to help them minimise the impact of their condition on their daily lives. Interventions aimed at the cognitive level emphasise the importance of providing new information about the illness or its management. Cognitive behavioural techniques are also implemented to modify the underlying core beliefs that people have about their condition which may cause psychological impairments. Interestingly, Tan and Bruni's (1986) use of group-based cognitive behavioural therapy resulted in an increase in ratings of well-being in patients with epilepsy. This author has found that short-term cognitive behavioural treatment can be particularly helpful in assisting people with epilepsy come to terms with their diagnosis, particularly when this is accompanied by clear and precise information about the condition. Families should also be considered as important targets for modifying beliefs about the epilepsy, its cause and its management.

While the general practitioner will be able to provide some information regarding the nature and management of epilepsy, counselling is likely to be undertaken by paramedical staff. Where the psychological consequences of the epilepsy are disabling for the individual, then referral to a clinical psychologist is likely to be the most appropriate referral.

Family therapy

For some families, education and counselling may be sufficient, but for others, where the impact of the epilepsy and its treatment are significant, formal family therapy may be necessary. With this approach, the role of the family is seen as important in the development and maintenance of psychological problems that may have arisen for many reasons, including overprotection, rejection and concealment by family members. In family therapy, the whole of the family are invited to explore and modify communication systems and behavioural functioning in order to minimise the negative aspects of the epilepsy. While there is little evidence of the efficacy of this approach in families with epilepsy, there is substantial evidence of its usefulness in other conditions (Minuchin 1974).

SUMMARY

While much is known about the clinical course of epilepsy, less is understood about the aetiology and prognosis of behavioural problems associated with it. More knowledge is required in order to disentangle the various contributory factors. It is only by increasing our understanding in this area that specific treatment programmes can be designed to ameliorate the often disabling psychological consequences of this condition.

It is clear from recent studies that a significant number of people with epilepsy will have well-controlled seizures with minimum side effects and few behavioural consequences (Jacoby *et al.* 1996). For this group of patients, the need for psychological input will be minimal. For those with behavioural problems associated with the diagnosis of epilepsy, there is evidence to suggest that not enough attention is given to the non-pharmacological management of their condition (Jacoby, personal communication). Evidence from single case and group studies have highlighted the benefits of using psychological techniques, including anxiety management, counselling and psychotherapy (Helgeson *et al.* 1990). Addressing the psychological consequences of this condition will undoubtedly help to improve the quality of life of people with epilepsy, although there is still a need for randomised clinical trials to demonstrate the efficacy of the various behavioural treatment strategies.

ACKNOWLEDGEMENTS

I would like to thank Ann Jacoby for her helpful comments on an earlier draft of this manuscript.

REFERENCES

Aldenkamp, A. P., Baker, G. A., Pieters, M. S. M., Schoemaker, H. C., Cohen, A. F. and Schwabe, S. (1995) 'The Neurotoxicity Scale: the validity of a patient-based scale, assessing neurotoxicity', *Epilepsy Research* 20: 229–39.

Arnston, P., Drodge, D., Norton, R. and Murray, E. (1986) 'The perceived psychosocial consequences of having epilepsy', in S. Whitman and B. P. Hermann (eds) *Psychopathology in Epilepsy*, New York and Oxford: Oxford University Press.

Baker, G. A., Jacoby, A. and Chadwick, D. W. (1996) 'The associations of psychopathology in epilepsy. A community study', *Epilepsy Research* 25: 29–39.

Betts, T. (1981) 'Depression, anxiety and epilepsy', in E. H. Reynolds and M. R. Trimble (eds) *Epilepsy and Psychiatry*, New York: Churchill Livingstone.

—— (1992) 'Epilepsy and stress', *British Medical Journal* 305: 378–9.

Collings, J. (1990) 'Epilepsy and well being', *Social Science and Medicine* 31: 165–70.

—— (1995) 'The impact of epilepsy on self-perceptions', *Journal of Epilepsy* 8: 164–71.

Conrad, P. and Schneider, J. W. (1992) *Deviance and Medicalisation: From Badness to Sickness*, Philadelphia: Temple University Press.

Cull, C. A. and Trimble, M. R. (1989) 'Effects of anticonvulsant medication on cognitive functioning in children with epilepsy', in B. Hermann and M. Seidenberg (eds) *The Childhood Epilepsies: Neuropsychological, Psychosocial and Intervention Aspects*, New York: Wiley.

Currie, S., Heathfield, K. W. G., Henson, R. A. and Scott, D. F. (1971) 'Clinical course and prognosis of temporal lobe epilepsy: A survey of 666 patients', *Brain* 94: 173–90.

Devinsky, O. (1992) *Behavioural Neurology: 100 Maxims*, London: Edward Arnold.

Dikmen, S., Hermann, B., Wilensky, A. and Rainwater, G. (1983) 'Validity of the MMPI to psychopathology in patients with epilepsy', *Journal of Nervous and Mental Disease* 171: 114–22.

Dodrill, C. B. and Batzel, L. W. (1986) 'Interictal behavioural features of patients with epilepsy', *Epilepsia* 27 (Suppl. 2): S64–72.

Fenwick, P. (1986) 'Aggression and behaviour', in M. R. Trimble and T. G. Bolwig (eds) *Aspects of Epilepsy and Psychiatry*, Chichester: Wiley.

Gastaut, H., Morrin, G. and Leserve, N. (1955) 'Study of the behaviour of psychomotor epileptics during the interval between seizures', *Annals of Medicine and Psychology* 113: 1–27.

Gehlert, S. (1994) 'Perceptions of control in adults with epilepsy', *Epilepsia* 31: 81–8.

Gibbs, F. A., Gibbs, E. L. and Fuster, B. (1948) 'Psychomotor epilepsy', *Archives of Neurology and Psychiatry* 60: 331–9.

Gloor, P., Olivier, A., Quesney, L. F., Andermann, F. and Horowitz, S. (1982) 'The role of the limbic system in experiential phenomena of temporal lobe epilepsy', *Annals of Neurology* 12: 129–44.

Goldstein, L. H. (1990) 'Behavioural and cognitive-behavioural treatments for epilepsy: a progress review', *British Journal of Clinical Psychology* 29: 257–69.

Hauser, W. A. and Hessdorfer, D. C. (1990) *Epilepsy, Frequency, Causes and Consequences*, Maryland: Epilepsy Foundation of America.

Helgeson, D. C., Mittan, R., Tan, S. A. and Chayasirisobhon, A. (1990) 'Sepulveda epilepsy education: the efficacy of a psychoeducational treatment programme in treating medical and psychosocial aspects of epilepsy', *Epilepsia* 31: 75–82.

Hermann, B. P. and Whitman, S. (1986) 'Psychopathology in epilepsy: a multiaetiological model', in S. Whitman and B. P. Hermann (eds) *Psychopathology in Epilepsy: Social Dimensions*, Oxford: Oxford University Press.

—— (1991) 'Neurobiological, psychosocial and pharmacological factors underlying interictal psychopathology in epilepsy', in D. Smith, D. Treiman and M. Trimble (eds) *Advances in Neurology. Vol 55: Neurobehavioural Problems in Epilepsy*, New York: Oxford University Press.

Hills, M. D. and Baker, P. G. (1992) 'Relationships among epilepsy, social stigmas, self-esteem and social support', *Journal of Epilepsy* 5: 231–8.

Illis, L. S. (1994) *Neurological Rehabilitation*, Oxford: Blackwell Scientific.

Jacoby, A. (1994) 'Felt versus enacted stigma: a concept revisited', *Social Science and Medicine* 38: 269–4.

Jacoby, A., Baker, G. A., Smith, D. F., Dewey, M. and Chadwick, D. W. (1993) 'Measuring the impact of epilepsy: the development of a novel scale', *Epilepsy Research* 16: 83–8.

Jacoby, A., Baker, G. A., Steen, A., Potts, P. and Chadwick, D. W. (1996) 'The clinical course of epilepsy and its psychosocial correlates: findings from a UK community study', *Epilepsia* 37: 148–61.

Landolt, H. (1958) 'Serial electroencephalographic investigations during psychotic episodes in epileptic patients during schizophrenic attacks', in L. de Haas (ed.) *Lectures on Epilepsy*, New York: Elsevier.

Lefcourt, H. (1976) *Locus of Control: Current Trends in Research and Theory*, New York: Wiley.

Leiderman, D. B., Csernanky, J. G. and Moses, J. A. (1990) 'Neuroendocrinology and limbic epilepsy: relationship to psychopathology, seizure variables and neuropsychosocial function', *Epilepsia* 31: 270–4.

McNair, D., Lorr, N. and Dropplemann, L. (1981) *Manual for the Profile of Mood States*, San Diego: Educational and Industrial Testing Service.

Matthews, W. S. and Barabas, G. (1981) 'Suicide and epilepsy: a review of the literature', *Psychosomatics* 22: 515–24.

Matthews, W. S., Barabas, G. and Ferari, M. (1982) 'Emotional concomitants of childhood epilepsy', *Epilepsia* 23: 671–81.

Mendez, M. F., Cummings, J. L. and Benson, D. F. (1986) 'Depression in epilepsy. Significance and phenomenology', *Archives of Neurology* 43: 766–70.

Minuchin, S. (1974) *Families and Family Therapy*, London: Tavistock Publications.

Mittan, R. J. (1986) 'Fear of seizures', in S. Whitman and B. P. Hermann (eds) *Psychopathology in Epilepsy: Social Dimensions*, New York: Oxford University Press.

Mittan, R. J. and Locke, G. E. (1982) 'Fear of seizures: epilepsy's forgotten symptom', *Urban Health* 11: 30–2.

Moos, R. and Moos, B. (1981) *The Family Environment Scale Manual*, Paolo Alta CA: Consulting Psychologists Press.

Pearlin, L. and Schooler, C. (1978) 'The structure of coping', *Journal of Health and Social Behaviour* 19: 2–21.

Perez, M. M. and Trimble, M. R. (1980) 'Epileptic psychosis-diagnostic comparison with process schizophrenia', *British Journal of Psychiatry* 137: 245–50.

Pond, D. A. and Bidwell, B. H. (1959) 'A survey of epilepsy in 14 general practices. II. Social and psychological aspects', *Epilepsia* 1: 285–9.

Robertson, M. M., Trimble, M. R. and Townsend, H. R. A. (1987) 'Phenomenology of depression in epilepsy', *Epilepsia* 28: 364–72.

Rosenberg, M. (1965) *Society and the Adolescent Self-image*, Princeton NJ: Princeton University Press.

Rousseau, A., Herman, B. P. and Whitman, S. (1985) 'Effects of progressive relaxation on epilepsy: analysis of a series of cases', *Psychological Report* 57: 1203–12.

Ryan, R., Kempner, K. and Emlen, A. C. (1980) 'The stigma of epilepsy as a self concept', *Epilepsia* 21: 433–44.

Scambler, G. (1989) *Epilepsy*, London: Tavistock.

—— (1993) 'Coping with epilepsy', in J. Laidlaw, A. Richens and D. W. Chadwick, D. W. (eds) *A Textbook of Epilepsy* (4th edn), Edinburgh: Churchill Livingstone.

Scambler, G. and Hopkins, A. (1986) 'Being epileptic: coming to terms with stigma', *Social Health and Illness* 8: 26–43.

Slater, E. and Beard, A. W. (1963) 'The schizophrenic-like psychosis of epilepsy', *British Journal of Psychiatry* 109: 95.

Smith, D. F., Baker, G. A., Dewey, M., Jacoby, A. and Chadwick, D. W. (1991) 'Seizure frequency, patient perceived seizure severity and the psychosocial consequences of intractable epilepsy', *Epilepsy Research* 9: 231–41.

Stanley, P. J. and Tillotson, A. (1982) *Epilepsy in the Community*, Leeds, UK: Leeds School of Social Studies, Leeds Polytechnic.

Sullivan, M. D. (1995) 'Depression and disability from chronical medical illness', *European Journal of Public Health* 5: 40–5.

Tan, S-Y. and Bruni, J. (1986) 'Cognitive-behavioural therapy with adult patients with epilepsy: a controlled outcome study', *Epilepsia* 27: 225–33.

Thompson, P. J. (1988) 'Methods and problems in the assessment of behaviour disorders in epileptic patients', in M. R. Trimble and E. H. Reynolds (eds) *Epilepsy, Behaviour and Cognitive Function*, Chichester: Wiley.

Toone, B. K. (1981) 'The psychosis of epilepsy', in E. H. Reynolds and M. Trimble (eds) *Epilepsy and Psychiatry*, Edinburgh: Churchill Livingstone.

Treiman, D. M. (1990) 'Epilepsy and aggression', in D. B. Smith (ed.) *Epilepsy: Current Approaches to Diagnosis and Treatment*, New York: Raven Press.

Trimble, M. R. (1988) 'Anticonvulsant drugs mood and cognitive function', in M. R. Trimble and E. H. Reynolds (eds) *Epilepsy, Behaviour and Cognitive Function*, Chichester: Wiley.

Waxman, S. G. and Geshwind, N. (1975) 'The interictal behaviour syndrome of temporal lobe epilepsy', *Archives of General Psychiatry* 32: 1580.

Wallaston, K. A. B. S. and De Villas, R. (1980) 'Development of multidimensional health locus of control scale', *Health Education Monograph* 6: 160–70

West, P. (1986) 'The social meaning of epilepsy. Stigma as a potential explanation for psychopathology in children', in S. Whitman and B. P. Hermann (eds) *Psychopathology in Epilepsy: Social Dimensions*, New York: Oxford University Press.

Zeigler, R. G. (1982) 'Epilepsy: individual illness, human predicament and family dilemma', *Family Relations* 31: 435–44.

Zigmond, A. S. and Snaith, R. P. (1983) 'The Hospital Anxiety and Depression Scale', *Acta Psychiatrica Scandinavica* 67: 361–70.

Chapter 7

Psychological control of seizures

Laura H. Goldstein

In recent years a major development of the role of clinical psychologists working with people with epilepsy has been in psychological management of seizures including spontaneous, self induced and non-epileptic (or pseudo) seizures.

THE BEGINNINGS OF A PSYCHOLOGICAL UNDERSTANDING OF SEIZURE OCCURRENCE

Fenwick and Brown (1989) adopt a model whereby epileptic seizures are precipitated or inhibited depending upon the relative excitation of groups of neurones in and around the damaged area of brain. Group One (G1) neurones, at the centre of an epileptic focus, are damaged and show continuously abnormal patterns of activity. Surrounding these are Group Two (G2) neurones, which are only partially damaged and function either normally or abnormally in terms of paroxysmal epileptic activity. During a focal seizure, G1 neurones recruit G2 neurones into their abnormal pattern of activity. If G2 neurones then recruit normal neurones into their abnormal firing, the seizure generalises. Fenwick and Brown (ibid.) state that the level of electrophysiological activation of G2 neurones, and of normal brain tissue surrounding the focus, determines whether seizure activity is subsequently inhibited or enhanced. There appears to be a relationship between behavioural, physiological and psychological states and the probability of seizure occurrence such that seizures do not occur in a vacuum (ibid.).

Epileptic seizures that are associated with psychological events are called 'psychogenic' seizures by Fenwick and Brown (1989) and are divided into two broad classes.

Primary psychogenic seizures are triggered by the individual engaging deliberately in an activity which they have previously found induces a seizure. For example, a 36-year-old man had learned that by allowing feelings of sadness (which had developed when his father had died during his adolescence) to persist, a seizure would occur; he used this phenomenon to induce seizures in later life when facing personal difficulties.

Secondary psychogenic seizures (Fenwick and Brown 1989) are precipitated by attending to a specific mental task which activates a local epileptogenic brain area without the deliberate intention on the part of the subject to cause a seizure and without an evoking peripheral stimulus. These are also referred to as the 'thinking epilepsies' (Fenwick 1994). Fenwick and Brown (1989) describe a 23-year-old woman with a left temporal lobe epileptic focus, who often experienced auras when doing crossword puzzles and other word retrieval tasks. Other examples include four people whose generalised seizures were triggered by mental or written calculations, card games or board games (Striano *et al.* 1993; see also Goossens *et al.* 1990). Game playing and tasks requiring strategic thinking produced significant EEG changes in a woman with generalised seizures (Siegel *et al.* 1992).

Fenwick and Brown (1989) also discuss 'evoked seizures'. These have external precipitants and include the reflex epilepsies (musicogenic, photogenic, movement evoked seizures, somatosensory evoked seizures and pattern stimulation). Such epilepsies may be very trigger-specific; a 20-year-old man experienced seizures during a hot bath, and on one occasion during a hot shower, but neither heat nor steam alone would provoke a seizure if he was not bathing (Lisovoski *et al.* 1992). Photosensitivity may be relevant in cases of video-game induced seizures (Ferrie *et al.* 1994). However non-photic factors such as excitement, tiredness, lack of sleep and cognitive processing may be relevant especially in non-photosensitive subjects, indicating that sometimes it may be difficult to distinguish between psychogenic and evoked seizures.

Cutting across these classifications of seizures, Cull (in preparation) discusses the self-induction of seizures that occurs in a small percentage of people with epilepsy. Most often reported for individuals with photosensitive epilepsy, seizures may be induced by a number of motor behaviours (e.g. blinking, deliberately looking at vertically striped objects, and waving fingers in front of the eyes in bright sunlight). These methods of seizure induction involve both evoking stimuli and the knowledge that certain actions in the presence of such stimuli will induce seizures (see also Chapter 11).

Extending the idea of predicting seizure occurrence, several studies have considered whether people with epilepsy can identify high and low risk situations for epileptic activity, seizure provoking factors, and whether they could self-induce or abort seizures. The pattern of results is similar across different studies. Thus, Antebi and Bird (1993) and Spector *et al.* (1994) found that the most common factor associated with an increase in seizure frequency was tension/anxiety. Løyning *et al.* (1993) also indicated that stress was the most common 'high-risk-for-seizure occurrence' situation. Spector *et al.* (1994) documented the negative effect of anger and unhappiness on seizure occurrence, happiness being associated with decreased seizure occurrence (Antebi and Bird, 1993). Of interest also are those individuals who can induce seizures at will. Of Løyning *et al.*'s sample, nearly 8 per cent said they could produce seizures, 3 per cent of Antebi and Bird's sample (1993) claimed they could produce a seizure at will and nearly 23 per cent of patients attending a psychiatric clinic for their epilepsy reported deliberately inducing seizures (Finkler *et al.* 1990). Seventeen per cent of patients attending a psychiatry clinic and over 12 per cent attending a neurology clinic reported sometimes being able to induce a seizure. In contrast, nearly 53 per cent and 39 per cent of these groups respectively could sometimes abort seizures; 88 and nearly 81 per cent respectively could identify at least one high risk-for-seizure occurrence situation (Spector *et al.* 1994). The ability to self-manage seizures (e.g. Pritchard *et al.* 1985) is not limited to adults (Cull *et al.* 1996) and has the potential to be formalised into systematic treatment plans.

APPROACHES TO THE PSYCHOLOGICAL MANAGEMENT OF SEIZURES

Clinical seizure frequency (sometimes including auras as evidence of ongoing seizure activity) has been used as the most common target of intervention (Goldstein 1990). Self-control approaches using cognitive-behavioural techniques are directed at psychogenic seizures, whereas classical conditioning procedures have been used successfully with evoked seizures (e.g. Forster 1969, 1972; Forster *et al.* 1969).

Early studies suffered from methodological problems (Mostofsky and Balaschak 1977; Krafft and Poling 1982) and even more recent studies (see Goldstein 1990) demonstrate persisting difficulty in matching treatments to seizure types, being able to make comparisons across different studies in terms of techniques and outcome measures, and rely on self-report of seizure frequency when considering effectiveness. The following sections will review the various cognitive and/or behavioural approaches that have been applied to seizure management, but they should be considered in the light of previous criticisms. For reviews of reward management approaches, see Powell (1981) and Mostofsky (1993).

Altering levels of arousal

Given the self-reported high association between seizure occurrence and stressful situations, it is informative that a number of published studies have used relaxation training as their therapeutic intervention.

Studies employing Progressive Muscular Relaxation (PMR) have varied in sample size and complexity of design, but have shown a similar tendency to produce a decrease in seizure frequency (Rousseau *et al.* 1985; Whitman *et al*, 1990; Puskarich *et al.* 1992). In all cases, subjects were not trained to use the relaxation in stressful situations, although at least twice daily practice was required. The question remains as to which patients will benefit most from relaxation training (Goldstein 1990; Puskarich *et al.* 1992).

Relaxation has been included in the treatment interventions examined by Dahl and colleagues, who have used variants of systematic desensitisation. Her group emphasised the need to train people to become accurately aware of seizure occurrence in order for treatment to be effective. Dahl *et al.* (1987) compared the use of 'contingent relaxation' (CR) to an attention placebo and waiting-list control group. CR involved the application of PMR in each individual's own high-risk-for-seizure-occurrence situations and when they were aware of early signs of an impending seizure. In addition, subjects identified low-risk-for-seizure-occurrence situations. Subjects were trained in fantasy, role play and *in vivo* to imagine or experience high-risk situations and then switch to a relaxed state combined with imagining a low-risk scene. Only subjects trained in CR showed a significant reduction in seizure frequency, with effects being maintained after thirty weeks. The mechanism behind the seizure reduction remained unclear.

Dahl *et al.* (1988) suggested that not only might the absolute level of arousal be important for seizure genesis but so might be a sudden change in arousal. Three children with refractory epilepsy underwent training that included CR, biofeedback training in early awareness of seizure signals, countermeasures for arousal level, and positive reinforcement for appropriate behaviour. Countermeasures (see below), which were designed to reverse the arousal level experienced at seizure onset were more effective than the CR and positive reinforcement in reducing seizures. Overt seizure behaviour and EEG paroxysmal activity were reduced by countermeasures. The rather intrusive and intensive treatment package, however, may only be justifiable with individuals with very frequent seizures.

In terms of long-term effectiveness of treatment, Dahl *et al.* (1992) evaluated children who had been studied eight years following a behavioural intervention, which comprised teaching the children, their parents and teachers to recognise pre-seizure events and to reinforce seizure control techniques and appropriate behaviour (Dahl *et al.* 1985). The children were also taught to apply CR in high-risk-for-seizure situations. Only those in the treatment group had shown a reduction in seizure index (frequency x duration of seizures) which was maintained at the eight-year follow-up; the control groups showed no change from baseline.

None of the studies that have employed relaxation indicate whether *inter alia* relaxation training focused on breathing patterns (Goldstein 1990). Fried (1993) explained how hyperventilation induces epileptic seizures, and the role that stress may play in this. Fried *et al.* (1984) employed diaphragmatic breathing with biofeedback of the per-cent-end tidal level of carbon dioxide in subjects with refractory generalised tonic-clonic, absence and psychomotor seizures, who also demonstrated chronic hyperventilation. Eight of their ten subjects showed normalisation of their EEG power spectra and reduction in the severity and frequency of seizures. Simply adjusting the rate of respiration via diaphragmatic breathing was insufficient to produce lasting seizure reduction; it was the knowledge of the effect that such breathing produces on blood carbon dioxide levels that was necessary for improvement to be maintained (Fried 1993). The unavailability of biofeedback should not, however, discourage the teaching of diaphragmatic breathing as part of a relaxation training programme; hyperventilation may be associated with other symptoms of anxiety and possibly with EEG dysrhythmia (ibid.).

Brown and Fenwick (1989) successfully combined the use of cue-controlled relaxation with systematic desensitisation in imagination. They exposed individuals to an aura in imagination, and while in a relaxed state they were then taught to associate the relaxed state with a cue word which could subsequently be used to recreate the feeling of relaxation, thereby preventing the development of a seizure and, by association, the aura.

As noted earlier, for some people it is a change in arousal that may precipitate a seizure (e.g. from an aroused to a relaxed state, such as after a day's work or after strenuous exercise). Such people may need to arouse themselves when a seizure is imminent. This would concur with some self-reported strategies for seizure abatement (Pritchard *et al.* 1985). Brown and Fenwick (1989) have successfully combined cue-controlled arousal with relaxation.

Thus while relaxation, either alone or in combination with other approaches, can be effective, the opposite may sometimes be required. Consequently, a detailed analysis of the seizure precipitants for a particular individual is essential.

Countermeasures

If cue-controlled (or contingent) relaxation or arousal serve to reduce the likelihood of seizure occurrence by altering states of arousal in pools of neurones, then other activities may also serve to counteract a seizure if they can alter the activity of the G2 and surrounding neurones. Dahl *et al.* (1988) have termed these actions countermeasures, which may include shouting aloud, increasing physical activity or concentrating on something such as the last thing that has been seen or said (Pritchard *et al.* 1985: 266; Fenwick 1994). Dahl *et al.* (1987) noted that thirteen of their eighteen subjects had spontaneously developed countermeasures. It is not clear whether the spontaneous development of these techniques interacts positively with other treatment techniques, or whether their use was discouraged during treatment studies (Goldstein 1990). It is also unclear why these self-generated techniques do not always seem to work, and why people persist in trying to use them (Betts *et al.* 1995a).

Betts *et al.* (1995b) used aromatherapy as a countermeasure. Here, an oil selected by the patient was initially paired with an autohypnotic suggestion to relax or to become more aroused. Subsequently, the oil was used in relaxing or arousing situations. Smelling the oil and, subsequently, the memory of the oil's smell were later used as countermeasures. Of thirty patients, at one year's follow-up, nine had complete seizure control and thirteen had achieved at least 50 per cent reduction in seizure occurrence. These promising findings require replication.

Multi-component psychological approaches

Gillham (1990) administered a short out-patient treatment package to individuals with inadequately controlled seizures. She examined the effectiveness of two treatment approaches, self-control of seizures and alleviation of psychological disorder, applied in a counterbalanced order. Each was undertaken over a five-week period, involving four hours of patient contact. Self-control of seizures focused on factors that might be involved in precipitating seizures; avoidance strategies, seizure interruption, countermeasures or use of relaxation and breathing exercises were encouraged. Alleviation of psychological disorder focused on problems such as anxiety associated with phobic avoidance of leaving home, mild depression and family disagreements. Relaxation training was not used to help alleviate these problems. Both groups showed a significant decrease in seizure frequency that was maintained after six months, with significantly reduced self-ratings of anxiety and depression.

The two treatments, which were equally effective, both taught subjects coping skills. Gillham (1990) suggested that the reduction in anxiety following from the improved sense of self-control is probably more important than whether the coping skill derived from treatment is primarily concerned with seizures or with psychological difficulties. She concluded that brief psychological treatments aimed at developing coping skills can be offered on an out-patient basis for people without marked psychopathology.

The importance of teaching coping mechanisms has been considered by other researchers. Tan and Bruni (1986) focused on the use of cognitive-behaviour therapy (CBT) because of the extent to which anxiety and depression are commonly associated with epilepsy. Their group-based CBT was applied over eight, two-hour-long weekly sessions and was directed towards training in coping skills for stress and seizure control. Their Supportive Counselling control group had a similar number of sessions of supportive and non-directive group counselling which did not encourage the use of coping strategies. A waiting list control group was also included. Therapists' global ratings of patients' adjustment improved for both active intervention groups, pre- to post-treatment, although the CBT group also maintained this difference after four months. There was only a non-significant tendency for improvement in seizure frequency to have been most sensitive to CBT. Tan and Bruni suggested that CBT might be more effective on an individual basis and that their coping-skills-based group therapy might only be effective for people already predisposed towards self-help skills. With respect to the former point, Brown and Fenwick (1989) report a single case in which the use of CBT for depression was accompanied by an abatement of seizure activity. It is also possible that a more focused approach, as used by Gillham (1990), is a more effective means of reducing seizure frequency.

A comprehensive self-control of seizures programme, with a very strong emphasis on coping strategies, was developed by Reiter *et al.* (1987) for individual patients. There are twelve stages in their programme, intrinsic to which is record-keeping, both in terms of seizures and thoughts associated with the programme requirements. Having decided at the outset that taking control is what the person wants to do, the patient has to identify a support person who will accompany them to some sessions and facilitate the process of taking control, which includes the patient fully understanding the consequences of taking anti-convulsants. Learning to identify seizure precipitants, pre-seizure auras and prodromes is emphasised. Participants are trained to deal with negative emotions and situations, external stresses and internal conflicts. The element of the programme not readily available in all settings is the use of biofeedback to train the brain to produce alpha waves, which in many cases will be incompatible with seizure genesis.

Individuals may proceed through the programme at different rates (Reiter *et al.* 1987). Andrews and Schonfeld (1992) evaluated retrospectively the records of eighty-three adults with initially uncontrolled seizures who underwent their treatment programme between 1980–5. Of these, sixty-nine achieved control of their seizures by the time treatment ended. An initially low seizure frequency was an important positive predictor of ultimate seizure control. Earlier age at onset of epilepsy, more years during which the person suffered uncontrolled seizures and higher seizure frequency at treatment onset, predicted the need for a greater number of treatment sessions. Overall, however, the ability to predict the number of sessions required was poor. Andrews and Schonfeld (ibid.) stress the continuing need to determine why the programme works and who might benefit in particular.

Our own preliminary attempts at reducing seizure frequency have adopted a group format, and have essentially followed Reiter *et al.*'s (1987) programme. For practical reasons, we omitted the biofeedback component, yet, with a total of eight, two-hour-long weekly highly-structured sessions run by a psychologist and a senior occupational therapist, we have shown a reduction in mean seizure frequency in seven adults with epilepsy who had a mean epilepsy duration of over nineteen-and-a-half years, in comparison to waiting list controls (Spector *et al.* 1995). Although the participants were a highly selected sample of our clinic population, in terms of motivation and availability to participate in the group, findings suggest that even chronic epilepsy may be amenable to self-control.

Biofeedback

A relatively brief account of the use of EEG biofeedback in the control of seizures will be given, since this is unlikely to be available for use by many clinical psychologists. Its relevance, however, is that it relates well to the model of seizure genesis expounded above and deals directly with the alteration of electrical activity in the brain. Sterman (1993) reviews his centre's work in training patients to alter the sensorimotor rhythm (SMR: 12–16 Hz) to normalise EEG patterns. Enhancement of this EEG activity can increase seizure threshold and reduce clinical and EEG epileptic activity. His review indicates the success of this method over placebo treatments; successful SMR training may also result in improved cognitive and motor functioning. Particular anti-convulsants and the nature of the epileptic pathology may render the process more difficult, but the crucial factor in undertaking such training is its very intensive nature and the commitment required from the patient. This applies to the training of other EEG patterns as well.

Reiter *et al.*'s (1987) biofeedback training of alpha activity in their self-control programme was facilitated by relaxation training. They suggest that training will require anything from four weeks to two months of weekly thirty-minute biofeedback sessions for alpha control to be achieved, with subsequent 'refresher' sessions as required. Their programme does not permit the specific evaluation of this form of biofeedback on treatment outcome.

NON-EPILEPTIC SEIZURES

The clinical psychologist's contribution to the management of seizure disorders also includes non-epileptic seizures (NESs). As with epileptic seizures, terminology has been confusing, and 'psychogenic seizures', 'hysterical seizures', and 'pseudoseizures' have been used to describe 'paroxysmal episodes of altered behaviour resembling epileptic attacks but devoid of characteristic epileptic clinical and electrographic features' (Liske and Forster 1964). Most NESs resemble tonic-clonic seizures, but there is also confusion between seizures arising from the frontal lobes and NESs. It is also important to distinguish between NESs that are thought to have an emotional basis (which are the subject of present interest) from disorders that have other medical causes (see Betts and Boden 1991).

Diagnosis of NESs requires a combination of video/EEG monitoring, blood prolactin and careful clinical observations, combined with the use of 'seizure' recording systems (see below). The diagnostic induction of NESs by suggestion can be a relatively sensitive procedure, although many ethical issues are raised (Lancman *et al.* 1994).

As many as 37 per cent of patients admitted for investigation of epilepsy may have NESs (Betts and Boden 1992a). However, many such patients will have a concomitant diagnosis of either a history of, or active, epilepsy (see also Scheepers *et al.* 1994) so that 20–24 per cent have only NESs (Ramani 1986; Betts and Boden 1992a, but see Montgomery and Espie 1986). With time and further clinical information, diagnoses may change, with major implications for management of such individuals.

A history of sexual abuse is likely to be found more often in females with NESs than with epilepsy or other psychiatric disorders (Betts and Boden 1992b; Litwin and Cardena 1993), which may explain the higher prevalence of NESs among females (Kristensen and Alving 1992; Betts and Boden 1991, but see McDade and Brown 1992). The development of NESs after rape has been conceptualised as an example of Post Traumatic Stress Disorder (e.g. Cartmill and Betts 1992) with the paroxysmal behaviour representing the acting out of intrusive, vivid memories of the rape. Other women with NESs and a history of abuse may have characteristic flashbacks of the abuse or may be reminded of it by external cues. Betts and Boden (1991, 1992a, b) describe different forms of NESs. They call these 'Swoons', 'Tantrums' and 'Abreactive Attacks'. This last type of attack is said to be particularly common in sexually-abused women. However, not all authors (see Scheepers *et al.* 1994) have been able to associate these types of NESs with the precipitants or psychopathology suggested by Betts and Boden. This may reflect how the history of abuse is elicited. The role of sexual abuse in precipitating NESs may need to be disentangled from the role of such abuse in the aetiology of genuine epilepsy in predisposed individuals (Betts and Boden 1991; Greig and Betts 1992).

Management of NESs is poorly described in terms of details of therapeutic intervention, but similar themes emerge. Scheepers *et al.* (1994) counsel against treating these patients as a homogeneous group. An eclectic approach to treatment is recommended since patients' responses to diagnosis will vary considerably. Scheepers *et al.* (1994) and Betts and Boden (1992a, b) stress above all that the patient must not feel rejected once the diagnosis is made, and should preferably be treated in the same service as people with epileptic seizures. Hostile reactions from staff must be avoided (Ramani and Gumnit 1982). No doubt must remain over diagnosis, since this is easily communicated to the patient and will undermine treatment. Some individuals may lose their NESs once diagnosis has been made; others may show 'symptom substitution'. Reactions of families should also be taken into account, since family pathology may well be involved in the development and maintenance of NESs (Moore *et al.* 1994). Understanding the functions of the seizures and their maintaining factors, as well as what was happening to the person when the NESs first started, is important since this may reveal unresolved stresses. Potential interventions include anxiety management, relaxation, and marital therapy, family therapy or individual supportive psychotherapy or counselling, operant conditioning and the occasional use of tranquilisers as appropriate (Betts and Boden 1992a, b; Scheepers *et al.* 1994). Anxiety management directed towards recognising and, in particular, predicting the occurrence of NESs may be beneficial as may cognitive-behaviour therapy to assist patients modify thought patterns which may predispose towards NES occurrence. In all of these respects, treatment of NESs is similar to the treatment of epileptic attacks.

In terms of direct treatment of NESs, minimal attention is given to the NESs without appearing uncaring, accompanied by reinforcement of 'seizure' free behaviour with early generalisation to the family (Ramani and Gumnit 1982). McDade and Brown (1992) explain to patients that a way of helping bring the attacks under control is to start by others paying as little attention to them as possible and by dealing with any emotional problems.

Families must avoid scapegoating the patient, even if they feel that the patient has been 'putting it on', since the lack of recrimination, and the ability of the person to 'save face' will affect outcome. Families may need assistance in coming to terms with a new lifestyle once the person no longer experiences NESs. When discussing the treatment of NESs sufferers with a history of sexual abuse, Betts and Boden (1992a, b) emphasise the need for the disclosure to come from the patient; treatment may need to continue on an out-patient basis for a long time.

Good prognosis with respect to outcome may depend upon having a history of epilepsy and anxiety attacks alongside the NESs (rather than the 'tantrum' or 'abreactive' types of NESs [Betts and Boden 1992a]), or on having an IQ of above eighty and no past history of violent behaviour (McDade and Brown 1992, but see Montgomery and Espie

1986). Almost two-thirds of Betts and Boden's (1991) patients were 'seizure' free on discharge from hospital, but relapses were common. Krumholz and Niedermeyer (1983) found complete absence of NESs after a five-year follow-up in 29 per cent of patients, whereas Kristensen and Alving (1992) noted that, with a median follow-up of nearly six years, 45 per cent of patients became free from NESs and epileptic seizures, compared to 64 per cent of patients with only epileptic seizures. Of Ramani and Gumnit's (1982) nine patients, one of whom was lost to follow-up, seven showed a marked reduction in NES frequency over a four-year period. Future evaluations require comparisons to be made across very different treatment settings having different referral biases and philosophies regarding aetiology and treatment.

PRACTICAL GUIDE

Whether one is formulating a treatment plan for spontaneous or self-induced epileptic or non-epileptic seizures, detailed behavioural analysis of the seizure behaviour will be required.

Identification of seizure occurrence and recording the antecedents and consequences of the seizure should form the first stage in seizure management. Dahl *et al.* (1985) recommended that treatment methods be developed for the type and function of epilepsy as revealed by careful *functional analysis* of seizure behaviour. Seizure logs or charts or structured interviews have been described by Dahl (1992) and Reiter *et al.* (1987) but can be developed by any practitioner who is skilled in assessing problem behaviours. The practitioner should not predict in advance what factors are likely to increase seizure frequency (e.g. Webster and Mawer 1989; Neufeld *et al.* 1994).

Seizure recording systems should include assessment of the following points:

(a) *The antecedents to the behaviour*, i.e. where the person was, who they were with, what they were doing, thinking, feeling, the time and day on which the seizure occurred, useful medical information such as whether the person was ill, or if female, whether they were pre- or peri-menstrual, whether they had not been sleeping well or have missed a dose of anti-convulsant medication or have been drinking alcohol. Antecedents may be construed as relating to events or feelings occurring in the immediate run-up to a seizure, such as during a thirty minute pre-ictal period.

Premonitory symptoms such as irritability, depression, headache and 'funny feelings' may occur more than thirty minutes before a seizure in patients with partial epilepsy (and possibly to a lesser extent in patients with generalised seizures) and can last for anything between ten minutes and three days (Hughes *et al.* 1993). Here, an informant's view may be crucial in identifying a seizure prodrome. The identification of such premonitory symptoms may provide an opportunity for a therapeutic intervention to counter the prevailing mood preceding the seizure.

(b) *What the seizure was like* (with a detailed description if there was an independent witness). This is important since many people have different types of seizures. Auras without subsequent full seizures must be recorded in addition to full seizures. Seizure duration should also be recorded if possible since a seizure index (*frequency x duration*; Dahl *et al.* 1985, 1987, 1988) may be a more sensitive treatment outcome measure. For NESs the nature of the attack may provide some clue as to its aetiology (Betts and Boden 1991, 1992a, b).

(c) *What happened after the seizure.* This should include the person's own, as well as other people's, reactions to the seizure, how he/she felt, whether additional medication was given, and how long it took the person to recover.

It may be necessary to train patients in record keeping. The clinician must also be fully conversant with the patient's recording system; one of our patients recorded his complex partial seizures as HPOs, which stood for 'Harry passes out'. Since seizure recording is a crucial part of both assessment and treatment, it may need to continue for some weeks before the clinician is satisfied that it will provide the information that is required to formulate a treatment plan.

It may be easier to work with people who have clear auras at their seizure onset, especially if one is attempting to train the person in the use of countermeasures, but the identification of a prodromal mood change may also permit a successful treatment plan to be developed. Even the more general use of relaxation training, however, has proved effective (e.g. Puskarich *et al.* 1992).

The clinical assessment of both epileptic and non-epileptic seizures should also address wider issues such as the impact of the person's epilepsy on their lifestyle and the lifestyle of those with whom they live or have close contact, support from others for the current treatment programme (Reiter *et al.* 1987), resources that are present for planning a life without (or with less severe) epilepsy, as well as the person's general perception of what constitute high- and low-risk situations for seizure occurrence, and whether avoidance of high-risk situations places undesirable restrictions on the person's lifestyle (Taube and Calman 1992). The guidelines about providing careful reassurance to patients and family about the meaning of gaining control will apply irrespective of the type of seizure.

CONCLUSIONS

Clinical psychology has a key role to play in the non-medical treatment of epilepsy, a role which is likely to increase as more sophisticated therapeutic techniques are developed. The effectiveness of the treatment, however, will depend on the inclusion in the programme of all interested and significant people in the person's life (Mostofsky 1993) to ensure complete generalisation of the treatment approach to everyday life.

REFERENCES

Andrews, D. J. and Schonfeld, W. H. (1992) 'Predictive factors for controlling seizures using a behavioural approach', *Seizure* 1: 111–16.

Antebi, D. and Bird, J. (1993) 'The facilitation and evocation of seizures. A questionnaire study of awareness and control', *British Journal of Psychiatry* 162: 759–64.

Betts, T. and Boden, S. (1991) 'Pseudoseizures (non-epileptic attack disorder)', in M. R. Trimble (ed.) *Women and Epilepsy*, Chichester: Wiley.

—— (1992a) 'Diagnosis, management and prognosis of a group of 128 patients with non-epileptic attack disorder. Part I', *Seizure* 1: 19–26.

—— (1992b) 'Diagnosis, management and prognosis of a group of 128 patients with non-epileptic attack disorder. Part II. Previous childhood sexual abuse in the aetiology of these disorders', *Seizure* 1: 27–32.

Betts, T., Fox, C. and MacCallum, R. (1995a) 'Assessment of countermeasures used by people to attempt to control their own seizures', *Epilepsia* 36 (Suppl. 3): S130.

—— (1995b) 'An olfactory countermeasures treatment for epileptic seizures using a conditioned arousal response to specific aromatherapy oils', *Epilepsia* 36 (Suppl 3): S130–1.

Brown, S. W. and Fenwick, P. B. C. (1989) 'Evoked and psychogenic epileptic seizures: II. Inhibition', *Acta Neurologica Scandinavica* 80: 541–7.

Cartmill, A. and Betts, T. (1992) 'Seizure behaviour in a patient with post-traumatic stress disorder following rape'. Notes on the aetiology of 'pseudoseizures', *Seizure* 1: 33–6.

Cull, C. A. (in preparation) 'Self-induction of seizures: the nature of the problem and a model of the development and maintenance of behaviour'.

Cull, C. A., Fowler, M. and Brown, S. W. (1996) 'Perceived self-control of seizures in young people with epilepsy', *Seizure*, 5: 131–8.

Dahl, J. (1992) *Epilepsy. A Behaviour Medicine Approach to Assessment and Treatment in Children. A Handbook for Professionals Working with Epilepsy*, Göttingen: Hogrefe and Huber.

Dahl, J., Brorson, L-O. and Melin, L. (1992) 'Effects of a broad-spectrum behavioural medicine treatment program on children with refractory epileptic seizures: an 8 year follow-up', *Epilepsia* 33: 98–102.

Dahl, J., Melin, L. and Leissner, P. (1988) 'Effects of a behavioural intervention on epileptic behaviour and paroxysmal activity: a systematic replication of three cases with intractable epilepsy', *Epilepsia* 29: 172–83.

Dahl, J., Melin, L. and Lund, L. (1987) 'Effects of a contingent relaxation treatment program on adults with refractory epileptic seizures', *Epilepsia* 28: 125–32.

Dahl, J., Melin, L., Brorson, L-O. and Schollin, J. (1985) 'Effects of a broad spectrum behavior modification treatment programme on children with refractory epileptic seizures', *Epilepsia* 26: 303–9.

Fenwick, P. B. C. (1994) 'The behavioral treatment of epilepsy generation and inhibition of seizures', *Neurologic Clinics* 12: 175–202.

Fenwick, P. B. C. and Brown, S. W. (1989) 'Evoked and psychogenic seizures: I. Precipitation', *Acta Neurologica Scandinavica* 80: 541–7.

Ferrie, C. D., De Marco, P., Grunewald, R. A., Giannakodimos, S. and Panayiotopoulos, C. P. (1994) 'Video game induced seizures', *Journal of Neurology, Neurosurgery and Psychiatry* 57: 925–31.

Finkler, J., Lozar, N. and Fenwick, P. (1990) 'Der Zusammenhang zwischen spezifischen Situationen emotionalen Zuständen und Anfallshäufigkeit: Vergleich einer psychiatrischen mit einer nichtpsychiatriaschen Population von Epilepsiepatienten', in D. Scheffner (ed.) *Epilepsie 90*, Berlin: Einhorn Presse.

Forster, F. M. (1969) 'Conditional reflexes and sensory-evoked epilepsy: the nature of the therapeutic process', *Conditional Reflex* 4: 103–14.

—— (1972) 'The classification and conditioning treatment of the reflex epilepsies', *International Journal of Neurology* 9: 73–86.

Forster, F. M., Hansotia, P., Cleeland, C. S. and Ludwig, A. (1969) 'A case of voice-induced epilepsy treated by conditioning', *Neurology* 19: 325–31.

Fried, R. (1993) 'Breathing training for the self-regulation of alveolar CO_2 in the behavioural control of idiopathic epileptic seizures', in D. I. Mostofsky and Y. Løyning (eds) *The Neurobehavioral Treatment of Epilepsy*, New Jersey: Lawrence Erlbaum.

Fried, R., Rubin, S. R., Carlton, R. M. and Fox, M. C. (1984) 'Behavioural control of intractable seizures: I. Self-regulation of end-tidal carbon dioxide', *Psychosomatic Medicine* 46: 315–31.

Gillham, R. (1990) 'Refractory epilepsy: an evaluation of psychological methods in out-patient management', *Epilepsia* 31: 427–32.

Goldstein, L. H. (1990) 'Behavioural and cognitive-behavioural treatments for epilepsy: a progress review', *British Journal of Clinical Psychology* 29: 257–69.

Goossens, L. A. Z., Andermann, F., Andermann, E. and Remillard, G. M. (1990) 'Reflex seizures induced by card or board games, and spatial tasks: a review of 25 patients and delineation of the epileptic syndrome', *Neurology* 40: 1171–6.

Greig, E. and Betts, T. (1992) 'Epileptic seizures induced by sexual abuse. Pathogenic and pathoplastic factors', *Seizure* 1: 269–74.

Hughes, J., Devinsky, O., Feldmann, E. and Bromfield, E. (1993) 'Premonitory symptoms in epilepsy', *Seizure* 2: 201–3.

Krafft, K. M. and Poling, A. D. (1982) 'Behavioural treatments of epilepsy: methodological characteristics and problems of published studies', *Applied Research in Mental Retardation* 3: 151–62.

Kristensen, O. and Alving, J. (1992) 'Pseudoseizures – risk factors and prognosis. A case-control study', *Acta Neurologica Scandinavica* 85: 177–80.

Krumholz, A. and Niedermeyer, E. (1983) 'Psychogenic seizures: a clinical study with follow-up data', *Neurology* 33: 498–502.

Lancman, M. E., Asconape, J. J., Craven, W. J., Howard, G. and Penry, J. K. (1994) 'Predictive value of induction of psychogenic seizures by suggestion', *Annals of Neurology* 35: 359–61.

Liske, E. and Forster, F. (1964) 'Pseudoseizures: a problem in the diagnosis and management of epilepsy patients', *Neurology* 14: 41–9.

Lisovoski, F., Prier, S., Koskas, P., Dubard, T., Stievenart, J. L., Dehen, H. and Cambier, J. (1992) 'Hot-water epilepsy in an adult: ictal EEG, MRI and SPECT features', *Seizure* 1: 203–6.

Litwin, R. G. and Cardena, E. (1993) 'Dissociation and reported trauma in organic and psychogenic seizure patients', *Psychological Hypnosis* 2.

Løyning, Y., Bjørnæs, H., Larsson, P. G., Areng, S., Aronsen, R., Bragason, A., Kloster, R. and Lossius, R. (1993) 'Influence of psychosocial factors on seizure occurrence', in D. I. Mostofsky and Y. Løyning (eds) *The Neurobehavioral Treatment of Epilepsy*, New Jersey: Lawrence Erlbaum.

McDade, G. and Brown, S. W. (1992) 'Non-epileptic seizures: management and predictive factors of outcome', *Seizure* 1: 7–10.

Montgomery, J. M. and Espie, C. (1986) 'Behavioural management of hysterical pseudo seizures', *Behavioural Psychotherapy* 14: 334–40.

Moore, P. M., Baker, G. A., McDade, G., Chadwick, D. and Brown, S. W. (1994) 'Epilepsy, pseudoseizures and perceived family characteristics: a controlled study', *Epilepsy Research* 18: 75–83.

Mostofsky, D. (1993) 'Behavior modification and therapy in the management of epileptic disorders', in D. I. Mostofsky and Y. Løyning (eds) *The Neurobehavioral Treatment of Epilepsy*, New Jersey: Lawrence Erlbaum.

Mostofsky, D. and Balaschak, B. A. (1977) 'Psychobiological control of seizures', *Psychological Bulletin* 84: 723–50.

Neufeld, M. Y., Sadeh, M., Cohn, D. F. and Korczyn, A. D. (1994) 'Stress and epilepsy: the Gulf War experience', *Seizure* 3: 135–39.

Powell, G. E. (1981) *Brain Function Therapy*, Hampshire: Gower.

Pritchard, P. B. III, Holstrom, V. L. and Giacinto, J. (1985) 'Self-abatement of complex partial seizures', *Annals of Neurology* 18: 265–7.

Puskarich, C. A., Whitman, S., Dell, J., Hughes, J., Rosen, A. J. and Hermann, B. P. (1992) 'Controlled examination of progressive relaxation training of seizure reduction', *Epilepsia* 33: 675–80.

Ramani, V. (1986) 'Intensive monitoring of psychogenic seizures, aggression and dyscontrol syndromes', in R. Gumnit (ed.) *Advances in Neurology. Vol. 46: Intensive Neurodiagnostic Monitoring*, New York: Raven Press.

Ramani, V. and Gumnit, R. J. (1982) 'Management of hysterical seizures in epileptic patients', *Archives of Neurology* 39: 78–81.

Reiter, J., Andrews, D. and Janis, C. (1987) *Taking Control of Your Epilepsy. A Workbook for Patients and Professionals*, Santa Rosa: The Basics Publishing Company.

Rousseau, A., Hermann, B. and Whitman, S. (1985) 'Effects of progressive relaxation on epilepsy: analysis of a series of cases', *Psychological Reports* 57: 1203–12.

Scheepers, B., Budd, S., Curry, S., Gregory, S. and Elson, S. (1994) 'Non-epileptic attack disorder: a clinical audit', *Seizure* 3: 129–34.

Siegel, M., Kurzrok, N., Barr, W. B. and Rowan, A. J. (1992) 'Game-playing epilepsy', *Epilepsia* 33: 93–7.

Spector, S., Foots, A. and Goldstein, L. H. (1995) 'Reduction in seizure frequency as a result of group intervention for adults with epilepsy', *Epilepsia* 36 (Suppl. 3): S130.

Spector, S., Goldstein, L. H., Cull, C. A. and Fenwick, P. B. C. (1994) Precipitating and inhibiting epileptic seizures: a survey of adults with poorly controlled epilepsy. London: International League against Epilepsy.

Sterman, M. B. (1993) 'Sensorimotor EEG feedback training in the study and treatment of epilepsy', in D. I. Mostofsky and Y. Løyning (eds) *The Neurobehavioural Treatment of Epilepsy*, New Jersey: Lawrence Erlbaum.

Striano, S., Meo, R., Bilo, L., Soricellis, M. and Ruosi, P. (1993) 'Epilepsia arithmetices: study of four cases', *Seizure* 2: 35–43.

Tan, S-Y. and Bruni, J. (1986) 'Cognitive-behaviour therapy with adult patients with epilepsy: a controlled outcome study', *Epilepsia* 27: 255–63.

Taube, S. L. and Calman, N. H. (1992) 'The psychotherapy of patients with complex partial seizures', *American Journal of Orthopsychiatry* 62: 35–43.

Webster, A. and Mawer, G. E. (1989) 'Seizure frequency and major life events in epilepsy', *Epilepsia* 30: 162–7.

Whitman, S., Dell, J., Legion, V., Eibhlyn, A. and Statsinger, J. (1990) 'Progressive relaxation for seizure reduction', *Journal of Epilepsy* 3: 17–22.

Chapter 8

Quality of life

Anna Kendrick

INTRODUCTION

Quality of Life (QoL) is a generic term encompassing an individual's feelings of satisfaction with a complex amalgam of areas of functioning. It is broadly accepted that QoL needs to address (at a minimum) satisfaction with physical, cognitive, emotional, social and economic functioning (WHO 1980; Hornquist 1982; Wenger *et al.* 1984, Spitzer 1987; Ware 1987; Fallowfield 1990).

The way in which an individual determines their level of satisfaction within these key areas remains a matter for debate. The philosophical approach to QoL introduces concepts such as the attainment of life goals (Hornquist 1982; Cohen 1982), achievement–aspiration discrepancy (Campbell *et al.* 1976; Calman 1984; Staats and Stassen 1987) and social–relational models (WHO 1980). It is beyond the scope of this chapter to cover such issues in detail. A full review of these concepts can be found in Kendrick (1993). Such concepts are pertinent to the clinician as they provide practical ways of improving a person's perception of their QoL, for example, through increasing patient self-awareness, adjusting patient goals and ensuring that patients set realistic expectations. For example, the achievement–aspiration discrepancy model suggests that it is the discrepancy between actual achievements and aspirations/expectations that play a critical role in determining an individual's feelings of satisfaction with their QoL. Health professionals can temper patient expectations and prepare them for changes and limitations that will occur as disease progresses, thus avoiding frustration and maximising QoL.

QoL is a complex phenomenon with the following key attributes: it is a multidimensional concept influenced by performance in, and satisfaction with, a number of life domains; it is an individual phenomenon in which an individual's beliefs, desires and perceptions play an integral role; it is a relational phenomenon in which an individual makes comparisons (conscious or unconscious) between their current life situation and some external criteria (for example, past abilities, peers); the discrepancy between actual situation and expectations or aspirations is an important component in the determination of QoL by an individual, and it is a fluctuating phenomenon, with changes being related both to objective circumstances (for example, deteriorating physical health) and subjective perceptions (for example, changing expectations).

QUALITY OF LIFE AND THE PATIENT WITH EPILEPSY

There are various medical (Duncan 1990), social (Thompson and Oxley 1988; Scambler 1990) and psychological factors (Vining 1987; McGuire and Trimble 1990) which may influence the QoL of the person with epilepsy (see Table 8.1).

The occurrence of recurring, unpredictable seizures is undoubtedly a major factor affecting the life of a person with epilepsy. Seizure frequency, fear of seizures and self-perception of epilepsy have been shown to be predictors of well-being in people with epilepsy (Leonard 1989; Collings 1990a, b, c; Chaplin *et al.* 1990). These findings are supported by research showing that health is an important mediator of QoL (Edwards and Klemmack 1973; Campbell 1981; Okun *et al.* 1984; Levitt *et al.* 1987) and, in particular, that self-rated health appears to be more predictive of QoL than objective health (Diener 1984). It is

Table 8.1 Contributory factors to impaired QoL in people with epilepsy

Factor	*Specific items*
Medical	Seizure occurrence (frequency, severity) Medication (intrusion/side effects) Hospitalisation (in-patient/out-patient)
Social	Stigmatisation (felt/enacted) Family dynamics (overprotection) Employment difficulties Legal restrictions (driving)
Psychological	Cognitive deficits (memory, concentration) Intellectual decline Psychiatric (depression, anxiety, behaviour disturbance)

unclear, however, whether ill-health directly affects life satisfaction or whether the association is due to the secondary effects of ill-health on other aspects of life that are important to QoL – for example, not being able to work, having reduced activity levels and limited social opportunities.

The diagnosis of epilepsy can bring with it many problems over and above that of experiencing recurrent seizures. Stigmatization, social isolation, psychological problems, educational and employment difficulties have all been documented in people with epilepsy (Dodrill *et al.* 1984a; Scambler and Hopkins 1986; Thompson and Oxley 1988; Levin *et al.* 1988). It is of interest that many of these areas have been shown to be predictive of QoL. Factors associated with increased feelings of well-being include being married (Cameron 1975; Campbell 1981; Costa *et al.* 1987; Mookherjee 1987), having high social status (Cameron 1975; Potter and Coshall 1987), having high levels of social support (Levitt *et al.* 1987), having high levels of activity – with activities involving a high degree of social integration which are in the individual's control being particularly desirable (Steinkamp and Kelly 1987; Reich *et al.* 1987) – and feelings of personal control and high self-esteem (Campbell 1981; Lewis 1982; Diener 1984; Levitt *et al.* 1987). Disadvantage in any of these areas is likely to result in lower feelings of satisfaction with QoL.

In summary, the person with epilepsy may face psychosocial difficulties in a range of areas of life-functioning that are likely to adversely influence feelings of satisfaction with their QoL. Given the far-reaching consequences that the diagnosis of epilepsy may have on a patient's QoL, it is interesting that few studies have attempted to objectively examine the impact of epilepsy on QoL. Whilst there has been a long-standing interest among researchers in areas relevant to quality of life (for example, adequacy of cognitive, emotional and behavioural status, ability to work, social functioning, self-esteem), research work has tended to concentrate on assessing the incidence of these problems and their relationship with epilepsy-related variables (seizure frequency, medication, seizure type – Harrison and Taylor 1976; Rodin *et al.* 1979; Dodrill *et al.* 1984b) rather than the impact of these difficulties on the individuals QoL. Hermann (1992) provides a review of QoL work in epilepsy and a useful summary can be also be found in Meador (1993).

Recent years have, however, seen an increased interest in formal studies of QoL in this group of patients (Hermann 1992), as evidenced by increased attempts to develop epilepsy-specific measures (Vickrey *et al.* 1992; Baker *et al.* 1993; Perrine 1993) and to examine determinants of QoL in this group of patients (Leonard 1989; Chaplin *et al.* 1990; Collings 1990a, b, c).

The development of epilepsy-specific scales is reviewed later in this chapter. In relation to the areas of functioning considered important to (or predictive of) QoL in patients with epilepsy, a number of recent studies have produced some interesting findings. Leonard (1989) used a fifty-item questionnaire to determine which items were considered most important to the QoL of patients living in a residential centre. Opinions were sought from twenty-five relatives, 135 staff and twenty-five residents. In general, broad agreement across the three groups was seen, with the greatest importance being given to:

1 basic physical needs (warm, dry accommodation, adequate diet, clothing, availability of medical care);
2 seizure frequency;
3 independence (having personal possessions, opportunity for privacy, being ambulant);
4 social relationships/occupation (availability of close friends, facilities to encourage socialising);
5 intellectual/creative needs.

Some interesting differences, however, were apparent. Residents themselves placed greater importance on being in good spirits, being able to get out of the centre (for shopping/day trips, etc), having close friends, having the opportunity for sexual relationships and having their own room than the other groups surveyed (relatives and staff).

Chaplin *et al.* (1990) interviewed patients about the impact and consequences of epilepsy and its treatment on their lives. They identified twenty-one areas of concern to people with epilepsy, covering medical, emotional, social and employment aspects (see Table 8.2).

Collings (1990a, b, c), in a study of factors related to general well-being in a group of patients with epilepsy, found that it was patients' perceptions of themselves (their self-image) and their epilepsy that were more predictive of overall well-being. In addition, he noted that it was the discrepancy between an individual's perception of their current self (with epilepsy) and an anticipated self (without epilepsy) that was important in producing a greater sense of well-being. Other factors that were important to well-being were employment status, seizure control, diagnostic certainty and age.

In summary, the person with epilepsy may face difficulties in a range of areas of life-functioning pertinent to QoL. To date, however, little is known about the impact that these problems have on the quality of

Table 8.2 Areas of concern identified by patients with epilepsy

Area	*Specific concern*
Medical	Attitude towards accepting epileptic attacks Attitude towards label 'epilepsy' Fear of having seizures Problems with chronic medication Misconceptions about epilepsy Lethargy/lack of energy Sleep disturbance Distrust of the medical profession
Emotional	Lack of confidence in the future Change of outlook on life/self Depression of emotional reactions
Social	Concern about sexual relationships Concern about housing Lack of confidence surrounding travel Adverse reactions in social life Adverse reactions in leisure pursuits Difficulty in communicating with family Feelings of increased isolation Concern about platonic relationships
Employment	Fear of stigma in employment Concern about performance at work

(Source: Chaplin *et al.* 1990)

everyday life of the individual with epilepsy. One of the major obstacles to answering these questions has been the lack of a QoL measure designed specifically for use in patients with epilepsy.

MEASUREMENT OF QOL IN PATIENTS WITH EPILEPSY

Recent years have seen increasing attempts to measure QoL as an outcome measure for clinical interventions. This has been paralleled by an increasing sophistication in our understanding of the QoL concept and measurement methods, as evidenced by the reviews of Najman and Levine (1981) and Hollandsworth (1988).

While there is a wide acceptance of the need to assess QoL in patients with epilepsy, there is no 'gold standard' measure in existence for so doing. Although there are a myriad of generic and disease-specific measures of QoL in existence (see Clark and Fallowfield 1986; McDowell and Newell 1987; Fletcher *et al.* 1987; Fallowfield 1990 for reviews), it is only in the past five years that a number of epilepsy-specific measures have been developed and these are reviewed here.

Washington Psychosocial Seizure Inventory – WPSI (Dodrill *et al.* 1980)

The WPSI was developed in the 1970s as a measure of the impact of epilepsy on a patient's psychosocial functioning. The original scale is a 132-item questionnaire covering seven areas of functioning: family background, emotional adjustment, interpersonal adjustment, vocational adjustment, financial status, adjustment to seizures and medical management. It is based on patient self-perceptions using self-report assessment and has been widely used both to define psychosocial problems in patients with epilepsy (Dodrill 1983; Dodrill *et al.* 1984a, b; Tan 1986) and to examine the influence of epilepsy-related and other variables on psychosocial functioning (Dodrill 1984; 1986). It has demonstrated acceptable levels of internal reliability, test–retest reliability and validity (Dodrill *et al.* 1980). A WPSI QoL scale has recently been developed (Dodrill and Batzel 1995) consisting of thirty-six items of the WPSI which correlated significantly with an independent QoL measure (the QoLIE-31 Inventory: Cramer 1995).

The WPSI, however, was not designed to provide as broad an assessment of areas of life-functioning important to QoL as generic measures of this concept (for example, the Sickness Impact Profile: Bergner *et al.* 1981), and its use as a measure of the broad impact of epilepsy on QoL has been questioned (Langfitt 1995). This scale is likely to be most appropriate in situations where information about the psychological and social facets of QoL is of primary importance.

The Liverpool Initiative (Baker *et al.* 1993)

This is a battery of measures developed specifically to assess QoL in patients with epilepsy. The battery covers physical, social and psychological functioning and incorporates previously validated measures including the Nottingham Health Profile (Hunt *et al.* 1980), a measure of activities of daily living (Brown and Tomlinson 1984), the Social

Problems Questionnaire (Corney and Clare 1985), the Hospital Anxiety and Depression scale (Zigmond and Snaith 1983), the Profile of Mood States (McNair *et al.* 1981), and measures of self-esteem (Rosenberg 1965) and mastery (Pearlin and Schooler 1978). In addition, three novel epilepsy-specific scales have been developed: a Seizure Severity Scale (Baker *et al.* 1991), an Impact of Epilepsy Scale (Jacoby *et al.* 1993) and a Life Fulfilment Scale (Baker *et al.* 1994). This approach has been used successfully to examine the effects of anti-epileptic treatment (Smith *et al.* 1993) and seizure severity (Smith *et al.* 1991) on the quality of life of patients with epilepsy. Other applications include when to start medication, when to discontinue medication, which medication to prescribe and how best to deliver medical services to people with epilepsy (Jacoby *et al.* 1995).

The Epilepsy Surgery Inventory – ESI-55 (Vickrey *et al.* 1992; Vickrey 1993)

This scale has been developed in the USA specifically to assess changes in QoL following epilepsy surgery. It is a self-report measure covering eleven dimensions of health-related QoL. It consists of a generic core of thirty-five items (covering eight dimensions: general health perceptions, energy/fatigue, social function, emotional well-being, role limitations due to emotional problems, physical function, role limitations due to physical problems, pain) based on the RAND thirty-six item Health Survey (SF-36: Ware and Sherbourne 1992). The SF-36 is a generic measure of functional status and well-being and has been subjected to extensive psychometric development. This is supplemented by nineteen epilepsy-specific items covering three dimensions (cognitive function, role limitations due to memory problems and overall QoL). In addition, the scale includes one item relating to change in health. Data from 200 patients who had undergone surgery for their epilepsy provide evidence of internal consistency and validity (content, construct, convergent) (Vickrey *et al.* 1992).

The Quality of Life in Epilepsy – QOLIE Project (Perrine 1993)

This is a USA-based, multicentre study which began in late 1991 with the aim of developing and validating an epilepsy-specific inventory for patients with mild to moderate epilepsy.

The test battery is based on the ESI-55 (Vickrey *et al.* 1992), but expanded to have a broader application. The initial inventory consisted of ninety-eight items, with the RAND 36-item Health Survey (SF-36) (Ware and Sherbourne 1992) forming a generic core to which epilepsy-specific items were added (based on a literature review and expert opinion as to the areas of importance to people with mild to moderate epilepsy). The epilepsy-specific items added covered ten dimensions: specific health perceptions, worry about seizures, attention and concentration, memory, language, working and driving limitations, medication effects, social support, social isolation and overall QoL. This ninety-eight-item scale was tested in 304 adults with epilepsy and also completed by patient proxies on two occasions with a one month test–retest interval. Patients also completed tests of neuropsychological function and mood status. The initial scale was reduced to eighty-nine items using multitrait scaling analysis methods.

The final version (QOLIE-89) consists of seventeen scales covering four domains (derived by factor analysis): epilepsy-targeted (seizure worry, medication effects, health discouragement, work/driving/social function), cognitive (language, attention/concentration, memory), mental health (overall QoL, emotional well-being, role limitations – emotional, social isolation, social support, energy/fatigue) and physical health (health perceptions, physical function, role limitations – physical, pain). Preliminary data suggest this scale is reliable and valid (Hermann 1995).

Two further versions have been developed: a 31-item version (QoLIE-31), which consists of seven scales focusing on those areas most pertinent to the person with epilepsy (seizure worry, cognitive function, work, energy, emotional well-being, driving, medication effects) and excluding some of the more general QoL scales covered by the QoLIE-89 (physical function, role limitations, pain, health perception, social support and social isolation). The QoLIE-31 takes less time to complete than the QoLIE-89 and is therefore particularly suited to research protocols in which multiple scales and tests are to be used. A QoLIE-10 version is also available, designed as a quick screening tool for use in clinical practice (Cramer 1995).

Quality of Life Assessment by Construct Analysis – QoLASCA, (Kendrick 1993)

This is a 70-item questionnaire based on repertory grid technique. Five areas of life functioning are covered (physical, cognitive, emotional, social and economic/employment). Within these areas, specific items are elicited for each respondent via a semi-structured interview.

Respondents are then asked to rate how much of a problem they view each item at the moment, using a five-point rating scale ranging from 'not a problem' to 'a severe problem'. In addition, patients are asked to rate a variety of situations ('as you were before having epilepsy', 'as you would like to be', 'as you expect to be', 'a close friend', 'the best possible life', 'the worst possible life'). This approach enables the relational aspects of QoL to be tapped. Scoring is based on the discrepancy between current situation ('as you are now') and expectations ('as you would like to be'), with aggregate and profile scores available. The psychometric properties of this scale were established in a group of patients with chronic epilepsy who were assessed on several occasions over a six-month period. Analysis of these data suggest that this scale is reliable, sensitive, valid and acceptable to patients (McGuire 1991; Kendrick 1993).

A cardinal feature of this scale is that it allows an individualised assessment of QoL. Two case histories are presented here to illustrate the benefit of an individualised approach to the assessment of quality of life.

Case history 1: EE

At the time of initial assessment, EE was a 66-year-old gentleman who had lived at a residential centre for a number of years. He had not had a seizure for seven years and led a relatively independent life, living in one of the houses for more able residents. In the ensuing six months he experienced a further seizure. He commented 'I had forgotten that I had epilepsy. This has made me realise that it is still there'. Figure 8.1 shows his overall QoL scores (a high score indicates greater dissatisfaction with QoL). A clear deterioration is seen. During interview the individualised areas he considered important to his quality of life were: to be seizure free, not to be tired, to be able to remember things, to be able to think quickly, to be in control of temper, not to be anxious, not to be lonely, to have confidence, to have job satisfaction and to have enough money for basic needs. Figure 8.2 plots the scores for these areas at the initial assessment and six months later. These profile scores show that the decrease in his overall satisfaction with life (Figure 8.1) seems to be primarily due to the occurrence of a seizure after being seizure free for a number of years. This is evidenced by higher scores (hence greater dissatisfaction) for the areas of seizures (being seizure free) and anxiety (not being anxious). These objective data fit well with his subjective reports of being worried about having another seizure.

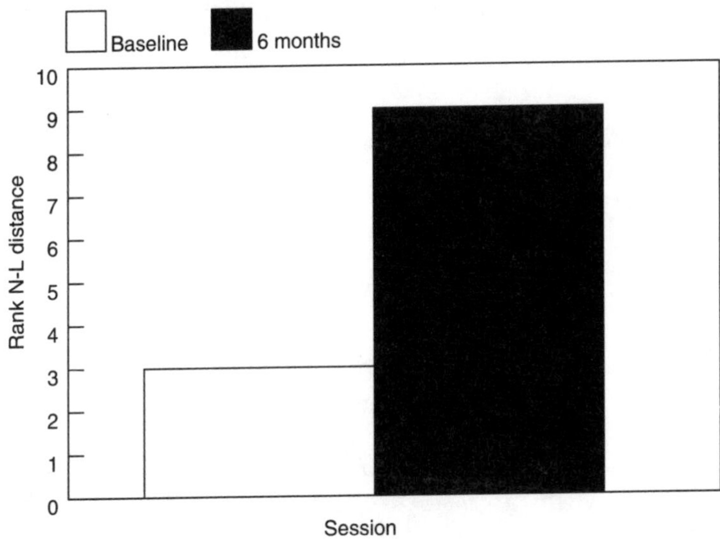

Figure 8.1 Global evaluation (Case 1)

Case history 2: SR

SR was a 27-year-old man who was resident at an independent hostel for people with epilepsy. At initial assessment he was very concerned about his lack of a girlfriend and felt that his lack of confidence and shyness would prevent him from forming such a relationship. He was also unhappy in his job. The specific areas he considered important to his QoL were: his seizures being under control, having a good memory, being able to concentrate, not being aggressive, overcoming shyness, having confidence, having a girlfriend, not being lonely, having job satisfaction and having sufficient money. Figure 8.3 shows the change in his overall evaluation of his QoL six months later. The improvement seen corresponds with major changes in his lifestyle. During these six months he achieved full independence, moving to living in private rented accommodation. He felt that this move noticeably increased his confidence. During the same period he also formed a close relationship with a girl and was given more responsibility at work. These changes are highlighted in his profile scores (Figure 8.4) where the largest changes (in terms of increased satisfaction) can be seen for shyness, confidence, lack of partner and job satisfaction.

A shorter version of the QoLASCA scale has been developed and has been used to compare drug treatments and evaluate surgery

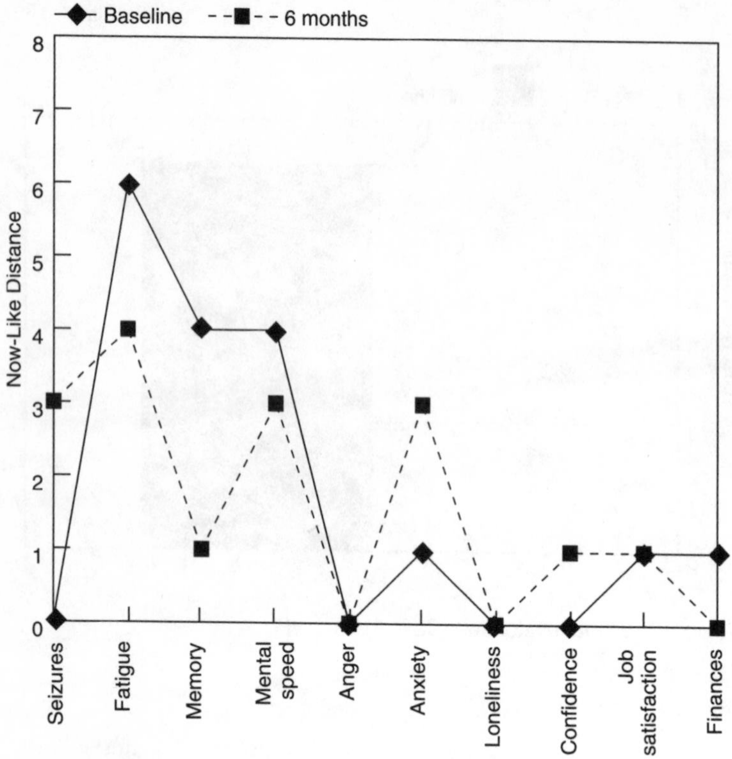

Baseline
6 months
8
7
6
5
4
3
2
1
0
Now-Like Distance
Seizures
Fatigue
Memory
Mental speed
Anger
Anxiety
Loneliness
Confidence
Job satisfaction
Finances

Figure 8.2 Individual profile (Case 1)

Baseline
6 months
10
9
8
7
6
5
4
3
2
1
0
Rank N-L Distance
Session

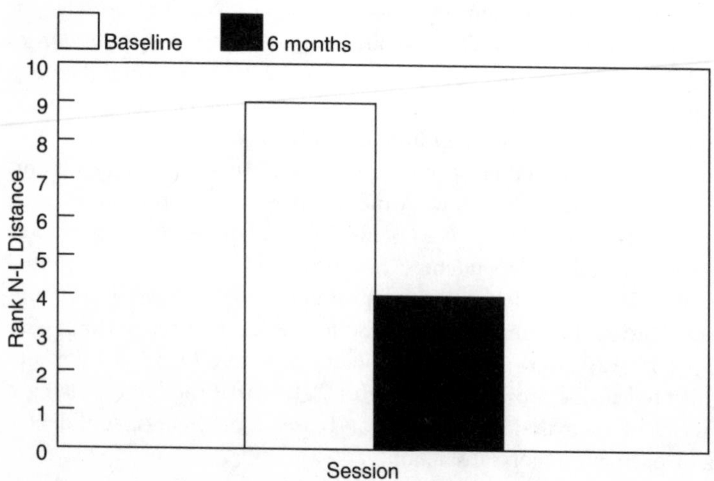

Figure 8.3 Global evaluation (Case 2)

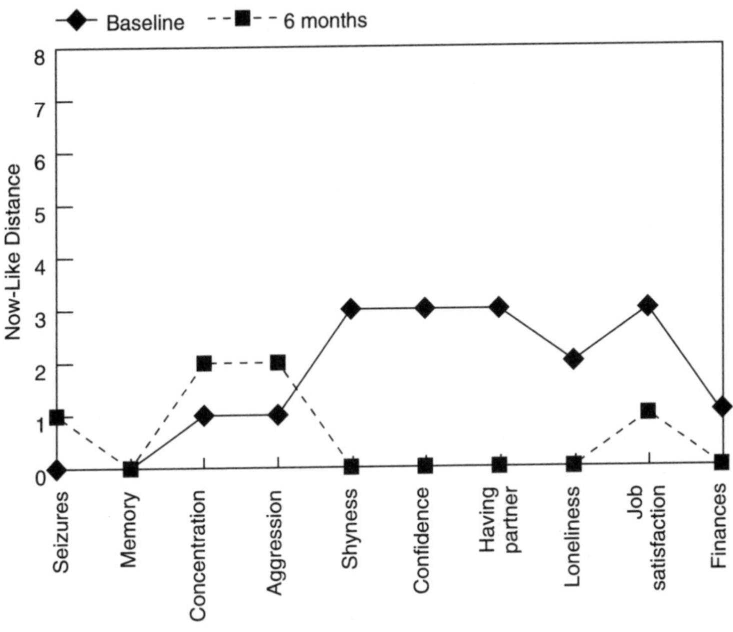

Figure 8.4 Individual evaluation (Case 2)

has been used to compare drug treatments and evaluate surgery outcome in patients with epilepsy (Selai and Trimble 1995).

Non-epilepsy-specific measures of QoL

There are a number of existing QoL measures which may be suitable for use in patients with epilepsy. One of the main advantages of using an older, existing measure is the increased availability of psychometric data relating to reliability, validity and sensitivity allowing increased confidence in interpreting data. Their obvious drawback is that they do not include items specific to the patient with epilepsy.

Psychosocial Adjustment to Illness Scale – PAIS (Morrow *et al.* 1978; Derogatis 1986)

The PAIS is a 45-item questionnaire which assesses adjustment to illness in seven domains: health care orientation (attitude/expectations of doctors and treatments), vocational environment (disruption to job performance, satisfaction with job and adjustment to work following illness), domestic environment (family relationships, communication and impact on finances), sexual relationships (quality, frequency, sexual satisfaction), extended family relationships (communication, interaction, degree of dependency), social environment (level of participation, level of interest) and psychological distress (anxiety, depression, guilt, hostility). Ratings are made on a four-point scale and summed to give scores for the seven domains as well as an overall adjustment score based on the forty-five items. Scores are converted to standardised T-scores (given in the PAIS handbook) which can be compared to published norms. Norms are available for the PAIS in four patient groups: lung cancer, renal dialysis, acute burns and hypertensive patients. Psychometric data is available to support internal consistency, inter-rater reliability, content validity, construct validity and predictive validity (Morrow *et al.* 1978).

This scale is of possible use in patients with epilepsy due to its comprehensiveness. However, its current use is limited by the unavailability of norms for epilepsy patients.

Nottingham Health Profile – NHP (Hunt and McEwen 1980; Hunt *et al.* 1985)

The NHP was designed to measure perceived health problems and the extent to which these impinge on the everyday activities of the patient (Hunt 1984). There are two parts to the questionnaire. Part I consists of thirty-eight statements grouped into six areas of functioning: sleep (five items), physical mobility (eight items), energy level (three items), pain (eight items), emotional reactions (nine items) and social isolation (five items). All statements require a yes or no response from the respondent. A weighted score (patient-based) is obtained for each of these areas with a high score indicating greater problems/difficulties. A simpler, unweighted scoring system is also used in which the number of affirmative responses in each area is counted (McDowell and Newell 1987). Part II consists of seven statements relating to areas of life most often affected by health. Patients are asked (using a yes/no response format) whether their health is causing problems with their paid employment, social life, home life, looking after the home, interests and hobbies, sex life or holidays. Statements in Part II are scored one for an affirmative response and zero for a negative reply. This measure has undergone extensive psychometric testing and has been used in a variety of patient populations (Hunt *et al.* 1985).

The main drawback to its use in patients with epilepsy is the large proportion of statements relating to physical problems (mobility, pain, etc). Such concerns are not usually considered to predominate the life of the patient with epilepsy, who is more likely to experience difficulties with social and emotional aspects of functioning. It may, however, be of value as an assessment of the impact of physical functioning on QoL in the patient with epilepsy as suggested by the Liverpool Initiative (Baker *et al.* 1993), which includes the NHP as a validated measure within the physical functioning domain.

Sickness Impact Profile – SIP (Bergner *et al.* 1981)

This is a comprehensive, generic, 136-item scale covering twelve areas of functioning: sleep and rest, eating, work, home management, recreation and pastimes, ambulation, mobility, bodycare and movement, social interaction, alertness behaviour, emotional behaviour and communication. Patients are asked to tick any item which describes them as they are today and is related to their health. Scores are weighted then summed and transformed to a percentage score to provide individual category scores. In addition, composite scores of physical, psychosocial and overall functioning can be computed. The higher the score on the SIP, the more dysfunctional the patient.

This scale has been widely used in a variety of patient populations and it is well researched with a wealth of published data relating to reliability and validity (Bergner *et al.* 1976; Pollard *et al.* 1976; Carter *et al.* 1976, Bergner 1988). It provides a good coverage of cognitive, emotional and social aspects of functioning, areas likely to be of concern for the person with epilepsy. In addition, internal consistency, reliability and validity have been established in a group of patients with epilepsy (Langfitt 1995).

SUMMARY

Epilepsy is a heterogeneous disease which can affect an individual's life in a variety of ways. The use of QoL as a health status indicator is of particular importance in epilepsy where treatment is often not curative and can be associated with adverse side effects. Information concerning an individual's QoL may be of value to the clinician in a number of ways. At the individual level, it can provide relevant information about how the illness and its treatment impacts on the QoL of the individual. Assessment of QoL can allow areas of concern to a patient to be identified and treatment planned accordingly. In addition, it may be used to monitor over time a patient's response to treatment or reaction to the illness. At group level, it may be used to compare the intrusiveness of different treatments on the individual's everyday life, thus providing a scientific rationale in the choice of treatment enabling a balance between seizure reduction and QoL to be achieved.

The availability of rigorously tested, epilepsy-specific measures of QoL will enable clinicians and researchers to assess the impact of epilepsy and its treatment on the QoL of the person with epilepsy in greater detail. Such measures have already been used to evaluate the impact of novel medication in adults (Smith *et al.* 1993) and children with epilepsy (Smith *et al.* 1995), to examine the relationship between QoL and seizure severity (Smith *et al.* 1991) and other epilepsy variables (age of onset, duration of epilepsy, seizure type) (Kendrick 1993) and to investigate agreement between patient and patient-proxy reports of QoL (Hays *et al.* 1995). It is hoped that wider use of these measures will improve our understanding of the factors relevant to QoL in people with epilepsy and ensure that treatment is tailored to maximise the QoL of all people with epilepsy.

REFERENCES

Baker, G. A., Jacoby, A., Smith, D. F., Dewey, M. E. and Chadwick, D. W. (1994) 'The development of a novel scale to assess life fulfilment as part of the further refinement of a quality-of-life model for epilepsy', *Epilepsia* 35: 591–6.

Baker, G. A., Smith, D. F., Dewey, M., Morrow, J., Crawford, P. M. and Chadwick, D. W. (1991) 'The development of a seizure severity scale as an outcome measure in epilepsy', *Epilepsy Research* 8: 245–51.

Baker, G. A., Smith, D. F., Dewey, M., Jacoby, A. and Chadwick, D. W. (1993) 'The initial development of a health-related quality of life model as an outcome measure in epilepsy', *Epilepsy Research* 16: 65–81.

Bergner, M. (1988) 'Development, testing and use of the Sickness Impact Profile', in S. R. Walker and R. M. Rosser (eds) *Quality of Life: Assessment and Application*, Lancaster: MTM Press.

Bergner, M., Bobbitt, R. A., Carter, W. B. and Gilson, B. S. (1981) 'The Sickness Impact Profile: development and final revision of a health status measure', *Medical Care* 19: 787–805.

Bergner, M., Bobbitt, R. A., Pollard, W. E., Martin, D. P. and Gilson, B. S. (1976) 'The Sickness Impact Profile: validation of a health status measure', *Medical Care* 14: 57–67.

Brown, S. W. and Tomlinson, L. L. (1984) 'Anticonvulsant side effects: a self-report questionnaire for use in community surveys', *British Journal of Clinical Practice* 18: S147–9.

Calman, K. C. (1984) 'Quality of life in cancer patients: an hypothesis', *Journal of Medical Ethics* 10: 124–7.

Cameron, P. (1975) 'Mood as an indicant of happiness: age, sex, social class and situational differences', *Journal of Gerontology* 30: 216–24.

Campbell, A. (1981) *The Sense of Well-Being in America: Recent Patterns and Trends*, McGraw-Hill: New York.

Campbell, A., Converse, P. E. and Rodgers, W. L. (1976) *The Quality of American Life*, New York: Russell Sage Foundation.

Carter, W. B., Bobbitt, R. A., Bergner, M. and Gilson, B. S. (1976) 'Validation of an interval scaling: the Sickness Impact Profile', *Health Services Research* 11–12: 1976–7.

Chaplin, J. E., Yepez, R., Shorvon, S. and Floyd, M. (1990) 'A quantitative approach to measuring the social effects of epilepsy', *Neuroepidemiology* 9: 151–8.

Clark, A. and Fallowfield, L. J. (1986) 'Quality of life measurements in patients with malignant disease: a review', *Journal of the Royal Society of Medicine* 79: 165–9.

Cohen, C. (1982) 'On the quality of life: some philosophical reflections', *Circulation* 66 (5 Part 2): III 29–33.

Collings, J. A. (1990a) 'Epilepsy and well-being', *Social Science and Medicine* 31: 165–70.

—— (1990b) 'Psychosocial well-being and epilepsy: an empirical study', *Epilepsia* 31: 418–26.

—— (1990c) 'Correlates of well-being in a New Zealand epilepsy sample', *New Zealand Medical Journal* 103: 301–3.

Corney, R. H. and Clare, W. (1985) 'The construction, development and testing of a self-report questionnaire to identify social problems', *Psychological Medicine* 15: 637–49.

Costa, P. T., Jr, McCrae, R. R. and Zonderman, A. B. (1987) 'Environmental and dispositional influences on well-being: longitudinal follow-up of an American national sample', *British Journal of Psychology* 78: 299–306.

Cramer, J. (1995) 'Development of the Quality of Life in Epilepsy Scales', *Epilepsia* 36: S219.

Derogatis, L. R. (1986) 'The Psychosocial Adjustment to Illness Scale (PAIS)', *Journal of Psychosomatic Research* 30: 77–91.

Diener, E. (1984) 'Subjective well-being', *Psychological Bulletin* 95: 542–75.

Dodrill, C. B. (1983) 'Psychosocial characteristics of epileptic patients', *Research Publication of the Association for Research into Nervous and Mental Disorders* 61: 341–53.

—— (1984) 'Number of seizure types in relation to emotional and psychosocial adjustment in epilepsy', in R. J. Porter and A. A. Ward Jnr (eds) *Advances in Epileptology. The XXth Epilepsy International Symposium*. New York: Raven Press.

—— (1986) 'Correlates of generalised tonic-clonic seizures with intellectual, neuropsychological, emotional and social function in patients with epilepsy', *Epilepsia* 27: 399–411.

Dodrill, C. B. and Batzel, L. W. (1995) 'The Washington Psychosocial Seizure Inventory: new developments in the light of the quality of life concept', *Epilepsia* 36: S220.

Dodrill, C. B., Batzel, L. W., Queisser, H. R. and Temkin, N. R. (1980) 'An objective method for the assessment of psychological and social problems among epileptics', *Epilepsia* 21: 123–35.

Dodrill, C. B., Beier, R., Kasparick, M., Tacke, I., Tacke, U. and Tan, S. Y. (1984a) 'Psychosocial problems in adults with epilepsy: a comparison of findings from four countries', *Epilepsia* 25: 176–83.

Dodrill, C. B., Breyer, D. N., Diamond, M. B., Dubinsky, B. L. and Geary, B. B. (1984b) 'Psychosocial problems among adults with epilepsy', *Epilepsia* 25: 168–75.

Duncan, J. S. (1990) 'Medical factors affecting quality of life in patients with epilepsy', in D. Chadwick (ed.) *Quality of Life and Quality of Care in Epilepsy*, Royal Society of Medicine Round Table Series 23, Oxford: Alden Press.

Edwards, N. J. and Klemmack, D. L. (1973) 'Correlates of life satisfaction: a re-examination', *Journal of Gerontology* 28: 134–43.

Fallowfield, L. (1990) *The Quality of Life. The Missing Measurement in Health Care*, London: Souvenir Press.

Fletcher, A. E., Hunt, B. M. and Bulpitt, C. D. (1987) 'Evaluation of quality of life in clinical trials of cardiovascular disease', *Journal of Chronic Disease* 40: 557–66.

Harrison, R. M. and Taylor, D. C. (1976) 'Childhood seizures: a 25 year follow-up: social and medical prognosis', *Lancet* 1: 948–51.

Hays, R. D., Vickrey, B. G., Hermann, B., Perrine, K., Cramer, J., Meador, K., Spritzer, K. and Devinsky, O. (1995) 'Agreement between self reports and proxy reports of quality of life in patients with epilepsy', *Quality of Life Research* 4: 159–68.

Hermann, B. P. (1992) 'Quality of life in epilepsy', *Journal of Epilepsy* 5: 153–65.

—— (1995) 'The evolution of health-related quality of life assessment in epilepsy', *Quality of Life Research* 4: 87–100.

Hollandsworth, J. G., Jr, (1988) 'Evaluating the impact of medical treatment on the quality of life: a 5-year update', *Social Science and Medicine* 26: 425–34.

Hornquist, J. O. (1982) 'The concept of quality of life', *Scandinavian Journal of Social Medicine* 10: 57–61.

Hunt, S. M. (1984) 'Nottingham Health Profile', in N. K. Wenger, M. E. Mattson, C. D. Furberg and J. Elinson (eds) *Assessment of Quality of Life in Clinical Trials of Cardiovascular Therapies*, New York: Le Jacq Publishing.

Hunt, S. M. and McEwen, J. (1980) 'The development of a subjective health indicator', *Sociology, Health and Illness* 2: 231–46.

Hunt, S. M., McEwen, J. and McKenna, S. (1985) 'Measuring health status: a new tool for clinicians and epidemiologists', *Journal of the Royal College of General Practitioners* 35: 185–8.

Hunt, S. M., McKenna, S. P., McEwen, J., Backett, E. M., Williams, J. and Papp, E. (1980) 'A qualitative approach to perceived health status: a validation study', *Journal of Epidemiology and Community Health* 34: 281–6.

Jacoby, A., Baker, G. A., Smith, D. F. and Chadwick, D. W. (1995) 'Quality of life in epilepsy: the Liverpool initiative'. *Epilepsia* 36: S219.

Jacoby, A., Baker, G., Smith, D., Dewey, M. and Chadwick, D. (1993) 'Measuring the impact of epilepsy: the development of a novel scale', *Epilepsy Research* 16: 83–8.

Kendrick, A. M. (1993) 'Repertory grid technique in the assessment of quality of life in patients with epilepsy', unpublished PhD thesis, University of London.

Langfitt, J. T. (1995) 'Comparison of the psychometric characteristics of three quality of life measures in intractable epilepsy', *Quality of Life Research* 4: 101–14.

Leonard, I. (1989) 'Quality of life in a residential setting', *Psychiatric Bulletin* 13: 492–4.

Levin, R., Banks, S. and Bero, B. (1988) 'Psychosocial dimensions of epilepsy: a review of the literature', *Epilepsia* 29: 805–16.

Levitt, M. J., Clark, M. C., Rotton, J. and Finley, G. E. (1987) 'Social support, perceived control and well-being: a study of an environmentally stressed population', *International Journal of Aging and Human Development* 25: 247–57.

Lewis, F. M. (1982) 'Experienced personal control and quality of life in late-stage cancer patients', *Nursing Research* 31: 113–9.

McDowell, I. and Newell, C. (1987) *Measuring Health: A Guide to Rating Scales and Questionnaires*, Oxford: Oxford University Press.

McGuire, A. M. (1991) 'Quality of life in women with epilepsy', in M. R. Trimble (ed.) *Women and Epilepsy*, Chichester: Wiley.

McGuire, A. M. and Trimble, M. R. (1990) 'Quality of life in patients with epilepsy: the role of cognitive factors', in D. Chadwick (ed.) *Quality of Life and Quality of Care in Epilepsy*, Royal Society of Medicine Round Table Series 23, Oxford: Alden Press.

McNair, D. M., Lorr, N. and Droppleman, L. F. (1981) *Manual for the Profile of Mood States*, San Diego: Education and Industrial Testing Service.

Meador, K. J. (1993) 'Research use of the new Quality of Life in Epilepsy Inventory', *Epilepsia* 34 (Suppl. 4): S34–8.

Mookherjee, H. N. (1987) 'Perception of life satisfaction in the United States: a summary', *Perceptual and Motor Skills* 65: 218.

Morrow, G. R., Chiarello, R. J. and Derogatis, L. R. (1978) 'A new scale for assessing patients' psychosocial adjustment to medical illness', *Psychological Medicine* 8: 605–10.

Najman, J. M. and Levine, S. (1981) 'Evaluating the impact of medical care and technologies on the quality of life: a review and critique', *Social Science and Medicine* 15F: 107–15.

Okun, M. A., Stock, W. A., Haring, M. J. and Witter, R. A. (1984) 'Health and subjective well-being. A meta analysis', *International Journal of Aging and Human Development* 19: 111–31.

Pearlin, L. and Schooler, C. (1978) 'The structure of coping', *Journal of Health and Social Behaviour* 19: 2–21.

Perrine, K. R. (1993) 'A new quality-of-life inventory for epilepsy patients: interim results', *Epilepsia* 34 (Suppl. 4): S28–33.

Pollard, W. E., Bobbitt, R. A., Bergner, M., Martin, D. P. and Gilson, B. S. (1976) 'The Sickness Impact Profile: reliability of a health status measure', *Medical Care* 14: 146–55.

Potter, R. B. and Coshall, J. T. (1987) 'Socio-economic variations in perceived life domain satisfactions: a South-West Wales case study', *Journal of Social Psychology* 127: 77–82.

Reich, J. W., Zautra, A. J. and Hill, J. (1987) 'Activity, event transactions and quality of life in older adults', *Psychology and Aging* 2: 116–24.

Rodin, E. A., Shapiro, H. L. and Lennox, K. (1979) 'Epilepsy and life performance', *Rehabilitation Literature* 38: 34–9.

Rosenberg, M. (1965) *Society and the Adolescent Self-Image*, Princeton NJ: Princeton University Press.

Scambler, G. (1990) 'Social factors and quality of life and quality of care in epilepsy', in D. Chadwick (ed.) *Quality of Life and Quality of Care in Epilepsy*, Royal Society of Medicine Round Table Series 23, Oxford: Alden Press.

Scambler, G. and Hopkins, A. (1986) 'Being epileptic: Coming to terms with stigma', *Sociology, Health and Illness* 8: 26–43.

Selai, C. E. and Trimble, M. R. (1995) 'Quality of life based on repertory grid technique', *Epilepsia* 36: S220.

Smith, D. F., Baker, G. A., Jacoby, A. and Chadwick, D. W. (1995) 'The contribution of the measurement of seizure severity to quality of life research', *Quality of Life Research* 4: 143–58.

Smith, D. F., Baker, G. A., Dewey, M., Jacoby, A. and Chadwick, D. W. (1991) 'Seizure frequency, patient-perceived seizure severity and the psychosocial consequences of intractable epilepsy', *Epilepsy Research* 9: 231–41.

Smith, D. F., Baker, G. A., Davies, G., Dewey, M. and Chadwick, D. W. (1993) 'Outcomes of add-on treatment with lamotrigine in partial epilepsy', *Epilepsia* 34: 312–22.

Spitzer, W. O. (1987) 'State of science 1986: quality of life and functional status as target variables for research', *Journal of Chronic Disease* 40: 465–71.

Staats, S. R. and Stassen, M. A. (1987) 'Age and present and future perceived quality of life', *International Journal of Aging and Human Development* 25: 167–76.

Steinkamp, M. W. and Kelley, J. R. (1987) 'Social integration, leisure activity and life satisfaction in older adults: activity theory revisited', *International Journal of Aging and Human Development* 25: 293–307.

Tan, S. Y. (1986) 'Psychosocial functioning of adult epileptic and MS patients and adult normal controls on the WPSI', *Journal of Clinical Psychology* 42: 528–34.

Thompson, P. J. and Oxley, J. (1988) 'Socioeconomic accompaniments of severe epilepsy', *Epilepsia* 29 (Suppl. 1): S9–18.

Vickrey, B. G. (1993) 'A procedure for developing a quality of life measure for epilepsy surgery patients', *Epilepsia* 34 (Suppl. 4): S22–7.

Vickrey, B. G., Hays, R. D., Graber, J., Rausch, R., Engel, J. E. and Brook, R. H. (1992) 'A health-related quality of life instrument for patients evaluated for epilepsy surgery', *Medical Care* 30: 299–319.

Vining, E. P. G. (1987) 'Cognitive dysfunction associated with anti-epileptic drug therapy', *Epilepsia* 28 (Suppl. 2): S18–22.

Ware, J. E. (1987) 'Standards for validating health measures: definition and content', *Journal of Chronic Disease* 40: 473–80.

Ware, J. E. and Sherbourne, C. D. (1992) 'The 36 item short-form health survey (SF-36). I. Conceptual framework and item selection', *Medical Care* 30: 473–83.

Wenger, N. K., Mattson, M. E., Furberg, C. D. and Elinson, J. (eds) (1984) *Assessment of Quality of Life in Clinical Trials of Cardiovascular Therapies*, New York: Le Jacq Publishers.

World Health Organisation (1980) *International Classification of Impairments, Disabilities and Handicaps*, Geneva: WHO.

Zigmond, A. S. and Snaith, R. P. (1983) 'The Hospital Anxiety and Depression Scale', *Acta Psychiatrica Scandinavica* 67: 361–70.

Chapter 9

Neuropsychological and cognitive assessment of children with epilepsy

Maria Fowler

The assessment of neuropsychological and cognitive function of children with epilepsy is complicated by alterations in consciousness, drug side-effects and emotional factors. For every one of these children there is a set of intricately linked parameters affecting their cognitive function and test performance. This chapter will address this relationship, its importance and how it influences the choice of methods of assessment and interpretation of test results.

COGNITIVE FUNCTION OF CHILDREN WITH EPILEPSY

General intellectual ability

Many studies have addressed the question of the effects of seizures on children's ability to learn and on their general intellectual development (see Cull 1988; Seidenberg 1989). The overall agreement is that there is wide variability in intellectual ability among children with epilepsy, and having epilepsy is not an adequate predictor of future academic performance on its own. The National Child Development Study (Ross *et al.* 1980) found that two-thirds of the children with epilepsy were in mainstream schools, and a number of other studies have found average or higher than average IQ scores in children with epilepsy who were no different from matched controls in this respect (Bourgeois *et al.* 1983; see also Cull 1988).

Academic achievement

Although most children with epilepsy are of average intelligence, evidence suggests that they underachieve in comparison with their peers in mainstream schools. Indeed, as many as 50 per cent of children with epilepsy have been found to be seriously underachieving to a greater degree than their peers without epilepsy (Holdsworth and Whitmore 1974).

Farwell *et al.* (1985) found that the academic achievement of a group of children with epilepsy (aged six to fifteen years) was behind grade placement more often than in a control group. Similarly, Seidenberg *et al.* (1986) reported that 122 children with epilepsy were making less academic progress than expected for their age and IQ.

Most studies have found reading to be an area where these children often underachieve (see Aldenkamp *et al.* 1990a). For example, in the Isle of Wight Study, Rutter *et al.* (1970) found that a group of fifty-nine children with 'uncomplicated' epilepsy (i.e. with no identifiable brain pathology) had a mean average IQ, but their reading age was about twelve months behind their chronological age. Further, 18 per cent were two, or more, years behind in their reading as compared to 6 per cent of children without epilepsy. Corbett and Trimble (1983) suggested that about one in five children with seizures was likely to show a severe reading deficit.

In their study, Seidenberg *et al.* (1986) found that academic weaknesses were greatest in arithmetic, followed by spelling, reading, comprehension and word recognition. Thompson (1987) reported that only 17 per cent of those with epilepsy in ordinary schools were rated by their teachers as high in mathematical skills compared to 31 per cent of those with no seizures.

Areas of specific cognitive impairment

Aldenkamp *et al.* (1990a) have suggested that the cognitive deficits seen in children with epilepsy fall into three wide but specific categories: (a) 'memory deficit' group, implicating short-term memory and memory span impairments, usually related to temporal lobe dysfunction; (b) the 'attention deficit' group, underachieving in several academic skills and associated with high-frequency tonic-clonic seizures; and (c) a 'speed factor' category which is associated with slowing of information processing and which also affects arithmetic skills. This last group also lacked ability to 'problem-solve', which is a higher order skill associated with verbal reasoning and logical thinking. Indeed, most of the studies highlight that academic underachievement is related to language difficulties, memory and attention deficits. The importance of these findings is not in any way disputed, but it would appear that they may, to some extent, have perhaps overshadowed the existence of other cognitive deficits of equal importance, i.e. perceptual and visuospatial problems. Focal discharges often result in differential influences on cognitive dysfunction. Morgan and Groh (1980) suggested that children with partial seizures are at a greater risk of having impaired visuoperceptual abilities than those children with primary generalised seizures. Such deficits, of course, may play a very important role in reading acquisition skills and in learning from 'doing' or observing, affecting academic skills and scholastic performance in a variety of different ways. They may also cause a child to become 'awkward' in games and sport activities, underachieving in physical education and missing out in peer interaction.

THE MULTIFACTORIAL FRAMEWORK OF DISABILITY

The task of explaining the cognitive and academic difficulties in childhood epilepsy is a complex one as many factors may be involved. These factors could be directly or indirectly related to the condition and these will now be addressed under the following headings:

(a) Aetiology;
(b) Epilepsy-related factors;
(c) Treatment-related factors;
(d) Factors indirectly-related to epilepsy.

Aetiology

One very important single factor in influencing cognitive development in childhood epilepsy is the presence or absence of coexisting brain damage and its severity (Rodin 1989). In general, children with seizures associated with an identifiable brain pathology i.e. 'symptomatic' or 'complicated' epilepsy, tend to show greater impairment of cognitive function than those with seizures without underlying brain damage or identifiable cause, that is those with 'idiopathic' or 'uncomplicated' epilepsy (Dikmen 1980; Cull 1988). Children with 'symptomatic' epilepsy therefore, tend to be at a disadvantage regarding the prognosis of intellectual ability and have significantly lower IQs, than those with 'idiopathic' epilepsy (Sofijanov 1982; Bourgeois *et al.* 1983). The literature is well in agreement that neurological as well as psychosocial variables are very important in influencing the cognitive development of children with epilepsy (Bourgeois *et al.* 1983; Rodin *et al.* 1986; Thompson 1987; Seidenberg 1989; Sabers 1990). The effects are often complex and multifactorial and a serious attempt to identify these factors is extremely important for the formulation of intervention programmes and for rehabilitation.

Epilepsy-related factors

Factors directly related to the condition affecting cognitive functioning in children with seizure disorders may include age at onset of epilepsy, frequency of seizures, type of seizure, localisation of epileptic focus and epileptic syndrome. It should be understood, however, that these factors are more likely to affect function in combination with each other and with other factors to be discussed later, rather than in isolation.

Age at onset

The literature is in agreement that early onset of seizures is associated with a poor intellectual prognosis (O'Leary *et al.* 1981; Corbett *et al.* 1985; Cull 1988; Aldenkamp *et al.* 1990a; Hermann 1991). However, although early onset is implicated in cognitive difficulties it is not quite clear whether the deficits may also be the result of a combination of factors such as seizure severity, chronicity and polypharmacy. The chronicity of the condition in itself may, of course, be an indication of its severity and the need for polypharmacy when the seizures remain difficult to control. All of these factors will have an accumulative negative effect on cognitive function.

An early onset of seizures can be detrimental to the acquisition of functions as they start to develop and may become implicated in a reorganisation of some of these functions within the young brain. The 'relateralisation' of function and the effects of the plasticity of the brain (Rourke *et al.* 1983) have important implications, particularly for the assessment of children with epilepsy being considered for neurosurgery.

Seizure frequency

As with adults, studies of children have observed a steady rise in IQ for those persons whose seizures are controlled, with the opposite effect for those with poor seizure control (Rodin 1968; Seidenberg *et al.* 1981; Bourgeois *et al.* 1983; Rodin *et al.* 1986). Evidence tends to indicate that good seizure control is important for improved learning ability and that seizure frequency may be related to educational attainment (Cull 1988; Marston *et al.* 1993).

Type of seizures and epileptic syndrome

Both of these factors have been found to influence intellectual ability to various degrees. Dam (1990) concluded that seizures can affect the intellectual ability of children with epilepsy when they occur continuously (*status epilepticus*) and when they occur singly. Frequent and prolonged seizures are typically linked with more severe cognitive deficits, especially in the presence of brain damage associated with specific epileptic syndromes such as the West and the Lennox-Gastaut syndromes (Guzzetta *et al.* 1993). Poor prognosis associated with these syndromes is again linked to pre-existing brain pathology (Dam 1990).

Research has also shown that left-sided foci are associated with verbal deficits, right hemisphere foci with spatial problems, centrencephalic foci with attentional deficits and memory problems are linked to psychomotor seizures (Binnie *et al.* 1990; Piccirilli *et al.* 1994).

Transitory cognitive impairment (TCI)

One other interesting disturbance in cognitive functioning, which is also rather difficult to observe, is caused by the effects of subclinical epileptic discharges and has been termed transitory cognitive impairment (TCI). These are very brief disruptions in attending to incoming information. TCI can disrupt cognitive processing in a significant way affecting attention, immediate memory and speed of reaction (Binnie *et al.* 1990; Marston *et al.* 1993).

Treatment-related factors

These are usually factors involving anti-epileptic medication (AED) and surgery. Most studies are in agreement that some drugs such as phenytoin may impair cognitive function in children with epilepsy (Trimble and Thompson 1985). Forsythe *et al.* (1991), investigating a group of sixty-four children with newly diagnosed epilepsy, reported a clear impairment in memory skills and specifically in 'recent recall' after the children had been taking carbamazepine for six months. Speed of information processing was also found to be affected after only one month on carbamazepine and phenytoin. However, these effects were transitory and reversible. The importance of this with regard to assessment will be discussed later.

Anti-epileptic drugs differ in the way they may affect cognitive function. The most important issue, nevertheless, as far as drug treatment and cognitive function is concerned, appears to be not so much which drugs are used, but rather how they are used (Cull and Trimble 1989). It is now universally accepted that dose, absence of toxicity and monotherapy are very important for avoiding adverse effects of the drugs on cognition and behaviour. The improvement that often occurs in attention and learning when epileptic activity is suppressed (Marston *et al.* 1993) suggests that these deficits are linked primarily to seizure occurrence and their control. The suggestion then is that a delicate balance exists between medication, seizure control and cognitive function. A recent study of the neuropsychological effects of anti-epileptic drugs (Nichols *et al.* 1993) confirms that polypharmacy and higher AED blood levels can upset the balance between the beneficial results of the reduction of seizures and the detrimental side effects on cognitive function. In the treatment of children in particular, the effects of the drugs on learning may have an especially negative effect on the development of cognitive skills, and may result in these children becoming delayed at school. Although this may well be a reversible process, the damage might take a long time to be corrected and the psychological scars might be even more long-lasting. Some drugs produce fewer side effects than others (Cull 1988) and, with the newer AEDs such as lamotrigine being increasingly widely used, further studies in this field are certainly needed.

Although the primary treatment of epilepsy in childhood consists of the control of seizures by AEDs, an increasing number of children with difficult-to-control epilepsy however are now being considered to be suitable for surgical treatment (see Chapter 4). Improved and more sophisticated surgical techniques make it more likely that children with difficult-to-control epilepsy will benefit from neurosurgery. Most studies emphasise the importance of presurgical evaluation and agree that the improvement in seizure control achieved by surgical treatment is usually reflected in improvement in cognitive function (Wyler 1989; Dreifuss 1992).

Factors indirectly related to epilepsy

Psychosocial factors are well recognised as influencing the educational achievement of children with epilepsy (Hartlage and Green 1972; Long and Moore 1979; Seidenberg 1989). The literature confirms and emphasises the impact of the lowered expectations of teachers and parents, which may be producing a 'self-fulfilling' prophecy and also influence the children's self-concept, their self-esteem, attitudes to learning, acceptance of failure and general aspirations. The author's own experience is that many of these children often underachieve in formal psychometric assessments because of a readiness to accept failure and to give up all too easily, without even trying.

Other equally important factors affecting scholastic performance associated with the condition, but not neurologically linked, include the actual loss of schooling due to hospitalisation or poor health, the child being sent home from school after a seizure because of the teacher's anxiety and/or ignorance (Stores 1980; Gadow 1982) and last, but not least, the effects of labelling and isolation from the peer group. School then becomes an unpleasant and negative environment, generating a number of damaging effects on the child's well-being. Academic and interpersonal difficulties often generate anxiety, which may cause more seizures leading to more social isolation, rejection, school problems and damaged self-esteem. A number of children could get trapped in a vicious circle of seizures leading to social and learning problems, in turn leading to more seizures.

ASSESSMENT OF CHILDREN – PRACTICAL CONSIDERATIONS

So far we have examined the factors which influence cognitive function in children with epilepsy and the complex relationship between these parameters. The literature agrees that for these children there is a greater than expected prevalence of learning difficulties (Madge *et al.* 1993), and that detailed assessment of specific learning profiles is beneficial both as a diagnostic measure and as a basis for rehabilitation programmes. Full details of test publishers are given in the Appendix.

Why assess?

It is apparent that the cognitive development of children with epilepsy depends on a multitude of factors and there is no specific pattern of neuropsychological dysfunction (Seidenberg 1989). Psychological assessment is invaluable, therefore, in terms of establishing the child's strengths and weaknesses. The findings can then be utilised to put together individual learning programmes so that those strengths can become the main pathways for more effective learning. Assessments of cognitive function are also important for monitoring development and the effects of treatment, for determining the impact of seizures on performance, and for evaluating specific learning and functional deficits.

Issues in the assessment of cognitive function and interpretation of results

Variability in repeated test administration

With respect to the test–retest variability of psychometric testing of children with epilepsy, Rodin *et al.* (1986) found that test results may fluctuate widely over time, and in some there may be a trend towards deterioration. A ten-point change, up or down, was not unusual and verbal and performance changes were not necessarily in the same direction. This may indicate that because differential gains and losses in scores may offset each other, Full Scale IQ might not be a reliable measure and that study of the detailed profile of scores will provide a far more reliable measure of function. In a later study on the test–retest reliability of WISC-R subtest profiles, Aldenkamp *et al.* (1990b) found a relatively stable pattern of cognitive performance over, on average, a four-year period. The increased stability in scores may have been partly due to fewer subjects than in previous studies being on the older drugs such as phenytoin and phenobarbital. This last study reported a specific pattern of cognitive weakness consistently reflected on the Vocabulary, Coding, Information and Digit Span subtests.

Deterioration versus slow learning

Besag (1988) suggested that for a small sub-group of children with epilepsy who show cognitive deterioration, the severity of the condition and pre-existing cerebral pathology are almost always contributing factors. However, a progressive fall in IQ scores does not necessarily indicate a deterioration or loss of skills. In many cases, it is the result of a slowing down in developmental progress, indicating a slower than normal rate of learning. Since scaled scores are age-correlated, a decrease in IQ scores may have arisen because the child, although still progressing, is a slow learner and has failed to acquire the new skills at a normal rate. It is extremely important, therefore, to examine carefully the raw scores and compare them over time in order to determine whether a child has continued to learn, albeit at a slow pace, has reached a plateau, or has lost abilities.

Developmental delay

In trying to examine the relationship between epilepsy and cognitive function, it is important to assess the extent to which cognitive impairment may be permanent, transient or state-dependent or due to a developmental delay. In the assessment of children with epilepsy, the latter is of particular importance and may present a special problem as one sometimes might be making assumptions about abilities that are not as yet fully developed, and whose deficits are due to a rather more global cognitive delay. The particular considerations for this group are not only related to the interpretation of the results, but also to the choice of tests to be used. Neuropsychological assessments are often regarded as a measurement of change from a premorbid state, and they are also used as a diagnostic measure of specific brain dysfunction. For this particular group, however, it is important to differentiate between whether a deficit is due to a specific and localised brain impairment or whether it is reflecting the absence of abilities which have never been developed. This delay, of course, may almost certainly be due to a pre-existing impairment, but not necessarily be indicative of a specific or localised lesion.

Impact of seizures

It is imperative that the skills of children with epilepsy are not judged lightly and only on the strength of one isolated assessment, often given by a professional who may have little prior knowledge of the child. Careful consideration is required in examining whether any deficit registering on any one assessment is of a transient or state-dependent nature due to seizure related (peri-ictal) influences affecting awareness and/or alertness. Such a state may vary tremendously between individuals, and temporary disturbances in cognitive functioning may be either very brief, or they may last for hours or even days and to varying degrees of intensity (Deonna 1993). These cognitive difficulties do not represent a permanent deficit and they should not be interpreted as such. Prior knowledge of a child's pattern of any pre or post-seizure difficulties would be beneficial in determining the best time for conducting assessments. Nevertheless, it would be interesting to ascertain whether such a transitory deficit may exist which could explain the occurrence of some day-to-day problems, and which, if anticipated and understood, may be of great help in the planning of interventions.

The role of EEG

Epileptic activity in the brain can affect functioning without any obvious seizures, as in the case of 'absence' epilepsy. Failure to perform then may be due to a temporary disturbance of information processing skills and not a real loss of skill. The use of split-screen video/EEG recording during psychometric testing can detect subtle epileptiform discharges as they occur and point to how they may be affecting cognitive function and task performance, even in the absence of obvious seizures. A small portable EEG cassette recorder is now available for use in 'real life' situations, such as a classroom, and can record spike-wave discharges over longer periods (Besag *et al.* 1989). The EEG recording can be analysed later and compared with activities occurring during that period, enabling a comparison of fluctuations in performance with discharges during the recording. Although such intensive assessments are not always possible, and perhaps are only done in special epilepsy centres, it is important that the professionals involved with these children are aware of such changes in cognitive function and performance. Psychologists should always be alert to any small tell-tale signs of brief changes in attention, blank expression or gaps in the reception of auditory information, which may be indicative of subtle seizure activity interfering with attention and response execution. This may also partly explain the variability in test performance mentioned earlier.

The influence of drugs

The transient and reversible side-effects of anticonvulsants on aspects of cognitive functioning (Forsythe *et al.* 1991) should be kept in mind when assessing children with epilepsy, especially when evaluating changes in performance, given the many transitory factors related to the condition and its treatment. It will be helpful for the psychologist to be aware of any specific effects of anti-epileptic drugs on performance, and take that into consideration when interpreting results.

Motivation and test behaviour

In addition to assessing cognitive function through psychometric testing, direct observation of the test behaviour is extremely important in order to evaluate any interaction between epilepsy and cognitive deficit, as well as reactions to the problem-solving situation of the assessment. As mentioned earlier, it is important that the assessor remains sensitive to any signs of possible subtle epileptic activity. Other factors equally important which can influence test performance are whether the child is motivated to work on the tasks and is willing to try without excessive sensitivity to failure. Motivation is also important in ensuring cooperation and gaining reliable results.

Throughout this discussion, the deficits in cognitive functioning and the academic underachievement of the children with epilepsy have been discussed. For the children themselves, however, it is of extreme importance that we pay at least equal, if not more, attention to their cognitive strengths. It cannot be emphasised enough how important it is to identify and to capitalise on the talents of the child – however small these may be – and help him or her celebrate success. Neuropsychological assessments can be a valuable guide to the areas of function most likely to help these children succeed.

The choice of measurements

The majority of the tests used to assess cognitive function in children with epilepsy are the traditional intelligence test batteries and tests of specific cognitive skills. For the younger children and for those whose cooperation is difficult to engage or sustain, developmental checklists may be a more appropriate tool. An important consideration when choosing assessments, is whether the tests to be used are sensitive enough to the needs of the child. A test must start at the level where it is easy for the child to achieve. This will boost his or her self-confidence and make the child try harder and for longer. It will also serve to establish a baseline of success. For the younger children, or those with limited concentration, very short tasks are essential to capture their potential within their brief attention span. An assessor may often use a variety of subtests taken from different batteries of tests to try and tap as accurately as possible the strengths and deficits within a child's cognitive development.

General ability

The Wechsler Intelligence Scale for Children (WISC-III UK) is always a useful tool, provided that attention is focused on the results of the individual subtests and their sensitivity to the various cognitive areas of function, rather than to the overall IQ score. The independent measurement of verbal and performance skills can potentially indicate differential development of skills and their effects on cognitive function.

One other quite useful measure of specific cognitive impairment, and one particularly related to the measurement of attention, is that of the distractibility factor (Gilandas *et al.* 1984). The Freedom from Distractibility index (FD) for the WISC-III is calculated from the Arithmetic and Digit Span scores (Kaufman 1994). As attention is sensitive to seizure activity, such an index can be a useful measure of the interaction between seizures and cognitive deficits. The Leiter International Performance Scale is another useful tool for measuring cognitive development. It covers a wide spectrum of developmental levels starting at two years. It is a non-verbal test and can be used with children who have language and speech problems or do not have a good command of the English language. The purely visual format of the test is useful with children whose attention may be disrupted by frequent epileptic activity. A particularly 'child-friendly' non-verbal measure of general ability is the Draw-a-Person test which provides a quick, efficient and fun way for screening a child's cognitive skills and general development.

Language skills / development

The Test for Reception of Grammar (TROG) assesses language comprehension and is of value in screening language disorders in children. Other assessments investigating language and verbal communication skills include:

(a) The British Picture Vocabulary Scale which is an easy-to-administer test measuring receptive vocabulary;
(b) The Token Test for Children which is a useful test for identifying the presence of subtle receptive language dysfunction within a good range of developmental levels;
(c) The Children's Category Test, which is a measure of more complex intellectual functioning such as concept formation, memory and learning from experience, and is easy and quick to administer.

It is important, however, that examiners make sure that language tests using visual materials do not yield results which may be contaminated through any visuo-perceptual difficulties which may be present in the child.

Visuo-perceptual skills

Tests for the measurement of perceptual and visual skills include the Bender Visual Motor Gestalt Test, which is a diagnostic evaluation of developmental deficits in children. The Benton Visual Retention Test has norms for children of eight and above and assesses visual perception and visual memory. The WISC-III and British Ability Scales subtests also provide good measures for the assessment of visuo-perceptual skills.

Memory

Memory deficits feature highly in childhood epilepsy and the assessment of memory problems is important. Some of the tests mentioned earlier provide scores for verbal or visual memory. Some specific subtests from the Wechsler series, the British Ability Scales or the Luria-Nebraska Battery children's version can be useful for screening for memory difficulties. The new California Verbal Learning Test for Children measures verbal learning and memory in children aged five years and older. The children's version of the Rivermead Behavioural Memory Test assesses functional memory, and was also standardised on a group of children with epilepsy. Rourke *et al.* (1986) give a comprehensive list of tests used with children (see also Chapter 4).

The assessment of children with developmental delay

As mentioned earlier, it is very important to choose the right tests to suit the needs of the child. Children with developmental delay present some special problems regarding the choice of assessments, as they usually have limited attention span and attend best to short, simple and mostly visual tasks. The Griffiths Mental Development Scales is a good comprehensive test for this group. The Stanford-Binet (Form L-M), although generally considered old-fashioned nowadays, is useful in the assessment of more severely delayed children as it has tasks which are short, change in quick succession, and keep the interest of the developmentally young. The Symbolic Play Test, which assesses early concept formation and abilities developing alongside early language, is suitable for special needs assessment for such children. Developmental checklists, like the Portage, may also be of use for assessing the general development of those who may not be able to cooperate effectively within a test situation. The Pre-Verbal Communication Schedule assesses communication skills of children who are either non-verbal or scarcely verbal and is valuable when working with severely delayed individuals. Finally, observation of the child's interaction with his or her environment and information from parents/carers will help to complete the picture.

Real-life measures of functioning

These are important supplementary measures to help identify any discrepancies between potential and performance, or gaps in children's functioning. Apart from measures of academic performance, i.e. reading, spelling, arithmetic, real-life measures of children's function are few. The Vineland Adaptive Behaviour Scales, scored through information given by a respondent, are useful in identifying areas of strength and need in four areas of development (communication, socialisation, daily living skills and motor skills) measuring personal and social sufficiency from birth to adulthood.

Computerised assessment

Computerised assessments have become much more available and are used for neuropsychological evaluation in epilepsy (Aldenkamp *et al.* 1990a; Thompson 1991). They may include measures of visual and auditory reaction, speed processing, vigilance and speed of learning as in Corsi-type blocks tests. Rugland and her colleagues have developed a computerised neuropsychological test battery to assess the impact of subclinical EEG discharges in patients with epilepsy. The same battery of tests has been useful in examining attention deficit in children with epilepsy (Rugland *et al.* 1991). One of the main advantages of these tests is that most children are well motivated by computer game-like assessments and enjoy doing them. The timing and scoring are also more accurate. Disadvantages include the fact that these tests are not, as yet, adequately validated and more reliability studies are needed (Alpherts and Aldenkamp 1990). Nevertheless, this is an exciting new area in cognitive testing, with potential to develop and expand its application.

CONCLUSION

Neuropsychological and cognitive assessments in children with epilepsy are useful, not only for the identification of strengths and weaknesses and evaluation of potential academic achievement, but also for developing interventions and rehabilitation programmes. The process of this evaluation, however, is complicated by different variables directly and indirectly linked to the epilepsy which have to be taken into consideration. For every child with epilepsy, there is a wide variation in the type of seizures, degree and nature of their learning disability, and psychosocial experiences which affect their cognitive function. This relationship should be investigated and understood for the evaluation to be as accurate as possible. Global measures such as IQ are not usually totally appropriate for evaluating the presence of specific cognitive deficits and more detailed investigation is required. The most difficult task for the examiner is to decide how these multifactorial influences affect performance.

The choice of measures should be flexible and adapted to suit the needs of the individual. New technology is useful in detecting deficits caused by transient or prolonged states of altered abilities due to the epilepsy.

REFERENCES

Aldenkamp, A. P., Alpherts, W. C. J., Dekker, M. J. A. and Overweg, J. (1990a) 'Neuropsychological aspects of learning disabilities in epilepsy', *Epilepsia* 31 (Suppl. 4): S9–20.

Aldenkamp, A. P., Alpherts, W. C. J., De Brune-Seeder, D. and Dekker, M. J. A. (1990b) 'Test–retest variability in children with epilepsy – a comparison of WISC-R profiles', *Epilepsy Research* 7: 165–72.

Alpherts, W. C. J. and Aldenkamp, A. P. (1990) 'Computerized neuropsychological assessment of cognitive functioning in children with epilepsy', *Epilepsia* 31 (Suppl. 4): S35–40.

Besag, F. M. C. (1988) 'Cognitive deterioration in children with epilepsy', in M. R. Trimble and E. H. Reynolds (eds) *Epilepsy, Behaviour and Cognitive Function*, Chichester: Wiley.

Besag, F. M. C., Mills, M., Wardale, F., Andrew, C. M. and Craggs, M. D. (1989) 'The validation of a new ambulatory spike and wave monitor', *Electroencephalography and Clinical Neurophysiology* 73: 157–61.

Binnie, C. D., Channon S. and Marston, D. (1990) 'Learning disabilities in epilepsy: Neurophysiological aspects', *Epilepsia* 31 (Suppl. 4): S2–8.

Bourgeois, B. F. D., Presky, A., Palkes, H. S., Talent, B. K. and Busch, S. G. (1983) 'Intelligence in epilepsy: a prospective study in children', *Annals of Neurology* 14: 438–44.

Corbett, J. A. and Trimble, M. R. (1983) 'Epilepsy and anti-convulsant medication', in M. Rutter (ed.) *Developmental Neuropsychiatry*, New York: Guilford Press.

Corbett, J. A., Trimble, M. R. and Nicol, T. C. (1985) 'Behavioural and cognitive impairments in children with epilepsy: the long term effects of anticonvulsant therapy', *Journal of the American Academy of Child Psychiatry* 24: 17–23.

Cull, C. A. (1988) 'Cognitive function and behaviour in children', in M. R. Trimble and E. H. Reynolds (eds) *Epilepsy, Behaviour and Cognitive Function*, Chichester: Wiley.

Cull, C. A. and Trimble, M. R. (1989) 'Effects of anticonvulsant medications on cognitive functioning in children with epilepsy', in B. P. Hermann and M. Seidenberg (eds) *Childhood Epilepsies: Neuropsychological, Psychological and Intervention Aspects*, Chichester: Wiley.

Dam, M. (1990) 'Children with epilepsy: the effect of seizures, syndromes and etiological factors on cognitive functioning', *Epilepsia* 31 (Suppl. 4): S26–9.

Dikmen, S. (1980) 'Neuropsychological aspects of epilepsy', in B. P. Herman (ed.) *A Multidisciplinary Handbook of Epilepsy*, Springfield IL: Charles C. Thomas.

Deonna, T. (1993) 'Cognitive and behavioural correlates of epileptic activity in children', *Journal of Child Psychology and Psychiatry* 34: 611–20.

Dreifuss, F. E. (1992) 'Cognitive function – victim of disease or hostage to treatment?', *Epilepsia* 33 (Suppl. 1): S7–12.

Farwell, J. R., Dodrill, C. B. and Batzel, L. W. (1985) 'Neuropsychological abilities of children with epilepsy', *Epilepsia* 26: 395–400.

Forsythe, I., Butler, R., Berg, I. and McGuire, R. (1991) 'Cognitive impairment in new cases of epilepsy randomly assigned to carbamazepine, phenytoin and sodium valproate', *Developmental Medicine and Child Neurology* 33: 524–34.

Gadow, K. D. (1982) 'School involvement in the treatment of seizure disorders', *Epilepsia* 23: 215–24.

Gilandas, A., Touyz, S., Beumont, P. J. V. and Greenberg, H. P. (1984) *Handbook of Neuropsychological Assessment*, Sydney: Grune and Stratton.

Guzzetta, F., Crisafulli, A. and Isaya-Crino, M. (1993) 'Cognitive assessment of infants with West Syndrome: how useful is it for diagnosis and prognosis?' *Developmental Medicine and Child Neurology* 35: 379–87.

Hartlage, L. C. and Green, J. B. (1972) 'The relation of parental attitudes to academic and social achievement in epileptic children', *Epilepsia* 13: 21–6.

Hermann, B. P. (1991) 'Contributions of traditional assessment procedures to an understanding of the neuropsychology of epilepsy', in W. E. Dodson, M. Kinsbourne and B. Hiltbrunner (eds) *The Assessment of Cognitive Function in Epilepsy*, New York: Demos Publications.

Holdsworth, L. and Whitmore, K. (1974) 'A study of children with epilepsy attending ordinary school. Their seizure patterns, progress and behaviour in school', *Developmental Medicine and Child Neurology* 16: 746–58.

Kaufman, A. S. (1994) *Intelligent Testing with the WISC-III*, New York: Wiley.

Long, C. G. and Moore, J. R. (1979) 'Parental expectations for their epileptic children', *Journal of Child Psychology and Psychiatry* 20: 299–312.

Madge, N., Diamond, J., Miller, D., Ross, E., McManus, C., Wadsworth, J. and Yule, W. (1993) 'Children with persisting convulsive disorders', *Developmental Medicine and Child Neurology* 35 (Suppl. 68): 78–88.

Marston, D., Besag, F., Binnie, C. D. and Fowler, M. (1993) 'Effects of transitory cognitive impairment on psychosocial functioning of children with epilepsy: a therapeutic trial', *Developmental Medicine and Child Neurology* 35: 574–81.

Morgan, A. M. B. and Groh, C. (1980) 'Visual perceptual deficits and young children with epilepsy', in B. M. Kulig, H. Meinardi and G. Stores (eds) *Epilepsy and Behaviour 79*, Lisse: Swets and Zeitlinger.

Nichols, M. E., Meador, K. J. and Loring, D. N. (1993) 'Neuropsychological effects of anti-epileptic drugs: a current perspective', *Clinical Neuropharmacology* 16: 471–84.

O'Leary, D. S., Seidenberg, M., Berent, S. and Boll, T. J. (1981) 'Effects of age of onset of tonic-clonic seizures on neuropsychological performance in children', *Epilepsia* 22: 197–204.

Piccirilli, M., D'Alessandro, P., Sciarma, T., Cantoni, C., Dioguardi, M. S., Giuglietti, M., Ibba, A. and Tiacci, C., (1994) 'Attention problems in epilepsy: possible significance of the epileptogenic focus', *Epilepsia* 35: 1091–6.

Rodin, E. A. (1968) *The Prognosis of Patients with Epilepsy*, Springfield IL: Charles C. Thomas.

—— (1989) 'Prognosis of cognitive functions in children with epilepsy', in B. P. Hermann and M. Seidenberg (eds) *Childhood Epilepsies: Neuropsychological, Psychosocial and Intervention Aspects*, Chichester: Wiley.

Rodin, E. A., Schmaltz, S. and Twitty, G. (1986) 'Intellectual functions of patients with childhood onset epilepsy', *Developmental Medicine and Child Neurology* 28: 25–33.

Ross, E. M., Peckham, C. S., West, P. B. and Butler, N. R. (1980) 'Epilepsy in childhood: findings from the national child development study', *British Medical Journal* 1: 207–10.

Rourke, B. P., Fisk, J. L. and Strang, J. D. (1986) *Neuropsychological Assessment of Children*, New York: Guildford Press.

Rourke, B. P., Bakker, D. J., Fisk, J. L. and Strang, J. D. (1983) *Child Neuropsychology – An Introduction to Theory, Research and Clinical Practice*, New York: Guilford Press.

Rugland, A-L., Henriksen, O. and Bjørnæs, H. (1991) 'Computer-assisted neuropsychological assessment in patients with epilepsy', in W. E. Dodson, M. Kinsbourne and B. Hiltbrunner (eds) *The Assessment of Cognitive Function in Epilepsy*, New York: Demos Publications.

Rutter, M., Graham, P. and Yule, W. (1970) 'A neuropsychiatric study in childhood', *Clinics in Developmental Medicine* 35/36, London: Heineman.

Sabers, A. (1990) 'Cognitive function and drug treatment', in M. Sillanpaa, S. Johannessen, G. Blennow and M. Dam (eds) *Paediatric Epilepsy*, Petersfield: Wrightson Biomedical Publishing.

Seidenberg, M. (1989) 'Academic achievement and school performance of children with epilepsy', in B. Hermann and M. Seidenberg (eds) *Childhood Epilepsies: Neuropsychological, Psychosocial and Intervention Aspects*, Chichester: Wiley.

Seidenberg, M., O'Leary, D. S., Berent, S. and Boll, T. (1981) 'Changes in seizure frequency and test–retest scores on the WAIS', *Epilepsia* 22: 75–83.

Seidenberg, M., Beck, N., Geisser, M., Giordani, B., Sackellares, J. C., Berent, S., Dreifuss, F. E. and Boll, T. J. (1986) 'Academic achievement of children with epilepsy', *Epilepsia* 27: 753–9.

Sofijanov, N. G. (1982) 'Clinical evolution and prognosis of childhood epilepsies', *Epilepsia* 23: 61–9.

Stores, G. (1980) 'Children with epilepsy: psychosocial aspects', in B. P.

Hermann (ed.) *A Multidisciplinary Handbook of Epilepsy*, Springfield IL: Charles Thomas.

Thompson, P. J. (1987) 'Educational attainment in children and young people with epilepsy' in J. Oxley and G. Stores (eds) *Epilepsy and Education*, London: Medical Tribute Group.

—— (1991) 'Integrating computerised and traditional neuropsychological assessment techniques' in W. E. Dodson, M. Kinsbourne and B. Hiltbrunner (eds) *The Assessment of Cognitive Function in Epilepsy*, New York: Demos Publications.

Trimble, M. R. and Thompson, P. J. (1985) 'Anticonvulsant drugs, cognitive function and behaviour', in E. Ross and E. Reynolds (eds) *Paediatric Perspectives on Epilepsy*, Chichester: Wiley.

Wyler, A. R. (1989) 'The surgical treatment of epilepsy', in B. P. Hermann and M. Seidenberg (eds) *Childhood Epilepsies: Neuropsychological, Psychosocial and Intervention Aspects*, Chichester: Wiley.

Chapter 10

Assessment and management of behaviour problems in children

Christine Cull

Behaviour problems are frequently associated with a diagnosis of epilepsy in children who are not intellectually impaired (for review, see Cull 1988). Significantly more children with epilepsy display behaviour disorders than do their own siblings (Epir *et al.* 1984), same age and ability peers (Clement and Wallace 1990), and children with other chronic diseases such as diabetes (Hoare and Mann 1994). Recent studies of children of normal intellectual ability attending epilepsy out-patient clinics suggest that approximately 50 per cent display some degree of behavioural disturbance as assessed by rating scales (Hoare and Kerley 1991; Austin *et al.* 1992). However, these rates can be even higher for children in specialist residential schools (Stores 1982).

In the literature, the terms 'behaviour disorder/problem/disturbance' and 'psychiatric disorder' have all been used interchangeably. This is in part a function of the measures used, which invariably have been broad-based rating scales or checklists. Thus, in talking about behaviour problems, many authors are making reference to the frequency and intensity of behaviours rather than to particular behaviours. Specific problems have been identified and include: poor self-esteem, excessive dependency, immaturity (Lothman and Pianta 1993); neurotic disorders, hyperactive disorders (Hoare and Kerley 1991), mixed conduct/emotional disorders (Harvey *et al.* 1988); anxiety and depression (Urion 1991); and autistic features (Harvey *et al.* 1988). Conversely, it has been suggested that children with epilepsy are less likely to show antisocial (Hoare and Kerley 1991) or delinquent (Rantakallio *et al.* 1992) behaviour although physical and verbal aggression, self-injurious behaviour, non-compliance, and disinhibition have all been reported (Besag 1995). It is clear, however, that specific 'epileptic behaviours' do not exist (ibid.).

The reasons for this increased risk of behaviour disorder are difficult to determine as epilepsy is not a unitary disorder, but may differ along a number of dimensions. Thus, Besag (1995) suggests that possible epilepsy-related causes may include: the seizure disorder itself, its treatment, the impact of associated brain damage, and the reactions to a diagnosis of epilepsy. Hermann and Whitman (1991) have proposed a multi-aetiological model for considering the role of epilepsy-related risk factors associated with the development of behaviour disorders, which fall into three main categories: neurobiological, pharmacological and psychosocial. Cull and Brown (1992), in contrast, have emphasised the importance of environmental factors in the development and maintenance of behaviour problems.

In order to explore this further, a brief review of the literature pertaining to the impact of different epilepsy-related factors on behaviour will be considered, using Herman and Whitman's (1991) framework, which also encompasses the potential causes suggested by Besag (1995). This will concentrate in the main on studies published since 1988, as studies up to this time have been reviewed by Cull (1988) and this review will be referred to as necessary.

NEUROBIOLOGICAL FACTORS

Included in this category are any variables pertaining to the biological status of the individual, as follows.

Aetiology

It has previously been concluded that 'the little available evidence shows only trends in the direction of an association between organic aetiology and behaviour disturbance' (Cull 1988), and that would still seem to be the case. In more recent studies, where aetiology has been investigated, it does not appear as a significant contributory factor to the development of behaviour disorder (Clement and Wallace 1990; Austin *et al.* 1992).

Age at onset of epilepsy

Studies reviewed up to 1988 yielded conflicting findings (Cull 1988), as do more recent investigations. Thus, it has been reported that children with onset of epilepsy before four years of age are more likely to show behaviour disturbance than those with a later age at onset (Hoare and Kerley 1991; Hoare and Mann 1994). In other studies, however, age at onset has not been found to be a significant factor, either individually (Clement and Wallace 1990; Austin *et al.* 1992), or as part of an overall medical risk score (Lothman and Pianta 1993). There are also conflicting findings with respect to the duration of epilepsy (Cull 1988).

Seizure/epilepsy type

In the past, claims have been made for an association between a particular seizure type and an increased rate of behavioural problems, although these have not been fully substantiated (Cull 1988). There is still uncertainty as to whether some seizure types predispose to behaviour problems while others do not, and this is reflected in the literature. Thus, there may be no relationship between seizure type and scores on a behaviour rating scale (Clement and Wallace 1990; Austin *et al.* 1992; Lothman and Pianta 1993; Hoare and Mann 1994).

More in the way of positive results appear when the epilepsy syndrome, rather than just the seizure type are considered, such that children with Temporal Lobe Epilepsy may show more psychopathology than healthy children, but this may be no different to children with asthma (Apter *et al.* 1991). Further, identification of the relevant epilepsy syndrome may well be of prognostic significance with respect to behaviour disorder. For example, Nolte and Wolf (1992) studied fifteen children with Myoclonic Astatic Epilepsy, which typically starts between the ages of 2 and 5 years and is characterized by the presence of primary generalized seizures (myoclonic or astatic) in children who are thought to be genetically predisposed. They reported that in the majority behavioural problems were apparent before seizure onset; these increased with seizure onset and frequent seizures, but decreased after seizure remission, and further decreased or disappeared after the cessation of medication.

Seizure frequency

In keeping with the contradictory findings of past studies (Cull 1988), more recent investigations are also conflicting in that some studies have reported a clear association between frequent/uncontrolled seizures and more behavioural problems (Hoare and Kerley 1991; Austin *et al.* 1992; Nicholas and Pianta 1994), whereas others have found no such relationship (Clement and Wallace 1990; Hoare and Mann 1994).

EEG activity

An abnormal EEG per se does not seem to be implicated in an increased rate of behaviour disturbance, but the type of abnormality may be a factor (Cull 1988). It has been suggested that focal abnormalities are more likely to be associated with behaviour disturbance than generalised ones (Hoare and Kerley 1991), although no significant relationship has also been reported (Clement and Wallace 1990).

Subclinical EEG discharges which result in Transitory Cognitive Impairment may contribute to impaired psychosocial performance and behaviour problems (Marston *et al.* 1993). Behaviour problems have also been found to be associated with continuous spike-and-wave activity during sleep in a small sample of children with severe learning disabilities and a frontal epileptic focus (Roulet Perez *et al.* 1993).

Other behaviour disorders

In trying to tease out the impact of epilepsy on functioning, an alternative approach is to look at the impact of epilepsy on behaviour within the confines of a particular syndrome. Thus, Kinney *et al.* (1990) compared children with attention deficit disorder with and without epilepsy and found no difference between the two groups with respect to the occurrence of behaviour disorder.

Seizure/behaviour relationship

What is at times confusing about many of the studies investigating the relationship between behaviour and epilepsy is that they do not make clear whether or not the behaviour is inter-ictal and/or ictal, i.e. directly related in some way to the ictus or seizure itself. Such a distinction is important in terms of differentiating whether the aberrant behaviour is part of the seizure and possibly less likely to be under an individual's control, or whether it may be more related to the sequelae of having a diagnosis of epilepsy, since this may well have implications for treatment.

Behavioural changes that are intimately linked with seizure occurrence can occur at any point in the seizure's progress, although, to the untrained eye, it will not necessarily be clear whether seizure activity is imminent, ongoing, or has just ceased. In this respect, Besag (1995) has produced a useful aetiological classification of ictally-related behaviour changes as follows:

- Behavioural changes including, for example, irritability or changes in mood may be observed in the *prodrome* (that period of time leading up to the seizure) which invariably remit once the seizure has occurred.
- The *aura* (a form of simple partial seizure) may affect behaviour if the subjective experience is of an unpleasant emotional sensation such as extreme fear or anxiety.
- *Automatisms* are movements or actions occurring in the ictal or post-ictal phase of which the individual is unaware, and over which he or she has no voluntary control.
- *Focal discharges* may be manifest as odd and apparently bizarre behaviours which are not within the individual's control.
- *Frequent subtle seizures* may not be accompanied by any obvious clinical manifestations, but will inevitably interrupt an individual's stream of consciousness and impair their ability to make sense of what is going on around them and to respond appropriately.
- In the *post-ictal* phase a child may remain in a confused or sleepy state for some considerable period of time, as a result of which their powers of reasoning and understanding may be much reduced.

It is likely that the above variables may have some combined effect, rather than operating in isolation. Therefore, rather than asking whether one factor – for example, seizure frequency – exerts an effect, a more appropriate question may be to ask what is the effect of seizure frequency in children with X seizure type who have Y epilepsy syndrome. Such studies remain to be undertaken.

PHARMACOLOGICAL FACTORS

The majority of children with epilepsy will share in common the taking of anti-epileptic medications (AEDs) to control their epilepsy, and may well be affected by the type of medication they are taking, its relative effective strength as determined by dose and blood level, and the number of different medications taken. This is a major area of research in its own right, and unfortunately space does not allow for a comprehensive review of the literature. The reader is directed to a review by Cull and Trimble (1989); in the space available here the focus will be on more recent findings.

Type of AED

The current literature is remarkably consistent with that reviewed by Cull and Trimble (1989) in that behaviour disorders are more likely to be found with phenobarbitone (Domizio *et al.* 1993) and phenytoin (Clement and Wallace 1990), although adverse responses to primidone and sodium valproate have also been reported (Nolte and Wolf 1992). Interestingly, in newly diagnosed children, phenytoin was not found to affect behaviour significantly after six months of treatment (Berg *et al.* 1993) suggesting that time may be a factor in the development of adverse effects. By contrast, in the same study, those children on carbamazepine or sodium valproate displayed some minor behavioural difficulties after one month of treatment, which was resolved by six months (ibid.). Clonazepam has been associated with behavioural deterioration in some children (Commander *et al.* 1991), and aggressive behaviours have been observed in some children taking clobazam (but predominantly in those with learning disabilities) (Sheth *et al.* 1994). However, it would appear that in all cases such adverse effects are reversible on cessation of the medication (Commander *et al.* 1991; Domizio *et al.* 1993; Sheth *et al.* 1994). It is also possible that a small number of children may display a quite idiosyncratic adverse response to an AED – as, for example, carbamazepine (Silverstein *et al.* 1982).

The impact of the newer AEDs, in particular vigabatrin, lamotrigine and gabapentin, needs to be fully evaluated. Thus far, vigabatrin has been associated with behavioural disturbance in some children, while the behaviour of children taking lamotrigine improved (Besag 1995), although the mechanism by which this was brought about was not clear.

Number of AEDs

Although it has been asserted that combined drug treatments are likely to be more behaviourally toxic than treatment with a single drug (Cull and Trimble 1989; Hermann *et al.* 1989; Hoare and Kerley 1991), a recent report has found that a monotherapy/polytherapy distinction was not of any predictive value with regard to the occurrence of child behaviour problems (Austin *et al.* 1992). However, further research is clearly needed here, as this may well depend on the total number of drugs used and their interactions.

As was mentioned in Chapter 1, there is now a move towards rational polypharmacy in the treatment of epilepsy, the impact of which on behaviour has yet to be evaluated.

Dose/serum level

Drugs given at doses that are too high, or at body concentrations that are toxic may well adversely affect behaviour too, although these effects should be reversible (Cull and Trimble 1989).

PSYCHOSOCIAL FACTORS

The focus of attention in this section are the psychosocial sequelae of a diagnosis of epilepsy. Included are the psychological characteristics of the child with epilepsy, and the impact of the diagnosis on the family.

Child

Children with epilepsy are reported to have a self-image and self-esteem which is significantly poorer than healthy controls or children with diabetes (Matthews *et al.* 1982; Hoare and Kerley 1991), and an external locus of control (Matthews *et al.* 1982), all of which may be associated with behavioural disturbance (Matthews and Barabas 1986). Thus, the lower a child's own rating of self-esteem, the more behaviourally disturbed the child is, as rated by the parent (Hoare and Mann 1994). In respect of skills, children who have good academic performance do not differ from their healthy peers, whereas poor school performance can be associated with behaviour disorder (Sturniolo and Galletti 1994).

Family

A range of family-related variables have been associated with behavioural problems and emotional disturbance in the child with epilepsy. These include: stresses and strains within the family (Hoare and Kerley 1991; Austin *et al.* 1992), a past history of maternal psychiatric treatment (Hoare and Kerley 1991), ill-health among siblings (Hoare and Kerley 1991); a lack of support from relatives (Austin *et al.* 1992), and a perceived lack of control over family events and outcomes (Austin *et al.* 1992). See also Cull 1988.

Interactions

Child–parent relationships are claimed to be important predictors of adjustment (Lothman and Pianta 1993). Indeed, it has been further asserted that these relationship variables are predictive of behaviour problems independently of, and to a greater extent than, epilepsy variables (Pianta and Lothman 1994).

The question then arises as to what are the factors that may impinge on this relationship. Perhaps, first and foremost, there is the epilepsy itself. Parents may feel anxious and uncertain about how to deal with the occurrence of seizures, or even fearful of provoking seizures. The pervasive nature of the perceived stigma associated with epilepsy has been emphasised, as it impinges on the functioning of the whole family (Ziegler 1981; Bagley 1986; West 1986). In addition, it would seem that parents expect different things of a child with epilepsy than of their siblings. For example, they anticipate that the child with epilepsy will be less reliable, less able to make friends, perform more poorly at school, and is more likely to be unpredictable, moody and to develop emotional problems (Long and Moore 1979; Ferrari 1989).

Given the above, it is not surprising perhaps that parents respond differently to their child with epilepsy. Thus, they may become overprotective (Munthe-Kaas 1981; Ritchie 1981), restrict the child's social activities (Long and Moore 1979; Munthe-Kaas 1981; West 1986), exert control over the child in a strict and autocratic manner (Long and Moore 1979; Ritchie 1981), and behave in a more dominant fashion towards the child with epilepsy than to other offspring (Long and Moore 1979).

By contrast, good adjustment in the child is more likely to be associated with parental responses that are, for example, contingent on the child's behaviour and that display warmth, sensitivity and positive regard for the child (Pianta and Lothman 1994).

Additional factors

Thus far, the literature review has been concentrating on those variables that are directly related to the seizure disorder itself and its psychosocial sequelae. What has not been considered here are all the possible explanations for the occurrence of behaviour/psychiatric disorders in children who do not have epilepsy. This is not within the scope of this chapter; however, as has been stressed by Besag (1995), the reader should remember that these factors may be just as relevant for the child with epilepsy, separate from or in combination with the epilepsy-related variables.

THE MULTI-AETIOLOGICAL APPROACH

From the foregoing review, it would appear that at least one variable within each of the dimensions considered may be an important contributor to the development of behaviour disorder in the child with epilepsy. The aim of the multi-aetiological approach is to identify the relative contributions of a variety of individual variables. For example, in an earlier study of their model, Hermann and Whitman (1986) reported that the biological variable (in this instance, seizure control) was the most predictive, followed by psychosocial factors and then medication-related variables. Demographic variables did not have any predictive value at all. Seizure frequency (as one of four epilepsy-related variables) was also found to be predictive of behaviour disorder by Austin *et al.* (1992), whereas two out of three family-related variables (family stress and family mastery) were also predictive, suggesting that much greater weight should be attached to these. It is of interest that, in their study, one demographic variable – female gender – also had a predictive role; this is in contrast to much of the literature regarding gender effects, which, if anything, have implicated boys (Cull 1988). Lothman and Pianta (1993) also highlight the importance of parent–child interactions over and above the impact of biological variables.

Reasons for disparate findings in studies

It is hard to draw any conclusions regarding the reasons for the high rate of behavioural problems found in children with epilepsy, given that there are some inconsistent and conflicting findings with respect to potential aetiological factors. There are a number of possible reasons for such discrepancies, as follows:

- Source of subjects is an important factor, with some subject groups coming from neurology out-patient clinics and others coming from specialist epilepsy out-patient clinics. It is likely that such groups may well differ with respect to the severity and complexity of their seizure disorder, and the results thus obtained are unlikely to be generalisable to other groups of children with epilepsy.
- The presence, absence, or indeed, severity of intellectual impairment may be another confounding factor, and while some studies restrict themselves to children who do not have global intellectual impairments (Apter *et al.* 1991; Clement and Wallace 1990; Lothman and Pianta 1993; Nicholas and Pianta 1994), others are more wide-ranging and do include children with intellectual disabilities

(Clement and Wallace 1990; Hoare and Kerley 1991; Hoare and Mann 1994). The inclusion of those with learning disabilities is rarely, if ever, controlled for.

- Further, many studies fail to be explicit about whether they are looking at all aberrant behaviours, ictally-related behaviours only, or inter-ictal behaviours only. These are important distinctions to make when it comes to thinking about assessment and treatment, as we shall see later.

It is apparent that these factors may well operate together and their relative contribution is hard to disentangle. For example, children with difficult-to-control epilepsy are likely to have multiple seizure types, occurring frequently. When asked to complete questionnaires pertaining to their behaviour, it is likely that some of what is reported will be concerned with ictally-related behaviours unless the respondent is asked specifically about inter-ictal behaviours. Conversely, in children whose seizures are well controlled, ictally-related behaviours will not be an issue, and the resulting information will be largely concerned with inter-ictal behaviours. Consequently it is hard to draw overall conclusions.

ASSESSMENT AND TREATMENT: CLINICAL CONSIDERATIONS

In this respect, the available literature has little to offer. The course of action depends, in part, on how one attributes any presenting problem.

Assessment of potential aetiological factors

Thus, the first step is to attempt to distinguish between medical and psychological factors. If it can be clearly established that the aberrant behaviour is in some way directly related to the seizure disorder itself, and/or is part of the seizure (as in Besag's (1995) classification system), and/or is related to medication variables, intervention should fall within the remit of the physician responsible for the management of the child's epilepsy. It is also important to exclude the possibility of any formal psychiatric disorder which may require additional pharmacological treatment. In this respect, the clinical psychologist can contribute much to such an assessment by undertaking a thorough behavioural analysis of the situation in collaboration with other professionals. The purpose of such an assessment would be to develop some hypotheses concerning the relative contributions of different variables, which can then be tested. Such a procedure is essential as there are dangers in making assumptions about causes of the behaviour. Thus, some parents report that their child's disruptive behaviour is wholly attributable to the epilepsy, implicit in which is the belief that nothing further can be done to change this until the epilepsy stops. Alternatively, carers may discount the impact of the seizure disorder, in their belief that X is just being difficult. One consequence of this may be the inappropriate punishment of a behaviour that is ictally-related, or unsuccessful attempts to reason with a child who is in an ictally-related state, for example, post-ictal confusion. It is possible that it may not be an all-or-nothing phenomenon, and consequently it would be important to distinguish between ictally-related and inter-ictal behaviours.

Typically, however, one may be confronted by a child whose behaviour disorder persists in the presence of a well-controlled seizure disorder and optimal medical treatment (Cull and Brown 1992) or, alternatively, where a potentially behaviourally-toxic drug is being used, but because the seizure disorder is well controlled, it is unlikely that any drug change will take place. The question arises as to what then?

Clearly, it is important to identify those areas which are amenable to change and for which, as a clinical psychologist, one has the necessary assessment and intervention skills. In this respect, the literature has quite a lot to offer with regard to potential targets for intervention.

For example, the importance of environmental factors in the development and maintenance of inter-ictal behaviour disorders has been emphasised by Cull and Brown (1992) with respect to the contingencies that operate around the behaviour. From this perspective, the logical target for intervention is the behaviour itself, using procedures derived from a behaviour-analytic framework. Alternatively, other investigations have concluded that family-related variables are of particular importance, and their recommendations for intervention include family work and, more specifically, dealing with family stress (Austin *et al.* 1992), family counselling (Sturniolo and Galletti 1994) and targeting aspects of the child–parent relationship (Lothman and Pianta 1993; Nicholas and Pianta 1994).

These different approaches will now be discussed in more detail.

Behaviour analysis

The effectiveness of behaviour-analytic approaches has been amply demonstrated in individuals with learning disabilities, but, as yet, its value for children with epilepsy has not really been explored. The essence of behaviour-analytic approaches is to arrive at as detailed an understanding of a behaviour as possible, incorporating its parameters and contingencies, and identifying its purpose for the individual concerned. This is combined into what is called 'Functional Analysis', which, as the name suggests, is aimed at understanding the function(s) or purpose of a particular behaviour (e.g. to escape from an unpleasant activity or to gain access to desired objects or activities). The methods of assessment are many and varied and will probably be familiar to most readers. A useful overview of the method and summary of approaches is available in a chapter by Durand and Crimmins (1991), which, although concerned mainly with individuals with severe learning disabilities, is clearly applicable in a wider range of settings. In brief, the assessment may involve interviews with the child and teachers/carers, direct observation, completion of questionnaires and checklists, and possibly the use of analogue investigations as originally described by Iwata *et al.* (1982). As part of such an assessment, it would be important to explore carers' attributions of the behaviour, as this itself may need to be a target for intervention and may have implications for the success of any intervention.

Within the field of behaviour analysis, it is now accepted that interventions should be constructional (Goldiamond 1974), focusing on developing skills, incorporating reward-based strategies and other non-aversive procedures, rather than punishment (LaVigna and Donellan 1986), in order to equip the individual with behaviours which will fulfil the same functions as the undesirable behaviour – i.e. developing functionally equivalent responses (Durand and Crimmins 1991).

Such an approach may need to be carried out in combination with some contingency management (i.e. rewarding the occurrence of appropriate behaviours), ecological management (i.e. changes in the environment), and some means of dealing with the problem behaviours when they occur (McGill and Toogood 1994). Cull and Brown (1992) have reported on the successful application of a simple contingency management scheme in two adolescent males, whereby tangible rewards of each boy's choosing were given for an absence of inappropriate behaviours. In both cases the behaviours were of long-standing duration, seizures were few, and the resulting improvements were of such a degree that medication used for controlling behaviour (haloperidol and thioridazine) was completely withdrawn within one year of the scheme starting.

While intervention strategies may vary, one common feature is the involvement of the child's parents/carers in the assessment of the behaviour and planning and carrying out the intervention. The need to involve parents/carers is clear from the perspective of treatment generalisation and maintenance and the prevention of future problems, not to mention enabling the stretching of scarce professional resources (Cunningham 1985; Callias 1987). In cases where there are clearly difficulties within the parent–child relationship, however, it may be important for these to be addressed initially, either alone, or as part of a more comprehensive approach.

Parent–child relationships as a target for change

Parent–child relationships are probably best assessed by means of direct observation, for example, during the course of a problem-solving task (e.g. Lothman and Pianta 1993), or within a less structured free-play setting (e.g. Forehand and McMahon 1981), which would also yield information about parent behaviours and child behaviours.

Subsequent interventions would focus on parental behaviour towards their child, attitudes and feelings about their child and ways in which these are communicated, and their response to the child and child-initiated behaviours. One such technique – the Parent/Child Game – was pioneered in the UK at the Maudsley Hospital and is based on the work of Forehand and McMahon (1981) with non-compliant children. The aim of this approach is to modify maladaptive parental interactions with their child by teaching more effective reinforcement strategies, how to use commands appropriately, and the use of behaviour contingent time-out procedures (Jenner 1988). Such an approach has been found to be of value in improving the skills of parents of non-compliant children (Forehand and McMahon 1981), parents who have abused their children (Jenner 1988), and the parent of a child with learning disabilities (Rix 1988); the behaviours of the children also improved.

Parents' groups

An alternative approach to working with parents has been in the use of parent groups as a forum for providing education and counselling regarding their potential role as behaviour-change agents for their child (Callias 1987), particularly for the parents of children with a chronic illness or disability. It would seem that such an approach might well be applicable to the families of children with epilepsy. However, in one recent study attempting to evaluate such an approach, the outcome was highly disappointing because of the very small number of parents who actually participated. Hoare and Kerley (1992) hoped to investigate the impact of a 'parents group counselling programme' on the 'psychosocial morbidity of children with epilepsy and their families' (ibid.: 760). However, of the 108 families who originally expressed an interest in such an intervention only fourteen attended the first session, with an increasing attrition rate as the sessions progressed. Consequently, the authors were unable to evaluate the intervention. It is of interest that the parents themselves subsequently said that they would have preferred individual counselling. It remains to be seen whether other parents of children with epilepsy share this reticence to participate in a group.

Family interventions

The prominent role that family variables appear to play in multi-aetiological models of behaviour disturbance in children with epilepsy (Austin *et al.* 1992) suggests that this may be another target for intervention. Indeed, the potentially useful role of family-centred interventions has been stressed by a number of authors (Austin *et al.* 1992; Sturniolo and Galletti 1994). However, at this time, published studies regarding the efficacy of family-based interventions are distinctly lacking. In order to explore the range of possible models on which to base such an intervention, the interested clinician need look no further than the wealth of material available within the family therapy field.

FUTURE DEVELOPMENTS

Clearly there is much scope for further work that aims to identify those children who are most at risk for developing behavioural disorders. If this were possible, then a range of early intervention-type programmes could be developed, aimed at the child, parents and/or family, with a view to preventing the development of further problems. Improved counselling of the child and parents following the initial diagnosis of epilepsy may well have a role to play in this. Investigations of the prevalence of specific disorders would be of value.

As has been made clear above, there is also an outstanding need for much more in the way of evaluative research of differing interventions for behaviour problems in childhood epilepsy.

To date, much of the literature has concentrated on children of at least average intellectual ability. Further work is clearly needed in exploring the presence (or otherwise) of behaviour problems in children who have learning disabilities.

REFERENCES

Apter, A., Aviv, A., Kaminer, Y., Weizman, A., Lerman, P. and Tyano, S. (1991) 'Behavioral profile and social competence in temporal lobe epilepsy of adolescence', *Journal of the American Academy of Child and Adolescent Psychiatry* 30: 887–92.

Austin, J. K., Risinger, M. W. and Beckett, L. A. (1992) 'Correlates of behavior problems in children with epilepsy', *Epilepsia* 33: 1115–22.

Bagley, C. (1986) 'Children with epilepsy as a minority group: evidence from the National Child Development Study', in S. Whitman and B. P. Hermann (eds) *Psychopathology in Epilepsy: Social Dimensions*, New York: Oxford University Press.

Berg, I., Butler, A., Ellis, M. and Foster, J. (1993) 'Psychiatric aspects of epilepsy in childhood treated with carbamazepine, phenytoin or sodium valproate: a random trial', *Developmental Medicine and Child Neurology* 35: 149–57.

Besag, F. M. C. (1995) 'Epilepsy, learning and behavior in childhood', *Epilepsia* 36 (Suppl. 1): S58–63.

Callias, M. (1987) 'Teaching parents, teachers and nurses', in W. Yule and J. Carr (eds) *Behaviour Modification for People with Mental Handicaps* 2nd edn, London: Croom Helm.

Clement, M. J. and Wallace, S. J. (1990) 'A survey of adolescents with epilepsy', *Developmental Medicine and Child Neurology* 32: 849–57.

Commander, M., Green, S. H. and Prendergast, M. (1991) 'Behavioural disturbances in children treated with clonazepam', *Developmental Medicine and Child Neurology* 33: 362–4.

Cull, C. A. (1988) 'Cognitive function and behaviour in children', in M. R. Trimble and E. H. Reynolds (eds) *Epilepsy, Behaviour and Cognitive Function*, Chichester: Wiley.

Cull, C. A. and Brown, S. W. (1992) 'A socio behavioural perspective for understanding and managing behaviour problems in children with epilepsy', *Behavioural Neurology* 5: 47–51.

Cull, C. A. and Trimble, M. R. (1989) 'Effects of anticonvulsant medications on cognitive functioning in children with epilepsy', in B. P. Hermann and M. Seidenberg (eds) *Childhood Epilepsies: Neuropsychological, Psychosocial and Intervention Aspects*, Chichester: Wiley.

Cunningham, C. C. (1985), 'Training and education approaches for parents of children with special needs', *British Journal of Medical Psychology* 58: 285–305.

Domizio, S., Verrotti, A., Ramenghi, L. A., Sabatino, G. and Morgese, G. (1993) 'Anti-epileptic therapy and behaviour disturbances in children', *Child's Nervous System* 9: 272–4.

Durand, V. M. and Crimmins, D. (1991) 'Teaching functionally equivalent responses as an intervention for challenging behaviour', in B. Remington (ed.) *The Challenge of Severe Mental Handicap*, Chichester: Wiley.

Epir, S., Renda, Y. and Baser, N. (1984) 'Cognitive and behavioural characteristics of children with idiopathic epilepsy in a low-income area of Ankara, Turkey', *Developmental Medicine and Child Neurology* 26: 200–7.

Ferrari, M. (1989) 'Epilepsy and its effects on the family', in B. P. Hermann and M. Seidenberg (eds) *Childhood Epilepsies: Neuropsychological, Psychosocial and Intervention Aspects*, Chichester: Wiley.

Forehand, R. and McMahon, R. (1981) *Helping the Non-compliant Child: A Clinician's Guide to Parent Training*, New York: Guilford Press.

Goldiamond, I. (1974) 'Toward a constructional approach to social problems', *Behaviorism*, 2: 1–84.

Harvey, I., Goodyer, I. M. and Brown, S. W. (1988) 'The value of a neuropsychiatric examination of children with complex severe epilepsy', *Child: Care, Health and Development* 14: 329–40.

Hermann, B. P. and Whitman, S. (1986) 'Psychopathology in epilepsy: a multietiologic model', in S. Whitman and B. P. Hermann (eds) *Psychopathology in Epilepsy: Social Dimensions*, New York: Oxford University Press.

—— (1991) 'Neurobiological, psychosocial, and pharmacological factors underlying interictal psychopathology in epilepsy', in D. Smith, D. Treiman and M. Trimble (eds) *Advances in Neurology* vol. 55, New York: Raven Press.

Hermann, B. P., Whitman, S. and Dell, J. (1989) 'Correlates of behavior problems and social competence in children with epilepsy, aged 6–11', in B. P. Hermann and M. Seidenberg (eds) *Childhood Epilepsies: Neuropsychological, Psychosocial and Intervention Aspects*, Chichester: Wiley.

Hoare, P. and Kerley, S. (1991) 'Psychosocial adjustment of children with chronic epilepsy and their families', *Developmental Medicine and Child Neurology* 33: 201–15.

—— (1992) 'Helping parents and children with epilepsy cope successfully: the outcome of a group programme for parents', *Journal of Psychosomatic Research* 36: 759–67.

Hoare, P. and Mann, H. (1994) 'Self-esteem and behavioural adjustment in children with epilepsy and children with diabetes', *Journal of Psychosomatic Research* 38: 859–69.

Iwata, B. A., Dorsey, M. F., Slifer, K. J., Bauman, K. E. and Richman, G. S. (1982), 'Toward a functional analysis of self-injury', *Analysis and Intervention in Developmental Disabilities* 2: 3–20.

Jenner, S. (1988) 'Assessing parenting skills', paper presented at a conference held December 1988 entitled *When Families Fail: Research and Practice in Child Abuse*, London: Institute of Psychiatry.

Kinney, R. O., Shaywitz, B. A., Shaywitz, S. E., Sarwar, M. and Holahan, J. M. (1990), 'Epilepsy in children with attention deficit disorder: cognitive, behavioral, and neuroanatomic indices', *Paediatric Neurology* 6: 31–7.

LaVigna, G. W. and Donnellan, A. M. (1986) *Alternatives to Punishment: Solving Behaviour Problems with Non-Aversive Strategies*, New York: Irvington Publishers.

Long, C. G. and Moore, J. R. (1979) 'Parental expectations for their epileptic children', *Journal of Child Psychology and Psychiatry* 20: 299–312.

Lothman, D. J. and Pianta, R. C. (1993) 'Role of mother–child interaction in predicting competence of children with epilepsy', *Epilepsia* 34: 658–69.

McGill, P. and Toogood, S. (1994) 'Organizing community placements', in E. Emerson, P. McGill and J. Mansell (eds) *Severe Learning Disabilities and Challenging Behaviours: Designing High Quality Services*, London: Chapman and Hall.

Marston, D., Besag, F., Binnie, C. D. and Fowler, M. (1993) 'Effects of transitory cognitive impairment on psychosocial functioning of children with epilepsy: a therapeutic trial', *Developmental Medicine and Child Neurology* 35: 574–81.

Matthews, W. S. and Barabas, G. (1986) 'Perceptions of control among children with epilepsy', in S. Whitman and B. P. Hermann (eds) *Psychopathology in Epilepsy: Social Dimensions*, New York: Oxford University Press.

Matthews, W. S., Barabas, G. and Ferrari, M. (1982) 'Emotional concomitants of childhood epilepsy', *Epilepsia* 23: 671–81.

Munthe-Kaas, A. W. (1981) 'Education of the family', in M. Dam, L. Gram and J. K. Penry (eds) *Advances in Epileptology: XIIth Epilepsy International Symposium*, New York: Raven Press.

Nicholas, K. K. and Pianta, R. C. (1994), 'Mother–child interactions and seizure control: relations with behavior problems in children with epilepsy', *Journal of Epilepsy* 7: 102–7.

Nolte, R. and Wolff, M. (1992) 'Behavioural and developmental aspects of primary generalized myoclonic-astatic epilepsy', *Epilepsy Research* Suppl. 6: 175–83.

Pianta, R. C. and Lothman, D. J. (1994) 'Predicting behavior problems in children with epilepsy: child factors, disease factors, family stress, and child–mother interactions', *Child Development* 65: 1415–28.

Rantakallio, P., Koiranen, M. and Möttönen, J. (1992) 'Association of perinatal events, epilepsy, and central nervous system trauma with juvenile delinquency', *Archives of Disease in Childhood* 67: 1459–61.

Ritchie, K. (1981) 'Research note: interaction in the families of epileptic children', *Journal of Child Psychology and Psychiatry* 22: 65–71.

Rix, K. (1988) 'Teaching a mother to attend differentially to her mentally handicapped child's behaviour', *Behavioural Psychotherapy* 16: 122–32.

Roulet Perez, E., Davidoff, V., Despland, P. A. and Deonna, T. (1993) 'Mental and behavioural deterioration of children with epilepsy and CSWS: acquired epileptic frontal syndrome', *Developmental Medicine and Child Neurology* 35: 661–74.

Sheth, R. D., Goulden, K. J. and Ronen, G. M. (1994) 'Aggression in children treated with clobazam for epilepsy', *Clinical Neuropharmacology* 17: 332–7.

Silverstein, F. S., Parrish, M. A. and Johnson, M. V. (1982) 'Adverse behavioural reactions in children treated with carbamazepine (Tegretol)', *Journal of Paediatrics* 101: 785–7.

Stores, G. (1982) 'Psychosocial preventive measures and rehabilitation of children with epilepsy', in H. Akimoto, H. Kazamatsuri, M. Seino and A. Ward (eds) *Advances in Epileptology: XIIIth Epilepsy International Symposium*, New York: Raven Press.

Sturniolo, M. G. and Galletti, F. (1994) 'Idiopathic epilepsy and school achievement', *Archives of Disease in Childhood* 70: 424–8.

Urion, D. K. (1991) 'Psychiatric aspects of epilepsy in children', in O. Devinsky and W. H. Theodore (eds) *Epilepsy and Behavior*, New York: Wiley.

West, P. (1986) 'The social meaning of epilepsy: stigma as a potential explanation for psychopathology in children', in S. Whitman and B. P. Hermann (eds) *Psychopathology in Epilepsy: Social Dimensions*, New York: Oxford University Press.

Ziegler, R. G. (1981) 'Impairments of control and competence in epileptic children and their families', *Epilepsia* 22: 339–46.

Chapter 11

Epilepsy and learning disabilities

Colin A. Espie and Audrey Paul

The co-presentation of epilepsy and learning disabilities is a very neglected area in respect of both research and clinical expertise. This chapter attempts to highlight some key issues in this complex area. However, other parts of this handbook also have much to contribute to understanding in this specialist field.

THE PREVALENCE OF EPILEPSY IN LEARNING DISABILITIES

There are few problems associated with learning disabilities which present as commonly and as persistently as seizure disorders. Around 20 per cent of people with learning disabilities have epilepsy, with prevalence rates rising sharply to 50 per cent where learning disabilities are severe or profound (Bicknell 1985; Coulter 1993). In terms of numbers, it has been estimated that 200 people per 100,000 population will have a learning disability and epilepsy (Brown *et al.* 1993). Furthermore, the administration of anti-epileptic drugs remains very high. A recent large national survey reported that approximately 53 per cent of children and adults with a learning disability were receiving at least one anti-epileptic drug (Hogg 1992). Whereas monotherapy is the treatment of choice in epilepsy, practice in learning disabilities demonstrates that 40 per cent of people are on polytherapy (Espie *et al.* 1990; Singh and Towle 1993). Encouragingly, where practices have been revised, there is evidence both of improved seizure control and of reductions in behavioural and social problems (e.g. Fischbacher 1985).

This tendency to over-medicate is in part due to the intractability of seizures in this population. Although it has long been recognised that the presence of additional neurological, psychological and social handicaps is associated with a more adverse prognosis (Rodin 1968), it is only recently that formal definition of complex presentations has been attempted. The term *epilepsy plus* has now been applied to those 30–40 per cent of patients who continue to require access to specialist services because of seizures continuing at an unacceptably high rate, despite treatment or the diagnosis remaining uncertain, or having additional neurological problems or psychiatric illness or learning difficulties (Brown *et al.* 1993). People with severe learning disabilities may present with all of these additional problems.

THE SEQUELAE OF EPILEPSY IN LEARNING DISABILITIES

Any significant degree of learning disability is invariably associated with permanent cerebral damage. Although brain damage is not a necessary precondition for the development of epilepsy, it is nonetheless a sufficient one. Thus, epilepsy and learning disabilities may be regarded as synergistic.

The coexistence of learning disabilities and epilepsy presents a particular challenge to the practitioner who is seeking to identify and resolve problems, or at least to reduce their impact. Answers to certain key questions are required. Does a person with learning disabilities and epilepsy necessarily have significant additional problems and, if so, what are they? What are the effects of seizures and of their treatment in day-to-day life? How can seizure events be differentiated from other behaviours, and what does this imply for management? In addition, self-induction of seizures and non-epileptic events may be a greater problem in people with learning disabilities. The following sections will review the available literature in each of these areas, prior to more specific guidelines for good practice in epilepsy and learning disabilities being presented and discussed.

Behaviour and psychological well-being

Rates of behavioural disturbance and psychiatric disorder are significantly elevated in populations of people with epilepsy (Hoare 1984; Lund 1985) and in populations of people with learning disabilities (Bouras and Drummond 1992; Mansell 1993). Although the presentation of a 'dual disability' might increase the frequency and/or severity of such problems, very few studies of this area have been undertaken.

Our earlier studies reported that people with a 'dual disability' demonstrated poorer life-skills than their peers with no epilepsy, particularly on measures of independent functioning and language development. Behavioural disturbance (aggression, inappropriate social manners, self injury) was particularly associated with frequent seizures and with anti-epileptic polytherapy (Espie *et al.* 1989, 1990; Gillies *et al.* 1989).

Despite the enormous research and clinical interest in 'challenging behaviours' over the past two decades very little specific attention has been directed to this sizeable sub-group of people to investigate possible relationships between epileptic phenomena and behaviour. Equally, interest in the social 'meaning' of epilepsy, clients' perceptions of themselves and of 'control', their coping strategies and the interrelations of all these with the functional analysis of behaviour patterns could be extremely productive.

Learning potential

An information-processing model is useful when considering learning processes of people with intellectual impairments (see Figure 11.1). In this model, deficits in performance of day-to-day tasks are mediated by prior states of arousal and selective attention. The integration of the individual's central nervous system and its capacity to respond to the external environment, the quality of his or her stream of consciousness and the overall capacity and efficiency with which the processing system works, will affect the desired learning and performance.

People with learning disabilities have particular problems, both with the sufficiency of the attentional resources available to them and with

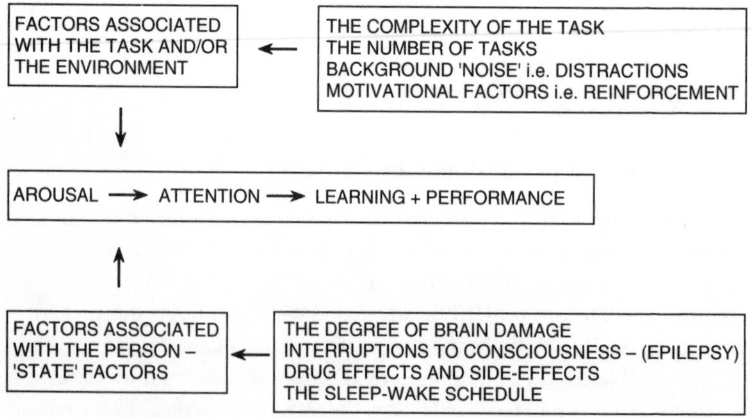

Figure 11.1 A conceptual model of factors influencing learning

the allocation of such resources, particularly when in competition with distracting environmental factors (Carr 1984; Merrill 1990). Figure 11.1 illustrates the interaction between a stimulus-control paradigm and an information-processing model whereby task/environment factors and central-state factors both influence the selective attention processes. Thus, conditions are favourable for attention and learning when the individual is wakeful, with senses focused and engaged on a task, in an environment with minimal competing stimulation. Epilepsy may be a significant contributory factor to the process for a number of reasons.

First, epilepsy typically interrupts consciousness, both during the seizure itself (the ictus) and probably during the interictal period. Although loss of consciousness may be characteristic of some types of seizures, an altered state of consciousness features in other seizure types. It should also be noted that absence seizures, sometimes regarded in clinical practice as relatively less important, may be extremely disruptive, since brief but recurring gaps in awareness may completely destroy the quality of attention available, as our example illustrates.

C was a 42-year-old woman with severe learning disabilities. Lengthy ambulatory EEG assessment revealed numerous bursts of epileptiform activity, ranging from one to thirty-two seconds in duration. Detailed examination of several random hours from the waking trace revealed an average of fifty-five bursts per hour.

The preoccupation with seizure frequency as an outcome measure, both in pharmacological research and in clinical practice, has led to a lack of recognition of the potential importance of interictal well-being, (see Espie *et al.* under review (a), for detailed discussion). 'Sub-clinical' activity may be of considerable qualitative importance in relation to the maintenance of a satisfactory stream of awareness and consciousness. Similarly, post-ictal adjustment and recovery time may be critical variables in determining suitable care plans.

Second, anti-epileptic drugs have an impact upon arousal. Each of the established anti-epileptic drugs (carbamazepine, sodium valproate, phenytoin) is regarded as predictably causing drowsiness (Brodie 1990); polypharmacy produces further cognitive impairment (Reynolds and Shorvon 1981). This should be viewed against the possibility that people with epilepsy already have an enhanced daytime sleep tendency (Palm *et al.* 1992).

Finally, it is important to recognise that the majority of both clinical and educational practice is based upon observation of clients, without access to EEG facilities to permit extrapolation of epileptic or sleep phenomena. With this fact in mind, the growing amount of work done in recent years on 'behaviour state analysis' may in time prove invaluable. Coding systems with behavioural criteria have been developed to define and discriminate between various states of optimal and sub-optimal functioning ranging from 'sleep states' to 'preferred awake states' (Guess *et al.* 1990). In these analyses, behavioural evidence of arousal and orientation is seen as indicating alertness and greater receptivity to learning, although Green *et al.* (1994) have indicated that apparently non-alert students will not necessarily be unresponsive to training. Behaviour state coding systems include seizures as a separate category, perhaps because seizures are regarded as relatively uncommon. Indeed, in our own studies of twenty-eight adults with severe learning disabilities and epilepsy, we observed only eleven seizures during 1,388 one-minute videotaped observation samples. However, such data almost certainly reflect some actual failure to detect or discriminate and, therefore, underestimate the true frequency of epileptic events in this population.

In conclusion, epilepsy potentially constrains learning potential and learning outcome. An information-processing model may be uniquely adapted to the profiling of neuropsychological status in people with epilepsy and learning disabilities, and assessment may be complemented by the use of behaviour state analysis, particularly if it develops greater assessment reliability and attested validity in the classification of interictal arousal states.

Quality of life

Epilepsy and quality of life (QoL) is discussed in Chapter 8 of this book. Little is known about the perceived importance of factors such as social stigma, difficulty in obtaining paid employment and driving restrictions to people with learning disabilities or to their carers. Attempts have been made to define, describe and quantify QoL for people with epilepsy, but it may not be valid to extrapolate themes or norms from such assessment scales to those with learning disabilities. Furthermore, the published measures are in self-report format and they require literacy skills, in addition to comprehension generally beyond those with intellectual disability.

Under the auspices of the West of Scotland Epilepsy Research Group, we ran a series of recent carers' workshops to identify what carers wanted from epilepsy services for people with learning disabilities. Thirty-nine participants, nineteen of whom were family carers, took part in four workshops. Carers were first asked to consider and write down their three main concerns about their family member/client having epilepsy. Second, small groups were formed to enable carers to share these concerns. The small groups then reported their findings to the entire workshop. The final stage in the process was for carers to consider revising their personal lists in the light of hearing how others felt. In this way, we hoped to distil the most strongly felt personal concerns affecting carers' quality of life.

The main themes which emerged were medication and side effects, further damage caused by seizures, risk of injury, client independence, social restrictions, mood change and carer responsibility. From the carer's perspective, 'quality of life' reflected concerns over some very basic issues. An Epilepsy Outcome Scale has now been developed and tested (Espie *et al.*, under review (b)).

Differentiating seizure behaviour from other behaviours

Questions arise in clinical practice about whether a behaviour could be seizure-related. Simple partial and absence seizures may be missed altogether, as of course may nocturnal seizures; myoclonic seizures may be difficult to differentiate from habits and stereotypies. Complex partial seizures are most likely to be labelled 'behavioural'. Primary and secondary generalised tonic-clonic seizures may be less ambiguous but can pass unobserved by carers. Non-epileptic seizures may present and these usually occur in people who also have genuine epileptic attacks. None of these problems is unique to learning disabilities, but three important factors contribute to additional difficulties in detection and classification.

First, clinical practice generally relies heavily upon the patient's self-report. Even when detailed EEG assessment has been conducted, actual seizures are rarely observed by the clinicians. However, patients may have unusual sensations, or be aware of altered consciousness immediately prior to attacks. They may be able to identify seizure events which can be verified electrophysiologically, but which involve extremely modest behavioural change, for example, a chewing movement or a blank stare. Furthermore, many seizures last only a matter of seconds but may be perceptible to patients in retrospect. They may conclude that they must have had a seizure because they dropped something, stumbled, or are in a recognisable post-ictal recovery state. The person with learning disabilities is likely to be less able to interpret and communicate any of this information effectively.

The second factor is the high rate of presentation of other similar behaviours such as movement disorders, automatisms, tics and tremors and drug-induced (especially neuroleptic) movements and postures. Stereotyped behaviours, which have been reported to be present in up to two-thirds of institutionalised people with severe learning disabilities (Berkson and Davenport 1962; Repp and Barton 1980), perhaps best illustrate the differential classification problems. The essential defining features of stereotypy are idiosyncratic, repetitive, invariant and frequent movements. They range in form from body rocking and pacing to more complex fine motor movements, posturing and vocalisation. Head jerking and arm waving are common characteristics, but the range of potential behaviours is quite extensive, particularly in specific disorders such as Rett Syndrome and autism (Paul, 1997).

Third, seizure events have to be differentiated from 'challenging behaviours' where the individual's actions are difficult to manage effectively in the care setting (Emerson *et al.* 1987; Mansell 1993). The usual assessment methodology here is functional analysis (e.g. Owens and Ashcroft 1982), a data gathering and hypothesis-testing approach designed to establish the setting conditions and maintaining factors for the behaviour. Self-injurious behaviour, for example, can be stereotyped and confused with ictal movement.

Another area of overlap is in the expression of emotionality. Although the association of aggression with temporal lobe epilepsy (complex partial seizures) remains speculative (Fenwick 1991), displays of emotion post-ictally are common and there is some evidence that maintenance of a steady state of emotion and avoidance of excitation can abate seizures for some (Betts 1989; Devellis *et al.* 1980). We have noted anecdotally that some carers try to avoid upsetting or pressuring clients in the belief that such emotional states can precipitate seizures. There are clear parallels in the relationship between challenging behaviours and mood (e.g. Novaco 1975).

Non-epileptic events

This topic is addressed in more detail in Chapter 7. Non-epileptic seizures may be symptomatic of other physical or psychological disorders, such as cardiogenic syncope, metabolic disorder and transient ischaemic attacks. The great majority of research work in this area has been on non-learning disabled populations (Stephenson 1990; Porter 1991) and the prevalence is not known for people with learning disabilities.

The association between psychological trauma and pseudo-neurological presentation has been summarised elsewhere (Gates *et al.* 1991).

There is evidence that non-epileptic seizures may represent emotional distress such as sexual abuse (Cascino *et al.* 1987), and this area continues to be an active focus of clinical research in general psychiatry (Greig and Betts 1992). In spite of a burgeoning literature in the learning disabilities field on the identification and management of sexual abuse, the authors are unaware of specific references to non-epileptic seizures within this literature.

Non-epileptic seizures may also represent a reinforced behaviour pattern where 'illness behaviour' has acquired the capacity to provide secondary gain (Gates *et al.* 1991). Montgomery and Espie (1986) describe in detail a case study of a woman with learning disabilities whose 'seizure' frequency was markedly reduced after behavioural intervention. Clearly, the treatment approach will vary markedly between these types of psychologically-based non-epileptic seizures. A psychotherapeutic approach is preferred for the former with a more strictly behavioural regime being advocated for the latter (Gates *et al.* 1991). Further research-based study is required to identify accurately prevalence rates amongst people with learning disabilities and also the efficacy of treatment outcomes.

Self-induced seizures

A small proportion of people with epilepsy demonstrate unambiguous seizure activity in response to sensory stimulation. The most studied area has been that of photosensitivity which occurs in 2–5 per cent of all individuals with epilepsy (Kasteleijn-Nolst Trenité 1989). It has been suggested that people with learning disabilities may be more likely to engage in self-stimulatory behaviour leading to photosensitive seizures. Kasteleijn-Nolst Trenité (ibid.) reported that eleven out of sixteen subjects with significant learning disabilities evidenced self-induction. Despite this small sample, the potential importance of the phenomenon is amply illustrated and beckons further systematic research study. Other forms of self-stimulation have also been reported in the literature, for example, hyperventilation (Fabisch and Darbyshire 1965), bilateral compression of the carotid arteries (Lai and Ziegler 1983) and chewing (Binnie 1988). The most promising avenue to an explanation of these phenomena would be through functional analysis to identify possible determinants and/or consequences of the behaviour for the individual. It would also be useful to consider the hypothesis that people with learning disabilities fail to inhibit behaviours liable to trigger seizures, rather than 'actively' engaging in them. The arousal mediation hypothesis (after Leuba 1955) may be an explanation for a number of poorly understood behavioural patterns, such as stereotyped behaviours, self-injurious behaviours, other challenging behaviours, and potentially self-induced seizures.

Summary

People with learning disabilities often present with epilepsy. This co-presentation potentially affects the individual's learning, behaviour, mood and their quality of life and that of their carers. A more sophisticated conceptual understanding of the mechanisms underlying co-morbidity and behavioural presentation is required. Methodologies of assessment and intervention in previous research have often been crude, and it continues to be an understudied area which is managed largely on a pragmatic basis. We hope the next section will guide practitioners towards improved assessment and treatment practices.

THE ROLE OF THE CLINICAL PSYCHOLOGIST IN THE PRACTICAL MANAGEMENT OF PEOPLE WITH EPILEPSY AND LEARNING DISABILITIES

It has been suggested that clinical psychologists and neuropsychologists should be core members of an 'epilepsy plus' team (Brown *et al.* 1993). Indeed, clinical psychologists see many people with epilepsy and learning disabilities within a general caseload, although rarely does the epilepsy, or the issues arising from a dual disability, become the focus of intervention. However, skilled input is required in each of the areas of diagnosis and classification, assessment methodology, the monitoring of treatment effects, preparation for surgery and evaluation of its outcome, adjunctive behavioural management and carer support. Each of these areas will be addressed briefly in turn.

Diagnosis, classification and behavioural analysis

A diagnosis of epilepsy is commonly a product of clinical observation and EEG confirmation; such observations should be structured and recorded by an agreed method. Behavioural descriptors should be written for each of the common seizure presentations exhibited by an individual on the front page of a seizure diary, which then requires carers only to enter a code letter and time at each presentation of the seizure, rather than having to make a classification decision. An example may be helpful to explain the use of this coding system.

W was a 25-year-old man with severe learning disabilities. His epilepsy started with infantile spasms and he had chronic, refractory seizures of four differing types. These could be described behaviourally for recording purposes and they reflect tonic-clonic, atonic, myoclonic and absence attacks respectively.

Code Behavioural Description

A W suddenly collapses, his whole body jerks quite violently, his eyes may appear to 'roll' and he will vocalise quite loudly.
B W's whole body becomes rigid, he shrieks and he falls either backwards or forwards (still upright) on to floor.
C There is an abrupt brief jerking of one or more limbs.
D W stares straight ahead without blinking for a short period (appears quite vacant).

Given that many carers are informal and are not trained in the classification of epilepsy, such a simple system would appear to be accurate, reliable and economical. The seizure diaries can then be presented to clinicians and are likely to provide the critical information required for diagnostic and treatment purposes.

The psychologist is uniquely placed to develop such systems and can relate these to parallel systems recording other behaviours which may be non-epileptic in origin, such as stereotyped behaviours. Thus, the hypothesis-testing model employed in the functional analysis of behaviour can be extended to include epileptic behaviours and to differentiate their nature and function. Where possible, recording of events on videotape can be extremely helpful in functional analysis and diagnosis. Indeed, many EEG departments make use of video telemetry in order to correlate clinical evidence with EEG deflections. There is tremendous scope, therefore, for closer collaboration between clinical psychologists and EEG specialists in the interpretation of data. The use of ambulatory monitoring equipment with event-marking facilities also has distinct advantages in that it allows the client to remain in the natural environment, thus facilitating behavioural analysis of any setting conditions, triggers or responses which affect the presentation of the disorder.

Assessment and management of challenging behaviours

Whilst this chapter will not concentrate upon challenging behaviour per se, several helpful parallels may be drawn between the study of challenging behaviour and the study of epilepsy.

First, challenging behaviour is 'behaviour which is likely to seriously limit or delay access to and use of ordinary community facilities' (Emerson *et al.* 1987). There has been a marked shift away from the concept of 'behavioural problem', which tended to ascribe responsibility for the behaviour to the individual concerned, towards an interactional view where context has to be taken into account. 'Seizure behaviours' often represent challenging behaviours which similarly restrict access to experience and to ordinary settings. There is a disproportionately high prevalence of severe epilepsy in institutionalised populations of people with learning disabilities (Corbett 1981) and epilepsy continues to represent a foremost health concern in community care planning (Welsh Health Planning Forum 1992; Department of Health 1995). The wide range of behavioural and emotional triggers and sequelae, coupled with these service issues, suggests that, for at least a proportion of people, epilepsy constitutes a 'challenging behaviour'.

Second, methods of assessment, developed in relation to behavioural analysis, may be readily applicable to the study of seizure behaviour, its antecedents and its consequences. Examples are functional analysis (Iwata *et al.* 1990), naturalistic observation (Repp and Felce 1990), analogue methodology (Oliver 1991) and validated questionnaires (Durand and Crimmins 1988). Relevant here is the earlier discussion of the use of behavioural descriptors with coding systems to minimise the inaccuracy of misclassifying seizures as they occur.

Third, conceptual models of challenging behaviour and the treatment techniques emanating from them have, potentially, much to offer to the understanding and management of those seizure disorders which are related to a stimulus control or instrumental learning model. Furthermore, effective treatment of challenging behaviours often depends upon providing services which are able to maintain the individual in the long term, and to support carers adequately. Similarly, people with learning disabilities and epilepsy often depend upon such a management strategy, rather than a curative one.

Assessment and monitoring of neuropsychological functions

The psychologist's potential assessment role does not end with diagnosis and need not be confined to the measurement of seizures alone. As previously stated, epilepsy affects the stream of consciousness and it can be useful to measure the individual's cognitive functioning in relation to the information-processing model presented in Figure 11.1. For example, what is an individual's span of attention in a given circumstance, and does it change for the better (or worse) with the prescription of an anti-epileptic drug? Although seizure control may improve, drowsiness may increase. Another example would be to monitor the impact of a change to anti-epileptic monotherapy from polytherapy, or the implementation of a new anti-epileptic, over a range of cognitive functions (see also Chapter 5).

The particular tools for assessment must be selected on an individual basis since conventional neuropsychological tests may prove either inappropriate due to the degree of learning disability, or insensitive as repeated measures to monitor the specific functions which are of interest. The most accurate assessments here are likely to be quite labour-intensive but may yield useful results. For example, we have found that a simple choice-reaction timer can be used even with people with severe learning disabilities to provide information on vigilance, attention span and eye–hand coordination. Similarly, behaviour state, as defined earlier, can be sampled to provide information on arousal and alertness levels.

Carers are often highly motivated to participate in monitoring changes in neuropsychological status. Side-effect profiles of anti-epileptic drugs should be regularly rated, and targeted outcomes can be derived for 'quality of life' dimensions on an individual basis. In our experience, visual analogue scales are user-friendly for these purposes.

Formal neuropsychological tests usually cannot be used with reference to published norms. However, as part of the clinical appraisal process, and for monitoring of change over time, we would recommend using appropriate sub-tests from the Wechsler Scales or the British Abilities Scales which will not yield floor and ceiling effects for the client in question. The development of standardised instruments for the assessment of cognitive functions in people with severe intellectual impairments is long overdue.

Monitoring drug treatment

Psychologists are commonly involved in clinical trials of new anti-epileptic drugs. Clinical psychologists working in the field of learning disabilities should become familiar with these studies, since changes in status or function may disproportionately affect the person with learning disabilities whose intellectual resources are intrinsically less. Monotherapy is generally the treatment approach of choice, with the discontinuation of all anti-epileptic medication where possible. (Alvarez 1989; Collaborative Group for the Study of Epilepsy 1992). The benefits of rationalisation of drug treatment are social, cognitive and medical, making it important for the psychologist to be in a knowledgeable enough position to advocate for improved functioning in these respects. The profiles of the newer anti-epileptic drugs (especially lamotrigine) appear more favourable in protecting psychological functions (Brodie 1996), although vigabatrin has been associated with psychotic phenomena, which may present as behaviour disturbance in people with learning disabilities (Grant and Heel 1991). The authors are unaware of any sizeable well-controlled comparative trial of anti-epileptic drugs specifically in people with learning disabilities.

Surgery

Surgical intervention for patients with refractory epilepsy has greatly increased in recent years (see Chapter 4). Although, currently, selection criteria for surgical treatment would generally exclude people with severe learning disabilities (Turmel *et al.* 1992), cases of corpus callosotomy in people with mild learning difficulties have been reported (Sass *et al.* 1992). The primary indication for the procedure appears to be for atonic seizures. Psychologists working in learning disabilities should be aware, therefore, of potential future involvements in the work-up to surgical procedures and in the monitoring of post surgical well-being.

Psychological treatment of seizures

There is some evidence that patients can learn seizure abatement strategies to control, or at least delay, the presentation of seizures (see Chapter 7). Such procedures are generally dependent upon the existence of an aura and the individual's ability to intervene prior to the development of the full seizure. Little is presently known about the potential for such an approach in people with learning disabilities, but a preliminary starting point would be to gather information on the frequency with which auras are recognised. Anecdotally, we can report on one man with severe learning disabilities, with no speech, who routinely sat down on the floor or on a couch immediately prior to a seizure to reduce injury. This was initially thought to be evidence of non-epileptic seizure behaviour, but it transpired (after ambulatory EEG monitoring and videotape analysis) that he did this in response to an aura.

Reference was made earlier to non-epileptic seizures evoked by psychological factors, or maintained as illness behaviours, that presumably attract some secondary gains. The psychologist's role in assessment (Hermann and Connell 1992) and treatment have been reviewed elsewhere (Gates *et al.* 1991). However, little of this pertains directly to people with learning disabilities. Further well-documented reports and controlled trials are needed. Similarly, the possible self-induction of seizures would fit well within a behavioural paradigm since the function(s) of such apparently self-stimulatory behaviours might be established through detailed observational analysis and pave the way for intervention using, for example, stimulus control models.

There is an outstanding need to consider the relationship between emotional state, thinking and behavioural response in the care and management of people with learning disabilities plus epilepsy. Cognitive (schema-based) theory potentially has much to offer with its emphasis upon 'internal states'. It does not seem unreasonable to hypothesise that people with learning disabilities will have greater than usual difficulty in understanding their epilepsy, its symptoms and its effects and in developing appropriate coping strategies. However, recently, concepts such as epilepsy knowledge, self-efficacy and locus of control orientation have been touched upon within this client group (Espie *et al.* 1990; Jarvie *et al.* 1993 a, b; Jarvie 1994). There is available a video-based training package which is the first to be designed specifically for use with people with learning disabilities (Paul, 1996). The field is wide open to consider the adaptation of models and methods from general adult psychology.

Carer support and management

Frequent seizures and anti-epileptic polytherapy tend to be associated with poorer social outcomes in people with learning disabilities, including lower levels of independence and higher levels of behavioural difficulty (Espie *et al.* 1989; Espie *et al.* 1990). Many adults with learning disabilities have difficulties in achieving their optimal level of independence from carers, and it seems likely that the added complication of epilepsy is associated with a strengthening of this dilemma.

From our studies it seems clear that carers are looking for improved control over epilepsy, reductions in side effects, reassurance that further damage is not taking place, limitation to the risk of injury, and, against the background of these, an increase in client independence and a reduction in social restriction. Carers experience difficulty in coping with post-ictal aggression or fear. A very common finding, however, was the sense of personal responsibility and anxiety which many carers felt they had and were likely to keep indefinitely. Common views were that other people were unable or unwilling to cope, and were liable either not to react or to over-react. Services must therefore face up to the reality of such consistently expressed concerns and provide psychological support and help to carers.

A therapeutic service to carers could start with information and education, provide training in anxiety management strategies, develop buddy systems between paid and family carers, and support groups, and could involve more specific individually-tailored help during times of social transition. Meeting these needs, along with the specific needs of the individual with epilepsy, will probably interact to produce the best outcomes since family dynamics can prove powerful inhibitors or facilitators of positive change.

CONCLUSION

Psychological factors play an important part in the presentation, assessment and care management of the person with epilepsy and his or her family. The psychologist can apply conceptual models which shed light upon the overall integration of the individual's personal functioning, and of their functioning within a social context. Importantly, the psychologist potentially has more to contribute to working with people with epilepsy than has traditionally been thought. There remains an outstanding need for well-documented clinical research to evaluate both theoretical and practical aspects of such psychological work.

REFERENCES

Alvarez, N. (1989) 'Discontinuance of anti-epileptic medications in patients with developmental disability and diagnosis of epilepsy', *American Journal on Mental Retardation* 93: 593–9.

Berkson, G. and Davenport, R. K. (1962) 'Stereotyped movements in mental defectives. I: Initial survey', *American Journal of Mental Deficiency* 66: 849–52.

Betts, T. A. (1989) 'Psychological aspects of epilepsy', in J. Marshall (ed.) *Focus: Epilepsy in Childhood*, St Ives: Chase Webb.

Bicknell, D. J. (1985) 'Epilepsy and mental handicap', in C. Wood (ed.) *Epilepsy and Mental Handicap. Royal Society of Medicine Round Table Series* No. 2, London: RSM.

Binnie, C. D. (1988) 'Self induction of seizures: the ultimate non-compliance', *Epilepsy Research* 1 (Suppl.): 153–8.

Bouras, N. and Drummond, C. (1992) 'Behaviour and psychiatric disorders of people with mental handicaps living in the community', *Journal of Intellectual Disability Research* 36: 349–57.

Brodie, M. J. (1990) 'Established anti-convulsants and treatment of refractory epilepsy', *Lancet* (Review): 20–5.

—— (1996) 'Lamotrigine – an update', *Canadian Journal of Neurological Sciences* 23 (Suppl. 2): S6–S9.

Brown, S., Betts, T., Chadwick, D., Hall, B., Shorvon, S. and Wallace, S. (1993) 'An epilepsy needs document', *Seizure* 2: 91–103.

Carr, T. H. (1984) 'Attention, skill and intelligence: some speculations on extreme individual differences in human performance', in P. H. Brooks, R. Sperber and C. McCauley (eds) *Learning and Cognition in the Mentally Retarded*, New Jersey: Lawrence Erlbaum.

Cascino, G., Woodward, A. and Johnson, M. (1987) 'Sexual and/or physical abuse occurring in association with psychogenic seizures', *Epilepsia* 28: 632.

Collaborative Group for the Study of Epilepsy (1992) 'Prognosis of epilepsy in newly referred patients: a multicenter prospective study of the effects of monotherapy on the long-term course of epilepsy', *Epilepsia* 33: 45–51.

Corbett, J. A. (1981) 'Epilepsy and mental retardation', in: E. H. Reynolds and M. R. Trimble (eds) *Epilepsy and Psychiatry*, London: Churchill Livingstone.

Coulter, D. L. (1993) 'Epilepsy and mental retardation: an overview', *American Journal on Mental Retardation* 98: S1–11.

Department of Health (1995) *The Health of the Nation; A Strategy for People with Learning Disabilities*, Wetherby: Department of Health.

Devellis, R. F., Devellis, B. M., Wallston, B. S. and Wallston, K. A. (1980) 'Epilepsy and learned helplessness', *Basic and Applied Social Psychology* 1: 241–53.

Durand, V. M. and Crimmins, D. B. (1988) 'Identifying the variables maintaining self-injurious behaviour', *Journal of Autism and Developmental Disorders* 18: 99–117.

Emerson, E., Barratt, S., Bell, C., Cummings, R. G., McCool, C., Toogood, A. and Mansell, J. (1987) *Developing services for people with severe learning disabilities and challenging behaviours*, University of Kent at Canterbury: Institute of Social and Applied Psychology.

Espie, C. A., Gillies, J. B. and Montgomery, J. M. (1990) 'Anti-epileptic polypharmacy, psychosocial behaviour and locus of control orientation among mentally handicapped adults living in the community', *Journal of Mental Deficiency Research* 34: 351–60.

Espie, C. A., Kerr, M., Paul, A., O'Brien, G., Betts, T., Berney, T., Clark, J.,

Jacoby, A., and Baker, G. (under review (a)), *Learning disabilities and epilepsy 2: A review of available outcome measures and position statement on development priorities.*

Espie, C. A., Pashley, A. S., Bonham, K. G., Sourindhrin, I. and O'Donovan, M. (1989) 'The mentally handicapped person with epilepsy: a comparative study investigating psychosocial functioning', *Journal of Mental Deficiency Research* 33: 123–35.

Espie, C. A., Paul, A., Graham, M., Sterrick, M., Foley, J. and McGarvey, C. (under review (b)) 'The Epilepsy Outcome Scale: the development of a measure for use with carers of people with epilepsy plus learning disabilities.'

Fabisch, W. and Darbyshire, R. (1965) 'Report on an unusual case of self-induced epilepsy with comments on some psychological and therapeutic aspects', *Epilepsia* 6: 335–40.

Fenwick, P. (1991) 'Aggression and epilepsy', in O. Devinsky and W. H. Theodore (eds) *Epilepsy and Behaviour; Frontiers of Clinical Neuroscience* Vol. 12, New York: Wiley-Liss.

Fischbacher, E. (1985) 'Mental handicap and epilepsy: are we still over treating?' in C. Wood (ed.) *Epilepsy and Mental Handicap. Royal Society of Medicine Round Table Series* No. 2, London: RSM.

Gates, J. R., Luciano, D. and Devinsky, O. (1991) 'The classification and treatment of non-epileptic events', in O. Devinsky and W. H. Theodore (eds) *Epilepsy and Behaviour, Frontiers of Clinical Neuroscience* Vol. 12, New York: Wiley-Liss.

Gillies, J. B., Espie, C. A. and Montgomery, J. M. (1989) 'The social and behavioural functioning of people with mental handicaps attending adult training centres: a comparison with those with and without epilepsy', *Mental Handicap Research* 2: 129–36.

Grant, S. M. and Heel, R. C. (1991) 'Vigabatrin: a review of its pharmacodynamic and pharmacokinetic properties, and therapeutic potential in epilepsy and disorders of motor control', *Drugs* 41: 889–926.

Green, C. W., Gardner, S. M., Canipe, V. S. and Reid, D. H. (1994) 'Analyzing alertness among people with profound multiple disabilities: implications for provision of training', *Journal of Applied Behavior Analysis* 27: 519–31.

Greig, E. and Betts, T. (1992) 'Epileptic seizures induced by sexual abuse. Pathogenic and pathoplastic factors', *Seizure* 1: 269–74.

Guess, D., Siegel-Causey, E., Roberts, S., Rues, J., Thompson, B. and Siegel-Causey, D. (1990) 'Assessment and analysis of behavior state and related variables among students with profoundly handicapping conditions', *Journal of the Association for Persons with Severe Handicaps* 15: 211–30.

Hermann, B. P. and Connell, B. E. (1992) 'Neuropsychological assessment in the diagnosis of non-epileptic seizures', in T. L. Bennett (ed.) *The Neuropsychology of Epilepsy*, New York: Plenum Press.

Hoare, P. (1984) 'The development of psychiatric disorder among school children with epilepsy', *Developmental Medicine and Child Neurology* 26: 3–13.

Hogg, J. (1992) 'The administration of psychotropic and anti-convulsant drugs to children with profound intellectual disability and multiple impairments', *Journal of Intellectual Disability Research* 36: 473–88.

Iwata, B. A., Vollmer, T. R. and Zarcone, J. R. (1990) 'The experimental (functional) analysis of behaviour disorders; methodology, applications and limitations', in A. C. Repp and N. N. Singh (eds) *Perspectives on the Use of Nonaversive and Aversive Interventions for Persons with Developmental Disabilities*, Sycamore IL: Sycamore Publishing Company.

Jarvie, S. (1994) 'Self-perception and psychosocial functioning in people with intractable epilepsy', unpublished Ph.D thesis, University of Glasgow.

Jarvie, S., Espie, C. A. and Brodie, M. J. (1993a) 'The development of a questionnaire to assess knowledge of epilepsy. 1: General knowledge of epilepsy', *Seizure* 2: 179–85.

—— (1993b) 'The development of a questionnaire to assess knowledge of epilepsy. 2: Knowledge of own condition', *Seizure* 2: 187–93.

Kasteleijn-Nolst Trenité, D. G. A. (1989) 'Photosensitivity in epilepsy: electrophysiological and clinical correlates', *Acta Neurologica Scandinavica* 80 (Suppl. 125): 1–149.

Lai, C. W. and Ziegler, D. K. (1983) 'Repeated self-induced syncope and subsequent seizures', *Archives of Neurology* 40: 820–3.

Leuba, C. (1955) 'Toward some integration of learning theories: the concept of optimal stimulation', *Psychological Reports* 1: 27–33.

Lund, J. (1985) 'Epilepsy and psychiatric disorder in the mentally retarded adult', *Acta Psychiatrica Scandinavica* 72: 557–62.

Mansell, J. L. (1993) *Services for People with Learning Disabilities and Challenging Behaviour or Mental Health Needs*, London: HMSO.

Merrill, E. C. (1990) 'Attentional resource allocation and mental retardation', *International Review of Research in Mental Retardation* 16: 51–88.

Montgomery, J. M. and Espie, C. A. (1986) 'Behavioural management of hysterical pseudoseizures', *Behavioural Psychotherapy* 14: 334–40.

Novaco, R. W. (1975) *Anger Control: The Development and Evaluation of an Experimental Treatment*, Lexington MA: Lexington Books.

Oliver, C. (1991) 'The application of analogue methodology to the functional analysis of challenging behaviour', in B. Remington (ed.) *The Challenge of Severe Mental Handicap: A Behaviour Analytic Approach*, Chichester: Wiley.

Owens, R. G. and Ashcroft, J. E. (1982) 'Functional analysis in applied psychology', *British Journal of Clinical Psychology* 21: 181–9.

Palm, L., Anderson, H., Elmqvist, D. and Blennow, G. (1992) 'Daytime sleep tendency before and after discontinuation of anti-epileptic drugs in preadolescent children with epilepsy', *Epilepsia* 33: 687–91.

Paul, A. (1996) *Epilepsy and You*, Brighton: Pavilion Publishing.

—— (1997) 'Epilepsy or stereotypy? Diagnostic issues in learning disabilities', *Seizure* 6 (in press).

Porter, R. J. (1991) 'Diagnosis of psychogenic and other non-epileptic seizures in adults', in O. Devinsky and W. H. Theodore (eds) *Epilepsy and Behaviour: Frontiers of Clinical Neuroscience* Vol. 12, New York: Wiley-Liss.

Repp, A. C. and Barton, L. E. (1980) 'Naturalistic observations of institutionalized retarded persons: a comparison of licensure decisions and behavioral observations', *Journal of Applied Behavior Analysis* 13: 333–41.

Repp, A. C. and Felce, D. (1990) 'A microcomputer system used for evaluative and experimental behavioural research in mental handicap', *Mental Handicap Research* 3: 31–2.

Reynolds, E. H. and Shorvon, S. D. (1981) 'Monotherapy or polytherapy for epilepsy?', *Epilepsia* 22: 1–10.

Rodin, E. A. (1968) *The Prognosis of Patients with Epilepsy*, Springfield IL: Charles C. Thomas.

Sass, K. J., Spencer, S. S., Westerveld, M. and Spencer, D. D. (1992) 'The neuropsychology of corpus callosotomy for epilepsy' in T. L. Bennett (ed.) *The Neuropsychology of Epilepsy*, New York: Plenum.

Singh, B. K. and Towle, P. O. (1993) 'Anti-epileptic drug status in adult outpatients with mental retardation', *American Journal on Mental Retardation* 98: S41–6.

Stephenson, J. (1990) 'Fits and faints', *Clinics in Developmental Medicine* No. 109, Oxford: MacKeith Press.

Turmel, A., Giard, N., Bouvier, G., Labrecque, R., Veilleux, F., Rouleau, I. and Saint-Hilaire, J. N. (1992) 'Frontal lobe seizures and epilepsy: indications for cortectomies or callosotomies', in P. Chauvel, A. V. Delgado-Escueta, E. Halgren and J. Bancaud (eds) *Frontal Lobe Seizures and Epilepsies, Advances in Neurology* Vol. 57, New York: Raven Press.

Welsh Health Planning Forum (1992) *Protocol for Investment in Health Gain: Mental Handicap (Learning Disabilities)*, Welsh Office: NHS Directorate.

Chapter 12

The way forward

Laura H. Goldstein and Christine Cull

The aforegoing chapters of this volume have laid out for the reader the current state of knowledge and practice of psychological matters that relate to epilepsy. It will be patently clear, however, that there is scope for enormous development in terms of the research and clinical practice that could be undertaken by clinical psychologists. This is essential in order for practitioners to be able to work from a sound evidence base.

The purpose of this final chapter, therefore, is to look at the role that psychologists can play in furthering our understanding of epilepsy and its sequelae by highlighting gaps in our present level of knowledge. Much of this will have been alluded to in the previous chapters and our task here is to pull that information together, as well as to add some thoughts of our own.

Neuropsychology

As will have been seen from Chapters 2, 3 and 4 (with respect to adults) and Chapter 9 (regarding children), much work has been undertaken to document the neuropsychological sequelae of epilepsy and how these might relate to outcome following neurosurgery. As will also have been apparent, however, it has been difficult to describe an entirely consistent pattern of cognitive deficits in patients with epilepsy who have not received, or who have not been candidates for, surgical treatment for their seizures. Whether this is the result of inconsistent criteria for subject or test selection, or is inherent in the disorder itself, is not clear; certainly there is a need for clinical psychologists working in the field to continue the painstaking process of neuropsychological test development, with rigorous test standardisation and validation (e.g. Baxendale and Thompson 1996; Walton *et al.* 1996). This is in order for the process of corroborating cognitive profiles with the results of neuroimaging and neurophysiological test data to be most beneficial for the patient, and to permit accurate descriptions of cognitive strengths and weaknesses to be made. More work is needed to compare the sensitivity of existing tests to detect neuropsychological deficits in patients along the lines of that undertaken by Randolf *et al.* (1994). Such work needs to be done equally in the field of computerised assessments as in the field of standardised pen and paper tests.

An increasing amount of neuropsychological work has involved the correlation of neuropsychological test performance with volumetric measures of temporal lobe structures using Magnetic Resonance Imaging (MRI). Some of this work has been discussed in passing in Chapters 2 and 4. Since the practice of neuropsychology is increasingly less diagnostic and increasingly more descriptive and corroborative, the scope for clinical psychologists working in the field of epilepsy to become involved in neuroimaging work is growing. Thus, for example, Kirkpatrick *et al.* (1993) have used a combination of verbal recognition memory testing and single photon emission computerised tomography (SPECT) to determine the locus of mediation of verbal recognition memory, in patients being worked-up for epilepsy surgery. This study served to demonstrate the difficulty in trying to make a simple localisation of cognitive function in people with epilepsy and demonstrates the value of having clinical psychologists involved in the design and interpretation of neuroimaging studies. With the development of functional MRI, the need for well-designed cognitive paradigms has become even more important, especially given the potential for repeated testing of patients with this technique, in contrast to the restrictions imposed when using scanning procedures involving radiation such as SPECT and Positron Emission Tomography. Thus, imaging during the performance of a neuropsychological test could be undertaken pre- and post-epilepsy surgery, providing the opportunity to monitor the effects of surgery on the mediation of cognitive function. The value of other types of neuroimaging techniques such as Magnetic Resonance Spectroscopy has already been demonstrated in providing an understanding of unexpected patterns of cognitive abilities following surgery (Incisa della Rochetta *et al.* 1995).

The neuropsychological investigation of children is a relatively recent development; however, there is a great need for refined assessment measures to enable us to fully understand the neuropsychological profiles of children with epilepsy. This also applies to those (adults and children) with learning disabilities and epilepsy. Clearly, this is not just an issue for clinical psychologists working in epilepsy but for those working in learning disabilities, since few of the assessment measures usually used to assess patients with epilepsy have norms that are appropriate for people with learning disabilities. It may be that the clinical psychologist with an interest in epilepsy has much to offer to the development of such measures.

Thompson (see Chapter 3), has outlined some approaches to cognitive rehabilitation; these are largely concerned with memory training procedures and, like Aldenkamp and Vermeulen (1991), Thompson has begun to discuss their use for people with epilepsy. Whilst this is a valuable contribution, strategies also need to be developed to help people with epilepsy to overcome significant cognitive impairments other than memory, for example language (see Chapter 2) or executive functions. In view of the possible existence of deficits in executive functioning in patients (see Chapters 2 and 4 in particular), which may be manifested for example in planning and reasoning deficits and also in response disinhibition, it will also be important for clinical psychologists to assess the applicability to patients with focal epilepsy of behavioural management techniques (e.g. von Cramon *et al.* 1991; von Cramon and Matthes-von Cramon 1994; Alderman 1996) which have recently been developed in other fields of neuropsychological rehabilitation. This may be especially relevant in view of the potentially negative cognitive–behavioural consequences of frontal lobe epilepsy surgery (e.g. Goldstein *et al.* 1993). The interaction between treatment designs and epilepsy variables (e.g. seizure type, frequency, age at onset) needs to be defined, as does the potential contribution, positive or negative, posed by anti-epileptic medication. The interaction between one particular anti-epileptic drug, carbamazepine, and behaviour modification techniques has been discussed in the field of head injury (e.g. Wood and Eames 1981). The importance of rehabilitative programmes in children has been alluded to in Chapter 9, but this is an area that has yet to be developed.

If it is possible to identify prospectively those individuals (children or adults) who are likely to experience difficulties in cognitive functions, it may be feasible to establish early intervention programmes that would aim to help individuals develop appropriate strategies and hopefully modify the sequelae of any serious cognitive dysfunction.

Psychological interventions – for patients with epilepsy and associated psychological disturbance and/or to reduce seizure frequency

People with epilepsy are at risk from developing any one of a variety of psychological problems. However, what has yet to be determined are the vulnerability factors that make it more likely that an individual will develop particular problems.

Despite the range of psychological problems that may accompany a diagnosis of epilepsy (see Chapter 6), the range of studies that have considered the value of psychological interventions in alleviating such disorders is remarkably small. Indeed, most accounts of psychological interventions are with single patients (adults and children), are largely psychodynamic in treatment orientation (e.g. Ragan and Seides 1990; Mathers 1992; Miller 1994) or have used counselling approaches (e.g. Usiskin 1993), and have little if any formal evaluation to indicate the rigour of treatment success. However, some attempt has been made to evaluate the effect of educational or self-help epilepsy groups on psychological disorders and psychosocial status (Helgeson *et al.* 1990; Becu *et al.* 1993). There is also some evidence that, as a spin-off of psychological interventions designed to reduce seizure frequency, patients' psychological state may improve (e.g. Rousseau *et al.* 1985; Tan and Bruni 1986; Gillham 1990). The lack of literature dealing with the treatment of seizure-related phobias and anxieties remains of concern, and is a clear area of potential work for clinical psychologists working with patients with epilepsy. It will be important to identify those factors that hinder or facilitate the use of psychological treatment programmes for each individual. For example, what impact would frequent seizures have? Would it matter what the seizure type was? Would the type of AED be of relevance (particularly in view of some of the reported well-being enhancing effects of the newer drugs, see Chapter 5)? Equally, if it is possible to identify those individuals who are most at risk of developing psychological problems, there is scope for developing early intervention programmes which aim to help people with recently diagnosed epilepsy to cope with the disorder, and hopefully avoid the development of more serious psychological disorders. A further area to be developed is the facilitation of adjustment to life without epilepsy for patients whose previously intractable seizures have relatively suddenly become well controlled through neurosurgical or pharmacological means.

In Chapter 7, we have illustrated the range of studies that have been undertaken to demonstrate the effectiveness of psychological interventions in reducing seizure frequency. Many questions remain untackled, most notably the identification of particular patient subgroups most likely to benefit from psychological interventions for seizure control. Although literature exists on issues of self-control in patients with epilepsy, there is only now some attempt being made to identify any personal characteristics that might single out those patients with epilepsy who believe they can control their seizures from those who do not (Spector-Oron *et al.* 1993). DiIorio *et al.* (1994) have considered the role of self-esteem, self-efficacy, social support and regimen-specific support in epilepsy self-management, and Gehlert (1994) has looked at the relationship between attributional style and seizure control; Tan and Bruni (1986) suggested that individuals predisposed to self-control approaches in their everyday lives might respond to a cognitive–behavioural treatment approach geared towards encouraging self-control of seizures, but as yet no study has set out to determine which personal characteristics offer good prognosis for response to cognitive–behavioural interventions to reduce seizures. Even Andrews and Schonfeld (1992), reviewing patients' progress in their self-control-of-seizures treatment approach, only investigated seizure variables as predictors of success in the programme; despite their findings (see Chapter 7), they indicated that seizure-related predictors were only weak. Thus, by conducting well-designed treatment trials that include, as independent variables, psychological characteristics of patients as well as seizure variables, clinical psychologists could contribute enormously to this area of research and lead to the development of evidence-based treatments which could be targeted at particular individuals. Important here, too, is the need for clear demonstration of which psychological seizure-reduction techniques can be applied to children and to people with learning disabilities; many of the published studies referred to in Chapter 7 have included individuals with learning difficulties, but it would be helpful ultimately for there to be guidelines as to which treatment approaches might optimally be used with children or with people with learning disabilities.

Within the area of psychological treatment of seizures also, clinical psychologists have an important educational role to play, not only in terms of the potential benefit of such treatments, but also in highlighting other factors in the patients' ongoing care that may jeopardise the success of such interventions. Clearly, the use of self-control strategies by patients requires them to take responsibility for actions related to seizure management, over and above remembering to take their anti-epileptic drugs, and places on them the onus for change. Families, too, need to be receptive and readily able to support the individual in their endeavours and share the same attributional framework for the genesis of seizures (e.g. Reiter *et al.* 1987). In addition, if, while engaging in a psychological treatment approach, the patient is simultaneously being investigated for their suitability for epilepsy surgery, they may well see the locus for seizure control as residing primarily in the neurosurgeon. These 'mixed messages' to the patient (i.e. that they are on the one hand considered to be able to gain control of seizures, whereas on the other hand the implication of surgery is that they are unable to control their seizures) may make it less likely that the person will feel motivated to change their behaviour with respect to their seizures, unless they are not in favour of having neurosurgery. The clinical psychologist working in an epilepsy service is in an ideal position to identify these possible treatment conflicts and help streamline patient care so that treatment approaches can be attempted in a more scientific and rational manner.

Anti-epileptic drugs (AEDs)

It is clear that the evaluation of anti-epileptic drug effects on cognition and behaviour will continue, but the way in which the issue is addressed would benefit from some considerable refinement. Studies need to be more specific about the particular population they are involving with respect to age, ability level, seizure type, epilepsy syndrome, etc. As far as contributing to the debate about which drug is best to use and least likely to impair cognition/behaviour, this sort of information will only come from studies comparing one drug with another.

Perhaps, more importantly, clinical psychologists need to be able to make an informed opinion about the impact of an AED on the individual, as well as the effect of changes in medication regimens.

Quality of life (QoL)

We can anticipate that studies relating to QoL will burgeon in the coming years. Issues that we would like to see addressed would include the relationship between psychological disorder and QoL in people with epilepsy, the relationship between different types of service provision and QoL, and some investigation of the factors that are important to the QoL in people who have learning disabilities and epilepsy – not to mention children, who so far have not featured in any of the QoL studies reviewed by Kendrick (Chapter 8). The relationship between a successful outcome of psychological intervention and quality of life for the individuals concerned would be an interesting study. It is hoped that the QoL of life work will also be used to inform new service developments for people with epilepsy.

Behaviour problems in children

The intervention approaches outlined in Chapter 10 have yet to be evaluated in this clinical group. In many respects, it is essential that intervention/management programmes are developed and evaluated in order to enhance further our understanding of the nature of such problems in epilepsy.

The literature exploring the risk factors for the development of behaviour problems in children with epilepsy has highlighted possible approaches to intervention; these now need to be put to the test in order to determine both the appropriateness of the model and the efficacy of the treatment. As yet, we are not in a position to identify those children who are most likely to develop behaviour problems, but even without this knowledge, there is scope for developing early intervention programmes by looking, for example, at parental management.

Learning disabilities

We can only emphasise again how sadly neglected the area of learning disabilities has been in the epilepsy literature as a whole. As has been described in Chapter 11, we know very little about the impact of epilepsy in people with learning disabilities, or the significance of this to their carers. Is the concept of stigma applicable here? As yet, it is unclear whether there is a greater prevalence of behaviour problems in people with epilepsy and learning disabilities than in their counterparts without epilepsy. While Espie *et al.* (1989) suggest that there is, this is refuted by Deb and Hunter (1991) and in our own work in children (Jones and Cull 1993).

Indeed, in the latter two studies, adaptive behaviours were poorer in people with epilepsy, but there was no difference in respect of behaviour problems. This work needs to be expanded, as it may well be that there are differences between people with mild, and those with severe, learning disabilities in this respect.

At the time of writing, a growing interest in the needs of people with learning disabilities and epilepsy is very much in evidence and has been highlighted by Brown *et al.* (1993). It is hoped that this will have a major impact on both research opportunities and clinical practice.

Family issues

It is evident to the clinician that a diagnosis of epilepsy does not solely effect the individual concerned, but can have a major impact on their family, as has been described for children (West 1986) and for the families of adults with epilepsy (Thompson and Upton 1992). However, these effects have been the subject of very little systematic research interest, and the work that has been done has focused predominantly on children with epilepsy (see Chapter 10).

Questions that need to be addressed include how the family and/or other carers adapt to the diagnosis; whether the type of response depends on whether the diagnosis is made in childhood, or in adulthood, or whether the epilepsy is idiopathic or acquired following a brain injury; how parents, siblings and children react to the diagnosis, and how this affects their interactions with the person with epilepsy. While there is some limited information in this area, there is even less on family responses to the occurrence of non-epileptic seizures, although this is a developing field (see Moore *et al.* 1994). However, whether seizures are epileptic or non-epileptic, it is clearly important to have some understanding of families' attributions of seizure genesis and seizure control. Such information is essential for the practising clinician who may need to work in collaboration with the family when looking at the management of childhood behaviour problems, psychological approaches to seizure control, interventions for serious psychological disorders, and post-surgery adjustment. There is also a need to consider whether epilepsy presents an additional stressor in families caring for someone who also has learning disabilities, has suffered a traumatic brain injury, or has a neurodegenerative illness such as Alzheimer's Disease.

CONCLUSIONS

We hope that we have demonstrated how significant the contribution of clinical psychologists has been to date, and will be in the future, in furthering our understanding of the nature of epilepsy. In view of this, they need to be considered as essential members of any epilepsy service. In order to further develop the role of the clinical psychologist in this area, psychologists need to be undertaking relevant clinical work, but within the framework of formal research protocols based on sound experimental design, with a view to publishing findings in order to better inform subsequent clinical practice.

REFERENCES

Aldenkamp, A. P. and Vermeulen, J. (1991) 'Neuropsychological rehabilitation of memory function in epilepsy', *Neuropsychological Rehabilitation* 1: 199–214.

Alderman, N. (1996) 'Central executive deficit and response to operant conditioning methods', *Neuropsychological Rehabilitation* 6: 161–86.

Andrews, D. J. and Schonfeld, W. H. (1992) 'Predictive factors for controlling seizures using a behavioural approach', *Seizure* 1: 111–16.

Baxendale, S. and Thompson, P. (1996) 'Test of spatial memory and its clinical utility in presurgical assessment', *Epilepsia* 37 (Suppl. 4): S32.

Becu, M., Becu, N., Menzur, G. and Kochen, S. (1993) 'Self-help epilepsy groups: an evaluation of the effect on depression and schizophrenia', *Epilepsia* 34: 841–5.

Brown, S., Betts, T., Chadwick, D., Hall, B., Shorvon, S. and Wallace, S. (1993) 'An epilepsy needs document', *Seizure* 2: 91–103.

Deb, S. and Hunter, D. (1991) 'Psychopathology of people with mental handicap and epilepsy. I: Maladaptive behaviour', *British Journal of Psychiatry* 159: 822–6.

DiIorio, D., Faherty, B. and Manteuffel, B. (1994) 'Epilepsy self-management: partial replication and extension', *Research in Nursing and Health* 17: 167–74.

Espie, C. A., Pashley, A. S., Bonham, K. G., Sourindhrin, I. and O'Donavan, M. (1989) 'The mentally handicapped person with epilepsy: a comparative study investigating psychosocial functioning', *Journal of Mental Deficiency Research* 33: 123–35.

Gehlert, S. (1994) 'Perceptions of control in adults with epilepsy', *Epilepsia* 31: 81–8.

Gillham, R. (1990) 'Refractory epilepsy: an evaluation of psychological methods in out-patient management', *Epilepsia* 31: 427–32.

Goldstein, L. H., Bernard, S., Fenwick, P. B. C., Burgess, P. W. and McNeil, J. (1993) 'Unilateral frontal lobectomy can product strategy application disorder', *Journal of Neurology, Neurosurgery and Psychiatry* 56: 274–6.

Helgeson, D. C., Mitan, R., Tan, S-Y. and Chayasirisobhon, S. (1990) 'Sepulveda epilepsy education: the efficacy of a psychoeducational treatment program in treating medical and psychosocial aspects of epilepsy', *Epilepsia* 31: 75–82.

Incisa della Rochetta, A., Gadian, D. G., Connelly, A., Polkey, C. E., Jackson, G. D., Watkins, K. E., Johnson, C. L., Mishkin, M. and Vargha-Khadem, F. (1995) 'Verbal memory impairment after right temporal lobe surgery: role of contralateral damage as revealed by 1H magnetic resonance spectroscopy and T2 relaxometry', *Neurology* 45: 797–802.

Jones, S. and Cull, C. A. (1993) 'Behavior in children with a severe learning difficulty and epilepsy', *Epilepsia* 34 (Suppl. 2): S22.

Kirkpatrick, P. J., Morris, R., Syed, G. M. S. and Polkey, C. E. (1993) 'Cortical activation during a cognitive challenge in patients with chronic temporal lobe epilepsy – a dynamic SPECT study', *Behavioural Neurology* 6: 187–92.

Mathers, C. B. (1992) 'Group therapy in the management of epilepsy', *British Journal of Medical Psychology* 65: 279–87.

Miller, L. (1994) 'Psychotherapy of epilepsy: seizure control and psychosocial adjustment', *Journal of Cognitive Rehabilitation* 12: 14–30.

Moore, P. M., Baker, G. A., McDade, G., Chadwick, D. and Brown, S. W. (1994) 'Epilepsy, pseudoseizures and perceived family characteristics: a controlled study', *Epilepsy Research* 18: 75–83.

Ragan, C. and Seides, M. (1990) 'The synthetic use of movement and verbal psychoanalytic psychotherapies', *Journal of the American Academy of Psychoanalysis* (Special issue: 'Psychoanalysis and severe emotional illness') 18: 115–30.

Randolf, C., Golds, J. M., Zorora, E., Cullum, C. M., Hermann, B. P. and Wyler, A. (1994) 'Estimating memory function disparity of Wechsler Memory Scale–Revised and California Verbal Learning Test indices in clinical and normal samples', *Clinical Neuropsychologist* 8: 99–108.

Reiter, J., Andrews, D. and Janis, C. (1987) *Taking Control of Your Epilepsy. A Workbook for Patients and Professionals*, Santa Rosa: Basics Publishing Company.

Rousseau, A., Hermann, B. and Whitman, S. (1985) 'Effects of progressive relaxation on epilepsy: analysis of a series of cases', *Psychological Reports* 57: 1203–12.

Spector-Oron, S., Goldstein, L. H. and Cull, C. A. (1993) 'Self-control of seizures in adults with epilepsy', *Epilepsia* 34 (Suppl. 2): S79.

Tan, S-Y. and Bruni, J. (1986) 'Cognitive-behaviour therapy with adult patients with epilepsy: a controlled outcome study', *Epilepsia* 27: 255–63.

Thompson, P. J. and Upton, D. (1992) 'The impact of chronic epilepsy on the family', *Seizure* 1: 43–8.

Usiskin, S. (1993) 'The role of counselling in an out-patient epilepsy clinic: a three year study', *Seizure* 2: 111–14.

von Cramon, D. Y. and Matthes-von Cramon, G. (1994) 'Back to work with a chronic dysexecutive syndrome? (A case report)', *Neuropsychological Rehabilitation* 4: 399–417.

von Cramon, D. Y., Matthes-von Cramon, G. and Mai, N. (1991) 'Problem-solving deficits in brain injured persons; a therapeutic approach', *Neuropsychological Rehabilitation* 1: 45–64.

Walton, N. H., Goodman, C. S., Bird, J. M., Sandeman, D. R., Butler, S. R. and Curry, S. H. (1996) 'The Burden maze as a measure of nonverbal memory in epilepsy', *Epilepsia* 37 (Suppl. 4): S30.

West, P. (1986) 'The social meaning of epilepsy: stigma as a potential explanation for psychopathology in children', in S. Whitman and B. P. Hermann (eds), *Psychopathology in Epilepsy: Social Dimensions*, New York: Oxford University Press.

Wood R. Ll. and Eames, P. (1981) 'Applications of behaviour modification in the rehabilitation of traumatically brain-injured patients', in G. Davey (ed.) *Applications of Conditioning Theory*, London: Methuen.

Appendix

NEUROPSYCHOLOGICAL, COGNITIVE AND DEVELOPMENTAL TESTS

The tests listed below were referred to in Chapters 2, 3, 4, 5 and 9. The purpose of this appendix is to provide ease of access to these tests; dates of publication are given where indicated in publishers' catalogues, etc. The tests are listed in alphabetical order of test names, rather than authors.

'The Abilities of Young Children', (Griffiths, R. 1986) High Wycombe: Test Agency Limited.

'Adult Memory and Information Processing Battery (AMIPB)', (Coughlan, A. J. and Hollows, S. 1985), Leeds: St James' University Hospital, A. J. Coughlan.

'Autobiographical Memory Interview (AMI)', (Kopelman, M. D., Wilson, B. A. and Baddeley, A. D. 1990) Bury St Edmunds, Suffolk: Thames Valley Test Company.

'Bayley Scales II', (Bayley, N. 1993) Sidcup: Psychological Corporation.

'Behavioural Assessment of Dysexecutive Syndrome (BADS)', (Wilson, B. A., Alderman, N., Burgess, P., Emslie, H. and Evans, J. J. 1996) Bury St Edmunds, Suffolk: Thames Valley Test Company.

'Bender Visual Motor Gestalt Test', (Bender, E. 1946) Sidcup: Psychological Corporation.

'Benton Visual Retention Test, 5th edn', (Benton-Sivan, A. 1992) Sidcup: Psychological Corporation.

'Boston Naming Test, 2nd edn', (Kaplan, E. F., Goodglass, H. and Weintraub, S. 1983) Philadelphia: Lea and Febiger.

'British Ability Scales', (Elliot, C. D., Murray, D. J. and Pearson, L. S. 1983) Windsor UK: NFER-Nelson.

'British Picture Vocabulary Scale', (Dunn L. M., Dunn, L. M., Whetton C. with Pintilie D. 1983) Windsor UK: NFER-Nelson.

'California Verbal Learning Test for Children', (Delis, D. C., Kramer, J., Kaplan, E. and Ober, B. A. 1993) Sidcup: Psychological Corporation.

'California Verbal Learning Test (CVLT) Research Edition', (Delis, D. C.,

Kramer, J., Kaplan, E., Ober, B. A. and Fridlund, A. 1986) Sidcup: Psychological Corporation.

'Children's Category Test (CTT)', (Boll T. 1993) Sidcup: Psychological Corporation.

'Clinical Evaluation of Language Fundamentals' (revised edn, UK adaptation, CELF-R^{UK}), (Wiig, E. H. 1994) Sidcup: Psychological Corporation.

'Controlled Oral Word Association Test', (Benton, A. L. and Hamsher, K. deS. 1989) in Multilingual Aphasia Examination, Iowa City IA: AJA Associates.

'Diagnostic and Attainment Testing' (including 'Graded Word Vocabulary Test' and 'Graded Word Spelling Test'), (Schonell, F. J. and Schonell, F. E. 1956) Edinburgh: Oliver and Boyd Limited.

'Doors and People Test', (Baddeley, A. D., Emslie, H. and Nimmo-Smith, I. 1994) Bury St Edmunds, Suffolk: Thames Valley Test Company.

'Draw-a-Person. A Quantitative Scoring System', (Naglieri, J. A. 1987) Sidcup: Psychological Corporation.

'FePSY The Iron Psyche' v.5.0A, (Alpherts W. C. J. and Aldenkamp A. P. 1995) Instituut voor Epilepsiebestrijding, Achterweg 5, 2103 SW Heemstede, Netherlands.

'Graded Naming Test', (McKenna, P. and Warrington, E. K. 1983) Windsor UK: NFER-Nelson.

'Halstead-Reitan Neuropsychological Test Battery: Theory and Clinical Interpretation', (Reitan, R. M. and Wolfson, D. 1993) Tucson AZ: Neuropsychological Press.

'Leiter International Performance Scale', (Leiter, R. G. 1969) Florida: Psychological Assessment Resources.

'Luria-Nebraska Neuropsychological Battery', (Golden, C. J., Hammeke, T. A. and Purish, A. D. 1983) USA: Western Psychological Services.

'Multilingual Aphasia Examination', (Benton, A. L. and Hamsher, K. deS. 1989) Iowa City: AJA Associates.

'National Adult Reading Test' 2nd edn, (Nelson, H. with Willison, J. 1991) Windsor UK: NFER-Nelson.

'Oldfield-Wingfield Naming Test', (Oldfield, R. C. and Wingfield, A. 1965) MRC Psycholinguistical Research Unit Special Report No PLU/65/19: London: Medical Research Council.

'Pre-Verbal Communication Schedule (PVCS)', (Kiernan, C. and Reid, B. 1987) Windsor UK: NFER-Nelson.

'Recognition Memory Test', (Warrington, E. K. 1984) Windsor UK: NFER-Nelson.

'Revised Token Test', (McNeil, M. M. and Prescott, T. E. 1978) Windsor UK: NFER-Nelson.

'Rey Auditory Verbal Learning Test', in 'Neuropsychological Assessment' 3rd edn, (Lezak, M. D. 1995) New York: Oxford University Press.

'Rey Complex Figure Test and Recognition Trial (RCFT)', (Meyers, J. E. and Meyers, K. R.) Florida: Psychological Assessment Resources.

'Rivermead Behavioural Memory Test', (Wilson, B. A., Coburn, J. and Baddeley, A. D. 1995) Bury St Edmunds, Suffolk: Thames Valley Test Company.

'Rivermead Behavioural Memory Test for Children Aged 5–10', (Wilson, B. A.,

Ivani-Chalian, R. and Aldrich, F. 1991) Bury St Edmunds, Suffolk: Thames Valley Test Company.

'Speed and Capacity of Language Processing (SCOLP)', (Baddeley, A. D., Emslie, H. and Nimmo-Smith, I. 1992) Bury St Edmunds, Suffolk: Thames Valley Test Company.

'Standford-Binet Intelligence Scale – Manual (Form L-M)', (Terman, L. M. and Merrill, M. A. 1972) Trowbridge: Redwood Press Limited.

'Stroop Colour and Word Test', (Golden, C.) Florida: Psychological Assessment Resources.

'Stroop Neuropsychological Screening Test', (Trenerry, M. R., Crosson, B., DeBoe, J. and Leber, W. R. 1989) Windsor UK: NFER-Nelson.

'Symbolic Play Test' 2nd edn, (Lowe, M. and Costello, A. J. 1988) Windsor UK: NFER-Nelson.

'Test of Everyday Attention (TEA)', (Robertson, I. H., Ward, T., Ridgeway, V. and Nimmo-Smith, I. 1994) Bury St Edmunds, Suffolk: Thames Valley Test Company.

'Test for Reception of Grammar (TROG)' 2nd edn, (Bishop, D. 1989) Manchester: Age and Cognitive Performance Research Centre, University of Manchester M13 9PL, UK.

'Token Test for Children', (Disimoni, F. 1978) Allen TX: DLM Teaching Resources.

'Visual Object and Space Perception Battery (VOSP)', (Warrington, E. K. and James, M. 1991) Bury St Edmunds, Suffolk: Thames Valley Test Company.

'Vineland Adaptive Behaviour Scales', (Sparrow, S. S., Balla, D. A. and Cicchetti, D. V. 1984) Minnesota: American Guidance Services.

'Wechsler Adult Intelligence Scale', revised UK edn (WAIS-R^{UK}), (Wechsler, D. 1986) Sidcup: Psychological Corporation.

'Wechsler Intelligence Scale for Children', 3rd UK edn (WISC-III^{UK}), (Wechsler, D. 1991) Sidcup: Psychological Corporation.

'Wechsler Memory Scale', revised (WMS-R), (Wechsler, D. 1987) Sidcup: Psychological Corporation.

'Wechsler Pre-School and Primary Scale of Intelligence' revised UK edn (WPPSI-R^{UK}), (Wechsler, D. 1990) Sidcup: Psychological Corporation.

'Wide Range Assessment of Memory and Learning (WRAML)', (Adams, W. and Sheslow, D.) Florida: Psychological Assessment Resources.

'Winconsin Card Sorting Test' (Grant, D. A. and Berg, E. A. 1981, 1993) Windsor UK: NFER-Nelson.

CONTRIBUTORS' ADDRESSES

Gus A. Baker
Lecturer in Clinical Neuropsychology and Health Psychology
University Department of Neurosciences
Walton Centre for Neurology and Neurosurgery
Rice Lane, Liverpool L9 1AE

Christine Cull
Clinical Psychologist, Learning Disabilities Service
Mid Anglia Community Health NHS Trust, Haverhill Health Centre
Camps Road, Haverhill, Suffolk CB9 8HF

Colin A. Espie
Professor of Clinical Psychology, Department of Psychological Medicine
Gartnavel Royal Hospital (Academic Centre)
1055 Great Western Road, Glasgow G12 0XH

Maria Fowler
Principal Psychologist, St Piers Lingfield
St Piers Lane, Lingfield, Surrey RH7 6PW

Ruth Gillham
Consultant Clinical Psychologist, Southern General Hospital
1345 Govan Road, Glasgow G51 4TF

Laura H. Goldstein
Senior Lecturer in Neuropsychology, Institute of Psychiatry
De Crespigny Park, London SE5 8AF

Anna Kendrick
Associate Lecturer, The Open University
24 Cathedral Road, Cardiff CF1 9SL

Susan Oxbury
Consultant Clinical Psychologist, Radcliffe Infirmary NHS Trust
Woodstock Road, Oxford OX2 6HE

Audrey Paul
Research Psychologist, Epilepsy Research Unit
Western Infirmary
Glasgow G11 6NT

Pamela J. Thompson
Head of Psychology Services, The National Society for Epilepsy
Chalfont St. Peter, Gerrards Cross, Bucks SL9 0RJ

Index

Adams, C.B.T. *et al* 63, 64
Adult Memory Information Processing Battery 28, 37, 45, 46
agression 100–1
Aldenkamp, A.P., *et al* 26, 85, 90, 150, 152, 156, 162; and Vermeulen, J. 44, 82, 205
Alderman, N. 205
Alpherts, W.C.J. and Aldenkamp, A.P. 29, 162
Alvarez, N. 196
Alzheimer's disease 7, 210
Aman, M.G. *et al* 83, 84
Anderson, V.E. and Hauser, W.A. 5
Andrews, D.J. and Schonfeld, W.H. 120, 207
Antebi, D. and Bird, J. 115
anti-epileptic drugs (AEDs) 13–15, 77, 177, 178, 184, 187, 205, 208; for children 153–4, 158, 171–3; comparisons 88–90; dose-serum level 173; implications for clinical practice 91–2; influence of 158; investigation of effects 77–82; and memory 40; monitoring of treatment with 196; monotherapy v. polytherapy 90, 184, 195; newer types 85–8, 196; number of 172; older types 82–5; and QoLASCA scale 139, 141; review of effects 82–90; type of 172
anxiety 98–9, 206; management of 105–6; and non-epiletic seizures 123; and seizures 115, 117, 119
Apter, A. *et al* 169, 175
Arnett, J.L. and Dodrill, C.B. 88
Arnston, P. *et al* 98
aromatherapy 118
assessment of cognitive function in children 155–62; choice of measurements 159–60; and computerised assessment 162; deterioration v. slow learning 156; and developmental delay 157, 161–2; general ability 159–60; and impact of seizures 157–9; and influence of drugs 158; issues in 156–7; and language skills/development 160–1; and memory 161; and motivation and test behaviours 158–9; and real-life measures of functioning 162; reasons for 155; and role of EEG 158; variability in repeated test administration 156; visuo-perceptual skills 161
Atkinson, L. 28
Auras 9, 117, 125
Austin, J.K. *et al* 167, 168, 169, 172, 173, 175, 177, 180
autism 190
Autobiographical Memory Interview (AMI) 41–2, 47

Baddeley, A.D. *et al* 36, 45, 48
Bagley, C. 174
Baker, G.A. *et al* 98, 99, 132, 135–6, 136, 143
Banks, G.K. and Beran, R.G. 87
Barr, W. *et al* 41

Baxendale, S.A. 60; and Thompson, P. 203
Bayley Development Scales 69
Beardsworth, E.D., and Adams, C.B.T. 65; and Bishop, D. 69
Becu, M. *et al* 206
behaviour: challenging 190, 194; differentiating seizures from other behaviours 189–90; and drugs 154; effect of LTG on 88; effect of VGB on 86–7; and link with seizures 113; problems of 96–109; and psychological well-being 185–6; *see also* cognitive-behavioural therapy
behaviour in children 167–8, 209, 210; assessment and treatment (clinical considerations) 176–80; future developments 180; multi-aetiological approach 175; neurobiological factors 168–71; pharmacological factors 171–3; psychosocial factors 173–5
behaviour state analysis 187–8
behavioural analysis 177–9, 192–3; Code Description 193; and learning disabilities 192–3
Behavioural Assessment of Dysexecutive Syndrome 29
Bender Visual Motor Gestalt Test 161
Bennett-Levy, J. *et al* 29, 43
Benton Visual Retention Test 21, 61, 68, 161
Benzodiazepines 85
Berent, S. *et al* 19
Berg, I. *et al* 172
Bergin, P.S. *et al* 39, 42
Bergner, M. *et al* 135, 143
Berkson, G. and Davenport, R.K. 190
Besag, F.M.C. 156, 167, 168, 170, 172, 174, 176; *et al* 158
Betts, T.A. 98, 99, 100, 190; and Boden, S. 11, 122, 123–4, 125; *et al* 118
Bicknell, D.J. 184
Binnie, C.D. 12, 26, 27, 87, 191; *et al* 153; and Marston, D. 26
biofeedback 116, 117, 120, 121
Bittencourt, P.R.M. *et al* 86, 90
Boniface, S.J. *et al* 27
Boston Naming Test (BNT) 21, 58, 59, 67
Bouras, N. and Drummond, C. 185
Bourgeois, B.F.D. *et al* 149, 151, 152
brain imaging 13, *56*; *see also* Magnetic Resonance Imaging (MRI)
Bridgeman, P.A. *et al* 38
British Ability Scales 69, 161, 195
British Picture Vocabulary Scale 160
Broadbent, D.E. *et al* 29
Brodie, M.J. 78, 187, 196; and McKee, P.J.W. 87
Brooks, J. *et al* 88
Broughton, R.J. *et al* 35
Brouwer, O.F. *et al* 84
Brown, S.W., and Betts, T. 4, 14–15; *et al* 4, 184, 185, 191, 210; and Fenwick, P.B.C. 117, 118, 119; and Tomlinson, L.L. 135; and Vaughan, M. 24
Buschke, H. 20

Calev, A. *et al* 41
California Verbal Learning Test (CVLT) 20, 46, 68, 161
Callias, M. 179
Calman, K.C. 130
Cameron, P. 132
Campbell, A. 132; *et al* 130
Carbamazepine (CBZ) 14, 84–5, 153, 172, 205
carers, support and management 197–8
Carpenter, K.N. *et al* 70
Carr, T.H. 187
Carter, W.B. *et al* 143
Cartmill, A. and Betts, T. 122
Cascino, G. *et al* 191
Chadwick, D. 5, 8, 9
Chaplin, J.E. *et al* 131, 133
Chataway, J. *et al* 85
Chelune, G.J., and Bornstein, R.A. 19; *et al* 62
children 205; assessment of cognitive function in 155–62; behaviour in

167–80, 209, 210; cognitive function of 149–51; and drugs 89–90, 153–4, 158; and multifactorial framework of disability 151–5; neuropsychological assessment 68–9, 149, 151, 154, 155, 157, 162–3, 204; and relaxation technique 116–17; and surgery 54, 63–6
Children's Category Test 160
Choice Reaction Time test 89
Clark, A. and Fallowfield, L.J. 135
Clement, M.J. and Wallace, S.J. 167, 168, 169, 170, 172, 175–6
Clinical Evaluation of Language Fundamentals (CELF) 69
clinical psychologist 196, 207, 210; and anxiety management 105–6; and cognitive-behavioural therapy 107–8; contribution of 104–8, 176–7; and family therapy 108; and individual counselling and education 106–7; and psychological assessment 105; role of in management of people with learning disabilities 192–8
Clobazam 14, 85, 172
Clonazepam 14, 85, 172
cognition: deterioration in 24; effect of LTG on 87; effect of VGB on 86; and learning disabilities 197; and neuropathology 25; rehabilitation 205; and seizure-related variables 25–7; *see also* cognitive-behaviour therapy
Cognitive Estimates 67
Cognitive Failures Questionnaire 29
cognitive function of children 149–51; academic achievement 149–50; aetiology 151–2; areas of specific impairment 150–1; assessment of 155–62; epilepsy-related factors 152–3; factors indirectly related to epilepsy 154–5; general intellectual ability 149; treatment-related factors 153–4
cognitive-behaviour therapy (CBT) 119, 107–8, 205, 207; and altering levels of arousal 116–18; and control of seizures 119–20, 123
Cohen, C. 130
Cohen, M. 37
Collaborative Group for the Study of Epilepsy 196
Collings, J.A. 98, 102, 131, 133
Commander, M. *et al* 85, 172
Committee on Drugs 82
Computerised Tomography (CT) scans 13
Conrad, P. and Schneider, J.W. 97
Controlled Oral Word Association test 21
coping skills 119–21, 186
Corbett, J.A. 194; *et al* 152; and Trimble, M.R. 150
Corcoran, R., and Thompson, P. 29, 38, 43, 44; and Upton, D. 22, 23, 24
Corney, R.H. and Clare, W. 135
corpus callosotomy 66; for adults 66; for children 67
Corsi block tests 68, 162
Costa, P.T. Jr. *et al* 132
Coulter, D.L. 184
Cowan, L.D. *et al* 4
Craig, I. and Tallis, R. 89
Cramer, J. 137
Crawford, P. 8
Creutzfeldt-Jakob disease 7, 10
Cull, C.A. 114, 149, 151, 152, 154, 167, 168, 169, 173, 175; and Brown, S.W. 168, 177, 178; *et al* 115; and Trimble, M.R. 97, 154, 171, 172, 173
Cunningham, C.C. 179
Currie, S. *et al* 99, 101

Dahl, J. 124; *et al* 116–17, 118, 124, 125
Dam, M. 153
Davies, K.G. *et al* 58, 59
Dead or Alive Test 48
Deb, S. and Hunter, D. 209
Delaney, R.C. *et al* 38

Deonna, T. 157
Department of Health 194
depression 99–100
Derogatis, L.R. 141–2
Design Learning test 37
Devellis, R.F. *et al* 190
Devinsky, O. 82, 101, 102
DEX 29
Diener, E. 131, 132
Digit Span test 80, 83, 84, 89, 156
Digit Symbol Substitution Test 81, 83, 89
Dikmen, S. 151; *et al* 38; and Matthews, C.G. 26
Dilorio, D. *et al* 207
Dodrill, C.B. 26, 40, 80, 81, 82, 135; and Batzel, L.W. 97; *et al* 59, 70, 71, 86, 87, 132, 135; and Temkin, N.R. 83
Domizio, S. *et al* 172
Doors and People Test 28, 47
Draw-a-Person Test 160
Dreifuss, F.E. 24, 82, 154; and Henriksen, O. 9, 11–12
drugs *see* anti-epileptic drugs (AEDs)
Duncan, J.S. *et al* 83, 84, 89
Durand, V.M. and Crimmins, D. 178, 194

education 106–7; and academic achievement of children 149–50, 154–5, 156, 159, 173; *see also* learning disabilities
Edwards, N.J. and Klemmack, D.L. 131
electroencephalogram (EEG) 12, 121, 158, 170, 187, 189, 193
Ellis, A.W. *et al* 20, 21
Emerson, E. *et al* 190, 194
Engel, J. 54; and Ojemann, G.A. 55
environmental factors 177, 178
Epanutin 14
epilepsy: adjustment to 106–7; age at onset 38, 152, 168–9; areas of concern; causes of 5–8; defined 4; diagnosis, classification and behavioural analysis 132, 192–3; epidemiology of 4–5; investigations 12–13; precipitating factors 7–8; predisposing factors 5–7; prognosis 8–9; treatment 13–16; *see also* non-epileptic seizures; seizures
epilepsy plus 185, 192
Epilepsy Surgery Inventory (ESI-55) 136
Epilim 14
Epir, S. *et al* 167
Espie, C.A. *et al* 184, 186, 189, 197, 209
Ethosuximide 14
Everyday Memory Questionnaire (EMQ) 43
executive functions, and frontal lobe lesions 22–4
Executive Test of Everyday Attention 28

Fabisch, W. and Darbyshire, R. 191
Fallowfield, L. 130, 135
families 180, 210; and non-epiletic seizures 123; therapy for 108
Farwell, J.R. *et al* 150
Fenwick, P.B.C. 100, 114, 190; and Brown, S.W. 27, 113–14
FePSY 29
Ferrie, C.D. *et al* 114
Finger Tapping test 89
Finger Tip Number Writing 84
Finkler, J. *et al* 115
Fischbacher, E. 184
Fletcher, A.E. *et al* 135
Forehand, R. and McMahon, R. 179
Form Sequence Learning 19
Forster, F.M. 115; *et al* 115
Forsythe, I. *et al* 89, 153, 158
Fowler, M. *et al* 88
Freedom from Distractibility (FD) index 160
Fried, R. 117
Frisium 14
Frisk, V. and Milner, B. 59
frontal lobe (FL) lesions: excisions 64–5; and executive functions 22–4
functional analysis 178, 191, 193, 194

functional imaging 56

Gabapentin 14, 88
Gadow, K.D. 155
Gallassi, R. *et al* 82, 83, 84
Gardenal 14
Gastaut, H. 4; *et al* 96
Gates, J.R. *et al* 190, 191, 197
Gehlert, S. 104, 207
Gibbs, F.A. *et al* 96
Gillham, R.A. 118–19, 120, 206; *et al* 86, 88, 89
Gillies, J.B. *et al* 186
Giordani, B. *et al* 25
Gloor, P. *et al* 96
Goldiamond, I. 178
Goldstein, L.H. 18, 19, 20, 25, 28, 104, 115, 116, 117, 118; *et al* 26, 68, 205; and Polkey, C.E. 24, 28, 29, 44, 62
Goossens, L.A.Z. *et al* 114
Graded Naming Test 67
Grant, S.M. and Heel, R.C. 196
Green, C.W. *et al* 188
Greig, E. and Betts, T. 122, 191
Griffiths Mental Development Scales 69, 161
Grooved Pegboard test 89
Grunewald, R.A. *et al* 86–7
Guess, D. *et al* 188
Guzzetta, F. *et al* 153

Halgren, E. 36; *et al* 38, 39
Halstead-Reitan battery 26, 80, 82
Harrison, R.M. and Taylor, D.C. 132
Hartlage, L.C. and Green, J.B. 154
Harvey, I. *et al* 167
Hauser, W.A., and Annegers, J.F. 4–5; and Hesdorffer, D.C. 102
Hays, R.D. *et al* 144
Head Injury Postal Questionnaire 29
Helgeson, D.C. *et al* 105, 109, 206
Helmstaedter, C. *et al* 20, 37
hemispherectomy 65; for early static damage 65
Hermann, B.P. 43, 70, 132, 137, 152; and Connell, B.E. 197; *et al* 21–3, 25, 37, 38, 58, 59, 62, 71, 172; and Whitman, S. 96, 103, 107, 168, 175; and Wyler, A.R. 58, 59
Hills, M.D. and Baker, P.G. 102, 107
hippocampal sclerosis (HS) 58, 59, 60–1, 62, 63
Hirtz, D.G. and Nelson, K.B. 82
Hoare, P. 185; and Kerley, S. 167, 168, 169, 170, 172, 173, 176, 180; and Mann, H. 167, 168, 169, 173, 176
Hogg, J. 184
Holdsworth, L. and Whitmore, K. 150
Hollandsworth, J.G. Jr. 134
Hopkins, A. 5
Horner, M.D. *et al* 23
Hornquist, J.O. 130
Hosking, G. *et al* 87
Hospital Anxiety and Depression (HAD) Scale 28, 45, 98, 99, 135–6
Hughes, J. *et al* 125
Hunt, S.M., *et al* 135, 142–3; and McEwen, J. 142–3
Huntington's disease 7
hyperventilation 117
hysterical seizures *see* non-epileptic seizures

Illis, L.S. 105
Impact of Epilepsy Scale 136
Incisa della Rochetta, A. *et al* 6, 204
Intellectualability 24
intelligence: and children 150, 156, 159–60, 163; effect of surgery on 57–8; tests 69, 156, 159–60
International League Against Epilepsy (ILAE) 9, 11
intracarotid sodium amytal (ISA) 58, 63, 70, 71
Iwata, B.A. *et al* 178, 194

Jacoby, A. 97, 100, 102; *et al* 98, 108, 136
Jarvie, S. 197; *et al* 197
Jenner, S. 179
Jennett, B. 6
Jones, S. and Cull, C.A. 209

Jones-Gotman, M. 19, 59, 61, 64, 67, 70

Kalska, K. 38, 39
Kälviäinen, R. *et al* 26, 82
Kapur, N. 39; *et al* 48
Kasteleijn-Nolst Trenité, D.G.A. 191; *et al* 26–7
Katz, A. *et al* 62
Kaufman, A.S. 160
Kendrick, A.M. 130, 137–8, 144
Kinney, R.O. *et al* 170
Kirkpatrick, P.J. *et al* 204
Kopelman, M.D. *et al* 41
Krafft, K.M. and Poling, A.D. 115
Kristensen, O. and Alving, J. 122, 124
Krumholz, A. and Niedermeyer, E. 124

Lafora Body disease 24
Lai, C.W. and Ziegler, D.K. 191
Lamictal 14
Lamotrigine (LTG) 14, 196; behavioural effects of 88, 172; cognitive effects of 87
Lancman, M.E. *et al* 122
Landau-Kleffner syndrome 11
Landolt, H. 101
Langfitt, J.T. 135, 143
language: effect of surgery on 58–9, 63; skills/development of 160–1; tests of function 69
Lassonde, M. *et al* 67
LaVigna, G.W. and Donellan, A.M. 178
learning disabilities 207, 209–10; behaviour and psychological well-being 185–6; differentiating seizure behaviour from other behaviours 189–90; and learning potential 186–8; and neuropsychology 204–5; and non-epileptic events 190–1; and prevalence of epilepsy 184–5; and quality of life 188–9; and self-induced seizures 191–2; sequelae of epilepsy in 185–92; *see also* education
Lee, G.P. *et al* 19, 20
Lefcourt, H. 103
Leiderman, D.B. *et al* 96
Lencz, T. *et al* 60, 61
Lennox Gastaut syndrome 10, 11, 153
Leonard, I. 131, 133
Letter Cancellation Task 83
Leuba, C. 191
Levitt, M.J. *et al* 131, 132
Lewis, F.M. 132
Løyning, Y. *et al* 115
Life Fulfilment Scale 136
Lindsay, J. *et al* 71
Lishman, W.A. 5, 6–7
Liske, E. and Forster, F. 121
Lisovoski, F. *et al* 114
Litwin, R.G. and Cardena, E. 122
locus of control *see* mastery
Logical Memory 20
Loiseau, P. *et al* 19, 36, 38, 39
Long, C.G. and Moore, J.R. 154, 174
Loring, D.W. *et al* 19, 58, 63
Lothman, D.J. and Pianta, R.C. 167, 169, 173, 175, 177, 179
Ludgate, J. *et al* 90
Lund, J. 185
Luria-Nebraska Battery 161

McDade, G. and Brown, S.W. 122, 123
McDowell, I. and Newell, C. 135, 142
McGill, P. and Toogood, S. 178
McGlone, J. 29
McGuire, A.M. 138; and Trimble, M.R. 131
McKee, P.J. *et al* 88
McMillan, T.M. *et al* 25, 26, 60
McNair, D.M. *et al* 136
Madge, N. *et al* 155
Magnetic Resonance Imaging (MRI) 13, 60, 61, 62, 204; *see also* brain imaging
Mansell, J.L. 185, 190
Marston, D. *et al* 152, 153, 154, 170
mastery (locus of control) 103–4
Mathers, C.B. 206
Matkovic, Z. *et al* 60, 61

Matthews, W.S., and Barabas, G. 99, 103, 173; *et al* 103, 173
Mayeux, R. *et al* 21
Meador, K.J. 86, 90, 91, 132; *et al* 89
memory: aetiology 37; and age at onset of epilepsy and duration 38; and anti-epileptic drugs 40; assessment of 45–8; and children 150, 153, 161; complaints 35–6, 49–50; and intervention 48–9; and mood 41; prospective 42–3; questionnaires 29, 43–4, 48; rehabilitation of 44–5, 50–1; remote 41–2, 47–8; risk factors 37–41; and seizures 38–40; and surgery 41, 59–62; systems *36*; and temporal lobe lesions 18–22; tests 69; and type of epilepsy 37
Mendez, M.F. *et al* 100
Merrill, E.C. 187
Meyer, F.B. *et al* 63
Miller, L.A. 64, 206; *et al* 60
Milner, B. 64
Minuchin, S. 108
Mittan, R.J. 107; and Locke, G.E. 98
Montgomery, J.M. and Espie, C.A. 122, 123, 191
Mookherjee, H.N. 132
Moore, P.M. *et al* 123, 210
Morgan, A.M.B. and Groh, C. 151
Morris, R.G.M. *et al* 28
Morrow, G.R. *et al* 141–2
Mostofsky, D. 116; and Balaschak, B.A. 115
Multilingual Aphasia Examination (MAE) 58–9, 67, 68
Multiple Ability Self-Report Questionnaire (MASQ) 29
Mungas, D. *et al* 21
Munthe-Kaas, A.W. 174
Myoclonic Astatic Epilepsy 169
Mysoline 14

Najman, J.M. and Levine, S. 134
National Adult Reading Test 21
National Child Development Study 149
Neppe, V.M. and Tucker, G.J. 9
Neufeld, M.Y. *et al* 124
neurobiological factors and behaviour: aetiology 168; age at onset of epilepsy 168–9; EEG activity 170; other behavioural disorders 170; seizure frequency 169; seizure/behaviour relationship 170–1; seizure/epilepsy type 169
Neurontin 14
neuropsychological assessment 18, 195, 203–5; for adults 67–8; for children 68–9, 149, 151, 154, 155, 157, 162–3; cognitive deterioration 24; executive functions and frontal lobe lesions 22–4; factors influencing cognitive performance 25–7; intellectual ability 24; memory and temporal lobe lesions 18–22; practical guide to 27–9; and surgery 55, *56*, 57
Nicholas, K.K. and Pianta, R.C. 169, 175, 177
Nichols, M.E. *et al* 154
Nolte, R. and Wolff, M. 169, 172
non-epileptic seizures (NESs) 121–4, 185, 189, 190–1, 197; and anxiety 123; and cognitive-behaviour therapy 123; and families 123; and lifestyle 125–6; management of 122–3; and QoL measures 141; and sexual abuse 122; *see also* epilepsy; seizures
Nottingham Health Profile (NHP) 142–3
Novaco, R.W. 190

Okun, M.A. *et al* 131
Oldfield-Wingfield Object Naming 63, 67
O'Leary, D.S. *et al* 152
Oliver, C. 194
Olivier, A. and Awad, I.A. 64
Owens, R.G. and Ashcroft, J.E. 190
Oxbury, J.M. 69; *et al* 62, 65; and Oxbury, S.M. 58, 60, 62
Oxcarbazepine 88

Paired Associates 69
Palm, L. *et al* 187
Parent/Child Game 179
parents: and children 173–4, 179; groups 179–80
Pearlin, L. and Schooler, C. 136
Perez, M.M. and Trimble, M.R. 101
Perrine, K.R. 132, 136
Petrides, M. 64
Phelps, E.A. *et al* 66
Phenobarbitone (PHB) 14, 82, 172
Phenytoin (PHT) 14, 82–3, 153, 172
Pianta, R.C. and Lothman, D.J. 174
Piccirilli, M. *et al* 153
Pilcher, W.H. *et al* 59, 66
Polkey, C.E. and Binnie, C.D. 13, 16
Pollard, W.E. *et al* 143
Pond, D.A. and Bidwell, B.H. 101
Porter, R.J. 190
Positron Emission Tomography (PET) 13, 204
Post Traumatic Stress Disorder 122
Potter, R.B. and Coshall, J.T. 132
Powell, G.E. 116; *et al* 58
Pre-Verbal Communication Schedule 161
Primidone 14
Pritchard, P.B. *et al* 115, 118
Profile of Mood States 136
Progressive Muscular Relaxation (PMR) 116
Provinciali, L. *et al* 26
pseudoseizures *see* non-epileptic seizures
psychogenic seizures *see* non-epileptic seizures
psychological responses 96–8, 108–9; interventions 206–8; multi-component approach 118–21; prevalence of 98–104; and treatment of seizures 196–7; and understanding of seizures 113–15
psychosis 101–2
Psychosocial Adjustment to Illness Scale (PAIS) 141–2
psychosocial factors 71–2; and child-parent interaction 173–4, 179; and children 173–4; and education 154–5; and the family 173
Pulliainen, V. and Jokelainen, M. 90
Puskarich, C.A. *et al* 116, 125

Quality of Life Assessment by Construct Analysis (QoLASCA) 137–8; case studies 138–9, 140–1, 141
Quality of Life in Epilepsy (QOLIE) project 136–7
Quality of Life (QoL) 130–1, 208–9; and learning disabilities 188–9; measurement of 134–43; non-epilepsy-specific measures 141; and patient with epilepsy 131–4; use of questionnaires 133; *see also* named measurement scales

Ragan, C. and Seides, M. 206
Ramani, V. 122; and Gumnit, 123
RAND Health Survey 137
Randolf, C. *et al* 28, 204
Rantakallio, P. *et al* 167
Rasmussen's syndrome 24, 65–6
Ratti, M. *et al* 41
Rausch, R., and Babb, T.L. 60; *et al* 70
Reaction Time Task 84
Recognition Memory Test 20, 37, 45, 46
Reich, J.W. *et al* 132
Reinvang, I. *et al* 84
Reiter, J. *et al* 120, 121, 124, 125
relaxation techniques 116–18, 119; and breathing patterns 117; contingent relaxation (CR)/cue-controlled 116–17, 118; Progressive Muscular Relaxation (PMR) 116
Remote Memory 47
Repp, A.C., and Barton, L.E. 190; and Felce, D. 194
Rett Syndrome 190
Rey Auditory Verbal Learning 22, 46, 61, 68
Rey-Osterreith 19, 68

Reynolds, E.H. and Shorvon, S.D. 187
Ribbler, A. and Rausch, R. 20
Richens, A. and Perucca, E. 13–15
Ritchie, K. 174
Rivermead Behavioural Memory Test 28, 47, 161
Rivotril 14
Rix, K. 179
Robertson, M.M. *et al* 99
Rodin, E.A. 151, 184; *et al* 132, 151, 152, 156
Rosenberg, M. 136
Ross, E.M. *et al* 149
Roulet Perez, E. *et al* 170
Rourke, B.P. *et al* 152, 161
Rousseau, A. *et al* 105, 116, 206
Rugland, A.-L. *et al* 29, 162
Russell, W.R. and Whitty, C.W.M. 6
Rutter, M. *et al* 150
Ryan, R. *et al* 102

Sabers, A. 151
Sabril 14
Sagar, H.J. and Oxbury, J.M. 59, 62
Saling, M. *et al* 20, 22, 25, 60
Sander, J.W.A.S., *et al* 8; and Hart, Y.M. 87
Sass, K.J. *et al* 20, 21, 60, 61, 196
Scambler, G. 98, 102, 106, 107, 131; and Hopkins, A. 97, 98, 99, 132
Scheepers, B. *et al* 122, 123
Schonell Graded Word Reading test 67
Schonell Graded Word Spelling test 67
Scott, D.F. and Moffett, A. 85
Scoville, W. and Milner, B. 59, 63
Seidenberg, M. 154, 155; *et al* 20, 23, 25, 26, 29, 150, 151
Seizure Severity Scale 136
seizures: absence 10; approaches to psychological management of 115–21; atonic 10; and behaviour 170–1; and biofeedback 121; classification of 9–12; and cognitive impairment 25–7; complex partial 9, 125, 190; countermeasures for 118; evoked 114; focal 54, 113, 205; frequency of 115, 152–3, 169, 187; generalised 10–12, 25; impact of on children 157–9; and lifestyle 125–6; and memory loss 38–40; multi-component psychological approaches to 118–21; myoctonic 10; partial 9–10, 25; practical guide to 124–6; psychogenic, primary and secondary 113–14; psychological treatment of 196–7; psychological understanding of 113–15; psychomotor 117, 153; recording systems 124–5; refractory 116, 196; and relaxation techniques 116–18; self-induced 114, 115, 185, 191–2, 197; simple partial 9; stress-induced 115, 117; tension/anxiety-induced 115, 117; tonic-clonic 10; *see also* epilepsy
Selai, C.E. and Trimble, M.R. 141
selective amygdalohippocampectomy (SAH) 57, 59, 62
Selective Reminding Test (SRT) 20, 60, 61, 68, 89
self-esteem 102–3
Selwa, L.M. *et al* 24, 26
Serial Subtraction 83
serum drug levels 14–15
sexual abuse 122, 191
Sheth, R.D. *et al* 85, 172
Shortened Token Test 63
Shorvon, S.D. 7
Sickness Impact Profile (SIP) 135, 143
Sieblink, B.M. *et al* 27
Siegel, M. *et al* 114
Sieveking, E.H. 35
Silverstein, F.S. *et al* 172
Singh, B.K. and Towle, P.O. 184
Single Photon Emission Computerized Tomography (SPECT) 13, 204
Slater, E. and Beard, A.W. 101
Smith, D.F. *et al* 87, 88, 98, 99, 136, 144
Smith, M.L. and Milner, B. 59
Snyder, P.J. *et al* 58

Social Problems Questionnaire 135
sodium amytal tests 56, 58, 63, 70, 71
Sodium valproate (VPA) 14, 84, 172
Sofijanov, N.G. 151
Spector, S. *et al* 115, 120
Spector-Oron, S. *et al* 207
Speed and Capacity of Language processing 28
Spitzer, W.O. 130
Spreen, O. and Strauss, E. 69
Staats, S.R. and Stassen, M.A. 130
Stafiniak, P. *et al* 59
Stanford-Binet 161
Stanley, P.J. and Tillotson, A. 102
status epilepticus 11, 25, 26
Steinkamp, M.W. and Kelly, J.R. 132
Stephenson, J. 190
Sterman, M.B. 121
Stores, G. 155, 167; *et al* 89
Strauss, E. *et al* 23, 25, 26, 27
stress 115, 117
Striano, S. *et al* 114
Stroop Test 22, 67, 81, 90
Sturniolo, M.G. and Galletti, F. 173, 177, 180
Subjective Memory Questionnaire (SMQ) 29, 43
Sullivan, M.D. 99
Sunderland, A. *et al* 29, 43, 48
surgery 15–16; cerebral dominance and language function 58–9; on children 54, 63–4, 154; corpus callosotomy 66–7; frontal lobe (FL) and other extra-temporal excisions 64–5; hemispherectomy 65; and intelligence 57–8; and learning disabilities 196; and memory 41, 59–62; and neuropsychological assessment 55, 56, 57, 67–71; and post-operative assessment 70–1; and pre-operative investigations 55; and psychosocial issues 71–2; and QoLASCA scale 139, 141; and Rasmussen's syndrome 65–6; and severe amnesia 63; specific interventions 57–67; temporal lobe (TL) excisions 57, 63–4; types of 54–*5*
Sveinbjornsdottir, S. *et al* 88
Symbolic Play Test 161

Tan, S.-Y. and Bruni, J. 107, 119, 206, 207
Tapping rate 83
Taube, S.L. and Calman, N.H. 126
Taylor, J. 4
Tegretol 14
temporal lobe (TL) lesions 169, 190; excisions 57–60, 62–4; and language functions 21–2; and memory 18–21
Test for Reception of Grammar (TROG) 21, 63, 69, 160
Thompson, P.J. 29, 101, 150, 151, 162; and Corcoran, R. 35, 36; and Oxley, J. 131; and Trimble, M.R. 40, 41, 83; and Upton, D. 210
Tiagabine 88
Token Test for Children 160
Toone, B.K. 101
Topamax 14
Topiramate 14, 88
Trail Making Test 23, 67, 69, 82, 84
Transitory Cognitive Impairment (TCI) 26, 87, 153
Treiman, D.M. 11, 101; and Delgado-Escueta, C.G. 40
Trenerry, M.R. *et al* 60, 61, 62
Trimble, M.R. 102; and Thompson, P.J. 153
Turmel, A. *et al* 196

Upton, D., *et al* 41; and Thomson, P.J. 23
Urion, D.K. 167
Usiskin, S. 206
Uvebrant, P. and Bauziene, R. 87, 88

Verbal and Visual Memory Indices 19
Verbal/Performance IQ 58, 63
Verma, N.P. *et al* 89
Vickrey, B.G. 136; *et al* 132, 136
Vickrey, R.D. *et al* 71
Victor, M. and Agamamolis, D. 40
Vigabatrin (VGB) 14; behavioural

effects of 86–7, 172; cognitive effects of 86
Vineland Adaptive Behaviour Scales 162
Vining, E.P.G. 131
Visual Object and Space Perception Battery (VOSP) 67
Visual Paired Associates 19
von Cramon, D.Y., *et al* 205; and Matthes-von Cramon, G. 205

Wallaston, K.A.B.S. and De Villas, R. 103
Walton, N.H. *et al* 203
Ware, J.E. 130; and Sherbourne, C.D. 136, 137
Warrington, E.K. and Duchen, L.W. 63
Washington Psychosocial Seizure Inventory (WPSI) 135
Waxman, S.G. and Geshwind, N. 101
Webster, A. and Mawer, G.E. 124
Wechsler scales 19–21, 26, 39, 46, 63, 67–8, 80–2, 159–61, 195
Welsh Health Planning Forum 194
Wenger, N.K. *et al* 130
West, P. 97, 174, 210
West of Scotland Epilepsy Research Group 188
West syndrome 153
Whitman, S. *et al* 116
WHO 130
Wide Range Assessment of Memory and Learning (WRAML) 69
Williams, J. and Rausch, R. 70
Williamson, P.D. *et al* 19
Wisconsin Card Sorting Test (WCST) 22–3, 67, 69
Wolf, R.L. *et al* 62
Wood, R.Ll. and Eames, P. 205
Wyler, A.R. 154

Zarontin 14
Ziegler, R.G. 103, 174
Zigmond, A.S. and Snaith, R.P. 28, 45, 98, 136

SOLVING PREACHING PROBLEMS

Preaching with All Ages

Twelve ways to grow your skills and confidence

Ally Barrett

The all-age talk is a task guaranteed to give preachers sleepless nights! Very few people feel they have a gift for it, and most lack confidence. This reflective and practical guide addresses these concerns, and aims to build a sure theological understanding, develop skills and grow confidence.

978 1 78622 171 1 • £14.99

Holy Attention

Preaching in today's church

Ed. Richard Sudworth and Frances Ward

This collection from the Littlemore Group of theologians explores the role of preaching in today's Church. Experienced contributors from a wide range of backgrounds - catholic, evangelical and liberal – weave together theology, anecdote and reflection on practice as they share their passion for preaching.

Contributors include Rachel Mann, Paula Gooder, Donna Lazenby, Sr Judith SLG, Edmund Newey, Anderson Jeremiah and Joel Love.

978 1 78622 165 0 £16.99

www.canterburypress.co.uk

The Canterbury Preacher's Companion 2020

Sermons for Sundays, Holy Days, Festivals and Special Occasions
Year A

Edited by Roger Spiller

First published in 2019 by the Canterbury Press Norwich
Editorial office
3rd Floor, Invicta House
108–114 Golden Lane
London EC1Y 0TG, UK
www.canterburypress.co.uk

Canterbury Press is an imprint of Hymns Ancient & Modern Ltd
(a registered charity)

Hymns Ancient & Modern® is a registered trademark of
Hymns Ancient & Modern Ltd
13A Hellesdon Park Road, Norwich,
Norfolk NR6 5DR, UK

British Library Cataloguing in Publication data

A catalogue record for this book is available from the British Library

978 1-78622-186-5

Typeset by Manila Typesetting Company

Printed and bound by CPI Group (UK) Ltd, Croydon, CR0 4YY

Contents

Preface	**xvii**
The Form that Makes Preaching Compelling	**xix**
Contributors	**xxviii**

SUNDAYS AND MAJOR FESTIVALS

Unless otherwise stated, the readings and the verse numbers of the psalms are taken from *Common Worship: Services and Prayers for the Church of England* (Church House Publishing, 2000), with revisions, and are for Year A.

2019

1 Dec.	**First Sunday of Advent**	
	Principal Service: Isa. 2.1–5 Living between Promise and Fulfilment	2
	Second Service: Isa. 52.1–12 Just How Beautiful are the Feet?	4
8 Dec.	**Second Sunday of Advent**	
	Principal Service: Matt. 3.1–12 Signposts	6
	Second Service: 1 Kings 18.17–39 Prepare the Way	9
15 Dec.	**Third Sunday of Advent**	
	Principal Service: Matt. 11.2–11 Rejoice and Blossom!	11
	Second Service: Acts 13.13–41 'They went on from Perga and came to Antioch in Pisidia'	13

22 Dec. **Fourth Sunday of Advent**
Principal Service: Matt. 1.18–end Prepare to be Dazzled 16
Second Service: Luke 1.39–45 Encounters with the Word 18

25 Dec. **Christmas Day**
Set I: Isa. 9.2–7 The Birth of the Light 21
Set II: Luke 2.[1–7] 8–20 The Shepherds' Point of View 23
Set III: John 1.1–14 The Old Made New: Hearing Christmas in New Ways 25
Second Service: Phil. 2.5–11 The Mind of Christ 28

29 Dec. **First Sunday of Christmas**
Principal Service: Matt. 2.13–end A Spiritual Geography to Bring us Home! 30
Second Service: Phil. 2.1–11 A Hymn to Jesus 33

2020
5 Jan. **Second Sunday of Christmas** (Epiphany)
Principal Service: John 1.[1–9] 10–18 Life Beyond Christmas 35
Second Service: John 4.7–26 First EP of Epiphany 37

12 Jan. **Baptism of Christ** (First Sunday of Epiphany)
Principal Service: Matt. 3.13–end No Turning Back 39
Second Service: Ps. 46 Bold Speech for Turbulent Times 42

19 Jan. **Second Sunday of Epiphany**
Principal Service: John 1.29–42 The One to Know 44
Second Service: Ezek. 2.1—3.4 'Is there anybody there?' 46

26 Jan. **Third Sunday of Epiphany**
Principal Service: 1 Cor. 1.10–18 Church Unity 49
Second Service: Eccles. 3.1–11 God in Time 51

2 Feb.	**Presentation of Christ in the Temple** (Candlemas)	
	Principal Service: Luke 2.22–40 Candlemas Bells	54
	Second Service: Hag. 2.1–9 The Latter Glory	56
9 Feb.	**Third Sunday before Lent** (Proper 1)	
	Principal Service: Isa. 58.1–9a A Watered Garden	58
	Second Service: Eph. 4.17–end How to Live a Good Life	61
16 Feb.	**Second Sunday before Lent** (Proper 2)	
	Principal Service: Matt. 6.25–end Lift Up Your Eyes	62
	Second Service: Prov. 8.1, 22–31 Root and Branch	65
23 Feb.	**Sunday next before Lent**	
	Principal Service: Matt. 17.1–9 The Mountain and the Plain	67
	Second Service: 2 Kings 2.1–12 Rule of Three	70
26 Feb.	**Ash Wednesday**	
	Matt. 6.1–6, 16–21 Lent Backstage	73
1 Mar.	**First Sunday of Lent**	
	Principal Service: Rom. 5.12–19 Adam	75
	Second Service: Deut. 6.4–9, 16–end Love God	77
8 Mar.	**Second Sunday of Lent**	
	Principal Service: Rom. 4.1–5, 13–17 Abraham	79
	Second Service: Num. 21.4–9 The Bronze Serpent	82
15 Mar.	**Third Sunday of Lent**	
	Principal Service: John 4.5–42 Moses	84
	Second Service: Eph. 6.10–20 The Power of Lists	86
22 Mar.	**Fourth Sunday of Lent** (Mothering Sunday)	
	Principal Service: John 19.25b–27 Christ's Body, the Church, Called to Love	89
	Second Service: Micah 7 From Despair to Hope	91

29 Mar.	**Fifth Sunday of Lent (Passiontide)**	
	Principal Service: John 11.1–45 If Only . . .	94
	Second Service: Lam. 3.19–33 The Need for Lament	96
5 Apr.	**Palm Sunday**	
	Principal Service: Matt. 21.1–11 Jesus Becomes King	99
	Second Service: Isa. 5.1–7 Rejection and Restoration	101
6–8 Apr.	**First Three Days of Holy Week**	
	John 12.1–11 Poured Out for Love's Sake	103
9 Apr.	**Maundy Thursday**	
	John 13.1–17, 31b–35 Handed Over	106
10 Apr.	**Good Friday**	
	John 18.1—end of 19 'I find no case against him'	108
11–12 Apr.	**Easter Vigil**	
	Rom. 6.3–11 Discovering Infinity	111
12 Apr.	**Easter Day**	
	Principal Service: John 20.1–18 Risen Yet Hidden	113
	Second Service: Song of Sol. 3.2–5; 8.6–7 Ardent Desire	116
19 Apr.	**Second Sunday of Easter**	
	Principal Service: John 20.19–end Faithful Enough to Doubt	118
	Second Service: Dan. 6.1–23 [or 6.6–23] Happy Endings	121
26 Apr.	**Third Sunday of Easter**	
	Principal Service: Luke 24.13–35 The Journey of Discipleship	124
	Second Service: 1 Cor. 3.10–17 Living Temple	126

3 May	**Fourth Sunday of Easter**	
	Principal Service: John 10.1–10 Called for Life	129
	Second Service: Ezra 3.1–13 Beginning Again	131
10 May	**Fifth Sunday of Easter**	
	Principal Service: John 14.1–14 Stilling Troubled Hearts	133
	Second Service: Rev. 21.1–14 A New Heaven and a New Earth	136
17 May	**Sixth Sunday of Easter** (Rogation Sunday)	
	Principal Service: John 14.15–21 Another Advocate	138
	Second Service: Rev. 21.22—22.5 A New City	140
21 May	**Ascension Day**	
	Principal Service: Luke 24.44–end Take Authority!	143
	Second Service: Song of the Three 29–37 Glory Be!	146
24 May	**Seventh Sunday of Easter** (Sunday after Ascension Day)	
	Principal Service: John 17.1–11 Overhearing Jesus' Intercession	149
	Second Service: Mark 16.14–end Correct Endings?	151
31 May	**Day of Pentecost** (Whit Sunday)	
	Principal Service: Acts 2.1–21 The Mightiest Festival of Them All	154
	Second Service: Joel 2.21–end 'Your sons and your daughters shall prophesy'	157
7 June	**Trinity Sunday**	
	Principal Service: Matt. 28.16–20 A Christian Identity Test	159
	Second Service: Isa. 6.1–8 The Power of Three	161

14 June	**First Sunday after Trinity** (Proper 6)	
	Principal Service: Rom. 5.1–8 Original Sin?	164
	Second Service: 1 Sam. 21.1–15 Refugee Crises	166
21 June	**Second Sunday after Trinity** (Proper 7)	
	Principal Service: Matt. 10.24–39 Counting the Cost	169
	Second Service: 1 Sam. 24.1–17 Anointed for Generosity	172
28 June	**Third Sunday after Trinity** (Proper 8)	
	Principal Service: Matt. 10.40–end The Kindness of Strangers	174
	Second Service: 1 Sam. 28.3–19 Ultimate Loyalty	176
5 July	**Fourth Sunday after Trinity** (Proper 9)	
	Principal Service: Matt. 11.16–19, 25–end Finding Peace in Complexity	179
	Second Service: Luke 18.31—19.10 20:20 Vision	181
12 July	**Fifth Sunday after Trinity** (Proper 10)	
	Principal Service: Matt. 13.1–9, 18–23 Hear!	183
	Second Service: 2 Sam. 7.18–end Jerusalem: House and Temple	186
19 July	**Sixth Sunday after Trinity** (Proper 11)	
	Principal Service: Matt. 13.24–30, 36–43 Weeding or Waiting	188
	Second Service: Acts 4.1–22 Pipsqueaks and Giants	191
26 July	**Seventh Sunday after Trinity** (Proper 12)	
	Principal Service: Matt. 13.31–33, 44–52 Inhabiting the World of the Parables	193
	Second Service: Acts 12.1–17 Faith in Dark Places	196

2 Aug. **Eighth Sunday after Trinity** (Proper 13)
Principal Service: Matt. 14.13–21
You Give Them Something to Eat! 198
Second Service: Acts 13.1–13 Holy Spirit: Director and Principal Actor 201

9 Aug. **Ninth Sunday after Trinity** (Proper 14)
Principal Service: Matt. 14.22–33
Between the Shores 203
Second Service: Acts 14.8–20 Seeing Right 205

16 Aug. **Tenth Sunday after Trinity** (Proper 15)
Principal Service: Matt. 15.[10–20] 21–28
Revealing Encounters 208
Second Service: Acts 16.1–15 Mission: God's Business, God's Church 210

23 Aug. **Eleventh Sunday after Trinity** (Proper 16)
Principal Service: Matt. 16.13–20
What Future for the Church? 213
Second Service: Acts 17.15–end Evangelism: Why Can't We Just Be a Bit More Normal? 215

30 Aug. **Twelfth Sunday after Trinity** (Proper 17)
Principal Service: Rom. 12.9–end
St Paul's Tweets 217
Second Service: Acts 18.1–16 'Do not be afraid, for I am with you' 220

6 Sept. **Thirteenth Sunday after Trinity** (Proper 18)
Principal Service: Matt. 18.15–20
Binding and Loosing 222
Second Service: Acts 19.1–20
The Spirit's Insider Work 224

13 Sept. **Fourteenth Sunday after Trinity** (Proper 19)
Principal Service: Matt. 18.21–35
Lightning Strikes Twice 227
Second Service: Acts 20.17–end
A Fond Farewell 230

20 Sept. **Fifteenth Sunday after Trinity** (Proper 20)
Principal Service: Matt. 20.1–16
Incongruous Grace 232
Second Service: Acts 26.1, 9–25 Rise Up,
Good Shepherd 235

27 Sept. **Sixteenth Sunday after Trinity** (Proper 21)
Principal Service: Matt. 21.23–32
What is Your Authority? 236
Second Service: Ezekiel 37.15–end
Better Together 239

4 Oct. **Seventeenth Sunday after Trinity** (Proper 22)
Principal Service: Ps. 19 [or 19.7–end]
The Heavens are Telling the Glory of God 242
Second Service: Mark 10.2–16 Take What You
Want, Says God . . . 244

11 Oct. **Eighteenth Sunday after Trinity** (Proper 23)
Principal Service: Matt. 22.1–14 Dressing Up 247
Second Service: Prov. 3.1–18
Wisdom's Source and Power 249

18 Oct. **Nineteenth Sunday after Trinity** (Proper 24)
Principal Service: Matt. 22.15–22
What's In Your Pocket? 252
Second Service: Prov. 4.1–18 Get Wisdom 254

25 Oct. **Last Sunday after Trinity** (Proper 25)
Principal Service: Matt. 22.34–end
Love Yourself 256
Second Service: 2 Tim. 2.1–7 Strong in Grace 258

25 Oct. **Bible Sunday**
Col. 3.12–17 Signpost, Spectacles
and Talking Book 261

1 Nov. **All Saints' Day**
Principal Service: Matt. 5.1–12 People of an
Alternative Culture 263
Second Service: Heb. 11.32—12.2
A Cloud of Witnesses 266

8 Nov. **Third Sunday before Advent** (Remembrance Sunday)
Principal Service: Matt. 25.1–13
Wait. Watch. Prepare 268
Second Service: Judg. 7.2–22 What God Does 271

8 Nov. **Remembrance Sunday**
(The readings of the day or those for 'The Peace of the World' or 'In Time of Trouble' can be used. These are for 'The Peace of the World'.)
Phil. 4.6–9 273

15 Nov. **Second Sunday before Advent**
Principal Service: Matt. 25.14–30 Monologue: The Man with Few Talents 276
Second Service: Rev. 1.4–18 The Blessing of Naming and Being Named 278

22 Nov. **Christ the King**
(Sunday next before Advent)
Principal Service: Matt. 25.31–end
Jesus, Hidden King 281
Second Service: 2 Sam. 23.1–7 The Last Words 283

SERMONS FOR SAINTS' DAYS AND SPECIAL OCCASIONS

2019
26 Dec. **St Stephen, Deacon, First Martyr**
Acts 7.51–end Faithful unto Death 286

27 Dec. **St John, Apostle and Evangelist**
1 John 1 Seeing and Believing 289

28 Dec. **Holy Innocents**
Matt. 2.13–23 Innocents: Catching the Reflections of Christ 291

2020
1 Jan. **Naming and Circumcision of Jesus**
Luke 2.15–21 Name Above All Names 293

6 Jan.	**Epiphany** *Matt. 2.1–12 From Fate to Freedom*	296
18–25 Jan.	**Week of Prayer for Christian Unity** *2 Cor. 5.19 Think Big and Act Boldly*	298
25 Jan.	**Conversion of St Paul** *Gal. 1.11–16a The Shock, Surprise and Singularity of Grace*	300
19 Mar.	**St Joseph of Nazareth** *Matt. 1.18–end Trouble!*	303
25 Mar.	**Annunciation of our Lord to the Blessed Virgin Mary** *Luke 1.26–38 'How can this be?'*	305
25 Apr.	**St Mark the Evangelist** *Mark 13.5–13 'Get behind me!'*	307
1 May	**SS Philip and James, Apostles** *Isa. 30.15–21 The Divine Love that Calls Us Back*	309
14 May	**Matthias the Apostle** *Acts 1.15–end A Forgotten Disciple with a Stand-in Part*	312
1 June	**Visit of the Blessed Virgin Mary to Elizabeth** *Luke 1.39–49 [50–56] Run to the Hills!*	315
11 June	**Day of Thanksgiving for the Institution of Holy Communion** (Corpus Christi) *1 Cor. 11.23–26 Taken, Blessed, Broken and Distributed*	317
12 June	**St Barnabas the Apostle** *Acts 11.19–end Cheerleader in Tough Times*	319
24 June	**Birth of John the Baptist** *Luke 1.57–66, 80 A Prophet for a Priest*	321

29 June **SS Peter and Paul, Apostles**
Acts 12.1–11 Bound Together by the Love of God 324

3 July **St Thomas the Apostle**
John 20.24–29 Seeing with the Heart 326

22 July **St Mary Magdalene**
John 20.1–2, 11–18 Loving the Lord 328

25 July **St James the Apostle**
Matt. 20.20–28 Costly, Clear-eyed Service 331

6 Aug. **Transfiguration of Our Lord**
Luke 9.28–36 The 'Story' of Transfiguration Retold 333

15 Aug. **The Blessed Virgin Mary**
Luke 1.46–55 Life at Its Most Unlikely 335

24 Aug. **St Bartholomew the Apostle**
Acts 5.12–16 Firmly I Believe and Truly 338

14 Sep. **Holy Cross Day**
John 3.13–17 Lift High the Cross 340

21 Sep. **Matthew, Apostle and Evangelist**
2 Cor. 4.1–6 What is Truth? 342

29 Sep. **St Michael and All Angels**
Rev. 12.7–12 Time for Angels? 344

18 Oct. **St Luke the Evangelist**
Acts 16.6–12a Luke, Evangelist of the Written Word 347

28 Oct. **SS Simon and Jude, Apostles**
Eph. 2.19–end On Firm Foundations 350

2 Nov. **Commemoration of the Faithful Departed**
(All Souls' Day)
John 6.37–40 'I am the resurrection and the life' 353

30 Nov. **St Andrew the Apostle**
Matt. 4.18–22 Apprentice to Jesus 355

Harvest Festival
Deut. 8.7–18 'Do not forget the Lord your God' 358

All-Age Services 361
Crib Service: Room for Everybody 361
Christingle Service: A Christingle for Life 363
Mothering Sunday: Kept Safe by Love 366

Notes 369
Acknowledgements of Sources 372
Index of Names and Subjects 373

Preface

A former spiritual director of mine used to draft sermons for the Archbishop of Canterbury. He was, apparently, among a circle of writers for Robert Runcie. I was somewhat shocked that an archbishop needed help to produce sermons, not least since Runcie himself had a lucid and persuasive way with words. But then I discovered the reason behind this curious episcopal collaboration. The Archbishop was conscious that as a preacher he was a representative figure and needed to include others in the process of discerning not so much what to say as what he *should* say.

All we who are preachers must feel the weight of responsibility to speak not just for ourselves but *to* and *for* the Church of God. Some preachers meet periodically just to chew over the readings for future sermons. Volumes of sermons, of which it seems there is no shortage but rather an apparent increase, can, like the *Preacher's Companion*, also assist in helping us to speak more representatively as well as owning our own words. Preachers can be immeasurably helped by hearing other voices, sharing with critical friends and tough interlocutors. But where this is not practicable, reading a few sermons by others can provide the grit that can bring our thoughts to speech. I hope the diversity of voices and perspectives in this volume prove to be a reliable and critical friend.

The introductory essay focuses attention on the forms or shapes of the sermon. I have included a number of sermons in the form of story, monologue, argument, journey and so on, to illustrate some of the styles that may be used. I hope that the forms may be usable with other texts. I realize that preachers looking for a 'straightforward' sermon on one text may be disappointed but, as I've discovered myself and heard from many other preachers, when we dare to change our style and confound our congregation the reaction can surprise us.

If we need authoritative encouragement for a different and more daring approach to preaching, let me cite words from *Common*

Worship (there is likely to be an equivalent in other church traditions): 'The "sermon" can be done in many different and adventurous ways.' It then proposes that this 'includes less formal exposition, the use of drama, interviews, discussion, audio-visuals and the insertion of hymns or other sections of the service between parts of the sermon'.[1]

Roger Spiller

The Form that Makes Preaching Compelling

Busy preachers can breathe a sigh of relief when we have discerned the content and message for our next sermon, jotted down the ideas and 'points' we want to make, and found what we hope will be an appetizing introduction. But, according to some of the leading gurus on preaching, we may be overlooking a further stage in preparing to preach, the form of preaching. The aim of this introduction is to suggest that the form of preaching deserves the same attention as the content if our preaching is to enact the surprise and thrill of the gospel rather than merely report it. The form, too, can engage its hearers on a journey in which they are given the freedom, resources and responsibility to undertake their own learning. I have cited sermons in this Companion to illustrate some of the forms that are available to us.

It's said that what's wrong with sermons is that too many sermons sound like sermons. Once past the brief interest-grabbing introduction, which too often bears little or no relationship to what follows, we fall back on a fixed pattern that is as predictable as the weather. It is ordered more like a logical sequence of 'points' and a stream of propositions or ideas. This resembles the regurgitation of an essay, more suited to the written word than to the spoken word. The points are like 'three pegs in a board, equal in height and distance from each other', as one of the great teachers of preaching, Fred Craddock, expressed it.[2] It's been said that the intellectual demands of this approach to preaching exclude 95 per cent of the population. 'Does the sermon say and do what the biblical text says and does?' asks Craddock, for if it doesn't it is keeping faith neither with Scripture nor with our hearers.

> It is possible that a sermon that buries itself in the text, moves through it phrase by phrase, may prove to be 'unbiblical' in the

> sense that it fails to achieve what the text achieves. On the other hand, a sermon may appear to be walking alongside rather than through a text, or may seem to pause now and then at the lofty peak of a text so extraordinarily as to defy the skills of the most experienced preacher, and yet be quite 'biblical' in the sense of releasing that text to do its work among the listeners.

If the preacher has invested all their time in discerning the content of the preaching, but has not given thought to the form by which it can be received by its hearers, they will have failed to deliver the self-involving and surprising good news. The form of preaching, then, is more than the ordering of material, more than a compilation of ideas and 'points'. It is a form chosen and sometimes created by the preacher to express what a particular text and message says and does. The form is not the fixed vessel in which the wine of the gospel is to be poured but the shape that the impact of the gospel makes upon our preaching.

A form that enables hearers to be active participants in the preaching

'A sermon form is a plan for the experience of listening, not merely shaping information.'[3] So wrote Tom Long, who has called the choice of the form of the sermon 'an act of pastoral care'.[4] That is achieved when the form of preaching encourages the hearers to listen with a sense of discovery and adventure. They do not merely hear the conclusions the preacher has already arrived at in their study, but hearers are encouraged to be active participants in a guided exploration of the territory of the text according to their capacity. Where possible, alternative interpretations and problems with the text are not passed over but highlighted to enable the hearers to participate in the interpretative process. Hearers not only follow the movement of the text but are also given space to complete the sermon for their own lives. The form of the sermon takes account of the way most people hear, which is laterally, intuitively and narratively. The sermon then flows in the way in which most people experience reality, which is less about 'points' and more about plot, progression and direction. Many preachers start their sermons inductively, from the particularities of the text and human experience to the general, but do not follow it through. The form has to shape the sermon as a whole if attention and participation is to be maintained. Such a form dispenses with the need for a discrete 'application' or for a peppering of illustrations, since the form itself is designed to maintain the interest of the hearers. It also dispenses with the need for a discrete 'application' to conclude the sermon since the preacher will have enlisted the hearers in their own individual applications of the sermon, not just at the end but throughout the preaching.

The form of the preaching is ideally developed and determined by the character and purpose of the particular text before us and by the particular character, stage of faith and perceived needs of the hearers. This will require a plurality of forms: some well-tried forms that we can adapt and some that we might need to create for ourselves. To explore further how the form functions to bring preaching to life, we look now at the generative form of narrative. This is well established and has spawned a wide range of other adaptive forms that can enrich the preacher's repertoire.

A form that keeps faith with Scripture and gospel

'Narrative', it has been said, is 'the central, foundational, and all-encompassing genre of the Bible'.[5] 'Nine-tenths of our preaching is verbal exposition and argument, but not one tenth of the gospel is exposition. Its ideas are mainly in the form of a story told.'[6] Thus to reduce the gospel message to abstract ideas is a betrayal of the creative, imaginative character of the biblical witnesses. The Christian message is predominantly narrative and requires to be told in narrative form. The greatest truths can only be told indirectly, as stories or pictures. How can we preach the incarnation or resurrection except by images and stories? We can seem more adept at turning biblical stories into exhortations to do and to believe rather than inhabiting them and allowing them to interrogate our own human stories.

Narrative preaching

Narrative is concerned with setting, characters and moves that involve a plot. The basic narrative plot is a movement from a problem to a solution, a need to a fulfilment; an ambiguity to a clarification, a question to an answer. The movement from the one to the other proceeds not by 'points' but by 'moves'. The sermon form 'presents a picture, a plan, a map . . . of a sermon's itinerary showing each step to be taken along the journey'.[7] These 'moves' are not linear, the shortest distance between two points, but like any story, discussion, journey or experience they are meandering and circuitous.

An example of a narrative form: Lowry's Loop

One of the most influential models of the narrative approach is by the American homiletician Eugene Lowry, known as 'Lowry's Loop'. Narrative preaching is still characterized by ordering the ideas or 'moves' in terms of a plot. It involves a strategic delay in the preacher's meaning and embodies a story-like process moving from conflict, through complication, towards a reversal and resulting in a resolution of thought and experience. The gospel comes, however, as it must, as a surprise and a 'sudden shift' that delivers us to a different place.

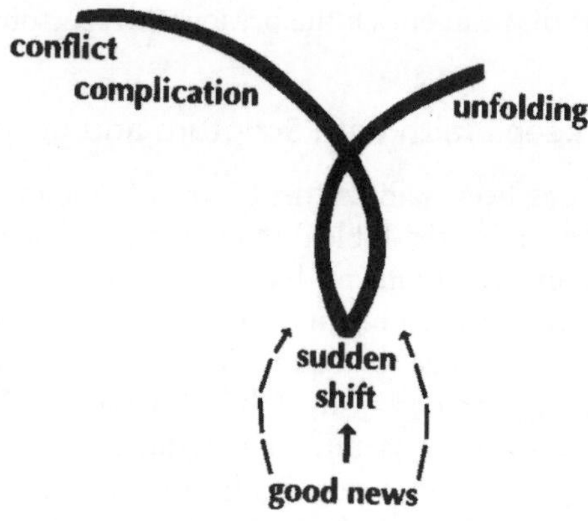

Narrative preaching can be expressed as an argument, or as an image or cluster of images, as well as story, provided there is a particular conflict, problem, issue or need that is being pursued through the sermon. Is that condition applicable to all the biblical material and all gospel preaching? It must, I think, be acknowledged that the testimony of Scripture witnesses to the discrepancy between promise and reality, between the existing reality and God's alternative world, and the litany of conflict, questions, ambiguity and needs are partial, personal manifestations of the divine trajectory to the kingdom.

Story

Preaching on the text as a story or parable that has already been read out requires a particular approach if it is to replicate something of the surprise that was originally inherent in the story. There are at least four options suggested by Lowry[8] to include in our repertoire of sermon forms. These will be illustrated by reference to some of the sermons in the *Companion.*

Running the story

This is the most straightforward, a running of the story as it is. The description of the event of the transfiguration is well known, so an attempt has been made to tell it as a story, as on page 333. Like the story, the account doesn't explain the meaning of the event or proclaim a message, but leaves it to the hearers to make sense of it for themselves. The preacher engages the imagination to fill out the story and take the congregation on a journey that they can make their own. Preachers who decry their own storytelling skills are, in my experience, often surprised by the warm response they receive when they do 'take the plunge' and offer the congregation a new experience.

Delaying the story

The preacher may begin the sermon with an extended current story or issue and then introduce a biblical text to provide some response or resolution to what has been raised. The predominance of stories in the Bible should encourage and authorize us to work with our own stories and reflect on using appropriate biblical material. Our example depicts a memorable story, which is then 'responded to by a gospel text' (p. 227, Fourteenth Sunday after Trinity). The awkward juxtaposition of story and text compels hearers to work out connections for themselves.

Suspending the story

The preacher has to decide at what point to bring the congregation into the story. In suspending the story, the preaching starts not where the parable starts but where the biblical story 'runs into trouble', takes a strange turn, registers a comment or provokes the preacher to raise an issue.

The parable of the wedding feast (p. 247) for the Eighteenth Sunday after Trinity is reflected in other versions of the parable. However, what in Matthew's Gospel snatches our interest and arouses our senses of bemusement and outrage is the treatment of the man without a wedding garment. Most sermons only get to him briefly at the end of a lengthy exposition of the mission to the Gentiles, or pass over him altogether on the grounds that by citing scholarly opinion this may not have been part of the original parable. But here the attempt is made to suspend much of the story so as to focus all the attention on the 'complication' facing the congregation. The preacher need not bring closure or resolution if the text itself has not brought closure, and the effect of the sermon will be prolonged in the minds of the hearers. Another form for stories that raises difficulties may also be handled in terms of argument.

Alternating the story

Here the biblical text may be used in sections interlaced with non-biblical material so that the preacher can enable their hearers to share in the dialogue that is set up between the disparate witnesses. The sermon for the Second Sunday of Epiphany (p. 44) combines different material, all of which is bound together with a repeated refrain. This can be an effective way of persuading a congregation to think theologically as the story proceeds.

Argument

The narrative form is as applicable to argument as it is to story when the congregation is brought face to face with disturbance, conflict, tension or ambiguity as a result of the text or the preacher's introduction of the text, or the experience of the congregation brought to the surface by the text. That condition determines the trajectory of the whole sermon. The conflict, problem or disturbance shared by the preacher becomes the problem that the congregation take on board as their problem for which they seek some resolution.

A Palm Sunday sermon (p. 99) precipitated 'conflict' or disorientation when the presence of palms and other usual accoutrements of the idealized Palm Sunday was challenged and forced the question as to how this strange event was understood.

A sermon on the mustard seed and leaven (p. 193) for the Seventh Sunday after Trinity deploys biblical references to subvert the usually settled interpretation of the components of the parable. This produces the experience of facing the unsettling, interrogative and heuristic function that could be applied to a number of other parables. The intent is to help the congregation to discover its own capacity for living and growing with and through the complexity and ambiguity inherent in the Christian message.

In the sermon on the parable of the labourers (p. 232) for the Fifteenth Sunday after Trinity, the congregation faces both unexplained generosity and also apparent unfairness. The sermon moves slowly through several possible solutions by way of trying to nail down the ambiguity freighted by this familiar account. It has the form 'Not this, or this, or this, or this, but that'. A strategic suspense gives space for the congregation to do their own thinking in tandem with the preacher.

Narrative in argument form is particularly suitable for apologetic, that is, explanatory or polemical sermons. There are examples of this form on 'why?' questions on the Seventh Sunday after Trinity (p. 196), on 'original sin' on the First Sunday after Trinity (p. 164), and a sermon on 'Why did Jesus Die?', assigned here to Good Friday (p. 108). Why was Jesus killed? He was crucified, so was he guilty of an offence against Rome? No, but why then was he not given a capital sentence of stoning by the Jewish authorities?

Monologue

A monologue form of sermon can also be conscripted to create shock and surprise, when a person takes on the part of a disfavoured biblical character and tells their side of the story. This is intended to create the ideological vacuum that gives space for the congregation to work out their own response in relation to the judgement made against some of the people. A sermon on the man who received one talent (p. 276) for the Second Sunday before Advent illustrates this. The monologue may benefit from commentary interspersed with the monologue proper, as in the sermon on the Fifth Sunday of Lent (p. 94) where Mary asks 'If only' in respect to the death of her brother Lazarus. There are other splendid examples of this approach collected in David Day's *A Preaching Workbook*.[9]

Image

The treasury of images and metaphors we have in the Scriptures provides a rich resource for preachers. Jesus preached in images and avoided abstractions. Besides, images have the capacity to lodge in the mind and fuel the imagination. Many of the abstract theological concepts like grace, judgement and forgiveness began life as concrete, visual images and remain for the preacher to unpack. Staying with one image can make for a memorable sermon. See the sermon on the 'cloak' for the Sunday next before Lent (p. 70). But a series of images can also be deployed in different ways, as the homiletician David Schlafer has suggested.

Juxtaposing of images

The discreet conduct expected of those who give, pray and fast, contrasting with the public parade of the Pharisees, seemed limited for the Ash Wednesday sermon. Instead, however, the text led to the contrast between the images of the front stage and back stage already implicit in the text being exploited more fully (p. 73). These images seemed to give the message in the text a new and immediate resonance, whatever our practice on fasting or giving may be.

Succession of images

A Bible Sunday sermon on the use of the Bible (p. 261) lent itself naturally to a succession of images none more important than the other, but which conveyed, more clearly than theological argument, how the Bible may be used in private study and contemplation.

Progression of images

A sermon on 'seeing', based on Luke's account of Paul's seeing the faith of a paralytic man, is set for the Ninth Sunday after Trinity (p. 203). A sermon on 'A Watered Garden', for the Third Sunday before Lent (p. 58), draws together the rich and progressive way this archetypal image is used throughout Scripture to carry the development of grace and faith in the human life.

I trust that these examples show how a judicious use of a biblical image deserves to be added to our repertory of preaching forms. There are clearly many different ways of forming a sermon other than those mentioned here. I have included some that have proved fruitful so as to stimulate preachers to develop their own forms when they come to prepare to preach. In conclusion, we might summarize the considerations we can keep in mind when finding a form for our sermon.

Choosing a form for our preaching

1 Keep faith with the text and the message.
   - What does this text say? What does it do?
   - Does this text primarily address the mind, the senses or the imagination?
   - Does the form keep faith with the intended purpose of the text and message?
   - What form best serves to recreate the original (intended) impact of the text?
   - Is the message best suited to story, image or argument?

2 Enable the congregation to engage with the preaching.
   - What sermon forms are the congregation likely to find refreshing and appropriately challenging but not disabling?
   - What anticipated congregational responses to the text should be challenged and what should be supported?
   - How much of the complexity and ambiguity found in the text will the congregation be able to handle and accept in developing their own mature handling of Scripture?

Contributors

The Revd Paul Ballard, a Baptist minister, is Professor Emeritus at Cardiff University where he taught Practical Theology. He is an Honorary President of the British and Irish Association for Practical Theology, associate of Workplace Chaplaincy Mission UK, and member of Green Christian and Peterborough Eco-faith Network, where he lives in retirement.

The Revd Dr Stuart Blythe is an ordained Scottish Baptist minister. He has pastored two churches in Scotland, taught at the Scottish Baptist College and was Rector of the International Baptist Theological Study Centre in Amsterdam. He currently lives with his wife Susanne in Nova Scotia, Canada, where he is Associate Professor in the John Gladstone Chair of Preaching and Worship.

The Revd Dr Kate Bruce is an RAF Chaplain and Visiting Fellow of St John's College, Durham. She is the author of *Igniting the Heart* (SCM Press) on preaching and imagination.

The Revd Christopher Burdon grew up in Essex and studied languages at Cambridge. Before ordination in 1974 he was engaged in reconciliation work in Northern Ireland, and after 18 years in Anglican parish ministry moved into theological education: first in lay adult education, then as Principal of the Northern Ordination Course, and later as Canon Theologian of St Edmundsbury with responsibility for continuing ministerial development. Chris's research and publications have been mainly in the reception history of Mark's Gospel and the Revelation to John. Now retired in Wiltshire, he is involved in spiritual direction and in work with homeless and vulnerable adults.

The Revd Paul Burdon is the Coordinator of the Sarum Centre for Formation in Ministry and Director of Contextual Learning at Sarum College, Salisbury, involved in training for ordination and lay ministry primarily in the Church of England. Previously, he worked in engineering before 22 years in parish ministry. Paul researches and leads training on preaching.

The Revd Canon Dr Christopher Burkett is Director of Ministry for Chester Diocese; he is editor of *The Preacher* and a sociologist.

The Revd Mary Cotes is a Baptist minister. Following pastorates in Devon and South Wales, she served as ecumenical moderator in Milton Keynes and now exercises an itinerant ministry in Britain and further afield. Over the years, she has been chaplain to a community centre, a night shelter and a psychiatric hospital, and is currently chair of the Milton Keynes Christian Foundation. She writes for the French website Servir Ensemble and is also a keen musician, enjoying both teaching and performing.

The Revd Dr Megan Daffern is Diocesan Director of Ordinands for Ely Diocese, former Chaplain of Jesus College, Oxford, and lecturer and tutor in the university Theology Faculty. She published her first book, *Songs of the Spirit* (IVP), in 2017.

Fr Rob Esdale, Parish Priest of Our Lady of Lourdes RC Church, Thames Ditton, Surrey, was ordained in 1991 and was Catholic Chaplain at the University of Sussex from 1996 to 2006.

The Rt Revd Dr Christopher Herbert, former Bishop of St Albans and currently a Trustee of the Royal Hospital for Neuro-disability, Putney, is a lecturer for the Arts Society and Visiting Professor of Christian Ethics in the University of Surrey.

The Revd Dr Victoria Johnson is a Residentiary Canon at Ely Cathedral and a Tutor for the College of Preachers. She studied Homiletics at Yale Divinity School and teaches preaching for those training for ministry.

The Revd Dr Deirdre Brower Latz is the Principal of Nazarene Theological College, Manchester, UK. Ordained in 1996, she went on to pastor in urban communities in the United Kingdom. Principal since 2012, she continues to serve among local congregations in urban environments. She teaches in the area of practical theology with an emphasis on social justice.

The Revd Dr Wendy Kilworth-Mason is a Methodist presbyter and a former Theological Tutor and Mission Partner with an interest in preaching the Old Testament.

The Revd Canon Dr Sandra Millar heads up national work for the Church of England on life events, leading work that helps the whole Church think about how it can engage more effectively with people around weddings, funerals and christenings. She was ordained in July 2000 after a career in retail marketing, and currently lives in Gloucester. Sandra is also the author of several books on families and worship.

The Very Revd David Monteith has been Dean of Leicester since 2013. Originally from Enniskillen, Northern Ireland, he shares long-term interests in music, poetry and the visual arts, with a commitment to living with diversity.

The Revd Dr Donald Norwood is a United Reformed Church Minister who has served in congregations in Windsor, Oxford and Bossey, and as Ecumenical Consultant to Students at Bossey in 2007–08. He is currently engaged in ecumenical research in Oxford and is the author of *Reforming Rome: Karl Barth and Vatican II* (2015); *Pilgrimage of Faith: Introducing the World Council of Churches* (2018); *Democracy and the Christian Churches: Ecumenism and the Politics of Belief* (2018), as well as a chapter on 'Reformed Reception' in the forthcoming Oxford Handbook on Vatican II.

The Rt Revd Dr John Perumbalath has been Suffragan Bishop of Bradwell since 2018. John hails from the ancient Syrian Christian community in Kerala, India, and trained for ministry at Union Biblical Seminary, Pune. Before his ordination, he was a youth worker among university students for two years and a theological educator for three years. He holds postgraduate degrees in philosophy and biblical studies and a doctorate in hermeneutics. He chairs the Committee for Minority Ethnic Anglican Concerns and sits on the Appointment Committee of the Church of England, Mission and Public Affairs Council.

The Revd Dr John Pridmore was Vicar of Hackney until his retirement. John was also a regular columnist for the *Church Times*, a lecturer at Ridley Hall, Cambridge, with one of his specialisms being the place of children in the Church.

The Revd Carey Saleh's first career was in nursing, specializing in haematology, oncology and palliative care. She later trained for the ministry at Queens Theological Foundation and went on to study for an MA in Transformative Practice of Theology. She is a published writer, married to a licensed Reader, mother of two sons and is an ordained priest in Worcester Diocese.

The Revd Canon Roger Spiller is Chair of Trustees of the College of Preachers and convenor of tutors. He was Director of Ministry for Coventry Diocese and Chair of the Church of England Continuing Ministerial Development Panel. He is a theological educator and is Chair of the UK Bossy (Ecumenical Institute), Geneva.

The Revd Emma Sykes has been ordained since 2008 and served her curacy at St Martin in the Bull Ring in Birmingham where she became Associate Rector. In 2014 she took a break from full-time ministry to finish her masters degree in theology, and since then has been engaged in a variety of different roles. Emma currently works part time for Church Pastoral Aid Society as a leadership specialist (with a focus on young vocations) as well as being an Assistant Diocesan Director of Ordinands for Birmingham Diocese and is licensed as an Associate Missioner to her local parish church.

Fr Terry Tastard is a priest in the Diocese of Westminster with a parish in north London and is a contributor to *The Preacher*.

The Revd Brett Ward is Parish Priest of Eltham in the Anglican Diocese of Southwark. He holds an MTh in preaching from the College of Preachers and has recently been a sermon commissioner for *The Preacher*.

The Revd Catherine Williams is an Anglican priest, previously working as a National Adviser for Selection for the Ministry Division of the Archbishops' Council. She is licensed to the Bishop of Gloucester as a Public Preacher.

The Revd Dr Stephen Wright is Vice-Principal and Academic Director of Spurgeon's College, London, former Director of the College of Preachers and author of a number of books on preaching.

Year A, the Year of Matthew

(Year A begins on Advent Sunday in 2019, 2022, 2025, etc.)

First Sunday of Advent 1 December

Principal Service **Living between Promise and Fulfilment**

Isa. 2.1–5; Ps. 122; Rom. 13.11–end; Matt. 24.36–44

It's becoming harder to guard Advent from the remorseless advance of Christmas. The festive season encroaches more and more on the weeks and months that precede it. The columnist Caitlin Moran has suggested that we're drunk from the very anticipation of Christmas and recommends that we should bring Christmas forward to 19 November. Even those of us who love this season of Advent know it can be displaced by the pressures of festive preparations.

This foreshortening of time squeezes out study, waiting and reflection, and Christmas and planning for the summer holidays become the limit of our hopes. But Advent isn't merely the countdown to Christmas. It's the space the Church guards in order for us to explore promises that take us far beyond Christmas and that help us to reckon with the ultimate longings, hopes and fears that lurk half buried within us.

Back to the future

We make a start on the First Sunday of Advent with an audacious promise from the Old Testament. This is made on the back of the fulfilment of God's earlier promise; not a welcome promise but a promise of judgement and one that those who heard it didn't want to hear and hoped would not be fulfilled. That was the promise of God's punishment on Israel that led to the destruction of the nation, its city and Temple, and the forced removal of its citizens into exile in Babylon.

But amid the rubble and devastation of the city God's prophet delivers a lyrical, daring message of transformation to his bewildered and demoralized people. The earth will be serviceable once more, human history will be consummated, and the God who can give enduring peace to humanity will deliver justice. Weapons will voluntarily be renounced, and nations will freely give up war so that peace will break out across the world.

Doesn't this ancient poetry voice our own deepest longing and hopes for that eventual transformation, for the restoration of justice, where lawlessness and terror have gone on unimpeded and where the depredations of the natural world and the environment pose immediate threats to the future of human life on the planet?

Future from the past

When hope had collapsed, the city been destroyed, Temple worship ceased and even belief in God was under strain and close to collapse, this seemed to be a remote and inconceivable promise. The new future promised in our readings can have no basis in the prevailing historical situation. We know that we cannot deliver newness but only more of the same, the predictable cycle of cause and effect, a future predicated on the tired old order. God's message always transcends the reality on the ground.

That's why our Gospel reading is framed in such apocalyptic, dramatic form, because it is exclusively about the activity and agency of God, outside and beyond history even as it determines history. It had addressed those who thought the end of the world had already arrived, but now it admonishes those who think, perhaps like us, that judgement and justice won't ever come. Instead, it declares that, as before, we are ultimately accountable, justice and judgement will come, and there will be no escape, extending to individuals, dividing even between couples working in the kitchen or the field. Doesn't the exalted poetic promise echo and awaken our deepest longings and intuitions for our ultimate deliverance and transformation?

Past hope for the future

Why trust in God? Because of promises fulfilled in the past. We're soon to be celebrating Christmas. If we haven't heard the hints and hopes and promises of the One who is to come, the Messiah, we might think Christ's coming was inevitable or a sudden one-off event. But the hope, intuition and promise of his coming seemed as unlikely and inconceivable as any other such divine promise. All the evidence that could be found for so great a claim was a 'stump', a 'stump of Jesse', from which, in the fullness of time, came Jesus of Nazareth, in whom the 'hopes and fears of all the years' are met.

Sacred time

Advent is sacred time, time to be with God, time to read the prophecies and promises, and mark their fulfilment, a time of forced inactivity in which to adjust to the vision of God's coming, again and again. Miss Advent and we miss out on the meaning of Christmas, and we miss the promises that lie beyond it. If we reckon with the future, we reclaim the hope that renews our resolve and energy to live, pray and work for the present. In the words of our prophet, we are to rise up and 'walk in the light of our God'; because our hope is in God, the Word made flesh, and in nothing else. And it is that Word coming to us again and again, as we inhabit the stories of his birth and the messengers of his grace, that seals our hope in the ultimate redemption of the world.

Roger Spiller

Suggested hymns

Lo, he comes with clouds descending; Hills of the North, rejoice; Longing for light, we wait in darkness; People, look east to see at last.

First Sunday of Advent 1 December

Second Service Just How Beautiful are the Feet?

Ps. 9; **Isa. 52.1–12**; Matt. 24.15–28

I've always known that my (maternal) grandfather and great-grandfather were both in the shoe industry. My mother told of how her father had lasts in the factory for both her mother and herself and so the first shoes from his designs would be made to fit one or other of them. Sometimes the shoes would then go into production, but other designs would not be approved, hence some of their shoes would be unique designer originals. Having 'good' shoes always mattered in our family, maybe because the family fortunes had depended upon footwear.

However, even though I'm going to admit that the verse within our Old Testament that really captured my attention was that which alludes to the beauty of the feet of the messenger, please don't assume that this is a sermon from a foot fetishist! Shoes can be beautiful: but I'm not so sure about feet. Furthermore, I don't know about you, but I usually look at someone's face, not their feet, especially if they are talking to me.

So, I wonder whether the passage is not so much about the feet as it is about the message that the herald comes to convey. In an era when you couldn't send a tweet or an email, or post it on Facebook, messages had to be conveyed by word of mouth, so the messenger had to make the physical commitment to travel from the originator to the recipient(s) of the message, and, depending upon the content of the message, he couldn't always be assured of a warm welcome following a wearisome journey.

A wake-up call

Let's return to the opening of the passage, where the prophet calls upon God's people to 'Awake'. They are to put on their glad rags and go out and 'party'. Of course there is debate about what the historical context of the original prophecy might be, whether or not the prophet is in exile, living in Babylon and encouraging his people as they are about to return to Jerusalem.

Hidden in the background to the passage may also be allusions to a well-known Ancient Near Eastern myth about the warrior God who slays the chaos monster (sometimes called the Leviathan). This God is their all-powerful, victorious God who has returned to Jerusalem and is summoning his people.

The people are told that now is the time to shake off the dust, loosen their bonds and rise up! However, as in much biblical prophecy, there are reminders of all that Judah has undergone through the experience of the exile and warnings that Jerusalem has been wasted and its sacred places defiled. Though they are being called to return, there is the warning that doing so will not be without its challenges.

Maybe everything good in life has to be worked for? People of faith must not assume that faith will cushion them from life's realities.

Cue the messenger

Awake and listen: to a people in exile, God's herald has come, the herald of good tidings, assuring them (despite any evidence to the contrary) that their God reigns. He says that the people's negative experiences of enslavement and exile were part of God's plan. Now, says the messenger, God has redeemed them and they have been set free. The people are to process back to Jerusalem, making the journey that their forebears made when they travelled from

Egypt to the land of promise, making the return journey of those who were dragged from the city into exile.

The message offers hope in despair. It has similar nuances to those of other passages that we read during the Advent season, passages that offer to us the promise of the Messiah.

Just how beautiful are the feet?

I suspect that the feet of the herald would have been hot, sweaty and dusty: hardly things of beauty, but they are made beautiful because they represent the work of a servant of God who has made every effort to bring a message of hope.

How beautiful are your feet? I wonder. Will you use them this Advent to go out and offer the message that our God reigns? God has redeemed us (bought us and brought us back from the brink of whatever self-engineered disasters we confront) and offers hope to all the world; salvation is not just for Jerusalem (either the city or Jerusalem meaning God's people) but for all the nations.

As we await and prepare for the coming of Jesus Christ our Lord, our God reigns.

Wendy Kilworth-Mason

Suggested hymns

How lovely on the mountains (Our God reigns); Hark the glad sound; Light of the world; Long ago, prophets knew.

Second Sunday of Advent 8 December

Principal Service **Signposts**

Isa. 11.1–10; Ps. 72.1–7, 18–19 (*or* 72.1–7); Rom. 15.4–13; **Matt. 3.1–12**

What gets in your way? When I drive to work there are different routes I can take – depending on the weather, or the time I have, or where I'm starting from. One of my favourite routes runs through pretty villages with narrow country lanes. But recently a new building site has opened up and there's always something in the way. Lorries, diggers and all sorts of heavy vehicles travel along those tiny lanes and I'm forever having to back up, or squeeze my car into the ditches and hedgerows. I've given up going that way because, though the signposts still point the right way, the road is impassable.

God's signpost

John the Baptist was one of God's signposts – a marker on the way – pointing to the Messiah. John's whole life and ministry witnessed to the one who was to come. The Jewish people were waiting for the Messiah – the one from King David's line, the stump of Jesse – who would be filled with the Spirit, who would judge with righteousness and equity and bring the nations and the whole of creation to reconciliation and harmony. The kingdoms of Israel and Judah would be reunited. Wolves and lambs would live side by side, and even children and snakes would be friends – all symbols of peace and restoration. When the Messiah came, he was expected to come from the desert and so various Jewish groups went to live in the wilderness in readiness to meet the Messiah. John the Baptist was one of these – God's signpost pointing to the desert, pointing to the Messiah, calling people to repentance, to turn their lives around so that they were ready to receive the Messiah when he came. Matthew describes John as dressing and living simply – in the model of Elijah, that great prophet from the Old Testament. The return of Elijah would herald the coming of the Messiah. People came out to the desert from Jerusalem and all around to meet John, to confess their sins and be baptized. All sorts of people came, including the religious leaders of the day – and even Jesus himself.

Pointing the way

John does not set himself up as the Messiah – he points the way, pointing beyond himself to the one who is to come. From his very first meeting with Jesus, when Mary visits Elizabeth and both boys are still in the womb, John points the way to Jesus, jumping for joy. Later, when baptizing him, John announces Jesus as the Lamb of God, who takes away the sins of the world. John points the way to Jesus – but never gets in the way. He knows that Jesus is much more powerful then he: 'I am not even worthy to carry his sandals.' Jesus is the one who will baptize with the Holy Spirit and with fire – a purifying baptism like none other, a gesture that will separate the wheat from the chaff, that will gather together what is good and wholesome and burn that which is useless, the dross. The Messiah will bring both peace and harmony but also a sword – what's good news for some will be bad news for others, declares John.

Ourselves as signposts

As Christians today, how do we signpost others to Jesus? How can we *point the way* rather than *get in the way* for those seeking God? Our lives are everyday pointers for others. What we buy, what we eat, the way we use our money – our day-to-day lifestyle is a pointer, especially at this time of year when the world goes mad for excess. We don't have to 'do' Christmas like everyone else, but as Christians we do need to prepare ourselves to celebrate again with great mystery and awe the wonder of Christ's birth among us. So, while everyone else is as busy as can be, our pointer to Christ might be to stop, sit still and be with God – to be a prayerful presence for those who are driven. The way we do our churchgoing and our worship should be a pointer to God, not a barrier. If we are always complaining about our church or sniping at fellow Christians, people get the impression that we worship a mean, tight, aggressive little God whose followers are miserable, pious and dull. Never be afraid to tell people you've been to church, and how good it is – that you're a faithful Christian and what a difference it makes to your life. Point the way – be a helpful signpost – but don't get in the way. Leave room for the Holy Spirit to work in God's own unique and extraordinary way, and then celebrate when you see the fruit of that. So, during Advent – these weeks before Christmas – consider how you can be God's signpost to Jesus. How can you point to God in a way that sparks interest? It could be as simple as sending Christmas cards with a religious picture on them, or saying to a neighbour, 'I'm going to a carol service – why not come too?' Pray that God will enable us all to be signposts this Christmas, and in the years to come. Amen.

Catherine Williams

Suggested hymns

On Jordan's bank; Hark, a thrilling voice is sounding; Days of Elijah; Jesus, name above all names.

Second Sunday of Advent 8 December

Second Service **Prepare the Way**

Ps. 11 [28]; **1 Kings 18.17–39**; John 1.19–28

Are you a prophet?

The Oratorio, *Messiah*, by George Frederick Handel, begins with the words from the book of the prophet Isaiah quoted by John the Baptist. 'I am the voice of him that crieth in the wilderness, prepare ye the way of the Lord, make straight in the desert a highway for our God.' The scene is set for the coming Messiah – the glory of the Lord shall be revealed, and, reaching back to the prophets of old, we hear how the world is making itself ready to behold its God. John is a prophetic figure who emerges from the wilderness in a strange way, wearing camel hair and eating locusts and wild honey. His appearance causes a stir and the priests and Levites send a delegation to investigate who he is representing and by what authority he makes these claims.

He is mistaken for Elijah, the prophet who reveals the coming Messiah to the people of Israel. Elijah was known for bearing the stark truth to the people of Israel and challenging them to make plain their allegiances. It is no surprise that John the Baptist, with his words and his appearance, causes people to recall the prophet Elijah.

Who do you worship?

In the episode recounted in the first book of Kings, Elijah seeks to convince the people to denounce their worship of Baal, and instead worship the one true God. He calls them to turn away from 850 false prophets and listen to him instead. Elijah calls upon the Lord to make himself known and reveal himself upon the altar he has created. Whereas Baal does not respond to the calls of the Israelites – Elijah mocks them, suggesting that perhaps their God Baal is asleep or has wondered off – the God of Abraham, Isaac and Jacob is made known by sending down fire and consuming the burnt offering. The people fall on their faces and worship; they now know that the Lord indeed is God, and no other.

Both Elijah and John the Baptist were figures who called the people to make their choices and live. They both prepared the way and pointed people to the truth. Whereas Elijah calls people away from the worship of Baal, John the Baptist calls people away from the worship of themselves and calls them towards repentance and the forgiveness of sins in anticipation of the coming kingdom. John and Elijah represent a voice crying out in the wilderness, prepare the way of the Lord.

Come among us, we pray

The Collect for the Second Sunday of Advent calls upon God in the same way that Elijah and John the Baptist did. It petitions: 'O Lord, raise up, we pray, your power and come among us.' As Elijah called upon God to make himself known to the Baal-worshippers, so John the Baptist tells people that, such is the power of the one who is to come, he is unworthy even to untie the thong of his sandal.

During this season of Advent, we prepare our hearts and minds to receive the coming Messiah. We are called to turn away from the false gods that we worship and fall down on our faces before the one true God in penitence and in faith. We also look towards the time when Christ, the Messiah, will come again. When that day comes, will we be ready or will we be worshipping the false Gods of our own day, whatever they may be?

Just as the people of Israel were told to clear a path for God, so we are also called to make a way for God to come into our lives, to open up our hearts to a transforming grace, to repent and turn to God with our whole being. What is uncertain is not that Christ *has come* or *will come* again, but whether we will be ready to receive him when he does. Like the prophets of old, we are to prepare the way for God's Messiah, so when Christ does come again we will be ready to greet him.

At the end of Part One of Handel's *Messiah*, after we have been called to prepare the way, we are greeted with a great affirmation of faith in the revelation of God to his people. A huge chorus rejoices that the glory of the Lord shall be revealed, and all flesh shall see it together. This is the vision to which we now turn and for which we prepare during this season of Advent.

Victoria Johnson

Suggested hymns

Hark, a herald voice is calling; On Jordan's bank the Baptist's cry; Long ago, prophets knew; Ye servants of the Lord.

Third Sunday of Advent 15 December

Principal Service **Rejoice and Blossom!**

Isa. 35.1–10; Ps. 146.4–10, *or Canticle*: Magnificat; James 5.7–10; **Matt. 11.2–11**

Today we pause in the tension of Advent and we 'rejoice'. This Sunday is *Gaudete Sunday* in the Church's calendar. If you are a church that wears vestments you might be wearing rose today, rather than purple. If you have a pink candle in your Advent wreath, it will be lit today. I like to think of it as 'being in the pink' – getting excited about Christmas – just a fortnight away. Some churches use the liturgy of 'asperges' this Sunday – sprinkling the congregation with water to remind them of their baptism and turning to Christ.

God in the desert

Today's readings tell of the transformation and new life that God brings. The prophet writing in the book of Isaiah captures our senses and stretches our imaginations. He urges us to look forward to a time when everything will be renewed: 'The wilderness and the dry land shall be glad, the desert shall rejoice and blossom.' Dry and dusty places will be bursting with flowers, all creation will break into song, humanity will be restored, people healed, fear taken away. God will return to save his people who will walk on a high road out of danger into Zion, the holy city, Jerusalem: the symbol for all that is good and pure, holy and eternal. This prophecy led the Israelites to believe that the Messiah, God's chosen rescuer, would come into the desert places. And so, for some, they went out literally into the desert to prepare for the Messiah. The Essene community, who wrote the Dead Sea Scrolls, was one such group. John the Baptist exercised his ministry of calling people to turn their lives around – by baptizing them into new life – in the desert region around the Jordan river. He was preparing the way of the Lord and found his identity as the Lord's messenger in the desert. Jesus too found his identity as the Son of God during his 40 days of temptation in the desert. So, it's into a place of extremes, of emptiness, dryness and isolation, that God comes – coming to transform, to renew and to save both individuals and communities. Desert places are places of stripping away, of getting below the froth on the surface and looking at the deep realities within.

John the Baptist

In the Gospel we meet John the Baptist again this week, but in a very different place to last week. Now he is watching and waiting in prison. He sends his disciples to find out who Jesus is – is this the Messiah or should we wait for someone else? Jesus urges them to look at what's happening around and through him: the blind see, the deaf hear, lepers are cleansed – creation is being renewed by his very presence. The prophecy of Isaiah is being fulfilled. The Messiah, the Saviour, is come, the kingdom of God is breaking in all around, renewing and transforming the desert places, so that even the least will be greater than John, the messenger of the Lord. It's in Jesus Christ that we see the glory of God fully revealed. Remember how the angels announce Christ's birth to the shepherds by bursting into song: 'Glory to God in the highest – peace to God's people on earth.'

Bursting into song

Many of us have desert places in our lives – times when we feel lonely, desperate, dry, bored, anxious, ashamed of the past, fearful of the future. Times when we're not sure where God is, or even if God exists. And it's into those places that Jesus wishes to come, to be born again, to bring new life, and to call you into life in all its fullness – life filled with blossom, where you will flourish, and where, like the angels, you just cannot help but sing. We can be in danger – particularly at this time of the year – of covering up or hiding away the very places where the Lord longs to come. While the world is rushing around, buying and selling, and going to parties and decorating madly, Advent calls us to get back to basics – to prepare for Christ to come, to strip everything down, to be still and silent, to watch and wait. If you are feeling a bit behind in your preparations for Christmas, don't worry – that's probably a good thing. We need to be still and watchful and patient, like the farmer waiting for the cycle of the harvest to be fulfilled, waiting and allowing God to be born again into those desert places in our lives and in the world, transforming us and our communities so that we can proclaim the glory of the Lord with integrity. We can say, 'Here is your God' – and show others the difference God makes. Then people will sit up, take notice and yearn to be part of God's transforming work. Imagine Jesus filling the desert places of your life and our world. Invite him to renew and heal and transform, so that we may all blossom and burst into song to the glory of God. Amen.

Catherine Williams

Suggested hymns

Rejoice in the Lord always; Long ago, prophets knew; Come, thou long expected Jesus; Rejoice, rejoice, sing with the angel voices.

Third Sunday of Advent 15 December

Second Service **'They went on from Perga and came to Antioch in Pisidia'**

Ps. 12 [14]; Isa. 5.8–end; **Acts 13.13–41**; *Gospel at Holy Communion*: John 5.31–40

Designing new towns

In the twentieth century no fewer than five new towns were created in the small (English) county of Hertfordshire. The first of those new towns was Letchworth Garden City, which was modelled on the ideas of Ebenezer Howard. He had pioneered the notion that new towns should be carefully planned and designed so that they could combine the best of rural life with the best of urban life. Letchworth was soon followed in 1920 by Welwyn Garden City. And here's a bit of useless information: Letchworth has the first roundabout in the United Kingdom, built in 1909.

Of course, the custom of purposefully designing cities and towns was nothing new. Scroll back through the centuries and just 25 years before the birth of Jesus, the Emperor Augustus refounded what is known in the Bible as Pisidian Antioch. It was created as part of the military process of subduing that part of Anatolia. At its heart as a new city was, unsurprisingly, a temple to Augustus. If this was like other temples to Augustus, it would have been about 26 feet wide x 57 feet long and would have been 46 feet high. On the front of the temple would have been a prominent notice stating its dedication: *To Roma and Augustus Caesar, son of the deity, father of the fatherland.*

Somewhere in this newly refounded town there was a synagogue. It was probably not very large, but acted as the meeting place for the Jewish community. It may even have been nothing more than an enlarged room in the house of one of the Jewish traders who lived there. Whatever its physical characteristics might have been, it was the place to which Paul and Barnabas went on the Sabbath. As was the custom in synagogues, strangers who were thought to have something to say were invited by the president to speak. And so, according to the account written by Luke, Paul launched into his sermon. It was that sermon that was read to us today.

The story of Israel

Paul rehearses the story of the people of Israel: from God's choice of them as his favoured people; the Exodus from Egypt; the initial appointment of judges as rulers, followed by the call of Saul to be King, and the rise, as a result, of King David.

At which point, Paul has reached the turning point of his sermon because he then leaps through history (he doesn't even mention the exile in Babylon), and brings the story up to date by exclaiming that Jesus of Nazareth, descended from David, is the promised Messiah. And through the resurrection of Jesus, he says, forgiveness of sins is now available to all.

Now, whether or not these were the actual words of Paul, we cannot know. Perhaps Luke had heard Paul's sermon so many times on other occasions that he was able to imagine accurately what Paul might have said: it was the core of Paul's message.

It is not difficult to picture in our minds the small synagogue, the crowded meeting room, and Paul, with an exciting charismatic authority, proclaiming his radical message – which some would have found offensively heretical.

Life goes on as normal

And meanwhile, out in the Forum with the temple of Augustus dominating the sight-lines, the multicultural life of Pisidian Antioch would have been carrying on as normal. Yet in a house not far away a new message was being preached.

Luke points out that the effect of Paul's preaching was such that some of the members of the synagogue asked him to speak again the following week – which he did. But this time, trouble was stirred up. It was, after all, a radical, subversive message that Paul had preached to the Jews and the Gentile God-fearers who were part of the synagogue community. As a result, Paul and Barnabas were expelled from the city. And life in the Forum returned to conversations about the weather and the price of vegetables and who was about to marry whom, and how you couldn't get the right kind of slaves any more.

Nothing had changed.

From small beginnings . . .

We, of course, with the benefit of knowing how the story developed, also know that it was from such tiny, apparently inconsequential beginnings that the good news of Jesus spread and within three hundred years Christianity had begun to usurp the place of the older Roman religions.

But pause for a moment. Place yourselves in your imagination in that Anatolian Forum two thousand years ago. You would not have known that something momentous was under way very close by. Now, translate that into our own age and times.

There can be no doubt that our Christian beliefs are not as widely shared in our society as used to be the case. There is, understandably, therefore, much noisy talk about mission and strategies for growth – and who doesn't want to see our faith and our churches grow? But inside all of this we should not lose sight of the patience of God, working out his mission in the world in ways that we might not yet recognize.

Perhaps, in our current circumstances, we are simply required to keep the faith, which in itself is a form of witness; we should rest in the powerful, overarching providence of God, and wait to see how God will bring about his kingdom.

When Paul and Barnabas were unceremoniously hustled out of Pisidian Antioch, leaving the temple of Augustus in their wake, they too could not have imagined what the future would bring. And nor can we. But God knows what he is doing, and in him we can place our trust.

Christopher Herbert

Suggested hymns

God is working his purpose out; Put thou thy trust in God; O happy band of pilgrims; Filled with the Spirit's power.

Fourth Sunday of Advent 22 December

Principal Service **Prepare to be Dazzled**

Isa. 7.10–16: Ps. 80.1–8, 18–20 (*or* 80.1–8); Rom. 1.1–7; **Matt. 1.18–end**

To talk about religion is to risk being seen as soft headed, credulous. The pressure from our culture and media is increasingly hostile to religion and to Christianity in particular. Royal mail postage stamps, Christmas nativity scenes, carol singing, the very celebration of Christmas have all been challenged by a tide of unbelief in the name of political correctness. But in case we think this is all entirely new, it's the case that from the very first God's dealings have caused embarrassment and awkwardness. What do you think people would have thought of Joseph telling Mary that he had a dream last night in which an angel told him to take Mary as his wife and that she will have a Son, Jesus? What might Mary herself have thought of Joseph's claim that she is to have a unique child as a result of a miraculous birth?

Credulity?

The expectation of Jesus according to Matthew is outside all of our normal categories. It's the very ordinariness focused on these two figures, Mary and Joseph, that confounds us, especially when it is through them that we dare to claim that the universal God entered our human history, shared our DNA and took on our flesh with all its vulnerability and its potential. And in the night, we're told, the angel came and said to this fearful peasant craftsman, 'Do not be afraid . . . for the child conceived in her is from the Holy Spirit.' Our business is not to explain the story – stories resist being reduced to explanations. Our business is to be dazzled that at Christmas something is happening beyond all our conceptions and calculations. This is a baby and a wonder and a gift that is designed to move us beyond ourselves.

But this is a baby that has no father, and in this family, like every family, it's a scandal when a baby has no father. But the story is concerned less with the scandal visited upon Joseph and more on the action of the Holy Spirit. Whatever you make of the virgin birth as a fact of history, there is no denying the fact that the incarnation of Jesus comes through God's Spirit – at his birth, at his baptism, at his death and resurrection. Whatever the human process God used, the source and originator was God's Spirit. And throughout the Bible God's Spirit is shown to be making things new. Matthew is saying that God's Spirit has stirred and caused something utterly new in the world. God has caused this new baby who will change everything among us.

Names

And this child is given two names, names that testify to his character. 'You are to name him Jesus, for he will save his people from their sins.' Imagine that on Christmas day we have a baby named 'Save'. And Jesus will save from sin and guilt, from death and destruction, from despair and hopelessness, from poverty and sickness. Advent is being ready for the saving one, who will come when we cannot save ourselves.

But there is another name: 'Emmanuel, God with us'. So what we see in the crib at Christmas is none other than God born into the world. The claim is too scandalous for some, too incredible. If they believe in God at all, they may be willing to concede that Jesus was inspired by God, was like God, the exemplar of God, the human face of God. But if we have only our human resources to make sense of things and to face evil and suffering, then there can't be salvation.

But what if our resources for making sense of suffering and evil and confusion and life now include the very being of God, one in whom all the fullness of God was pleased to dwell? Well, then, God's newness can promise change and redemption. When we see in the face of the Christ-child the very reality of God beckoning us beyond the horizons of our own humanity to a place where the Light of the World shines full of grace and truth, then we can glimpse some healing of the tragedies of human life. We can see sense in what seems senseless, and meaning in what defies human understanding.

Compelling belief?

If we read the story in the light of our canons of understanding, in terms of what is comprehensible to us, then we won't make progress. But for those of us willing to ponder the complexity of our existence and the competing demands of faith and unbelief, this was the point of the Christmas story – that God would choose to come among us in such a way that is so strange, so inexplicable, so unbelievable that it compels us to believe.

And so in these frenetic hours right on the cusp of Christmas, St Matthew challenges us to be credulous if that's what happens when we receive the angel's message in a dream that is beyond our control or expectation. That God's Spirit makes all things new through this baby. And that Jesus saves us from all that is destructive and joyless and hopeless and tells us that we are not alone. Unlike the demands we put upon ourselves, this story doesn't ask us to do anything. It invites us to be dazzled and to be prepared to have our lives contradicted by this gift from God.

Roger Spiller

Suggested hymns

Into the darkness of this world; Earth was waiting, spent and restless; Longing for light, we wait in darkness; Sing we of the blessed Mother.

Fourth Sunday of Advent 22 December

Second Service **Encounters with the Word**

Ps. 113 [126]; 1 Sam. 1.1–20; Rev. 22.6–end; *Gospel at Holy Communion*: **Luke 1.39–45**

'And why has this happened to me, that the mother of my Lord comes to me?'

In the south aisle of Westminster Abbey near the west end is a small wooden door. If you go through the door (actually, you are not allowed to do so, because this is a private part of the Abbey . . . but imagine, for the moment, that you have been invited), you will climb some steps. At the top of the steps is a small room known as the Jericho Parlour. It was built in the sixteenth century by the Abbot, John Islip who jokingly left a pun on his name in the small panes of glass in the window. There's an image of an eye and next to it an image of a small slip of a branch: 'I' 'Slip'.

The Jerusalem Chamber

Leave that parlour, turn to your right and you will find yourself in a beautiful, large room known as the Jerusalem Chamber. It was the room in which in 1611 the committee met to begin the painstaking task of creating the Authorised (King James') Version of the Bible. It's a translation that has helped to shape the English language. The scholars who worked on it did so with immense care and skill, but there must have been times when they debated long and hard about the meaning of the text they were translating. For example, those translating the Gospel of Luke from the original Greek were faced with a problem in finding the right words for the story that we heard in today's Gospel.

The King James' version of the text is as follows: 'And whence is this to me, that the mother of my Lord should come to me?'

It is an accurate and literal translation of the Greek words written by St Luke. But it doesn't quite make sense, at least not to us in the twenty-first century. So more recent translators have tried to create a better and more understandable version: for example, the people who worked on the New Revised Standard Version, published in 1989, translated the phrase in this way: 'And why has this happened to me, that the mother of my Lord comes to me?' You'll note that instead of the word 'whence', they have used the word 'why'. It has to be admitted that that makes more sense: it captures the spirit of the words rather than being literally accurate; which all goes to show that translation is an art as well as a science.

Listening is an art and a science

But that has important implications for us as we listen to the Gospel being read. We need to bring to our listening the same skills as translators bring to their work, for listening is also both an art and a science. If we are only concerned to capture the precise and accurate meaning of individual words we shall miss the overall meaning; and if we concentrate solely on the meaning we shall miss the strength of individual words. In other words (forgive the pun), translating and listening are dynamic processes. They require a toing and froing between the text and us, and between us and the text.

Now, let's return to the Gospel story – because this too involves a dynamic, interactive activity.

There are two main characters in what we might describe as this tiny play: there is Mary and there is Elizabeth. A conversation takes place involving question and answers. Elizabeth is portrayed as the junior partner: she realizes that Mary is bearing the Christ-child in her womb and therefore she gives honour to her. So far, so straightforward. But let's pause for a moment – because, when you think about it, there are not just two characters in this play, there are three: we, the listeners to the dialogue, are also present. In fact, it's even more complex than that, for we are privileged to know the stories that lie behind the encounter. We have met Elizabeth before and we have met Mary before. And we bring that knowledge to our understanding of this little play.

The miracle of imagination

We are actually involved – not by being there, in the sense of witnessing the historical moment of the encounter, but through the intricate relationship between the text and our imaginations we are caught up into the action and into the dialogue.

The process is a minor miracle in itself. As we give attention to the words, our imaginations can help us understand the meanings of the encounter. We can imagine what we might have said, had we been there. We can imagine what our first reaction to seeing Mary might have been. We can go deeper still and imagine what it would be like to be in the presence of a woman who is radiant with the promise of God.

If we approach the story in this way, endless possibilities emerge. It's very like the images created by John Islip's pun on his own name, which we saw in the Jericho Chamber. It involves a kind of wit, a joy in creation, a playfulness with words in which new meanings are revealed.

And so it is with Mary meeting Elizabeth. Through humdrum words, the joy and pleasure of the courteous presence of God are made visible – and that is a gift of great and humble beauty.

Christopher Herbert

Suggested hymns

With Mary let my soul rejoice; Her virgin eyes saw God incarnate born; Tell out, my soul, the greatness of the Lord.

Christmas Day 25 December

Any of the following sets of readings may be used on the evening of Christmas Eve and on Christmas Day. Set III should be used at some service during the celebration.

Set I **The Birth of the Light**

Isa. 9.2–7; Ps. 96; Titus 2.11–14; Luke 2.1–14 [15–20]

What does darkness look like?

What does darkness look like? I don't suppose you found that out on your way to church tonight. Headlights and streetlights and the parish Health & Safety rep. ensured you got here without fear of stumbling or losing your way. Even in the most remote rural location, torchlight would have guided you safely to the church door. And when we're safely back at home, we know that darkness is what happens when we choose to switch out the light. It isn't the inevitable result of the fire burning down and the embers dying.

The full power of Isaiah's words is probably lost to us, therefore: 'The people who walked in darkness have seen a great light; those who lived in a land of deep darkness – on them light has shined.' And it is the same when we turn to the scene in the shepherds' fields outside Bethlehem: 'The angel of the Lord stood before them and the glory of the Lord shone around them.' Let's just say that it had better be a good light show if St Luke expects twenty-first-century children to be impressed.

What does darkness feel like?

We can't go back to life before electricity, when darkness ruled our world each day from dusk to dawn. Some of us can scarcely glimpse the night sky, after all, because of the perpetual neon glow of our horizon. So perhaps we need to ask another question: what does darkness feel like? We all get glimpses of that, sometimes in faraway places where violent deeds are done; sometimes in the stories of private miseries exposed in criminal courtrooms (just think back over the news in recent days); sometimes in our own lives when we are gripped by hurt or fear or loss of hope. It's that feeling of moral darkness that we must connect with in order to hear the prophet's proclamation in all its power.

That is the realm of shadows where a light has shone: not with the million-lumen dazzle of stadium displays, but through the birth cry of a little child, born in the obscurity of a cave burrowed deep into a Bethlehem hillside. That's the light we celebrate tonight, amid the dark and cold of a northern hemisphere winter.

The birth of the light

That light shines in utter wordless vulnerability, a newborn infant in the arms of an exhausted teenage mum; wrapped in the conventions of his time, swaddling clothes, of course; and sheltered in a borrowed space, owning nothing, dependent for everything. Why this way? Because only through this fragility and littleness can he burrow into our darkness – our wrongs and fears and hurts and despairs – and bring his light. But it is in that darkness that today 'a child has been born for us, a son given to us'.

I hope that sometime you've been in the presence of a newborn infant. And I hope you'll always bear within you the memory of that moment and of how it touched you. Words fail us. It's the same with the birth of the Word-made-flesh. Words fail us here as well. And yet the words bubble up, nonetheless – 'Wonderful Counsellor, Mighty God, Everlasting Father, Prince of Peace'. This is our sign – the vulnerability of love, entrusted to us. Here, as Paul tells Titus, 'the grace of God has appeared, bringing salvation to all, training us to renounce impiety and worldly passions'.

Hurrying to Bethlehem

That is the holiness of this night: the invitation to leave everything behind, if only for a moment (even the preparations for tomorrow), so as to focus on the gift given us in Christ. We find ourselves following the shepherds to Bethlehem – to go and 'see this thing that has taken place, which the Lord has made known to us'. He it is who has brought us here tonight, whether we are fervent in our faith or 'just looking', or somewhere in between, wondering and watching.

Whatever our story, wherever we are on our own journey, we're led beyond our preoccupations, our plans, our 'flocks'. We're brought to the darkness of a stable, to a newborn child and to utter wonder. We glimpse not just the birth of hope but the beginning of the healing of our world, the lifting of the yoke of oppression, the rejection of the way of violence – the very tasks Christ gives to his followers; for the whole gospel message is already there in that manger, in such littleness and peace.

Rob Esdaile

Suggested hymns

The people that in darkness sat; It came upon the midnight clear; Let all mortal flesh keep silence; O come, all ye faithful.

Christmas Day 25 December

Set II The Shepherds' Point of View

Isa. 62.6–end; Ps. 98; Titus 3.4–7; **Luke 2.[1–7] 8–20**

In the Museum of Fine Art in Dijon there is a sparkling jewel of a painting. It was created in the fifteenth century by an artist called Robert Campin and is an image of Christ's nativity. (*You might find it helpful to print off a copy of the painting from the internet and offer one to each member of the congregation.*) The painting is crowded with fascinating detail: four angels hover above the broken-down stable; Mary kneels on the ground; she is dressed in white. Joseph, clothed in a red woollen tunic, holds a lighted candle. There are two midwives present wearing sumptuous dresses made from brocades and satins, highlighted with pearls. In the background, in tiny detail, the artist has painted pollarded trees and people going to market, one of whom has a basket of eggs on her head. In the far distance is a lake on which a small galley and a rowing boat are sailing; nearer to hand is a walled city with a fortified castle towering above it on a precipitous bluff. And the sun rises above the surrounding mountain tops.

The shepherds at the door

But it's one of the details that I want to concentrate on just for a moment. Leaning in across the half-door of the stable are three shepherds. The eldest one is bearded and with split-mitten gloves holds his felt hat against his chest; his close companion is much younger. He holds a small set of bagpipes in his hand, and the third, looking over the shoulders of the other two, holds in his left hand a wooden staff, on the top of which is a kind of bill-hook called a 'slasher'. They could not be more typical of medieval shepherds – but it is the look of wonder on their faces that is so engrossing. This is not a 'Wow!' moment of over-exuberant, phony excitement such as you see in television game shows; it's much quieter than that. These shepherds are simply contemplating the Christ-child and his family gathered on a dirt floor in a rickety, tumble-down barn.

The painting has many layers of meaning. The sun rising over the hills, for example, is an obvious reference to a new age dawning; the broken-down stable symbolizes the old giving way to the newness of the Christ-child; Mary kneeling on the ground symbolizes her humility.

Luke's story of the nativity

In exactly the same way, when Luke created his gorgeous and delicate story of the nativity he layered that story with meaning. It's a kind of painting, but a painting with words. Consider the shepherds: they not only represent ordinary humanity but they are a reference backwards in time to the story of the famous shepherd-king of Israel, David; they rush to adore the miracle of a newborn child, but in doing so they are also gazing at the child who will be called the Lamb of God; they lean on the stable door and see the child who, much later, will refer to himself as a 'good shepherd'.

All of these layers of meaning are woven into the story, which is partly why it is such a delight. Luke could have written something totally banal, such as 'Some shepherds had a vision of angels and hurried to Bethlehem to look for a child', but by shaping the event in story form he captures our imaginations. Through his careful construction of the narrative, he engages our minds and our imaginations and we are taken through the layers into the very depths of the event. Our emotions are as engaged as our intellects are. It's why carols are written; it's why poems sing off the page; it's why, as you hear the story read, accompanying music (probably from Handel) pops into your head. We are taken down to a level in which the very core of our humanity is involved. This is a story that tugs at our souls, for it is trying to explore the outrageous idea that God, the Creator of the infinite reaches of the universe, could have come to earth in sweet and disarming humility.

How does Luke's story speak to us?

Faced with that possibility, how might we react?

Let us be clear: each one of us will react in different ways – which is exactly what one would expect, for this is how stories work. They capture us, they refresh our perceptions and they shift our understanding of the world. They leave us wondering.

But this is not simply another story among all the stories that have ever been written. This is a story that faces us with a startling possibility: that there is a God; that that God revealed himself in Jesus of Nazareth; that in taking this initiative God approaches humanity in a way that courteously seeks a loving response and that takes us mortals, our hopes and our fears, our doubts and our dreams, very seriously.

This is a story in which the deepest joys one could ever imagine are held in front of our eyes, a story whose potential truth each one of us, like the shepherds in the painting, should ponder in the days ahead. We have no idea what happened to those shepherds after they left the manger. But the birth of Christ must have made an amazing impact upon them.

And so too for us: this Christmas, may we have the courage to allow ourselves to let go of our carefully constructed personal defences and, instead, let our imaginations soar: let us imagine that the truths hidden in the layers of Luke's story were written not only for an audience two thousand years ago but were written especially for us in this place, at this particular time – how shall we respond?

Christopher Herbert

Suggested hymns

While shepherds watched; See amid the winter's snow; See him lying on a bed of straw; It came upon the midnight clear.

Christmas Day 25 December
Set III **The Old Made New: Hearing Christmas in New Ways**

Isa. 52.7–10; Ps. 98; Heb. 1.1–4 [5–12]; **John 1.1–14**

It's an old story – 'long ago' God spoke it – it was spoken in hushed tones, in loud ones, in hope-filled ones, in glorious declaratives. The problem with old stories is that we feel like we know them so well, they can become tired old stories – we hear, but don't hear. We know, but know so well they become almost ignorable. We are jaded by them, they have become so familiar to us that we forget to listen with new ears, and our eyes can't see beyond the expected, the obvious, the old. Poor Christmas – poor Jesus – to be so easily made into nothing but gifts and stuffed turkeys.

I wonder if the book of Hebrews offers us a new way of thinking about the familiar stories of Christmastide? Instead of the mangered recitals we're so used to, or the begetting of this and that person whose fecundity results in Jesus (basically, fertility has mattered through the ages!), or, in place of the angel visitations and the loud 'Do not fears' accompanied by humble 'Here I am's, instead of shepherds and wonky angels' wings, or instead even of the poem John teaches, that densely laden recital of who Jesus is, how he is to be known, what he does, where he enters the world . . . I wonder if we can think together today about the beginning of Hebrews and try and see our lives in faith through its startling hymn?

All things held together

First, the long ago-ness matters: God has been sending a message repeatedly, through the ages, in lots of ways, and always with the same intent, it seems. God's message is a clear and simple one: that people may know God's desire for the world that God created, founded, set in place – that people may understand that this place that we are inhabiting, this earth, at this time, will end (whatever that may look like). That people may understand that the earth and heavens are care-worn and tattered, that they will fade, that we will die, but that although the earth is time-bound, God's hopes, dreams, vision, purpose, Godself is unchanging, unbound by time. Beyond time and above time, before time – before the foundation of the world – all things held together in God.

The message of Christmas in its core is that God speaks the world into existence and that, in speaking, breathing, loving, creating, the world itself in all its fullness – from creation to created – is designed to respond to God, to lean towards God, to praise, sing, dance, recite, make things, celebrate who God is – and God-is-love. This message, this inviting, banquet-feasting message has been repeated, retold, reframed over and over again. And the timelessness of God's call, the ceaseless and perseverance of God – who sends messengers of love – is at its climax here. God's final Word made flesh, God's heir, God's co-creating, exact-likeness, only Son, is here. HERE HE IS!

God's Son, God's glory

This seems so dense. It would be so much easier to riff on the Christmas story, or on light and darkness – but if we ignore Hebrews here we miss so much of the essence of the reason why the Christmas story and the in-fleshing of God's Son-only-begotten matters. God's Son sent, birthed, firstborn of God, lover of the world, anointed for saving us – God's only son – demonstrates exactly, *exactly,* God's very being, reflects exactly God's glory, God's beauty, God's grace, God's mercy, God's joy, God's love, God's desires to be above all. God's Son is come among people as the only living, breathing, imprint of the way God is. Of who God is. How do we know God – LOOK! Look at all the messengers God's sent – and here, here is the final messenger, the truest, the brightest, the Son!

This story, old though it may be, repeated as it is, needs to be heard in fresh ways. Gone the idea of presents and tinsel. Replaced instead by the ideas of presence and speaking-hope-of-life into the world. Gone the idea of a once-a-year event (although the Christmas story is unique and unrepeatable in its history, it is remembered every year), but, instead, this Jesus is all-time, all-time – the incarnate one who IS, is co-eternal. This Son is sustaining – bearing along the world itself. This Son is so like the Father-God that this Son is the heartbeat of all the world. This is mystery. This is beauty. This is Christmas in a whole new way.

This changes everything

When I think in this way about our faith-story, the pulse that beats through this time of year, it matters that we hear in a whole new way that this truth changes everything. This truth – testified to through the years – that Jesus is light and life, that with the Word becoming flesh God's hopes for the world have entered into it in a whole new way, that Jesus is God demonstrating that God is *for* all the earth, that God is about presence, with-ness, that God's very *being* is about love – and that the prophets have declared this kind of good news from the beginning of time. So, in the passages today – from Isaiah's messenger of peace, to John the Baptist's witness to light, to the Psalms' new song declaring God's marvel and victory, steadfast love and faithfulness – Christmas is a time of remembering that a son is the Son that shines into the world. Glory to God!

Deirdre Brower Latz

Suggested hymns

Of the Father's love begotten; Let all mortal flesh keep silence; The Servant King; Once in Royal David's city.

Christmas Day 25 December

Second Service The Mind of Christ

Morning Ps. 110, 117; Evening Ps. 8; Isa. 65.17–25; **Phil. 2.5–11**, *or* Luke 2.1–20 (*if it has not been used at the Principal Service of the day*)

The trouble began earlier on Christmas morning. Mother was knitting a nice jumper for her daughter. I say 'she was knitting' because it wasn't quite ready in time for Christmas. But she wasn't alone in thinking that her daughter needed a jumper. So also did her mother-in-law, who was sharing Christmas with the family. But hers was finished, ready to be worn, delivered on time. This generated competitiveness between the two mothers. This grew when the slow-knitting mother handed over one present of a large soft toy for her granddaughter, who quickly forgot about it when the other grandmother produced a dozen little toys. When the two families sat down for lunch together, the husband felt he needed to warn his mother-in-law that she needed to handle their best bone china with a little more care. But she, already feeling sore, ignored the warning, and their costly vegetable dish dropped into pieces on to the pristine carpet. The husband found comfort in alcohol and, losing his inhibitions, he told his mother-in-law plainly what he really felt about her. This merely confirmed her long-held but erroneous view that he was an alcoholic and a bad influence on the family. It's a true account, of course, and competes with other stories of family divisions.

A drama in three acts

Divisions were part and parcel of the domestic life of God's family at Philippi: pride, squabbles and vanity. Paul's response to unacceptable conduct is to invoke the 'mind of Christ', pointing to his humility and self-effacing character. This is in the form of a hymn and widely believed to be an early description of Jesus that predated St Paul himself. It depicts Jesus in three acts in the drama of salvation, forming a parabola, a move from his celestial home downwards to earth, and then back to where he came from. First as Son of God, he is in glory with the Father. Then he comes down to earth to a life of servitude, humiliation and death. Then, third, he returns to whence he came but is now exalted and glorified by his Father, given the divine name, having accomplished his redeeming purposes. Let's look very briefly at each of them in turn.

Glory

The Son of God shares the glory that befits God's Son. He has the 'form' of God, which is the 'state' of the first man, Adam, at his creation. So there is the possibility that the Son might act like Adam and snatch at equality with God. It's not that he didn't already have equality with God. It's that he had the choice of displaying and exploiting the glory that belonged to his divine nature and rejected it.

Humiliation

The scene now moves to earth and to the earthly phase of Christ's mission. He freely came down to earth and set aside his divine glory in order to tread the pathway of lowly obedience. He took the 'form of a slave'. In becoming human he divested himself of his visible glory and endured the shame of rejection and crucifixion. Mention of death, believed to be added by Paul, drives home the lesson that his identification with humanity had reached the lowest rung on the ladder.

Exultation

At this stage, attention moves from the Son of God to God, who becomes the chief actor in the drama. God raises his Son from the depth and elevates him to the place of honour, the honour that he refused to grasp for himself. The Son is given the 'name' of Lord, the name of God in the Old Testament. This means that Jesus Christ is installed in the place that rightfully belongs to God himself. And he assumes cosmic sovereignty.

'Let the same mind be in you that was in Christ Jesus,' says Paul. This is the attitude of mind we are to have in our personal relations. It's the way to put our house in order. It's the only attitude appropriate to those who are 'in Christ'. The downward path of dispossession is the path to elevation and blessing. It could be a glorious legacy after Christmas and result in a fulfilling New Year.

Roger Spiller

Suggested hymns

May the mind of Christ my Saviour; Thou didst leave thy throne and thy kingly crown; At the name of Jesus; Joy to the world, the Lord has come.

First Sunday of Christmas 29 December
Principal Service A Spiritual Geography to Bring us Home!

Isa. 63.7–9; Ps. 148 [*or* 148.7–end]; Heb 2.10–end;
Matt 2.13–end

In these quieter days after the frenetic social celebrations that occupy so many of us at the festive season, there is hopefully space for us to re-engage with the wonder of Christ's birth. Today in our Gospel, St Matthew offers an unusual way of helping us to enter into that birth so as to discover its meaning for our lives. He gives us an itinerary, place names visited by the infant Jesus with his parents. These are places that trigger associations with significant events in Jewish history. Jesus is reliving them, and in doing so Matthew is showing us how he is fulfilling and redeeming the hopes and promises that God made to his people.

Today's Gospel starts with a departure from Bethlehem, it takes us to Egypt, escaping a massacre in Bethlehem, takes us out of Egypt, back to the Land of Israel, bypasses Judaea and settles down in Nazareth in Galilee, where Jesus will begin his public ministry.

Bethlehem

We all know that Jesus was born in Bethlehem. Luke has it that the holy family went to Bethlehem, only briefly, for the purpose of the census. There they found temporary, makeshift accommodation and returned to their home in Nazareth. Matthew is emphatic, however, that Bethlehem was home to the holy family at least for the first few years of Jesus' infancy. Why was it so important for this most Jewish and royalist writer Matthew to emphasize Bethlehem?

It was, of course, the birthplace of David, the anointed, first and greatest king of Israel. And then when the monarchy finally collapsed and the country was disbanded, what better model was there for a future messianic deliverer than David, and how important that he too should come from Bethlehem. Joseph, the adopted father of Jesus, provides Jesus with his legal ancestry to David and his birthplace in Bethlehem. The Gentile magi affirm Jesus as king. By contrast the Jewish King Herod rejected the kingship of Jesus and forced the infant Jesus to find refuge in Egypt and thus, unwittingly, strengthen the claims made for Jesus as the answer to his enslaved people.

Egypt

Jesus, just like his ancestors in Canaan, was saved by a flight to Egypt. Joseph, Jesus' father, is divinely guided by angels and by dreams, and Matthew intends to remind us of another Joseph, the patriarch long ago, who was also guided by dreams to bring his people to safety in Egypt. In taking us to Egypt, it's Moses, above all, whom Matthew wants us to see as the prefiguring of Jesus. Like Jesus, Moses was a fugitive, with a price on his head. But as the death of the pharaoh freed Moses to begin his mission to return to the Promised Land, so the death of Herod enabled Jesus to return from Egypt in preparation for his own mission. Matthew is keen for us to see Jesus as the New Moses. Jesus replicates in his own life the temptations in the wilderness, and in the Sermon on the Mount he compares and contrasts himself with Moses, who received the commandments on a mountain. Matthew cites the words of Hosea: 'Out of Egypt I have called my son.' That originally referred to the great deliverance of the Exodus from Egypt, but Matthew shows that it is the pattern for the new covenant and the new 'exodus' from slavery that Jesus will accomplish in his life and death.

If Jesus is connected to the Exodus, and the second section of Matthew's Gospel parallels the second book of the Old Testament that we call Exodus, what of the other supreme miraculous deliverance, that from the exile? Can Matthew squeeze that in too?

Matthew cites Jeremiah's reference to Ramah, the mourning place of the exile. Its brutalities are relived in Herod's massacre of the infants. Jesus too is exiled from his homeland. In revisiting Exodus and Exile, Matthew is declaring the implicit hope and promise of salvation that God made through the ministry of another King, one Jesus.

Nazareth

When Herod dies, Joseph is instructed in a dream to return to Israel with a view to returning to Judaea and Bethlehem. But Bethlehem is too close for comfort. Another dream directed him instead to bypass Judaea for the independent northern state of Galilee, and thence to the small village of Nazareth, where his family made their home. There's no trace of the text that Matthew cites in support of the belief that the Messiah would be a Nazarene. And opponents of Jesus, when he was conducting his public ministry, ridiculed the very idea that Jesus was from Nazareth in Galilee because it undermined the claims made for his royal and divine origin. But this too was countered in John's Gospel by others who claimed that the origins of the Messiah would be a mystery, and that claims to know the human origins of Jesus would serve only to count against his divine claims. But the care with which Joseph was divinely led to Nazareth of Galilee stands to tantalize and subvert all human attempts to construct a saviour and king in our own likeness.

The itinerary that Matthew has offered for the infant Jesus has shown the vast context in which we must set our understanding of Jesus. He is the one on whom all the lines, hopes, fears and promises converge. On him the formative events of Jewish history are re-membered and fulfilled. A journey that began in the exclusive soil of Judaism is led by the Gentile visitors from the East to the Galilee of the Gentiles and to Jesus' universal kingship. Readers of Matthew and John thought the place names of Bethlehem and Nazareth pointed to two different identities for Jesus. Either he was a prophet, from Nazareth, or, if he was from Bethlehem, he was the Messiah. But that wasn't and isn't a real choice at all. The only real choice is the one that Matthew's Gospel so skilfully tries to set before us. It's the question that faces us before the Christmas story recedes from view. Is Jesus from an earthly home, or is he from God, and is he Emmanuel, God with us?

Roger Spiller

Suggested hymns

Bethlehem of noblest cities; The Son of God his glory hides; A man there lived in Galilee; Thou who wast rich beyond all splendor.

First Sunday of Christmas 29 December

Second Service A Hymn to Jesus

Ps. 132; Isaiah 49.7–13; **Phil. 2.1–11**; *Gospel at Holy Communion*: Luke 2.41–52

Do you ever feel that Advent has ceased to be a penitential season, both in our culture and in our churches, and has become an extended period of expectation or even of joyful anticipation? By the time Christmas Day arrived we had already heard the biblical lessons, attended the nativity plays and sung all the best-known carols, and now, just a few days after Christmas Day, it is as if we have galloped on in time as we have among our readings a passage that succinctly offers a theologically profound, post-resurrection, christological formula. We must shake off our post-Christmas sluggishness and shift our thinking because the babe of Bethlehem has become Jesus the Christ, the one through whom we know God.

It's the general scholarly consensus that Paul wrote this letter from his prison cell to encourage the Christian community in Philippi. In this section of the letter, Paul in effect poses two questions: 'Who is Jesus?' and 'Who are we?'

Who is Jesus?

In the extended passage, of which our reading forms a part, Paul is encouraging the recipients of his letter to come together, to be united in Christ. Jesus is represented as the model for unity. So, particularly in the latter part of our reading, in the so-called hymn to Jesus, we learn who Jesus was.

Jesus was in the form of God; he was in fact equal to God, but he didn't use his status for his own ends. He was in the form of a slave: the servant-God (I hear echoes of Isaiah's prophecies here). He was in human likeness. This God-slave-human form humbled himself and was obedient, to the point of death on a cross. Then God exalted him so that all in heaven and earth should bow at the sound of his name and every tongue should confess him as Lord. God, slave, human who died a criminal's death upon the cross, he is our Lord.

For someone steeped in the Jewish tradition this would have been a revolutionary statement, even a potentially blasphemous one (how could a mere man claim equality with God?). This understanding of who and what Jesus was was certainly both new and shocking. Beyond the Jewish diaspora, would not the peoples of the ancient world, who were accustomed to martial gods, have asked, 'What kind of god would humble himself not just to live among us but to be one of us, one with the lowliest of stations in life?' Who would want a weak god?

Maybe the passage of time has desensitized us to how radical the teaching is. Is then this five-verse passage a 'hymn'? When I think back, I realize how much of the Church's teaching became embedded in me through song. And I have certainly sung hymns based upon this passage. Perhaps my problem is that as a Christian from my church tradition I'm listening for a tune! Therefore, I find it easier to understand this as an early creed, a succinct statement of the faith of the early Church. Did Paul write it, or had he heard it spoken in the churches, then, having valued and remembered it, he wrote it down? Even at the time of his writing it, the Gospels had yet to be composed. Hence, it is one of the earliest known statements of the faith of the Church and is something that might have been learned by initiates as they became grafted into the new community of faith.

Who are we?

Like those early Christians, we are called into the community of faith, which confesses the faith in statements of belief and in the theologies of our prayers, hymns and sermons. We, too, are called to be Christ-like. That is a call to a life not of status but of humility. We are told to set aside ambition and conceit, and to regard others as better than ourselves. We are challenged to live selflessly, always looking out for others.

So how are we doing? Hard, isn't it? I know I pride myself on what I would regard as goodness and decency. Sometimes I take pride in my particular tradition, wearing it as a badge of honour. Just what kind of Christian exemplar am I? What would it mean for all of us truly to be of the same mind that was in Jesus? That is our challenge.

Finally, it is relatively easy, here in this place, to bend the knee and worship the Lord, but how will we go from here to live to his glory?

Wendy Kilworth-Mason

Suggested hymns

At the name of Jesus; He came to earth in poverty; He is Lord; Jesus is the name we honour.

Second Sunday of Christmas 5 January

(*or* Ephiphany; see p. 296)

Principal Service **Life Beyond Christmas**

Jer. 31.7–14, Ps. 147.13–end; *or* Ecclus. 24.1–12, *Canticle:* Wisd. 10.15–end; Eph. 1.3–14; **John 1.[1–9] 10–18**

Today is the twelfth day of Christmas, the final day of festivities. It's the day, after all, when 'my true love' sends her final and most ludicrous gift: 'twelve Lords a leaping', a sight that is hard to credit when we see some of the inhabitants of our second chamber visibly expiring before the television cameras. For the rest of the world, Christmas is truly over and we're into a new year.

Into the future

We may, however, ask wistfully if there is anything that we can hold on to and carry forward into the new year from the Christmas event. What of the claims, the promises, the stupendous Bible readings that hinted at some 'out of this world' hope and experience? And as if to remind us, verses from the first chapter of John are visited upon us once more, for the second or possibly third time over this season. John's isn't a birth story at all, at least in the form given to us by Matthew and Luke; there are no angels, no shepherds, no kings, no Christ-child, no parents. In fact the life of Jesus doesn't begin on earth, but in and with the Father, God, before time and before the world itself was created. Jesus has a divine origin and has come down to earth 'from a far country', from the Father's side, in order to become flesh and to 'pitch his tent with us'.

Children of God?

John doesn't give us a birth story. He doesn't provide a birth story because, for John, Jesus pre-existed his life on earth. Again, he doesn't give us a birth story because he's really only interested in our birth or, more precisely, the difference the coming of Jesus makes to us. And he sums this up in two remarkable verses:

> He was in the world, and the world came into being through him; yet the world did not know him. He came to what was his own, and his own people did not accept him. But to all who received him, who believed in his name, he gave power to become children of God, who were born, not of blood or of the will of the flesh or of the will of man, but of God.

Jesus came so that we might become children of God. Are we not already all children of God? That is contradicted, in part, by the fact that Jesus' own people had rejected him. If the idea of God as Father is sometimes implied in Scripture, it is, nevertheless, noticeably reluctant to call all people God's children. Being a child of God involves nothing less than a personal, mutual, affective relationship with the Father. And that has to be God's work not ours; the result of an interior change, whether gradual or dramatic, that may be likened to a 'second birth', to a process of adoption into God's family. It's this change that reconstitutes our lives so that they begin to reflect a family likeness to our divine Father.

Our choice

The work, the gift, the power, the will is God's alone, but it waits upon our receiving Jesus into our lives. That is all that is required of us. But what does that add up to? John speaks of the need to believe in the name of Jesus. And we may well ask, why this curious expression? It means that we need to believe that Jesus bears the divine name. That involves a practical trust in the one we believe to have come from God.

That is the only ultimate choice we're asked to make. There are no other grounds on which God judges us – it is our response to his Son, Jesus Christ, that determines everything. It determines whether we prefer light or darkness, truth or falsehood.

St John says, 'We have seen his glory, full of grace and truth.' We can only catch a glimpse of his glory – too much would blow our fuse, we couldn't take it. But this much we can receive. We can receive power to become children of God; God's Spirit occupies us, fashioning us into our Father's likeness.

Grounds for hope

Today we're not celebrating a world magically altered once and for all. We are claiming that the Word was made flesh – God is caught up in, identified with, all our life, even the most appalling and brutal parts, and he is working to transform it through love. How do we know that the world will be remade? Because we can know ourselves to be remade. To all who received him, who believed in his name, he gave power to become children of God.

What stronger ground is there for hope, what greater resource for lasting transformation, and what greater cause for joy and thanksgiving could we have than that we might behold his glory, the glory of the Father's only Son, full of grace and truth; and that we might be enlisted in making him known and working with him in the slow, costly project of renewing his world?

Roger Spiller

Suggested hymns

Word of God, come down on earth; Praise to you, O Christ, our Saviour, Word of the Father, calling us to life; Word that formed creation, earth and sea and sky; Thou didst leave thy throne and thy kingly crown.

Second Sunday of Christmas 5 January

Second Service **First EP of Epiphany**

Ps. 96, 97; Isa. 49.1–13; **John 4.7–26**

Gathering waters

We often think of water only as being something that quenches thirst – something to drink. And though that is very true, water has many meanings and uses, and another quality of water is its ability to neutralize, as a solvent, or, in everyday language, to make all things equal – to calm, or to heal, to salve, to reconcile or restore.

So water, as well as being thirst-quenching, is restorative, healing and life-giving. It is able of its own energy to bring about new life and new possibilities. Water always finds a way.

The prophet Isaiah speaks of the coastlands and those who live at the edge of the water. They are called to listen, they are being gathered in from the north, and the south, the west and the east. Those who are hungry and thirsty will be guided by springs of water. Water moves things along – always flowing, never still – and with God's life-giving water, people are moved through situations whatever they may be, into something which can ultimately be life-giving.

Throughout the history of the people of Israel, water had brought people together. Flowing water was the miracle from the side of a rock, and through that water the people are reconciled to God. Water washes away and cleans, and water is transformed into wine at the wedding in Cana. Here by the well, Jesus speaks to a Samaritan woman about the kind of water which will quench her thirst for eternity, but the water is also revealing its other properties too.

The living water

Our Gospel reading is about more than thirst-quenching water. We are given an image of the water of wisdom, coming from a deep, deep well. This water reveals the true identity of the woman who came to fetch it, and through her reveals the identity of Christ. This water heals the rifts that have divided communities; this water equals out the Samaritan and the Jew, the male and the female, the slave and the free, and gathers people together from the ends of the earth. This water is like a great tide of love drawing all things to itself.

Jesus is crossing every social boundary by talking to the Samaritan woman. Nevertheless, through his conversation, he speaks of his hope that one day all will worship together on the holy mountain. Jesus is the water of life that will make this happen.

As the water from the stone brought the Israelites together, so Jesus, the living water, is seeking to restore and reconcile all things to himself, to bring the whole of humanity through the wilderness of doubt and fear into the promised land of joy and gladness and complete unification with God.

Healing waters

What does this kind of reconciliation mean in today's world? Can people who are different be gathered together in unity? Can individuals burdened with guilt and anger find peace? Can arguments and feuds and old hatreds between peoples and nations, and chasms within the Church, be soothed by the water that is from God?

Many of these big questions that we face start in the simple act of seeking reconciliation with God, and many of the big questions about the world that we face together start in the simple act of seeking reconciliation with our neighbour. There are many more situations in which the living water of God can bring harmony out of discord. As well as quenching thirst, water also provides the opportunity for healing. Throughout the Gospels, Jesus constantly challenges us by asking us to consider who is 'included' and who is 'excluded'. Who do we need to be reconciled with? What situations need healing? He always turns our assumptions on their head. Where is our hope in the living water? What does being reconciled in and through Christ mean for us today, at the beginning of this new year?

The story of the woman at the well shows us that Christ, the living water, shows no partiality. We are all one in Christ Jesus. Though the disciples were clearly uncomfortable about Jesus talking to a Samaritan woman, *who has had many husbands, you know,* Jesus breaks down their fears, and makes this woman of ill repute a prophet, a messenger, an evangelist, for the good news.

Who is worthy of tasting the living water, and who does God turn away? We might be surprised to find that God turns no one away – the water is there for all of us, freely given. We might be surprised at who we meet at the living well, gathering water.

Water has this amazing knack of making all things equal, of reconciling us with one another and bringing us back to God's generous heart. This year, we too are invited to taste of this living water and there find healing and restoration, and new life in all its fullness.

Victoria Johnson

Suggested hymns

I heard the voice of Jesus say; Glorious things of thee are spoken; As the deer pants for the water; God is working his purpose out.

Baptism of Christ (First Sunday of Epiphany)

12 January

Principal Service **No Turning Back**

Isa. 42.1–9; Ps. 29; Acts 10.34–43; **Matt. 3.13–end**

Waters of a new creation

After years of reflection and worry no doubt, Jesus is in the water with John, the famous baptizer. John himself is all too conscious of the momentous action this baptism might be – 'I need to be baptized by you, and do you come to me?' Jesus comes to the moment of disclosure, showing himself after all those hidden years in the carpenter's shop. What it must have taken to bring him to this act.

Neither his nor John's high expectations were disappointed. And the divine voice was heard to say, 'This is my Son, the Beloved, with whom I am well pleased.' A dove hovered over the waters just as the Spirit of God hovered over the waters of creation in the first days. Here was the sign of a new creation, and Jesus could not mistake it. Yet coming out of the waters of this new creation it is not adulation that greets him but the terrible loneliness of self-doubt. Read on to the verse after the story of the baptism: 'Jesus was led up by the Spirit into the wilderness to be tempted by the devil.' What a let-down!

Real intensity

This is a word of comfort and support for us: even the Son of God knows that sense of let-down. He enters the troughs and peaks of living, and he doesn't stand aloof when that same experience is ours. Too often we imagine that if we could only get our faith right then we would be carried along on a height of experience that will push all the troubles and doubts of life out of the way. Or, conversely, we think that if our faith comes as a struggle and we have to grit our teeth and grind away at it, then somehow we have failed as Christians. Both outlooks are wrong. It wasn't like that for Christ, and it won't be for his followers.

Notice the intensity of the experience described. The implication is, I think, that only Jesus himself sees the heavens opened and hears the divine voice. Is the Gospel-writer telling us this was a special and profound experience for Jesus? Such a moment of intensity is hard to share; other people often can't recognize it. I found viewing the Victoria Falls a life-changing experience, but no one else seemed to understand. No one else until that day I met a person who had also stood where I had stood next to the thundering waters. People describe a similar sense of isolation and being unable to communicate the experience when it comes to birth and bereavement.

Ultimate consequence

Yet that very sense of isolation isn't itself true. The experience goes beyond the self and inevitably touches other lives. The baptism of Jesus means that the Spirit of God is with him, his life has taken a new direction, as it was always meant to. From now on there is no going back. The ultimate consequence of this baptism is the redemption of the world!

Our early Christian forebears had real difficulty with the fact that Jesus submitted himself to a baptism of repentance and the forgiveness of sins. He who was sinless makes himself one with the sinful. Hence the appeal in Matthew to the inscrutable will of God: 'Let it be so now; for it is proper for us in this way to fulfil all righteousness.' In John's Gospel there is no direct reference to the baptism at all. Yet this is the moment when Christ's individual act becomes the falling domino that will lead to so many other acts.

Bible echoes

The early Christians used characters from the Hebrew Bible to interpret what was going on in this act and to make plain the connection between the personal and the social. So, Jesus is the new David, anointed to kingship in order to ransom his people Israel. Jesus is the new Noah who will carry his people through the destructive waters of death and sin. Jesus is the new Moses, who will lead his people beyond the reach of their enemies through the waters of the Red Sea of despair and power's abuse And Jesus is the new Joshua who will lead his people over the troubled Jordan to the promised land of God's kingdom. All these things begin in the waters of baptism.

Shock or destiny

And finally, this is all part of the gracious activity of God – it is God's plan and purpose. Jesus leaves the carpenter's shop and suddenly sets about his mission, his destiny. Prepared for and expected in some ways, but in others a shock that leads John the Baptist to wonder what is going on and sends Jesus' family after him to curb his supposed madness. Deep questions are being raised; some greet what's happening with joy, but others with hostility. Suddenly everyone has to have an opinion about this carpenter.

What begins in the waters of the Jordan must go on until the Friday of Calvary and the Sunday in the Garden. There can be no turning back. The story of Jesus becomes our story also: for we are marked by God, though too often others claim not to notice the sign. We also must contend with the spiritual high spots that so soon leave us to the struggles of living the faith. We also must live the choosing so that personal faith has social consequences. Like our Saviour, once touched by the hand of God there is no turning back.

Christopher Burkett

Suggested hymns

At the dawning of creation; When Jesus came to Jordan; Jesus calls us o'er the tumult; The sinless one to Jordan came.

Baptism of Christ (First Sunday of Epiphany)

12 January

Second Service **Bold Speech for Turbulent Times**

Ps. 46, 47; Josh. 3.1–8, 14–end; Heb. 1.1–12; *Gospel at Holy Communion*: Luke 3.15–22

What can be said as Christians when our world seems to be caving in? When there is political unrest and uncertainty about the future? What can be said with an objectivity that won't trivialize or deny the mood that is engulfing us? New minted words can sound fresh but can unwittingly reveal a partisan stance. Perhaps lofty, lyrical speech that has worked its passage and proved its worth over long years in testing conditions may at least help to recalibrate our condition by placing it in a larger, cosmic and eternal framework.

'God is our refuge and strength, a very present help in trouble. Therefore we will not fear, though the earth should change.' What is that ancient poetic line from Psalm 46 meant to achieve? We live in 'worlds' that are formed by language. Learning French or Mandarin, for example, means far more than discovering a new vocabulary. Language forms us in a whole new way of seeing things, enabling us to inhabit another world. And when we read such a line of poetry the fixed, fated, hopeless world view is challenged. There is an alternative 'world' in which the God who has been a 'present' help through thousands of adversities remains active and available.

Creation

The Psalmist doesn't go in for half measures. He envisages a time when the earth could be changed, the mountains shaking, the waters roaring and cosmic disorder heralding the dissolution of the world. It's cathartic to posit the very worst that can be pitted against even the seeming enormity of our present troubles. It appeals to any residual pessimism we may have, facing the worst that can happen; and after all, God seems to specialize in setting himself hard tasks, acting in extreme conditions when human options seem to have dried up. Abraham is promised a vast family when his wife is childless; the future of God's chosen people goes right to the wire, leaving only a 'stump' from which a Messiah is promised; and a rejected, suffering and crucified man is revealed as saviour of world.

This psalm was the basis for Luther's great battle hymn of the Reformation, *Ein feste Burg*. Saying or singing that 'God is our hope and strength' like a mantra evokes not merely the transformative power of the poetic word; it summons the written memory of defeats and disasters that have been overcome by God's power, and breaks open a space in our lives for a sudden infilling of hope, courage and defiance. Those who allow themselves to be dominated by thoughts of God, for whom God is the ultimate goal, can begin to face even the collapse of the world order and hope and wait for its renewal.

History

The first of three sections of the psalm was preoccupied with the creation and destruction of the natural world. In the second strophe, it is history that claims our attention. The raging of the nations from fierce waves of destruction now gives way to a peaceful picture of the river in Jerusalem. Although Jerusalem has no actual river, we're meant to imagine links with the Garden of Eden, and the vision that, notwithstanding limitations of geography, a miraculous river would flow out of the city of God to the whole world. Since the security of the city depended on a supply of water, with God in the frame, its populace experienced protection and gladness. But these verses also represent history at its worst, living in a war zone. And when the people wake up in the morning they see the alarming sight of a city that has been assailed, assaulted like the roar of the sea we heard before. But because God is in the midst of her, God needs only to let his voice be heard and the city will remain firm, unmoved, a 'safe stronghold'.

Future

So now in the final section of the psalm, readers are invited to see the completion of God's work of deliverance. The broken bows, shattered spears and burned shields lie all around, but they speak about God's will for peace. 'Be still, and *know* that I am God!' God's mission is that people should *know* God and submit to him. And the God whom we're to know is 'exalted among the nations' and 'exalted in the earth'. This is the God who has form, the God of patriarchs like Jacob, who oversaw the fortunes of God's people from their early formative years.

If we reckon without God, the present sight of wars, division and destruction are all there is to shape our mood, belief and hope. But if, instead, we reckon with the fact and presence of God, Immanuel, with us, then we are led towards the future that God is bringing, just as he did in the past. We put our faith, then, not in outward appearances, but in the God whose will is to make all things new, and 'therefore we will not fear'. Act, engage in political argument, mobilize public opinion, yes, but with an ultimate source of hope that refuses to incapacitate us. The psalm evokes the destructive and the saving power of water. That chimes in with the day's theme, the baptism of Jesus. Let us be immersed in the life of God that we may be renewed by hope.

Roger Spiller

Suggested hymns

God is our strength and refuge; Be still and know; Be still, for the presence of the Lord; Our God stands like a fortress rock/A mighty fortress is our God.

Second Sunday of Epiphany 19 January

(For Week of Prayer for Christian Unity, see p. 298.)

Principal Service The One to Know[10]

Isa. 49.1–7; Ps. 40.1–12; 1 Cor. 1.1–9; **John 1.29–42**

You could have been rubbing shoulders in Palestine with the quiet carpenter's son and not known who he was. You could have jostled with him on the muddy banks of the River Jordon and not known that this young man was the Son of God. Even John didn't know who Jesus was – at least, not until after he had been baptized. We complain, rightly, about churches baptizing people indiscriminately, but this was the most indiscriminate baptism there ever was. John baptizing people he didn't know. No wonder he said, 'Among you stands one whom you do not know.'

If the Son of God, the Word of God, who was with God in the beginning, and through whom all things were made, was walking the soil of his own creation, wouldn't you expect that everybody would know his identity? Shouldn't everybody be able to tell, immediately, unmistakably, at a glance, who he was? But you could stand right behind him in a crowd, you could be at a dinner party with him and have no idea that the hands that were passing the Merlot were the same hands that once sent galaxies spinning in space.

'Among you stands one whom you do not know.'

Once when the Queen was walking around the village of her home in Balmoral, in head scarf and country casuals, she was accosted by a woman. 'You look just like the Queen,' she told her. To which the Queen is reported to have replied, 'How very reassuring.' She remained unrecognized.

Churches in every village of the land, the bestselling book of all time, the rituals in national and local celebrations and tragedies, some of the finest music, exalted language, greatest paintings and the loftiest edifices all witness to his stupendous person and life. And prayers offered up every day in Parliament, at great banquets, retreat houses and thousands of churches and chapels attest and invoke his contemporary, living presence and power to shape our world, and yet . . .

'Among you stands one whom you do not know.'

Did you see the TV series on millionaires who go undercover? They work in needy communities and support-agencies, so that they can discover the real needs, where they can target their wealth. And the unrecognized Jesus lifts up, and gives succor to, the invisible, overlooked people who stand among us, whom society doesn't know. And who are they? They are the sons and daughters of God, children of the one heavenly Father, the people whom Jesus came to rescue. They are the poor to whom Jesus came to preach good news and the release of captives. Lord, when did we see you hungry . . . when did we see you naked? When did we see you in prison?

'Among you stands one whom you do not know.'

> He comes to us as One unknown, without a name, as of old, by the lake-side, He came to those men who knew Him not. He speaks to us the same word: 'Follow thou me!' and sets us to the tasks which He has to fulfil for our time. He commands. And to

> those who obey Him, whether they be wise or simple, He will reveal Himself in the toils, the conflicts, the sufferings which they shall pass through in His fellowship, and, as an ineffable mystery, they shall learn in their own experience Who He is.[11]

If this day you do know him, if through the gift of faith you can recognize him – rejoice and be thankful. It's not obvious, or natural. But if by the gift of grace you can see the Lamb of God who takes away the sin of the world, you can also see all those other people among us for whom Jesus is still unknown, who sorely need to know the Lamb of God, and you too can tell them what you have discovered about Jesus. He is among us still, he is the one to know.

Roger Spiller

Suggested hymns

Christ is the world's light; Jesus Christ is waiting, waiting in the streets; Dear Lord, we long to see your face; Jesus, come, for we invite you.

Second Sunday of Epiphany 19 January
Second Service 'Is there anybody there?'

Ps. 96; **Ezek. 2.1—3.4**; Gal. 1.11–end; *Gospel at Holy Communion*: John 1.43–end

It's sometimes claimed that the notion of God is an invention, a human construct. There's nothing outside us, only our language, we're told. The experience of the silence and hiddenness of God can lead believers themselves to ask, 'Is there anybody there?' That's not, of course, a new question. Ezekiel and St Paul, whose callings are set out in our readings, provide testimony that seems to defy the sense that we are alone in an alien universe.

Commission

Ezekiel was a young man of some 30 years when he felt overpowered by a calling from God. He was newly deported to Babylon as a result of a fresh military challenge to his country's independence. His prospects for a priestly vocation and his hopes for the security of his nation were abruptly terminated. At the 'appearance of the likeness of the glory of the LORD', Ezekiel fell on his face. God summons him, 'O mortal'. The voice orders him to 'stand up' on his feet and the divine spirit penetrates his feeble body. This direct, dynamic apprehension of God owes nothing to his own spiritual power. It gives him over to a new divine reality which puts question marks over all he previously believed and shakes him to the core of his being. Ezekiel's experience has obvious parallels in St Paul's conversion experience.

Task

The prophet Ezekiel was himself called to establish God's existence to a humanity estranged from him. Ezekiel began his ministry in exile, just seven years before the destruction of the capital city of Judah. The prospect of a final destruction of Jerusalem seemed inconceivable to God's own people. Its inviolability seemed guaranteed by God's covenant with his people. But the waves of destruction by the Babylonians and the experience of exile precipitated a spectacular collapse of faith in God. Ezekiel had to warn of impending danger before the final assault, then interpret God's action when disaster came, and invite that same inward renewal by the Spirit that he himself had experienced at his call. His task was daunting and unlikely to bear fruit. His people were a 'rebellious house'. That became the title of a Church of England report that illustrated the slowness of working together in world mission. Ezekiel would face opposition, contempt and even bodily attacks. But God promised him just one thing: that people would recognize that God's prophet had appeared among the exiles and that where God's rule was thought to have died out it will nevertheless be heard afresh.

Embodiment

Ezekiel is commanded by God to eat the scroll inscribed with the message he is to relay. This performance art, and prophetic symbolism, indicates that he is to be totally consumed by the words that he is given; God is making a total claim that extends to the prophet's physical body. He must be one with his people, in their own dis-ease and desolation, just as St Paul spoke of bearing in his own body the sufferings of Christ. Eating the scroll also tells us that God's message has its own existence, independent of the judgement of the prophet, and that it is divine in origin. Paul too makes clear that the gospel message that came to him was no human product but he 'received it through a revelation of Jesus Christ'. It followed, therefore, that Paul saw no need to report to the key 'pillars' of Christianity in Jerusalem, at least for three years. There must be no reason to question the divine origin of the good news. Ezekiel, too, demonstrated that his gospel owed nothing to himself, and indeed overturned much of his priestly training. For Ezekiel, as for Paul, God's message is embodied. For Paul, there is the unidentified, painful, physical affliction and bodily weakness. Ezekiel would experience paralysis and numbness, mental breakdown and the loss of intimacy with the death of his wife.

Light to Gentiles

Both Paul and Ezekiel had commissions that served the Epiphany promise that God would bring light to all people, including the Gentiles. Ezekiel taught that God's presence was not tied to any place and is present even in the unclean land of exile. God has come out of hiding and seeks a personal relationship with individuals and nations; a new birth for each individual through the Spirit. Paul, too, challenges the racial and religious separation and superiority of his own nation. Called the apostle to the Gentiles, he prefers to be the apostle to all nations, serving the one gospel, sharing table fellowship with all people, and in one church for Christians of all complexions. Both he and Ezekiel had a vision for the salvation of the world.

Divine reality

The doubts that circle around the silence of God are confronted by the direct, dynamic apprehension of God. Ezekiel, called the father of Judaism, restored confidence in God for a new generation after the shock and desolation of their national and religious life. God is not, it seems, a talkative, loquacious God; he acts through climactic events and speaks representatively through the people he calls, and they in turn testify to the impact he makes upon them. We may recoil from the cost of the vocation that God demands of his servants, but can we dismiss the invasive, generative power of a mind and will that prevailed over characters like Ezekiel and Paul? And their witness to God's action in human history and in the words that confronted them have power to address us afresh. When we read their accounts, we find they speak to our condition, beckon us from our sense of aloneness and draw us into the story of redemption.

Roger Spiller

Suggested hymns

Come, living God, when least expected; Hear me, O Lord, in my distress; From the deep places, hear my cry; We turn to Christ, anew.

Third Sunday of Epiphany 26 January

Principal Service Church Unity

Isa. 9.1–4; Ps. 27.1, 4–12 [*or* 27.1–11]; **1 Cor. 1.10–18**; Matt. 4.12–23

As soon as Jesus called not just Andrew but Peter, and then James and John, there was potential for division in the Church. This is human nature. You don't need a big group to have squabbles. You just need a minimum of two people.

And so the problem that Paul identifies among the Christians at Corinth is familiar:

> For it has been reported to me by Chloe's people that there are quarrels among you, my brothers and sisters. What I mean is that each of you says, 'I belong to Paul', or 'I belong to Apollos', or 'I belong to Cephas' (that's Peter), or 'I belong to Christ.'

From difference to division

People are different – in appearance, character, interests, beliefs and many other ways. And different people attract different people. But sadly, difference easily becomes division. The existence of other groups is seen as a threat to my group. Power struggles follow on. And when one group gets so big that it's hard for individuals to feel allegiance to it, it often splits apart and the process multiplies. It's happening all over the world. And it's not too surprising that it was happening in Corinth.

What troubled Paul, of course, was that it was happening in the church, the body of Christ. Because Paul believed that the church was called to be not just like society at large, but to offer a radical alternative model of human relationship. We can be thankful for all the signs that the Church is indeed offering an alternative vision of unity. And we would do well to heed the positive arguments Paul gives as to why division among Christians is not only wrong, but fundamentally illogical, a denial of the truth of Jesus Christ.

He presents two key reasons why the Christians in Corinth should be 'all of you . . . in agreement and that there be no divisions among you, but that you should be united in the same mind and the same purpose'.

Jesus Christ is one

The first reason is simply that the Lord Jesus Christ is one. Our divisions obscure that. Paul makes his appeal *in the name of Jesus Christ*. In his name they have been baptized. And has he, Christ, been divided? Has he split himself up into parties or factions or personality cults? No, the very idea is absurd. For Paul, Christ is not just another leader. He is God's unique gift of himself to the world. No one is beyond the reach of his care and interest. So to put up walls between us and square off against each other is to obscure the nature of the Lord we claim to serve. It's to draw a veil over the amazing love which alone has power to unite human beings, to lift them beyond their rivalries and hostilities.

The trouble is that, in practice, this radical oneness is often forgotten. Whether we think of relationships between churches or within churches, some other allegiance often threatens to become more important than our allegiance to Christ. So an individual or group who seems 'not like me' or 'not like us' in some way, or who clearly has different views from 'me' or 'us', or different ideas about how the church should operate, becomes a person or group whom we avoid, ignore or, at worst, see as a rival. The truth is that we don't need to deny the fact of difference – indeed, we can celebrate it – but we recognize that in Christ we are united even with those from whom we differ.

The message not the messenger

Paul's second argument for the importance of unity is that the good news of Jesus Christ will be obscured if people concentrate their attention on its messengers. The Corinthian Christians, like people generally in the classical world, loved a fine speaker. Indeed, public speakers fulfilled to some extent the role of the entertainers of their age. Paul does not want the church to regard its various leaders in that way. He doesn't want to become a focus of attention in himself, or have a personality cult grow up around him.

What had happened to Jesus was so shocking that the stark facts would only be obscured if people tried to dress them up in clever entertaining language. Speakers like that would end up drawing attention to themselves rather than to the message. And so, inevitably, there would be division, because what people focused on would not be the story of Christ but the talents of the speaker.

'The message about the cross is foolishness to those who are perishing.' But, he goes on to say, it's the power of God to save and to unify the human race, as he takes the sting of all our hatred and hostility and gives himself for us all. As we focus on *that* remarkable story we stay united ourselves and become a sign and foretaste of that unity for all people.

Week by week, as we gather round this table as people who are in many ways very different in background, opinions, character and experience, and share bread and wine, the signs and presence of the Christ who unites us across all those differences, our unity in him is strengthened and renewed.

Stephen Wright

Suggested hymns

Living God, your word has called us; Let us build a house where love is found; I come with joy, a child of God; Filled with the Spirit's power, with one accord.

Third Sunday of Epiphany 26 January

Second Service God in Time

Ps. 33 [*or* 33.1–12]; **Eccles. 3.1–11**; 1 Peter 1.3–12; *Gospel at Holy Communion*: Luke 4.14–21

If you want a tract warning against a driven, frantic, workaholic lifestyle, then the book of Ecclesiastes is the text to turn to. It points to the arbitrariness and absurdity of life, our ignorance about the future and the futility of seeking after the meaning and future of life. A hedonistic lifestyle is the recommended choice. Of course, this needs the counterbalance of the rest of Scripture, but as it stands it delivers a timely challenge to so much speculative theology that risks losing touch with the sharp realities of human life.

One such challenge reads: God 'has put a sense of past and future into [our] minds, yet [we] cannot find out what God has done from the beginning to the end'.

Living in time

We live in time, time that was created with the world, and time that scientists think is real and physical and not merely the invention of our minds. In his posthumously produced book, Stephen Hawkins makes explicit that time had a beginning in the Big Bang and will end in black holes. Our subjective sense that time has a relentless forward movement is also shared by physics. We experience time to use, to kill, to fill, to make, to keep. But as our writer reminds us, time isn't undifferentiated but tensed, past, present and future. The past can be accessed, not just our own past, but the corporate memory of past peoples that is handed down to us. Christian belief tells us that the past can be re-membered in the present, notably at the Eucharist but also as we inhabit the Scriptures. Although the calumnies of the past cannot be reversed, their effects can be redeemed and their destructive cycle broken, so we need not be held captive by our past.

Time present

Our writer takes the present for granted, as well he might. But the present is the time when God and God's kingdom, present though hidden in our world, encounter us in myriad guises, faces, voices, crises and other events. Such moments have the features of timelessness or, as the New Testament calls it, 'kairos' time, rather than our more usual 'chronos' time. This kairos time intersects ordinary time and generates surprise and newness that cannot be accounted for by antecedent causes.

Time future

We, too, have a prevailing sense of future time, which can squeeze out living in the present moment. But the future is also the repository of our hopes and projections generated by the supreme religious faculty of the imagination, and this can in turn give us space to shape and inform our present. We can even grasp the future, which is not-yet, and put one foot in its alternative 'world', even as we keep one foot in the present world.

Instead of 'past and future', the translation may read that God has 'set *eternity* in our hearts'. That vastly expands the ordinary 'future' dimension of time and reflects the widespread impulse that our destiny and time is beyond and different from the one we currently occupy. We have a sense of restlessness, homelessness, exile, longing for a new home.

Beginning time

The writer of Ecclesiastes says: '[We] cannot find out what God has done from the beginning to the end.' He rightly identifies the mystery that attends the beginning and end of earthly life, which now has to reckon with the scientific world view. The major religions all affirm God's agency in creation, but, in the nature of the case, the God we posit to have created the causal process of creation cannot himself be an identifiable cause like the physical causes recognized by science. But it remains the case that a personal mind, a mind infinitely greater than our own, but still a mind able to relate to us, is likely to go on being a credible explanatory force in our understanding of creation.

End-time

The 'end' in which God is also mysteriously active is perhaps more challenging for us. It's usual for us to catch the inexorable movement to the future that is a major theme of the Scriptures. A sense of goal, aspiration or what the biblical writers call 'telos' runs parallel with the thermodynamic arrow of time recognized by modern physics. While the expansion of the universe supplied the conditions for human life to emerge, the scientific expectation is that the universe is destined to contract and to end in black holes. But then, too, we learn from St Paul that creation is in 'bondage to decay', but will be redeemed.

The God in whom we believe is Lord of time and history, but he is not above and outside time as we know it. He subjects himself to the limitations of time so that he can accompany us as we pass from past into present and then embrace the future in imagination. He addresses us in time, but creates moments of transcendence and timelessness. We accept the mystery of God's works but know him as he is in Jesus Christ, and that is ground enough for our living in the present and for our hope for the future.

Roger Spiller

Suggested hymns

When all thy mercies, O my God; To everything turn, turn, turn; Just for today; Beyond all mortal praise.

Presentation of Christ in the Temple (Candlemas) 2 February

Principal Service **Candlemas Bells**

Mal. 3.1–5; Ps. 24 [*or* 24.7–end]; Heb. 2.14–end; **Luke 2.22–40**

From winter to spring

The humble snowdrop peeps out into the world just as we experience the last throws of winter. They are the first heralds of spring. Something of beauty; so precious and small, yet steely enough to burst through ice, snow and earth as hard as iron. For centuries, Christian folk have seen in the snowdrop a sign of hope and new life, and also something bitter-sweet. Their beauty is fading and fleeting. When each flower raises its head above the earth there is no fanfare, no great trumpeting of spring like the loud and confident daffodils. The snowdrop emerges somewhat forlorn, bowing her pale head.

They were once commonly known as 'Candlemas Bells', and in one folk rhyme we are told that 'The Snowdrop, in purest white array, First rears her head on Candlemas day.' They were often planted around churchyards and at vestry doors, and this simple flower, because of its annual life cycle, chimes in with the churches' festival of Candlemas. This might explain the meaning that people have ascribed to this perfect, delicate, little flower, which holds within each petal a sad farewell and a remarkable rebirth. A death and a resurrection.

Looking back and looking forward

The festival of Candlemas falls halfway between the winter solstice and spring equinox. Liturgically, the Presentation of Christ in the Temple falls 40 days after Christmas, signalling the end of the season of Christmas and Epiphany and the beginning of our turn towards Lent, Passiontide and Easter. Candlemas marks a turning away from the nativity of Christ to consider his suffering and death. But we are also given hope of what is beyond.

Our Gospel reading recalls the time when Mary and Joseph took their child to the Temple for the ceremonies of ritual purification. It is there that they meet the old man Simeon and the elderly woman Anna, both of whom, nearing the end of their lives, rejoice that they have at last seen God's Messiah. Simeon and Anna have been waiting years for this day. It's as if they have been stuck in an eternal winter. Perhaps they had begun to wonder if God's promises would be fulfilled. Then into the Temple comes someone so small, pure and full of light that they can hardly believe their eyes. A child, like a tiny flower, just a few months old. A child who is powerless and cannot speak for himself, but is a sure sign of God's grace.

The only way Simeon can express himself is through song, and after a lifetime of waiting he can at last face his own mortality and be released into eternal life. Spring has come. But he also sees suffering, betrayal and pain. This child, almost unbelievably, will cause division even within households. No one will be able to hide from the purity that this child will bring, and the inner thoughts of many will be revealed.

Mary would not have been consoled by Simeon's words in the Temple that day. He was warning her of a future grief, before life had even begun. There was no promise in this child of an easy life for anyone; there was no promise that we would be free from sorrow, struggle and anguish. And yet in this child there was light and life surging through every bone in his body; this child was so full of the spirit that through him, even in the darkest moments, hope would emerge and love would overcome everything.

Like a beam of pure light, this child will expose sin and hatred and injustice, and witness against all those who oppress the orphan, the widow, the alien. He will comfort the afflicted and afflict the comfortable. His breath will turn hearts of stone into hearts of flesh; all desires will be known and no secrets hidden from his gaze. Like a refiner's fire, like fuller's soap, this child will cleanse and purify and re-create us in his image. It is no consolation to stand before this child, for we will be transformed; we will all be changed. He comes to dispel the shadows and make the whole universe brilliant with his eternal light.

Love will come again

Within the festival of Candlemas we find our own stories of loss and longing and grief. We yearn for the light to once again dispel the darkness that lingers over our world today. We each know that we are battling through our own winters and waiting for the spring. We hope for new life and new beginnings, but often struggle to rise above the frozen earth.

The story of Simeon and Anna, and the story of the Candlemas Bells, might give us hope that the Sun of Righteousness will arise with healing in his wings, to soften the earth and call the flowers from their slumber. We come with the light of our candles in procession, but also with the whole of our lives, seeking God's blessing and trusting in God's promise as Simeon and Anna did. For every winter we face we will be given the strength, like the snowdrop, to emerge from the stone cold earth. When our hearts are wintry, grieving or in pain, the love of God will call us back to life again.

Victoria Johnson

Suggested hymns

Now the green blade riseth; Faithful vigil ended; Hail to the Lord's anointed; Shine, Jesus, shine!

Presentation of Christ in the Temple (Candlemas) 2 February

Second Service The Latter Glory

Morning Ps. 48, 146; Evening Ps. 122, 132; **Hag. 2.1–9**; John 2.18–22

When the new Coventry Cathedral was consecrated in 1962, the Archbishop took his text from the book of the prophet Haggai. It was Haggai who, some 520 years before Christ, had been the prime mover in rebuilding the Temple in Jerusalem. And now, two and a half thousand years later, his words were chosen to mark the celebrations of the newly built cathedral: 'The latter splendour of this house shall be greater than the former, says the LORD of hosts; and in this place I will give prosperity.' 'Greater than the former'? Was the latter building greater than the one that it replaced?

It didn't seem that it was, from the wave of controversy and disappointment that stretched over the city. For those who remembered the much loved gothic edifice that was destroyed in the German bombing, the new building was no match for the one it replaced. 'More like an aircraft hangar than a place of worship' was one of the unfavourable comparisons. Since then, it has grown on people. Simon Jenkins awards it three stars in his book on England's cathedrals, but, for all that, he concludes that it should be knocked down and rebuilt as it was before!

The second Temple

But did the latter, second Temple in Jerusalem fare better and prove more splendid than the one that preceded it? Not for those who were about 70 years of age or more and had memories of the glorious, lavish Temple, built by Solomon. By comparison, the latter house was a pale and pathetic shadow of its former edifice. One Ezra chronicles that 'old men who had seen the first house, wept with a loud voice when they saw the foundation of this house being laid'. The prophet Isaiah had raised expectations of the new Temple: 'I will make your pinnacles of rubies, your gates of jewels, and all your wall of precious stones'. Such grandiose promises fired up the returning exiles, inflated their expectations and fuelled their negative response. It was analogous to the disappointment that greeted the soldiers returning from the world wars. For the exiles there were vivid reminders of the catastrophe of war everywhere they looked. And there were younger people returning to their homeland who hadn't seen the earlier Temple and saw no need for one now.

Hope or fulfilment?

What reason could there be for the claim that 'the latter splendour of the temple would be greater than the former', or was this grandiosity only a ruse to inspire and encourage the builders? Solomon's Temple was a lavish building worthy of God's abode. But it fed the idea that God was somehow localized in his house, and guaranteed that the Temple would be inviolable against the warnings of judgement and destruction by the prophets. The people had learnt in exile that they could worship God even without a temple.

So the reason for rebuilding was more intentionally to serve God's mission to other peoples and nations. What did it say about God, whose house lay in ruins, while the people were living in their own elaborate homes? God's house needed to be a witness, a public statement, a physical declaration of her universal Lordship, and that was the driving force behind Haggai's enterprise.

Prosperity and well-being

The promise God made through his prophet wasn't just about the splendour of the building, nor even the restoration of God's honour. It was a promise, ultimately, of prosperity and well-being. Haggai believed that the ancient covenant with God was still in force, despite his people's disobedience. The Temple was proof that the old order remained and God still had a claim on his people. The country was languishing economically and psychologically. The building would bring material and psychological benefit. It would be the first step in a struggle that would take another hundred years, in which Judaea would gain some autonomy and independence. And it marked the restoration of civil order.

But the promise of Haggai was not exhausted. Twenty years before Christ's birth, in an initiative to gain popularity among the Jews and redeem his brutal regime, King Herod rebuilt the Temple associated with Haggai. His was on a monumental scale whose splendour was believed to have far exceeded Solomon's Temple itself. But this was a self-glorifying, self-serving edifice, whose imminent destruction was foretold by Jesus himself within the Temple area: 'Destroy this temple, and in three days I will raise it up.' Jesus would in his own body replace the temple built by hands, and his Spirit would create a living temple in the people of God.

With God, the latter splendour will always be greater than the former. But not because of human development but because God's glorious future invades our present. And as for the cathedral in Coventry, it has become a great international centre, drawing people from all nations to build peace and reconciliation across the world.

Roger Spiller

Suggested hymns

O thou not made with hands; Christ is our cornerstone; Let us build a house; Be still, for the presence of the Lord.

Third Sunday before Lent (Proper 1) 9 February

Principal Service **A Watered Garden**

Isa. 58.1–9a [9b–12]; Ps. 112 [*or* 112.1–9]; 1 Cor. 2.1–12 [13–end]; Matt. 5.13–20

Storyteller, midwife, herald, gardener, choreographer, host, conductor – these are just some of the metaphors that enable ministers and priests to reimagine their vocation. Consultants to business, schools, even churches try to help us to identify the often secret, root metaphors that subliminally shape organizations. And therapies that offer to change our outlook on life do so by offering fresh metaphors. Even the ubiquitous C. S. Lewis in an early scholarly paper acknowledged that it's not possible to think meaningfully without using metaphors. Science, too, has its metaphors: 'string theory', 'black holes', 'God particles'. Metaphors lodge in the mind, enable leaps of the imagination to take place, and inspire and envision us, in ways that rational logical speech cannot match. It's often more enriching and life-changing for us to inhabit fresh metaphors in worship and preaching than to learn arcane facts from the Scriptures.

Images that defy explanation

'You shall be like a watered garden, like a spring of water' – a verse from Isaiah, also repeated in Jeremiah. What on earth does that mean? I was a young teenager when a bishop preached on that verse. I was none the wiser when he had stopped talking. But the image took root in my imagination. It helped that the bishop didn't kill the metaphor by attempting to explain it. And so it remained, present throughout my life, collecting around it other rich metaphors of water in the Bible, metaphors that between them just about cover the whole story of our salvation. The 'watered garden' served as a mantra whose repetition nourished and irrigated my parched soul in some subliminal way. The text is a promise, and the metaphor is the form by which God can fructify our lives.

Not long after, I took part in the annual Boys' Brigade parade around the city centre of Birmingham, which concluded with worship and a sermon on a reading that held me captivated and enthralled. The preacher took the vision of Ezekiel chapter 47: of water rising uncontrollably around the Temple and flowing out in all directions around it. At first it was just toe deep, then ankle deep, then knee deep, then waist deep, and finally deep enough to swim in. That would be more than enough to give any churchwarden, steward or treasurer cause for apoplexy. I learnt the fear of water when our home was flooded, and the carpet made a brave attempt to embrace the ceiling. Here, Ezekiel offers us an unforgettable metaphor for mission – wild, uncontrollable, outgoing, renewing everything in its path.

Water and Spirit

Water is one of the essential metaphors for the Spirit. It needs the great archetypal, elemental metaphors of fire and wind and breath to convey its power as well as its subtlety. And when in the 1960s the Church rediscovered the Spirit, we looked to the words John records of Jesus at the great feast at the Temple, where he promises that out of the hearts of those who believe in him 'shall flow rivers of living water', or as Jesus promises after giving 'living water' to the Samaritan woman, 'a spring of water welling up to eternal life'.

This is picked up in our second epistle of St Paul to Corinth, where he speaks of God's grace overflowing into the human situation as a transforming excess, like a stream or fountain that cannot cease, but must endlessly flow out of itself even to remain itself. So also in Paul's second letter to the Corinthians those who perpetuate God's overflowing are not impoverished but enriched. What is received must be given away or else it will block the flow of ever more gifts from God. As R. S. Thomas puts it: 'Some ask for the world, / and are diminished / in the receiving / of it. You gave me / only this small pool / that the more I drink / from, the more overflows / me with sourceless light.'[12]

Concrete metaphors

The baptismal font can be a restrictive dispenser of water if Philip Larkin's liberating advice is not heeded. Attending church would involve 'A furious devout drench'.[13] Still, in some churches the font is encircled by a channel of water pumped forcefully around it, and baptism candidates cross over to reach it. That is meant to recall the way the Israelites crossed over the Red Sea to find deliverance, and this is used to prefigure baptism. In a church in Plymouth, water pours down from its source where the Bible is read and is sent forcibly moving around the circumference of the church, encircling the whole congregation. It declares that God's people are 'a watered garden, like a spring of water'.

The Bible is a treasure store of metaphors that have the power to expand, excite, connect, transform, delight, re-imagine and nourish our lives. What are the root metaphors that shape how you live? What are the metaphors that shape your church, your place of work, your hopes and dreams? My metaphor flows into prayer: 'Deliver me from the long drought / of the mind. Let leaves / from the deciduous Cross / fall on us, washing / us clean, turning our autumn / to gold by the affluence of their fountain.'[14] So says R. S. Thomas. Gerard Manley Hopkins says, 'send my roots rain'.[15]

Roger Spiller

Suggested hymns

Glorious things of thee are spoken; As the deer pants for the water; In water we grow, safe in the womb; As water to the thirsty.

Third Sunday before Lent (Proper 1) 9 February
Second Service **How to Live a Good Life**

Ps. [1, 3] 4; Amos 2.4–end; **Eph. 4.17–end**; *Gospel at Holy Communion*: Mark 1.29–39

A rule for a new life

How do you live a good life? If you go into any bookshop you can find shelves upon shelves of self-help books which claim to help us live a good and fulfilling life. It seems many in our world today are yearning to live an authentic and value-driven life in which they can be honest about themselves and respect and care for those around them. But sometimes people don't know where to look or where to go for advice, so the self-help shelf is an obvious place to begin. There is a desire to be good in all of us, but we are often blown off track in pursuit of that cause and get dragged back into selfish and destructive behaviours that diminish ourselves and those closest to us. The Christian might describe this as our human propensity to sin.

The quest for self-improvement is often focused inwards to the self, whereas paradoxically it may be that we actually become who we are called to be by being attentive to the needs of others and putting the self to one side. The more we turn away from self and towards others and towards God, the more likely we are to find out who we really are.

Amos, the prophet of justice and mercy, has a hard message for those who fail to be attentive to the needs of others. He pronounces judgement upon Judah and upon Israel, among others, for their selfish behaviour. Their actions have been exploitative and selfish and they have trampled over the poor and needy in favour of personal and communal gain. His judgement is made upon communities who have transgressed the commandments of God.

Identity found in community

Community has long been the place where we find out who we really are, and throughout Christian history community is the place where people have found their true identity and their ultimate purpose.

St Benedict wrote his monastic rule for those living in community; it is in effect a guide to how to live a good life by being attentive to the needs of others. Within the Rule of St Benedict every detail of community life is examined and the thread running throughout the rule is that of obedience and attentiveness to one another. In popular terms, St Benedict affirms that there is no 'I' in 'team'!

Similarly, Paul's advice in the letter to the Ephesians draws upon examples born of being in Christian community. We are advised to build each other up, to work honestly, not to let the sun go down on our anger and to speak truth to our neighbours. We can understand our life by measuring the impact that it has on others and the legacy we leave behind in our wake. We are members of one another, we are together one body and we need one another to complete the whole.

Those of us who have been part of a church community understand that this manifestation of Christian community is very much a place where virtues are learnt by living alongside others in good times and in bad. Churches are places that, at their very best, image the kind of community where we can learn about ourselves by being part of a diverse family. We know also that churches can be challenging places for the same reasons, but in a world often devoid of community they can be a gift and a place where people find the freedom to develop and grow in themselves.

Living in community is a formational experience, meaning we are often changed by it and through it. We can grow into people shaped by Christ and so put on a new 'self' by the renewing of our minds. Our old self is cast away and we are in a sense reborn in Christ. If we listen to his commandments and are obedient to his word, we begin to embody in our own lives what it means to be good in his name.

Victoria Johnson

Suggested hymns

Brother, Sister, let me serve you; Help us to help each other, Lord; For ourselves no longer living; Forgive our sins as we forgive.

Second Sunday before Lent (Proper 2) 16 February

Principal Service **Lift Up Your Eyes**

Gen. 1.1—2.3; Ps. 136 [*or* 136.1–9, 23–end]; Rom. 8.18–25; **Matt. 6.25–end**

Back to the beginning

It is sometimes good to go back to the very beginning and remember there is a bigger picture. It is good for us to lift up our eyes from the small worlds that we sometimes inhabit and see that we are part of a greater narrative. The first chapter of the book of Genesis establishes the greatest story ever told. We hear tell of God's creative act, which begins with a formless void and leads us through the creation of night and day, the heavens and the earth, the land and the sea, the sun, the moon, the stars, the creeping things that creep upon the earth, vegetation, the birds of the air, the wild animals and then, to crown it all, humankind made in the image of God the Creator. God then blesses humankind and looks upon all that has been created, and it was very good indeed.

The Psalmist echoes this theme of journeying through creation step by step and responds to each creative moment by reminding us all that *God's steadfast love endures for ever.* The writers of Genesis and Psalm 136 proclaim a God who is intimately connected to the earth and continuously engaged in the world that has been created. Creation progresses and evolves, but God is still there, attentive to the sparrow, as much as he is attentive to every hair of our head. As the story continues, we repeat again and again, *God's steadfast love endures for ever*. We are children of this creation and if we gaze on this history, if we look upon this magnificent beauty and endless bounty and recognize that we are part of it, we might also gain the confidence to hope on God's amazing providence. If God can do all this, surely anything is possible?

Do not worry

Thousands of years after this story was written, Jesus finds himself among those who seem to have lost faith in what is possible. Their eyes are downcast, their hearts are fearful. Worry clouds their thoughts. His disciples may well have given up homes and jobs and families to follow him; successful fishermen put down their nets and gave up everything for this charismatic rabbi from Nazareth. Understandably, they are now uncertain of the future and anxious about how they will survive. What will they eat? What will they drink? What will they wear? Perhaps after the thrill of making a new start and the novelty of being on the road, the realities of an itinerant life were now becoming apparent. They are suddenly dependent on the generosity of the earth and the generosity of those around them. So what does Jesus do? Jesus reminds them of their ultimate origin and encourages them to consider that their horizons are much broader than they imagine. He suggests they lift up their eyes and look at the birds of the air, the same birds of the air that flew above the earth across the dome of the sky, on the fifth day. He then suggests they look to the lillies of the field, adorned like kings, a sign of splendour. 'If they are clothed in such a fashion, how much more will God clothe you?' he asks the disciples, 'you of little faith'.

Looking to the future

Jesus calls his disciples back to the beginning and to the utter, life-giving generosity of God. He offers a bigger picture, a grander narrative. When our worlds become too small it is natural to worry about the little things, but Jesus always calls us to see things differently and to put our hope in him. This, of course, is where faith comes in. And even a little faith can work wonders.

We are challenged to put our faith in God, to trust and be unafraid. We believe in the God of past, present and future, who holds all things in his mighty hands. In the midst of our uncertainties and worries, we might remind ourselves of what God has already done for us. For the disciples, on that particular day, the fullness of God's plan in Christ was yet to be revealed to them but, for us looking back, we are those who have not seen and yet have come to believe through the power of the cross and the glorious resurrection. On the third day, two thousand years ago, there was a new beginning, a new creation, as mighty and as miraculous as the first, and we, through faith, are part of that story.

It is in this context that we can then look to the future with confidence, and not only to our immediate future, but towards the ultimate future in Christ to which we are all called. This is the vision to which St Paul directs us in the letter to the Romans. We are reminded that the suffering of the present time is nothing compared to the glory that will be revealed. It is not only we who wait, it is creation itself that waits with eager longing until that day when all things are consummated by the love of God, which was from the beginning, which is now, and for ever shall be. With that truth in mind, with God's promises held in our hearts, our worries should melt away, for God's steadfast love endures for ever.

Victoria Johnson

Suggested hymns

Have faith in God, my heart; Put thou thy trust in God; Thou, whose almighty word; All my hope on God is founded.

Second Sunday before Lent (Proper 2) 16 February
Second Service **Root and Branch**

Ps. 148; **Prov. 8.1, 22–31**; Rev. 4; *Gospel at Holy Communion*: Luke 12.16–31

At this time of year in the fields root vegetables are growing silently, deliciously, beneath the surface. Some may have their leaves and stalks covered with hay or sacking to keep the frosts out, and there may even be little sign of the carrots ripening underneath. It is only when they are harvested that we see tender and nutritious food that has not only survived but miraculously been helped by the cold winter's weather.

Surface appearances

Sometimes it's hard to know exactly how wonderful our creation is. We don't see everything. Today's psalm celebrates creation with a universal imagination. The Psalmist thinks of the heavens, the earth, the seas, the skies, the fields, the animals that live in them all, and the people. The writer probably hasn't seen those sea monsters, or the waters above the heavens, but he is looking at the fullness of God's creation. These are all God's creatures: they are to look up to God, who gave them life and put them in order. The Psalmist knows that God's power goes beyond what he can see, and that his fellow creatures and other parts of God's creation are more numerous and varied than he can even imagine.

The Old Testament reading today, also Hebrew poetry, celebrates God's creation again. But this time, it doesn't so much call us to praise, like the psalm does, as invite us to wonder at God's creativeness. Proverbs 8 is a well-loved passage because of its imagery. Wisdom is personified, and that Wisdom-person is there alongside God throughout the acts of his creation. That Wisdom-person is sometimes understood by Christians to be the image of Jesus, who would similarly be written about in the Gospel of John as the 'Logos', the word, the reason, the logic, of God. Put this next to the better-known creation accounts of Genesis, where there's that 'Spirit of God' right at the start, and there's a sense that even the idea of creation-from-nothing involved a sense of teamwork in God. That's one of the ways that the Church began to think about God as Trinity.

It's such an attractive image in Proverbs: that Wisdom-person dancing around alongside God, laughing, pointing, delighting in every detail of the creation. Again, it's not something we think of when we think of God's creative act. But what a beautiful thought: that God had a partner in creation, someone to share his pleasure and joy in the new things that were given life. When we go deeper beneath the surface – which is, after all, one of the special gifts of God's wisdom – there is so much more to see.

Beyond experience

So much of the Bible challenges us, makes us go beyond what we already know, see and experience. It helps us dig out those root vegetables: things deeper than our understanding, nutritious, life-giving, miraculous. It helps us look past what we know every day, to an imagining of what lies behind, beneath, beyond.

Revelation 4 is another example of the wonder that comes through our heart's imagining of God. The whole book is mind-blowing in its creative, colourful imagination. St John the Divine wrote down his visions as best as he could in words, but we are left with the feeling that there was and is always so much more to them than meets the eye. Here in chapter 4, John is invited – and carried in the Spirit – to the doorway where he could peek at heaven. Utter stillness and perpetual movement go hand in hand. There's the jewel-like throne and the enthroned one – 'like rock' in the Greek – and the vast surrounding crystal: such solidity, preciousness and stability. Next there are the 24 elders who fall before the one on the throne and worship, and the four wondrous living creatures who, never stopping for a second, are singing God's name: naming his holiness and power and eternity. The stillness in the centre is surrounded by lightning, rumblings of thunder, bright flaming torches, and all this movement and worship. It is, literally, other-worldly and awesome.

Seeking first the kingdom of heaven

The Gospel reading for the Eucharist reminds us to keep our visions of heaven central in our lives – so that bigger are our thoughts of heaven than our thoughts of food and of what we should wear today. If we are filled with that awesome wondrousness of a heavenly vision like St John the Divine's revelation, then we will think less about our stocks and shares (or whatever is for us the bigger barn of the rich man). Our greed will lessen, and our interest will be more in the things of God than our own day-to-day worries.

Getting things in the right order echoes the divine creativeness. In Proverbs 8, Wisdom repeatedly sings of how she was there 'first', 'at the beginning'. She was 'brought forth' before even the greatest bits of creation, she was present at the very earliest moments in creation. Finally, she witnessed God setting in stone the limits of the sea and the earth: the Hebrew word here is not just about a boundary line, but the word used elsewhere of 'statutes' or 'decrees': lines not to be crossed. Wisdom was there first, and she knows the divine orders of creation.

So, first things first: let's make sure we have a vision of heaven as the foundation stone in our lives, in the forefront of our field of sight.

Megan Daffern

Suggested hymns

Glory, honour and endless praises; Let all creation dance; How shall I sing that majesty; Seek ye first the kingdom of God.

Sunday next before Lent 23 February

Principal Service The Mountain and the Plain

Ex. 24.12–end; Ps. 2, *or* Ps. 99; 2 Peter 1.16–end; **Matt. 17.1–9**

Lent is a season destined to be spent on the plain, in sombre, austere mood. But just days before we embark upon that wilderness journey, the pattern is interrupted and our attention is directed to a mountain-top spectacular. The innermost circle of disciples are with Jesus. But this time they're afforded a unique preview of Jesus' unique destiny. His face is radiant, luminous; his garments are covered in gleaming iridescence. Moses and Elijah appear, saluting him, deferring to him as the fulfiller of both law and prophets

In the clouds

The disciples are up in the clouds, they hear the confirmation of God's voice. They are mystified, elated, fearful by turns. They see their familiar friend, Jesus, in a new light – in the glory that belongs to him. They discover him not as a religious solitary but as one who has a cosmic role, linked to the great stream of history.

The disciples want to linger, to prolong the vision, to continue to bathe in this new light, staying on the mountain above the growing hostility of the plain. Peter offers to make a structure to contain the dramatis personae. And now, perhaps, like Elijah, Jesus will avoid the suffering and death he had spoken of and ascend directly to heaven. But the vision fades; they have to come down, back to the plain, to the harsh, hostile terrain, where Jesus is still seen as a dark and enigmatic figure, left alone to struggle to win men and women to his cause. Soon those same people will agonize over the contrast they wouldn't have imagined to have existed.

On the plain

There, on the plain, their companions had been engaged in a taxing problem, presented by a father. His son was sick and was brought for healing. He had faith enough, but the disciples couldn't match it; they turn him away, and the man appeals directly to Jesus. Those other disciples are blind to the light and power that was so close to them.

So the contrast is made by Matthew of the mountain and the plain. People are drawn to one or other of these conditions. There are those who expect Christianity to consist of peak experiences and to be permanently 'high and lifted up'. They become disappointed and feel deficient if they are not in a near perpetual state of elation, ecstasy and triumph, with the wilderness and the plain safely behind them.

But there are others, who endure the heat of the battle on the plain; they expect no more than the harsh, hostile, testing conditions of the plain.

There isn't much traffic between the mountain and the plain. People like to stick where they are. Those on the mountain top are as unwilling to leave it as Peter, James and John, and those on the plain are as blind to the mountain as the rest of the disciples.

The need for the peak experience

The mountain is the indispensable venue of all creative religious experience. It was the venue for all the nodal experiences of Israelite life, the giving of the Law and sealing of the covenant, the place of God's epiphanies, the ground where God's honour was decisively vindicated. Jerusalem, the Temple mount, was the focus of worship and praise to which pilgrims had to ascend. And for Jesus, the mountain was the place of the new covenant, the scene of transfiguration, the mount of crucifixion.

The mountain experience is crucial but still exceptional; it breaks the monotony of the plain that it relates to. It was the exception for Moses, for Elijah and for Jesus. Between those high points were spread out years and miles of flat land and sinking hearts. If the vision of the mountain top were to be prolonged, then it would become an indulgence rather than an inspiration. Transfiguration is the pledge that the people and problems and conditions that now exist can be reconfigured, that they are the raw ingredients of transfiguration. They can be seen in a fresh light, not as they are but as they are being shaped and will one day become.

The need to return to the plain

Cling to the peak experience for its own sake, build experience on experience, and we will forfeit our chance to realize change right here in our midst. We're not at risk of indulging in too rich a fare of religious experience. We're more likely to prefer the life of the plain, reliant upon our own meagre resources, comfortable and undemanding.

That too is deficient. No more than Alice in Wonderland can we know what to do, what route to take, unless we have seen a glimpse of our ultimate hope and destiny. So Christians need to be tomorrow's people, forward-looking, seeing the end from the beginning, having a perspective that determines the choices we make and the route that we follow.

A man came to the disciples of Jesus and they were impotent to meet his need, even to match his faith. How they needed to be overwhelmed by the power that God makes available to those who trust him! So men and women come to us, they come even today, to our church, casual, fleeting, for mixed reasons, but they come, and we need the fresh experience of the God who meets us from the future to raise their sights and enlarge their horizons, if they are to leave fulfilled and joyful.

But there's one more reason why we need the mountain-top experience. For we need our trust in Jesus to be certain and sure, we need to see a glimpse of his glory and grace. As the old chorus has it: 'Turn your eyes upon Jesus, Look full in his wonderful face, And the things of earth will grow strangely dim, In the light of his glory and grace.'[16]

Roger Spiller

Suggested hymns

Jesus on the mountain peak; Christ pours his grace upon his own; Look, ye saints, the sight is glorious; Christ, whose glory fills the sky.

Sunday next before Lent 23 February

Second Service **Rule of Three**

Ps. 84; Ecclus. 48.1–10, *or* **2 Kings 2.1–12**; Matt. 17.9–23 [*or* 17.1–23]

There was an Englishman, an Irishman and a Scotsman. They went into a pub . . .

The formula for the telling of jokes is well known. It's a similar formula when it comes to fairy stories. Those stories begin with the time-honoured phrase of 'Once upon a time . . . ', and then the story often reveals three characters. Think of the story of Goldilocks, for example: Daddy Bear, Mummy Bear and Baby Bear . . . or perhaps, the Norwegian story of the Three Billy-Goats Gruff – 'Who's that trip-trapping over my bridge?'

Why 'three'? Because it makes the story memorable; it sets up a recognizable pattern and a rhythm. It's sometimes called the 'Rule of Three'.

And if you want an example from more contemporary literature, think of the three main characters in the Harry Potter series: Harry Potter himself, Ron Weasley and Hermione Granger.

The Rule of Three

Today's reading from the second book of Kings also employs the Rule of Three: three times a memorable phrase occurs in the dialogue between Elisha and Elijah. Elisha says: 'As the LORD lives, and as you yourself live, I will not leave you.'

Which gives us an important clue about the kind of story this is: it's more like a folk tale or a fairy story than it is like a piece of historical reportage. It's a story that through the Rule of Three lends itself to easy repetition. And it has another element within it that can also be found in fairy and fantasy stories: an apparently ordinary object which actually has magical powers. In this story the ordinary object is a cloak. Elijah strikes the water of the River Jordan with the cloak and amazingly the waters roll back on either side so that he and Elisha can cross on dry land.

So: Rule of Three, and a cloak that has magical properties. It's no wonder that it was such a popular story in biblical times. It has all the ingredients you might expect. But then the story ends with an even more extraordinary episode, an episode worthy of J. K. Rowling. A chariot of fire and horses of fire suddenly appear and whisk Elijah up to heaven, leaving Elisha clutching the abandoned mantle. Will it work for him? Well, it does, because he comes to the banks of the River Jordan, strikes the water with the cloak and the waters divide right and left so that he can walk through.

It's a story that, perhaps surprisingly, remains embedded in ordinary, everyday discourse. Sports writers, for example, talk about a new manager of a football team taking on the mantle of the previously successful manager. Putting on that mantle carries implications about exercising leadership in such a way that the great traditions of the football club will be respected and even enhanced. Putting on the mantle also conveys the notion that with leadership comes a weight of responsibility. Suddenly, the magic of the mantle has disappeared (there's no further mention of the cloak in the rest of the stories about Elisha) and the new leader has to search his or her own resources to cope and thrive.

The mantle placed on our shoulders

Now let's bring the story closer to home, closer to ourselves.

Here are some rhetorical questions: what cloak has been put around your shoulders? By whom? When? For what purpose?

The questions are easier to pose than to answer, but for sure, as disciples of Christ in our generation, we might expect that a mantle has indeed been placed around our shoulders. Think of it this way: we became disciples of Christ at our baptism, and from then on it is likely that we have been nurtured and challenged in our discipleship by older people who themselves were wearing the cloak of faith that had been passed on to them by their forebears. And now it's your turn . . . our turn.

No doubt you feel entirely inadequate – that is true for all of us. We might jib at putting on the cloak. We might be very reluctant to do so. We might not want the responsibility. But if not us, who?

The mantle as a gift

Let's not suggest that the cloak is an easy one to wear and let's not pretend that it fits us perfectly. But it has been handed to us and so we need to pray for grace and strength that we may have the courage and the resilience to wear the cloak with confidence, and with the assurance that our risen Lord walks with us, sharing the task with us, holding us up when the responsibility feels altogether too heavy for us to bear and knowing that nothing, not even our failures, can separate us from his love and compassion.

To wear that kind of cloak is certainly a responsibility, but it is also a very beautiful and life-enriching gift.

Christopher Herbert

Suggested hymns

O, let the Son of God enfold you; Awake, awake, fling off the night; And can it be; God is working his purpose out.

Lent

Ash Wednesday 26 February

Lent Backstage

Joel 2.1–2, 12–17, *or* Isa. 58.1–12; Ps. 51.1–18;
2 Cor. 5.20b—6.10; **Matt. 6.1–6, 16–21**, *or* John 8.1–11

'All the world's a stage and all the men and women merely players.' In a single sentence our greatest playwright summed up the essential character and vocation of human beings. We are destined to perform on the public stage and play many parts. Whether we are natural or reluctant players, there's no escaping the repertory of roles we have to perform throughout our lives.

Playing roles

Our Ash Wednesday reading acknowledges that we play roles. It refers to 'hypocrites', which literally means actors, but the word is used here and elsewhere in the Gospels to refer to people who act falsely because they want to be seen to be good and virtuous in the eyes of others, and are not concerned or content to be good and virtuous for its own sake.

Giving, praying and fasting, three practices of piety, once stable Lenten disciplines, have been turned by these hypocrites into public performances, so that they can be seen and praised by other people. These performers have chosen to occupy the public places where they can be best seen; they are intent on self-advertising, 'blowing their own trumpet'; some are even dressing up, and others are using grease paint to 'disfigure their faces', so as to extract every ounce of sympathy and praise from their audience.

The figures in the Gospel were called hypocrites because they were more concerned about how they were perceived by other people than how they were seen by God. More concerned about winning public adulation for their performance than by cultivating their own virtue in secret, behind closed doors. Giving, praying and fasting are hidden activities. They're not to be flaunted before other people in order to elicit a favourable response.

Today in the secularized western world those who pursue church-going, fasting, almsgiving or other ascetic activities are more likely to keep it to themselves than to risk ridicule. But that doesn't negate the force of our reading. In fact, it liberates it from a narrow focus on a few religious observances. Broadened in scope, it challenges all activities played on the front stage, which are driven simply by the need to secure respect and recognition; by the need to satisfy and secure the adulation of others; by playing our audience rather than finding our true selves.

Front and back stage[16]

If we have a front stage we also have a back stage to relate to. Our back stage is the secret, hidden, locked room of the Gospel reading. It's the space and place where we learn, prepare and rehearse for our part on the front stage. It's where we face and work with our anxieties, wounds, losses and uncertainties. When we don't occupy our back stage we risk acting out the expectations of others and suppressing our own, and when we don't allow space to reckon with our anxieties and wounds, they are likely to leak out on our front stage.

Living from the back stage

This is a tough and far-reaching challenge in a culture that insists that everything is played out on the front stage and often wishes to invade or dismiss the back stage. The people called hypocrites in our reading ignored their back stage. They resemble those for whom the front stage is all that matters, doing everything for the sake of a headline or a good story.

Lent is the season the Church sets aside for us to spend an extended time at the back stage of our lives. It's the environment in which, in the bleak, scarce, wilderness experience, we allow our illusions and pretences to be challenged. It's the place when we decide to let ourselves be defined no longer by the allure of the front stage but by the struggle of the back stage, not from the outside but from within, not from the shallows but from the depths. It's the space where we allow ourselves to be persuaded that, as someone put it, 'what you are always comes out, what you project rarely comes off'.[17] Lent is the season not for gestures of self-denial that may feed our self-satisfaction but for abandoning ourselves in the self-sustaining love that God has for us. As we emerge from Lent, may we too experience some echo of the experience of Jesus himself, as he returned to the public, front stage of his ministry, and hear the most important affirmation that we can and need to know: 'You are my son, my daughter; with you I am well pleased.'

Roger Spiller

Suggested hymns

Will you come and follow me; Dust and ashes touch our face; Forty days, and forty nights; Rock of ages, cleft for me.

First Sunday of Lent 1 March

Principal Service **Adam**[18]

Gen. 2.15–17; 3.1–7; Ps. 32; **Rom. 5.12–19**; Matt. 4.1–11

There's just been another one of these indestructible television series to get viewers to identify the greatest figures in the last hundred years. *Icons* it was called. It's a tough choice between people like Martin Luther King, Gertrude Bell, Alan Turing and Nelson Mandela. The series makes us realize that it's usually individuals, not groups of people, who really make a difference and shape and define an era.

This is never truer than when we try to understand the great story of the Old Testament. As we journey through the first three weeks of Lent, the Old Testament readings show Jewish history focusing on outstanding figures and representative figures. Between them, they not only remind us of our religious ancestors but they also represent us and help us to interpret our own selves.

First Adam

Adam is the obvious starting point. But his is not a personal name, as if he were the first figure to enter human history. Adam means 'man', and in the primordial story he was given dominion over creation, and 'placed in the garden of delights'. But not content to be obedient to his Maker and to adhere to the one simple prohibition placed upon him, he challenged God and subverted his creation. The promise of the serpent, 'You will be like God', was too much for him to resist, and so he revolted against God. The face-to-face relationship that God intended for Adam became strained, subverted, broken. Adam became a fugitive, hiding from God out of his shame and guilt. In revolting against God, he set off a chain of self-destruction that extends to every one of us. We're in a state of enmity before God, says Paul. And that is echoed in the fear, awkwardness and antipathy that talk of God can elicit.

Luther said we cannot know God as a friend until we have known him as our enemy. Yes, but that doesn't mean that God is our enemy, because 'while we were enemies, we were reconciled to God through the death of his Son'. It wasn't after we were reconciled to him that God began to love us, said Augustine, because God loved us, even when we 'practised enmity towards him and committed wickedness'. He loved us 'before the foundation of the world', and his love doesn't change. He loved us, paradoxically, as Augustine went on to say, 'when we practised wickedness', he 'loved us even when he hated us', hating 'in each one of us what we had made' and loving 'in us what he had made'.[19]

Second Adam

How then does the God who loves us reconcile us to himself? St Paul tells us in today's Epistle that Adam is a type of Christ, the one to come. Christ is the new Adam, whom he compares and contrasts with the old Adam. The one made the wrong choice; the other made the right choice. Adam was tempted by the serpent to disobey and act independently of God. In Christ's temptations, the tempter again tried to sow doubt and disobedience: 'If you are the Son of God . . . '. While Adam, was disobedient, Christ, the Second Adam, was obedient. And his obedience even to death justifies us, so that we don't have to justify ourselves.

Adam precipitated a cycle of sin and death. Jesus is the one representative of our humanity whose indefectible obedience to God breaks the cycle of sin and death and reverses our condition. The relentless destructiveness of Adam's act is outmatched by the superabundant, extravagant, incongruous grace of God. It's not merely the action of 'one man', Jesus, the Second Adam, great as that is, but the action of God in 'one man' that results in the reversal of the reign of sin. The relentless momentum of sin isn't just stopped in its tracks. It is reversed by a counter momentum that leads us into life and freedom. The dominion that Adam forfeited is restored to us.

Can we really believe that God's love is for us, for me? The good news is as wide as the human race. Wherever there is sin, there is always more grace. There is room for everyone. No one is left out. There is room even for me. Anyone who knows themselves to be in need of grace and healing can be sure that God's grace is for them.

Roger Spiller

Suggested hymns

Praise to the Holiest in the height; Lord, your voice in Eden's Garden; From heaven you came; How can it be that I should gain.

First Sunday of Lent 1 March

Second Service **Love God**

Ps. 50.1–15; **Deut. 6.4–9, 16–end**; Luke 15.1–10

There's a great loss of national identity, after the heady years of the empire, a severe moral collapse, a permissiveness where everyone does what is right in their own eyes, a breakdown of national institutions and the collapse of trust. The place of religion in public life is relegated to the margins, and there's an intense interest in idolatrous religions and weird rites instead of the traditional belief in God.

No, I'm not speaking of today. That's the situation that pertained in Israel approximately seven hundred years before Christ. How, then, could such a condition be addressed? What cure was available for the nation's ills? Did they lack leadership, military strength, a government tough on crime and the causes of crime? Were they needing a new economic policy, a stronger alliance with the adjacent countries? What was the one thing necessary to halt the Gadarene rush into chaos and oblivion?

Belief and national fortune

'Hear, O Israel: The LORD is our God, the LORD alone.' The words are spoken as coming from Moses, recalling people back to God. 'You shall Love the LORD your God with all your heart, and with all your soul, and with all your might.' The nation's future rests upon its love of the one God. The writer of the book of Deuteronomy, which is not exactly bedtime reading, sets out to show how the welfare of the country is directly related to its faith in God: its changes of fortune, its alliances, its wealth, its building programmes, they are all shown to depend directly upon the nation's capacity to love God.

Now, is this too ridiculous to be believed? After all we're in a pluralist society, we've grown up to throw off old gods, to reclaim our own autonomy, to take responsibility for ourselves and not defer to some remote, doubtful, mysterious force we call God.

And yet there's no escaping the claim that love of God has been the central truth about the character of humankind. Once love of God is lost, no civilization is safe and free. Instead, people worship the idols of power, the stupidity of force and the list of cruelty and barbarism. Where love for God is denied, we don't have no gods but we divinize human beings. The divinity accorded to the Roman emperors, the hysterical worship of the Führer, the worship at Lenin's tomb, the adulation of Stalin at a time when he was murdering millions of Russians, the worship of Mao Tse-tung all illustrate this. The most evil and destructive societies of the twentieth century have all been idolatrous. Unless we appreciate this we won't appreciate the Old Testament emphasis on the evil of idolatry. So belief and practice of the love of God is not only the basis of all major religions, it is the basis of any human society that is fit for human beings to live in.

Reciting the Shema

When devout Jews recite this daily prayer, the Shema, they feel they are harnessing themselves to God's chariot, putting themselves at God's disposal to do whatever God demands, and letting God take them where he chooses. It's a love that engages heart, soul, mind and strength. It's where you put your energy; where you focus your hard thinking; where you orientate your life. Practising Jews have it tied to their bodies, so that they are reminded of it every moment of the day. If it is pressed on your flesh, if it is declared to everyone who passes through your door, so much the better.

Today, not merely love of God but the very existence of God is questioned. We have become half-believers. Atheism lurks in all our lives. We struggle to make sense of competing beliefs. We have only to ask ourselves, when and where does our love of God determine our choices, our decisions, our attitudes, our conduct, our way of living? Where does it gain a foothold in the commerce of life? Where does it impact and make itself felt now, today? Instead, perhaps, religion and the attendant panoply of churches, services, hymns, vicars, risks consuming the remnant of religious people rather than love for God.

Losing and finding our love for God

Have we lost our first love, lost, as a nation, as a religious community, our religious past, our corporate memory? That's where our second lesson comes in. What has a woman with a lost coin, or a farmer with lost sheep, to do with belief in God? It's simply this, that the God who commands our love has, in our day, to be re-sought, searched for, rediscovered. We have got to sense what we've lost, what we ourselves have lost. When the people of Israel heeded the command to love God, they underwent a radical reform and entered upon a period of peace and stability. And there's no telling what would happen if as people, faith communities and nations we heeded the commandment to 'love the LORD your God with all your heart, and with all your soul, and with all your might'.

Roger Spiller

Suggested hymns

God is love, let heaven adore him; O, for a closer walk with God; Lord of our life and God of our salvation; Lead us, heavenly Father, lead us.

Second Sunday of Lent 8 March

Principal Service Abraham

Gen. 12.1–4a; Ps. 121; **Rom. 4.1–5, 13–17**; John 3.1–17

We think of Abraham as the great father figure of the Jewish people, the first person who gives his name to the unlikely beginnings of God's Chosen People. Jewish people have valued him highly for his virtue and piety. If Adam was a sinner, Abraham was a believer. But what kind of believer was he? Was he a person who secured his faith by keeping the law, anticipating it even before it was revealed? On this basis, Jewish people referenced him in their argument to enforce strict racial and religious differences between

Jews and Gentiles. Jews insisted that Gentiles referred to Abraham when speaking of Jews as 'your father', but, emphatically not as '*our* father'.

But Paul saw things differently. The passage from Romans gets to the heart of the matter, although it's open to different interpretations. But if we attend to it, we get a glorious and far-reaching grasp of the good news that can help to undermine the fierce racial and tribal divisions that disfigure our world and demonize religion.

The grounds for God's promises to Abraham

Abraham received the gift and favour of God. Paul argues that Abraham did absolutely nothing to make him worthy of the favour of God. Was his belief something that could be banked so that God was obliged to reward him? No, goodness was the natural, minimal acceptance of a gift that was and is always utterly incongruous and undeserving. Paul strengthens his argument further elsewhere. If Abraham had made himself worthy, he would surely have been circumcised before he received God's promise, but that came later so it was not the result of Abraham's actions. Why was Abraham called and blessed by God? Not, as Paul argues, because of human initiative or human capacity, but for reasons that lie in God's inscrutable will.

When Abraham received God's promise, it appeared to be ludicrous, unbelievable: the promise of a vast family made to a man of a great age and a wife long since beyond the age of childbearing. But Abraham accepted the promise against all evidence simply because it was given by the God who does the impossible. Nothing, not our unworthiness, our unpromising physical conditions, nor all the reasonable factors that we can muster against it can hinder God's promise. Abraham's hope against all reasonable expectations reflects his faith that owes nothing to a person's goodness or achievements. And the God in whom Abraham trusted, and in whom we too are invited to trust is, as Paul goes on to remind us, the God who 'gives life to the dead, and calls into existence the things that do not exist'.

The surprise and incredulity of grace

We meet more surprise and incredulity in our Gospel from the Jewish leader Nicodemus, who meets Jesus under cover of darkness.

He at least recognizes that Jesus is performing signs that simply cannot be accounted for except by the presence of God in him. But Nicodemus is 'astonished' by the invitation of Jesus that seems counter to all that he can expect from God. 'How can anyone be born after having grown old? Can one enter a second time into the mother's womb and be born?' And after further explication by Jesus, Nicodemus is no further forward: 'How can these things be?' he asks.

We have no less than the event of the death and resurrection of Jesus and the gift of the Spirit to persuade us to embrace the free, unconditional, incongruous, generous grace of God. What was written for Abraham, as Paul says, was written also 'for us', because we too are expected to live by an identical faith, that the God who does the impossible and raises the dead brings us a spiritual rebirth and 'newness of life'.

The promise of God's inclusive future

But it also has far-reaching consequences for our tolerance of racial and religious divisions. Paul's exposition of Abraham shows that the one God justifies both Jews and Gentiles. The difference between Jews and non-Jews is relativized. Why? Because from the beginning the blessing to Abraham was blind to every token of worth or human achievement or initiative. Grace through faith is the one and only criterion of God's universal family. So Abraham is destined to be not simply the father of Judaism but the father of the whole human family, a multi-ethnic family. That convinced Paul that God's mission extended to all people, to the Gentiles as well as to Jews. That's why he insisted against other leaders that his mission was to 'the nations' and not merely to the Gentiles. If we're to be faithful successors of Abraham and Paul, we will allow ourselves to be defined and united around the particular historical event of Jesus Christ. That is the hope and promise for the future of the world and for the salvation of all God's people.

Roger Spiller

Suggested hymns

The God of Abraham, praise; Gracious God, in adoration; I cannot tell; To God be the glory.

Second Sunday of Lent 8 March

Second Service **The Bronze Serpent**

Ps. 135 [*or* 135.1–14]; **Num. 21.4–9**; Luke 14.27–33

I don't know about you, but I've not often found myself reading the book of Numbers. Not being much of a mathematician, the very name of the book doesn't readily attract my interest. Yes, twice in the book there are records of a census of the people of Israel, at the beginning of the book (counting the generation that escaped from Egypt) and then in chapter 26 (a record of those of the next generation who are about to enter the Promised Land), and from those two censuses the book acquired its name in the Latin Bible. However, there's far more to Numbers than lists of names. It's the story of Israel's complaints and discontent. Maybe we would have a different response to the book if it had a title derived from that in the Hebrew Bible where it is the book of in-the-wilderness. Perhaps some of its stories would then speak to us when we feel that we are undergoing a 'wilderness experience'.

Have you ever felt that you are wandering through life on a circuitous route, without a clear sense of your destination? In such a situation, isn't it natural to remember instances of the past with affection? Maybe you can empathize with the children of Israel at this stage in their journey through the wilderness.

Israel's story

The people of Israel leave Hor, where they have buried Aaron, and head southwards, taking something of a detour around the border of Edom. Maybe their sense of loss and the seeming aimlessness of their journey fuels their frustration and they begin again to voice their perennial complaint. 'Why have you brought us up out of Egypt to die in the wilderness?'

This is the last complaint story in Numbers and it is also the most serious one because the Israelites don't just become impatient and complain against Moses, they complain directly about and to God. They call manna, God's gift that has kept them alive, worthless food. They sin by their unwillingness to believe that God can deliver them.

The people's grumbling is nothing new; sometimes God hears and is merciful but sometimes he says, 'Enough'. God, who has so often treated them mercifully, now chooses to mete out summary justice.

Fiery serpents and a serpent of bronze

The Lord sends snakes to attack the Israelites, fiery serpents, perhaps so-called because they had a venomous, burning bite. There's carnage as many of the Israelites die. Immediately, the people realize the gravity of their sin (wouldn't you?). Apologizing to both Moses and their God, they beg Moses to pray to God on their behalf for the removal of the serpents.

When Moses prays to Yahweh, the response he receives from God is the surprising command to make a poisonous serpent, a bronze representation, and set it upon a pole. When the people are bitten, if they look at the serpent of bronze they will live. The bronze serpent will remind each individual of the need to turn to the God who still loves them, despite their constant ungrateful whingeing and despite their sin.

In the surrounding cultures of the Ancient Near East, the serpent was usually a symbol of power and chaos, whereas in the religion of the people of Israel chaos is neutralized as the serpent becomes the symbol of life. The serpent symbolizes both life and death – choose life.

Wait a minute, isn't this a strange story? Doesn't one of the ten commandments expressly prohibit the making of idols? The God who spoke the commandments is now saying something very different to Moses, in this context. Here in Numbers we are made aware of the importance of ritual actions and of symbols. God encourages the use of a physical sign as a means to a spiritual end. The bronze serpent will act as a reminder of this incident in the story of Israel and it will recall them to faithfulness.

Surely God is taking a risk here in establishing a visual symbol. It's possible that it could be understood as a sort of magic wand, to be used in a healing ritual. Its use is reminiscent of sympathetic magic (as in alternative medicine, where a little of the 'complaint' is also the cure). Such practices do seem to sit strangely in the Hebrew Bible.

In the later story of Israel, the Israelites do begin to use a bronze serpent as an idol, burning incense before it, so Hezekiah, in his religious reform, orders what is supposedly Moses' serpent to be broken up.

The bronze serpent and the Gospel

In the Christian tradition the bronze serpent is remembered because Jesus makes reference to the story, using the image of the serpent in his discussion with Nicodemus, proclaiming that 'just as Moses lifted up the serpent in the wilderness, so must the Son of Man be lifted up'. Just like the bronze serpent, Christ will be raised up, on his cross. As the serpent symbolized the choice between death and life, so the cross symbolizes both death and life.

God calls us to turn our backs on sin and disobedience, look to the cross of Christ and choose life.

Wendy Kilworth-Mason

Suggested hymns

Jesu, lover of my soul; Guide me, O thou great Redeemer; Lift high the cross; To God be the glory.

Third Sunday of Lent   15 March

Principal Service   **Moses**

Ex. 17.1–7; Ps. 95; Rom. 5.1–11; **John 4.5–42**

Without air, you die within three minutes; without water, you die within three days. Water is the source on which all life depends. And today we find the Israelites on their journey in the wilderness in parched, scorched, dry land, thirsting for water. 'Give us water to drink', they shouted at Moses, and their cries echo to the millions of people in Somalia, South Sudan, Ethiopia, Yemen and Kenya crying desperately for fresh, clean water in regions that have experienced months and sometimes years of drought. For them, as for the Israelites under Moses, it's not merely a physical or economic issue. It's a religious issue, which raises acutely the question, 'Is the Lord among us or not?'

And if we think providing water is God's responsibility, we have to reckon with the fact that in our Gospel it is Jesus himself who is in need of a drink. He is tired, and while the disciples have gone off to buy food, he rests at Jacob's well. It's a place you can visit to this day, as I've done, and it goes right back to the earliest history of the Jews.

The Samaritan woman

It's remarkable that Jesus is there at all; Jews would normally avoid Samaritan territory. But Jesus not only doesn't avoid it, he strikes up a conversation with one of the natives. And he asks for a drink.

It's a deceptively simple request but far reaching, boundary breaking, revolutionary. It causes the woman to say, 'How is it that you, a Jew, ask a drink of me, a woman of Samaria?' Jewish men were supposed to avoid contact with women because they were seen to pose a threat of seduction. But worse, this woman has a disreputable past and would contaminate anyone in close contact with her.

Why does she come to draw water at the hottest time of the day? She's avoiding all human contact. Her multiple marriages and her current non-marital state have alienated her from even her own people and she feels ostracized, ashamed, wanting to hide away. And it gets worse; she's a Samaritan – branded a heathen as far as religion is concerned, and politically a sworn enemy of the Jews. Samaritans had even aided the Syrians in wars against the Jews.

And there's yet another problem, as the woman rightly recognizes: 'Sir, you have no bucket.' Since she's got a bucket, why does she think this is a problem. Because she knew that Jews might contract ritual impurity by using a common vessel to draw water.

The *Good News Bible* has line drawings to illustrate the text, and they printed 40,000 copies depicting Jesus with a bucket before someone noticed that the text says that Jesus doesn't have a bucket!

Jesus and the living water

In his request to this woman for water, Jesus broke through all the barriers of race, religion, ethnicity, gender and morality. Here was a Jew who did not stereotype people, not as a woman, nor as a Samaritan, nor as a sinner. He saw her as a person who had come to draw water but was herself in need of much more than Jacob's well could provide.

Jesus then tells her about a different kind of water, water as an image or analogy for something greater. But she misunderstands Jesus and thinks he's just recommending a better source of water, like, we might say, Malvern water. But what Jesus is offering is the Spirit, the divine life. And, says Jesus, it's 'a spring of living water gushing up to eternal life'. Jesus has no less than seven exchanges with the woman, but, as he speaks, that living water begins to well up inside her; the water that alone can address her needs, the water of inclusion and embrace and generosity and hospitality, the water that can't be contained.

The Samaritan women brings salvation to her people

There's so much more that could be said about this passage, but the sequel is amazing. The woman leaves her water jar at the well and goes back into the city. What need is there for a water jar when she has drunk the living water that makes one never thirst again? And now she walks tall, full of confidence, regaining her voice in the community. She goes boldly to her fellow Samaritans to tell the good news of Jesus to the very people who were ostracizing her. We're told the city believed because of the woman's testimony. The one whom they marginalized has become the one through whom they believed. And now, the Samaritans press Jesus to stay with them.

That is the woman's story, but John invites us to make it our story too; to own our own thirst, dryness, unsatisfied longing.

Jesus' thirst for the world

Jesus was to acknowledge his thirst just once more. On the cross that dark Friday afternoon, Jesus cries out, 'I thirst'. He who is the source of living water cries out in thirst, not on his own account but thirsting for men and women who themselves are thirsty and unfulfilled. Jesus must die before he can dispense this living water: 'If I do not die, the Spirit will not come.' But now that living water of the Spirit is poured out to all who seek it.

Are you thirsty? Does your thirst have a name or a source? Or is it deeper and unsatisfied? Maybe we know we have a deep need for God, a yearning for renewal and refreshment. We too may echo the Psalmist: 'O God, you are my God, I seek you . . . as in a dry and weary land.' If you're really thirsty, yearning, dry, then here is the good news that you've been waiting for: God thirsts for you, and, as John's Gospel says, 'Out of the believer's heart shall flow rivers of living water.'

Roger Spiller

Suggested hymns

Rock of ages; Jesus, thou joy of loving hearts; As the deer pants; As water to the thirsty.

Third Sunday of Lent 15 March

Second Service The Power of Lists

Ps. 40; Josh. 1.1–9; **Eph. 6.10–20**; *Gospel at Holy Communion*: John 2.13–22

There are some people who love making lists. Perhaps you're one of them? So, let's try making a collective list today – this, by the way, is an entirely rhetorical suggestion.

Our imaginary task is to write a list in answer to the question, 'Who do you think were the ten most powerful people in history?'

At which point we might need to pause while names pop into our heads. Would you, for instance, include in your list Genghis Khan? Would you include Hitler? Gandhi? Nelson Mandela? Plato? Florence Nightingale? Queen Elizabeth I? Madame Curie? Catherine the Great? Julius Caesar? Cleopatra? Tim Berners-Lee?

As soon as you try to create such a list you can see that all kinds of caveats enter your thinking. Should the list of the powerful be confined to politicians and military leaders? Are there not forms of power that have changed the world but have been exercised not by politicians but by mathematicians such as Einstein? And what about the power exercised by writers of genius such as Shakespeare, or composers such as Bach? Would you include artists who have shaped how we perceive the world, such as Michelangelo or Picasso?

You might well have noticed that the list I began to create a few moments ago did not include any religious leaders. So, in your imaginary list of the ten most powerful people in history, where would you place Moses or Jesus of Nazareth or the Buddha or the Prophet Muhammad or Guru Nanak? Should they not have a place?

What all of this goes to show is that the making of lists can be a way of making very complex issues appear simple, but actually it does not achieve much. In fact, it prevents us from considering far bigger questions.

Power in the Bible

Instead of making a list of the ten most powerful people in the world, let's try to go deeper and look at the underlying question: what does power consist of?

This is where we turn to the author of the letter to the Ephesians. In today's reading he begins by saying, 'Be strong in the Lord and in the strength of his power.' But then almost immediately he moves to a description of those crafty powers that seem to exist in opposition to God:

> Put on the whole armour of God, so that you may be able to stand against the wiles of the devil. For our struggle is not against

> enemies of blood and flesh, but against the rulers, against the authorities, against the cosmic powers of this present darkness, against the spiritual forces of evil in the heavenly places.

Note who the struggle is against. It's against the Enemy (capital 'E'); an enemy who infects not just the way the world is, but infects the whole cosmos. The follower of Christ, the author says, is up against a negative, annihilating force that has a universal dimension.

Now, this is not a comfortable or an easy idea to grapple with. We can just about understand how evil might be personal, in the sense that it can affect individuals. One person murdering another, while horrible, is within our capacity to imagine. And we know too, if we are honest, of the ways in which we ourselves have the capacity to commit individual evil acts. But evil as a *cosmic* force? That stretches our thinking almost to breaking point.

But bring to mind the Holocaust. Was that not an evil event that had a dimension larger and more horribly insidious than the individuals who began it? Or, in England in the sixteenth century, think of the burning alive of people for their religious beliefs. Was that pitiless brutality the result simply of individual actions, or did it have a wider dimension? Or, think of the horrific pogroms carried out by Josef Stalin, Chairman Mao and Pol Pot. Were those cruelties the result of an individual's evil or was there, in some sense, a larger dimension? Or, to bring us up to date, consider the way the Internet is used in creating child abuse on a terrible, industrial scale. Is that the result of individual acts of evil or is it the evil of a much larger, far-reaching, non-human kind?

Sometimes the sheer depth and reach of evil is almost beyond comprehension. And so perhaps, in such cases, to talk of evil in cosmic terms is the only way we can make sense of the scale and destructive absurdity of it.

It is this that the author of Ephesians has in mind when he tells us that we need heavenly armour to withstand its attacks: 'Put on the whole armour of God . . .'

So, in the light of this, maybe we should forget lists of the ten most powerful people in the world (that's far too trivial and pointless an exercise), and contemplate instead, when faced with the enormity of evil, the kind of power to combat it that is offered to us by God. In Jesus Christ we are given the sword of truth, the breastplate of righteousness and the shield of faith, and, above all else, the gift of love.

When we are faced with evil on a massive scale, we must pray that those gracious gifts from God will protect and guide us, and pray too that God will give us the courage to enter the battle.

Christopher Herbert

Suggested hymns

Jesus is Lord! Creation's voice proclaims it; Meekness and majesty; Before the throne of God above; How deep the Father's love for us.

Fourth Sunday of Lent (Mothering Sunday)

22 March

Principal Service **Christ's Body, the Church, Called to Love**

Ex. 2.1–10, *or* 1 Sam. 1.20–end; Ps. 34.11–20, *or* Ps. 127.1–4; 2 Cor. 1.3–7, *or* Col. 3.12–17; Luke 2.33–35, *or* **John 19.25b–27**

The dean of a cathedral in Catherine Fox's novel looks out across her congregation and realizes that a service that just gives thanks for mothers isn't going to cut it. She sees pain. *You have lost a child*, she thinks, *you are infertile, you have never been a mother, you have never had a mother, your mother is wandering in dementia, you are grieving for your mother, you are a single father of small children.* And seeing this she knows that every person in her congregation is in deep need of those flowers traditionally given out on Mothering Sunday.

Being human, being made for love as we are, makes us vulnerable. And family life can be complicated. Oh, how God knows that! Parent of us all, in whom every family in heaven and earth is named, God who gave his son and watched him die, knows that.

In the words of a priest in Dunblane, preaching the Sunday after the shootings in his local school, 'When the gunshots rang out in that school hall, God was the first to weep.'

Scripture

Today's lectionary readings don't give us a picture of nice, uncomplicated family life. Exodus tells of a mother forced to hide her child from the anger of Pharaoh and watch another woman lift him from the water and claim him. For her child to live, the mother gives him up. Our Gospel reading shows us a mother who also had to save her baby from the wrath of a jealous king by fleeing to Egypt, the place that had put her people in slavery yet lifted Moses from the water. History comes full circle. Mary's son survived infancy but years later she must watch his slow, agonizing death at the hands of a Roman executioner. Beside her is someone else, who has no recognized family ties or status but loves and grieves nonetheless deeply. And the dying man looks down with the compassion born of God and gives them to one another. Behold your mother. Behold your child.

God understands the often unspoken and unsung loves and griefs of being human; sometimes a longing to mother and to be mothered, or to love and belong to someone whatever our age or gender. Family, like love, can be unconventional in the journey of our human experience.

Mothering Sunday is so much more than an opportunity for grateful children to give their mother flowers. We can enjoy that, of course, but it isn't the sum total of this day. Mothering Sunday grew from a tradition of the Church as mother. During the eighteenth and nineteenth centuries, when many young people were in service away from home and had few Sundays off, Mothering Sunday was the day they returned to their 'mother' Church, the Body of Christ that had baptized them. As the Body of Christ, the Church's role is to nurture our faith, enable us to grow into maturity and to enfold us in the love that God has for us through all the changing scenes of life; enable us to recognize in the God we worship the compassion and life-giving nurture and grace without which we could not survive or mature as human beings.

Divine heart

In its original Aramaic, the opening word of the Lord's Prayer is *Abwoon*. It means birth giver, source of being, womb. From that divine creative love we are brought into being. When Jesus asked, 'Who is my mother?' he meant no disrespect to the woman who bore him, whose very soul would be pierced in her love for him. But he enabled those he knew and loved to belong in ways that were not always conventional. It reminds me of Augustine's prayer, 'Lord, you have made us for yourself and we are restless until we find ourselves in you.' We are made for love by love. And as human beings the first experience we have of God's love is through human love. We come into the world, as Christ did, among people to whom we matter, who will love us unconditionally. And if those basic relationships of our core family break down, we mourn something deeply. Sometimes there are people in our lives who at different times have mothered us, or whom we for a while have mothered. This is part of our discipleship, our ministry, our calling to be fully human and therefore an awesome responsibility; one we know the Church has not always fulfilled in the past.

Christ's call to the Church

So as we mark Mothering Sunday in our journey through Lent, may we reflect on our calling to love, to nurture, to find that which is creative and abundant, so that children of all ages might find their hearts leap, the barren woman sing for joy and the widow and orphan, the single and separated, the lonely and the grieving find solace. For we are the Church called to be Christ's love in the world. Those offered flowers should say to all, whatever their experience, 'See, the winter is past, the rain is over and gone, the flowers appear in the earth, and the time of singing has come.' And even if it hasn't come for all of us, though our loneliness and loss may still be hard to bear, the promise of spring in the middle of Lent is part of our gospel hope.

Carey Saleh

Suggested hymns

Jesus call us here to meet him; Faithful God so unchanging; Father Lord of all creation; God, you search me and you know me; God is love, let heaven adore him.

Fourth Sunday of Lent (Mothering Sunday)

22 March

Second Service **From Despair to Hope**

Ps. 31.1–16; **Micah 7**, *or* Prayer of Manasseh; James 5; *Gospel at Holy Communion*: John 3.14–21

(If the Principal Service readings for the Fourth Sunday of Lent are displaced by Mothering Sunday provisions they may be used at the Second Service.)

Who was Micah? Actually, we don't know much about him, in large part because he tells us little about himself in the book that bears his name. However, based upon the social context that he describes (as evidenced in our passage), it is generally accepted that he was an eighth-century BC contemporary of (First) Isaiah and Amos.

Despair

In our passage, Micah speaks of a time of economic affluence when, enjoying their sense of security and well-being, the people have turned away from their commitment to their God. Micah despairs because he is living in a spiritual wasteland. At the beginning of our reading he tries to find upright and righteous men, but none remain. Even the justice system is tainted by bribery and corruption, which are rife, he says. So 'justice' can be manipulated to favour the wealthy. Everyone's 'virtue' is questionable. In short, civil society is completely breaking down. Furthermore, family life is under threat; you can't trust your own flesh and blood, he warns, indeed, your enemies may be members of your own household. The situation is so severe that trust itself is dead.

The prophet maintains that the state of the nation, as he describes it, is the product of the materialism and godlessness that he decries. 'The city' represents sin and godlessness.

Do we have such experiences today? I can recall sitting for hours awaiting my turn to speak with a government official, seeking to clear my belongings through customs. I'd taken a book to read, knowing that I'd have a long wait. When I was ushered into the inner office (accompanied by an officer from the Church's Central Office) the government official, impeccably garbed in a smart white shirt and tie, a business suit and well-polished shoes, asked what I was reading and subtly made it clear that he wanted my book (I do wonder what he made of the novel *A Short History of Tractors in Ukrainian*). When we left the office, with the assurance that my belongings would be released, the official's secretary followed us out and negotiated with the Church's officer the bribe we would have to pay. The experience did not augur well for my time in that country, the most blatantly corrupt one in which I have ever lived.

Surrounded by and immersed in corruption, in the depths of despair, what can a righteous person do? Micah declares that he will wait for the God of his salvation. He will watch and pray. God will answer his prayer and will vindicate him.

When God intervenes

From verse 8 the tone of the chapter changes somewhat. There have been prophecies that Jerusalem will fall. Indeed, the city will be destroyed by foreign invaders, who are the means by which God's plan can be brought to fruition. However, the victors will not long enjoy their victory, they in turn suffer defeat.

Though the city falls, her God has not been defeated. From the depths of despair and destruction Micah looks forward to the rebuilding of the city. Because though sin and disobedience caused the downfall of the city, God will come and plead his people's case.

Hope

Micah (or, as some commentators would have it, a disciple of the earlier prophet) offers a 'myth' of the return. Their faithful God will not fail them because beyond or behind the judgement of God is God's compassion. So, a faithful remnant will triumph because of their relationship with God. They will find true life in him. Their good shepherd will restore them. There is reference in the text to the fertile pasture lands of Bashan and Gilead: rich farmlands beyond the city walls. The hoped-for restoration will incorporate not just the rebuilt city but the surrounding lands. 'The countryside' represents godliness and hope.

The city will be redeemed and the nations will come to Jerusalem in fear of God.

What is Micah's message to us?

Do we live in a time of affluent godlessness? Do we observe corruption, selfishness and sin? Is the grime of our city streets representative of the degradation of society?

Perhaps, like Micah, we struggle to find righteous men and women.

If our cultural context is analogous to that of Micah, then the message holds true: God is in control of our destiny and he will destroy and rebuild. The faithful should wait upon the God of their salvation.

Wendy Kilworth-Mason

Suggested hymns

Come, let us sing of a wonderful love; The Kingdom of God is justice and joy; Great God, your love has called us here; To God be the glory.

Fifth Sunday of Lent (Passiontide) 29 March

Principal Service **If only . . .** [20]

Ezek. 37.–14; Ps. 130; Rom. 8.6–11; **John 11.1–45**

My brother is dead. He has lain in his tomb for four days; all that is left is his lifeless body, a shell of who he was, All I am left with is a shadow and a pain in my heart that will not go away. A pain that consumes me, a pain that is reflected in those around me and in my dear sister Mary. Of course I have some comfort in those around me and there is some vague future hope that I can cling on to that in the end times he will be resurrected as all of us Jews will be. But what good is that to me now, for in this moment I am left with no brother.

Where was Jesus? Where was he? I sent word to him several days ago that his dear friend Lazarus was ill and yet he delayed and by the time he got here, Lazarus, my brother, was dead. My friend Jesus who has performed so many miraculous signs could not come soon enough to heal my brother. If only he had come as soon as I sent word, if only he had not delayed. Even if he came a day after his death there may have been hope of resuscitation of his body, but now four days dead there is no hope of that, his soul has gone. If only Jesus had come sooner . . . If only . . .

Commentary

When was the last time you had an 'if only' moment? A moment like Martha here in the first part of our reading today who was re-playing events in her mind in an attempt to change the devastating circumstances that she was faced with. 'If only we hadn't argued before he left that day . . .' 'If only she had worked harder and passed her exams . . .' 'If only he had never got in with the wrong crowd . . .' 'If only we had seen the signs sooner . . .' It's nostalgia for a life that could have been, a bitter-sweet feeling that can lead to the realms of fantasy. And to keep dwelling on these things can lead to living a life in the past.

Martha was dreaming of what might have been. Then Jesus shows up . . . and does what Jesus is best at doing, turning every-thing on its head.

Jesus has finally arrived. I heard he was coming, I couldn't wait inside patiently like my sister, I had to run out and meet him. I also wanted to be with him, to find some comfort from his closeness.

I couldn't help blurting out that I thought he could have prevented my brother's death.

But he said the strangest thing to me. He said: 'I am the resurrection and the life. Anyone who believes in me will live, even though they die; and whoever lives by believing in me will never die.' He asked if I believed this. But what does he mean? All I could say is that Jesus is the Messiah, the Son of God, who was to come into the world. But what does it mean? Will there be hope for my brother sooner than expected? Can Jesus do something greater than I have ever seen before?

Commentary

And here our story breaks off, we are left with the tantalizing thoughts of what might happen. Jesus has come in, has moved Martha from her 'If only' to ask herself, 'If Jesus . . .'.

What of our 'if only' situations? What if we are moved by Jesus to dare to think 'if Jesus . . .'? For Jesus has come from God's future, to the here-and-now. He has broken into the mess and the muddle of the world we know. The future hope of the resurrection is no longer a far-off distant promise, but it is here, now, for everyone of us who believe in Jesus as the Son of God.

For the key to what Jesus does and says is the *faith* of the grieving woman, Martha. It is her faith that Jesus is the Messiah, the promised one, that led to Jesus doing something beyond her expectations.

Of course this does not mean that there will be no death or suffering for those who believe in Jesus; Lazarus does eventually die an earthly death.

But hope in the risen Jesus gives hope in even the most desperate of situations. Even when we cannot see how there is hope, Jesus takes us beyond ourselves and leads us to himself.

Is there an 'if only' in your heart? Run to Jesus like Martha and share it with him. Tell him your fears, disappointments and desires. And in doing so be prepared for a surprising response. I don't know what it will be, but Jesus promises to meet our problems with some new part of God's future that will burst into this present time, into the mess and the grief, with hope and new possibilities. And that hope begins with us. If we dare to believe and have faith in Jesus then we will be a witness and an encouragement to others to dare to believe that Jesus is indeed the resurrection and the life.

Emma Sykes

Suggested hymns

Jesus the Lord said; I danced in the morning; I am the Light whose brightness shines; Now is eternal life.

Fifth Sunday of Lent (Passiontide) 29 March

Second Service **The Need for Lament**

Ps. 30; **Lam. 3.19–33**; Matt. 20.17–end

Lamentations is one of the shortest yet one of the most powerful books in the Bible. The setting is almost certainly the collapse of Jerusalem in 587 BC and the exile in Babylon. The book is written with an intensity that suggests some terrible catastrophe has just overtaken the people. It's really a requiem over a city.

Requiem over a city

Lamentations describes a horrific scene of urban devastation and destruction – the pall of disease and death hanging over the whole city, bodies piled high, people, even small children, scavenging, and mothers forced to cannibalism, eating their own children. Women are raped by the invading army, children are abused and their rulers are strung up by the hands. The skin of the people is described as being 'as black as an oven and dry as wood from scorching heat'.

It's a book that has been used ever since then within Jewish history to commemorate a special day, the ninth day of Arv when the Temple of Solomon fell to the Babylonians. And it has been the source book for language appropriate to express the loss of the second Temple in AD 70. And yet again to interpret the Holocaust. And it's used liturgically in many funeral services.

Lamenting the world's pain

But, you may ask, what is its relevance to us today? Lamentations supplies memorable quotations that interpret the passion of Jesus. 'All who pass by clap their hands; they hiss and wag their heads.' 'Is it nothing to you, all you who pass by. Look and see if there is any sorrow like my sorrow.' And the book of Lamentations has inspired many musical settings for the late evening service in Holy Week called Tenebrae, in which the lights are extinguished and we are plunged into darkness. And that edges us towards a reason for lingering with this unique book. As we enter into Passiontide, it serves to invite us to attend to the dark, tragic features of human existence and gives us permission, indeed requires of us, that we make our lament against the world's pain as well as our own.

A cry against God

The book is a cry against God – an unstructured cry. Yet the form of the book is one of the most structured in the Bible. Each verse starts with a letter of the alphabet of the Hebrew Bible, an acrostic. Even the metre of the verses in Hebrew reflects the mood:

di-da di-da, di-da
di-da, di-da.

You notice it misses a beat, the rhythm isn't resolved, because the pain isn't resolved. This is communal poetry – shared chanting and ritual. Shared lament on the Temple ruins after its loss. It may have started as a liturgy – people wrestling with their grief, who have come together to articulate their calamitous condition. There's a sense of urgency and immediacy. The people are all over the place, typical of how people deal with suffering: shock, control, regression, bargaining, adaptation, denial, isolation. A crisis destabilizes meaning and defies explanation.

Hard-won hints of hope

Our passage implies hope after all. It appears for the first time in the third chapter, only to be abruptly extinguished. It reappears again in a single verse in the last chapter, which then goes on to ask why God has forgotten his people so completely. At the end is a prayer to restore the people to God and an open-ended question, 'unless you have utterly rejected us, and are angry with us beyond measure'. Again we read: 'I called on your name, O Lord, from the depths of the pit; you heard my plea, "Do not close your ear".' But then we read this: 'You have wrapped yourself with a cloud so that no prayer can pass through.' We are told the Lord does not willingly afflict or grieve anyone, but then we're told that both good and bad come from the Lord. Everything is related to God, the text refuses to hive off the nasty things and dump them on a devil figure.

Language for voicing pain

Pain, whether personal or communal, is not far from the surface for many of us. I'd just announced the first hymn to a musical accompaniment – and a solo bassoonist made the first entry, a rich guttural sound from the bowels of life. Then a 50-year-old woman, a clinical psychologist, who was so self-assured and intimidating, started to cry. What had happened so suddenly to ignite this pain that had so suddenly welled up in her? It was, as I was to discover later, the sound of the bassoon that brought her in touch with all the pain of her clients that she was carrying.

The language of lament is the speech pattern by which our pain and loss can be called out, voiced and owned. It's like the effect of a Shakespearean tragedy or a great symphony. You feel you've been put through the ringer. On Passion Sunday we are on the dark side of Calvary, called to enter into the fellowship of Christ's sufferings and to name our own pains, losses and experiences of abandonment and forsakenness, before we can even hear, still less embrace, the hope on the other side.

Roger Spiller

Suggested hymns

Lead, kindly light, amid the encircling gloom; This is the night of new beginnings; By gracious powers, so wonderfully sheltered; Within our darkest night.

Holy Week

Palm Sunday 5 April

Principal Service **Jesus Becomes King**

Liturgy of the Palms: **Matt. 21.1–11**; Ps. 118.1–2, 19–end [*or* 118.19–24]; *Liturgy of the Passion*: Isa. 50.4–9a; Ps. 31.9–16 [*or* 31.9–18]; Phil. 2.5–11; Matt. 26.14 —end of 27, *or* Matt. 27.11–54

What's Palm Sunday without palms? But there's no mention of palms in Matthew's Gospel. Only an improvised red carpet of clothing and branches. And we like to think of Jesus riding on a donkey – but Matthew tells us he sits on both a donkey and a colt. Are we really expected to believe that he's riding both at the same time? And we think of it as a triumphal entry into Jerusalem, but it was a procession that began in Bethphage, a place we can't locate, and it was hardly triumphal with the crowd shrieking, 'Save us', 'Help us'. And what of the crowd, which is called fickle when a few days later they cry, 'Crucify'? But the crowd that flanks Jesus consists of the country yokels from tiny rural villages far away from the capital. Their voices won't be heard in Pilate's courts on Good Friday, in the places where power and decision-making is exercised. As always they will be silenced by the metropolitan elite. But these common folk have experienced a presence so powerful, and a love so amazing, that they are willing to make the arduous journey and put their heads above the parapet, despite the risk.

Street theatre

It's clear, then, that Jesus choreographed everything very deliberately. So his procession begins at the Mount of Olives, the place linked to King David and where the Messiah is expected to appear and where leading Jews like President Peres are buried, so they're first in the queue when the Messiah returns. Jesus rides a donkey, which is associated with the coronation of kings at the same time as being a beast of burden, and which speaks of service. Jesus isn't riding a stallion, a war horse, as if he were leading troops into battle. Jesus seems to be parodying those who rule by force and their accoutrements of power, and pouring scorn on the idea of coercion as the means to get things done. Jesus is engaging in street theatre, a surprise, comedic, satirical exercise in unmasking the futility of self-centred living.

A fateful challenge

So what are we to make of it? Why in fact did Jesus go up to Jerusalem? He went, first of all, as a pilgrim. It was the Passover festival, when the nation celebrated God's liberation from oppressors in Egypt and kept alive their hopes that God would act again, finally to rescue his people from Roman occupation. There's a swirl of expectation in the air, like a tinder box ready to ignite, with religious hotheads always ready to inflame a dangerous situation in the hope of a showdown with the authorities or an attempt to force God to show his hand.

Jesus went to Jerusalem as a pilgrim, but it seems too that he went up to Jerusalem on that final, fateful journey to present his nation with one last challenge – to make a final bid to save them from the disastrous course on which they had embarked, politically and religiously. Jesus didn't seek death – in fact, right at the last he recoiled from it – but he did pursue with inflexible devotion a way of life that inevitably led to his death. Jesus came into the world, went up to Jerusalem, to call Israel to prepare for the inauguration of God's kingdom. Being with Christ leads us into a topsy-turvy world that confounds and unsettles us, and on the first Palm Sunday he will convulse and shake the whole ruling establishment and force them to act.

Becoming king

In his passion and death, Jesus becomes king. God takes back authority. He establishes his kingdom and saves and renews his people. His death was the only way by which he could defeat the principalities and powers of the world. There's a cost for reversing the malign, pernicious forces of evil and it will be met by the death of the unique and incomparable Son of God.

Palm Sunday is the first day in a week in which Jesus became our rightful king. He will be decked in royal purple, wearing a crown, albeit of thorns, enthroned on a cross. And the greatest power on earth unwittingly proclaims him 'King of the Jews'. That's the strange way in which God restores his sovereignty: suffering love, self-sacrifice, self-emptying.

'Here might I stay and sing'

So the man who will be hanging on a cross at the end of the week is God's answer to the problems of the world; God's rescue plan for our human plight? It can seem that our faith is hanging by a thread. But the thread is Jesus. And to come to know that he loves us and gave himself for us defies comprehension. So how can we keep Holy Week in a way that keeps company with Christ's cross?

> Here might I stay and sing,
> No story so divine;
> Never was love, dear King,
> Never was grief like Thine.
> This is my Friend,
> In whose sweet praise,
> I all my days
> Could gladly spend.

Jesus went to the cross and made his way through death to something beyond life. Let him take our hand, empty, weak and worn, and his journey will be ours too.

Roger Spiller

Suggested hymns

All glory, laud and honour; Ride on, ride on, in majesty; Make way, make way, for Christ the King; My song is love unknown.

Palm Sunday 5 April

Second Service Rejection and Restoration

Ps. 80; **Isa. 5.1–7**; Matt. 21.33–end

The themes of rejection and restoration run through these readings on Palm Sunday. This theme is also present in the reading of the Passion from earlier in the day, when we first hear of Christ riding triumphantly into Jerusalem and the crowds praising him. In this narrative we begin with a restoration of sorts, Christ acclaimed as the people's king, but this is quickly followed soon after by the crowd rejecting him, baying for his life and shouting, 'Crucify him!'

The beginning of Holy Week takes us from one extreme to another, we are drawn into a story that began with contradictions. The Lord of heaven and earth stooped to redeem our humanity in the cry of a baby, and then that innocent baby was revealed to be the cause of grief and the falling and rising of many. The contradictions continue as we journey inexorably towards the cross where, like a lamb to slaughter, the Son of God is nailed to hard wood and left to die. He is mocked and crowned with thorns on a throne of suffering.

Jesus is not unaware of his destiny. In his ministry he has turned all worldly assumptions upside down, he has challenged the rich and powerful, he has raised up the fallen and the vulnerable. He has spoken hard words to the entitled and words of compassion to those whom the world has rejected. With such radical actions and prophetic speech, he was always heading towards confrontation and conflict with the political and religious establishment of the day.

A vineyard ruined

The image of the vineyard is often used throughout Scripture to represent God's people. God is the careful owner, tending for it as a loving gardener even when the vines bear little or no fruit and grow wild. Jesus tells the chief priests and the Pharisees the parable of the Wicked Tenants. He wants them to understand the meaning of the gift that they are turning away. In the Gospel reading from Matthew, Jesus picks up on the language and imagery of the vineyard which is well understood in the history of his people.

A generous landowner trusts in the tenants to whom he has left his land, a vineyard. When the harvest is ready, the tenants reject his generosity by killing first his slaves, and then most horrifically, his son. They are not only rejecting the landowner, they are rejecting the possibility of a good harvest which would benefit everyone. The analogy is too close for comfort for the religious leaders of the day who are not only rejecting Jesus and his teaching, but also plotting to have him killed.

Jesus then quotes from Psalm 118, calling to mind that the stone that the builders rejected has, and will, become the cornerstone; the one who is rejected will be restored, the one who is despised will become honoured, the one who is tortured and killed will live, and through him the vineyard will be restored to its former glory.

A vineyard restored

In all these readings we hear of the potential of a vineyard to produce fruit, fruit for feasting and fellowship, fruit for joy and consolation, but in each case the vineyard is ruined by neglect and pride and greed. The prospect of sharing in the bountiful harvest is undermined because the vine itself is rejected. I am the true vine, says Jesus in the Gospel of John. No good fruit can come unless we have a share in him.

The reading from Isaiah reminds us of the origin and meaning of this offer. It all begins in a love song for a beloved and for his vineyard. God desires to give everything in love and to restore all things to himself. In the gift of his Son, he is seeking to build a new temple, a new vineyard, and inaugurate a new creation.

The Psalmist understands the possibility that God may indeed turn away and so pleads with God to look kindly upon them, and restore them. This is the hope that we must hold on to as we journey to the cross. We pray that God's face may shine upon us, as the sun shines on the vineyard and causes the fruit to grow, and as rain falls and waters the earth making it bring forth and bud.

We too are called to bear fruit as a choice vine, fruit that can be transformed into wine for feasting and celebration, but as part of that restoration process we must first taste the bitter wine on the lips of the Son who was sent to save us.

Victoria Johnson

Suggested hymns

I am the vine, you are the branches; Restore, O Lord; My song is love unknown; Christ is made the sure foundation.

First three days of Holy Week 6–8 April
Poured Out for Love's Sake

(*These are the readings for Monday of Holy Week but the sermon may be used on any day.*)

Isa. 42.1–9; Ps. 36.5–11; Heb. 9.11–15; **John 12.1–11**

We move into Holy Week to keep company with Jesus and follow the story that will unfold during the late, fateful days of his life on earth. We may well approach it with some trepidation, not knowing quite how the story may affect us. We will once again be confronted by the extremities of the human condition, the injustice and brutality that has free reign on Good Friday, contrasting with the costly love of Mary in today's Gospel. Staying close to Jesus and following his story during this week, we discover the cost that Jesus met in order to secure our salvation. And we are made to feel the force of his passion in our own lives and open ourselves to the love that he expended in order to rescue, redeem and restore us to God.

Bethany

We begin in Bethany, the home of Lazarus. John tells us that it is six days before the Passover, and that frames this momentous week. It alerts us to the fact that the inevitable showdown with Jesus and the Jewish authorities is imminent. The presence of Lazarus, recently raised from the dead, makes this dinner a special celebration, a dinner to celebrate Lazarus' restoration to life by Jesus. But even as they celebrate, the storm clouds are already enveloping them. The miracle had precipitated a deep division among the people and led to an unplanned meeting of the Jewish council, the Sanhedrin. They decided to get rid of Jesus, not this time on religious grounds but out of fear that his actions could incite the Romans to move against the Jews. As Caiaphas the high priest had said, 'it is better for you to have one man die for the people than to have the whole nation destroyed.' There speaks the voice of political opportunism and expedience. But he spoke better than he knew. The death of Jesus might placate the Romans, but his death would also neutralize all the enmity that separated humankind from God. However, this was not the 'hour' for Jesus to face his future. Instead he had been forced to withdraw and avoid capture by fleeing with his disciples to relative safety close to the wilderness. But by restoring Lazarus, Jesus' gift of life will lead to his own death.

Anointing

Now Jesus has surfaced at the home of his friends, before crowds arrive to satisfy their curiosity and besiege the house. Bethany is the point of departure for Jesus' final journey. It's a steep climb up from the valley below, but at the top on the Mount of Olives there is a staggering backward view of Jerusalem the golden. This is the reunion meal. Martha is graciously on hand, ready to serve the guests, while Mary performs one final act of devotion. The custom was for feet to be washed, but instead Mary anoints the feet of Jesus. Oil is for anointing the head. Only the dead have their feet anointed. This is Mary's prophetic sign of Jesus' impending death. And in a personal and intimate act, which was frowned on in the society when in the company of men, Mary wipes his feet with her hair. The ointment is costly but so is her love. She won't be at Jesus' burial; the wealthy and powerful Nicodemus will take care of all that. And he has a disgustingly vast supply of oil ready for the burial. But Mary has poured out not merely her precious oil, but her own love for her Lord, and her love, like the fragrance of the perfume, spreads far and wide, right down to us today.

Rejection

But now the malign presence of Judas makes itself felt. Long before, John told us that Jesus called Judas a 'devil', and yet he's still in this select group sitting close to Jesus. He's the treasurer, and there's always a prominent place reserved for those who keep the purse strings. But he's in an indignant mood and complains that the money, the equivalent of a year's wages, could have been given to benefit the poor. He really cares only for himself and for lining his own pocket, and makes 'the poor' the excuse for his own greed and dishonesty. The poor are often made a cover for those who want to exploit the poor to win honour and respectability while caring only for themselves.

The devotion of Mary exposes the cold formality of Judas, who knows the cost of everything but the value of nothing. Jesus doesn't dismiss the value of helping the poor; he affirms it. But Judas is wrong to set costly acts of love and devotion in opposition to the welfare of the poor.

Mary recognizes that Jesus is worth everything she has got. She realizes that the love of her Lord is free and unconditional. Jesus will, like the Suffering Servant, pour himself out to death. How then could she withhold anything? How, indeed, can we? 'Love so amazing, so divine, demands my soul, my life, my all.'

Roger Spiller

Suggested hymns

A prophet-woman broke a jar; When I survey; All for Jesus, all for Jesus; Take my life and let it be.

Maundy Thursday 9 April

Handed Over

Ex. 12.1–4 [5–10] 11–14; Ps. 116.1, 10–end [*or* 116.9–end]; 1 Cor. 11.23–26; **John 13.1–17, 31b–35**

The Last Supper, whose institution we remember tonight, was the turning point in the life of Jesus. Jesus, says St John, 'knew that his hour had come'. And it was the deed of Judas that signalled the turning point.

We know Judas as the betrayer. But of the 33 occasions in the New Testament where the deed of Judas is mentioned, or where it is attributed to 'one of the twelve', only once is Judas said to betray Jesus. Instead the Gospel writers use a colourless, neutral word to describe what Judas did – they say that Jesus was 'handed over'. It is surprising that they didn't use a stronger word to describe Judas' dastardly deed. But the Gospel writers weren't particularly interested in Judas as such – who he was and how he handed over Jesus. They were more interested in the fact that Jesus allowed himself to be handed over, to put himself in the hands of evil men.

Activity

In the Gospels it's always the activity of Jesus that is described. He's shown to be purposeful, constantly moving from place to place; packing so many things into every moment; always ready to intervene, leaving behind him a trail of transformed scenes and changed lives. Jesus isn't an observer of a scene, one who waits upon events. He's the initiator, the master of every situation. When his enemies try to corner him or plan his death, he simply walks clean out of their hands.

It's remarkable then that at a certain point, the point we remember tonight, all this dramatic activity ceases. This is the point at which Jesus is handed over by Judas in the garden to the authorities. Jesus who has been the subject of every activity now becomes the object of the activities of others. He no longer does – he is done to.

Passion

St Mark's Gospel shadows Jesus. He looks at everything through the eyes of Jesus, telling us what Jesus felt and thought. Now, suddenly, this changes. Jesus is handed over, men appear out of the wings and take the initiative. They make decisions about Jesus, they send him hither and thither. And when Jesus does speak, it no longer appears to be with his usual power and authority. More often the emphasis is on his silence. And when he does speak his words are disregarded, ridiculed or misunderstood.

St John makes the same point differently. One short pregnant sentence sums up the mood. 'It was night.' He signals that the daylight period is over: 'Night comes when no man can work.' It's the start of Christ's passion. It's not just his suffering and death, passion means 'being done to', you are in the hands of others. It isn't necessarily malign. A person who is in hospital experiences passion, the loss of control.

But the astonishing thing is that for the Gospel writers it isn't his teaching or miracles or any other activity of Jesus that discloses his deepest glory. It's the fact that Jesus, of his own volition, places himself in human hands and allows himself to be used and abused according to their will. So for John, the crucifixion is the hour of Christ's glorification. He is reigning from the throne. 'Of all that God has done in and for the world,' one writer said, 'the most glorious thing is this, that he has handed himself over to the world; that he has given the world, not only the power of being but also the power to affect himself.'[21]

Letting be

Isn't this waiting, this letting be, allowing ourselves to be vulnerable, what love requires? So the lover is shown to be a waiting figure, waiting for the phone to ring, for a bunch of flowers, for a text message that never seems to come. And the lover is meanwhile powerless, open to rejection, betrayal, suffering. And isn't that how God loves us, by handing over his own dear Son so as to face and absorb and outlive all their hatred and malice?

If we're to follow Christ, who was handed over, is there not need for us too to hand ourselves over to God; to listen as well as to speak; to wait as well as to work; to accept service as well as to give service.

At the Last Supper, Jesus donned a towel and proceeded to wash his disciples' feet. Peter protested. He'd rather serve than be served.

But he had to learn to let Christ serve him, before his service could be of any value.

So for us too, may we be ready to watch and wait through the hours of Christ's passion and to wonder at the God who puts himself into the hands of cruel men; at the Lord who, for our sakes, allows himself to be handed over unto death so that we can be made clean.

Roger Spiller

Suggested hymns

Great God, your love has called us here; Jesus, in dark Gethsemane; This is the night, dear friends, the night for weeping; Love is his word, love is his way.

Good Friday 10 April

'I find no case against him'

Isa. 52.13—end of 53; Ps. 22 [*or* 22.1–11, *or* 22.1–21]; Heb. 10.16–25, *or* Heb. 4.14–16; 5.7–9; **John 18.1—end of 19**

Jesus was crucified. But no Jew ever crucified anyone. Crucifixion was a Roman penalty inflicted on rebels against the state. But must we then conclude that Jesus planned to lead an armed revolt against Rome? This isn't supported by the teaching of Jesus in the Sermon on the Mount, and nothing that we know of Jesus gives grounds for this conclusion. So we must come back to the Jews. After all, the witness of the New Testament is that the Jews killed the Lord Jesus. But on what charge did the Jews find him guilty? Jesus had spoken of the son of man sitting on the right hand of 'the Power'. He had pronounced the forgiveness of sins, which was a prerogative of God, he put his own authority above that of Moses, and he had spoken of destroying and rebuilding the Temple in three days. None of these claims strictly constituted blasphemy, but they did pose a threat to Judaism and its leaders and left open the possibility that someone would try to use Jesus to trigger an uprising that would draw in the Romans. It suited the Jewish authorities to press charges with the Romans against Jesus. Securing the penalty of crucifixion rather than their own penalty of stoning would avoid stirring up opposition to the Jewish leaders from the supporters of Jesus.

Jewish leaders bring judgement on themselves

Pilate has no appetite for subtle religious arguments, so the Jewish leaders have to work hard to convince him to take action. And they do so by appealing to his naked self-interest. 'If you release this man, you are no friend of the emperor.' But not even questioning his loyalty to Caesar makes him cave in to their demands. So they take the ultimate, fateful step: 'We have no king but Caesar.' They have judged themselves, they have condemned themselves. In defence of their religion they have forfeited the basis of all religion. In misreading a charge of blasphemy, they have not only murdered the Son of God, they have perpetrated the ultimate and final act of idolatry. Jesus, the one on whom their hopes depended, was himself being expelled in the name of Israel's faith. But in what they do they are meeting the condition of showing to the world that God is the victim, the rejected one, the one in our midst whom we cast out.

John's claim of Jesus is fulfilled

This fateful renunciation of all their religious legitimacy, this ultimate religious treachery, takes place at noon on the eve of Passover, the very hour when the priests have begun to slaughter the pascal lambs in the Temple precincts. The Jews renounce the covenant at the very moment when their priests are beginning the feast that recalls God's deliverance of his people. They think of Passover as the time for God's judgement on the world, and on the eve of Passover they have judged themselves by condemning the one whom God sent into the world. The claim of John the Baptist at the beginning of the Gospel, 'Behold the Lamb of God who takes away the sins of the world', is now fulfilled. Jesus is the Passover lamb, whose blood sets them free from the world of sin and death, and transfers them to the kingdom of God.

'Only doing what our religion tells us to do'

The religious leaders weren't wicked. They were acting as they thought best to protect their religion. But they exposed the dangers of religion, the dangers when we are too certain of our perceptions of God and our beliefs about God, that they become a substitute for trust in God's self. Religion can lead us to trust in our beliefs about God, rather than in the God of surprises, who confounds our logic and breaks free of the religion in which we try to confine him.

The failure of the religious people who had their way with Jesus on the first Good Friday was their unwillingness to reckon with the surprising otherness and difference of God. And so they made God's son a victim of their religious bigotry and narrowness. They are a warning that religion can be used to exclude and marginalize and so make victims of those for whom Christ died.

Pilate's unwitting proclamation

Pilate has been weak, cowering to the demands of the Jews, but he will cower no longer. His final words in the Gospel are defiant. Could any playwright have given Pilate a more impressive final line? He writes the title on the cross: 'Jesus of Nazareth, the King of the Jews'. Jesus' kingship is acknowledged by the representative of the greatest power on earth. Written in the three great languages of the world, Hebrew, Latin and Greek, it is a proclamation of the kingship of Jesus to all nations. Salvador Dali painted the cross of Christ across the whole world, and that's where Jesus is. For John, the triumph of the resurrection comes precisely as Jesus hangs on the cross. For when he is lifted on the cross, he is being exalted, enthroned; he reigns from the cross and begins to draw all people to himself.

The cross, Christ's meeting place

It's at the cross of Christ, like the old market crosses, that God intersects with all human experience. It's God's meeting place. He says he will meet us there. For nowhere is God more characteristically himself than in the suffering figure who hangs there, and will be so until the end of time. Today, the towering figure of Jesus stands over us from the cross. Most people whom the world has thought great have their greatness diminished as the distance grows from us, but Jesus' influence grows, drawing people from all points in the compass, bringing the true life that sets us free.

Roger Spiller

Suggested hymns

O sacred head, sore wounded; Morning glory, starlit sky; My song is love unknown; When I survey the wondrous cross.

Easter

Easter Vigil 11–12 April

Principal Service **Discovering Infinity**

(*A minimum of three Old Testament readings should be chosen. The reading from* Ex. 14 *should always be used.*)
Gen. 1.1—2.4a *and* Ps. 136.1–9, 23–end; Gen. 7.1–5, 11–18; 8.6–18; 9.8–13 *and* Ps. 46; Gen. 22.1–18 *and* Ps. 16; Ex. 14.10–end; 15.20–21 *and Canticle*: Ex. 15.1b–13, 17–18; Isa. 55.1–11 *and Canticle*: Isa. 12.2–end; Baruch 3.9–15, 32—4.4 *and* Ps. 19, *or* Prov. 8.1–8, 19–21; 9.4b–6 *and* Ps. 19; Ezek. 36.24–28 *and* Ps. 42, 43; Ezek. 37.1–14 *and* Ps. 143; Zeph. 3.14–end *and* Ps. 98; **Rom. 6.3–11** *and* Ps. 114; Matt. 28.1–10

John Wallis was a seventeenth-century clergyman who was born in Ashford, Kent. He was a gifted and talented mathematician who has been credited with creating the mathematical symbol for infinity: it's like the number 8 lying on its side.

Circles and octagons

Whether consciously or not, John Wallis was following a long tradition of creating symbols for eternity, one of which was a circle; that is, a line that has no beginning and no end. In architecture the shape of a circle was used for high-status tombs in Classical times; for example, the fourth-century church of Santa Costanza in Rome has a circular dome and was traditionally regarded as the burial place of the daughter of the Emperor Constantine, though that is now disputed. What is not disputed, however, is the shape of the rotunda created above the tomb of Christ in the Church of the Holy Sepulchre in Jerusalem. That too is circular in form. Eternity, symbolized by a circle, is an appropriate architectural motif for a building that encloses the tomb from which Christ rose from the dead.

There were slight architectural variations on this theme in the early centuries of the Church. In Ravenna, for instance, the baptistery called the Orthodox Baptistery was built at the end of the fourth or the beginning of the fifth century, not in a circular but in an octagonal form. That too was a deliberately symbolic choice. The baptistery was designed as an Octagon because it represented the seven days of creation plus the eighth day, the day of the new creation in Christ. And if you step inside this wonderful building you will see that high above your head is a mosaic image of Jesus being baptized by John the Baptist. In other words, circular and octagonal shapes were created to symbolize the powerful relationship between baptism, death, new life and eternity.

In many churches that same symbolism is found in our fonts, which are often circular or octagonal in shape.

And just to heighten the symbolism, in the early Church new Christians, having been instructed in the Christian faith during Lent, were baptized on Easter Eve: leaving their old lives behind, they went down into the waters of baptism (which symbolized the death of Jesus), and were then raised up out of the waters into their new lives.

So, the symbolism of circles, octagons and baptism in the early days of the Church were all of a piece.

But let's move away from those historical times and instead concentrate on our own lives now.

Easter Eve and baptism

This Easter Eve is a moment when we ought to recall our own baptism. Think of the church where you were baptized; think of the people who were with you then. Pray for that church and pray for those people.

But now let's do one thing more. Let's try to consider how far our own lives have been shaped by our baptism. Have we grasped the gift of new life offered to us in that sacrament? Have we lived up to our calling to be disciples of Christ? During our baptism the priest would have placed on our foreheads an invisible sign of the cross, and, whether we have been aware of it or not, that is a sign we have worn ever since.

The trouble is that if we aren't careful we might regard the fact of our baptism in an almost magical way; as though once we have received baptism, all will be well. One second's thought will remind us that that over-simple idea does not bear scrutiny. Do not baptized Christians suffer, as they always have done? Are not

Christians subject to the stresses and strains and agonies of human life just like everyone else?

The gift of new life

So what's all this about a new life? Well, perhaps we may consider it this way. At our baptism we are indeed granted new life through Jesus Christ, but it's a life that has to be lived in the everyday turmoil of the world. We aren't spared that. But what God promises us is that his Holy Spirit will be with us, no matter what happens. As Paul wrote, 'nothing can separate us from the love of God in Christ Jesus our Lord'.

And if that is true, it does indeed hint at a way in which our perceptions of life can be changed. The change might take a lifetime to happen, but if we come to realize that God's gift to us can never be revoked; if we realize that the strength and grace of God are always with us; if we realize that death itself has been defeated, then that is indeed new life, for our perspective is changed, our lives can be seen to have purpose, our future in God is absolutely secure.

In short, the truths and beauties of eternity are ours to enjoy now. For our baptism, therefore, let us this Easter night give God thanks and praise.

Christopher Herbert

Suggested hymns

This is the night of new beginnings; Within our darkest night; Firmly I believe and truly; I will sing the Lord's high triumph.

Easter Day 12 April

Principal Service **Risen Yet Hidden**

Acts 10.34–43, *or* Jer. 31.1–6; Ps. 118.1–2 [*or* 118.14–24]; Col. 3.1–4, *or* Acts 10.34–43; **John 20.1–18**, *or* Matt. 28.1–10

Where is he?

He'd gone.

Mary came to the tomb, and he was not there.

Peter and John came to the tomb, and he was not there.

But when John went in, and saw his absence, he believed.

Yes, he would appear. To ones and twos, to groups of friends, even to 500 at once. But not to everyone: to those chosen by God as witnesses.

And those witnesses were to proclaim that God had raised him; that God had appointed him judge of the living and the dead; that release from the heavy chains of sin was promised in his name.

How could they do this, when Jesus, risen from the dead, was not there, visible, obvious, to be paraded in front of the crowds as God's great Exhibit A?

How could they do this, when only a few had seen him?

How could they do this, when he had publicly died the most shameful of deaths?

Maybe it goes back to that early moment in the still-darkened garden, when John saw – not his risen body, but his absence – and believed.

The story and memory of Jesus evoke faith

The faith that Jesus had been raised by God; that he was the crowning fulfilment of God's promises and plans; that he was the key to a liberated future for all – that faith is not evoked through dramatic signs alone. It is evoked by the story and the memory of one who went about doing good and healing all who were oppressed by the devil; by the sense that this, supremely, was a life God blessed, a life God approved, a life God attested, a life that could never be finished by death.

That story, so near, that memory, so raw, must have combined in that moment with the sight of the absence of Jesus: and John saw, and believed. And that story, and that memory, would be told to hundreds and thousands and millions who had never seen Jesus: and even in his absence, they, and we, would believe too.

Where are we?

And in believing, be caught up into his life. Strangely enough, we in a sense become hidden as the risen Jesus is hidden. Remember Paul's words: 'You have died, and your life is hidden with Christ in God.' Yes, people can still see us. But there is a secret, a mystery to us, like the secret and mystery of the risen but invisible Christ. We live like others around us: we eat and sleep and dress and work and play. But our *real* life is not what people see on the surface. It doesn't belong to this temporary, finite world. Our *real* life is hidden with Christ in God. It is safe in God's eternal sphere.

And so we dance to a different music and march to a different drumbeat. We go the way of the one whose life God approved, and raised never to die again. And as we do, mysteriously, others may encounter the hidden Christ whose secret life we share.

The world around us dances to the music of money, marches to the drumbeat of the dollar. Life revolves around the cuts and the mortgages and the debts and the bills, if you're poor. Life revolves around the holidays and the dividends and the luxury homes, if you're rich.

But *our* life revolves around neither. Our life is hidden, with Christ, in God. People may look at us, as John looked at the linen wrappings and the cloth rolled up, and think: 'She's gone', 'She's not here', and yet believe: because somehow they grasp that the source of our life is elsewhere, guarded in God's eternal sphere.

Anticipating the final revelation

One day, though, Christ our eternal life will be revealed. The curtain will be pulled back on his splendour. And there, with him, will be his friends, those who have died to this world-bound existence and found their true life in him.

And till then?

Till then, we enter day by day as Jesus taught us into the secret place of prayer, where we revel again in our roots in eternity; where we open wide the channels through which the fresh springs of true life can pass from Christ.

Till then, we live each day in *this* world as those who have a compass and light from another. We live trusting that the way of *Jesus* is the way of the future: not the way of the dictators or the suicide bombers, not the way of those who amass wealth to themselves without care for the hungry, not the way of the small-hearted and hard-hearted and bitter-hearted.

Till then, we pass on the memory; we tell the story. We don't allow the news of Jesus to be silenced by vague religiosity, or embarrassment, or ignorance, or the tragic failings of his followers. We share it simply, straightforwardly, not raucously, not defensively. We have no Exhibit A to parade before people. We have ourselves, as the channels of his hidden but risen and eternal life.

And till then, we gather round his table, where we remember his life and his death, find his absence and his presence, and eagerly anticipate the day when the curtain is drawn back.

And we see, and believe.

Stephen Wright

Suggested hymns

Hail, festival day; Teach me to dance to the beat of your heart; Alleluia, alleluia, hearts to heaven and voices raise; Jesus Christ is risen today.

Easter Day 12 April
Second Service **Ardent Desire**

Morning Ps. 114, 117; Evening Ps. 105, *or* Ps. 66.1–11; **Song of Sol. 3.2–5; 8.6–7**; John 20.11–18 *if not used at the Principal Service, or* Rev. 1.12–18

Have you ever really wanted someone or something? Someone you have fallen in love with, a new job or house? Unstoppable feelings of desire can be exciting, energizing; but they can also be dangerous to both ourselves and those around us. Except when it's about God. Then the good news is that when such burning yearnings are simply, wholly desiring God who is unquenchable Love, they lead to purity and peace beyond words.

Looking for the one 'whom my soul loves'

Desire burns fiercely throughout the Song of Solomon. This Hebrew love song doesn't in fact mention God by name at all (so some Christians throughout the centuries have chosen to set it aside). It's particularly challenging because it tells of experiences of love and desire in often intense, sometimes erotic, terms. The poetry just can't get over the power of love: it keeps repeating words and phrases, sounding like an obsession. Obsessions for sure can be bad news: when we are obsessed with someone or something we can get very stuck, unable to get it or them out of our minds. But here the one who's so full of desire is consumed instead with the one 'whom my soul loves'. When you take this as a pointer to God (as most interpreters of the Song of Solomon have done for generations) then you hear the voice of someone who is simply full of desire for the God who is Love.

'I will seek him whom my soul loves,' says that person who is seeking God. We probably don't as yet know quite how much our souls desire God, but let's stop to notice that desire for God in our lives and in our world. So many people today might say they are 'spiritual' but not 'religious'. They have noticed a deep yearning to connect with something bigger, someone Other. We might notice in ourselves a desire for the world to be a better place, for people to be kinder, for ourselves to be more compassionate. When we are looking for a 'more' that is not about 'stuff' or 'things' for the sake of our own greed, then we are in fact looking beyond ourselves. We are looking for the divine Other who is God.

That desire is bright in today's Old Testament reading. It sends the seeker all round the houses looking for the known object of that love. And on finding the one 'whom my soul loves', the singer of the song does not want to let go.

To let go or not to let go?

These verses in the Song of Solomon look like a prototype of the Easter story in John's Gospel. When Mary Magdalene first gets to the tomb, she doesn't go in. She realizes that something's happened, because the stone (which is like the door to the tomb) is not where they left it on Friday night. She has run back to get a couple of the disciples; they've gone into the empty tomb, and gone home again. And here she is, loitering still, not knowing what to think.

But she knows what she wants. She wants Jesus back. Now she looks into the tomb. It is she, not the two disciples, who sees the two angels sitting where Jesus' body had been laid; and then she turns and sees Jesus (although she doesn't yet recognize him). The angels and Jesus have both asked her why she is weeping. It is Jesus who asks her who she is looking for. (Note that Jesus knows it's a person she is looking for: he knows she's seeking him.) And when he addresses her by name, she knows she's found him.

She was wanting Jesus back; now she learns that she hasn't got Jesus back again, *but she's found the risen Jesus*. It's not the old Jesus: not someone she can hold on to. This risen Jesus' divine qualities are now becoming clear. The moment she truly recognizes Jesus, she calls him 'Teacher'. He is showing her, the one who most desired to find him, what new life is like. It doesn't involve going back to how things were, it's not about clinging on to the past.

She can't hold on to him any more than you can hold on to what's past and gone. He's teaching her to realize that her deepest desire is in fact the risen version of him.

What's stopping you?

No one, not even Mary Magdalene, the greatest seeker of Jesus in the Gospels, can stop the risen Jesus. And no one can stop us in our search for God. Psalms 105 and 114 echo this as they remember the Exodus, that Jewish story remembered at the Passover, which was the feast Jesus and his disciples celebrated the night he was arrested. The Red Sea couldn't stop the Israelites escaping Egypt and getting to the Promised Land, which they so desired. The soldiers and guards, Herod and Pilate, couldn't stop Jesus on his journey through death. And no one, nothing, can hold you back from your own ardent search for the love of God.

Even if you don't think you do 'desire God' right now, you can *want* to look for God, you can entertain the idea that it is God whom your soul loves above all. Or you can *want to want* to look for him . . . and so on. Just ask in prayer. Seek the One whom your soul most truly, most ardently, desires.

I want doesn't get? It does if it is God you're talking about.

Megan Daffern

Suggested hymns

Now the green blade rises from the buried ground; Jesus lives! Thy terrors now; Alleluia! Alleluia! Hearts to heaven and voices raise; Now is eternal life.

Second Sunday of Easter 19 April

Principal Service Faithful Enough to Doubt

Ex. 14.10–end; 15.20–21 (*if used, the reading from Acts must be used as the second reading*), *or* Acts 2.14a, 22–32; Ps. 16; 1 Peter 1.3–9; **John 20.19–end**

Torrential rain poured upon a summer holiday. Sunshine spirits were crushed as the pool overflowed and the empty beach turned sodden and unwelcoming. The excitement which had greeted the holiday was rapidly swamped and it was hard to regain momentum.

Dampening doubts

As we imagine that sense of gloomy disappointment, it's not terribly difficult to imagine that something like this was the experience of the ten disciples.

First their sorrow-filled hearts had been rejuvenated when the risen Lord appeared to them. It's John's Gospel's version of Pentecost, emphasizing the power of their experience behind those locked doors.

But Thomas wasn't there. And when he arrived, the joyful eagerness of the ten was seriously rained on by Thomas' adamant refusal to believe what they were telling him.

This was far more important than a soggy holiday, and it's unlikely the ten allowed their resurrection experience to be completely overwhelmed by Thomas' doubt. But there must have been real disappointment. We can only guess what the dynamics between them were like over the course of the next week. It was probably a week of wondering and attempted persuasion. One week later the doors were still locked, which is a strong hint that none of them yet had a clear vision of what should happen next. Perhaps Thomas' doubtful dampening of their excitement had created not only disappointment but some necessary space for further reflection.

Faithful doubts

Doubt can do that. Reflection is important. Fairly early in the film *The Life of Pi*, there's a conversation between the adult Pi and a young writer. Pi comments: 'Faith is a house with many rooms.' The writer asks him if there is room for doubt, and Pi replies, 'Oh plenty, on every floor. Doubt is useful; it keeps faith a living thing. After all, you cannot know the strength of your faith until it is tested.'

It could almost have been a post-resurrection conversation with Thomas. Thomas' frequently negative press as 'the doubter' does no credit to the gospel account of his discipleship. Nor does it do credit to the holiness of doubt as one element of a living faith.

Through the years, many people of faith have decried doubt as a terrible thing, a weakness, an opponent of holiness, a sin. It isn't. And Thomas' role in the resurrection narrative helps us see why.

Honest doubts

But we need first to pause and think through our definitions of doubt and faith. Doubt isn't the opposite of faith. The opposite of faith is certainty. Certainty is one of humanity's great perils. Certainty, not faith, is the food that nourishes the fanaticism of terrorists and extremists. It's certainty, not faith, that builds separation walls and locks people into the rhythms of violence and hatred that scar generations of God's children.

With his honestly spoken doubt, Thomas stands in the centre of the great tradition of God's faithful people. He reminds us of the truth that faith is a process of exploration, of belief that is testing and being tested. Thomas wasn't a morally feeble figure from the shadows. Earlier, when the disciples knew that by going to Bethany where Lazarus had died, Jesus risked the murderous intentions of his enemies, it was Thomas who courageously stirred the disciples, 'Let us also go, that we may die with him.'

To doubt, then, is not to be weak. On the contrary, doubt can be an expression of strong character and vibrant faith. When Thomas utters those forceful, visceral words about putting his finger in the mark of the nails and his hand in the speared side, we're not merely overhearing understandable scepticism. We're listening to a strength of character that refuses to be bullied into belief. We're listening to someone who inhabits – comfortably – the many-roomed house of faith. We're listening to someone who is honest.

It's in Thomas' honesty that we can find good news. Our focus is not on encouraging doubt but on acknowledging doubt. He was confronted with a group of excited, overjoyed friends bursting with an extraordinary message. Most of us would find little surprise in Thomas' incredulous reaction. Most of us probably suspect a similar reaction in ourselves had we been in his place.

But would we have been as honest? Indeed, how honest are we (with ourselves or anyone else) about the doubts we experience in the life of faith?

Transformed doubts

Thomas doesn't shut the door on faith and lock himself into the stuffy air of a closed-minded room. Instead, with his blunt honesty, he throws the door open and looks for the fresh air of conviction. It was not least because of that very openness that the risen Lord was most effectively able to work with him. A closed mind will never see the truth because it's convinced it already knows it. An open mind is a room into which the Spirit can come with fresh insight, into which the risen Lord himself can come, confronting, enlightening, expanding.

It was from the doubting, open mind that we then heard that joyful exclamation: 'My Lord and my God!' Not only had Thomas' honesty created the space for our Lord to transform his doubt, but he transformed Thomas' doubt into a confession that was to be the climax of John's Gospel.

'Blessed are those who have not seen and yet have come to believe,' concludes the risen Lord with words directed at each of us. John takes his climax and grounds it in his readers' lives. Doubts have been honestly spoken and magnificently transformed. As for Thomas, Easter also breathes new life into us. That enlivening breath draws us from honest and holy doubt into the resurrection experience of a faith made all the deeper for the struggle.

Brett Ward

Suggested hymns

O sons and daughters, let us sing; Christ the Lord is risen again; Jesus, these eyes have never seen; Now is eternal life.

Second Sunday of Easter 19 April

Second Service **Happy Endings**

Ps. 30.1–5; **Dan. 6.1–23** [*or* 6.6–23]; Mark 15.46—16.8

There's something so appealing about the 'and they all lived happily ever after' ending to a children's story. But our life stories, our news headlines, don't always – don't often – seem to fit this model. We sometimes seem to survive one hard chapter of our lives only to face another one. So where, realistically, can we find the happy ending we can trust?

Where does it end?

Daniel and his friends came to Babylon because they were effectively prisoners of war. Babylon had first attacked Jerusalem in 605 BC, and the people in charge of Jerusalem – the royal family, the well educated, the officers of the state – were slowly but surely carted off to Babylon, particularly in 597 BC and again in 586 BC. Daniel, Hananiah, Mishael and Azariah are some of those who were carried off to Babylon as young men and integrated as Babylonian courtiers. They were even given Babylonian names: Belteshazzar, Shadrach, Meshach and Abednego. The book of Daniel itself is written partly in Hebrew and partly in Aramaic, which hints at its complicated history as a text, and how it was passed down through different people with different languages.

So Daniel and friends survive the Babylonian attack, only to be persecuted for their faith – because they hold on to their customs and beliefs even in exile. One edict commanding worship of a golden statue sends Shadrach, Meshach and Abednego to the fiery furnace, but thanks to God they walk out unharmed. A second edict commanding worship of the king Darius consigns the similarly law-breaking Daniel to the lions' den – as in our reading today.

Daniel's story is one of faithfulness rewarded. The whole tale is told as the result of the jealousy of the Babylonian chiefs towards the unfailingly wise Daniel; they set the king up, apparently against his will, to bring about Daniel's punishment. The king himself seals up the den with a stone rolled against the entrance. It's a happy ending for Darius, who is so relieved that Daniel's God has brought him deliverance; it's a happy ending for Daniel, who survives; and it's a happy ending for those who therefore come to know God through Daniel.

But it doesn't end here. The rest of the book, from chapter 7 onwards, turns into something that sounds more like the book of Revelation: Daniel prophesies and has visions about his people, Jerusalem and the end of times.

Foreshadow of the resurrection

That tomb-like sealing of the lions' den, and the amazement that Daniel can walk out alive in the morning, makes us think of that first Easter Day. But Mark's telling of the Easter story is much more faltering. It's full of perplexity, confusion, mystery, as well as raw and immediate power.

Mark – the shortest, fastest paced, simplest of the Gospels – shows an unadorned version of the bare bones of the story. Perhaps that tells us it's the earliest. There's no splendour here. Just sleep-deprived women trying to do their domestic task for the one they loved; just an already-moved sealing stone; just a young man dressed in a white robe. And just an empty tomb. The young man tells them simply not to be alarmed (probably something they needed to hear but couldn't believe): that the Jesus of Nazareth who was crucified has been raised, he is not there, and they are to go off and tell the disciples. The plain details make it more believable than the most fantastic of storytellings.

And probably what makes it most believable as a story is its ending. For there really isn't one. Mark's final sentence ends with a very odd word in Greek, which is about the last word you would ever end a sentence with. It would be like just finishing with 'for' or 'because'. This doesn't just end a sentence, or a story. It closes a whole Gospel.

Some Christians in the earliest times after Jesus didn't think this was plausible, so they wrote different endings, and that's probably how we have both a shorter and longer ending offered after verse 8. But none have the same ancient weight of originality. Mark, it seems, wanted his Gospel to end with 'because . . . '.

The sense of an ending

Neat endings, fairy-tale conclusions, aren't the stuff of the real Christian message. We might think they are – 'happily ever after' endings are the straightforward way of giving hope – but there's something much more down to earth going on. And it's way more powerful.

Because it really makes us ask – does it end here? And Mark wants us to know that it doesn't. His story does; but for Christ this is just a turning point in the story. The empty tomb isn't so much a happy ending as a happy beginning. And a challenging one at that. Daniel's survival of a near-death experience was part of a journey towards awesome visions of the end-times, a future beyond time, a vision of heavenly power. Jesus' resurrection, for Mark, is about a journey onward, deeper into life for him, deeper into faith for us.

It can make us reread Mark's Gospel, or look at the other Gospels. It can make us ask questions, think about the sense of it, and what it means for the Christian. Because nothing just ends here – despite our daily losses and bereavements and endings of one kind or another. This is always just a turning point, even a beginning. The best is always yet to come.

Megan Daffern

Suggested hymns

Christ is alive! Let Christians sing; Breathe on me, breath of God; Jesus, these eyes have never seen; Love's redeeming work is done.

Third Sunday of Easter 26 April

Principal Service The Journey of Discipleship

Zeph. 3.14–end (*if used, the reading from Acts must be used as the second reading*), *or* Acts 2.14a, 36–41; Ps. 116.1–3, 10–end [*or* 116.1–7]; 1 Peter 1.17–23; **Luke 24.13–35**

The Pilgrim's Way stretches from England to Compostella in Spain, or from Canterbury to Rome, or from Jerusalem to Emmaus. Our life is one journey in itself, but there are shorter journeys through school or employment, smaller journeys still, which can prove significant for the shape of our journey through life as a whole.

The journey of two disciples to Emmaus is an exquisite story. Journeys, for Luke, are an image of discipleship. His Gospel is shot through with the language of journey. We can enter it imaginatively, but it serves to illuminate the journey that we ourselves make. Journeys, whether or not we call them pilgrimages, open us up to new experience and meeting with new people who share our route. There's no knowing in advance what will happen on the journey. Most will be uneventful, but we can't know when our journey will be unforgettable and change our lives for ever. No wonder the regular showing of people from different walks of life and faith backgrounds makes for compelling television.

Inward

The journey of the two disciples from Jerusalem is triggered by loss and desolation. Their hopes and expectations have been dashed, their world has caved in. And now they want only to turn their backs on Jerusalem and move hastily into a fresh environment. But the loss is all-consuming. They are caught up in a frenetic discussion and, as typical of newly bereaved people, they need to go over and over the details in microscopic detail, hoping to find some sense in the tragedy that has overtaken them.

Alongside

And then a stranger crosses their path, a pilgrim presumed to be returning from the festival, but a stranger nevertheless. The stranger is a disquieting figure in the modern world; he or she keeps us in suspense. It's a strange irony that Luke casts Jesus as a stranger – and so he remains to this day to most of our friends and acquaintances. They and we miss Jesus if we misread the Gospel, and our conceptual framework is too rigid to countenance a God who is incognito and is met as a stranger. 'Never talk to strangers.' But some strangers can be 'angels unawares'. And the sense of loss is the one condition when even the most private of people are ready to open up to strangers, as do the erstwhile disciples of Jesus.

The stranger listens and then asks the most naive question. He sustains the cheeky suggestion that he, Jesus above all people, is out of touch with news that concerns his own misfortune. In playing along with them, Jesus always draws people out of themselves, and he draws out of those two bewildered, disillusioned disciples all their pent-up feelings. That's what friends are for, but sometimes strangers, with their critical distance, can give us a clearer perspective.

But faith isn't recycling our feelings or securing clarification by a stranger. There has to be something outside ourselves to enlarge our scope. And that's the purpose of Scripture; Jesus explains it, he's the critical interpreter who teaches his people how to read the Scriptures. Understanding the Scriptures is critical to recognizing who Jesus is.

Outward

The journey can end there. It often does. We learn a bit more of the Bible to store away, but that's as far as it goes. The stranger makes as if to go on. He won't make them feel they have to invite him in; after all, it's late and they weren't prepared for visitors. But the disciples prevail upon the stranger to stay with them. If they hadn't, he would have passed on and the opportunity would have been lost. No wonder hospitality is a great theme of the Christian faith, which St Luke draws attention to in his Gospel.

They sit for supper. It's not a special festival meal, like Passover. But then for Oriental people no meal is ordinary. There's a great respect for bread. The stranger takes it, blesses it and breaks it. That's exactly what he's done with his own life. Then, we're told, only when he took bread were their eyes opened and they recognized him. Their eyes were opened – that is, God opened their eyes, enabling them to see. And what they saw was not merely that the stranger was really Jesus – but, much more important, that Jesus the stranger was the crucified and glorified Messiah. A discovery then, which was too rich to be lived at the time it occurred. A journey to shape all journeys and one to blaze the trail on the journey of life itself.

Return

Their journey from disbelief to faith involves a journey back to Jerusalem and a journey into mission and worship. And when they get back to the rest of the disciples, they find they too have heard that Jesus is alive and has appeared to Simon Peter. So, whatever the journey, whoever the travellers, however preoccupied, there is always the possibility that a stranger will emerge from the shadows, cross our path and show himself as the Lord of life.

Roger Spiller

Suggested hymns

The peace of God comes close; Come, living God, when least expected; O changeless Christ, for ever new; Come, O thou Traveller unknown.

Third Sunday of Easter 26 April

Second Service Living Temple[22]

Ps. 48; Hag. 1.13—2.9; **1 Cor. 3.10–17**; *Gospel at Holy Communion*: John 2.13–22

What metaphor would you choose for the Church? I know T. S. Eliot's image of the Church of England was of a hippopotamus. It was a satire and it doesn't take much imagination to think of reasons why that might be a reasonable comparison! Those working in management and organizational leadership encourage their colleagues to identify the images that influence people and can bring about change. Some think of the Church as 'family', and that carries with it a host of expectations, not all of which are deliverable, and so it can help us to identify the limitation of this metaphor and search for another; perhaps one that is inclusive of single people.

The New Testament was in the business of metaphor-making long before management gurus, and it has a large spectrum of images that overlap, clash, support or challenge one another. And there are new metaphors that can be introduced. No one metaphor will suffice, but the attempt to identify and agree what might be the core metaphors for our times can sharpen and drive our church life forward. Others mentioned in the New Testament include a boat, a letter, a fish net, a loaf, branches, a vineyard, a bride, a pillar, a buttress, exile.

People of God, Body of Christ and temple of the Holy Spirit are three core images in the New Testament, but the one mentioned by St Paul in his first letter to the Corinthians is the temple of the Holy Spirit. Here he uses it of the local church, but he uses it elsewhere also for the individual Christian. What connections, associations, implications can be drawn from the metaphor of the temple of the Holy Spirit?

Urban

The Temple was inseparable from the city of Jerusalem, and so also was the health and destiny of both institutions; in most New Testament passages, the thought of the Temple evoked the thought of the city. This image, then, mandates us to ask in what ways is the presence of the Spirit in the life of God's living temple evident and active in our cities and urban areas. What is the mission of the Church, not merely to people and homes but also to the institutions of power and decision-making to which we relate? Food banks, shelters for the homeless, street pastors, credit unions and advice centres are some of the ways in which churches have expressed this aspect of ministry.

Visible

The image of the temple suggests high visibility and provokes thought as to how this might be translated. What, to co-opt other images, does it mean for a city set on a hill, that gives light to all? How can the light of Christ be manifest in the dark, sleazy, anonymous and apparently godforsaken margins of city life? What are the appropriate and effective means for debating and presenting the gospel in our public squares?

Growing

The building 'not made with hands' consists of 'living stones' which are joined together 'into a holy temple in the Lord, in whom you also are built together spiritually into a dwelling place for God', says Ephesians. It compels us to visualize the process of construction rather than the completed edifice. The emphasis on the process of growth rather than on completion prompted Peter to refer to individual Christians as 'living stones', who are shaped and moulded into a spiritual house, joined to Jesus Christ, the stone that serves as the corner of the entire edifice. What provision are we making for the growth and learning of followers of Jesus? This image allows for differentiations between those who laid the foundations and those who come after, who are stones. But we might also co-opt the other New Testament images and ask who are the pillars and who the buttresses. What kind of relationship should we develop between those who are the flying buttresses, as Churchill defined himself, who support from the outside, and those who are inside and at its core?

Dwelling

The most obvious and defining characteristic of the temple is as the dwelling place of God. The early Christian writers deliberately rejected the word for temple that denoted a physical building, choosing instead the word that suggests a temple, 'not made with hands', one that is created by the very fact that God chooses to dwell or camp with us and move among us. Where God's Spirit is, there the temple is present. Every congregation is thus a temple. Are we then being shaped by his presence or by the exigencies of maintaining a building? Is the fact of God moving, tenting, travelling with his people exerting its rightful pressure on an excessive attachment to buildings? Are we prepared to recognize God's withdrawal from some of our earthly edifices and the relocation of his presence in many new expressions and dwelling places among us? What other ideas does the image of the temple yield?

Metaphors provide a feast for the imagination and a fund of ideas. They can lead to transformation. We can try them out, playfully, imaginatively, to see which bear fruit, and then let them work on the debates, programmes and restructuring of our existing churches and congregations, reconfiguring them so that they are more truly living sacraments of God's presence in our world today.

Roger Spiller

Suggested hymns

O thou not made with hands; Let us build a house where love can dwell; Christ is made the sure foundation; Come build the Church – not heaps of stone.

Fourth Sunday of Easter 3 May

Principal Service **Called for Life**

Gen. 7 (*if used, the reading from Acts must be used as the second reading*), *or* Acts 2.42–end; Ps. 23; 1 Peter 2.19–end; **John 10.1–10**

You may, like me, not wish to be compared to sheep, who as slobbering, timid creatures only exist to be shorn and slaughtered. In one island in the South Pacific, the populace has no experience of sheep. But they have pigs, so instead of the Good Shepherd, the Gospel speaks of the Good Herdsman who looks after the swine. I'd prefer to be a sheep rather than swine, but I can be both.

Jesus is using the favoured Old Testament image of shepherd used for kings, prophets and priests, most of whose self-serving and faithless service brought the nation to its knees. He is the Good Shepherd who cares for his sheep and calls them all by name. Sheep can recognize a voice they trust and know, and still in Palestine today, when shepherds issue their distinctive calls, the sheep withdraw from their shared pasture to follow their own shepherd home.

Called to be

Today the Church gives particular attention to God's call upon our lives. We are all called by God as our primary vocation. Our vocation to Jesus Christ isn't something that is added on like Lego bricks as an extra to what we do. God's call is not just vocation, but evocation, a drawing out and intensification of our truest self, like the restoration of an old master whose distinctive features have been buried under layers of grime. Discipleship to Jesus Christ is meant to be the most fundamental thing about us. It's not what we do, but who we are, that defines us. The call to discipleship is our primary call, around which every aspect of our lives – work, family, recreation – has to be shaped and reconfigured. It's a call to full-time service, whatever the paid work we may do. It can be lived out with equal and complete commitment, whether as lay or ordained, provided we are obedient to the particular character of the call God makes to us.

'I can't wait to get to work tomorrow morning. I'm so excited, it's just like the day I first started work,' said one man to me after a service at which I'd been asked to preach on vocations. He said he'd been exploring ordained ministry for many years but he'd never before heard anybody say that you can be called to stay where you are, and so his exploration was at an end. God's call was all that mattered to him.

Called to serve

We can be discouraged from exploring God's call through a sense of unworthiness or some other deficit or inadequacy. But we don't discern our call by seeing how our innate gifts and strengths align against some job description or person specification. The people God called and the disciples Jesus called seemed ludicrously unsuitable at the time of their call. And we may even be wondering why on earth some of our clergy have been called! But God calls, to discipleship or to a particular vocation, not as recognition of existing natural gifts but because God's call promises and brings with it the empowering and anointing that are needed.

A young woman in the congregation of which I was a member experienced a call to be a doctor. But she was sickened by the sight of blood and felt temperamentally unsuited. These impediments were overcome once she surrendered to the call. The Church of England, for one, states in respect of ordained ministry that 'without a convincing sense of vocation – a candidate cannot be recommended, however skilled, gifted or experienced'. Why this strange departure from shared employment practice? It's because the initiative has to rest in God and his inscrutable will. But also because, in choosing weak, human vessels, as St Paul says, 'It may be made clear that this extraordinary power belongs to God and does not come from us.'

Whether a person is pope, lay person, bishop or priest, the one and only thing that counts is if God's call is being heard and obeyed. That call is usually too persistent and powerful to be ignored, even if we wished to do so. And it can come in many and sometimes surprising ways. Friends and sometimes strangers can help us to see it more clearly than we can ourselves.

Hearing aids

So what are we to think if God hasn't called us? Jesus says that our capacity to hear is amplified if we are in his flock. It's through practising hearing and being exposed to God's written word in the faith community that we come to recognize the voice of the Good Shepherd. When our community is focused on the development of its members, it can help us to discern our gifts and amaze and surprise us by extending us in ways we'd never imagined. Where any of the myriad jobs and duties in the local church are shared, tasks accepted in the church can awaken us to our primary call and lead us to renew or reconfigure the vocation that God intends for us. It's in responding to the call of Christ that we discover who we are and allow Christ to be formed in us.

Roger Spiller

Suggested hymns

Will you come and follow me if I but call your name; O for a thousand tongues to sing; Loving Shepherd of thy sheep; I, the Lord of sea and sky.

Fourth Sunday of Easter 3 May

Second Service Beginning Again

Ps. 29.1–10; **Ezra 3.1–13**; Eph. 2.11–end; *Gospel at Holy Communion*: Luke 19.37–end

Rebuilding the Temple

How would you feel if your church burnt down? Imagine how it might be if you were then taken away into captivity and unable to worship faithfully in the way laid down by your ancestors. The Israelites went through these traumatic experiences. The Temple was set ablaze in AD 587 and the people taken to Babylon to live as aliens in a strange land. The book of Ezra records the return from exile, the restoration of ordered worship and the rebuilding of the Temple in Jerusalem. In the passage set for today the leaders and the people are 'making a beginning'. They are about to lay the foundations of the new Temple: it's a momentous time. And although its billed as a 'beginning', in reality, there's been a lot of preparation to reach this point. The first year has been spent setting up an altar, praying and sacrificing to God – giving regular offerings, including each month at the new moon, and celebrating a variety of festivals. In the Festival of Booths, the Exodus from Egypt is remembered and the Israelites relive the story, reminding themselves that Yahweh is a God who rescues and saves. The rebuilding of the Temple includes deciding who is going to do what, making detailed plans, and sending out beyond the confines of the faith to find experts and resources – the Sidonians and Tyrians bring cedar from Lebanon. There's great excitement as the beginning is made. There are trumpets and cymbals and fine vestments, and a psalm is sung with the refrain 'his steadfast love endures for ever'– it could be Psalm 118, maybe its Psalm 136. It's a new beginning, but one that builds on the Law of Moses and the words of King David – so it's by way of continuation too: past, present and future held together. And, as often with new things, some people are very excited and others are distraught – those who remember the first Temple weep; those who are looking forward to the new one give shouts of joy. Change always elicits a variety of responses.

Building another Temple

The Temple that the Israelites rebuild in Jerusalem is a massive, physical, material structure: a building bringing glory to God. In the letter written to the Ephesians we hear of the new temple. This one is not made of stones but of flesh. This temple is built not *by* people, but *of* people, raised on the foundation of the prophets and apostles, with the risen Christ as the corner or key stone – the central block in which all hold together within Christ's body. Through Christ's resurrection, all are redeemed and built into a holy temple in the Lord. This temple is fully inclusive – everyone is welcome. Through the shedding of Christ's blood on the cross both Gentiles and Jews – those who are far off and those who are near – have been brought together to form a single humanity. The barriers have been removed and no one is now a stranger or an alien – everyone is a 'citizen' in the kingdom of God, and Christ is the Prince of Peace for all. Worship in this temple is about discipleship: following in the footsteps of Jesus, being alive to the movement of the Holy Spirit, who dwells within each person. The sacrifices now are not burnt animals, but the remembrance of the sacrifice of Jesus on the cross, once and for all, celebrated in the Eucharist. The psalms of David are still sung, but they are joined by newer hymns and songs written by more recent lovers of God. The Law of Moses is read alongside the words of the apostles and the Gospel writers. The importance of regular, ordered, beautiful and joyous worship remains, because God is constant, universal and faithful, loving each and all, without beginning or end.

Temple worship and witness

Today is Vocations Sunday, the particular day in the Church's year when we remember that God calls each of us into discipleship and ministry, equipping us to be his witnesses and ambassadors to those with whom we share our lives, wherever we find ourselves. Whatever God is calling you to be and do in his service, it will need to be underpinned with faithful, regular and committed worship. We don't serve in our own strength, but through the power of the Holy Spirit dwelling within us – leading, inspiring and empowering. In worship, we declare our love for God, we lay ourselves before God, we are restored and renewed through the power of God and we are built up as the Body of Christ – the new temple – to witness to God's love and power throughout the world. The Israelites worked tirelessly to restore worship and rebuild the Temple in Jerusalem after their exile. Jesus gave up his life in order that a new temple might be built through his resurrected body – one that is universal and has the power to bring all people together for eternity. We are part of that body today – let's give thanks that God has found us and loves us, and commit ourselves again to faithful worship and witness, that the world might see and believe. Amen.

Catherine Williams

Suggested hymns

God is here, as we his people; Let us build a house; Christ is made the sure foundation; In Christ there is no East or West.

Fifth Sunday of Easter 10 May

Principal Service Stilling Troubled Hearts

Gen. 8.1–19 (*if used, the reading from Acts must be used as the second reading*), *or* Acts 7.55–end; Ps. 31.1–5, 15–16 [*or* 31.1–5]; 1 Peter 2.2–10; **John 14.1–14**

'In my Father's house there are many mansions' or 'dwelling places' as the new version has it. Generations of people have found comfort in those words usually used at funerals. I, or was it a colleague, used it at the funeral of a publican – a man who kept a pub, with all the separate rooms, the smoking room, the lounge, the bar, the snug

(I can't imagine what that was for . . .). It's comforting to think that death is like a relocation, house-moving from one place to another, going upmarket, say, from Studley to Surrey, and we have in mind a sort of National Trust house, hopefully without stamp duty or community charge or local income tax.

There's an old joke. A man died and was ushered into heaven, which appeared to be an enormous house. An angel began to escort him down a long hallway, past 'many rooms'. 'What's in that room? That's the Roman Catholic, said the angel. And that room, who's in that room? That's the Orthodox. Now, said the angel, we have to be very quiet as we go past the fundamentalist Christians, because they think they're the only ones here.

Mansions in the sky?

It's a quaint idea, of course. But the idea of mansions in the sky stretches our credulity. Heaven never was a location on a map. It's beyond space and time, not even in outer space. And its not all that comforting anyway. Moving house is one of the most stressful experiences. And we can barely get our minds around the idea that we relocate ourselves from terra firma to some other location beyond space. In fact, what we're given here is far richer and more reassuring.

'Do not let your hearts be troubled.' This is part of Jesus' farewell speech. At one level it is addressed to the disciples in the upper room. On another level it's addressed to Christ's followers living on the other side of his death and resurrection and ascension. And it answers the question: why did Jesus leave us? Why couldn't he have stayed around after the resurrection? That's not a question the disciples in the upper room would have asked. It is a concern for the believers who came later, including ourselves.

Why 'troubled'?

What might cause our hearts to be troubled? What might cause people to stop believing? John's immediate readers are a small church, facing suffering and persecution, frightened at being left alone when Jesus is no longer there. It would also be the sense of the loss, absence of Christ, a feeling that we are on our own, abandoned, deserted, forgotten by God. It could be the continuing threat of terrorism; the victims of the wars in Afghanistan and Iraq – any of the circumstances in our lives that undermine our faith and peace.

How can our troubled hearts be stilled?

Jesus' departure and return to God after his death makes possible the return to us of Jesus' spiritual presence and the ministry of the Holy Spirit. That would not be possible without the death and departure of Jesus. His crucifixion, although a staggering blow, is in fact a blessing. Jesus' return to his Father has made all the difference in the world. Not only has Jesus got a dwelling place with the Father, but the Father has a dwelling place in the Son. Father and Son mutually relate. 'I am in the Father and the Father is in me.'

But, in departing, Jesus is preparing (not a spot in a physical dwelling but) a place in God's family, a place where one can be related to and remain with the Father as closely as Jesus, the Son. And the place that he prepares, the relationship that he opens up, is not something that only begins after we die. The preparation was the short interval between Jesus' departure and the coming of the Spirit of Jesus.

It happens when we enter into a relationship with Jesus through his Spirit and in his family. What is required is belief in Jesus – not believing doctrines, not simply intellectual assent. More like trust. But it's deeper even than that. It's long-term solidarity with, abiding in, Jesus and in one another.

Travel directions?

Thomas says they do not know where Jesus is going, so how can they know the way. He's thinking about travel directions and maps and destinations. But Jesus answers, 'I am the way.' You don't need directions to find me because I'm your destination. I am the truth. I don't have truths to share, because I embody truth. I am the life. I don't make provision for you to have life. Knowing me brings life because I and the Father are one. Now, what Jesus offers is not a physical place but a relational state. Not a house or mansion but a household – a community of people.

Heaven is not a place, but a relationship. We are not left alone, because the Spirit of Jesus is with us. He is not preparing a place; the place is prepared and we are invited to enter. And that's why St Peter can ascribe all God's dazzling blessings to his people: 'You are a chosen race, a royal priesthood, a holy nation, God's own people.' And what is the reason for this relationship to Jesus, this incorporation into the Christian family? It is 'in order that you may proclaim the mighty acts of him who called you out of darkness into his marvellous light'.

Roger Spiller

Suggested hymns

Good Christians all, rejoice and sing; Come, my Way, my Truth, my Life; O Lord, we long to see your face; Christ is the world's light.

Fifth Sunday of Easter 10 May

Second Service A New Heaven and a New Earth

Ps. 147.1–12; Zech. 4.1–10; **Rev. 21.1–14**; *Gospel at Holy Communion*: Luke 2.25–32 [33–38]

There's a longing among people to discuss what believing in heaven means and yet often a resistance to do so. This reluctance to discuss one of the greatest questions of our existence is due to the inherent mystery surrounding the subject and the recognition that there is little that can be said with any certainty about it. It is brought to our attention in our reading from the book of Revelation, and we may be surprised and reassured by the light it can throw on our thinking and living.

Heaven and earth

The very first verse of the Bible declares that 'God created the heavens and the earth', both created in the Genesis myth, in time and at the 'beginning'. Heaven and earth are connected in the same world. There's just one word in Hebrew that has to serve both for the sky and for the location of God's presence. We don't share the triple-decker cosmology of our biblical ancestors, but thanks to modern astronomy we're very conscious of the distance between 'earth' and 'sky' in the vastness of the universe. But alongside the 'distance' there is a closeness. In picture language, if 'heaven is God's throne, earth is his footstool'. If you have the luxury of a footstool, you know it goes with your chair, distinct but in the same space, not in a different room. God himself bestrides and connects heaven and earth.

Heaven is a discrete dimension. It's the supreme reality where God's writ rules. It's the repository for all our glorious, hopeful human projects that have been licensed by the biblical promises of God. Heaven is the generative image and present reality of what life on earth was intended to be after its 'good' creation. And meanwhile we hope and pray that God's will will come 'on earth as it is in heaven'.

A new heaven and new earth

But there is the promise of a new heaven and new earth, both renewed together. This doesn't mean that heaven and earth will be destroyed and replaced. It means the miraculous transformation and renewal of heaven and earth. There will be a continuity between the old and the new, and not just spiritual but material too. Even a 'new Jerusalem' will come down from heaven like a bride, to be joined to earth in the form of her husband. Heaven and earth will be joined together in eternity and God's presence will be among his people. The human life that began in a garden is now consummated in the city. That signals enchantment, liberation and expansiveness. And in the new earth there will be no mourning, crying, pain or death.

John tells us that human destiny isn't a realm characterized only by heaven. It's a kingdom that also embraces earth. It suggests a physical existence of created beings, and it implies that eternity won't be a timeless monotone but an eternity with time at the heart of it. Some people imagine that in eternity all personalities are swallowed up and lost in God, all temporal distinctions cease, and all finite and human life melt into the infinite. But we're given a promise of physical continuity with the best features of our existing condition. We aren't promised that we will be snatched up out of earth into heaven, but raised on a new earth, joined as it will be in the new heaven. A new heaven and a new earth. That is yet to be achieved, but it comes with the final coming of Jesus.

The vision of a new earth

John wrote to strengthen and give comfort to his beleaguered people. So what assurance does it give for us? Heaven is not just a future destiny but a picture of present reality, the divine dimension of our present life. Heaven is close, it's God's space, and it intersects with our space in a variety of ways. The earth is not a disposable part of God's creation. That would undermine the material, incarnational character of our faith and provide an excuse for those who wish to abdicate responsibility for the welfare not only of the people but also for the sustainability of the planet. Our world may be mired in sinfulness, but it is still good enough to be instrumental in God's redemptive purpose.

The worship of a new heaven

If the reality of heaven strengthens our commitment to life on earth, then, too, our earthly life can be the gate or vestibule of heaven. The boundaries between heaven and earth are permeable, and there is movement between them. This can be experienced supremely in worship when we respond to the summons to 'Lift up your hearts' and 'Lift them to the Lord', where he reigns in heaven. What passes for worship can become earthbound and hollow until it is suffused by the anticipation of being gathered up in praise together with 'the whole company of heaven'.

Roger Spiller

Suggested hymns

Come, let us join our cheerful songs; Now from the heavens descending; Let all creation dance; To you, O Christ, the Prince of Peace.

Sixth Sunday of Easter (Rogation Sunday) 17 May

Principal Service **Another Advocate**

Gen. 8.20—9.17 (*if used, the reading from Acts must be used as the second reading*), *or* Acts 17.22–31; Ps. 66.7–end; 1 Peter 3.13–end; **John 14.15–21**

Jesus said, 'I will ask the Father, and he will give you another Advocate, to be with you for ever.' He was referring of course to the gift of the Holy Spirit who would come on the disciples after he himself had finally disappeared from their sight. And this was all part of that precious final conversation he had with his close-knit group of followers before he died, in which he explained to them that his death would not end up being the disaster it would seem at the time, but would lead them to a new era of life and closeness to God.

An advocate is someone who stands up for someone else. It might be in a court of law, where you stand accused of some crime and a professional barrister takes your side. But we can be advocates in many other ways too, for example when we take someone's side, particularly in a situation where the odds seem stacked against them. Perhaps you've been asked to testify on behalf of a colleague appealing against unfair dismissal. People write references for us, or we for them, in support of job applications.

An advocate stands up for you, and the best advocates are true friends who will stand by you and respect you and value you and love you even when you have messed things up badly. It is always moving to see when spouses and children and parents stand beside those charged and even those convicted of serious crimes, despite the shame that brings on them as well. How often have we needed an advocate ourselves?

Jesus said, 'I will ask the Father, and he will give you another Advocate, to be with you for ever.' *Another* Advocate. He was saying that he himself had been his disciples' advocate. He had been *for* them. He had been on their side, their strong cheerleader, as it were. The way he had lived and acted and spoken had given them worth and built their confidence and promoted their well-being. And he was acutely conscious that with his death they would feel as if all those solid foundations he had given them had been swept away. So he explains that actually, wonderfully, that would not happen.

Imagine Jesus speaking, and later go back and read the words of the Gospel.

'We've been really close, the twelve of you and me. I know that you love me: well, the way that you can go on showing that you *really* love me is not to collapse in despair when I've been killed, but to go on keeping to my way – the Jesus way you've all been learning. And you know what? You won't be on your own. I've supported you and stuck up for you and stood by you the last three years as I've tried to show you this way – though you've tested my patience at times! Well, I'm praying to God that there'll be no break in that support. Although I won't be around, I'm asking God to give you his own Spirit, the Spirit of truth, the Spirit who keeps us grounded in the reality of God's awesome holiness and love. He'll be your new supporter. And don't worry, he's no stranger to you. Actually, you know him well already, because he's been in me. Now he's going to be in you! Unfortunately, you can't expect that the world at large will recognize this, or come on to your side, because at the moment it seems to be set against him, just as on the whole it's been set against me.

'But the thing is that you won't be bereft, like children without parents or refugees without a defence lawyer. In fact, God is going to make sure that the handover from one advocate to another is as smooth as possible. Because after I've died you'll see me again. You'll realize that I'm not dead any more, in the only sense that matters. And that means that you won't feel abandoned. In fact, your life will grow stronger and you will gain in confidence, not lose it. Because I live, you also will live!

'When that happens, things will at last fall into place for you. You'll see that I've brought you into that same amazing intimate relationship with God that I've always had myself, brought you into a place where you are safe and utterly supported, no matter how much you are betrayed by circumstances or people or even your own foolishness.

'Yes, I won't be walking around on earth in the old way any more, after tomorrow. But my death will be the gateway to new life, for me and for you. And I will have many ways of showing myself. Sometimes in special dreams and visions, but more often, I expect, in the glint of others' eyes, or in a strange an unexpected turn of events, or in a puzzle falling into place, and especially when you gather to break bread with each other as we've done so often over these last years. Yes, I'll show myself, your old advocate, still the same, 100 per cent on your side, whoever you are, whatever you've done, whatever you will do. And God's own Spirit who has been in me will be in you.'

Stephen Wright

Suggested hymns

Alleluia, sing to Jesus; Holy Spirit, come, confirm us; Today I awake and God is before me; Filled with the Spirit's power.

Sixth Sunday of Easter (Rogation Sunday) 17 May
Second Service **A New City**

Ps. 87, 36.5–10; Zech. 8.1–13; **Rev. 21.10, 22—22.5**; *Gospel at Holy Communion*: John 21.1–14

Introduction part 1 – cities

Cities are interesting places. Even if you don't live in one, and I'm a small-town boy at heart, cities are fascinating. I love taking a few days to visit a city, particularly in a new country, to sense the atmosphere, to eat the food, to visit the glories of the place, yes, but also to explore the back streets and find something of the real life there. Cities show off the riches of a nation and declare something of what that nation aspires to be. However, they also hold the scars of history, the story of their people, which is important to tell. They point to the future in new investment and new building, in contemporary culture and art. And, as we know only too well in our world today, they can become the focus of conflict, a place for demonstrations, atrocities and all-out destruction, which again speaks loudly of the passions of the place and the future that is being fought for. Cities say something profound, of where a nation comes from, of who it is and of where it is headed.

And when we experience that, even in the difficult places, it may be that we fall in love with that city, or the idea of what it aspires to be. We want to visit again, and we may want to be part of the vision it calls us into.

Introduction part 2 – visiting the Holy City

With that in mind, let's visit a city, a city that I pray we'll fall in love with and wish to visit over and over again, so the journey it calls us to will be our journey, and its aspirations become our aspirations. It's the Holy City at the end of our Bibles in Revelation. The city of Babylon is fallen, now a New Jerusalem is unveiled, seemingly balanced halfway between earth and heaven where the two meet, a city that shows off all that God wants this earth to be. So we pick up the guidebook to visit this city, to get a sense of what it stands for and the vision it gives.

Buildings: the walls

Where do we start? Let's look at the buildings first – they always say so much about a city. It's a walled city – the Hebrew for city means 'an enclosed place' – and although 12 gates give plenty of access, ultimately this is a city that exudes safety from those who would attack. As we go in, we enter into a safe place, on to a glorious main street, and we look around.

Buildings: no temple

Now, in a city there are usually churches and marketplaces to look at, grand buildings displaying the glories of the nation. But we look around and there's no temple, no churches, no division between worship and the marketplace. No division between sacred and secular here. This whole city is bathed in the presence of God, the whole of life is sanctified and lived out in the light of God, every task is worship and every joy is praise. This is wholeness of life. Think what that means for a city.

Buildings: the kings of the earth

But the glory of God doesn't eclipse everything. The kings of the earth, all the powerful, the influential, the movers and the shakers, have brought their riches into the city – their art, their culture, their science, their invention. So this city rings in a celebration both of the glory of God and of the splendour of human endeavour, gathered into this one place.

People: from every nation

It's a walled city, gloriously built, but with gates that never close. People are at peace, moving freely to visit and trade. If we spend a few moments just to watch the people and the buzz around us, we see people from every nation coming in, knowing they're honoured. This is not a place where people are rolled into one, this is a place where difference is glorious. And so there's work here too, humanizing work done in the service of God, and where each one knows they are known by God and named by him.

People: the best of human life

But what's absent are the lies and secrets, the dark places of city life, dispersed by God as day chases out night. I wonder what a city without the shame and the deceit is like – surely we can hear the banter, the parties, the joking in the streets that mark out the best of human life, people alive in this place?

Life: the river of life

Water always speaks of life, and we have water here. Down the main street of the city there's a river, a river of life flowing, clear and unpolluted, and across it is a tree, a tree of life, continually producing fruit. This place is life-giving. Water moves and refreshes, and the fruit is of different types, so there's the variety of life here, different things to eat and savour.

Life: the tree of life

And movement of the leaves on the tree gives life. With these different people together, coming together in life-giving variety, so often that difference divides and injures, rather than beautifying and strengthening. Adam and Eve used leaves to hide behind. But these leaves, leaves from the tree of life, heal the injuries by binding people together, not hiding them. They bring life in variety. Why? Because we are all being brought into the light of the throne of God and of the Lamb.

Conclusion

This is an exciting city. It's a city that stands for something, that gives us vision. It's our desire for what can be and, in God's grace, what will be as we pray 'Your kingdom come'. It's a city to excite us, all of us, just as it excited Lydia on the banks of the river in Philippi, as she opened her heart. It's a city we are called to as we hear Jesus promising the Holy Spirit in our lives, promising that he and the Father will make their home with us. It's a city where we glimpse aspects already among us, so we praise God and rejoice and affirm what's good. And where we see this Holy City violently absent, we pray and work that it may come, in the grace of God. Let's visit the Holy City. Let's look for it, pray for it, work for it, to glimpse the glory of God in our day.

Paul Burden

Suggested hymns

Christ is made the sure foundation; Blest are the pure in heart; Here is love, vast as the ocean; Glorious things of thee are spoken.

Ascension Day 21 May

Principal Service Take Authority!

Acts 1.1–11 (*must be used as either the first or second reading*), *or* Dan. 7.9–14; Ps. 47, *or* Ps. 93; Eph. 1.15–end; **Luke 24.44–end**

The picture of the ascension is an awkward, perhaps embarrassing, image. The idea of someone levitating upwards, with feet poking below the clouds, arouses incredulity from minds attuned to the modern scientific world view. The story is found only in Luke's writings and without Luke it is doubtful if there would have been an Ascension Day at all, nor for that matter a separate day and season of Pentecost, as well as other feast days to do with the birth and infancy of Jesus.

Luke's clothes line

Most sermons sidestep Luke's description of the ascension but we at least should pause to acknowledge the educational and spiritual benefits of what he has left to us. Luke has spaced out the one explosive event as it appears in the other Gospels, the resurrection, coming of the Spirit, the return of Jesus to the Father, and arguably the return of the son of man. Luke has separated them out in time, putting forty days between the resurrection and ascension and ten days between that and Pentecost. Like clothes on a washing line, he has pegged out each event so that we can attend to them separately. The spy writer John le Carré said: 'There are moments which are made up of too much stuff for them to be lived at the time they occur.' So we can be grateful for Luke giving space for us to give serious attention to the different dimensions of Christ's work separately from one another.

But even on his own terms, Luke is not quite able completely to tidy up and reorder the events, and appears to leave us with two accounts of Christ's ascension, one on Easter Day at the end of his Gospel, and the other at the beginning of the book of Acts.

John's spin-drying

Jesus was exalted to be with his Father after the resurrection, but did it need to be the grand and decisive exit that Luke painted? Not for the other evangelists. For St John, Jesus' exaltation is there on Good Friday, reigning from the cross. The meeting of the risen Lord with Mary suggests his return to the Father is imminent, but that didn't mean the end of the post-resurrection appearances. Of course, there came a time when the physical presence of Jesus was no longer available to his followers, but it might well have been more obscure and complicated than Luke's clear-cut programme suggests. It always is. But first we need the clarity, simplicity and space that Luke's story gives us.

Kingdom restored

So what does it say to us? Here the witness of the Gospel writers is unanimous. Ascension is not a negative experience, the termination of Christ's earthly, physical presence. Instead, we should see it as the start of God's worldwide mission and the witness by the Church through the power of the Spirit. The disciples ask Jesus before he departs whether this is the time 'when you will restore the kingdom to Israel'. After telling them that the times are set by his Father and are not their concern, he appears to answer affirmatively. Yes, this is the time when the kingdom will be restored, but more than that. The disciples are the first generation who will receive power to be his witnesses, not merely to restore Israel, but to witness to the ends of the earth.

You may think it puzzling that at the point at which Jesus is set to inaugurate his worldwide kingship, he hands the task over. It's been described as the 'most spectacular case of voluntary redundancy in human history'. Why does he entrust it to us? Why not do the work himself? And as we look over the troubled chapters of the history of the Church, we are bound to ask why the task was entrusted to feeble men and women.

A world re-created

The resurrection affirmed God's re-creation of the world. The appearances in the garden, especially in John's Gospel, are there to bring to our minds the story of creation. The resurrection is to be recognized as the start of a new era, God's work of re-creation. In the death and resurrection of Jesus the first creation is recapitulated, and its destructive features are already reversed in Jesus Christ, the second Adam. But in that story humankind was brought into the picture and given dominion or, we might now say, stewardship over all of creation. Speaking of human beings, the Psalmist says, 'Yet you (God) have made them a little lower than God and crowned them with glory and honour.' Well, if God is re-creating the world, how does he make good on and extend the authority given to human beings? Jesus, who receives all authority in heaven and earth, commits to humans the awesome task of realizing his kingdom because that was always the divine intention anyway. The authority that Jesus gives to his disciples to proclaim and be agents of the kingdom is an authority restored, not newly created. From the creation, God committed humans to be stewards of his kingdom. And now, through Jesus and by the outpouring of the Spirit, he restores to us our divine vocation: 'Take authority.' The Spirit of Jesus is with us. Wherever we go, Jesus will have been before us, preparing a way. We go in his name and bear his authority.

Roger Spiller

Suggested hymns

Hail, festival day; All together in one place; Clap your hands, all you nations; Ascended Christ who gained.

Ascension Day 21 May

Second Service **Glory Be!**

Morning Ps. 110, 150; Evening Ps. 8; **Song of the Three 29–37**, *or* 2 Kings 2.1–15; Rev. 5; *Gospel at Holy Communion*: Mark 16.14–end

Do you have a usual expression of surprise or shock when you're with other people? The phrase 'Glory be!' is quite an old-fashioned one. It's a bit like 'O, Lord!', 'Heavens!', 'Gracious!', or 'My goodness!' Stronger exclamations we might keep to ourselves. But notice how all these idioms are in fact something to do with faith, or God. Surprise, the unexpected, the miraculous: we often subtly connect our response to those moments with the language of faith, whether we mean to or not.

Surprised by faith

Surprise can be a great asset to a faithful ministry. It leads people to ask questions, to be open, to engage. There's lots about Ascension Day that could cause people to ask questions. Perhaps, earlier today, you've already thought about that shock of the Ascension

Day story – some churches and chapels like to mark the feast by a service on top of a tower or a roof. Now, that really will draw attention to this day in our faith calendar, and make people on the ground say, 'But what are they doing up there?' Ministry and discipleship can be about asking questions, or inviting others to ask questions, about God and faith; and then they're open to hear your answer.

There's a good deal to be surprised about in our readings in this service too. The Song of the Three is an apocryphal text – a later addition passed down only in Greek versions of the Bible. It is fitted into the story in Daniel of his three companions when they are thrown into the fiery furnace in Babylon. Shadrach, Meshach and Abednego are the names given to them by their Babylonian overlords; their Hebrew names were Hananiah, Mishael and Azariah. Once in the furnace, first there is the Prayer of Azariah, then the tale of the angel of the Lord coming down to calm the flames, and lastly there is this song glorifying God in response to their rescue. It's a very simple song: it repeats 'Blessed are you, Lord God of our ancestors!' or 'Bless the Lord!' throughout. It's very like Psalm 150, which praises God repetitively, but in different contexts, which echo throughout all creation.

A glorious response

To be saved from such a fiery furnace is something that calls for, first, surprise and then praise. Similarly, there's surprise in Elisha's voice, and then glorification in the actions of the 50 prophets who are looking on, when Elijah is taken from them up into heaven in the whirlwind. Elijah doesn't die (tradition had it that he would return to herald the Messiah; an extra seat is put out at some Jewish celebrations in expectation of him). Elisha exclaims, 'My Father, father! The chariots of Israel and its horsemen!', an image of mightiness, which reminds us both of God's great power and also the power of Elijah's prophetic ministry. The prophets looking on recognize something of Elijah's spirit now in Elisha, and they bow down before him. Glorification is the only response they can give.

Revelation 5 says something similar about glorification. There's this awesome image of heaven, angels and elders, and the sealed scroll in the hand of the one who sits on the throne. When the Lamb has triumphed – the only one worthy to take and break open the scroll – the whole gathering falls down and worships, with musical instruments, incense and great choruses of song. The only response to seeing Jesus the Lamb who was slain, who alone is worthy, is to glorify God.

Starting with glory

Glory is sometimes the only real response. If we spend time in meditation, or study the Bible, or notice the creation around us, the deepest response of our souls may well be to sing God's glory. Ascension Day is a day of glory. Christ is glorified. And through Christ, God is glorified.

It's certainly a pretty astonishing thing to picture: the risen Christ being taken into heaven. This is the ending we have to two of the Gospels. Luke's Gospel speaks of the ascension plainly, as Jesus being simply 'taken into heaven', something the disciples react to by worshipping him. In the longer (and probably later) ending of Mark's Gospel, the simplicity of Christ being taken into heaven is then crowned with the statement 'and [he] sat down at the right hand of God'. Christ's glory is made plain.

But this isn't about finishing the story on a glorious note. This is starting the story with glory. While there are two Gospels that have endings with the ascension, Luke's next book, Acts, starts with it. Acts perhaps gives the most star-struck account, with a cloud hiding Jesus from sight, and two angels coming to talk with the disciples who are left staring up at heaven. Here, this starts them praying fervently: a good way to prepare for Pentecost in ten days' time.

And actually, although it's at the end of Mark, that too is a starting point: it is after this ascension that they go out and proclaim the good news, with the Lord present with them and giving more miraculous signs to help it all sink in. If this ending *was* added a little later, then it really does represent less of an ending and more of a beginning.

God is glory from start to finish. Glory may be the result of our growing deeper in God; and knowing the glory of God can only start us glorifying him again. Or, as the poet John Donne (Dean of St Paul's Cathedral in the early seventeenth century) put it, 'no ends nor beginnings, but one equal eternity, in the habitations of thy majesty and glory'.

Megan Daffern

Suggested hymns

Rejoice, the Lord is King; Christ triumphant, ever reigning; The head that once was crowned with thorns; Come ye faithful, raise the anthem.

Seventh Sunday of Easter
(Sunday after Ascension Day) 24 May
Principal Service Overhearing Jesus' Intercession

Ezek. 36.24–28 (*if used, the reading from Acts must be used as the second reading*), *or* Acts 1.6–14; Ps. 68.1–10, 32–end [*or* 68.1–10]; 1 Peter 4.12–14; 5.6–11; **John 17.1–11**

Sometimes you have no choice. People are talking to one another as though they are addressing a public meeting and you cannot help overhearing. At other times, a quiet bit of conversation catches your attention and you listen in to what's being said. You may initially feel bad at overhearing private conversations, but then notice they're talking about a book or person or event that interests you. Perhaps they're struggling and you feel tempted to chip in and come to their rescue.

Overhearing has a respectable Christian pedigree. Augustine indicated that we're more likely to listen to what we overhear accidentally than to what is addressed directly to us, advice he gave to preachers. Speaking ostensibly to one audience while knowing that he would be overheard by another was an art form perfected by Jesus.

Overhearers

We're overhearers of the prayer of Jesus. For once the disciples fade into the background and we are invited to overhear Jesus' intimate conversation with his Father. We're not being addressed, of course, but we're included in Jesus' intercessions. This is a curtain raiser to the continuing life of God. The themes pick up those already present in the Gospels as a whole. Its centrepiece is Jesus' prayer to his Father, that after his physical departure from the world, God will protect them.

This, for the writer, is Jesus' final word, although it is placed before Jesus' passion and death. Jesus, it seems, has already crossed the threshold, beginning his journey back to his Father. His hour has arrived. We could easily be misled by Jesus' request for 'glory', as we would in human terms for anyone seeking 'their own glory'. But this human idea is turned on its head because the supreme act of glorification will be his death. Jesus reigns not from a throne in a celestial palace. He reigns and is glorified when he is suspended on the shameful cross. The action that most fully expresses God is Jesus' death. That is his hour, the hour for which his whole life waited – and is the conclusive manifestation of divine glory.

The cross of glory

The work of the Son is to glorify his Father. And what work does he do to glorify the Father? He makes God known. Once asked to summarize his mission, a church leader replied: 'To create opportunities for God'. Yes, that reflects the mission of Jesus.

But it's not just the intention to make God known that brings glory. Glory comes when people respond. So Jesus can say of his disciples, 'they have kept your word. Now they know that everything you have given me is from you ... they have received [your words] and know in truth that I came from you; and they have believed that you sent me.' In other words, what glorifies God is when Jesus is recognized as coming from God, as sent by God, and that everything received from Jesus comes from God.

In the second part of the prayer, Jesus, anticipating his imminent departure, is praying for the future welfare of his disciples. They are to be left in the world, but they don't belong to the world, because they have been born from above. So they are aliens in the world, and their very presence provokes trouble. He asks not that they will be taken out of the world but that they might be protected in God's name. And they are sent into the world to fulfil the same purpose for which Jesus was sent into the world – to challenge the world.

Jesus' intercession

Jesus' work doesn't stop with the ending of his earthly life. It now takes a decisively new phase. Only by being lifted up on the cross can he draw all people to himself. Only now can he pray that his disciples will be one, because he has laid down his life for his friends.

One in Christ

His prayer is part of the unity that Jesus shares with his Father: that 'they may be one'. That's a text often cited to encourage us to pursue church unity, but of course that wasn't in the mind of St John. It's a prayer that the followers of Jesus should be part of the unity that exists between Jesus and his Father. Just as the Father gives life to the Son, so Christians are one with one another and with the Father and the Son because they have received this life. Christ is not merely telling his disciples about life in union with him and how to attain it. He is actually imparting it to them. Christians are being incorporated with Christ in the life of God. And all of this is based on Jesus' relationship with his Father. That is the model of our own relationship to God. And Jesus brings this about – he draws all people after him into the sphere of eternal life, which is union with God. It's not tacked on after death, it begins here and now.

However diffident we may feel about overhearing conversations, the prayer of Jesus to his Father is one that we must hear and hear again to hear afresh the commission he gives to us and to rejoice in his continuing intercession for our protection and strengthening.

Roger Spiller

Suggested hymns

At the name of Jesus; Before the throne of God above; How deep the Father's love for us; The head that once was crowned with thorns.

Seventh Sunday of Easter
(Sunday after Ascension Day) 24 May
Second Service **Correct Endings?**

Ps. 47; 2 Sam. 23.1–5; Eph. 1.15–end; *Gospel at Holy Communion*: **Mark 16.14–end**[23]

It is generally agreed among most biblical scholars that Mark's Gospel originally ended like this: 'they went out and fled from the tomb, for terror and amazement had seized them; and they said nothing to anyone, for they were afraid.'

Scholars have debated long and hard about such an unusual concluding sentence. After all, in a book labelled 'Good News', you would not expect such a curiously downbeat ending. Some have suggested that a dramatic intervention might have caused Mark suddenly to end his Gospel in this fashion. Perhaps, they say (with a twinkle in their eye), some soldiers burst into his room to arrest him before he could write another sentence. Others, less dramatically, have speculated that perhaps the original bit of the scroll on which he was writing was accidentally torn off. And yet others have made a strong case for saying that this is exactly the kind of ending Mark would have intentionally created. It is certainly strange, but it fits in with one of the motifs of Mark's Gospel – that people simply did not always recognize Jesus for who he was, and exactly the same sense of bewilderment and awe overtook the women at the resurrection.

Alternative endings

This is not the time to debate the question, fascinating though it is. What we can say is that the earliest surviving texts of Mark's Gospel do indeed end in this strangely abrupt way. But it wasn't long before other anonymous writers tried to offer alternative endings. One of those was our Gospel reading for today. It's fairly clear that someone, or perhaps a number of people, had a go at tidying up Mark's original ending and they did this by paraphrasing some of the resurrection stories in the other Gospels to give Mark's Gospel what they believed to be a more orthodox conclusion.

Unfortunately, what they also did was to leave us with a set of further problems. Having outlined the appearances to Mary Magdalene and to the disciples, the authors of these extra verses added this:

> And these signs will accompany those who believe: by using my name they will cast out demons; they will speak in new tongues; they will pick up snakes in their hands, and if they drink any deadly thing, it will not hurt them; they will lay their hands on the sick, and they will recover.

The idea that there was a direct link between preaching and miracles was made even more explicit in the final verse: 'the Lord worked with them and confirmed the message by the signs that accompanied it.'

It would of course be an absolute delight if stupendous miracles accompanied without fail the preaching of the gospel, but, if we are honest, we have to admit that such a cause-and-effect link is not often seen. Yet, without doubt, across our nation, in one way or another, the gospel is preached daily – though obvious miracles don't necessarily follow.

Cause and effect?

Let's be clear. There are some very, very rare instances where what we might ordinarily describe as 'miracles' do occur, but for the most part, even though the good news is preached, miracles simply do not happen.

What can we make of this? It's where unscrupulous preachers can make outrageous claims, either that they themselves are somehow extra-special and therefore miracles happen, or they suggest that all other preachers are less than perfect, in which case miracles don't happen. But that's too simple and is, in any case, harshly judgemental.

We need quietly to return to our sources – to the Gospel of Mark – to see what happened when Jesus himself began to preach. There is no doubt that what were termed 'miracles' took place, and they were frequently associated with the onlookers regarding Jesus as having a compelling, numinous authority. But there were also times when he told the recipients of a miracle of healing to tell no one about it. The miracles seemed to be not only about the well-being of the recipient but were regarded as prophetic signs of the in-rush of the kingdom of God. The miracles were not magic; they did not rely upon an over-simple cause-and-effect, and the disciples themselves, in spite of being trained by Jesus, did not always share his astonishing, overarching power. The miracles of Jesus were certainly signs, but they also have an elusive quality. The one thing the miracle stories of Jesus have in common is that they were occasioned by his presence: it was the profound encounter with Jesus himself that led to the miracles occurring.

Unobtrusive miracles

Now let's translate that into our own context. There can be no doubt that some people have such an intense encounter with Christ that their lives are completely and immediately turned around: the sinner knows him- or herself saved and healed; the anguished person suddenly finds peace. Sometimes such radical changes seem to happen instantaneously. But, for most of us, our encounters with Christ in word, in sacrament and in prayer have an impact that is gradual, long term and slow. Nevertheless, the reshaping of our lives goes on, but that too is miraculous in its own way, isn't it?

It is in our growing relationship with Christ that these tiny, gradual miracles occur. We are people to whom quiet and unobtrusive miracles happen, and for that gentle and powerful grace we should give our heartfelt thanks to God.

Christopher Herbert

Suggested hymns

Rejoice, the Lord is King!; Christ triumphant, ever reigning; The head that once was crowned with thorns; Jesus shall reign where'er the sun.

Day of Pentecost (Whit Sunday) 31 May

Principal Service ***The Mightiest Festival of Them All***

Acts 2.1–21 (*must be used as either the first or second reading*), *or* Num. 11.24–30; Ps. 104.26–36, 37b [*or* 104.26–end]; 1 Cor. 12.3b–13; John 20.19–23, *or* John 7.37–39

Today we celebrate Pentecost, the mightiest Christian festival of them all. We have relived the cycle of Christ's life in our church calendar – his birth, life, ministry, death, resurrection and ascension, but we are at best detached admirers without the Spirit.

Archbishop William Temple put it like this:

> It is no good giving me a play like *Hamlet* or *King Lear* and telling me to write a play like that. Shakespeare could do it. I can't. And it is no good showing me a life like the life of Jesus and telling me to live a life like that. But if the genius of Shakespeare could come and live in me, then I could write plays like this. And if the Spirit could come into me, then I could live a life like that.

Jesus is history until the Spirit makes Jesus part of *my* history. And the Spirit does that because the Spirit is the Spirit of Jesus, the Spirit sent by Jesus, the memory of Jesus for us.

The Church espouses its beliefs, its doctrines and teachings week by week, but they can wash right over us until they are brought alive by the Spirit. Our beliefs are no more useful than a route map unless we have power in our car. It's the Spirit that makes it possible for us to move ahead in our Christian lives.

Transforming presence

Worship, church, Bible, prayer – these can be tedious, laborious and routine until the Spirit quickens us. We hear some Christians say how exciting it is to pray, to read the Bible, to come to church. We wonder what's wrong with them or with us! Are they reading the same book, sharing the same experience, going to the same church? Yes, and the difference is down to the Spirit, who is activating and enlivening. The Spirit wants to extend his influence, to speed up his reforming work, to shower upon us more of his gifts, to draw us into his magnetic field where we can produce more of the Christ-like life and display more fruits of the Spirit.

All this the Spirit can do. That's why Pentecost should excite us and give us the thrill of the explorer – because the presence of the Spirit gives us access to new horizons, new summits to climb, new tasks to be attempted. Pentecost celebrates the possibility of transformation. The life-giving Spirit, the Spirit of Christ, is the whirlwind of grace and the fire of love whose glory shines in lives marked by the fruits of the Spirit. At Pentecost we acknowledge God as a transforming presence, whose grace is a resource of love to change the world. No wonder, then, the Spirit is like the great mighty elemental forces of wind, fire and water, by which the world was made and is sustained.

Some hold back, because they fear that their individuality would be lost if they opened themselves up to the Spirit. They fear they might find themselves transformed into hand-waving, foot-tapping, exuberant Christians who set a pace that they find terrifying. But we need have no fear. The Spirit is indeed unpredictable. But for all that the Spirit works unpredictably, he also works gently with us; he uncovers our real selves, he intensifies our individualities. The Spirit differentiates us from each other by his gifts. It's sin that creates sameness and dull conformity. The diversity of languages on the day of Pentecost wasn't set aside. It was affirmed when people of many languages heard the good news in their own language.

Gift of communication

But there's one more gift of the Spirit that we need to discover. On the day of Pentecost, the disciples received the gift of tongues – the gift of communication. Pentecost reverses the confusion of languages in the wake of the hubristic attempt to build a bridge to God, the Tower of Babel. There have been other vanity projects in recent years! Then communication was broken. It is, of course, always broken when people act in the single-minded pursuit of their own interests and are deaf to the voices of others. So the Spirit on the day of Pentecost restores God's people with the gift of communication. The Spirit acts like the quiet whisper from the director's control room, whispering in our ear the edifying words that open the channels of communication between us. He will, as Jesus said, give us words to say when we are in a tight corner, threatened, on trial for Jesus' sake, or wanting healing words to speak in hard times. As the Spirit of love, the Spirit will purify the toxic, fake, violent and self-destructive speech that is permeating our public discourse.

W. H. Auden said that on the day of Pentecost we are given the gift of ears. For the first time, Parthians and Medes and Elamites and strangers from Rome, Jews and proselytes were able to listen when a foreigner was speaking. Whether tongues or ears, the Spirit is the communicative as well as creative activity of God.

Pentecost, then, celebrates the possibility of transformation and communication. The Spirit brings us into God's vitalizing field of energy. God's Spirit is the power of the new life in us and space of the new life around us.

All that's needed for us to move forward is a sense of dissatisfaction, dryness, emptiness, to be open and broken and in crisis. Revival happens not when we raise the roof but when the floor caves in. So we have in our Gospel that picture of a river of living water, bubbling up to eternal life. Water that once flowed from the Temple in Jerusalem like a flood, can now flow through our lives, bringing us to new life. Pentecost is the potential not yet realized, the life not yet embraced, the spiritual high not yet climbed, the God who is nearer than breathing, indeed in our breathing, whose Spirit is the source of love and power to change the world.

Roger Spiller

Suggested hymns

Come down, O love divine; Come, Holy Spirit, come; O Spirit of the living God; There's a spirit in the air.

Day of Pentecost (Whit Sunday) 31 May

Second Service **'Your sons and your daughters shall prophesy'**

Morning Ps. 87; Evening Ps. 67, 133; **Joel 2.21–end**; Acts 2.14–21 [22–38]; *Gospel at Holy Communion*: Luke 24.44–end

Do you remember a time when the noticeboards outside our churches would often display not only the name of the next Sunday's preacher but also the title of their sermon? Often the title would be similar to that offered in the lectionary that was published in our service book and would be rather humdrum. Sometimes the intended title would catch my eye because it had an element of challenge.

I was serving overseas when the (current) Revised Common Lectionary was being introduced. Soon the preachers complained that they were no longer being advised as to which was the 'controlling lesson' and there was no title to guide their thinking, so, as a new member of staff at the theological college, I was tasked to provide a title and suggest a controlling lesson. I can remember that for Pentecost Sunday I suggested the title I have chosen for this sermon and that the controlling lesson should be that from Joel. I did this because I wanted to challenge preachers to look beyond the Acts account of the Pentecost event and explore the potentially revolutionary impact of Joel's prophecy. (However, when the guide to the lectionary was published, the Acts reading was designated as the controlling lesson and the title was a bland one.)

Joel's prophecy in context

We don't know precisely when Joel lived and prophesied. However, in the book that bears his name, he describes how a plague of locusts has devastated the crops and that there has been a drought. Joel believes that these catastrophes have occurred because God is angry with his people, so he says that if they then repent the same God who has punished them will repay and restore them. Joel promises not just like-for-like restoration, but abundance.

The former and latter rains will fall, replenishing the earth, showing God's blessings. After the abundance of crops will come the gift of the abundance of the Spirit.

'Your sons and your daughters shall prophesy'

The Spirit is God's gift, the Spirit is not a gentle comforter: it's a breath or wind, which blows where it will; it is a powerful storm wind that's beyond human control. It can't be domesticated. It's the same breath or wind that blew over the waters of chaos: God's creative and creating force.

The Spirit comes as a gift to recipients who would not expect to receive it. Remember how, in the Old Testament, God often chooses to favour those who are of lesser rank or significance: for example, younger sons like Jacob, Joseph and David. Joel goes beyond offering hope to noteworthy younger sons. He says to the people, 'your sons and your daughters shall prophesy, your old men shall have dreams and your young men shall see visions.' In other words, the Spirit will be poured out on all flesh, irrespective of gender or age.

After this amazing outpouring there will be signs and portents. The Day of the Lord will come, a great and terrible day. (Remember, the Spirit is no gentle agent.) Only those who truly call on the Lord will be saved.

In Acts 2, Peter refers to this prophecy as he preaches to the crowd that has gathered on the day of Pentecost; he proclaims that Joel's prophecy has been fulfilled. That is to say, at Pentecost God's revolution began.

A world turned upside down

Today, on Pentecost Sunday, we can seek the presence of the Spirit, if we dare. Are we waiting for the Day of the Lord?

In this interim period, when we struggle to identify true prophets, do we accept that God's Spirit speaks to and inspires the forgotten and the insignificant? Are our sons and daughters recipients of the Spirit?

Do we live in a culture where the younger generation are truly encouraged to speak out and share their vision of how God sees the future? My observation would be that even in churches where there is a considerable commitment to youth work it is seldom the case that youth are encouraged to have a significant say in the life of the church. Their place is not to lead but to learn!

What has happened to the dreams of the old and the visions of the young? I wonder what our churches would be like if we truly looked to the youth to lead us? Would there be a more positive, outward-looking and visionary understanding of the nature of church?

Wendy Kilworth-Mason

Suggested hymns

Born in song; Breathe on me, breath of God; O breath of life, come sweeping through us; Spirit of God, unseen as the wind.

Trinity Sunday 7 June

Principal Service A Christian Identity Test?

Isa. 40.12–17, 27–end; Ps. 8; 2 Cor. 13.11–end; **Matt. 28.16–20**

I'm half tempted to put the congregation through a brief test of Christian identity this morning; nothing too arduous, just one simple question from a list of questions used by the UK immigration authority to determine eligibility for asylum seekers to the UK. Explain the Trinity!

We may well feel that it's not a fair test of identity for asylum seekers, or for British citizens, or even for Christians. Yet the doctrine of the Trinity safeguards all that is crucial in thinking about and living the Christian life. The Trinity is not a puzzle to be explained, a mathematical conundrum to be solved; it is an experience to be embraced and a mystery to be explored. We can't simply invoke mystery to call a halt to our exploration before it has begun. We hold that the Trinity has been revealed to us and we are therefore constrained to explore the nature and wonder of that mystery and to be able to give an account of the dynamic way in which the Triune God is at work in his world.

We depend on analogies when we think about the Trinity. Many simple analogies have emphasized the oneness and unity of God, but often at the cost of the difference and plurality of God. Let's explore whether the image of the musical trio might prove to be a suggestive image for exploring the concept of the Trinity.

'Persons'

It is sound more than sight that is the preferred sense for God's self-disclosure. Speech is attributed to each of the Persons of the Trinity. As each member of a trio has their own distinctive 'voice', so too the divine 'Persons' have their distinctive range and timbre. We're given one set of defining characteristics that are attributed to the Persons of the Trinity in the familiar words of 'the grace'. But it's in the nature of their interactions that we see most clearly the natures of their distinctive characters.

Relationships

In a musical trio each instrumentalist makes their own contribution. Attentiveness and mutual subordination are required and are the perfect cue for the different musical lines to be relayed from one player to another. Each player may in turn be assigned the melody line, then passing it on, sometimes supporting the main tune, at other times diverging from it, at times offering a counter-melody as if they're doing their own thing but then surrendering it to another player and yielding a supportive and unobtrusive harmony. Individual interests are subordinated to the whole in order for perfect unity, community, to be achieved.

Comm-unity

In the divine Trinity, John's Gospel shows the mutual attentiveness and perfect reciprocity between the Persons: 'The Son can do nothing on his own, but only what he sees the Father doing,' but, says Jesus, 'The Father and I are one.' There is mutual self-surrender and subordination that makes space for the Other. Scripture depicts the Father as having handed over his people to Jesus for salvation and the world for judgement. In turn, Jesus hands back his followers to the Father during his passion and death. The Father passes on all authority to the risen Jesus, and Jesus will in turn pass back to the Father his renewed creation at the consummation.

The unity of the divine Trinity that is to be inferred from the New Testament isn't static or inevitable but one that is dynamic and lets itself be open to the possibility of disruption. The unity was worked out and achieved, not predetermined in advance. The Gospels seem to suggest real potential for Jesus to take independent action. He could have submitted to temptation, he could have called down divine assistance, he did not 'snatch at equality with God', but that course was surely open to him, as was the chance to refuse the cup of suffering offered to him. Did the cry of godforsakenness on the cross infer that the divine life itself may be under pressure and could even potentially unravel? We approach with awe and wonder, but are we not duty bound to take up the hints in the New Testament that at least awaken us to the cost and love of the divine life and allow it free rein in our thinking, worship and adoration?

We've used the image of the musical trio to help explore the Trinity. Some informed people may well be thinking that the greatest music has been produced not by a trio but by a quartet, supremely, say, Beethoven's (late) quartets. So where does that leave our image?

The divine life of the Trinity isn't a community to admire from afar, nor a model that we can or should try to emulate. It is a life in which God makes room for *us*. As St John's Gospel makes clear, at every point the unity of Father and Son is reproduced in the unity of Christ and believers. We become united with Christ in the Spirit and share in his life and form with him, like a musical quartet. We have the self-same relationship Jesus had with his Father and the Spirit. And that is because the divine life is not self-contained or self-preserving but open-ended, the divine community that makes room for people created in God's image.

The Trinity is not, then, a puzzle to solve, but a community to be drawn into. Not so much an article of belief as a way of life; the sublime demonstration of the full panoply of God's dynamic, communal life, reaching down and through and into every life, that we too might share the wonders of his divine life.

Roger Spiller

Hymn suggestions

Father of heaven, whose love profound; Restore in us, O God; All-creating heavenly Giver; Father, Lord of all creation.

Trinity Sunday 7 June

Second Service The Power of Three

Morning Ps. 86.8–13; Evening Ps. 93, 150; **Isa. 6.1–8**; John 16.5–15

The triangle has great strength as a shape in construction. There is a kind of mutuality, between the length of its sides and the angles at its corners that holds it firm. Threeness and strength go hand in hand.

Threefold fullness

In the Hebrew Bible (the Old Testament), the number three was held to signify perfection or completeness. There are three patriarchs (Abraham, Isaac and Jacob), three visitors to Abraham; Jonah was in the belly of the whale for three days and three nights, and so on. This tradition carries on in the New Testament: Jesus rose from the dead on the third day; he was tempted three times; Peter denied Jesus three times (and is asked to affirm his love for Jesus three times after the resurrection); and Jesus' ministry lasted three years.

Sometimes, Isaiah chapter 6 is taken to 'prove' that the Holy Trinity – a Christian doctrine – existed even in the Old Testament. As the seraphim (mysterious, heavenly creatures that are literally 'burning ones') sing to one another, their song is, 'Holy, holy, holy is the LORD of hosts (literally, 'armies'): the whole earth is full of his glory!' Could the threefold repetition of 'holy' point to the three persons of the Holy Trinity – Father, Son and Holy Spirit? Probably not, to be honest, since three was already a very significant number, so it's natural the praise would be threefold.

What the threefold 'holy, holy, holy' is telling us is that God's holiness is perfect, complete, unsurpassable, beyond even our imagination. After all, that picture of God's robe as so big that even its edge or circumference 'filled the temple' is an image of fullness, perfection, unimaginable majesty. If the Temple is the very holiest of places, there is no single corner of holy place in the world where God and his glory does not come. God has the monopoly on holiness. The language of fullness is repeated: the earth is filled with God's glory. It's not just the holy places that God fills: it's the whole earth, the whole of our possible spatial experience.

And then there's a third fullness, as the Temple is 'filled with smoke'. This fullness is about mystery: God's glory is the fullness of holiness, the fullness of the created world. Now we have a glimpse of something even more fully glorious than all that. This kind of mind-expanding fullness is explored by St Augustine in just the third paragraph of his great work, *Confessions*. He meditates on how everywhere God wholly fills all things, yet neither heaven nor earth contain God. So, in a sense, there's always more: we can never grasp the fullness of God and his glory.

The only response to such fullness of glory is one that echoes as best as possible that perfection, that completeness. The only way is: 'Holy, holy, holy!'

Divine simplicity

Perfect fullness, though, also has a sense of oneness about it. Nothing more is needed. God fills all. There is only one God. That's something else that the Hebrew Bible says. The first of the Ten Commandments in Deuteronomy says, 'You shall have no other gods before me.' Then almost straight after the Ten Commandments have been given, there is the verse that our Jewish brothers and sisters have always held dear, the *Shema* (so-called because that's the first word of the Hebrew phrase) in Deuteronomy 6.4. It says 'Hear, O Israel: The LORD is your God, the LORD alone.' There's only one God (a message that the Israelites would have needed to hear time and again as they lived and moved among other Ancient Near Eastern peoples who worshipped many gods). And God is perfect in himself. God – alone – is. Nothing more, nothing less.

Psalm 86.8 pictures this Ancient Near Eastern context: 'There is none like you among the gods, O Lord; nor are there any works like yours.' And 86.10 echoes the *Shema:* 'You alone are God.' In the next verse, the Psalmist prays for 'an undivided heart'. God's perfection, his fullness in himself, can be understood by a heart that is whole – and so the Psalmist prays that his own innermost being can reflect that simple, undivided oneness that is of God. So it is with the 'whole heart' that the Psalmist worships, and he glorifies God's name 'for ever'. In full singleness of heart, the Psalmist's worship transcends even the fullness of time – and so goes beyond human limitations to the eternity of the divine. In mystical terms, that's like seeking union with God.

Perfect union

On Trinity Sunday we are inspired by our God who is both Trinity and unity. We worship the fullness of the Trinity, and the simplicity of the one God. Putting them both together, we get a vision of relationship that is complete and simple in itself. At one, unified.

It's because there is perfect relationship between the three and the one – Father, Son and Holy Spirit, and the one God – at the heart of our God that we can be called into that relationship too. Remember the call to Isaiah in verse 8? We too are invited to say, 'Here am I', and join worshipping in the words of 'Holy, holy, holy!' – to be fully, wholly at one with our God. Simple, really.

Megan Daffern

Suggested hymns

Holy, holy, holy; Affirm anew the threefold name; Firmly I believe and truly; Father of heaven, whose love profound.

First Sunday after Trinity (Proper 6) 14 June

Principal Service Original Sin?

(*Continuous*): Gen. 18.1–15 [21.1–7]; Ps. 116.1, 10–17 [*or* 116.9–17]; *or* (*Related*): Ex. 19.2–8a; Ps. 100; **Rom. 5.1–8**; Matt. 9.35—10.8 [9–23]

Before Charles Darwin put forward his theory about the origin of species, theology was relatively straightforward. The Bible provided the textbook of the way the world worked. It demonstrated that history began in the Garden of Eden with Adam and Eve but, once they had disobeyed God's commandments, sin and death entered the world; that original sin infected everything. It was a kind of unstoppable and contagious virus that burrowed its way into humanity. The created order changed from the perfections of Paradise to a world in which cruelty, disease, murder, mayhem, power-struggles and death disfigured everything. Humankind had 'fallen'. It was a state both pitiful and terrible, for there was no solution to the existential agonies of the world.

St Paul's thinking

That overarching story about the way sin had entered the world was one that St Paul shared.

Let there be no mistake: his thinking was immense, noble and wonderfully radical – but it was shaped by the categories of his time, just as our thinking is shaped and constrained by the categories of our own age. For Paul, sin was a given and derived directly from the disobedience of the first man and the first woman.

However, as Paul taught, the life, death and resurrection of Jesus provided the solution. He wrote: 'But God proves his love for us in that while we still were sinners Christ died for us.' Which is a wonderful declaration of faith for those able to share Paul's world view, but, probably for the majority of people today, that world view is not one they can believe. They don't believe in a historical Adam and Eve. They don't necessarily believe in a divine act of creation. They don't believe in the Fall.

This, at first sight, makes Paul's statement about Christ being the answer to sin a kind of non-sequitur. It simply does not fit with the way people today view the world.

Perhaps a long and wistful sigh of resignation is called for from those of us who are Christian believers. Have we got it all wrong? Are we deluding ourselves?

Approaching from a different angle

Let's approach this from a different angle to see if we can work out an answer.

There can be no doubt that as we look back over the twentieth century there is plenty of evidence of cruel and merciless human behaviour. Think of the Holocaust; think of Stalin's killing of millions; think of the pitiless regime of Pol Pot. Only one word will do for that terrible list of politically motivated slaughter. That word is 'evil' and we haven't even included in our list those vast numbers of individuals murdered, tortured, starved, bullied, enslaved and raped in what we might call 'ordinary' life. It is simply not possible to look at any newspaper on any day and not read about profoundly evil and unethical behaviour at both a communal and personal level.

So, what are the causes of our inhumanity to one another? Some, of course, will reply that it's a result of injustice in society; others will cite early childhood damage in the lives of the perpetrators; others will blame economic factors; yet others will talk about the insatiable desire some people have to exercise power over their fellow human beings. Some will blame religion; some will blame political corruption. The possible answers are many. But what cannot be denied are the horrors to which many of our fellow citizens of the world are subjected.

Somehow, our contemporary response to these horrors, it seems to me, does not have sufficient depth or magnitude. Certainly, outrage is expressed, but those expressions are so frequent and so hackneyed that they are beginning to lose their force. We have individualized everything to such an extent that the communal dimension of our lives has been pushed to the margins. In other words, we have lost any sense of an overarching moral dimension in our world, a dimension that includes both the individual and the communal.

And without that, all we can do is wring our hands in sorrow, offer our condolences to the victims, make statements about 'learning lessons', and, as is said nowadays, work for 'closure'.

Abandon the megaphones

In these confusing times it probably will not be at all effective to use Christian megaphones to shout louder. We have to think deeply about the way the world is and to see if within such a world the Christian Church has any answers.

In doing so, let us admit we cannot entirely share the thought-world of Paul, nor, come to that, can we share the thought-world of our Victorian forebears before Darwin. We have to find ways of expressing the depths of our faith that are true to the ways we do our thinking. One of the challenges for us might be that we have to re-explore and reinvent the concept of 'sin'. Why? Because it is the only word that will do that encompasses both individual and communal acts of evil.

If we can reinvent that idea of sin then perhaps the concept of Jesus dying on the cross for our redemption can get a greater imaginative purchase on the minds of our fellow citizens. For his death revealed the overarching purposes of God – to save and heal the brokenness of our world. Universal propensity for sin requires a universal solution, and God-in-Christ provides just that.

Christopher Herbert

Suggested hymns

All my hope on God is founded; All praise to Christ, our Lord and King; Draw nigh and take the body of the Lord; Forth in the peace of Christ we go.

First Sunday after Trinity (Proper 6) 14 June

Second Service **Refugee Crises**

Ps. [42] 43; **1 Sam. 21.1–15**; Luke 11.14–28

It is sad that the only time a country really seems to think hard about refugees is when they end up seeking asylum in that country. Then the question is whether they should be given refuge there or elsewhere – if indeed they are considered 'worthy' of asylum. Did you know that World Refugee Day is on 20 June this coming Saturday? Did you know that in 2019 the largest refugee camp in the world, in Bangladesh, was bigger than the third most populated city in the UK? And that no European state was among the top ten refugee-hosting countries in the world?

Refugees in the Bible

Christians who know the story of the 'Flight into Egypt' of Joseph, Mary and the newborn Jesus may remember that the holy family were refugees from the earliest days of Jesus' life, fleeing Herod's slaughter of young boys, the 'Holy Innocents'. And there is the Old Testament story of the Israelites' flight *from* Egypt, led by Moses, which came to be known as the Exodus. Fleeing is a significant part of many faith stories.

In our Old Testament reading today we heard of David's flight from Saul. David had been in Saul's royal household from boyhood, and he had been a great warrior for Saul ever since his youth. Saul was the first king of Israel, when all the 12 tribes of Israel were ruled together (they split into a northern and southern kingdom after the death of David's son Solomon). And Saul felt increasingly threatened by this popular young man whom he had taken from his simple life as a shepherd to be soldier and singer in the royal court. David was best friends with his brother-in-law, Saul's son Jonathan, the one who confirmed to David that Saul wanted to kill David just before today's passage begins. David flees, and this is the story of his first few days or weeks as a fugitive.

David in need

Back in 1 Samuel 15, Samuel the prophet has already begun to see that Saul can longer continue as king due to his disobedience to God. Samuel anointed David as king in 1 Samuel 16. It's not surprising that Saul sees David as a rival and wants to kill him. David has suspected the worst of Saul for a little while, but now in 1 Samuel 21 he not only needs to keep his distance but avoid Saul knowing where he is. So he begins a flight from Saul's base in Gibeah that will take him all around the local lands, in and out of Saul's kingdom. David's first refuge has been with Samuel in Ramah, but that's too obvious a hiding place. He heads to the nearby settlement of Nob.

David needs bread. The priest Ahimelech in Nob only has available the consecrated bread that has just been replaced by freshly baked bread. Ahimelech wants to make sure that he is not giving such holy bread lightly, so asks questions about David's ritual purity. David answers his questions appropriately so that Ahimelech feels he can give it to David. Centuries later, Jesus would use this story to argue that human need must come before religious rules, even though David has given satisfactory answers to Ahimelech.

And David needs a weapon. This is perhaps why he came to Nob – because he knew that's where he would find the great sword of Goliath that David himself had won as a boy, bringing him fame and popularity in Saul's kingdom. Ahimelech is proud of how carefully it has been kept safe, and is happy to give it back to the man who won it.

David receives his daily bread and his means of self-defence. There is a real sense that if anyone had a right to the sacred bread and the holy sword it is David.

A telling story

The way this story is told tells us a lot about David and his journey from danger to power.

That David can demand and receive the sacred bread paints the picture that here is a man in favour with God, a man who is entitled to God's nourishment. And that David can demand and receive the sword of Goliath shows that here is a man who is a warrior for God. It's OK to give David these holy things. Although Ahimelech doesn't know about Samuel anointing David, David acts with both the confidence and desperation of one who knows he is destined by God for greatness. He *must* survive.

There is a clear sense of danger. In between these two crucial gifts, a single verse has noted the presence of one of Saul's servants, Doeg the Edomite. It's as if this is the catalyst for David asking for the sword. He knows what grave danger he is in. So David is also shown to be intelligent and observant, a man with realistic expectations. And conversely, Saul is again hinted at as a dangerous man now obsessed with killing this anointed man of God. David's departure from Ahimelech seems very rapid, as soon as the sword is handed over. He flees beyond Saul's own lands, where again his cunningness is displayed in the lengths he'll go to in order to survive.

Desperate measures

Not only does this bit of the story of David's flight from Saul tell us about David and Saul, painting David as the rightful king, but it also reminds us of the desperation of the refugee. David will use both bluntness and clever persuasion with Ahimelech, and will feign madness with King Achish of Gath, complete with the dribbling of an incontinent man. All in a few speedy verses.

He *must* survive. God's plan needs him to survive. How do we respond to those who are truly desperate? How might their survival too be part of God's plan?

Megan Daffern

Suggested hymns

Once to every life and nation; Down the road run refugees; Heaven shall not wait; God's Spirit is in my heart.

Second Sunday after Trinity (Proper 7) 21 June

Principal Service **Counting the Cost**

(*Continuous*): Gen. 21.8–21; Ps. 86.1–10, 16–end [*or* 86.1–10]; *or* (*Related*): Jer. 20.7–13; Ps. 69.8–11 [12–17] 18–20 [*or* 69.14–20]; Rom. 6.1b–11; **Matt. 10.24–39**

Although Jesus instructed us to 'count the cost' before following him as his disciple, I've heard few sermons or teaching on what that cost might involve. Today, however, in our Gospel reading, that cost is set out in dramatic form and leaves little scope for misunderstanding: 'whoever does not take up the cross and follow me is not worthy of me'.

But before we dare to speak of the cost of discipleship and the cross we have to carry we have first to make clear that Christ has taken on our cross as his own. His cross is unique, borne not on his own account but for 'us' and for 'the whole world'. We are but followers of the one Lord Jesus who poured out his life for us.

Christ's cross

The call to follow Jesus is a call to share his suffering, the suffering that comes our way as a result of serving the mission of Christ. We often hear people say that we all have our own cross to bear, and by that is meant the deck of cards we've been dealt, the aches and pains and bodily afflictions and tribulations and losses that may come our way. But that is not what Jesus intended here. Anyone who suffers pain is connected to the one who died on the cross, but the suffering Jesus speaks of is the suffering that comes as the by-product of living intentionally as his disciple.

Cognitive dissonance

We're bound to find the idea that a man hanging on a cross as God's plan for the salvation of the world stretches credulity. It sounded foolish in the early Church and it does so no less today. If we believe it, we nevertheless know we're likely to be met with ridicule from those who do not share our belief. We don't want to look foolish, and so when we're at the tennis club, golf club or enjoying a relaxing drink with friends, the easiest course is to keep quiet and avoid the division and possible rejection that speaking up for our faith might bring. This is the first example in Jesus' teaching of what suffering might mean. We might call it cognitive dissonance or distress. Our Christian convictions are counter-intuitive, and yet we will not be recognized by Christ as his disciples if we refuse to witness to them in the public square.

Challenging the powers

At least all people can coalesce around the peace-loving, moderate, popular view of Christianity, can't they? No, Jesus declares that he hasn't come to bring peace but a sword. The world's powers are being contested by the invasive power of the kingdom. Disciples of Christ are expected to mobilize and follow Jesus into the courts, debating chambers, political forums and social media channels to expose, ridicule and disarm the coercive, self-serving, idolatrous forces that have free reign across the world. We must expect that when powerful vested interests are challenged, they will abuse, threaten and seek to silence those who call them to account.

Domestic conflict

But now Jesus turns to the domestic arena: conflict within families, between children and parents, not because of hormonal excesses but because a family member has become a Christian and follows a changed lifestyle that others find disturbing. Harry and his family had led a relaxed, indulgent life. But when he became a Christian, all that changed. As someone half his age, I would often be called on to adjudicate by his family on the perceived reasonableness of the new Christian regime he wanted to impose. He was now purposeful and driven by his faith, no longer the carefree man his wife had married, and he suffered the fallout from the reaction to his new-found faith and the struggle to keep his family on side.

First in my heart

Jesus now focuses down on the individual. Where in the pecking order do our nearest and dearest come in relation to Jesus? You may have been involved in a group exercise in which you're asked to write on small cards the five or so most prized things in your life, putting them in order from the least on the top to the most valued hidden on the bottom. People are then invited to give up their choices, beginning with the least painful loss, placing the cards to one side or on the altar. Even this ritual action becomes unbearably hard, but that's the cost Jesus asks his disciples to reckon with if they wish to be his followers. Jesus as king must reign pre-eminent in our hearts.

Absorbing hostility

The manner of Jesus' own living and dying presents one further way in which Christ's disciples must suffer. We are expected to emulate the love, life and service we find in Jesus Christ. But love exacts a cost; it can tear our heart in pieces; it can bring the pain of rejection. But even when we're rejected, subjected to abuse and hardship, we're to act to absorb the hostility and not pass it on, and to call down God's Spirit so that we can be forgiving and help to break the downward spiral of hate and evil.

We are not promised protection from the pain – emotional, physical and intellectual – that comes from following a crucified king. But we are promised freedom from fear. We're not offered deliverance from pain, but we do believe that dying to self is the necessary cost of coming alive.

Roger Spiller

Suggested hymns

Take up thy cross and follow me; Will you come and follow me if I but call your name; Take my life and let it be; In the cross of Christ I glory.

Second Sunday after Trinity (Proper 7) 21 June

Second Service **Anointed for Generosity**

Ps. 46 [48]; **1 Sam. 24.1–17**; Luke 14.12–24

Mercy matters

Have you ever been told you are too nice? I was worried once when two of my pupils came to me at the end of their course and brought me a large box of chocolates: they said I was their 'nicest tutor'. Had I let them get away with things? Have I not been strict enough with them? I later found out that they had both excelled in their exams and were both going to continue with their studies after their course. Perhaps it was just the right amount of 'nice' after all.

Conscientious to a fault?

In today's Old Testament reading is the story of how David, who by now had been pursued far and wide by Saul, could have killed his enemy but chose not to. Instead, he cuts off a corner of Saul's robe without Saul noticing, and later shows Saul. Saul then knows that David has been merciful to him.[24]

David's men would have attacked Saul. It's often easier to get angry or fight on behalf of someone else than we might for ourselves. David is a picture of self-control. With Saul vulnerable – he has gone to relieve himself in the cave where David is hiding, and presumably Saul's eyes don't have a chance to adjust to the darkness – David makes a point.

Perhaps this particular act is even more significant. There's a reminder of Samuel's prophetic words to Saul back in chapter 15, when Saul tore a corner from Samuel's robe, and Samuel used it as a sign that God has torn the kingdom from Saul. Some say that the emphasis on David's act of 'cutting off' stands for how David could also have 'cut off' Saul's life, or even 'cut off' his family line (had David taken fuller advantage of Saul's nakedness to castrate him). Maybe David felt he *had* to do something to restrain his men, and this was the smallest 'cutting off' he could have done.

Even this causes David to feel bad. Literally, 'his heart struck him'. He speaks to his men in penitence – how could he think of doing something to Saul? After all, Saul is God's anointed one – a phrase David says twice in this one verse.

The anointed one

The Hebrew for 'anointed one' is 'Messiah' (in Greek, it is *Christos*, so we can see why Jesus is later called 'the Christ'). Saul has hardly been acting like God's anointed: he has been chasing David all over, trying to kill him. He seems hysterical and obsessed with eliminating his rival, David. Yet Saul had nevertheless been anointed by Samuel the prophet and nothing can change that past fact. So David still has the highest regard for Saul as the anointed one of God.

Maybe this is because David himself has also been anointed by Samuel the prophet, after Saul started going off the rails. No one but Samuel and David's family appears to know about this anointing. David seems to strive to act in line with his anointed identity. It is because he has the 'spirit of the Lord' that he can kill Goliath the great Philistine enemy and have so many military successes. And in today's story we also see how, military skills aside, David can further act with mercy and avoid killing.

After the episode in the cave, David calls after Saul, to make known how he has just spared him. David addresses Saul as 'My lord the king' and bows down before him. Not only did he just choose to spare Saul's life, but he shows considerable respect for the anointed king. By telling Saul of how he had been merciful to him, David argues that Saul should never have doubted David's allegiance and loyalty to the king. Saul may continue to hunt David down, but David has shown he would not reciprocate. Later, when Saul is killed after he is mortally wounded in battle, David even kills the messenger who proudly reports how he helped end Saul's life. David lives with full regard for the Lord's anointing.

Righteous generosity

David has proved himself before Saul, and now he prays that God would judge between the two of them. David has shown he would not harm God's anointed, but Saul has shown time and again that he is fixated on killing David. David has demonstrated his righteousness, and Saul now admits it. David's sparing of Saul has been merciful, and Saul knows it. Saul knows that, of the two of them, David is by far the most righteous.

The anointed David shows his righteousness through repeated acts of mercy towards Saul. David is not just 'too nice' because he stands up for himself and makes a point of his mercy. It's a similar tale again when David once more has the chance to kill Saul but chooses not to do so. David is generous, and he wants that generosity to be known.

In stories like these in 1 and 2 Samuel, David is a prototype for righteousness by a firm and intentional display of generosity towards Saul – someone whose own righteousness, generosity and mercy will never match up to David's.

In the Gospel of Luke, Jesus is sometimes referred to as 'son of David'. The merciful, righteous, intentional generosity of David looks like the kind of generosity that we see in the verses from Luke today – a generosity that knowingly invites to a feast those who will never be in a position to reciprocate.

How can we live as generous, merciful children of God? If we call ourselves 'Christians', we are literally connected to 'the anointed one'. How can we reflect the power of God's anointing – at our baptism, confirmation or ordination – on our lives?

Megan Daffern

Suggested hymns

There's a wideness in God's mercy; Touch the earth lightly; Take this moment, sign and space; How deep the Father's love for us.

Third Sunday after Trinity (Proper 8) 28 June

Principal Service **The Kindness of Strangers**

(*Continuous*): Gen. 22.1–14; Ps. 13; *or* (*Related*): Jer. 28.5–9; Ps. 89.1–4, 15–18 [*or* 89.8–18]; Rom. 6.12–end; **Matt. 10.40–end**

I wish I could wind back the clock and energetically thank the elderly woman who, when hearing that I liked to read reviews of classical music, painstakingly cut them out and gave them to me as she was saying goodbye week by week for four years as I stood at the cathedral door after the service. I wish I could have been more vocal with my gratitude to the couple who heard me when in the course of a sermon on the Spirit I said as an aside that I'd been looking over a big new book on the Spirit in the Christian bookshop for so long that they brought me a chair, and who then decided to buy it for me. Then there were the elderly sisters who provided Sunday lunch for a fellow single clergyman and me, which we washed down with the now notorious Blue Nun. And as to the gift of money put through my door on Christmas Eve when I was in Stratford, well, there were no clues as to the identity of this anonymous giver, but like those and other gifts it was a blessing that far exceeded its monetary value.

Receiving

In what must be the shortest Gospel reading, Jesus concludes his second mission address not by espousing the importance of practising hospitality but of receiving it. It's addressed to the disciples, then and now. It's taken only two verses to express this but it's perhaps more than a life's work to accept the hospitality and generosity of others. As Peter showed at the foot-washing by Jesus, it is sometimes harder to receive service than to give it.

You may know the famous closing line spoken by the character Blanche DuBois in the play *A Streetcar Named Desire*: 'I have always relied on the kindness of strangers.' In our Gospel, Jesus tells his disciples that they too must rely on the 'kindness of strangers' when they go out into the wider world to proclaim the good news of the kingdom. He told them earlier that they were to travel light. That is, they should not carry with them all the supplies that they may need as those who wish to be self-sufficient. Instead, they should make themselves dependent upon the kindness of the hosts they would encounter on the way.

Giving or receiving

Why do we find it easier to render service than to accept service? Is it because when we have something that others want we remain in control and being in control we avoid leaving ourselves open to the uncertain treatment and possible rejection that we might receive at the hands of others? But then the sheer dependency of Jesus' disciples creates the opportunity for strangers to provide sustenance and hospitality to the messengers of Christ and in turn to experience the blessing of God for the generosity they have offered.

The promise that those who bless God's messengers will themselves be blessed goes right back to the promise made to Abraham, and is reiterated in our Old Testament lesson for today. That promise is now being fulfilled in Jesus through the treatment received by his disciples. They are not merely to deliver their message and withdraw. They are to embody the message they bring because they are filled with the life of Jesus. Commenting on his own missionary experience, St Paul in his first letter to the Thessalonians said: 'we are determined to share with you not only the gospel of God but also our own selves.'

Acknowledging blessings

A few years ago, Lord Jonathan Sacks, former Chief Rabbi, filled his Saturday article 'Credo', in *The Sunday Times*, with a paean of thanks for all that he had received, whether through other people or through his birth, upbringing or faith. It was a splendidly comprehensive list, including thanks for 2B pencils and wide-lined notepads, right up to the gift of faith itself, with some surprising causes for thanksgiving, including for atheists and agnostics, on the way. It gave me the cue to compile my own litany of thanks and then to invite ordinands on their ordination retreat to do the same. In the Christian dispensation we are blessed not merely by our preaching and service to others, but by the response of hospitality that we receive from others, who may have come to us as complete strangers. That is the way of grace: it spreads, it cascades down, in and among us, so that giver and receiver are indiscernible or, better, that we become simultaneously givers and receivers.

I'm not comfortable with Matthew's emphasis on rewards, but when I think of my own failure to express my gratitude to others, I am thankful that those who have blessed me without hope or expectation of any acknowledgement or thanks will have experienced the blessing of God.

Roger Spiller

Suggested hymns

Brother, sister, let me serve you; Put peace into each other's hands; We are not our own; When I needed a neighbour, were you there?

Third Sunday after Trinity (Proper 8) 28 June

Second Service **Ultimate Loyalty**

Ps. 50 [*or* 50.1–15]; **1 Sam. 28.3–19**; Luke 17.20–end

Today's passage from Luke reminds us that Jesus was a rabbi, a respected Jewish teacher. He is on his way to Jerusalem and a great range of different people come to talk with him, for all sorts of different reasons. Some want to test him, some want to follow him, and I'd imagine some aren't sure what they want but are drawn to his charismatic and challenging teachings about God and the kingdom of heaven. His teaching is based not only on his relationship with God, but also on his learning of the Hebrew Scriptures. Today we see Jesus linking his contemporary society with the people we read about in the Old Testament, Noah and Lot. We're reminded that he would have known the Old Testament thoroughly, and that he would have been able to understand his own ministry in the light of the traditional Jewish teachings.

Establishing the kingdom

Jesus would have known the historical teachings of the Hebrew Scriptures. The two books of Samuel turn a corner in Israelite history. They describe the transition of Israel from 12 tribes to a kingdom under its first king, Saul, to its establishment and unity under the great King David, Jesus' ancestor. This is the beginning of kingship in Israel. While it would not physically last throughout the centuries, the language and idea of godly, holy kingship would live on, and Jesus would have the inscription 'This is the King of the Jews' above him on the cross.

This Old Testament reading tells of the end of Saul's reign. It describes a frantic man who has lost control of both himself and his kingdom – someone who is no longer fit for kingship. While he has been pursuing his rival (and future king), David, Saul has also been at war with the Philistines. Now on the eve of battle, he is scared, and rightly so.

He has disobeyed God time and again, and because of this he has fallen out with the prophet Samuel who anointed him. Samuel had died a few chapters back; we are reminded of this at the beginning of this portion of text. Saul is trying to be the holy man, the follower of Yahweh, that both God and Samuel had wanted him to be: he has banned those who aren't Yahwists, namely the mediums and witches and so on. But when he is so afraid of the Philistines, and he doesn't hear an answer to his prayers in the ways he is expecting, Saul turns to those very same kinds of people and religion that he had banned. He goes in disguise to a witch and asks her to bring Samuel back, to make Samuel talk to Saul.

The outcome is as sure as ever it was: Saul and his family will die. God has already left him and given his kingdom to David.

The narrator leaves the reader in no doubt that David, not Saul, is the righteous king, and that God will achieve his purposes.

God in your pocket?

Samuel's speech is awe-inspiring. He's deeply angry with Saul for trying to manipulate him and God in this way. Saul's action of going undercover to use banned religious practices shows how unsteady his own faith is. Once again, he doesn't live up to his role as ruler of Yahweh's people. At the first sign of danger, and without an immediate response from God in the ways his narrow vision can perceive, Saul has turned away from the true God again. He has failed to demonstrate loyalty and obedience to God so many times before; his fate was decided back in chapter 15. Now he tries to summon up that divine power at his own bidding.

But God will not be manipulated. He is not to be got out as and when it suits someone. He is to be obeyed unswervingly, especially by an anointed king who should be being an example of this to his people! It's God who calls the shots, and anyone who thinks or pretends otherwise is seriously mistaken. The awesome, God-inspired power of Samuel even in death, his strong words, his blunt truth-telling to Saul, is enough to make anyone tremble.

Awesome forebodings

A prophet isn't just someone who tells the future; a prophet also speaks 'truth to power' or tells it as it really is, right now. Samuel is clearly doing just that. This time tomorrow, Saul and his sons will be dead. The kingdom will be David's. It's already David's, truth be told.

This kind of fearsome, honest talk is a mark of the strong Jewish teacher Jesus. He also has prophetic qualities, and he certainly doesn't shirk from speaking truth to power. Nor does he mince his words when talking of the kingdom of God. Especially not to those Pharisees who are blinkered about the kingdom of God in Luke 17. They will not see the kingdom of God, just as Saul did not hear an answer to his prayer, because they are only looking for it in their own narrow understanding. They are not ready to let the raw power of God – as blatant as a blaze of lightning – enter their lives.

Their loyalty is to their ideas, to their religious constructs, to themselves. Saul's only real loyalty was to himself and his own ideas of what God should be like, even on the eve of his death. Jesus challenges his hearers to put God first. We could all, like in the days of Noah, and of Lot, be distracted by everyday life. What happens if we die suddenly, if the King comes to his kingdom when we aren't expecting it? We are to make sure that our loyalty is always to God, and not to our own religious constructs. That's what will then turn out to be our truly ultimate loyalty.

Megan Daffern

Suggested hymns

Seek ye first the kingdom of God; Put thou thy trust in God; Be thou my vision; All for Jesus, all for Jesus.

Fourth Sunday after Trinity (Proper 9) 5 July

Principal Service **Finding Peace in Complexity**

(*Continuous*): Gen. 24.34–38, 42–49, 58–end; Ps. 45.10–end; *or* (*Related*): Zech. 9.9–12; Ps. 145.8–15; Rom. 7.15–25a; **Matt. 11.16–19, 25–end**

Conflicts and contradictions

Life can be full of conflicts and contradictions. Opposing events, actions and words each challenging the other, each presenting an alternative view. Life is complicated, and often a muddle of decisions made with insufficient preparation or information. It feels like we are swayed in one direction and then the other, always having to compromise.

Even within our own being we are sometimes at war with ourselves. Our feelings pull us from one thing to another and our best intentions are often undermined by our own decisions and actions. St Paul speaks of this struggle in his letter to the Romans. He says he can will what is right, but he cannot do it. He wants one thing but does another, he expects one thing to happen and the opposite comes to pass, he is captive to the will of his body when perhaps his mind and his heart are pulling him in another direction. He may desire to follow in the law of the Lord, but he is blown off track again and again by his propensity to be drawn into sin; it almost seems like one step forward and two steps back. Paul acknowledges that there is an answer to the contradictions and conflicts that each of us may be fighting within and without, and the answer is Jesus

Christ. We are called to follow him and learn from him, as he is the one who can keep us on the straight and narrow way.

Courting controversy

There is much about the Christian faith that also contradicts the expected order of the world. That a king should come riding on donkey, as described in the book of the prophet Zechariah, is an image that immediately contradicts worldly expectations of what power is and what power does. Of course, this prophecy comes to pass in the person of Jesus Christ who turned the world upside down and inside out. As we know, his words and his actions brought him into conflict with the political and religious authorities of the day. That God should send his Son to be crucified as a common criminal is also an image that challenges human expectations of authority. To the unseeing eye it seems that in the crucifixion God has lost all power and authority, but for those with eyes to see, power and glory come through vulnerability. Jesus also said of himself that his actions would cause division, even within the same household. But, at the same time, Jesus is the one who will command peace to the nations, and offer all people that peace that the world cannot give, if they choose to accept it.

Both Jesus and his forerunner John the Baptist court controversy. John comes to herald the kingdom of God and promote devout aestheticism and the repentance of sins, and yet people said he had a demon. Jesus comes to eat with those on the edge of society, so that they might be brought back into the fold, and he is called a glutton and a drunkard. Can anyone do right for doing wrong? It seems that John and Jesus enter into a world where people are not ready to listen to what they have to say. Like children sitting in the marketplace, they did not dance to the joyful music that was being played by the Son of God, they did not mourn when there was wailing. They were obviously conflicted as to which way to turn, so they chose to sit passively and do nothing.

The path towards peace

Jesus then looks up to heaven and prays to his Father. In his prayer he gives thanks that there are some who respond wholeheartedly to his message. As life gets more and more complicated and conflicted, people find it harder to respond to him. But those who are as pure in heart as a mere infant are able to respond with joy to the good news of salvation and see God the Father who is revealed to them through the Son.

It can be tiring living with conflict and navigating contradictions. It can feel like living on the edge trying to discern what to do, where to go, how to live, and there are daily decisions for all of us, which can try us and challenge us and disrupt our spiritual well-being. We can often feel torn in two about any number of issues: what is the best route to take through any given situation?

Jesus offers a solution through this moral and spiritual maze. Interestingly, he doesn't say that he can make conflict, complexity, contradiction and challenge disappear altogether, but he does promise rest for our souls and refreshment for our hearts. He promises an oasis of calm where we can offload our burdens and find a new kind of peace, which may then help us navigate and understand a complex and challenging world. Ultimately, we are to put our life in his hands with the simple trust of a child.

Victoria Johnson

Suggested hymns

When all thy mercies, O my God; Peace, perfect peace, in this dark world of sin; O Jesus, I have promised; All you who seek a comfort sure.

Fourth Sunday after Trinity (Proper 9) 5 July

Second Service **20:20 Vision**

Ps. 56 [57]; 2 Sam. 2.1–11; 3.1; **Luke 18.31—19.10**

Are you one of those fortunate people who still has 20:20 vision? Or are you perhaps long- or short-sighted? Maybe you have astigmatism, or cataracts. I'm very short-sighted. Without the everyday miracle of contact lenses, I can barely see in focus. But now I'm middle-aged, I'm becoming long-sighted too – and that means I have to juggle lenses and glasses in order to see properly when driving or reading. The optician is training my eyes so that one sees distance and one sees close – it's amazing what's possible these days. Our reading from Luke's Gospel has three episodes – one after the other. All are related to vision.

Tunnel vision

Jesus and the disciples are on their way to Jerusalem. Jesus says that once there, the prophesises about the Son of Man will come to fruition. He lists the violence that will happen to him. He anticipates being mocked and flogged, spat on and insulted, handed over and killed. He says that after three days he will rise again. Luke has Jesus rehearse the unfolding of God's plan – it's a spoiler alert, but the disciples simply don't get it. Even though they have journeyed with Jesus and been his closest companions they don't understand what's coming – they can't grasp either the details or the importance of it. They are still hoping that the Messiah will overthrow the Roman occupation and restore the people of Israel to their rightful place. They have tunnel vision – they are unable to see or grasp that God might act in a different way to bring about the kingdom.

Inner vision

On the approach to Jericho, Jesus and the disciples encounter a blind man begging by the roadside. The man can't see Jesus so the people tell him who it is that is passing by. He calls out, 'Jesus, Son of David, have mercy on me!' The crowd try to shut him up but he just shouts louder, until Jesus stops and attends to him. Asked what he'd like Jesus to do for him, the man doesn't ask for money, or food. He asks instead for his deepest desire: 'Lord, let me see again.' While the man may not be able to physically see, he has great inner vision. He senses the power of God and reaches out with faith and trust. Jesus heals him, and the man – now able to see – rejoices and gives glory to God. The kingdom of God is breaking in through Jesus: those with faith and vision are experiencing it. The blind man recognized the Son of Man in a way that the disciples could not.

Clear vision

The journey continues – the disciples and Jesus enter Jericho and the crowd accompanying them grows. Now it's so large that Zacchaeus – the chief tax-collector – who isn't very tall, can't see Jesus. But he is longing to do so. He uses his initiative and climbs a tree so that he has a clear vision of this incredible teacher and healer. Jesus has a clear vision of Zacchaeus too – he spots him in the tree and invites himself to Zacchaeus' home. The crowd are annoyed. Tax-collectors were not popular – being seen to be in collaboration with the Romans.

The town's *chief* tax-collector would have been the most hated of all – impure, a sinner. But the Son of Man has come to rescue and save sinners. Just a few verses earlier, Jesus had remarked on how hard it is for those with wealth to enter the kingdom. Now he's going to show that nothing is impossible with God. Being seen and recognized by Jesus, welcoming Jesus into his home, enables the beginnings of transformation in Zacchaeus. Ripe for salvation, he gives away half his possessions and offers to repay fourfold those he has defrauded. What an extraordinary effect this would have had on the people of Jericho. The ripples of this would have touched many lives and the salvation of this one person would have been the catalyst for much restoration and redemption throughout the area. The Son of Man is changing the world – person by person. The coming events in Jerusalem will enable all humanity to see clearly who Jesus is and embark on the path of salvation opened up by his living, dying and rising among us.

20:20 vision

Who do you identify with most in these stories? Are you a close follower of Jesus who has seen God work in extraordinary ways, but you struggle sometimes to believe in God's plans? Do you have inner vision – a strong sense of who Jesus is? Do you have faith and trust that he will answer your deepest desire if you ask him? Are you longing to see Jesus? Would you do anything to reach out – to have a clear vision of him? Are you prepared to invite him into your home, and allow him to change your heart and your character? God calls us to have 20:20 vision – to see Jesus in full focus and to trust and believe in his saving power for all humanity. Amen.

Catherine Williams

Suggested hymns

Be thou my vision; Take my life, and let it be; As the deer; Will you come and follow me?

Fifth Sunday after Trinity (Proper 10) 12 July

Principal Service **Hear!**

(*Continuous*): Gen. 25.19–end; Ps. 119.105–112; *or*

(*Related*): Isa. 55.10–13; Ps. 65 [*or* 65.8–end]; Rom. 8.1–11;

Matt. 13.1–9, 18–23

What words have changed your life in some way? What have you heard in a classroom, in a talk, lecture, sermon, in the theatre, in conversation, that has made a difference to you?

A new hearing

Once as a 14-year-old I came into the classroom after the mid-morning break, and the English master had written on the blackboard: 'Give me my Romeo and, when he shall die, take him and cut him out in little stars, and he will make the face of heaven so fine that all the world will be in love with night and pay no worship to the garish sun.' That was it, that was all it took to drive me to bury myself in an old mildewed copy of Shakespeare and to devour long speeches and give little recitals to amuse family and friends. Other young people had better homes, wealthier parents, but I had been given the key to a treasury that 'shut me up in measureless content', and I looked out with sadness on my peers who didn't hear what I had been given to hear.

What powerful words have sunk right down into your soul like a drill to reach oil in some deep-sea exploration? It might just be a throwaway line, a comment, a story, a piece of music. It doesn't have to be fully understood.

Words to hear and bring change

Words bring change; they change the world, change situations, change people's lives. 'Today we are in a state of war with Germany', 'I love you', 'Will you marry me?' 'I declare you to be husband and wife.' 'Your sins are forgiven you', 'Go in peace.'

Words change us, but some words change us fundamentally. And the words that change us more fundamentally than any others are words that come from our ultimate and complete lover, whom we call God. It's when we hear God speaking for the first time his word of love and grace that we are changed for ever, set in a new relationship, on a new path. And we begin to recognize his voice, and listen out when he speaks to us again.

St Teresa of Avila was a formidable woman, charged to reform the order of Carmelites in Spain, which had become decadent and self-serving. Once she said of God: 'Just these two words he spoke changed my life: "Enjoy me." After a night of prayer, he changed my life when he sang: "Enjoy me."'

Hearing difficulties

Hearing is everything. The parable Jesus told is an analysis of the difficulties of hearing. The first is that we decide not to hear. Hearing can be as impossible as sowing seed on a newly tarmacked road if we aren't prepared even to try to hear what may be said. Now it's reasonable to cut dead all the telephone salespeople from the subcontinent trying to sell us things. But we may dismiss the one voice among the myriad voices that can deliver us blessing.

Sometimes we do hear, and catch a vision; we get excited, decide to follow up what we have heard, and start to act differently, whether, for example, to get more exercise, take up drawing, spend more time in prayer or visit neighbours we don't know too well. We make a decent start, but soon our enthusiasm has dissipated. We haven't prepared the ground and reclaimed the congested spaces in our lives, and so our short-lived signs of growth wither away.

Sometimes we do better. We hear something and we register it, plan to give ourselves the time to 'process it', as we say. But we also feel the pressure to rattle through books, articles, programmes, reports that squeeze out the few messages that are really worth living with. In his diary, the priest and writer Henri Nouwen admits to God:

> I am so busy with other things, that I cannot hear you; so preoccupied with what to read, what to write, what to say or what to do that I do not realize that all those problems would not exist if I listened to you and stopped listening to my own inner turmoil.[25]

We're distracted by words – good, interesting, wholesome words – and unintentionally miss the Word.

Jesus is offering us a lesson in processing the word of life. We've heard it many times over, in different forms. But it can sail past us. Or can just touch the surface of our lives but not go where it can form us.

I was walking back with my host to the bar feeling disappointed with the sermon I'd just preached at a university college. But then a young woman ran to my host, with tears rolling down her face. She asked the Warden to direct her to the preacher, not realizing at first that I was alongside him. She told me that she was a theology student, and that she wanted to tell me that she'd just heard for the very first time that God loved her. Of course she'd heard the message a thousand times, but it remained on the surface, she hadn't heard it as a message for her. But now she knew it was.

Is there a line of a hymn, a verse, a Bible story, a parable, a prayer, that is a word of God, good news, that you can hold on to and take into yourself?

Roger Spiller

Suggested hymns

I heard the voice of Jesus say; Will you come and follow me if I but call your name; Lord, you sometimes speak in wonders; Lord, speak to me, that I may speak.

Fifth Sunday after Trinity (Proper 10) 12 July

Second Service **Jerusalem: House and Temple**

Ps. 60 [63]; **2 Sam. 7.18–end**; Luke 19.41—20.8

Today, all the Abrahamic religions and many of their various denominations or sects have a stake in Jerusalem. It makes it an exciting place, a holy place, but also a place that knows danger. Jerusalem in the time of Jesus as well was central to religious observance. It was the place that good Jews went to if they could for the pilgrimage festivals. These were Passover (remembering the escape from slavery in Egypt and the crossing of the Red Sea), Shavuot (originally the first fruits of the harvest, it evolved into a commemoration of God giving the Torah to Moses) and Sukkot (just after the Day of Atonement, a week-long autumn festival memorializing God sheltering his people in the wilderness after the Exodus). Jesus the observant Jew is going to Jerusalem for the Passover; and he knows it will also bring his death.

Holy place

Perhaps you have a particular place where you feel close to God. It may be a pilgrimage site or a retreat house, a local church or a small prayer corner in your home. Interestingly, in the New Testament, the Greek word *hieros* is both an adjective and a noun, meaning either holy or holy thing: something set apart for God. It is this word that is translated here in Luke's Gospel today as 'Temple'. It is good to remember the sacred background to a place. Otherwise, cathedrals risk becoming simply tourist venues, and ancient churches only heritage sites.

Jesus has just wept over Jerusalem as he looks down upon it from a viewpoint near the Mount of Olives. Like an Old Testament prophet of doom, he can see what they could become, but he also knows what disasters will face them. Some see his words to be referring to the great wars that would happen in AD 66–70 between the Jewish people and the Roman authorities, which would result in the destruction of the Temple – again – as in the Old Testament before the exile in the sixth century BC. The Temple is central.

So it's no surprise that Jesus goes straight there. He goes to teach, but when he finds it full of traders at perhaps their peak season for sacrificial offerings, he has to clear it of those religious exploiters first. (Luke's account of the cleansing of the Temple is shorter than all the other Gospels – compare Matthew 21.12–27, Mark 11.15–19 and John 2.13–16.) That done, he can turn to what this place should really be about: getting closer to God.

God's house

Jesus immediately quotes from the Hebrew Scriptures – from Isaiah and Jeremiah. He describes the Temple now in the words of Jeremiah as a 'den of robbers', but in Isaiah as it should be, a 'house of prayer'. Notice how he naturally refers to the Temple as 'a house of prayer'.

Today's Old Testament reading described God's promise to David that he would make Jerusalem his house, his holy dwelling place. There are the first signs of real peace between the tribes of Israel making up the kingdom over which David was now settling down as ruler. The south-eastern part of Jerusalem is still today called 'City of David' and archaeologists think that is the ancient core of Jerusalem. David's martial progress has ended with the conquering of the Jebusites who lived in Jerusalem. He then took his time to prepare carefully before bringing the Ark of the Lord (the special tabernacle or tent structure that had been carried around from the time of the Exodus, housing various ancient holy things, including the tablets of the Ten Commandments) into Jerusalem. It is when the Ark has been safely brought into Jerusalem that David and his people can at last settle down.

It's not long, though, before David contrasts his grand palace with the travelling tent of God. Should he make a grand palace for God too? He consults the great prophet Nathan, who reports God's response to David. God has declared himself a God who has been content to be on the move with his people, who doesn't need a house like David does. It will be for David's son to build God a house, and God will build up the house of David, David's family and descendants. (Christians see the fulfilment of this in Jesus, born of the 'house of David'.)

David responds to this news with the prayer and praise we heard earlier. He thanks God for the blessings he has given to David's house, or family. He rejoices that God has settled his people Israel in safety, and then he turns to his own line of descendants, praying for God's continued blessing on David's house. The futures of God's house and David's house are intertwined.

Holy dwellings

The Hebrew word built up from the three Hebrew letters *q-d-sh* can mean holy, holy thing or holiness. In both psalms today this word occurs, meaning 'sanctuary'. Psalms 60 and 63 both have introductory headings linking them with David and parts of his life before he made it to Jerusalem. There were always holy things, and their physicality made places holy. They could be visited spiritually as well as physically: both psalms visualize imaginatively those holy sanctuaries.

Some people are called to pilgrimages; some to retreats; some to work in churches. But whatever we do or wherever we are, we are all called to let ourselves become dwelling places for God. Let us pray that even our hearts and souls may be sanctuaries, places of still holiness where God can speak and bless, be heard and praised.

Megan Daffern

Suggested hymns

Blessed city, heavenly Salem; Church of God, elect and glorious; O thou not made with hands; We love the place, O God.

Sixth Sunday after Trinity (Proper 11) 19 July

Principal Service Weeding or Waiting[26]

(*Continuous*): Gen. 28.10–19a; Ps. 139.1–11, 23–24 [*or* 139.1–11]; *or* (*Related*): Wisd. 12.13, 16–19, *or* Isa. 44.6–8; Ps. 86.11–end; Rom. 8.12–25; **Matt. 13.24–30, 36–43**

There was a farmer in India with a small plot of land. Every year it yielded a good crop of rice, enough to feed himself and his family and have a little to sell on the open market.

One day he was talking to his neighbour, who told him he'd had a visit from an agent of a large American company. The agent offered to sell him some special grains, modified by inserting a wheat gene into the rice. The agent promised that he would get a significantly higher yield, and the crop would be more resistant to pests. The neighbour said he had signed a contract.

But the first farmer was worried. He had heard about this new kind of grain, and he had a lot of questions. Since he had the next plot, some of the new grains could easily end up taking root over on his patch. Would he be able to tell the difference between the new crop and the old? Might they take over completely? Would he still be able to use the grains from one year's crop to grow the next year's? Or would he keep needing to buy new grains from the big American company? Would his family be safely nourished by the new kind of rice as they had been for generations by the old kind? What about his daughter, who had an allergy to wheat? Would she still be able to eat rice if it had a wheat gene inserted? Would he be able to go back to the old ways, the old grains? Or would they just not survive in that soil any more? And if he had to go on buying the new grains, would he get back the money he spent on them from the increased yield that was promised? What about the animals and birds that were a familiar and important part of daily life and work on his land? Would they still be there?

The two farmers decided to consult a community leader. The community leader told them that nobody really knew the answers to those questions yet. In two or three years' time, perhaps they would know whether the new seeds were a good idea or not. Until then, they would just have to wait.

Wait

Now that's hard advice to follow for farmers around the world who may sense instinctively that genetic technology may have tremendous potential both for evil and for good. An end to freedom and the natural balance of the earth? Or an end to hunger and poverty?

Wait: hard advice to follow for slaves who could see the weeds sprouting up among the wheat.

Wait: hard advice for all concerned people who can see the growth of good and evil side by side, and don't know how it will turn out. The danger is that when well-meaning people try to root out evil, they root out much that is good at the same time.

Yet there's encouragement here too. 'The field is the world' – this baffling blend of beauty and brokenness: and one day there will be a universal sifting. Then it won't be a matter of introducing a good kingdom that was not there before, but of collecting out of God's world 'all causes of sin and all evildoers'. This isn't a picture of a mean and spiteful God pouncing on every human peccadillo. It is a picture of a God who comes down hard on everything and everyone who deliberately causes others to fall into sin, and on those who persistently initiate and perpetrate wickedness. Such a God is good news for the sinned against, and for those who sense their moral weakness, who find themselves longing for the good and bewailing how they fall short.

Waiting with others

Let's say a young man unburdens himself to me as a pastor, or to you as a friend. He is troubled about his sexuality. He has been hurtfully treated by his church. As he talks to me about the lifestyle he has chosen to adopt, I cannot reconcile it with my understanding about how God has intended us to live. But he also talks to me about his faith. About his struggles to understand himself. About his deep concern for spiritual growth and his visits to a spiritual director. As I listen to him and look at his situation, I cannot be simplistic about it. I cannot say everything is right. Nor can I possibly say, here is a plant that's got to be uprooted and destroyed. What must I do? I must wait. I cannot see how it will turn out. But I wait *with him*. I let him know that there is in me no ounce of condemnation for him. At the same time, I let him know that I'm not trying to pretend that all is as it should be. And in that waiting together there is opportunity for us both to see more clearly: gradually to see through all the entanglement that which is good, distinguished from that which is evil: and how it is that the good may be allowed to flourish and claim him completely.

What of those who can't wait for the sifting to begin?

The trouble is – as I guess Matthew knew – those who follow Jesus may be tempted to be more impatient than anyone else for the sifting process to begin. Disciples are often the ones most tempted to premature and zealous weeding – secure in the supposition that they are 'wheat' themselves! But that in itself is to be a stumbling block. Jesus in Matthew has harsh words for stumbling blocks – who destroy the possibility of good in others instead of nursing it along. In the words of one commentator, the kingdom of God as Jesus announced it was not, like some of the sectarian groups of the time, 'the exclusive coterie of self-elected saints'.

But that's the glory and relief of knowing that the kingdom belongs to God: knowing that it is his business to sift the good from the bad. Knowing that restrained waiting can enable the good to grow – in all sorts of surprising places, even ourselves.

Stephen Wright

Suggested hymns

The kingdom of God is justice and joy; Judge eternal, throned in splendour; What shall our greeting be? Jesus is Lord!; Let us build a house where love can dwell.

Sixth Sunday after Trinity (Proper 11) July 19

Second Service **Pipsqueaks and Giants**

Ps. 67 [70]; 1 Kings 2.10–12; 3.16–end; **Acts 4.1–22**; *Gospel at Holy Communion*: Mark 6.30–34, 53–end

Do you ever feel like you are too small, too insignificant to have much impact on anything; a pipsqueak among giants? It's easy to slip into despair in the face of sickness, grief, misery, worry, pain, political instability, fear and all the various trials that afflict our frail humanity. Our vision can become distorted when all we see are the things that frighten or overwhelm us. Today's reading from Acts comes as a form of corrective laser eye surgery, restoring right seeing and offering terrific hope.

A picture of opposition

Picture the scene: in the red corner stand the representatives of the Establishment, smart, powerful people who are used to running the show: priests, temple big wigs, the whole 'high priestly family', and they are pretty brassed off with the disruptive behaviour of a couple of mere pipsqueaks causing trouble in their domain. In the blue corner stand two simple men, Peter and John, uneducated, unsophisticated, ordinary blokes. If I were a gambling woman, I wouldn't be backing them.

Luke offers us a picture of opposition. At first glance it looks like two pipsqueaks coming face to face with a tribe of giants. But look a bit closer. Our 'pipsqueaks' Peter and John proclaim that in Jesus 'there is the resurrection of the dead'. People believe them. Five thousand people. When they are challenged in whose name they act, Peter responds with eloquence and clarity, pointing to the man who had been healed at the Beautiful Gate, declaring that it is by the name of Jesus Christ that this man is healed. Peter goes further, 'whom you crucified, whom God raised from the dead . . . There is salvation by no one else under heaven given among mortals by which we must be saved.'

An attempt to silence the pipsqueaks

The Temple powers see the boldness and recognize Peter and John as having been companions of Jesus. Rather than asking where this boldness has come from and what it means for the man to have been healed, they are more concerned with closing things down and bolstering the status quo. So, in the time-honoured fashion of all bullying giants, they try to shut the little guys up, imprisoning them and forbidding them to speak. But our pipsqueaks are having none of it: 'we cannot keep from speaking about what we have seen and heard.' The giants' hands are tied, at least for now. The people are praising God; news of the healing has spread. There is no way to silence the little guys without creating more trouble. Round one to the pipsqueaks.

Remarkably obtuse giants

So how come ordinary people can face down giants? This is a key question for any of us who have ever fled the giants in our lives, or been pinned down in terror of them. The answer is simple. In the blue corner stand two ordinary men. With them, in them and surrounding them stands the power of God the Holy Spirit. They are not alone. Peter speaks eloquently because he is filled with the Holy Spirit. The men are bold because God is with them and they trust this. The giants look to their power, position and privilege. These things distort their vision. They are so hell-bent on holding on to their power that they completely miss the significance of the lame man being healed, of news of resurrection of the dead, of the statement that salvation is in Jesus Christ. Salvation – which is hope, healing, forgiveness, wholeness and completeness. They miss all of this. They want to stamp their authority and grasp on to their position. They will know no other power, yield to no other power. Salvation for them is by their own hands, in their own authority and strength. They might be giants, but they are remarkably obtuse giants.

From pipsqueaks to giant-slayers

And what of our pipsqueaks? The truth is that God works in our frailty and fragility, transforming hesitant speech into bold declaration, strengthening feeble knees, giving hope and confidence in place of despair and fear. We see it here in Acts: in the power of God, two pipsqueaks face down a horde of giants, two pipsqueaks who know where their hope is, where their salvation lies, where their shalom is. Two pipsqueaks who see with holy clarity. Two pipsqueaks become giant-slayers.

Have the giants got hold of you?

Have you adopted the giants' outlook – trying to wield your own power? Save yourself?

Have you forgotten where hope lies?

In the name of Jesus and by the power of his Spirit, may we know that mere pipsqueaks, like us, in God's strength, are giant-slayers. Therein lies all our hope. Amen

Kate Bruce

Suggested hymns

Faithful one (so unchanging); Breathe on me, breath of God; When a knight won his spurs; Fight the good fight with all thy might.

Seventh Sunday after Trinity (Proper 12) 26 July

Principal Service Inhabiting the World of the Parables

(*Continuous*): Gen. 29.15–28; Ps. 105.1–11, 45b (*or* 105.1–11), *or* Ps. 128; (*or Related*): 1 Kings 3.5–12; Ps. 119.129–136; Rom. 8.26–39; **Matt. 13.31–33, 44–52**

A woman asked T. S. Eliot, 'What do you mean in your poem "Ash-Wednesday" by the line: "Lady, three white leopards sat under a juniper-tree"?'[27] 'Yes, Madam, I can give you a straight answer. I mean "Lady, three white leopards sat under a juniper tree".' In the same way, followers of Jesus have been seeking for clear, direct, satisfying interpretations of his parables from the time he first uttered them down to the present. But the parables can't simply be translated once and for all, into direct, plain speech without loss. If we're to try to uncover the meaning and the experience of the parables we must be prepared to struggle and be unsettled and confounded by these pregnant texts.

A clear meaning?

The meaning of today's pair of short, familiar parables about mustard seed and leaven, however, seem pretty obvious. 'Little and large' is surely what they are about, not, of course, an old television comedy duo, but two images of massive growth from miniscule and unpromising beginnings. The parable of the mustard seed, with its image of a glorious future, serves as an encouragement to Christians struggling in the meantime. The parable of the leaven tells us that the kingdom is immersed and present, though hidden, in all aspects of human life for those with eyes to see, and that 'seeing' sustains our hope that God's kingdom will come 'on earth as it is in heaven'. That's about as much as we can and need to say about the text and its meaning for us today. An obvious point to bring this short sermon to a close.

Confusion and complication

Except that those of you who know your Bibles and the customs of the time will recognize that mustard trees and leaven were known for their negative and destructive characteristics and seem an odd choice here. Why did Jesus cite the mustard tree as a source of blessing when it was more usually despised as a voracious weed? Why did he refer to the picture of the birds of the air nesting in its branches when this, as his hearers would have known, had already been used to condemn the proud cedar tree in the Old Testament that gave succour to the enemies of God's kingdom? And, to deepen the puzzle, why were these two parables placed in Matthew's Gospel immediately after the parable where good and bad, wheat and tares are permitted to co-exist until the harvest?

What's going on here?

Do these parables have a subversive counter-argument, a counter melody? Are we being offered a satire, in the parable of the mustard seed, a savage mockery of triumphalist dreams, projects and institutions, including the Church, when they succumb to secular power, built on collusion and competition and are too impressed by strength, success and size? The image of the kingdom at the end of the old Testament period was that of a pitiable tree stump or branch. Now Matthew in his Gospel seems to be hedging his bets as to whether the tiny seed will become a great shrub or a modest tree.

The parable of the leaven involves the agency of a woman who collects a small portion of leaven from the mouldy remainder of the last bake and sneaks it into a vast quantity of new, pure flour. That homely image seems obvious enough until we recall that leaven is an image of corruption all through the Bible. Its use here in this passage seems consistent with that. We're told that the woman had 'three measures' of pure flour, a precise note that indicates a sacred amount that underlines the purity of the flour in stark contrast to the leaven with which it was corrupted. Is the parable, perhaps, inviting us to transcend the category of pure and impure, by detoxifying the latter in the service of the gospel? Is it hinting at a more glorious redemption than our plain, direct speech can contain, one that is experienced in Jesus sharing bread with sinners?

Confounding curiosity but opening us to a new world

We've seen that even the briefest of parables can unsettle, intrigue and confound us. We'd hope to distil their meaning in the plain, ordered, rational, controlling language by which we try to master the world we normally inhabit. But, as T. S. Eliot's woman inquisitor was hopefully to discover, poetic language, and notably that of the parables, has the capacity to ambush and interrogate us, opening us up to the possibility of a new, alternative world that can only be accessed by the faculty and language of the imagination. Where 'The Word made flesh here is made word again', as the poet Edwin Muir reminds us,[28] our faith in the kingdom becomes impoverished. We have not merely to translate the parables into meaningful language. We have to immerse ourselves in their strange world, let them seep through and strike up new and conflicting ideas, images, ways of thinking in our lives. The parables invite us to inhabit the regular, mundane world of planting, pruning, breadmaking, eating and celebrating, but to see through it the signs of the kingdom that prefigure a glorious, if not triumphalist, consummation.

Roger Spiller

Suggested hymns

The kingdom of God is justice and joy; Put peace into each other's hands; Jesu, priceless treasure; How shall we sing God's kingdom here.

Seventh Sunday after Trinity (Proper 12) July 26

Second Service **Faith in Dark Places**

Ps. 75 [76]; 1 Kings 6.11–14, 23–end; **Acts 12.1–17**; *Gospel at Holy Communion*: John 6.1–21

When you heard the reading from Acts today, I wonder if you were drawn to anyone in particular? Maybe you are with those praying for Peter – hoping against hope that, somehow, he will be all right. Perhaps you are with Peter, wide-eyed and open-mouthed, as the chains fall from his wrists and an angel leads him past the prison guards to freedom. Do you stand with Rhoda the maid who hears Peter's voice and is so overcome she leaves him standing alone in her haste to tell the others he is at the gate? Perhaps you align yourself with those who told Rhoda she was out of her mind until the gate swings open and you see Peter standing there. Maybe you ponder the difference between Herod – all blatant self-assertion, violence, bullying and self-aggrandisement – and the church gathered to pray. The power of the tyrant meets the power of trust in God. Herod is autocratic, he acts alone, ordering his soldiers to do his will. The church operates together, drawing in close as community – humble, hopeful, faithful. What are you drawn to? Where do you stand?

Standing with John

I keep coming back to John. His brother James is murdered by the sword. Notwithstanding resurrection hope, John has lost his sibling in a brutal, needless act of violence. We aren't told how he reacts. Did he wonder to himself, 'Um, an angel appears to Peter, Peter's chains fall off, he walks passed heavily armed guards . . . to freedom. Great. Where was the angel when they came for James?' It would be an understandable question.

There is a danger in a reading of this passage, which cheers the power of the church at prayer, sees the connection between prayer and freedom, champions the victory of God (all these things are undoubtedly true), but airbrushes out the pain of John's loss. That too is real. There are no easy answers here. We must balance the sense of victory with deep compassion.

Living in the tension of the 'why' questions

We must live in the tension of the 'why' questions, holding faith in the God who opens locked doors, but who sometimes does not intervene in the ways we hope for. James bled out at Herod's hands. There was no divine reprieve. John grieves. Peter is freed, but surely he grieves too. Peter, James and John had shared so much together. Now James is murdered. How do we handle this tension between God's clear activity and the apparent absence of God?

Yes, rejoice in the God who comes and breaks the chains, who sets the prisoner free. Laugh at the comedy of Peter left knocking on the gate. Rejoice in the healing in intensive care. Rejoice with the couple blessed with a child when all seemed lost. Rejoice in the freedom of the oppressed. But remember too those who struggle with the tension between their faith in God who does act, heal and restore, when their own personal experience does not bear this out, at least not in the way they desire.

Faith in the dark places

Faith in God is easy when the chains break and the prison doors open, when we witness the powerful brought down from their thrones and the lowly lifted high, when we read of tyrants trounced and the hungry filled with good things. Faith is obvious. But what does faith in God look like when the doors remain locked, when God's people are murdered, when there is no apparent reprieve from suffering? What does faith in God mean when the Herods throw their weight about and inflict terrible pain on the powerless? This is flinty faith. Steely faith. Faith hammered out on the anvil of suffering. Faith in the dark places. It's a million miles from simplistic triumphalism that lacks intelligence and compassion – flabby faith. It's a million miles from despair – stick-like faith, starved of remembrance of the goodness of God, and the power of divine love.

Faith in the dark places takes courage. The willingness to wrestle with hard questions, choosing to believe in God's overriding goodness and the longevity of his promises. Faith in hard times takes patience, the decision to trust that ultimately God's power will triumph over all forms of darkness, degradation and death. Faith in the wilderness is full of compassion: the willingness to cop an earful from those who grieve and rage, without defensiveness. The willingness to simply stay present, living with courage, compassion, patience, trust, doubt, question, hope and love. Love for those who suffer. Love for those who know blessing. Love for God who is always present, when the doors are locked and barred, and when they swing wide open.

At any point in the life of the Church there will be those experiencing a sense of blessing, an awareness of the wonderful active power and love of God; those who see doors unlock and chains fall off. Rejoice with them. There will also be those experiencing grief, doubt, question, those who are in dark places. Sit with them, keep watch with them. Don't airbrush them out. Faith is expressed in dark places, as well as in the light.

Kate Bruce

Suggested hymns

Blessed be your name (In the land that is plentiful); Empty, broken, here I stand (Kyrie Eleison); Jesus Christ is waiting; And can it be that I should gain? Watch and pray.

Eighth Sunday after Trinity (Proper 13) 2 August

Principal Service **You Give Them Something to Eat!**

(*Continuous*): Gen. 32.22–31; Ps. 17.1–7, 16 [*or* 17.1–7]; *or* (*Related*): Isa. 55.1–5, Ps. 145.8–9, 15–end [*or* 145.15–end]; Rom. 9.1–5, **Matthew 14.13–21**

Have you ever been hungry? *Really* hungry! Not 'hungry' as in 'it's about 10 o'clock, I didn't have any breakfast and I'm feeling a bit peckish'. Hungry in the sense of stomach cramps, light-headedness and fatigue when you haven't eaten for a day or so. Have you ever gone a day or two or even three without solid food? Many of us have never had that experience – and we don't really know what it's like to go without food for days or even weeks and to have no idea when or where the next meal is coming from. Seeing on the news the desperate hunger in famine-stricken places I'm embarrassed when I hear myself or others saying, 'I'm starving!' As hungry as you and I might ever have been, there is nothing that can compare to the sight of mothers carrying dying children, standing in line at feeding centres. As we think about that we should be struck by the full force of Jesus' words to his disciples in today's Gospel: 'You give them something to eat!'

Compassion

The feeding of the five thousand appears in all four Gospels. In Matthew's account, Jesus has withdrawn in a boat to a deserted place where he can pray and grieve in private. He's just had news that his cousin, John the Baptist, has been brutally beheaded by Herod, on the whim of Herod's wife and daughter. Jesus needs to be alone. However, the plan doesn't work. As he sails across the lake the people rush round on foot and get to the other side first. He arrives to a great crowd. Jesus isn't annoyed and irritated. The Gospel says he has compassion on the people – this crowd who are hungry for help and hope. He doesn't just see huge numbers of anonymous people; he sees individuals, and teaches and heals them. And when they become hungry for physical food, he reaches out with surprising abundance. Jesus is compassionate. Every encounter with hurting people in the Gospels is characterized by Jesus' compassionate touch. It is this compassion that draws the hurting crowds. Outreach and evangelism, from God's perspective, begin with compassion. Jesus shapes his disciples into compassionate people who will carry the ministry and message of Christ to a hungry world.

Feeding the hungry

When the time comes for the crowd to eat, the disciples want Jesus to send the people away to the nearby villages to buy supplies. Jesus responds with these words: 'You give them something to eat!'

The disciples are not equipped. They have no idea how to feed such a vast crowd. What they have to offer is pitiful. Five loaves and two fish – nearly nothing! But Jesus uses the little they have to offer help and hope to the hungry crowd. In the hands of Jesus, the loaves and fishes go a very long way. Feeding the hungry is a powerful symbol in Scripture. In the Magnificat, Mary praises God who 'has filled the hungry with good things, and sent the rich empty away'. In our reading from Isaiah, God calls out to Israel, 'Everyone who thirsts, come to the waters . . . come, buy and eat! Come, buy wine and milk without money and without price.' In years to come, the prophet Amos will warn the people that they will experience a spiritual famine because they have resisted this very invitation from God.

A serious issue for us in the modern world is 'compassion fatigue' – 'compassion burn-out'. We see so many horrors in the news that we become immune to the true human element of suffering. It's how we protect ourselves – but it can paralyse us into apathy and non-action. We say to ourselves, 'I'm just one person. What can I possibly do in the light of such overwhelming need?' Or in terms of the Gospel, 'We have nothing here but five loaves and two fish.'

More than enough

Jesus never has compassion fatigue: his love for individuals and crowds is eternal. One of the central propositions in our Gospel is that God can take our 'not enough' and turn it into 'more than enough'. Amazing things can happen when we see with the eyes of compassion and make ourselves available as God's agents. So, it doesn't matter how much you have. What matters is what God can do with what you have. And the God of Isaiah, and Paul and Jesus and us, is a God of love and faithfulness who has promised never to let us go.

Very small amounts of money can save lives, can feed starving people, and clothe and care for those in the hurting and broken places of our world. Prayers and action can transform desperate situations. Somewhere in your experience this week you will see a person or a situation where compassion is needed. If you are open to it, you will know in your spirit that God needs an agent of compassion and that the agent he chooses is you. When you begin to wonder what can be done for this person – or in this situation – then remember that your 'not enough' can be 'more than enough' in the hands of God, and may you be empowered to 'give them something to eat!' Amen.

Catherine Williams

Suggested hymns

Guide me, O thou great Redeemer; Where is bread?; Broken for me, broken for you; There's a wideness in God's mercy.

Eighth Sunday after Trinity (Proper 13) 2 August

Second Service **Holy Spirit: Director and Principal Actor**

Ps. 80 [*or* 80.1–8]; 1 Kings 10.1–13; **Acts 13.1–13**; *Gospel at Holy Communion*: John 6.24–35

The Holy Spirit is the director and principal actor behind all the action in the book of Acts. This is really clear in today's reading. We see the Spirit calling and commissioning through the church community, guiding and inspiring Saul and Barnabas as they come into contact with forces opposed to God's work. Just in case we think this is an ancient text about the good old days, we should remember that nothing has changed. The Holy Spirit has always been, and still is, the director and principal actor in the life of the Church.

'Unless the LORD builds the house, those who build it labour in vain'

Saul and Barnabas are called by the Spirit, in the context of the worshipping life of the church. The Holy Spirit speaks to those gathered together and instructs them to set aside both men to the work he has called them. The Spirit is not a vague entity, or a distant deity. Rather, we see the Spirit involved in the specific details of the life and mission of the Church, calling certain people to particular tasks. Are we seeking God in prayer and worship as we develop plans for the future of the Church, or for the next step in our lives? It's easy to make plans and forge ahead with good ideas – but 'unless the LORD builds the house, those who build it labour in vain'. So, wherever we are in our ministry of bright ideas, the reading from Acts calls us to worship and in so doing to submit our planning to the judgement and oversight of the Holy Spirit.

The Spirit works through the context of the Church not because God is in any way limited but because God chooses to work with people; the divine will is earthed in the ordinariness of human life. Note that Saul and Barnabas are commissioned by the call of the

Spirit and the actions of the church. The church engages with prayer and fasting before laying hands on the men's heads and sending them off. In short, the church orientates itself around God and acts from that starting point. If we base our ideas around human plans devoid of the call of God, we have set something else up in God's place – and we will labour in vain.

We are not in this alone

As Saul and Barnabas set out for Cyprus, Luke clearly states that they are sent out by the Holy Spirit. Though they are setting out into the unknown, they are not alone. God has called, commissioned and sent them; they have the companionship of the Spirit as they journey to and through Cyprus, travelling from one end of the island to the other, proclaiming God's word in the synagogues. The Spirit's presence is a constant source of comfort and cheer, sustaining them in the inevitable snags of day-to-day travel, and being an invaluable source of wisdom and insight when they encounter opposition. The knowledge of God's clear calling is a source of hope, energy, direction and purpose. They are not in this alone, and it doesn't all depend on their efforts. Worth remembering.

The Spirit gives insight

In Paphos they come face to face with evil in the form of Elymas, who seeks to prevent the proconsul from engaging with faith. The proconsul is a key source of political power, well placed to demonstrate the effect of the life of faith to men and women of influence. Faced with the magician's hostility, Paul (now named as such in the text) is able to see through to the heart of the man's opposition. How? Luke is clear that Paul, being 'filled with the Holy Spirit', is able to see the truth that Elymas is a 'son of the devil', 'enemy of all righteousness', 'full of all deceit and villainy', one who makes crooked the straight paths of the Lord. Elymas is an agent of unholiness, seeking to unravel God's work. Paul sees this quite clearly and states it boldly. Ironically, Elymas, having tried to prevent the proconsul from seeing the light, finds himself condemned to mist and darkness. He experiences blindness and needs someone to guide him. The sight of this judgement quickens the insight of the proconsul who is astonished at the teaching about the Lord. Through Paul, God turns the evil back on itself by using the judgement against Elymas as a means of opening the proconsul's eyes. Nothing stands in the way of the will of God.

Expect to encounter

Our reading comes with challenge. Are we expectant? Have we lost a sense that the Church belongs to God? Have we become burdened by a sense that we are in this alone and it's all down to us? Remember, the Spirit is director and principal actor, overseeing the work of the Church and acting in the earthy, everyday details.

The reading today comes as a reminder to us to seek God in worship, to listen to the Spirit's guidance in very specific ways. We are to expect God to be alive and active in the Church, working through people, calling, commissioning, guiding, inspiring. The reading asks us to raise our expectations. To seek God's guidance and expect to encounter it. To be confident that God who begins good works always sees them through to the end.

Kate Bruce

Suggested hymns

Holy Spirit, living breath of God; Breathe on me, breath of God; Guide me, O thou great redeemer; Spirit of the Living God, fall afresh on me.

Ninth Sunday after Trinity (Proper 14) 9 August

Principal Service Between the Shores

(*Continuous*): Gen. 37.1–4, 12–28; Ps. 105.1–6, 16–22, 45b [*or* 105.1–10]; *or* (*Related*): 1 Kings 19.9–18; Ps. 85.8–13; Rom. 10.5–15; **Matt. 14.22–33**

This is a story not just about Jesus and his disciples, but also about a boat that is forging its way in a terrible storm across the Sea of Galilee with the disciples on board. Matthew paints a terrifying picture of waves lashing wildly at the boat, and of a raging headwind impeding progress. It's dark too, and barely possible to make out what is ahead. Out in the middle of the lake, the disciples are suspended between one shore and another – one place of safety and another – having left Jesus on the shore behind them. In the thinking of ancient Israel, the sea was a place of chaos, and here with the water billowing around them the disciples may well and truly feel that their boat is offering but little protection against such chaos.

No safe space

For the disciples in this story there is no really easy or comfortably safe space. There is only the boat battling the storm and the storm itself, and we might readily understand that, given the option, the disciples would prefer to cling to the protection that the boat affords rather than step out on to the water. Jesus, however, is not so fearful of the chaos. He chooses the sea, walking over the water with the ease of walking on dry land. Matthew offers an inspiring picture of the Christ, in the midst of a storm that cannot overcome him.

Meanwhile the disciples, blinded by darkness and whirling water, don't even recognize who this figure is. Peter asks him to prove his identity by telling him to walk on the water. Is Peter calling a ghost's bluff here, hoping to stay inside the boat? But Jesus responds to Peter's request, commanding him to confront the chaos. The real Jesus does not invite us to stay clinging on to our security for dear life, but calls us to be bold and step out into the waves of our chaotic world in order to recognize and meet him there.

Obedience and discipleship

Peter's action as he steps out of the boat is not a great feat of bravery or even foolhardiness, but, first, simply an act of obedience. Jesus commands, and Peter responds. His obedience becomes an act of discipleship: Peter walks on water as Jesus does. As long as he keeps his eyes on Jesus, he steps across the waves with assurance. But as soon as he looks at the overwhelming chaos around him, he starts to go under and cries out, 'Lord, save me.' At this point Peter's experience becomes one of trust and faith. He discovers himself held and supported by his Lord, and together they return to the boat. There all kneel in worship, recognizing the identity of Jesus as the Son of God.

So what was the point of getting out of the boat if in the end Peter was going to end up back in it? Couldn't Peter have stayed relatively safe in the boat all along and never bothered to confront the waves? Well, yes; but by staying in the boat he would have been disobedient, and would never have discovered that Jesus was strong when he was weak. By getting out of the boat, Peter learns that Jesus is truly in the midst of the storm; Jesus calls his disciples to be there with him, and never abandons them. Perhaps it isn't surprising that some days later it's Peter who responds in faith when Jesus asks, 'Who do you say that I am?'

The boat as the image of the Church

In telling his story, Matthew has painted a profound picture not just of Jesus and his disciples but also of the boat, which down the centuries has been seen as an image of the Church, called to navigate stormy waters often in great times of darkness. In a world torn by divisions of all kinds, in a changing society in which religious believers are thought to be at best quirky and eccentric, and at an unsettling time in which our nation is journeying from one political set-up to another, as yet mostly unknown, we might feel as though we in the Church are having to forge a way through the storm. We don't quite know where we are going; we can long for the secure shores of the past when we knew who we were as the Church in society and felt more confident to speak of faith to the people around us. Equally, we may long for the security of the new shores to come – even though we may not yet know what they will be.

But our story suggests that the Church doesn't offer us a place to hide in and cling to. It's the place to which we come and return to, again and again, having encountered the living Christ in the midst of the chaos of everyday life. We return to recognize the authority of the one who meets us and holds us when we step into the storm in faithful obedience to his call. And it's the place where we bow down, and discover that the storm no longer actually threatens: because Christ is Lord over it.

Mary Cotes

Suggested hymns

Put thou thy trust in God; O sing a song of Bethlehem; Put your trust in the man who tamed the sea; Eternal Father, strong to save.

Ninth Sunday after Trinity (Proper 14) 9 August

Second Service Seeing Right

Ps. 86; 1 Kings 11.41—12.20; **Acts 14.8–20**; *Gospel at Holy Communion*: John 6.35, 41–51

The other week I experienced a miracle. It involved SpecSavers (other opticians are available). I went to collect my new glasses – first time wearing specs. Immediately, I noticed that trees in the far distance are not, in reality, blurry. I wandered around taking the glasses off and putting them on, marvelling at the difference in my field of vision, reading distant signs clearly. Clear vision. Like I said – a miracle.

'I see what you mean.' It's a common idiom. It means 'I get your point, I understand, I view this as you do, I've got the picture . . .' Our reading from Acts today is full of this theme of seeing. How do we frame things? How do we understand them? What's our vision like? Luke presents us with a picture of a man crippled from birth – he'd never been able to walk. I guess many people framed his life by the limitations of his condition. We see the man listening to Paul as he speaks. We don't know what Paul says, but it's a fair inference that he was talking about God, about good news of faith and hope. As he listened, was the man reframing his life, beginning to believe that there might be new possibilities for him?

Seeing in depth

It seems so, since, Luke says, Paul looked intently at him and saw that he had faith to be healed. What did Paul see as he looked at the man? He sees past the externals, into the man's desire and hope. He sees the man as he truly is. Seeing past the externals, seeing in depth, is a work of deep discernment, guided by the Holy Spirit.

As a chaplain I often listen to people's stories, which are frequently complex and messy. My hope is to have the discernment to see through the extraneous details, to grasp the heart of the matter, to see the other person clearly. Seeing people as they are is at the heart of all ministry, and ministry is the work of the whole Church. When was the last time we really gave ourselves to another, to see them as they truly are? Deeply listening to a person helps us to fully see them, and being seen is a crucial part of any act of healing.

Paul sees the man's need and desire and is straight in: 'Stand upright on your feet!' Bearing in mind this guy had never stood on his feet, and never walked, Paul's faith and courage is astounding, as is the man's! The man doesn't fumble his way to his feet, he jumps up and begins to walk. Paul's vision is 20:20, such that his faith is deep and rich and there is no gap between his command to the man and the man's obedient response.

Incorrect framing

The locals see this healing and see it as a divine act. So far so good; they are right. The man's healing is a divine act. Then their seeing falters, and they frame the healing quite incorrectly. They slot it into pre-existing categories they can grasp. They have a Temple to Zeus just outside the city, so they decide Barnabas is Zeus and Paul is Hermes, 'because he was the chief speaker'. It is so easy to slot experiences into pre-existent frameworks. We do it all the time. It's an exercise in assumption, which is a sign of faulty vision.

In the case of the people of Lystra, their religious framework makes gods of two men, potentially elevating them and missing the truth of the one God who acts through human agents. In our own time, how often does the Church elevate cult figures – top speakers on the circuit, musicians, writers, spiritual gurus – running the risk of worshipping them rather than the God who gives the gifts? We need to check our eyesight.

Paul's speech to them is the equivalent of giving them glasses to correct their faulty vision. He points to his ordinary mortality, and then points to God. He calls them to turn away from worthless things, to the living God. God is the creator of all things, provider of rain, crops, food and joy. Paul offers them corrective vision. The problem is, you can give people glasses but you can't make folk keep them on, and he is barely able to stop them offering sacrifice to him and Barnabas.

Things get worse as a mob from Antioch and Iconium blind the crowds to the truth. In their distorted vision they drag Paul out and stone him. Seeing him as dead, they leave him outside the city. But, their seeing is wrong again. The disciples surround Paul, and he can get up and go on to Derbe.

Restored vision

How often have we seen this? New possibility arising from seeming dead ends. Lazarus, Mary Magdalene, Peter, Paul – all seemingly facing the end, all restored, lives reframed in the resurrecting, restorative power of God.

What are you facing today? Have you limited your picture by airbrushing God out? Has despair blurred the clarity of your hope? Do we need restored vision? Jesus came to bring sight to the blind. Let's pray for clarity of sight, insight and foresight in all we are experiencing and in all we offer to our communities.

Kate Bruce

Suggested hymns

Open the eyes of my heart, Lord; God, whose almighty word; Amazing grace; Light of the world (you stepped down into darkness).

Tenth Sunday after Trinity (Proper 15) 16 August

Principal Service **Revealing Encounters**

(*Continuous*): Gen. 45.1–15; Ps. 133; *or* (*Related*): Isa. 56.1, 6–8; Ps. 67; Rom. 11.1–2a, 29–32; **Matt. 15.[10–20] 21–28**

Leicester is one of the most diverse places in the UK. Over 50 per cent identify from a faith background other than Christianity. Many of our Christians come from across the globe. Conscious of many displaced people, we have become more aware of strangers. Some find these outsiders frightening. This Gospel reminds us that, like the poor, outsiders are part of our story. How should we react?

The contours of outsiders

This vignette from Matthew is also told in Mark. Both writers place it adjacent to a discourse about purity and therefore about true belonging. This is a story about a woman who approaches Jesus directly. He is a Jewish rabbi. This is a meeting fraught with purity taboos. The story is set in Tyre and Sidon, north of Galilee in modern Lebanon. Such places beyond Jewish territory were diverse as a result of being centres of trade and travel. The woman was a Canaanite. She was a Gentile whose culture and faith was shaped by the land of her birth as a kind of 'first nation' inhabitant.

So this key encounter takes place between Jesus and a female, with a non-Jew beyond Jesus' routine territory. He is prepared to travel both physically and socially in order to meet. This woman may have been every bit as strange or frightening as some see refugees and asylum seekers in our culture. Jews and Canaanites are living adjacent, but it is Jesus who crosses over into their territory in order to have a real encounter with difference.

We may well live adjacent to people from cultures and faiths different from our own, but do we ever decide to 'cross over'? How can we help our communities have real encounters that move us beyond what we read in the media? This suggests real encounter with outsiders can be transformative.

Unexpected faith

The woman uses two surprising phrases to address this rabbi. She recognizes him as 'Son of David', so she spots his Jewish credentials (very important for Matthew) and can speak respectfully to him. This affirms his ethnic and cultural identity. In dialogue with other faiths and cultures, I invariably experience this kind of respect. Second, she uses the word 'Lord'. This is also translated as 'Messiah'. Understanding more than the so-called 'disciples', she recognizes divine authority in Jesus. She asks him to make a difference in her child's life. She recognizes that a promised future is becoming present through this encounter. This is a future that no longer is configured by the unruly forces summed up by the word 'demon'.

Faith in a diverse church

This woman is ahead of the game. Only when Jesus faces death in Jerusalem do we see the full impact of his coming and the sheer extent of his realm. The early Christians will begin to explore this as the mission extends into Gentile territory. Here this woman already recognizes the answer to which the Council of Jerusalem will attend decades later – all are welcome through faith.

We meet people on a journey of faith with complex sets of identities. I meet people who offer me insights into Jesus who are still identifiably a member of another faith. In India I have met people who are Hindus by practice but hold a more secret Christian affiliation and deep discipleship.

This encounter invites us to be attentive to the people we meet and to be prepared to have our categories about faith challenged by their witness.

Persistence

Some find the way Jesus acts to be very shocking. There is no getting out of the fact that he likens the woman to a dog that only gets the scraps. The word used for dog is diminutive, used perhaps for a household pet. Nevertheless, it is still a dog. Some people would like to airbrush this out. Hard sayings in the New Testament make the likelihood of authenticity greater. Why else would the early Church have left it there, since it unsettles the picture of a 'nice Jesus'? This woman, like so many, recognizes that she does not fully belong; yet even a scrap is better than nothing. She knows that even dogs find a place within the household.

There is something within her rising up, which not only names her needs but which fires her with persistence until she gets answers. I am forever meeting people in our asylum system caught between rocks and hard places who show me the true nature of persistence. They are outsiders like her who will not be silenced by their demons. She will not go away until she receives a sign of the future.

Conclusion

The Church is invited like Jesus to engage in unfamiliar territory with unfamiliar people. We are asked to notice who is an insider and who an outsider. We are asked to really trust that God's kingdom does extend far beyond our categories. We are invited to engage in persistent, truthful, yet even bluntly honest conversations. Despite discomfort, such encounters still reveal faith, persistence and ultimately the breaking in of the kingdom of heaven.

David Monteith

Suggested hymns

There's a wideness in God's mercy; Down the road run refugees; Brother, sister, let me serve you; When I needed a neighbor.

Tenth Sunday after Trinity (Proper 15) 16 August

Second Service Mission: God's Business, God's Church

Ps. 90 [*or* 90.1–12]; 2 Kings 4.1–37; **Acts 16.1–15**; *Gospel at Holy Communion*: John 6.51–58

Read all about it: 'Church Strengthened in Faith and Increasing in Numbers Daily'. Wouldn't that be a fantastic headline, especially when so many churches are experiencing decline and many leaders are burnt out? 'Strengthened in faith.' The Church in Acts is growing in depth as well as in numbers. It's worth reflecting on what is happening in these verses as we think about the contemporary mission of the Church.

Leaders for seasons

First, notice how God raises up leaders for seasons. Timothy, well thought of by many, is the son of a Jewish mother and a Greek father. In his genes he unites the division between the Jewish and Greek factions. He is the right leader for this particular period in the life of the church. As a pragmatic move, rather than a sell-out to legalism, Timothy is circumcised.

Where do we look for leadership in the Church? Are we open to leaders being raised up from backgrounds that might not have been expected or once accepted? Do we limit the effectiveness of the Church by limiting the pool of acceptable leaders – lay and ordained? Do we assume that leadership must look a certain way, come from the right side of the tracks? Do we allow age, gender, ethnicity, educational background, sexual orientation, looks or accent to proscribe the pool of leaders God might raise up? God raises up leaders for particular seasons in the mission of the Church. Are we guilty of getting in God's way by our assumptions about what leadership should look like? We need to be careful of turning the Church into a club for those whose faces fit.

Beware the Ministry of Bright Ideas

Second, notice how Paul and Timothy are listening to the Spirit's guidance about where they should and should not focus their efforts. They can't be everywhere and do everything. Perhaps the Church that is exhausted from a huge programme of bright ideas might find instruction here. The Holy Spirit forbids them to speak the word in Asia, and the Spirit of Jesus doesn't allow them to go into Bithynia. Then there's the vision of the man from Macedonia asking them to come and help them. To say yes to the right things means saying no to other things to release energy and resource. Paul and Timothy are deeply attuned to God. How often do we head off down a path that seems like a good idea, without having sought God's guidance? Successful mission is a work of God. There is comfort here. It is not about our efforts alone, we are not left to our own devices and we don't have to do everything, or say 'yes' to everything. That way burn-out lies.

Genuine inclusiveness

Third, notice how God builds the church in Acts. He draws in people from different cultural backgrounds and different economic backgrounds. This is not a church for men. Full stop. Or a church for the poor. Full stop. Or a church for Jewish converts. Full stop. There is no full stop, more a divine plus sign. In Philippi, Paul and Timothy go and speak to women gathered by the river, at a place of prayer. It's remarkable that Paul, given his background as a strict Jew, is willing to tear down previous assumptions and approach these women. In a culture where women are way down in the pecking order, this is a remarkable sign of the inclusive nature of God's Church. Notice too that Lydia is a wealthy businesswoman, running a business dealing in purple cloth. Today she'd be the equivalent of a CEO. You don't get to be a dealer in cloth without being smart. This wealthy, intelligent woman is drawn to Paul's message, because, Luke tells us, God opened her heart. She and her household are baptized. In return, she opened her home to Paul and Barnabas. Generous and faithful, Lydia. God's Church should be a remarkable tapestry of variety, with a place for all. In Acts we see God drawing together rich and poor, Greek and Jew, men and women. There is a radical freedom here, and a genuine inclusiveness. Full stop.

Openness, discernment and inclusion

Our reading today offers us food for thought as we reflect on the mission of the contemporary Church: God raises leaders for seasons in the mission of the Church. Do we get in the way of God's choice of leaders by erecting barriers based on our internal assumptions of worth and suitability?

Do we set off on mission schemes without asking God first? Are we overburdened by the ministry of good ideas and therefore doing too much of the wrong things? Is it time to start saying no?

Are we genuinely open to being a church that crosses societal and cultural boundaries in welcoming all people, or do we want to belong to a cosy club of people like us?

If we want to see the Church growing in faith and numbers there is much worth pondering in this passage from Acts: openness to a range of people in leadership, discernment in focus, and radical inclusiveness.

Kate Bruce

Suggested hymns

Let us build a house where love can dwell; The Church's one foundation; She sits like a bird brooding on the waters; In Christ there is no east or west.

Eleventh Sunday after Trinity (Proper 16)
23 August
Principal Service **What Future for the Church?**

(*Continuous*): Ex. 1.8—2.10; Ps. 124; *or* (*Related*): Isa. 51.1–6; Ps. 138; Rom. 12.1–8; **Matt. 16.13–20**

Today's Gospel has unwittingly given rise to all those jokes about Peter and the pearly gates. One of my favourites was the story of Ian Paisley getting to the pearly gates, and being asked by St Peter why he should be let into the kingdom. Ian Paisley replies, 'I've kept the Protestant faith.' 'Yes, but what else have you done?' says Peter. 'I marched down O'Connell Street in Dublin with the Union Jack.' 'When was that?' Peter asked. 'Two minutes ago!'

Church

Well, before we look at Peter's role, we need to backtrack, because Jesus tells Peter that he is the rock on which Jesus will build his Church. Did Jesus intend to found a church? Alfred Loisy famously said that 'Jesus preached the kingdom and it was the Church that came'. Matthew's Gospel alone of the Gospels makes a direct reference to the church, twice using the word *ecclēsia*, and so it's been dubbed the ecclesiastical Gospel, the Gospel most beloved by Roman Catholics, for its emphasis on the Church and on discipline and order. Some argue that if Jesus was expecting the coming of the kingdom in his lifetime, there would be no need of a church and that accounts for the paucity of allusions to it in the Gospels. But, at least by the time he wrote his Gospel, Matthew was convinced of the necessity for the church in the purpose of God.

What church endures?

The church envisaged by Matthew was very different from the great, bulky, bureaucratic, hippopotamus figure, as T. S. Eliot called it, that we know today. If Peter is a rock, then the church is living stones. It isn't a building, but an assembly; not a thing, but an event; not a place to visit, but a community to belong to; the community gathers around Jesus, and to Matthew Jesus matters decisively. The promise Jesus makes is that the church will endure and that 'the gates of Hades will not prevail against it'. This may seem unlikely in the face of the decline of church attendance in the UK. But it is not a claim for the numerical size of the church – not that my church, our church, will continue unchanged. It's a claim that the 'living stones' that gather faithfully around Jesus will remain the witness of God to the world.

Gatekeeper: keys and rope

Peter is entrusted with a responsible role in the new ecclesia. He is the gatekeeper who holds the keys. His authority is not for the afterlife but for oversight of the infant church. And so the keys are not to the gate to control admission, but to the storehouse to enable him to make provision for the household. Peter isn't there to block access, and so far from excluding people it was he who felt God's pressure to open the gates to the Gentiles.

But as well as keys, there is the image of rope. It's not for tying people up. Nor need it be about the right to forgive sins. It's most likely to be about issues being tied up or loosened. Peter is being entrusted to know when to constrain people and when to let them go, when to shape the church along well-worn paths and when to set it free to explore boundless possibilities in the life of the Spirit.[29] The decisions taken by Peter were not just underwritten by heaven. Peter is promised divine guidance, so that decisions taken are in accord with decisions already made in heaven.

Binding and loosing

Our deep divisions in the Church come down to binding and loosing. One group argues that the Church is doing too much binding, expecting people to believe and to live in a certain way. Others claim that the Church is doing too much loosing and that it's time that people were bound to more rigid beliefs and conduct. The answer to that issue relates to the purpose for the Church and especially to who Jesus is.

'Who do you say that I (Jesus) am?' Peter trotted out a formulaic reply, but we have each to answer for ourselves. One answer given by a church leader sounds refreshing and accurate: 'You are the epicentre of the universe, the purpose of creation, the meaning of existence, the bond that joins humanity to God forever.'[30] It's our vocation to say who we believe Christ is. It's our Church's vocation to help us to learn and know who Jesus is and then to provide the safe space where we can practise voicing our convictions and hammering out our beliefs. And we do so in the assurance that the Church will not cease until the gospel is known in all the world.

Roger Spiller

Suggested hymns

The Church of God a kingdom is; Thou art the Christ, O Lord; There's a wideness in God's mercy; Forth in the peace of Christ we go.

Eleventh Sunday after Trinity (Proper 16)

23 August

Second Service **Evangelism: Why Can't We Just Be a Bit More Normal?**

Ps. 95; 2 Kings 6.8–23; **Acts 17.15–end**; *Gospel at Holy Communion*: John 6.56–69

Evangelism. How do you respond to that word? I was chatting with a friend about this recently. We imagined writing a book called 'Evangelism: Why Can't We Just Be a Bit More Normal?' The fantasy title stems from our reflections that somehow evangelism often feels forced and awkward. Instead of making our hearts sing, it made our toes curl as we shared memories of forced, unnatural, intense conversations and events. I have listened to some gospel presentations that made me feel I was being bullied into the arms of a loving God: believe in God or else he'll get you. This sounds rather like Bad News to me.

Welcome to Athens

Paul's visit to Athens in Acts 17 offers much to ponder on the theme of faith sharing. We find him on the tourist trail, taking in Athens, a city of culture with a rich heritage. This is the city of Socrates, Plato and Aristotle: a metropolis for the intelligentsia. This is a city of hot debate, full of the latest ideas. Welcome to Athens.

Paul gets a feel for the place, and his feelings are pretty distressed. The place is chock full of statues to this, that and the other god – gold, silver, ivory, marble – statues, temples, shrines. Paul is angry, irritated, shaken. What does he do? He begins to talk, to build relationships and to make connections. He goes where the people are, to the religious folk in the synagogue, to the marketplace where he talks to passers-by. He speaks with people who think God is distant and uninterested (the Epicureans) and to people who think God expresses himself in all kinds of forms (Stoics). He even gets an invitation to speak before the council of the great and the good of Athens – known as the Areopagus. He's hooked people's interest, in the church, the marketplace and the academy.

When he speaks at the Areopagus, he doesn't tell them how bad they are. He addresses them with knowledge and respect, and not a little canny flattery. 'Athenians, I see how extremely religious you are.' Who could resist an opener like that? He builds on what he has seen, using the altar to an unknown God as a way of connecting with them. 'Let me tell you a bit about this unknown God'. . . and away he goes.

Engaging with the God-thinking

Paul engages with the God-thinking going on around him. What kind of God-thinking is going on around us? We might encounter: atheism (that's a kind of God-thinking); lack of interest – thinking God doesn't matter; anger – if God is so loving why did this happen? Curiosity – what's the meaning of life? Interest – do you really believe that? Let's open our ears, tune in to what people say about God and join in the conversation.

When Paul addresses the view point of the Epicureans (those who think God is distant and uninterested) he uses the lyrics from their own poetry to help his argument: 'In him we live and move and have our being' and 'we too are his offspring'. Paul uses the cultural landscape of the Athenians to connect with them. What can we learn from this? Big questions resonate out from contemporary films, books, songs, the news – let's join in the conversation.

Back to Paul's speech: he doesn't duck out of the difficult bits in his faith sharing. He refers to the resurrection, which is scandalous to reason, an offence to many. Some scoffed, but some were intrigued and wanted to hear more, and some believed. His attempts at connecting are not wasted. They never are.

Mission to the church, marketplace and academy

Paul speaks about God in the church, the marketplace and the academy. How do we take the opportunities to do just that? Talking about God in the Church is perhaps easiest as we are generally among people of faith. But let's beware the tendency to live split lives – God in church but not at work or around the dinner table. Let's not be churchy people, but God's people.

What for us is the marketplace? The pub? The gym perhaps, the mums and tots group, school, an evening class? There are all kinds of contenders. Do we ever speak of God in these places?

How about faith sharing in the academy – the contemporary Areopagus – in the places of learning. Let's pray for our schoolteachers and lecturers, especially for professors in theology departments, and students in schools, colleges and universities – for the courage and wisdom, strength and gentleness to speak of God.

Invite hearts to sing

'Evangelism: Why Can't We Just Be a Bit More Normal?' – I doubt the book will ever be written, but if it was it would look at how Paul speaks of God through his personality, his intelligence, his experiences. It would ask us to think about our God-talk in church, in the marketplace and in the academy. It would take inspiration from Paul's boldness, and from the way he makes connections between the gospel and culture – without gimmicks, or high-pressure spiels. It would reflect on how Paul's God-talk flows out of his life lived with God, loving God – natural, powerful and real. Let's speak of God not in ways that curl the toes but in cadences that invite hearts to sing.

Kate Bruce

Suggested hymns

Come, people of the risen King; Shout to the north; All people that on earth do dwell; Be thou my vision.

Twelfth Sunday after Trinity (Proper 17) 30 August

Principal Service **St Paul's Tweets**

(*Continuous*): Ex. 3.1–15; Ps. 105.1–6, 23–26, 45b, *or* Ps. 115; *or* (*Related*): Jer. 15.15–21; Ps. 26.1–8; **Rom. 12.9–end**; Matt. 16.21–end

St Paul would have been entirely at ease sending tweets. He naturally condenses his thinking into short memorable phrases. Not for him the 280-character limit of Twitter – he could get below that limit quite easily, as you can see in the text chosen for this sermon.

The curious and troubling thing about this particular technology is that while it is undoubtedly useful for sending brief messages might it be having the long-term effect of harming our human capacity for creating long and thoughtful pieces of writing?

The growth of Big Brother

It isn't just Twitter that we need to be aware of. More and more articles are appearing in the press highlighting the gigantic power of some of the world's major technology companies and raising ethical questions about their behaviour. Some of those companies, for example, have wealth that far exceeds the wealth of small nation-states and yet they do not appear to have robust systems of accountability, nor are they subject to much regulation – though that appears to be gradually changing. One of the results of this technology is that as these companies harvest more and more data about all of us, their power grows. Big Brother is getting bigger and bigger and more and more intrusive and exploitative. These companies understand in considerable detail what our consumerist needs and desires are and work closely with advertisers to ensure that we are ever more precisely targeted.

If you don't believe this, try a little experiment. Type the name and model of a car into Google and see how long it is before advertisements about that particular car appear on your screen. It will probably be within minutes, if not seconds.

Does this combination of speed and intrusiveness mean that our humanity is gradually being redefined? We are in danger (aren't we?) of becoming unthinking machines programmed just to consume. As a result, the consumerist engine revolves at faster and faster speeds because our wants are constantly in a state of frenzied and heightened distraction and can only be satisfied by our possession of the latest gizmo. And ironically, the latest gizmo soon becomes obsolete and we want an even later model.

'I did it my way'

The powerful belief that underlies all of this is that it is only our individuality with its needs and desires that matters. 'I did it my way' is our anthem and our credo.

One of the disturbing consequences, as Umberto Eco has written in his book *Chronicles of a Liquid Society*, is that our default position is to be indignant; we are indignant about anything that harms or limits our individualism. Then, to make matters worse, we discover on Twitter or Facebook, or one of the other social media platforms, that there are countless others who feel exactly as we do. Indignation and discontent grow in an incoherent, chaotic and unstructured way – and who can foretell the social results?

This is not a plea to turn the clock back. That is impossible anyway. Nor is this an anguished cry from the heart of a Luddite, but the issues are ones about which we need to be aware. Our society, our politics and our culture are under intense and massive onslaught.

Is there an answer?

So what is to be done?

The first thing is to take a deep breath, stand back for a while from the onslaught, and with our neighbours, friends and colleagues in church consider whether the analysis offered in this sermon has any truth within it.

We should be quite good at this because our churches are perhaps the only publically accessible places left in society where careful reflection is part of the way we do things. But we need consciously to practise our reflective skills, not least because our churches can themselves be seduced into thinking that modish relevance is all that is needed.

Second, we might want to reflect on what it means to be a disparate group of people who nevertheless choose to worship together on a regular basis and who share a common prayer that begins with the words 'Our Father'. In other words, in spite of all our failures, we do try, under the grace of God, to create some sense of community not only with each other but with our wider society. We do not buy into the rampant individualism of our world for we believe that it is in our relationships with each other that the purpose and meaning of our human lives can be discovered.

Third, we have a gospel and a set of teachings delivered to us by our Lord that ensure that our eyes and hearts are focused not simply on the things of this world but on eternal values and upon words like 'grace' and 'forgiveness' and 'compassion' and 'hope' and 'truth'.

We are so richly blessed by God, do we not have a duty therefore to listen deeply to the concerns of our neighbours and together with them share some of our thinking and insights so that our world can become a less restless and a more healing place?

Christopher Herbert

Suggested hymns

Dear Lord and Father of mankind; The peace of Christ comes close; We have a gospel to proclaim; Forth in thy name.

Twelfth Sunday after Trinity (Proper 17) 30 August

Second Service 'Do not be afraid, for I am with you'

Ps. 105.1–15; 2 Kings 6.24–25; 7.3–end; **Acts 18.1–16**; *Gospel at Holy Communion*: Mark 7.1–8, 14–15, 21–23

Paul is a man who has experienced terrific hardship. He has been flogged, stoned, insulted, vilified, accused and imprisoned. We don't often think of him as a man who knew fear. He seems such a spiritual black belt! In this passage he boldly opposes those who revile him and therefore the message of the gospel, declaring, 'Your blood be on your own heads! I am innocent. From now on I will go to the Gentiles.' Many in the community in and around the synagogue do come to faith. Paul seems, at least externally, to be bold, strong, successful and fearless. However, the divine word to Paul suggests a different picture may have been going on in Paul's inner world. Externally, he is the confident man of God, but internally what is going on? His night-time vision seems to infer that he is experiencing the temptation to adopt a pragmatic silence, fear of spiritual abandonment, and fear of physical attack. God says to Paul: 'Do not be afraid, but speak and do not be silent; for I am with you, and no one will lay a hand on you to harm you, for there are many in this city who are my people.'

God's words are never random, so it seems reasonable to see this message as speaking into turmoil going on within Paul. Into this maelstrom, God encircles Paul with words of deep comfort and reassurance.

'Do not be afraid'

Frequently, in the Scriptures we read of God telling people not to be afraid. In Isaiah 43.1–2 the Lord instructs Israel not to fear because he has summoned them by name and promises to be with them in difficulties: when they pass through water or fire they will neither be swept away nor burned. A cursory glance through the Scriptures will find many references to God's instruction not to be afraid. Perhaps the most well-known example of this comes in Luke's Gospel, when the angel Gabriel speaks into Mary's troubled state with the words, 'Do not be afraid.' These examples, from Isaiah, Luke and Acts, present situations in which, humanly speaking, there is very good reason to fear. Water is a metaphor for chaos, and no one wants to be up to their neck in that; fire has a nasty habit of burning; an unmarried, expectant woman could expect to be stoned to death; and Paul's enemies have previous form for violence. There may well be trouble ahead. God's assurance and presence, and the call not to fear, does not magic away the danger.

Paul could have been forgiven for thinking, 'Here we go again, another kicking coming my way.' The risk of physical harm is real; this time Sosthenes the synagogue official takes the brunt of it, as we read if we venture beyond the end of today's passage.

God in the boat with us

God's reassurance comes into the midst of a genuinely dangerous situation. The divine word does bring promise of protection for Paul, but it also seeks to alter his perception. So often we want God to take away the source of our fears, be that illness, loneliness or hostility in whatever form. The human response is quite understandable: 'God, please fix this.' However, the divine call of encouragement generally does not fix the immediate problem we face. It does not come and transport us into a Pollyanna-ish Utopia. Rather, it comes as a reminder that God is in the boat with us. Sometimes the storms are calmed and sometimes they rage around us – but whatever, God is a present reality within the trouble. Paul, we can infer from God's word, was considering shutting up shop, yet he stays in Corinth faithfully teaching the word of God among the people, for a further year and a half. He faces hostility, and opposition, he is hauled before the proconsul, Gallio, and accused. Gallio dismisses the complaint as a matter of Jewish law, but Paul still has to face the trouble and stress of accusation and dissension.

So often, when we face recurrent problems, opposition, ill health and so on, we want God to come and heal by taking away the source of pain and discomfort. Yet, God does not often lift us away from our troubles; rather, he strengthens us to journey through them with him. The things that we are afraid of are relocated against the broad backdrop of God's loving presence. The situations often don't change, but we do. Paul is not whisked away and promised a trouble-free future. He is reminded that he is not alone; God is with him and there are people of God around him.

The divine presence brings protection to Paul, in the sense that on this occasion he does not receive physical abuse. Yet, he is still in a hostile situation. The reminder of God's presence, the call not to fear, gives him the strength to keep on keeping on, and he stays a further year and a half.

God does not promise to inoculate us against trouble. He does not helicopter in to airlift us out of the struggles we face. The word is 'Do not be afraid, for I am with you.' I AM is with you. We are called to relocate our fears and struggles against the backdrop of God's intimate and loving presence. Amen.

Kate Bruce

Suggested hymns

Do not be afraid (for I have redeemed you); Change my heart, O Lord; Through all the changing scenes of life; The Lord's my shepherd.

Thirteenth Sunday after Trinity (Proper 18)
6 September
Principal Service **Binding and Loosing**

(*Continuous*): Ex. 12.1–14; Ps. 149; *or* (*Related*): Ezek. 33.7–11; Ps. 119.33–40; Rom. 13.8–end; **Matt. 18.15–20**

'Binding and loosing': the keys of the kingdom given to Peter in Matthew chapter 16 and then, in today's Gospel, to all disciples. As Christians, we all have authority from Jesus to bind and to loosen: to hold things together and to let things go. This is how we should live together as a Christian community. Today's Gospel is not a discipline manual for excommunicating those causing bother. It's important to remember that before this passage comes the exhortation to become like children in order to enter the kingdom; not to be a stumbling block for others; that God searches for the lost sheep and receives it with joy – and then following our passage the reminder to Peter that forgiveness is limitless: seventy times seven.

Binding

In that light, how is it that we are to hold together? What binding should happen for loving community to grow? Jesus says that if anyone sins against us, we are to go privately to that person and point out the fault. We are not to grumble, we are not to sulk or nurse grudges. We are not to undermine each other. We are not to set up factions and power bases – alienating those we find difficult. Our first step is to attempt reconciliation privately. Then, if that fails, we are to take others with us to try again. The whole Church should work together to turn someone around – working at listening to one another. This passage has Jesus say 'listen' four times in quick succession. If none of that works, says Jesus, then that person becomes like a Gentile or a tax-collector – someone who needs extra care – who needs to go back to basics with God. Sometimes reconciliation isn't possible and we have to let people walk away for them to find new life in Christ in a new place. Binding is about holding things together. Books are bound so that all the pages remain in the right order. Bias binding is sown on to seams so that fabric doesn't fray under stress. Binding for the Christian is not about handcuffing the enemy: Christ has done that already. We are to bind ourselves and one another to Jesus – being in loving covenant with God who has bound himself to us – through the creation of the world, through the incarnation, death and resurrection of Christ, and through the sending of the Holy Spirit. In the words of St Patrick, 'I bind unto myself today the strong name of the Trinity.'

Loosing

Loosing is about liberation – about letting things go and setting people free. Tackling disputes in a mature Christian way, we dare to do things differently from our natural inclinations. We can break the circles of violence, revenge and stored-up animosity. We set people free to start again just as God has set us free. The crucified Christ takes the sins of the world to liberate creation into full and loving relationship with God. In Ezekiel, God says that he does not want to destroy the wicked – or fight evil with evil – but he longs for people to turn from their wickedness and live. When we loosen someone, we give them space to be themselves. We remove all that shackles them, and they are free. Those chains might be fear, anger, grief, envy, poverty, ignorance, discrimination, oppression – any number of forces that besiege people, both within and without.

Liberating people means they are truly free to walk away if they choose. The good news of the Christian faith declares that God loves everyone and calls and longs for them to be where they can live life in all its fullness. God desires a loving, flourishing, faithful humanity, and the Christian community is called to model this to the world.

Christ before us

Jesus took as his manifesto Isaiah's words about binding up the broken hearted and setting the captives free: 'binding and loosing'. St Paul urges us to 'put on the Lord Jesus Christ'. Clothing ourselves in Christ reminds us to take up responsibility for binding and loosing – being part of the transforming work of Christ in the world. In Greek, Matthew 18.18 reads: 'whatever you bind on earth is already bound in heaven and whatever you loose on earth is already loosed in heaven'. We are called to mirror on earth the wholeness and healing of heaven. So then – how shall we bind ourselves closer to one another, to the world, to God? What bridges can we build? What reconciliation do we need to initiate? What can we hold together that is falling apart? How can we bind people closer to Christ? What might we each do to liberate another? What do we need to let go of for flourishing to happen? The Eucharist binds us to Christ. The Eucharist loosens us to be God's agents in the world. Go then in the power of the Holy Spirit to bind and to loosen on earth that which is already bound and loosened in heaven. Amen.

Catherine Williams

Suggested hymns

I bind unto myself today; Bind us together, Lord; All my hope on God is founded; As we are gathered.

Thirteenth Sunday after Trinity (Proper 18)
6 September
Second Service **The Spirit's Insider Work**

Ps. 108 [115]; Ezek. 12.21—13.16; **Acts 19.1–20**; *Gospel at Holy Communion*: Mark 7.24–end

'Did you receive the Holy Spirit when you became believers?' is the surprising question St Paul asked of some 'disciples'. A poll across the American nation concluded that there is no such thing as the Holy Spirit. And six out of ten 'born again' Christians concluded that the Holy Spirit is a symbol of God's presence and power but is not a living entity. So, perhaps St Paul's question isn't so strange after all. He spoke to people whom he expected to be disciples of Jesus and they replied: 'No, we have not even heard that there is a Holy Spirit.' They soon had, with Paul's instruction and after receiving baptism in the name of Jesus.

The inward zone

The Spirit can seem like a shadowy figure and, like its cognate 'spirituality', gives little indication of its identity. In reality, that is bound to be how it seems because the Spirit functions hidden in the recesses of our lives, like God's secret agent, persuading, nudging, interpreting. His particular zone of activity is inward, contrasting with the 'alongsideness' of Jesus' incarnate life and the 'aboveness' or 'transcendence' of the Father's natural ambit.

Law internalized

The Spirit fulfils the glorious promise that the new covenant will be written on the heart, that indeed there will be a new heart, and that the law 'of the Spirit of life' will 'set us free from the law of sin and death'. In other words, the Spirit internalizes the law and covenant, which would otherwise have continued to be an unnatural and external reference point, powered by self-will and heroic effort.

Words to speak

In keeping with the inwardness of the Spirit, Jesus promises his disciples that the Spirit will give them the words to speak when facing opposition and trial. And even when the words they speak are their own, the Spirit promises empowerment and anointing, so as to speak boldly and truthfully. We see in the book of Acts how Peter and John speak boldly, whereas only days before they received the gift they were tongue-tied by fear. It is but an extension of this to recognize the Spirit's activity in directing the route of travel for missionaries. When the Spirit did take control over the missionary operation from

Peter, John or Paul, they experienced a commanding force that they were in no position to overrule, however much they were tempted to do so. We too may seek and sometimes discover a clear sense of the path we ought to follow, or at least the path we should avoid.

Spirit and baptism

Anyone who has been baptized in his name has received the Spirit. St Paul said that 'no one can say "Jesus is Lord" except by the Holy Spirit'. It can be said as a mantra, but the confession is so awesome that it's hard to imagine it getting across the lips of anyone who has not received the Spirit and is not a Christian. The Spirit is sometimes called the Spirit of Jesus, as he is the Spirit of God, for he is present not on his own account but to witness and represent the life of Jesus. When the physical presence of Jesus was withdrawn from us, the Spirit of Jesus ensured the continuing presence of Jesus. That can be more real than the Jesus who was limited by space and time. He's the invasive force who works to bring Jesus Christ to us, by making him real and interpreting afresh his teaching in our changed situation.

Gospel and Spirit

If we ask how the Spirit comes to us, one answer would be that he comes through the word of the gospel. The gospel and Spirit are inseparable, so that to receive the gospel is synonymous with receiving the Spirit. The Spirit comes to us not only when we receive the gospel. He comes to us to enable us to receive it. The faith by which we hear is itself a gift of the Spirit in the gospel.

Family likeness and glorious liberty

And what can we expect of his presence within us? We can answer in two ways. The work of the Spirit is to effect our rebirth or adoption so as to become children of God, born by his Spirit, who is at work to create the family resemblance in our lives. The other is compatible with this. The Spirit is to rescue and restore our true nature and glory, which our alienation from the Father has obscured and which has been defaced by the homogenizing effect of sin. As the monk Harry Williams put it, 'the chief work of the Holy Spirit is to reconcile what I think I am with what I really am, what I think I believe with what I really feel; to liberate what fear compels me to suffocate . . . to introduce this very me to the glorious liberty of the children of God.'[31]

Roger Spiller

Suggested hymns

Come down, O love divine; All together in one place; Come, Holy Spirit, come!; There's a spirit in the air.

Fourteenth Sunday after Trinity (Proper 19)
13 September
Principal Service **Lightning Strikes Twice**

(*Continuous*): Ex. 14.19–end; Ps. 114, *or Canticle*: Ex. 15.1b–11, 20–21; *or* (*Related*): Gen. 50.15–21; Ps. 103.1–13 [*or* 103.8–13]; Rom. 14.1–12; **Matt. 18.21–35**

They say lightning never strikes twice. John Rogers knew better. Everyone said how amazingly he had coped with redundancy. It is no easy task to begin again, aged 55, after a lifetime working for the same company. With a lightness of heart, he sank all his redundancy money into his new enterprise. If his wife thought it foolhardy, she didn't say so. Just a few said, 'What an idiot to blow it all, he'll be bankrupt in a year', though never to his face.

He rented a unit at the new Craft Park, one of those out-of-town shopping sites with a large car park, a cafe and a play area for the kids. The unit was really an elaborate shed, one of about thirty on the site. Equipping it with tools, buying in wood and creating a display and sales area took all his cash, but it didn't matter. What was important was that he could now make things. His speciality: wooden toys. Sometimes very traditional things – rocking horses, the grain of the wood dictating the racing shape of the animal. Sometimes new things that seemed strange as wooden toys—alien space creatures that came apart, and docking satellite stations with flashing lights.

The business advice woman at the bank said his margins weren't large enough. He was covering his costs and making enough to live on – just – but he'd never be able to expand, and if supplies and sales got too out of kilter he'd have cash-flow problems. He nodded and made some encouraging noises, but in his heart he didn't care. He was making things. He was happy, perhaps the happiest he'd been in his whole life.

Fire!

The arson attack was so mindless. A teenager fooling about, oblivious to just how paint, wood and varnish would blaze. He was a lad newly come to the area, in a foster home to prepare him for life on his own. John knew nothing of him. He was pleased that the magistrate thought the matter so serious; pleased that the sullen youth got a custodial sentence. But that didn't make up for what he'd lost; somehow all his motivation had gone up in flames.

The insurance company paid out. The site manager was efficient in the rebuilding of the unit. Customers urged him on. But as the smell of the burning lingered about the place, so did the dead weight of John's wounding. It was as if the fire had burnt from him all the enjoyment he'd once had. He was a victim, and he couldn't shake it off.

And sure enough the business began to fail. His toys didn't have the same originality about them any more. The first Christmas after the fire John just got by. The second Christmas was a disaster. 'It'll not survive,' they said. 'It was obvious from the first that it wasn't a sensible thing to do with his redundancy money.'

He really lost it!

The last thing people expected was that he would take on staff: a young fella called Andy with a beard and a pony tail, a ring in his nose and in one of his ears. No one knew where John found him. It was all so unlikely; another indication that John had really lost it.

How surprised the scoffers were when the business started to turn around. Andy had a talent for working wood, and John was soon able to build on it. Teaching Andy rekindled his enthusiasm. For the first time for two years he had ideas for new toys.

And Andy brought something new to the business as well. Computers were his thing. Before joining John, he'd been on an intensive course and he put his learning to good use. When their work featured in a Sunday supplement, orders started to come thick and fast. They started selling from their own website. The woman at the bank was impressed. 'The business has turned a corner,' she said. When people asked John, 'Are you thinking of retiring?', 'Never' was the reply.

Lightning strikes twice!

But lightning can strike twice. The lad who broke into the workshop was after the computer. Why then did he smash the rest of the place up? Wrecking the stock, smashing the lathe, throwing customer files everywhere, and pouring varnish over the lot. The police seemed to know who he was, but there wasn't enough proof to arrest him. 'We'll start again. There's nothing here that a few weeks' effort won't put to rights.' But John's optimism found no echo in Andy. The younger man burned with anger.

John had no idea how Andy knew who the suspect was. He had no idea either of the revenge he intended. It wasn't until the police came to tell him that Andy was charged and in the cells that he knew anything was going on. Andy had followed the suspect to a local pub, cornered him in the toilets, and beaten him until an arm and a nose were broken.

Minutes after the police left, John put the notice on the door. It simply said, 'Closed down'. With a heavy heart he turned off the lights and locked his workshop for the last time.

A few days later the site manager came to see him. 'Don't you realize how much money you're going to lose giving up the lease without notice? The business has got such prospects, why end it now? You recovered after the fire, you can recover now.' And sensing the real cause of John's hurt, he added, 'Surely the court will take into account why Andy did it? They'll be lenient with him. After all, it was his first offence.'

'No, not his first,' said John. 'He's already served time for arson.'

Jesus ended his story, 'In his anger his lord handed [his servant] over to be tortured until he should pay his entire debt.' And he added, 'So my heavenly Father will also do to every one of you, if you do not forgive your brother or sister from your heart.'

Christopher Burkett

Suggested hymns

Forgive our sins as we forgive; Dear Lord and Father of mankind; Just as I am, without one plea; Who can sound the depths of sorrow.

Fourteenth Sunday after Trinity (Proper 19)

13 September

Second Service **A Fond Farewell**

Ps. 119.41–48 [49–64]; Ezek. 20.1–8, 33–44; **Acts 20.17–end**; *Gospel at Holy Communion*: Mark 8.27–end

Can you remember a time when you had to say goodbye to someone inspirational, whom you might never see again? Perhaps it was a teacher at school, a minister, a work colleague, or a relative. Do you remember that last meeting and what it was like to bid them farewell? I can remember getting very upset when I left primary school, knowing that chapter was over. It's also very difficult to leave a parish when you've lived among people for years and worked closely with them – it can be hard too for parishioners to let go of their clergy and move into God's future, working with a new minister. We have the luxury of phone and email today: easy and swift communication. In the ancient world it was much harder to keep in touch.

Remember

In our reading from Acts, Paul is taking his leave of the church elders at Ephesus. He and Luke are making their way to Jerusalem, hoping to be there for the festival of Pentecost. From there Paul is planning to go to Rome and then Spain – fulfilling the Lord's command to take the gospel to 'the ends of the earth'. Paul doesn't expect to come to the eastern Mediterranean again – so this really is goodbye. In fact, he hasn't come back to Ephesus – he's taken the route from Troas to Miletus and is waiting 30 miles south of Ephesus to meet with the church elders: the pastoral leadership team. Paul delivers his farewell speech. All Paul's other speeches in the book of Acts are evangelistic outreach or legal defence – this is the only one given to a Christian community. He urges the elders to remember the time he has spent with them, establishing the Ephesian church – teaching and preaching: everything to everyone, everywhere. He has served with humility, energy, commitment and without pay, supporting himself by making tents. His ministry has been faithful in public and private, and all of it in the name of Jesus Christ.

Watch for wolves

Paul's final words to the Ephesian elders are an encouragement and a warning. There are tough times ahead. They are to keep watch – first over themselves and then over the flock. Good pastors take care of themselves: praying, growing, learning and resting. The elders can have confidence that they have been given oversight by the Holy Spirit, but they are to remember always that every member of the flock is precious to God and has been bought with the blood of Jesus. We still use these words and images at ordination services today. Paul tells the elders to keep watch for wolves – who are out to savage the flock. Ephesus was a very powerful and wealthy city with many cults and a deep focus on magic. Even today if you visit the ruins you get a sense of a very powerful place – with marble pavements and vast buildings to a variety of gods and goddesses. Paul had made enemies with his preaching and teaching: there were many who would have liked to destroy the Ephesian church. Paul warns that the wolves don't just come from outside – they can come from inside the flock too, distorting the truth, or picking arguments over secondary matters, blowing everyone off course. And this is exactly what happened. In chapter two of the book of Revelation the message given by the angel to the church in Ephesus praises their patient endurance but chastises them for abandoning their first love. It's a warning for us too. Are we in danger of spending so much time taking sides over various issues that we neglect our love and worship of Jesus and our service to others in his name? What is our 'first love'?

Onwards

Finally, Paul shares his future with the Ephesians. The Holy Spirit is calling him onwards and he knows that hardship, persecution and prison await him – but he is compelled to keep going: to complete the race and finish the task. He knows he is not coming back. They all kneel and pray together, hug and kiss one another and take Paul to his ship – it must have been a very tearful farewell. The Ephesians have said goodbye to their mentor and friend – they must rely on the Holy Spirit from now on: to counsel, to guide and to lead them into grace and truth. There are many more adventures for Paul ahead. Once he gets to Jerusalem he will be arrested and then, as prophesied by Jesus in Matthew 10.18, he will be brought before governors and kings: Festus, Felix, Agrippa. He will eventually make it to Rome – but only after spending years in custody, getting shipwrecked in the Mediterranean and being bitten by a Maltese viper. It's a gripping story – if you don't know it, read from Acts chapter 21 onwards to find out what happens.

The Christian journey is rarely dull. What adventures is God calling you to? Trust the Holy Spirit to guide and lead you – watch for wolves and hold on tightly to your first love! Go with Paul's exhortation ringing in your ears: 'I commend you to God and to the message of his grace, a message that is able to build you up and to give you the inheritance among all who are sanctified.'

Catherine Williams

Suggested hymns

Forth in thy name, O Lord, I go; One more step along the world; For all the saints; Go forth and tell.

Fifteenth Sunday after Trinity (Proper 20)
20 September

Principal Service **Incongruous Grace**

(*Continuous*): Ex. 16.2–15; Ps. 105.1–6, 37–end [*or* 105.37–end]; *or* (*Related*): Jonah 3.10—end of 4; Ps. 145.1–8; Phil. 1.21–end; **Matt. 20.1–16**

The action happens at the wages office as the workers line up. Most of us have waited to be paid, perhaps after undertaking seasonal or vocational work, where the pay was less clear than it might be. Or perhaps as children, we've done little jobs for friends and family and have made our own calculation as to what we might hope to be paid, based upon previous experience.

Justice for some, generosity for others

In the parable, those who had worked for only the last hour or two of the day were called first to the pay checkout. They expected to receive a proportion of the usual wage and were therefore surprised to receive instead a full day's wage. We know only that those who had worked a full day from early morning, facing the heat and physical exertion, received the usual pay that had been agreed beforehand. We're not told what the other three groups, hired at intervals between the two, received but it makes no difference to the story. The day workers received justice, as they were promised. The workers who were enlisted at the end of the day received not justice but generosity. Equal pay for unequal work hardly seemed fair to those who had worked hard in the heat of the day. Was there a more acceptable outcome, we ask ourselves? What could the landowner have done differently? What other choices could he have made?

Justice for all

The most obvious strategy was to pay everyone in proportion to the time they spent at work. That at least was what the day workers had expected and agreed with their employer. That would have been fair and be seen to be fair to all parties, including those who were the last recruits to be employed. It would have been fair and been seen as acceptable to both parties and avoided resentment that groups were treated unequally.

Generosity congruent with effort for all

The landowner, having decided to pay the full daily rate to those who had worked only for the last few hours of the day, might, instead, have given a proportionate increase to all the workers, even to those who worked for the whole day. That would have seemed generous as well as fair to all, since all workers would be rewarded for the amount of work they had done and treated generously as well. Those who had worked only for a few hours would have felt compensated for the shame and indignity they had suffered waiting around anxiously for work. And it would have given them some financial security to set against further risk of unemployment in the days ahead. Reward would still be linked to effort and achievement but it would also show unexpected generosity to all the workers, not only to a few.

With two options to act fairly and generously, while avoiding any grounds for complaint or resentment, why did the landowner act in the way he did and trigger resentment? He was, of course, mirroring the kingdom of heaven and not contributing to the theory and practice of industrial relations. But what was he mirroring about the kingdom that could have only been demonstrated in these terms?

Undeserved, incongruous generosity

God plays by different rules. 'Am I not allowed to do what I choose with what belongs to me?' His sovereign freedom will not be trapped into fixed, impersonal, predetermined rules that reward the 'haves', the achievers, the virtuous. Instead, God gifts the 'have-nots' and those who have no claim to make on others. His undeserved generosity is destined for all people, but it can only be embraced by those who renounce all claims to rewards on their own account, and who abandon all attempts to justify themselves by their own effort, work, achievements and goodness. But, then, does effort, duty, service, virtue count for nothing? It counts as evidence of our disposition towards God but not as the basis of a claim upon God. Every instinct for self-preservation protests against the upside-down world of grace, where non-achievers are blessed, first-comers come last, the poor are filled and the rich are left empty-handed.

All latecomers

To experience grace we have to recognize that we are all, without a single exception, latecomers to God's kingdom. The difference between any of us is as inconsequential as whether, when we've missed the train for a crucial meeting, we missed it by only ten seconds or by a whole hour. Do you love the nine-year-old three times as much as the three-year-old because he's been around to help three times as long? Of course not. The labourers who were late to work received generosity because they were called. It was the employer, not the workers, who determined the generosity of their reception. And there is no other basis on which our relationship to God and to friends can be established.

Roger Spiller

Suggested hymns

Rock of ages; Father, who in Jesus found us; Amazing grace; Put thou thy trust in God.

Fifteenth Sunday after Trinity (Proper 20)

20 September

Second Service **Rise Up, Good Shepherd**

Ps. 119.113–136 (*or* 119.121–128); Ezek. 33.23, 30—34.10; **Acts 26.1, 9–25**; Gospel at Holy Communion: Mark 9.30–37

Beware false shepherds

The prophet Ezekiel offers a stark warning to the false shepherds of Israel. For those who hold positions of authority and then abuse their position for their own gain, God has little patience. The shepherds have fed themselves and not their flock, they have clothed themselves with wool, they have not healed the sick or bound up the injured. They have abnegated all responsibility and neglected their duty. The shepherds of Israel have failed to seek out the lost and bring them back to the fold. Altogether, they have not lived up to their name. Ezekiel tells them that God will raise up a new shepherd, who will lay down his life for the sheep, bind up the broken and seek out the lost.

Of course, we identify Christ as the good shepherd, and throughout his ministry he lives up to the name, binding up the brokenhearted, feeding the flock and seeking out the lost. The extent to which Christ will seek out the lost sheep of the house of Israel becomes apparent in the conversion of Paul.

A shepherd of the people

Paul, as he himself states in the Acts of the Apostles, begins his journey persecuting the followers of Jesus. He is given authority to do so and he does it with great zeal. But the Good Shepherd speaks from out of a dazzling light and seeks out Saul, as he was at the time, to set him on a new mission to the Gentiles and gather them into the family of God. Saul the persecutor becomes Paul the missionary, who will become one of the pillars of the early Church, a shepherd in his own right.

What is interesting about Paul's story is that he is an unlikely shepherd to begin with. In many ways he acts more like a ravenous wolf towards the followers of Jesus, but then the power of God in Christ, revealed in flashing lights and voices on the road to Damascus, sets his life on a different course. It is clear that redemption and forgiveness is available to all, and there is potential for anyone to be converted into the newness of life that the resurrection of Christ makes possible. This might give us hope when we feel let down by those in positions of power. Both readings suggest that power can corrupt but in Christ anything is possible. It also offers guidance to anyone who has to take on a position of responsibility and power, whether as a parent, teacher, priest, business leader or politician, or any number of roles where the care and nurture of others falls under our remit.

The Psalmist pleads with God to be delivered from earthly oppressors, and we might pray that those with power and responsibility in our world today may exercise their authority with mercy and wisdom, perhaps with the pastoral sensitivity of a good shepherd.

A good shepherd

We have an example in Christ of what it means to be a good shepherd. The Scriptures reveal to us the many qualities of Christ throughout his ministry, which embody the words of the prophet Ezekiel. Jesus will lay down his life for the sheep; they are nurtured and fed in green pasture and beside still water; the lost sheep are sought out and carried home on his shoulders; they are protected from wolves and from false shepherds who are only interested in what they can gain from exploiting the sheep. Jesus calls himself the good shepherd; he knows his sheep and his sheep know his voice. In contrast to the false shepherds, Jesus is attentive to every sheep and its needs. He is concerned for the individual as well as the flock. Indeed, so great is his concern that he will go after the one sheep who is in danger. He will not abandon even one, and with him there is no lost cause.

Victoria Johnson

Suggested hymns

Amazing Grace; The King of love, my shepherd is; The Lord's my shepherd, I'll not want; Great Shepherd of thy people, hear.

Sixteenth Sunday after Trinity (Proper 21)
27 September

Principal Service **What is Your Authority?**

(*Continuous*): Ex. 17.1–7; Ps. 78.1–4, 12–16 [*or* 78.1–7]; *or* (*Related*): Ezek. 18.1–4, 25–end; Ps. 25.1–8; Phil. 2.1–13; **Matt. 21.23–32**

God's commandments are not set in stone

Our readings are a range of summits. The prophet Ezekiel, pioneering the path that John Milton will follow in *Paradise Lost*, seeks 'to justify the ways of God to men'. Paul 'unfolds the mystery of the incarnation'. Matthew requires us to reckon with the authority of Jesus – and not to play games with him.

Ezekiel and his contemporaries – in exile far from their homeland – have much in common with my grandson Alex. 'It's not fair!' shouts Alex, aged seven. It is our earliest moral utterance. To be sure, Alex is more alert to the injustices he thinks have been done to him than to those done to his younger brother Max, aged five. But as he grows older, Alex will notice that Max, too, is sometimes hard done by. Then one day he will come to see that inequity is more widespread still. 'It's not fair!' Alex cries today when refused an ice cream. 'It's not fair!' he will cry tomorrow when contemplating the moral order of the universe.

'It's not fair!' they cry. Their complaint is that God allows children to suffer as a consequence of their parents' wrongdoing. They quote the bitter biblical proverb, 'The parents have eaten sour grapes, and the children's teeth are set on edge.' What makes matters worse is that God has apparently *decreed* that that is how things should be. For generation after generation, God has punished children for their parents' sins.

Ezekiel has to learn that, if that's how things always were, it's not how they always will be. God's commandments, even the top ten, are not set in tablets of stone. From now on, Ezekiel is told, individuals will suffer only for their own sins, not for what their forebears did.

The gasman, the bishop and the Christ of God

Then one greater than Ezekiel appears. Very soon, Jesus says, God's kingdom will come. Then at long last God's justice will be done. The religious leaders ask Jesus the one question we all ask, when someone makes extravagant claims about themselves or makes excessive demands on us. 'What's your authority?' 'Who gave you the right', they ask, 'to do what you do and to say what you say?'

They had to learn, as we all must, that there are different kinds of authority. On the one hand, there is the authority of the gasman and the bishop. On the other hand, there is the authority of Jesus.

The gasman calls. He has a laminated card, dangling from a ribbon round his neck, confirming his authority to read your gas meter. The bishop emerges from the vestry. He is wearing a mitre, the sign of his authority to conduct the service about to start. The gasman's authority and the bishop's authority have been conferred on them by others. They may or may not be in themselves authoritative figures. The gasman may be a coward and the bishop a wimp, but the former is still entitled to inspect the dials under your stairs and the latter to confirm you.

The clergy who question Jesus' authority are not asking about his character. They are asking about his credentials. For 'the chief priests and the elders', Jesus is a maverick cleric whose orders are probably invalid and who anyway has no 'permission to officiate'. But the claim of Jesus doesn't need supporting paperwork. He doesn't have a card dangling from a ribbon round his neck. Nor, for that matter, does he wear a mitre. He needs no human endorsement or validation. The authority of Jesus is his own.

All he will show us will be his wounds

That authority was clear from the start. The fishermen dropped their nets at his command and followed him. Mark, the earliest Gospel writer, tells us that when Jesus began his public ministry everyone was astounded at his authority. He made an immediate impact. 'For he taught as one having authority and not as the scribes.' Jesus made his mark well before he worked his miracles.

'What's your authority?' the priests and elders ask, hoping to trap him. Jesus declines to give them the straight answer they hope for. As so often is Jesus' way, he returns their question with one of his own. He asks them about John the Baptist and what they make of him. However they answer, they're skewered. If they condemn John, they will alienate the many who hang on John's words. If they give John their approval, they will have to explain why they don't accept what John says about Jesus.

The authority of Jesus has always been questioned. The Jewish readers of Matthew's Gospel had many doubts about him, doubts that Matthew seeks to settle by his frequent appeals to the 'Old Testament', as we call it. The Gospel writers present the miracles as signs to the sceptical that Jesus wields authority over all that challenges the reign of God. 'Who is this,' the disciples ask, 'that even the wind and the sea obey him?'

But we badly misunderstand the nature of Jesus' claim on us if we suppose that it stands or falls by this or that proof-text, or by 'signs and wonders', however impressive. Christ's glory is revealed in his humanity. That is 'the divine divestiture' of which Paul speaks in his letter to the Philippians. Jesus' authority does not depend on any kind of external endorsement. If, like Thomas, we insist on verification, all he will show us will be his wounds.

Jesus invites me to trust and follow him. If, in my pride, I ask what right he has to do so, his response will be what it was to those in his own day who demanded to see his credentials: 'I won't tell you.' Jesus' only authorization is who he is.

John Pridmore

Suggested hymns

When to our world the Saviour came; Light of the minds that know him; Dear Lord, we long to see your face; At the name of Jesus.

Sixteenth Sunday after Trinity (Proper 21)

27 September

Second Service **Better Together**

Ps. [120, 123] 124; **Ezekiel 37.15–end**; 1 John 2.22–end;
Gospel at Holy Communion: Mark 9.38–end

Sometimes togetherness sounds threatening: like a business merger, there's the risk that the bigger partner will simply take over the smaller one. But many partnerships – social, romantic, professional, political – flourish because of their togetherness. Togetherness works when it is done in love. Togetherness works when it is done with God.

But for the grace of God

How often have you had pity on someone, and then checked yourself, realizing that what has happened to them could so easily have happened to you or someone you love? We live fragile existences and often the things that affect us are way beyond our control. Psalm 124 reminds us that if it wasn't for God's help, disaster could have happened. If God hadn't been with us, we could have been destroyed.

It's a way of giving God the credit when life is good. It's a way of recognizing that we need God – that we can't do it by ourselves.

Is God really with *him*?

Sometimes we're also tempted to judge others and in so doing think that the conclusion we reach about them is the conclusion God has reached too. But God isn't so easily tamed. In fact, he's not tamed at all – and he can surprise us again and again in the people he *does* work with. The Gospel reading today describes the disciples trying to stop some kind of a magician who is not (yet) a true follower of Christ from using the power of Christ's name. But Jesus reassures them: if they achieve anything in the name of Christ, they will soon come to know Christ. Our pre-judgement is as nothing compared with the power of God at work in others too. So we can set our prejudice aside and be open to meeting God in surprising people.

Surprising togetherness

There is much that would have been surprising in Ezekiel's prophetic act and teaching in the first reading today. The northern and southern kingdoms, Israel and Judah, at the time when the book of Ezekiel was composed, had been separate for at least three centuries. More than that, the northern kingdom, Israel, had been conquered by Assyria in 722 BC, well over a century earlier. So it's hard to think how Ezekiel could even have imagined Israel and Judah coming together again. But that's what he prophesies.

Coming straight after the mind-blowing prophecy of the dry bones coming together in the valley and having new life breathed into them, maybe this message of togetherness between Israel and Judah doesn't require quite as much imagination. Ezekiel is particularly good at dramatic acting out of his prophecies to help get his point over. He does it again here, bringing two sticks together in his hand to look like one. God's instructions to Ezekiel in this enactment make every detail clear. Not only is Ezekiel to say what the two sticks signify, he's even to *write* on them. There's no doubting what they stand for. The language of writing is of inscribing, enrolling, registering; a lasting communication and relationship between writer and reader. There is the branch of Joseph (and the northern tribes), and then the branch of Judah: the two will become one. The northern tribes – lost so long ago – will be joined to the one tribe of Judah, King David's tribe. More than this: even though King David, under whose rule the tribes were united, himself died even before the separation, it is David, that very same servant of God, who will be their king.

Signs of unity

The symbolic acts of Ezekiel, and the colourful scene of expectation he paints, aren't to be taken as literal, pedestrian prose so much as a beautiful poetic invitation to dream, to engage in such clear-cut and significant hopes. It's not a going-back-to-how-it-all-was-before. It's an attractive image of two great but now separate branches of a massive family tree being as one. Better still, they are reunited under the one, best ever, king. A king who is prince, shepherd and servant all at the same time.

Powerful partnerships of peoples or groups will require strong leaders. For a partnership to flourish fully, that leader needs qualities not only of nobility but also of care and humility. And David's servanthood signifies humility not under human agendas but under the aegis of God. The one who will be best placed to fulfil that will be none other than the Messiah, the Christ, who in Jesus is of the house of David, the branch of Judah.

God's dwelling place will be with his united people: they will be his people, and he will be their God. This is the sense that a faithful Christian can draw from this extraordinary image: that in Jesus is the dwelling place of God, and through Jesus all are invited to dwell in God and to let God dwell in them.

Abiding together

The letters that make up many books in the New Testament suggest that the early Christians had a range of different views about God and Jesus. The great teachers among them – whose letters would be kept, gathered together until the collection formed what we know as the Epistles of the New Testament – had to work hard to keep them together. We see this in the first letter of John: he's trying to undo some of the misleading work of another preacher. He wants the most basic teaching about God and Jesus Christ to remain at the heart of his flock.

And if we with them keep such teaching in mind, God will abide in us and we will abide in him. Or, in the words of Ezekiel, he will be our God and we will be God's people.

Megan Daffern

Suggested hymns

Jesus calls us here to meet him; Breathe on me, breath of God; Living God, your word has called us; Thanks be to God whose love has gathered us today.

Seventeenth Sunday after Trinity (Proper 22)

4 October

Principal Service **The Heavens are Telling the Glory of God**

(*Continuous*): Ex. 20.1–4, 7–9, 12–20; **Ps. 19 [*or* 19.7–end]**; *or* (*Related*): Isa. 5.1–7; Ps. 80.9–17; Phil. 3.4b–14; Matt. 21.33–end

The mystery of beauty

Here's a challenge. Think of the most beautiful place you know. That's the easy bit. Here's the more difficult part: now try to find the words to describe its beauty.

The chances are that as soon as you try to describe that place, words will be almost impossible to find. And, if you are like me, you will splutter to a halt, saying apologetically, 'I can't describe it. It's just beautiful.'

There's no need for apologies. It's in the nature of beauty to be beyond plodding, clumsy words. We know beauty when we see it. By contrast, think of a really ugly place and now you'll find that the words aren't at all elusive, they come flooding out: 'brutal', 'out of proportion', 'foul', 'horrible', 'disgusting'.

It's time for a quick burst of philosophy. In an article about beauty and buildings, Roger Scruton, the philosopher, wrote this: 'It is, in my view, the commandment to love your neighbour as yourself that is most evidently violated by the uglifying blocks that are being dumped on our cities.' Now, he's talking about town design and architecture but his words could be translated into thinking about beauty in nature. We know almost instinctively when a place of natural beauty is beautiful. It seems to have a number of qualities: first, it is profoundly good in and of itself; second, it points beyond itself to that which is greater; third, it reminds us of our place in the order of things; fourth, it reminds us of our relatedness to the world and to other people.

End of the philosophical detour.

The heavens are telling . . .

Let's return to the Psalms and in particular to the opening verses of Psalm 19: 'The heavens are telling the glory of God; and the firmament proclaims his handiwork.'

It is an outburst of poetry created by the author as he gazes up at the sky at night. All those stars . . . all that space. His mind reels at the beauty and immensity of it all. Unfortunately, our contemporary lives are so pervaded by artificial street lighting that we rarely glimpse the stars. We are the poorer for it. We might get closer to a sense of the enormousness of it via astronomical mathematics: there are about 250 billion stars in our Milky Way. And how many galaxies are there in the universe? At least 2 trillion.

Even without our knowledge, the poet, two or three thousand years ago, looking up at the stars was not only bowled over by their beauty. He went one step further and suggested that the stars somehow had their own form of communication.

> There is no speech, nor are there words;
>   their voice is not heard;
> yet their voice goes out through all the earth,
>   and their words to the end of the world.

It's a wonderful idea, but note that in order to express it the Psalmist-poet had to resort to paradox: the stars have neither voices nor language, yet 'their voice . . . and their words go out to the end of the world'. It's a mind-boggling idea and an idea, if you'll excuse the phrase, of very great beauty. There is something about the glory of the universe that means that our ordinary means of discourse are humbled towards incoherence. And we, gazing up at the stars, can only catch our breath and allow our minds to be expanded by the wonder of it all.

God: the source of all?

Now take this one stage further: suppose that all this immensity, all this beauty, has its source in God. This is not a rehearsal of one of the traditional arguments for the existence of God. Such design, says those arguments, implies a Designer. No. This is about our minds being open to the possibility, no more than that, of One who brought all of this into being and continues to hold it in being. If that might be the case, what is our relationship with him? Is our being part of the underlying being of God?

Press this idea even harder. Is the beauty that we experience in our world somehow a fragment of the beauty of God? Is it a revelation of the truth at the heart of God?

There are, of course, no definitive answers. We can only pose the questions, but such questions at the very least ensure that we remain open to new possibilities, to new ways of thinking about the world. The questions expand the imaginative capacities of our souls. They help us to approach the potential of eternity with humility.

St Augustine, when contemplating his relationship with God, said in a stunningly haunting phrase: 'Late have I loved you Beauty so old and so new, late have I loved you.'

Just like the Psalmist with his outburst of joy, the elusive and gracious truth of Augustine's words seem to me to point towards the possibility and the beauty of God. And for that I give heartfelt thanks.

> The heavens are telling the glory of God;
>   and the firmament proclaims his handiwork.
> Day to day pours forth speech,
>   and night to night declares knowledge.
> There is no speech, nor are there words;
>   their voice is not heard;
> yet their voice goes out through all the earth,
>   and their words to the end of the world.

Christopher Herbert

Suggested hymns

The spacious firmament on high; Let all creation dance; Creating God, we bring our song of praise; Lord of all worlds, we worship and adore you.

Seventeenth Sunday after Trinity (Proper 22)

4 October

Second Service Take What You Want, Says God . . .

Ps. 136 [*or* 136.1–9]; Prov. 2.1–11; 1 John 2.1–17; *Gospel at Holy Communion*: **Mark 10.2–16**

'Truly I tell you, whoever does not receive the kingdom of God as a little child will never enter it.'

There is a harsh proverb that several sites on Google suggest comes from Spain. It goes like this: 'Take what you want and pay for it, says God. You can have anything you want, as long as you accept that there is a price and you will have to pay it.'

Now, whether or not that particular proverb actually comes from Spain, who can tell? It is undoubtedly hard-hearted and tough, but does it contain an element of realism? It argues in a pithy way, rather like the English saying that was particularly popular in the years of Margaret Thatcher's premiership, that there is no such thing as a free lunch.

But the proverb ignores human generosity. It fails to acknowledge that, for example, good parents love their children unconditionally, they are a gift beyond price; it ignores the outstanding philanthropy of people such as Bill and Melinda Gates; it fails to see that some things in life are indeed free, like, the view across a valley bathed in sunshine that takes your breath away by its beauty.

Receiving gifts: receiving the kingdom

And then there is the saying by Jesus about the kingdom, which we have just heard. It too is breathtaking. It implies that the kingdom of God is not something that is built; it is not something that is extended. It is a gift from God to be received, and to be received in the way a child receives gifts; that is, with open arms and a radiant joy (remember watching children at Christmas receiving gifts – the excitement and the happiness are palpable).

The difference, of course, between the excitement of receiving gifts at Christmas and Jesus' saying about the kingdom is that the kingdom gift is not a singular, once-a-year event. The gift is continuous. It is a daily process.

And what do I mean by this?

We can get a clue from the delightful prayer found in Morning Prayer in *Common Worship*.

> The night has passed and the day lies open before us . . .
> As we rejoice in the gift of this new day,
> so may the light of your presence, O God,
> set our hearts on fire with love for you;
> now and for ever.[32]

It is a simple statement, but to recognize that each new day is a gift is a life-changing experience. It means that we take nothing for granted; we keep our eyes attuned; we live with gratitude as a foundational principle of our lives.

And if each new day is a gift, what about considering the possibility that, even with all our flaws, fears, weaknesses and foibles, each of us exists as a gift from God. We did not create our own lives; we are emphatically not self-made human beings; we came into being as a gift, unique and precious in the sight of God.

It's within you

What follows from these two principles – that each new day is a gift and that our lives are a gift – is that we can glimpse within the daily run of our existence the presence of God. The kingdom is around us, and, as Luke says in his Gospel, it is within us:

> Once Jesus was asked by the Pharisees when the kingdom of God was coming, and he answered, 'The kingdom of God is not coming with things that can be observed; nor will they say, "Look, here it is!" or "There it is!" For, in fact, the kingdom of God is among [or within] you.'

It is a timely reminder that the kingdom of God is like no other created thing: it does not have shape or boundaries; it is not like a parcel wrapped in shiny paper that we can tear off to see what's inside; it is not limited by time or space; it is elusively but constantly present. And, if we so choose, the kingdom can be at the very core of our being.

Living with thankfulness

But this is the question: are we willing to recognize the fact that the kingdom really is a gift? We need to be aware that our pride, our egos, can get in the way. But think back to Jesus referring to accepting the kingdom like a child. When children receive gifts, they are sublimely indifferent to their own egos. What exists for them is the gift itself and their excited enjoyment of it. They are not playing to any galleries; they have not yet created defensive walls around themselves; they are, in the strict sense of the word, innocent of all of that. For a few moments they are experiencing the pureness of joy.

We cannot pretend that as adults we can re-enter that state of unmitigated child-like joy, but through changing our perceptions and changing our inner attitudes, and, perhaps above all, by living with deep thankfulness, we can find moments in our lives when the very presence of God brings peace to our souls.

Christopher Herbert

Suggested hymns

Praise the One who breaks the darkness; We bring our children, Lord, today; Lord of all hopefulness; Songs of thankfulness and praise.

Eighteenth Sunday after Trinity (Proper 23)
11 October
Principal Service **Dressing Up**

(*Continuous*): Ex. 32.1–14; Ps. 106.1–6, 19–23 (*or* 106.1–6);
or (*Related*): Isa. 25.1–9; Ps. 23; Phil. 4.1–9; **Matt. 22.1–14**

It's not the people who refused the initial invitation to a wedding feast, nor even the second invitation to an odd assortment of people, good and bad, rounded up from the street, that gets our attention. It's the harsh treatment meted out to the man without a wedding garment, which provokes a sense of outrage and incredulity. The man seems to have committed a minor infringement of the dress code. And he is excluded, tied up and punished in a way that seems out of all proportion to his misconduct.

Dressing inappropriately

We can all sympathize with the guest in the parable who was unsuitably dressed. Have we not ourselves struggled to know what to wear for a special event, not wanting to be overdressed or under-dressed, and not knowing until we arrive whether or not our attire is appropriate?

When I attended the marriage service of my patron's daughter in an unfamiliar church, I was shocked to realize that I was the only male in the large congregation, sprinkled with royalty, celebrities and government ministers, not wearing full morning dress! That made me more determined to slip quietly away after the service and decline the open invitation to the buffet meal that followed. But the host saw me and graciously insisted that I join the rest of the celebrations.

Dress codes are still important even in these sartorially relaxed times. Complying shows effort and respect, and dressing up helps to engender a mood of anticipation and celebration. But what could be expected from the man who was invited at short notice to this wedding party? Was he supposed to keep a designer-label suit with him in case he received an unexpected invitation?

Banquet

A banquet or meal is a picture of the kingdom. Those on the original guest list who refused the invitation stood for the Jewish people who had rejected Jesus. We're told in the parable that the king responded by burning their city, which might be a reference to the actual burning of Jerusalem that occurred when the Gospel was being written, and as a divine punishment for the rejection of God's invitation. But now, through their rejection, an invitation is made to Gentiles. This time it's broad and indiscriminate, extending to good and bad alike. So why then is exception taken to the man without a wedding garment?

Strict dress code

It's been suggested that it was the king who provided the wedding garment and the man had only to wear it, but refused. But there's no evidence for this or for some other such explanations. More likely the wedding garment wasn't a special dress for the occasion but decent, clean white clothes such as anyone would have owned. All that was asked of the man was to go home, wash and have a change of clothes. A simple task that involved no cost and minimum effort was all that was required in order to express the gratitude that was rightfully due to the host and to clinch the invitation.

The dress code of the kingdom

What does this parable say to those who have received God's gracious invitation? The invitation is unconditional, offered to bad people as well as to good. Recognizing the invitation and embracing its grace cannot but usher in conformity to the kingdom's values. It can't leave us unchanged, if we have appropriated it for ourselves. Our response retains the joy of the parable. It's no sacrifice to change clothes in order to go to a banquet we've been looking forward to for ages. The dressing up and preparation is part of the celebration and honours the host and the other guests.

God provides the 'garments of salvation' and 'robe of righteousness'. After all, he even made garments for Adam and Eve. The gift is given, we're invited to the banquet, included in the kingdom. But to come to the feast in response to the gracious initiative of Christ and then not to conform our lives to his gracious will is to exclude ourselves. St Paul said, 'put on the Lord Jesus Christ, and make no provision for the flesh'. Putting on Christ, symbolized in baptism, means being transformed, becoming who we really are. It means being conformed to Christ in every aspect of our lives, so that though we're conspicuous in the world we are at home in God's kingdom.

Roger Spiller

Suggested hymns

At the Lamb's high feast we sing; The trumpets sound; My God, and is thy table spread; Deck thyself, my soul, with gladness.

Eighteenth Sunday after Trinity (Proper 23)
11 October
Second Service **Wisdom's Source and Power**

Ps. 139.1–18 [*or* 139.1–11]; **Prov. 3.1–18**; 1 John 3.1–15; *Gospel at Holy Communion*: Mark 10.17–31

What proverbs do you know? Here are a few: 'A bird in the hand is worth two in the bush', 'Absence makes the heart grow fonder', 'An army marches on its stomach', 'The best things in life are free'. Proverbs are pithy sayings that contain insight. They are memorable. You can call them to mind when you need them. Such sayings have been popular down the ages. Some are biblical, some are from Shakespeare, or Chaucer – some origins are lost in the midst of time. The book of Proverbs in the Bible is part of the Old Testament Wisdom literature, which is made up of

Proverbs, Job, Psalms, Ecclesiastes and Song of Songs. Proverbs contains short verses of wisdom that can help with our faithful living as Christians on a daily basis. In the passage from Proverbs set for today I've picked out three themes that should underpin our Christian lives.

Remembering God

Solomon urges his child to remember all that he has been taught about God – and to rehearse it regularly, so that when difficulties arise he will be able to hold onto the reality of God's faithfulness to Israel in the past, as evidence of God's continual love and favour. One of the reasons that we use a liturgical calendar in the Church is to remind ourselves of the story of our faith. We hear over and over again, down the years, the stories of God's creation and sustaining of the universe, Christ's incarnation, sacrifice and resurrection, and the new life lived in the Holy Spirit, which is available to all who believe. It's important that we keep the narrative of our faith alive and lively, not just in church but throughout our communities, so that people don't become disconnected from their Christian heritage. We are entrusted to keep the rumour of God alive – not just for ourselves but for everyone. Recent research from the Bible Society has indicated that many Christian parents are reluctant to share their faith with their children even in very committed Christian homes. The book of Proverbs urges us to be loyal and faithful to God and to one another. We are to wear loyalty and faithfulness like a scarf or a necklace, and have these attributes carved on our hearts like the commandments were carved on tablets of stone. So, remember all that God has done and pass the message on.

Giving generously

Solomon also reminds his child to give to God the first fruits of his produce. The Law of Moses required the Israelites to tithe to God – to give 10 per cent of their produce, flocks and goods each year. The 'first fruits' meant both that which is produced, grown or birthed first as well as the 'best' of the crop. Giving to God is to come before anything else, and once this giving is in place and adhered to faithfully then we can be assured of God's provision towards us, often shown in extraordinary ways. Barns filled with plenty and vats overflowing with wine are the illustrations given here. You may have more contemporary examples. As Christians, we are beyond the Law of Moses and so our giving to God should increase beyond a tithe, to include recognition of and response to God's extraordinary grace shown in Jesus Christ. We're called to offer '10 per cent + grace' to God. If we all responded in that way, the Church's money issues would be resolved overnight. Jesus encourages a faithful, rich man to sell all he has and give to the poor. The rich man is deeply challenged and saddened by this request and Jesus has some sharp things to say about those who have wealth but are not generous towards God and others. Might God be asking you to review your charitable giving and the destination of your 'first fruits'?

Seeking wisdom

Solomon also recommends to his child that he seek for wisdom and understanding. These things are much more precious than gold, silver or jewels, says Solomon – who was famed for his wisdom. He knows what he is talking about! This is wisdom that comes from God, not from oneself. We're urged not to rely on our own wisdom but to trust in the Lord who will lead and guide us in the ways we should go. Wisdom's ways lead to peace, long life and happiness. This is the wisdom that founded the heavens and the earth – divine wisdom that holds all things together and leads to knowledge and understanding. In Colossians we hear that all the treasures of wisdom and knowledge are hidden in Christ. Our discipleship and faithfulness to him will lead to the wisdom and understanding we seek. This may look very different from what the world applauds as cleverness or brilliance. The wisdom of the world is foolish in God's sight, says Paul writing to the church at Corinth. Where do you seek for wisdom – are you looking in the right place? So, the book of Proverbs challenges us today to remember the teachings of God and pass them on to others, to give to God generously, joyfully and wholeheartedly, and to seek life in Christ that is shaped by wisdom and understanding. Amen.

Catherine Williams

Suggested hymns

Be thou my vision; Take my life; I vow to thee, my country; Indescribable.

Nineteenth Sunday after Trinity (Proper 24)
18 October
(For St Luke, see p. 347.)

Principal Service **What's In Your Pocket?**

(*Continuous*): Ex. 33.12–end; Ps. 99; *or* (*Related*): Isa. 45.1–7; Ps. 96.1–9 [10–13]; 1 Thess. 1.1–10; **Matt. 22.15–22**

Tax is always going to be a contentious issue, dividing political parties as well as public opinion, and, like the poll tax, it can bring down a government while the debate about how far tax-raising powers should be devolved rages on. Coinage is a powerful symbol of political power. Our nation kept the pound, refusing to join the euro, in order to keep control of its finances. For Jewish people, the hated tax was paying for the army and government that occupied their country; taxes were supporting the occupation. And they were required to be paid in Roman coinage. So if you wanted to ambush Jesus, a question about taxes was a perfect catch question.

Enemies united against a greater threat

The Pharisees, supported by the Herodians, sought Jesus to put to him their question. The two politico-religious groups were diametrically opposed to one another; the Pharisees resented the tax, the Herodians supported it. The Pharisees were the pragmatists, they followed rather than led public opinion. The Herodians were the hard-line ideologues, collaborators, who were hated by pious Jews. They worked out of the court of Herod for the Roman government. But though they differed on everything else, they had one thing in common – opposition to Jesus. They united against someone who threatened them both more even than they threatened each other.

Trick question

'Is it lawful to pay taxes?' they ask. If Jesus says yes, he's a collaborator; if he says no, he's a seditionist. If he says it is lawful to pay taxes to Caesar, he becomes instantly unpopular with the people, oppressed by their Roman overlords, and colludes with the pagan, tyrannical powers that are occupying his own country. But if he says no, it is not lawful to pay taxes, he's playing right into the hands of his enemies. And he's seen to be defining his kingdom in merely human, earthbound political terms, in terms of political activism. You have to give it to them, it's a masterly question, a catch question, Jesus is condemned if he says 'yes', and condemned if he says 'no'.

Letting others judge themselves

Jesus singles out the Pharisees as prime movers of this trap. Although he had less in common with the Herodians, they at least were consistent, but these Pharisees were playing their Jewish audience and thus were literally 'actors', hypocrites, whose hypocrisy Jesus in a masterstroke is now about to expose.

Jesus doesn't just talk theoretically, abstractly, in generalities. He brings things down to earth with unsettling precision. 'Show me the coin used for the tax,' says Jesus. Why this sudden interest in numismatics? Isn't the fact of Roman taxation the issue, not the coinage? Well, 'they brought him a denarius'. But now Jesus asks them whose head and title is inscribed upon the coin. And they produce a coin that has on it the image of the Roman emperor Tiberias or possibly Augustus. And on the one side of the coin are the words '*divi filius* – Son of God – Son of divine Augustus'. The coin is a violation of the first two commandments, which forbid graven images, the likeness of anything else, idolatry. And for this reason no strictly pious Jew would ever carry a coin bearing Caesar's image with its inscription proclaiming Caesar to be king and God. So in reaching into their pockets and being found carrying a graven image, they unwittingly produce the evidence that condemns them.

Jesus offers no guidance on tax; he's not primarily concerned with economic relationships to government but with our existential relationship to God. Some have mistakenly taken this episode as the basis for a separation of powers – political and religious – for a split-level view of life. Instead, it points to the fact that God claims the whole of our life, and from that commitment we can work out questions about taxes and other issues of conduct.

Whose image do we carry?

Whose image do we bear? Whose face and superscription is there? On the imperial coins there's a uniformity that makes clear the limitations of the power of the emperor. But the diversity of human faces shows the unity and infinity of God. The coins with Caesar's image belong to Caesar, but human beings, created in God's image, belong to God. Whose face do we bear? Whose face do we see in each other? What is rendered to God is whatever bears the divine image. Every life is marked with that inscription. When we see in others the face of God, we will treat people with love, care and respect.

A young girl kept a coin in her pocket, just like the Pharisees. She recalls how her mother encouraged her as a child to keep a small coin, a sixpence, in her pocket so that she could have it available to give to homeless people she saw in the street. When she was 15 years old, she lived and worked with homeless people on the streets of London and later founded homes for homeless children, around the world. Sally Trench founded some 600 homes for vulnerable young people. Rendering to God requires us to see God's face in others, to face all that defaces God's image in us and destroys our humanity.

Roger Spiller

Suggested hymns

When I needed a neighbour; All to Jesus I surrender; In the streets of every city; Father, I place into your hands.

Nineteenth Sunday after Trinity (Proper 24)
18 October

Second Service **Get Wisdom**

Ps. 142 [143.1–11]; **Prov. 4.1–18**; 1 John 3.16—4.6

Information or insight?

There is an argument that we live in an information-based economy. Data is king, knowledge is power, information is instant and we see the manipulation and abuse of personal and public data to influence society and shape opinion. We have also seen the proliferation of false information and fake news being disseminated. Sometimes it is difficult to know who or what to believe and who or what to listen to.

More positively, we can also retrieve information at the touch of a button, or the swipe of a screen, and we have access to knowledge that our forebears could only have dreamt of accessing. However, with all of this information and with all of this knowledge, are we any better for it? Are we any wiser than those who have gone before us? How can we discern what is good news and what might be fake news? How can we use the information available to us in a positive way for the common good of all and in the service of the gospel?

Learning for life

In the book of Proverbs, we are given the example of a parent teaching a child. We are told of a father's instruction which represents a patient bearing with someone else in order that wisdom can be passed on from one generation to another. Here Wisdom is also personified, Wisdom is one whom we are told to prize highly, to embrace and indeed to love. When Wisdom speaks, we are called to listen.

Wisdom presents a very different kind of knowledge acquisition to fact-based data collection and instant information. Wisdom offers a different kind of education. Wisdom teaches us how to live well and stay on the right path. Wisdom is learning for life. There are some forms of knowledge that cannot be acquired instantly but require a good and patient teacher to help us learn by example and through practice. Not all things worth learning are instantaneous, not all information reveals the truth. To gain wisdom requires discipline, trust and commitment, and a willingness to listen.

Wisdom is therefore a practical thing. It is not just a theory or a paper exercise. Gaining wisdom and insight will bear tangible fruits in our lives; it will shape who we are and how we respond to the world around us. In the first letter of John, we are again presented with a lesson in how to discern different kinds of knowledge. Someone who is attentive to the wisdom that comes from God is able to transform words that are said into positive action and truth. It seems the quality of information can be judged by its fruits.

We are also reminded that God knows everything, and part of our discipleship is to follow the commandments of God in thought and word and deed, for, in the commandments of God, true wisdom is to be found.

Listen and learn

Belief in Christ and in his commandment to love one another bestows upon us another kind of wisdom. Knowledge of Christ gives us confidence to discern and test what is good in the world around us and where we may need to exercise caution. If we are open to the wisdom of God in Christ, and if we carry Christ with us at all times, we may see more clearly how to discern between the spirits of truth and the spirits of error. If we are committed to following Christ and learning from him, the path towards wisdom is made open to us.

Through his teaching and his example, Jesus showed us how to live well. He taught his disciples where true wisdom is to be found. Because he laid down his life for us, we ought to lay down our lives for one another. Wisdom is to be found in service, in love and in discipleship. None of those things are quick fixes, all must be learned and discerned over time. In a world swamped by information and knowledge, and in a world overloaded with many competing voices, we would do well to listen more attentively to the wisdom that comes from Christ, hearing his voice above all others and learning from him.

Victoria Johnson

Suggested hymns

Be thou my guardian and my guide; Light of the minds that know him; Rise and hear, the Lord is speaking; Thy way, not mine, O Lord.

Last Sunday after Trinity (Proper 25) 25 October

Principal Service **Love Yourself**

(*Continuous*): Deut. 34.1–12; Ps. 90.1–6, 13–end [*or* 90.1–6];
or (*Related*): Lev. 19.1–2, 15–18; Ps. 1; 1 Thess. 2.1–8;
Matt. 22.34–end

It was said of the nationally known trio of Methodist leaders that were around after the war: Dr Sangster loved God, Dr Weatherhead loved humanity, and Lord Soper loved an argument! An oversimplification, of course, like all shorthand attempts to categorize people. But, as Scripture testifies, there will be some people who find it easier to love the neighbour they see than the God they don't, and others who find it easier to love God rather than the neighbour they see too closely for comfort. Of course, love of God, love of neighbour and love of self aren't alternatives. The command to love God and to love neighbour are distinct but equally mandatory. But what of the third member of the trio, love of self? That is to be the model for the way we should love our neighbour – 'as ourselves'. Might not a healthy love of self turn out to be the source and starting point for the way we love both God and neighbour? If love of God has primacy, might not a love of self have priority in love's journey?

Fear of self-love

But isn't a love of self precisely the corrosive force that defeats both love of God and love of neighbour? A crude reading of St Paul and St John has misled us into an indiscriminate condemnation of the self. Our humanity has thus to be chastened, denied and sacrificed rather than be celebrated and enjoined in love's service. But the self that is to be loved is not the self we present to the outside, the public self we feel we have to adopt in order to win the love and acceptance of others. That false self is an interloper. The bigger the space we make for it, the less we love our true selves. And the less we love our true selves, the more distorted will be our love for others. Jung said:

> That I feed the hungry, that I forgive an insult, that I love my enemy in the name of Christ – all these are undoubtedly great virtues. What I do to the least of my brethren, that I do unto Christ. But what if I should discover that the least amongst them all, the poorest of all the beggars . . . [is] within me, and that I myself am the who that must be loved – what then?[33]

Cherishing the self

There is a real self waiting to be loved and cherished. This self is the imprint of God's own self within us. The love of self cannot contradict our love for God because it is God's own creation. We love God by loving ourselves as his creation. After all, we cannot give ourselves in love either to God or to others until we have discovered a self to give. If we fail to love ourselves, our relationships will be distorted because they will be used only to satisfy our unmet needs. When we fail sufficiently to love and embrace our true selves, relationships with others risk becoming possessive or manipulative.

Deposing the false self

The false self does, indeed, need to be deposed and decentred, but the treatment of self-denial and sacrifice has so often suffocated the real self as well. So how can the true self be loved back into health and vitality? How can the self-image be restored, and self-confidence as God's creation be established? It's sometimes said that until we experience God's love for us we cannot properly love ourselves. But until we love ourselves, we may find it impossible to accept that God loves us. We can't love others until we love ourselves, but we need to experience the love of others before we can love them or ourselves. We face a conundrum. As Bruce Avery, a psychologist, put it, 'The key that unlocks the safe is in the safe.'

Nurturing the true self

But the door that is locked against logic can be opened by the multiple strategy of Spirit-inspired relationships. The true self is, after all, conceived and kept in being through relationships, whereas the false self is false because it is self-centred and closed to relationships. Falling in love, forming a close relationship, discovering a personal faith in God – any such decisive relationship can cast out fear and make it safe for the real self to come out of the closet and be brought to life. Friendship, spiritual direction and sometimes therapy can help to uncover the paved areas of our lives and retrieve the hidden pearl of infinite value buried within us. These may be the voices that mediate to us the voice of God, that tells us, 'You are my beloved son, daughter, in whom I am well pleased.'

Love of self frees us from self-preoccupation, frees us to reach out to greet the world with delight and love, and thereby to begin to change it. It frees us to love our neighbour and to love God with God's own love. Love for self, neighbour and God is an unbroken threefold cord with which to embrace our fractured, love-starved world.

Roger Spiller

Suggested hymns

How deep the Father's love for us; It is a thing most wonderful; O love, how deep, how broad, how high! O love that wilt not let me go.

Last Sunday after Trinity (Proper 25) 25 October

Second Service **Strong in Grace**

Ps. 119.89–104; Eccles. 11; 12; **2 Tim. 2.1–7**; *Gospel at Holy Communion*: Mark 12.28–34

Last words?

If I played a recording of a piece of music by Eric Coates to you, I am sure you would recognize it. It's not his 'Dam Busters March', nor is it his 'Knightsbridge March', which was the signature tune of an old BBC radio programme, *In Town Tonight*. It is, however, the tune that introduces *Desert Island Discs*. And it's called, as you may well know, 'By the sleepy lagoon'. It's the perfect introduction – at ease, relaxed, welcoming. Just the thing you might need to steady your nerves before the interview begins and your choice of eight records is steadily revealed. You will know that the interviewees, in addition to their eight records, also have a choice of a book and one luxury item. The format is simple. It enables the interviewer gently to take a walk through the guest's life, picking out the highlights.

For some people, that process of looking back over their lives is nothing like so relaxed. Think of those people facing execution who are allowed to write one last letter that can be sent to their loved ones. The last letter from the Lutheran pastor Dietrich Bonhoeffer to his fiancée, which he wrote when he was held in prison by the Nazis in Germany in 1944, was deeply poignant, yet filled with hope. It is dated Christmas 1944. This is what he wrote:

> These will be quiet days in our homes. But I have had the experience over and over again that the quieter it is around me, the clearer do I feel the connection to you. It is as though in solitude the soul develops senses we hardly know in everyday life. Therefore I have not felt lonely or abandoned for one moment. You, the parents, all of you, the friends and students of mine at the front, all are constantly present to me. Your prayers and good thoughts, words from the Bible, discussions long past, pieces of music, and books – [all these] gain life and reality as never before. It is a great invisible sphere in which one lives and in whose reality there is no doubt.[34]

He was executed four months later.

Paul's last words?

The letter that we heard read today was written in a similarly uncertain situation. Paul was in prison in Rome and was awaiting his fate. He decided to write to one of his young companions, Timothy: 'I am reminded of your sincere faith, a faith that lived first in your grandmother Lois and your mother Eunice and now, I am sure, lives in you.'

It is a letter of loving encouragement to a young man whom Paul regarded as a kind of adopted son. In it he emboldens Timothy in his Christian faith. He reminds him that he has had Paul's hands laid upon him and as a result he has received God's gift. 'Hold to the standard of sound teaching that you have heard from me, in the faith and love that are in Christ Jesus. Guard the good treasure entrusted to you, with the help of the Holy Spirit living in us.'

Paul then goes on a little detour and tells Timothy of the way that he was let down by some of his companions, but states that he has been supported by others, including a man called Onesiphorus who visited Paul in his Roman prison.

For a final letter it is quite chatty. Almost, in our terms, like something on social media but interspersed with theological reflection. One of those reflections opened today's reading: 'You then, my child, be strong in the grace that is in Christ Jesus . . .'

Strong in grace

It is a curious choice of words. In what sense can one be strong in the grace that is in Christ? Perhaps it is based on a recognition that as fallible human beings our natural inner strength can sometimes fail us. We make terrible mistakes as a result. Our relationships may be damaged. We may cause hurt to others. We might be plagued by a sudden loss of confidence. We may have feelings of worthlessness and end up metaphorically covered in mud in what John Bunyan so accurately called the 'slough of despond'. Those feelings are common to us all. So what is to be done?

Perhaps the answer lies in the way we treat those awful times. We can wallow in them, we can ignore them, we can, in a resigned kind of way, accept them – or, we might want to lift our eyes from a preoccupation with ourselves and instead look at Christ. Easily said, but isn't there a truth lurking in there somewhere? If Christ has risen from the dead there is nothing – as Paul said in another letter he wrote – there is nothing that can separate us from the love of God in Christ Jesus. That is the foundation of our hope, that God really is God, and that as we turn towards him and towards our fellow human beings we will feel God's arms under us, lifting us out of the depths, or, if you prefer, God walking with us through those depths, holding us by the hand until we find ourselves on solid ground. It is what Bonhoeffer felt. It is what St Paul felt.

Grace is not an added human extra that we can create by our own effort. It is precisely not that. But it is – it really is – the very life and love of God that always, in all circumstances, upholds us, surrounds us and walks with us.

Christopher Herbert

Suggested hymns

In our darkest night; Lead, kindly light, amid the encircling gloom; O changeless Christ, for ever new; Sing my soul, when hope is sleeping.

Bible Sunday 25 October
(*May be celebrated in preference to the Last Sunday after Trinity.*)

Signpost, Spectacles and Talking Book

Neh. 8.1–4a [5–6], 8–12; Ps. 119.9–16; **Col. 3.12–17**; Matt. 24.30–35

The Bible is the bestselling book of the year, every year, of all time. That's based upon the number of copies sold, though there's no knowing how many people actually read it. Callum Brown, a distinguished sociologist of religion, has argued in his book *The Death of Christian Britain* that the collapse of faith in our country can be attributed directly to the decline in the practice of Bible stories being read by parents to their children from the 1960s. But why should we adults read the Bible in our homes? What benefits should we expect it to bring us? And how should we set about reading it?

Signpost

Most people I guess would say, if asked, that the Bible is a source of knowledge, good for a general knowledge quiz and more seriously as teaching, instruction, for living. Who could possibly disagree with that? Other great religious leaders have left holy books that instruct their followers in the way they should live. But try doing that with the Bible and you get into difficulties. Of course we're exhorted to love our enemies, do good to those who wrong us, turn the other cheek and so on. But you soon find you're running out of fuel and can't keep it up because it's the *person* of Jesus who is our living Word, and, as he said, without him 'you can do nothing'. So the Bible is inseparable from the living Lord Jesus.

But how do we come to know Jesus? What do we need to know about him in order to answer our questions and help us come to a decision? Where are the indicators as to how we might see the one who is no longer physically visible? The Bible is first and foremost the signpost that points us to Jesus. Jesus is promised and foreshadowed in the Old Testament. Its characters, people like Adam, Abraham, Moses and Elijah, prefigure him, and the promises made by the prophets point to and converge on him. In the Gospels we have four portraits of Jesus that reveal more than a photograph ever could, supposing it had been available at the time: the impression Jesus made on different people, and the words and teaching Jesus gave as they recorded and interpreted it. The Bible, then, is a signpost. It's not a map, and Jesus warns those who are tempted to treat it as a masterplan or route map, 'You search the scriptures because you think that in them you have eternal life . . . Yet you refuse to come to me to have life.' When the Bible draws us to the towering figure of Jesus, as we seek him we find that he has already set out to meet us.

Spectacles

You know how it is, you read a great story or see a powerful play and it stays with you; you can't get it out of your mind, it causes you to see things differently. Enabling us to see the world and ourselves differently is another reason for reading the Bible. Reading the Bible, we find that it critiques and contradicts our world view. It can't do otherwise because it depicts the transcendent God as the chief actor. So the Bible offers an alternative view of the world and its future to the prevailing, fixed, expiring world view that we normally inhabit. So, for example, the secular world view focuses on self-fulfilment, attainment, possessiveness, and sees other people as potential competitors in a fierce market. The biblical world view sees us as dependent on God's grace, called to love and serve others and to defuse the weakness of power through the power of weakness.

This alternative perspective is only glimpsed and hinted at in the present, but the Bible fuels our imagination to see the future kingdom that God set in train through the death and resurrection of Jesus Christ. Some readers use the Bible like a telescope, to help us peer right back to the earliest years of Jewish Christian history. But our priority is to see through the Bible into the present and future in clear focus. We have an example of this in our reading from Nehemiah. 'Let the word of Christ dwell in you richly,' says Paul in our Epistle. When we're immersed in Scripture and inhabit its world, then the ideas and images of the Bible fund this alternative imagination and fuel a hopeful, grace-filled way of living.

Talking book

When I've seen a Shakespeare play at the RSC, I've been tempted to accuse the director of tampering with the author's text because the references and sometimes the place names seem to refer to a major current news item. Of course no such changes have been made. Great literature, art and music speak beyond their own time. And better than its creator could ever know. And this is truer of the Bible because the Spirit is promised to us as the interpreter of the Bible. So the Bible is our interlocuter, our critical friend, and if we listen we will discover that the ancient words of Scripture address us even more directly than a message from a close friend.

No wonder this book 'contains all things necessary for salvation', or, in the words used at the Coronation when the Bible is presented to the Sovereign, 'We present you with this book, the most valuable thing this world affords. Here is wisdom, this is the royal law, these are the lively oracles of God.' The bestselling book of all time is not to be shelved – it demands to be read!

Roger Spiller

Suggested hymns

God in his wisdom, for our learning; Thanks be to God whose word was spoken; O Christ the Word incarnate.

All Saints' Day 1 November

Principal Service **People of an Alternative Culture**

Rev. 7.9–end; Ps. 34.1–10; 1 John 3.1–3; **Matt. 5.1–12**

A festival to celebrate 'all saints' is a reminder to the faithful in Christ about their collective identity, existence and mission. We are not celebrating the life and faith of any particular individual, or group of individuals, but the whole body of saints and so are reaffirming the connectedness in the Body of Christ that transcends the limitations of time and space.

No celebration of heroes

No one is named in today's feast. There is no one lesser or greater here. In fact the focus here is on those who were never named. Those who could not make it to the church calendars and lectionaries. Or those who did not catch the attention of the church hierarchy. And this group surely includes those faithful who were rejected and even tortured by ecclesial authorities. The accent is not on the canonized saints, but on all the baptized and redeemed people of God. If we survey the list of the saints named in the Church's calendar we will find the diversity and variety of people – women and men, noble and lowly – breathtaking in its range. They come from all sorts of conditions and are of various types – the poor, the hungry, the meek and so on. This is a source of hope for us all and is tremendously encouraging. There is a place for everyone! And a special place for the lowly and the humble.

Celebrating God's achievement

Then what unites them all, and of course us, together? Each one of them was unique and different. But they were all related to God. Or God found favour in them. It was not their achievements or qualities but God's grace, and grace alone. This feast day comes to us with an invitation to recover the vision of the Church that is God's and not ours, and to rejoice in the abundant mercy in Christ that accepts us just as we are. We are celebrating God's achievement, not ours or our forebears' in faith.

God's achievement is all about empowering and reversing. The persecuted ones are still seeking to make peace and those mourning are still showing mercy. They do not give up. God has transformed them. In their weakness they are safe, because they know that 'they will see God'. Normal human standards and assumptions are turned around. In Christ, God reverses the values of the world and so 'the saints' are not heroes of holiness, but the poor who simply hold on to God. God achieves all these through the Lordship of Christ. In him, God has won the world.

Recapturing our vision

The agenda in our reading today takes us quite outside and beyond the Church, to the world and its peoples, to the desperate needs and longings of so many – those who have become victims of the widening gap between the rich and poor, international debt, economic injustice, the violation of women and children, fundamentalism, racism and so on. And it is that call and its fulfilment in the lives of the saints that we celebrate at this feast. This feast confronts the mediocre nature of our own discipleship today.

A sincere reflection on the good news of JesusChrist can move us from terror and dejection to hope and commitment. The saints do not just march on through this world merely celebrating their privileges and hope, but by their very character and behaviour become agents of God's transforming mission in this world.

Sanctifying our lives

The vision reflected in Matthew's beatitudes is essentially tied up with our expected character. In laying out some snippets of blessedness and accursedness, these readings offer a foundation for the kind of holy living that is celebrated on All Saints' Day. The saints are those whose lives bear witness to suffering and struggle, demonstrating life on the margins and fulfilling the prophetic role that this world so badly demands. Luke understands that the poor and hungry, the sad and the scorned are special objects of God's love. Matthew preserves the eschatological ('end time') dimension while placing due emphasis on saints' current ways of living. This holy way of living consists of our absolute trust in God, commitment to peace and justice in our world, and our active involvement in God's compassionate and transforming mission in this world of injustice and inequalities. We are challenged on this day to eagerly press on being sanctified by the unmerited and persistent love of God and the hope that it brings to ourselves and our world.

Matthew portrays what life is like in the reign of God in a subversive and threatening way. Blessings and woes are placed side by side. The reading does not exalt poverty or grief as if they are virtues. And they pity those who are benefited and honoured by the present system. God's reign calls for an alternative manner of life that swims against the stream, or for embracing a counterculture. The saints are those who struggle to live out this alternative manner of life. They belong to the past, present and the future of God's kingdom, including all of us who struggle to practise the Christian counterculture today. And today's feast is an occasion to celebrate faith and hope – ours and God's.

John Perumbalath

Suggested hymns

Rejoice in God's saints, today and all days!; Let saints on earth in concert sing; We sing for all the unsung saints; For all the saints.

All Saints' Day 1 November
Second Service A Cloud of Witnesses

Morning Ps. 15, 84, 149; Evening Ps. 148, 150; Is. 65.17–end; **Heb. 11.32—12.2**

The trouble with saints is that they shame us with their faith; they separate us by their death, and we're not all quite sure what we have to do with them, on the other side of the divide. A roll call of some 16 heroes of faith has been read out to us from Hebrews and, having told us of the lack of time to speak of others, the writer proceeds regardless to add another nine examples to his tally. There are some of the obvious names and some that may surprise us. It's been said that 'a saint is a sinner whose life has been insufficiently researched', and from what we know of some of them, they may not have passed closer scrutiny. But for all that, they are people of faith or, better, people for whom faith won out over the less glorious features of human conduct.

Supporters

They are summoned as a 'great cloud of witnesses' to give us encouragement in running our race. The author of the letter to the Hebrews compares them to sports fans in the stands of a vast stadium. Their race is over but they've not lost interest in those who are still struggling and running. They urge us on and applaud us. And that is how they support our faith.

If you've run a marathon or even been present to support a friend, you'll know that supporters are strategically placed along the route to be ready to give a sharp audible burst of encouragement just at the stages when the energy of the competitors may be evaporating.

Our gallery of faith

Saints are not just the people approved by the Church. They include people we've known and loved and whose faith supports our own race. We tried to bring this home to people once at a summer school. In the chapel, people were given a coloured acetate square on which to draw or name a person in our own personal cloud of witnesses. These were then inserted into a large frame like a stained-glass window. As a hymn was being sung before the preaching, strobe lights illuminated this modern stained-glass window and an ice machine on overdrive filled the chapel with a cloud like smoke.

The particular people whose memory lights up our lives and energizes us to press forward to the prize also need including in our own personal gallery of saints. There aren't fixed frontiers between us. We believe in the 'communion of saints'. Departed saints and we ourselves are in Christ, who is Lord of the living and the dead. When we celebrate the Eucharist they are there with us, along with 'angels and archangels and all the company of heaven'.

Making communion

We sense the reality of this in her published letter by the wife of a late husband sent to her daughter.

> It is hard to believe a year has really gone. Cambridge, the river, the trees, are still there, but none of them will ever look quite as they did. I look at the trees as I walk across Christ's Piece, at their yellow autumn leaves, and can't really yet believe that he and I will never walk there and look at them again together; and yet the darkness and loss are beginning to go, because I'm beginning to know with increasing certainty that part of him is still with us. I only know it sometimes – when I listen to very beautiful music in Caius chapel, or sometimes at Communion, when I know quite unmistakably that he is there.
>
> Death could not separate us from him. I know that increasingly, as life begins to come back into perspective. Because he is part of God's spirit, his own serenity comes through more and more, and his light shines more easily through the slight barrier

of death. Because he was always so much a part of God, he comes back into our lives very easily, as easily as he left us in the summer afternoon at Papworth, content, confident and at peace.[35]

Looking to Jesus

The closer we come to Christ, the more deeply we enter into communion with the saints and all the faithful departed. The practice in some churches of naming our departed friends and family serves to remind us of this connection. Churches in Latin America have a more memorable way of doing the same thing. When the roll of those who've died is called, the congregation calls out 'Present!'[36] It serves as a reminder that it's through Christ, and Christ alone, that we have this communion.

The witness of the saints declares that God's people are not left alone in a climate that is increasingly antagonistic to the idea of a life and 'world' beyond our existing home. The saints are our supporters, but it is Jesus himself who is the pioneer and perfecter of our faith. It's to his living presence that we're called to set our sights and focus our eyes in running the race to which he himself has called us.

Roger Spiller

Suggested hymns

In heavenly love abiding; When human voices cannot sing; O love that wilt not let me go; Glory to you, O God, for all your saints in light.

Third Sunday before Advent   8 November

(For Remembrance Sunday, see p. 273.)

Principal Sunday   **Wait. Watch. Prepare**

Wisd. 6.12–16, *and Canticle*: Wisd. 6.17–20; *or* Amos 5.18–24, *and* Ps. 70; 1 Thess. 4.13–end; **Matt. 25.1–13**

When did you last have to wait for something? Perhaps you're waiting for something now – maybe it's a long time coming. My generation are not very good at waiting. We're used to having things when we want them, and we find waiting for something, even when we know it's going to happen, quite difficult – because we're not in control. Waiting for something when you have no idea when or if it's coming is even harder. It requires patience, endurance and trust.

Wait

Our passages today are addressed to the early Church who were waiting for the return of Jesus. They expected it to be imminent – certainly in their lifetimes – and as the time moved on and there was no sign of Jesus returning, they were getting despondent and confused. In Thessalonians, Paul writes to set their minds at rest: some will die before Jesus returns, but its okay – God has a plan for raising the dead, so that no one will miss the Second Coming. They are to encourage one another in this hope. The parable of the ten bridesmaids also encourages the Church to remain faithful and watchful for the Lord – to be prepared for the coming of God's kingdom among them and not to be caught out and miss the party. Nearly two thousand years on from the early Church, Jesus is yet to return. We are still waiting, and that makes it all the harder for us to comprehend and to heed the warnings about being watchful and prepared for Christ's return. The Church is currently in the kingdom season. It's a thoughtful season of remembering and of pondering God's kingdom. We are mistaken if we think God's kingdom is only in the future, that it will only be established when Christ returns. The kingdom of God is breaking in around all the time, and we need to have eyes of faith to see it, hearts of faith to celebrate it and patient faith to wait for it.

Watch

Our parable warns us what can happen if we're not prepared to see God around us. Ten bridesmaids are watching for the bridegroom. All ten have been chosen: part of his entourage. The bridegroom is delayed, and all ten fall asleep. When the bridegroom arrives, the bridesmaids wake and prepare, but only five are adequately prepared – having brought sufficient oil to light their lamps. The Greek word here is 'torches' – long sticks wrapped in rags, dipped in oil and lit. Such torches require you to keep dipping the rags in the oil about every 15 minutes. The foolish bridesmaids rush off to buy more oil, and while away they miss the bridegroom. Those who are ready and prepared enter the banquet and the doors are shut. When the foolish girls come back, they find themselves shut out and the bridegroom says he doesn't know them. It's a harsh warning! We need to watch for God – to recognize the signs of God at work and be prepared to join in with them as part of God's working. Often God acts when we're not expecting it, when we're half-asleep, or when we've almost given up hope. God acts in places we don't expect, through surprising people, and in ways that startle and puzzle us. Too often in the Church we are anxious and weary. We look at what's not going well; we criticize, and put down rather than build up. We hold on to the familiar and safe rather than look to God's new thing. Sometimes our apathy and negativity kill new initiatives before they've even begun. But this parable teaches us that we are to be expectant, to watch and wait and be filled with hope for that which God is doing among us. We are to be ready to move forward with God when the time is right, and the time is in God's hands not ours.

Prepare

What is God going to do in this church and in this community? We need to be ready and prepared, so that we don't miss God's calling, don't miss the signs of God working and moving among us. Part of the being ready, part of the process of waiting and watching, is about being regular at worship. Part is about being faithful in prayer. Part is about being in touch with God through the Bible. Part is about being aware of God in those around us – in all whom we meet. Part is about recognizing that with God new things are likely to happen, and change is often a requirement of faithful living for the Christian. Here's a spiritual exercise to do through this kingdom season. Write down every night three ways that you have been aware of God working during the day. Three ways in which the kingdom of God has broken in around you. You might read something in the paper. You might have a conversation where you are aware of the Holy Spirit in the dialogue. Something good might take you by surprise. Remember, God works mightily in the world not just in the Church. Be prepared and expectant for the signs of God at work and celebrate them, when you recognize them. Even better – tell each other what you've seen and discovered. Wait, watch and prepare for God. Don't miss the signs, or the party! Amen.

Catherine Williams

Suggested hymns

Hark, what a sound, and too divine for hearing; Jesus Christ is waiting; Give me oil in my lamp; Wait for the Lord.

Third Sunday before Advent 8 November

Second Service What God Does

Ps. [20] 82; **Judg. 7.2–22**; John 15.9–17

When we're preparing for a job interview, we may have to work at selling ourselves. It's not necessarily easy if we have the typical English reserve or low self-confidence. On the other hand, we also need to make sure we don't claim achievements as our own, but rather give credit to members of a team whose contributions have really brought success to our work.

Issues of trust

Gideon's story is told in Judges 6—8. It's a tale about confidence. Gideon's response to his calling shows his doubt that God is with the people of Israel, or that Gideon can really do anything to help. It's not attractive modesty – it's a reaction of fear and unbelief: Gideon is not satisfied until he gets a sign from the Lord. He follows God's first command but only by night because he is afraid. Next, before he leads the armies of Israel, he asks God to reassure him further, by making a fleece heavy with dew while keeping the rest of the threshing floor dry. Still not content, he asks God to repeat it a second time. Before the beginning of today's reading, God has already been remarkably generous in giving Gideon all the reassurances he needs – a pattern that continues.

God, it seems, is unafraid to demonstrate his strength, so that it is simply unquestionable who actually *does* bring about the victory in the end. It's all about what *God* does; apart from God, they stand no chance! God makes the most of Gideon's lack of confidence to show an unbelieving people precisely who's behind Israel's successes. God doesn't hesitate to make victory look totally improbable (unless it's with divine help). First, he cuts down the size of Gideon's army, by sending away those who are afraid. Second, he cuts them down further by distinguishing between those who are shown to be alert and ready by the way they take a drink (with cupped hands enabling them to be more observant). Gideon is left with 300 men and lots of provisions and trumpets.

God is realistic when he speaks to Gideon. God knows that, regardless of what he says to Gideon, Gideon will *still* be afraid. So God sets up yet another encounter to build Gideon's confidence. There's such irony that Gideon is encouraged more by overhearing the conversation of strangers and enemies than by the direct address of God to him! Yet it's hardly, as they say, 'the sword of Gideon' that gains the victory.

Credit where it's due?

It seems that Gideon's 300 men are victorious against the 135,000 enemy forces simply in the act of causing confusion in the camp with their trumpets, torches and jars. Their enemies are in chaos, woken abruptly, and they turn on one another. The enemy soldiers are routed magnificently. But at no point does Gideon lead the Israelites in thanking God. Rather, it seems, this has boosted his own confidence rather than his faith in God. After this seemingly absurd victory, he simply boasts to his allies the Ephraimites of what he has done and what he will do. His ego is all over the place in the text. There are no more scenes of divine reassurance. Gideon, by the end of his life, is seen to have led Israel astray by worshipping idols. He has led people to put their confidence in the wrong things.

A bigger story

Gideon's story, like most of the book of Judges (so-called because it tells heroic stories of different 'Judges' or 'Deliverers of Justice' among the tribes of Israel), shows God's people again and again falling away from the covenant. Will they trust in God, and in God alone? No. Idolatry and disobedience are pictured even when God's people should be most thankful for deliverance.

The book as a whole was probably drawn together in the form we have it today as a piece of political propaganda that gave good reasons for the setting up of King David's monarchy. The people of Israel seemed unable to commit solely to God as sovereign, to trust in him and obey him exclusively. And the stories show how God acts in the particular: he has chosen this people, but despite this particular choice, they don't mirror that in their relationship. They need a kind of leadership that will help them to choose the Lord and keep to the particular promises he has given to his chosen people.

All about God?

Perhaps this story lends new light to Jesus' words in the Gospel of John today. 'You did not choose me, but I chose you.' At baptism, new Christians have a number of questions to answer, called 'The Decision'. They *decide* for God. They choose Christ.

We aren't always very good at keeping on choosing God, choosing Jesus Christ as our way, our truth and our life. But our saving grace lies in the fact not that we chose Jesus but that he chose us. It would be easy to feel special because of this, as we receive the particular grace of God; but obedience to God means that we realize *it's not about us, it's about God*. It's God who achieves victories and successes; we can't do that apart from him. It's God who achieves our salvation; we can't do that by ourselves. We aren't chosen because of who we are; we are chosen because of who God is.

So it's not for us to judge others according to whether or not we think God has or hasn't chosen them. It is for us to be truly confident in a God who chooses simply because of who he is, a God who will have improbable patience, generosity and power. That's the choice that ultimately matters.

God's decisions for us, and our decisions for God, are rooted in love.

Megan Daffern

Suggested hymns

There is a land of pure delight; Guide me, O thou great Redeemer; God is working his purpose out; O God of Bethel, by whose hand.

Remembrance Sunday 8 November
(The readings of the day or those for 'The Peace of the World' or 'In Time of Trouble' can be used. These are for 'The Peace of the World'.)

Isa. 9.1–6; Ps. 40.14–17; **Phil. 4.6–9**; Matt. 5.43–48

> Do not worry about anything, but in everything by prayer and supplication with thanksgiving let your requests be made known to God. And the peace of God, which surpasses all understanding, will guard your hearts and your minds in Christ Jesus. (Phil. 4.6–7)

Imaginative remembering

In 2003 the world was introduced for the first time to a man called Matthew Shardlake. He is the main protagonist in a series of novels written by C. J. Sansom set in London during the reign of Henry VIII, and a wonderful creation Shardlake is too. He is a barrister at the Inns of Court, a man physically handicapped by being a hunchback, who finds himself caught up in the dark and murky political life of the capital. He navigates his way through it, and with skill and integrity solves crimes and murders en route. If you haven't read any of the Shardlake novels, I commend them to you. They are brilliant.

One of the great things about the novels is their historical accuracy. C. J. Sansom has a PhD in history from Birmingham University and trained as a solicitor, so his research for each novel is meticulous. He not only gives his readers an insight into the political complexities of Tudor England, but in the details about the streets of the City of London, its dockyards, ale-houses and celebrations, he enables his readers to get a real feel for the times.

It's so real it's almost as though he himself were there. But here's a conundrum: how does a writer of historical novels go about his work?

Well. There has to be careful research and there has to be the capacity to tell a good story, but above all there has to be the ability to imagine. The word 'immersive' is nowadays overdone, but in C. J. Sansom's case no other word will do. Clearly, he has completely immersed himself in his characters and in Tudor England, and we his readers are more richly informed as a result.

But why on a Remembrance Sunday am I drawing your attention to C. J. Sansom? It's all to do with the process of 'imaginative remembering'.

When we meet, as we have done today, to remember those from our country who gave their lives in armed conflicts we are impelled to use our imaginations. Very few of us nowadays have direct experience of war, and the numbers who can tell us about the huge military conflicts of the twentieth century are inevitably diminishing as time rolls on.

What is remembering?

In these circumstances, how can we talk of 'remembering'?

Let's look at what we actually do on a Remembrance Sunday. We speak aloud the names of the dead, and so we should. We take part in time-honoured rituals: ‘They shall grow not old as we that are left grow old . . .’ We keep two minutes of silence. We lay wreaths. But within this, we are engaging our imaginations so that we can picture the kind of people our predecessors and ancestors might have been, the horrors they experienced, the pain, the misery, the sense of bewilderment, the anguish and boredom, the bravery and heroism. Imaginatively we try to place ourselves in their shoes. But we are going even deeper than that: we are rehearsing and exploring our own humanity. Could we have done what they did? Would we have been heroes? Would we have coped with the fear? When we remember the fallen we are, as it were, recognizing our own potential limitations and perhaps promising ourselves to try to overcome them. By remembering, therefore, we not only bring the past to life, we are implicitly testing ourselves morally and spiritually.

A holy act of remembering

At the very heart of our Christian faith there is also a great and holy act of remembrance that has nothing to do with war. It is an act of remembering that we carry out whenever the Holy Communion, the Eucharist, the Lord’s Supper, the Mass, takes place. When Jesus was at the Last Supper with his friends he broke bread, blessed God and gave the bread to his disciples, saying, ‘Take, eat. This is my body which is given for you. Do this in remembrance of me.’ Ever since, for the best part of two thousand years, the Church has followed that command, and in doing so has discovered that somehow the risen Christ himself, in and through the breaking of the bread, is present with us, in our very midst.

None of us, of course, were present at that last meal in Jerusalem, so how can we talk authentically and honestly about remembering? Again, it is about entering the past imaginatively in such a way that the past becomes present to us. But it has a deeper dimension. We also are involved in testing ourselves morally and spiritually. We are brought face to face with who we are. We recognize our frailty, we seek forgiveness and we receive the gift of God’s grace.

At the heart of all remembering, whether that be the special form of remembering on Remembrance Sunday, or the act of remembering associated with the Last Supper, God himself is present. He holds all time in his hands, past, present and future. He holds us, his creation, in his hands. And, therefore, we are caught up with him and with each other in the mysteries of life.

We give thanks for the gift of imagination and pray that through our imaginations we may be so inspired by God that we become more compassionate, more honest and more devoted to that love and peace that passes all understanding.

Christopher Herbert

Suggested hymns

O God, our help in ages past; Hope for the world's despair; Awake, awake, to love and work; Dear Lord and Father of mankind.

Second Sunday before Advent 15 November

Principal Service **Monologue: The Man with Few Talents**

Zeph. 1.7, 12–end; Ps. 90.1–8 [9–11] 12 [*or* 90.1–8]; 1 Thess. 5.1–11; **Matt. 25.14–30**

Well, I'm the unlucky servant, given just one talent by my master, and it's time you heard my side of the story. Still, I'm rather chuffed that I got a mention by Jesus in one of his stories. And now I'm immortalized, and people will be discussing me for generations. I'm not sure what Jesus intended in telling my story, but when I've had my say you can decide for yourselves.

My story began when my master was about to go off on another so-called business venture. It might be to join a big yacht moored off the Italian coast for all I know. Well, before he goes he makes arrangements so that he can maximize his income while he's away. He's got spare cash, eight talents in all. Spare change for him, but do you know how long it takes to earn one single talent? It's what a labourer working all year round at the grape harvest would earn in 15 years!

And let me tell you another thing. He amassed all this fortune by exploiting the poor. If the peasant farmers needed a loan, when, say, there's a crop failure, he can fix them up with a loan, but the interest repayments are exorbitant, and if they fall behind with their repayments, he seizes their land. You know how he summed up his business practice? 'I reap where I do not sow and gather where I do not scatter.' Seizing or squeezing, we call it. He takes what doesn't belong to him and benefits from the labours of others. And, of course, he expects us, his retainers, to copy him and become richer through taking advantage of even less fortunate people, making a healthy profit for ourselves on the side. Well, he knows us to be shrewd operators so he distributes his talents on the basis of our previous performance. I didn't mind; in fact, I was relieved just to receive one; after all, that alone is worth £300,000 in today's money. And it carries a lot of responsibility.

My lord returns and summons us. And, of course, the only thing that matters to him is profit and managing money. Amassing wealth like the other two stewards is all he cares about, and so they get enthusiastic, back-slapping plaudits. But then it's my turn to hand over the money and it's the moment I've been dreading. But I've at least kept the money safe and I've got good reasons for what I did. But I wasn't expecting the tirade of abuse that he delivered as he snatched the coins off me. 'You wicked and lazy servant.' He tells me that at the very least I should have invested it in a bank. A bank! Hasn't he heard how unreliable they've become? Merchants of greed. Hasn't he heard of HBOS, Royal Bank of Scotland, Lehman Brothers? Besides, there are treasures that have come to light that were buried and kept safe for 15,000 years. If you'd left that in a bank vault, it would either have been forgotten or seized by the treasury.

Well, I know what my employer thinks about me, but what does Jesus think about me? Well, strike me down, but he doesn't say anything. He just tells the story and leaves it to his hearers to work it out for themselves. But one thing's for sure, he can't approve of my master's dishonest and greedy conduct, not when he's teaching about the danger of riches, the abuse of authority and respect for the poor and exploited. But where does that leave me?

Some of my mates who heard Jesus thought he might be citing me not for doing anything wrong but simply for doing nothing. I was just too lazy or fearful to carry out my responsibilities. I needed to maximize my opportunities and not waste them, maintain business as usual in my master's absence and be ready to give a good account when he returned. Apparently, my story follows another story about being ready and responsible, which concerned wise and foolish virgins.

Jesus could be citing me to warn people that they all have gifts and opportunities, but they are not the same for everybody. But we have to use what we've been given in such a bold and enterprising way that when the king of all the world comes, we will be ready to enter his kingdom.

Others who had heard Jesus tell my story thought I was shown to have made myself a fool by jeopardizing my own prospects.

They thought Jesus was using me to warn his followers not to try to pretend they could withdraw from the messy, murky business of trade and markets and commerce, as if they could escape from the real world. They heard him say on another occasion that we have to make friends with money, and that children who live in the real world are often wiser than those who live in the other world.

Just when I felt I was being condemned, set up for all time as a lazy, good-for-nothing fool, it was suggested that Jesus might be giving me praise for publicly exposing my master's exploitative and corrupt practices and for putting the talent right out of circulation so that it could not be used to tempt people to take out loans that would condemn them to a lifetime's unpayable debt and crippling interest repayments. So, did Jesus intend my story to show my courage as a whistle-blower, who turned his back on ill-gotten gains and rising prospects and security?

Well, that's it really. Did Jesus take me for a fool for not grasping the opportunities I had, or some kind of moral hero, for daring to expose corrupt practices that deny his kingdom? It's really for you to decide.

Roger Spiller

Suggested hymns

Take this moment, sign and space; Take my life and let it be; Let us talents and tongues employ; O Lord my God, when I in awesome wonder.

Second Sunday before Advent 15 November
Second Service The Blessing of Naming and Being Named

Ps. 89.19–37 [*or* 89.19–29]; 1 Kings 1.15–40 [*or* 1–40];
Rev. 1.4–18; *Gospel at Holy Communion*: Luke 9.1–6

> 'I am the Alpha and the Omega', says the Lord God, who is and who was and who is to come, the Almighty.'

'Today we have naming of parts'

The Jewish authors of the books of the Old Testament were fascinated by names. Take, for instance, the delightful story in Genesis in which Adam names all the creatures on earth. This is what the author wrote:

> So out of the ground the LORD God formed every animal of the field and every bird of the air, and brought them to the man to see what he would call them; and whatever the man called every living creature, that was its name. The man gave names to all cattle, and to the birds of the air, and to every animal of the field.

It's the kind of whimsical fairy story in which you wonder how Adam might have come up with names such as aardvark, or ant, or armadillo. By the way, and this is totally useless information, the name 'aardvark' comes from Afrikaans and means 'earth pig'. Which all goes to prove that it wasn't just Adam who loved naming things – so do we all. Think, again whimsically, of the name 'Eeyore' in the Winnie the Pooh stories. It's a clever name for a character that captures the braying sound made by a donkey but also somehow embraces the melancholy nature of the character itself.

The joy of naming

Naming things seems to be a characteristic of all human beings. But let's return to the Old Testament, for there we find not only the joy in naming things but the joy in naming places. Here's an example: Jacob, on one of his journeys, had an encounter with a man who wrestled with him throughout the night. At daybreak the man said to Jacob, 'Let me go.' But Jacob replied that he would not cease from his wrestling match unless the man blessed him.

> So he said to him, 'What is your name?' And he said, 'Jacob.' Then the man said, 'You shall no longer be called Jacob, but Israel, for you have striven with God and with humans, and have prevailed.' Then Jacob asked him, 'Please tell me your name.' But he said, 'Why is it that you ask my name?' And there he blessed him. So Jacob called the place Peniel, saying, 'For I have seen God face to face, and yet my life is preserved.'

Genesis

In that story not only is Jacob renamed. He is given the name 'Israel', which means 'the one who strives with God', but he also names the place where the encounter took place. He called it 'Peniel', which means 'the face of God'.

Sometimes names in the Old Testament are used as warnings. Hosea the prophet named his children in just such a way: one he called 'Jezreel', which means 'God sows'; his daughter he named Lo-ruhamah, which means 'Not loved' (you can imagine what that did for her mental well-being as she grew up); and the next son he called 'Lo-ammi', which means 'Not my people'. What terrible names to inflict on children.

The renaming of people also continued in the New Testament: Jesus called James and John 'Boanerges', that is, 'Sons of thunder', because of their fiery dispositions, and famously he drew attention to the name 'Peter', which means 'rock', and said, 'On this rock I will build my church.'

The naming of God

But perhaps the most significant story about names comes in the account of Moses at the burning bush where Moses bravely asks God what his name is, and God replies 'I AM WHO I AM', which can also be translated as 'I am what I am' or 'I will be what I will be'. That was one of the greatest of insights, for the name contained both present and future, and also implied that God was Being itself, the source and ground of all being.

In the first chapter of the book of Revelation, which we heard read earlier, a similar brilliant and profound insight is offered by the author. He describes God as being the Alpha and the Omega. Alpha is the first letter of the Greek alphabet and Omega is its last letter. The more you think about it, the richer such an idea is. It implies that all words come from God. Everything that has ever been named, every thought that has ever been uttered, everything that is described within the words composed from the letters of the alphabet, are held in being by God. God is the divine Word that contains all words.

It's a stunning thought. Now, whether the author of Revelation had the Moses story in mind when he wrote his book, who can tell? But he ensured that not only the 'I AM' version of God's name was remembered but also the alternative translation, 'I will be who I will be'. In short, not only all the things that can be named or uttered are within God's being but so also is all time: time past, time present and time future.

And if that is true, then it follows that we too are held within the boundless infinity of God. Our own past is hidden with him, so is our present, and so will our future be. And our own names, composed of the letters of the alphabet, are also known and cherished by God. What a blessing.

Christopher Herbert

Suggested hymns

Thine arm O Lord in days of old; When all thy mercies, O my God; God is working his purpose out; Before Jehovah's aweful throne.

Christ the King 22 November (Sunday next before Advent)

Principal Service **Jesus, Hidden King**

Ezek. 34.11–16, 20–24; Ps. 95.1–7; Eph. 1.15–end; **Matt. 25.31–end**

One of the features of our recent society is the pervasive introduction of tests, assessments, reviews and appraisals. Tiresome and unwelcome they might be, but how can we know where we stand without feedback? How can we have the satisfaction of monitoring our progress or attainments without the judgement of exams or appraisals? Judgement has come to have a negative meaning, but in the Jewish Christian context it comes close to a process of 'discernment'. On that understanding, judgement was usually a welcome event for Judaism. It couldn't come soon enough for many people, because it would cause wrongs and injustices to be righted and the hopes of the Messiah to be realized. God's people were often deluded in putting themselves on the right side of judgement, but at least the fact of judgement served to reset the pattern of life that was expected of them.

Today the festival of Christ the King comes at the end of the Church's year and the onset of the penitential season of Advent, and so it is well placed to help us to review our lives afresh and to prepare us to make good use of the new year.

A puzzling text

The judgement scene from Matthew's Gospel makes for a puzzling read, for which scholars have been debating for more than

1,700 years and still with varied and inconclusive results. It depicts the Last Judgement, but is that intended to be a description or a parable? What shocks us is that the basis of judgement is quite simply how we respond to the poor and needy. That would seem at variance with the fundamental teaching of Paul and of Jesus in the parables, where the judgement goes in favour of all those who acknowledge their culpability, plead the death of Jesus and trust in the gift of faith.

Now with Matthew the goal posts seem to have changed and there's uncertainty as to the basis of the final judgement ahead of us. We must at once acknowledge with James that 'faith without works is dead', and that if the grace and generosity that we have received at God's hands doesn't compel us to offer generosity in turn to others, then our claim to have appropriated God's grace is mistaken and we are deluded.

Another interpretation of the story suggests that it's not the generality of the poor and needy of the world that Mathew intends. It's the more restricted group of needy disciples, hounded, rejected and persecuted Christian missionaries. These are the ones referred to as 'one of the least of these who are members of my family'. If it's the disciples who are cast as needy, then it's the non-Christian world that is being judged for its rejection of their message and its hard-heartedness to the messengers. On this showing, the story is intended to be an encouragement to those Christian disciples who suffer for their faith.

The needy make Christ visible

On either view, the story identifies Jesus with people. Jesus is King, we declare, but what king is hidden, incognito, in his poor and needy people? Today we expect high visibility, accessibility, immediate action and responsiveness from those we put in authority. We infer absence from those who are not grabbing the headlines, occupying the limelight. But our King, though hidden, is present. Jesus Christ is not only at the right hand of God. He comes to us again and again in the flesh of individual men, women and children, in their wretchedness and need. He is really present in daily life by means of the men and women who need our succour. If they are Christ's ambassadors, how then can we feel superior and resentful of their presence? The eyes of the world may see them as beggars who need to crave our help, but we are to see in them the Lord Jesus Christ and their right to be served as we would serve an earthly king.

Serving Jesus in the other

There was a monastery that had fallen on hard times and was likely to close, so the guardian asked the advice of a rabbi. And he said, tell the monks that one of them is the Messiah. And word went round that one of them is God's emissary. Who could it be? Not that crotchety old monk Titus? Not Brother James? But since it could be any one of them, they treated each other with great respect and care. And soon the monastery became healthy, and people came to it, to discover the secret of its new life.

The challenge and tension of our Gospel remains. But, as one scholar suggests, we 'need the idea of judgement because, without it, we would be unable to take God seriously as God'.[37] And heroic action isn't being asked for. Even a cup of water or a discarded item of clothing is sufficient for us to be serving the world's unknown King.

Although now hidden, we can declare to the world and to our own troubled hearts that Christ is King. This is the counter rhetoric to the false perspective that there is no alternative to the fixed, fated, expiring and menacing world in which we live. We know that God's kingdom will come on earth as it is in heaven, because its king, Jesus, has begun his reign on earth and acts in and with his needy people.

And so, as we move into the glorious season of Advent, we learn again what it means for us to wait and work and pray, and look forward to Christ's just and gentle rule, and prepare to open ourselves so as to enthrone him in our lives.

Roger Spiller

Suggested hymns

Brother, sister, let me serve you; When I needed a neighbour were you there?; Jesus Christ is waiting; Gracious God, in adoration.

Christ the King 22 November
(Sunday next before Advent)
Second Service The Last Words

Morning Ps. 29, 110; Evening Ps. 93 [97]; **2 Sam. 23.1–7**, *or* 1 Macc. 2.15–29; Matthew 28.16–end

Famous last words

On 24 June AD 79, the dying Emperor Vespasian is reputed by Suetonius to have said, 'Oh dear, I think I am becoming a god.' Given that he ruled during an era when deceased emperors were often, posthumously, declared to have been divine, he could be fairly certain that, once dead, he would be so elevated.

Throughout history there has been a fashion for recording the last words of the famous (and the infamous). So I must admit that one such quotation that I prefer to recall is, 'The best of all is, God is with us,' which were the last words of John Wesley, as he lay on his deathbed, surrounded by his friends, on 2 March 1791.

Somehow, last words resonate with us. Hence, even those of us of less significance than an emperor of Rome, or the founder of a religious movement, might hope that our last recorded words or wishes should leave a legacy to the world. However, I doubt that I'll have the wit to come up with anything memorable and I don't intend to leave too convoluted a will.

The last words of David

We've heard the 'last words' of David from 2 Samuel. In the Hebrew Bible the books we know as First and Second Samuel form one book, which is named for Samuel, who anointed both kings Saul and David, hence how David refers to himself as 'the man whom God exalted'. Samuel was the last great judge of Israel. The book covers the period from about 1075 to 975 BC. In our Bible, 2 Samuel recounts the reign of David. David was popular, and in folk memory he was remembered as *the* great king. He was a man of great faith, but he was flawed, far from perfect: from the story of his affair with Bathsheba we know that he could be ruthless. However, given his status in Jewish memory, his last words would be regarded as noteworthy.

According to the first words of our text itself, these are the last words of David. Wait a minute, though; there are further words from him in the remaining chapter of 2 Samuel – so, in what respect are these, indeed, last words? Are they those of David as an inspired author rather than some last will and testament?

Surely the best way to appreciate these words is to examine them a bit more closely. David says that they're the words the spirit of the Lord has spoken through him; he's God's mouthpiece. They take the literary form of a brief poem. As to the content of the poem, it's a summary of the ideology of kingship. Remember, David was not only a faith leader, he was also the king.

David acknowledges that all power derives from God. When God permitted his people to have a king, that form of social order became part of his plan. As the story of David reveals, kingship was a gift from God (he had done nothing to deserve to be king), so David was the king only by God's will. As king he was required to be faithful: we know of David that he didn't serve other gods, but he sometimes failed in his faithfulness to Yahweh. The safety and security of the nation was rooted in faith in God, whose anointed was the king.

God has spoken, and his chosen king is to reign justly, for the sake of the weak and the poor. David compares the justice of a king with the fruitfulness that will arise from the mixture of sun and rain (in the previous chapters there's reference to the problem of drought).

In the closing verses there's a reminder that the relationship between Yahweh-God, David (the king) and the people is grounded in the everlasting covenant that God has made. The Davidic covenant is a promise to the house of David. It's a gift from God to which the king (and the people) must respond with faithfulness. Through the covenant, the safety and security of the faithful people is secured, but in the final verses we learn that the godless will perish.

Getting the last word

In the Christian tradition so much of the language that is used about Jesus is derived from that about his forebear David. Jesus is the flawless, faithful King who will bring God's justice.

Does our God reign here? If the measure of any society is how it treats its most vulnerable citizens, then surely we too should be concerned about the nature of our society. Do we experience leadership that understands that it must rule with justice and equity, or are those we elect to office still more flawed than David? Can we reintroduce the notion of faithfulness?

Let's listen to the voices of those who speak the truth. Who will be God's mouthpiece now? It is God who, ultimately, will have the last word.

Wendy Kilworth-Mason

Suggested hymns

Rejoice, the Lord is King; Thou didst leave thy throne; Christ whose glory fills the skies; Majesty; King of kings, majesty.

Sermons for Saints' Days and Special Occasions

Stephen, Deacon, First Martyr 26 December

Faithful unto Death

2 Chron. 24.2–22, *or* **Acts 7.51–end**; Ps. 119.161–168 (*if the Acts reading is used instead of the Old Testament reading, the New Testament reading is* Gal.2.16b–20); Matt. 10.17–22

The commemoration of the first Christian martyr the day after we celebrate the birth of Jesus emphasizes the sacrifice that is part of the Christian's vocation. This was memorably described in the Christmas sermon that T. S. Eliot wrote for his play *Murder in the Cathedral*, commemorating the Christian martyr Thomas à Becket:

> At this same time of all the year that we celebrate at once the Birth of Our Lord and His Passion and Death upon the Cross. Beloved, as the World sees, this is to behave in a strange fashion. For who in the World will both mourn and rejoice at once and for the same reason? For either joy will be overborne by mourning, or mourning will be cast out by joy; so it is only in these our Christian mysteries that we can rejoice and mourn at once for the same reason.[38]

Serving at tables

Stephen is first heard of when chosen with six others to solve a minor administrative problem. In the church community in Jerusalem, there were Christians, widows who had come from Greek centres to spend their last days in or near Jerusalem, probably without family and so in need of support. They felt neglected, as distinct from the native Hebrew, Judaean Christians, in the daily provision of care and charity. When the need for additional assistance was required, the 12 disciples said, 'It is not acceptable that we should forsake the word of God and serve at tables', and so the decision was to made to select 'men of good repute and full of the Spirit and wisdom' to handle this issue.

Stephen was one, and seems to have headed up the group of seven, all with Greek names, who might have hailed from Greek cities. It's likely that choosing people with Greek affiliations to serve widows who were also Greek-speaking reflected the recognition that mission is always assisted by matching people of similar backgrounds. These men were probably evangelists and not just social workers.

Establishing Christian identity

St Luke gives his customary report on the numerical growth of the church and reports on the signs and wonders made at Stephen's hands. But these were early days for the fledgling Christians, as they had yet to define themselves in relation to Judaism from which they had sprung and also to the Gentile and Greek Christians who lacked a background in Judaism. Were Christians a development of Judaism, so that they might remain as a sect within it? And where would that leave Gentile Christians? Might they too need to embrace some aspects of Judaism, and if so, which laws: table fellowship, circumcision? Or was Christianity destined to break free of Judaism altogether? This was clearly a fundamental question for Christians that would take time to resolve. It remains a big question today, in a multi-faith society, although not in the same terms. At stake was not merely a theological dispute but, as we shall see, an issue that could lead to persecution and death. Jews who did not become Christians would understandably be incensed with those of their number who had become Christians and had, in their view, betrayed the ancestral faith. Their angst was focused on Stephen in particular and he was carried off by a mob to the authorities. He was arrested on the charge that he blasphemed God and attacked the institution of the Temple. This is reminiscent of the trial of Jesus, where false witnesses testify and make slanderous and trumped-up charges.

The case for the prosecution

In a court scene, the High Priest put the charges to Stephen and got more than he bargained for. Stephen responded by giving a long speech setting out a potted history of the Jews, from the call of Abraham. He showed that his opponents were wrong in suggesting he was opposed to Moses and the law. In fact Stephen spoke well of Moses and valued the law. In this he, and probably Luke, held a different view of the law from Paul, whose gospel arguably marginalized the place given to the law in Judaism.

The witness statement

As Stephen got into his stride, he became more offensive to the Jews. He claimed that the Israelites were idolaters during their time in the wilderness, but when it came to the Temple, Stephen was to bring fierce opposition on his head. In this, at least, his opponent's accusation was correct. Stephen had no love of the Temple regime and seems to have identified with Jesus' foretelling of its destruction. He claimed that the Temple should not have been built and cited some of the few Old Testament passages that supported his view. He appeared also to have denied, in step with Jeremiah, that God required sacrificial worship at all.

His rejection of the Temple was a view not shared by all other Christians, including St Paul, who continued to use the Temple. Stephen concluded that throughout their history Jewish people were in the habit of disobeying the messages addressed by God to his people. The die was cast, but even under pressure Stephen's accusers noted that they 'saw his face as if it had been the face of an angel'. Stephen was thrown out of the city and stoned to death. This might be a judicial murder, but equally it is suggestive of a mob lynching.

Stephen has rejected at least some aspects of Judaism. Now, in killing Stephen, the Jews have shown Judaism's own rejection of the gospel. Stephen in his dying claimed to have a vision of heaven opened and the Son of Man standing at the right hand of God, standing as in readiness to welcome him.

There's a tantalizing mention of a young man in the crowd who witnessed the killing. His name was Saul, and he probably cast his vote in favour of Stephen's martyrdom.

We mistake the Christian faith if we separate birth and dying, death and resurrection, discipleship and sacrifice. Today we have to reckon with the news that Christians are the most persecuted religious group in the world. 'An estimated one in three people suffer from religious persecution and the persecution of Christians in parts of the world is at near "genocide" levels.'[39] We cannot forget the cost of discipleship, not even at Christmas.

Roger Spiller

Suggested hymns

Stephen, first of Christian martyrs; Take my life, and let it be; Sing my song when faith is sleeping; Be still, my soul: the Lord is on your side.

St John, Apostle and Evangelist 27 December

Seeing and Believing

Ex. 33.7–11a; Ps.117; **1 John 1**; John 21.19b–end

> We declare to you what was from the beginning, what we have heard, what we have seen with our eyes, what we have looked at and touched with our hands, concerning the word of life.

So there he sits. He's at his desk with a blank sheet of papyrus in front of him. He gazes through the window, which is framed by the tendrils of a vine dappled in sunlight. Its leaves tremble in the soft breeze of the early morning. In the far distance is a range of hills, on the top of which he can see the outlines of a temple dedicated to Zeus.

He dips his stylus in the inkwell, pauses and then scratches a few words on to the papyrus. He writes: 'We declare to you what was from the beginning . . .'

He is not quite certain why he has written these particular words. Perhaps it was looking at the temple of Zeus. He knew that he wanted to make as strong a statement as possible about Jesus of Nazareth, and that proud and beautiful temple of Zeus spurred him to write a sentence that set Jesus not only as a complete contrast to the Greek gods in the neighbourhood but stated with absolute conviction that because Jesus was the Logos, he had existed from the very beginnings of time.

To make sure that the power of his belief struck home, he scribbled a few more words, but, this time, words that conveyed that Jesus was utterly real. He was not a figment of the luxuriant imagination of his Greek neighbours. Jesus was not a fickle god playing carelessly with the lives of mortals, nor was he just one god among many. He was unique. He had come to earth. He was the Word from the very heart of the universe, from the centre of the being of God.

The imaginary author

Now, of course, this picture of the author of the Epistle is entirely imaginary. The situation of the act of writing could have been very different. It might have been, for example, that if the author of the Epistle was the same man who wrote the Gospel of John – and biblical scholars disagree about who the author of the Epistle was – then the idea of Jesus as the Word, the Logos, would have been an idea he had been pondering for a very long time. You will recall that the Gospel of John begins with the sonorous lines, 'In the beginning was the Word . . .'

But if the author was not John the Evangelist we can suppose that, whoever the author might have been, he had been profoundly influenced by the thought of John. Might he have been an acquaintance, or perhaps someone who had heard John speak? The fact is, we cannot know.

All that we have is the text in front of us. We can surmise that that text was written at a time when what is called the Docetic heresy was in full flow. This was a belief that Jesus was, as it were, only a virtual human; he was not real flesh and blood. The author of our Epistle sets out to counter that heresy. He writes in his very first sentence his counterblast: 'what we have heard, what we have seen with our eyes, what we have looked at and touched with our hands, concerning the word of life. . .'.

The belief that Jesus was fully human and fully God

He is adamant that Jesus of Nazareth was completely real, completely human – but equally adamant that he was also the Logos, the one through whom the whole of creation had come into being; the one who had become incarnate; the one who had returned in resurrection glory to God. The claims are stupendous and stretch our minds to breaking point. Questions pile in upon each other: how can the infinite become finite? What happens to what we might term God's infinite-ness when he walked the earth? How can the one who is all-knowing become a fallible human being, susceptible like all human beings to making mistakes? How can the divine step away from his own divinity? How can the timeless become bounded by time? How can an immortal being suffer?

Now, of course, in the Greek world the gods in the mythologies descended from the heavens and walked the earth, but on earth they behaved in fickle and arbitrary fashion. Was not Hermes, for example, known as a trickster? Did not Dionysus have a reputation for encouraging loss of self-restraint and drunkenness? Was not Aphrodite, born full-grown from the head of Zeus, known for her wisdom but was also the goddess of war?

The cultural context of the Epistle

It is against this kind of mythological and cultural background that the Epistle of John needs to be read. Its strong, powerful and simple message is about the very essence of God. God, according to the author, has revealed to humankind the deep truths of his own nature.

Such a theological statement has consequences for those of us who are the followers of Jesus, the Logos. If we follow the Word, do we not have a moral obligation to live as children of the Word? To be a disciple of Christ is to choose a way of living that necessarily challenges the beliefs and behaviours of our own age and culture, in the same kind of way that the author of the Epistle, when he was choosing the words to speak of God, challenged the behaviours and beliefs of his own age.

Are we up for that? If you were asked to write a letter to our own age about God, a letter that had punch and dynamism, what would your opening sentence be?

Christopher Herbert

Suggested hymns

Come, thou Redeemer of the earth; A great and mighty wonder; Word that formed creation, earth and sea and sky; Christ is the world's light.

Holy Innocents 28 December

Innocents: Catching the Reflections of Christ

Jer. 31.15–17; Ps. 124; 1 Cor. 1.26–29; **Matt. 2.13–18**

Jolted out of our comfort zone

Of all the images we have in our minds of Christ, which dominate? The good shepherd? The healer? The crucified Christ? Christ risen from death? Perhaps at Christmas we've been imagining Jesus as a plump baby surrounded by festive trimmings! If so, today's Gospel reading jolts us out of our cocoon and shines a spotlight upon the stark and painful realities of our human life that God in Christ entered and shared. Here is a ruler incited to acts of violence even against his own people. Here are tiny babies and small infants slaughtered in the name of a supposed political stability. And here is the plight of a displaced family, fleeing violence and seeking refuge in a foreign country – not just on one occasion, but twice over. It is striking that Matthew makes no reference to Nazareth in his account of the birth of Jesus. Unlike Luke, he neither writes that Mary came originally from Nazareth, nor tells a story of Mary and Joseph travelling to Behlehem.

The infant Jesus: a refugee

Matthew's drama of Jesus' birth begins in Bethlehem, in Judaea, and it is here that wise men come bringing gifts. And when violence threatens, it is from here that the family flees south into neighbouring Egypt, seeking refuge there. But the story of flight does not finish here. When Herod's reign of terror comes to an end, an angel appears to Joseph in a dream instructing him to go back to the land of Israel. It is still dangerous there, however: Herod's son Archelaus has come to the throne, and Joseph is frightened of settling in Bethlehem. So what instead? The angel commands Joseph to seek refuge yet somewhere else: in Nazareth in Galilee, to the north. So they move on again. And there Jesus grows up – in a different community, far from Bethlehem.

God with us in a violent world

This text offers us a strong image of the infant Christ as a refugee in a very insecure and dangerous world – not a million miles from our own. Until we stare into this Gospel and face both its horror and the uncomfortable image of Christ that it offers, we aren't ready even to begin to grasp the magnificent and frightening truth of the incarnation – God with us: with us here in this complex, unjust and war-torn world. We proclaim God in Christ, Emmanuel, God with us, and we catch his reflection in the faces of the most vulnerable of our world.

The murder of innocents and the crucified Christ

Matthew speaks not only of the holy family who flee, but also of those for whom there is no escape from violence, and in this passage those victims are infants. Still arguably today, but even more so in the ancient world, small children were considered to be the most powerless in society. There is a raw irony in the way in which Herod, the king maintained and protected by the power of the Roman Empire, is so frightened of losing power that he turns to murdering the most powerless in society – small children – in order to shore himself up. Matthew speaks movingly of the nature of unquenched sorrow felt by those whose children have died. He quotes Jeremiah, declaring that there is 'loud lamentation' and 'weeping'. The tears of Rachel, who for Matthew represents all the mothers of Israel, will not dry.

Traditionally this story has been referred to as the flight into Egypt and the slaughter of the holy innocents. In its wisdom, the Church has often seen in the massacre of these children a foreshadowing of the death of Christ. Even if the innocents, unlike Christ himself, had no choice in the matter, the Church has traditionally wanted to see in the face of these little ones a picture of Christ himself, saving others by his death.

How can these images change us?

So this passage offers us two images of Christ. First, we have the picture of the infant Christ fleeing violence and seeking refuge in foreign lands. And second, we have an invitation to see a reflection of the crucified Christ in the life of each massacred infant.

This text challenges us to ask ourselves what images of Christ we are most ready to hold. What if, when we prayed 'Jesus Christ, forgive us', we imagined Christ not as the kindly elder brother or the victorious king in glory, but as the one dying on the cross, or as the small innocent child screaming as the bombs fall? What if, when we prayed, 'Have mercy on us sinners', we imagined Christ not as the one seated in pomp in the Temple, but as the vulnerable child seeking hope and security far from home? With such images, how might our prayer be deepened? How might God challenge us and change our lives?

Mary Cotes

Suggested hymns

O little Love, who comes again; The tyrant issues his decree; Inspired by love and anger; Father Eternal, ruler of creation.

Naming and Circumcision of Jesus 1 January

Name Above All Names

Num. 6.22–end; Ps. 8; Gal 4.4–7; **Luke 2.15–21**

Happy New Year! What New Year's resolutions have you made? Mine tend to be the same most years and run along the lines of:

get thinner, get fitter, read *Remembrance of Things Past* by Proust, visit the Taj Mahal and acquire a Mini Cooper. Needless to say, I never manage any of them! A new year is a liminal moment – a time of transition from one year to the next, an opportunity to look both backwards and forwards. January gets its name from the double-faced Roman god Janus who looked in both directions at once. The turning of the year is an important moment for many people. It's a point of reference for the beginning of new things, for fresh hope in a similar but maybe shallower way to the new birth and hope we experience as Christians with the coming of the Christ-child. Today we celebrate that child's naming and circumcision.

Looking back

Eight days after his birth, using the age-old Jewish ritual, Jesus is named and circumcised. The ritual of male circumcision, called *brit milah* in Hebrew, dates back to Abraham, and is a sign of the covenant between God and God's people, recorded in Genesis. God declared to Abraham that he would be the founder of a vast nation, which would be a great blessing for the entire world. Our Old Testament passage today from Numbers is the Aaronic blessing: 'The Lord bless you and keep you.' It indicates that God is pleased with us, and shows us his special regard. It's a blessing that bestows well-being and is also part of the prayer that Hannah used to dedicate her son Samuel to God. Pregnant with Jesus, while visiting her cousin Elizabeth, Mary sang her great song of praise and revolution indicating that all generations would call her blessed because of God's favour towards her. It's important that Luke records the naming and circumcision of Jesus because, through it, Jesus is fulfilling the Law of Moses: he is a Jew, 'born under the law', as St Paul writes.

The name given to Mary's son is 'Jesus' – the name indicated by Gabriel at the Annunciation. Jesus means 'saviour', 'salvation' or 'God saves'. Names are very important – they are indicative of character. Sometimes they require quite a bit of growing into or living up to! But in his meeting with Mary, Gabriel has already told us that this baby will be great. He will be the 'Son of the Most High'. He will be the one to take the throne of David and reign over the house of Jacob. Luke is tying Jesus tightly into Jewish history. Looking back, we see a clear and strong line, a solid heritage and pedigree.

Looking forward

But as well as being rooted in history, this is a liminal moment – a new beginning. It's a new beginning for Mary and Joseph who are celebrating their first child. Already they are realizing that this is no ordinary baby. Both he and his cousin John have been produced by miracle. Jesus' birth has been announced by angels, and shepherds have visited the manger. Mary ponders and treasures all that is happening. There will be many more surprises and challenges for her to process through this baby's life. Born under the law, Jesus will, through his life, death and resurrection, set free those under the law so that all can be adopted as children of God. St Paul writes that through the Spirit living within us, made possible through Jesus' resurrection, we are all children and heirs of God. The medieval Church made much of the circumcision of Jesus and there are many Renaissance paintings showing this ritual. This is because theologians at the time saw Jesus' circumcision as the first shedding of the Messiah's blood – and therefore the beginning of the redemption of the world. This comes to fruition on the cross when Jesus fulfils his given name: 'God saves'. All this is waiting in the wings as the young couple celebrate the birth of their first child – this is what they have to look forward to, though they don't know it yet. As Christians we were baptized into the name of Jesus and we are part of the Body of Christ. This celebration today is not just marking an episode recorded by the Gospels, it's our celebration too – of the name of 'Jesus' that we all carry. Instead of those 'get thinner', 'get fitter' resolutions, how about making some resolutions this year that build our faith. Put in place a resolution that will strengthen your relationship with God and enable you to carry the name of Jesus confidently and faithfully into the future – so that you may be a blessing to many.

> The LORD bless you and keep you;
> the LORD make his face to shine upon you, and be gracious to you;
> the LORD lift up his countenance upon you, and give you peace.

Catherine Williams

Suggested hymns

While shepherds watched; In the bleak mid-winter; At the name of Jesus; Jesus, name above all names.

Epiphany 6 January

From Fate to Freedom

Isa. 60.1–6; Ps. 72.[1–9] 10–15; Eph. 3.1–12; **Matt. 2.1–12**

The Magi who followed the star that led them to the infant Jesus can get short shrift in our worship. It is, after all, Luke's shepherds that take centre stage in our Christmas carols, readings and cribs. The Magi don't really belong in the crib, which is already packed with shepherds, sheep and maybe other incongruous figures. One American minister recommended installing figures like Homer Simpson in our cribs to give them a more contemporary flavour!

Much time has elapsed by the time the Magi arrive. The holy family has relocated from the stable to a home, Jesus is no longer a baby, and for us Christmas is over, the crib is packed away, and our principal Gospel reading faces us with the man Jesus at his baptism. But then, with Jewish antipathy to magic, it's surprising that the story of the Magi made its way into the gospel story at all!

Astrologer

The Magi were most likely to have been astrologers. Their assiduous habit of surveying the heavens, keeping track of the stars, was what drew them to Judaea. As the word *magos* originally suggests, they might well also have been advisers to the royal court of Persia. They were men who specialized in the interpreting of dreams, and probably also dabbled in the magical arts. Frankincense and myrrh were the stocks in trade of magicians, used in incantations and potions for discerning the future. They were the sort of people who might write a horoscope column for the *Baghdad Gazette*.

Credibility

There's nothing in the story to make us question its credibility. The trade routes from Persia to Palestine were well travelled. Herod's paranoia on hearing the talk of a new king fits what we know of his character from independent sources. And there are explanations for the phenomenon that appeared in the night sky. The star, if it was a star, didn't conform to the usual rules. But then there was a star a few years ago which didn't play by the rules and caused consternation within the astro-physics community. But Jewish writers like Matthew also wanted to show how Jesus was the fulfilment of Jewish predictions and stories. He may well have taken his inspiration from the Old Testament story of Balaam, a man with magical powers, who came from the East and predicted that a star would rise from Jacob.

Determinists

Why then does this story of astrologers and magic men appear in the gospel? The Magi were members of a caste in Persia who believed in determinism, that life was pre-ordained, fixed, fated, and functioned according to immutable laws. That's why they were prepared to invest so much toil and trouble in investigating a new heavenly body that was acting strangely. But Judaism had no truck with astrology and magic. The idea that human destiny is fixed and unalterable contradicts the Jewish belief in the sovereign freedom and providence of God and his gift of freedom and responsibility that he gave to humankind at creation. As one rabbi shortly before the time of Jesus warned, 'He who learns from the magi is worthy of death.' So it would be astonishing for people who were regarded as charlatans and quacks, foolish rather than wise men, to be keeping company with Jesus.

Challenge

Judaism disapproved of magic, but in common with our own society it was fascinated by it. The deterministic, rigid mindset infests public discourse: 'There's no alternative'; 'Nothing has changed'; 'What will be, will be'; 'We've tried all this before'; 'What goes around comes around'. It's a cyclical view of time, one thing after another, and it exercises a moratorium on new, bold, imaginative initiatives. The stoical view of life leads us to abdicate the God-given responsibility we have received as co-creators with God and stewards of his creation. It can drain the will to challenge and precipitate change. The primordial sin may not be pride but apathy, the failure to take responsibility and act freely.

The Magi do something right. They are attentive interpreters of nature, they read the signs, 'they represent the best of pagan lore and religious perceptivity which has come to seek Jesus through revelation in nature'.[40] And the gifts of frankincense and myrrh that were used as auguries and their ill-gotten gold when offered to the Christ sealed their renunciation of their old ways. They were changed, as T. S. Eliot's poem declares, 'no longer at ease . . . in the old dispensation'.[41] Once foolish, now they have become wise, citizens of a universal King.

The choice we face

Embarking upon a new year faces us with a stark choice. We can choose to live like the changed Magi, responsively, intuitively, generously, or like Herod, by exerting control and coercion. We can live like the Magi, with openness to all that is new and challenging and adventurous, or guardedly, defensively and suspiciously like Herod. We can live with risk and daring and vulnerability, like the eastern travellers, or we can imitate the self-preserving, safe, secure path of Herod. We are, after all, invited to attend to and follow Jesus, who is himself the bright and morning star.

Roger Spiller

Suggested hymns

O worship the Lord in the beauty of holiness; How brightly gleams the morning star; As with gladness, men of old; Brightest and best.

Week of Prayer for Christian Unity 18–25 January
(For an alternative, see the sermon for the Third Sunday of Epiphany, Principal Service.)
Think Big and Act Boldly
2 Cor. 5.19

Here in Oxford five denominations worship together, Sunday by Sunday, and can't see what keeps Anglicans and Baptists, Methodists, Moravians and the United Reformed Church apart. On a new and relatively poor estate, built originally to help house the 25,000 car workers at Cowley, it was economic to be ecumenical. Only the Church of England had the resources and the national obligation to provide for a new parish. The rest might not find enough folk of their own kind to warrant such a venture. Besides, there was now the official recommendation from national church leaders that there was no need to go it alone. Form a Local Ecumenical Partnership was the big idea that came from the first ever British

Faith and Order Conference at Nottingham in 1964. We took up the challenge in 1965 and still can't see what keeps other congregations apart even when we are told that single-congregation LEPs are no longer the flavour of the month.

Official rules that separate

Baptists could criticize the rest of us for baptizing infants, but down the road, in the centre of the city, New Road Baptists decided years ago that there were good arguments on either side as to when to baptize, so such disagreements need not be divisive. Officially the Church of England still says that other ministers are not proper ministers because they have not been ordained by bishops in the apostolic succession. But then Rome says the same about Anglicans, so such appeals help no one. As for that other claim that Christ is not present in our communions, who dare not give permission to the good Lord to preside where he please or presume to know where the wind of God's Spirit may choose to blow? We note, too, that the founders of Methodism never intended to set up a new church but wanted freedom to preach across rigidly controlled parish boundaries. As for the Moravians, John Wesley learned much from them, so can we all. They place more emphasis than many of us on frequent communion and a more corporate understanding of ministry. As for the United Reformed, my own tradition, we had hoped in 1972 that our union of Congregationalists and Presbyterians and later members of the Churches of Christ would give the lead to other reunions. It was not to be, except in Local Partnerships. So here we are. But where should we be?

The fact of war

Our text summons us to think big and act boldly! 'In Christ God was reconciling *the world* to himself,' says Paul. Paul is the great apostle of reconciliation. Reconciling is what God does – not just for us but for the whole world. It was a favourite text for Reformed theologian Peter Taylor Forsyth, and it led him to be active in projects for unity even before the modern ecumenical movement had really begun. It was also a costly concern, since many of his best friends were Germans, and Britain and Germany had grown apart and were soon at war. In a profound sense, though not in so many words, Forsyth placed the cross of Christ in the centre of the battle field because God himself was not at war with any of us but had made peace through the shedding of Christ's blood on the cross. He had done so to reconcile the whole world to himself.

A strong case can be made for saying that the ecumenical movement was an answer to the tragedy and travesty of war. Another great theologian, William Temple, said so too. At his enthronement sermon as Archbishop of Canterbury in 1942, he described the ecumenical movement as 'the great new fact of our time'. Hitler was trying to divide the world. Christ, through the churches, could bring us together. It was a bold vision, but still not as bold as Paul's: 'In Christ God was reconciling the [whole] world to himself.' The great cosmos of all creation!

God chooses to work with us

But being God, he chooses to work with us. Hence the bringing together of five divided denominations in one church near Cowley, and our close friendship with the Roman Catholic Church of Sacred Heart round the corner is the work of Christ, the Reconciler. All Christians acknowledge Christ's saving work when they gather round Christ's cross. Thank God we are not divided in faith, we say. So the challenging question remains: What keeps us apart? Don't ask me!

Donald Norwood

Suggested hymns

Living God, you word has called us; We need each other's voice to sing; O thou, who at thy Eucharist didst pray; Filled with the Spirit's power, with one accord.

Conversion of St Paul 25 January
The Shock, Surprise and Singularity of Grace

Jer. 1.4–10; Ps. 67; Acts 9.1–22 (*if the Acts reading is used instead of the Old Testament reading, the New Testament reading is* **Gal. 1.11–16a**); Matt. 19.27–end

We are often struck by the brutal conduct of those we call religious fanatics who misguidedly act in the name of their god. Such was the man Saul, whose formidable energy, scrupulous attention to the law and zeal for his privileged ancestral religion made him a notorious opponent of the fledgling followers of Jesus. He was acting, as he believed, out of good motives, not bad, out of the highest principles, obeying his religion and God as best he knew how.

Shock

But the dramatic divine voice and light stopped him dead in his tracks. It was outside his control and the implications were far reaching and would take time to work through. His conversion demanded far more than a change of mind. It required a drastic abandonment of all the norms, values and beliefs to which he had adhered with such passion and conviction. It required a mental change that was so momentous that it constituted an unparalleled demand on a human being. He was being asked to trample all over his most sacred convictions and instead embrace the incredible, unprecedented notion of a suffering God newly revealed to him in a vision of Jesus Christ.

Surprise

But there was something still more astonishing with which Saul, now Paul, had to reckon. He was experiencing not only his conversion but a call and commissioning to be an apostle to the Gentiles, to be the missionary to the people he had moments before believed could have no stake in the promises of God, the very people he had been persecuting and bringing to their deaths.

Judaism had a rich notion of grace, as we have come to recognize afresh in recent years. Grace was lavish and superabundant, but it was generally thought to be given selectively in relation to a person's goodness, virtue, conduct and ethnicity. But now Paul had to reckon with a grace that was incongruous, indiscriminate, given alike to the bad and reprehensible as to the good and virtuous. Judaism could just recognize that a person might die for a good person, but there was nothing that could prepare Jews to accept that a good person might die for a bad person. But as Paul was later to affirm in his letter to the church at Rome, echoing his own experience, 'When we were yet sinners, Christ died for us.' And to show that God's grace and Christ's calling are independent of a person's virtue, conduct, effort or achievement, Paul asserts that God 'set me aside from my mother's womb'. Paul's call rested entirely on God's call before and quite independent of the manner of his life. This is the unexpected, unconditioned character of grace that Paul brings to us with a unique clarity and persuasiveness. It was the sole ground for his conversion and for his commission to be the apostle to the Gentiles.

Singularity

How could Paul accept a mission to the Gentiles? How could he *not* with the logic of grace that had brought about his conversion? If no one is granted God's grace on the grounds of their worth, goodness, social standing or achievements, then no one is excluded from its reach. And so it proved. In his experience in founding churches, Paul discovered that even Gentile Christians had already been miraculously endowed with the Spirit to fulfil God's will and had the law 'written on their hearts'.

It's the event of Christ crucified, not some general teaching, that alone transformed Paul's identity and in the light of which he reappraised and redefined his life and conduct. And that is the one and only gospel that has transformative power. That is the gospel that must determine our identity, values, beliefs and conduct. But there is always the risk that grace will be restricted by our customs, traditions, rules and practices. That was so in the Galatian church, whose reading is set for today. Paul had a mammoth struggle with those who, having found freedom from the law, were beginning to forfeit that freedom by re-adopting Jewish laws. The only values that count are those that arise from the gospel.

St Paul epitomises in his life journey as well as in his letters the core truth of the gospel. And he challenges all our attempts to make criteria other than the cross of Christ the basis of membership, of access to the Church's sacraments and ministrations or to its fellowship. He exposes the hierarchies we build and rely on. We have differences – ethnic, gender, ideological and belief. These are not, of course, to be eliminated; they will, indeed, be cherished. But through Christ they are now shown to be relative and subservient to the gospel. The difference that counts, that changes us, is the difference of knowing Christ. And so, following Paul, there is scope to form innovative communities to span the dividing lines and demonstrate the power of the gospel, which this 'least of all the apostles' displayed with such transcendent power.

Roger Spiller

Suggested hymns

Amazing grace; Make me a captive, Lord; I stand amazed in the presence; And can it be.

St Joseph of Nazareth 19 March

Trouble!

2 Sam. 7.4–16; Ps. 89.27–36; Rom. 4.13–18; **Matt. 1.18–end**

If Matthew wants to tell us anything through these verses it is this: God is at work in the birth of Jesus of Nazareth. The pregnancy is the result of the working of the Holy Spirit. The one conceived 'will save his people from their sins'. He is the fulfilment of Old Testament prophecy. The child conceived is Emmanuel, 'God with us'.

Trouble in the text: God is at work

All well and fine. But as the story begins, Joseph does not have the benefit of our knowledge, reciting Christian creeds or years of singing Advent and Christmas carols. He appears initially unaware of the working of God in these events. Or if Mary has talked to him about it he is at best sceptical of her claims. Accordingly for him the news of the pregnancy must have been a gut-wrenching moment. This was not the way he saw his life working out. We are told little of his emotions but suspect anger, disappointment and confusion. He proposes breaking off the betrothal, a legal engagement, but not exposing Mary to public disgrace. This indicates a good man, a kind man, a loving man – indeed, a man in love. It also indicates, however, that from Joseph's perspective Mary's pregnancy was an act of moral failure and personal betrayal. The working of God in Mary's life hidden was for Joseph the source of confusion, deep personal pain and the cause of a potentially fatal disruption in their relationship.

Trouble in the world: God is at work

Yet the working of God and its outcomes in a person's life may not always be apparent to or welcomed by others. Not every parent welcomes their child's announcement that they intend to spend their lives serving God instead of following other more secure if not lucrative career plans. The working of God in a person's life may not always be apparent to or welcomed by others – including us.

Grace in the text: God is at work

This is the message that, if nothing else, Matthew wants to tell us in these verses. It is also the message that an angel brought to Joseph in a dream. This dream encounter transforms Joseph. It changes his perspective on the situation. It changes his proposed actions from divorce to marriage. In the light of the message he receives, rather than separating from her he aligns his own future with the working of God in Mary's life and becomes supportive of it. This transformation in Joseph could be explained by the 'miraculous' nature of the 'angelic message'. It was, however, only a dream, and we can all have strange dreams that mean nothing more than that we should avoid cheese at supper time! Perhaps, then, it is better to see the transformation in Joseph as being the result of the hopeful and inspiring content of the message centred on Jesus Christ. For it is here in the dream that we, along with Joseph, get to hear that what is happening to Mary is that God is at work. The pregnancy is the result of the working of the Holy Spirit. The one conceived 'will save his people from their sins'. He is the fulfilment of Old Testament prophecy. The child conceived is Emmanuel, 'God with us'. God is at work in the event of Jesus Christ. Joseph's subsequent obedience to the angel's command and commitment to Mary is the commitment of faith to the message that God is at work in Mary in the child conceived within her. It is this now shared appreciation of the working of God that unites them.

Grace in the world: God is at work

God is at work not least in the way of Jesus Christ embodied in his people. At work in the lives of those who see in Jesus 'God with us' and who in turn seek to apply that to their own believing and behaving in relation to the world around them. Paraphrasing the writer Glen Stassen, 'History is the laboratory in which their lives were tested and their faithfulness validated.'[42] Here, as with Joseph, therefore, we are offered a message in which we can put our faith, causes to which we can commit, a solid ground on which we can take our stand. For God is at work in the way of Jesus Christ in the world. Joseph got it. Do we?

Stuart Blythe

Suggested hymns

O blessed St Joseph, how great is your worth; Let saints on earth in concert sing; Thanks to God whose word was spoken; The kingdom of God is justice and joy.

Annunciation of Our Lord to the Blessed Virgin Mary 25 March

'How can this be?'

Isa. 7.10–14; Ps. 40.5–11; Heb. 10.4–10; **Luke 1.26–38**

'In the sixth month the angel Gabriel was sent by God to a town in Galilee called Nazareth, to a virgin engaged to a man whose name was Joseph, of the house of David. The virgin's name was Mary.' What have we here? What we have is a story of stupendous, unimaginable divine intervention. The place Nazareth is insignificant; the peasant woman, inconsequential; her status, 'betrothed to a man', is socially awkward; that God's future is made to depend upon her is inconceivable. 'How can this be?'

A class of 9-year-olds wrote a church nativity play. Joseph and Mary ask for a room overlooking Bethlehem. The inn displays a 'No vacancy' sign. But Joseph persists. 'Can't you see that my wife's expecting a baby any minute?', he says. 'That's not my fault,' snaps the innkeeper. 'It's not mine either,' retorts Joseph!

'How can this be?'

'How can this be?' Mary articulates the dislocation between the old order and the new. Such things don't happen in real life. Women simply don't get pregnant just by kissing the man they're engaged to without sexual relations. No: 'The Holy Spirit will come upon you, and the power of the Most High will overshadow you.' When God acts, there can only be surprise and consternation: 'How can this be?' Surely this is impossible. It's one more of the long list of promises that challenge credulity.

'How can this be?' That was Mary's puzzled question when she was promised a gift that lay beyond what was currently possible. How can there be anything different from the grim perspective that we've been conditioned to accept? But then this is typical of all the stories about Jesus himself.

Is there an alternative perspective, a different scenario, a more hopeful, more truthful way of reconceiving ourselves, our future? Is there a hope and promise that can gladden our hearts and mobilise our wills? If there is, then there's nothing that could make a greater difference to the way we live and no greater gift for the people of the world.

Human story

Is it believable, a story to trust and to live by, or is it only an escape and pretence, a story so at variance with the fixed experiences of life as to be discredited? After all, people like stories with a happy ending, and you can even get videos of dramas offering a choice of ending. The human story of Mary ends with a crucifixion, not just a resurrection. And portents of disturbance, brutality and death accompany the birth of Jesus: Herod's paranoia and massacre, the flight into Egypt, the appointment of another king no better than the last. So the story embraces the dark and sordid along with the new and hopeful. And the fact that at Christmas we join millions of worshippers around the globe in worship, and that people of all beliefs and none get caught up in the celebration, testifies to the power of the Christian story.

Universal story

We're not just eavesdropping on a private, personal story. The story of the annunciation has become a public, universal story. It's a story that Christians live by because it's a story that is radical and hopeful, promising an alternative to the sombre scenario of the myth of human progress. This story tells us that we're not alone, that hope isn't measured by our experience of the world, but that God intervenes to surprise and confound us; he turns the ordinary into the extraordinary. It's a paradigm through which we're to refocus on our world. It's as if through this story we're given the chance to have our sight restored and to begin to see properly. The world can't give birth to new life, but God can and does and will. And he can bring you to new life and hope. God can change the ordinary into the extraordinary, he can disturb and surprise and confound, and if we cooperate with him, like Mary, we can let his glory through.

It's a story, not because it isn't true but because it's a truth so explosive that it cannot be expressed in any other way. It's a story that is too good not to be true, because it declares the deepest intuition of truth that we have. And it's a hopeful story because it's rooted in the action of the transcendent God who brought the world's salvation through the death of this Jesus and lives in our hearts through his Spirit.

Roger Spiller

Suggested hymns

Long ago, prophets knew; The angel Gabriel from heaven came; Sing we of the blessed Mother; Of the Father's heart begotten.

St Mark the Evangelist 25 April

'Get behind me!'

Prov. 15.28–end, *or* Acts 15.35–end; Ps. 119.9–16; Eph. 4.7–16; **Mark 13.5–13**

The Gospel writers all have their feast days: Matthew and Luke in the autumn, John just after Christmas. But St Mark's day comes towards the end of April, so it always falls in Eastertide.

And isn't that proper for the writer of our first Gospel? As we celebrate Mark's story of good news and new life, the flowers of spring are budding in our gardens; the alleluias of Easter are echoing in our churches; Christ's victory over death is trumpeted in our world.

Except that the story Mark wrote doesn't end in a very victorious way. Far from it: the women 'went out and fled from the tomb, for terror and amazement had seized them; and they said nothing to anyone, for they were afraid'. Almost certainly this is how Mark ended his book, in the middle of a sentence. Any verses that may be printed after it in our Bibles were written by other hands, trying to rectify this unsatisfactory conclusion.

Absent or behind?

And unsatisfactory it is, for anybody seeking comfort or closure. Flight, terror, silence. No appearances of the risen and glorious Christ that we read about in the other Gospels. Not his presence but his *absence*: the message from the tomb that 'he is not here'. What kind of Easter, what kind of good news, is that?

But the mysterious young man has more to say. 'Go, tell his disciples and Peter that he is going ahead of you to Galilee; there you will see him . . .'

Jesus is absent *because he is the one who goes ahead.* And his followers are, by definition, those who go behind. 'Come behind me,' says Jesus to the fishermen at the start of Mark's story. They and the others tag along behind their tantalizing teacher: blundering, quarrelling, but still trying to catch up. And still *he* goes ahead, exhausting their bodies and their minds.

Who is this difficult leader? Halfway through the story, Simon Peter blurts out the correct answer: 'You are the Messiah.' But no sooner are the words out of his mouth than he gets it wrong again, rebuking the Messiah for his negative talk about suffering and death. Jesus' rebuke in turn is severe: 'Get behind me, Satan.'

'Behind' again – for behind is the place of the disciple in Mark's world. A little later, it gets harder still. 'They were on the road,' writes Mark, 'going up to Jerusalem, and Jesus was walking ahead of them; they were amazed, and those who followed were afraid.' This scene is the opposite of what most religious people look for in the comfort of faith: being beside your Saviour, of one mind or face to face with him.

The one ahead

Those followers in Mark's story – and we readers of it, if we're alert – find that Jesus is constantly a move ahead. When you think you've got your head round his parables or riddles, he's on the move again. It's like the walker in R. S. Thomas's poem 'Pilgrimages', trudging up the arduous path to the holy place to find – well, nothing:

> There
> is no body in the stained window
> of the sky now. Am I too late?
> Were they too late also, those
> first pilgrims? He is such a fast
> God, always before us and
> leaving as we arrive.[43]

Always before us – on the road up to Jerusalem, to Golgotha, to the tomb, going ahead to Galilee. And from there, if we haven't lost our breath or our patience, ahead into all the world where the story of this difficult Messiah is told and lived.

In that telling and living over the centuries, his followers have devised many pictures of Christ, many hymns to Christ, many doctrines of Christ. But I wonder whether, for all their beauty, these may be an attempt to *arrest* Jesus. Arresting is, literally, what Judas and the soldiers and priests do, stopping him from going ahead. But the disciple's place is *behind* – where, perhaps, now and again we might catch just a glimpse of his heels, as he turns the next corner and dreams up a new riddle for us.

How can you call this stark story 'good news'? Isn't it discouraging?

Well, I actually find it quite *encouraging* that those apostles, those heroes of the faith, stumbled and misunderstood. Doesn't that give hope for us at the back of the class? And encouraging too that, despite *their* failure, there are *other* characters in Mark's story who humbly but instinctively get it right. A woman, with a disease that excludes her from society, comes up behind Jesus in the crowd and touches his cloak and is healed. A blind beggar, annoying people with his shouts for attention, receives his sight from Jesus and follows him on the road.

That 'road' is the way winding through Mark's story and on through its abrupt ending into the world we inhabit. Easter doesn't mark its end; nor does Easter obliterate the suffering that precedes it. The road isn't easy, nor is it predictable. But it's not unmarked or untrodden, for our Pioneer is asking us to follow. Yes, he is not here. But he is risen and going ahead of us. Alleluia!

Christopher Burdon

Suggested hymns

The Saint who first found grace to pen; One more step along the road I go; Can we by searching find out God?; Sing my song backwards.

SS Philip and James, Apostles 1 May

The Divine Love that Calls Us Back

Isa. 30.15–21; Ps. 119.1–8; Eph. 1.3–10; John 14.1–14

> And when you turn to the right or when you turn to the left, your ears shall hear a word behind you, saying, 'This is the way; walk in it.'

The nature of God's call

The strange joy of human language is the way in which a language other than our own can create a word for which English has no equivalent. But in discovering and using that foreign word we are introduced to new and enlightening ways of looking at things. Let me give an example. In German, the word *umwelt* was developed by a twentieth-century German scientist called Jakob von Uexkül who studied animal behaviour. He came to the conclusion that each species of animal had its own way of negotiating the world, its own way, if you like, of interpreting and using the data that it encountered. He described this capacity that each species had as its *umwelt*. The word can be defined as 'the world as it is experienced by a particular organism'. What did he mean by this?

Consider, for instance, a great seabird such as an albatross. It inhabits a mental and social world, an *umwelt*, which is almost beyond our comprehension. An albatross can navigate across vast distances of the ocean without apparently using the earth's magnetic field to do so, nor does it seem to use the sun as its guide. Nor, as far as we can tell, when it forages for food as much as 20 days' flight away from its nesting site, does it use any landmark clues to navigate itself home. How it navigates its incredible journeys is still being investigated. If it were possible to launch a human being into flight from the middle of an ocean without a compass, GPS or telecommunication system and instruct that person to find their way home, the result would be disastrous. In other words, the *umwelt* of the albatross is amazing and very, very different from our own.

Now bring the idea of *umwelt* much closer to our own experience. If you have taken a dog for a walk you will know that once it is let off the lead it will race away from you and go scampering hither and yon. But, when it is ahead of you it will stop and look back to check on your whereabouts, and only when it has located where you are will it set off on another mini-exploration. A dog's mental and social world, its *umwelt*, can only be partly known by us, but it certainly contains some vestiges of what one might call a homing instinct, even if on a walk 'home' is temporarily a person rather than a place.

Isaiah and the right path

Well. Here is an absurd, silly and unanswerable question: when Isaiah wrote the words we heard in our reading, might he have had a dog's *umwelt* behaviour in mind? Look again at what he wrote: 'And when you turn to the right or when you turn to the left, your ears shall hear a word behind you, saying, "This is the way; walk in it."'

In this verse, Isaiah is making the assumption that we humans seem to have an inbuilt capacity to wander away from our main moral path. Our human *umwelt* involves the desire and the capacity to stray from the right way, to go 'walkabout'.

Isaiah was writing over two thousand five hundred years ago, so does what he wrote ring any bells with us in the twenty-first century? Is what he is saying about human behaviour true in our own experience? More than likely it is. All of us will have learnt from perhaps sad and bitter experience how damaging wandering away from the right moral path can be. But suppose Isaiah is right not only about human behaviour but right too about the nature of God.

'And when you turn to the right or when you turn to the left, your ears shall hear a word behind you, saying, "This is the way; walk in it."'

Vocation?

Suppose, when we are tempted to wander away, we pause and look about us; might we discover that God is calling us to come back to a path of *his* choosing, not ours? That certainly is true of very many of us who have explored a vocation.

First, there was a time of deliberately not listening – the challenge was unwelcome, too daunting, too impossible. Questions and doubts poured in: who, me? Why? What for? Then came a gradual realization that listening to the call of God, hard though it was, was necessary; and then, often after months or even years of pondering, the small and insistent voice of God could be ignored no longer. God was telling us the way we should go; which is not to say that everything thereafter was plain sailing. For most people, including clergy and Readers, the decision to try to listen to God is a lifetime's activity with serious mistakes and calamitous diversions along the way. But the underlying reality of our humanity is one of grace: even when the voice of God is heard but ignored, God sets us back eventually on the right road.

The ability and the willingness to listen to the voice of God was a characteristic of the first disciples, and, of course, their response was often as incoherent and as puzzled as ours. But on this day when we celebrate two of the first disciples, Philip and James, about whom in historical terms we know very little, we would do well to reflect on God's call to each of us, calling us gently and insistently to follow his way and to do his will. Our natural *umwelt* includes the capacity to stray from the right path, but God in his infinite love and forgiveness calls us back to his way.

And for such a blessing and grace, we should give God thanks and praise.

Christopher Herbert

Suggested hymns

Rejoice in God's saints, today and all days; Give us the wings of faith to rise; For all thy saints, O Lord; Give to God, the source of all our mission.

St Matthias the Apostle 14 May

A Forgotten Disciple with a Stand-in Part

Isa. 22.15–end, *or* Acts 1.15–end; Ps. 15; **Acts 1.15–end**, *or* 1 Cor. 4.1–7; John 15.9–17

> And they cast lots for them, and the lot fell on Matthias; and he was added to the eleven apostles.

Resting in God's faithfulness

Imagine this. You have just got on to a train to go to visit a friend when a young and vivacious woman comes to sit opposite you. You soon get into conversation, and when you ask her what she does for a living she explains that she has just started out in publishing. As you love books too, the conversation flows and before long you explain that you really enjoy history, especially the history of Victorian Britain.

'Golly!' says the young woman. 'Let me make a suggestion. I have just been asked to create a series of small books about British history. Would you be interested in seeing what you might put together about Victoria?'

How might you react? Would you demurely turn down the offer, or would you rise to the challenge?

You ask for a few more details. Each book in the series, the young woman explains, needs to be about forty thousand words long.

At which point we must leave this fantastical conversation – because the likelihood of something like this happening in reality is virtually nil.

However, it's a way of trying to think about how the authors of the books of the New Testament set about their task. After all, they had a story that they wanted to tell. And like all authors, especially historians, they had to consider how they would give shape to their narrative.

Shaping the story

When Luke wrote his two books, the Gospel and the Acts, he opened each book with an explanation about what he was intending to do. At the beginning of his Gospel he wrote this:

> Since many have undertaken to set down an orderly account of the events that have been fulfilled among us, just as they were handed on to us by those who from the beginning were eyewitnesses and servants of the word, I too decided, after investigating everything carefully from the very first, to write an orderly account for you, most excellent Theophilus, so that you may know the truth concerning the things about which you have been instructed.

And he opens the second part of his book, the Acts of the Apostles, in a similar fashion.

> In the first book, Theophilus, I wrote about all that Jesus did and taught from the beginning until the day when he was taken up to heaven, after giving instructions through the Holy Spirit to the apostles whom he had chosen.

So, it looks as though Luke had a particular person in mind as his reader; someone called Theophilus. That might have been the name of a real person, but because the name means 'lover of God' it might be a kind of corporate name, like addressing the book to everyone who loves God. We simply don't know.

What we do know is that Luke gave his combined book a narrative shape. In the first book he takes the story from the birth of Jesus up to Jesus' death and resurrection in Jerusalem. In the second half of the book he begins in Jerusalem and traces the way the message spreads from that city throughout the Middle

Eastern region. So far, so good. And, by the way, his combined book, Luke-Acts, consists of about forty thosand words in total, or about sixty pages.

But here is something odd. At the beginning of the second part of his book he introduces us to a new character, Matthias (we heard about his appointment in the lesson). You might expect that, by introducing him, Luke would go on to tell us more about him and all that he did in spreading the message. In fact, he doesn't. We are given the story of how he was elected to make up the Twelve, and after that, silence.

The forgotten apostle

Even early legends in the Church tell us little. Some stories claim that Matthias went to the Caspian Sea area and preached the gospel in Georgia. Others say that he lived and died in Jerusalem. Yet others say that he worked in Cappadocia in what is now Turkey. And sadly, he didn't even get given his own feast day in the Roman Calendar until the eleventh century.

He is the forgotten apostle.

So why did Luke make such a thing about his appointment? Perhaps it was because the method of his appointment was so unusual. After all, although Matthias had apparently been among those who had followed Jesus, he had not been chosen by Jesus himself. Perhaps Luke simply included the details to show that after Judas' betrayal the number of apostles had to be 12 again because that reflected the number of the tribes of Israel.

It's impossible to know what Luke's reasons were. Matthias has a tiny walk-on part in Luke's sweeping narrative but is then heard of no more. He has fulfilled the author's purpose and the story can move on.

Any message in that for us?

Perhaps simply that our part in God's story as it works itself out across the centuries is also unknown to many. We shall not be remembered for long after we have died, but if we have been faithful to God, maybe that is enough. We are in his hands, and how he will weave us into his narrative of salvation is known to him alone.

Maybe, then, Matthias is as good a saint for us as any, and resting in the faithfulness of God is what we are called to do.

Christopher Herbert

Suggested hymns

Take up thy cross, the Saviour said; Blessed are the pure in heart; I, the Lord of sea and sky; All my hope on God is founded.

Visit of the Blessed Virgin Mary to Elizabeth

1 June (transferred)

Run to the Hills!

Zeph. 3.14–18; Ps. 113; Rom. 12.9–16; **Luke 1.39–49 [50–56]**

Have you ever wanted to run away? If you have it might have been because you were frightened about something or someone. Or maybe because you needed to take time out to reassess the direction your life might take? Have you ever needed to retreat for a while to rest, take stock and regain your energy and motivation? Today we're celebrating the visit of Mary to Elizabeth. Some of those things might have been going on for Mary following her amazing meeting with the angel Gabriel, and her courageous and obedient response to the news that she is to conceive the Messiah in a miraculous way.

Retreating

Luke tells us that Mary goes 'with haste' to the house of Zechariah, up in the Judaean hills. Perhaps she needs to get away – away from the extraordinary events that are unfolding. Being pregnant and unmarried was not just a scandal in first-century Jewish society, it was punishable by death. And so, Mary's 'yes' to God is fraught with danger – well beyond her comfort zone, and open to misunderstanding from every side. What an extraordinary way for God to bring about the salvation of the world – through a teenage, unmarried mum. Mary's obedience to God requires courage, recklessness and deep faith. No wonder she chooses to get out of the limelight for a while – to retreat. She runs to her cousin Elizabeth, who is in a similar predicament. Unable to have children and now in old age, she too is experiencing a miraculous pregnancy – she will understand. Elizabeth is further ahead in her pregnancy than Mary – she will have wisdom to share. Here is solidarity. Here is support and comfort. Here is time and space to reflect, to get used to the extraordinary things that are happening, to take stock.

Taking stock

When Mary arrives to stay with her cousin, the baby inside Elizabeth – John the Baptist – leaps for joy at this first meeting with Jesus (*in utero*!). Elizabeth is filled with the Holy Spirit and calls Mary 'blessed' and the 'Mother of my Lord'. Elizabeth's holy intuition recognizes and proclaims that the longed-for fulfilment of God's promises is breaking into the present. It's confirmation for Mary that the extraordinary and miraculous things that are happening around and through her really are from God and not just a young girl's fantasy. Sometimes it can be really helpful to speak to those who are wise and experienced – who have been faithful for a long time – about the things we believe God may be up to in our lives and in the world. In our reading from Romans today, St Paul gives simple, practical advice about day-to-day Christian living. He shows that love isn't about a warm glow and fuzzy feelings, but is exercised through solid, thoughtful, practical care. He encourages us to honour each other; to be patient with one another; to share joys and sorrows together; to extend hospitality, and to bless. It sounds like the quality of love Mary and Elizabeth shared in the three months they lived together as their pregnancies progressed and they prepared for the demands of the future.

Advancing

As Mary meets with Elizabeth she celebrates with a great song of revolution – the Magnificat. Drawing on Scriptures and imagery deeply known and loved, Mary stitches together a song that is very similar to that sung by Hannah when celebrating the gift of her son Samuel. Mary declares that her whole being praises God. She is confident that God will restore order, save the poor, act with strength and mercy, and keep his promises. Mary is the new daughter of Zion spoken of by the prophet Zephaniah. She proclaims salvation for her people Israel. She declares the good news of God, and shows that the lowly can indeed 'rejoice'. Her time apart with Elizabeth helps her to advance in her calling – to grow into that which God is asking of her, even as God in Jesus is growing within her. And this advancing in faith isn't just for Mary. Bearing Christ doesn't just make Mary 'full of grace' – it changes the people around her. Mary's soul magnifies the Lord: the person she is, brings God into focus for others. Christ within

Mary gives Joseph generosity of spirit. Christ within Mary makes John the Baptist in Elizabeth's womb jump for joy. Christ within Mary brings a Pentecost experience for Elizabeth as she is filled with the Holy Spirit. The Lord is truly in the midst of his people: the prophecy of Zephaniah is fulfilled.

God calls each of us – as individuals and as a Church – to costly, surprising, risky, adventurous living, which may be open to misunderstanding and ridicule. Obedience to God's call requires courage – no wonder we sometimes want to run away. It's good to take time out to consider, think through and really grasp what we're being called to do, before we're ready to move forward. Let's recall Mary when we're responding to God's call on our lives. Remember her time of retreating and taking stock with the wise and holy Elizabeth, so that by the power of the Holy Spirit she could grow into all that God was asking of her. Amen.

Catherine Williams

Suggested hymns

For Mary, mother of our Lord; Tell out my soul; Brother, sister, let me serve you; Let there be love shared among us.

Day of Thanksgiving for the Institution of Holy Communion (Corpus Christi) 11 June

Taken, Blessed, Broken and Distributed

Gen. 14.18–20; Ps. 116.10–end; **1 Cor. 11.23–26**; John 6.51–58

> Jesus told his friends to do this, and they have done it always since. Was ever another command so obeyed? For century after century, spreading slowly to every continent and country and among every race on earth, this action has been done, in every conceivable human circumstance, for every conceivable human need, from infancy and before it, to extreme old age and beyond it; from the pinnacles of earthly greatness to the refuge of fugitives in the caves and dens of the earth.[44]

These well-known and thanks-inducing lines were written by the theologian Dom Gregory Dix and we can only garner still more reasons to be thankful for the Holy Communion.

Invitation

It would seem remarkable, if we weren't already so familiar with it, that it was the drama and physicality of a meal that Jesus commanded us to enact in order to carry his memory. Who cannot have been stirred and elated by the opportunity to choose to respond to the gracious invitation to come out, to stand in a queue, waiting, and soon to be opening empty hands to receive the bread of life, and to be flanked around us by fellow Christians making their own public declaration of their faith and their need of grace.

The enormity of the invitation can make us flinch with unease and shame. How can we dare to present ourselves at the Lord's table? The invitation is itself sufficient to bring our unworthiness to the surface. But we recollect words drawn originally from the Prayer Book: 'We are not worthy to eat the crumbs from under your table, but you are the same Lord whose nature is always to have mercy.' And the lines of George Herbert's exquisite poem, 'Love bade me welcome', may come to mind to persuade us that we are indeed welcomed for love's sake. So we cultivate an expectant, attentive inner centredness so that we can 'lift up' our hearts and be transported inwardly in heart and mind to the throne of grace. We need the gravitas of the moment to envelop us, reminding us that by our participation in the Eucharist we are acknowledging our complicity in the death of the Saviour. And in accepting his table fellowship we are entering into a binding covenant to be in 'love and peace with all people'.

'The Lord is here'

It's the Holy Communion whether in a country church or a great cathedral. Words and speech alone can't satisfy our hunger. But the multisensory and repeated plain dramatic act can feed and fill our hungry lives at our Lord's love-feast.

'The Lord is here,' we boldly acclaim. We believe the real presence of Christ is with us, at least in the sense that we must deny that he could be really absent, even though we cannot circumscribe his ineffable being in our feeble verbal categories. Bread and wine 'become for us the body and blood of our Lord Jesus Christ'. And the defining actions of breaking the bread and pouring the wine and blessing them evoke in us 'love's expense', as the cost of our salvation. Christ is in the whole drama from the beginning, and there, not merely as an offering, but as the celebrant.

Jesus, now liberated from space and time, is not restricted in the way he can communicate himself. This is, after all, where Christ has pledged himself to be. We know we can meet him anywhere, but this is the appointed time and place where we can be certain we can meet him. Here is the visible preaching that can settle and soothe and ground us. We don't need an explanation to iron out the wonder and the mystery of the celebration. Michael Ramsay got the heart of the matter when he said: 'The question is not what we make of the Eucharist but what the Eucharist is making of us.'

Becoming his Body

We eat the food and we become what we eat: the Body of Christ. Through the Eucharist, Christ is 'transubstantiated' in us – made substantial in his Body, the Church. And we behold and greet fellow members of his Body. In their flesh and blood we too encounter the real presence of Christ.

As we conclude, we know we do this as an anticipation of the banquet that is being prepared for us in heaven. We have received an aperitif, a first course, to set us longing and hoping for that fulfilment when all creation will gather round the Lord's feast. Meanwhile, we know what it is to be broken, but now we know too what it is to be blessed. Now then, like the bread, we are ready to be distributed, as the agents of Christ, to feed and clothe the needy and to pass on the invitation to the Lord's Supper, so that all God's people will be gathered around his table.

Roger Spiller

Suggested hymns

Rock of ages, cleft for me; Let all mortal flesh keep silence; Now my tongue the mystery telling; Soul of my Saviour, sanctify my breast.

St Barnabas the Apostle 12 June (transferred)
Cheerleader in Tough Times

Job 29.11–16; Ps. 112; **Acts 11.19–end** (*if the Acts reading is used instead of the Old Testament reading, the New Testament reading is* Gal. 2.1–10); John 15.12–17

Son of Encouragement

We all need a cheerleader. Someone who builds us up and gets us going. Someone who enthuses us and in the face of adversity keeps people buoyant. From all that we know, Barnabas, the apostle, was someone like this. Indeed, one of his nicknames was 'Son of Encouragement'. One can't help thinking that Barnabas was a cup half-full kind of person. Barnabas was the kind of person you wanted by your side; he was in essence everything a good friend should be. Barnabas was the kind of person who could be sent on your behalf to share good news and build up community. This is exactly how Barnabas is portrayed in Scripture. In the book of Acts, he is sent to Antioch to visit the fledgling community of faith. He then sets out to find Paul. Together they teach and preach, and we are told a 'great many people were brought to the Lord'. Obviously, Barnabas' attitude was attractive and infectious. The writer of the Acts of the Apostles also notes that it was in Antioch at this time that the disciples were first called 'Christians'.

So there we find Barnabas at the very beginning, when people were trying to work out what it meant to be called a Christian and belong to the Church of Christ. He is perhaps an exemplar of what it means to live a good life. He is described as a good man, full of the Holy Spirit and of faith, and we also know that he was generous, attentive to the needs of the poor, selling his own goods for the benefit of others. He lived up to the words of Job: he took on the suffering and needs of others and attended to them, leading them through their time of trouble. He could be said to have caused the widow's heart to sing for joy and became eyes for the blind and as feet for the lame. Barnabas became a father for the needy and championed the cause of the stranger. There is no sense in what we read that Barnabas was trying to promote himself. He led by example and this is how he became a pillar of the church. His actions and his words were all for Christ. He was one of the first Christians.

All for Christ

One of Barnabas' particular strengths seems to have been in promoting the idea that all are one in Christ. Whatever background, whatever history, whether slave or free, male or female, Jew or Gentile, circumcised or uncircumcised. He takes the commandment of Christ to its natural conclusion. This is what it means to *love one another* in the name of Christ, to love as he loved and bear fruit in his name.

As friends of Christ, we are chosen in this age to encourage one another, to exhort, praise and give thanks. We are to rejoice in the love of God, and through our actions, as well as our words, make that love visible, becoming generous people of God, fully alive in Christ.

In a world of cynicism and judgement, to live in this way was a risk and indeed it still is. According to tradition, Barnabas was martyred for his faith in the year 61. It is sometimes dangerous to be generous. The natural propensity of humans is to exclude and to condemn, to turn inwards to ourselves and our own needs – an attitude prevalent in many societies today. Barnabas, through Christ, shows us another way. However countercultural this may be, we are encouraged always to err on the side of generosity, to put self aside in the service of all, even to lay down one's life for one's friends. We are encouraged to build up community, and to live, breathe and speak good tidings to a world that longs to hear of joy, gladness and unity.

When Barnabas saw the grace of God at work in the newly emerging Christian communities to which he was sent, it is said he rejoiced and encouraged the community to remain faithful. His uplifting message is one that we might hold on to today as we seek to love God and to love our neighbour in the name of Christ.

Victoria Johnson

Suggested hymns

All for Jesus; Christians, lift up your hearts; Rejoice, the Lord is King; Thy hand, O God, has guided.

Birth of John the Baptist 24 June
A Prophet for a Priest

Isa. 40.1–11; Ps. 85.7–end; Acts 13.4b–26, *or* Gal. 3.23–end; **Luke 1.57–66, 80**

It was a shock when John the Baptist arrived on the scene. There hadn't been a prophet in the land for some five hundred years. The last great prophets – Isaiah, the writer of chapters 40—55 of the book of his name, Jeremiah and Ezekiel – functioned at or before the devastating event of the exile. After them there were a number of 'minor prophets', but the spirit of prophecy was already beginning to wane. This was in part seen as the judgement of God on a people who had ignored the prophetic warnings. In place of the prophets, a priestly movement centred on the rebuilt Temple emerged and a long period of soul-searching began, looking back into God's laws and creation stories for clues for what had gone wrong and how faith in God and God's demands could be renewed. This tension between priests and prophets is enacted in John's upbringing and development.

People used to speak of their sons or, for that matter, daughters 'following in their father's footsteps'. Some careers were particularly thought appropriate to be handed down in a family succession. Not only crafts learnt and handed down by families, but legal, army and priestly vocations were often thought to be 'kept in the family'. In Old Testament times the priesthood, or to be specific, the Levitical priesthood, was largely a hereditary office.

Prophet versus priest

How was it then that John 'changed sides' and became a prophet, and withstood pressure to follow his father and become a priest? We might well imagine household arguments that reflect the passion and disappointment when children stake out their plans in defiance of the hopes and advice of their parents. Zechariah made sure he had his way in choosing the name 'John' for his son, but the choice of career was not his, but God's.

Priests were deputed by the state to handle the mysterious, irrational and religious dimension of life on its behalf. They insisted that God dwelt only in the holiest inner sanctum of the Temple, over which they presided, perpetuating their power and control. They were close to the court and usually de facto functionaries of the king and government. Their life ran smoothly on secure tracks, avoiding trouble and certainly not creating a showdown with the authorities. How then did Zechariah's son become the fearless, free-spirited person that launched a national renewal movement? There were no shoes for him to fill, no vacant job prospectus to inform this wholly novel ministry. Of course his own view of priesthood at close quarters helped inform and define his future, if only by contrast to his father. But it couldn't have been attempted without the call and empowering of God. How could John have had the will or strength to renew the prophetic ministry after half a century without the direct, intervention of Israel's God and king? What experience led him to exchange the God who was confined to the Temple for the travelling God, who could just as well be found in the wilderness, as he was when the nation was being formed?

Wilderness training

The wilderness became again the formative ground for John's own divine call to be forged and fashioned to his time. The wilderness dispossesses us of all the clutter and commerce that distract us from separating what is ultimate from what is mundane. Its horizons are vast and expansive, and nurture the far-sighted visionary utterances that have always characterized the great prophets. The priests could be too close to power to dare to challenge it. The prophets, in the marginal and powerless places, see things more clearly and voice them without fear. Wilderness experiences have also been available through the monastic movement, where we are set aside from everyday preoccupations so that we can listen to God without distraction.

Era of fulfilment

John's sudden and surprising appearance signalled a new era. He at once took up the promises voiced by Isaiah long before him and declared that their long-awaited fulfilment was now at hand. He was the 'voice of one crying in the wilderness'. It was hardly likely to be evident to him how precisely this fulfilment would be initiated. Meanwhile, we suspect, like prophets before him, he gathered around him a band of disciples who would wait for signs of the coming kingdom and prepare people for the kingdom when it came. It was then that John saw and identified Jesus as the instrument of God's deliverance.

No one who has seen in pictures or in real life Matthias Grünewald's famous painting of John the Baptist at the foot of the cross pointing at Jesus, with the Lamb of God looking on, in the Isenheim Altarpiece, can fail to be moved. His is the hand of 'judgement and grace', as Karl Barth describes it. John renounces all the titles that are put to him: Elijah, Messiah or the great final prophet. He characterizes himself merely as a 'voice', a voice that

God borrows and possesses so that his Son Jesus can be introduced and identified for his mission in the world.

Now, through the coming of the Spirit, we too can be a voice to the world, a voice that speaks of judgement and grace, a voice that is vigilant and keeps watch on the maladies that deface God's creation and, supremely, to point to Jesus where he comes 'in the faces of people not his own' and feeds us by word and sacrament.

Roger Spiller

Suggested hymns

On Jordan's bank the Baptist's cry; The great forerunner of the morn; Wait for the Lord, whose day is near; Sing we the praises of the great forerunner.

SS Peter and Paul, Apostles 29 June
Bound Together by the Love of God

Zech. 4.1–6a, 10b–end, Ps. 125; **Acts 12.1–11** (*if the Acts reading is used instead of the Old Testament reading, the New Testament reading is* 2 Tim. 4.6–8, 17–18); Matt. 16.13–19

To be a Christian is to participate. To be a Christian is to be part of something bigger than just yourself. To be a Christian is to be bound together with others. By virtue of our baptism we are made members of a new family, a new community, the Body of Christ. That family, that community, that body, is called the Church.

Sometimes people criticize the Church, and very often it deserves that criticism, but there does come a point when every one of us has to realize that we are the Church: you are the Church, I am the Church. If we want the Church to change and grow and develop, we who call ourselves Christians and members of the Body of Christ have to step up and take some responsibility. We are called to be active participants not passive observers; we are sent by the Lord to participate in his work to the world. We are called to be apostles, those who are sent in the name of Christ, just as much as Peter and Paul were.

Jesus famously says to Peter that he is the rock on which the Church will be built. He has a part to play, an offering to give.

Peter is nevertheless imperfect in many ways, as we all are. He proclaims Christ as Lord, and then betrays him. He is reluctant to let Christ wash his feet and he sets his mind on earthly things rather than heavenly things. But despite everything, Simon becomes Cephas, the 'rock', and Peter proclaims Christ as his Lord and his God.

Paul, too, is not an easy character. His story begins as someone who persecutes Christians with great zeal, but an encounter on the road to Damascus changes all that and his life is turned around completely. Saul becomes Paul, and Paul spends the rest of his days helping the early Church live out its calling and live into its identity.

Very different characters with very different gifts, but made one in Christ. They have been remembered jointly on this day since the very early days of the Church and they can be imagined, as the prophet Zechariah imagines them, as two olive trees standing to right and to left of the light of Christ, pillars of the Church.

What can we give?

Peter and Paul participate fully in the life of Christ and so build up the life of his Church. In spite of their differences, they are bound together by the love of God in which they live and move and have their being. By their example we can have hope that a church made up of diverse opinions and personalities can witness together to the love of God in Christ Jesus.

Everyone has gifts to share, something to offer. However inadequate we feel, God can take us and use us whatever our backgrounds, whoever we are, in our diversity and with all our imperfections. This is no clearer than in the lives of Peter and Paul, these two towering figures of the early Church, apostles, with differing roles and personalities but bound together in Christ. Peter and Paul help us realize that we are the Church. We are the rocks that help build the Church of today, the living stones that have so much more potential than bricks and mortar. We make our church buildings come to life; we are today's apostles sent out into the world in the name of Christ.

Your calling?

Building community is not always easy, building the Church is not always easy, but we don't build anything by stepping away from the action. Around the country at this time of year, around the time of the feast day of Saints Peter and Paul, often on or near 29 June, many churches make new deacons and priests. People from all walks of life take a step forward for Christ into an unknown future and put themselves forward for all kinds of ministries according to their God-given gifts. It's appropriate that we remember Peter and Paul at such a time, people who stepped forward and said, 'We are the Church.' We too are members of the Church, through our prayer, through acts of service, through worship and through our community life. We are not all called to be ordained, but we are called by virtue of our baptism to be a living stone. We have a part to play, something to offer. Inspired by the teaching and the example of Peter and Paul, perhaps today is a good time to think about our contribution to the life of the Church and consider what God is calling us to be and to do in his name.

Victoria Johnson

Suggested hymns

Christ is made the sure foundation; All my hope on God is founded; Christ is our cornerstone; The Church's one foundation; Bind us together.

St Thomas the Apostle 3 July
Seeing with the Heart

Hab. 2.1–4; Ps. 31.1–6; Eph. 2.19–end; **John 20.24–29**

St Thomas, with his doubts and his rigorous demand for evidence, has come into his own. In an age when Christianity is widely thought to be a matter of private opinion rather than laying claim to public truth, Thomas has become a role model and polemicist for a reasoned approach to faith. No longer castigated for his doubts, Thomas himself reflects the scepticism of the age and shows that doubts can be voiced and answered.

But legitimate as that is, might we not also ask whether Jesus or John is approving Thomas or rebuking him. Have we been keener to listen to Thomas than to hear the words John attributes to Jesus? What can the interchange with Thomas say to us who, unlike Thomas, can't see Jesus?

Blessed are those who have not seen

'Blessed are those who have not seen and yet have come to believe.' Was that a reproof to Thomas? John saw only the empty grave clothes but did not see Jesus, and yet he believed. Mary of Magdala 'saw' Jesus but it didn't get her very far; only when Jesus spoke to her did she 'see' and believe. The disciples believed when they saw Jesus, but Thomas dismissed their testimony and demanded both to see and to touch. John couches Jesus' reproof of Thomas in language that recalls his saying: 'Unless you can see signs and wonders you will not believe.' So it seems likely that Thomas is being rebuked for refusing to accept the word of the other disciples and for being caught up with the miraculous aspect of Jesus' appearance and an over-reliance on the faculty of sight.

When seeing is not believing

The Queen is known to have said, 'I have to be seen to be believed.' We know what she means. But is the popular mantra 'Seeing is believing' so obvious, as if the evidence of the eye is sufficient to settle all the claims that come our way? It's not surprising then that non-believers ask, 'Why doesn't Jesus show himself again?'

But the demand is not only theologically ludicrous but also philosophically untenable. Seeing isn't self-authenticating, since what we see has to be interpreted. As those visual puzzle pictures show, there is always an ambiguity and subjectivity in how we see. 'Two men looked through prison bars; one saw mud, the other stars.' We sometimes hear it said that we see what we believe. Belief is always at work, influencing if not determining what we actually see and how we interpret it. Would you have expected any other comment from the first Russian astronaut Juri Gagarin when he declared that he didn't find God in outer space? As well as Mary Magdalene, Jesus drew alongside the two disciples travelling to Emmaus; but they too failed to see him. Sight alone cannot settle our doubts, and can't by itself settle the question of Jesus' post-resurrection reality and identity.

'Looking with the heart'

If John suggests the limits of sight, he doesn't dismiss it altogether. It met Thomas' demands, but his sublime confession of Jesus far exceeded what sight or sound or evidence and argument could have drawn from him. If we use the language of sight, we are on safer ground with Saint Exupery's Little Prince, who tells us 'to look with the heart'. 'Come and see' is the invitation to immerse ourselves in the household of those who know and love Jesus until we know and love him for ourselves.

At the time John was writing, fewer witnesses of Jesus' resurrection were alive. John's primary concern is for those, like us, who cannot 'see' but who come to believe by hearing the testimony of the disciples and experiencing the presence of Jesus in his body the Church. But this is St Thomas' day and we give thanks that 'But for the fact that Thomas and the other apostles saw the incarnate Christ there would have been no Christian faith at all'.[45] And we are thankful, too, that he is written into the story as a stooge who sets up the scene and creates the opportunity for Jesus to speak to us and teach us a surer way to be blessed. 'Blessed are those who have not seen and yet have come to believe.' Or, as St Peter expresses it: 'Although you have not seen him, you love him; and even though you do not see him now, you believe in him and rejoice with an indescribable and glorious joy.'

Roger Spiller

Suggested hymns

Dear Lord, we long to see your face; Come, living God, when least expected; Year by year, from past to future; All my hope on God is founded.

St Mary Magdalene 22 July
Loving the Lord

Song of Sol. 3.1–4; Ps. 42.1–10; 2 Cor. 5.14–17; **John 20.1–2, 11–18**

Today we're celebrating Mary Magdalene. Many of the followers of Jesus in the Gospels are very human figures: they're easy to identify with. We can be like impetuous Peter, jumping ahead only to trip up. Like James and John, we can hanker after status and honour. Like Thomas, we all have our moments of doubt. And we can even sometimes identify with Judas – and teeter on the brink of betrayal. But, what do we identify with in the person of Mary

Magdalene? This is a hard question to answer because in Mary's case we have to sift the fact from fiction. What we know about Mary from the Scriptures bears little resemblance to the myths and fantasy that have surrounded her for centuries. At different times she has been seen as a prostitute, a mystic, a feminist icon, and most recently in Dan Brown's fiction as the matriarch of divinity's secret dynasty. Who was she?

Mary

From the Gospels we know that Mary almost certainly came from the wealthy city of Magdala on the west bank of the Sea of Galilee. St Luke tells us that Jesus cast out seven demons from Mary, so it seems she had been very sick, both mentally and physically, at the time of her first meeting with Jesus. Mary may have come from a wealthy family herself. She certainly had the freedom to follow Jesus and to support his work from her own funds. She was fully included as an integral member of the emerging Jesus movement. Mary – alone of the women in the Gospels – has her own name. She is not Mary, mother of anyone. She is not Mary, wife of so and so. She is Mary, called Magdalene. She is named 12 times in the Gospels and her presence is implied on two more occasions. Most importantly, Mary is the first to encounter the risen Christ following his resurrection. Jesus calls her by her name, 'Mary', as a close friend might. And Mary was close not just to Jesus but to all the apostles. In greeting her so lovingly in the garden, Jesus affirms her status as the 'apostle to the apostles' – a term that's been used of Mary for centuries. It's remarkable that Jesus revealed the resurrection first to a woman. Women in first-century Judaism generally ranked far behind men. Jesus always subverts the hierarchical order of things – turns the world upside down – he is making all things new. Mary is confident to join in with this subversion. She is so affirmed by Jesus that she is able to embody the message that the kingdom of God is available to all, regardless of any human constructs that try to put people down. Is this a trait in Mary with which we can identify?

Love

Perhaps Jesus chose to reveal himself first to Mary Magdalene because she, over and above all the characters in the gospel stories, is the one who dared to truly love him. That love took her beyond fear to stand at the foot of the cross and watch Jesus die, to go to the tomb to anoint him, to hold on to his risen body, and to tell everyone the good news of his resurrection. Our reading today from the Song of Solomon has long been spiritually linked with Mary seeking for Jesus after the resurrection and longing to find him. Did you spot the parallels between the questioning of the sentinels and Mary's questioning of the angels at the tomb? The Song of Solomon clearly expresses the kind of love that Mary Magdalene shows: 'I will rise now and go about the city, in the streets and in the squares; I will seek him whom my soul loves.' Do we seek such love? Do we find such love in the person of Jesus? Will we allow this love to overcome any fear we may have? Will we let this love heal and restore us? Is this Mary's challenge to us?

Witness

Today Jesus calls you by your name just as he did when he spoke to Mary Magdalene. He sends you, like her, to announce the good news that Jesus has died and is risen: to offer forgiveness and hope to the world. He calls all of us to tell others the Christian story. Not just the story of the cross and resurrection but also our story of meeting with the risen Jesus and the difference that has made in our lives. You may not feel very confident to do that but I'm guessing Mary Magdalene had tons of questions; vast amounts that she didn't understand, and she certainly couldn't explain it all. Jesus simply asked her to go and tell others, and she told what she could. Jesus asks the same of you, and me: go and tell others what you can about the risen Jesus, the love you've found, and the difference it makes. So, here's how we can identify with Mary Magdalene. We can accept that we are dearly loved by God – whoever we are. We can challenge the status quo and work for inclusivity and equality. We can love and adore Jesus by accepting his presence with us through the work of the Holy Spirit. Filled with that Spirit we can confidently tell others the good news of Jesus Christ. Amen.

Catherine Williams

Suggested hymns

Led like a lamb; My song is love unknown; I am a new creation; Walking in a garden.

St James the Apostle 25 July

Costly, Clear-eyed Service

Jer. 45.1–5; Ps. 126; Acts 11.27—12.2 (*if the Acts reading is used instead of the Old Testament reading, the New Testament reading is* 2.Cor 4.7–15); **Matt. 20.20–28**

Poor St James, the only thing we know about him is the unedifying story of personal ambition, and the request to be awarded superior status over others. In Matthew's Gospel it's not James and John who make the request to Jesus, it's their mother. But the fact that Jesus replies to James and John suggests that they put their mother up to it.

On the face of it, it wasn't an unreasonable request. James and John were, after all, two of the first disciples, just after Andrew and Peter, and, together with Peter, the brothers formed an inner circle chosen by Jesus to be with him at important times. They were the only ones Jesus took with him to witness the transfiguration, and they were the ones he asked to keep company with him in the Garden of Gethsemane. Why shouldn't they ensure that they would have superior status when Jesus comes into his kingdom?

This comes hard on the heels of Jesus telling them that he is about to be mocked, flogged, condemned to death and crucified. The first time he told them, Peter objected, 'God forbid it, Lord, this will never happen to you.' The second time he told them, they argued among themselves as to which of them was the greatest. Now he tells them for the third time, and James and John get their mother to speak up for them and put in a claim for them to occupy the best seats in the kingdom.

And when he was crucified, the religious leaders mocked him: 'He saved others; he cannot save himself.' They spoke better than they knew. James and John might have hoped that service with and for Jesus was part of the cost of following him on a triumphal journey leading straight into the kingdom when Jesus takes his rightful place. But the way of costly service is never compatible with service of self. Ambition isn't wrong if it is set upon the service of others; the ambition of James and John was wrong because it was self-serving and would always be at the expense of others.

The serving Church

This story inspired fresh thinking on the relationship between the Church and the wider world. The recovery of the image of 'the servant Church' encourages Christians to model themselves on service. This can, unwittingly, keep church members in a state of submission to the institution while leaving the old hierarchical structures unchanged. It can also be a way of reacting and responding to the needs and agendas of people and communities while the Church remains torn and uncertain about its priorities and mission. With no clear agenda ourselves, we're more than happy to meet the expectations that other people put upon us. But there's a tough, hard-headed quality about the servant image.

Being a servant doesn't mean that we come with no agenda except to fulfil the agendas and demands of others. Jesus himself had priorities – he knew when to turn his back on a crowd, to let the dead bury their dead. He spoke of pruning as well as planting. Service needs to have a tough edge. He acts gently or toughly as best serves the need of the individual or group. He has a repertoire of styles, and because he's free in himself he can adopt the stance that most fulfils the true interests of the other person or situation.

Service from strength

Service comes from strength, not weakness and fragility. Being a servant doesn't mean keeping the peace at all costs. You don't serve anybody if you tolerate everything, certainly not the people who need you to help them grow and develop their ego strength, their character.

Service, then, can look as tough and abrasive as the exercise of power that it replaces. The difference is that service is constrained by love, not power. It acts out of a secure sense of self-love and for the well-being of the other, not necessarily as they see it, but as it may be seen within the context of God and his kingdom. We won't always get it right, but service will be good enough if it is not self-serving.

When Jesus addressed James and John, he asked them if they were able to undergo death and they replied that they were. That, not any exalted place in the kingdom, was all that Jesus promised. James must have learnt that the way of the cross is sacrificial service of others. He is the only one of the 12 disciples whose murder, by King Herod, is recorded in the New Testament. And that's as good a reason as any to remember him today, and why we remember saints, not only exceptional people we idealize through stained-glass windows but people who recognize their fallibility and weakness and are ready to change.

Roger Spiller

Suggested hymns

Brother, sister, let me serve you; By contact with the crucified, we all are gathered, called and named; Ye servants of God; Christ is the world in which we move.

Transfiguration of Our Lord 6 August

The 'Story' of Transfiguration Retold

For an alternative sermon, see the Principal Service for the Sunday next before Lent (p. 67).

Dan. 7.9–10, 13–14; Ps. 97; 2 Peter 1.16–19; **Luke 9.28–36**

It's very early in the morning, the darkness slowly giving way to the first light of day; three of us friends are at the foothills of one of the rugged peaks you can see for miles around. We're beginning a gradual ascent. The wind is blowing, casting a thin spray of sand around our feet. He usually goes alone, early, to be still, to converse with the one he calls his father. But this time he's invited us to join him. He's setting a brisk pace, and we're struggling to keep him in our sights. We're chuffed that he's asked us to accompany him. It makes us feel rather special, but still you can't be sure what to expect when you're with this man. It's never easy, but he's so compelling. Especially those long searing conversations that show he reads us like a book. And just six days ago, he put my brother on the spot and wouldn't let up until he got him to say who he thought he was. And then he rebuked him as a devil when he tried to lift his spirits and poo-poo all this talk of suffering! But today I don't think he's got anything in mind for us – but just to keep awake and join him on his long and lonely vigil. It's getting steep now, we're gasping for air, we can feel our pulses racing. We're a little distance behind him. We daren't take our eyes off him.

Strange light and sight

Then, just as we're struggling up the last steep, craggy ascent, something extraordinary is happening. His whole face is suddenly lit up, as it were, from inside. He looks different, and yet the same, and his clothing is becoming luminous, with a whiteness I've never seen before. My eyes are dazzled, burning, stopping me from seeing clearly. Suddenly two other figures are appearing out of nowhere, coming into focus, standing with our master, flanking him on both sides. We know enough about them to recognize them: great figures representing law and prophets from the past, whose great activities were on mountains just like this one. One of them had been up on the mountain for so long, conversing with God, that his people wondered whether they'd ever see him again. But when he came down, his face shone with light too bright to behold. And there's the other figure, the mighty prophet who did battle with and destroyed all the false prophets. It's a pity we didn't experience this before he asked us who we thought he was.

Listen!

Now there's a murmur of sound. They're talking. We can just about overhear snippets of conversation. It's about our master's departure, once again, something that my brother won't hear of. It's hard for us to keep awake. It's not just the exercise; it's facing all the strangeness of this person. And now my brother chips in: 'Master, it is good for us to be here.' My brother will say anything to fill an awkward silence. And what's he saying now: 'Let us make three dwellings.' What! A building programme up here! He doesn't know what he's saying. But the other two figures are disappearing, so he's got that wrong again. Suddenly the temperature drops and we're terrified, enveloped in a great cloud. And we're just standing still, too petrified to move, not knowing where to go. But now there's a voice that comes out of the cloud: 'This is my Son, my Chosen; listen to him.'

What a story!

That's spoken to us, yes, to us! My brother told him who he was and now we know. 'This is my Son' – God's son. There were rumours that he'd heard those very words, when he was baptized by that wild, wilderness figure called John, but it made no sense. And what does the voice say to us: 'listen to him'. That's all: listen to him. And now, quick as a flash, we're back to normal, with the one figure, standing alone, just as he always was, now purposefully leading us back down. What a story to tell our friends. But no, it's too amazing, indescribable, incredible to be shared with others. So we've got to sit on this story. But, as the voice said in the cloud, 'listen to him'. We've got to start listening.

Optional explanation

The story of Jesus can't be explained. It can only be accessed by the imagination. It has to be felt, smelt, heard, seen – all our senses conscripted at fever pitch, so that we can be part and parcel of Jesus' story. Followers of Christ say that the meaning of this world is found outside it; the meaning of human history cannot be known in history itself. It is found at the end of history, beyond history, and all things are converging on that point when God's purpose will become transparent. Other people increasingly believe the opposite, that either there is no meaning, no point to the human story, to my life and to yours, or that we are left to draw whatever meaning we can salvage from the fragments of our own stories. Believers say that God is the story-maker and all will be revealed in the last chapter. But, in the story of Jesus, including, and perhaps especially, in his transfiguration, death and resurrection, we are given a sneak preview of the final scene. If we ascend above the immediate day-to-day episodes of our lives, inhabit Jesus' story, let it illuminate and fill and feed our imaginations as well as our minds and hearts, then we will be able to recognize his transforming presence in the midst and muddle of our lives. For, Christians stake their lives on the fact that Jesus, known by his story, is the best clue we have to the meaning of life and human history. And if we're serious, really serious, then we too must obey the divine voice and 'listen to him', make Jesus the source and reference point for all that we are and do. As the inscription on the recent memorial stone to C. S. Lewis in Westminster Abbey has it, 'I believe in Christianity as I believe that the Sun has risen, not only because I see it but because by it I see everything else.'

Roger Spiller

Suggested hymns

Christ, whose glory fills the sky; Christ is the world's light; Longing for light; O Morning Star, how fair and bright.

The Blessed Virgin Mary 15 August

Life at Its Most Unlikely

Isa. 61.10–end, *or* Rev. 11.19—12.6, 10; Ps. 45.10–end; Gal. 4.4–7; **Luke 1.46–55**

I recently watched (again) the film *Mama Mia!* Its delightful, if ridiculous, storyline is little more than an excuse to get a varied list of stars to show off their very varied singing talents. And to entertain us with a stream of Abba songs sung in the tradition of the classic musicals. The links are often thin, but then they usually are. Life isn't like a musical – the dramas of everyday encounters don't find us bursting into song, fun as it is to see it all implausibly assembled on the screen. So if real life isn't like that, it seems rather peculiar that we find our Lady bursting forth into the Magnificat during her visit to Elizabeth.

Life turns to poetry

Universal Pictures gives us a hardly challenging script, but Luke's description of the Visitation of Mary to Elizabeth offers us something much more. He offers us poetry. Some events are so pregnant with mystery and wonder that ordinary language is incapable of rendering them. One of the gifts poetry is to us is that it conveys profound truths without the descent into cliché it would be hard otherwise to avoid.

How might Mary respond to the build-up of events that have transposed her life into a higher key? How might she respond to the series of messages and reactions that promise something so terrifying and yet so tremendous? As Luke relates the story, it all grows until nothing but an outburst into the poetry of Magnificat can really express it. Indeed, we find the same poetic gift as we listen to St John the Divine's apocalyptic vision: here is a birth-giving woman clothed with the sun and crowned with 12 stars. Visions aren't the stuff of ordinary experience and certainly not of ordinary, prosaic language. Poetry alone can help us enter something of its wonder and make connections with other parts of life and other parts of the story.

Certainly, when we come to today's feast, we can enter it most helpfully by seeing it as belonging to faith's poetry. However we want to explain what happened at the end of our Lady's earthly life, normal words will inevitably fail us, so we hold on to words of poetry: falling asleep, assumption or, more grandly, 'dormition'. Whatever the term, it points us not to a scientific explanation but to a life uniquely lived and gloriously captured into the resurrection life God offers in Christ.

Mary's Magnificat is embedded in the religious consciousness of many of us. Thanks to some of the soaring musical settings of choral evensong, the poetry has been enriched by music and we can easily find ourselves settling into it with a sense of comfortable luxury as the beautiful cadences wash around us.

Life gains an unexpected edge

If that's where the poetry leaves us, however, we have missed it. If the Magnificat only leaves us aesthetically pleased, we haven't listened. Mary's words demand much more of us than pleasure. This is poetry with a sharp, radical edge. This is poetry that calls for revolution. This is poetry that points us to the demanding words about the kingdom that would be revealed in word and action by Jesus in his ministry. So already we discover that, even as he is moulded in her womb, Mary's words lead us to her Son.

Life turns to discipleship

And that is Mary's vocation. Mary is the one who not only bears the Lord: she directs us to him in everything she does, in everything she says, in everything she is. Mary is often called first among the disciples, not because she always understood her Son but because she had the fullness of grace to respond even when she didn't understand. We remember her response to Gabriel's annunciation: 'Here am I, the servant of the Lord . . .' Long before comprehension came, Mary modelled trustful obedience and faithful trust. She directs us to the Lord by modelling something of what the call to discipleship is for each of us.

And as we listen to the poetry of the Magnificat, we encounter another vital dimension of that discipleship. Following our Lord is not a passive occupation. It's a challenge that engages us in ways that are spiritual but also deeply practical. We might describe it as 'living the Magnificat'. To do that is to recognize that the world is not yet how God intends it to be; what's more, it's to recognize that we're the ones he calls to bring about that change. We must imagine that this youthful Mary had little idea of the rich implications of the poetry we hear placed in her mouth. In her simple humanity, she became a revolutionary: not only did she offer her womb to bear the fruit which was God's greatest gift to us; but she offered her voice to sing of God's greatest aspirations for us.

Thank goodness life is never like a Broadway musical. Perhaps we should also be relieved that life isn't like choral evensong either. It's a beautiful part of our religious tradition. The rhythmic majesty of the poetry and the beauty of much of the music will often stir our hearts. But, much as we might love the Magnificat, if we don't let it stir our consciences and our actions, it's poetry we have failed to hear.

Brett Ward

Suggested hymns

Sing we of the blessed Mary; For Mary, mother of our Lord; Lord Jesus Christ; Tell out, my soul, the greatness of the Lord.

St Bartholomew the Apostle 24 August

Firmly I Believe and Truly

Isa. 43.8–13; Ps. 145.1–7; **Acts 5.12–16** (*if the Acts reading is used instead of the Old Testament reading, the New Testament reading is* 1 Cor. 4.9–15); Luke 22.24–30

Though Bartholomew was one of the Twelve, we know relatively little about him, but he is named as an apostle in the Gospels of Matthew, Mark and Luke. He is often portrayed by the side of Philip, and there is a tradition that puts forward the idea that Bartholomew is the very same as Nathanael, the man who was brought to Jesus by Philip in the Gospel of John. Nathanael is at first rather cynical about Jesus of Nazareth, and utters those infamous words, 'Can anything good come out of Nazareth?' Nathanael does then recognize Jesus as the Son of God and the King of Israel, and his life is changed for ever. Jesus comments that Nathanael is one in whom there is no deceit, he is true to himself and true to his word.

There is scholarly disagreement about whether Nathanael and Bartholomew are one and the same person, but what really matters is Bartholomew's witness to Christ, the Son of God, through his life and through his gruesome death. He was martyred for his faith and according to tradition he was skinned alive. In art he is depicted often as wearing his flayed skin like a garment over his arm or around his neck.

Whatever his origins, Bartholomew left his home, his work, his ordinary life to follow Jesus around the Galilean countryside. He was called and he responded. Whenever we hear tell of the apostles in the Gospels, we can be sure Bartholomew was there, not necessarily up front with a speaking part, but in the background, loyal and steadfast to the very end.

Confidence in Christ

According to the early church historian Eusebius of Caesarea, Bartholomew set out after being a witness to the ascension to proclaim the good news of Jesus Christ in India. He then went on to Armenia where he gained many disciples for Christ. As he was brought to Christ, so he went on to bring others, and, like all the apostles, he was so changed by the events he witnessed that he could do no other than go forth and tell of them. We don't know whether he was indeed a great orator like St Paul, but we can be sure that there was something about what he said and what he did that made people sit up and listen.

For someone apparently in the background, for someone with little to say in the Gospels, the passion, death and resurrection of Christ gave Bartholomew confidence to journey into unknown regions and share his experiences and beliefs with others.

Bartholomew's story, like the story of many saints throughout history, reminds us what faith can do and how faith can transform each one of us into the people God calls us to be. We might feel weak, weary, inadequate and underprepared; we may even have our doubts; we might feel a fool; we may just be shy – but our little bit of faith can give us great confidence to speak out in the name of Christ to those who have not seen and those who have not heard. Whether people hear or choose not to hear, we are nevertheless called to proclaim Christ not only with our lips but with our lives.

Go forth and tell

One common misconception about Christianity is that it is a private affair, and polite people do not talk about their faith. This is not what Bartholomew lived and died for. We are each called to give an account of the faith that is within us, but we don't have to give a lecture or stand on a street corner to do this. We just have to be true to ourselves and true to Christ. It is all right to discuss and grapple with our faith, and talk about it with others, telling them what it means to us in our daily lives and how it shapes who we are and what we do. We just need to be honest and speak as people in whom there is no deceit. In the book of Acts, many people became believers because of what they saw the apostles doing. In the Gospel for St Bartholomew's day, we are told that we can witness to Christ through service; we become great by becoming as one who serves. We can witness to Christ by our actions as well as our words. Sometimes we don't need words at all to tell of his love for the world.

Victoria Johnson

Suggested hymns

Go forth and tell; Firmly, I believe and truly; Blessed are the pure in heart; Give us the wings of faith.

Holy Cross Day 14 September

Lift High the Cross

Num. 21.4–9; Ps. 22.23–28; Phil. 2.6–11; **John 3.13–17**

Today is Holy Cross Day. It's an ancient festival in the Church's calendar which is associated with St Helena's visit to the Holy Land in the fourth century and her discovery of pieces of the true cross of Christ. Helena was the mother of the Roman Emperor Constantine whose conversion to Christianity made it the official religion of the Roman Empire. On 14 September 335, the great Church of the Holy Sepulchre in Jerusalem was dedicated and Holy Cross Day has been celebrated ever since. Cross-shaped cakes or even hot cross buns are eaten on this day, and some cultures use basil to flavour special dishes to signify the basil growing where Helena found the fragments of the cross. One of the churches in which I used to serve has a medieval Holy Cross window, set high towards the roof. If the sun is shining on 14 September, shafts of sunlight pour down upon the cross of Christ set on the rood beam – it can be very dramatic!

Healing

Unlike the more sombre Good Friday, this is a day when Christians have traditionally celebrated the cross as the symbol of God's victory over sin and death, and God's love for the world. Our Old Testament passage looks back to the Israelites in the wilderness. They are discouraged and miserable. There's nothing to drink, and they moan about how terrible the food is. They don't seem to be getting anywhere. Worst of all, God sends a plague of snakes: people get bitten and die.

It's all going horribly wrong. The people realize they have sinned, and they ask Moses to intervene and pray for the snakes to be taken away. The Lord instructs Moses to make a bronze serpent and raise it high on a pole so that when people are bitten by a snake they can look to the symbol and live. The snake is a powerful and mixed symbol in many cultures – it can be both dangerous and positive; it can bring both death and life. The symbol with the snake on a pole – or sometimes a double snake and staff – has been used down the centuries to indicate healing. The health professions still use it today. Look out for it – it's often on pharmacy signs.

Life

John refers to this episode of the bronze snake and links it with the cross of Christ. Just as Moses lifted up the snake in the desert, so the Son of Man must be lifted up, says John. When we look to and believe in Christ on the cross we will receive not just healing, but life – eternal life. The cross is a bridge or a ladder between heaven and earth – the connecting piece that holds all things together. The Father has sent the Son not to berate us for our waywardness and lack of faith but to save us and to bring us to reconciliation and oneness with God. And this giving of God's self in Jesus on the cross is for the whole world: not just for individuals, not just for the Church, but for everyone, throughout all time. God loves us so much that he sacrificed himself for us in Jesus. There is nothing any of us can do that can make God love us any more than he already does – he loves us completely and utterly, without beginning or end. And there is nothing in all creation that can separate us from that love, shown in the crucified Christ. So, when we look at the cross we are looking at the extraordinary and overwhelming love of God for the entire world.

Lifting high

No wonder the medieval stonemasons built special Holy Cross windows in our churches to illuminate the cross. They wanted the world to see the power and beauty of the cross. So many people in our world today need to hear the message that God loves them unconditionally, forgives their sins and longs for them to come to know and love him in return. So many people need to hear that they can turn their lives around, start again and be saved – rescued – by looking to and believing in Jesus Christ. When I visit in hospitals or hospices, I sometimes take a holding cross to leave with someone who is anxious or fearful about their future. It's a cross designed to fit snugly into your hand so that you can hang on to Jesus at a difficult time. As individuals and as a church, we're called to 'lift high the cross', to reveal the loving, saving power of God to our neighbours, so that we may all learn to bow the knee at the name of Jesus Christ and enter into life in all its fullness. So, today, consider what the cross means to you. Do you wear a cross? Do you have a cross in your home or on your desk? In what ways can you raise the profile of Jesus for those around you? How might you show people the difference believing in Jesus makes in your life? On this Holy Cross Day, let's make a resolution to 'lift high the cross' so that God's love for the world can be seen and experienced by all. Amen.

Catherine Williams

Suggested hymns

Lift high the cross; At the name of Jesus; The wonder of the cross; When I survey the wondrous cross.

Matthew, Apostle and Evangelist 21 September
What is Truth?

Prov. 3.13–18; Ps. 119.65–72; **2 Cor. 4.1–6**; Matt. 9.9–13

> We have renounced the shameful things that one hides; we refuse to practise cunning or to falsify God's word; but by the open statement of the truth we commend ourselves to the conscience of everyone in the sight of God.

You may (or may not) know the song from the musical *Gigi* entitled 'I remember it well'. It was sung by Maurice Chevalier and Hermione Gingold. The lyrics are a conversation between a couple talking about their first date: they met at nine/no, it was eight; he was on time/no, he was late; they dined with friends/no, they dined alone; a tenor sang/no, a baritone. Undaunted, the man muses, 'Ah, yes, I remember it well.'[46]

It's a tender love song sung by an elderly man and woman, which captures a kind of wistful human reality but also accepts the fallibility of memory. If you had to decide which of the two characters was actually speaking the truth and remembering things accurately, you'd be hard pressed to do so.

It's a reminder that one of the strange characteristics of we humans is that we can each witness a single event and yet see and remember it differently. It raises a serious question: what is truth?

Let's try approaching the question from a different angle.

We hear much these days about 'fake news'. It's thrown around by politicians whenever a journalist writes or broadcasts a piece being critical of the politician. It's a very dangerous game because it's based on the assumption that the journalist is lying (and has some ulterior motive for doing so) whereas the politician is speaking the truth. The net result is that all of us are becoming more and more cynical. Who, if anyone, can we trust to speak the truth?

Jesting Pilate

Well. The question is not as contemporary as we might like to think it is. Remember Pontius Pilate at Jesus' trial asking the question, 'What is truth?'

And in today's reading we come across another reference to 'truth'. Paul claims that 'by the open statement of the truth we commend ourselves to the conscience of everyone in the sight of God'. To what truth is he referring? Is it simply a reference to his personal view about the nature of Jesus? Because if that is what it is, then it is open to challenge. Put crudely: how can we know that Paul's view of the truth is the same as ours? Does his view have an authenticity that other people's views of truth do not have?

Now, as we follow this argument we are approaching difficult territory. Bring to mind the Gospel of John in which Jesus refers to himself as 'the truth'. In John 14, verse 6, he states, 'I am the way, and the truth, and the life.' What are we to make of this? Is that all that needs to be said about truth?

It is worth noting that John's Gospel has over twenty references to 'truth' whereas, by contrast, Matthew has just one. It would seem, therefore, that the concept of truth was one with which John genuinely struggled. It was presumably one of the central concepts of his mental world view by which he made sense of things. And, as a result, he found that he could approach the elusive figure of Jesus by using the concept of 'truth' as his guide. If that is what he did, then the words that Jesus said about 'truth' are of great importance.

Jesus and 'truth'

So, let's dig even deeper. In what sense was or is Jesus the 'truth'? The answer to that question depends on whether or not you believe that God disclosed himself to us in Jesus. If Jesus was and is God's epiphany, and if we can also assume that the ultimate truth of all things is found in God, we can, with John, talk confidently of Jesus as 'truth', can't we?

That is a bit of a convoluted way of putting it, but in a world where all things described as 'true' are up for discussion, and in a world where one person's view of truth is considered as valid as any other person's, perhaps John was on to something that can help us.

Maybe this can be put in a simpler way: if God is Truth and if all that we regard as true emanates from God, then we can begin to find a way out of our philosophical quagmire. Perhaps we can say that things are true the more they resemble God. This is not to claim that we as Christians have a monopoly on truth; far from it, for which of us can say that we completely know God? The search for truth, therefore, necessarily requires humility. But that search for truth, wherever it is to be found, is one of the greatest and noblest challenges any of us can undertake.

Let us pray that God will grant us the grace and strength to continue on the quest.

Christopher Herbert

Suggested hymns

I will sing the wondrous story; Christ is the one who calls; We turn to Christ anew.

St Michael and All Angels 29 September
Time for Angels?

Gen. 28.10–17, *or* Rev. 12.7–12; Ps. 103.19–end; **Rev 12.7–12**, *or* Heb. 1.5–end; John 1.47–end

Today's Feast of St Michael and All Angels surely belongs to the margins of Christian life. Weird, winged creatures have their place in fiction but surely not in the real world of sight and sound and touch? Well, it may come as a surprise that the time for angels has come. *Time Magazine* found that 70 per cent of Americans believe that angels exist. In the UK, recent opinion polls suggest that one in three people believe that they have a guardian angel, including one in six who describe themselves as atheists. The wave of interest in angels in our society shows no sign of slowing. But we don't hear much about it because there is a reluctance for people to share their experiences and beliefs about angels – perhaps because of the risk of being thought of or called a 'nutter'.

Angels

The Bible is more selective and restrained in its presentation of angels than what we infer from the popular mind. We think, for example, of Jacob the patriarch fleeing from his angry brother and dreaming of a ladder reaching up into heaven with angels ascending and descending. There is Isaiah, in his vision in the Temple, having his lips purified by a seraph. And twice Jesus was attended by angels, once at his temptation and again in his agony in the Garden of Gethsemane.

Angels are literally 'messengers', divine messengers close to the courts of heaven. Wings and blond hair are not obligatory. One of their functions is, like Gabriel and the angels at the tomb of Jesus, to pass on messages. Then there are angels who serve around God's throne, as in the book of Revelation They conduct the praise of God. At every Eucharist we get close to them as we in our praise join with 'angels and archangels and all the company of heaven'.

Guardians

But it's the guardian role that is the most characteristic function of angels in the popular mind. Angels are trusted to have the capacity to see further back and further forward, with expanded horizons, and to be available and present at critical stages such as birth, danger and death. The evidence for guardian angels is slender in the Bible. There is the promise in Psalm 91 that the devil invoked when he tempted Jesus to rely on supernatural power. And when in Gethsemane Peter acts with force to protect Jesus, Jesus reminds him that he could have commanded the protection of legions of angels if he had chosen to do so. And in the book of Daniel we hear of the angel Michael, later to be promoted archangel, who is deputed to be the protector of God's people. These were the few seeds from which the idea of a guardian angel that was assigned to individuals began to be developed in the first few centuries of the Church.

If the weight of evidence suggests that people find help and protection from angels, whether as a symbol or as a physical reality, there is reason to rejoice. If angels make unexpected appearances, we may have to consider that they are more present than we can know, and become visible only when they need to do so to deliver a message or bring assurance or protection.

Warrior angel

Michael stands for the great warrior angel who is recognized by Jews, Muslims and Christians alike. There was 'war in heaven', declares the book of Revelation, and Michael with his angelic host overcame and expelled the powers of evil, symbolized in the dragon. The Epstein sculpture of Michael defeating the dragon outside the Cathedral of St Michael, Coventry, is a well-placed visual declaration of the power of evil that was also unleashed around the cathedral space during the war. But the 'war in heaven' attests the superhuman forces, what St Paul calls the 'principalities and powers' and hosts of wickedness that defy human power and can only be fought with spiritual forces on a cosmic plane.

Healer

There's more to Michael than military might. He's venerated less as a warrior than as a protector and healer. Celtic Christianity built shrines to St Michael, whether from the sea at Mont St Michael, Brittany, and St Michael's Mount in Cornwall, or from evil spirits at Glastonbury Tor. Michael was also invoked against pestilence and disease in the town of Houghton-le-Spring in County Durham.

The celebration of St Michael and All Angels draws our attention to the invisible world. It challenges the simplistic view that only what is seen and heard and sensed *is*. It says, in Hamlet's words to Horatio, 'There are more things in heaven and earth, than are dreamt of in your philosophy.'

Jesus is himself the ladder between earth and heaven. But, still, is there not room in that vast celestial space for intermediary, angelic messengers and guardians as God's secret agents? Can we not rejoice in the comfort and reassurance they bring as expressed in that funeral favourite, the Robbie Williams' hit single, 'Angels'. We believe that the decisive battle was fought and won by Jesus himself when he defeated death on the cross. But his rule has still to be implemented and it's to St Michael and the invisible host that we look to champion us against evil, assure us that we don't fight alone, and that we are under the protection of a power beyond our own. And there's nothing more that we can do to get closer to the angels than to join them and all God's people in worship.

Roger Spiller

Suggested hymns

Come, let us join our cheerful song; Christ the fair glory of the holy angels; Songs of praise the angels sang; Ye holy angels bright.

St Luke the Evangelist 18 October

Luke, Evangelist of the Written Word

Isa. 35.3–6 *or* **Acts 16.6–12a**; Ps. 147.1–7; 2 Tim. 4.5–17; Luke 10.1–9

Luke is known to us chiefly through his writings. With John and Paul he is one of the great and extensive writers in the New Testament. St Luke was a second-generation Christian, like St Paul, and probably also St John. Not one of the early band of Jesus, Luke had ample opportunity to associate with them, and as he said in the foreword to his book, he deliberately sought out those who had been with Jesus from the beginning. Unlike all other contributors to the New Testament, he was not a Jew. He was a lay Christian, well versed in Judaism, yet an outsider, writing for non-Jewish lay people.

His education is self-evident, a professional man, widely travelled, with an international perspective. What St Mark calls the sea of Galilee is for Luke the seasoned traveller only an inland 'lake'. And Luke ties the birth and baptism of Jesus to the dates of the Roman emperors and to world events. In both his Gospel and the Acts, he supports the claim that the era of Jesus and the Spirit are world events and that they can thrive even within the Roman Empire.

Marginalized

More interested in people than ideas, Luke's sympathies are with the sinners, the outcasts, the powerless, the sick, women and children.

Not for him the prosperous Magi, but the shepherds; not the protective figure of Joseph, as in Matthew's Gospel, but the vulnerable young woman Mary. And his stories are laced with grace and forgiveness. A penitent prostitute anoints Jesus' head; Zacchaeus is noticed by Jesus and brought to new life; the dying thief on the cross is forgiven and is received into heaven.

Parables

Luke's Gospel abounds with vivid pen portraits of characters. He notices little details that other Gospel writers overlook. And he preserves some of the best-loved parables: the good samaritan; the prodigal son; the lost sheep. St Paul is at one with the gospel of grace, but while he prefers to make the argument for the good news, Luke prefers to paint us pictures. He loves the dramatic effect of drawing sharp contrasts: Mary and Martha, rich man and Lazarus, Pharisee and publican. The stories he selects grab attention and keep us listening, and then, suddenly, we discover that we are unwittingly identifying with censorious or hard-hearted people and become ourselves the intended subjects of Christ's teaching.

Luke was a doctor, as is well known, and has no qualms about repeating Mark's note of the failure of doctors to cure a woman's condition. True to form, he collected stories showing Jesus the healer, characteristically tender, intimate stories: the healing of the only son of the widow of Nain; Peter's mother-in-law's fever; the little daughter of Jairus. And when that little child is healed, Luke records that Jesus told her parents to bring her something to eat!

Spirit and prayer

Although more interested in people than in ideas, Luke gives special emphasis to the work of the Spirit. Little scope was given for the work of the Spirit in the light of the expected imminent end of the world and the coming of the kingdom. But Luke ensures the Spirit has a commanding role, as the Spirit does in the later Gospel of John, and there are two accounts of the coming of the Spirit in the day of Pentecost unique to his Gospel. The Acts is really the Acts of the Spirit. Luke hasn't developed the profounder understanding of the Spirit as an indwelling, personal presence, but he shows the Spirit to be a powerful guiding sign giving miraculous force. With the emphasis on the Spirit, there is a similar emphasis on prayer. Luke collected more about Jesus' practice and teaching on prayer than is to be found in any other Gospel. He records seven instances of Jesus at prayer and preserves some of the parables on prayer, in the Acts as well as the Gospel.

Church's year

There is something else for which Luke deserves our gratitude. He gives us all we know about the rituals that followed Jesus' birth, and the account of the 12-year-old boy in the Temple. And he spaces out the resurrection, Pentecost and ascension – which were hardly separate events at all, so that we can properly revisit them and enter into the experience afresh. In that way Luke laid the groundwork for the Church's year, so that we can ourselves move through the birth, boyhood, ministry, death, resurrection, sending of the Spirit and ascension of Jesus.

A Christian defence

Luke's writing doesn't end with his Gospel. He continues the exciting story on which he embarked in his second volume, the Acts of the Apostles, which charts the story of the emerging church. His aim is not primarily to provide a historically accurate record. His account doesn't tally with St Paul's record, notably in his letter to the Galatians. But Luke has a more immediate and important task if the small, vulnerable following of Jesus is to survive the threats made against it. So where Peter, Paul and other apostles are brought before the Jewish and Roman authorities, Luke skilfully shows how the defence is made, that this new movement called 'the Way' should be treated as an extension and fulfilment of Judaism, and therefore deserves the protection afforded to it.

In a number of places in Acts, Luke abruptly changes from the 'they' of a detached observer to the 'we' of an eyewitness. And we know that he was sometimes present as companion and doctor to St Paul. We catch the strong affection and respect that he has for Paul, and so it's somewhat puzzling that Luke won't admit him to the status of an apostle in his writing. Luke is perhaps too concerned to restrict the status of an apostle to those who were 'with Jesus from the beginning'.

Luke has shown us that Christianity has permeated the whole known world. And when Paul has arrived in Rome, the very citadel of world power, Luke puts down his pen. It's an abrupt and tantalizing ending. But Luke has shown that the fledgling Christian movement has flourished through the support of Rome. There remains one thing for us to do: read Luke, read it and rejoice in the compelling narrative left us by Luke.

Roger Spiller

Suggested hymns

God in his wisdom for our learning; Break thou, the bread of life; Thanks to God whose word was spoken; How beauteous are their feet.

SS Simon and Jude, Apostles 28 October

On Firm Foundations

Isa. 28.14–16; Ps. 119.89–96; **Eph. 2.19–end**; John 15.17–end

> [You are] built upon the foundation of the apostles and prophets, with Christ Jesus himself as the cornerstone.

If you wander around towns keeping your eyes peeled, you might well spot on the lower levels of older public buildings foundation stones. Often these are inscribed with the name of the local worthy who, with a silver trowel, laid the stone on its bed of mortar. The act of laying foundation stones has now largely gone out of fashion. Instead, we bury time capsules in the foundations of buildings in the romantic hope that archaeologists of the future will be fascinated by the hoard we have left. It's perhaps a more imaginative way of doing things.

When the author wrote his letter to the Ephesians (as we have seen in today's Epistle), he used metaphors from building processes to describe early Christian communities. He refers to foundations, cornerstones (or key-stones) and temples. So it's worth speculating what he had in mind when he chose the metaphor. Was it perhaps a Greek temple, with its colonnades and soaring, decorated pillars? There were some of those temples in Ephesus itself, whose remains we can still see today. Or was it a more modest Palestinian house with small rooms, where the room sizes were dictated by the strength and length of timber beams used to support the upper storeys and the roof? Or was he thinking of something much more stunning, like the Temple in Jerusalem with its huge courtyards and massive supporting walls?

We cannot know, of course, which of those examples he had in mind, but it is highly likely that he was basing the building metaphor on his own visual experience.

The limitations of the building metaphor

The difficulty with the idea of the Christian community being like a building is that it can mislead us. We may find ourselves imagining that, like a building, the community has boundaries, outsides and insides. But the author of the letter presses on with his metaphor: 'In him the whole structure is joined together and grows into a holy temple in the Lord.' And with a rhetorical flourish he concludes, 'in whom you also are built together spiritually into a dwelling-place for God'.

But that metaphor, like many metaphors, raises an interesting question: how can a building, which of necessity has limitations of height and breadth and depth, contain the infinite glory and power of God? Patently, the idea is absurd. But pause for a moment. What happens if God takes the initiative, as it were, to limit himself? We find that idea pushed to its fascinating extreme in Paul's letter to the Philippians where he refers to God's self-emptying.

> Let the same mind be in you that was in Christ Jesus, who, though he was in the form of God, did not regard equality with God as something to be exploited, but emptied himself, taking the form of a slave, being born in human likeness. And being found in human form, he humbled himself and became obedient to the point of death – even death on a cross.

Clearly, what was going on in those early letters to the young churches in Ephesus and Philippi was that the authors were struggling to convey the enormity, beauty and complexity of their beliefs: God was infinitely powerful and glorious, yet limited himself; the followers of Jesus were not simply disciples, they were being re-created by God into new ways of living, just as a building has to grow in order to accommodate new uses. Metaphors tumbled over themselves. The new Christians were not only compared with buildings, they were also compared with foreigners in a strange land who had been brought to their rightful home; they were compared with members of a household. They were told that they were members of the Body of Christ; they were like released slaves; they were inheritors of riches; they were heirs of heavenly glory – the similes and metaphors are like a torrent in spate. It's all thoroughly exhilarating. This is not carefully worked-out, dry, academic prose; it is a kind of song of joy, more like a love letter than a report from a Synod, which means that we should treat such writing with deft delight, not expecting it to make coherent or logical sense.

Truth within metaphors

And yet each metaphor has within it much truth. It is true, for example, that without firm foundations a building will be unstable. The building metaphor created by the author of the letter to the young church in Ephesus is therefore useful. It is indeed accurate to say that the foundation of the Christian faith is not only Jesus but also his first disciples – disciples such as Simon and Jude – though if we go digging around to find much about those particular disciples and their roles as foundation stones of the Church we shall not find anything substantial. Legends suggest that they went off on missionary journeys to Persia and Armenia. Other bits of the legend say that they were martyred.

From a historical perspective the lack of reliable documentary evidence about them is frustrating. All that we can safely say is that they were members of the Twelve. Yet, in the epistle to the Ephesians, while they are not named, they are nevertheless seen as part of the foundation of Christianity.

However, that is a comfort. It's a reminder that our worldly status or success, or lack of it, does not matter in the eyes of God. What matters is our faithfulness to our calling. It's through that that we, under God's grace and in our turn, can be foundations of the future Church. And that's enough to be going on with, isn't it?

Christopher Herbert

Suggested hymns

Ye that know the Lord is gracious; Blessed are the pure in heart; For all thy saints, O Lord; Glory to God, the source of all our mission.

Commemoration of the Faithful Departed (All Souls' Day) 2 November

'I am the resurrection and the life'

Lam. 3.17–26, 31–33, *or* Wisd. 3.1–9; Ps. 23, *or* 27.1–6, 16–end; Rom. 5.5–11, *or* 1 Peter 1.3–9; John 5.19–25, *or* **John 6.37–40**

I wonder why you've come to church today. It could be that you're a committed member of this church and come every week, and join in all the celebrations and festivals. But it could be that you are here today because you've come to remember someone you've been very close to who has recently died, or whose memory you've been keeping down the years. The Church sets aside this day – following the great festival of All Saints – in order to remember and pray for those who have died in the faith of Christ, and those whose faith is known to God alone. Whenever we remember we become aware again of our loss and our grief, and it hurts. One of the good things about coming into church to do our remembering is that it reminds us that God is with us: to comfort, to support and to bring hope for the future. Not just here – but in each moment, wherever we find ourselves.

Holding on to God

In our British culture there is a tendency to put on a brave face, to keep a stiff upper lip. We often praise those who suppress their emotions, who don't show their wounds, their hurting. I expect some of you have been praised for being strong, or brave, or for coping. But just because we don't show it, it doesn't mean that the pain has gone away. In our reading from the book of Lamentations, the writer cries out to God. He says that he can't find any peace, he has forgotten what happiness is, and all his hopes and dreams are shattered. However, in the midst of his pain he holds on tightly to God and remembers that God's love never stops. God is faithful to us whatever we're going through, and shows compassion towards us. God is to be trusted and will never let us go. And if you are very angry with God at the moment, that's fine, and completely natural. Shout at God as much as you like – he's big enough to take it, and his love towards you won't stop, even if you can't feel it at the moment.

Death is not the end

We know that God loves us without beginning or end, because he gave his Son Jesus for us. Jesus died on the cross in order that we could be reconciled to God – be friends with God once again. When Jesus rose from the dead, he opened a gate that will never be closed. He showed that there is life beyond death, and promised those who love God that they would one day be with him in heaven. Death is not the end, but the beginning of a new and changed life, a fuller life with God in a new place. Jesus promises that he has prepared a place for us when we die, a place where we can experience peace as we are loved and held by God. Therefore, we have hope for our loved ones who've died and for ourselves – our future is secure in Christ. Nothing that any of us can do can separate us from God's eternal love. We can let go of our loved ones, knowing they are safe with God.

Wounds of grief

Our wounds of grief are nothing to be ashamed of. Our tears and our pain are signs and proof of our love for those who have died. It is precisely because we loved those who've died that we are wounded by their passing from this life. When Jesus was raised from the dead, he didn't hide the wounds of his crucifixion – he still carried the scars, and his disciples saw them. Why did he keep those wounds on his risen body? Why wasn't the flesh made new? Maybe it's because those wounds represent how much God loves us. God in Jesus was prepared to die for us on the cross – his wounds are nothing to be ashamed of. You never fully recover from deep grief – there are always some scars left, and sometimes grief gets worse before it gets better. The pain doesn't just vanish, though in time it does get less. The marks on your wounded heart will remain, though they will hurt less as you move on.

Faith in Jesus

Faith helps that process of moving on and letting go. Jesus broke the chains of death and rose from the tomb to demonstrate to us that God never lets us go, whoever we are. The Christian faith teaches us that our departed ones are not lost, or dead and gone, but alive and safe with God – in a place beyond our understanding. Jesus calls us to be filled with peace, at peace with ourselves, with each other and with God. Jesus calls us not to doubt but to believe. Don't be afraid to show your wounds – your grief and pain. Don't be afraid to hold on to God who loves you more than you could ever know. Don't be afraid to believe that in Jesus Christ life beyond the grave is assured. Trust that – in God – all things will be well. Amen.

Catherine Williams

Suggested hymns

All my hope on God is founded; The Lord's my shepherd; Great is thy faithfulness; Abide with me.

St Andrew the Apostle, 30 November
Apprentice to Jesus

Isa. 52.7–10; Ps. 19.1–6; Rom. 10.12–18; **Matt. 4.18–22**

It's one of the quirks of the lectionary compilers that the Gospel reading set for St Andrew's day tells us nothing (about him) that differentiates him from the three other fishermen who were called by Jesus in close proximity to follow him. If we know anything of Andrew it is that he first identified Jesus as Messiah and then told his brother Peter and brought him to Jesus. That comes from John's Gospel, where it provides the basis for the missionary character attributed to Andrew. But Matthew's Gospel cuts across that tradition and tells us nothing to enable us to latch on to St Andrew as a distinctive disciple.

Always communal

Perhaps that is no bad thing, because Jesus didn't call a set of individualists or prima donnas to be his disciples. He gathered together a group of followers, the core of whom were four people engaged in the fishing trade. Jesus' first recorded action, after his baptism and temptation, was to call disciples whose number, 12, would indicate his intention that they would represent the 12 tribes of Israel and fulfil his nation's promised destiny.

Andrew and the other fishermen have no pre-theological training. Not for Matthew the preliminary initiation as a disciple of

John the Baptist that the Fourth Gospel suggests. They ply their trade as fishermen and respond to Jesus' call with immediate effect. Poor Zebedee is left holding the business as his two sons abandon him to follow Jesus. But as if to anticipate the callous abandonment of an elderly man, the author tells us that he had hired men to take the place of his sons. The call is a sudden and complete change of lifestyle, a radical disruption and reordering of work, relationships, geography and family life with an uncertain future.

Only by being called

Why are they or any of the disciples called? We may well wonder in view of their slow progress and eventual desertion of their master at the end of the story. They were disciples for no other reason than that Jesus called them. They are not selected for their suitability, prior learning and life experience, leadership qualities, stability, adaptability and resourcefulness. They are disciples *only* because of Jesus and his call, and not for any qualities that we could discern in them. There were just 12 disciples; the number counted for more than the character of the disciples themselves. There were other would-be disciples caught up with Jesus, and at the end of the Gospel all people were given an open invitation to become his disciples. And so what Andrew and the other disciples reveal of their call is addressed to us too.

'Followership'

Discipleship meant 'followership', simply being with Jesus. And we can't exaggerate the extent and range of the time the disciples spent with Jesus. They are his support group, but he is their trainer. From this point on, we don't come across stories about Jesus alone, but always stories of Jesus together with his disciples. Wherever he goes they go, and we shall not see him alone again until the disciples desert him in the garden of Gethsemane. Matthew's story is not just that of the Messiah. It's about a messianic community that is coming into being around him. The positioning of this incident right at the beginning leaves no doubt but that this is Jesus' intention. The corporate, communal character of Christian discipleship is an essential and obligatory claim on Jesus' followers, and should contest the atomistic, individualistic, self-serving tendencies that weaken the intrinsic communal witness of the Church.

Apprenticeship

In Ursula Le Guin's Earthsea books,[47] Ged began his apprenticeship in magic with a great magician, Ogion. He expected that he would soon enter into the mysterious arts and gain mastery of nature. But day after day nothing happened. Ogion hadn't shared a single charm or taught him a single name or spell. Finally, Ged became emboldened to ask his master: 'When will my apprenticeship begin, Sir?' 'It has begun,' said Ogion. There was a silence, as if Ged was keeping back something he had to say. Then he said it: 'But I haven't learnt anything yet!' 'Because you haven't found out what I am teaching,' replied the magician.

There were signs of impatience among the disciples, for they too were apprenticed to Jesus. But there was no three-year programme, no long list of learning goals to work through, no assessments and credentials to acquire. Growth is slow and imperceptible. Apprenticeship with Jesus is destined to be lifelong, communal and holistic. It's learning more by engagement than by withdrawal; it's a practical activity; it's more like learning to lay bricks than to live in a library, as the American theologian Stanley Hauerwas observed. And those who pay attention to the way people learn recognize that an apprenticeship to Jesus engages all learning styles: example, experience, observation, interaction, reflection, questions, life-skills, case studies, directive and non-directive learning. Jesus prepares his disciples for mission by preparing people for living. Mission is not a separate department, a discrete project, but the natural and inevitable response of the life he is shaping his disciples to inhabit.

Living mission

Jesus extends the image of fishing to the new life to which he calls them. Nothing is lost, there is always some continuity, however unpromising, between old and new, the known that takes us to the threshold of the unknown and the new challenge before us. The analogy of the fish, considering their destiny and the process by which they are ensnared, is not easily transferable to Christ's mission. But it expresses the relentless, strenuous and intentional activity that is required of all who make disciples of Jesus Christ. The calling of Andrew and the other disciples serves to show us that it's the communal, corporate being together with Jesus, feasting on his word and sacraments, rejoicing in the fellowship that the Spirit creates among his people, and growing together through the Church's apprenticeship in discipleship and learning, that we are called to be and become.

Oh yes, there is one feature that distinguishes Andrew after all, in Matthew's Gospel. He alone has a Greek, not Jewish, name. We know he moved to border territory in Galilee and perhaps his name and pedigree prepared him for the cross-cultural mission for which he is honoured!

Roger Spiller

Suggested hymns

Jesus calls us, o'er the tumult; Take up thy cross, the Saviour said; Will you come and follow me; Go forth, and tell! O Church of God, awake!

Harvest Festival

'Do not forget the Lord your God'

Deut. 8.7–18, *or* Deut. 28.1–14; Ps. 65; 2 Cor. 9.6–end; Luke 12.16–30, *or* Luke 17.11–19

Harvest Festival is the culmination of the agricultural year, celebrating the yields of field and orchard, of river and ocean, of mine and forest.

In Deuteronomy, the children of Israel are poised to enter a land of fertile hills and valleys, a 'land flowing with milk and honey'. But each year they were to remember the source of their prosperity: 'Take care that you do not forget the LORD your God . . . who brought you out of the land of Egypt, out of the house of slavery.'

For us, too, it is good to ask again how we, in our society, with all its pressures, demands and opportunities, relate to the creation in which and out of which we live.

All is gift

Harvest is, first of all, a time of thanksgiving. To give thanks is to acknowledge a gift. For the ancient Israelites this was to remember that they were utterly dependent on the bounty and faithfulness of God, mediated through the gifts of creation. As Psalm 67 says:

The earth has yielded its increase;
  God, our God, has blessed us.
May God continue to bless us;
  let all the ends of the earth revere him.

We are totally dependent and must receive all that sustains us as gift. Especially is this true of the natural world. The mysteries of our environment are now being revealed in ways hitherto hardly imagined. We look into space and vast aeons of time, probing the origins of the universe. We discern the very structure of matter and even the origins of life itself. Increasingly we are masters of our world. But all these must be received as gift, manifestations of God's wisdom, grace and love. So, with St Francis we say: 'Praised be my Lord God with all his creatures. Praise and bless the Lord and give thanks to him, and serve him with great humility.'

Receiving and responsibility

There is, however, also that which we receive from each other. Humanity's privilege and responsibility has been to create a social existence. As Deuteronomy reminds us: the land and its resources enabled the Israelites to eat, be housed, possess flocks and draw riches out of the earth.

A country vicar, greeting a parishioner who was tending his garden, said, 'You and God have brought forth a beautiful display.' 'You should have seen it when God had it to himself,' came the reply. Indeed, the skill and care of the farmer are to be received with thanksgiving, as are those that make things out of the resources of the earth, with all who contribute to the common life, in industry and commerce, in health and welfare, in education and law and order, in governance and public service, as family or in friendship. All this, too, is gift, which we offer to God with thanksgiving. This is reflected in the Eucharist. Bread and wine are brought to the table as God's gift.

> Blessed are you, Lord God of all creation. Through your goodness we have this bread to set before you, which earth has given and human hands have made. It will become the bread of life . . . we have this wine to set before you, fruit of the vine and work of human hands. It will become for us the cup of salvation.[48]

Thanksgiving as responsibility

Harvest comes with a health warning. The words of Deuteronomy: 'Do not say to yourself, "My power and the might of my own hand have gotten me this wealth."'

Similarly, Jesus saw how gift so easily slips into possession. The rich farmer assumed that the burgeoning barns were all his. All too often, creation is thought of as being there simply to exploit or to absorb our waste. We consume the earth's resources faster than can be sustained, through pollution, deforestation, desertification, endangering species, global warming. In the words of Gerard Manley Hopkins:

> Generations have trod, have trod, have trod;
> And all is smeared with trade; bleared, smeared with toil;
> And wears man's smudge, and shares man's smell: the soil
> Is bare now, no feet can foot feel, being shod.[49]

It is true that, slowly, a more responsible use of the natural environment is emerging. For this, too, it is proper to give thanks.

But ecological sustainability cannot happen without a huge cultural change, a 'paradigm shift' in our perspectives on human existence, that includes at its heart not only our own welfare but that of the whole of creation, which limits our demands to what the planet can supply. This is a tall order.

'Do not forget' means recovering a sense of belonging to and responsibility for each other and the natural world, remembering that all is gift.

In the Gospel reading, Jesus tells his disciples, 'Do not worry.' Jesus does not mean, 'Do not care', or, 'Simply assume it will all come right.' He is saying 'trust'; get things into perspective; put God first. 'Strive first for the kingdom of God and his righteousness, and all these things will be given to you as well.'

The fundamental question is, 'Do we trust Jesus?' Can we follow in the path of grateful thanksgiving? The future of the planet demands it.

Paul Ballard

Suggested hymns

Come, ye thankful people, come; For the fruits of all creation; Praise and thanksgiving; We plough the fields and scatter.

All-Age Services

Crib Service: Room for Everybody

Preparation

You will need a reasonable-sized toy that would not usually feature in a crib scene and that could have been bought at a garden centre. This story features Pete the Purple Reindeer.

Who is in the story?

We all know the characters in the crib scene: we can see them here today. There are shepherds and kings, angels, sheep, cows, a donkey – oh, and Mary, Joseph. I guess there might be a dog or a cat or a mouse or a bird. Can anyone think of anything I have missed out?

Oh yes, there is a baby – the Christ-child lying in a manger.

(*Reveal the purple reindeer.*)

But a purple reindeer? There is definitely no place for a purple reindeer in the crib scene. Everyone knows that.

This is Pete, the purple reindeer. Pete lived in a garden centre – I expect you've been to one. You might have gone with grandma or grandad, had a cup of tea, looked at the fish (if they have them).

Has anyone been Christmas shopping at a garden centre?

The garden centre dream

The garden centre where Pete the purple reindeer lived had the most wonderful Christmas shop.

There were trees and baubles, treats and tinsel, owls and robins, penguins, squirrels, angels and fairies. Oh, and of course an elf or two as well. And all of them had tinsel and snowflakes all over.

And then there was Pete the purple reindeer. He is a bit sparkly. He is a bit Christmassy. Pete used to look around the Christmas shop at all the things that were going to be part of the parties and the presents, and he used to feel a bit sad. Because he only wanted one thing to happen. Pete wanted to be part of the crib scene. He wanted to be there with the angels and the star, the shepherds and the kings, the sheep and the cows, and above all he wanted to see the Christ-child, lying in the manger.

But all the others – can you remember them? The owls and the robin, the snowmen, the angels, the penguins and the squirrels, just laughed at him. You can't go there, they said. You're a purple reindeer and everyone knows that only shepherds and angels, sheep, donkey, cows – oh, and kings – can go there. Never, ever, ever can a purple reindeer be in a crib scene.

And they laughed at Pete the purple reindeer, laughed at his silly dream.

But every day Pete thought about it. How much he wanted to be there, and take his place at the manger, looking at the Christ-child with the sheep, the cows, the shepherds and the kings. But he knew that it would never happen. After all, who would want a purple reindeer to spoil everything?

Everything changes

Then one day someone came walking round the Christmas shop at the garden centre. They looked at the angels, the snowmen, the robins and the penguins. She walked past all of them. And then saw Pete the purple reindeer, picked him off the shelf and took him home.

Pete thought he was going to sit under a Christmas tree, or welcome visitors in the hallway, perhaps even sit in a garden. But the buyer had a really, really, really special job for Pete.

Perhaps you've guessed.

Who do you think was doing the shopping? It's me! I bought Pete the purple reindeer and today the impossible is going to happen. I'm going to place Pete right here in the crib. He is going to stand next to the manger, right by the Christ-child, with the sheep, the cows, the donkey, the shepherds and the kings.

Room for everyone

Pete the purple reindeer reminds us that there is room for everyone at the manger. Jesus came to show us that there is no one who is left out of God's love. The Christmas story isn't just for children, or for 'good' people, people who come to church, who wear nice clothes and who never make mistakes. Jesus came because God loves all of the world that he made, every part of it, and every single person. We all have a place in God's heart, and we can all draw close to the manger and look at the baby who is the Christ-child, the Saviour of the world.

The story of the crib can change everyone. No one is left out – and Pete the purple reindeer is going to stay right here to remind me and to remind you of God's great love for each and every one of us.

Merry Christmas!

Sandra Millar

Christingle Service: A Christingle for Life

Preparation

No props are needed except your hands.

How quickly do you eat yours?

There may be some of you here who have never been to a Christingle service before. You are probably looking forward to getting your orange and I just wonder whether the whole Christingle will make it home with you. Maybe you could turn to people near you who have been to Christingle before and ask them for how long their Christingle is complete.

The first thing to go – sometimes even before you have got back to your seat – is the sweets or the raisins. Then we are left with the pointy sticks to deal with. Maybe we then manage to get the now bare-looking orange home. Perhaps the candle falls out on the way. And even if you do get it home fairly intact, it will just be a few days before the orange starts to look a bit withered, maybe even a bit mouldy, and it has to be thrown in the bin.

Yet Christingle has been celebrated across churches in England for over fifty years. And the message is one that can change lives and last a lifetime. So I am going to show you how to make a Christingle that will last not just for today, not just through all of next year, but for your whole life.

The orange

First, I want you to make a circle with your hands. An upright circle, touching your thumbs and first fingers together – fold your other fingers out of the way.

This circle represents the orange. And the orange reminds us of our world, our great big beautiful world that God created in all its wonder and variety. God gave us huge mountains and enormous rivers, great big elephants and giant trees. He gave us tiny insects invisible to you and me, and all the wonders of the ocean depths. You might have favourite things in creation. And all of this wonderful world is for us and future generations to enjoy and to take care of. So when you see the orange, when you make the circle, you can give thanks to God for everything you love and remember that you have a part to play in taking care of our planet.

The ribbon

Now tip your circle from vertical to horizontal, so it looks like a big ring.

This reminds us of the red ribbon that goes round the Christingle. Red is an interesting colour – red often makes us think of warnings and danger, or people who are hurting or suffering. But red is also the colour of love – you might think about balloons for Valentine's day, or roses or hearts that are red. And the red ribbon of the Christingle reminds us of God's great love for us stretching all the way round our world, and all the way round all the people of the world. God's love is big enough to hold us in our good times and in our sad and difficult times. And our job is to help show that love to other people just as Jesus showed God's love to us through his life and death.

(*Repeat the first two gestures.*)

The sweets

Now place the heels of your palms together and spread your fingers out – as if you were holding an orange in between them. Wriggle your fingers if you want.

This reminds us of the sticks with all the fruits and sweets – everybody's favourite bit of Christingle! These treats remind us of all the good gifts that God has given to us, but not just the things we enjoy each day – like food, water and shelter – but the gifts and talents that you and I have been given. You might be good at speaking or drawing, at listening or telling jokes; you might be good at fixing things or running; at science or art or cooking. God has given all of us gifts that we can use to make a difference in the world.

The treats on the Christingle remind us that we can do things that help others – and we can also say thank you for our own gifts and the gifts that our friends and family have as well. We can encourage each other to speak or act in a way that helps others and reflects love into the world.

(*Repeat the first three gestures.*)

The candle

Now fold your hands together, and simply put your index fingers pointing upwards, like a tower, or like the candle in the Christingle.

The candle is there to remind us that Jesus came into the world to be light in everybody's darkness. The thing about candlelight is that it is always the winner. The darkness can never beat it, however hard it tries. Even a tiny light makes a big difference. So the candle reminds us that Jesus came into the world to show us the light of God's love, and every time we do something that is good or kind or helpful we are helping to bring light into the world.

And, finally, I want you to imagine that you are lighting your candle. Use a finger as if it were a match alongside the finger that is representing the candle. And as you light your candle make that your prayer for God's world.

(*Repeat all five gestures.*)

Now you have a Christingle that will last you not just till you get home but for your whole lifetime. You can remember God's wonderful world, God's love that wraps around every situation, the gifts and talents that you have that will make a difference, Jesus who came to bring light. And you can pray for that light and love to be known everywhere.

Soon we will be holding our real Christingles. We will light the candles – carefully – and we will pray for the work of the Children's Society and for others who help in our world. We will think about how we can play our part by giving generously, speaking up, listening well and praying. And we will be glad that there is love and light in our world today.

Later, when you have eaten the sweets, and the candle is lost, and the orange is mouldy, you can make the Christingle with your hands. And you can remember the great story of God's love for always.

Sandra Miller

Mothering Sunday: Kept Safe by Love

Preparation

You will need a wicker basket, a doll and some blue/silvery fabric to represent water.

A big river and a special child

(*Begin by unrolling the fabric down the central nave/space.*)

I wonder what this makes you think about? Blue is the colour that we use to remind us of water, and today it makes us think not of the sea but of a river. Rivers also make us think of journeys, even the journey through life, and that's a really good thing to think about on this Mothering Sunday – or Mother's Day – and whatever you call it, it's a day for all of us to give thanks. Whether we are just setting out on life's journey or have been travelling a long time, all of us had a bit of help and support to see us on our way. I wonder who has been involved in your journey?

The reading from the book of Exodus also featured a big, big river and the beginning of someone's journey through life. And this story is going to help us think not just about mothers but about all the other people who get involved in supporting and helping mothers, children and families.

Put your hand up if you have or have ever had a mother? That's all of us, and although some of us may be sad because our mums are not here, we can all be thankful. Our story has a mum at the heart of it. A mum and her baby son. So I'm going to place this doll into the basket to represent the baby at the heart of this story. Before this baby even arrived in the world, there were some special people who helped his mum and all the families from his people.

Moses was a special child – centuries later the writer to the Hebrews would describe him as 'no ordinary child'. How did you feel when you first saw a new child in your family? I think everyone – especially grandmas! – looks at a child and thinks they are special, extraordinary really.

Brave midwives

But, like countless pregnant women in the world today, Moses' parents and family lived in a high state of anxiety, not just because of the physical risks of a pregnancy, but because they lived in a cruel and pitiless political regime that persecuted them. But that's where the midwives came in: Shiprah and Puah were very clever. They stepped in to make sure the baby was delivered safely and kept alive.

I wonder if there is anyone here who is or has ever been a midwife or a children's nurse? Lots of people get involved in making sure babies make it safely into the world – and there are midwives in today's story too. Is there a midwife here or someone who would like to be a midwife who will stand next to the baby?

Brave mums

But the dangers were everywhere. So, this time, Mum makes a plan to keep her baby safe. She risks herself and her family to save this special child. She makes a basket and places him in it, and then hides him in the river. The river has risks too – but because everyone is scared of it, it's a good place to hide. Even today, mums take risks and make hard decisions for the sake of their children. The world a child is born into is difficult and full of dangers ahead – and mums want to find a place of safety for their little one.

Is there a mum here or someone who would like to represent mums who will stand in the river with the basket?

Sassy sisters

And then something extraordinary happens. The princess from the palace sees the basket, opens it and decides to do something about it, but before that happens there is someone who speaks up. Someone who makes a suggestion, speaks for the child who has no voice. In our story, that person is the baby's sister. But there are lots of people who speak up for children – you might work as a social worker, or campaign for better healthcare, or give advice as a school nurse. How else might people today speak and act so that children have a sure future?

Is there a big sister here, or someone who would like to represent all those who speak up for children at risk? Come and stand next to the basket.

Caring princesses

And then there is the princess, who gladly takes on a child who is not her own. She brings him up in the palace, looks after him, makes wise decisions and gives him an opportunity to grow up safely. There are so many people in our world who do that for children. Some do it alongside mums and dads and families – teachers, childminders and others. And some make the decision to foster or adopt a child, providing a place of safety for a short time or a lifetime. These are the princesses of our world.

Is there anyone here who knows about adopting and fostering, or would represent them, to come and stand by the basket?

There are four people here, all providing support for Moses' mum and for baby Moses. It takes more than just mums to be mums! It takes midwives and sisters and princesses. It takes lots of people who help children and help families. But there is more for all of us to do today.

Would everyone who can, please stand up?

Praying communities

There is one more thing that we can all do – remember where Moses' parents placed him for safety? In a basket. And to this day people place newborn babies into 'Moses baskets'. But I like to think that our prayers are like a huge cradle of love holding the children of our world, supporting them so that they grow up safely and peacefully. That's how we all get involved – and if you are comfortable you might like to hold hands and imagine you are cradling the mums, families, children you care about today.

Our second reading reminded us that Jesus taught us a new way of being family. Even as he was dying, he invited one of his disciples, John, and his own mum to care for each other. Mary could be a mother to John, and John could take care of Mary – a new way of being family. Jesus reminds us that as a church we can reach out and make new kinds of relationships, relationships that support and love and help to show God's great mothering love in our world.

Thank God for mothers and children and families today.

Sandra Millar

Notes

1 *Common Worship: Services and Prayers for the Church of England*, London: Church House Publishing, 2000, pp. 21 and 27 (note 7).
2 Fred B. Craddock, *As One Without Authority*, Nashville, TN: Abingdon Press, 1971, pp. 173f.
3 Tom Long, *The Witness of Preaching*, Louisville, KY: Westminster John Knox Press, 1989, p. 96.
4 Long, *The Witness of Preaching*, p. 132.
5 Sidney Greidanus, *The Modern Preacher and the Ancient Text*, Grand Rapids, MI: Eerdmans, 1988, p. 188.
6 H. Grady Davis, *Design for Preaching*, Philadelphia, PA: Fortress Press, 1958, p. 157.
7 Long, *The Witness of Preaching*, p. 122.
8 Eugene L. Lowry, *How to Preach a Parable: Designs for Narrative Sermons*, Nashville, TN: Abingdon Press, 1989.
9 David Day, *A Preaching Workbook*, London: SPCK, 2004.
10 Although John 1.26b, here used as a refrain, is not included in our Gospel, it is integral to it and sets up John's view that the baptism of Jesus is intended to reveal his identity. I am indebted to American homiletician Scott Hoezee for inspiration for this sermon although I bring it to a somewhat different conclusion.
11 A. Schweitzer, *The Quest for the Historical Jesus*, New York: Macmillan, 1956, p. 403.
12 R. S. Thomas, 'Gift', in R. S. Thomas, *Experimenting with an Amen*, London: Macmillan, 1986, p. 15.
13 Philip Larkin, 'Water', in Philip Larkin, *Collected Poems*, London: Faber & Faber, 1988.
14 R. S. Thomas, 'The Prayer', in R. S. Thomas, *Laboratories of the Spirit*, London: Macmillan, 1975, p. 10.
15 G. M. Hopkins, 'Thou art indeed just', in G. M. Hopkins, *The Poems of Gerard Manley Hopkins*, ed. W. H. Gardner and N. H. MacKenzie, Oxford: Oxford University Press, 1977.
16 Helen H. Lemmel, 'Turn Your Eyes Upon Jesus', first published 1918.
17 Erving Goffman, *The Presentation of Self in Everyday Life*, New York: Anchor Books, 1959.

18 Donald Nicholl, *Holiness*, London: Darton, Longman & Todd, 2004, p. 54.
19 The readings for the first three Sundays offer the preacher the opportunity to make links between the Old Testament and Epistle and/or Gospel. I have used this opportunity to build a series on Adam, Abraham and Moses.
20 Cited approvingly by J. Calvin, *Institutes*, II.16.4.
21 The writer acknowledges her inspiration to write a narrative-style sermon after reading Tom Wright's comment on Martha's 'If only', in his book *John for Everyone Part 2* (London: SPCK, 2002).
22 W. A. Vanstone, *The Stature of Waiting* (London: Darton, Longman & Todd, 1982), to whom the editor is indebted for inspiration for this sermon.
23 See also for Haggai 2.1–9, Presentation of Christ in the Temple (Candlemas), Second Service, 2 February. On the use of images, see also Third Sunday before Lent, Principal Service (p. 58).
24 See also Second Sunday of Easter, Second Service (p. 121).
25 There's a similar story in 1 Samuel 26.
26 Henri J. M. Nouwen, *A Cry for Mercy: Prayers from the Genesee*, New York: Doubleday, 1981.
27 The opening story is fictitious, but based upon research and news stories at the time; it could be adapted in the light of further developments in this area.
28 T. S. Eliot, 'Ash-Wednesday', in T. S. Eliot, *The Waste Land and Other Poems*, London: Faber and Faber, 1999, p. 47.
29 Edwin Muir, 'The Incarnate One', in Edwin Muir, *Collected Poems*, London: Faber and Faber, 1960, p. 228.
30 Sam Wells, *Power and Passion: Six Characters in Search of Resurrection*, Grand Rapids, MI: Zondervan, 2006, p. 138.
31 Wells, *Power and Passion*, p. 139.
32 H. A. Williams, *The True Wilderness*, London: Constable & Co., 1965.
33 *Common Worship*, p. 32.
34 C. G. Jung, *Modern Man in Search of a Soul*, Abingdon: Routledge, 2001, pp. 200–1.
35 D. Bonhoeffer, *Letters and Papers from Prison*, ed. E. Bethege, New York: Touchstone, 1970, p. 419.
36 C. F. D. Moule (ed.), *G. W. H. Lampe: Christian Scholar, Churchman – A Memoir by Friends*, London: Mowbray, 1982, pp. 122f.
37 J. Moltmann, *The Coming of God*, London: SCM Press, 1996, p. 108.
38 U. Luz, *The Theology of the Gospel of Matthew*, Cambridge: Cambridge University Press, 1995, p. 132.
39 T. S. Eliot, *The Complete Plays of T. S. Eliot*, New York: Harcourt, Brace and World, 1935.
40 From an interim report of a review led by the Bishop of Truro, 2019.

41 R. E. Brown, *The Birth of the Messiah*, New York: Doubleday, 1999, p. 168.
42 T. S. Eliot, 'Journey of the Magi', in Eliot, *The Waste Land and Other Poems*, p. 62.
43 G. Stassen, *A Thicker Jesus*, Louisville, KY: Westminster John Knox Press, 2012.
44 R. S. Thomas, 'Pilgrimages', in R. S. Thomas, *Frequencies*, London: Macmillan, 1978, p. 51.
45 Dom Gregory Dix, *The Shape of the Liturgy*, London: Dacre Press, 1945.
46 C. K. Barrett, *The Gospel According to St John*, London: SPCK, 1958, p. 477.
47 Alan Jay Lerner and Frederick Loewe, 'I remember it well', from *Gigi*. Lyrics © Warner/Chappell Music, Inc.
48 Ursula Le Guin, *The Earthsea Quartet*, London: Puffin Books, 1993, p. 25.
49 *Common Worship*, p. 291.
50 G. M. Hopkins, 'God's Grandeur', in Hopkins, *The Poems of Gerard Manley Hopkins*.

Acknowledgements of Sources

Permission to use extracts from the following publications is acknowledged with thanks.

'Ash-Wednesday' by T. S. Eliot, in *The Waste Land and Other Poems*, London: Faber and Faber, 1999, p. 47.

Common Worship: Services and Prayers for the Church of England, London: Church House Publishing, 2000, pp. 32 and 291.

'Gift' by R. S. Thomas, in *Experimenting with an Amen*, London: Macmillan, 1986, p. 15. Used by permission of the estate of R. S. Thomas.

'The Incarnate One' by Edwin Muir, in *Collected Poems*, London: Faber and Faber, 1960, p. 228.

Murder in the Cathedral by T. S. Eliot, in *The Complete Plays of T. S. Eliot*, New York: Harcourt, Brace and World, 1935.

'Pilgrimages' by R. S. Thomas, in *Frequencies*, London: Macmillan, 1978, p. 51. Used by permission of the estate of R. S. Thomas.

'The Prayer' by R. S. Thomas, in *Laboratories of the Spirit*, London: Macmillan, 1975, p. 10. Used by permission of the estate of R. S. Thomas.

'Turn Your Eyes Upon Jesus' by Helen H. Lemmel (1961). Copyright renewal 1950 © 1950 New Spring Publishing, Universal Music (Adm UK&Eire Song Solutions, www.songsolutions.org). All rights reserved. Used by permission.

'Water' by Philip Larkin, in *Collected Poems*, London: Faber & Faber, 1988.

Index of Names and Subjects

Note: Entries in italics are titles of sermons.

20:20 Vision 181–3, 206

Abraham 79–81
Acts of the Apostles 148, 201–3, 349–50
Adam 75–7, 164–5
 Second Adam 76–7, 145
Advent 2–20, 33
Advent Sunday 2–6
All Saints' Day 263–6, 266–8
All Souls' Day 353–5
all-age services 361–8
Amos (prophet) 200
Andrew, St (apostle) 355–8
angels 344–7
Anna 55–6
Annunciation to the Blessed Virgin Mary 305–7
Anointed for Generosity 172–4
Another Advocate 138–40
Antioch (Pisidian) 13–14
Antony of Egypt, St
Apprentice to Jesus 355–8
Ardent Desire 116–18
ascension 144
Ascension Day 143–8
Ash Wednesday xxvi, 73–5
asylum seekers 159, 166–7, 210
atheism 78
Auden, W.H. 156
Augustine of Hippo 76, 90, 149, 162, 244
authority 143–6, 235–6, 236–9
Avery, Bruce 258

Ballard, Paul 358–60
baptism:
 at Easter 112–13
 of Christ 39–42, 42–44, 44–6, 112, 334
 and decision 273
 and Holy Spirit 226
Barnabas, St (apostle) 207, 212, 319–21
 call 201–2
Barth, Karl 323
Bartholomew, St (apostle) 338–9
Beatitudes 265
beauty 242–4
Beginning Again 131–3
Benedict, St 62
Bethlehem 21–2, 24, 30–2
Better Together 239–41
Between the Shores 203–5
Bible, and problems of translation 19
Bible Sunday xxvi, 261–3
Binding and Loosing 222–4
The Birth of the Light 21–3
Blessed Virgin Mary *see* Mary, Blessed Virgin
The Blessing & Naming and Being Named 278–81
Blythe, Stuart 303–4

body of Christ, church as 49–51, 90, 127, 132–3, 264, 295, 319, 324, 352
Bold Speech for Turbulent Times 42–4
Bonhoeffer, Dietrich 259, 260
Bound Together by the Love of God 324–6
The Bronze Serpent 82–4
Brower Latz, Deirdre 25–7
Brown, Callum 261
Brown, Dan 329
Bruce, Kate xxvi, 191–3, 196–8, 201–3, 205–7, 210–12, 215–17, 220–2
building metaphor 350–2
Bunyan, John 260
Burden, Paul 140–3
Burdon, Christopher 307–9
Burkett, Christopher xxiii, 39–42, 227–9

Called for Life 129–31
Campin, Robert, *Nativity* 23–4
Candlemas Bells 54–6
Cheerleader in Tough Times 319–21
children of God 36–7, 45, 226–7, 295
Christ the King 32, 281–3, 283–5
christening *see* baptism
A Christian Identity Test? 159–61
Christians and Jews 287–8
Christingle service 363–5
Christmas Day 21–3, 23–5, 25–8, 28–30
Christmas season 30–9
Christ's Body, the Church, Called to Love 89–91
Church:
 as body of Christ 49–51, 90, 127, 132–3, 264, 295, 319, 324, 352
 and God's mission 210–12
 and Holy Spirit 127–8, 132–3, 201–3
 leadership 211–12
 metaphors for 126–9, 205
 and Peter 213–15, 324–6
 as servant 332, 339
Church Unity 49–51
circumcision of Jesus 293–5
cities 140–3
A Cloud of Witnesses 266–8
Commemoration of the Faithful Departed 353–5
communion of saints 267–8
community 61–2
compassion:
 of disciples 117, 197–8, 200
 of God 72, 90, 93, 265, 353
 of Jesus 102, 199–200
contradiction 18, 36, 102
controversy 180–1
Conversion of St Paul 300–2
Corpus Christi 317–19
Correct Endings? 151–4
Costly, Clear-eyed Service 331–2
Cotes, Mary 203–5, 291–3
Counting the Cost 169–71
covenant 285, 294, 318
Coventry Cathedral 56–8, 346
Craddock, Fred B. xix–xx
creation 43, 53, 63, 65–7, 358–60, 364
 new 145–6
crib service 361–3
cross *see* crucifixion; Holy Cross Day
crucifixion 84, 100–1, 102, 107, 108–10, 135, 180
Cyprian of Carthage, St

Daffern, Megan 65–6, 116–18, 121–3, 146–8, 161–3, 166–9, 172–4, 176–9, 186–8, 239–41, 271–3
Dali, Salvador 110
Daniel 121–3
darkness:
 and faith 196–8
 and light 21–3, 27, 55–6

Darwin, Charles 164, 166
David (king of Israel) 7, 24, 187, 240–1, 272, 284–5
Jesus as new David 14, 31, 41, 99, 188, 241, 285, 294
and Saul 167–8, 172–3, 177–8
Davis, H. Grady xxi, 369 n.6
Day, David xxv
Day of the Lord 158
desire 116–18
despair 17, 92–3, 191–3, 198, 207
disciples of Jesus 63–4, 67–8, 145–6, 150, 308–9, 311–12, 327
calling 355–6
and journey to Jerusalem 182
and kindness of strangers 175–6
and storm on Sea of Galilee 203–5
discipleship:
as communal 356–8
cost 169–71, 255–6, 264, 287–8, 331–2
as journey 124–6, 209
and obedience 204–5, 315–17, 337
Discovering Infinity 111–13
The Divine Love that Calls Us Back 309–12
Dix, Dom Gregory 317
'Do not be afraid, for I am with you' 220–2
'Do not forget the Lord your God' 358–60
Donne, John 148
dress codes 247–9
Dressing Up 247–9

earth, new 136–7
Easter, Sundays after 118–54
Easter Day 113–18
Easter Vigil 111–13
Eco, Umberto 219
ecumenism 298–300
Elijah 8, 9–10, 12, 70–1, 79, 147, 156, 326, 334
Eliot, T.S. 126, 194, 195, 213, 286, 298
Elisha 70–1, 147
Elizabeth (mother of John the Baptist) 7, 19–20, 315–17, 336
Emmanuel, Jesus as 17, 32, 292, 303, 304
Emmaus, journey to 124–6, 327
Encounters with the Word 18–20
Ephesus 230–2
Epiphany 296–8
Epiphany season 39–54
Esdaile, Rob 21–3
eternity 137, 244
symbols 111–12
Eusebius of Caesarea 338–9
Evangelism: Why Can't We Just be a Bit More Normal? 215–17
evil 87–9, 165–6, 190, 202, 346–7
exile 2, 5–6, 31–2, 47–8, 57, 96, 121–2, 131
Exodus from Egypt 14, 31–2, 89–90, 118, 131, 167
Ezekiel (prophet) 46–8, 235–6, 237, 240–1

faith:
and doubt 119–21, 125–6, 326–8
and grace 81
and obedience 204–5, 315–17, 338–9
and saints 265–6, 266–7
sharing 215–17
Faith in Dark Places 196–8
Faithful Enough to Doubt 118–21
Faithful unto Death 286–8
family life 89–91, 92, 170–1, 368
fasting 73–4
fear 220–2
Finding Peace in Complexity 179–81
Firmly I Believe and Truly 338–9
first fruits 250–1
A Fond Farewell 230–2
foot-washing 107–8, 175
forgiveness 108, 228–9, 235–6, 348
Forsyth, Peter Taylor 299–300

Fox, Catherine 89
From Despair to Hope 91–3
From Fate to Freedom 296–8
fruits of the Spirit 155

Gagarin, Juri 327
Gaudete Sunday 11–13
generosity 73, 172–4, 232–4, 250–1, 321
Gentiles 48, 80–1, 300–2
'Get behind me!' 307–9
Get Wisdom 254–6
Gideon 271–3
glorification 146–8, 150, 163
Glory Be! 146–8
God in Time 51–3
Good Friday xxv, 108–10
Good Shepherd 129–31, 235–6
grace xxv, 22, 55, 90, 143, 219, 264, 311
  and faith 81
  and glory 69
  incongruous 76–7, 80–1, 232–4, 301–2
  in Luke 348
  in Old Testament 247–8
  in Paul 17, 60, 232, 348
  singularity 300–2
  strength in grace 72, 113, 258–61
  as transformative 10, 155, 184, 304, 335
  and truth 36–7, 46, 231
Greidanus, Sidney xxi, 369 n.5
grief 353–5
Grünewald, Matthias 323
guardian angels 345–6

Handed Over 106–8
Handel, George Frederick, *Messiah* 9, 10, 24
Happy Endings 121–3
Harvest Festival 358–60
Hauerwas, Stanley 357
Hawkins, Stephen 52
healing 206, 340–1, 348
Hear! 183–6
heaven 66–7, 133–5, 136–8
The Heavens are Telling the Glory of God 242–4
Herbert, Christopher 13–15, 18–20, 23–5, 70–2, 86–9, 111–13, 151–4, 164–6, 217–20, 242–4, 245–7, 258–61, 273–6, 278–81, 309–12, 312–14, 342–4, 350–2
Herbert, George 318
Herod (king of Judaea) 31, 292, 296, 298, 306
Herodians 252–3
heroes and saints 264
history 43–4
holiness 162, 188
Holocaust 88, 96, 165
Holy Communion, and remembering 275
  see also Corpus Christi
Holy Cross Day 340–2
Holy Innocents 167, 291–3
holy living 265
Holy Spirit: Director and Principal Actor 201–3
Holy Spirit:
  as advocate 138–40
  and baptism 226
  and baptism of Jesus 40–1
  and birth of Jesus 16–17, 303, 304, 305
  and Day of Pentecost 154–6, 157–8, 192–3
  fruits of 155
  in Luke 348–9
  metaphors for 60, 84–6
  and Paul (apostle) 211, 225–7, 230–2
Holy Week 99–110
  first three days 103–5
hope 2–4, 6, 22, 37, 44, 56, 91, 93, 95, 97–8, 260, 265–6
Hopkins, Gerard Manley 60
  'God's Grandeur' 360
hospitality 85, 125, 175–6

How to Life a Good Life 61–2
Howard, Ebenezer 13
humankind, in image of God 63, 145, 253–4
hunger 198–200
A Hymn to Jesus 33–5
hypocrisy 73–4, 253

'I am the resurrection and the life' 353–5
'I find no case against him' 108–10
identity 61–2
idolatry 83, 253, 272
If only . . . 94–5
imagery:
 of church 126–8, 350–2
 of Trinity 159–61
 of vineyard 102–3
 of vision xxv–xxvi, 63–4, 181–3, 205–7
 of water 59–60, 84–6, 156
imagination, and remembering 275–6
inclusion 81, 85, 126, 132, 211–12, 329–30, 362–3
Incongruous Grace 232–4
individualism 218–19
Inhabiting the World of the Parables 193–6
Innocents: Catching the Reflections of Christ 291–3
intercession of Jesus 149–51
'Is there anybody there?' 46–8
Isaiah (prophet) 11–12, 187, 200, 310–11
Islip, John (Abbot of Westminster) 18, 20

James, St (apostle; brother of John) 196–7, 331–2
Jenkins, Simon 57
Jeremiah (prophet) 187
Jerusalem 7, 43
 destruction 47, 93, 96
 Holy Sepulchre Church 340
 Jesus' final journey to 99–101, 176–7, 182
 New 141–3
 return to 5–6, 11, 56–7
 see also Temple
Jerusalem: House and Temple 186–8
Jesus:
 authority 237–8
 birth 16–17, 21–3, 23–5, 25–7, 30–2, 35–6, 292, 347, 349
 as Emmanuel 17, 32, 292, 303, 304
 as Good Shepherd 129–31, 235–6
 as image of God 26–7
 and John the Baptist 7–8, 12, 40–1, 109, 112, 180, 238, 323–4
 as king 100–1, 102, 110, 338
 as Lamb of God 46, 109, 148
 as Messiah 3, 6, 12–13, 14, 32, 55, 95, 99–100, 125, 173, 182, 209, 241, 308, 355
 as new David 14, 31, 41, 99, 188, 241, 285, 294
 as new Moses 31–2, 41
 as Prince of Peace 132
 as Redeemer 17, 32
 as refugee 292
 as Second Adam 76–7, 145
 Second Coming 269–70
 as son of David 174, 182, 209
 as Son of God 11, 28–9, 40, 45, 76, 95, 100, 109, 204, 338
 as Son of Man 83–4, 108, 182–3, 288
 as teacher 176–8, 208, 356–7
 temptation 11, 40, 76
 as true vine 103
 as the truth 135, 139, 273, 306–7, 343–4
 walking on the water 203–5
 as Word 18–20, 37, 45, 65–6, 261–2, 289–91
 see also baptism, of Christ; Christ the King; resurrection

Jesus Becomes King 99–101
Jesus, Hidden King 281–3
Jews:
  and Christians 287–8
  and Jesus 108–10
Joel (prophet) 157–8
John (apostle and evangelist) 196–7, 289–91, 316
  and ascension of Jesus 144–5
  and intercession of Jesus 149–51
  and the Trinity 160–1
John the Baptist 10–12, 109, 180, 238
  and baptism of Jesus 39–42, 42–4, 44–6, 112, 334
  birth 321–4
  death 199
John the Divine 336
Johnson, Victoria 9–10, 37–9, 54–6, 61–2, 62–4, 101–3, 179–81, 235–6, 254–6, 319–21, 324–6, 338–9
Joseph of Nazareth 16, 23, 31–2, 55, 303–4
The Journey of Discipleship 124–6
Judas Iscariot 105, 106
judgement 281–2, 323–4
Jung, C. G. 257
Just How Beautiful are the Feet? 4–6

Kept Safe by Love 366–8
Kilworth-Mason, Wendy 4–6, 33–5, 82–4, 91–3, 157–8, 283–5
kindness 174–6
The Kindness of Strangers 174–6
kingdom of God 15, 41, 100, 183, 191, 237
  as banquet 247–9
  on earth 52, 132, 137, 194, 246
  and Jewish authorities 178–9, 182
  and John the Baptist 10, 12, 109, 180
  and miracles 153–4
  and parables 193–6
  receiving 245–6
  and role of followers 145–6, 170, 175
kingdom of heaven 66–7, 137–8, 210, 233–4
kingdom season 269–70
knowledge, and wisdom 255

labourers, parable xxv, 232–4
Lamentations (book) 96–8
language 19, 42–3, 155–6, 184, 195, 309–10, 336
Larkin, Philip, 'Water' 60
Last Judgements 281–3
Last Supper 106–9, 275
The Last Words 283–5
The Latter Glory 56–8
Lazarus of Bethany 94–5, 104, 120
Le Carré, John 144
Le Guin, Ursula 357
leadership 211–12
leaven, parable xxiv–xxv, 194–6
Lemmel, Helen Haworth 69
Lent 73–98
Lent Backstage 73–5
Lewis, C.S. 59, 335
liberation 223–4
life:
  family life 89–91, 92, 170–1
  as gift 245–6
  good life 61–2
  new life 11–12, 38–9, 54, 56, 112–13, 117–18
  real life 114–15
Life at Its Most Unlikely 335–7
Life Beyond Christmas 35–7
Lift High the Cross 340–2
Lift Up Your Eyes 62–4
light, and darkness 21–3, 27, 55–6
Lightning Strikes Twice 227–9
lists 86–9
Living between Promises and Fulfilment 2–4
Living Temple 126–8
Loisy, Alfred 213

Long, Tom xx, xxi, 369 nn.4,7
love:
divine 56, 63–4, 76–7, 83, 90–1, 116–18, 185, 257–8, 260–1, 330, 341, 354–5, 362–3, 364–5
for God 77–9, 133, 256–7
human 89–91, 255–6
for neighbour 256–7
Love God 77–9
Love Yourself 256–8
Loving the Lord 328–30
Lowry, Eugene L., 'Lowry's Loop' xxii–xxiii
Luke, St (evangelist) 347–50
and ascension of Jesus 144–5, 148
and birth of Jesus 347, 349
intention in writing 323–4
and mission of Paul 202, 288, 349–50
Luke, Evangelist of the Written Word 347–50
Luther, Martin 43, 76

magi 31, 32, 296–8
Magnificat 200, 316, 336–7
Mark (evangelist) 238, 307–9
gospel ending 122–3, 148, 151–4, 307
Martha of Bethany 94–5, 105
Mary of Bethany 105
Mary, Blessed Virgin 55, 90, 335–7
Annunciation to 305–7
and birth of Jesus 23–4
Visit to Elizabeth 7, 19–20, 315–17, 336
Mary Magdalene 328–30
as apostle 329
and resurrection of Christ 117–18, 144, 152, 327, 329
Matthew (apostle and evangelist) 342–4
and Andrew 355–8
and the Church 213–14
and Joseph 303–4
and Old Testament 238
Matthias, St (apostle) 312–14
Maundy Thursday 106–8
mercy 172–4
messengers 5–6, 11, 27
Messiah 7–8, 9–10, 11–12, 32, 57, 95, 99–100, 125, 173, 182, 308
and Andrew 355
and David 14, 99, 209, 241
metaphors 59–60, 126–8
Micah (prophet) 92–3
Michael, St, and All Angels 344–7
The Mightiest Festival of Them All 154–6
Millar, Sandra 361–3, 363–5, 366–8
Milton, John 237
miracle 238
and preaching 152–3
mission:
of God 44, 81, 145, 210–12, 265
as spreading water 59–60
Mission: God's Business, God's Church 210–12
Monologue: The Man with Few Talents 276–8
monologue sermon xxv, 276–8
Monteith, David 208–10
Moran, Caitlin 2
Moses 31–2, 41, 82–3, 334, 366–8
Moses 84–6
Mothering Sunday 89–93, 366–8
The Mountain and the Plain 67–9
Muir, Edwin 195
mustard seed, parable xxiv–xxv, 194–6

Name Above All Names 293–5
names and naming 278–81
Naming and Circumcision of Jesus 293–5
narrative preaching xxi–xxiv
argument xxiv–xxv
story xxiii–xxiv
Nathaniel *see* Bartholomew
Nazareth 30, 32

The Need for Lament 96–8
A New City 140–3
A New Heaven and a New Earth 136–8
New Year 293–5
Nicholl, Donald 74–5, 369 n.17
Nicodemus 80–1, 83–4, 105
No Turning Back 39–42
Norwood, Donald 298–300
Nouwen, Henri 185

The Old Made New: Hearing Christmas in New Ways 25–8
On Firm Foundations 350–2
The One to Know 44–6
Original Sin? 164–6
outsiders 208–10

pain 96–8
Palm Sunday xxiv, 99–103
parables xxiv–xxv, 193–6, 348–9
Passiontide 94–8
Passover 100, 104, 109, 118, 186
Paul (apostle) 13–15, 47–8, 53, 126–8, 193, 316
  and Abraham 80–1
  in Athens 215–17
  call 201–2, 301–2
  and Christian unity 49–51, 300
  conversion 235–6, 300–2, 325
  and Ephesians 230–2, 350–2
  and evil 87–9, 202
  and fear 220–2
  and grace 17, 60, 232, 301–2
  healing of crippled man 206
  and Holy Spirit 211, 225–7, 230–2
  hymn to Jesus 28–30, 33–5
  missions 210–12, 302
  and Second Coming 269
  and sin 164–6, 179–81
  and Timothy 211–12, 259–61
  and truth 343
  see also Peter and Paul, SS (apostles)
Pentecost 144, 154–8
People of an Alternative Culture 263–6
persecution of Christians 288
Perumbalath, John 263–6
Peter (apostle) 193, 196–8, 204
  and the Church 213–15, 324–6
Peter and Paul, SS (apostles) 324–6
Pharisees 252–3
Philip and James, SS (apostles) 309–12
Pilate, Pontius 109, 110
Pipsqueaks and Giants 191–3
poetry 42–3, 65, 97, 116–17, 195, 243, 336–7
Poured Out for Love's Sake 103–5
The Power of Lists 86–9
The Power of Three 161–3
prayer, in Luke 349
preaching:
  essential points xix, xxvii
  and miracle 152–3
  narrative xxi–xxiv
Prepare to be Dazzled 16–18
Prepare the Way 9–10
Presentation of Christ in the Temple 54–6, 56–8
Pridmore, John 237–9
priests 322–3
promises and fulfilment 2–4, 30, 32, 80, 114, 175, 316, 323–4
A Prophet for a Priest 321–4
prophets 178, 321–3
  see also Elijah; Elisha; Isaiah; Joel; Micah; Samuel
proverbs 249–51
Proverbs (book) 249–51, 255
providence, divine 63, 297

Ramsay, Michael 319
reconciliation 38–9, 76, 223–4, 299–300, 354
Redeemer, Jesus as 17, 32
redemption 235–6
Refugee Crises 166–9
refugees 139, 166–9, 208–9

Rejection and Restoration 101–3
Rejoice and Blossom! 11–13
Remembrance Sunday 273–6
resurrection 14, 95, 113–16, 116–18, 119–21, 121–3, 124–6, 132, 144–6, 192, 216, 354
  and Mary Magdalene 117–18, 144, 152, 327, 329
Revealing Encounters 208–10
Rise Up, Good Shepherd 235–6
Risen Yet Hidden 113–19
Rogation Sunday 138–43
Root and Branch 65–7
Rule of Three 70–2
Run to the Hills! 315–17

Sacks, Lord Jonathan 176
St Paul's Tweets 217–20
saints 263–6, 266–8
Saleh, Carey 89–91
salvation 17, 29, 32, 48, 59, 85–6, 104, 160, 170
  for all 6, 22, 81, 183
  in Old Testament 92–3, 193
Samaritans 38, 60, 84–6
Samuel (prophet) 167, 168, 172–3, 177–8, 284–5
Sansom, C. J. 274
Saul, and David 167–8, 172–3, 177–8
Schlafer, David xxvi
Schweitzer, A. 45–6
Scruton, Roger 242
Sea of Galilee, storm 203–5
seeing *see* vision
Seeing and Believing 289–91
Seeing with the Heart 326–8
Seeing Right 205–7
self, love of 256–8
self-sacrifice 101, 257, 286
sermon forms xix–xxvii
  apologetic xxv
  argument xxiv–xxv
  and listeners xx–xxi, 19–20
  monologue xxv
  narrative preaching xxi–xxiv
  story xxiii–xxiv
Sermon on the Mount 31, 108
Shakespeare, William 73, 87, 98
Shardlake, Matthew 274
Shema 78
The Shepherds' Point of View 23–5
The Shock, Surprise and Singularity of Grace 300–2
Signpost, Spectacles and Talking Book 261–3
Signposts 6–8
Simeon 55–6
Simon and Jude, SS (apostles) 350–2
sin 76, 82–4, 179–80, 190
  forgiveness 108, 228–9, 235–6, 348
  original sin 164–6
  of parents 237
Song of Solomon 115–18, 330
Song of the Three 146–8
Spiller, Roger 2–4, 16–18, 28–30, 30–2, 35–7, 42–4, 44–6, 46–8, 51–3, 56–8, 58–60, 67–9, 73–5, 75–7,77–9, 79–81, 84–5, 96–8, 99–101, 103–5, 106–8, 108–10, 125–6, 126–8, 129–31, 133–5, 136–8, 143–6, 149–51, 154–6, 159–61, 169–71, 174–6, 183–6, 193–6, 213–15, 224–7, 232–4, 247–9, 252–4, 256–8, 261–3, 266–8, 276–8, 281–3, 286–8, 296–8, 300–2, 305–7, 317–19, 321–4, 331–2, 333–5, 344–7, 347–50, 355–8
The Spirit's Insider Work 224–7
A Spiritual Geography to Bring us Home! 30–2
Stassen, Glen 304
Stephen, St 286–8
Stilling Troubled Hearts 133–5
stories xxii–xxv
The 'Story' of Transfiguration Retold 333–5

strangers 124–6, 132, 208–10
'Strong in Grace' 258–61
suffering, and faith 196–8
surprise 146–8
Sykes, Emma 94–5

Take Authority! 143–6
Take What You Want, Says God . . . 244–7
Taken, Blessed, Broken and Distributed 317–19
talents, parable xxv, 276–8
tax 252–4
Temple:
Herodian 58, 108, 187, 288
as house of prayer 187
Second 54–5, 56–8, 131–2, 322
Solomonic 57–8, 96–7, 131
Temple, William 154, 300
temptation of Jesus 11, 40, 76
ten bridesmaids, parable 269–70, 277
Tenebrae 96–7
Teresa of Avila, St 184
thankfulness 246–7
thanksgiving 358–60
Thanksgiving for the Institution of Holy Communion 317–19
'They went on from Perga and came to Antioch in Pisidia' 13–15
Think Big and Act Boldly 298–300
Thomas, R.S.:
'Gift' 60
'Pilgrimages' 308
'The Prayer' 60
Thomas, St (apostle) 119–21, 135, 239, 326–8
time 52–3, 137
Time for Angels? 345–7
Timothy, St 211–12, 259–61
tithes 250–1
togetherness 239–41
tongues 155–6
Transfiguration of Christ xxiii, 67–9, 333–5
translation 19
Trench, Sally 254
Trinity 66
Trinity Sunday 159–63
Sundays after 164–261
trio, musical, as image of Trinity 159–61
Trouble! 303–4
truth 135, 139, 219, 255–6, 342–4
and grace 36–7, 46, 231

Ultimate Loyalty 176–9
umwelt 309–12
unity and division 49–51, 151, 179–81, 214, 320–1

Vanstone, W.E. 107, 370 n.21
vineyard imagery 102–3
virgin birth 16
vision imagery xxvi, 63–4, 181–3, 205–7
Visit of the Blessed Virgin Mary 7, 19–20, 315–17, 336–7
vocation 129–31, 133, 214–15, 286, 311–12, 322

Wait. Watch. Prepare 268–70
Wallis, John 111
Ward, Brett 118–21, 335–7
water xxvi, 11, 37–9, 44, 84–6
in baptism 60
as metaphor of Spirit 60, 84–6, 156
A Watered Garden 58–60
Wedding Feast, parable xxiii–xxiv, 247–9
Weeding or Waiting 188–91
Week of Prayer for Christian Unity 298–300
What Future for the Church? 213–15
What God Does 271–3
What is Truth? 342–4
What is Your Authority? 236–9
What's in Your Pocket? 252–4

Whit Sunday 154–8
Wicked Tenants, parable 102
wilderness 7, 9–10, 11, 38, 67–8, 74, 82
and temptations of Jesus 11, 40, 76
Williams, Catherine 6–8, 11–13, 131–3, 181–3, 198–200, 222–4, 230–2, 249–51, 268–70, 293–5, 315–17, 328–30, 340–2, 353–5
Williams, Harry 226–7
Williams, Robbie, 'Angels' 346
wisdom 66–7, 249–51, 254–6
Wisdom's Source and Power 249–51
witnesses, saints as 266–8
Word 18–20, 37, 45, 65–7, 185–6, 261–2, 289–91
Wright, Stephen 49–51, 113–16, 138–40, 188–91

You Give Them Something to Eat! 198–200
'Your sons and your daughters shall prophesy' 157–8

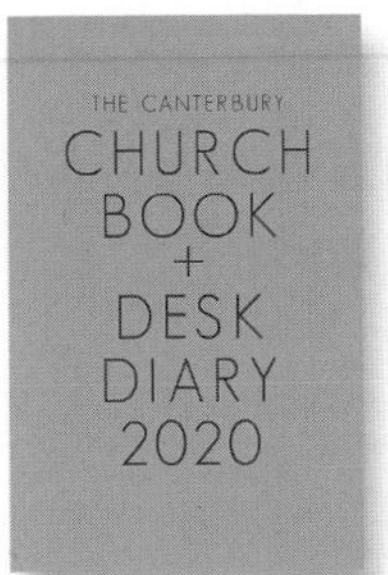

Advance order for the 2021 editions *(available May 2020)*

quantity

Prices are subject to confirmation and may be changed without notice

CANTERBURY CHURCH BOOK & DESK DIARY 2021 *Hardback* **£19.99** + p&p* ....

CANTERBURY CHURCH BOOK & DESK DIARY 2021 *Personal Organiser* *(A5)* **£19.99** + p&p* ....

CANTERBURY PREACHER'S COMPANION 2021 *Paperback* **£19.99** + p&p* ....

For details of special discounted prices for purchasing the above in any combinations or in bulk, please contact the publisher's Norwich office as shown below.

Order additional copies of the 2020 editions

Subject to stock availability

Hardback Diary **£19.99***............

Preacher's Companion **£19.99***............ A5 Personal Organiser **£19.99***............

Ask for details of discounted prices for bulk orders of 6+ copies of any individual title when ordered direct from the Publisher.

Sub-total £................

*Plus **£2.50** per order to cover post and packing (UK only): £................

All orders over £50 are sent POST FREE to any UK address.
Contact the Publishers office for details of overseas carriage.

TOTAL AMOUNT TO PAY: £................

I wish to pay by ...

... **CHEQUE** for £ .... made payable to **Hymns Ancient and Modern Ltd**

... **CREDIT CARD** All leading credit and debit cards accepted (*not American Express or Diners Club*)
Your credit card will not be debited until the books are despatched.

Card number: .... Expiry: ____ /____

Issue No: ____ Valid from: ____ /____

Switch or *Maestro* only

Signature of cardholder: .... Security code:________

Last three digits on signature panel

Please PRINT all details below.

Title: .... Name: ....

Delivery address: ....

....

....

.... Post Code: ....

Telephone or e-mail: .... Date: ....

Please ensure you have ordered the edition you require for the correct year. No liability will be accepted for incorrect orders

Return this order form or a photocopy – with details of payment – to

Norwich Books and Music, 13A Hellesdon Park Road, Norwich NR6 5DR

Telephone: 01603 785900 Fax: 01603 785915 Website: www.canterburypress.co.uk